Synonyms and Antonyms

Chambers Dictionary of Synonyms and Antonyms

Edited by
Martin H. Manser

CAMBRIDGE EDINBURGH
NEW YORK NEW ROCHELLE MELBOURNE SYDNEY

Published jointly by W & R Chambers Limited
43-45 Annandale Street, Edinburgh EH7 4AZ, and
The Press Syndicate of the University of Cambridge
The Pitt Building, Trumpington Street, Cambridge CB2 1RP
32 East 57th Street, New York, NY 10022, USA
10 Stamford Road, Oakleigh, Melbourne 3166, Australia.

Reprinted 1989

British Library Cataloguing in Publication Data

Chambers dictionary of synonyms and antonyms.
1. English language. Synonyms and antonyms. Dictionaries
I. Manser, Martin H. 423'. 1

ISBN 1-85296-350-6

Typeset by Pillans & Wilson Specialist Litho Printers Ltd, Edinburgh
Printed in Great Britain by Richard Clay Ltd, Bungay, Suffolk

Introduction

A synonym is a word that means something similar to another word. This dictionary lists the synonyms for common English words. In many entries, antonyms—words that mean the opposite of another word—are also shown.

Chambers Dictionary of Synonyms and Antonyms is based on *Chambers Thesaurus,* which itself is drawn from the extensive *Chambers English Dictionary* database.

How to use this book

Suppose you want to find a synonym for the word *interesting*. You may have used this word already or you may want to vary the style of what you are writing or saying. If you look up the entry **interesting,** after the part-of-speech marker *adj.* you will see a list of synonyms in alphabetical order: *absorbing, appealing, attractive, compelling,* etc. Antonyms are given at the end of many entries, for example at **interesting***: boring, dull, monotonous, tedious.*

Many entries are divided into numbered sections. This means that the word has several meanings. See, for example, the entry **vain,** which is divided into two parts:

> **1** abortive, empty, fruitless, futile . . . **2** affected, arrogant, bigheaded, conceited . . .

Words in the first part could replace *vain* in the phrase *a vain attempt;* words in the second part describe someone who is very proud. The numbered sections are usually given in order of frequency.

The numbers for the antonyms at the end of such entries refer to the numbered meanings of the synonyms. For example, some opposites of the first meaning of **vain** are given: *fruitful, successful;* and of the second meaning: *modest, self-effacing.*

At the end of some entries, some phrases that use the main headword are included. For example, *at once* is given at **once** and *in order to* at **order.**

Some entries have small raised numbers, for example **lock**[1] (a bolt) and **lock**[2] (of hair). This means that the words have a different history.

Note that no one word can be used in place of another word in every context. So if you are not sure of the meaning or use of one of the words included as a synonym, ask someone, or look the word up in a good dictionary such as *Chambers English Dictionary* or *Chambers Concise Dictionary*.

Two other points:

1. The oblique stroke / is used to show alternatives. For example at **clarify** *shed/throw light on* means both *shed light on* and *throw light on.*
2. Round brackets ( ) are used to enclose optional information. For example, at **everything** *the (whole) lot* means both *the lot* and *the whole lot.*

This dictionary has been compiled to help you find the most appropriate word for a particular occasion. You will be able to include a more exact term in a report, a livelier phrase in a speech, a simpler expression in a letter. We hope that, not only will your skills in using English improve, but that you will enjoy sampling more of the varied delights of the English language.

Appendix

There are lists of related words on pages 403–5.

Abbreviations

adj.	adjective	*n.*	noun
adv.	adverb	*prep.*	preposition
conj.	conjunction	®	trademark
interj.	interjection	*v.*	verb

Acknowledgements

The editor would like to thank Peter Schwarz for his technical expertise and for his assistance in the production of this book, and Rosalind Desmond for her invaluable editorial assistance.

A

abandon *v.* desert, ditch, drop, forgo, forsake, give up, jilt, leave, leave behind, leave in the lurch, quit, relinquish, renounce, resign, scrap, sink, surrender, vacate, waive, withdraw from, yield.
antonyms continue, persist, support.
n. dash, recklessness, wantonness, wildness.
antonym restraint.

abandoned *adj.* **1** derelict, deserted, desolate, forlorn, forsaken, neglected, unoccupied. **2** dissolute, uninhibited, wanton, wicked, wild.
antonyms **1** kept. **2** restrained.

abandonment *n.* desertion, discontinuation, dropping, forsaking, giving up, jilting, leaving, neglect, relinquishment, renunciation, resignation, sacrifice, scrapping, surrender, waiver.

abase *v.* belittle, cast down, debase, degrade, demean, discredit, disgrace, dishonour, humble, humiliate, lower, malign, mortify, reduce.
antonyms elevate, honour.

abashed *adj.* ashamed, bewildered, confounded, confused, discomposed, disconcerted, dismayed, dum(b)founded, embarrassed, floored, humbled, humiliated, mortified, nonplussed, perturbed, shamefaced, taken aback.
antonyms at ease, composed.

abate *v.* alleviate, decline, decrease, deduct, diminish, discount, dull, dwindle, ease, fade, fall off, lessen, let up, mitigate, moderate, pacify, quell, rebate, reduce, relieve, remit, sink, slacken, slow, subside, subtract, taper off, wane, weaken.
antonyms increase, strengthen.

abbey *n.* cloister, convent, friary, monastery, nunnery, priory, seminary.

abbot *n.* abbé, head, prior, superior.

abbreviate *v.* abridge, abstract, clip, compress, condense, contract, curtail, cut, digest, lessen, précis, reduce, shorten, shrink, summarise, trim, truncate.
antonyms amplify, extend.

abbreviation *n.* abridgement, abstract, abstraction, clipping, compression, contraction, curtailment, digest, précis, reduction, résumé, shortening, summarisation, summary, synopsis.
antonyms expansion, extension.

abdicate *v.* abandon, cede, forgo, give up, quit, relinquish, renounce, repudiate, resign, retire, surrender, vacate, yield.

abdomen *n.* belly, guts, midriff, paunch, stomach, tummy.

abdominal *adj.* gastric, intestinal, ventral, ventricular, visceral.

abduct *v.* abduce, appropriate, carry off, kidnap, make off with, run away with, run off with, seduce, seize, snatch, spirit away.

aberration *n.* anomaly, defect, delusion, deviation, divergence, eccentricity, freak, hallucination, illusion, irregularity, lapse, nonconformity, oddity, peculiarity, quirk, straying, wandering.
antonym conformity.

abet *v.* aid, assist, back, encourage, goad, help, incite, promote, prompt, sanction, second, spur, succour, support, sustain, uphold, urge.
antonyms discourage, hinder.

abhor *v.* abominate, despise, detest, hate, loathe, recoil from, shrink from, shudder at, spurn.
antonyms adore, love.

abhorrence *n.* abomination, aversion, disgust, distaste, enmity, hate, hatred, horror, loathing, malice, repugnance, revulsion.
antonyms adoration, love.

abide *v.* **1** accept, bear, put up with, stand, stomach, tolerate. **2** continue, endure, last, persist, remain.
abide by acknowledge, acquiesce in, adhere to, agree to, carry out, comply with, conform to, discharge, follow, fulfil, go along with, hold to, keep to, obey, observe, stand by, submit to.

abiding *adj.* constant, continual, continuing, enduring, eternal, everlasting, firm, immortal, immutable, lasting, permanent, persistent, stable, steadfast, surviving, tenacious, unchangeable, unchanging, unending.
antonyms ephemeral, transient.

ability *n.* adeptness, aptitude, capability, capacity, competence, deftness, dexterity, endowment, expertise, facility, faculty, flair, forte, genius, gift, knack, know-how, potentiality, power, proficiency, qualification, skill, strength, talent, touch.
antonyms inability, incompetence, weakness.

abject *adj.* contemptible, debased, degenerate, degraded, deplorable, despicable, dishonourable, forlorn, grovelling, hopeless, humiliating, ignoble, low, mean, miserable, outcast, pathetic, pitiable, servile, slavish, sordid, submissive, vile, worthless, wretched.
antonyms exalted, proud.

ablaze *adj.* **1** aglow, alight, blazing, burning, flaming, flashing, glaring, gleaming, glowing, ignited, illuminated, lighted, luminous, on fire, radiant, sparkling. **2** angry, aroused, brilliant, enthusiastic, excited, exhilarated, fervent, fiery, frenzied, furious, impassioned, incensed, passionate, raging, stimulated.

able *adj.* accomplished, adept, adequate, adroit, capable, clever, competent, deft, dexterous, effective, efficient, experienced, expert, fit,

fitted, gifted, ingenious, masterly, powerful, practised, proficient, qualified, skilful, skilled, strong, talented.
antonyms incapable, incompetent, ineffective.

able-bodied *adj.* fit, hale, hardy, healthy, hearty, lusty, powerful, robust, sound, stalwart, staunch, stout, strapping, strong, sturdy, tough, vigorous.
antonyms delicate, infirm.

ablutions *n.* bath, bathing, cleansing, purgation, purging, purification, shower, wash, washing.

abnormal *adj.* aberrant, anomalous, curious, deviant, different, divergent, eccentric, erratic, exceptional, extraordinary, irregular, odd, paranormal, peculiar, queer, singular, strange, uncanny, uncommon, unexpected, unnatural, unusual, wayward, weird.
antonyms normal, straight, typical.

abnormality *n.* aberration, anomaly, bizarreness, deformity, deviation, difference, divergence, eccentricity, exception, flaw, irregularity, oddity, peculiarity, singularity, strangeness, unnaturalness, unusualness.
antonym normality.

abolish *v.* annul, blot out, cancel, destroy, do away with, eliminate, end, eradicate, get rid of, invalidate, nullify, obliterate, overthrow, overturn, put an end to, quash, repeal, repudiate, rescind, revoke, stamp out, subvert, suppress, terminate.
antonyms authorise, continue, retain.

abolition *n.* abrogation, annulment, cancellation, dissolution, end, ending, eradication, extinction, invalidation, nullification, obliteration, overturning, quashing, repeal, repudiation, subversion, suppression, termination.
antonyms continuance, retention.

abominable *adj.* abhorrent, accursed, appalling, atrocious, contemptible, despicable, detestable, disgusting, execrable, foul, hateful, heinous, horrible, horrid, loathsome, nauseating, nauseous, obnoxious, odious, repellent, reprehensible, repugnant, repulsive, revolting, terrible, vile, wretched.
antonyms delightful, desirable, pleasant.

abominate *v.* abhor, condemn, despise, detest, execrate, hate, loathe.
antonyms adore, love.

abomination *n.* abhorrence, anathema, aversion, bête noire, curse, disgrace, disgust, distaste, evil, hate, hatred, horror, hostility, loathing, offence, outrage, plague, repugnance, revulsion, torment.
antonyms adoration, delight.

aboriginal *adj.* ancient, domestic, earliest, first, indigenous, native, original, primal, primary, primeval, primitive, primordial, pristine.

aborigine *n.* aboriginal, native.
antonyms immigrant, incomer.

abort *v.* arrest, call off, check, end, fail, frustrate, halt, miscarry, nullify, stop, terminate, thwart.
antonym continue.

abortion *n.* failure, frustration, misadventure, misbirth, miscarriage, termination.
antonyms continuation, success.

abortive *adj.* barren, failed, failing, fruitless, futile, idle, ineffective, miscarried, sterile, unavailing, unproductive, unsuccessful, useless, vain.
antonyms fruitful, successful.

abound *v.* be plentiful, flourish, increase, overflow, proliferate, run riot, superabound, swarm, swell, teem, thrive.
antonym be in short supply.

about *prep.* **1** as regards, concerned with, concerning, connected with, referring to, regarding, relating to, with reference to, with regard to, with respect to. **2** adjacent to, beside, close to, near, nearby. **3** all over, around, encircling, encompassing, round, surrounding, throughout.
adv. **1** almost, approaching, approximately, around, in the region of, more or less, nearing, nearly, roughly. **2** active, from place to place, here and there, present, to and fro.
about to all but, intending to, on the point of, on the verge of, preparing to, ready to.

about-turn *n.* about-face, apostasy, backtrack, reversal, right-about (face), turnabout, turn(a)round, U-turn, volte-face.

above *prep.* before, beyond, exceeding, higher than, in excess of, on top of, over, prior to, superior to, surpassing, upon.
antonyms below, under.
adv. aloft, earlier, on high, overhead.
antonym below.
adj. above-mentioned, above-stated, earlier, foregoing, preceding, previous, prior.

above-board *adj.* candid, fair, fair and square, forthright, frank, guileless, honest, honourable, legitimate, on the level, open, reputable, square, straight, straightforward, true, trustworthy, truthful, upright, veracious.
antonyms dishonest, shady, underhand.

abrade *v.* chafe, erase, erode, grind, rub off, scour, scrape, wear away, wear down.

abrasion *n.* abrading, chafe, chafing, erosion, friction, grating, graze, grinding, rubbing, scouring, scrape, scraping, scratch, scratching, wearing away, wearing down.

abrasive *adj.* annoying, biting, caustic, chafing, frictional, galling, grating, harsh, hurtful, irritating, nasty, rough, scraping, scratching, sharp, unpleasant.
antonyms pleasant, smooth.

abreast *adj.* acquainted, au courant, au fait, conversant, familiar, in the picture, in touch, informed, knowledgeable, up to date.
antonyms out of touch, unaware.

abridge *v.* abbreviate, abstract, compress, concentrate, condense, contract, curtail, cut (down), decrease, digest, lessen, précis, prune, reduce, shorten, summarise.
antonyms amplify, expand, pad out.

abridgement *n.* abstract, concentration, contraction, cutting, decrease, digest, diminishing, epitome, limitation, outline, précis, reduction, restriction, résumé, shortening, summary, synopsis.

antonyms expansion, padding.

abroad *adv.* **1** extensively, far and wide, in foreign parts, out of the country, overseas, widely. **2** about, around, at large, circulating, current.
antonym **1** at home.

abrupt *adj.* blunt, brief, brisk, broken, brusque, curt, direct, disconnected, discontinuous, gruff, hasty, hurried, impolite, irregular, jerky, precipitate, precipitous, quick, rapid, rough, rude, sharp, sheer, short, snappy, steep, sudden, surprising, swift, terse, uncivil, uneven, unexpected, unforeseen.
antonyms ceremonious, expansive, leisurely, polite.

abscond *v.* bolt, clear out, decamp, disappear, escape, flee, fly, make off, quit, run off, take French leave.

absence *n.* dearth, default, defect, deficiency, lack, need, non-appearance, non-attendance, non-existence, omission, scarcity, truancy, unavailability, vacancy, want.
antonyms appearance, existence, presence.

absent *adj.* **1** away, gone, lacking, missing, not present, out, truant, unavailable. **2** absent-minded, day-dreaming, distracted, dreamy, elsewhere, faraway, inattentive, oblivious, preoccupied, unaware, unheeding, vacant, vague.
antonyms **1** present. **2** alert, aware.

absent-minded *adj.* absent, absorbed, abstracted, distracted, dreaming, dreamy, engrossed, faraway, forgetful, heedless, impractical, inattentive, musing, oblivious, pensive, preoccupied, scatterbrained, unaware, unconscious, unheeding, unthinking, withdrawn.
antonyms attentive, matter-of-fact, practical.

absolute *adj.* **1** categorical, certain, complete, conclusive, consummate, decided, decisive, definite, definitive, downright, entire, exact, exhaustive, final, flawless, free, full, genuine, out-and-out, outright, perfect, positive, precise, pure, sheer, supreme, sure, thorough, total, undivided, unequivocal, unmixed, unqualified, unquestionable, utter. **2** autocratic, despotic, dictatorial, omnipotent, sovereign, totalitarian, tyrannical, unlimited, unrestricted.

absolutely *adv.* categorically, certainly, completely, conclusively, dead, decidedly, decisively, definitely, entirely, exactly, exhaustively, finally, fully, genuinely, infallibly, perfectly, positively, precisely, purely, supremely, surely, thoroughly, totally, truly, unambiguously, unconditionally, unequivocally, unquestionably, utterly, wholly.

absolve *v.* acquit, clear, deliver, discharge, emancipate, excuse, exempt, exonerate, forgive, free, justify, let off, liberate, loose, pardon, ransom, redeem, release, remit, set free, vindicate.
antonym charge.

absorb *v.* assimilate, consume, devour, digest, drink in, engross, engulf, enthral, exhaust, fascinate, fill (up), hold, immerse, involve, monopolise, occupy, preoccupy, receive, retain, soak up, submerge, suck up, take in, understand.
antonyms dissipate, exude.

absorbing *adj.* amusing, captivating, compulsive, diverting, engrossing, entertaining, enthralling, fascinating, gripping, interesting, intriguing, preoccupying, riveting, spellbinding, unputdownable.
antonyms boring, off-putting.

abstain *v.* avoid, cease, decline, deny, desist, forbear, forgo, give up, keep from, refrain, refuse, reject, renounce, resist, shun, stop.
antonym indulge.

abstemious *adj.* abstinent, ascetic, austere, disciplined, frugal, moderate, restrained, self-denying, self-disciplined, sober, sparing, temperate.
antonyms gluttonous, intemperate, luxurious.

abstention *n.* abstaining, abstinence, avoidance, forbearance, frugality, non-indulgence, refraining, refusal, restraint, self-control, self-denial, self-discipline, self-restraint, sobriety.

abstinence *n.* abstemiousness, asceticism, avoidance, forbearance, frugality, moderation, non-indulgence, refraining, self-denial, self-discipline, self-restraint, sobriety, teetotalism, temperance.
antonyms indulgence, self-indulgence.

abstract *adj.* abstruse, academic, complex, conceptual, deep, general, generalised, hypothetical, indefinite, intellectual, metaphysical, non-concrete, philosophical, profound, subtle, theoretical, unpractical, unrealistic.
antonyms actual, concrete, real.
n. abridgement, compression, digest, epitome, essence, outline, précis, recapitulation, résumé, summary, synopsis.
v. abbreviate, abridge, compress, condense, detach, digest, dissociate, extract, isolate, outline, précis, remove, separate, shorten, summarise, withdraw.
antonyms expand, insert.

abstracted *adj.* absent, absent-minded, distrait(e), dreamy, faraway, inattentive, pensive, preoccupied, remote, withdrawn.
antonym alert.

abstraction *n.* **1** concept, conception, formula, generalisation, generality, hypothesis, idea, notion, theorem, theory, thought. **2** absent-mindedness, absorption, distraction, dream, dreaminess, inattention, pensiveness, preoccupation. **3** extraction, isolation, separation, withdrawal.

abstruse *adj.* abstract, cryptic, dark, deep, difficult, enigmatic, hidden, incomprehensible, mysterious, mystical, obscure, occult, perplexing, profound, puzzling, subtle, tortuous, unfathomable, vague.
antonyms concrete, obvious, simple.

absurd *adj.* comical, crazy, daft, derisory, fantastic, farcical, foolish, funny, humorous, idiotic, illogical, implausible, incongruous, irrational, laughable, ludicrous, meaningless, non-sensical, paradoxical, preposterous, ridiculous, risible, senseless, silly, stupid, unreasonable, untenable.

antonyms logical, rational, sensible.
abundant *adj.* ample, bountiful, copious, exuberant, filled, full, generous, in plenty, lavish, overflowing, plentiful, profuse, rank, rich, teeming, well-supplied.
antonyms scarce, sparse.
abuse *v.* damage, deceive, defame, disparage, exploit, harm, hurt, ill-treat, injure, insult, libel, malign, maltreat, misapply, misuse, molest, oppress, revile, scold, slander, smear, spoil, swear at, take advantage of, upbraid, violate, wrong.
antonyms care for, cherish, praise.
n. cursing, damage, defamation, disparagement, exploitation, harm, hurt, ill-treatment, imposition, injury, insults, libel, maltreatment, misconduct, misuse, offence, oppression, reproach, scolding, sin, slander, spoiling, swearing, tirade, upbraiding, violation, wrong, wrong-doing.
antonyms attention, care.
abusive *adj.* censorious, cruel, defamatory, derogatory, destructive, disparaging, harmful, hurtful, injurious, insulting, libellous, maligning, offensive, pejorative, reproachful, reviling, rough, rude, scathing, scolding, slanderous, upbraiding, vilifying.
antonyms complimentary, polite.
academic *adj.* abstract, bookish, conjectural, educational, erudite, highbrow, hypothetical, impractical, instructional, learned, literary, notional, pedagogical, scholarly, scholastic, speculative, studious, theoretical, well-read.
n. don, fellow, lecturer, man of letters, master, pedant, professor, scholar, student, tutor.
academy *n.* college, institute, school, university.
accelerate *v.* advance, expedite, facilitate, forward, further, hasten, hurry, pick up speed, precipitate, promote, quicken, speed, speed up, step up, stimulate.
antonyms decelerate, delay, slow down.
accent *n.* accentuation, articulation, beat, cadence, emphasis, enunciation, force, inflection, intensity, intonation, pitch, pronunciation, pulsation, pulse, rhythm, stress, tone.
v. emphasise, stress, underline.
accentuate *v.* accent, deepen, emphasise, highlight, intensify, strengthen, stress, underline.
antonyms play down, weaken.
accept *v.* **1** acquire, gain, obtain, receive, secure, take. **2** acknowledge, admit, adopt, agree to, allow, approve, believe, consent to, recognise, take on. **3** abide by, bear, face up to, put up with, stand, stomach, tolerate, yield to.
antonyms **1** refuse, turn down. **2** reject.
acceptable *adj.* adequate, admissible, all right, conventional, correct, desirable, grateful, gratifying, moderate, passable, pleasant, satisfactory, suitable, tolerable, unexceptionable, welcome.
antonyms unacceptable, unsatisfactory, unwelcome.
acceptance *n.* accepting, acknowledgement, acquiring, admission, adoption, affirmation, agreement, approval, assent, belief, concession, concurrence, consent, credence, gaining, getting, having, obtaining, OK, permission, ratification, receipt, recognition, securing, stamp of approval, taking, tolerance, toleration, undertaking.
antonyms dissent, refusal, rejection.
accepted *adj.* acceptable, acknowledged, admitted, agreed, approved, authorised, common, confirmed, conventional, correct, customary, established, normal, ratified, received, recognised, regular, sanctioned, standard, time-honoured, traditional, universal, unwritten, usual.
antonyms controversial, unorthodox.
access *n.* admission, admittance, approach, course, door, entering, entrance, entry, gateway, key, passage, path, road.
antonyms exit, outlet.
accessible *adj.* achievable, approachable, attainable, available, exposed, friendly, get-at-able, handy, informal, near, nearby, obtainable, on hand, open, possible, reachable, ready, sociable.
antonyms inaccessible, remote, unapproachable.
accession *n.* acquisition, addition, agreement, assumption, attainment, consent, enlargement, entering upon, increase, installation, purchase, submission, succession, taking over, yielding.
accessory *n.* accompaniment, accomplice, addition, adornment, aid, appendage, assistant, associate, attachment, colleague, component, confederate, convenience, decoration, extension, extra, frill, help, helper, partner, supplement, trimming.
accident *n.* blow, calamity, casualty, chance, collision, contingency, crash, disaster, fate, fluke, fortuity, fortune, hazard, luck, misadventure, miscarriage, mischance, misfortune, mishap, pile-up, prang, serendipity, shunt.
accidental *adj.* casual, chance, fluky, fortuitous, haphazard, inadvertent, incidental, random, uncalculated, uncertain, unexpected, unforeseen, unintended, unintentional, unlooked-for, unplanned.
antonyms calculated, intentional, premeditated.
acclaim *v.* announce, applaud, approve, celebrate, cheer, clap, commend, crown, exalt, extol, honour, praise, salute, welcome.
n. acclamation, applause, approval, celebration, cheering, clapping, commendation, eulogising, eulogy, exaltation, honour, ovation, praise, welcome.
antonym criticism.
acclamation *n.* acclaim, applause, approbation, cheer, cheering, cheers, commendation, declaration, enthusiasm, homage, ovation, praise, shouting, tribute.
antonym disapproval.
acclimatise *v.* accommodate, accustom, adapt, adjust, attune, conform, familiarise, get used to, habituate.
accolade *n.* award, honour, laurels, praise.
accommodate *v.* **1** board, house, lodge, put up, shelter. **2** aid, assist, comply, conform, help, oblige, provide, serve, supply. **3** acclimatise,

accustom, adapt, adjust, compose, fit, harmonise, modify, reconcile, settle.

accommodating *adj.* considerate, co-operative, friendly, helpful, hospitable, indulgent, kind, obliging, polite, sympathetic, unselfish, willing.
antonyms disobliging, rude.

accommodation *n.* bed and breakfast, billet, board, digs, domicile, dwelling, harbouring, house, housing, lodgings, quarters, residence, shelter.

accompaniment *n.* accessory, background, back-up, complement, concomitant, support.

accompany *v.* attend, belong to, chaperon, co-exist, coincide, complement, conduct, convoy, escort, follow, go with, occur with, supplement, usher.

accomplice *n.* abettor, accessory, ally, assistant, associate, collaborator, colleague, confederate, conspirator, helper, helpmate, henchman, mate, participator, partner.

accomplish *v.* achieve, attain, bring about, carry out, complete, conclude, consummate, discharge, do, effect, engineer, execute, finish, fulfil, manage, obtain, perform, produce, realise.

accomplished *adj.* adept, adroit, consummate, cultivated, expert, gifted, masterly, polished, practised, professional, proficient, skilful, skilled, talented.
antonyms incapable, inexpert, unskilled.

accomplishment *n.* ability, achievement, aptitude, art, attainment, capability, carrying out, completion, conclusion, consummation, deed, discharge, doing, execution, exploit, faculty, feat, finishing, forte, fruition, fulfilment, gift, management, perfection, performance, production, proficiency, realisation, skill, stroke, talent, triumph.

accord *v.* agree, allow, bestow, concur, confer, conform, correspond, endow, give, grant, harmonise, match, render, suit, tender.
antonyms deny, disagree.
n. accordance, agreement, assent, correspondence, harmony, sympathy, unanimity, unity.
antonyms conflict, discord, disharmony.

accordance *n.* agreement, concert, conformity, correspondence.

according to after, after the manner of, commensurate with, consistent with, in accordance with, in conformity with, in keeping with, in line with, in proportion to, in relation to, in the light of, in the manner of, obedient to.

accordingly *adv.* appropriately, as a result, consequently, correspondingly, hence, in accord with, in accordance, in consequence, properly, so, suitably, therefore, thus.

accost *v.* approach, button-hole, confront, detain, halt, importune, salute, solicit, stop, waylay.

account *n.* **1** chronicle, communiqué, description, explanation, ground, history, memoir, narrative, note, portrayal, presentation, record, report, sketch, statement, story, tale, version, write-up. **2** balance, bill, book, books, charge, check, computation, inventory, invoice, ledger, reckoning, register, score, statement, tab, tally, tick.

account for answer for, clear up, destroy, elucidate, explain, illuminate, incapacitate, justify, kill, put paid to, rationalise, vindicate.

accountable *adj.* amenable, answerable, bound, charged with, liable, obliged, responsible.

accredited *adj.* appointed, approved, attested, authorised, certified, commissioned, empowered, guaranteed, licensed, official, qualified, recognised, sanctioned, vouched for.
antonym unauthorised.

accrue *v.* accumulate, amass, arise, be added, build up, collect, emanate, enlarge, ensue, fall due, gather, grow, increase, issue, proceed, result, spring up.

accumulate *v.* accrue, aggregate, amass, assemble, build up, collect, cumulate, gather, grow, hoard, increase, multiply, pile up, stash, stockpile, store.
antonym disseminate.

accumulation *n.* assembly, build-up, collection, conglomeration, gathering, growth, heap, hoard, increase, mass, pile, reserve, stack, stock, stockpile, store.

accuracy *n.* authenticity, carefulness, closeness, correctness, exactness, faithfulness, fidelity, precision, truth, veracity.
antonym inaccuracy.

accurate *adj.* authentic, careful, close, correct, exact, factual, faithful, faultless, just, mathematical, meticulous, minute, nice, perfect, precise, proper, regular, right, rigorous, scrupulous, sound, spot-on, strict, true, truthful, unerring, veracious, well-directed, well-judged, word-perfect.
antonyms imprecise, inaccurate, inexact, wrong.

accusation *n.* allegation, charge, complaint, denunciation, impeachment, imputation, incrimination, indictment, recrimination.

accuse *v.* allege, arraign, attribute, blame, censure, charge, cite, criminate, denounce, impeach, impugn, impute, incriminate, indict, inform against, recriminate.

accustomed *adj.* acclimatised, acquainted, adapted, confirmed, conventional, customary, disciplined, established, everyday, expected, familiar, fixed, general, given to, habitual, in the habit of, normal, ordinary, prevailing, regular, routine, seasoned, traditional, trained, used, usual, wonted.
antonyms unaccustomed, unusual.

ache *v.* agonise, crave, desire, grieve, hanker, hunger, hurt, itch, long, mourn, need, pain, pine, pound, smart, sorrow, suffer, throb, twinge, yearn.
n. anguish, grief, hurt, itch, misery, mourning, need, pain, pang, pounding, smarting, soreness, sorrow, suffering, throb, throbbing, yearning.

achieve *v.* accomplish, acquire, attain, bring about, carry out, complete, consummate, do, earn, effect, execute, finish, fulfil, gain, get, manage, obtain, perform, procure, produce,

reach, realise, strike, succeed, win.
antonyms fail, miss.

achievement *n.* accomplishment, acquirement, act, attainment, completion, deed, effort, execution, exploit, feat, fruition, fulfilment, performance, production, qualification, realisation, stroke, success.

acid *adj.* acerbic, biting, bitter, caustic, corrosive, cutting, harsh, hurtful, ill-natured, incisive, mordant, morose, pungent, sharp, sour, stinging, tart, trenchant, vinegary, vitriolic.

acknowledge *v.* **1** accept, admit, allow, concede, confess, declare, grant, recognise. **2** address, greet, notice, recognise. **3** answer, confirm, reply to, respond to.

acknowledged *adj.* accepted, accredited, answered, approved, attested, avowed, conceded, confessed, confirmed, declared, professed, recognised, returned.

acknowledgement *n.* **1** acceptance, admission, confession, declaration, profession, recognition. **2** greeting, notice, recognition, salutation. **3** affirmation, answer, appreciation, gratitude, reaction, reply, response, thanks, tribute.

acquaint *v.* accustom, advise, announce, brief, disclose, divulge, enlighten, familiarise, inform, notify, reveal, tell.

acquaintance *n.* associate, association, awareness, chum, colleague, companionship, contact, experience, familiarity, fellowship, friend, intimacy, knowledge, relationship, understanding.

acquiesce *v.* accede, accept, agree, allow, approve, assent, comply, concur, conform, consent, defer, give in, submit, yield.
antonyms disagree, object.

acquiescence *n.* acceptance, accession, agreement, approval, assent, compliance, conformity, consent, deference, giving in, obedience, sanction, submission, yielding.
antonyms disagreement, rebelliousness.

acquire *v.* achieve, appropriate, attain, buy, collect, cop, earn, gain, gather, get, net, obtain, pick up, procure, realise, receive, secure, win.
antonyms forfeit, forgo, relinquish.

acquisition *n.* accession, achievement, appropriation, attainment, buy, find, gain, learning, possession, procurement, property, purchase, pursuit, securing, take-over.

acquisitive *adj.* avaricious, covetous, grabbing, grasping, greedy, insatiable, possessive.
antonym generous.

acquit *v.* absolve, bear, behave, clear, conduct, deliver, discharge, dismiss, excuse, exonerate, free, fulfil, liberate, release, relieve, repay, reprieve, satisfy, settle, vindicate.
antonym convict.

acquittal *n.* absolution, clearance, deliverance, discharge, dismissal, exculpation, excusing, exoneration, freeing, liberation, release, relief, reprieve, vindication.
antonym conviction.

acrid *adj.* acerbic, acid, acrimonious, biting, bitter, burning, caustic, cutting, harsh, incisive, irritating, malicious, nasty, pungent, sarcastic, sardonic, sharp, stinging, trenchant, venomous, virulent, vitriolic.

acrimonious *adj.* abusive, biting, bitter, censorious, cutting, ill-tempered, severe, sharp, spiteful, trenchant, virulent.
antonyms irenic, kindly, peaceable.

acrimony *n.* acerbity, astringency, bitterness, gall, harshness, ill-temper, ill-will, irascibility, mordancy, petulance, rancour, resentment, sarcasm, trenchancy, virulence.

acrobat *n.* balancer, gymnast, somersaulter, stunt-girl, stuntman, tumbler.

act *n.* **1** accomplishment, achievement, action, deed, doing, enterprise, execution, exploit, feat, manoeuvre, move, operation, step, stroke, undertaking. **2** affectation, dissimulation, fake, feigning, front, make-believe, pretence, sham, show. **3** bill, decree, edict, law, measure, ordinance, resolution, statute. **4** gig, performance, sketch, turn.
v. **1** behave, carry out, conduct, do, execute, exert, function, make, operate, work. **2** assume, enact, feign, imitate, impersonate, mime, mimic, perform, play, portray, pretend, put on, represent, simulate.
act up carry on, cause trouble, give bother, give trouble, malfunction, mess about, misbehave, muck about, play up, rock the boat.
act (up)on 1 carry out, comply with, conform to, follow, fulfil, heed, obey, take. **2** affect, alter, change, influence, modify, transform.

acting *adj.* interim, provisional, reserve, stand-by, stop-gap, substitute, supply, temporary.
n. artistry, characterisation, dramatics, imitating, impersonation, melodrama, performance, performing, play-acting, portrayal, stagecraft, theatre, theatricals.

action *n.* **1** accomplishment, achievement, act, activity, agency, cause, deed, effect, effort, endeavour, energy, enterprise, exercise, exertion, exploit, feat, force, functioning, influence, liveliness, mechanism, motion, move, movement, operation, performance, power, proceeding, process, spirit, undertaking, vigour, work. **2** battle, clash, combat, conflict, contest, engagement, fight, fray, skirmish, warfare. **3** case, lawsuit, litigation, prosecution, suit.

activate *v.* animate, arouse, energise, excite, fire, galvanise, impel, initiate, mobilise, motivate, move, prompt, propel, rouse, set in motion, set off, start, stimulate, stir, switch on, trigger.
antonyms arrest, deactivate, stop.

active *adj.* **1** activist, ambitious, assertive, busy, committed, devoted, diligent, engaged, enterprising, enthusiastic, forceful, forward, full, hard-working, industrious, involved, militant, occupied, on the go, spirited, vital. **2** agile, alert, animated, energetic, light-footed, lively, nimble, quick, sprightly, vigorous. **3** functioning, in operation, running, working.
antonyms **1** passive. **2** dormant, inert. **3** inactive.

activity *n.* **1** action, activeness, bustle, commotion, deed, exercise, exertion, hustle, industry, interest, labour, life, liveliness, motion, movement. **2** act, endeavour, enterprise, hobby, job, occupation, pastime, project, pursuit, scheme, task, undertaking, venture, work.

actor *n.* actress, artist, comedian, ham, impersonator, masquerader, mime, participant, participator, performer, play-actor, player.

actual *adj.* absolute, authentic, bona fide, certain, concrete, confirmed, current, definite, existent, factual, genuine, indisputable, legitimate, live, living, material, physical, positive, present, present-day, prevailing, real, realistic, substantial, tangible, true, truthful, unquestionable, verified, veritable.
antonyms apparent, imaginary, theoretical.

actuality *n.* fact, factuality, historicity, materiality, reality, realness, substance, substantiality, truth, verity.

actually *adv.* absolutely, as a matter of fact, as it happens, essentially, in fact, in reality, in truth, indeed, really, truly.

actuate *v.* activate, animate, arouse, cause, circulate, dispose, drive, excite, impel, incite, induce, influence, inspire, instigate, lead, mobilise, motivate, move, prod, prompt, propel, quicken, rouse, spur, stimulate, stir, urge.

acumen *n.* astuteness, cleverness, discernment, discrimination, ingenuity, insight, intelligence, intuition, judgement, keenness, penetration, perception, quickness, sense, sharpness, shrewdness, wisdom, wit.
antonym obtuseness.

acute *adj.* **1** crucial, cutting, dangerous, decisive, distressing, extreme, grave, intense, poignant, serious, severe, sharp, urgent, violent, vital. **2** astute, discerning, incisive, judicious, keen, observant, penetrating, perceptive, sharp, shrewd. **3** keen, powerful, sensitive.
antonyms **1** mild, slight. **2** obtuse. **3** poor.

adamant *adj.* determined, firm, fixed, hard, immovable, inflexible, insistent, intransigent, resolute, rigid, set, stiff, stubborn, tough, unbending, uncompromising, unrelenting, unshakable, unyielding.
antonyms flexible, hesitant, yielding.

adapt *v.* acclimatise, adjust, alter, apply, change, comply, conform, convert, customise, familiarise, fashion, fit, harmonise, match, modify, prepare, qualify, remodel, shape, suit, tailor.

adaptable *adj.* adjustable, alterable, amenable, changeable, compliant, conformable, convertible, easy-going, flexible, modifiable, plastic, resilient, variable, versatile.
antonyms inflexible, refractory.

adaptation *n.* accommodation, adjustment, alteration, change, conversion, modification, refitting, remodelling, reshaping, revision, reworking, shift, transformation, variation, version.

add *v.* affix, annex, append, attach, augment, combine, count, include, join, reckon, sum up, supplement, tack on, tot up, total.
antonyms subtract, take away.
add up 1 add, count (up), reckon, sum up, tally, tot up, total. **2** amount, come to, constitute, indicate. **3** be consistent, be plausible, be reasonable, fit, hang together, make sense, mean, signify.

addict *n.* adherent, buff, devotee, enthusiast, fan, fiend, follower, freak, junkie, mainliner, tripper, user.

addicted *adj.* absorbed, accustomed, dedicated, dependent, devoted, disposed, fond, hooked, inclined, obsessed.

addiction *n.* craving, dependence, habit, monkey, obsession.

addition *n.* **1** accession, accessory, addendum, adding, additive, adjunct, annexation, appendage, appendix, attachment, enlargement, extension, extra, gain, inclusion, increase, increasing, increment, supplement. **2** counting, reckoning, summing-up, totalling, totting-up.
antonyms **1** removal. **2** subtraction.
in addition additionally, also, as well, besides, further, furthermore, moreover, over and above, too.

additional *adj.* added, additive, appended, extra, fresh, further, increased, more, new, other, spare, supplementary.

address *n.* **1** abode, department, direction, dwelling, home, house, inscription, location, lodging, place, residence, situation, whereabouts. **2** discourse, dissertation, lecture, sermon, speech, talk.
v. **1** accost, approach, button-hole, greet, hail, invoke, lecture, salute, speak to, talk to. **2** apply (oneself) to, attend to, concentrate on, devote (oneself) to, engage in, focus on, take care of, turn to, undertake.

adept *adj.* able, accomplished, adroit, deft, experienced, expert, masterly, nimble, polished, practised, proficient, skilled, versed.
antonyms bungling, incompetent, inept.
n. dab hand, expert, genius, maestro, master, old hand, pastmaster, wizard.
antonyms bungler, incompetent.

adequate *adj.* able, acceptable, capable, commensurate, competent, enough, fair, fit, passable, presentable, requisite, respectable, satisfactory, serviceable, sufficient, suitable, tolerable.
antonyms inadequate, insufficient.

adhere *v.* **1** attach, cement, cleave to, cling, coalesce, cohere, combine, fasten, fix, glue, hold, join, link, paste, stick. **2** abide by, agree, comply with, follow, fulfil, heed, keep, obey, observe, respect, stand by.

adherent *n.* admirer, advocate, devotee, disciple, enthusiast, fan, follower, freak, hanger-on, henchman, nut, partisan, satellite, supporter, upholder, votary.

adhesion *n.* adherence, adhesiveness, attachment, bond, cohesion, grip, holding fast, sticking.

adhesive *adj.* adherent, adhering, attaching, clinging, cohesive, gluey, gummy, holding, sticking, sticky, tacky.
n. cement, glue, gum, paste, tape.

adjacent *adj.* abutting, adjoining, alongside,

beside, bordering, close, contiguous, juxtaposed, near, neighbouring, next, touching.
antonyms distant, remote.

adjoin *v.* abut, add, annex, approximate, attach, border, combine, connect, couple, interconnect, join, link, meet, neighbour, touch, unite, verge.

adjourn *v.* continue, defer, delay, discontinue, interrupt, postpone, put off, recess, retire, stay, suspend.
antonyms assemble, convene.

adjournment *n.* break, deferment, deferral, delay, discontinuation, dissolution, interruption, pause, postponement, putting off, recess, stay, suspension.

adjudicate *v.* arbitrate, decide, determine, judge, pronounce, settle, umpire.

adjunct *n.* accessory, addendum, addition, appendage, appendix, auxiliary, complement, extension, supplement.

adjust *v.* acclimatise, accommodate, accustom, adapt, alter, arrange, balance, change, compose, concert, conform, convert, dispose, fine-tune, fit, fix, harmonise, jiggle, measure, modify, reconcile, rectify, regulate, remodel, set, settle, shape, square, suit, temper, tune.
antonyms disarrange, upset.

adjustable *adj.* adaptable, alterable, flexible, modifiable, movable.
antonyms fixed, inflexible.

adjustment *n.* acclimatisation, accommodation, adaptation, alteration, arrangement, arranging, conforming, conversion, fitting, fixing, harmonisation, modification, naturalisation, ordering, orientation, reconciliation, rectification, regulation, remodelling, setting, settlement, shaping, tuning.

ad-lib *v.* extemporise, improvise, invent, make up.
adj. extempore, impromptu, improvised, made up, off-the-cuff, spontaneous, unpremeditated, unprepared, unrehearsed.
antonym prepared.
adv. extemporaneously, extempore, impromptu, impulsively, off the cuff, off the top of one's head, spontaneously.

administer *v.* **1** conduct, control, direct, govern, head, lead, manage, officiate, organise, oversee, preside over, regulate, rule, run, superintend, supervise. **2** apply, contribute, disburse, dispense, dispose, distribute, dole out, execute, give, impose, measure out, mete out, provide, supply.

administration *n.* administering, control, direction, directorship, execution, executive, governing, governing body, government, leadership, management, ministry, organisation, overseeing, performance, regime, ruling, running, settlement, superintendence, supervision, term of office.

administrative *adj.* authoritative, directorial, executive, governmental, legislative, management, managerial, organisational, regulatory, supervisory.

administrator *n.* boss, controller, curator, custodian, director, governor, guardian, leader, manager, organiser, overseer, ruler, superintendent, supervisor, trustee.

admirable *adj.* choice, commendable, creditable, deserving, excellent, exquisite, fine, laudable, praiseworthy, rare, respected, superior, valuable, wonderful, worthy.
antonyms deplorable, despicable.

admiration *n.* adoration, affection, amazement, appreciation, approval, astonishment, delight, esteem, idolism, pleasure, praise, regard, respect, reverence, surprise, veneration, wonder, worship.
antonym contempt.

admire *v.* adore, applaud, appreciate, approve, esteem, idolise, laud, praise, respect, revere, value, venerate, worship.
antonyms censure, despise.

admirer *n.* adherent, boyfriend, devotee, disciple, enthusiast, fan, follower, idoliser, lover, suitor, supporter, sweetheart, worshipper.
antonyms critic, opponent.

admissible *adj.* acceptable, allowable, allowed, justifiable, lawful, legitimate, passable, permissible, permitted, tolerable, tolerated.
antonyms illegitimate, inadmissible.

admission *n.* **1** acceptance, acknowledgement, affirmation, allowance, concession, confession, declaration, divulgence, exposé, granting, initiation, introduction, profession, revelation. **2** access, admittance, disclosure, entrance, entry, inclusion.
antonyms **1** denial. **2** exclusion.

admit *v.* **1** accept, acknowledge, affirm, agree, allow, concede, confess, declare, disclose, divulge, grant, initiate, introduce, profess, receive, recognise, reveal. **2** allow to enter, give access, let in, permit, take in.
antonyms **1** deny. **2** exclude, shut out.

admittance *n.* acceptance, access, admitting, allowing, entrance, entry, letting in, reception.

adolescence *n.* boyhood, boyishness, childishness, development, girlhood, girlishness, immaturity, minority, puberty, teens, transition, youth, youthfulness.
antonym old age.

adolescent *adj.* boyish, girlish, growing, immature, juvenile, maturing, puerile, teenage, young, youthful.
n. juvenile, minor, teenager, youth.

adopt *v.* accept, appropriate, approve, assume, back, choose, embrace, endorse, follow, foster, maintain, ratify, select, support, take in, take on, take up.
antonyms disown, repudiate.

adorable *adj.* appealing, attractive, captivating, charming, darling, dear, delightful, enchanting, fetching, lovable, pleasing, precious, sweet, winning, winsome.
antonyms abominable, hateful.

adoration *n.* admiration, esteem, exaltation, glorification, honour, idolatry, love, reverence, veneration, worship.
antonyms abhorrence, detestation.

adore *v.* admire, cherish, dote on, esteem, exalt,

glorify, honour, idolatrise, idolise, love, revere, venerate, worship.
antonyms abhor, hate.

adorn *v.* bedeck, crown, deck, decorate, doll up, embellish, enhance, enrich, garnish, gild, grace, ornament, trim.

adulation *n.* acclaim, fawning, flattery, idolisation, personality cult, worship.
antonym abuse.

adult *adj.* developed, full-grown, fully grown, grown-up, mature, of age, ripe, ripened.
antonym immature.

adulterate *v.* contaminate, corrupt, debase, defile, deteriorate, devalue, dilute, pollute, taint, water down, weaken.
antonym refine.

advance *v.* **1** ameliorate, flourish, go ahead, go forward, improve, move on, proceed, progress, prosper. **2** accelerate, hasten, send forward, speed. **3** assist, benefit, facilitate, foster, further, grow, increase, promote, support, upgrade. **4** allege, bring forward, cite, furnish, offer, present, provide, submit, suggest, supply. **5** lend, pay beforehand, profit.
antonyms **1** retreat. **3** impede, retard.
n. **1** amelioration, breakthrough, development, furtherance, growth, headway, improvement, increase, progress, step. **2** credit, deposit, down payment, gain, loan, prepayment, profit, rise.
antonyms **1** recession, retreat.
adj. beforehand, early, foremost, forward, in front, leading, preliminary, prior.
in advance ahead, beforehand, earlier, early, in front, in the forefront, in the lead, previously, sooner.
antonyms behind, later.

advanced *adj.* ahead, avant-garde, extreme, foremost, forward, forward-looking, higher, leading, original, precocious, progressive.
antonyms backward, elementary, retarded.

advancement *n.* advance, betterment, development, forward movement, furtherance, gain, growth, headway, improvement, maturation, onward movement, preferment, progress, promotion, rise.
antonyms demotion, retardation.

advances *n.* approaches, attentions, moves, overtures, proposals, proposition.

advantage *n.* aid, asset, assistance, avail, benefit, blessing, convenience, edge, fruit, gain, good, help, hold, interest, lead, precedence, preeminence, profit, purchase, service, start, superiority, sway, upper hand, use, usefulness, utility, welfare.
antonyms disadvantage, drawback, hindrance.

advantageous *adj.* beneficial, convenient, favourable, gainful, helpful, opportune, profitable, remunerative, rewarding, superior, useful, valuable, worthwhile.
antonyms adverse, damaging, disadvantageous.

adventure *n.* chance, enterprise, experience, exploit, hazard, incident, occurrence, risk, speculation, undertaking, venture.

adventurer *n.* daredevil, fortune-hunter, gambler, hero, heroine, opportunist, speculator, venturer, voyager, wanderer.

adventurous *adj.* audacious, bold, daring, enterprising, headstrong, impetuous, intrepid, plucky, reckless, risky, venturesome.
antonyms cautious, chary, prudent.

adversary *n.* antagonist, assailant, attacker, competitor, contestant, enemy, foe, opponent, opposer, rival.
antonyms ally, supporter.

adverse *adj.* antagonistic, conflicting, contrary, counter, counter-productive, detrimental, disadvantageous, hostile, hurtful, inauspicious, injurious, inopportune, negative, noxious, opposing, opposite, reluctant, repugnant, uncongenial, unfavourable, unfortunate, unfriendly, unlucky, unwilling.
antonyms advantageous, favourable.

adversity *n.* affliction, bad luck, calamity, catastrophe, disaster, distress, hard times, hardship, ill-fortune, ill-luck, misery, misfortune, reverse, sorrow, suffering, trial, tribulation, trouble, woe, wretchedness.
antonym prosperity.

advertise *v.* announce, blazon, broadcast, declare, display, herald, inform, make known, notify, plug, praise, proclaim, promote, publicise, publish, push, trumpet.

advertisement *n.* ad, advert, announcement, bill, blurb, circular, commercial, display, handbill, handout, hype, leaflet, notice, placard, plug, poster, promotion, propaganda, publicity.

advice *n.* caution, communication, counsel, direction, do's and don'ts, guidance, help, information, injunction, instruction, intelligence, memorandum, notice, notification, opinion, recommendation, suggestion, view, warning, wisdom.

advisable *adj.* appropriate, apt, beneficial, correct, desirable, fit, fitting, judicious, profitable, proper, prudent, recommended, sensible, sound, suggested, suitable, wise.
antonyms foolish, inadvisable.

advise *v.* acquaint, caution, commend, counsel, forewarn, guide, inform, instruct, make known, notify, recommend, report, suggest, teach, tell, tutor, urge, warn.

adviser *n.* aide, authority, coach, consultant, counsel, counsellor, guide, helper, instructor, lawyer, mentor, monitor, righthand man, teacher, tutor.

advisory *adj.* advising, consultative, consulting, counselling, helping, hortatory, recommending.

advocate *v.* adopt, advise, argue for, campaign for, champion, countenance, defend, encourage, endorse, favour, justify, patronise, plead for, press for, promote, propose, recommend, subscribe to, support, uphold, urge.
antonyms deprecate, disparage, impugn.
n. **1** campaigner, champion, defender, pleader, promoter, proponent, speaker, spokesman, supporter, upholder, vindicator. **2** attorney, barrister, counsel, counsellor, lawyer, mediator, solicitor.

antonyms **1** critic, opponent.

affable *adj.* agreeable, amiable, amicable, approachable, benevolent, congenial, cordial, courteous, expansive, free, friendly, genial, good-humoured, good-natured, gracious, kindly, mild, obliging, open, pleasant, sociable, warm.
antonyms cool, reserved, reticent, unfriendly.

affair *n.* **1** activity, business, circumstance, concern, connection, episode, event, happening, incident, interest, matter, occurrence, operation, proceeding, project, question, reception, responsibility, subject, topic, transaction, undertaking. **2** amour, intrigue, liaison, relationship, romance.

affect *v.* **1** act on, afflict, alter, apply to, attack, bear upon, change, concern, disturb, grip, impinge upon, impress, influence, interest, involve, modify, move, overcome, penetrate, perturb, prevail over, regard, relate to, seize, soften, stir, strike, sway, touch, transform, trouble, upset. **2** adopt, aspire to, assume, contrive, counterfeit, fake, feign, imitate, pretend, profess, put on, sham, simulate.

affectation *n.* act, airs, appearance, artificiality, façade, imitation, insincerity, mannerism, pose, pretence, pretentiousness, sham, show, simulation.
antonyms artlessness, ingenuousness.

affected *adj.* artificial, assumed, contrived, counterfeit, fake, feigned, insincere, mannered, phoney, pompous, precious, pretentious, put-on, sham, simulated, stiff, studied, unnatural.
antonyms genuine, natural.

affection *n.* attachment, care, desire, devotion, favour, feeling, fondness, friendliness, good will, inclination, kindness, liking, love, partiality, passion, penchant, tenderness, warmth.
antonyms antipathy, dislike.

affectionate *adj.* amiable, attached, caring, cordial, devoted, doting, fond, friendly, kind, loving, responsive, tender, warm, warm-hearted.
antonyms cold, undemonstrative.

affilliation *n.* alliance, amalgamation, association, coalition, combination, confederation, connection, federation, joining, league, merger, relationship, syndication, union.

affirm *v.* assert, certify, confirm, corroborate, declare, endorse, maintain, pronounce, ratify, state, swear, testify, witness.
antonyms deny, reject.

affirmation *n.* affirmance, assertion, attestation, certification, confirmation, corroboration, declaration, endorsement, oath, pronouncement, ratification, statement, testimony, witness.

affirmative *adj.* agreeing, approving, assenting, concurring, confirming, corroborative, emphatic, positive.
antonyms dissenting, negative.

affix *v.* add, annex, append, attach, bind, connect, fasten, glue, join, paste, pin on, stick, tack, tag.
antonym detach.

afflict *v.* beset, burden, distress, grieve, harass, harm, hurt, oppress, pain, plague, strike, torment, torture, trouble, try, visit, wound, wring.
antonyms comfort, solace.

affliction *n.* adversity, calamity, cross, curse, depression, disaster, disease, distress, grief, hardship, illness, misery, misfortune, ordeal, pain, plague, sickness, sorrow, suffering, torment, trial, tribulation, trouble.
antonyms blessing, comfort, consolation, solace.

affluence *n.* abundance, fortune, opulence, plenty, profusion, property, prosperity, riches, substance, wealth, wealthiness.
antonym poverty.

affluent *adj.* comfortable, flush, loaded, moneyed, opulent, prosperous, rich, wealthy, well-off, well-to-do.
antonyms impoverished, poor.

afford *v.* **1** allow, bear, have enough for, manage, spare, sustain. **2** furnish, generate, give, grant, impart, offer, produce, provide, supply, yield.

affront *v.* abuse, anger, annoy, displease, incense, insult, irritate, offend, outrage, provoke, slight, snub, vex.
antonyms appease, compliment.
n. abuse, discourtesy, disrespect, indignity, injury, insult, offence, outrage, provocation, rudeness, slight, slur, snub, vexation, wrong.
antonym compliment.

afoot *adv.* about, afloat, brewing, circulating, current, going about, in preparation, in progress, in the air, in the wind.

afraid *adj.* alarmed, anxious, apprehensive, cowardly, distrustful, faint-hearted, fearful, frightened, intimidated, nervous, reluctant, scared, sorry, suspicious, timid, timorous, unhappy.
antonyms bold, confident, unafraid.

after *prep.* as a result of, behind, below, following, in consequence of, later, subsequent to.
antonym before.

aftermath *n.* after-effects, consequences, effects, end, outcome, repercussion, results, upshot, wake.

afternoon *n.* after lunch, siesta, tea-time.

again *adv.* **1** afresh, also, another time, besides, encore, furthermore, in addition, moreover, once more. **2** conversely, however, on the contrary, on the other hand, yet.

against *prep.* abutting, across, adjacent to, close up to, confronting, facing, fronting, hostile to, in contact with, in contrast to, in defiance of, in exchange for, in opposition to, in the face of, on, opposed to, opposing, opposite to, resisting, touching, versus.
antonyms for, pro.

age *n.* **1** (a)eon, date, day, days, duration, epoch, era, generation, period, span, time, years. **2** decline, dotage, elderliness, maturity, old age, senility, seniority.
antonym **2** youth.
v. decline, degenerate, deteriorate, grow old,

mature, mellow, ripen, season.

agency *n.* **1** bureau, business, department, office, organisation, work. **2** action, activity, effect, force, influence, instrumentality, intervention, means, mechanism, medium, operation, power, workings.

agent *n.* **1** actor, agency, delegate, deputy, doer, emissary, envoy, functionary, go-between, intermediary, middleman, mover, negotiator, operative, operator, performer, rep, representative, substitute, worker. **2** cause, channel, force, instrument, means, vehicle.

aggravate *v.* **1** exacerbate, exaggerate, heighten, increase, intensify, magnify, worsen. **2** annoy, exasperate, harass, incense, inflame, irk, irritate, pester, provoke, tease, vex.
antonyms **1** alleviate, improve. **2** appease, mollify.

aggregate *n.* accumulation, amount, collection, combination, entirety, generality, sum, total, totality, whole.
adj. accumulated, added, collected, collective, combined, complete, composite, cumulative, mixed, total, united.
antonyms individual, particular.
v. accumulate, add up, amount to, assemble, cluster, collect, combine, conglomerate, heap, mix, total.

aggression *n.* anger, antagonism, assault, attack, belligerence, combativeness, destructiveness, hostility, incursion, injury, intrusion, invasion, militancy, offence, offensive, onslaught, provocation, raid.
antonyms gentleness, passivity, peace, resistance.

aggressive *adj.* argumentative, assertive, belligerent, bold, contentious, destructive, forceful, go-ahead, hostile, intrusive, invasive, offensive, provocative, pushy, quarrelsome, ruthless, vigorous, zealous.
antonyms friendly, peaceable, submissive, timid.

aggrieved *adj.* distressed, harmed, hurt, ill-used, injured, insulted, maltreated, offended, pained, resentful, saddened, unhappy, wronged.
antonym pleased.

aghast *adj.* afraid, amazed, appalled, astonished, astounded, confounded, dismayed, frightened, horrified, horror-struck, shocked, startled, stunned, stupefied, terrified, thunder-struck.

agile *adj.* active, acute, adroit, alert, brisk, clever, fleet, flexible, limber, lively, mobile, nimble, prompt, quick, quick-witted, sharp, sprightly, spry, swift.
antonyms clumsy, stiff.

agitate *v.* alarm, arouse, beat, confuse, convulse, discompose, disconcert, disquiet, distract, disturb, excite, ferment, flurry, fluster, incite, inflame, rattle, rouse, ruffle, shake, stimulate, stir, trouble, unnerve, unsettle, upset, work up, worry.
antonyms calm, tranquillise.

agitated *adj.* anxious, discomposed, disturbed, feverish, flurried, flustered, insecure, jumpy, nervous, restless, ruffled, twitchy, uneasy, unsettled, upset, wrought-up.
antonyms calm, composed.

agitator *n.* inciter, instigator, rabble-rouser, revolutionary, stirrer, troublemaker.

agonise *v.* strive, struggle, suffer, worry, wrestle, writhe.

agony *n.* affliction, anguish, distress, misery, pain, spasm, suffering, throes, torment, torture, tribulation, woe, wretchedness.

agree *v.* **1** accord, concur, conform, correspond, fit, match, see eye to eye, settle, suit, tally. **2** accede, admit, allow, assent, comply, concede, consent, grant, permit, yield.
antonyms **1** conflict, differ, disagree. **2** refuse.

agreeable *adj.* **1** acceptable, appropriate, attractive, congenial, consenting, consistent, delightful, enjoyable, fitting, gratifying, in accord, likeable, palatable, pleasant, proper, satisfying, suitable. **2** amenable, complying, responsive, sympathetic, well-disposed, willing.
antonyms **1** disagreeable, distasteful, nasty.

agreement *n.* **1** arrangement, bargain, compact, contract, covenant, deal, pact, settlement, treaty, understanding. **2** acceptance, accord, adherence, affinity, compatibility, compliance, concord, concurrence, conformity, consistency, correspondence, harmony, similarity, sympathy, unanimity, union.
antonym **2** disagreement.

agricultural *adj.* agrarian, agronomic, farming.

agriculture *n.* agronomics, cultivation, culture, farming, husbandry, tillage.

ahead *adj., adv.* advanced, along, at an advantage, at the head, before, earlier on, forwards, in advance, in front, in the forefront, in the lead, leading, onwards, superior, to the fore, winning.

aid *v.* accommodate, assist, boost, ease, encourage, expedite, facilitate, favour, help, oblige, promote, rally round, relieve, second, serve, subsidise, succour, support, sustain.
antonyms hinder, impede, obstruct.
n. assistance, benefit, contribution, donation, encouragement, favour, help, helper, patronage, prop, relief, service, sponsorship, subsidy, support, supporter.
antonyms hindrance, impediment, obstruction.

ailing *adj.* diseased, failing, feeble, frail, ill, indisposed, infirm, invalid, languishing, off-colour, out of sorts, poorly, sick, sickly, suffering, under the weather, unsound, unwell, weak.
antonyms flourishing, healthy, thriving.

ailment *n.* affliction, complaint, disability, disease, disorder, illness, infection, infirmity, malady, sickness, weakness.

aim *v.* aspire, attempt, design, direct, endeavour, intend, level, mean, plan, point, propose, purpose, resolve, seek, sight, strive, take aim, target, train, try, want, wish, zero in on.
n. ambition, aspiration, course, design, desire, direction, dream, end, goal, hope, intention, mark, motive, object, objective, plan, purpose, scheme, target, wish.

aimless *adj.* chance, directionless, erratic, frivolous, haphazard, irresolute, pointless, pur-

poseless, rambling, random, stray, undirected, unguided, unmotivated, unpredictable, wayward.
antonyms determined, positive, purposeful.
air *n.* **1** atmosphere, blast, breath, breeze, draught, heavens, oxygen, puff, sky, waft, wind. **2** appearance, aspect, aura, bearing, character, demeanour, effect, feeling, impression, look, manner. **3** melody, song, strain, theme, tune.
v. **1** aerate, freshen, ventilate. **2** broadcast, circulate, communicate, declare, disclose, display, disseminate, divulge, exhibit, expose, express, give vent to, make known, make public, parade, publicise, publish, reveal, tell, utter, voice.
airless *adj.* breathless, close, heavy, muggy, musty, oppressive, stale, stifling, stuffy, suffocating, sultry, unventilated.
antonyms airy, fresh.
airman *n.* ace, aviator, flyer, pilot.
air-tight *adj.* closed, impenetrable, impermeable, sealed, tight-fitting, wind-tight.
airy *adj.* **1** aerial, blowy, breezy, draughty, gusty, open, roomy, spacious, vaporous, well-ventilated, windy. **2** cheerful, happy, high-spirited, light-hearted, lively, nonchalant, offhand.
antonyms **1** close, heavy, oppressive, stuffy. **2** serious.
aisle *n.* alleyway, corridor, division, gangway, lane, passage, passageway, path, walkway.
akin *adj.* affiliated, alike, allied, analogous, cognate, comparable, congenial, connected, consonant, corresponding, like, parallel, related, similar.
antonyms alien, different.
alacrity *n.* briskness, cheerfulness, dispatch, eagerness, enthusiasm, haste, liveliness, promptness, quickness, readiness, speed, swiftness, willingness, zeal.
antonyms dilatoriness, reluctance, slowness.
alarm *v.* agitate, daunt, dismay, distress, frighten, give (someone) a turn, panic, put the wind up (someone), scare, startle, terrify, terrorise, unnerve.
antonyms calm, reassure, soothe.
n. **1** anxiety, apprehension, consternation, dismay, distress, fear, fright, horror, nervousness, panic, scare, terror, trepidation, uneasiness. **2** alarm-bell, alert, bell, danger signal, distress signal, siren, warning.
antonyms **1** calmness, composure.
alarming *adj.* daunting, dismaying, distressing, disturbing, dreadful, frightening, ominous, scaring, shocking, startling, terrifying, threatening, unnerving.
antonym reassuring.
alcohol *n.* hard stuff, intoxicant, liquor, spirits.
alcoholic *adj.* brewed, distilled, fermented, hard, intoxicating, strong.
n. dipsomaniac, drunk, drunkard, hard drinker, tippler.
alcoholism *n.* alcohol-addiction, dipsomania, drunkenness.
alcove *n.* bay, booth, carrel, compartment, corner, cubby-hole, cubicle, niche, nook, recess.
alert *adj.* active, agile, attentive, brisk, careful, circumspect, heedful, lively, nimble, observant, on the ball, on the lookout, perceptive, prepared, quick, ready, sharp-eyed, sharp-witted, spirited, vigilant, wary, watchful, wide-awake.
antonyms listless, slow, unprepared.
n. alarm, signal, siren, warning.
v. alarm, forewarn, inform, notify, signal, tip off, warn.
alias *n.* assumed name, false name, nickname, nom de plume, pen name, pseudonym, soubriquet, stage name.
prep. also called, also known as, formerly, otherwise, otherwise called.
alibi *n.* cover-up, defence, excuse, explanation, justification, plea, pretext, reason, story.
alien *adj.* adverse, antagonistic, conflicting, contrary, estranged, exotic, extraneous, foreign, incompatible, incongruous, opposed, outlandish, remote, separated, strange, unfamiliar.
antonym akin.
n. emigrant, foreigner, immigrant, newcomer, outsider, stranger.
antonym native.
alienate *v.* antagonise, divert, divorce, estrange, separate, set against, turn away, turn off, withdraw.
antonyms disarm, unite.
alight[1] *v.* come down, come to rest, descend, disembark, dismount, get down, get off, land, light, perch, settle, touch down.
antonyms ascend, board, rise.
alight[2] *adj.* ablaze, blazing, bright, brilliant, burning, fiery, flaming, flaring, ignited, illuminated, lighted, lit, lit up, on fire, radiant, shining.
antonym dark.
align *v.* affiliate, agree, ally, associate, co-operate, co-ordinate, even (up), join, line up, make parallel, order, range, regularise, regulate, side, straighten, sympathise.
alignment *n.* adjustment, affiliation, agreement, alliance, arrangement, association, conformity, co-operation, co-ordination, evening up, line, lining up, order, ranging, regulating, regulation, sequence, straightening, sympathy, union.
alike *adj.* akin, analogous, comparable, corresponding, duplicate, equal, equivalent, even, identical, parallel, resembling, similar, the same, uniform.
antonyms different, dissimilar, unlike.
adv. analogously, correspondingly, equally, evenly, identically, in common, similarly, uniformly.
alive *adj.* **1** active, animate, breathing, existent, having life, in existence, live, living, real. **2** alert, animated, awake, brisk, eager, energetic, lively, quick, spirited, vibrant, vigorous, vital, vivacious, zestful.
antonyms **1** dead, extinct. **2** apathetic, lifeless.
alive with abounding in, bristling with, bustling with, buzzing with, crawling with, crowded with, infested with, overflowing with, overrun by, swarming with, teeming with.

all *adj.* complete, each, each and every, entire, every, every bit of, every one of, every single, full, greatest, gross, outright, perfect, the complete, the entire, the sum of, the total of, the totality of, the whole of, total, utter.
antonym none.
n. aggregate, comprehensiveness, entirety, everything, sum, total, total amount, universality, utmost, whole, whole amount.
antonym nothing.
adv. altogether, completely, entirely, fully, totally, utterly, wholesale, wholly.
all right *adj.* acceptable, adequate, allowable, average, fair, healthy, OK, passable, safe, satisfactory, secure, sound, standard, unharmed, unhurt, unimpaired, uninjured, unobjectionable, well, whole.
antonyms inadequate, unacceptable.
adv. acceptably, adequately, appropriately, OK, passably, reasonably, satisfactorily, suitably, unobjectionably, well enough.
antonyms unacceptably, unsatisfactorily.
allay *v.* alleviate, blunt, calm, check, diminish, ease, lessen, moderate, mollify, pacify, quell, quiet, reduce, relieve, smooth, soften, soothe, tranquillise.
antonyms exacerbate, intensify.
allegation *n.* accusation, affirmation, assertion, charge, claim, declaration, plea, profession, statement, testimony.
allege *v.* affirm, assert, attest, avow, charge, claim, contend, declare, hold, insist, maintain, plead, profess, put forward, reckon, state.
alleged *adj.* affirmed, claimed, declared, described, designated, doubtful, dubious, inferred, ostensible, professed, reputed, so-called, stated, supposed, suspect, suspicious.
allegiance *n.* adherence, constancy, devotion, duty, faithfulness, fidelity, friendship, loyalty, obedience, obligation, support.
antonyms disloyalty, enmity.
allegorical *adj.* figurative, parabolic, representative, significative, symbolic, symbolising, typical.
allegory *n.* analogy, comparison, fable, metaphor, myth, parable, story, symbol, symbolism, tale.
allergic *adj.* affected, averse, disinclined, hostile, hypersensitive, opposed, sensitive, susceptible.
antonym tolerant.
allergy *n.* antipathy, aversion, dislike, hostility, loathing, opposition, sensitivity, susceptibility, vulnerability, weakness.
antonyms affinity, tolerance.
alleviate *v.* abate, allay, check, cushion, deaden, diminish, dull, ease, lessen, mitigate, moderate, modify, reduce, relieve, soften, soothe, subdue, temper.
antonym aggravate.
alliance *n.* affiliation, affinity, agreement, association, bloc, bond, cartel, coalition, combination, compact, confederation, conglomerate, connection, consortium, federation, guild, league, marriage, pact, partnership, syndicate, treaty, union.
antonyms divorce, enmity, estrangement, hostility.
allocate *v.* allot, apportion, appropriate, assign, budget, designate, disperse, distribute, earmark, mete, ration, set aside, share out.
allocation *n.* allotment, allowance, apportionment, appropriation, budget, grant, lot, measure, portion, quota, ration, share, stint.
allot *v.* allocate, apportion, appropriate, assign, budget, designate, dispense, distribute, earmark, grant, mete, render, set aside, share out.
allotment *n.* allocation, allowance, apportionment, appropriation, division, grant, lot, measure, partition, percentage, portion, quota, ration, share, stint.
all-out *adj.* complete, determined, exhaustive, full, full-scale, intensive, maximum, no-holds-barred, optimum, powerful, resolute, thorough, thoroughgoing, total, undivided, unlimited, unrestrained, utmost, vigorous, wholesale.
antonyms half-hearted, perfunctory.
allow *v.* **1** afford, approve, authorise, enable, endure, let, permit, put up with, sanction, tolerate. **2** acknowledge, admit, concede, confess, grant. **3** allocate, allot, apportion, assign, give, provide.
antonyms **1** forbid, prevent. **3** deny.
allow for arrange for, bear in mind, consider, foresee, include, keep in mind, make allowances for, make provision for, plan for, provide for, take into account.
antonym discount.
allowable *adj.* acceptable, admissible, all right, appropriate, approved, apt, legal(ised), legitimate, permissible, suitable, tolerable.
antonyms inadmissible, unacceptable.
allowance *n.* allocation, allotment, amount, annuity, concession, deduction, discount, grant, lot, pension, portion, quota, ration, rebate, reduction, remittance, share, stipend, subsidy, tolerance, weighting.
alloy *n.* amalgam, blend, coalescence, combination, composite, compound, fusion, mix, mixture.
allure *v.* attract, beguile, cajole, captivate, charm, coax, disarm, enchant, entice, entrance, fascinate, interest, lead on, lure, persuade, seduce, tempt, win over.
antonym repel.
n. appeal, attraction, captivation, charm, enchantment, enticement, fascination, glamour, lure, magnetism, persuasion, seductiveness, temptation.
ally *n.* accessory, accomplice, associate, collaborator, colleague, confederate, consort, co-worker, friend, helper, helpmate, leaguer, partner, side-kick.
antonyms antagonist, enemy.
v. affiliate, amalgamate, associate, band together, collaborate, combine, confederate, connect, fraternise, join, join forces, marry, team up, unify, unite.
antonyms estrange, separate.
almighty *adj.* **1** absolute, all-powerful, great,

invincible, omnipotent, supreme. **2** awful, desperate, enormous, intense, overpowering, overwhelming, severe, terrible.
antonyms **1** impotent, insignificant, weak.

almost *adv.* about, all but, approaching, approximately, as good as, close to, just about, nearing, nearly, not far from, not quite, practically, towards, virtually, well-nigh.

alone *adj., adv.* abandoned, apart, by itself, by oneself, deserted, desolate, detached, forlorn, forsaken, incomparable, isolated, lonely, lonesome, matchless, mere, on one's own, only, peerless, separate, simply, single, single-handed, sole, solitary, unaccompanied, unaided, unassisted, unattended, unconnected, unequalled, unescorted, unique, unparalleled, unsurpassed.
antonyms accompanied, escorted, together.

aloof *adj.* chilly, cold, cool, detached, distant, forbidding, formal, haughty, inaccessible, indifferent, offish, remote, reserved, stand-offish, supercilious, unapproachable, unforthcoming, unfriendly, uninterested, unresponsive, unsociable, unsympathetic.
antonyms concerned, friendly, sociable.

aloud *adv.* audibly, clearly, distinctly, intelligibly, loudly, noisily, out loud, plainly, resoundingly, sonorously, vociferously.
antonym silently.

already *adv.* at present, before now, beforehand, by now, by that time, by then, by this time, even now, just now, previously.

also *adv.* additionally, along with, and, as well, as well as, besides, further, furthermore, in addition, including, moreover, plus, too.

alter *v.* adapt, adjust, amend, change, convert, diversify, emend, modify, qualify, recast, reform, remodel, reshape, revise, shift, take liberties with, transform, transmute, transpose, turn, vary.
antonym fix.

alteration *n.* adaptation, adjustment, amendment, change, conversion, difference, diversification, interchanging, modification, reciprocation, reformation, remodelling, reshaping, revision, rotation, shift, transfiguration, transformation, transposition, variance, variation, vicissitude.
antonym fixity.

alternate *v.* alter, change, fluctuate, follow one another, interchange, intersperse, oscillate, reciprocate, rotate, substitute, take turns, transpose, vary.
adj. alternating, alternative, another, different, every other, every second, interchanging, reciprocal, rotating, second, substitute.

alternative *n.* back-up, choice, option, other, preference, recourse, selection, substitute.
adj. alternate, another, different, fringe, other, second, substitute, unconventional, unorthodox.

although *conj.* admitting that, conceding that, even if, even supposing, even though, granted that, notwithstanding, though, while.

altitude *n.* elevation, height, loftiness, stature, tallness.
antonym depth.

altogether *adv.* absolutely, all in all, all told, as a whole, completely, entirely, fully, generally, in all, in general, in toto, on the whole, perfectly, quite, thoroughly, totally, utterly, wholesale, wholly.

altruism *n.* considerateness, generosity, humanity, philanthropy, public spirit, self-sacrifice, social conscience, unselfishness.
antonym selfishness.

altruistic *adj.* benevolent, charitable, considerate, disinterested, generous, humane, humanitarian, philanthropic, public-spirited, self-sacrificing, unselfish.
antonym selfish.

always *adv.* consistently, constantly, continually, endlessly, eternally, ever, evermore, every time, forever, invariably, perpetually, regularly, repeatedly, unceasingly, unfailingly, without exception.
antonym never.

amalgamate *v.* alloy, ally, blend, coalesce, combine, commingle, compound, fuse, homogenise, incorporate, integrate, intermix, merge, mingle, synthesise, unify, unite.
antonym separate.

amateur *n.* buff, dabbler, dilettante, fancier, ham, layman, non-professional.
antonym professional.

amateurish *adj.* clumsy, crude, incompetent, inept, inexpert, unaccomplished, unprofessional, unskilful, untrained.
antonyms professional, skilled.

amaze *v.* astonish, astound, bewilder, confound, daze, disconcert, dismay, dumbfound, flabbergast, floor, shock, stagger, startle, stun, stupefy, surprise.

amazement *n.* admiration, astonishment, bewilderment, confusion, dismay, marvel, perplexity, shock, surprise, wonder, wonderment.

ambassador *n.* agent, apostle, consul, deputy, diplomat, emissary, envoy, legate, minister, plenipotentiary, representative.

ambiguity *n.* ambivalence, confusion, doubt, doubtfulness, dubiousness, equivocality, equivocation, obscurity, puzzle, uncertainty, unclearness, vagueness, woolliness.
antonym clarity.

ambiguous *adj.* ambivalent, confused, confusing, cryptic, double-barrelled, double-meaning, doubtful, dubious, enigmatic, enigmatical, equivocal, inconclusive, indefinite, indeterminate, multivocal, obscure, puzzling, uncertain, unclear, vague, woolly.
antonyms clear, definite.

ambit *n.* circuit, compass, confines, environs, precincts, scope.

ambition *n.* aim, aspiration, craving, design, desire, dream, drive, eagerness, enterprise, goal, hankering, hope, hunger, ideal, intent, longing, object, objective, purpose, push, striving, target, wish, yearning, zeal.

antonyms apathy, diffidence.
ambitious *adj.* arduous, aspiring, assertive, bold, challenging, demanding, desirous, difficult, driving, eager, elaborate, energetic, enterprising, enthusiastic, exacting, formidable, go-ahead, hard, hopeful, impressive, industrious, intent, keen, pretentious, purposeful, pushy, severe, strenuous, striving, zealous.
antonyms lazy, modest, unassuming, uninspiring.
ambivalence *n.* ambiguity, clash, conflict, confusion, contradiction, doubt, equivocation, fluctuation, inconsistency, indecision, instability, irresolution, opposition, uncertainty, vacillation, wavering.
antonym certainty.
ambivalent *adj.* ambiguous, clashing, conflicting, confused, contradictory, debatable, doubtful, equivocal, fluctuating, hesitant, inconclusive, inconsistent, irresolute, mixed, opposed, uncertain, undecided, unresolved, unsettled, unsure, vacillating, warring, wavering.
antonym unequivocal.
amble *v.* drift, meander, promenade, ramble, saunter, stroll, toddle, walk, wander.
antonyms march, stride.
ambush *n.* cover, hiding, snare, trap, waylaying.
v. ensnare, surprise, trap, waylay.
amenable *adj.* accountable, agreeable, answerable, chargeable, conformable, flexible, open, persuadable, responsible, responsive, submissive, susceptible.
antonym intractable.
amend *v.* adjust, alter, ameliorate, better, change, correct, emend, enhance, fix, improve, mend, modify, qualify, rectify, redress, reform, remedy, repair, revise.
antonyms impair, worsen.
amendment *n.* addendum, addition, adjunct, adjustment, alteration, change, clarification, correction, corrigendum, emendation, improvement, modification, qualification, rectification, reform, remedy, repair, revision.
antonyms deterioration, impairment.
amends *n.* atonement, compensation, expiation, indemnification, indemnity, recompense, redress, reparation, requital, restitution, restoration, satisfaction.
amenity *n.* advantage, attraction, charm, comfort, convenience, facility, pleasantness, refinement, service.
antonyms eyesore, inconvenience.
amiable *adj.* affable, agreeable, approachable, attractive, charming, cheerful, companionable, congenial, delightful, engaging, friendly, genial, good-natured, good-tempered, kind, likable, obliging, pleasant, pleasing, sociable.
antonyms curt, hostile, unfriendly.
amid *conj.* amidst, among, amongst, in the middle of, in the midst of, in the thick of, surrounded by.
amnesty *n.* absolution, dispensation, forgiveness, immunity, indulgence, lenience, mercy, oblivion, pardon, remission, reprieve.
among *prep.* amid, amidst, amongst, between, in the middle of, in the midst of, in the thick of, midst, surrounded by, together with, with.
amoral *adj.* abandoned, free-living, loose, uninhibited, unprincipled, unrestrained.
antonym moral.
amorphous *adj.* chaotic, featureless, formless, indeterminate, indistinct, irregular, nebulous, nondescript, shapeless, undefined, unformed, unstructured, vague.
antonyms definite, distinctive, shapely.
amount *n.* addition, aggregate, bulk, entirety, expanse, extent, lot, magnitude, mass, measure, number, quantity, quota, sum, sum total, supply, total, volume, whole.
amount to add up to, aggregate, approximate to, be equivalent to, be tantamount to, become, come to, equal, grow, mean, run to, total.
ample *adj.* abundant, big, bountiful, broad, commodious, considerable, copious, expansive, extensive, full, generous, great, handsome, large, lavish, liberal, munificent, plenteous, plentiful, plenty, profuse, rich, roomy, spacious, substantial, sufficient, unrestricted, voluminous, wide.
antonyms inadequate, insufficient, meagre.
amplitude *n.* abundance, bigness, breadth, bulk, capacity, compass, completeness, copiousness, dimension, expanse, extent, fullness, greatness, largeness, magnitude, mass, plentifulness, plethora, profusion, range, reach, richness, scope, size, spaciousness, sweep, vastness, volume, width.
amputate *v.* curtail, cut off, dissever, dock, excise, lop, remove, separate, sever, truncate.
amuse *v.* absorb, charm, cheer (up), delight, divert, engross, enliven, entertain, enthral, gladden, interest, occupy, please, recreate, regale, relax, slay, tickle.
antonyms bore, displease.
amusement *n.* delight, distraction, diversion, enjoyment, entertainment, fun, game, hilarity, hobby, interest, joke, laughter, pastime, pleasure, prank, recreation, sport.
antonyms bore, boredom, monotony.
amusing *adj.* amusive, charming, comical, delightful, droll, enjoyable, entertaining, facetious, funny, hilarious, humorous, interesting, jocular, jolly, killing, laughable, ludicrous, pleasant, witty.
antonyms boring, dull.
anachronism *n.* antique, archaism, back number, fogey, fossil.
anaemic *adj.* ashen, bloodless, chalky, colourless, dull, enervated, feeble, frail, ineffectual, infirm, insipid, pale, pallid, pasty, sallow, sickly, wan, weak, whey-faced.
antonyms full-blooded, ruddy, sanguine.
anaesthetic *n.* analgesic, narcotic, pain-killer, sedative.
anaesthetise *v.* deaden, desensitise, dope, dull, lull, mull, numb, stupefy.
analogous *adj.* agreeing, akin, alike, comparable, correlative, corresponding, equivalent, like, matching, parallel, reciprocal, related,

resembling, similar.
antonyms different, disparate.
analogy *n.* agreement, comparison, correlation, correspondence, equivalence, likeness, parallel, relation, resemblance, similarity.
analyse *v.* anatomise, break down, consider, dissect, dissolve, divide, estimate, evaluate, examine, interpret, investigate, judge, reduce, resolve, review, scrutinise, separate, sift, study, test.
analysis *n.* breakdown, dissection, division, enquiry, estimation, evaluation, examination, explanation, explication, exposition, interpretation, investigation, judgement, opinion, reasoning, reduction, resolution, review, scrutiny, separation, sifting, study, test.
analytic *adj.* anatomical, critical, detailed, discrete, dissecting, enquiring, explanatory, expository, inquisitive, interpretative, investigative, logical, methodical, questioning, rational, searching, studious, systematic.
anarchic *adj.* anarchistic, chaotic, confused, disordered, disorganised, lawless, libertarian, nihilist, rebellious, revolutionary, riotous, ungoverned.
antonyms orderly, submissive.
anarchist *n.* apostate, insurgent, libertarian, rebel, revolutionary, terrorist.
anarchy *n.* anarchism, apostasy, chaos, confusion, disorder, insurrection, lawlessness, misrule, mutiny, pandemonium, rebellion, revolution, riot, unrule.
antonyms control, order, rule.
anathema *n.* abhorrence, abomination, aversion, bane, bugbear, curse, object of loathing, proscription, taboo.
anatomy *n.* analysis, build, composition, constitution, construction, frame, framework, make-up, structure, vivisection.
ancestor *n.* antecedent, antecessor, forebear, forefather, forerunner, precursor, predecessor, progenitor.
antonym descendant.
ancestral *adj.* familial, genealogical, genetic, hereditary, lineal, parental.
ancestry *n.* ancestors, antecedents, antecessors, blood, derivation, descent, extraction, family, forefathers, genealogy, heredity, heritage, line, lineage, origin, parentage, pedigree, progenitors, race, roots, stock.
anchor *n.* mainstay, pillar of strength, prop, security, staff, support.
v. affix, attach, fasten, fix, make fast, moor.
ancient *adj.* aged, age-old, antediluvian, antiquated, antique, archaic, bygone, early, fossilised, immemorial, obsolete, old, old-fashioned, original, out-of-date, prehistoric, primeval, time-worn.
antonyms contemporary, modern, recent.
ancillary *adj.* accessory, additional, auxiliary, contributory, extra, secondary, subordinate, subsidiary, supplementary.
anecdote *n.* fable, reminiscence, sketch, story, tale, yarn.
angel *n.* archangel, backer, benefactor, cherub, darling, divine messenger, fairy godmother, guardian spirit, ideal, paragon, principality, saint, seraph, supporter, treasure.
antonyms devil, fiend.
angelic *adj.* adorable, beautiful, celestial, divine, heavenly, holy, innocent, lovely, pious, pure, saintly, unworldly, virtuous.
antonyms devilish, fiendish.
anger *n.* annoyance, antagonism, bitterness, displeasure, exasperation, fury, gall, indignation, irritability, irritation, outrage, passion, pique, rage, rancour, resentment, temper, vexation, wrath.
antonyms forbearance, forgiveness.
v. affront, aggravate, annoy, antagonise, bother, displease, enrage, exasperate, frustrate, gall, incense, infuriate, irk, irritate, madden, miff, needle, nettle, offend, outrage, provoke, rile, ruffle, vex.
antonyms appease, calm, please.
angle *n.* approach, aspect, bend, corner, crook, crotch, direction, edge, elbow, facet, flexure, hook, nook, outlook, perspective, point, point of view, position, side, slant, standpoint, turn, viewpoint.
angle for aim for, be after, be out for, contrive, fish for, have one's beady eye on, hunt, invite, scheme, seek, solicit.
angry *adj.* aggravated, annoyed, antagonised, bitter, displeased, enraged, exasperated, furious, heated, hot, incensed, indignant, infuriated, irate, irritated, mad, outraged, passionate, raging, resentful, uptight.
antonyms calm, content, happy.
anguish *n.* agony, angst, anxiety, distress, dole, dolour, grief, heartache, heartbreak, misery, pain, pang, rack, sorrow, suffering, torment, torture, tribulation, woe, wretchedness.
antonyms happiness, solace.
animal *n.* barbarian, beast, brute, creature, cur, hound, mammal, monster, pig, savage, swine.
adj. bestial, bodily, brutish, carnal, fleshly, gross, inhuman, instinctive, physical, piggish, savage, sensual, wild.
animate *v.* activate, arouse, encourage, energise, enliven, excite, fire, galvanise, goad, impel, incite, inspire, instigate, invest, invigorate, kindle, move, quicken, reactivate, revive, rouse, spark, spur, stimulate, stir, suffuse, urge, vitalise.
antonyms dull, inhibit.
adj. alive, breathing, conscious, live, living.
antonyms inanimate, spiritless.
animated *adj.* active, alive, ardent, brisk, buoyant, eager, energetic, enthusiastic, excited, fervent, glowing, impassioned, lively, passionate, quick, radiant, spirited, vehement, vibrant, vigorous, vital, vivacious, vivid.
antonyms inert, lethargic, sluggish.
animosity *n.* acrimony, antagonism, bitterness, enmity, feud, hate, hatred, hostility, ill-will, loathing, malevolence, malice, malignity, rancour, resentment, spite.

antonym goodwill.
annex *v.* acquire, add, adjoin, affix, append, appropriate, attach, connect, conquer, fasten, incorporate, join, occupy, seize, take over, unite, usurp.
annexe *n.* addition, attachment, expansion, extension, supplement, wing.
annihilate *v.* abolish, assassinate, destroy, eliminate, eradicate, erase, exterminate, extinguish, liquidate, murder, obliterate, raze, thrash, wipe out.
annotate *v.* comment, elucidate, explain, gloss, interpret, note.
annotation *n.* comment, commentary, elucidation, exegesis, explanation, footnote, gloss, note.
announce *v.* advertise, blazon, broadcast, declare, disclose, divulge, intimate, leak, make known, notify, proclaim, promulgate, propound, publicise, publish, report, reveal, state.
antonym suppress.
announcement *n.* advertisement, broadcast, bulletin, communiqué, declaration, disclosure, dispatch, divulgence, intimation, notification, proclamation, publication, report, revelation, statement.
announcer *n.* broadcaster, commentator, compère, crier, herald, messenger, newscaster, news-reader, reporter.
annoy *v.* aggravate, anger, bother, displease, disturb, exasperate, harass, harm, irk, irritate, madden, molest, pester, plague, provoke, rile, ruffle, tease, trouble, vex.
antonyms comfort, gratify, please.
annoyance *n.* aggravation, anger, bind, bore, bother, displeasure, disturbance, exasperation, fash, harassment, headache, irritation, nuisance, pain, pest, plague, provocation, tease, trouble, vexation.
antonym pleasure.
annoyed *adj.* bored, displeased, exasperated, harassed, irritated, piqued, provoked, vexed.
antonym pleased.
annoying *adj.* aggravating, boring, displeasing, disturbing, exasperating, galling, harassing, irksome, irritating, maddening, offensive, provoking, teasing, troublesome, vexatious.
antonyms pleasing, welcome.
annual *n.* almanac, annal, year-book.
annul *v.* abolish, abrogate, cancel, countermand, invalidate, negate, nullify, quash, recall, repeal, rescind, retract, reverse, revoke, suspend, void.
antonyms enact, restore.
annulment *n.* abolition, abrogation, cancellation, countermanding, invalidation, negation, quashing, recall, repeal, rescindment, retraction, reversal, revocation, suspension, voiding.
antonyms enactment, restoration.
anoint *v.* bless, consecrate, daub, dedicate, embrocate, grease, lard, lubricate, oil, rub, sanctify, smear.
anomalous *adj.* abnormal, atypical, deviant, eccentric, exceptional, freakish, incongruous, inconsistent, irregular, odd, peculiar, rare, singular, unusual.
antonyms normal, ordinary, regular.
anomaly *n.* aberration, abnormality, departure, deviation, divergence, eccentricity, exception, freak, incongruity, inconsistency, irregularity, misfit, oddity, peculiarity, rarity.
anonymous *adj.* faceless, impersonal, incognito, nameless, nondescript, unacknowledged, unattested, unexceptional, unidentified, unknown, unnamed, unsigned, unspecified.
antonyms distinctive, identifiable, named.
anorak *n.* blouson, golf-jacket, jerkin, parka, waterproof, windcheater.
answer *n.* acknowledgement, comeback, defence, explanation, outcome, plea, reaction, rebuttal, rejoinder, reply, response, retaliation, retort, riposte, solution, vindication.
v. **1** acknowledge, react, refute, reply, respond, retaliate, retort, solve. **2** agree, balance, conform, correlate, correspond, fill, fit, fulfil, match up to, meet, pass, satisfy, serve, succeed, suffice, suit, work.
answer back argue, contradict, disagree, dispute, rebut, retaliate, retort, riposte, talk back.
answerable *adj.* accountable, amenable, blameworthy, chargeable, liable, responsible, to blame.
antagonise *v.* alienate, anger, annoy, disaffect, embitter, estrange, incense, insult, irritate, offend, provoke, repel.
antonym disarm.
antagonist *n.* adversary, competitor, contender, contestant, enemy, foe, opponent, opposer, rival.
antonyms ally, supporter.
antagonistic *adj.* adverse, at variance, averse, belligerent, conflicting, contentious, hostile, ill-disposed, incompatible, inimical, opposed, unfriendly.
antonyms friendly, sympathetic.
antecedents *n.* ancestors, ancestry, background, blood, descent, extraction, family, forebears, forefathers, genealogy, history, line, lineage, past, pedigree, progenitors, record, stock.
anthem *n.* canticle, chant, chorale, hymn, psalm, song.
anthology *n.* collection, compendium, compilation, digest, miscellany, selection, treasury.
anticipate *v.* **1** forestall, intercept, pre-empt, prevent. **2** await, bank on, count upon, expect, forecast, foresee, hope for, look for, look forward to, predict.
anticlimax *n.* comedown, disappointment, fiasco, let-down.
antics *n.* buffoonery, capers, clowning, doings, escapades, foolery, frolics, mischief, monkey tricks, playfulness, pranks, silliness, skylarking, stunts, tricks.
antidote *n.* corrective, counter-agent, countermeasure, cure, neutraliser, preventive, remedy.
antipathy *n.* abhorrence, allergy, animosity, antagonism, aversion, bad blood, disgust, dislike, distaste, enmity, hate, hatred, hostility, ill-will, incompatibility, loathing, opposition,

repulsion, resentment.
antonyms affection, rapport, sympathy.

antiquated *adj.* anachronistic, ancient, antediluvian, antique, archaic, dated, fossilised, obsolete, old, old-fashioned, outdated, out-of-date, outworn, quaint, unfashionable.
antonyms fashionable, forward-looking, modern.

antique *adj.* aged, ancient, antiquarian, archaic, obsolete, old, old-fashioned, outdated, quaint, vintage.
n. antiquity, bygone, curio, curiosity, heirloom, museum-piece, period piece, rarity, relic.

antiquity *n.* age, agedness, ancient times, antique, distant past, old age, oldness, time immemorial.
antonyms modernity, novelty.

antiseptic *adj.* clean, disinfectant, germ-free, hygienic, medicated, pure, sanitary, sanitised, sterile, uncontaminated, unpolluted.
n. cleanser, disinfectant, germicide, purifier.

antisocial *adj.* alienated, antagonistic, asocial, belligerent, disorderly, disruptive, hostile, rebellious, reserved, retiring, unacceptable, unapproachable, uncommunicative, unfriendly, unsociable, withdrawn.
antonyms gregarious, sociable.

anxiety *n.* apprehension, care, concern, craving, desire, distress, dread, foreboding, fretfulness, impatience, misgiving, nervousness, restlessness, suspense, tension, uneasiness, worry.
antonyms calm, composure, serenity.

anxious *adj.* afraid, apprehensive, concerned, disquieted, distressed, disturbed, fearful, fretful, impatient, in suspense, nervous, on tenterhooks, restless, taut, tense, tormented, tortured, troubled, uneasy, worried.
antonyms calm, composed.

apart *adv.* afar, alone, aloof, aside, away, by oneself, cut off, distant, distinct, divorced, excluded, in bits, in pieces, independently, individually, into parts, isolated, on one's own, piecemeal, privately, separate, separated, singly, to bits, to one side, to pieces.
antonyms connected, together.

apartment *n.* accommodation, chambers, compartment, condominium, flat, living quarters, lodgings, maisonette, pad, penthouse, quarters, room, rooms, suite, tenement.

apathetic *adj.* cold, cool, emotionless, impassive, indifferent, listless, numb, passive, unambitious, unconcerned, unemotional, unfeeling, uninterested, uninvolved, unmoved, unresponsive.
antonyms concerned, enthusiastic, feeling, involved, responsive.

apathy *n.* coldness, coolness, impassivity, indifference, inertia, insensibility, lethargy, listlessness, passiveness, sluggishness, torpor, unconcern, uninterestedness.
antonyms concern, enthusiasm, interest.

ape *v.* affect, caricature, copy, counterfeit, echo, imitate, mimic, mirror, mock, parody, parrot, take off.
n. baboon, chimpanzee, gibbon, gorilla, monkey, oaf, orang-utan.

aplomb *n.* assurance, audacity, balance, calmness, composure, confidence, coolness, equanimity, poise, self-assurance.
antonym discomposure.

apocalyptic *adj.* ominous, portentous, prophetic, revelational, revelatory, signal, threatening.

apocryphal *adj.* concocted, doubtful, dubious, equivocal, fabricated, fictitious, imaginary, legendary, mythical, questionable, spurious, unauthenticated, unsubstantiated, unsupported, unverified.
antonyms authentic, true.

apologetic *adj.* conscience-stricken, contrite, penitent, regretful, remorseful, repentant, rueful, sorry.
antonyms defiant, impenitent.

apology *n.* **1** acknowledgement, confession, explanation, justification, plea, vindication. **2** defence, excuse, substitute, travesty.
antonym **1** defiance.

appal *v.* alarm, astound, daunt, disconcert, disgust, dishearten, dismay, frighten, horrify, intimidate, outrage, scare, shock, terrify, unnerve.
antonyms encourage, reassure.

appalling *adj.* alarming, astounding, awful, daunting, dire, dismaying, dreadful, frightening, frightful, ghastly, grim, harrowing, hideous, horrible, horrid, horrific, intimidating, loathsome, scaring, shocking, terrible, terrifying, unnerving, wretched.
antonyms encouraging, reassuring.

apparatus *n.* appliance, bureaucracy, contraption, device, equipment, framework, gadget, gear, hierarchy, implements, machine, machinery, materials, means, mechanism, network, organisation, outfit, set-up, structure, system, tackle, tools, utensils.

apparent *adj.* clear, declared, distinct, evident, manifest, marked, noticeable, obvious, on paper, open, outward, patent, perceptible, plain, seeming, unmistakable, visible.
antonyms obscure, real.

apparently *adv.* clearly, it appears, manifestly, obviously, ostensibly, outwardly, patently, plainly, seemingly, superficially.

apparition *n.* chimera, ghost, manifestation, materialisation, phantom, presence, spectre, spirit, vision.

appeal *n.* **1** application, entreaty, imploration, invocation, petition, plea, prayer, request, solicitation, suit, supplication. **2** allure, attraction, attractiveness, beauty, charisma, charm, enchantment, fascination, interest, magnetism, winsomeness.
v. **1** address, apply, ask, beg, beseech, call, call upon, entreat, implore, invoke, petition, plead, pray, refer, request, resort to, solicit, sue, supplicate. **2** allure, attract, charm, draw, engage, entice, fascinate, interest, invite, lure, please, tempt.

appear *v.* act, arise, arrive, attend, be published,

come into sight, come into view, come out, come to light, crop up, develop, emerge, enter, issue, leak out, look, loom, materialise, occur, perform, play, rise, seem, show (up), surface, take part, turn out, turn up.
antonyms disappear, vanish.

appearance *n.* **1** appearing, arrival, coming, début, emergence, introduction. **2** air, aspect, bearing, demeanour, expression, face, figure, form, front, guise, illusion, image, impression, look, looks, manner, semblance, show.
antonym **1** disappearance.

appendix *n.* addendum, addition, adjunct, appendage, codicil, epilogue, postscript, rider, supplement.

appetiser *n.* apéritif, cocktail, foretaste, hors d'oeuvre, preview, sample, taster, titbit.

appetising *adj.* appealing, delicious, inviting, mouthwatering, palatable, piquant, savoury, scrumptious, succulent, tasty, tempting.
antonyms disgusting, distasteful.

appetite *n.* craving, desire, eagerness, hunger, inclination, liking, longing, passion, propensity, relish, stomach, taste, yearning, zeal, zest.
antonym distaste.

applaud *v.* acclaim, approve, cheer, clap, commend, compliment, congratulate, eulogise, extol, laud, praise.
antonyms censure, disparage.

applause *n.* acclaim, acclamation, accolade, approval, cheering, cheers, commendation, congratulation, ovation, praise.
antonyms censure, criticism, disparagement.

appliance *n.* apparatus, contraption, contrivance, device, gadget, implement, instrument, machine, mechanism, tool.

applicable *adj.* apposite, appropriate, apt, fit, fitting, legitimate, pertinent, proper, relevant, suitable, suited, useful, valid.
antonyms inapplicable, inappropriate.

applicant *n.* aspirant, candidate, competitor, contestant, enquirer, interviewee, petitioner, suitor.

application *n.* **1** appeal, claim, enquiry, petition, request. **2** function, pertinence, purpose, relevance, use, value. **3** assiduity, attentiveness, commitment, dedication, diligence, effort, industry, keenness, perseverance. **4** balm, cream, dressing, emollient, lotion, medication, ointment, preparation, salve.

apply *v.* **1** appeal, ask for, claim, enquire, indent for, petition, put in, request, requisition, solicit, sue. **2** address, buckle down, commit, concentrate, dedicate, devote, direct, give, persevere, settle down, study, throw. **3** administer, assign, bring into play, bring to bear, direct, employ, engage, execute, exercise, harness, implement, ply, practise, resort to, set, use, utilise, wield. **4** be relevant, fit, have force, refer, relate, suit. **5** anoint, cover with, lay on, paint, place, put on, rub, smear, spread on, use.

appoint *v.* allot, arrange, assign, charge, choose, command, commission, constitute, decide, decree, delegate, designate, destine, detail, determine, devote, direct, engage, equip, establish, fix, furnish, install, name, nominate, ordain, outfit, provide, select, set, settle, supply.
antonyms discharge, dismiss, reject.

appointment *n.* **1** arrangement, consultation, date, engagement, interview, meeting, rendezvous. **2** job, office, place, position, post, situation. **3** choice, choosing, commissioning, delegation, election, naming, nomination, selection.

appraisal *n.* appreciation, assessment, estimate, estimation, evaluation, examination, inspection, judgement, once-over, opinion, rating, reckoning, review, survey, valuation.

appreciable *adj.* apparent, clear-cut, considerable, definite, discernible, distinguishable, evident, marked, material, noticeable, obvious, perceivable, perceptible, pronounced, recognisable, significant, substantial, visible.
antonyms imperceptible, negligible.

appreciate *v.* **1** acknowledge, admire, be sensitive to, cherish, comprehend, do justice to, enjoy, esteem, estimate, know, like, perceive, prize, realise, recognise, regard, relish, respect, savour, sympathise with, take kindly to, treasure, understand, value, welcome. **2** enhance, gain, grow, improve, increase, inflate, mount, rise, strengthen.
antonyms **1** despise, overlook. **2** depreciate.

appreciation *n.* **1** acclamation, acknowledgement, admiration, assessment, awareness, comprehension, enjoyment, esteem, estimation, gratefulness, gratitude, indebtedness, judgement, knowledge, liking, notice, obligation, perception, praise, realisation, recognition, regard, relish, respect, responsiveness, sensitivity, sympathy, thankfulness, tribute, understanding, valuation. **2** enhancement, gain, growth, improvement, increase, inflation, rise.
antonyms **1** ingratitude, neglect. **2** depreciation.

appreciative *adj.* admiring, conscious, encouraging, enthusiastic, grateful, indebted, knowledgeable, mindful, obliged, perceptive, pleased, respectful, responsive, sensitive, supportive, sympathetic, thankful, understanding.
antonym ungrateful.

apprehension *n.* alarm, anxiety, concern, disquiet, doubt, dread, fear, foreboding, misgiving, mistrust, qualm, suspicion, uneasiness, worry.

apprehensive *adj.* afraid, alarmed, anxious, concerned, distrustful, disturbed, doubtful, mistrustful, nervous, suspicious, uneasy, worried.
antonyms assured, confident.

apprentice *n.* beginner, learner, newcomer, novice, probationer, pupil, recruit, starter, student, trainee.
antonym expert.

approach *v.* advance, appeal to, apply to, approximate, be like, begin, catch up, come close, come near to, commence, compare with, draw near, gain on, introduce, meet, mention, near, reach, resemble, set about, sound out, undertake.
n. **1** advance, arrival. **2** access, avenue, doorway, entrance, passage, road, threshold, way. **3**

application, motion, proposal, proposition. **4** attitude, manner, means, method, procedure, style, technique.

approachable *adj.* accessible, congenial, conversable, cordial, easy, friendly, informal, open, reachable, sociable.
antonym unapproachable.

appropriate *adj.* applicable, apt, befitting, congruous, correct, fit, fitting, meet, opportune, pertinent, proper, relevant, right, seasonable, spot-on, suitable, timely, to the point, well-chosen, well-suited.
antonyms inappropriate, irrelevant, unsuitable.
v. allocate, allot, apportion, assign, assume, commandeer, confiscate, devote, earmark, embezzle, filch, misappropriate, pilfer, pocket, purloin, seize, set apart, steal, take, usurp.

approval *n.* acclaim, acclamation, admiration, agreement, applause, appreciation, approbation, assent, authorisation, blessing, certification, commendation, concurrence, confirmation, consent, esteem, favour, go-ahead, good opinion, green light, honour, leave, licence, liking, mandate, OK, permission, praise, ratification, recommendation, regard, respect, sanction, support, validation.
antonyms condemnation, disapproval.

approve *v.* accede to, accept, acclaim, admire, adopt, advocate, agree to, allow, applaud, appreciate, assent to, authorise, back, bless, commend, comply with, confirm, consent to, countenance, endorse, esteem, favour, like, mandate, OK, pass, permit, praise, ratify, recommend, regard, rubber-stamp, sanction, second, support, uphold, validate.
antonyms condemn, disapprove.

approved *adj.* accepted, authorised, correct, favoured, official, permitted, preferred, proper, recognised, recommended, sanctioned.
antonym unorthodox.

approximate *adj.* close, estimated, guessed, inexact, like, loose, near, relative, rough, similar, verging on.
antonym exact.
v. approach, be tantamount to, border on, resemble, verge on.

approximation *n.* approach, estimate, estimation, extrapolation, guess, guesswork, likeness, proximity, resemblance, rough calculation, rough idea.
antonyms exactitude, precision.

apropos of in connection with, in relation to, in respect of, on the subject of, regarding, with reference to, with regard to, with respect to.

apt *adj.* **1** accurate, applicable, apposite, appropriate, correct, disposed, fair, fit, fitting, given, liable, likely, prone, proper, ready, relevant, seasonable, seemly, spot-on, suitable, timely. **2** clever, expert, gifted, intelligent, quick, sharp, skilful, talented.
antonyms **1** inapt. **2** stupid.

aptitude *n.* ability, bent, capability, capacity, cleverness, disposition, facility, faculty, flair, gift, inclination, intelligence, leaning, proficiency, quickness, talent, tendency.
antonym inaptitude.

arbitrary *adj.* **1** capricious, chance, discretionary, inconsistent, instinctive, random, unreasonable, unreasoned. **2** absolute, autocratic, despotic, dictatorial, dogmatic, domineering, high-handed, imperious, magisterial, overbearing, tyrannical.
antonyms **1** circumspect, rational, reasoned.

arbitrate *v.* adjudicate, decide, determine, judge, pass judgement, referee, settle, umpire.

arbitration *n.* adjudication, decision, determination, intervention, judgement, negotiation, settlement.

arbitrator *n.* adjudicator, intermediary, judge, mediator, moderator, negotiator, referee, umpire.

arcade *n.* cloister, colonnade, covered way, gallery, mall, portico, precinct.

arch[1] *n.* arc, archway, bend, bow, concave, curvature, curve, dome, semicircle, span, vault.
v. arc, bend, bow, camber, curve, extend, vault.

arch[2] *adj.* **1** accomplished, chief, consummate, expert, finished, first, foremost, greatest, highest, leading, main, major, master, pre-eminent, primary, principal, top. **2** mischievous, playful, provocative, sly.

archaic *adj.* ancient, antiquated, antique, bygone, obsolete, old, old hat, old-fashioned, outdated, outmoded, out-of-date, passé, primitive, quaint.
antonyms modern, recent.

archetype *n.* classic, conception, form, idea, ideal, model, original, paradigm, pattern, precursor, prototype, standard, type.

architect *n.* artist, author, constructor, creator, designer, deviser, engineer, fashioner, founder, instigator, inventor, maker, master builder, originator, planner, prime mover, shaper.

architecture *n.* arrangement, building, composition, construction, design, framework, make-up, planning, structure, style.

archives *n.* annals, chronicles, deeds, documents, ledgers, memorials, papers, records, registers, roll.

ardent *adj.* **1** dedicated, devoted, eager, enthusiastic, fervent, fierce, fiery, impassioned, intense, keen, spirited, vehement, warm, zealous. **2** amorous, lusty, passionate.
antonyms **1** apathetic, unenthusiastic.

arduous *adj.* backbreaking, difficult, exhausting, fatiguing, formidable, gruelling, hard, harsh, laborious, onerous, punishing, rigorous, severe, strenuous, taxing, tiring, tough, troublesome, trying, uphill.
antonym easy.

area *n.* arena, breadth, canvas, compass, department, district, domain, environs, expanse, extent, field, locality, neighbourhood, part, patch, portion, province, range, realm, region, scope, section, sector, size, sphere, stretch, terrain, territory, tract, width, zone.

arena *n.* amphitheatre, area, battlefield, battleground, bowl, coliseum, field, ground, park, ring, scene, stadium, stage.

argue *v.* assert, bicker, claim, contend, convince, debate, demonstrate, denote, disagree, discuss, display, dispute, evidence, exhibit, fall out, fence, feud, fight, haggle, hold, imply, indicate, join issue, maintain, manifest, persuade, plead, prove, quarrel, question, reason, remonstrate, show, squabble, suggest, talk into, wrangle.

argument *n.* **1** clash, conflict, disagreement, dispute, feud, fight, quarrel, row, squabble, wrangle. **2** assertion, case, claim, contention, controversy, debate, defence, demonstration, discussion, logic, reason, reasoning, summary, synopsis, theme.

argumentative *adj.* belligerent, contentious, contrary, opinionated, perverse, polemical, quarrelsome, wranglesome.
antonym complaisant.

arise *v.* appear, ascend, begin, climb, come to light, commence, crop up, derive, emerge, ensue, flow, follow, get up, go up, grow, happen, issue, lift, mount, occur, originate, proceed, result, rise, set in, soar, spring, stand up, start, stem, tower, wake up.

aristocracy *n.* élite, gentility, gentry, nobility, peerage, quality, ruling class, upper class.
antonym the plebs.

aristocrat *n.* lady, lord, noble, nobleman, noblewoman, peer, peeress.
antonym commoner.

aristocratic *adj.* blue-blooded, courtly, dignified, elegant, élite, fine, gentle, haughty, highborn, lordly, noble, polished, refined, supercilious, thoroughbred, titled, upper-class, well-born, well-bred.
antonyms plebeian, vulgar.

arm[1] *n.* **1** appendage, bough, branch, department, detachment, division, extension, limb, offshoot, projection, section, upper limb. **2** channel, estuary, firth, inlet, sound, strait, tributary.

arm[2] *v.* ammunition, brace, equip, forearm, fortify, furnish, gird, issue with, munition, outfit, prepare, prime, protect, provide, reinforce, rig, steel, strengthen, supply.

armaments *n.* ammunition, arms, artillery, cannon, guns, munitions, ordnance, weapons.

armed *adj.* armoured, braced, briefed, equipped, fitted out, fortified, furnished, girded, guarded, prepared, protected, provided, steeled, strengthened, thorny.
antonyms unarmed, unprepared.

armour *n.* armature, chain-mail, iron-cladding, shell, steel-plating.

armoured *adj.* armour-plated, bomb-proof, bullet-proof, protected, steel-plated.

armoury *n.* ammunition dump, arsenal, depot, magazine, ordnance depot, repository, stock, stockpile.

arms *n.* **1** armaments, firearms, guns, instruments of war, ordnance, weaponry, weapons. **2** armorial bearings, blazonry, crest, heraldry, insignia, shield.

army *n.* armed force, cohorts, horde, host, land forces, legions, military, militia, multitude, soldiers, troops.

aromatic *adj.* balmy, fragrant, perfumed, pungent, redolent, savoury, spicy, sweet-smelling.
antonym acrid.

around *prep.* about, approximately, circa, encircling, enclosing, encompassing, more or less, on all sides of, on every side of, roughly, surrounding.
adv. about, all over, at hand, close, close by, everywhere, here and there, in all directions, in the air, near, nearby, on all sides, to and fro.

arouse *v.* agitate, animate, awaken, call forth, evoke, excite, foster, galvanise, goad, incite, inflame, instigate, kindle, move, prompt, provoke, quicken, rouse, sharpen, spark, spur, startle, stimulate, stir up, summon up, wake up, waken, warm, whet, whip up.
antonyms calm, lull, quieten.

arrange *v.* **1** adjust, align, categorise, class, classify, construct, contrive, co-ordinate, design, determine, devise, dispose, distribute, file, fix, form, group, lay out, marshal, methodise, order, organise, plan, position, prepare, project, range, regulate, set out, settle, sift, sort (out), style, systematise, tidy. **2** adapt, harmonise, instrument, orchestrate, score, set.
antonyms **1** disorganise, muddle, untidy.

arrangement *n.* **1** array, classification, construction, design, display, disposition, form, grouping, layout, line-up, marshalling, method, order, ordering, organisation, plan, planning, preparation, provision, schedule, scheme, set-up, structure, system, tabulation, terms. **2** agreement, compromise, contract, settlement. **3** adaptation, harmonisation, instrumentation, interpretation, orchestration, score, setting, version.

array *n.* **1** arrangement, assortment, collection, display, exhibition, exposition, formation, line-up, marshalling, order, parade, show, supply. **2** apparel, attire, clothes, dress, finery, garments, regalia, robes.
v. **1** align, arrange, assemble, display, dispose, draw up, equip, exhibit, group, line up, marshal, muster, order, outfit, parade, range, show, supply. **2** adorn, clothe, deck, decorate, dress, robe.

arrest *v.* **1** apprehend, capture, detain, run in, seize. **2** absorb, catch, engage, engross, fascinate, grip, occupy. **3** block, check, delay, halt, hinder, hold, impede, inhibit, interrupt, obstruct, restrain, retard, slow, stall, stem, stop.

arrival *n.* advent, appearance, approach, coming, entrance, occurrence.
antonym departure.

arrive *v.* appear, come, enter, happen, materialise, occur, reach, show up, turn up.
antonyms depart, leave.

arrogant *adj.* assuming, conceited, condescending, contemptuous, disdainful, haughty, high and mighty, high-handed, imperious, insolent, lordly, overbearing, presumptuous, proud,

scornful, supercilious, superior.
antonyms bashful, humble, unassuming.

arrow *n.* bolt, dart, flight, indicator, pointer, shaft.

arsenal *n.* ammunition dump, armoury, depot, magazine, ordnance depot, repository, stock, stockpile, store, storehouse, supply, warehouse.

art *n.* **1** artwork, craft, craftiness, craftsmanship, draughtsmanship, drawing, painting, sculpture, visuals. **2** aptitude, dexterity, expertise, facility, finesse, ingenuity, knack, knowledge, mastery, method, profession, skill, trade. **3** artfulness, astuteness, cunning, deceit, guile, shrewdness, slyness, trickery.

artful *adj.* clever, crafty, cunning, deceitful, designing, devious, dexterous, foxy, ingenious, masterly, resourceful, scheming, sharp, shrewd, skilful, sly, smart, subtle, tricky, wily.
antonyms artless, ingenuous, naïve.

article *n.* **1** account, commentary, composition, essay, feature, paper, report, review, story. **2** commodity, constituent, division, item, object, part, piece, portion, thing, unit. **3** clause, paragraph, section.

articulate *adj.* clear, coherent, comprehensible, distinct, expressive, fluent, intelligible, lucid, meaningful, understandable, vocal, well-spoken.
v. breathe, enunciate, express, pronounce, say, speak, state, talk, utter, verbalise, vocalise, voice.

articulated *adj.* attached, connected, coupled, fastened, hinged, interlocked, joined, linked.

articulation *n.* delivery, diction, enunciation, expression, pronunciation, saying, speaking, talking, utterance, verbalisation, vocalisation, voicing.

artificial *adj.* affected, assumed, bogus, contrived, counterfeit, fake, false, feigned, forced, hyped up, imitation, insincere, made-up, man-made, mannered, manufactured, mock, non-natural, phoney, plastic, pretended, pseudo, sham, simulated, specious, spurious, synthetic, unnatural.
antonyms genuine, natural, real, true.

artillery *n.* battery, cannon, field-guns, field-pieces, guns, heavy metal, ordnance.

artisan *n.* artificer, craftsman, expert, journeyman, mechanic, operative, technician, workman.

artist *n.* craftsman, draughtsman, expert, maestro, master, painter, portrait-painter, sculptor.

artiste *n.* actor, comedian, comedienne, comic, entertainer, performer, player, trouper, variety artist, vaudevillian.

artistic *adj.* aesthetic, beautiful, creative, cultivated, cultured, decorative, elegant, exquisite, graceful, harmonious, imaginative, ornamental, refined, sensitive, skilled, stylish, talented, tasteful.
antonyms inelegant, tasteless.

artistry *n.* accomplishment, brilliance, craft, craftsmanship, creativity, deftness, expertise, finesse, flair, genius, mastery, proficiency, sensitivity, skill, style, talent, taste, touch, workmanship.
antonym ineptitude.

as *conj., prep.* because, being, considering that, for example, for instance, in that, in the character of, in the manner of, in the role of, inasmuch as, like, seeing that, since, such as, that, what, when, which, while.
as for as regards, in connection with, in relation to, on the subject of, with reference to, with regard to, with relation to, with respect to.

ascend *v.* climb, float up, fly up, go up, lift off, mount, move up, rise, scale, slope upwards, soar, take off, tower.
antonyms descend, go down.

ascent *n.* ascending, ascension, climb, climbing, elevation, escalation, gradient, hill, incline, mounting, ramp, rise, rising, scaling, slope.
antonym descent.

ascetic *n.* abstainer, celibate, hermit, monk, nun, puritan, recluse.
adj. abstemious, abstinent, austere, celibate, frugal, harsh, plain, puritanical, rigorous, self-controlled, self-denying, self-disciplined, severe, stern, strict, temperate.
antonym voluptuous.

asceticism *n.* abstemiousness, abstinence, austerity, celibacy, continence, frugality, harshness, moderation, monasticism, plainness, puritanism, rigorousness, rigour, self-control, self-denial, self-discipline, temperance.
antonym voluptuousness.

ascribe *v.* accredit, assign, attribute, chalk up to, charge, credit, impute, put down.

ashamed *adj.* abashed, apologetic, bashful, blushing, confused, conscience-stricken, crestfallen, discomposed, distressed, embarrassed, guilty, hesitant, humbled, humiliated, modest, mortified, prudish, redfaced, reluctant, remorseful, self-conscious, sheepish, shy, sorry.
antonyms defiant, proud, shameless.

aside *adv.* alone, apart, away, in isolation, in reserve, on one side, out of the way, privately, secretly, separately.
n. departure, digression, parenthesis, soliloquy, whisper.

ask *v.* appeal, apply, beg, beseech, bid, claim, clamour, crave, demand, enquire, entreat, implore, interrogate, invite, order, petition, plead, pray, press, query, question, quiz, request, require, seek, solicit, sue, summon, supplicate.

askance *adv.* contemptuously, disapprovingly, disdainfully, distrustfully, doubtfully, mistrustfully, sceptically, scornfully, suspiciously.

asleep *adj.* dormant, dozing, fast asleep, inactive, inert, napping, numb, resting, sleeping, snoozing, sound asleep, unconscious.

aspect *n.* air, angle, appearance, attitude, bearing, condition, countenance, direction, elevation, exposure, expression, face, facet, feature, look, manner, outlook, point of view, position, prospect, scene, side, situation, standpoint, view.

aspirant *n.* applicant, aspirer, candidate, competitor, contestant, hopeful, seeker, striver, suitor.

aspiration *n.* aim, ambition, craving, desire, dream, eagerness, endeavour, goal, hankering, hope, ideal, intent, longing, object, objective, purpose, wish, yearning.

aspire *v.* aim, crave, desire, dream, hanker, hope, intend, long, purpose, pursue, seek, wish, yearn.

aspiring *adj.* ambitious, aspirant, eager, endeavouring, enterprising, hopeful, keen, longing, optimistic, striving, wishful, would-be.

ass *n.* **1** donkey, hinny, jackass, jenny, mule. **2** blockhead, fool, idiot, nincompoop, twit.

assassin *n.* bravo, cut-throat, executioner, hatchet man, hit-man, killer, liquidator, murderer, slayer, thug.

assassinate *v.* dispatch, eliminate, hit, kill, liquidate, murder, slay.

assault *n.* attack, blitz, charge, incursion, invasion, offensive, onset, onslaught, raid, storm, storming, strike.
v. attack, charge, fall on, hit, invade, lay violent hands on, set upon, strike.

assemble *v.* **1** accumulate, amass, bring together, collect, congregate, convene, flock, gather, group, join up, marshal, meet, mobilise, muster (up), rally, round up, summon. **2** build, compose, construct, fabricate, make, manufacture, piece together, put together.
antonyms **1** disperse, scatter.

assembly *n.* **1** assemblage, body, building, collection, company, conference, congregation, congress, convocation, council, crowd, flock, gathering, group, meeting, multitude, rally, reception, throng. **2** construction, fabrication, manufacture.

assert *v.* advance, affirm, allege, attest, claim, contend, declare, defend, insist, lay down, maintain, press, profess, promote, pronounce, protest, state, stress, swear, testify to, thrust forward, uphold, vindicate.
antonyms deny, refute.

assertion *n.* affirmance, affirmation, allegation, claim, contention, declaration, profession, pronouncement, statement, vindication, vouch, word.
antonym denial.

assertive *adj.* aggressive, assuming, bold, confident, decided, dogmatic, domineering, emphatic, firm, forceful, forward, insistent, opinionated, overbearing, presumptuous, pushy, self-assured, strong-willed.
antonyms diffident, timid.

assess *v.* compute, consider, demand, determine, estimate, evaluate, fix, gauge, impose, investigate, judge, levy, rate, review, size up, tax, value, weigh.

assessment *n.* appraisal, calculation, consideration, determination, estimate, estimation, evaluation, gauging, judgement, opinion, rating, review, taxation, valuation.

asset *n.* advantage, aid, benefit, blessing, help, plus, resource, service, strength, virtue.
antonym liability.

assets *n.* capital, estate, funds, goods, holdings, means, money, possessions, property, reserves, resources, securities, wealth.

assign *v.* accredit, allocate, allot, appoint, apportion, ascribe, attribute, choose, consign, delegate, designate, determine, dispense, distribute, fix, give, grant, name, nominate, put down, select, set, specify, stipulate.

assignment *n.* allocation, appointment, charge, commission, consignment, delegation, designation, distribution, duty, errand, giving, grant, job, nomination, position, post, responsibility, selection, task.

assimilate *v.* absorb, accept, acclimatise, accommodate, accustom, adapt, adjust, blend, conform, digest, fit, incorporate, integrate, learn, merge, mingle, take in, tolerate.
antonym reject.

assist *v.* abet, accommodate, aid, back, benefit, boost, collaborate, co-operate, enable, expedite, facilitate, further, help, rally round, reinforce, relieve, second, serve, support, sustain.
antonyms hinder, thwart.

assistance *n.* aid, backing, benefit, boost, collaboration, comfort, co-operation, furtherance, help, reinforcement, relief, support, sustainment.
antonyms hindrance, resistance.

assistant *n.* abettor, accessory, accomplice, aide, ally, ancillary, associate, auxiliary, backer, collaborator, colleague, confederate, co-operator, helper, helpmate, partner, right-hand man, second, subordinate, subsidiary, supporter.

associate *v.* accompany, affiliate, ally, amalgamate, combine, company, confederate, connect, consort, correlate, couple, fraternise, hang around, identify, join, league, link, mingle, mix, pair, relate, socialise, unite, yoke.
n. affiliate, ally, assistant, collaborator, colleague, companion, compeer, comrade, confederate, co-worker, fellow, follower, friend, mate, partner, peer, side-kick.

association *n.* **1** alliance, band, cartel, clique, club, coalition, combination, company, confederacy, confederation, consortium, corporation, federation, fellowship, fraternity, group, league, organisation, partnership, society, syndicate, union. **2** affiliation, bond, companionship, connection, correlation, familiarity, friendship, intimacy, involvement, relation, relationship, tie.

assorted *adj.* different, differing, diverse, heterogeneous, manifold, miscellaneous, mixed, several, sundry, varied, various.

assortment *n.* arrangement, choice, collection, diversity, grouping, jumble, medley, miscellany, mixture, pot-pourri, selection, variety.

assume *v.* **1** accept, believe, deduce, expect, fancy, guess, imagine, infer, postulate, presume, suppose, surmise, take for granted, think, understand. **2** affect, counterfeit, feign, pretend to, put on, simulate, take on. **3** acquire, adopt, appropriate, arrogate, commandeer, embrace, seize, take over, undertake, usurp.

assumed *adj.* affected, bogus, counterfeit, fake, false, feigned, fictitious, hypothetical, made-up,

phoney, presumed, pretended, pseudonymous, sham, simulated, supposed.
antonyms actual, real, true.
assumption *n.* **1** belief, conjecture, fancy, guess, hypothesis, idea, inference, notion, postulate, premise, presumption, supposition, surmise, theory. **2** acceptance, adoption, seizure, taking.
assurance *n.* **1** affirmation, assertion, declaration, guarantee, oath, pledge, promise, vow, word. **2** aplomb, audacity, boldness, certainty, confidence, conviction, courage, firmness, nerve, self-confidence, sureness.
antonyms **2** doubt, shyness, uncertainty.
assure *v.* affirm, boost, comfort, confirm, convince, encourage, ensure, guarantee, hearten, persuade, pledge, promise, reassure, secure, soothe, strengthen, swear, tell, vow, warrant.
assured *adj.* assertive, audacious, bold, certain, confident, confirmed, definite, fixed, guaranteed, indisputable, irrefutable, positive, secure, self-assured, self-confident, self-possessed, settled, sure.
antonyms shy, uncertain.
astonish *v.* amaze, astound, baffle, bewilder, confound, daze, dumbfound, flabbergast, floor, shock, stagger, startle, stun, stupefy, surprise.
astonishment *n.* amazement, bewilderment, confusion, consternation, dismay, shock, surprise, wonder.
astound *v.* amaze, astonish, baffle, bewilder, confound, daze, dumbfound, flabbergast, overwhelm, shake, shock, stagger, stun, stupefy, surprise.
astray *adv.* adrift, amiss, lost, off course, off the mark, off the rails, to the bad, wrong.
astringent *adj.* acerbic, acid, austere, biting, caustic, exacting, grim, hard, harsh, rigorous, scathing, severe, stern, strict, stringent, trenchant.
antonym bland.
astronomical *adj.* astrophysical, celestial, cosmological, enormous, high, huge.
asylum *n.* **1** hospital, institution, mental hospital. **2** haven, refuge, retreat, safety, sanctuary, shelter.
asymmetrical *adj.* asymmetric, awry, crooked, disproportionate, irregular, unbalanced, unequal, uneven, unsymmetrical.
antonym symmetrical.
asymmetry *n.* disproportion, imbalance, inequality, irregularity, misproportion, unevenness.
antonym symmetry.
atheism *n.* disbelief, free-thinking, godlessness, heathenism, impiety, infidelity, irreligion, nonbelief, paganism, rationalism, scepticism, unbelief, ungodliness.
atheist *n.* disbeliever, free-thinker, heathen, infidel, non-believer, pagan, sceptic, unbeliever.
atheistic *adj.* disbelieving, free-thinking, heathen, impious, irreligious, irreverent, rationalistic, sceptical, unbelieving, ungodly, unreligious.
antonym religious.
athlete *n.* agonist, competitor, contender, contestant, gymnast, jock, runner, sportsman, sportswoman.
athletic *adj.* active, brawny, energetic, fit, husky, muscular, powerful, robust, sinewy, strapping, strong, sturdy, vigorous, well-knit, well-proportioned, wiry.
antonym puny.
athletics *n.* agonistics, contests, events, exercises, games, gymnastics, races, sports, track events.
atmosphere *n.* **1** aerospace, air, climate, heavens, sky. **2** ambience, aura, character, environment, feel, feeling, flavour, mood, quality, spirit, surroundings, tenor, tone.
atmospheric *adj.* aerial, climatic, meteorological.
atom *n.* bit, crumb, grain, hint, iota, jot, mite, molecule, morsel, particle, scintilla, scrap, shred, speck, spot, trace, whit.
atrocious *adj.* abominable, appalling, dreadful, fiendish, ghastly, grievous, heinous, hideous, horrible, monstrous, ruthless, savage, shocking, terrible, vicious.
antonyms admirable, fine.
atrocity *n.* abomination, atrociousness, barbarity, brutality, cruelty, enormity, evil, heinousness, hideousness, horror, monstrosity, outrage, savagery, viciousness, vileness, villainy, wickedness.
attach *v.* add, adhere, affix, annex, articulate, ascribe, assign, associate, attract, attribute, belong, bind, captivate, combine, connect, couple, fasten, fix, impute, join, link, place, put, relate to, secure, stick, tie, unite, weld.
antonyms detach, unfasten.
attached *adj.* affectionate, associated, connected, fond, loving.
attachment *n.* **1** accessory, addition, adjunct, appendage, codicil, extension, extra, fastener, fitting, fixture, supplement. **2** affection, affinity, attraction, bond, devotion, fondness, friendship, liking, link, love, loyalty, partiality, regard, tenderness, tie.
attack *n.* **1** abuse, aggression, assault, battery, blitz, bombardment, censure, charge, criticism, foray, incursion, invasion, offensive, onslaught, raid, rush, strike. **2** convulsion, fit, paroxysm, seizure, spasm, stroke.
v. abuse, assail, assault, blame, censure, charge, criticise, denounce, do over, fake, fall on, invade, lash, lay into, make at, malign, raid, revile, set about, set on, storm, strike.
antonyms defend, protect.
attacker *n.* abuser, aggressor, assailant, assaulter, critic, invader, mugger, persecutor, raider, reviler.
antonyms defender, supporter.
attain *v.* accomplish, achieve, acquire, arrive at, complete, earn, effect, fulfil, gain, get, grasp, net, obtain, procure, reach, realise, secure, touch, win.
attainable *adj.* accessible, achievable, available, feasible, manageable, obtainable, possible,

potential, practicable, probable, reachable, realistic, within reach.
antonym unattainable.

attainment *n.* ability, accomplishment, achievement, aptitude, art, capability, competence, completion, consummation, facility, feat, fulfilment, gift, mastery, proficiency, reaching, realisation, skill, success, talent.

attempt *n.* attack, bash, bid, effort, endeavour, experiment, go, move, push, shot, stab, struggle, trial, try, undertaking, venture.
v. aspire, endeavour, experiment, have a go, seek, strive, tackle, try, undertake, venture.

attend *v.* **1** be present, frequent, go to, visit. **2** accompany, care for, chaperon, escort, follow, guard, help, look after, minister to, nurse, serve, take care of, tend, usher, wait upon. **3** hear, heed, listen, mark, mind, note, notice, observe, pay attention. **4** appear, arise from, result from.
attend to concentrate on, control, cope with, deal with, direct, look after, manage, oversee, see to, supervise, take care of.

attendance *n.* appearance, assistance, audience, crowd, gate, house, presence, turn-out.

attendant *n.* aide, assistant, auxiliary, companion, custodian, escort, follower, guard, guide, helper, marshal, page, retainer, servant, steward, usher, waiter.
adj. accessory, accompanying, associated, attached, consequent, incidental, related, resultant, subsequent.

attention *n.* alertness, awareness, care, concentration, concern, consideration, contemplation, heed, mindfulness, notice, observation, recognition, regard, service, thought, treatment, vigilance.
antonyms carelessness, disregard, inattention.

attentive *adj.* accommodating, alert, awake, careful, concentrating, conscientious, considerate, courteous, devoted, heedful, kind, mindful, obliging, observant, polite, studious, thoughtful, vigilant, watchful.
antonyms heedless, inattentive, inconsiderate.

attitude *n.* approach, aspect, bearing, condition, disposition, feeling, manner, mood, opinion, outlook, perspective, point of view, pose, position, posture, stance, view.

attract *v.* allure, appeal to, bewitch, captivate, charm, draw, enchant, engage, entice, excite, fascinate, incline, induce, interest, invite, lure, pull, seduce, tempt.
antonyms disgust, reject, repel.

attraction *n.* allure, amenity, appeal, bait, captivation, charm, draw, enchantment, entertainment, enticement, fascination, inducement, interest, invitation, lure, magnetism, pull, seduction, show, temptation.
antonyms rejection, repulsion.

attractive *adj.* agreeable, appealing, beautiful, captivating, charming, engaging, enticing, fair, fascinating, fetching, glamorous, good-looking, gorgeous, handsome, interesting, inviting, lovely, magnetic, pleasant, pleasing, pretty, seductive, stunning, tempting, winning, winsome.
antonyms repellent, unattractive.

attribute *v.* accredit, apply, ascribe, assign, blame, charge, credit, impute, put down, refer.
n. affection, aspect, character, characteristic, facet, feature, idiosyncrasy, mark, note, peculiarity, point, property, quality, quirk, sign, symbol, trait, virtue.

attune *v.* acclimatise, accustom, adapt, adjust, familiarise, reconcile, regulate, set, tune.

au fait abreast of, acquainted, clued-up, conversant, in the know, in touch, knowledgeable, on the ball, posted, up-to-date, well up, well-informed.

auburn *adj.* chestnut, copper, red, russet, rust, tawny.

audacious *adj.* adventurous, bold, brave, brazen, cheeky, courageous, daring, dauntless, enterprising, fearless, forward, insolent, intrepid, plucky, rash, reckless, risky, rude, shameless, unabashed, valiant.
antonyms cautious, cowardly, reserved, timid.

audacity *n.* adventurousness, boldness, brass neck, bravery, brazenness, cheek, chutzpah, courage, daring, defiance, disrespectfulness, enterprise, fearlessness, forwardness, gall, guts, impertinence, impudence, insolence, intrepidity, nerve, presumption, rashness, recklessness, rudeness.
antonyms caution, reserve, timidity.

audible *adj.* appreciable, clear, detectable, discernible, distinct, perceptible, recognisable.
antonyms inaudible, quiet, unclear.

audience *n.* assemblage, assembly, auditorium, congregation, crowd, devotees, fans, following, gallery, gathering, hearing, listeners, meeting, onlookers, public, reception, regulars, spectators, turn-out, viewers.

audit *n.* analysis, balancing, check, examination, inspection, investigation, review, scrutiny, statement, verification.
v. analyse, balance, check, examine, inspect, investigate, review, scrutinise, verify.

auditor *n.* accountant, actuary, analyst, examiner, inspector, scrutiniser.

augur *v.* bode, forebode, herald, portend, predict, presage, promise, prophesy, signify.

aura *n.* air, ambience, aroma, atmosphere, feeling, hint, mood, quality, scent, suggestion.

auspices *n.* aegis, authority, backing, care, charge, control, guidance, influence, patronage, protection, sponsorship, supervision, support.

auspicious *adj.* bright, cheerful, encouraging, favourable, fortunate, happy, hopeful, lucky, opportune, optimistic, promising, prosperous, rosy, white.
antonyms inauspicious, ominous.

austere *adj.* **1** bleak, economical, forbidding, plain, simple, stark, unadorned. **2** abstemious, ascetic, chaste, cold, exacting, formal, grave, grim, hard, harsh, puritanical, restrained, rigid, rigorous, self-denying, self-disciplined, serious, severe, sober, solemn, stern, strict.

antonyms **1** elaborate, extravagant. **2** genial.

austerity *n.* abstemiousness, abstinence, asceticism, coldness, economy, formality, hardness, harshness, plainness, puritanism, severity, simplicity, solemnity.
antonyms elaborateness, materialism.

authentic *adj.* accurate, actual, bona fide, certain, factual, faithful, genuine, honest, legitimate, original, pure, real, reliable, true, true-to-life, trustworthy, valid, veritable.
antonyms counterfeit, fake, false, spurious.

authenticate *v.* accredit, attest, authorise, certify, confirm, corroborate, endorse, guarantee, validate, verify, vouch for, warrant.

authenticity *n.* accuracy, authoritativeness, certainty, correctness, dependability, faithfulness, fidelity, genuineness, honesty, reality, reliability, trustworthiness, truth, truthfulness, validity, veracity.
antonyms invalidity, spuriousness.

author *n.* architect, composer, creator, designer, fabricator, fashioner, founder, framer, initiator, inventor, maker, mover, originator, parent, pen, penman, penwoman, planner, prime mover, producer, writer.

authorisation *n.* approval, certification, credentials, go-ahead, green light, leave, licence, permission, permit, sanction, warrant.

authorise *v.* accredit, allow, approve, commission, confirm, consent to, empower, enable, entitle, legalise, license, permit, ratify, sanction, validate, warrant.

authoritarian *adj.* absolute, autocratic, despotic, dictatorial, disciplinarian, doctrinaire, dogmatic, domineering, harsh, heavy, imperious, inflexible, oppressive, repressive, rigid, severe, strict, tyrannical, unyielding.
antonym liberal.
n. absolutist, autocrat, despot, dictator, disciplinarian, fascist, Hitler, tyrant.

authoritative *adj.* accepted, accurate, approved, assured, authentic, authorised, commanding, confident, convincing, decisive, definitive, dependable, factual, faithful, learned, legitimate, masterly, official, reliable, sanctioned, scholarly, sound, sovereign, true, trustworthy, truthful, valid, veritable.
antonym unreliable.

authority *n.* **1** administration, control, dominion, force, government, influence, officialdom, power, rule, sovereignty, supremacy, sway. **2** authorisation, justification, licence, permission, permit, prerogative, right, sanction, warrant. **3** connoisseur, expert, judge, master, professional, pundit, scholar, specialist.

autocracy *n.* absolutism, authoritarianism, despotism, dictatorship, fascism, totalitarianism, tyranny.
antonym democracy.

autocrat *n.* absolutist, authoritarian, despot, dictator, fascist, Hitler, totalitarian, tyrant.

autocratic *adj.* absolute, all-powerful, authoritarian, despotic, dictatorial, domineering, imperious, overbearing, totalitarian, tyrannical.
antonyms democratic, liberal.

automatic *adj.* automated, certain, inescapable, inevitable, instinctive, involuntary, mechanical, mechanised, natural, necessary, push-button, reflex, robot, routine, self-activating, self-propelling, self-regulating, spontaneous, unavoidable, unconscious, unthinking, unwilled.

autumn *v.* fall, harvest.

auxiliary *adj.* accessory, aiding, ancillary, assistant, assisting, back-up, emergency, helping, reserve, secondary, subsidiary, substitute, supplementary, supporting, supportive.
n. accessory, accomplice, ally, ancillary, assistant, associate, companion, confederate, helper, partner, reserve, subordinate, supporter.

available *adj.* accessible, at hand, attainable, convenient, free, handy, obtainable, on hand, on tap, ready, to hand, vacant, within reach.
antonym unavailable.

avalanche *n.* barrage, cascade, deluge, flood, inundation, landslide, landslip, torrent.

avant-garde *adj.* advanced, enterprising, experimental, far-out, forward-looking, innovative, innovatory, inventive, pioneering, progressive, unconventional, way-out.
antonyms conservative, dyed-in-the-wool.

avarice *n.* acquisitiveness, covetousness, greed, greediness, rapacity.
antonyms generosity, liberality.

avaricious *adj.* acquisitive, covetous, grasping, greedy, mean, rapacious.
antonym generous.

avenge *v.* punish, repay, requite, take revenge for, take vengeance for, vindicate.

average *n.* mean, mediocrity, medium, midpoint, norm, par, rule, run, standard.
antonyms exception, extreme.
adj. common, everyday, fair, general, indifferent, intermediate, mean, medial, median, mediocre, medium, middle, moderate, normal, ordinary, passable, regular, run-of-the-mill, satisfactory, so-so, standard, tolerable, typical, undistinguished, unexceptional, unremarkable, usual.
antonyms exceptional, extreme.

averse *adj.* antagonistic, disapproving, disinclined, hostile, ill-disposed, loath, opposed, reluctant, unfavourable, unwilling.
antonyms keen, sympathetic, willing.

aversion *n.* abhorrence, abomination, animosity, antagonism, detestation, disapproval, disgust, disinclination, dislike, distaste, hate, hatred, horror, hostility, loathing, opposition, phobia, repugnance, repulsion, revulsion, unwillingness.
antonyms desire, liking, sympathy.

avert *v.* avoid, deflect, evade, fend off, forestall, frustrate, obviate, parry, prevent, stave off, turn aside, turn away, ward off.

aviation *n.* aeronautics, flight, flying.

avid *adj.* ardent, covetous, dedicated, devoted, eager, earnest, enthusiastic, fanatical, fervent, grasping, greedy, hungry, insatiable, intense, keen, passionate, ravenous, thirsty, zealous.
antonym indifferent.

avoid *v.* abstain from, avert, balk, bypass, circumvent, dodge, duck, elude, escape, evade, get out of, prevent, refrain from, shirk, shun, side-step, steer clear of.

avoidable *adj.* escapable, preventable.
antonym inevitable.

avoidance *n.* abstention, abstinence, circumvention, dodge, eluding, elusion, escape, evasion, prevention, refraining, shirking, shunning.

avowed *adj.* acknowledged, admitted, confessed, declared, open, overt, professed, self-confessed, self-proclaimed, sworn.

awake *v.* arouse, awaken, rouse, wake, wake up.
adj. alert, alive, aroused, attentive, aware, conscious, observant, sensitive, vigilant, watchful, wide-awake.

awakening *n.* activation, animating, arousal, awaking, birth, enlivening, prompting, revival, rousing, stimulation, waking.

award *v.* accord, allot, allow, apportion, assign, bestow, confer, determine, dispense, distribute, endow, gift, give, grant, present.
n. adjudication, allotment, allowance, bestowal, conferral, decision, decoration, dispensation, endowment, gift, grant, judgement, order, presentation, prize, trophy.

aware *adj.* acquainted, alive to, appreciative, attentive, au courant, conscious, conversant, enlightened, familiar, heedful, informed, knowing, knowledgeable, mindful, observant, on the ball, sensible, sensitive, sentient, sharp, shrewd.
antonyms insensitive, oblivious, unaware.

awe *n.* admiration, amazement, apprehension, astonishment, dread, fear, respect, reverence, terror, veneration, wonder.
antonym contempt.

awe-inspiring *adj.* amazing, astonishing, awesome, awful, breathtaking, daunting, fearsome, formidable, impressive, intimidating, magnificent, overwhelming, wonderful.
antonyms contemptible, tame.

awesome *adj.* alarming, amazing, astonishing, awe-inspiring, awful, breathtaking, daunting, dread, dreadful, fearful, formidable, frightening, imposing, impressive, intimidating, magnificent, majestic, moving, overwhelming, solemn, stunning, stupefying, stupendous, terrifying, wonderful.

awe-struck *adj.* afraid, amazed, astonished, awe-inspired, awe-stricken, daunted, dumbfounded, fearful, frightened, impressed, intimidated, speechless, struck dumb, stunned, terrified, wonder-struck.

awful *adj.* abysmal, alarming, atrocious, dire, dread, dreadful, fearful, frightful, ghastly, gruesome, hideous, horrible, horrific, nasty, shocking, spine-chilling, terrible, tremendous, ugly, unpleasant.
antonyms astounding, fantastic, wonderful.

awkward *adj.* **1** bungling, clumsy, cumbersome, delicate, difficult, fiddly, gauche, graceless, ham-fisted, inconvenient, inelegant, inept, inexpert, perplexing, troublesome, unco-ordinated, ungainly, ungraceful, unskilful, unwieldy. **2** embarrassed, ill at ease, uncomfortable. **3** irritable, obstinate, prickly, rude, stubborn, touchy, unco-operative, unpleasant.
antonyms **1** convenient, elegant, graceful, handy. **2** comfortable, relaxed. **3** amenable, pleasant.

awry *adv., adj.* amiss, askew, asymmetrical, cock-eyed, crooked, misaligned, oblique, off-centre, skew-whiff, twisted, uneven, unevenly, wonky, wrong.
antonyms straight, symmetrical.

axe *v.* cancel, chop, cleave, cut (down), discharge, discontinue, dismiss, eliminate, fell, fire, get rid of, hew, remove, sack, split, terminate, throw out, withdraw.

axiom *n.* adage, aphorism, byword, dictum, fundamental, maxim, precept, principle, truism, truth.

axis *n.* axle, centre-line, longitude, pivot, plumb-line, shaft, spindle, vertical.

B

babble *v.* **1** cackle, chatter, gabble, jabber, mumble, murmur, mutter, prate. **2** burble, gurgle.
n. burble, clamour, gabble, gibberish, hubbub, murmur.
baby *n.* babe, child, infant, suckling, tiny, toddler.
adj. diminutive, little, midget, mini, miniature, minute, small, small-scale, tiny.
babyish *adj.* baby, childish, foolish, immature, infantile, juvenile, naïve, puerile, silly, sissy, soft, spoilt, young.
antonyms mature, precocious.
back *n.* backside, end, hind part, hindquarters, posterior, rear, reverse, stern, tail, tail end.
antonyms face, front.
v. **1** backtrack, recede, recoil, regress, retire, retreat, reverse, withdraw. **2** advocate, assist, boost, champion, countenance, countersign, encourage, endorse, favour, finance, sanction, second, side with, sponsor, subsidise, support, sustain, underwrite.
antonyms **1** advance, approach. **2** discourage, weaken.
adj. **1** end, hind, hindmost, posterior, rear, reverse, tail. **2** delayed, earlier, elapsed, former, outdated, overdue, past, previous, prior, superseded.
antonym **1** front.
back down back-pedal, concede, give in, retreat, submit, surrender, withdraw, yield.
back out abandon, cancel, chicken out, give up, go back on, pull out, recant, resign, withdraw.
back up aid, assist, bolster, champion, confirm, corroborate, endorse, reinforce, second, substantiate, support.
antonym let down.
backbiting *n.* abuse, bitchiness, cattiness, criticism, defamation, denigration, detraction, disparagement, gossip, malice, revilement, slander, spite, spitefulness.
antonym praise.
backbone *n.* **1** basis, character, core, foundation, mainstay, spine, vertebral column. **2** courage, determination, grit, mettle, nerve, pluck, power, resolve, stamina, steadfastness, strength, support, tenacity, toughness.
antonyms **2** spinelessness, weakness.
backbreaking *adj.* arduous, crushing, exhausting, gruelling, hard, heavy, laborious, punishing, strenuous, tiring, wearing.
antonym easy.
backfire *v.* boomerang, fail, flop, miscarry, rebound, recoil, ricochet.
background *n.* breeding, circumstances, credentials, culture, education, environment, experience, grounding, history, preparation, record, surroundings, tradition, upbringing.
back-handed *adj.* ambiguous, double-edged, dubious, equivocal, ironic, oblique, sarcastic, two-edged.
antonyms sincere, wholehearted.
backing *n.* accompaniment, advocacy, aid, assistance, championing, encouragement, endorsement, favour, funds, grant, helpers, moral support, patronage, sanction, seconding, sponsorship, subsidy, support.
backlash *n.* backfire, boomerang, kickback, reaction, recoil, repercussion, reprisal, resentment, response, retaliation.
backlog *n.* accumulation, excess, mountain, reserve, reserves, resources, stock, supply.
backsliding *n.* apostasy, defaulting, defection, desertion, lapse, relapse.
backward *adj.* bashful, behind, behindhand, dull, hesitant, hesitating, immature, late, reluctant, retarded, shy, slow, stupid, subnormal, underdeveloped, unwilling, wavering.
antonyms forward, precocious.
backwoods *n.* back of beyond, bush, outback, sticks.
bad *adj.* **1** adverse, damaging, detrimental, disagreeable, distressing, grave, harmful, harsh, injurious, serious, severe, undesirable, unfortunate, unpleasant. **2** corrupt, criminal, evil, immoral, sinful, vile, wicked. **3** defective, deficient, faulty, imperfect, inferior, poor, substandard, unsatisfactory, useless. **4** contaminated, decayed, mouldy, off, putrid, rancid, rotten, sour, spoilt. **5** disobedient, mischievous, naughty.
antonyms **1** good, mild, slight. **2** virtuous. **3** skilled. **4** fresh. **5** well-behaved.
badge *n.* brand, device, emblem, identification, insignia, logo, mark, sign, stamp, token, trademark.
badly *adv.* **1** acutely, bitterly, critically, crucially, deeply, desperately, exceedingly, extremely, greatly, intensely, painfully, seriously, severely. **2** carelessly, criminally, faultily, immorally, imperfectly, improperly, inadequately, incompetently, incorrectly, negligently, poorly, shamefully, unfairly, unfavourably, unfortunately, unsatisfactorily, unsuccessfully, wickedly, wrong, wrongly.
bad-tempered *adj.* crabbed, cross, crotchety, fractious, impatient, irritable, petulant, querulous, snappy, stroppy.
antonyms equable, genial.
baffle *v.* amaze, astound, bamboozle, bemuse,

bewilder, check, confound, confuse, daze, defeat, disconcert, dumbfound, flabbergast, flummox, foil, frustrate, hinder, mystify, perplex, puzzle, stump, stun, thwart, upset.
antonyms enlighten, help.

bag *v.* acquire, appropriate, capture, catch, commandeer, corner, gain, get, grab, kill, land, obtain, reserve, shoot, take, trap.
n. carrier, case, container, grip, handbag, haversack, hold-all, holder, pack, rucksack, sack, satchel, satchet, shoulder-bag, suit-case.

baggage *n.* bags, belongings, equipment, gear, impedimenta, luggage, paraphernalia, suitcases, things, traps.

baggy *adj.* billowing, bulging, droopy, floppy, ill-fitting, loose, pouchy, roomy, sagging, slack.
antonyms firm, tight.

bail *n.* bond, guarantee, pledge, security, surety, warranty.
bail out[1] aid, assist, finance, help, relieve, rescue.
bail out[2], **bale out** back out, cop out, escape, quit, retreat, withdraw.

bailiff *n.* agent, constable, deputy, factor, magistrate, office, sheriff.

bait *n.* allurement, attraction, bribe, enticement, incentive, inducement, lure, temptation.
antonym disincentive.
v. annoy, goad, harass, irk, irritate, needle, persecute, provoke, tease, torment.

balance *v.* **1** adjust, counteract, counterbalance, equalise, equate, level, match, neutralise, offset, poise, square, stabilise, steady. **2** compare, consider, estimate, weigh. **3** assess, calculate, compute, settle, tally, total.
antonyms **1** overbalance, unbalance.
n. **1** correspondence, equality, equilibrium, equity, equivalence, evenness, parity, stability, steadiness, symmetry. **2** composure, equanimity, poise, self-possession. **3** difference, remainder, residue, rest, surplus.
antonyms **1** imbalance, instability.

balanced *adj.* calm, equitable, even- handed, fair, impartial, just, self- possessed, sensible, unbiased, unprejudiced, well-rounded.
antonyms prejudiced, unbalanced.

balcony *n.* gallery, terrace, upper circle, veranda.

bald *adj.* **1** bald-headed, hairless, uncovered. **2** bare, barren, naked, plain, severe, simple, stark, treeless, unadorned. **3** direct, downright, forthright, outright, straight, straightforward.
antonyms **1** hairy, hirsute. **2** adorned.

bale *n.* bundle, pack, package, parcel, truss.
bale out *see* **bail out**[2].

balk, baulk *v.* baffle, bar, boggle, check, counteract, defeat, disconcert, dodge, evade, flinch, foil, forestall, frustrate, hesitate, hinder, jib, make difficulties, obstruct, prevent, recoil, refuse, resist, shirk, shrink, stall, thwart.

ball[1] *n.* bullet, conglomeration, drop, globe, globule, orb, pellet, pill, shot, slug, sphere.

ball[2] *n.* assembly, carnival, dance, dinner-dance, masquerade, party, soirée.

ballad *n.* carol, composition, ditty, folk-song, poem, shanty, song.

ballot *n.* election, plebiscite, poll, polling, referendum, vote, voting.

balm *n.* anodyne, balsam, calmative, comfort, consolation, cream, curative, embrocation, lotion, ointment, restorative, sedative, solace.
antonyms irritant, vexation.

balmy[1] *adj.* clement, gentle, mild, pleasant, soft, summery, temperate.
antonym inclement.

balmy[2] *adj.* barmy, crazy, daft, dotty, foolish, idiotic, insane, mad, nutty, odd, round the bend, silly, stupid.
antonyms rational, sane, sensible.

bamboozle *v.* baffle, cheat, con, confound, confuse, deceive, defraud, delude, dupe, fool, hoax, hoodwink, mystify, perplex, puzzle, stump, swindle, trick.

ban *v.* banish, bar, disallow, exclude, forbid, ostracise, outlaw, prohibit, restrict, suppress.
antonyms allow, authorise, permit.
n. boycott, censorship, condemnation, curse, denunciation, embargo, outlawry, prohibition, proscription, restriction, stoppage, suppression, taboo.
antonyms dispensation, permission.

banal *adj.* boring, clichéd, commonplace, corny, empty, everyday, hackneyed, humdrum, ordinary, stale, stereotyped, stock, threadbare, tired, trite, unimaginative.
antonyms fresh, imaginative, original.

band[1] *n.* bandage, belt, binding, bond, chain, cord, fetter, ligature, manacle, ribbon, shackle, strap, strip, tape, tie.

band[2] *n.* association, body, clique, club, company, crew, ensemble, flock, gang, group, herd, orchestra, party, range, society, troop.
v. affiliate, ally, amalgamate, collaborate, consolidate, federate, gather, group, join, merge, unite.
antonyms disband, disperse.

bandage *n.* compress, dressing, ligature, plaster, swaddle, swathe, tourniquet.
v. bind, cover, dress, swaddle, swathe.

bandit *n.* brigand, buccaneer, cowboy, desperado, gangster, gunman, highwayman, hijacker, marauder, outlaw, pirate, robber, thief.

bandy[1] *v.* barter, exchange, interchange, pass, reciprocate, swap, throw, toss, trade.

bandy[2] *adj.* bandy-legged, bent, bowed, bow-legged, crooked, curved.

bang *n.* blow, boom, bump, clang, clap, clash, collision, crash, detonation, explosion, hit, knock, noise, peal, pop, punch, report, shot, slam, smack, stroke, thud, thump, wallop, whack.
v. bash, boom, bump, burst, clang, clatter, crash, detonate, drum, echo, explode, hammer, knock, peal, pound, rap, resound, slam, stamp, strike, thump, thunder.
adv. directly, hard, headlong, noisily, precisely, right, slap, smack, straight, suddenly.

banish *v.* ban, bar, debar, deport, discard, dislodge, dismiss, dispel, eject, eliminate, eradi-

cate, evict, exclude, excommunicate, exile, expel, get rid of, ostracise, oust, outlaw, remove, shut out, transport.
antonyms recall, welcome.
banishment *n.* deportation, eviction, exile, expatriation, expulsion, ostracisation, outlawry, transportation.
antonyms recall, return, welcome.
bank[1] *n.* accumulation, cache, depository, fund, hoard, pool, repository, reserve, reservoir, savings, stock, stockpile, store, treasury.
v. accumulate, deposit, keep, save, stockpile, store.
antonym spend.
bank[2] *n.* earthwork, edge, embankment, heap, mass, mound, pile, rampart, ridge, shore, side, slope, tilt.
v. accumulate, amass, drift, heap, incline, mass, mound, pile, pitch, slant, slope, stack, tilt, tip.
bank[3] *n.* array, bench, group, line, rank, row, sequence, series, succession, tier, train.
bank-note *n.* bill, note, paper money, treasury note.
bankrupt *adj.* beggared, broke, depleted, destitute, exhausted, failed, impoverished, insolvent, lacking, ruined, spent.
antonyms solvent, wealthy.
n. debtor, insolvent, pauper.
bankruptcy *n.* beggary, disaster, exhaustion, failure, indebtedness, insolvency, liquidation, ruin.
antonyms solvency, wealth.
banner *n.* colours, ensign, flag, pennant, standard, streamer.
banquet *n.* dinner, feast, meal, treat.
banter *n.* badinage, chaff, chaffing, derision, jesting, joking, kidding, mockery, pleasantry, quiz, repartee, ribbing, ridicule, word play.
baptise *v.* call, christen, cleanse, enrol, immerse, initiate, introduce, name, purify, recruit, sprinkle, style, term, title.
baptism *n.* beginning, christening, début, dedication, immersion, initiation, introduction, launch, launching, purification, sprinkling.
bar *n.* **1** counter, dive, inn, lounge, pub, public house, saloon, tavern. **2** block, chunk, ingot, lump, nugget, slab, wedge. **3** barricade, barrier, batten, check, cross-piece, deterrent, hindrance, impediment, obstacle, obstruction, paling, pole, rail, railing, rod, shaft, stake, stanchion, stick, stop. **4** advocates, attorneys, barristers, bench, counsel, court, courtroom, dock, law court, tribunal.
v. ban, barricade, bolt, debar, exclude, fasten, forbid, hinder, latch, lock, obstruct, preclude, prevent, prohibit, restrain, secure.
barb *n.* **1** arrow, bristle, point, prong, quill, spike, stab, thorn. **2** affront, dig, gibe, home-thrust, insult, rebuff, sarcasm, sneer.
barbarian *n.* boor, brute, hooligan, ignoramus, illiterate, oaf, philistine, ruffian, savage, vandal.
barbaric *adj.* barbarous, brutal, brutish, coarse, crude, cruel, ferocious, fierce, inhuman, primitive, rude, savage, uncivilised, uncouth, vulgar, wild.
antonyms civilised, gracious, humane.
barbarity *n.* barbarousness, brutality, brutishness, cruelty, ferocity, inhumanity, rudeness, ruthlessness, savagery, viciousness, wildness.
antonyms civilisation, civility, humanity.
barbarous *adj.* backward, barbarian, brutal, coarse, crude, cruel, ferocious, heartless, heathenish, ignorant, inhuman, primitive, rough, rude, ruthless, savage, uncivilised, uncultured, unrefined, vicious, vulgar, wild.
antonyms civilised, cultured, educated.
barbed *adj.* **1** hooked, jagged, pointed, prickly, pronged, spiked, spiny, thorny, toothed. **2** acid, caustic, critical, cutting, hostile, hurtful, nasty, snide, unkind.
bare *adj.* **1** denuded, exposed, naked, nude, stripped, unclothed, uncovered, undressed. **2** bald, barren, basic, empty, essential, hard, plain, simple, stark, unfurnished.
antonyms **1** clothed. **2** decorated, detailed.
barefaced *adj.* arrant, blatant, bold, brash, brazen, flagrant, glaring, impudent, insolent, manifest, naked, obvious, open, palpable, patent, shameless, transparent, unabashed, unconcealed.
bargain *n.* **1** agreement, arrangement, contract, negotiation, pact, pledge, promise, stipulation, transaction, treaty, understanding. **2** discount, giveaway, reduction, snip.
v. agree, barter, buy, contract, covenant, deal, haggle, negotiate, promise, sell, stipulate, trade, traffic, transact.
bargain for anticipate, consider, contemplate, expect, foresee, imagine, include, look for, plan for, reckon on.
barge *v.* bump, butt in, collide, elbow, gatecrash, hit, impinge, interfere, interrupt, intrude, muscle in, push (in), shove.
n. canal boat, flatboat, house-boat, lighter, narrow-boat.
bark *n.* bawl, bay, growl, shout, snap, snarl, woof, yap, yell, yelp.
v. advertise, bawl, bay, bluster, growl, shout, snap, snarl, yap, yell, yelp.
barmy *adj.* balmy, crazy, daft, dotty, foolish, idiotic, insane, mad, nutty, odd, silly, stupid.
antonyms rational, sane, sensible.
baroque *adj.* bold, convoluted, elaborate, extravagant, exuberant, fanciful, fantastic, flamboyant, florid, grotesque, ornate, overdecorated, overwrought, rococo, vigorous.
antonyms plain, simple.
barracks *n.* accommodation, billet, camp, encampment, garrison, guard-house, lodging, quarters.
barrage *n.* assault, attack, bombardment, broadside, burst, cannonade, deluge, gunfire, hail, mass, onset, onslaught, profusion, rain, shelling, shower, storm, stream, torrent, volley.
barrel *n.* butt, cask, keg, tun, water-butt.
barren *adj.* arid, boring, childless, desert, desolate, dry, dull, empty, flat, fruitless, infertile, pointless, profitless, stale, sterile, unbearing,

unfruitful, uninformative, uninspiring, uninstructive, uninteresting, unproductive, unprolific, unrewarding, useless, waste.
antonyms fertile, fruitful, productive, useful.
barricade *n.* barrier, blockade, bulwark, fence, obstruction, protection, rampart, stockade.
v. bar, block, defend, fortify, obstruct, protect.
barrier *n.* **1** bar, barricade, blockade, boom, boundary, check, ditch, fence, fortification, railing, rampart, wall. **2** difficulty, drawback, handicap, hindrance, hurdle, impediment, limitation, obstacle, obstruction, restriction, stumbling-block.
barrow *n.* hand-barrow, wheelbarrow.
bartender *n.* bar-keeper, barmaid, barman, publican.
barter *v.* bargain, deal, exchange, haggle, negotiate, sell, swap, trade, traffic.
base *n.* basis, bed, bottom, camp, centre, core, essence, essential, foot, foundation, fundamental, groundwork, headquarters, heart, home, key, origin, pedestal, plinth, post, principal, rest, root, settlement, source, stand, standard, starting-point, station, support.
v. build, construct, depend, derive, establish, found, ground, hinge, locate, station.
baseless *adj.* gratuitous, groundless, unauthenticated, uncalled-for, unconfirmed, unfounded, unjustified, unsubstantiated, unsupported.
antonym justifiable.
bashful *adj.* abashed, backward, blushing, confused, coy, diffident, embarrassed, hesitant, inhibited, modest, nervous, reserved, reticent, retiring, self-conscious, shamefaced, sheepish, shrinking, shy, timid, unforthcoming.
antonyms aggressive, bold, confident.
basic *adj.* central, elementary, essential, fundamental, important, indispensable, inherent, intrinsic, key, necessary, primary, root, underlying, vital.
antonyms inessential, minor, peripheral.
basically *adv.* at bottom, at heart, essentially, fundamentally, inherently, intrinsically, primarily, principally.
basics *n.* bedrock, core, essentials, facts, fundamentals, grass roots, necessaries, practicalities, principles, rock bottom, rudiments.
basin *n.* bowl, cavity, crater, depression, dip, dish, hollow, sink.
basis *n.* approach, base, bottom, core, essential, footing, foundation, fundamental, ground, groundwork, heart, pedestal, premise, principle, support, thrust.
bask *v.* delight in, enjoy, laze, lie, lounge, relax, relish, revel, savour, sunbathe, wallow.
basket *n.* bassinet, creel, hamper, pannier, punnet.
bass *adj.* deep, grave, low, low-toned, resonant.
bastion *n.* bulwark, citadel, defence, fortress, mainstay, pillar, prop, rock, stronghold, support.
batch *n.* amount, assemblage, assortment, bunch, collection, consignment, contingent, group, lot, pack, parcel, quantity, set.
bath *n.* cleansing, douche, Jacuzzi®, scrubbing, shower, soak, tub, wash.
v. bathe, clean, shower, soak, wash.
bathe *v.* cleanse, cover, flood, immerse, moisten, rinse, soak, steep, stew, suffuse, swim, wash, wet.
n. dip, dook, rinse, soak, swim, wash.
battalion *n.* army, brigade, company, contingent, division, force, herd, horde, host, legion, mass, multitude, platoon, regiment, squadron, throng.
batten *v.* barricade, board up, clamp down, fasten, fix, nail down, secure, tighten.
batter *v.* abuse, assault, beat, bruise, buffet, crush, dash, demolish, destroy, disfigure, distress, hurt, injure, lash, maltreat, mangle, manhandle, maul, pelt, pound, pummel, ruin, shatter, smash, thrash, wallop.
battered *adj.* abused, beaten, bruised, crumbling, crushed, damaged, dilapidated, ill-treated, injured, ramshackle, tumbledown, weather-beaten.
battery *n.* artillery, assault, attack, barrage, beating, cannon, guns, onslaught, set, thrashing.
battle *n.* action, attack, campaign, clash, combat, conflict, contest, controversy, crusade, debate, disagreement, dispute, encounter, engagement, fight, fray, hostilities, row, skirmish, strife, struggle, war, warfare.
v. agitate, argue, campaign, clamour, combat, contend, contest, crusade, dispute, feud, fight, strive, struggle, war.
battle-cry *n.* catchword, motto, slogan, war cry, warsong, watchword.
bauble *n.* bagatelle, knick-knack, plaything, tinsel, toy, trifle, trinket.
baulk *see* **balk**.
bay[1] *n.* arm, bight, cove, gulf, inlet, voe.
bay[2] *n.* alcove, booth, carrel, compartment, cubicle, niche, nook, opening, recess, stall.
bay[3] *v.* bark, bawl, bell, bellow, cry, holler, howl, roar.
bayonet *v.* impale, knife, pierce, spear, stab, stick.
bazaar *n.* bring-and-buy, exchange, fair, fête, market, market-place, mart, sale.
be *v.* abide, arise, befall, breathe, come about, come to pass, continue, develop, dwell, endure, exist, happen, inhabit, last, live, obtain, occur, persist, prevail, remain, reside, stand, stay, survive, take place.
beach *n.* coast, sand, sands, seaboard, seashore, seaside, shingle, shore, strand, water's edge.
beachcomber *n.* forager, loiterer, scavenger, scrounger, wayfarer.
beacon *n.* beam, bonfire, flare, lighthouse, rocket, sign, signal, watch-fire.
bead *n.* blob, bubble, dot, drop, droplet, glob, globule, pearl, pellet.
beak *n.* bill, bow, nose, nozzle, projection, snout.
beam *n.* **1** gleam, glimmer, glint, glow, ray, shaft. **2** bar, board, boom, girder, joist, plank, rafter, spar, support, timber.
v. broadcast, emit, glare, glimmer, glitter, glow, grin, radiate, shine, smile, transmit.

bear *v.* **1** bring, carry, convey, move, take, transport. **2** hold, shoulder, support, sustain, uphold. **3** beget, breed, bring forth, develop, engender, generate, give birth to, give up, produce, propagate, yield. **4** cherish, harbour, maintain. **5** abide, admit, allow, endure, permit, put up with, stand, suffer, tolerate.
bear down advance on, approach, attack, close in, compress, converge on, encumber, near, oppress, press down, push, strain, weigh down.
bear on affect, concern, connect with, involve, refer to, relate to, touch on.
bear out confirm, demonstrate, endorse, justify, prove, substantiate, support, testify, uphold, vindicate.
bear up carry on, endure, persevere, soldier on, suffer, withstand.
bear with be patient with, endure, forbear, make allowances for, put up with, suffer, tolerate.

bearable *adj.* acceptable, endurable, manageable, sufferable, supportable, sustainable, tolerable.

beard *n.* goatee, moustache, sideburns, whiskers.

bearded *adj.* bristly, bushy, hairy, hirsute, shaggy, tufted, unshaven, whiskered.
antonyms beardless, clean-shaven, smooth.

bearer *n.* beneficiary, carrier, conveyor, courier, holder, messenger, porter, possessor, post, runner, servant.

bearing *n.* **1** connection, reference, relation, relevance, significance. **2** air, behaviour, carriage, comportment, demeanour, manner, mien, poise, posture. **3** aspect, attitude, course, direction.

bearings *n.* aim, course, direction, location, orientation, position, situation, track, way, whereabouts.

beast *n.* animal, ape, barbarian, brute, creature, devil, fiend, monster, pig, savage, swine.

beat *v.* **1** bang, bash, batter, bruise, buffet, cane, flog, hammer, hit, knock, lash, lay into, pelt, pound, punch, strap, strike, swipe, tan, thrash, wham, whip. **2** flutter, palpitate, pulsate, pulse, quake, quiver, race, shake, throb, thump, tremble, vibrate. **3** best, conquer, defeat, excel, hammer, outdo, outrun, outstrip, overcome, overwhelm, slaughter, subdue, surpass, trounce, vanquish.
n. **1** blow, hit, lash, punch, shake, slap, strike, swing, thump. **2** accent, flutter, measure, metre, palpitation, pulsation, pulse, rhyme, rhythm, stress, throb, time. **3** circuit, course, journey, path, round, rounds, route, territory, way.
adj. exhausted, fatigued, jiggered, tired, wearied, worn out.
beat up assault, attack, batter, do over, knock about, knock around, thrash.

beaten *adj.* fashioned, forged, formed, hammered, malleated, shaped, stamped, worked.

beating *n.* belting, caning, chastisement, conquest, corporal punishment, defeat, downfall, flogging, rout, ruin, slapping, smacking, thrashing, whipping.

beautician *n.* beauty specialist, cosmetician, friseur, hairdresser.

beautiful *adj.* alluring, appealing, attractive, charming, delightful, exquisite, fair, fine, good-looking, gorgeous, graceful, handsome, lovely, pleasing, radiant, ravishing, stunning.
antonyms hideous, plain, ugly.

beautify *v.* adorn, array, bedeck, deck, decorate, embellish, enhance, garnish, gild, glamorise, grace, improve, ornament, tart up, titivate.
antonyms disfigure, spoil.

beauty *n.* **1** allure, attractiveness, bloom, charm, elegance, excellence, fairness, glamour, grace, handsomeness, loveliness, pleasure, seemliness, symmetry. **2** belle, charmer, cracker, good-looker, lovely, Venus.
antonyms **1** repulsiveness, ugliness.

becalmed *adj.* at a standstill, idle, motionless, still, stranded, stuck.

because *conj.* as, by reason of, for, in that, inasmuch as, on account of, owing to, since, thanks to.

beckon *v.* allure, attract, call, coax, draw, entice, gesticulate, gesture, invite, lure, motion, nod, pull, signal, summon, tempt, waft.

become *v.* **1** change into, get, grow, turn. **2** befit, develop into, embellish, enhance, flatter, grace, harmonise, ornament, set off, suit.

bed *n.* **1** berth, bunk, cot, couch, divan, mattress, pallet, sack. **2** base, border, bottom, channel, foundation, garden, groundwork, layer, matrix, patch, plot, row, stratus, substratum, watercourse.
v. base, embed, establish, fix, found, ground, implant, insert, plant, settle.

bedclothes *n.* bedding, bed-linen, blankets, coverlets, covers, eiderdowns, pillows, quilts, sheets.

bedlam *n.* anarchy, chaos, clamour, commotion, confusion, furore, hubbub, hullabaloo, madhouse, noise, pandemonium, tumult, turmoil, uproar.
antonym calm.

bedraggled *adj.* dirty, dishevelled, disordered, messy, muddied, muddy, scruffy, slovenly, sodden, soiled, stained, sullied, unkempt, untidy.
antonyms clean, neat, tidy.

befitting *adj.* appropriate, correct, decent, fit, fitting, meet, proper, right, suitable, suited.
antonyms improper, unbecoming.

before *adv.* ahead, earlier, formerly, in advance, in front, previously, sooner.
antonyms after, later.
prep. ahead of, earlier than, in advance of, in anticipation of, in front of, in preparation for, previous to, sooner than.
conj. in case, rather than.

beforehand *adv.* already, before, earlier, in advance, preliminarily, previously, sooner.

befriend *v.* aid, assist, back, benefit, comfort, encourage, favour, help, stand by, succour, support, sustain, take a liking to, take under

one's wing, uphold, welcome.
antonyms neglect, oppose.

beg *v.* beseech, crave, desire, entreat, implore, petition, plead, pray, request, require, scrounge, solicit, sponge on, supplicate.

beggar *n.* cadger, down-and-out, mendicant, pauper, scrounger, sponger, supplicant, tramp, vagrant.

begin *v.* activate, appear, arise, commence, emerge, happen, initiate, instigate, institute, introduce, originate, prepare, set about, set in, spring, start.
antonyms cease, end, finish.

beginner *n.* amateur, apprentice, cub, fledgling, freshman, learner, novice, recruit, starter, student, tenderfoot, trainee.
antonyms expert, old hand, veteran.

beginning *n.* birth, commencement, establishment, fountainhead, inauguration, inception, initiation, introduction, onset, opening, origin, outset, preface, prelude, prime, rise, root, rudiments, seed, source, start, starting point.
antonyms end, finish.

begrudge *v.* covet, envy, mind, resent, stint.
antonym allow.

beguile *v.* amuse, charm, cheat, cheer, deceive, delude, distract, divert, dupe, engross, entertain, entice, fool, hoodwink, mislead, occupy, pass, trick.

beguiling *adj.* alluring, appealing, attractive, bewitching, captivating, charming, diverting, enchanting, entertaining, enticing, intriguing.
antonyms offensive, repulsive.

behalf *n.* account, advantage, authority, benefit, good, interest, name, profit, sake, side, support.

behave *v.* acquit, act, bear, conduct, function, operate, perform, react, respond, run, work.

behaviour *n.* action, actions, conduct, dealings, doings, functioning, habits, manner, manners, operation, performance, reaction, response, ways.

behead *v.* decapitate, execute, guillotine.

behind *prep.* after, backing, causing, following, for, initiating, instigating, later than, responsible for, supporting.
adv. after, afterwards, behindhand, following, in arrears, in debt, next, overdue, subsequently.
n. backside, bottom, butt, buttocks, posterior, rear, rump, seat, tail.

behind-hand *adj.* backward, delayed, late, remiss, slow, tardy.

beholden *adj.* bound, grateful, indebted, obligated, obliged, owing, thankful.

beige *adj.* buff, camel, cinnamon, coffee, cream, fawn, khaki, mushroom, neutral, sand, tan.

being *n.* **1** actuality, animation, entity, essence, existence, life, living, nature, reality, soul, spirit, substance. **2** animal, beast, body, creature, human being, individual, mortal, thing.

belated *adj.* behind-hand, delayed, late, overdue, retarded, tardy, unpunctual.
antonyms punctual, timely.

belch *v.* burp, discharge, disgorge, emit, hiccup, spew, vent.
n. burp, hiccup.

beleaguered *adj.* badgered, beset, besieged, bothered, harassed, hedged in, persecuted, plagued, surrounded, vexed, worried.

belief *n.* assurance, confidence, conviction, credit, creed, doctrine, dogma, expectation, faith, feeling, ideology, impression, intuition, judgement, notion, opinion, persuasion, presumption, principle, reliance, sureness, surety, tenet, theory, trust, view.
antonym disbelief.

believable *adj.* acceptable, authentic, authoritative, conceivable, credible, imaginable, likely, plausible, possible, probable, reliable, trustworthy.
antonyms doubtful, unconvincing.

believe *v.* accept, assume, be under the impression, conjecture, consider, count on, credit, deem, depend on, gather, guess, hold, imagine, judge, maintain, postulate, presume, reckon, rely on, speculate, suppose, swear by, think, trust, wear.
antonyms disbelieve, doubt.

believer *n.* adherent, convert, devotee, disciple, follower, proselyte, supporter, upholder, zealot.
antonyms apostate, sceptic, unbeliever.

belittle *v.* decry, deprecate, deride, detract, diminish, dismiss, disparage, lessen, minimise, ridicule, run down, scorn, underestimate, underrate, undervalue, vilipend.
antonyms exaggerate, praise.

belligerent *adj.* aggressive, antagonistic, argumentative, bullying, combative, contentious, forceful, militant, pugnacious, quarrelsome, violent, warlike, warring.
antonym peaceable.

bellow *v.* clamour, cry, howl, roar, scream, shout, shriek, yell.

belly *n.* abdomen, bowels, gut, guts, insides, paunch, pot, stomach, tummy.

belong *v.* attach to, be connected with, be part of, be relevant to, be tied to, fit, go with, link up with, relate to, tie up with.

belongings *n.* chattels, effects, gear, goods, paraphernalia, possessions, stuff, things, traps.

beloved *adj.* admired, adored, cherished, darling, dear, dearest, favourite, loved, pet, precious, prized, revered, sweet, treasured.
n. darling, dear, dearest, favourite, lover, pet, precious, sweet, sweetheart.

below *adv.* beneath, down, lower, lower down, under, underneath.
prep. inferior to, lesser than, subject to, subordinate to, under, underneath, unworthy of.

bemused *adj.* absent-minded, befuddled, bewildered, confused, dazed, distracted, muddled, perplexed, stunned, stupefied, tipsy.
antonyms clear, clear-headed, lucid.

bench *n.* **1** board, counter, form, ledge, pew, seat, settle, stall, table, terrace, tier, workbench, work-table. **2** court, courtroom, judge, judicature, judiciary, magistrate, tribunal.

bend *v.* **1** bow, buckle, contort, crouch, curve,

deflect, diverge, flex, incline, lean, squat, stoop, swerve, turn, twist, veer. **2** dispose, influence, mould, shape, subdue, sway.
antonym **1** straighten.
n. angle, arc, bow, corner, crank, crook, curvature, curve, elbow, hook, loop, turn, twist, zigzag.

beneath *adv.* below, lower, lower down, under, underneath.
prep. **1** below, lower than, subject to, subordinate to, under, underneath. **2** inferior to, unworthy of.

benefactor *n.* angel, backer, contributor, donor, endower, friend, helper, patron, philanthropist, promoter, provider, sponsor, subscriber, subsidiser, supporter, well-wisher.
antonyms opponent, persecutor.

beneficial *adj.* advantageous, edifying, favourable, helpful, improving, profitable, rewarding, useful, valuable, wholesome.
antonyms detrimental, harmful, useless.

beneficiary *n.* assignee, heir, heiress, inheritor, payee, receiver, recipient, successor.

benefit *n.* advantage, aid, asset, assistance, avail, betterment, blessing, favour, gain, good, help, interest, profit, service, use, welfare.
antonyms damage, disadvantage, harm.
v. advance, advantage, aid, assist, avail, better, enhance, further, improve, profit, promote, serve.
antonyms harm, hinder, undermine.

benevolence *n.* altruism, compassion, fellow-feeling, generosity, goodness, goodwill, humanity, kindness, munificence, sympathy.
antonyms malevolence, meanness, selfishness.

benevolent *adj.* altruistic, benign, caring, compassionate, considerate, generous, good-will, humane, humanitarian, kind, liberal, philanthropic, well-disposed.
antonyms malevolent, mean, selfish.

benign *adj.* **1** amiable, benevolent, friendly, genial, gentle, good, gracious, kind, obliging, sympathetic. **2** curable, harmless. **3** beneficial, favourable, mild, propitious, refreshing, restorative, temperate, warm, wholesome.
antonyms **1** hostile. **2** malignant. **3** harmful, unpleasant.

bent *adj.* **1** angled, arched, bowed, curved, doubled, folded, hunched, stooped, twisted. **2** criminal, crooked, dishonest, untrustworthy.
antonyms **1** straight, upright. **2** honest.
n. ability, aptitude, capacity, facility, faculty, flair, forte, gift, inclination, knack, leaning, preference, talent, tendency.
bent on determined, disposed, fixed, heading for, inclined, insistent, resolved, set on.

bequeath *v.* assign, bestow, commit, endow, entrust, gift, give, grant, hand down, impart, pass on, settle, transmit, will.

bequest *n.* bestowal, devisal, donation, endowment, estate, gift, heritage, inheritance, legacy, settlement, trust.

bereave *v.* afflict, deprive, dispossess, divest, orphan, rob, strip, widow.

bereavement *n.* death, deprivation, dispossession, loss.

bereft *adj.* deprived, destitute, devoid, lacking, minus, robbed, stripped, wanting.

berserk *adj.* crazy, demented, deranged, frantic, frenzied, furious, insane, mad, rabid, raging, raving, violent, wild.
antonyms calm, sane.

berth *n.* **1** bed, billet, bunk, hammock. **2** anchorage, dock, harbour, mooring, pier, port, quay, shelter, wharf.
v. anchor, dock, drop anchor, land, moor, tie up.
antonym weigh anchor.

beset *v.* afflict, assail, attack, bedevil, besiege, embarrass, harass, hassle, hem in, perplex, pester, plague, surround.

beside *prep.* abreast of, abutting on, adjacent, bordering on, close to, near, neighbouring, next door to, next to, overlooking.
beside oneself berserk, crazed, delirious, demented, deranged, distracted, distraught, frantic, frenzied, furious, insane, mad, unbalanced, unhinged.

besides *adv.* additionally, also, as well, further, furthermore, in addition, moreover, otherwise, too.
prep. apart from, in addition to, other than, over and above.

besiege *v.* assail, badger, belay, beleaguer, beset, blockade, bother, confine, encircle, harass, hound, importune, nag, pester, plague, surround, trouble.

besotted *adj.* doting, hypnotised, infatuated, intoxicated, obsessed, smitten.
antonyms disenchanted, indifferent.

best *adj.* advantageous, excellent, finest, first, first-class, first-rate, foremost, greatest, highest, incomparable, largest, leading, matchless, optimal, optimum, outstanding, perfect, superlative, supreme, unequalled, unsurpassed.
antonym worst.
adv. excellently, exceptionally, extremely, greatly, superlatively, surpassingly.
antonym worst.
n. choice, cream, élite, favourite, finest, first, hardest, pick, prime, top, utmost.
antonym worst.

bestow *v.* accord, allot, apportion, award, bequeath, commit, confer, donate, endow, entrust, give, grant, impart, lavish, lend, present, transmit, wreak.
antonyms deprive, withhold.

bet *n.* ante, bid, flutter, gamble, pledge, risk, speculation, stake, venture, wager.
v. bid, chance, gamble, hazard, lay, pledge, punt, risk, speculate, stake, venture, wager.

betray *v.* **1** abandon, desert, double-cross, forsake, inform on, sell (out), undo. **2** disclose, divulge, expose, give away, manifest, reveal, show, tell.
antonyms **1** defend, protect. **2** conceal, hide.

betrayal *n.* deception, disloyalty, double-dealing, duplicity, falseness, sell-out, treachery, treason, trickery, unfaithfulness.

antonyms loyalty, protection.
betrayer *n.* apostate, conspirator, deceiver, double-crosser, grass, informer, renegade, supergrass, traitor.
antonyms protector, supporter.
better *adj.* bigger, finer, fitter, greater, healthier, improving, larger, longer, on the mend, preferable, progressing, recovered, recovering, restored, stronger, superior, surpassing, worthier.
antonym worse.
v. ameliorate, beat, correct, enhance, forward, further, improve, mend, outdo, outstrip, overtake, promote, raise, reform, surpass, top.
antonyms deteriorate, worsen.
betterment *n.* advancement, edification, enhancement, furtherance, improvement.
antonyms deterioration, impairment.
between *prep.* amidst, among, amongst, inter-, mid.
between ourselves in confidence, in secret, privately, within these four walls.
bevel *n.* angle, bias, diagonal, mitre, oblique, slant, slope.
v. bias, cant, mitre, slant.
beverage *n.* draught, drink, liquid, liquor, poison.
bevy *n.* band, bunch, collection, company, crowd, flock, gaggle, gathering, group, pack, throng, troupe.
bewail *v.* bemoan, cry over, deplore, greet, grieve for, keen, lament, moan, mourn, regret, repent, rue, sigh over, sorrow over.
antonyms gloat, glory, vaunt.
beware *v.* avoid, guard against, look out, mind, shun, steer clear of, take heed, watch out.
bewilder *v.* baffle, bamboozle, confound, confuse, daze, disconcert, disorient, muddle, mystify, perplex, puzzle, stupefy.
bewildered *adj.* baffled, bamboozled, bemused, confused, disoriented, muddled, mystified, nonplussed, perplexed, puzzled, stunned, surprised, uncertain.
antonyms collected, unperturbed.
bewilderment *n.* confusion, daze, disorientation, mystification, perplexity, puzzlement, stupefaction, surprise, uncertainty.
antonyms composure, confidence.
bewitch *v.* allure, attract, beguile, captivate, charm, enchant, enrapture, entrance, fascinate, hypnotise, obsess, possess, spellbind.
beyond *prep.* above, across, apart from, away from, before, further than, out of range, out of reach of, over, past, remote from, superior to.
bias *n.* angle, bent, bigotry, distortion, favouritism, inclination, intolerance, leaning, one-sidedness, partiality, prejudice, slant, tendency, turn, unfairness.
antonyms fairness, impartiality.
v. distort, influence, load, predispose, prejudice, slant, sway, twist, warp, weight.
biased *adj.* angled, bigoted, blinkered, distorted, jaundiced, loaded, one-sided, predisposed, prejudiced, slanted, swayed, twisted, unfair, warped, weighted.
antonyms fair, impartial.
bicker *v.* argue, clash, disagree, dispute, feud, fight, quarrel, row, scrap, spar, squabble, wrangle.
antonym agree.
bicycle *n.* bike, cycle, penny-farthing, push-bike, racer, tandem, two-wheeler.
bid *v.* ask, call, charge, command, desire, direct, enjoin, greet, instruct, invite, offer, proclaim, propose, request, require, say, solicit, summon, tell, wish.
n. **1** advance, amount, offer, price, proposal, submission, sum, tender. **2** attempt, effort, endeavour, go, try, venture.
big *adj.* **1** bulky, burly, colossal, considerable, enormous, extensive, gigantic, great, huge, immense, large, mammoth, massive, sizable, spacious, substantial, vast, voluminous. **2** eminent, important, influential, main, momentous, principal, prominent, serious, significant. **3** generous, gracious, magnanimous, unselfish.
antonyms **1** little, small. **2** insignificant, unknown.
bigot *n.* chauvinist, dogmatist, fanatic, racist, religionist, sectarian, sexist, zealot.
antonyms humanitarian, liberal.
bigoted *adj.* biased, blinkered, chauvinist, closed, dogmatic, illiberal, intolerant, narrow, narrow-minded, obstinate, opinionated, prejudiced, sectarian, twisted, warped.
antonyms broad-minded, enlightened, liberal, tolerant.
bigotry *n.* bias, chauvinism, discrimination, dogmatism, fanaticism, ignorance, injustice, intolerance, jingoism, narrow-mindedness, prejudice, racialism, racism, sectarianism, unfairness.
antonym tolerance.
bile *n.* anger, bitterness, gall, ill-humour, irascibility, irritability, peevishness, rancour, spleen, testiness.
bilious *adj.* choleric, cross, crotchety, grouchy, grumpy, irritable, nauseated, out of sorts, peevish, queasy, sick, sickly, testy.
bill[1] *n.* **1** account, charges, invoice, reckoning, score, statement, tally. **2** advertisement, broadsheet, bulletin, card, catalogue, chit, circular, handbill, hand-out, leaflet, list, listing, note, notice, placard, playbill, poster, programme, roster, schedule, sheet, syllabus. **3** legislation, measure, proposal.
v. advertise, announce, charge, debit, invoice, list, post, reckon, record.
bill[2] *n.* beak, mandible, nib.
billet *n.* accommodation, barracks, berth, employment, housing, lodging, occupation, post, quarters.
v. accommodate, berth, lodge, quarter, station.
billow *v.* expand, fill out, flutter, heave, puff out, roll, seethe, spread, surge, swell, swirl, undulate.
bind *v.* **1** attach, bandage, clamp, cover, fasten, lash, seal, secure, stick, strap, tie, truss, wrap. **2**

compel, confine, constrain, detain, force, hamper, necessitate, oblige, prescribe, restrain, restrict.

binding *adj.* compulsory, conclusive, indissoluble, irrevocable, mandatory, necessary, obligatory, permanent, requisite, strict, unalterable, unbreakable.
n. bandage, border, covering, edging, tape, trimming, wrapping.

biography *n.* account, adventures, autobiography, curriculum vitae, fortunes, history, life, life story, memoir, memoirs, recollections, record.

birth *n.* ancestry, background, beginning, birthright, blood, breeding, childbirth, delivery, derivation, descent, emergence, extraction, family, genealogy, line, lineage, nativity, nobility, origin, parentage, pedigree, race, rise, source, stock.

birthday *n.* anniversary, day of birth.

birthmark *n.* mole, naevus.

birthplace *n.* fount, native country, native town, place of origin, provenance, roots, source.

biscuit *n.* cake, cookie, cracker, rusk, wafer.

bisect *v.* bifurcate, cross, divide, fork, halve, intersect, separate, split.

bishop *n.* archbishop, diocesan, metropolitan, patriarch, prelate, primate, suffragan.

bit *n.* atom, chip, crumb, fragment, grain, instant, iota, jot, mite, morsel, part, piece, scrap, segment, slice, speck, whit.
bit by bit gradually, little by little, piecemeal, step by step.
antonym wholesale.

bitchy *adj.* back-biting, catty, cruel, malicious, mean, nasty, snide, spiteful, venomous, vicious, vindictive.
antonym kind.

bite *v.* **1** champ, chew, crunch, crush, gnaw, masticate, munch, nibble, nip. **2** pierce, rend, seize, tear, wound. **3** smart, sting, tingle. **4** pinch, take effect.
n. **1** nip, smarting, sting, wound. **2** food, morsel, mouthful, refreshment, snack, taste. **3** kick, punch, pungency.

biting *adj.* bitter, caustic, cold, cutting, cynical, freezing, harsh, hurtful, incisive, penetrating, piercing, raw, scathing, severe, sharp, stinging, tart.
antonyms bland, mild.

bitter *adj.* **1** acid, harsh, sharp, sour, tart, unsweetened, vinegary. **2** acrimonious, embittered, hostile, resentful, sore, sullen. **3** biting, cruel, fierce, freezing, intense, painful, raw, severe. **4** distressing, heartbreaking, merciless, poignant, ruthless, savage, stinging, unpleasant.
antonyms **1** sweet. **2** contented. **3** mild. **4** genial.

bizarre *adj.* abnormal, comical, curious, deviant, eccentric, extraordinary, extravagant, fantastic, freakish, grotesque, ludicrous, odd, outlandish, peculiar, quaint, queer, ridiculous, strange, unusual, way-out, weird.
antonyms normal, ordinary.

blabber *v.* babble, blather, chatter, gab, gabble, jabber, natter, prattle, whitter.

black *adj.* **1** coal-black, dark, dingy, dusky, ebony, inky, jet, jet-black, moonless, murky, overcast, sooty, starless, swarthy. **2** depressing, dismal, gloomy, grim, hopeless, menacing, mournful, ominous, sad, sombre, sullen, threatening. **3** dirty, filthy, grimy, grubby, soiled, stained.
antonyms **1** white. **2** bright, hopeful. **3** clean.
v. ban, bar, blacklist, boycott, taboo.
black out 1 collapse, faint, flake out, pass out. **2** censor, conceal, cover up, darken, eclipse, extinguish, gag, suppress, withhold.

blacken *v.* **1** cloud, darken, dirty, smudge, soil. **2** besmirch, defame, defile, denigrate, detract, discredit, dishonour, malign, revile, slander, smear, stain, sully, taint, tarnish, vilify.
antonyms **2** enhance, praise.

blackmail *n.* blood-sucking, chantage, extortion, hush money, intimidation, pay-off, protection, ransom.
v. bleed, bribe, coerce, compel, demand, force, hold to ransom, lean on, milk, squeeze, threaten.

blackout *n.* **1** censorship, concealment, cover-up, oblivion, secrecy, suppression. **2** coma, faint, unconsciousness. **3** power cut.

blade *n.* dagger, edge, knife, rapier, scalpel, sword.

blame *n.* accountability, accusation, censure, charge, complaint, condemnation, criticism, culpability, fault, guilt, incrimination, liability, onus, rap, recrimination, reprimand, reproach, reproof, responsibility, stick.
v. accuse, admonish, censure, charge, chide, condemn, criticise, disapprove, find fault with, rebuke, reprehend, reprimand, reproach, reprove, tax, upbraid.
antonyms exonerate, vindicate.

blameless *adj.* above reproach, clear, faultless, guiltless, innocent, irreproachable, perfect, sinless, stainless, unblamable, unblemished, unimpeachable, upright, virtuous.
antonyms blameworthy, guilty.

blameworthy *adj.* at fault, culpable, discreditable, disreputable, guilty, indefensible, inexcusable, reprehensible, reproachable, shameful, unworthy.
antonyms blameless, innocent.

blanch *v.* bleach, blench, drain, fade, pale, whiten.
antonyms blush, colour, redden.

blank *adj.* **1** bare, clean, clear, empty, plain, unfilled, unmarked, void, white. **2** apathetic, deadpan, expressionless, glazed, impassive, poker-faced, staring, uncomprehending, vacant.
n. break, emptiness, gap, nothingness, space, vacancy, vacuity, vacuum, void.

blanket *n.* carpet, cloak, coat, coating, cover, covering, envelope, film, housing, layer, mantle, rug, sheet, wrapper, wrapping.
adj. across-the-board, all-embracing, all-inclusive, comprehensive, inclusive, overall, sweeping, wide-ranging.

v. cloak, cloud, coat, conceal, cover, deaden, eclipse, hide, mask, muffle, obscure, surround.

blare *v.* blast, boom, clamour, clang, honk, hoot, peal, resound, ring, roar, scream, shriek, toot, trumpet.

blarney *n.* blandishment, cajolery, coaxing, eloquence, flattery, persuasiveness, plausibility, smooth talk, soft soap, sweet talk.

blasé *adj.* apathetic, bored, cool, indifferent, jaded, nonchalant, offhand, unconcerned, unexcited, unimpressed, uninspired, uninterested, unmoved, weary.
antonyms enthusiastic, excited.

blaspheme *v.* abuse, curse, damn, defile, desecrate, imprecate, profane, revile, swear.

blasphemous *adj.* godless, impious, imprecatory, irreligious, irreverent, profane, sacrilegious, ungodly.

blasphemy *n.* curse, cursing, defilement, desecration, expletive, impiety, imprecation, irreverence, outrage, profanity, sacrilege, swearing, violation.

blast *n.* **1** bang, burst, clap, crack, crash, detonation, discharge, explosion, outburst, volley. **2** bluster, draught, gale, gust, squall, storm, tempest. **3** blare, blow, boom, hoot, peal, roar, scream, shriek, sound, wail.
v. **1** assail, attack, blow up, burst, castigate, demolish, destroy, explode, kill, lash, ruin, shatter, shrivel, storm at, wither. **2** blare, boom, hoot, peal, roar, scream, shriek, sound, wail.

blatant *adj.* arrant, barefaced, brazen, clamorous, conspicuous, flagrant, flaunting, glaring, harsh, loud, naked, noisy, obtrusive, obvious, ostentatious, outright, overt, prominent, pronounced, sheer, unmitigated.

blaze *n.* blast, bonfire, brilliance, burst, conflagration, eruption, explosion, fire, flame, flames, flare-up, flash, fury, glare, gleam, glitter, glow, light, outbreak, outburst, radiance, rush, storm.
v. beam, burn, burst, erupt, explode, fire, flame, flare (up), flash, fume, glare, gleam, glow, seethe, shine.

bleach *v.* blanch, decolorise, fade, lighten, pale, whiten.

bleak *adj.* bare, barren, blae, cheerless, chilly, cold, colourless, comfortless, depressing, desolate, discouraging, disheartening, dismal, dreary, empty, exposed, gaunt, gloomy, grim, hopeless, joyless, leaden, loveless, open, raw, sombre, unsheltered, weather-beaten, windswept, windy.
antonyms bright, cheerful, congenial.

bleed *v.* deplete, drain, exhaust, exude, flow, gush, haemorrhage, milk, ooze, reduce, run, sap, seep, spurt, squeeze, suck dry, trickle, weep.

blemish *n.* birthmark, blot, blotch, blur, botch, defect, deformity, disfigurement, disgrace, dishonour, fault, flaw, imperfection, mark, naevus, smudge, speck, spot, stain, taint.
v. blot, blotch, blur, damage, deface, disfigure, flaw, impair, injure, mar, mark, spoil, spot, stain, sully, taint, tarnish.

blend *v.* amalgamate, coalesce, combine, complement, compound, fit, fuse, harmonise, merge, mingle, mix, synthesise, unite.
antonym separate.
n. alloy, amalgam, amalgamation, combination, composite, compound, concoction, fusion, mix, mixture, synthesis, union.

bless *v.* anoint, approve, bestow, consecrate, countenance, dedicate, endow, exalt, extol, favour, glorify, grace, hallow, magnify, ordain, praise, provide, sanctify, thank.
antonyms condemn, curse.

blessed *adj.* adored, contented, divine, endowed, favoured, fortunate, glad, glorious, hallowed, happy, holy, joyful, joyous, lucky, prosperous, revered, sacred, sanctified.
antonym cursed.

blessing *n.* advantage, approval, authority, backing, benediction, benefit, commendation, concurrence, consecration, consent, countenance, dedication, favour, gain, gift, godsend, grace, help, invocation, kindness, leave, permission, profit, sanction, service, support, thanksgiving, windfall.
antonyms blight, condemnation, curse.

blight *n.* affliction, bane, cancer, check, contamination, corruption, curse, decay, depression, disease, evil, fungus, infestation, mildew, pest, pollution, rot, scourge, set-back.
antonyms blessing, boon.
v. annihilate, blast, crush, destroy, disappoint, frustrate, injure, mar, ruin, shatter, shrivel, spoil, undermine, wither, wreck.
antonym bless.

blind *adj.* **1** eyeless, purblind, sightless, unseeing, unsighted, visionless. **2** careless, hasty, impetuous, irrational, mindless, rash, reckless, unreasoning, unthinking. **3** ignorant, inattentive, inconsiderate, indifferent, insensitive, neglectful, oblivious, thoughtless, unaware, unconscious, unobservant. **4** closed, concealed, hidden, obscured, obstructed.
antonyms **1** sighted. **2** careful. **3** aware, sensitive.
n. camouflage, cloak, cover, cover-up, distraction, façade, front, mask, masquerade, screen, smoke-screen.

blindly *adv.* aimlessly, carelessly, frantically, headlong, heedlessly, impulsively, inconsiderately, indiscriminately, madly, passionately, precipitately, recklessly, thoughtlessly, unseeingly, wildly, wilfully.
antonyms carefully, cautiously.

blink *v.* bat, flash, flicker, flutter, gleam, glimmer, glimpse, peer, scintillate, shine, sparkle, squint, twinkle, wink.

bliss *n.* blessedness, blissfulness, ecstasy, euphoria, gladness, happiness, heaven, joy, paradise, rapture.
antonyms damnation, hell, misery.

blissful *adj.* delighted, ecstatic, elated, enchanted, enraptured, euphoric, happy, heavenly, joyful, joyous, rapturous.
antonyms miserable, wretched.

blister *n.* abscess, boil, canker, carbuncle, cyst,

pimple, pustule, sore, swelling, ulcer.
blistering *adj.* cruel, hot, intense, sarcastic, savage, scathing, scorching, strenuous, vicious, virulent, withering.
antonym mild.
blithe *adj.* animated, buoyant, carefree, careless, casual, cheerful, debonair, gay, happy, heedless, light-hearted, lively, merry, nonchalant, sprightly, thoughtless, unconcerned, untroubled, vivacious.
antonyms gloomy, morose, sullen.
blizzard *n.* snow-squall, snowstorm, squall, storm, tempest.
bloated *adj.* blown up, bombastic, dilated, distended, enlarged, expanded, inflated, sated, swollen, turgid.
antonyms shrivelled, shrunken, thin.
blob *n.* ball, bead, bobble, bubble, dab, dewdrop, drop, droplet, glob, globule, gob, lump, mass, pearl, pellet, pill, spot.
bloc *n.* alliance, axis, cartel, clique, coalition, combine, entente, faction, group, league, ring.
block *n.* bar, barrier, blockage, brick, chunk, cube, delay, hang-up, hindrance, hunk, impediment, jam, let, lump, mass, obstacle, obstruction, piece, resistance, square, stoppage.
v. arrest, bar, check, choke, clog, close, dam up, deter, halt, hinder, impede, obstruct, plug, scotch, stonewall, stop (up), thwart.
blockade *n.* barricade, barrier, closure, obstruction, restriction, siege, stoppage.
blockage *n.* block, blocking, clot, hindrance, impediment, jam, log-jam, obstruction, occlusion, stoppage.
blond, blonde *adj.* bleached, fair, fair-skinned, flaxen, golden-haired, light-coloured.
blood *n.* **1** ancestry, birth, descendants, descent, extraction, family, kindred, kinship, lineage, relations, relationship. **2** anger, bloodshed, murder, temper.
bloodcurdling *adj.* chilling, dreadful, fearful, frightening, hair-raising, horrendous, horrible, horrid, horrifying, scaring, spine-chilling, terrifying, weird.
bloodless *adj.* anaemic, ashen, cold, colourless, drained, feeble, insipid, languid, lifeless, listless, pale, pallid, passionless, pasty, sallow, sickly, spiritless, torpid, unemotional, unfeeling, wan.
antonyms bloody, ruddy, vigorous.
bloodshed *n.* bloodletting, butchery, carnage, gore, killing, massacre, murder, slaughter, slaying.
bloodthirsty *adj.* barbaric, barbarous, brutal, cruel, ferocious, inhuman, murderous, ruthless, savage, slaughterous, vicious, warlike.
bloody *adj.* bleeding, bloodstained, brutal, cruel, ferocious, fierce, murderous, savage.
bloom *n.* beauty, blossom, blow, blush, bud, flourishing, flower, flush, freshness, glow, health, heyday, lustre, perfection, prime, radiance, rosiness, vigour.
v. blossom, blow, bud, develop, flourish, grow, open, prosper, sprout, succeed, thrive, wax.
antonyms fade, wither.
blossom *n.* bloom, bud, flower.
v. bloom, blow, develop, flourish, flower, grow, mature, progress, prosper, thrive.
antonyms fade, wither.
blot *n.* blemish, blotch, defect, disgrace, fault, flaw, mark, patch, smear, smudge, speck, spot, stain, taint.
v. blur, disfigure, disgrace, mar, mark, smudge, spoil, spot, stain, sully, taint, tarnish.
blot out cancel, darken, delete, destroy, eclipse, erase, expunge, obliterate, obscure, shadow.
blotch *n.* blemish, blot, mark, patch, smudge, splash, splodge, spot, stain.
blotchy *adj.* blemished, patchy, reddened, smeary, spotted, spotty, uneven.
blow[1] *v.* bear, blare, blast, breathe, buffet, drive, exhale, fan, fling, flow, flutter, mouth, pant, pipe, play, puff, rush, sound, stream, sweep, toot, trumpet, vibrate, waft, whirl, whisk, wind.
n. blast, draught, flurry, gale, gust, puff, squall, tempest, wind.
blow over cease, die down, disappear, dissipate, end, finish, fizzle out, pass, peter out, subside, vanish.
blow up **1** blast, bomb, burst, detonate, erupt, explode, go off. **2** blow one's top, hit the roof, lose one's temper, rage. **3** bloat, dilate, distend, enlarge, expand, fill (out), magnify, puff up, pump up, swell.
blow[2] *n.* affliction, bang, bash, belt, biff, box, buff, buffet, calamity, catastrophe, clap, clip, clout, clump, comedown, concussion, disappointment, disaster, jolt, knock, misfortune, punch, rap, reverse, setback, shock, slap, slat, smack, stroke, swipe, thump, upset, wallop, whack.
blow-out *n.* **1** binge, feast, party, spree. **2** blast, burst, detonation, eruption, escape, explosion, fuse, leak, puncture, rupture.
blowy *adj.* blustery, breezy, draughty, fresh, gusty, squally, stormy, windy.
blowzy *adj.* bedraggled, dishevelled, flushed, frowzy, messy, ruddy, slatternly, slipshod, sloppy, slovenly, sluttish, tousled, ungroomed, unkempt, untidy.
antonyms neat, smart.
bludgeon *n.* baton, club, cosh, cudgel, truncheon.
v. badger, batter, beat, browbeat, bulldoze, bully, club, coerce, cosh, cudgel, force, harass, hector, intimidate, sap, strike, terrorise, torment.
blue *adj.* **1** aquamarine, azure, cobalt, cyan, indigo, navy, sapphire, turquoise, ultramarine. **2** black, bleak, dejected, depressed, despondent, dismal, dispirited, down in the dumps, downcast, down-hearted, fed up, gloomy, glum, low, melancholy, miserable, morose, sad, unhappy. **3** bawdy, coarse, dirty, improper, indecent, lewd, near the bone, obscene, offensive, pornographic, risqué, smutty, vulgar.
antonyms **2** cheerful, happy. **3** clean, decent.
blue-pencil *v.* bowdlerise, censor, clean up, correct, edit, expurgate, purge.

blueprint *n.* archetype, design, draft, guide, model, outline, pattern, pilot, plan, project, prototype, sketch.

blues *n.* dejection, depression, despondency, doldrums, dumps, gloom, glumness, melancholy, miseries, moodiness.
antonyms bliss, euphoria.

bluff[1] *n.* bank, brow, cliff, crag, escarpment, foreland, headland, height, peak, precipice, promontory, ridge, slope.

bluff[2] *v.* bamboozle, blind, deceive, defraud, delude, fake, hoodwink, humbug, lie, mislead, pretend, sham.
n. boast, bravado, deceit, deception, fake, fraud, humbug, idle boast, lie, pretence, sham, show, subterfuge, trick.

blunder *n.* bloomer, clanger, error, fault, faux pas, gaffe, howler, inaccuracy, indiscretion, mistake, oversight, slip, slip-up, solecism.
v. botch, bumble, bungle, err, flounder, fluff, miscalculate, misjudge, mismanage, slip up, stumble.

blunt *adj.* **1** dull, pointless, rounded, stubbed, stumpy, unsharpened, worn. **2** abrupt, brusque, candid, curt, direct, downright, explicit, forthright, frank, honest, impolite, insensitive, outspoken, plain-spoken, rude, tactless, unceremonious, uncivil, unpolished.
antonyms **1** pointed, sharp. **2** subtle, tactful.
v. abate, allay, alleviate, anaesthetise, dampen, deaden, dull, numb, soften, unedge, weaken.
antonyms intensify, sharpen.

blur *v.* becloud, befog, blear, blemish, blot, blotch, cloud, darken, dim, fog, mask, obscure, smear, soften, spot, stain.
n. blear, blot, blotch, cloudiness, confusion, dimness, fog, fuzziness, haze, indistinctness, muddle, obscurity, smear, smudge.

blurb *n.* advertisement, commendation, copy, hype, spiel.

blurred *adj.* bleary, blurry, clouded, confused, dim, faint, foggy, fuzzy, hazy, ill-defined, indistinct, misty, unclear, vague.
antonyms clear, distinct.

blurt *v.* babble, blab, cry, disclose, divulge, exclaim, gush, leak, let slip, reveal, spill, spill the beans, spout, utter.
antonyms bottle up, hush up.

blush *v.* colour, flush, glow, redden.
antonym blanch.
n. colour, flush, glow, reddening, rosiness, ruddiness.

blushing *adj.* confused, embarrassed, flushed, glowing, red, rosy, suffused.
antonyms composed, pale, white.

bluster *v.* boast, brag, bully, rant, roar, storm, strut, swagger, swell, talk big, vaunt.
n. bluff, boasting, bravado, crowing, racket, swagger.

blustery *adj.* boisterous, gusty, noisy, squally, stormy, tempestuous, violent, wild, windy.
antonym calm.

board *n.* **1** beam, clapboard, panel, plank, sheet, slab, slat, timber. **2** advisers, chamber, commission, committee, council, directorate, directors, jury, panel, trustees. **3** food, meals, provisions, rations.
v. **1** accommodate, bed, billet, feed, house, lodge, put up, quarter, room, table. **2** catch, embark, enter, entrain, mount.

boast *v.* be all mouth, blow, bluster, bounce, brag, claim, crow, exaggerate, exhibit, possess, show off, strut, swagger, talk big, trumpet, vaunt.
antonyms belittle, deprecate.
n. brag, claim, gem, joy, pride, swank, treasure, vaunt.

boastful *adj.* bragging, cocky, conceited, crowing, proud, puffed-up, self- glorious, swaggering, swanky, swollen-headed, vain.
antonyms humble, modest, self-effacing.

boat *n.* canoe, dinghy, gondola, punt, rowing-boat, speed-boat, water-craft.

boatman *n.* ferryman, gondolier, oarsman, rower, sailor, voyageur, waterman, yachtsman.

bob *v.* bounce, hop, jerk, jolt, jump, leap, nod, oscillate, quiver, shake, skip, spring, twitch, weave, wobble.
bob up appear, arise, arrive, crop up, emerge, materialise, pop up, rise, show up, spring up, surface.

bode *v.* augur, foreshadow, foreshow, foretell, forewarn, indicate, intimate, omen, portend, predict, presage, prophesy, signify, threaten, warn.

bodily *adj.* actual, carnal, concrete, corporeal, earthly, fleshly, material, physical, real, substantial, tangible.
antonym spiritual.
adv. altogether, as a whole, collectively, completely, en masse, entirely, fully, in toto, totally, wholly.
antonym piecemeal.

body *n.* **1** build, figure, torso, trunk. **2** cadaver, carcass, corpse. **3** association, band, bevy, bloc, cartel, collection, company, confederation, congress, corporation, crowd, group, mass, mob, multitude, society, syndicate, throng. **4** bulk, consistency, density, essence, firmness, fullness, mass, richness, solidity, substance.

bodyguard *n.* minder, protector.

boffin *n.* backroom-boy, brain, designer, egghead, engineer, genius, headpiece, intellect, intellectual, inventor, mastermind, planner, scientist, thinker, wizard.

bog *n.* fen, marsh, marshland, mire, morass, moss, quag, quagmire, quicksands, slough, swamp, swampland, wetlands.
bog down delay, deluge, halt, hinder, impede, overwhelm, retard, sink, slow down, slow up, stall, stick.

boggy *adj.* fenny, marshy, miry, muddy, oozy, quaggy, soft, spongy, swampy, waterlogged.
antonyms arid, dry.

bogus *adj.* artificial, counterfeit, dummy, fake, false, forged, fraudulent, imitation, phoney, pseudo, sham, spurious, unauthentic.

antonyms genuine, real, true, valid.
bohemian *adj.* alternative, artistic, arty, bizarre, eccentric, exotic, irregular, nonconformist, offbeat, unconventional, unorthodox, way-out.
antonyms bourgeois, conventional.
n. beatnik, drop-out, hippie, nonconformist.
antonyms bourgeois, conformist.
boil[1] *v.* agitate, brew, bubble, effervesce, erupt, explode, fizz, foam, froth, fulminate, fume, gurgle, rage, rave, seethe, simmer, sizzle, steam, stew, storm, wallop.
boil down abridge, abstract, concentrate, condense, decrease, digest, distil, reduce, summarise.
boil[2] *n.* abscess, blister, carbuncle, gumboil, inflammation, papule, pimple, pustule, tumour, ulcer.
boiling *adj.* angry, baking, blistering, bubbling, enraged, flaming, fuming, furious, gurgling, hot, incensed, indignant, infuriated, roasting, scorching, turbulent.
boisterous *adj.* bouncy, clamorous, disorderly, exuberant, impetuous, loud, noisy, obstreperous, raging, riotous, rough, rowdy, rumbustious, tumultous, turbulent, unrestrained, unruly, wild.
antonyms calm, quiet, restrained.
bold *adj.* **1** adventurous, audacious, brash, brave, brazen, cheeky, confident, courageous, daring, dauntless, enterprising, fearless, forward, gallant, heroic, impudent, insolent, intrepid, outgoing, plucky, shameless, showy, spirited, unabashed, valiant, venturesome. **2** bright, colourful, conspicuous, eye-catching, flamboyant, flashy, fresh, jazzy, lively, loud, prominent, pronounced, striking, strong, vivid.
antonyms **1** cautious, shy, timid. **2** faint, restrained.
bolt *n.* bar, catch, fastener, latch, lock, peg, pin, rivet, rod, shaft.
v. **1** bar, fasten, latch, lock, secure. **2** abscond, dash, escape, flee, fly, hurtle, run, rush, spring, sprint. **3** cram, devour, gobble, gorge, gulp, stuff, wolf.
bomb *n.* atom bomb, bombshell, charge, explosive, grenade, mine, missile, mortar-bomb, petrol bomb, projectile, rocket, shell, torpedo.
v. attack, blow up, bombard, collapse, destroy, fail, flop, misfire, shell, torpedo.
bombard *v.* assail, assault, attack, barrage, besiege, blast, blitz, bomb, harass, hound, pelt, pester, pound.
bombardment *n.* air-raid, assault, attack, barrage, blitz, bombing, cannonade, fire, flak, fusillade, salvo, shelling, strafe.
bombastic *adj.* bloated, grandiloquent, grandiose, high-flown, inflated, magniloquent, pompous, verbose, windy, wordy.
bona fide actual, authentic, genuine, honest, lawful, legal, legitimate, real, true, valid.
antonym bogus.
bond *n.* **1** affiliation, affinity, attachment, band, binding, connection, link, relation, tie, union. **2** agreement, contract, covenant, obligation, pledge, promise, word.
v. bind, connect, fasten, fuse, glue, gum, paste, seal, unite.
bondage *n.* captivity, confinement, enslavement, enthralment, imprisonment, incarceration, restraint, serfdom, servitude, slavery, subjection, subjugation, subservience, yoke.
antonyms freedom, independence.
bonny *adj.* attractive, beautiful, blooming, bouncing, cheerful, cheery, chubby, fair, fine, handsome, lovely, merry, pretty, wholesome, winsome.
antonym ugly.
bonus *n.* advantage, benefit, bribe, commission, dividend, extra, gift, gratuity, hand-out, honorarium, perk, perquisite, plus, premium, prize, profit, reward, tip.
antonyms disadvantage, disincentive, liability.
bony *adj.* angular, drawn, emaciated, gangling, gaunt, gawky, knobbly, lanky, lean, rawboned, scrawny, skinny, thin.
antonyms fat, plump.
book *n.* album, booklet, companion, diary, jotter, manual, manuscript, notebook, pad, paperback, publication, roll, scroll, textbook, tract, volume, work.
v. arrange, arrest, bag, charter, engage, enter, insert, list, log, note, organise, post, procure, programme, record, register, reserve, schedule.
antonym cancel.
boom *v.* **1** bang, blare, blast, crash, explode, resound, reverberate, roar, roll, rumble, sound, thunder. **2** develop, escalate, expand, explode, flourish, gain, go from strength to strength, grow, increase, intensify, prosper, spurt, strengthen, succeed, swell, thrive.
antonyms **2** collapse, fail, slump.
n. **1** bang, blast, burst, clang, clap, crash, explosion, reverberation, roar, rumble, thunder. **2** advance, boost, development, escalation, expansion, explosion, gain, growth, improvement, increase, jump, spurt, upsurge, upturn.
antonyms **2** collapse, depression, failure, slump.
boon *n.* advantage, benefaction, benefit, blessing, favour, gift, godsend, grant, gratification, gratuity, kindness, present, windfall.
antonyms blight, disadvantage.
boorish *adj.* awkward, coarse, crude, gross, oafish, rude, uncivilised, uncouth, uneducated, unrefined, vulgar.
antonyms cultured, polite, refined.
boost *n.* addition, advancement, ego-trip, encouragement, enhancement, expansion, fillip, heave, help, hoist, improvement, increase, increment, jump, lift, praise, promotion, push, rise, supplement, thrust.
antonyms blow, setback.
v. advance, advertise, aid, amplify, assist, augment, bolster, develop, elevate, encourage, enhance, enlarge, expand, foster, further, heave, heighten, hoist, improve, increase, inspire, jack up, lift, plug, praise, promote, push, raise, supplement, support, sustain, thrust.
antonyms hinder, undermine.

boot *n.* galosh, gumboot, overshoe, riding-boot, rubber, top-boot, wellington.
v. bounce, dismiss, eject, expel, fire, give the heave, kick (out), knock, oust, sack, shove.

booth *n.* carrel, compartment, hut, kiosk, stall, stand, ticket-office.

booty *n.* gains, haul, loot, pickings, pillage, plunder, spoil, spoils, swag, takings, winnings.

border *n.* borderline, bound, boundary, bounds, brim, brink, circumference, confine, confines, demarcation, edge, fringe, frontier, hem, limit, margin, perimeter, periphery, rim, skirt, surround, trimming, valance, verge.
adj. boundary, dividing, frontier, limitary, marginal, perimeter, separating, side.
border on abut, adjoin, appear like, approach, approximate, communicate with, connect, contact, impinge, join, march, resemble, touch, verge on.

borderline *adj.* ambivalent, doubtful, iffy, indefinite, marginal, problematic, uncertain.
antonyms certain, definite.

bore[1] *v.* burrow, countermine, drill, gouge, mine, penetrate, perforate, pierce, sap, sink, tunnel, undermine.

bore[2] *v.* annoy, bother, bug, fatigue, irk, irritate, jade, pester, tire, trouble, vex, weary, worry.
antonyms charm, excite, interest.
n. annoyance, bind, bother, drag, headache, nuisance, trial, vexation.
antonyms delight, pleasure.

boredom *n.* apathy, dullness, irksomeness, listlessness, monotony, tediousness, tedium, weariness, world-weariness.
antonyms excitement, interest.

boring *adj.* commonplace, dreary, dry, dull, flat, humdrum, insipid, monotonous, repetitious, routine, stale, tedious, trite, unamusing, uneventful, unexciting, unimaginative, uninspired, uninteresting.
antonyms appealing, exciting, interesting, original, stimulating.

borrow *v.* adopt, appropriate, cadge, copy, crib, derive, draw, echo, filch, imitate, list, mimic, obtain, pilfer, plagiarise, scrounge, sponge, steal, take, use, usurp.

bosom *n.* breast, bust, centre, chest, circle, core, heart, midst, protection, sanctuary, shelter.
adj. boon, cherished, close, confidential, dear, favourite, inseparable, intimate.

boss[1] *n.* administrator, captain, chief, director, employer, executive, foreman, gaffer, governor, head, leader, manager, master, overseer, owner, superintendent, supervisor, supremo.
boss around browbeat, bulldoze, bully, dominate, domineer, order about, order around, push around, tyrannise.

boss[2] *n.* knob, nub, point, protuberance, stud, tip.

bossy *adj.* arrogant, authoritarian, autocratic, demanding, despotic, dictatorial, domineering, exacting, high- handed, imperious, insistent, lordly, oppressive, overbearing, tyrannical.
antonym unassertive.

bother *v.* alarm, annoy, bore, concern, dismay, distress, disturb, harass, hassle, inconvenience, irk, irritate, molest, nag, pester, plague, trouble, upset, vex, worry.
n. aggravation, annoyance, bustle, difficulty, flurry, fuss, hassle, inconvenience, irritation, nuisance, perplexity, pest, problem, strain, trouble, vexation, worry.

bottle *n.* carafe, decanter, demijohn, flagon, flask.
bottle up conceal, contain, curb, enclose, hide, hold in, inhibit, quell, restrain, restrict, suppress.
antonyms unbosom, unburden.

bottleneck *n.* block, blockage, clogging, congestion, hindrance, hold-up, jam, obstacle, obstruction, snarl-up, traffic-jam.

bottom *n.* **1** base, basis, bed, depths, floor, foot, foundation, ground, pedestal, plinth, sole, substructure, support, underneath, underside. **2** backside, behind, buttocks, posterior, rear, rear end, rump, seat, tail.
antonym **1** top.

bottomless *adj.* boundless, deep, fathomless, immeasurable, inexhaustible, infinite, limitless, measureless, profound, unfathomed, unlimited, unplumbed.
antonyms limited, shallow.

boulevard *n.* avenue, mall, parade, promenade, prospect, row, street, terrace, thoroughfare.

bounce *v.* bob, bound, jump, leap, rebound, recoil, ricochet, spring.
n. animation, bound, ebullience, elasticity, energy, exuberance, give, go, liveliness, rebound, recoil, resilience, spring, springiness, vigour, vitality, vivacity, zip.

bouncing *adj.* blooming, bonny, healthy, lively, robust, strong, thriving, vigorous.

bound[1] *adj.* **1** bandaged, cased, chained, constrained, fastened, held, restricted, secured, tied, tied up. **2** certain, committed, compelled, destined, doomed, duty-bound, fated, fixed, forced, liable, obliged, required, sure.

bound[2] *v.* bob, bounce, caper, frisk, gambol, hurdle, jump, leap, lunge, pounce, prance, skip, spring, vault.
n. bob, bounce, caper, dance, frisk, gambol, jump, leap, lunge, pounce, prance, scamper, skip, spring, vault.

boundary *n.* barrier, border, borderline, bounds, brink, confines, demarcation, edge, extremity, fringe, frontier, junction, limes, limits, line, march, margin, perimeter, termination, verge.
adj. border, demarcation, frontier, perimeter.

boundless *adj.* countless, endless, immeasurable, immense, incalculable, indefatigable, inexhaustible, infinite, interminable, limitless, measureless, unbounded, unconfined, unending, unflagging, unlimited, untold, vast.
antonyms limited, restricted.

bounds *n.* borders, boundaries, circumference, confines, edges, extremities, fringes, frontiers, limits, marches, margins, periphery, rim, verges.

bounty *n.* allowance, almsgiving, annuity, assistance, beneficence, bonus, donation, generosity, gift, grace, grant, gratuity, kindness, largesse, liberality, philanthropy, premium, present, recompense, reward.

bouquet *n.* anthology, aroma, bunch, buttonhole, corsage, fragrance, garland, nosegay, odour, perfume, posy, savour, scent, smell, spray, wreath.

bourgeois *adj.* banal, commonplace, conformist, conservative, conventional, dull, hide-bound, humdrum, materialistic, middle-class, traditional, trite, trivial, unadventurous, unimaginative, uninspired, unoriginal.
antonyms bohemian, original, unconventional.
n. conformist, philistine, plebeian, stick-in-the-mud.
antonyms bohemian, nonconformist.

bout *n.* battle, competition, contest, course, encounter, engagement, fight, fit, go, heat, match, period, round, run, session, set-to, spell, spree, stint, stretch, struggle, term, time, turn, venue.

bovine *adj.* beefy, dense, dull, dumb, heavy, hulking, obtuse, slow, slow-witted, sluggish, stolid, stupid, thick.
antonym quick.

bow[1] *v.* accept, acquiesce, bend, bob, capitulate, comply, concede, conquer, consent, crush, curtsey, defer, depress, droop, give in, incline, kowtow, nod, overpower, stoop, subdue, subjugate, submit, surrender, vanquish, yield.
n. acknowledgement, bending, bob, curtsey, inclination, kowtow, nod, salutation.
bow out abandon, back out, chicken out, defect, desert, give up, opt out, pull out, quit, resign, retire, stand down, step down, withdraw.

bow[2] *n.* beak, head, prow, rostrum, stem.

bowdlerise *v.* blue-pencil, censor, clean up, cut, edit, excise, expunge, expurgate, modify, mutilate, purge, purify.

bowels *n.* belly, centre, core, depths, entrails, guts, heart, innards, inside, insides, interior, intestines, middle, viscera.

bowl[1] *n.* basin, dish, receptacle, sink, vessel.

bowl[2] *v.* fling, hurl, pitch, revolve, roll, rotate, spin, throw, trundle, whirl.
bowl over amaze, astonish, astound, dumbfound, fell, flabbergast, floor, stagger, startle, stun, surprise, topple, unbalance.

box[1] *n.* carton, case, chest, coffer, coffin, container, coop, fund, pack, package, present, receptacle, trunk.
v. case, encase, pack, package, wrap.
box in cage, circumscribe, confine, contain, coop up, cordon off, corner, enclose, hem in, imprison, restrict, surround, trap.

box[2] *v.* buffet, butt, clout, cuff, fight, hit, punch, slap, sock, spar, strike, thwack, wallop, whack.
n. blow, buffet, clout, cuff, punch, slap, stroke, thump, wallop, wham.

boxing *n.* fisticuffs, prize-fighting, pugilism, sparring.

boy *n.* fellow, junior, kid, lad, nipper, puppy, stripling, youngster, youth.

boycott *v.* ban, bar, black, blacklist, cold-shoulder, disallow, embargo, exclude, ignore, ostracise, outlaw, prohibit, refuse, reject, spurn.
antonyms encourage, support.

boyfriend *n.* admirer, bloke, date, fellow, fiancé, lover, man, sweetheart, young man.

brace *n.* **1** binder, bracket, buttress, corset, prop, reinforcement, shoring, stay, strap, strut, support, truss. **2** couple, duo, pair, twosome.
v. bandage, bind, bolster, buttress, fasten, fortify, prop, reinforce, shore (up), steady, strap, strengthen, support, tie, tighten.

bracing *adj.* brisk, crisp, energetic, energising, enlivening, exhilarating, fortifying, fresh, invigorating, refreshing, reviving, rousing, stimulating, strengthening, tonic, vigorous.
antonyms debilitating, weakening.

brackish *adj.* bitter, briny, saline, salt, saltish, salty.
antonym fresh.

braid *v.* entwine, interlace, intertwine, interweave, lace, plait, ravel, twine, twist, weave, wind.
antonyms undo, untwist.

brain *n.* **1** cerebrum, grey matter, intellect, mind. **2** boffin, egghead, expert, genius, highbrow, intellect, intellectual, mastermind, prodigy, scholar.
antonym **2** simpleton.

brains *n.* capacity, common sense, grey matter, head, intellect, intelligence, mind, reason, sense, shrewdness, understanding, wit.

brainy *adj.* bright, brilliant, clever, intellectual, intelligent, smart.
antonym dull.

brake *n.* check, constraint, control, curb, drag, rein, restraint, restriction, retardment.
v. check, decelerate, drag, halt, moderate, pull up, retard, slacken, slow, stop.
antonym accelerate.

branch *n.* **1** arm, bough, limb, offshoot, part, prong, shoot, sprig, wing. **2** chapter, department, division, office, section, subdivision, subsection.
branch out broaden out, develop, diversify, enlarge, expand, extend, increase, move on, multiply, proliferate, ramify, vary.

brand *n.* brand-name, class, emblem, grade, hallmark, kind, label, line, logo, make, mark, marker, quality, sign, sort, species, stamp, symbol, trademark, type, variety.
v. burn, censure, denounce, discredit, disgrace, label, mark, scar, stain, stamp, stigmatise, taint, type.

brandish *v.* display, exhibit, flash, flaunt, flourish, parade, raise, shake, swing, wave, wield.

brand-new *adj.* fire-new, fresh.

brash *adj.* assuming, assured, audacious, bold, brazen, cocky, foolhardy, forward, hasty, heedless, impertinent, impetuous, impudent, impulsive, incautious, indiscreet, insolent, precipitate, rash, reckless, rude.
antonyms cautious, reserved, unobtrusive.

brassy *adj.* **1** blatant, flashy, garish, gaudy, jazzy, loud, obtrusive, showy. **2** blaring, grating, harsh, jangling, noisy, piercing, raucous. **3** bold, brash, brazen, forward, loud-mouthed, pert, saucy.
antonyms **1** gentle, refined. **2** mellow, soft. **3** shy.

bravado *n.* bluster, boast, boastfulness, boasting, bombast, bragging, daring, parade, pretence, show, showing off, swagger, talk, vaunting.
antonyms modesty, restraint.

brave *adj.* audacious, bold, courageous, daring, dauntless, fearless, gallant, hardy, heroic, indomitable, intrepid, plucky, resolute, stalwart, stoical, stout-hearted, unafraid, undaunted, valiant.
antonyms afraid, cowardly, timid.
v. bear, challenge, confront, dare, defy, encounter, endure, face, face up to, stand up to, suffer, withstand.
antonyms capitulate, crumple.

bravery *n.* audacity, boldness, courage, daring, dauntlessness, fearlessness, fortitude, gallantry, grit, guts, hardiness, heroism, indomitability, intrepidity, mettle, pluck, resolution, spirit, stalwartness, stout-heartedness, valiance, valour.
antonyms cowardice, faint-heartedness, timidity.

brawl *n.* affray, altercation, argument, battle, broil, clash, disorder, dispute, dust-up, fight, fracas, fray, free-for-all, mêlée, punch-up, quarrel, row, rumpus, scrap, scuffle, squabble.
v. argue, battle, dispute, fight, quarrel, row, scrap, scuffle, squabble, tussle, wrangle, wrestle.

brawny *adj.* athletic, beefy, bulky, burly, fleshy, hardy, hefty, hulking, massive, muscular, powerful, robust, sinewy, solid, stalwart, strapping, strong, sturdy, vigorous, well-built.
antonyms frail, slight.

bray *v.* blare, hoot, roar, screech, trumpet.
n. bawl, bellow, blare, blast, cry, hoot, roar, screech, shout, shriek.

brazen *adj.* assured, barefaced, blatant, bold, brash, brassy, defiant, flagrant, forward, immodest, impudent, insolent, saucy, shameless, unabashed, unashamed.
antonyms modest, shamefaced, shy.

breach *n.* **1** contravention, disruption, infringement, lapse, offence, transgression, trespass, violation. **2** alienation, difference, disaffection, disagreement, dissension, dissociation, division, estrangement, parting, quarrel, rift, rupture, schism, separation, split, variance. **3** break, chasm, cleft, crack, crevice, disobedience, fissure, gap, hole, opening, rift, rupture.

bread *n.* **1** diet, fare, food, necessities, nourishment, nutriment, provisions, subsistence, sustenance. **2** cash, finance, funds, money, wherewithal.

breadth *n.* amplitude, area, broadness, bulk, compass, comprehensiveness, dimension, expanse, extensiveness, extent, latitude, magnitude, measure, range, reach, scale, scope, size, space, span, spread, sweep, thickness, vastness, volume, wideness, width.

break *v.* **1** crack, demolish, destroy, disintegrate, divide, fracture, rend, ruin, separate, sever, shatter, shiver, smash, snap, splinter, split. **2** breach, disobey, flout, infringe, violate. **3** discontinue, interrupt, pause, rest, stop, suspend. **4** demoralise, enfeeble, impair, subdue, tame, undermine, weaken. **5** announce, disclose, divulge, impart, inform, reveal, tell.
antonyms **1** mend. **2** abide by, keep, observe. **4** strengthen.
n. **1** breach, cleft, crack, crevice, fissure, fracture, gap, gash, hole, opening, rift, rupture, schism, separation, split, tear. **2** breather, holiday, interlude, intermission, interruption, interval, let-up, lull, pause, rest, time-out. **3** advantage, chance, fortune, opportunity.
break away depart, detach, escape, flee, fly, leave, part company, quit, revolt, run away, secede, separate, split.
break down 1 collapse, conk out, crack up, fail, give way, pack up, seize up, stop. **2** analyse, dissect, separate.
break in burgle, encroach, impinge, interfere, interject, interpose, interrupt, intervene, intrude, invade.
break off cease, detach, disconnect, discontinue, divide, end, finish, halt, interrupt, part, pause, separate, sever, snap off, splinter, stop, suspend, terminate.
break out 1 arise, begin, burst, commence, emerge, erupt, flare up, happen, occur, start. **2** abscond, bolt, escape, flee.
break through achieve, emerge, gain ground, make headway, pass, penetrate, progress, succeed.
break up adjourn, demolish, destroy, disband, dismantle, disperse, disrupt, dissolve, divide, divorce, finish, part, separate, sever, split, stop, suspend, terminate.
break with ditch, drop, finish with, jilt, part with, reject, renounce, repudiate, separate.

breakable *adj.* brittle, crumbly, delicate, flimsy, fragile, frail, insubstantial, murly.
antonyms durable, sturdy.

breakaway *adj.* apostate, dissenting, heretical, rebel, renegade, schismatic, seceding.

breakdown *n.* analysis, categorisation, classification, collapse, disintegration, disruption, dissection, failure, interruption, stoppage.

break-in *n.* burglary, housebreaking, intrusion, larceny, robbery, theft.

breakthrough *n.* advance, development, discovery, find, finding, gain, headway, improvement, invention, leap, progress, step.

break-up *n.* breakdown, crack-up, crumbling, disintegration, dispersal, dissolution, divorce, finish, parting, rift, separation, split, splitting, termination.

breakwater *n.* dock, groyne, jetty, pier, quay, wharf.

breast *n.* bosom, bust, chest, front.

breath *n.* air, animation, aroma, breathing, breeze, energy, exhalation, existence, flutter, gasp, gulp, gust, hint, inhalation, life, murmur, odour, pant, puff, respiration, sigh, smell, spirit, suggestion, suspicion, undertone, vapour, vitality, waft, whiff, whisper.

breathe *v.* articulate, exercise, exhale, expire, express, impart, infuse, inhale, inject, inspire, instil, live, murmur, pant, puff, respire, say, sigh, utter, voice, whisper.

breathless *adj.* **1** choking, exhausted, gasping, gulping, out of breath, panting, puffed (out), puffing, short- winded, wheezing, winded. **2** agog, anxious, eager, excited, expectant, feverish, impatient.

breathtaking *adj.* amazing, astonishing, exciting, impressive, magnificent, moving, overwhelming, stirring, stunning, thrilling.

breed *v.* arouse, bear, bring forth, bring up, cause, create, cultivate, develop, educate, engender, foster, generate, hatch, induce, instruct, make, multiply, nourish, nurture, occasion, originate, produce, propagate, raise, rear, reproduce, train.
n. family, ilk, kind, line, lineage, pedigree, progeny, race, sort, species, stamp, stock, strain, type, variety.

breeding *n.* ancestry, background, civility, culture, development, education, gentility, lineage, manners, nurture, polish, politeness, raising, rearing, refinement, reproduction, stock, strain, training, upbringing, urbanity.
antonym vulgarity.

breeding-ground *n.* hotbed, nest, nursery, school, training ground.

breeze *n.* air, breath, draught, flurry, gale, gust, waft, whiff, wind, zephyr.
v. flit, glide, hurry, sail, sally, sweep, trip, wander.

breezy *adj.* **1** airy, blowing, blustery, fresh, gusty, squally, sunny, windy. **2** animated, blithe, bright, buoyant, carefree, casual, cheerful, debonair, easy-going, exhilarating, informal, jaunty, light, lively, vivacious.
antonyms **1** calm. **2** serious, staid.

brevity *n.* abruptness, briefness, conciseness, crispness, curtness, impermanence, incisiveness, pithiness, shortness, succinctness, summariness, terseness, transience, transitoriness.
antonyms longevity, permanence, verbosity.

brew *v.* boil, build up, concoct, contrive, cook, develop, devise, excite, ferment, foment, gather, hatch, infuse, mix, plan, plot, prepare, project, scheme, seethe, soak, steep, stew.
n. beverage, blend, broth, concoction, distillation, drink, fermentation, gruel, infusion, liquor, mixture, potion, preparation, stew.

bribe *n.* allurement, back-hander, enticement, hush money, incentive, inducement, kickback, pay-off, protection money, refresher, slush fund, sweetener.
v. buy off, buy over, corrupt, reward.

bribery *n.* corruption, graft, greasing, inducement, lubrication, palm-greasing, protection.

bric-à-brac *n.* antiques, baubles, curios, curiosities, knick-knacks, ornaments, trinkets.

bridal *adj.* conjugal, marital, marriage, matrimonial, nuptial, wedding.

bridge *n.* arch, band, bond, causeway, connection, flyover, link, overpass, pontoon bridge, span, tie, viaduct.
v. attach, bind, connect, couple, cross, fill, join, link, span, traverse, unite.

bridle *v.* check, contain, control, curb, govern, master, moderate, repress, restrain, subdue.

brief *adj.* abrupt, blunt, brusque, compressed, concise, crisp, cursory, curt, ephemeral, fast, fleeting, hasty, laconic, limited, momentary, passing, pithy, quick, sharp, short, short-lived, succinct, surly, swift, temporary, terse, thumbnail, transient, transitory.
antonyms lengthy, long.
n. advice, argument, briefing, case, data, defence, demonstration, directions, directive, dossier, instructions, mandate, orders, outline, précis, remit, summary.
v. advise, direct, explain, fill in, gen up, guide, inform, instruct, prepare, prime.

briefing *n.* advice, conference, directions, filling-in, gen, guidance, information, instructions, intimation, low-down, meeting, notification, orders, preamble, preparation, priming.

brigade *n.* band, body, company, contingent, corps, crew, force, group, guard, outfit, party, squad, team, troop, unit.

brigand *n.* bandit, desperado, gangster, highwayman, marauder, outlaw, plunderer, robber, ruffian.

bright *adj.* **1** beaming, blazing, brilliant, dazzling, flashing, glaring, gleaming, glistening, glittering, glorious, glowing, illuminated, intense, luminous, radiant, resplendent, shimmering, shining, sparkling, splendid, twinkling, vivid. **2** cheerful, glad, happy, jolly, joyful, lively, merry, vivacious. **3** auspicious, encouraging, favourable, hopeful, optimistic, promising, propitious, rosy. **4** acute, astute, brainy, clever, intelligent, keen, perceptive, quick, quick-witted, sharp, smart. **5** clear, lucid, translucent, transparent. **6** breezy, cloudless, fine, sunny, unclouded.
antonyms **1** dull. **2** sad. **3** depressing. **4** stupid. **5** muddy. **6** dark.

brighten *v.* burnish, cheer up, clear up, encourage, enliven, gladden, gleam, glow, hearten, illuminate, light up, lighten, perk up, polish, rub up, shine.
antonyms darken, dull, tarnish.

brilliance *n.* **1** aptitude, braininess, cleverness, distinction, excellence, genius, greatness, inventiveness, talent, virtuosity. **2** brightness, dazzle, glamour, glory, gloss, intensity, lustre, magnificence, radiance, sheen, sparkle, splendour, vividness.

brilliant *adj.* **1** accomplished, astute, brainy, celebrated, clever, exceptional, expert, famous, gifted, illustrious, intellectual, intelligent, masterly, outstanding, quick, skilful, star, superb, talented. **2** blazing, bright, dazzling, glaring, glittering, glorious, glossy, intense, magnificent, scintillating, shining, showy, spark-

ling, splendid, vivacious, vivid.
antonyms **1** stupid, undistinguished. **2** dull, restrained.

brim *n.* border, brink, circumference, edge, lip, marge, margin, perimeter, periphery, rim, skirt, verge.

bring *v.* **1** accompany, bear, carry, conduct, convey, deliver, escort, fetch, guide, introduce, lead, take, transfer, transport, usher. **2** cause, create, engender, produce, put. **3** attract, draw, force, prompt, provoke.
bring about accomplish, achieve, cause, create, effect, engineer, fulfil, generate, manage, manipulate, manoeuvre, occasion, produce, realise.
bring down abase, break, debase, degrade, fell, floor, humble, lay low, level, lower, overthrow, overturn, reduce, ruin, shoot, topple, undermine.
bring forth afford, bear, engender, furnish, generate, produce, provide, supply, yield.
bring in accrue, earn, fetch, gross, introduce, net, produce, profit, realise, return, yield.
bring off accomplish, achieve, bring about, discharge, execute, fulfil, perform, rescue, win.
bring on accelerate, advance, cause, coach, expedite, generate, give rise to, induce, inspire, lead to, occasion, precipitate, prompt, provoke.
antonym inhibit.
bring out draw out, emphasise, enhance, express, highlight, introduce, issue, print, publish, utter.
bring up 1 educate, form, foster, nurture, raise, rear, support, teach, train. **2** broach, introduce, mention, propose, submit. **3** regurgitate, throw up, vomit.

brink *n.* bank, border, boundary, brim, edge, extremity, fringe, limit, lip, marge, margin, point, rim, skirt, threshold, verge, waterside.

brisk *adj.* **1** active, agile, alert, bustling, busy, energetic, lively, nimble, no-nonsense, quick, snappy, spirited, stimulating, vigorous. **2** bracing, bright, crisp, exhilarating, fresh, invigorating, nippy, refreshing.
antonyms **1** lazy, sluggish. **2** heavy.

bristle *n.* barb, hair, prickle, spine, stubble, thorn, whisker.
v. bridle, draw oneself up, prickle, react, rise, seethe, spit.

bristly *adj.* bearded, hairy, prickly, rough, spiky, stubbly, thorny, unshaven, whiskered.
antonyms clean-shaven, smooth.

brittle *adj.* **1** breakable, crisp, crumbling, crumbly, delicate, fragile, frail, shattery, shivery. **2** curt, edgy, irritable, nervous, nervy, short, tense.
antonyms **1** durable, resilient.

broad *adj.* all-embracing, ample, capacious, comprehensive, encyclopaedic, extensive, far-reaching, general, generous, inclusive, large, roomy, spacious, square, sweeping, universal, unlimited, unrefined, vast, wide, wide-ranging, widespread.
antonyms narrow, restricted.

broadcast *v.* advertise, air, announce, beam, cable, circulate, disseminate, promulgate, publicise, publish, radio, relay, report, show, spread, televise, transmit.
n. programme, relay, show, transmission.

broaden *v.* augment, branch out, develop, diversify, enlarge, enlighten, expand, extend, increase, open up, spread, stretch, supplement, swell, thicken, widen.

broad-minded *adj.* enlightened, flexible, free-thinking, liberal, open-minded, permissive, receptive, tolerant, unbiased, unprejudiced.
antonyms biased, intolerant, narrow-minded.

broke *adj.* bankrupt, bust, destitute, impoverished, insolvent, ruined.
antonyms affluent, rich, solvent.

broken *adj.* **1** burst, defective, demolished, destroyed, faulty, fractured, out of order, rent, ruptured, separated, severed, shattered. **2** disconnected, discontinuous, disjointed, erratic, fragmentary, halting, hesitating, imperfect, intermittent, interrupted, spasmodic, stammering. **3** beaten, crushed, defeated, demoralised, disturbed, down, exhausted, feeble, isolated, oppressed, run-down, weak. **4** betrayed, dishonoured, disregarded, ignored, infringed, transgressed, violated.
antonyms **1** mended. **2** fluent. **3** healthy, whole. **4** obeyed.

broken-down *adj.* collapsed, decayed, dilapidated, disintegrated, inoperative, out of order, ruined.

broken-hearted *adj.* crestfallen, dejected, desolate, despairing, despondent, devastated, disappointed, grief-stricken, heartbroken, inconsolable, miserable, mournful, prostrated, sorrowful, unhappy, wretched.

bronze *adj.* auburn, chestnut, copper, copper-coloured, reddish-brown, rust, tan.

brooch *n.* badge, breastpin, clasp, clip, pin, prop.

brood *v.* agonise, dwell on, go over, meditate, mull over, muse, ponder, rehearse, ruminate.
n. birth, chicks, children, clutch, family, hatch, issue, litter, offspring, progeny, young.

brook *n.* beck, burn, channel, rivulet, stream, watercourse.

broom *n.* besom, brush, sweeper.

brother *n.* associate, chum, colleague, companion, comrade, fellow, friar, friend, mate, monk, partner, relation, relative, sibling.

brotherhood *n.* affiliation, alliance, association, clan, clique, community, confederacy, confederation, fraternity, guild, league, society, union.

brotherly *adj.* affectionate, amicable, benevolent, caring, concerned, cordial, fraternal, friendly, kind, loving, neighbourly, supervisory, sympathetic.
antonyms callous, unbrotherly.

brow *n.* **1** eyebrow, face, forehead, front. **2** cliff, peak, summit, top.

browbeat *v.* awe, batter, bludgeon, bulldoze, bully, coerce, domineer, dragoon, hound, intimidate, oppress, overbear, threaten, tyrannise.
antonym coax.

brown *adj.* auburn, bay, bronze, bronzed, browned, brunette, chestnut, chocolate, coffee, dark, dusky, ginger, hazel, mahogany, russet, rust, rusty, sunburnt, tan, tanned, tawny, toasted, umber.

browse *v.* **1** dip into, flick through, leaf through, peruse, scan, skim, survey. **2** eat, feed, graze, nibble.

bruise *v.* blacken, blemish, crush, discolour, grieve, hurt, injure, insult, mark, offend, pound, pulverise, stain, wound.
n. blemish, contusion, discoloration, injury, mark, shiner, swelling.

brunt *n.* burden, force, impact, pressure, shock, strain, stress, thrust, violence, weight.

brush[1] *n.* besom, broom, sweeper.
v. **1** burnish, clean, flick, polish, rub, scrape, shine, stroke, sweep. **2** contact, graze, kiss, touch.
brush aside belittle, dismiss, disregard, flout, ignore, override, pooh-pooh.
brush off cold-shoulder, discourage, dismiss, disown, disregard, ignore, rebuff, refuse, reject, repudiate, repulse, scorn, slight, snub, spurn.
antonyms cultivate, encourage.
brush up 1 cram, improve, read up, relearn, revise, study, swot. **2** freshen up, refresh.

brush[2] *n.* brushwood, bushes, ground cover, scrub, shrubs, thicket, undergrowth, underwood.

brush[3] *n.* clash, conflict, confrontation, dust-up, encounter, fight, fracas, incident, scrap, set-to, skirmish, tussle.

brusque *adj.* abrupt, blunt, curt, discourteous, gruff, hasty, impolite, sharp, short, surly, tactless, terse, uncivil, undiplomatic.
antonyms courteous, polite, tactful.

brutal *adj.* animal, barbarous, beastly, bestial, bloodthirsty, callous, coarse, crude, cruel, ferocious, gruff, harsh, heartless, impolite, inhuman, inhumane, insensitive, merciless, pitiless, remorseless, rough, rude, ruthless, savage, uncivilised, unfeeling, vicious.
antonyms civilised, humane, kindly.

brutalise *v.* dehumanise, desensitise, harden, inure.
antonym civilise.

brutality *n.* atrocity, barbarism, barbarity, bloodthirstiness, callousness, coarseness, cruelty, ferocity, inhumanity, roughness, ruthlessness, savagery, viciousness, violence.
antonyms gentleness, kindness.

brute *n.* animal, beast, creature, devil, fiend, lout, monster, ogre, sadist, savage, swine.
adj. bodily, gross, mindless, physical, senseless, sensual, unthinking.
antonym refined.

bubble *n.* ball, bead, blob, drop, droplet, globule.
v. boil, burble, effervesce, fizz, foam, froth, percolate, ripple, seethe, sparkle, trickle.

bubbly *adj.* **1** carbonated, effervescent, fizzy, sudsy. **2** bouncy, elated, excited, happy, lively, merry.
antonyms **1** flat. **2** lethargic.

buck up brighten, cheer, cheer up, encourage, hearten, improve, perk up, rally, stimulate, take heart.
antonyms discourage, dishearten.

bucket *n.* bail, barrel, can, pail, vessel.

buckle *n.* catch, clasp, clip, fastener.
v. **1** catch, clasp, close, connect, fasten, hitch, hook, secure. **2** bend, bulge, cave in, collapse, crumple, distort, fold, twist, warp, wrinkle.

bud *n.* embryo, germ, shoot, sprig, sprout.
v. burgeon, develop, grow, shoot, sprout.
antonyms waste away, wither.

budding *adj.* burgeoning, developing, embryonic, flowering, growing, hopeful, intending, potential, promising.
antonyms experienced, successful.

budge *v.* bend, change, convince, dislodge, give (way), inch, influence, move, persuade, propel, push, remove, roll, shift, slide, stir, sway, yield.

budget *n.* allocation, allotment, allowance, cost, estimate, finances, funds, means, resources.
v. allocate, apportion, cost, estimate, plan, ration.

buff[1] *adj.* fawn, khaki, sandy, straw, tan, yellowish, yellowish-brown.
v. brush, burnish, polish, polish up, rub, shine, smooth.

buff[2] *n.* addict, admirer, connoisseur, devotee, enthusiast, expert, fan, fiend, freak.

buffer *n.* bumper, cushion, intermediary, pad, pillow, safeguard, screen, shield, shock-absorber.

buffet[1] *n.* café, cafeteria, counter, snack-bar, snack-counter.

buffet[2] *v.* bang, batter, beat, box, bump, clobber, clout, cuff, flail, hit, jar, knock, pound, pummel, push, rap, shove, slap, strike, thump, wallop.
n. bang, blow, box, bump, clout, cuff, jar, jolt, knock, push, rap, shove, slap, smack, thump, wallop.

bug *n.* **1** bacterium, disease, germ, infection, micro-organism, virus. **2** blemish, defect, error, failing, fault, flaw, gremlin, imperfection.
v. annoy, badger, bother, disturb, get, harass, irk, irritate, needle, vex.

build *v.* assemble, augment, base, begin, constitute, construct, develop, edify, enlarge, erect, escalate, establish, extend, fabricate, form, formulate, found, improve, inaugurate, increase, initiate, institute, intensify, knock together, make, originate, raise, strengthen.
antonyms destroy, knock down, lessen, weaken.
n. body, figure, form, frame, physique, shape, size, structure.
build up advertise, amplify, assemble, boost, develop, enhance, expand, extend, fortify, heighten, improve, increase, intensify, plug, promote, publicise, reinforce, strengthen.
antonyms lessen, weaken.

building *n.* architecture, construction, dwelling, edifice, erection, fabric, fabrication, house, structure.

build-up *n.* accumulation, development, enlarge-

ment, escalation, expansion, gain, growth, heap, increase, load, mass, plug, promotion, publicity, stack, stockpile, store.
antonyms decrease, reduction.

built-in *adj.* essential, fundamental, implicit, in-built, included, incorporated, inherent, inseparable, integral, intrinsic, necessary.

bulge *n.* bump, distension, hump, increase, intensification, lump, projection, protuberance, rise, surge, swelling, upsurge.
v. bulb, dilate, distend, enlarge, expand, hump, project, protrude, sag, swell.

bulk *n.* amplitude, bigness, body, dimensions, extensity, extent, generality, immensity, largeness, magnitude, majority, mass, most, plurality, preponderance, size, substance, volume, weight.

bulky *adj.* big, chunky, colossal, cumbersome, enormous, heavy, hefty, huge, hulking, immense, large, mammoth, massive, substantial, unmanageable, unwieldy, weighty.
antonyms handy, insubstantial, small.

bullet *n.* ball, missile, pellet, projectile, shot, slug, weight.

bulletin *n.* announcement, communication, communiqué, dispatch, message, newsflash, notification, report, statement.

bully *n.* bouncer, browbeater, bully-boy, intimidator, oppressor, persecutor, ruffian, tormentor, tough.
v. browbeat, bulldoze, bullyrag, coerce, cow, domineer, intimidate, oppress, overbear, persecute, push around, terrorise, tyrannise.
antonyms coax, persuade.

bumbling *adj.* awkward, botching, bungling, clumsy, incompetent, inept, maladroit, stumbling.
antonyms competent, efficient.

bump *v.* bang, bounce, budge, collide (with), crash, dislodge, displace, hit, jar, jerk, jolt, jostle, knock, move, rattle, remove, shake, shift, strike.
n. **1** bang, blow, collision, crash, hit, impact, jar, jolt, knock, rap, shock, smash, thud, thump. **2** bulge, hump, knot, lump, protuberance, swelling.
bump off assassinate, do in, eliminate, kill, liquidate, murder, remove, top.

bumper *adj.* abundant, bountiful, enormous, excellent, exceptional, great, large, massive.
antonyms miserly, small.

bumptious *adj.* arrogant, boastful, cocky, conceited, egotistic, forward, full of oneself, impudent, overbearing, over-confident, pompous, presumptuous, pushy, self-assertive, self-important, showy, swaggering.
antonyms humble, modest.

bumpy *adj.* bouncy, choppy, irregular, jerky, jolting, jolty, knobbly, knobby, rough, uneven.
antonyms even, smooth.

bunch *n.* assortment, band, batch, bouquet, bundle, clump, cluster, collection, crew, crowd, flock, gang, gathering, heap, lot, mass, mob, multitude, number, parcel, party, pile, quantity, sheaf, spray, stack, swarm, team, troop, tuft.
v. assemble, bundle, cluster, collect, congregate, crowd, flock, group, herd, huddle, mass, pack.
antonyms scatter, spread out.

bundle *n.* accumulation, assortment, bag, bale, batch, box, bunch, carton, collection, consignment, crate, group, heap, mass, pack, package, packet, pallet, parcel, pile, quantity, roll, shook, stack, swag.
v. bale, bind, fasten, pack, tie, truss, wrap.

buoy *n.* beacon, float, marker, signal.
buoy up boost, cheer, encourage, hearten, lift, raise, support, sustain.
antonyms depress, discourage.

buoyant *adj.* **1** animated, bouncy, bright, bullish, carefree, cheerful, happy, joyful, light-hearted, lively. **2** afloat, floatable, floating, light, weightless.
antonyms **1** depressed, despairing. **2** heavy.

burble *n.* babble, gurgle, lapping, murmur.
v. babble, gurgle, lap, murmur, purl.

burden *n.* affliction, anxiety, bear, care, cargo, dead weight, encumbrance, grievance, load, millstone, obligation, obstruction, onus, responsibility, sorrow, strain, stress, trial, trouble, weight, worry.
v. bother, encumber, handicap, lie heavy on, load, oppress, overload, overwhelm, strain, tax, worry.
antonyms lighten, relieve, unburden.

bureau *n.* agency, branch, counter, department, desk, division, office, service.

bureaucracy *n.* administration, city hall, civil service, directorate, government, ministry, officialdom, officialese, officials, red tape, regulations, the authorities, the system.

bureaucrat *n.* administrator, civil servant, functionary, mandarin, minister, office-holder, officer, official.

burglar *n.* house-breaker, pilferer, robber, thief.

burglary *n.* break-in, house-breaking, larceny, pilferage, robbery, stealing, theft, thieving.

burial *n.* burying, entombment, funeral, interment, sepulchre.

burly *adj.* athletic, beefy, big, brawny, bulky, heavy, hefty, hulking, husky, muscular, powerful, stocky, stout, strapping, strong, sturdy, well-built.
antonyms puny, slim, small, thin.

burn *v.* bite, blaze, brand, char, consume, corrode, desire, expend, flame, flare, flash, flicker, fume, glow, hurt, ignite, incinerate, kindle, light, parch, scorch, seethe, shrivel, simmer, singe, smart, smoulder, sting, tingle, toast, yearn.

burning *adj.* acute, ardent, biting, blazing, caustic, compelling, consuming, crucial, eager, earnest, essential, excessive, fervent, fiery, flaming, flashing, frantic, frenzied, gleaming, glowing, hot, illuminated, impassioned, important, intense, irritating, painful, passionate, piercing, pressing, prickling, pungent, reeking, scorching, significant, smarting, smouldering, stinging, tingling, vehement, vital, zealous.
antonyms apathetic, cold, mild, unimportant.

burrow *n.* den, earth, hole, lair, retreat, set(t), shelter, tunnel, warren.
v. delve, dig, earth, excavate, mine, tunnel, undermine.

burst *v.* blow up, break, crack, disintegrate, erupt, explode, fragment, gush, puncture, run, rupture, rush, shatter, shiver, split, spout, tear.
n. bang, blast, blasting, blow-out, blow-up, breach, break, crack, discharge, eruption, explosion, fit, gallop, gush, gust, outbreak, outburst, outpouring, rupture, rush, spate, split, spurt, surge, torrent.

bury *v.* **1** conceal, cover, entomb, hide, inter, lay to rest, shroud. **2** absorb, embed, enclose, engage, engross, engulf, enshroud, immerse, implant, interest, occupy, sink, submerge.
antonyms **1** disinter, exhume, uncover.

bush *n.* backwoods, brush, hedge, plant, scrub, scrubland, shrub, thicket, wilds, woodland.

bushy *adj.* bristling, bristly, fluffy, fuzzy, luxuriant, rough, shaggy, spreading, stiff, thick, wiry.
antonyms neat, tidy, trim, well-kept.

business *n.* **1** bargaining, commerce, dealings, industry, manufacturing, merchandising, selling, trade, trading, transaction(s). **2** company, concern, corporation, enterprise, establishment, firm, organisation. **3** calling, career, duty, employment, job, line, occupation, profession, pursuit, responsibility, task, venture, vocation, work. **4** affair, issue, matter, point, problem, question, subject, topic.

business-like *adj.* correct, efficient, formal, impersonal, matter-of-fact, methodical, orderly, organised, practical, precise, professional, regular, routine, systematic, thorough, well-ordered.
antonyms careless, disorganised, inefficient.

businessman *n.* capitalist, employer, entrepreneur, executive, financier, industrialist, merchant, trader, tycoon.

bust *n.* bosom, breast, carving, chest, head, statue, statuette, torso.

bustle *v.* dash, fuss, hasten, hurry, rush, scamper, scramble, stir.
n. activity, ado, agitation, commotion, excitement, flurry, fuss, haste, hurry, stir, tumult.

bustling *adj.* active, busy, crowded, energetic, eventful, full, hectic, lively, restless, rushing, stirring, swarming, teeming, thronged.
antonym quiet.

bust-up *n.* brawl, disruption, disturbance, quarrel, separation.

busy *adj.* active, diligent, employed, energetic, engaged, full, hectic, industrious, inquisitive, interfering, lively, occupied, persevering, restless, slaving, stirabout, stirring, strenuous, tireless, tiring, troublesome, unleisured, working.
antonyms idle, lazy, quiet.
v. absorb, bother, concern, employ, engage, engross, immerse, interest, occupy.

busybody *n.* eavesdropper, gossip, intruder, meddler, nosey parker, pry, snoop, snooper, troublemaker.

butt[1] *n.* base, end, foot, haft, handle, shaft, stock, stub, tail, tip.

butt[2] *n.* dupe, laughing-stock, mark, object, point, subject, target, victim.

butt[3] *v., n.* buffet, bump, hit, jab, knock, poke, prod, punch, push, ram, shove, thrust.
butt in cut in, interfere, interpose, interrupt, intrude, meddle.

butter up blarney, cajole, coax, flatter, soft-soap, wheedle.

buttocks *n.* backside, behind, bottom, hindquarters, posterior, rear, rump, seat.

button *n.* catch, clasp, fastening, knob.

buttonhole *v.* accost, catch, detain, grab, importune, nab, pin, waylay.

buttress *n.* brace, mainstay, pier, prop, reinforcement, shore, stanchion, stay, strut, support.
v. bolster up, brace, hold up, prop up, reinforce, shore up, strengthen, support, sustain, uphold.
antonyms undermine, weaken.

buy *v.* **1** acquire, get, obtain, procure, purchase. **2** bribe, corrupt, fix.
antonym **1** sell.
n. acquisition, bargain, deal, purchase.

buyer *n.* emptor, vendee.
antonyms seller, vendor.

buzz *n.* buzzing, drone, gossip, hearsay, hiss, hum, murmur, news, purr, report, ring, ringing, rumour, scandal, whir(r), whisper, whizz.
v. drone, hum, murmur, reverberate, ring, whir(r), whisper, whizz.

by *prep.* along, beside, near, next to, over, past, through, via.
adv. aside, at hand, away, beyond, close, handy, near, past.

bypass *v.* avoid, circumvent, ignore, neglect, outflank.
n. detour, ring road.

by-product *n.* after-effect, consequence, fall-out, repercussion, result, side-effect.

bystander *n.* eye-witness, looker-on, observer, onlooker, passer-by, spectator, watcher, witness.

byword *n.* adage, catch-word, epithet, maxim, motto, proverb, saw, saying, slogan.

C

cabin *n.* **1** berth, compartment, quarters, room. **2** chalet, cottage, hut, lodge, shack, shanty, shed.
cabinet *n.* case, closet, commode, cupboard, dresser, locker.
cable *n.* chain, cord, line, mooring, rope.
cadence *n.* accent, beat, inflection, intonation, lilt, measure, metre, modulation, pattern, pulse, rate, rhythm, stress, swing, tempo, throb.
cadge *v.* beg, hitch, scrounge, sponge.
cage *v.* confine, coop up, encage, fence in, impound, imprison, incarcerate, lock up, restrain, shut up.
antonyms free, let out, release.
n. aviary, coop, corral, enclosure, pen, pound.
cag(e)y *adj.* careful, chary, circumspect, discreet, guarded, non-committal, secretive, shrewd, wary, wily.
antonyms frank, indiscreet, open.
cajole *v.* beguile, coax, dupe, entice, entrap, flatter, lure, manoeuvre, mislead, seduce, soothe, sweet-talk, tempt, wheedle, wile.
antonyms bully, compel, force.
cake *v.* bake, coagulate, coat, congeal, consolidate, cover, dry, encrust, harden, solidify, thicken.
n. block, fancy, flan, gâteau, loaf, lump, madeleine, mass, pie, roll, slab.
calamitous *adj.* catastrophic, deadly, devastating, dire, disastrous, dreadful, fatal, ghastly, grievous, ruinous, tragic, woeful.
antonyms fortunate, good, happy.
calamity *n.* adversity, affliction, catastrophe, desolation, disaster, distress, downfall, misadventure, mischance, misfortune, mishap, reverse, ruin, tragedy, trial, tribulation.
antonyms blessing, godsend, help.
calculate *v.* aim, compute, consider, count, determine, enumerate, estimate, figure, gauge, intend, judge, plan, rate, reckon, value, weigh, work out.
calculated *adj.* considered, deliberate, intended, intentional, planned, premeditated, purposed, wilful.
antonyms unintended, unplanned.
calculating *adj.* contriving, crafty, cunning, designing, devious, manipulative, scheming, sharp, shrewd, sly.
antonyms artless, naïve, open.
calculation *n.* **1** answer, computation, deliberation, estimate, figuring, forecast, judgement, planning, reckoning, result, sum. **2** contrivance, cunning, manipulation, slyness.
calibre *n.* **1** bore, diameter, gauge, measure, size. **2** ability, capacity, character, distinction, faculty, force, gifts, merit, quality, scope, stature, strength, talent, worth.
call *v.* **1** christen, designate, dub, label, name, style, term. **2** cry, exclaim, shout, yell. **3** announce, assemble, bid, convene, invite, summon. **4** contact, phone, ring (up), telephone.
n. **1** cry, exclamation, scream, shout, yell. **2** invitation, ring, visit. **3** cause, demand, excuse, grounds, justification, need, occasion, plea, reason, request, right. **4** announcement, appeal, claim, command, order, signal, summons.
call for 1 demand, entail, involve, necessitate, need, occasion, require, suggest. **2** collect, fetch, pick up.
call off abandon, break off, cancel, desist, discontinue, drop, withdraw.
call on appeal (to), ask, bid, call round, entreat, go and see, invite, invoke, request, summon, visit.
calling *n.* business, career, employment, field, job, line, line of country, mission, occupation, profession, province, pursuit, trade, vocation, work.
callous *adj.* cold, hardened, hard-hearted, heartless, indifferent, insensitive, thick-skinned, uncaring, unfeeling, unresponsive, unsympathetic.
antonyms caring, kind, sensitive, sympathetic.
calm *adj.* **1** collected, composed, cool, dispassionate, impassive, imperturbable, laid back, placid, quiet, relaxed, restful, sedate, self-possessed, unapprehensive, undisturbed, unemotional, uneventful, unexcitable, unexcited, unflappable, unflustered, unmoved, unperturbed, unruffled, untroubled. **2** mild, peaceful, serene, smooth, still, tranquil, unclouded, windless.
antonyms **1** excitable, worried. **2** anxious, rough, stormy, wild.
v. compose, hush, pacify, placate, quieten, relax, soothe.
antonyms excite, irritate, worry.
n. calmness, hush, peace, peacefulness, quiet, repose, serenity, stillness.
antonyms restlessness, storminess.
camouflage *n.* blind, cloak, concealment, covering, deception, disguise, front, guise, mask, masquerade, screen.
v. cloak, conceal, cover, disguise, hide, mask, obscure, screen, veil.
antonyms reveal, uncover.
camp *n.* clique, crowd, faction, group, party, section, side.
campaign *n.* attack, battle, crusade, drive, expedition, movement, offensive, operation, promotion, push.
v. advocate, attack, crusade, fight, promote,

push.

can *n.* canister, container, jar, pail, receptacle, tin.

cancel *v.* abolish, abort, annul, compensate, countermand, delete, eliminate, erase, neutralise, nullify, obliterate, offset, quash, redeem, repeal, repudiate, rescind, revoke, strike.

cancer *n.* blight, canker, corruption, evil, growth, malignancy, pestilence, rot, sickness, tumour.

candid *adj.* blunt, clear, fair, forthright, frank, free, guileless, ingenuous, just, open, outspoken, plain, sincere, straightforward, truthful, unbiased, uncontrived, unequivocal, unprejudiced.
antonyms cagey, devious, evasive, guarded.

candidate *n.* applicant, aspirant, claimant, competitor, contender, contestant, entrant, nominee, possibility, pretender, runner, suitor.

candour *n.* artlessness, directness, fairness, franchise, frankness, guilelessness, honesty, ingenuousness, naïvety, openness, outspokenness, plain-dealing, simplicity, sincerity, straightforwardness, truthfulness, unequivocalness.
antonyms cageyness, deviousness, evasiveness.

canny *adj.* acute, artful, astute, careful, circumspect, clever, comfortable, harmless, judicious, knowing, perspicacious, prudent, sagacious, sharp, shrewd, skilful, sly, subtle, wise, worldly-wise.
antonyms foolish, imprudent, unskilled.

canon *n.* catalogue, criterion, dictate, formula, list, precept, principle, regulation, rule, standard, statute, yardstick.

canonical *adj.* accepted, approved, authorised, authoritative, orthodox, recognised, regular, sanctioned.
antonyms uncanonical, unorthodox.

canopy *n.* awning, covering, shade, sunshade, umbrella.

cant *n.* **1** humbug, hypocrisy, insincerity, pretentiousness. **2** argot, jargon, lingo, slang, vernacular.

cantankerous *adj.* bad-tempered, contrary, crabbed, crabby, crotchety, crusty, difficult, disagreeable, grouchy, grumpy, ill-humoured, ill-natured, irritable, peevish, perverse, piggish, quarrelsome, testy.
antonyms easy-going, good-natured, pleasant.

canvass *v.* agitate, analyse, ask for, campaign, debate, discuss, dispute, electioneer, examine, inspect, investigate, poll, scan, scrutinise, seek, sift, solicit, study.
n. examination, investigation, poll, scrutiny, survey, tally.

canyon *n.* gorge, gully, ravine.

cap *v.* beat, better, complete, cover, crown, eclipse, exceed, excel, finish, outdo, outstrip, surpass, top, transcend.
n. beret, boater, bonnet, deerstalker, fez, hat, skullcap, sou'wester, tam-o'-shanter, yarmulka.

capability *n.* ability, capacity, competence, facility, faculty, means, potential, potentiality, power, proficiency, qualification, skill, talent.
antonyms inability, incompetence.

capable *adj.* able, accomplished, adequate, apt, clever, competent, disposed, efficient, experienced, fitted, gifted, intelligent, liable, masterly, proficient, qualified, skilful, suited, talented.
antonyms incapable, incompetent, useless.

capacity *n.* **1** compass, dimensions, extent, magnitude, range, room, scope, size, space, volume. **2** ability, aptitude, brains, capability, cleverness, competence, efficiency, faculty, forte, genius, gift, intelligence, power, readiness, role. **3** appointment, function, office, position, post, service.

cape[1] *n.* head, headland, ness, peninsula, point, promontory.

cape[2] *n.* cloak, coat, poncho, robe, shawl, wrap.

capital *n.* assets, cash, finance, funds, investment(s), means, money, principal, property, resources, stock, wealth, wherewithal.

capitalise *v.* cash in on, exploit, profit, take advantage of.

capitulate *v.* give in, relent, submit, succumb, surrender, throw in the towel/sponge, yield.
antonym fight on.

caprice *n.* changeableness, fad, fancy, fickleness, freak, humour, impulse, inconstancy, notion, quirk, vagary, whim.

capsize *v.* invert, keel over, overturn, turn over, turn turtle, upset.

capsule *n.* lozenge, module, pill, pod, receptacle, sheath, shell, tablet, vessel.

captain *n.* boss, chief, commander, head, leader, master, officer, patron, pilot, skipper.

captivate *v.* allure, attract, beguile, bewitch, charm, dazzle, enamour, enchant, enrapture, enthral, fascinate, hypnotise, infatuate, lure, mesmerise, seduce, win.
antonyms appal, disgust, repel.

captive *n.* convict, detainee, hostage, internee, prisoner, slave.
adj. caged, confined, enchained, enslaved, ensnared, imprisoned, restricted, secure.
antonym free.

captivity *n.* bondage, confinement, custody, detention, duress, imprisonment, incarceration, internment, restraint, servitude, slavery.
antonym freedom.

capture *v.* apprehend, arrest, catch, secure, seize, take.
n. arrest, catch, imprisonment, seizure, taking, trapping.

carcass *n.* body, cadaver, corpse, framework, hulk, relics, remains, shell, skeleton.

care *n.* **1** affliction, anxiety, concern, distress, pressure, strain, stress, tribulation, trouble, vexation, worry. **2** attention, carefulness, caution, consideration, forethought, heed, interest, meticulousness, pains, prudence, regard, vigilance, watchfulness. **3** charge, control, custody, guardianship, keeping, protection, responsibility, supervision, ward.
antonyms **2** carelessness, inattention, neglect, thoughtlessness.

v. bother, mind, worry.
care for 1 attend, foster, look after, mind, nurse, protect, tend, watch over. **2** be keen on, delight in, desire, enjoy, like, love, take pleasure in, want.
career *n.* calling, course, employment, job, life-work, livelihood, occupation, passage, path, procedure, progress, pursuit, race, vocation, walk.
v. bolt, dash, gallop, hurtle, race, run, rush, shoot, speed, tear.
carefree *adj.* blithe, breezy, careless, cheerful, cheery, easy-going, happy, happy-go-lucky, laid-back, light-hearted, untroubled, unworried.
antonyms anxious, despondent, worried.
careful *adj.* **1** alert, attentive, cautious, chary, circumspect, judicious, mindful, prudent, vigilant, wary, watchful. **2** accurate, conscientious, detailed, meticulous, painstaking, particular, precise, punctilious, scrupulous, thorough, thoughtful, thrifty.
antonyms **1** careless, inattentive, reckless, thoughtless. **2** careless.
careless *adj.* **1** forgetful, hasty, heedless, inconsiderate, irresponsible, negligent, remiss, thoughtless, uncaring, unconcerned, unguarded, unmindful, unthinking. **2** casual, cursory, disorderly, inaccurate, messy, neglectful, offhand, slap-dash, slipshod, sloppy, untidy.
antonyms **1** prudent, thoughtful. **2** accurate, careful, meticulous.
caress *v.* canoodle, cuddle, embrace, fondle, hug, kiss, pet, rub, stroke, touch.
n. cuddle, embrace, fondle, hug, kiss, pat, stroke.
caretaker *n.* curator, custodian, janitor, keeper, porter, superintendent, warden, watchman.
cargo *n.* baggage, consignment, contents, freight, goods, haul, lading, load, merchandise, payload, shipment, tonnage, ware.
caricature *n.* burlesque, cartoon, distortion, farce, lampoon, mimicry, mockery, parody, representation, satire, send-up, take-off, travesty.
v. distort, mimic, mock, parody, ridicule, satirise, send up, take off.
carnage *n.* blood-bath, bloodshed, butchery, havoc, holocaust, massacre, murder, slaughter.
carnival *n.* celebration, fair, festival, fête, fiesta, gala, holiday, jamboree, jubilee, merrymaking, revelry, wassail.
carol *n.* canticle, chorus, hymn, noel, song, strain, wassail.
carousing *n.* celebrating, drinking, merrymaking, party, partying.
carping *adj.* biting, bitter, cavilling, critical, fault-finding, hypercritical, nagging, nit-picking, picky, reproachful.
n. censure, complaints, criticism, disparagement, knocking, reproofs.
antonyms compliments, praise.
carriage *n.* **1** coach, vehicle, wagon. **2** air, bearing, behaviour, conduct, demeanour, deportment, manner, mien, posture. **3** carrying, conveyance, delivery, transport, transportation.
carrier *n.* bearer, conveyor, courier, deliveryman, messenger, porter, runner, transporter.
carry *v.* accomplish, bear, bring, capture, conduct, convey, fetch, gain, give, haul, lift, maintain, move, offer, relay, release, secure, shoulder, stand, suffer, support, sustain, take, transfer, transport, underpin, uphold, win.
carry on administer, continue, endure, keep on, last, maintain, manage, misbehave, operate, persevere, persist, proceed, run.
antonyms finish, stop.
carry out accomplish, achieve, bring off, conduct, discharge, do, execute, fulfil, implement, perform, realise, undertake.
cart *n.* barrow, truck, wagon, wheel-barrow.
v. bear, carry, convey, haul, hump, jag, lug, move, transport.
carton *n.* box, case, container, pack, package, packet, parcel.
cartoon *n.* animation, caricature, comic strip, drawing, parody, representation, sketch, take-off.
cartridge *n.* canister, capsule, case, cassette, charge, container, cylinder, magazine, round, shell.
carve *v.* chip, chisel, cut, divide, engrave, etch, fashion, form, grave, hack, hew, incise, indent, make, mould, sculpt, sculpture, slice.
cascade *n.* avalanche, cataract, deluge, falls, flood, force, fountain, outpouring, rush, shower, torrent, waterfall.
antonym trickle.
v. descend, flood, gush, overflow, pitch, plunge, pour, rush, shower, spill, surge, tumble.
case[1] *n.* box, cabinet, canister, capsule, carton, cartridge, casing, casket, chest, compact, container, cover, covering, crate, envelope, folder, holder, jacket, receptacle, sheath, shell, showcase, suit-case, tray, trunk, wrapper, wrapping.
v. encase, enclose, skin.
case[2] *n.* **1** argument, circumstances, condition, context, contingency, dilemma, event, example, illustration, instance, occasion, occurrence, point, position, situation, specimen, state. **2** action, argument, cause, dispute, lawsuit, proceedings, process, suit, trial.
cash *n.* bank-notes, bullion, change, coin, coinage, currency, funds, hard currency, hard money, money, notes, payment, ready money, resources, wherewithal.
v. encash, liquidate, realise.
cashier *n.* accountant, assistant, banker, bursar, check-out girl, clerk, purser, teller, treasurer.
cask *n.* barrel, butt, firkin, hogshead, tub, tun, vat, wood.
casket *n.* box, case, chest, coffer, jewel-box.
cast *v.* **1** diffuse, direct, drive, emit, fling, hurl, impel, lob, pitch, project, scatter, sling, spread, throw, toss. **2** allot, appoint, assign, bestow, brand, choose, describe, label, name, pick, select. **3** form, model, mould, shape.
n. **1** actors, artistes, characters, company, dramatis personae, entertainers, performers,

players, troupe. **2** form, mould, shape.
cast down crush, deject, depress, desolate, discourage, dishearten, sadden.
antonyms encourage, lift up.
caste *n.* class, degree, estate, grade, order, position, race, rank, station, status.
castle *n.* château, citadel, fortress, keep, mansion, palace, schloss, stronghold, tower.
casual *adj.* **1** accidental, chance, cursory, fortuitous, incidental, irregular, occasional, random, superficial, unexpected, unforeseen, unintentional, unpremeditated. **2** apathetic, blasé, indifferent, informal, lackadaisical, negligent, nonchalant, offhand, relaxed, unconcerned.
antonyms **1** deliberate, painstaking, planned. **2** formal, involved.
casualty *n.* death, injured, injury, loss, sufferer, victim, wounded.
cataclysm *n.* blow, calamity, catastrophe, collapse, convulsion, debacle, devastation, disaster, upheaval.
catacomb *n.* burial-vault, crypt, tomb, vault.
catalogue *n.* directory, gazetteer, index, inventory, list, record, register, roll, roster, schedule, table.
v. alphabetise, classify, file, index, inventory, list, record, register.
catapult *v.* heave, hurl, launch, pitch, plunge, propel, shoot, throw, toss.
cataract *n.* cascade, deluge, downpour, falls, force, rapids, torrent, waterfall.
catastrophe *n.* adversity, affliction, blow, calamity, cataclysm, debacle, devastation, disaster, end, failure, fiasco, mischance, misfortune, reverse, ruin, tragedy, trial, trouble, upheaval.
catcall *n.* barracking, boo, gibe, hiss, jeer, raspberry, whistle.
catch *v.* **1** clutch, get hold of, grab, grasp, grip, seize, take. **2** apprehend, arrest, capture. **3** detect, discern, discover, expose, find (out), surprise, unmask. **4** contract, develop, go down with. **5** captivate, charm, enchant, fascinate. **6** hear, perceive, recognise, understand.
antonyms **1** drop. **2** free, release. **6** miss.
n. **1** bolt, clasp, clip, fastener, hasp, hook, latch. **2** disadvantage, drawback, hitch, obstacle, problem, snag.
catch up draw level with, gain on, make up leeway, overtake.
catching *adj.* **1** communicable, contagious, infectious, transmittable. **2** attractive, captivating, charming, enchanting, fascinating, fetching, winning, winsome.
antonyms **1** non-infectious. **2** boring, ugly, unattractive.
catchword *n.* byword, catch-phrase, motto, password, refrain, slogan, watchword.
catchy *adj.* attractive, captivating, confusing, deceptive, haunting, memorable, popular.
antonyms boring, dull.
categorical *adj.* absolute, clear, direct, downright, emphatic, explicit, express, positive, total, unconditional, unequivocal, unqualified, unreserved.
antonyms qualified, tentative, vague.
categorise *v.* class, classify, grade, group, list, order, rank, sort.
category *n.* chapter, class, classification, department, division, grade, grouping, head, heading, list, order, rank, section, sort, type.
cater *v.* furnish, indulge, pander, provide, provision, supply.
catholic *adj.* all-embracing, all-inclusive, broad, broad-minded, comprehensive, general, global, inclusive, liberal, tolerant, universal, whole, wide, wide-ranging.
antonyms limited, narrow, narrow-minded.
cattle *n.* beasts, cows, livestock, stock.
catty *adj.* back-biting, bitchy, ill-natured, malevolent, malicious, mean, spiteful, venomous, vicious.
antonyms kind, pleasant.
caucus *n.* assembly, clique, convention, gathering, get-together, meeting, session, set.
cause *n.* agency, agent, attempt, basis, beginning, belief, consideration, conviction, creator, end, enterprise, grounds, ideal, impulse, incentive, inducement, mainspring, maker, motivation, motive, movement, object, origin, originator, producer, purpose, reason, root, source, spring, stimulus, undertaking.
antonyms consequence, effect, result.
v. begin, bring about, compel, create, effect, generate, give rise to, incite, induce, motivate, occasion, precipitate, produce, provoke, result in.
antonyms hinder, prevent, stop.
caustic *adj.* acid, acrimonious, biting, bitter, burning, corrosive, cutting, keen, mordant, pungent, sarcastic, scathing, severe, stinging, virulent.
antonyms mild, soothing.
caution *n.* admonition, advice, alertness, care, carefulness, counsel, deliberation, discretion, forethought, heed, injunction, prudence, vigilance, wariness, warning, watchfulness.
antonyms carelessness, recklessness.
v. admonish, advise, urge, warn.
cautious *adj.* alert, cagey, careful, chary, circumspect, discreet, guarded, heedful, judicious, prudent, scrupulous, softly-softly, tentative, unadventurous, vigilant, wary, watchful.
antonyms heedless, imprudent, incautious, reckless.
cavalcade *n.* array, march-past, parade, procession, retinue, train, troop.
cavalier *n.* attendant, equestrian, escort, gallant, gentleman, horseman, knight, partner, royalist.
adj. arrogant, condescending, curt, disdainful, free-and-easy, haughty, insolent, lofty, lordly, off-hand, scornful, supercilious, swaggering.
cave *n.* cavern, cavity, grotto, hollow, pothole.
cave in collapse, fall, give way, slip, subside, yield.
caveat *n.* admonition, alarm, caution, warning.
cavern *n.* cave, cavity, grotto, hollow, pothole,

vault.
cavernous *adj.* concave, deep, echoing, gaping, hollow, resonant, sepulchral, sunken, yawning.
cavil *v.* carp, censure, complain, nit-pick, object, quibble.
n. complaint, criticism, objection, quibble.
cavity *n.* dent, gap, hole, hollow, pit, sinus, ventricle, well.
cavort *v.* caper, dance, frisk, frolic, gambol, prance, romp, skip, sport.
cease *v.* call a halt, conclude, culminate, desist, die, discontinue, end, fail, finish, halt, pack in, refrain, stay, stop, terminate.
antonyms begin, commence, start.
ceaseless *adj.* constant, continual, continuous, endless, eternal, everlasting, incessant, interminable, never-ending, non-stop, perpetual, persistent, unending, unremitting, untiring.
antonyms irregular, occasional.
cede *v.* abandon, abdicate, allow, concede, convey, give up, grant, relinquish, renounce, resign, surrender, transfer, yield.
celebrate *v.* bless, commemorate, commend, eulogise, exalt, extol, glorify, honour, keep, observe, perform, praise, proclaim, publicise, rejoice, solemnise, toast, wassail.
celebrated *adj.* acclaimed, distinguished, eminent, exalted, famed, famous, glorious, illustrious, notable, outstanding, popular, pre-eminent, prominent, renowned, revered, well-known.
antonyms forgotten, obscure, unknown.
celebration *n.* anniversary, commemoration, festival, festivity, gala, honouring, jollification, jubilee, merrymaking, observance, party, performance, rave-up, rejoicings, remembrance, revelry.
celebrity *n.* big name, dignitary, luminary, name, personage, personality, star, superstar, VIP.
antonyms nobody, nonentity.
celibacy *n.* bachelorhood, singleness, spinsterhood, virginity.
cell *n.* caucus, cavity, chamber, compartment, group, nucleus, unit.
cellar *n.* basement, crypt, store-room, vault, wine-store.
cement *v.* attach, bind, bond, cohere, combine, fix together, glue, gum, join, plaster, seal, solder, stick, unite, weld.
n. concrete, mortar, plaster, sealant.
cemetery *n.* burial-ground, churchyard, graveyard.
censor *v.* amend, blue-pencil, bowdlerise, cut, edit, expurgate.
censorious *adj.* carping, cavilling, condemnatory, critical, disapproving, disparaging, fault-finding, hypercritical, severe.
antonyms approving, complimentary.
censure *n.* admonishment, admonition, blame, condemnation, criticism, disapproval, rebuke, reprehension, reprimand, reproach, reproof, telling-off.
antonyms approval, compliments, praise.
v. abuse, admonish, blame, castigate, condemn, criticise, denounce, rebuke, reprehend, reprimand, reproach, reprove, scold, tell off, upbraid.
antonyms approve, compliment, praise.
central *adj.* chief, essential, focal, fundamental, important, inner, interior, key, main, mid, middle, primary, principal, vital.
antonyms minor, peripheral, secondary.
centralise *v.* amalgamate, compact, concentrate, condense, converge, gather together, incorporate, rationalise, unify.
antonym decentralise.
centre *n.* bull's-eye, core, crux, focus, heart, hub, mid, middle, mid-point, nucleus, pivot.
antonyms edge, outskirts, periphery.
v. cluster, concentrate, converge, focus, gravitate, hinge, pivot, revolve.
ceremonial *adj.* dress, formal, ritual, ritualistic, solemn, stately.
antonyms casual, informal.
n. ceremony, formality, protocol, rite, ritual, solemnity.
ceremonious *adj.* civil, courteous, courtly, deferential, dignified, exact, formal, grand, polite, pompous, precise, punctilious, ritual, solemn, starchy, stately, stiff.
antonyms informal, relaxed, unceremonious.
ceremony *n.* **1** celebration, commemoration, function, observance, parade, rite, service. **2** ceremonial, decorum, etiquette, form, formality, niceties, pomp, propriety, protocol, ritual, show, solemnities.
certain *adj.* **1** absolute, assured, conclusive, confident, convinced, convincing, incontrovertible, indubitable, irrefutable, plain, positive, sure, true, undeniable, undoubted, unquestionable. **2** bound, destined, fated, inevitable, known. **3** decided, definite, established, express, fixed, individual, particular, precise, settled, some, special, specific. **4** constant, dependable, reliable, stable, steady, trustworthy.
antonyms **1** doubtful, hesitant, uncertain, unsure. **2** unlikely. **4** unreliable.
certainly *adv.* absolutely, definitely, doubtlessly, for sure, naturally, of course, undoubtedly.
certainty *n.* assurance, authoritativeness, confidence, conviction, fact, faith, inevitability, positiveness, reality, sureness, trust, truth, validity.
antonyms doubt, hesitation, uncertainty.
certificate *n.* attestation, authorisation, award, credentials, diploma, document, endorsement, guarantee, licence, pass, qualification, testimonial, validation, voucher, warrant.
certify *v.* ascertain, assure, authenticate, authorise, confirm, corroborate, declare, endorse, guarantee, notify, show, testify, validate, verify, vouch, witness.
chain *n.* bond, coupling, fetter, link, manacle, progression, restraint, sequence, series, set, string, succession, train, union.
v. bind, confine, enslave, fasten, fetter, handcuff, manacle, restrain, secure, shackle, tether, trammel.
antonyms free, release.

chairman *n.* chair, chairperson, chairwoman, convenor, director, master of ceremonies, MC, president, presider, speaker, spokesman, toastmaster.

chalky *adj.* ashen, pale, pallid, powdery, wan, white.

challenge *v.* accost, brave, confront, dare, defy, demand, dispute, impugn, provoke, query, question, stimulate, summon, tax, test, throw down the gauntlet, try.
n. confrontation, dare, defiance, hurdle, interrogation, obstacle, poser, provocation, question, test, trial, ultimatum.

champion *n.* backer, challenger, conqueror, defender, guardian, hero, patron, protector, upholder, victor, vindicator, warrior, winner.
v. advocate, back, defend, espouse, maintain, promote, stand up for, support, uphold.

chance *n.* **1** accident, coincidence, destiny, fate, fortuity, fortune, gamble, likelihood, luck, odds, possibility, probability, prospect, providence, risk, speculation. **2** occasion, opening, opportunity, time.
antonyms **1** certainty, law, necessity.
v. gamble, happen, occur, risk, stake, transpire, try, venture, wager.
adj. accidental, casual, fortuitous, inadvertent, incidental, random, unforeseeable, unforeseen, unintended, unintentional, unlooked-for.
antonyms certain, deliberate, foreseen, intentional.

chancy *adj.* dangerous, dicey, dodgy, fraught, hazardous, problematical, risky, speculative, tricky, uncertain.
antonyms safe, secure.

change *v.* alter, alternate, convert, displace, diversify, exchange, fluctuate, interchange, moderate, modify, reform, remodel, remove, reorganise, replace, restyle, shift, substitute, swap, trade, transfigure, transform, transpose, vacillate, vary.
n. alteration, break, conversion, difference, diversion, exchange, innovation, interchange, modification, novelty, permutation, revolution, satisfaction, shift, substitution, transformation, transition, transposition, upheaval, variation, variety.

changeable *adj.* capricious, erratic, fickle, fitful, fluid, inconstant, irregular, kaleidoscopic, mobile, mutable, shifting, uncertain, unpredictable, unreliable, unsettled, unstable, unsteady, vacillating, variable, volatile, wavering.
antonyms constant, reliable, unchangeable.

channel *n.* approach, artery, avenue, canal, chamber, communication, conduit, course, duct, flume, furrow, gat, groove, gullet, gut, gutter, level, main, means, medium, overflow, passage, path, route, sound, start, strait, trough, watercourse, waterway, way.
v. conduct, convey, direct, force, furrow, guide, send, transmit.

chant *n.* carol, chorus, melody, psalm, slogan, song, war-cry.
v. chorus, croon, intone, recite, sing.

chaos *n.* anarchy, bedlam, confusion, disorder, disorganisation, lawlessness, pandemonium, tumult, unreason.
antonym order.

chaotic *adj.* anarchic, confused, deranged, disordered, disorganised, lawless, purposeless, riotous, topsy-turvy, tumultous, uncontrolled.
antonyms ordered, organised.

chap *n.* bloke, character, cove, fellow, guy, individual, person, sort, type.

chaperon *n.* companion, escort.
v. accompany, attend, escort, guard, protect, safeguard, shepherd, watch over.

chapter *n.* assembly, branch, chapel, clause, division, episode, part, period, phase, section, stage, topic.

character *n.* **1** attributes, bent, calibre, complexion, constitution, disposition, feature, honour, individuality, integrity, make-up, nature, peculiarity, personality, position, quality, reputation, stamp, status, strength, temper, temperament, type, uprightness. **2** cipher, emblem, figure, hieroglyph, ideograph, letter, logo, mark, sign, symbol, type. **3** fellow, guy, individual, person, role, sort, type.

characterise *v.* brand, distinguish, identify, indicate, inform, mark, represent, stamp, typify.

characteristic *adj.* distinctive, distinguishing, idiosyncratic, individual, peculiar, representative, special, specific, symbolic, symptomatic, typical, vintage.
antonyms uncharacteristic, untypical.
n. attribute, faculty, feature, hallmark, idiosyncrasy, mannerism, mark, peculiarity, property, quality, symptom, thing, trait.

charade *n.* fake, farce, mockery, pantomime, parody, pretence, travesty.

charge *v.* **1** ask, demand, exact, price. **2** accuse, blame, impeach, incriminate, indict. **3** assail, attack, rush, storm.
n. **1** amount, cost, expenditure, expense, fee, outlay, payment, price, rate. **2** accusation, allegation, imputation, indictment, injunction. **3** assault, attack, onslaught, rush, sortie. **4** care, custody, duty, mandate, office, order, responsibility, safekeeping, trust, ward.

charitable *adj.* accommodating, benevolent, benign, broad-minded, compassionate, considerate, favourable, forgiving, generous, gracious, indulgent, kind, lavish, lenient, liberal, magnanimous, mild, philanthropic, sympathetic, tolerant, understanding.
antonyms inconsiderate, uncharitable, unforgiving.

charity *n.* affection, alms-giving, altruism, assistance, beneficence, benevolence, benignness, bountifulness, clemency, compassion, endowment, fund, generosity, gift, goodness, handout, humanity, indulgence, love, philanthropy, relief, tender-heartedness.
antonyms malice, selfishness, stinginess.

charlatan *n.* cheat, con man, fake, fraud, impostor, phoney, pretender, quack, sham, swindler, trickster.

charm *v.* allure, attract, beguile, bewitch, cajole, captivate, delight, enamour, enchant, enrapture, fascinate, mesmerise, please, win.
antonym repel.
n. allure, amulet, appeal, attraction, desirability, enchantment, fascination, fetish, idol, magic, magnetism, sorcery, spell, talisman, trinket.

charming *adj.* appealing, attractive, captivating, delightful, fetching, irresistible, lovely, pleasant, pleasing, seductive, sweet, winning, winsome.
antonyms repulsive, ugly, unattractive.

chart *n.* blueprint, diagram, drawing, graph, map, plan, table.
v. delineate, draft, draw, graph, map out, mark, outline, place, plot, shape, sketch.

charter *n.* authorisation, bond, concession, contract, deed, document, franchise, indenture, licence, permit, prerogative, privilege, right.
v. authorise, commission, employ, engage, hire, lease, rent, sanction.

chary *adj.* careful, cautious, circumspect, guarded, heedful, prudent, reluctant, slow, suspicious, uneasy, unwilling, wary.
antonyms heedless, unwary.

chase *v.* course, drive, expel, follow, hunt, hurry, pursue, rush, track.
n. hunt, hunting, pursuit, race, run, rush, venery.

chasm *n.* abyss, breach, canyon, cavity, cleft, crater, crevasse, fissure, gap, gorge, gulf, hollow, opening, ravine, rift, split, void.

chassis *n.* anatomy, bodywork, bones, frame, framework, fuselage, skeleton, structure, substructure, undercarriage.

chaste *adj.* austere, immaculate, innocent, modest, moral, neat, pure, refined, restrained, simple, unaffected, undefiled, unsullied, virginal, virtuous, wholesome.
antonyms corrupt, indecorous, lewd, vulgar.

chasten *v.* admonish, afflict, castigate, chastise, correct, curb, discipline, humble, humiliate, repress, reprove, soften, subdue, tame.

chastise *v.* beat, berate, castigate, censure, correct, discipline, flog, lash, punish, reprove, scold, scourge, smack, spank, upbraid, whip.

chat *n.* chatter, gossip, heart-to-heart, natter, rap, talk, tête-à-tête.
v. chatter, crack, gossip, jaw, natter, rabbit (on), talk, visit.

chatter *n.* babble, chat, gossip, jabber, natter, prattle, tattle, twaddle.
v. babble, blather, chat, clatter, gossip, natter, prattle, tattle.

chatterer *n.* big mouth, blabber, chatterbox, gossip, loudmouth, windbag.

chatty *adj.* colloquial, familiar, friendly, gossipy, informal, newsy, talkative.
antonym quiet.

cheap *adj.* **1** bargain, budget, cut-price, dirt-cheap, economical, economy, inexpensive, knock-down, reasonable, reduced, uncostly. **2** common, contemptible, despicable, inferior, low, mean, paltry, poor, second-rate, shoddy, tatty, tawdry, vulgar, worthless.
antonyms **1** costly, expensive. **2** admirable, noble, superior.

cheapen *v.* belittle, degrade, demean, denigrate, depreciate, devalue, discredit, disparage, downgrade, lower.
antonyms enhance, improve.

cheat *v.* bamboozle, beguile, con, deceive, defraud, diddle, do, double-cross, dupe, fleece, fob, foil, fool, hoodwink, mislead, rip off, short-change, swindle, trick.
n. **1** artifice, deceit, deception, rip-off, swindle, trickery. **2** charlatan, cheater, con man, deceiver, dodger, double-crosser, extortioner, fraud, impostor, rogue, shark, swindler, trickster.

check *v.* **1** compare, confirm, examine, give the once-over, inspect, investigate, monitor, note, probe, research, scrutinise, study, test, verify. **2** arrest, bar, bridle, control, curb, damp, delay, halt, hinder, impede, inhibit, limit, obstruct, pause, repress, restrain, retard, stop, thwart.
n. **1** audit, examination, inspection, investigation, research, scrutiny, test. **2** bill, counterfoil, token. **3** blow, constraint, control, curb, damper, disappointment, frustration, hindrance, impediment, inhibition, limitation, obstruction, rejection, restraint, reverse, setback, stoppage.
check out examine, investigate, test.

cheek *n.* audacity, brazenness, disrespect, effrontery, gall, impertinence, impudence, insolence, nerve, temerity.

cheeky *adj.* audacious, disrespectful, forward, impertinent, impudent, insolent, insulting, pert, saucy.
antonyms polite, respectful.

cheer *v.* acclaim, applaud, brighten, clap, comfort, console, elate, encourage, exhilarate, gladden, hail, hearten, incite, uplift, warm.
antonyms boo, dishearten, jeer.
n. acclamation, applause, bravo, hurrah, ovation.

cheerful *adj.* animated, bright, buoyant, cheery, chirpy, contented, enlivening, enthusiastic, genial, glad, happy, hearty, jaunty, jolly, jovial, joyful, joyous, light-hearted, light-spirited, merry, optimistic, pleasant, sparkling.
antonyms dejected, depressed, sad.

cheery *adj.* blithe, breezy, bright, carefree, cheerful, good-humoured, happy, jovial, lively, merry, pleasant, sparkling, sunny.
antonyms downcast, sad.

chemical *n.* compound, element, substance, synthetic.

cherish *v.* comfort, encourage, entertain, foster, harbour, make much of, nourish, nurse, nurture, prize, shelter, support, sustain, tender, treasure, value.

chest *n.* ark, box, case, casket, coffer, crate, strongbox, trunk.

chew *v.* champ, crunch, gnaw, grind, masticate, munch.

chief *adj.* central, essential, foremost, grand, highest, key, leading, main, major, outstanding, predominant, pre-eminent, premier, prevailing, primary, prime, principal, superior, supreme, uppermost, vital.
antonyms junior, minor, unimportant.
n. boss, captain, chieftain, commander, director, governor, head, leader, lord, manager, master, principal, ringleader, ruler, superintendent, superior, supremo.

chiefly *adv.* especially, essentially, for the most part, generally, mainly, mostly, predominantly, primarily, principally, usually.

child *n.* babe, baby, descendant, infant, issue, juvenile, kid, minor, nipper, offspring, progeny, suckling, toddler, tot, youngster.

childbirth *n.* child-bearing, confinement, delivery, labour, lying-in.

childhood *n.* adolescence, babyhood, boyhood, girlhood, immaturity, infancy, minority, schooldays, youth.

childish *adj.* boyish, foolish, frivolous, girlish, immature, infantile, juvenile, puerile, silly, simple, trifling, weak, young.
antonyms mature, sensible.

childlike *adj.* artless, credulous, guileless, ingenuous, innocent, naïve, natural, simple, trustful, trusting.

children *n.* line, offspring, progeny.

chill *v.* **1** congeal, cool, freeze, refrigerate. **2** dampen, depress, discourage, dishearten, dismay, frighten, terrify.
n. bite, cold, coldness, coolness, crispness, frigidity, nip, rawness, sharpness.

chilly *adj.* **1** blowy, breezy, brisk, cold, crisp, draughty, fresh, nippy, sharp. **2** aloof, cool, frigid, hostile, stony, unfriendly, unresponsive, unsympathetic, unwelcoming.
antonyms **1** warm. **2** friendly.

chime *v.* clang, dong, jingle, peal, ping, ring, sound, strike, ting, tinkle, toll.

china *adj.* ceramic, earthenware, porcelain, pottery, terracotta.

chink[1] *n.* aperture, cleft, crack, crevice, cut, fissure, flaw, gap, opening, rift, slot, space.

chink[2] *n.* clink, ding, jangle, jingle, ping, ring, ting, tinkle.

chip *n.* dent, flake, flaw, fragment, nick, notch, paring, scrap, scratch, shaving, sliver, wafer.
v. chisel, damage, gash, nick, notch, whittle.
chip in contribute, donate, interrupt, participate, pay, subscribe.

chirp *v., n.* cheep, chirrup, peep, pipe, tweet, twitter, warble, whistle.

chirpy *adj.* bright, cheerful, cheery, happy, jaunty, merry, perky, sunny.
antonyms downcast, sad.

chivalrous *adj.* bold, brave, courageous, courteous, gallant, gentlemanly, heroic, honourable, polite, true, valiant.
antonyms cowardly, disloyal, ungallant.

chivalry *n.* boldness, bravery, courage, courtesy, gallantry, gentlemanliness, politeness.

chivvy *v.* badger, harass, hassle, hound, importune, nag, pester, plague, pressure, prod, torment, urge.

choice *n.* alternative, choosing, decision, dilemma, discrimination, election, opting, option, pick, preference, say, selection, variety.
adj. best, elect, excellent, exclusive, exquisite, fine, hand-picked, plum, precious, prime, prize, rare, select, special, superior, uncommon, unusual, valuable.
antonyms inferior, poor.

choke *v.* asphyxiate, bar, block, clog, close, congest, constrict, dam, gag, obstruct, overpower, reach, smother, stifle, stop, strangle, suffocate, suppress, throttle.

choose *v.* adopt, designate, desire, elect, fix on, opt for, pick, plump for, predestine, prefer, see fit, select, settle on, single out, take, vote for, wish.

choosy *adj.* discriminating, exacting, fastidious, finicky, fussy, particular, picky, selective.
antonym undemanding.

chop *v.* cleave, cut, divide, hack, hew, lop, sever, slash, slice, truncate.
chop up cube, cut (up), dice, divide, fragment, mince, slice (up).

choppy *adj.* blustery, broken, rough, ruffled, squally, stormy, tempestuous, wavy, white.
antonyms calm, peaceful, still.

chore *n.* burden, duty, errand, job, stint, task, trouble.

chorus *n.* call, choir, choristers, ensemble, refrain, response, shout, singers, strain, vocalists.

christen *v.* baptise, call, designate, dub, inaugurate, name, sprinkle, style, term, title, use.

Christmas *n.* Noel, Nowell, Xmas, Yule, Yuletide.

chronic *adj.* appalling, atrocious, awful, confirmed, deep-rooted, deep-seated, dreadful, habitual, incessant, incurable, ingrained, inveterate, persistent, severe, terrible.
antonyms mild, temporary.

chronological *adj.* consecutive, historical, ordered, progressive, sequential.

chubby *adj.* flabby, fleshy, paunchy, plump, podgy, portly, rotund, round, stout, tubby.
antonyms skinny, slim.

chuckle *v.* chortle, crow, exult, giggle, laugh, snigger, snort, titter.

chum *n.* companion, comrade, friend, mate, pal.
antonym enemy.

chunk *n.* block, chuck, dollop, hunk, lump, mass, piece, portion, slab, wad, wodge.

chunky *adj.* beefy, brawny, bulky, dumpy, fat, square, stocky, stubby, thick, thickset.
antonym slim.

church *n.* abbey, cathedral, chapel, house of God, house of prayer, minster, sanctuary.

cinema *n.* big screen, filmhouse, flicks, movies, picture-house, picture-palace.

cipher *n.* character, code, device, digit, figure, logo, mark, monogram, number, numeral, symbol, zero.

circle *n.* **1** circuit, circumference, coil, cycle, disc,

globe, hoop, loop, orb, orbit, perimeter, revolution, ring, round, sphere, turn. **2** band, clique, club, company, coterie, crowd, fellowship, fraternity, group, set, society.
v. **1** coil, compass, curve, encircle, enclose, encompass, envelop, gird, girdle, hem in, loop, pivot, revolve, ring, rotate, surround, whirl. **2** circumnavigate, tour.
circuit *n.* ambit, area, boundary, bounds, circumference, compass, course, district, journey, limit, orbit, range, region, revolution, round, route, tour, track, tract.
circuitous *adj.* devious, indirect, labyrinthine, meandering, oblique, periphrastic, rambling, roundabout, tortuous, winding.
antonyms direct, straight.
circular *adj.* annular, disc-shaped, hoop-shaped, ring-shaped, round.
n. advert, announcement, handbill, leaflet, letter, notice, pamphlet.
circulate *v.* broadcast, diffuse, distribute, flow, go around, gyrate, issue, pass round, propagate, publicise, publish, revolve, rotate, spread, swirl, whirl.
circulation *n.* blood-flow, circling, currency, dissemination, distribution, flow, motion, rotation, spread, transmission.
circumference *n.* border, boundary, bounds, circuit, edge, extremity, fringe, limits, margin, outline, perimeter, periphery, rim, verge.
circumstances *n.* conditions, details, elements, factors, facts, incidents, items, lifestyle, means, particulars, position, resources, situation, state, state of affairs, status, times.
circumstantial *adj.* conjectural, detailed, exact, hearsay, incidental, indirect, inferential, minute, particular, presumptive, provisional, specific.
antonyms hard, inexact, vague.
cistern *n.* basin, pool, reservoir, sink, tank, vat.
citadel *n.* acropolis, bastion, castle, fortification, fortress, keep, stronghold, tower.
citation *n.* **1** award, commendation. **2** cutting, excerpt, illustration, mention, passage, quotation, quote, reference, source.
cite *v.* adduce, advance, call, enumerate, extract, mention, name, quote, specify.
citizen *n.* burgher, city-dweller, inhabitant, ratepayer, resident, subject.
city *n.* conurbation, metropolis, municipality, town.
civic *adj.* borough, city, communal, community, local, municipal, public, urban.
civil *adj.* accommodating, affable, civic, civilised, complaisant, courteous, courtly, domestic, home, interior, internal, municipal, obliging, polished, polite, political, refined, temporal, urbane, well-bred, well-mannered.
antonyms discourteous, rude, uncivil.
civilisation *n.* advancement, cultivation, culture, development, education, enlightenment, progress, refinement, sophistication, urbanity.
antonyms barbarity, primitiveness.
civilise *v.* cultivate, educate, enlighten, humanise, improve, perfect, polish, refine, sophisticate, tame.
civilised *adj.* advanced, cultured, educated, enlightened, humane, polite, refined, sophisticated, tolerant, urbane.
antonyms barbarous, primitive.
civility *n.* affability, amenity, amiability, attention, breeding, courteousness, courtesy, graciousness, politeness, politesse, tact, urbanity.
antonyms discourtesy, rudeness, uncouthness.
claim *v.* affirm, allege, ask, assert, challenge, collect, demand, exact, hold, insist, maintain, need, profess, request, require, state, take, uphold.
n. affirmation, allegation, application, assertion, call, demand, insistence, petition, pretension, privilege, request, requirement, right.
claimant *n.* applicant, petitioner, supplicant.
clairvoyant *adj.* extra-sensory, prophetic, psychic, second-sighted, telepathic, visionary.
n. augur, diviner, fortune-teller, oracle, prophet, prophetess, psychic, seer, soothsayer, telepath, visionary.
clammy *adj.* close, damp, dank, heavy, moist, muggy, slimy, sticky, sweating, sweaty.
clamp *n.* brace, bracket, fastener, grip, press, vice.
v. brace, clinch, fasten, fix, impose, secure.
clan *n.* band, brotherhood, clique, confraternity, coterie, faction, family, fraternity, group, house, race, sect, set, society, tribe.
clang *v.* chime, clank, clash, jangle, peal, resound, reverberate, ring, toll.
n. clank, clash, clatter, jangle, peal.
clap *v.* acclaim, applaud, bang, cheer, pat, slap, smack, thrust, wallop, whack.
clarify *v.* define, explain, gloss, illuminate, purify, refine, resolve, shed/throw light on, simplify.
antonyms confuse, obscure.
clarity *n.* clearness, comprehensibility, definition, explicitness, intelligibility, lucidity, obviousness, precision, simplicity, transparency, unambiguousness.
antonyms imprecision, obscurity, vagueness.
clash *v.* bang, clang, clank, clatter, conflict, crash, disagree, feud, fight, grapple, jangle, jar, quarrel, rattle, war, wrangle.
n. brush, clatter, collision, conflict, confrontation, disagreement, fight, jangle, jar, noise, show-down.
clasp *n.* buckle, catch, clip, embrace, fastener, grasp, grip, hasp, hold, hook, hug, pin, snap.
v. attach, clutch, connect, embrace, enfold, fasten, grapple, grasp, grip, hold, hug, press, seize, squeeze.
class *n.* **1** category, classification, collection, department, description, division, genre, genus, grade, group, grouping, kind, league, order, quality, rank, section, set, sort, species, sphere, status, style, type, value. **2** course, lecture, seminar, teach-in, tutorial.
v. brand, categorise, classify, codify, designate, grade, group, rank, rate, sort.

classic *adj.* abiding, ageless, archetypal, best, characteristic, consummate, definitive, enduring, established, excellent, exemplary, finest, first-rate, ideal, immortal, lasting, master, masterly, model, regular, restrained, standard, time-honoured, traditional, typical, undying, usual.
antonyms second-rate, unrepresentative.
n. exemplar, masterpiece, masterwork, model, pièce de résistance, prototype, standard.

classical *adj.* elegant, established, excellent, harmonious, pure, refined, restrained, standard, traditional, well-proportioned.
antonyms inferior, modern.

classification *n.* analysis, arrangement, cataloguing, categorisation, codification, grading, sorting, taxonomy.

classify *v.* arrange, assort, catalogue, categorise, codify, digest, dispose, distribute, file, grade, pigeon-hole, rank, sort, systematise, tabulate.

classy *adj.* elegant, exclusive, exquisite, fine, gorgeous, grand, high-class, posh, select, stylish, superior, swanky, up-market.
antonyms dowdy, plain, unstylish.

clause *n.* article, chapter, condition, heading, item, paragraph, part, passage, point, provision, proviso, section, specification, subsection.

claw *n.* gripper, nail, nipper, pincer, pounce, talon, tentacle, unguis.
v. dig, graze, lacerate, mangle, maul, rip, scrabble, scrape, scratch, tear.

clean *adj.* **1** antiseptic, decontaminated, faultless, flawless, hygienic, immaculate, laundered, perfect, pure, purified, sanitary, spotless, sterile, sterilised, unadulterated, unblemished, uncontaminated, unpolluted, unsoiled, unspotted, unstained, unsullied, washed. **2** chaste, decent, guiltless, honest, honourable, innocent, moral, respectable, upright, virtuous.
antonyms **1** dirty, polluted, unsterile. **2** dirty, dishonourable, indecent.
v. bath, cleanse, deodorise, deterge, disinfect, dust, launder, mop, purge, purify, rinse, sanitise, scour, scrub, sponge, swab, sweep, vacuum, wash, wipe.
antonyms defile, dirty.
clean up sanitise, tidy, wash.

cleanse *v.* absolve, clean, clear, decontaminate, purge, purify, rinse, scavenge, scour, scrub, wash.
antonyms defile, dirty.

cleanser *n.* detergent, disinfectant, purifier, scourer, scouring-powder, soap, solvent.

clear *adj.* **1** apparent, coherent, comprehensible, conspicuous, distinct, evident, explicit, express, intelligible, lucid, manifest, obvious, patent, plain, unambiguous, unmistakable, unquestionable, well-defined. **2** certain, convinced, definite, positive, sure. **3** see-through, transparent, unclouded. **4** bright, cloudless, fine, light, luminous, sunny, undimmed, undulled. **5** empty, free, open, unblocked, unhindered, unimpeded, unobstructed. **6** audible, perceptible, pronounced, recognisable.
antonyms **1** ambiguous, confusing, unclear, vague. **2** muddled, unsure. **3** cloudy, opaque. **4** dull. **5** blocked.
v. **1** decongest, disentangle, extricate, free, loosen, rid, unblock, unclog, unload. **2** clean, cleanse, erase, refine, tidy, wipe. **3** absolve, acquit, emancipate, excuse, exonerate, free, justify, let go, liberate, release, vindicate. **4** acquire, earn, gain, make.
antonyms **1** block. **2** defile, dirty. **3** condemn.
clear up answer, clarify, elucidate, explain, order, rearrange, remove, resolve, solve, sort, tidy, unravel.

clearance *n.* **1** allowance, authorisation, consent, endorsement, go-ahead, leave, OK, permission, sanction, the green light. **2** gap, headroom, margin, space.

clear-cut *adj.* clear, definite, distinct, explicit, plain, precise, specific, straightforward, unambiguous, unequivocal, well-defined.
antonyms ambiguous, fuzzy, vague.

clearing *n.* dell, glade, hollow, opening, space.

clergy *n.* churchmen, clergymen, clerics, ministry, priesthood, the church, the cloth.

clergyman *n.* canon, chaplain, churchman, curate, deacon, dean, divine, father, man of God, minister, padre, parson, pastor, presbyter, priest, rabbi, rector, reverend, vicar.

clerk *n.* account-keeper, assistant, copyist, official, pen-pusher, receptionist, shop-assistant, writer.

clever *adj.* **1** able, adroit, apt, brainy, bright, capable, deep, discerning, expert, gifted, ingenious, intelligent, inventive, keen, knowing, knowledgeable, quick, quick-witted, rational, resourceful, sensible, witty. **2** cunning, shrewd, smart.
antonyms **1** foolish, naïve, senseless, stupid. **2** honest.

cliché *n.* banality, bromide, chestnut, platitude, stereotype, truism.

client *n.* applicant, buyer, consumer, customer, dependant, patient, patron, protégé, shopper.

cliff *n.* bluff, crag, escarpment, face, overhang, precipice, rock-face, scar, scarp.

climate *n.* ambience, atmosphere, country, disposition, feeling, milieu, mood, region, setting, temper, temperature, tendency, trend, weather.

climax *n.* acme, culmination, head, height, high point, highlight, peak, summit, top, zenith.
antonyms low point, nadir.

climb *v.* ascend, clamber, mount, rise, scale, shin up, soar, top.
climb down back down, eat one's words, retract, retreat.

clinch *v.* agree, conclude, confirm, decide, determine, embrace, fasten, seal, secure, settle, verify.

cling *v.* adhere, clasp, cleave, clutch, embrace, fasten, grasp, grip, hug, stick.

clinical *adj.* analytic, business-like, cold, detached, disinterested, dispassionate, emotionless, impersonal, objective, scientific, unemotional.

antonyms biased, emotional, subjective.

clip *v.* **1** crop, curtail, cut, dock, pare, poll, prune, shear, shorten, snip, trim. **2** box, clobber, clout, cuff, hit, knock, punch, slap, smack, sock, thump, wallop, whack.
n. blow, box, clout, cuff, hit, knock, punch, slap, smack, sock, thump, wallop, whack.

clipping *n.* citation, cutting, excerpt, extract, piece.

clique *n.* bunch, circle, clan, coterie, crew, crowd, faction, gang, group, mob, pack, set.

cloak *n.* cape, coat, cover, front, mantle, mask, pretext, shield, wrap.
v. camouflage, conceal, cover, disguise, hide, mask, obscure, screen, veil.

clog *v.* block, burden, congest, dam up, hamper, hinder, impede, jam, obstruct, shackle, stop up, stuff.
antonym unblock.
n. burden, dead-weight, drag, encumbrance, hindrance, impediment, obstruction.

close[1] *v.* **1** bar, block, clog, cork, lock, obstruct, plug, seal, secure, shut. **2** cease, complete, conclude, connect, end, finish, stop, terminate, wind up. **3** couple, fuse, join, unite.
antonyms **1** open. **2** start. **3** separate.
n. cessation, completion, conclusion, culmination, denouement, end, ending, finale, finish, junction, pause, stop, termination, wind-up.

close[2] *adj.* **1** adjacent, adjoining, at hand, impending, near, near-by, neighbouring. **2** attached, dear, devoted, familiar, intimate, loving. **3** airless, heavy, humid, muggy, oppressive, stifling, stuffy, suffocating, sweltering, unventilated. **4** mean, miserly, niggardly, parsimonious, stingy, tight. **5** confidential, private, secret, secretive, uncommunicative. **6** accurate, exact, faithful, literal, precise, strict. **7** concentrated, fixed, intense, keen. **8** compact, cramped, dense, packed, solid.
antonyms **1** distant, far. **2** cool, unfriendly. **3** airy, fresh. **4** generous. **5** open. **6** rough.

closure *n.* cessation, closing, conclusion, end, finish, lid, plug, seal, stoppage, stopper, stricture, winding-up.
antonym opening.

clot *n.* clotting, coagulation, curdling, lump, mass, occlusion, thrombus.
v. coagulate, coalesce, congeal, curdle, jell, thicken.

cloth *n.* dish-cloth, duster, fabric, face-cloth, material, rag, stuff, textiles, tissue, towel.

clothe *v.* apparel, attire, deck, dress, invest, outfit, put on, rig, robe, vest, wear.
antonyms disrobe, unclothe, undress.

clothes *n.* clothing, costume, dress, garments, gear, get-up, outfit, togs, vestments, wardrobe, wear.

cloud *n.* darkness, fog, gloom, haze, mist, obscurity, shower, vapour.
v. confuse, darken, dim, disorient, distort, dull, eclipse, impair, muddle, obfuscate, obscure, overcast, overshadow, shade, shadow, stain, veil.
antonym clear.

cloudy *adj.* blurred, blurry, confused, dark, dim, dismal, dull, hazy, indistinct, leaden, lightless, lowering, muddy, murky, nebulous, obscure, opaque, overcast, sombre, sullen.
antonyms bright, clear, sunny.

clout *v.* box, clobber, cuff, hit, slap, smack, sock, strike, thump, wallop, whack, wham.
n. **1** blow, cuff, slap, smack, thump, wallop, whack. **2** authority, influence, power, prestige, standing, weight.

clown *n.* buffoon, comedian, fool, harlequin, jester, joker.

cloying *adj.* excessive, nauseating, oversweet, sickening, sickly.

club *n.* **1** association, bunch, circle, clique, combination, company, fraternity, group, guild, league, order, set, society, union. **2** bat, bludgeon, cosh, cudgel, mace, stick, truncheon.
v. bash, batter, beat, clobber, clout, cosh, hit, pummel, strike.

clue *n.* evidence, hint, idea, indication, inkling, intimation, lead, notion, pointer, sign, suggestion, suspicion, tip, tip-off, trace.

clump *n.* bunch, bundle, cluster, mass, thicket, tuffet, tuft.
v. clomp, lumber, plod, stamp, stomp, thud, thump, tramp, tread.

clumsy *adj.* awkward, blundering, bumbling, bungling, clumping, crude, gauche, gawky, ham-fisted, heavy, hulking, ill-made, inept, lumbering, rough, shapeless, unco-ordinated, uncouth, ungainly, ungraceful, unhandy, unskilful, unwieldy.
antonyms careful, elegant, graceful.

cluster *n.* assemblage, batch, bunch, clump, collection, gathering, group, knot, mass.
v. assemble, bunch, collect, flock, gather, group.

clutch *v.* catch, clasp, embrace, fasten, grab, grapple, grasp, grip, hang on to, seize, snatch.

clutter *n.* confusion, disarray, disorder, jumble, litter, mess, muddle, untidiness.
v. cover, encumber, fill, litter, scatter, strew.

coach *n.* grinder, instructor, teacher, trainer, tutor.
v. cram, drill, instruct, prepare, teach, train, tutor.

coagulate *v.* clot, congeal, curdle, jell, solidify, thicken.
antonym melt.

coalition *n.* affiliation, alliance, amalgamation, association, bloc, combination, compact, confederacy, confederation, conjunction, federation, fusion, integration, league, merger, union.

coarse *adj.* **1** coarse-grained, rough, uneven, unfinished, unpolished, unprocessed, unpurified, unrefined. **2** bawdy, boorish, crude, earthly, foul-mouthed, immodest, impolite, improper, impure, indelicate, loutish, offensive, ribald, rude, smutty, vulgar.
antonyms **1** fine, smooth. **2** polite, refined, sophisticated.

coarsen *v.* blunt, deaden, desensitise, dull,

harden, roughen.
antonyms civilise, sensitise.

coast *n.* coastline, seaboard, seaside, shore.
v. cruise, drift, free-wheel, glide, sail.

coat *n.* cloak, coating, covering, fur, hair, hide, mackintosh, mantle, overlay, raincoat.
v. apply, cover, paint, plaster, smear, spread.

coating *n.* blanket, coat, covering, dusting, film, finish, fur, glaze, lamination, layer, membrane, sheet, skin, varnish, veneer, wash.

coax *v.* allure, beguile, cajole, entice, flatter, persuade, soft-soap, sweet-talk, wheedle.
antonyms browbeat, force.

cobble *v.* botch, bungle, knock up, mend, patch, put together, tinker.

cock-eyed *adj.* **1** askew, asymmetrical, awry, crooked, lop-sided, skew-whiff. **2** absurd, crazy, daft, ludicrous, nonsensical, preposterous.
antonyms **1** straight. **2** sensible.

cocky *adj.* arrogant, bouncy, brash, cocksure, conceited, egotistical, fresh, swaggering, swollen-headed, vain.
antonyms humble, shy.

coddle *v.* cosset, indulge, mollycoddle, nurse, pamper, pet, spoil.

code *n.* **1** convention, custom, ethics, etiquette, manners, maxim, principles, regulations, rules, system. **2** cipher, cryptograph.

coerce *v.* bludgeon, browbeat, bulldoze, bully, compel, constrain, dragoon, drive, drum, force, intimidate, press-gang, pressurise.
antonyms coax, persuade.

coercion *n.* browbeating, bullying, compulsion, constraint, duress, force, intimidation, pressure, threats.
antonym persuasion.

co-existent *adj.* co-existing, concomitant, contemporary, synchronous.

coffer *n.* ark, case, casket, chest, repository, strongbox, treasure, treasury.

cognition *n.* apprehension, awareness, comprehension, discernment, insight, intelligence, perception, reasoning, understanding.

cohere *v.* adhere, agree, bind, cling, coalesce, combine, consolidate, correspond, fuse, glue, hang together, harmonise, hold, square, stick, unite.
antonym separate.

coherence *n.* agreement, comprehensibility, congruity, connection, consistency, correspondence, intelligibility, meaning, rationality, sense, union, unity.
antonym incoherence.

coherent *adj.* articulate, comprehensible, consistent, intelligible, logical, lucid, meaningful, orderly, organised, rational, reasoned, sensible, systematic.
antonyms meaningless, unintelligible.

cohort *n.* band, company, contingent, division, legion, regiment, squadron, troop.

coil *v.* convolute, curl, entwine, loop, snake, spiral, twine, twist, wind, wreathe, writhe.
n. convolution, curl, loop, spiral, twist.

coin *v.* conceive, create, devise, fabricate, forge, form, formulate, frame, introduce, invent, make up, mint, mould, originate, produce, think up.
n. bit, cash, change, copper, loose change, lucky-piece, money, piece, silver, small change.

coincide *v.* accord, agree, co-exist, concur, correspond, harmonise, match, square, tally.

coincidence *n.* accident, chance, concurrence, conjunction, correlation, correspondence, eventuality, fluke, fortuity, luck.

coincidental *adj.* accident, casual, chance, coincident, concurrent, fluky, fortuitous, lucky, simultaneous, synchronous, unintentional, unplanned.
antonyms deliberate, planned.

cold *adj.* **1** arctic, biting, bitter, bleak, chill, chilled, chilly, cool, freezing, frigid, frosty, frozen, glacial, icy, nippy, parky, raw, shivery, unheated, wintry. **2** aloof, distant, indifferent, lukewarm, phlegmatic, reserved, stand-offish, stony, undemonstrative, unfeeling, unfriendly, unmoved, unresponsive, unsympathetic.
antonyms **1** hot, warm. **2** friendly, responsive.
n. catarrh, chill, chilliness, coldness, frigidity, hypothermia, iciness, inclemency.
antonym warmth.

cold-blooded *adj.* barbaric, barbarous, brutal, callous, cruel, dispassionate, heartless, inhuman, merciless, pitiless, ruthless, savage, stony-hearted, unemotional, unfeeling, unmoved.
antonyms compassionate, merciful.

collaborate *v.* collude, conspire, co-operate, co-produce, fraternise, participate, team up.

collaboration *n.* alliance, association, concert, co-operation, partnership, teamwork.

collaborator *n.* assistant, associate, colleague, confederate, co-worker, fellow-traveller, partner, team-mate, traitor, turncoat.

collapse *v.* crumple, fail, faint, fall, fold, founder, peg out, sink, subside.
n. breakdown, cave-in, debacle, disintegration, downfall, exhaustion, failure, faint, flop, subsidence.

collate *v.* arrange, collect, compare, compose, gather, sort.

collateral *n.* assurance, deposit, funds, guarantee, pledge, security, surety.

colleague *n.* aide, aider, ally, assistant, associate, auxiliary, collaborator, companion, comrade, confederate, confrère, helper, partner, team-mate, workmate.

collect *v.* accumulate, acquire, aggregate, amass, assemble, cluster, congregate, convene, converge, gather (together), heap, hoard, muster, obtain, raise, rally, save, secure, stockpile, uplift.
antonyms disperse, scatter.

collected *adj.* assembled, calm, composed, confident, cool, efficient, gathered, imperturbable, placid, poised, self-possessed, serene, together, unperturbed, unruffled.
antonyms agitated, anxious, troubled, worried.

collection *n.* accumulation, anthology, assemblage, assembly, assortment, cluster, company, compilation, conglomerate, conglomeration, congregation, convocation, crowd, gathering, group, harvesting, heap, hoard, ingathering, job-lot, mass, pile, set, stockpile, store.

collective *adj.* aggregate, combined, common, composite, concerted, co-operative, corporate, cumulative, joint, shared, unified, united.
n. aggregate, assemblage, corporation, gathering, group.

collide *v.* bump, clash, conflict, confront, crash, smash.

collision *n.* accident, bump, clash, conflict, confrontation, crash, impact, opposition, pile-up, skirmish, smash.

colloquial *adj.* controversial, everyday, familiar, idiomatic, informal, non-technical, vernacular.
antonym formal.

collusion *n.* artifice, complicity, connivance, conspiracy, deceit, fraudulent, intrigue.

colonise *v.* people, pioneer, populate, settle.

colonist *n.* colonial, coloniser, emigrant, frontiersman, immigrant, pioneer, planter, settler.

colony *n.* dependency, dominion, outpost, possession, province, settlement, territory.

colossal *adj.* enormous, gigantic, huge, immense, mammoth, massive, monstrous, monumental, vast.
antonyms minute, tiny.

colour *n.* **1** appearance, coloration, complexion, dye, hue, paint, pigment, pigmentation, shade, timbre, tincture, tinge, tint, tone, wash, watercolour. **2** animation, brilliance, glow, liveliness, vividness.
v. **1** crayon, dye, paint, stain, tinge, tint. **2** blush, flush, redden. **3** affect, distort, exaggerate, falsify, pervert.

colourful *adj.* bright, brilliant, distinctive, exciting, graphic, intense, interesting, jazzy, kaleidoscopic, lively, multicoloured, parti-coloured, picturesque, rich, stimulating, variegated, vivid.
antonyms colourless, drab, plain.

colourless *adj.* anaemic, ashen, bleached, characterless, drab, dreary, dull, faded, insipid, lacklustre, neutral, pale, plain, sickly, tame, transparent, uninteresting, unmemorable, washed out.
antonyms bright, colourful, exciting.

colours *n.* banner, colour, emblem, ensign, flag, standard.

column *n.* file, line, list, obelisk, pillar, post, procession, queue, rank, row, shaft, string, support, upright.

columnist *n.* correspondent, critic, editor, journalist, reporter, reviewer, writer.

coma *n.* drowsiness, hypnosis, insensibility, lethargy, oblivion, somnolence, stupor, torpor, trance, unconsciousness.

comb *v.* hunt, rake, ransack, rummage, scour, screen, search, sift, sweep.

combat *n.* action, battle, bout, clash, conflict, contest, duel, encounter, engagement, fight, hostilities, judo, karate, kung fu, skirmish, struggle, war, warfare.
v. battle, contend, contest, defy, engage, fight, oppose, resist, strive, struggle, withstand.

combination *n.* alliance, amalgamation, association, blend, coalescence, coalition, combine, composite, composition, compound, confederacy, confederation, connection, consortium, conspiracy, federation, merger, mix, mixture, syndicate, unification, union.

combine *v.* amalgamate, associate, bind, blend, bond, compound, connect, cooperate, fuse, incorporate, integrate, join, link, marry, merge, mix, pool, sythesise, unify, unite.
antonyms detach, divide, separate.

come *v.* advance, appear, approach, arrive, attain, become, draw near, enter, happen, materialise, move, near, occur, originate, reach.
antonyms depart, go, leave.
come about arise, come to pass, happen, occur, result, transpire.
come across bump into, chance upon, discover, encounter, find, happen on, meet, notice, unearth.
come along arise, arrive, develop, happen, improve, mend, progress, rally, recover, recuperate.
come apart break, crumble, disintegrate, fall to bits, separate, split, tear.
come between alienate, disunite, divide, estrange, interfere, part, separate, split up.
come down decline, degenerate, descend, deteriorate, fall, reduce, worsen.
come in appear, arrive, enter, finish, show up.
come off happen, succeed, take place.
come on advance, appear, begin, develop, improve, proceed, progress, take place, thrive.
come out conclude, end, result, terminate.
come out with affirm, declare, disclose, divulge, own, say, state.
come round 1 awake, recover, wake. **2** accede, allow, concede, grant, relent, yield.
come through accomplish, achieve, endure, prevail, succeed, survive, triumph, withstand.

come-back *n.* rally, re-appearance, rebound, recovery, resurgence, return, revival.

comedian *n.* clown, comic, funny man, humorist, joker, laugh, wag, wit.

come-down *n.* anticlimax, blow, decline, deflation, degradation, demotion, descent, disappointment, humiliation, let-down, reverse.

comedy *n.* clowning, drollery, facetiousness, farce, fun, hilarity, humour, jesting, joking, sitcom, slapstick, witticisms.

come-uppance *n.* chastening, deserts, dues, merit, punishment, rebuke, recompense, requital, retribution.

comfort *v.* alleviate, assuage, cheer, console, ease, encourage, enliven, gladden, hearten, invigorate, reassure, refresh, relieve, soothe, strengthen.
n. aid, alleviation, cheer, compensation, consolation, ease, encouragement, enjoyment, help, luxury, relief, satisfaction, snugness, support, well-being.
antonyms discomfort, distress, torment.

comfortable *adj.* **1** adequate, agreeable, convenient, cosy, delightful, easy, enjoyable, pleasant,

relaxing, restful, snug. **2** at ease, contented, happy, relaxed. **3** affluent, prosperous, well-off, well-to-do.
antonyms **1** uncomfortable, unpleasant. **2** nervous, uneasy. **3** poor.

comic *adj.* amusing, comical, droll, facetious, farcical, funny, humorous, joking, light, rich, witty.
antonyms serious, tragic, unfunny.
n. buffoon, clown, comedian, funny, gagster, humorist, jester, joker, man, wag, wit.

comical *adj.* absurd, amusing, comic, diverting, droll, entertaining, farcical, funny, hilarious, humorous, laughable, ludicrous, priceless, ridiculous, side-splitting, silly, whimsical.
antonyms sad, serious, unamusing.

coming *adj.* approaching, aspiring, due, forthcoming, future, imminent, impending, near, next, nigh, promising, rising, up-and-coming.
n. accession, advent, approach, arrival.

command *v.* bid, charge, compel, control, demand, direct, dominate, enjoin, govern, head, instruct, lead, manage, order, reign over, require, rule, supervise, sway.
n. **1** bidding, charge, commandment, decree, direction, directive, edict, injunction, instruction, mandate, order, precept, requirement. **2** authority, control, domination, dominion, government, grasp, leadership, management, mastery, power, rule, sway.

commander *n.* admiral, boss, captain, chief, commander-in-chief, commanding officer, director, general, head, leader, marshal, officer, ruler.

commanding *adj.* advantageous, assertive, authoritative, autocratic, compelling, controlling, decisive, dominant, dominating, forceful, imposing, impressive, superior.

commemorate *v.* celebrate, honour, immortalise, keep, mark, memorialise, observe, remember, salute, solemnise.

commemoration *n.* ceremony, honouring, observance, recordation, remembrance, tribute.

commemorative *adj.* celebratory, dedicatory, in memoriam, memorial.

commence *v.* begin, embark on, inaugurate, initiate, open, originate, start.
antonyms cease, end, finish.

commend *v.* acclaim, applaud, approve, commit, compliment, confide, consign, deliver, entrust, extol, praise, recommend, yield.
antonym criticise.

comment *v.* annotate, criticise, elucidate, explain, interpose, interpret, mention, note, observe, remark, say.
n. annotation, commentary, criticism, elucidation, explanation, exposition, footnote, illustration, marginal note, note, observation, remark, statement.

commentary *n.* analysis, critique, description, explanation, narration, notes, review, treatise, voice-over.

commentator *n.* annotator, commenter, critic, expositor, interpreter, reporter.

commerce *n.* business, communication, dealing(s), exchange, intercourse, merchandising, relations, trade, traffic.

commercial *adj.* business, exploited, mercenary, monetary, popular, profitable, profit-making, saleable, sales, sellable, trade, trading, venal.

commission *n.* **1** appointment, assignment, authority, charge, duty, employment, errand, function, job, mandate, mission, task, trust, warrant. **2** board, committee, delegation, deputation, representative. **3** allowance, cut, fee, percentage, rake-off.
v. appoint, ask for, authorise, contract, delegate, depute, empower, engage, nominate, order, request, select, send.

commit *v.* align, bind, commend, compromise, confide, confine, consign, deliver, deposit, do, enact, engage, entrust, execute, give, imprison, involve, obligate, perform, perpetrate, pledge.
commit oneself bind oneself, decide, pledge oneself, promise, undertake.

commitment *n.* adherence, assurance, dedication, devotion, duty, engagement, guarantee, involvement, liability, loyalty, obligation, pledge, promise, responsibility, tie, undertaking, vow, word.
antonyms vacillation, wavering.

committed *adj.* active, card-carrying, fervent, red-hot.
antonyms apathetic, uncommitted.

committee *n.* advisory group, board, cabinet, commission, council, jury, panel, task force, think-tank, working party.

commodities *n.* goods, merchandise, output, produce, products, stock, things, wares.

common *adj.* **1** accepted, average, collective, communal, conventional, customary, daily, everyday, familiar, frequent, general, habitual, mutual, ordinary, plain, popular, prevalent, public, regular, routine, run-of-the-mill, simple, social, standard, undistinguished, unexceptional, universal, usual, widespread, workaday. **2** coarse, flat, hackneyed, ill-bred, inferior, low, plebeian, stale, stock, trite, vulgar.
antonyms **1** noteworthy, rare, uncommon, unusual. **2** refined, tasteful.
common sense gumption, judgement, levelheadedness, practicality, prudence, soundness, wit.

commonplace *adj.* common, customary, everyday, humdrum, obvious, ordinary, pedestrian, stale, threadbare, trite, uninteresting, widespread, worn out.
antonyms exceptional, exciting, rare.
n. banality, cliché, platitude, truism.

common-sense *adj.* astute, common-sensical, down-to-earth, hard-headed, judicious, levelheaded, matter-of-fact, practical, pragmatic, realistic, reasonable, sane, sensible, shrewd, sound.
antonyms foolish, unrealistic, unreasonable.

commotion *n.* ado, agitation, ballyhoo, burst-up, bustle, bust-up, disorder, disturbance, excitement, ferment, fracas, furore, fuss, hubbub, hullabaloo, hurly-burly, racket, riot, rumpus, to-do, toss, tumult, turmoil, uproar.

communal *adj.* collective, common, community, general, joint, public, shared.
antonyms personal, private.

commune *n.* collective, colony, community, co-operative, fellowship, kibbutz, settlement.
v. communicate, confer, converse, discourse, make contact with.

communicate *v.* acquaint, announce, bestow, connect, contact, convey, correspond, declare, diffuse, disclose, disseminate, divulge, impart, inform, intimate, notify, proclaim, publish, report, reveal, signify, spread, transmit, unfold.

communication *n.* announcement, bulletin, communiqué, connection, contact, conversation, correspondence, disclosure, dispatch, dissemination, information, intelligence, intimation, message, news, report, statement, transmission, word.

communicative *adj.* candid, chatty, conversational, expansive, extrovert, forthcoming, frank, free, friendly, informative, open, outgoing, sociable, talkative, unreserved, voluble.
antonyms quiet, reserved, reticent.

communion *n.* **1** accord, affinity, agreement, closeness, communing, empathy, fellow-feeling, fellowship, harmony, participation, rapport, sympathy, togetherness, unity. **2** Eucharist, Holy Communion, Lord's Supper, Mass, Sacrament.

communism *n.* collectivism, Leninism, Marxism, socialism, sovietism, Stalinism, totalitarianism, Trotskyism.

communist *n.* collectivist, Leninist, Marxist, socialist, soviet, Stalinist, totalitarian, Trotskyist.

community *n.* agreement, association, brotherhood, colony, company, district, fellowship, fraternity, identity, kibbutz, locality, people, populace, population, public, residents, society, state.

commute *v.* **1** adjust, alter, curtail, decrease, lighten, mitigate, modify, reduce, remit, shorten, soften. **2** alternate, journey, travel.

compact *adj.* brief, close, compressed, concise, condensed, dense, firm, impenetrable, solid, stocky, succinct, thick, well-knit.
antonyms diffuse, rambling, rangy.

companion *n.* accomplice, aide, ally, assistant, associate, attendant, attender, buddy, chaperon, cohort, colleague, comrade, confederate, confidant, confidante, consort, counterpart, escort, fellow, follower, friend, intimate, mate, partner, twin.

companionable *adj.* affable, amiable, approachable, congenial, conversable, convivial, extrovert, familiar, friendly, genial, gregarious, informal, neighbourly, outgoing, sociable, sympathetic.
antonyms hostile, unfriendly.

companionship *n.* camaraderie, companionhood, comradeship, conviviality, esprit de corps, fellowship, fraternity, friendship, rapport, support, sympathy, togetherness.

company *n.* **1** association, business, cartel, concern, corporation, establishment, firm, house, partnership, syndicate. **2** assembly, band, circle, collection, community, consortium, crew, crowd, ensemble, fraternity, gathering, group, league, party, set, throng, troop, troupe. **3** attendance, callers, companionhood, companionship, fellowship, guests, party, presence, society, support, visitors.

comparable *adj.* akin, alike, analogous, cognate, commensurate, correspondent, corresponding, equal, equivalent, kindred, parallel, proportionate, related, similar, tantamount.
antonyms dissimilar, unequal, unlike.

compare *v.* balance, contrast, correlate, equal, equate, juxtapose, liken, match, parallel, resemble, vie, weigh.

comparison *n.* analogy, comparability, contrast, correlation, distinction, juxtaposition, likeness, parallel, parallelism, resemblance, similarity.

compartment *n.* alcove, area, bay, berth, booth, box, carrel, carriage, category, cell, chamber, cubby-hole, cubicle, department, division, locker, niche, pigeon-hole, section, stall, subdivision.

compassion *n.* commiseration, concern, condolence, fellow-feeling, humanity, kindness, mercy, pity, sorrow, sympathy, tenderness, understanding, yearning.
antonyms cruelty, indifference.

compassionate *adj.* benevolent, caring, clement, humane, humanitarian, kind-hearted, kindly, lenient, merciful, pitying, supportive, sympathetic, tender, tender-hearted, understanding, warm-hearted.
antonyms cruel, indifferent, ruthless.

compatible *adj.* adaptable, agreeable, conformable, congenial, congruous, consistent, consonant, harmonious, like-minded, reconcilable, suitable, sympathetic.
antonyms antagonistic, contradictory, incompatible.

compel *v.* browbeat, bulldoze, bully, coerce, constrain, drive, enforce, exact, force, gar, hustle, impel, make, necessitate, oblige, press-gang, pressurise, strongarm, urge.

compelling *adj.* binding, coercive, cogent, compulsive, conclusive, convincing, enchanting, enthralling, forceful, gripping, imperative, incontrovertible, irrefutable, irresistible, mesmeric, overriding, persuasive, powerful, pressing, spellbinding, telling, unanswerable, unavoidable, urgent, weighty.
antonyms boring, unconvincing, weak.

compensate *v.* balance, cancel, counteract, counterbalance, indemnify, offset, recompense, recover, redeem, redress, refund, reimburse, remunerate, repay, requite, restore, reward, satisfy.

compensation *n.* amends, comfort, consolation, damages, indemnification, indemnity, payment, recompense, redress, refund, reimbursement, remuneration, reparation, repayment, requital, restitution, restoration, return, reward, satisfaction.

compete *v.* battle, challenge, contend, contest, duel, emulate, fight, oppose, rival, strive, struggle, tussle, vie.

competent *adj.* able, adapted, adequate, appropriate, belonging, capable, clever, efficient, endowed, equal, fit, legitimate, masterly, proficient, qualified, satisfactory, strong, sufficient, suitable, trained, well-qualified.
antonyms incapable, incompetent, unable.

competition *n.* challenge, challengers, championship, combativeness, competitiveness, competitors, contention, contest, cup, event, field, match, opposition, quiz, race, rivalry, rivals, series, strife, struggle, tournament.

competitive *adj.* aggressive, ambitious, antagonistic, combative, contentious, cut-throat, keen, pushy.
antonyms sluggish, unambitious.

competitor *n.* adversary, antagonist, challenger, competition, contender, contestant, emulator, entrant, opponent, opposition, rival.

compilation *n.* accumulation, anthology, arrangement, assemblage, assortment, collection, composition, selection, thesaurus, treasury, work.

compile *v.* accumulate, amass, arrange, assemble, collect, compose, cull, garner, gather, marshal, organise.

complacency *n.* content, contentment, gloating, gratification, pleasure, pride, satisfaction, self-content, self-satisfaction, serenity, smugness, triumph.
antonyms diffidence, discontent.

complacent *adj.* contented, gloating, gratified, pleased, proud, satisfied, self-assured, self-contented, self-righteous, self-satisfied, smug, triumphant, unconcerned.
antonyms concerned, diffident, discontented.

complain *v.* beef, bemoan, bewail, carp, deplore, fuss, gripe, groan, grouse, growl, grumble, moan, whine.

complaint *n.* **1** accusation, annoyance, beef, censure, charge, criticism, dissatisfaction, fault-finding, grievance, gripe, grouse, grumble, moan, nit-picking. **2** affliction, ailment, disease, disorder, illness, indisposition, malady, malaise, sickness, trouble, upset.

complementary *adj.* companion, correlative, corresponding, fellow, interdependent, interrelated, interwoven, matched, reciprocal.
antonyms contradictory, incompatible, incongruous.

complete *adj.* **1** absolute, all, entire, full, intact, integral, out-and-out, perfect, thorough, total, utter. **2** accomplished, achieved, concluded, done, ended, finished. **3** unabbreviated, unabridged, undivided, unedited, unexpurgated, whole.
antonyms **1** partial. **2** incomplete. **3** abridged.
v. accomplish, achieve, clinch, close, conclude, consummate, crown, discharge, end, execute, finalise, finish, fulfil, perfect, perform, realise, settle, terminate, wind up.

completion *n.* accomplishment, achievement, attainment, close, conclusion, consummation, culmination, discharge, end, finalisation, finish, fruition, fulfilment, perfection, realisation, settlement, termination.

complex *adj.* circuitous, complicated, composite, compound, convoluted, elaborate, intricate, involved, mixed, multiple, ramified, tangled, tortuous.
antonyms easy, simple.
n. **1** aggregate, development, establishment, institute, network, organisation, scheme, structure, synthesis, system. **2** fixation, hang-up, obsession, phobia, preoccupation.

complexion *n.* appearance, aspect, character, colour, colouring, composition, countenance, disposition, guise, hue, kind, light, look, make-up, nature, pigmentation, skin, stamp, temperament, type.

complexity *n.* complication, convolution, deviousness, diversity, elaboration, intricacy, involvement, multiplicity, ramification, repercussion, tortuousness, variation, variety.
antonym simplicity.

compliance *n.* acquiescence, agreement, assent, concession, concurrence, conformability, conformity, consent, co-operation, deference, obedience, observance, passivity, submissiveness, yielding.
antonyms defiance, disobedience.

complicate *v.* compound, confuse, elaborate, entangle, foul up, involve, mix up, muddle, tangle.
antonym simplify.

complicated *adj.* ambivalent, complex, convoluted, difficult, elaborate, intricate, involved, perplexing, problematic, puzzling, tangled, tortuous, troublesome.
antonyms easy, simple.

complication *n.* aggravation, complexity, confusion, difficulty, drawback, elaboration, embarrassment, factor, intricacy, mixture, obstacle, problem, ramification, repercussion, snag, web.

compliment *n.* accolade, admiration, bouquet, commendation, congratulations, courtesy, eulogy, favour, flattery, honour, praise, tribute.
antonyms criticism, insult.
v. admire, applaud, commend, congratulate, extol, flatter, laud, praise, salute.
antonyms condemn, insult.

complimentary *adj.* admiring, appreciative, approving, commendatory, congratulatory, courtesy, eulogistic, favourable, flattering, free, gratis, honorary.
antonyms critical, insulting, unflattering.

compliments *n.* best wishes, congratulations, greetings, regards, respects.

comply *v.* accede, accommodate, accord, agree, assent, conform, consent, defer, discharge, fall in, follow, fulfil, obey, oblige, observe, perform, respect, satisfy, submit, yield.
antonyms disobey, resist.

component *n.* bit, constituent, element, factor,

ingredient, item, part, piece, spare part, unit.

compose *v.* **1** comprise, constitute, form. **2** adjust, arrange, build, construct, create, devise, fashion, frame, invent, make, produce, write. **3** calm, control, pacify, quell, quiet, regulate, settle, soothe, still, tranquillise.

composed *adj.* calm, collected, complacent, confident, cool, imperturbable, level-headed, placid, relaxed, self-possessed, serene, tranquil, unflappable, unruffled, unworried.
antonyms agitated, troubled, worried.

composer *n.* arranger, author, creator, maker, originator, poet, songwriter, writer.

composite *adj.* blended, combined, complex, compound, conglomerate, fused, mixed, patchwork, synthesised.
antonyms homogeneous, uniform.
n. agglutination, alloy, amalgam, blend, combination, compound, conglomerate, fusion, mixture, patchwork, synthesis.

composition *n.* arrangement, balance, combination, compilation, compromise, concord, configuration, consonance, constitution, creation, design, exercise, form, formation, formulation, harmony, invention, lay-out, make-up, making, mixture, organisation, piece, placing, production, proportion, structure, study, symmetry, work, writing.

composure *n.* aplomb, assurance, calm, confidence, coolness, dignity, dispassion, ease, equanimity, impassivity, imperturbability, placidity, poise, self-assurance, self-possession, serenity, tranquillity.
antonyms agitation, discomposure, nervousness.

compound *v.* **1** alloy, amalgamate, augment, blend, coalesce, combine, compose, concoct, fuse, intermingle, mingle, mix, synthesise, unite. **2** aggravate, complicate, exacerbate, heighten, increase, intensify, magnify, worsen.
n. alloy, amalgam, amalgamation, blend, combination, composite, composition, conglomerate, conglomeration, fusion, medley, mixture, synthesis.
adj. complex, complicated, composite, intricate, mixed, multiple.

comprehend *v.* appreciate, apprehend, assimilate, comprise, conceive, cover, discern, embrace, encompass, fathom, grasp, include, know, penetrate, perceive, realise, see, tumble to, understand.
antonym misunderstand.

comprehensible *adj.* clear, coherent, explicit, intelligible, knowable, lucid, plain, rational, simple, straightforward, understandable.
antonyms incomprehensible, obscure, puzzling.

comprehension *n.* appreciation, apprehension, conception, discernment, grasp, intelligence, judgement, knowledge, perception, realisation, sense, understanding.
antonyms incomprehension, unawareness.

comprehensive *adj.* across-the-board, all-embracing, all-inclusive, blanket, broad, compendious, complete, encyclopedic, exhaustive, extensive, full, general, inclusive, sweeping, thorough, wide.
antonyms incomplete, partial, selective.

comprise *v.* consist of, contain, cover, embody, embrace, encompass, include, incorporate, involve.

compromise *v.* **1** adapt, adjust, agree, arbitrate, bargain, concede, make concessions, negotiate, retire, retreat, settle. **2** discredit, dishonour, embarrass, expose, hazard, imperil, implicate, involve, jeopardise, prejudice, undermine, weaken.
antonyms **1** differ, quarrel.
n. accommodation, accord, adjustment, agreement, bargain, concession, co-operation, settlement, trade-off.
antonyms disagreement, intransigence.

compulsive *adj.* compelling, driving, hardened, hopeless, incorrigible, incurable, irredeemable, irresistible, obsessive, overmastering, overpowering, overwhelming, uncontrollable, unputdownable, urgent.

compulsory *adj.* binding, forced, imperative, mandatory, obligatory, required, requisite, stipulated, stipulatory.
antonyms discretionary, optional, voluntary.

computer *n.* adding machine, analogue computer, calculator, data processor, digital computer, mainframe, processor, word processor.

comrade *n.* ally, associate, brother, colleague, companion, confederate, co-worker, fellow, friend, mate, pal, partner.

con *v.* bamboozle, beguile, bluff, cheat, deceive, defraud, double-cross, dupe, fiddle, hoax, hoodwink, inveigle, mislead, rip off, rook, swindle, trick.
n. bluff, confidence trick, deception, fraud, swindle, trick.

concave *adj.* cupped, depressed, excavated, hollow, hollowed, indented, scooped, sunken.
antonym convex.

conceal *v.* bury, camouflage, cloak, cover, disguise, hide, keep dark, mask, obscure, screen, shelter, sink, smother, submerge, suppress, veil.
antonyms disclose, reveal, uncover.

concede *v.* accept, acknowledge, admit, allow, confess, forfeit, give up, grant, own, recognise, relinquish, sacrifice, surrender, yield.
antonyms deny, dispute.

conceit *n.* arrogance, assumption, cockiness, complacency, conceitedness, egotism, pride, self-conceit, self-importance, self-satisfaction, swagger, vanity.
antonyms diffidence, modesty.

conceited *adj.* arrogant, assuming, bigheaded, cocky, complacent, egotistical, self-important, self-satisfied, stuck-up, swollen-headed, toffee-nose(d), vain.
antonyms diffident, humble, modest, self-effacing.

conceivable *adj.* believable, credible, imaginable, likely, possible, probable, tenable, thinkable.
antonyms inconceivable, unimaginable.

conceive *v.* **1** appreciate, apprehend, believe, comprehend, envisage, grasp, imagine, realise, see, suppose, think, understand, visualise. **2** create, design, develop, devise, form, formulate, germinate, invent, originate, produce.

concentrate *v.* absorb, accumulate, attend, attract, centre, cluster, collect, condense, congregate, converge, crowd, draw, engross, focus, gather, intensify.
antonyms disperse, distract, separate.

concentrated *adj.* **1** compact, condensed, deep, dense, evaporated, reduced, rich, thickened, undiluted. **2** all-out, concerted, hard, intense, intensive.
antonyms **1** diluted. **2** half-hearted.

concentration *n.* absorption, accumulation, agglomeration, aggregation, application, centralisation, cluster, collection, combination, compression, conglomeration, consolidation, convergence, crowd, denseness, focusing, grouping, heed, intensity, mass, single-mindedness.
antonyms dilution, dispersal, distraction.

concept *n.* abstraction, conception, conceptualisation, construct, hyphothesis, idea, image, impression, invention, notion, pattern, picture, plan, theory, type, view, visualisation.

conception *n.* **1** concept, design, idea, knowledge, notion, plan, thought. **2** appreciation, apprehension, clue, image, impression, inkling, perception, picture, understanding, visualisation. **3** beginning, birth, formation, inauguration, initiation, invention, launching, origin, outset. **4** fertilisation, germination, impregnation, insemination.

concern *v.* **1** affect, bother, disquiet, distress, disturb, trouble, upset, worry. **2** interest, involve, refer to, regard, relate to, touch.
n. **1** anxiety, care, disquiet, distress, sorrow, unease, worry. **2** attention, consideration, heed, reference, relation, thought. **3** affair, bearing, business, charge, duty, field, importance, interest, involvement, job, matter, occupation, relevance, responsibility, task. **4** business, company, corporation, enterprise, establishment, firm, organisation.
antonyms **1** joy. **2** indifference.

concerned *adj.* active, anxious, apprehensive, attentive, bothered, caring, connected, distressed, disturbed, implicated, interested, involved, troubled, uneasy, unhappy, upset, worried.
antonyms apathetic, indifferent, unconcerned.

concerning *prep.* about, as regards, in the matter of, regarding, relating to, relevant to, respecting, with reference to, with regard to.

concerted *adj.* collaborative, collective, combined, co-ordinated, joint, organised, planned, prearranged, shared, united.
antonyms disorganised, separate, unco-ordinated.

concert-hall *n.* assembly room, auditorium, chamber, music hall, odeon, town hall.

concession *n.* acknowledgement, adjustment, admission, allowance, assent, boon, compromise, exception, favour, grant, indulgence, permit, privilege, relaxation, sacrifice, surrender, yielding.

conciliate *v.* appease, disarm, mollify, pacify, placate, propitiate, satisfy, soften, soothe.
antonym antagonise.

conciliation *n.* appeasement, indulgence, mollification, pacification, peace-making, propitiation, reconciliation, satisfaction.
antonyms alienation, antagonisation.

conciliatory *adj.* disarming, irenic, mollifying, pacific, peaceable, propitiatory, reconciliatory.
antonym antagonistic.

concise *adj.* abbreviated, abridged, aphoristic, brief, compact, compendious, compressed, condensed, pithy, short, succinct, summary, synoptic, terse.
antonyms diffuse, expansive, wordy.

conclude *v.* **1** assume, deduce, infer, judge, reckon, suppose, surmise. **2** accomplish, cease, close, complete, consummate, culminate, end, finish, terminate. **3** clinch, decide, determine, establish, resolve, settle.
antonyms **2** commence, start.

conclusion *n.* **1** assumption, conviction, decision, deduction, inference, judgement, opinion, resolution, verdict. **2** answer, close, completion, consequence, consummation, culmination, end, finale, finish, outcome, result, settlement, solution, termination, upshot.

conclusive *adj.* clear, clinching, convincing, decisive, definite, definitive, final, incontrovertible, indisputable, irrefutable, ultimate, unanswerable, unarguable, undeniable.
antonyms inconclusive, indecisive, questionable.

concoct *v.* brew, contrive, design, develop, devise, digest, fabricate, form, formulate, hatch, invent, mature, plan, plot, prepare, project, refine.

concoction *n.* blend, brew, combination, compound, contrivance, creation, mixture, potion, preparation.

concrete *adj.* **1** compact, compressed, conglomerated, consolidated, material, perceptible, physical, solid, solidified, substantial, tangible, touchable, visible. **2** actual, definite, explicit, factual, firm, real, specific.
antonyms **1** abstract. **2** vague.

concurrent *adj.* co-existing, coincident, coinciding, concerted, concomitant, confluent, consilient, convergent, converging, simultaneous, synchronous, uniting.

condemn *v.* ban, blame, castigate, censure, convict, damn, denounce, disapprove, disparage, doom, reprehend, reproach, reprove, revile, slam, slate, upbraid.
antonyms approve, praise.

condemnation *n.* ban, blame, castigation, censure, conviction, damnation, denunciation, disapproval, disparagement, judgement, reproach, reproof, sentence, thumbs-down.
antonyms approval, praise.

condensation *n.* abridgement, compression, concentration, consolidation, contraction, crystallisation, curtailment, digest, distillation, liquefaction, precipitation, précis, reduction, synopsis.

condense *v.* abbreviate, abridge, coagulate, compact, compress, concentrate, contract, crystallise, curtail, distil, encapsulate, evaporate, precipitate, précis, reduce, shorten, solidify, summarise, thicken.
antonyms dilute, expand.

condensed *adj.* abbreviated, abridged, abstracted, clotted, coagulated, compact, compressed, concentrated, concise, contracted, crystallised, curtailed, distilled, evaporated, reduced, shortened, summarised, thickened.
antonyms diluted, expanded.

condescend *v.* bend, deign, patronise, see fit, stoop, submit.

condescending *adj.* disdainful, gracious, haughty, imperious, lofty, lordly, patronising, snooty, stooping, supercilious, superior, unbending.
antonyms approachable, humble.

condescension *n.* affability, airs, civility, deference, disdain, haughtiness, loftiness, lordliness, superciliousness, superiority.
antonym humility.

condition *n.* **1** case, circumstances, plight, position, predicament, situation, state. **2** limitation, obligation, proviso, qualification, requirement, restriction, rule, stipulation, terms. **3** complaint, defect, disease, disorder, infirmity, problem, weakness. **4** fitness, health, shape, state.
v. accustom, adapt, adjust, educate, equip, groom, indoctrinate, influence, mould, prepare, prime, ready, restrict, season, temper, train, treat, tune.

conditional *adj.* contingent, dependent, limited, provisional, qualified, relative, restricted, tied.
antonyms absolute, unconditional.

conditions *n.* atmosphere, background, circumstances, context, environment, habitat, medium, milieu, setting, situation, state, surroundings.

condolence *n.* commiseration, compassion, condolences, consolation, pity, support, sympathy.

condom *n.* French letter, johnny, protective, rubber, sheath.

condone *v.* allow, brook, disregard, excuse, forgive, ignore, indulge, overlook, pardon, tolerate.
antonyms censure, condemn, disallow.

conducive *adj.* advantageous, beneficial, contributory, encouraging, favourable, helpful, leading, productive, tending.
antonyms adverse, detrimental, unfavourable.

conduct *n.* **1** actions, attitude, behaviour, manners, ways. **2** administration, control, direction, guidance, leadership, management, operation, organisation, running, supervision.
v. accompany, acquit, act, administer, attend, bear, behave, carry, chair, control, convey, direct, escort, govern, guide, handle, lead, manage, orchestrate, organise, pilot, regulate, run, steer, supervise, usher.

conduit *n.* canal, channel, chute, culvert, ditch, drain, duct, flume, gutter, main, passage, pipe, tube, water-course, waterway.

confer *v.* **1** consult, converse, deliberate, discuss, talk. **2** accord, award, bestow, give, grant, impart, lend, present.

conference *n.* congress, consultation, convention, convocation, debate, discussion, forum, meeting, seminar, symposium, teach-in.

confess *v.* acknowledge, admit, affirm, allow, assert, attest, betray, concede, confide, confirm, declare, disclose, divulge, expose, grant, manifest, own (up), profess, prove, recognise, reveal, show.
antonyms conceal, deny.

confession *n.* acknowledgement, admission, affirmation, assertion, declaration, disclosure, divulgence, exposé, exposure, profession, revelation, unburdening.
antonyms concealment, denial.

confide *v.* admit, breathe, confess, disclose, divulge, impart, reveal, unburden, whisper.
antonyms hide, suppress.

confidence *n.* **1** assurance, boldness, calmness, composure, courage, credence, dependence, faith, firmness, reliance, self-assurance, self-confidence, self-possession, self-reliance, trust. **2** communication, disclosure, secret.
antonyms **1** apprehension, diffidence, distrust.

confident *adj.* assured, bold, certain, composed, convinced, cool, dauntless, fearless, positive, satisfied, secure, self-assured, self-confident, self-possessed, self-reliant, sure, unabashed, unselfconscious.
antonyms diffident, sceptical.

confidential *adj.* **1** classified, closed, hush-hush, private, privy, secret. **2** faithful, familiar, intimate, trusted, trustworthy.
antonyms **1** common, public.

confidentially *adv.* behind closed doors, between you me and the bed-post, in confidence, in privacy, in private, in secret, on the quiet, personally, privately, within these four walls.
antonym openly.

confine *v.* bind, bound, cage, circumscribe, constrain, cramp, crib, enclose, immure, imprison, incarcerate, inhibit, intern, keep, keep prisoner, limit, repress, restrain, restrict, shackle, shut up, trammel.
antonym free.

confined *adj.* enclosed, housebound, limited, pokey, restricted.
antonyms free, open, unrestricted.

confinement *n.* **1** constraint, custody, detention, house-arrest, imprisonment, incarceration, internment. **2** birth, childbirth, labour.
antonyms **1** freedom, liberty.

confines *n.* border, boundaries, bounds, circumference, edge, frontier, limits, perimeter, periphery, precincts.

confirm *v.* approve, assure, authenticate, back, clinch, corroborate, endorse, establish, evidence, fix, fortify, prove, ratify, reinforce, sanction, settle, strengthen, substantiate, support, validate, verify, witness to.

antonyms deny, refute.

confirmation *n.* acceptance, agreement, approval, assent, attestation, authentication, backing, corroboration, endorsement, evidence, proof, ratification, sanction, substantiation, support, testimony, validation, verification, witness.
antonyms cancellation, denial.

confirmed *adj.* chronic, committed, corroborated, dyed-in-the-wool, entrenched, established, habitual, hardened, incorrigible, incurable, inveterate, long-established, long-standing, proved, proven, rooted, seasoned, substantiated.
antonyms uncommitted, unconfirmed.

confiscate *v.* appropriate, commandeer, impound, remove, seize, sequester.
antonyms restore, return.

conflict *n.* agony, antagonism, battle, brawl, clash, collision, combat, confrontation, contention, contest, difference, disagreement, discord, dispute, dissension, encounter, engagement, feud, fight, fracas, friction, hostility, opposition, quarrel, set-to, skirmish, strife, turmoil, unrest, variance, war, warfare.
antonyms agreement, concord, harmony.
v. battle, clash, collide, combat, contend, contest, contradict, differ, disagree, fight, interfere, oppose, strive, struggle, war, wrangle.
antonyms agree, harmonise.

conform *v.* accommodate, accord, adapt, adjust, agree, assimilate, comply, correspond, follow, harmonise, match, obey, square, suit, tally, yield.
antonyms conflict, differ, rebel.

conformist *n.* bourgeois, conventionalist, stick-in-the-mud, traditionalist, yes-man.
antonyms bohemian, eccentric, nonconformist.

conformity *n.* affinity, agreement, allegiance, compliance, congruity, consonance, conventionality, correspondence, harmony, likeness, observance, orthodoxy, resemblance, similarity, traditionalism.
antonyms difference, nonconformity, rebellion.

confound *v.* abash, amaze, astonish, astound, baffle, bamboozle, bewilder, confuse, contradict, demolish, destroy, dismay, dumbfound, flabbergast, mystify, nonplus, overthrow, overwhelm, perplex, ruin, startle, stupefy, surprise, thwart, upset.

confront *v.* accost, address, beard, brave, challenge, defy, encounter, face, front, oppose.
antonym evade.

confrontation *n.* battle, collision, conflict, contest, crisis, disagreement, encounter, engagement, fight, quarrel, set-to, showdown.

confuse *v.* baffle, bewilder, confound, darken, disarrange, discompose, disconcert, disorientate, embarrass, fluster, involve, jumble, maze, mingle, mistake, mix up, mortify, muddle, mystify, obscure, perplex, puzzle, tangle, tie in knots, upset.
antonyms clarify, enlighten, reassure.

confused *adj.* **1** chaotic, disarranged, disordered, disorderly, disorganised, higgledy-piggledy, jumbled, muddled, untidy. **2** baffled, bewildered, disorientated, flummoxed, nonplussed, perplexed, puzzled.
antonyms **1** clear, definite.

confusion *n.* **1** chaos, clutter, commotion, disarray, disorder, disorganisation, jumble, mess, mix-up, muddle, turmoil, untidiness, upheaval. **2** bewilderment, misunderstanding, mystification, perplexity, puzzlement.
antonyms **1** order. **2** clarity.

congeal *v.* clot, coagulate, coalesce, condense, curdle, freeze, fuse, harden, jell, set, solidify, stiffen, thicken.
antonyms dissolve, melt, separate.

congenital *adj.* complete, connate, constitutional, hereditary, inborn, inbred, inherent, inherited, innate, inveterate, natural, thorough, utter.

congested *adj.* blocked, clogged, crammed, full, jammed, overcharged, overcrowded, overflowing, packed, saturated, stuffed, swollen, teeming.
antonyms clear, unblocked.

congestion *n.* bottle-neck, clogging, fullness, gridlock, jam, mass, overcrowding, snarl-up, surfeit, traffic-jam.

conglomeration *n.* accumulation, agglutination, aggregation, assemblage, combination, composite, hotchpotch, mass, medley.

congratulate *v.* compliment, wish well.
antonym commiserate.

congratulations *n.* compliments, good wishes, greetings.
antonyms commiserations, condolences.

congregate *v.* accumulate, assemble, clump, cluster, collect, concentrate, conglomerate, converge, convoke, crowd, flock, gather, mass, meet, muster, rally, rendezvous, throng.
antonyms dismiss, disperse.

congregation *n.* assemblage, assembly, concourse, crowd, fellowship, flock, host, laity, multitude, parish, parishioners, throng.

congress *n.* assembly, conference, convention, convocation, council, forum, legislature, meeting, parliament, synod.

conical *adj.* cone-shaped, funnel-shaped, pointed, pyramidal, tapered, tapering.

conjecture *v.* assume, estimate, guess, hypothesise, imagine, infer, reckon, speculate, suppose, surmise, suspect, theorise.
n. assumption, conclusion, estimate, extrapolation, guess, guesswork, hypothesis, inference, notion, opinion, presumption, projection, speculation, supposition, surmise, theory.

conjunction *n.* amalgamation, association, coincidence, combination, concurrence, juxtaposition, unification, union.

conjure *v.* **1** do tricks, juggle. **2** bewitch, charm, compel, fascinate, invoke, raise, rouse, summon.
conjure up awaken, contrive, create, evoke, excite, produce, recall, recollect.

connect *v.* affix, ally, associate, cohere, combine,

couple, fasten, join, link, relate, unite.
antonyms cut off, detach, disconnect.

connected *adj.* affiliated, akin, allied, associate, associated, combined, coupled, joined, linked, related, united.
antonyms disconnected, unconnected.

connection *n.* acquaintance, affinity, alliance, ally, association, attachment, bond, coherence, commerce, communication, contact, context, correlation, correspondence, coupling, fastening, interrelation, intimacy, junction, link, relation, relationship, relevance, sponsor, tie, union.
antonym disconnection.

connive *v.* collude, conspire, intrigue, plot, scheme.
connive at abet, aid, blink at, condone, disregard, let go, overlook, turn a blind eye to.

connoisseur *n.* authority, buff, devotee, expert, judge, specialist, virtuoso.

connotation *n.* association, colouring, hint, implication, nuance, overtone, significance, suggestion, undertone.

conquer *v.* acquire, annex, beat, best, crush, defeat, get the better of, humble, master, obtain, occupy, overcome, overpower, overrun, overthrow, prevail, quell, rout, seize, subdue, subjugate, succeed, surmount, triumph, vanquish, win, worst.
antonyms give in, surrender, yield.

conqueror *n.* champ, champion, defeater, hero, lord, master, number one, subjugator, vanquisher, victor, winner.

conquest *n.* acquisition, appropriation, captivation, coup, defeat, invasion, mastery, occupation, overthrow, rout, seduction, subjection, subjugation, takeover, triumph, victory.
antonym defeat.

conscience *n.* ethics, morals, principles, scruples, standards.

conscience-stricken *adj.* ashamed, contrite, disturbed, guilt-ridden, guilty, penitent, regretful, remorseful, repentant, sorry, troubled.
antonyms unashamed, unrepentant.

conscientious *adj.* careful, diligent, faithful, hard-working, high-principled, honest, meticulous, painstaking, particular, punctilious, responsible, scrupulous, strict, thorough, upright.
antonyms careless, irresponsible, unreliable.

conscious *adj.* alert, alive, awake, aware, calculated, deliberate, heedful, intentional, knowing, mindful, premeditated, rational, reasoning, reflective, regardful, responsible, responsive, self-conscious, sensible, studied.
antonyms unaware, unconscious.

consciousness *n.* apprehension, awareness, intuition, knowledge, realisation, recognition, sensibility, sentience.
antonym unconciousness.

consecrate *v.* dedicate, devote, exalt, hallow, ordain, revere, sanctify, venerate.

consecutive *adj.* chronological, continuous, following, running, sequential, succeeding, successive, unbroken, uninterrupted.
antonym discontinuous.

consent *v.* accede, acquiesce, admit, agree, allow, approve, assent, comply, concede, concur, grant, permit, yield.
antonyms decline, oppose, refuse.
n. accordance, acquiescence, agreement, approval, assent, compliance, concession, concurrence, go-ahead, green light, permission, sanction.
antonyms disagreement, opposition, refusal.

consequence *n.* **1** effect, end, outcome, repercussion, result, side effect, upshot. **2** concern, distinction, eminence, importance, note, significance, value, weight.
antonyms **1** cause. **2** insignificance, unimportance.

consequent *adj.* ensuing, following, resultant, resulting, sequential, subsequent, successive.

conservation *n.* custody, ecology, husbandry, keeping, maintenance, preservation, protection, safeguarding, safe-keeping, saving, upkeep.
antonyms destruction, neglect, waste.

conservatism *n.* conventionalism, orthodoxy, traditionalism.
antonym radicalism.

conservative *adj.* cautious, conventional, diehard, establishmentarian, guarded, hidebound, middle-of-the-road, moderate, reactionary, right-wing, sober, Tory, traditional, unprogressive.
antonyms innovative, left-wing, radical.
n. diehard, moderate, reactionary, right-winger, stick-in-the-mud, Tory, traditionalist.
antonyms left-winger, radical.

conservatory *n.* academy, glasshouse, greenhouse, hothouse, institute.

conserve *v.* guard, hoard, husband, keep, maintain, nurse, preserve, protect, save.
antonyms squander, use, waste.

consider *v.* believe, consult, contemplate, count, deem, deliberate, discuss, examine, judge, meditate, mull over, muse, perpend, ponder, rate, reflect, regard, remember, respect, revolve, study, think, weigh.
antonyms ignore, neglect.

considerable *adj.* abundant, ample, appreciable, big, comfortable, distinguished, great, important, influential, large, lavish, marked, much, noteworthy, noticeable, plentiful, reasonable, significant, siz(e)able, substantial, tidy, tolerable.
antonyms insignificant, slight, small, unremarkable.

considerate *adj.* attentive, charitable, concerned, discreet, forbearing, gracious, kind, mindful, obliging, patient, tactful, thoughtful, unselfish.
antonyms selfish, thoughtless.

consideration *n.* **1** analysis, attention, contemplation, deliberation, examination, meditation, notice, reflection, regard, review, scrutiny, thought. **2** factor, issue, point, respect. **3** kindness, thoughtfulness. **4** fee, payment,

recompense, remuneration, reward.
antonyms **1** disregard. **3** disdain, thoughtlessness.

consign *v.* banish, commit, convey, deliver, devote, entrust, hand over, relegate, seal, ship, sign, transfer.

consignment *n.* assignment, batch, cargo, committal, delivery, dispatch, distribution, goods, load, relegation, sending, shipment, transmittal.

consist of amount to, be composed of, comprise, contain, embody, embrace, include, incorporate, involve.

consistency *n.* accordance, agreement, coherence, compactness, compatibility, congruity, constancy, correspondence, density, evenness, firmness, harmony, identity, regularity, sameness, steadfastness, steadiness, thickness, uniformity, viscosity.
antonym inconsistency.

consistent *adj.* accordant, agreeing, coherent, compatible, congruous, consonant, constant, dependable, harmonious, logical, persistent, regular, steady, unchanging, undeviating, unfailing, uniform.
antonyms erratic, inconsistent, irregular.

console *v.* calm, cheer, comfort, encourage, hearten, soothe.
antonyms agitate, upset.

consolidate *v.* affiliate, amalgamate, cement, combine, compact, condense, conjoin, fuse, harden, join, reinforce, secure, solidify, stabilise, strengthen, thicken, unify, unite.

conspicuous *adj.* apparent, blatant, clear, discernible, evident, flagrant, flashy, garish, glaring, manifest, noticeable, obvious, patent, showy, visible.
antonyms concealed, hidden, inconspicuous.

conspiracy *n.* collusion, fix, frame-up, intrigue, league, machination, plot, scheme, treason.

conspirator *n.* conspirer, intriguer, plotter, practisant, schemer, traitor.

conspire *v.* **1** collude, devise, hatch, intrigue, manoeuvre, plot, scheme. **2** combine, contribute, co-operate, tend.

constancy *n.* **1** firmness, permanence, perseverance, regularity, resolution, stability, steadiness, tenacity, uniformity. **2** devotion, faithfulness, fidelity, loyalty.
antonyms **1** change, irregularity. **2** fickleness.

constant *adj.* **1** ceaseless, changeless, continual, continuous, endless, eternal, even, everlasting, firm, fixed, habitual, immutable, incessant, interminable, invariable, never-ending, non-stop, permanent, perpetual, persevering, persistent, regular, relentless, resolute, stable, unalterable, unbroken, unchangeable, unfailing, unflagging, uniform, unremitting, unvarying, unwavering. **2** dependable, devoted, dogged, faithful, loyal, staunch, steadfast, true, trustworthy.
antonyms **1** fitful, irregular, occasional, variable. **2** fickle, undependable.

consternation *n.* alarm, amazement, anxiety, awe, bewilderment, confusion, dismay, distress, dread, fear, fright, horror, panic, shock, terror, trepidation.
antonym composure.

constituent *adj.* basic, component, essential, inherent, integral, intrinsic.
n. bit, component, element, essential, factor, ingredient, part, portion, principle, section, unit.
antonym whole.

constitute *v.* account for, compose, comprise, establish, form, make up, represent.

constitutional *adj.* chartered, congenital, inborn, inherent, innate, intrinsic, organic, statutory, vested.

constrain *v.* bind, chain, check, coerce, compel, confine, constrict, curb, drive, force, impel, necessitate, oblige, pressurise, railroad, restrain, urge.

constrained *adj.* embarrassed, forced, guarded, inhibited, reserved, reticent, stiff, subdued, uneasy, unnatural.
antonyms free, relaxed.

constraint *n.* check, coercion, compulsion, curb, damper, deterrent, duress, force, hindrance, limitation, necessity, pressure, restraint, restriction.

constrict *v.* choke, compact, compress, contract, cramp, inhibit, limit, narrow, pinch, restrict, shrink, squeeze, strangle, tighten.
antonym expand.

constriction *n.* blockage, compression, constraint, cramp, impediment, limitation, narrowing, pressure, reduction, restriction, squeezing, stricture, tightening.
antonym expansion.

construct *v.* assemble, build, compose, create, design, elevate, engineer, erect, establish, fabricate, fashion, form, formulate, found, frame, make, manufacture, model, organise, put together, raise, shape.
antonyms demolish, destroy.

construction *n.* assembly, building, composition, constitution, creation, edifice, erection, fabric, fabrication, figure, form, formation, model, organisation, shape, structure.
antonym destruction.

constructive *adj.* advantageous, beneficial, helpful, positive, practical, productive, useful, valuable.
antonyms destructive, negative, unhelpful.

construe *v.* analyse, decipher, deduce, explain, expound, infer, interpret, read, render, take, translate.

consult *v.* ask, confer, consider, debate, deliberate, discuss, interrogate, question, regard.

consultant *n.* adviser, authority, expert, specialist.

consultation *n.* appointment, conference, council, deliberation, dialogue, discussion, examination, hearing, interview, meeting, session.

consume *v.* **1** devour, drink, eat, gobble, swallow. **2** absorb, deplete, dissipate, drain, exhaust, expend, spend, squander, use (up), waste. **3** annihilate, demolish, destroy, devas

tate, ravage.
consumer *n.* buyer, customer, end-user, purchaser, shopper, user.
consuming *adj.* absorbing, compelling, devouring, dominating, engrossing, excruciating, gripping, monopolising, overwhelming, tormenting.
consumption *n.* consuming, depletion, exhaustion, expenditure, use, utilisation, waste.
contact *n.* acquaintance, approximation, association, communication, connection, contiguity, impact, junction, juxtaposition, meeting, touch, union.
v. approach, call, get hold of, notify, phone, reach, ring, telephone.
contagious *adj.* catching, communicable, epidemic, infectious, spreading, transmissible.
contain *v.* **1** accommodate, comprise, embody, embrace, enclose, have, hold, include, incorporate, involve, seat. **2** check, control, curb, limit, repress, restrain, stifle.
antonym **1** exclude.
container *n.* holder, receptacle, vessel.
contaminate *v.* adulterate, corrupt, debase, defile, deprave, infect, pollute, soil, stain, sully, taint, tarnish.
antonym purify.
contemplate *v.* behold, consider, deliberate, design, envisage, examine, expect, foresee, inspect, intend, mean, meditate, mull over, observe, plan, ponder, propose, reflect on, regard, scrutinise, study, survey, view.
contemporary *adj.* current, latest, modern, newfangled, present, present-day, recent, ultramodern, up-to-date, up-to-the-minute.
antonyms old-fashioned, out-of-date.
contempt *n.* condescension, derision, detestation, disdain, disgrace, dishonour, disregard, disrespect, humiliation, loathing, mockery, neglect, scorn, shame, slight.
antonyms admiration, regard.
contemptible *adj.* abject, degenerate, despicable, detestable, ignominious, loathsome, low, mean, paltry, pitiful, shameful, vile, worthless, wretched.
antonyms admirable, honourable.
contemptuous *adj.* arrogant, condescending, cynical, derisive, disdainful, haughty, high and mighty, insolent, insulting, scornful, sneering, supercilious.
antonyms humble, polite, respectful.
contend *v.* affirm, allege, argue, assert, clash, compete, contest, cope, debate, declare, dispute, grapple, hold, jostle, maintain, skirmish, strive, struggle, vie, wrestle.
content *v.* delight, enjoy, gratify, humour, indulge, pacify, please, reconcile, satisfy.
antonym displease.
n. burden, capacity, essence, gist, ideas, load, matter, meaning, measure, significance, size, subject matter, substance, text, thoughts, volume.
adj. agreeable, contented, fulfilled, happy, pleased, satisfied, untroubled, willing.
antonyms dissatisfied, troubled, unhappy.
contented *adj.* cheerful, comfortable, content, glad, happy, pleased, relaxed, satisfied, thankful.
antonyms annoyed, discontented, dissatisfied, unhappy.
contention *n.* affirmation, allegation, argument, assertion, belief, claim, competition, contest, controversy, debate, declaration, discord, dispute, dissension, hostility, idea, opinion, position, profession, rivalry, stand, strife, struggle, thesis, view, wrangling.
contentment *n.* comfort, complacency, ease, equanimity, fulfilment, gladness, gratification, happiness, peace, peacefulness, pleasure, satisfaction, serenity.
antonyms dissatisfaction, unhappiness.
contents *n.* chapters, divisions, elements, ingredients, items, load, parts, subjects, themes, topics.
contest *n.* battle, combat, competition, conflict, controversy, debate, discord, dispute, encounter, fight, game, match, set-to, shock, struggle, tournament, trial.
v. argue against, challenge, compete, contend, debate, deny, dispute, doubt, fight, litigate, oppose, question, refute, strive, vie.
antonym accept.
contestant *n.* aspirant, candidate, competitor, contender, entrant, participant, player.
context *n.* associations, background, circumstances, conditions, connection, frame of reference, framework, relation, situation.
contingent *n.* batch, body, bunch, company, complement, deputation, detachment, group, mission, quota, section, set.
continual *adj.* constant, frequent, incessant, interminable, oft-repeated, perpetual, recurrent, regular, repeated, repetitive.
antonyms intermittent, occasional, temporary.
continuation *n.* addition, development, extension, furtherance, maintenance, prolongation, resumption, supplement.
antonyms cessation, termination.
continue *v.* abide, carry on, endure, extend, go on, last, lengthen, maintain, persevere, persist, proceed, project, prolong, pursue, reach, remain, rest, resume, stay, stick at, survive, sustain.
antonyms discontinue, stop.
continuity *n.* cohesion, connection, extension, flow, interrelationship, linkage, progression, sequence, succession.
antonym discontinuity.
continuous *adj.* ceaseless, connected, consecutive, constant, continued, endless, extended, non-stop, prolonged, unbroken, unceasing, undivided, uninterrupted, unremitting.
antonyms broken, discontinuous, intermittent, sporadic.
contort *v.* convolute, deform, disfigure, distort, gnarl, knot, misshape, squirm, twist, warp, wrench, wriggle, writhe.
contour *n.* aspect, character, curve, figure, form, lines, outline, profile, relief, shape, silhouette.

contraband *adj.* banned, black-market, forbidden, hot, illegal, illicit, prohibited, proscribed, smuggled, unlawful.

contract *v.* **1** abbreviate, abridge, compress, condense, constrict, curtail, diminish, lessen, narrow, reduce, shorten, shrink, shrivel, tighten, wrinkle. **2** acquire, catch, develop, get, go down with. **3** agree, arrange, close, enter into, negotiate, pledge, stipulate, undertake.
antonyms **1** enlarge, expand, lengthen.
n. agreement, arrangement, bargain, bond, commission, commitment, compact, convention, covenant, deal, engagement, instrument, pact, settlement, stipulation, transaction, treaty, understanding.

contraction *n.* abbreviation, compression, constriction, diminution, elision, narrowing, reduction, shortening, shrinkage, shrivelling, tensing, tightening.
antonyms expansion, growth.

contradict *v.* challenge, contravene, counter, counteract, deny, disaffirm, dispute, impugn, negate, oppose.
antonyms agree, confirm, corroborate.

contradiction *n.* conflict, contravention, denial, incongruity, inconsistency, negation, opposite.
antonyms agreement, confirmation, corroboration.

contradictory *adj.* antagonistic, conflicting, contrary, discrepant, dissident, incompatible, inconsistent, irreconcilable, opposed, opposite, paradoxical, repugnant, unreconciled.
antonym consistent.

contraption *n.* apparatus, contrivance, device, gadget, mechanism, rig.

contrary *adj.* **1** adverse, antagonistic, clashing, counter, hostile, inconsistent, opposed, opposite. **2** awkward, cantankerous, difficult, disobliging, intractable, obstinate, perverse, stroppy, wayward.
antonyms **1** like, similar. **2** obliging.
n. converse, opposite, reverse.

contrast *n.* difference, differentiation, disparity, dissimilarity, distinction, divergence, foil, opposition.
antonym similarity.
v. compare, differ, differentiate, discriminate, distinguish, oppose, set off.

contravene *v.* break, contradict, cross, disobey, hinder, infringe, interfere, oppose, refute, thwart, transgress, trespass, violate.
antonym uphold.

contribute *v.* add, afford, bestow, conduce, donate, furnish, give, help, lead, provide, subscribe, supply, tend.
antonyms subtract, withhold.

contribution *n.* addition, bestowal, donation, gift, grant, gratuity, handout, input, offering, subscription.

contributor *n.* backer, benefactor, bestower, conferrer, correspondent, donor, freelance, freelancer, giver, journalist, patron, reporter, subscriber, supporter.

contrivance *n.* **1** apparatus, appliance, contraption, design, device, equipment, expedient, fabrication, formation, gadget, gear, implement, invention, knack, machine, measure, mechanism, project. **2** dodge, intrigue, machination, plan, plot, ploy, ruse, scheme, stratagem, trick.

contrived *adj.* artificial, elaborate, false, forced, laboured, mannered, overdone, planned, strained, unnatural.
antonyms genuine, natural.

control *v.* **1** command, direct, govern, lead, manage, oversee, rule, run, superintend, supervise. **2** monitor, regulate, verify. **3** check, curb, repress, restrain, subdue.
n. **1** authority, charge, command, direction, discipline, government, guidance, management, mastery, oversight, rule, superintendence, supervision. **2** check, curb, regulation, restraint. **3** dial, instrument, knob, lever, switch.

controller *n.* administrator, captain, director, executive, executor, governor, manager, marshal, navigator, pilot, ringmaster, ruler, steward.

controversial *adj.* contentious, debatable, disputable, disputed, doubtful, polemical, questionable.

controversy *n.* argument, contention, debate, disagreement, discussion, dispute, dissension, polemic, quarrel, squabble, strife, war of words, wrangle, wrangling.
antonyms accord, agreement.

convenience *n.* accessibility, accommodation, advantage, amenity, appliance, availability, benefit, chance, comfort, ease, enjoyment, facility, fitness, handiness, help, leisure, opportunity, satisfaction, service, serviceability, suitability, use, usefulness, utility.
antonyms discomfort, inconvenience.

convenient *adj.* accessible, adapted, advantageable, appropriate, at hand, available, beneficial, commodious, fit, fitted, handy, helpful, labour-saving, nearby, opportune, suitable, suited, timely, useful, well-timed.
antonyms awkward, inconvenient.

convention *n.* **1** code, custom, etiquette, formality, matter of form, practice, tradition, usage. **2** assembly, conference, congress, council, delegates, meeting, protocol, representatives, treaty.

conventional *adj.* accepted, arbitrary, common, commonplace, correct, customary, expected, formal, hidebound, normal, ordinary, orthodox, pedestrian, prevailing, prevalent, proper, regular, ritual, routine, run-of-the-mill, standard, stereotyped, straight, traditional, unoriginal, usual.
antonyms exotic, unconventional, unusual.

converge *v.* approach, coincide, combine, concentrate, concur, focus, gather, join, meet, merge.
antonyms disperse, diverge.

convergence *n.* approach, blending, coincidence, concentration, confluence, intersection, junction, meeting, merging, union.
antonyms divergence, separation.

conversant with acquainted with, at home with, experienced in, familiar with, informed about, knowledgeable about, practised in, proficient in, skilled in, versed in.
antonym ignorant of.

conversation *n.* chat, communication, communion, dialogue, discussion, exchange, gossip, talk.

converse *n.* antithesis, contrary, obverse, opposite, reverse.
adj. contrary, counter, opposite, reverse, reversed, transposed.

conversion *n.* adaptation, alteration, change, modification, rebirth, reconstruction, reformation, regeneration, remodelling, reorganisation, transformation.

convert *v.* **1** adapt, alter, change, interchange, modify, remodel, reorganise, restyle, revise, transform, turn. **2** convince, persuade, proselytise, reform.

convertible *adj.* adaptable, adjustable, exchangeable, interchangeable.

convex *adj.* bulging, protuberant, rounded.
antonym concave.

convey *v.* bear, bring, carry, communicate, conduct, deliver, devolve, fetch, forward, grant, guide, impart, lease, move, relate, reveal, send, steal, support, tell, transfer, transmit, transport, will.

convict *v.* condemn, imprison, sentence.
n. criminal, culprit, prisoner.

conviction *n.* assurance, belief, certainty, confidence, creed, earnestness, faith, fervour, firmness, opinion, persuasion, principle, reliance, tenet, view.

convince *v.* assure, confirm, persuade, reassure, satisfy, sway, win over.

convincing *adj.* cogent, conclusive, credible, impressive, incontrovertible, likely, persuasive, plausible, powerful, probable, telling.
antonyms dubious, improbable.

convoluted *adj.* complex, complicated, involved, meandering, tangled, twisting, winding.
antonyms straight, straightforward.

convolution *n.* coil, coiling, complexity, contortion, helix, intricacy, loop, spiral, tortuousness, twist, whorl, winding.

convoy *n.* attendance, attendant, escort, fleet, guard, protection, train.

convulsion *n.* agitation, commotion, contortion, contraction, cramp, disturbance, eruption, fit, furore, outburst, paroxysm, seizure, shaking, spasm, tremor, tumult, turbulence, upheaval.

convulsive *adj.* fitful, jerky, spasmodic, sporadic, violent.

cook *v.* bake, boil, braise, broil, fry, grill, heat, prepare, roast, sauté, simmer, steam, stew, toast.
cook up brew, concoct, contrive, devise, fabricate, improvise, invent, plan, plot, prepare, scheme.

cool *adj.* **1** breezy, chilly, fresh, nippy. **2** calm, composed, laid-back, level-headed, pleasant, quiet, relaxed, reserved, self-possessed, unemotional, unexcited, unruffled. **3** aloof, apathetic, cold, distant, frigid, half-hearted, lukewarm, stand-offish, uncommunicative, unconcerned, unenthusiastic, unfriendly, uninterested, unresponsive, unwelcoming.
antonyms **1** hot, warm. **2** angry, excited. **3** friendly, welcoming.
v. abate, allay, assuage, calm, chill, dampen, defuse, fan, freeze, lessen, moderate, quiet, refrigerate, temper.
antonyms excite, heat, warm.
n. calmness, collectedness, composure, control, poise, self-control, self-discipline, self-possession, temper.

co-operate *v.* aid, assist, collaborate, combine, concur, conspire, contribute, co-ordinate, help, play ball, work together.

co-operation *n.* assistance, collaboration, concurrence, give-and-take, helpfulness, participation, responsiveness, teamwork, unity.
antonyms discord, opposition, rivalry.

co-operative *adj.* accommodating, collective, combined, concerted, co-ordinated, helpful, joint, obliging, responsive, shared, supportive, unified, united.
antonyms rebellious, unco-operative.

co-ordinate *v.* arrange, correlate, harmonise, integrate, match, mesh, organise, regulate, relate, synchronise, systematise, tabulate.

cope *v.* carry on, get by, make do, manage, survive.
cope with contend with, deal with, encounter, grapple with, handle, manage, struggle with, weather, wrestle with.

cop-out *n.* alibi, dodge, evasion, fraud, pretence, pretext.

copy *n.* archetype, borrowing, carbon copy, counterfeit, crib, duplicate, facsimile, flimsy, forgery, image, imitation, likeness, loan-word, model, pattern, photocopy, Photostat®, plagiarisation, print, replica, representation, reproduction, tracing, transcript, transcription, Xerox®.
antonyms model, original, prototype.
v. ape, borrow, counterfeit, crib, duplicate, echo, emulate, exemplify, extract, facsimile, follow, imitate, mimic, mirror, parrot, personate, photocopy, plagiarise, repeat, reproduce, simulate, transcribe.

cord *n.* bond, connection, line, link, rope, strand, string, tie, twine.

core *n.* centre, crux, essence, germ, gist, heart, kernel, nitty-gritty, nub, nucleus, pith.
antonyms exterior, perimeter, surface.

corner *n.* angle, bend, cavity, cranny, hide-away, hideout, hole, joint, niche, nook, recess, retreat.

corny *adj.* banal, clichéd, commonplace, dull, feeble, hackneyed, old-fashioned, sentimental, stale, stereotyped, trite.
antonyms new, original.

corporate *adj.* allied, amalgamated, collective, combined, communal, concerted, joint, merged, pooled, shared, united.

corporation *n.* association, authorities, body,

combine, conglomerate, council, society.
corps *n.* band, body, brigade, company, contingent, crew, detachment, division, regiment, squad, squadron, team, troop, unit.
corpse *n.* body, carcass, remains, skeleton.
corpus *n.* body, collection, compilation, entirety, whole.
corral *n.* coop, enclosure, fold, pound, stall, sty.
correct *v.* **1** adjust, amend, debug, emend, improve, rectify, regulate, remedy, right. **2** discipline, punish, reform, reprimand, reprove.
adj. acceptable, accurate, appropriate, exact, faultless, fitting, flawless, just, OK, precise, proper, regular, right, standard, strict, true, well-formed, word-perfect.
antonyms inaccurate, incorrect, wrong.
correction *n.* adjustment, alteration, amendment, emendation, improvement, modification, rectification.
corrective *adj.* curative, disciplinary, medicinal, remedial, restorative, therapeutic.
correlate *v.* associate, compare, connect, coordinate, correspond, equate, interact, link, parallel, relate, tie in.
correspond *v.* accord, agree, answer, coincide, communicate, complement, concur, conform, correlate, dovetail, fit, harmonise, match, square, tally, write.
correspondence *n.* **1** communication, letters, mail, post, writing. **2** agreement, analogy, coincidence, comparability, comparison, conformity, congruity, equivalence, fitness, harmony, match, relation, resemblance, similarity.
antonyms **2** divergence, incongruity.
correspondent *n.* contributor, journalist, reporter, writer.
corresponding *adj.* analogous, answering, complementary, equivalent, identical, interrelated, matching, reciprocal, similar.
corridor *n.* aisle, hallway, lobby, passage, passageway.
corroborate *v.* authenticate, bear out, confirm, document, endorse, establish, prove, ratify, substantiate, support, sustain, underpin, validate.
antonym contradict.
corroborative *adj.* confirmative, confirmatory, supportive.
corrode *v.* consume, corrupt, crumble, deteriorate, disintegrate, eat away, erode, impair, oxidise, rust, waste, wear away.
corrosive *adj.* abrasive, acid, acrid, caustic, consuming, corroding, cutting, wasting, wearing.
corrugated *adj.* channelled, creased, crinkled, fluted, furrowed, grooved, ridged, rumpled, wrinkled.
corrupt *adj.* abandoned, bent, bribed, crooked, defiled, degenerate, depraved, dishonest, dissolute, fraudulent, rotten, shady, unethical, unprincipled, unscrupulous, untrustworthy.
antonyms ethical, honest, trustworthy, upright, virtuous.
v. adulterate, bribe, contaminate, debase, defile, demoralise, deprave, lure, pervert, spoil, taint.
antonym purify.
corruption *n.* bribing, crookedness, decay, degeneration, degradation, demoralisation, depravity, dishonesty, distortion, evil, extortion, falsification, fraud, immorality, impurity, iniquity, perversion, shadiness, unscrupulousness, vice, wickedness.
antonyms honesty, virtue.
corset *n.* belt, check, curb, curtailment, foundation garment, girdle, limit, limitation, restriction, stays.
cosmetic *adj.* non-essential, superficial, surface.
antonym essential.
cosmetics *n.* grease paint, make-up.
cosmopolitan *adj.* international, sophisticated, universal, well-travelled, worldly, worldy-wise.
antonyms insular, parochial, rustic.
cosset *v.* baby, cherish, coddle, cuddle, mollycoddle, pamper, pet.
cost *n.* **1** amount, charge, disbursement, expenditure, expense, figure, outlay, payment, price, rate, worth. **2** deprivation, detriment, harm, hurt, injury, loss, penalty, price, sacrifice.
costly *adj.* catastrophic, damaging, dear, disastrous, excessive, exorbitant, expensive, harmful, highly-priced, lavish, loss-making, precious, priceless, pricy, rich, sacrificial, splendid, valuable.
antonyms cheap, inexpensive.
costs *n.* budget, expenses, outgoings, overheads.
costume *n.* clothing, dress, garb, get-up, livery, outfit, robes, uniform, vestment.
cosy *adj.* comfortable, comfy, homely, intimate, secure, sheltered, snug, warm.
antonyms cold, uncomfortable.
cottage *n.* bungalow, cabin, chalet, hut, lodge, shack.
couch *v.* bear, cradle, express, frame, phrase, support, utter, word.
n. bed, chaise-longue, chesterfield, divan, lounge, ottoman, settee, sofa.
council *n.* assembly, board, cabinet, chamber, committee, conference, congress, convention, convocation, ministry, panel, parliament, syndicate.
counsel *n.* **1** advice, consideration, consultation, deliberation, direction, forethought, guidance, information, plan, recommendation, suggestion. **2** advocate, attorney, barrister, lawyer, solicitor.
v. admonish, advise, advocate, caution, direct, exhort, guide, instruct, recommend, suggest, urge, warn.
counsellor *n.* adviser, attorney, councillor, lawyer, representative.
count *v.* **1** add, calculate, check, compute, enumerate, estimate, include, list, number, score, tot up, total. **2** matter, signify, tell. **3** consider, deem, hold, impute, judge, qualify, reckon, regard, think.
n. addition, calculation, computation, enumeration, numbering, poll, reckoning, sum, tally, total.
count on believe, depend on, expect, reckon on,

rely on, trust.

counter *adv.* against, conversely, in opposition. *adj.* adverse, against, conflicting, contradictory, contrary, contrasting, obverse, opposed, opposing, opposite.
antonyms concurring, corroborating.
v. answer, meet, offset, parry, resist, respond, retaliate, retort, return.

counteract *v.* act against, annul, check, contravene, counterbalance, countervail, cross, defeat, foil, frustrate, hinder, invalidate, negate, neutralise, offset, oppose, resist, thwart, undo.
antonyms assist, support.

counterfeit *v.* copy, fabricate, fake, feign, forge, imitate, impersonate, pretend, sham, simulate. *adj.* bogus, copied, faked, false, feigned, forged, fraudulent, imitation, phoney, pretend(ed), pseudo, sham, simular, simulated, spurious.
antonyms authentic, genuine, real.
n. copy, fake, forgery, fraud, imitation, phoney, reproduction, sham.

counterpart *n.* complement, copy, duplicate, equal, equivalent, fellow, match, mate, opposite number, supplement, tally, twin.

countless *adj.* endless, immeasurable, incalculable, infinite, innumerable, limitless, measureless, myriad, uncounted, unnumbered, untold.
antonyms finite, limited.

country *n.* **1** kingdom, nation, people, realm, society, state. **2** backwoods, countryside, farmland, green belt, outback, provinces, sticks, wilds. **3** area, community, district, land, region, terrain, territory.
antonyms **2** city, town.
adj. agrarian, bucolic, landed, pastoral, provincial, rude, rural, rustic.
antonym urban.

countryman *n.* **1** compatriot, fellow countryman. **2** bumpkin, farmer, husbandman, peasant, provincial, rustic, yokel.

countryside *n.* country, farmland, green belt, landscape, outback, outdoors, sticks.

county *n.* area, district, province, region, shire.

coup *n.* **1** coup d'état, putsch, revolution. **2** accomplishment, action, blow, deed, exploit, feat, manoeuvre, masterstroke, stratagem, stroke, stunt.
coup d'état coup, overthrow, putsch, rebellion, revolt, revolution, takeover, uprising.

couple *n.* duo, pair, span, team, twosome.
v. accompany, buckle, clasp, connect, hitch, join, link, marry, pair, unite, wed, yoke.

courage *n.* boldness, bravery, daring, dauntlessness, fearlessness, firmness, fortitude, gallantry, guts, heroism, mettle, nerve, pluck, resolution, spirit, valour.
antonyms cowardice, fear.

courageous *adj.* audacious, bold, brave, daring, dauntless, fearless, gallant, hardy, heroic, high-hearted, indomitable, intrepid, lion-hearted, plucky, resolute, valiant.
antonyms afraid, cowardly.

courier *n.* bearer, carrier, emissary, envoy, guide, herald, legate, messenger, representative, runner.

course *n.* **1** classes, curriculum, lectures, lessons, studies, syllabus. **2** advance, current, development, flow, furtherance, movement, order, progress, progression, sequence, series, succession. **3** duration, passage, period, term, time. **4** channel, circuit, direction, flight-path, line, orbit, path, race, race-course, race-track, road, route, track, trail, trajectory, way. **5** method, mode, plan, policy, procedure, programme, schedule.

court *n.* **1** bar, bench, law-court, session, trial, tribunal. **2** cloister, courtyard, hall, plaza, quadrangle, square, yard. **3** attendants, cortège, entourage, retinue, suite, train.

courteous *adj.* affable, attentive, civil, considerate, courtly, debonair, elegant, gallant, gracious, obliging, polished, polite, refined, respectful, urbane, well-bred, well-mannered.
antonyms discourteous, impolite, rude.

courtesy *n.* attention, breeding, civility, consideration, elegance, gallantry, generosity, graciousness, kindness, manners, politeness, urbanity.
antonyms discourtesy, rudeness.

courtier *n.* attendant, chamberlain, follower, lady, lord, noble, nobleman, page, squire, steward, sycophant, toady.

courtly *adj.* affable, aristocratic, ceremonious, chivalrous, civil, dignified, elegant, flattering, formal, gallant, gracious, obliging, polished, polite, refined, stately.
antonyms inelegant, provincial, rough.

courtyard *n.* area, enclosure, patio, playground, quad, quadrangle, yard.

cove *n.* bay, bight, creek, estuary, fiord, firth, harbour, inlet, sound.

cover *v.* **1** camouflage, conceal, disguise, encase, hide, mask, obscure, screen, shroud, veil. **2** clothe, coat, daub, dress, envelop, spread, wrap. **3** defend, guard, protect, shelter, shield. **4** comprehend, comprise, consider, contain, deal with, describe, detail, embody, embrace, encompass, examine, include, incorporate, investigate, involve.
antonyms **1** uncover. **2** strip. **3** attack. **4** exclude.
n. **1** bedspread, canopy, case, clothing, coating, concealment, disguise, dress, envelope, façade, front, jacket, lid, mask, screen, top, veil, wrapper. **2** camouflage, defence, guard, protection, refuge, shelter, shield.
cover up conceal, dissemble, hide, hush up, repress, suppress, whitewash.
antonyms disclose, reveal, uncover.

coverage *n.* analysis, assurance, description, protection, reportage, reporting, treatment.

covering *n.* blanket, casing, cloak, clothing, coating, cover, housing, layer, mask, overlay, protection, shelter, top, wrapping.

cover-up *n.* complicity, concealment, conspiracy, front, pretence, smoke-screen, whitewash.

covet *v.* begrudge, crave, desire, envy, fancy, hanker, long for, lust after, thirst for, want, yearn for, yen for.

coward *n.* chicken, faint-heart, renegade, scaredy-cat, sneak.
antonym hero.

cowardice *n.* faint-heartedness, fear.
antonyms courage, valour.

cowardly *adj.* chicken, craven, faint-hearted, fearful, scared, shrinking, soft, spineless, timorous, unheroic, weak, weak-kneed, yellow.
antonyms bold, brave, courageous.

cower *v.* cringe, crouch, flinch, grovel, quail, shake, shiver, shrink, skulk, tremble.

coy *adj.* backward, bashful, coquettish, demure, diffident, evasive, flirtatious, kittenish, maidenly, modest, prudish, reserved, retiring, self-effacing, shrinking, shy, skittish, timid, virginal.
antonyms forward, impudent, sober.

crabby *adj.* acrimonious, bad-tempered, cross, crotchety, difficult, grouchy, harsh, ill-tempered, irritable, morose, prickly, snappy, sour, surly.
antonyms calm, placid.

crack *v.* **1** break, burst, chop, fracture, shatter, splinter, split. **2** burst, clap, crackle, crash, detonate, explode, pop, slap, snap, whack. **3** decipher, solve, work out.
n. **1** breach, break, chink, crevice, fissure, flaw, fracture, gag, gap, line, rift, split. **2** blow, burst, clap, crash, explosion, pop, slap, smack, snap, stab, whack. **3** dig, jibe, joke, wisecrack, witticism. **4** attempt, go, opportunity, try.
adj. choice, excellent, first-class, first-rate, hand-picked, superior, top-notch.
crack down on act against, check, clamp down on, end, put a stop to, stop.
crack up break down, collapse, go crazy, go to pieces.

crackdown *n.* clampdown, crushing, end, repression, stop, suppression.

cradle *n.* **1** bassinet, bed, cot, crib. **2** beginning, birthplace, fount, fountain-head, origin, source, spring, well-spring.
v. bear, couch, hold, lull, nestle, nurse, rock, support, tend.

craft *n.* **1** ability, aptitude, art, business, calling, cleverness, dexterity, employment, expertise, expertness, handicraft, handiwork, knack, mastery, occupation, skill, talent, trade, vocation, work. **2** aircraft, boat, ship, spacecraft, spaceship, vessel.

craftsman *n.* artisan, maker, master, smith, technician, wright.

craftsmanship *n.* artistry, expertise, mastery, technique, workmanship.

crafty *adj.* artful, calculating, canny, cunning, deceitful, designing, devious, fraudulent, scheming, sharp, shrewd, sly, subtle, wily.
antonyms naïve, open.

cram *v.* **1** compress, crowd, crush, force, glut, gorge, jam, overfill, pack, press, ram, squeeze, stuff. **2** mug up, study, swot.

cramp[1] *v.* check, clog, confine, constrain, frustrate, hamper, handicap, hinder, impede, inhibit, obstruct, restrict, shackle, thwart, tie.

cramp[2] *n.* ache, contraction, convulsion, crick, pain, pang, pins and needles, spasm, stiffness, stitch, twinge.

cramped *adj.* awkward, confined, congested, crowded, jam-packed, narrow, overcrowded, packed, restricted, squashed, squeezed, squeezy, tight, uncomfortable.
antonym spacious.

cranny *n.* chink, cleft, crack, crevice, fissure, gap, hole, nook, opening.

crash *n.* **1** accident, bump, collision, pile-up, smash, smash-up, wreck. **2** bang, boom, clang, clash, clatter, din, racket, thud, thump, thunder. **3** bankruptcy, collapse, depression, downfall, failure, ruin.
v. **1** bang, bump, collide, hit. **2** break, dash, disintegrate, fracture, fragment, shatter, shiver, smash, splinter. **3** collapse, fail, fall, fold (up), go bust, go under, lurch, pitch, plunge, topple.

crate *n.* box, case, container, packing case, packing-box, tea-chest.

crave *v.* ask, beg, beseech, desire, entreat, fancy, hanker after, hunger for, implore, long for, need, petition, pine for, require, seek, solicit, thirst for, want, yearn for.
antonyms dislike, spurn.

craving *n.* appetite, desire, hankering, hunger, longing, lust, thirst, urge, yearning.
antonyms dislike, distaste.

crawl *v.* **1** creep, inch, wriggle, writhe. **2** cringe, fawn, grovel.

craze *n.* enthusiasm, fad, fashion, frenzy, infatuation, mania, mode, novelty, obsession, passion, preoccupation, rage, thing, trend, vogue.

crazed *adj.* crazy, demented, lunatic, maddened, possessed.
antonyms sane, sensible.

crazy *adj.* **1** absurd, barmy, berserk, daft, demented, deranged, foolish, half-baked, idiotic, impracticable, imprudent, inappropriate, insane, irresponsible, ludicrous, lunatic, mad, nonsensical, odd, outrageous, preposterous, ridiculous, senseless, short-sighted, silly, unbalanced, unwise. **2** ardent, devoted, eager, enamoured, enthusiastic, fanatical, infatuated, mad, passionate, smitten, wild, zealous.
antonyms **1** sane, sensible. **2** indifferent.

creak *v.* grate, grind, groan, rasp, scrape, scratch, screak, screech, squeak, squeal.

creaky *adj.* creaking, grating, rasping, screaky, squeaking, squeaky, unoiled.

cream *n.* **1** cosmetic, emulsion, lotion, oil, ointment, paste, salve. **2** best, élite, pick, prime.

creamy *adj.* buttery, cream-coloured, creamed, lush, milky, off-white, oily, rich, smooth, soft, velvety.

crease *v.* corrugate, crimp, crinkle, crumple, fold, pucker, ridge, ruckle, rumple, wrinkle.
n. bulge, corrugation, crumple, fold, groove, line, overlap, pucker, ridge, ruck, tuck, wrinkle.

create *v.* appoint, beget, cause, coin, compose, concoct, constitute, design, develop, devise, engender, establish, form, formulate, found,

generate, hatch, initiate, install, institute, invent, invest, make, occasion, originate, produce, set up.
antonym destroy.

creation *n.* **1** achievement, brainchild, chef d'oeuvre, concept, conception, concoction, constitution, development, establishment, formation, foundation, generation, handiwork, institution, invention, making, origination, procreation, production. **2** cosmos, life, nature, universe, world.
antonym **1** destruction.

creative *adj.* adept, artistic, clever, fertile, gifted, imaginative, ingenious, inspired, inventive, original, productive, resourceful, stimulating, talented, visionary.
antonym unimaginative.

creativity *n.* artistry, cleverness, fertility, imagination, imaginativeness, ingenuity, inspiration, inventiveness, originality, resourcefulness, talent, vision.
antonym unimaginativeness.

creator *n.* architect, author, begetter, designer, father, framer, God, initiator, inventor, maker, originator.

creature *n.* animal, beast, being, bird, body, brute, character, fellow, individual, man, mortal, person, soul, woman.

credentials *n.* accreditation, attestation, authorisation, card, certificate, deed, diploma, endorsement, letters of credence, licence, passport, permit, recommendation, reference, testament, testimonial, title, voucher, warrant.

credibility *n.* integrity, plausibility, probability, reliability, trustworthiness.
antonym implausibility.

credible *adj.* believable, conceivable, convincing, dependable, honest, imaginable, likely, persuasive, plausible, possible, probable, reasonable, reliable, sincere, supposable, tenable, thinkable, trustworthy.
antonyms implausible, unbelievable, unreliable.

credit *n.* acclaim, acknowledgement, approval, commendation, distinction, esteem, estimation, fame, glory, honour, praise, prestige, recognition, reputation, thanks, tribute.
antonyms discredit, shame.
v. accept, believe, subscribe to, swallow, trust.
antonym disbelieve.

creditable *adj.* admirable, commendable, deserving, estimable, excellent, exemplary, good, honourable, praiseworthy, reputable, respectable, worthy.
antonyms blameworthy, shameful.

credulous *adj.* gullible, naïve, trusting, uncritical, unsuspecting, unsuspicious, wide-eyed.
antonyms sceptical, suspicious.

creed *n.* articles, belief, canon, catechism, confession, credo, doctrine, dogma, faith, persuasion, principles, tenets.

creek *n.* **1** bay, bight, cove, fiord, firth, inlet. **2** brook, rivulet, stream, tributary, watercourse.

creep *v.* crawl, dawdle, drag, edge, grovel, inch, scrape, slink, slither, sneak, squirm, steal, tiptoe, worm, wriggle.

creeper *n.* climber, plant, rambler, runner, trailing vine.

creepy *adj.* disturbing, eerie, frightening, gruesome, hair-raising, horrible, macabre, nightmarish, scary, sinister, spooky, terrifying, threatening, unpleasant.
antonyms normal, pleasant.

crest *n.* **1** apex, crown, head, peak, pinnacle, ridge, summit, top. **2** mane, plume, tassel, tuft. **3** badge, device, emblem, insignia, symbol.

crestfallen *adj.* dejected, depressed, despondent, disappointed, discouraged, disheartened, downcast, downhearted.
antonyms elated, exuberant.

crevice *n.* chink, cleft, crack, cranny, fissure, fracture, gap, hole, opening, rent, rift, slit, split.

crew *n.* assemblage, band, bunch, company, complement, corps, crowd, gang, hands, herd, horde, lot, mob, pack, party, set, squad, swarm, team, troop.

crime *n.* atrocity, corruption, fault, felony, guilt, iniquity, law-breaking, misconduct, misdeed, misdemeanour, offence, outrage, sin, transgression, trespass, vice, villainy, violation, wickedness, wrong, wrong-doing.

criminal *n.* con, convict, crook, culprit, delinquent, evil-doer, felon, law-breaker, offender, transgressor.
adj. bent, corrupt, crooked, culpable, deplorable, illegal, immoral, indictable, lawless, scandalous, unlawful, unrighteous, wicked, wrong.
antonyms honest, upright.

cringe *v.* bend, bow, cower, crawl, creep, crouch, flinch, grovel, kneel, quail, quiver, recoil, shrink, shy, sneak, start, stoop, submit, tremble, wince.

crinkle *n.* curl, fold, pucker, ruffle, scallop, twist, wrinkle.
v. crimp, crimple, crumple, curl, fold, pucker, ruffle, rumple, rustle, scallop, twist, wrinkle.

crinkly *adj.* curly, fluted, frizzy, furrowed, gathered, puckered, ruffled, wrinkled.
antonyms smooth, straight.

cripple *v.* cramp, damage, debilitate, destroy, disable, impair, incapacitate, injure, lame, maim, mutilate, paralyse, ruin, sabotage, spoil, weaken.

crippled *adj.* deformed, disabled, handicapped, incapacitated, invalid, lame, paralysed.

crisis *n.* catastrophe, confrontation, crunch, difficulty, dilemma, disaster, emergency, extremity, mess, predicament, quandary, trouble.

crisp *adj.* **1** brittle, crumbly, crunchy, firm. **2** bracing, brisk, fresh, invigorating, refreshing. **3** brief, clear, incisive, pithy, short, snappy, terse.
antonyms **1** flabby, limp, soggy. **2** muggy. **3** vague, wordy.

critic *n.* analyst, attacker, authority, carper, censor, censurer, commentator, connoisseur, expert, expositor, fault-finder, judge, reviewer.

critical *adj.* **1** all-important, crucial, decisive, essential, grave, momentous, pressing, serious, urgent, vital. **2** dangerous, perilous, precarious,

risky. **3** carping, censorious, derogatory, disapproving, disparaging, fault-finding, nit-picking, uncomplimentary. **4** accurate, analytical, diagnostic, discerning, penetrating, precise.
antonyms **1** unimportant. **2** safe. **3** appreciative, complimentary.

criticise *v.* **1** blame, carp, censure, condemn, disparage, knock, slate. **2** analyse, assess, evaluate, judge, review.
antonyms **1** commend, praise.

criticism *n.* **1** blame, brickbat, censure, disapproval, disparagement, fault-finding, flak, knocking. **2** analysis, appreciation, assessment, comment, commentary, critique, evaluation, judgement, review.
antonyms **1** commendation, praise.

croak *v.* gasp, grunt, squawk, wheeze.

crockery *n.* ceramics, china, dishes, earthenware, pottery, stoneware, whiteware.

crook *n.* cheat, criminal, robber, rogue, shark, swindler, thief, villain.

crooked *adj.* **1** angled, askew, asymmetric, awry, bent, bowed, crippled, crump, curved, deformed, deviating, distorted, hooked, irregular, lopsided, misshapen, off-centre, skew-whiff, slanted, slanting, squint, tilted, tortuous, twisted, uneven, warped, winding, zigzag. **2** bent, corrupt, crafty, criminal, deceitful, discreditable, dishonest, dishonourable, fraudulent, illegal, knavish, nefarious, questionable, shady, shifty, treacherous, underhand, unethical, unlawful, unprincipled, unscrupulous.
antonyms **1** straight. **2** honest.

crop *n.* fruits, gathering, growth, harvest, ingathering, produce, vintage, yield.
v. clip, curtail, cut, lop, pare, pick, prune, shear, shorten, snip, top, trim.
crop up appear, arise, arrive, emerge, happen, occur.

cross *adj.* **1** angry, annoyed, bad-tempered, contrary, crotchety, disagreeable, fractious, fretful, grouchy, grumpy, ill-tempered, impatient, irritable, shirty, short, snappish, snappy, sullen, surly, vexed. **2** crosswise, hybrid, interchanged, intersecting, oblique, opposite, reciprocal, transverse.
antonyms **1** calm, placid, pleasant.
v. **1** bridge, ford, go across, span, traverse. **2** criss-cross, intersect, intertwine, lace, meet. **3** blend, crossbreed, cross-fertilise, cross-pollinate, hybridise, interbreed, mix, mongrelise. **4** block, foil, frustrate, hinder, impede, obstruct, oppose, thwart.
n. **1** affliction, burden, grief, load, misery, misfortune, trial, tribulation, trouble, woe, worry. **2** amalgam, blend, combination, crossbreed, hybrid, intersection, mixture, mongrel. **3** crucifix.

cross-examine *v.* grill, interrogate, pump, question, quiz.

cross-question *v.* cross-examine, debrief, examine, grill.

crouch *v.* bend, bow, cower, cringe, duck, hunch, kneel, squat, stoop.

crowd *n.* army, assembly, attendance, audience, bunch, circle, clique, company, flock, gate, group, herd, horde, host, lot, mass, masses, mob, multitude, pack, people, populace, press, public, rabble, riff-raff, set, spectators, squash, swarm, throng.
v. bundle, compress, congest, congregate, cram, elbow, flock, gather, huddle, jostle, mass, muster, pack, pile, press, push, shove, squeeze, stream, surge, swarm, throng.

crowded *adj.* busy, congested, cramped, crushed, filled, full, huddled, jammed, jam-packed, mobbed, overflowing, overpopulated, packed, swarming, teeming, thronged.
antonyms deserted, empty.

crown *n.* **1** circlet, coronet, diadem, garland, tiara, wreath. **2** honour, laurels, prize, reward, trophy. **3** king, monarch, monarchy, queen, royalty, ruler, sovereign, sovereignty. **4** acme, apex, crest, pinnacle, summit, tip, top.
v. **1** adorn, dignify, festoon, honour, reward. **2** cap, complete, consummate, fulfil, perfect, top.

crowning *adj.* climactic, consummate, culminating, final, perfect, sovereign, supreme, top, ultimate, unmatched, unsurpassed.
n. coronation, installation.

crucial *adj.* central, critical, decisive, essential, important, key, momentous, pivotal, pressing, searching, testing, trying, urgent, vital.
antonyms trivial, unimportant.

crude *adj.* **1** natural, primitive, raw, rough, unfinished, unpolished, unprocessed, unrefined. **2** coarse, dirty, gross, indecent, lewd, obscene, rude, vulgar.
antonyms **1** finished, refined. **2** decent, polite.

cruel *adj.* atrocious, barbarous, bitter, bloodthirsty, brutal, callous, cold-blooded, cutting, depraved, excruciating, ferocious, fierce, flinty, grim, hard-hearted, harsh, heartless, hellish, implacable, inexorable, inhuman, inhumane, malevolent, merciless, murderous, painful, pitiless, relentless, remorseless, ruthless, sadistic, savage, severe, spiteful, stony-hearted, unfeeling, unkind, unnatural, unrelenting, vicious.
antonyms compassionate, kind, merciful.

cruelty *n.* barbarity, bestiality, bloodthirstiness, brutality, callousness, depravity, ferocity, hardheartedness, harshness, heartlessness, inhumanity, mercilessness, murderousness, ruthlessness, sadism, savagery, severity, spite, tyranny, venom, viciousness.
antonyms compassion, kindness, mercy.

crumble *v.* break up, collapse, crush, decay, decompose, degenerate, deteriorate, disintegrate, fragment, grind, pound, powder, pulverise.

crumbly *adj.* brittle, friable, powdery, short.

crunch *v.* champ, chomp, grind, masticate, munch.

crusade *n.* campaign, cause, drive, expedition, holy war, jihad, movement, push, undertaking.

crusader *n.* advocate, campaigner, champion, enthusiast, fighter, missionary, reformer, zealot.

crush *v.* **1** break, compress, crumble, crumple,

grind, pound, press, pulverise, quell, smash, squash, squeeze, wrinkle. **2** conquer, demolish, overcome, overpower, overwhelm, put down, quash, vanquish. **3** abash, devastate, humiliate, shame.

crust *n.* caking, coat, coating, concretion, covering, exterior, film, incrustation, layer, outside, rind, scab, shell, skin, surface.

crusty *adj.* brusque, crabbed, cross, curt, grouchy, gruff, ill-humoured, irritable, prickly, short-tempered, surly, touchy.
antonyms calm, pleasant, soft.

crux *n.* core, essence, heart, nub, vexed question.

cry *v.* **1** bawl, blubber, snivel, sob, wail, weep, whimper. **2** bellow, call, exclaim, roar, scream, screech, shout, shriek, yell.
n. **1** bawl(ing), blubber(ing), call, snivel(ling), sob(bing), wail(ing), weep(ing). **2** bellow, exclamation, plea, roar, scream, shout, shriek, yell.

crypt *n.* catacomb, mausoleum, tomb, undercroft, vault.

cryptic *adj.* abstruse, ambiguous, aprocryphal, bizarre, dark, enigmatic, equivocal, esoteric, hidden, mysterious, obscure, occult, perplexing, puzzling, secret, strange, veiled.
antonyms clear, obvious, straightforward.

crystallise *v.* appear, coalesce, emerge, form, harden, materialise, solidify.

cub *n.* babe, fledgling, offspring, pup, puppy, whelp, young.

cuddle *v.* canoodle, clasp, cosset, embrace, fondle, hug, nestle, pet, snuggle.

cuddly *adj.* cosy, cuddlesome, huggable, lovable, plump, soft, warm.

cue *n.* catchword, hint, incentive, key, nod, prompt(ing), reminder, sign, signal, stimulus, suggestion.

cuff *v.* bat, beat, belt, biff, box, buffet, clap, clobber, clout, knock, pummel, punch, slap, smack, strike, thump, whack.
n. belt, blow, box, clout, knock, punch, rap, slap, smack, swat, thump, whack.

culminate *v.* climax, close, conclude, consummate, end (up), finish, terminate.
antonyms begin, start.

culmination *n.* climax, completion, conclusion, consummation, crown, finale, height, peak, perfection, pinnacle, summit, top.
antonyms beginning, start.

culprit *n.* criminal, delinquent, felon, guilty party, law-breaker, miscreant, offender, sinner, transgressor, wrong-doer.

cult *n.* **1** body, clique, denomination, party, school, sect. **2** craze, fad.

cultivate *v.* **1** farm, fertilise, harvest, plant, plough, tend, till, work. **2** aid, cherish, develop, encourage, enrich, foster, further, help, improve, nurture, polish, prepare, promote, refine, support, train, work on.
antonym **2** neglect.

cultural *adj.* aesthetic, artistic, arty, civilising, developmental, edifying, educational, elevating, enlightening, enriching, humanising, liberal.

culture *n.* **1** civilisation, customs, lifestyle, mores, society, the arts. **2** breeding, cultivation, education, enlightenment, gentility, politeness, refinement, taste, urbanity. **3** agriculture, agronomy, farming, husbandry, tending.

culvert *n.* channel, conduit, drain, duct, gutter, sewer, watercourse.

cumbersome *adj.* awkward, bulky, burdensome, clumsy, embarrassing, heavy, inconvenient, onerous, oppressive, unmanageable, unwieldy, weighty.
antonyms convenient, manageable.

cumulative *adj.* accumulative, additive, aggregate, collective, increasing.

cunning *adj.* artful, astute, canny, crafty, deceitful, deep, deft, devious, dexterous, guileful, imaginative, ingenious, knowing, sharp, shrewd, skilful, subtle, tricky, wily.
antonyms gullible, ingenuous, naïve.
n. adroitness, artfulness, astuteness, cleverness, craftiness, deceitfulness, deviousness, guile, ingenuity, policy, sharpness, shrewdness, slyness, trickery.
antonyms openness, simplicity.

cupboard *n.* cabinet, closet, locker, wardrobe.

curb *v.* bit, bridle, check, constrain, contain, control, hamper, hinder, impede, inhibit, moderate, muzzle, repress, restrain, restrict, retard, subdue, suppress.
antonyms encourage, foster, goad.
n. brake, bridle, check, control, deterrent, hamper, hobble, limitation, rein, restraint.

curdle *v.* clot, coagulate, condense, congeal, earn, ferment, sour, thicken, turn.

cure *v.* **1** alleviate, correct, ease, heal, help, mend, rehabilitate, relieve, remedy, restore. **2** dry, kipper, pickle, preserve, salt, smoke.
n. alleviation, antidote, corrective, healing, medicine, panacea, recovery, remedy, restorative, specific, treatment.

curio *n.* antique, bygone, curiosity, knick-knack, object of virtu, trinket.

curiosity *n.* **1** inquisitiveness, interest, nosiness, prying, snooping, trinket. **2** bygone, curio, knick-knack, novelty, objet d'art, rarity. **3** freak, oddity, phenomenon, spectacle.

curious *adj.* **1** enquiring, inquisitive, interested, meddlesome, nosy, prying, puzzling, questioning, snoopy. **2** bizarre, exotic, extraordinary, funny, mysterious, novel, odd, peculiar, quaint, queer, rare, strange, unconventional, unexpected, unique, unorthodox, unusual.
antonyms **1** indifferent, uninterested. **2** normal, ordinary, usual.

curl *v.* bend, coil, corkscrew, crimp, crimple, crinkle, crisp, curve, frizz, loop, meander, ripple, scroll, spiral, turn, twine, twirl, wind, wreathe, writhe.
antonym uncurl.
n. coil, kink, spiral, swirl, tress, twist, whorl.

curly *adj.* crimped, crimpy, crinkly, curled, curling, frizzy, fuzzy, kinky, spiralled, waved, wavy, whorled, winding.
antonym straight.

currency *n.* **1** bills, coinage, coins, legal tender, money, notes. **2** acceptance, circulation, exposure, popularity, prevalence, publicity, vogue.

current *adj.* accepted, circulating, common, contemporary, customary, fashionable, general, on-going, popular, present, present-day, prevailing, prevalent, reigning, trendy, up-to-date, up-to-the-minute, widespread.
antonyms antiquated, obsolete, old-fashioned.
n. atmosphere, course, draught, drift, feeling, flow, inclination, jet, juice, mood, progression, river, stream, tendency, tide, trend, undercurrent.

curse *n.* **1** blasphemy, expletive, oath, obscenity, swearing, swear-word. **2** condemnation, denunciation. **3** affliction, anathema, bane, burden, calamity, disaster, evil, imprecation, jinx, misfortune, ordeal, plague, scourge, torment, tribulation, trouble, vexation, woe.
antonyms **3** advantage, blessing.
v. **1** blaspheme, swear. **2** damn, denounce, fulminate. **3** afflict, blight, burden, destroy, plague, scourge, torment, trouble, vex.
antonym **2** bless.

curtail *v.* abbreviate, abridge, contract, cut, decrease, lessen, pare, reduce, restrict, shorten, trim, truncate.
antonyms extend, lengthen, prolong.

curtain *n.* backdrop, drapery, hanging, tapestry, wall-hanging.

curve *v.* arc, arch, bend, bow, coil, hook, inflect, spiral, swerve, turn, twist, wind.
n. arc, bend, camber, curvature, loop, trajectory, turn.

curved *adj.* arched, bent, bowed, crooked, humped, rounded, sinuous, sweeping, turned, twisted.
antonym straight.

cushion *n.* bolster, buffer, hassock, headrest, pad, pillow, shock absorber, squab.
v. allay, bolster, buttress, dampen, deaden, lessen, mitigate, muffle, protect, soften, stifle, support, suppress.

custodian *n.* caretaker, curator, guardian, keeper, overseer, protector, superintendent, warden, warder, watch-dog, watchman.

custody *n.* **1** care, charge, custodianship, guardianship, keeping, possession, preservation, protection, safe-keeping, supervision, trusteeship, watch. **2** arrest, confinement, detention, imprisonment, incarceration.

custom *n.* convention, etiquette, form, formality, habit, manner, observance, observation, policy, practice, procedure, ritual, routine, rule, style, tradition, usage, use, way.

customary *adj.* accepted, acknowledged, common, confirmed, conventional, established, everyday, familiar, fashionable, favourite, general, normal, ordinary, popular, prevailing, regular, routine, traditional, usual.
antonyms occasional, rare, unusual.

customer *n.* buyer, client, consumer, patron, prospect, punter, purchaser, regular, shopper.

cut *v.* **1** bisect, carve, chisel, chop, clip, crop, dissect, divide, dock, engrave, excise, form, gash, hack, hew, incise, lacerate, lop, mow, nick, pare, part, penetrate, pierce, prune, score, sculpt, sever, shape, shave, shear, slash, slice, slit, split, trim, wound. **2** abbreviate, abridge, condense, curtail, decrease, delete, edit, lower, précis, reduce, shorten. **3** avoid, cold-shoulder, ignore, insult, rebuff, slight, snub, spurn.
n. **1** gash, incision, laceration, nick, rip, slash, slit, wound. **2** cutback, decrease, economy, lowering, reduction, saving. **3** percentage, portion, rake-off, share, slice.
cut back check, crop, curb, decrease, economise, lessen, lower, prune, reduce, slash, trim.
cut down decrease, diminish, fell, hew, lessen, level, lop, lower, reduce.
cut in interject, interpose, interrupt, intervene, intrude.
cut off **1** block, disconnect, excise, intercept, interrupt, intersect, isolate, obstruct, separate, sever. **2** discontinue, disinherit, disown, end, halt, stop, suspend.
cut out cease, contrive, debar, delete, eliminate, excise, exclude, extract, remove, sever, shape, stop, supersede, supplant.
cut out for adapted, adequate, competent, designed, equipped, fitted, made, qualified, right, suitable, suited.
cut up carve, chop, dice, divide, injure, knife, mince, slash, slice, wound.

cutback *n.* cut, decrease, economy, lessening, reduction, retrenchment.

cut-price *adj.* bargain, cheap, cut-rate, low-priced, reduced, sale.

cut-throat *adj.* barbarous, bloodthirsty, bloody, brutal, competitive, cruel, dog-eat-dog, ferocious, fierce, relentless, ruthless, savage, unprincipled, vicious, violent.

cutting *adj.* acid, biting, bitter, caustic, chill, incisive, keen, malicious, penetrating, piercing, pointed, raw, sarcastic, scathing, severe, sharp, stinging, wounding.
antonyms flattering, kind.
n. bit, cleavage, clipping, piece, scion, scission, slice.

cycle *n.* aeon, age, circle, epoch, era, period, phase, revolution, rotation, round, sequence.

cylinder *n.* barrel, bobbin, column, drum, reel, spindle, spool.

cynic *n.* doubter, killjoy, knocker, pessimist, sceptic, scoffer, spoilsport.

cynical *adj.* contemptuous, derisive, distrustful, ironic, mocking, mordant, pessimistic, sarcastic, sardonic, sceptical, scoffing, scornful, sharp-tongued, sneering.

cynicism *n.* disbelief, distrust, doubt, pessimism, sarcasm, scepticism.

D

dab *v.* daub, pat, swab, tap, touch, wipe.
n. bit, dollop, drop, fleck, flick, pat, peck, smear, smudge, speck, spot, stroke, tap, touch, trace.
dabble *v.* **1** dally, potter, tinker, toy, trifle. **2** moisten, paddle, splash, sprinkle, wet.
dabbler *n.* amateur, potterer, tinkerer, trifler.
antonyms connoisseur, expert, professional.
daft *adj.* absurd, berserk, crazy, dotty, foolish, giddy, hysterical, idiotic, inane, infatuated, insane, lunatic, mad, mental, silly, simple, stupid.
antonyms bright, sane, sensible.
daily *adj.* common, commonplace, customary, day-to-day, everyday, normal, ordinary, regular, routine.
dainty *adj.* charming, delectable, delicate, delicious, dinky, elegant, exquisite, fastidious, fine, fussy, graceful, neat, nice, particular, petite, pretty, refined, scrupulous, tasty, tender.
antonyms clumsy, gross.
dam *n.* barrage, barrier, blockage, embankment, hindrance, obstruction, wall.
v. barricade, block, check, choke, confine, obstruct, restrict, staunch, stem.
damage *n.* destruction, detriment, devastation, harm, hurt, impairment, injury, loss, mischief, mutilation, scathe, suffering.
antonym repair.
v. deface, harm, hurt, impair, incapacitate, injure, mar, mutilate, play havoc with, ruin, spoil, tamper with, weaken, wreck.
antonyms fix, mend, repair.
damages *n.* compensation, fine, indemnity, reimbursement, reparation, satisfaction.
damn *v.* abuse, blaspheme, blast, castigate, censure, condemn, criticise, curse, denounce, denunciate, doom, execrate, imprecate, revile, sentence, slam, slate, swear.
antonym bless.
damnation *n.* anathema, ban, condemnation, denunciation, doom, excommunication, perdition.
damning *adj.* condemnatory, damnatory, dooming, implicative, incriminating.
damp *n.* clamminess, dampness, dankness, dew, drizzle, fog, humidity, mist, moisture, muzziness, vapour, wet.
antonym dryness.
adj. clammy, dewy, dripping, drizzly, humid, misty, moist, muggish, muggy, soggy, sopping, wet.
antonyms arid, dry.
dampen *v.* **1** check, dash, deaden, decrease, depress, deter, diminish, discourage, dishearten, dismay, dull, lessen, moderate, muffle, reduce, restrain, smother, stifle. **2** moisten, spray, wet.
antonyms **1** encourage. **2** dry.
dance *v.* caper, frolic, gambol, hoof it, hop, jig, juke, prance, rock, skip, spin, stomp, sway, swing, whirl.
n. ball, hop, knees-up, shindig, social.
dancer *n.* ballerina, ballet dancer, prima ballerina, tap-dancer.
dandy *n.* beau, fop, popinjay, swell.
adj. excellent, fine, first-rate, great, splendid.
danger *n.* endangerment, hazard, insecurity, jeopardy, liability, menace, peril, precariousness, risk, threat, trouble, venture, vulnerability.
antonyms safety, security.
dangerous *adj.* alarming, breakneck, critical, daring, exposed, grave, hairy, hazardous, insecure, menacing, nasty, perilous, precarious, reckless, risky, serious, severe, threatening, treacherous, unsafe, vulnerable.
antonyms harmless, safe, secure.
dangle *v.* droop, flap, flaunt, flourish, hang, lure, sway, swing, tantalise, tempt, trail, wave.
dapper *adj.* active, brisk, chic, dainty, neat, nimble, smart, spruce, spry, stylish, trim, well-dressed, well-groomed.
antonyms dishevelled, dowdy, scruffy, shabby, sloppy.
dappled *adj.* bespeckled, checkered, dotted, flecked, freckled, mottled, piebald, speckled, spotted, stippled, variegated.
dare *v.* adventure, brave, challenge, defy, endanger, gamble, goad, hazard, presume, provoke, risk, stake, taunt, venture.
n. challenge, gauntlet, provocation, taunt.
daredevil *n.* adventurer, desperado, madcap, stuntman.
antonym coward.
daring *adj.* adventurous, audacious, bold, brave, dauntless, fearless, impulsive, intrepid, plucky, rash, reckless, valiant.
antonyms afraid, cautious, timid.
n. audacity, boldness, bravery, courage, defiance, fearlessness, gall, grit, guts, intrepidity, nerve, pluck, prowess, rashness, spirit.
antonyms caution, cowardice, timidity.
dark *adj.* **1** black, cloudy, dim, dingy, dusky, ebony, murky, overcast, shadowy, unilluminated, unlit. **2** bleak, cheerless, dismal, drab, forbidding, gloomy, grim, menacing, morose, mournful, ominous, sinister, sombre. **3** abstruse, cryptic, enigmatic, hidden, mysterious, obscure, occult, secret, unintelligible.
antonyms **1** light. **2** bright, happy. **3** comprehen-

sible.
n. concealment, darkness, dimness, dusk, evening, gloom, murk, murkiness, night, nightfall, night-time, obscurity, secrecy, twilight.
antonyms brightness, light.

darken *v.* blacken, cloud (over), deepen, deject, depress, dim, eclipse, obscure, overshadow, sadden, shadow.
antonyms brighten, lighten.

darling *n.* beloved, blue-eyed boy, dear, dearest, favourite, lady-love, love, pet, sweetheart.
adj. adored, beloved, cherished, dear, precious, treasured.

dart *v.* bound, dash, flash, fling, flit, fly, hurl, launch, propel, race, run, rush, scoot, send, shoot, sling, spring, sprint, start, tear, throw, whistle, whiz.
n. arrow, barb, bolt, flight, shaft.

dash *v.* **1** bolt, dart, fly, hurry, race, run, rush, sprint, tear. **2** crash, fling, hurl, slam, throw. **3** blight, confound, dampen, destroy, disappoint, discourage, foil, frustrate, ruin, shatter, smash, spoil.
n. **1** bit, drop, flavour, hint, little, pinch, smack, soupçon, suggestion, tinge, touch. **2** bolt, dart, race, run, rush, sprint, spurt.

dashing *adj.* bold, daring, dazzling, debonair, elegant, exuberant, flamboyant, gallant, impressive, jaunty, lively, plucky, showy, smart, spirited, sporty, stylish.
antonyms dowdy, drab.

data *n.* details, documents, facts, figures, info, information, input, materials, statistics.

date *n.* **1** age, epoch, era, period, point, point in time, stage, time. **2** appointment, assignation, engagement, escort, friend, meeting, partner, rendezvous, steady.
out-of-date *adj.* antiquated, archaic, dated, obsolescent, obsolete, old-fashioned, outdated, outmoded, passé, superseded, unfashionable.
antonyms fashionable, modern, new.
up-to-date *adj.* contemporary, current, fashionable, modern.
antonyms dated, old-fashioned.

dauntless *adj.* bold, brave, courageous, daring, fearless, gallant, heroic, indomitable, intrepid, lion-hearted, plucky, resolute, undaunted, unflinching, valiant.
antonyms cowardly, discouraged, disheartened.

dawdle *v.* dally, delay, dilly-dally, fiddle, fritter, hang about, idle, lag, loaf, loiter, lounge, potter, shilly-shally, trail.
antonym hurry.

dawn *n.* **1** cock-crow(ing), dawning, daybreak, daylight, morning, sunrise. **2** advent, beginning, birth, emergence, onset, origin, start.
antonyms **1** dusk, sunset.
v. appear, begin, break, brighten, develop, emerge, gleam, glimmer, hit, initiate, lighten, occur, open, originate, register, rise, strike, unfold.

day *n.* age, date, daylight, daytime, epoch, era, generation, height, period, time, young days, youth.
antonym night.
day after day continually, endlessly, forever, monotonously, perpetually, persistently, regularly, relentlessly.
day by day daily, gradually, progressively, slowly but surely, steadily.

daydream *n.* castles in Spain, castles in the air, dream, fantasy, figment, fond hope, imagining, musing, phantasm, pipe dream, reverie, vision, wish.
v. dream, fancy, fantasise, hallucinate, imagine, muse.

daze *v.* amaze, astonish, astound, baffle, bewilder, blind, confuse, dazzle, dumbfound, flabbergast, numb, paralyse, perplex, shock, stagger, startle, stun, stupefy, surprise.
n. bewilderment, confusion, distraction, shock, stupor, trance.

dazzle *v.* amaze, astonish, awe, bedazzle, bewitch, blind, blur, confuse, daze, fascinate, hypnotise, impress, overawe, overpower, overwhelm, scintillate, sparkle, stupefy.
n. brilliance, glare, glitter, magnificence, scintillation, sparkle, splendour.

dead *adj.* **1** breathless, deceased, defunct, departed, extinct, gone, inanimate, late, lifeless. **2** apathetic, cold, dull, frigid, indifferent, insensitive, lukewarm, numb, still, torpid, unresponsive. **3** dead-beat, exhausted, tired, worn out. **4** absolute, complete, downright, entire, outright, perfect, thorough, total, unqualified, utter.
antonyms **1** alive. **2** lively. **3** refreshed.

deaden *v.* abate, allay, alleviate, anaesthetise, benumb, blunt, check, cushion, damp, dampen, desensitise, diminish, hush, impair, lessen, muffle, mute, numb, paralyse, quieten, reduce, smother, stifle, suppress, weaken.
antonym enliven.

deadlock *n.* halt, impasse, stalemate, standstill.

deadly *adj.* **1** dangerous, destructive, fatal, lethal, malignant, mortal, murderous, pernicious, savage, venomous. **2** boring, dull, monotonous, tedious, uninteresting. **3** devastating, effective, true, unerring.
antonyms **1** harmless. **2** exciting.

deadpan *adj.* blank, dispassionate, empty, expressionless, impassive, inexpressive, inscrutable, poker-faced, straight-faced, unexpressive.

deaf *adj.* hard of hearing, heedless, indifferent, oblivious, stone-deaf, unconcerned, unmindful, unmoved.
antonyms aware, conscious.

deafening *adj.* booming, ear-splitting, piercing, resounding, ringing, roaring, thunderous.
antonym quiet.

deal *v.* allot, apportion, assign, bargain, bestow, dispense, distribute, divide, dole out, give, mete out, negotiate, reward, sell, share, stock, trade, traffic, treat.
n. **1** amount, degree, extent, portion, quantity, share. **2** agreement, bargain, buy, contract, pact, transaction, understanding. **3** distribution, hand, round.
deal with attend to, concern, consider, cope

with, handle, manage, oversee, see to, treat.
dealer *n.* marketer, merchandiser, merchant, trader, tradesman, wholesaler.
dealings *n.* business, commerce, trade, traffic, transactions.
dear *adj.* **1** beloved, cherished, close, darling, esteemed, familiar, favourite, intimate, loved, precious, respected, treasured, valued. **2** costly, expensive, high-priced, overpriced, pric(e)y.
antonyms **1** disliked, hated. **2** cheap.
n. angel, beloved, darling, loved one, precious, treasure.
dearly *adv.* affectionately, devotedly, extremely, fondly, greatly, lovingly, profoundly, tenderly.
dearth *n.* absence, barrenness, deficiency, famine, inadequacy, insufficiency, lack, need, paucity, poverty, scantiness, scarcity, shortage, sparsity, want.
antonyms abundance, excess.
death *n.* annihilation, bane, bereavement, cessation, curtains, decease, demise, departure, destruction, dissolution, downfall, dying, end, eradication, exit, expiration, extermination, extinction, fatality, finish, loss, obliteration, passing, release, ruin, undoing.
antonyms birth, life.
deathly *adj.* ashen, deadly, deathlike, fatal, ghastly, grim, haggard, intense, mortal, pale, pallid, terrible, wan.
debase *v.* abase, adulterate, allay, cheapen, contaminate, corrupt, defile, degrade, demean, devalue, diminish, disgrace, dishonour, humble, humiliate, impair, lower, pollute, reduce, shame, taint.
antonyms elevate, upgrade.
debatable *adj.* arguable, borderline, contentious, contestable, controversial, disputable, doubtful, dubious, moot, open to question, problematical, questionable, uncertain, undecided, unsettled.
antonyms certain, incontrovertible, questionable.
debate *v.* **1** argue, contend, discuss, dispute, question, wrangle. **2** consider, deliberate, meditate on, mull over, ponder, reflect, weigh.
n. argument, consideration, contention, controversy, deliberation, discussion, disputation, dispute, polemic, reflection.
debauchery *n.* carousal, decadence, depravity, dissipation, dissoluteness, excess, gluttony, immorality, indulgence, intemperance, lewdness, licentiousness, lust, orgy, overindulgence, revel, riot, wantonness.
debilitate *v.* enervate, exhaust, impair, incapacitate, relax, sap, undermine, unman, weaken, wear out.
antonyms energise, invigorate, strengthen.
debility *n.* enervation, enfeeblement, exhaustion, faintness, feebleness, frailty, incapacity, infirmity, languor, malaise, weakness.
antonyms strength, vigour.
debris *n.* bits, brash, drift, duff, fragments, litter, moraine, pieces, remains, rubbish, rubble, ruins, sweepings, trash, waste, wreck, wreckage.
debt *n.* arrears, bill, claim, commitment, debit, due, duty, indebtedness, liability, obligation, score.
antonyms asset, credit.
debtor *n.* bankrupt, borrower, defaulter, insolvent, mortgagor.
antonym creditor.
debut *n.* appearance, beginning, bow, entrance, inauguration, initiation, introduction, launching, première, presentation.
decadence *n.* corruption, debasement, decadency, decay, decline, degeneration, deterioration, dissipation, dissolution, fall, perversion.
antonyms flourishing, rise.
decadent *adj.* corrupt, debased, debauched, decaying, declining, degenerate, degraded, depraved, dissolute, immoral, self-indulgent.
antonym moral.
decamp *v.* abscond, bolt, desert, do a bunk, escape, flee, flit, fly, make off, run away, scarper, skedaddle.
decapitate *v.* behead, execute, guillotine.
decay *v.* canker, corrode, crumble, decline, decompose, degenerate, deteriorate, disintegrate, dissolve, dwindle, mortify, perish, rot, shrivel, sink, spoil, waste away, wear away, wither.
antonyms flourish, grow, ripen.
n. collapse, decadence, decline, decomposition, degeneration, deterioration, disintegration, dying, fading, failing, perishing, rot, rotting, wasting, withering.
decease *n.* death, demise, departure, dissolution, dying, passing, release.
deceased *adj.* dead, defunct, departed, expired, extinct, finished, former, gone, late, lost.
n. dead, departed.
deceit *n.* abuse, artifice, cheating, craftiness, cunning, deception, double-dealing, duplicity, fake, feint, fraud, fraudulence, guile, hypocrisy, imposition, misrepresentation, phenakism, pretence, ruse, sham, shift, slyness, stratagem, subterfuge, swindle, treachery, trickery, underhandedness, wile.
antonyms frankness, honesty, openness.
deceitful *adj.* counterfeit, crafty, deceiving, deceptive, designing, dishonest, double-dealing, duplicitous, false, fraudulent, guileful, hypocritical, illusory, insincere, knavish, prestigious, sneaky, treacherous, tricky, two-faced, underhand, untrustworthy.
antonyms honest, open, trustworthy.
deceive *v.* abuse, bamboozle, befool, beguile, betray, camouflage, cheat, delude, disappoint, dissemble, double-cross, dupe, ensnare, fool, gag, gull, have on, hoax, hoodwink, impose upon, lead on, mislead, outwit, seel, swindle, take for a ride, take in, trick, two-time.
antonym enlighten.
deceiver *n.* abuser, betrayer, cheat, con man, crook, deluder, diddler, dissembler, dissimulator, double-dealer, fake, fraud, hypocrite, impostor, inveigler, pretender, sharper, swindler, trickster.

decency *n.* civility, correctness, courtesy, decorum, etiquette, fitness, helpfulness, manners, modesty, propriety, respectability.
antonyms discourtesy, impropriety, indecency.

decent *adj.* acceptable, adequate, appropriate, becoming, befitting, chaste, comely, competent, courteous, decorous, delicate, fair, fit, fitting, generous, gracious, helpful, kind, modest, nice, obliging, polite, presentable, proper, pure, reasonable, respectable, satisfactory, seemly, sufficient, suitable, thoughtful, tolerable.
antonyms disobliging, indecent.

decentralisation *n.* delegation, development, devolution.
antonym centralisation.

deception *n.* artifice, bluff, cheat, craftiness, cunning, deceit, deceptiveness, decoy, dissembling, duplicity, feint, fraud, fraudulence, guile, hoax, hypocrisy, illusion, imposition, imposture, insincerity, leg-pull, lie, pretence, ruse, sham, snare, stratagem, subterfuge, treachery, trick, wile.
antonyms artlessness, honesty, openness.

deceptive *adj.* ambiguous, catchy, dishonest, fake, fallacious, false, fraudulent, illusive, illusory, misleading, mock, specious, spurious, unreliable.
antonyms artless, genuine, open.

decide *v.* adjudicate, choose, conclude, decree, determine, elect, end, fix, judge, opt, purpose, reach a decision, resolve, settle.

decided *adj.* absolute, categorical, certain, clear-cut, decisive, definite, deliberate, determined, distinct, emphatic, firm, forthright, indisputable, marked, positive, resolute, unambiguous, undeniable, undisputed, unhesitating, unmistakable, unquestionable.
antonyms indecisive, irresolute, undecided.

decipher *v.* construe, crack, decode, deduce, explain, figure out, interpret, make out, read, solve, transliterate, understand, unfold, unravel, unscramble.
antonym encode.

decision *n.* arbitration, conclusion, decisiveness, determination, finding, firmness, judgement, outcome, purpose, resolve, result, ruling, settlement, verdict.

decisive *adj.* absolute, conclusive, critical, crucial, crunch, decided, definite, definitive, determined, fateful, final, firm, forceful, forthright, incisive, influential, momentous, positive, resolute, significant, strong-minded, supreme.
antonyms inconclusive, indecisive, insignificant.

declaration *n.* acknowledgement, affirmation, announcement, assertion, attestation, disclosure, edict, manifesto, notification, proclamation, profession, promulgation, pronouncement, revelation, statement, testimony.

declare *v.* affirm, announce, assert, attest, aver, certify, claim, confess, confirm, convey, disclose, maintain, manifest, proclaim, profess, pronounce, reveal, show, state, swear, testify, validate, witness.

decline *v.* **1** avoid, balk, deny, forgo, refuse, reject. **2** decrease, diminish, dwindle, fall, lessen, sink, wane. **3** decay, degenerate, deteriorate, worsen. **4** descend, dip, sink, slant, slope.
antonyms **3** improve. **4** rise.
n. **1** abatement, decay, degeneration, deterioration, deviation, diminution, downturn, dwindling, failing, falling-off, lessening, recession, slump, weakening, worsening. **2** declination, declivity, descent, deviation, dip, divergence, hill, incline, slope.
antonyms **1** improvement. **2** rise.

decode *v.* decipher, interpret, translate, transliterate, uncipher, unscramble.
antonym encode.

decompose *v.* break down, break up, crumble, decay, disintegrate, dissolve, distil, fester, putrefy, rot, separate, spoil.

decomposition *n.* breakdown, corruption, decay, disintegration, dissolution, division, electrolysis, putrefaction, rot.

decontaminate *v.* clean, disinfect, freshen, fumigate, purge, purify.
antonyms contaminate, dirty, pollute.

décor *n.* colour-scheme, decoration, furnishings, ornamentation, scenery.

decorate *v.* **1** adorn, beautify, colour, deck, do up, embellish, enrich, grace, ornament, paint, paper, prettify, refurbish, renovate, tart up, trick out, trim, wallpaper. **2** bemedal, cite, crown, garland, honour.

decoration *n.* **1** adornment, bauble, beautification, elaboration, embellishment, enrichment, flourish, frill, garnish, ornament, ornamentation, scroll, trimming. **2** award, badge, colours, crown, emblem, garland, garter, laurel, medal, order, ribbon, star.

decorative *adj.* adorning, beautifying, embellishing, enhancing, fancy, non-functional, ornamental, ornate, pretty, rococo, superfluous.
antonyms plain, ugly.

decorum *n.* behaviour, breeding, decency, deportment, dignity, etiquette, grace, manners, modesty, politeness, protocol, respectability, restraint, seemliness.
antonyms bad manners, impropriety, indecorum.

decoy *n.* attraction, bait, ensnarement, enticement, inducement, lure, pretence, trap.
v. allure, attract, bait, deceive, draw, ensnare, entice, entrap, lead, lure, seduce, tempt.

decrease *v.* abate, contract, curtail, cut down, decline, diminish, drop, dwindle, ease, fall off, lessen, lower, peter out, reduce, shrink, slacken, slim, subside, taper, wane.
antonym increase.
n. abatement, contraction, cutback, decline, diminution, downturn, dwindling, ebb, falling-off, lessening, loss, reduction, shrinkage, step-down, subsidence.
antonym increase.

decree *n.* act, command, edict, enactment, interlocution, law, mandate, order, ordinance, precept, proclamation, regulation, ruling, statute.

v. command, decide, determine, dictate, enact, lay down, ordain, order, prescribe, proclaim, pronounce, rule.

decrepit *adj.* aged, antiquated, broken-down, debilitated, dilapidated, doddery, feeble, frail, infirm, rickety, run-down, tumble-down, worn-out.
antonyms fit, well-cared-for, youthful.

decry *v.* blame, censure, condemn, criticise, cry down, declaim against, denounce, depreciate, detract, devalue, discredit, disparage, rail against, run down.
antonyms appreciate, praise, value.

dedicate *v.* address, assign, bless, commit, consecrate, devote, give over to, hallow, inscribe, offer, pledge, present, sacrifice, sanctify, set apart, surrender.

dedicated *adj.* committed, devoted, enthusiastic, given over to, purposeful, single-hearted, single-minded, whole-hearted, zealous.
antonyms apathetic, uncommitted.

dedication *n.* **1** adherence, allegiance, attachment, commitment, devotion, faithfulness, loyalty, self-sacrifice, single-mindedness, whole-heartedness. **2** address, consecration, hallowing, inscription, presentation.
antonym **1** apathy.

deduce *v.* conclude, derive, draw, gather, glean, infer, reason, surmise, understand.

deduct *v.* decrease by, knock off, reduce by, remove, subtract, take away, withdraw.
antonym add.

deduction *n.* **1** assumption, conclusion, corollary, finding, inference, reasoning, result. **2** abatement, allowance, decrease, diminution, discount, reduction, subtraction, withdrawal.
antonyms **2** addition, increase.

deed *n.* **1** achievement, act, action, exploit, fact, feat, performance, reality, truth. **2** contract, document, indenture, record, title, transaction.

deem *v.* account, believe, conceive, consider, esteem, estimate, hold, imagine, judge, reckon, regard, suppose, think.

deep *adj.* **1** bottomless, dark, fathomless, hidden, immersed, profound, unplumbed. **2** abstruse, devious, difficult, esoteric, mysterious, obscure. **3** astute, discerning, learned, penetrating, profound, wise. **4** extreme, grave, intense, serious.
antonyms **1** open, shallow. **2** clear, distinct, open, plain. **3** superficial. **4** light.
n. briny, drink, high seas, main, ocean, sea.

deepen *v.* grow, hollow, increase, intensify, magnify, reinforce, scoop out, strengthen.

deep-seated *adj.* confirmed, deep, deep-rooted, entrenched, fixed, ingrained, settled, subconscious, unconscious.
antonyms eradicable, temporary.

deer *n.* buck, doe, hart, reindeer, roe, stag.

deface *v.* blemish, damage, deform, destroy, disfigure, impair, injure, mar, mutilate, obliterate, spoil, sully, tarnish, vandalise.
antonym repair.

defamation *n.* aspersion, disparagement, innuendo, libel, scandal, slander, slur, smear, vilification.
antonyms commendation, praise.

defamatory *adj.* abusive, denigrating, derogatory, disparaging, injurious, insulting, libellous, pejorative, slanderous, vilifying.
antonyms appreciative, complimentary.

defame *v.* blacken, denigrate, discredit, disgrace, dishonour, disparage, libel, malign, slander, smear, stigmatise, vilify, vituperate.
antonyms compliment, praise.

default *n.* absence, defect, deficiency, failure, fault, lack, lapse, neglect, non-payment, omission, want.
v. backslide, defraud, dodge, evade, fail, neglect, swindle, welsh.

defaulter *n.* non-payer, offender.

defeat *v.* baffle, balk, beat, checkmate, confound, conquer, disappoint, foil, frustrate, get the better of, outbargain, overpower, overthrow, overwhelm, quell, repel, rout, ruin, subdue, subjugate, thump, thwart, vanquish, vote down.
n. beating, conquest, disappointment, failure, frustration, overthrow, rebuff, repulse, reverse, rout, setback, thwarting, vanquishment.

defeatist *n.* futilitarian, pessimist, prophet of doom, quitter.
antonym optimist.
adj. despairing, despondent, fatalistic, gloomy, helpless, hopeless, pessimistic, resigned.
antonym optimistic.

defect *n.* absence, blemish, bug, deficiency, error, failing, fault, flaw, frailty, imperfection, inadequacy, lack, mistake, shortcoming, spot, taint, want, weakness.
v. apostatise, break faith, desert, rebel, renegue, revolt.

defective *adj.* abnormal, broken, deficient, faulty, flawed, imperfect, out of order, short, subnormal.
antonyms in order, normal, operative.

defence *n.* **1** barricade, bastion, bulwark, buttress, cover, deterrence, fortification, guard, immunity, munition, protection, rampart, resistance, safeguard, security, shelter, shield. **2** alibi, argument, case, declaration, denial, excuse, exoneration, explanation, justification, plea, pleading, testimony, vindication.
antonyms **1** assault, attack, raid.

defenceless *adj.* endangered, exposed, helpless, powerless, unarmed, undefended, unguarded, unprotected, vulnerable.
antonyms guarded, protected.

defend *v.* assert, champion, contest, cover, endorse, fortify, guard, justify, plead, preserve, protect, safeguard, screen, secure, shelter, shield, speak up for, stand by, stand up for, support, sustain, uphold, vindicate, watch over.
antonyms attack, invade.

defendant *n.* accused, defender, litigant, offender, prisoner, respondent.

defender *n.* advocate, bodyguard, champion, counsel, escort, guard, patron, protector, sponsor, supporter, vindicator.

antonyms attacker, invader.
defensive *adj.* apologetic, averting, cautious, defending, opposing, protective, safeguarding, self-justifying, wary, watchful.
defer[1] *v.* adjourn, delay, hold over, postpone, procrastinate, prorogue, protract, put off, shelve, suspend, waive.
defer[2] *v.* accede, bow, capitulate, comply, give way, respect, submit, yield.
deference *n.* civility, consideration, courtesy, esteem, honour, obedience, politeness, regard, respect, reverence, submission, submissiveness, thoughtfulness, veneration, yielding.
deferential *adj.* civil, considerate, courteous, dutiful, ingratiating, obedient, polite, respectful, reverential, submissive.
antonyms arrogant, immodest.
defiance *n.* challenge, confrontation, contempt, disobedience, disregard, insolence, insubordination, opposition, provocation, rebelliousness, spite.
antonyms acquiescence, compliance, submissiveness.
defiant *adj.* aggressive, audacious, bold, challenging, contumacious, daring, disobedient, insolent, insubordinate, intransigent, obstinate, provocative, rebellious, unco-operative.
antonyms acquiescent, compliant, submissive.
deficiency *n.* absence, dearth, defect, deficit, failing, fault, flaw, frailty, imperfection, inadequacy, insufficiency, lack, scantiness, scarcity, shortage, shortcoming, want, weakness.
antonyms abundance, excess, superfluity.
deficient *adj.* defective, faulty, flawed, impaired, imperfect, inadequate, incomplete, inferior, insufficient, lacking, meagre, scanty, scarce, short, skimpy, unsatisfactory, wanting, weak.
antonyms excessive, superfluous.
deficit *n.* arrears, default, deficiency, lack, loss, shortage, shortfall.
antonym excess.
defile *v.* abuse, contaminate, corrupt, debase, degrade, desecrate, disgrace, dishonour, molest, pollute, profane, soil, stain, sully, taint, tarnish, violate.
antonym cleanse.
definable *adj.* ascertainable, definite, describable, perceptible, specific.
antonym indefinable.
define *v.* bound, characterise, delimit, demarcate, describe, designate, detail, determine, explain, expound, interpret, limit, mark out, outline, specify, spell out.
definite *adj.* assured, certain, clear, clear-cut, decided, determined, exact, explicit, express, fixed, guaranteed, marked, obvious, particular, positive, precise, settled, specific, sure.
antonyms indefinite, vague.
definitely *adv.* absolutely, categorically, certainly, clearly, doubtless, doubtlessly, easily, finally, indeed, obviously, plainly, positively, surely, undeniably, unmistakably, unquestionably.
definition *n.* **1** clarification, delimitation, delineation, demarcation, description, determination, elucidation, explanation, exposition, interpretation. **2** clarity, clearness, contrast, distinctness, focus, precision, sharpness.
definitive *adj.* absolute, authoritative, complete, conclusive, correct, decisive, exact, exhaustive, final, perfect, reliable, standard, ultimate.
antonym interim.
deflate *v.* **1** collapse, contract, dash, debunk, disconcert, dispirit, empty, exhaust, flatten, humble, humiliate, mortify, press, puncture, put down, shrink, squash, squeeze, void. **2** decrease, depreciate, depress, devalue, diminish, lessen, lower, reduce.
antonyms **1** expand, inflate. **2** boost, increase.
deflect *v.* avert, bend, deviate, diverge, glance off, ricochet, sidetrack, swerve, turn (aside), twist, veer, wind.
deflection *n.* aberration, bend, deviation, divergence, drift, refraction, swerve, turning, veer.
deform *v.* corrupt, disfigure, distort, mar, pervert, ruin, spoil, twist, warp.
deformed *adj.* bent, buckled, contorted, corrupted, crippled, crooked, defaced, disfigured, distorted, maimed, mangled, marred, misshapen, mutilated, perverted, ruined, spoilt, twisted, warped.
deformity *n.* abnormality, corruption, defect, depravity, disfigurement, distortion, irregularity, malformation, misfeature, misproportion, misshapenness, ugliness.
defraud *v.* beguile, cheat, con, deceive, delude, diddle, do, dupe, embezzle, fleece, outwit, rip off, rob, sting, swindle, trick.
deft *adj.* able, adept, adroit, agile, clever, dexterous, expert, feat, handy, neat, nifty, nimble, proficient, skilful.
antonyms awkward, clumsy.
defunct *adj.* dead, deceased, departed, expired, extinct, gone, inoperative, invalid, non-existent, obsolete.
antonyms alive, live, operative.
defy *v.* baffle, beat, brave, challenge, confront, dare, defeat, despise, disregard, elude, face, flout, foil, frustrate, provoke, repel, resist, scorn, spurn, thwart, withstand.
antonyms flinch, quail, yield.
degeneracy *n.* corruption, debasement, decadence, decay, decline, decrease, degradation, depravation, depravity, deterioration, dissoluteness, falling-off, immorality, inferiority, meanness, poorness.
antonyms improvement, morality, uprightness.
degenerate *adj.* base, corrupt, debased, decadent, degenerated, degraded, depraved, deteriorated, dissolute, fallen, immoral, low, mean, perverted.
antonyms moral, upright, virtuous.
v. age, decay, decline, decrease, deteriorate, fall off, lapse, regress, rot, sink, slip, worsen.
antonyms improve, progress.
degradation *n.* abasement, decadence, decline, degeneration, deterioration, disgrace, dishonour, downgrading, humiliation, ignominy

mortification, perversion, shame.
antonyms enhancement, virtue.

degrade *v.* abase, adulterate, cheapen, corrupt, debase, demean, depose, deprive, deteriorate, discredit, disgrace, disgrade, dishonour, humble, humiliate, impair, injure, lower, pervert, shame, weaken.
antonyms enhance, exalt, improve.

degree *n.* **1** class, grade, order, position, standing, status. **2** extent, intensity, level, measure, range, stage, standard, step. **3** level, limit, mark, unit.

dehydrate *v.* desiccate, drain, dry out, dry up, evaporate, parch.

deify *v.* elevate, ennoble, enthrone, exalt, extol, glorify, idealise, idolise, immortalise, venerate, worship.

dejected *adj.* cast down, crestfallen, depressed, despondent, disconsolate, disheartened, dismal, doleful, down, downcast, downhearted, gloomy, glum, low, melancholy, miserable, morose, sad, spiritless, wretched.
antonyms bright, happy, high-spirited.

dejection *n.* depression, despair, despondency, doldrums, downheartedness, dumps, gloom, gloominess, low spirits, melancholy, sadness, sorrow, unhappiness.
antonyms happiness, high spirits, liveliness.

delay *v.* check, dawdle, defer, detain, dilly-dally, drag, halt, hinder, hold back, hold up, impede, linger, loiter, obstruct, postpone, procrastinate, prolong, protract, put off, set back, shelve, stall, stop, suspend, tarry.
antonyms accelerate, expedite, hurry.
n. check, dawdling, deferment, detention, hindrance, hold-up, impediment, interruption, interval, lingering, obstruction, postponement, procrastination, setback, stay, stoppage, suspension, tarrying, wait.
antonyms hastening, hurry.

delectable *adj.* agreeable, appetising, charming, delicious, delightful, enjoyable, enticing, flavoursome, gratifying, inviting, luscious, lush, palatable, pleasant, pleasurable, satisfying, tasty.
antonyms horrid, nasty, unpleasant.

delegate *n.* agent, ambassador, commissioner, deputy, envoy, messenger, representative.
v. appoint, assign, authorise, charge, commission, consign, depute, designate, devolve, empower, entrust, give, hand over, name, nominate, pass on, transfer.

delegation *n.* commission, contingent, deputation, embassy, legation, mission.

delete *v.* blot out, cancel, cross out, dele, edit (out), efface, erase, obliterate, remove, rub out, strike (out).
antonyms add, include.

deliberate *v.* cogitate, consider, consult, debate, discuss, meditate, mull over, ponder, reflect, think, weigh.
adj. advised, calculated, careful, cautious, circumspect, conscious, considered, designed, heedful, intentional, measured, methodical, planned, ponderous, prearranged, premeditated, prudent, slow, studied, thoughtful, unhurried, wary, wilful, willed.
antonyms accidental, chance, unintentional.

deliberation *n.* calculation, care, carefulness, caution, circumspection, consideration, consultation, debate, discussion, forethought, meditation, prudence, purpose, reflection, rumination, speculation, study, thought, wariness.

delicacy *n.* **1** daintiness, discrimination, elegance, exquisiteness, fineness, finesse, lightness, luxury, niceness, nicety, precision, purity, refinement, sensitivity, subtlety, tact. **2** dainty, relish, savoury, sweetmeat, taste, titbit, treat.
antonyms **1** indelicacy, roughness, tactlessness.

delicate *adj.* **1** dainty, elegant, exquisite, fine, flimsy, fragile, graceful. **2** ailing, faint, frail, weak. **3** accurate, careful, discriminating, precise, scrupulous, sensitive, weak.
antonyms **1** clumsy, harsh, robust, strong. **2** healthy, strong.

delicious *adj.* agreeable, appetising, charming, choice, dainty, delectable, delightful, enjoyable, exquisite, luscious, mouthwatering, palatable, pleasant, savoury, tasty.
antonyms unpalatable, unpleasant.

delight *n.* bliss, ecstasy, enjoyment, gladness, gratification, happiness, joy, jubilation, pleasure, rapture, transport.
antonyms disgust, dismay, displeasure.
v. charm, cheer, enchant, gratify, please, ravish, rejoice, satisfy, thrill, tickle.
antonyms dismay, displease.
delight in appreciate, enjoy, gloat over, glory in, indulge in, like, love, relish, revel in, savour, take pride in.
antonyms dislike, hate.

delighted *adj.* captivated, charmed, ecstatic, elated, enchanted, happy, joyous, jubilant, overjoyed, pleased, thrilled.
antonyms disappointed, dismayed, displeased.

delightful *adj.* agreeable, captivating, charming, enchanting, engaging, enjoyable, entertaining, fascinating, fetching, gratifying, pleasant, pleasing, pleasurable, thrilling.
antonyms horrible, nasty, unpleasant.

delinquency *n.* crime, criminality, fault, lawbreaking, misbehaviour, misconduct, misdeed, misdemeanour, offence, wrong-doing.

delinquent *n.* criminal, culprit, hooligan, lawbreaker, miscreant, offender, wrong-doer, young offender.
adj. careless, culpable, guilty, neglectful, negligent, remiss.

delirious *adj.* beside oneself, crazy, demented, deranged, ecstatic, excited, frantic, frenzied, hysterical, incoherent, insane, light-headed, mad, raving, wild.
antonym sane.

deliver *v.* **1** bring, carry, convey, direct, distribute, give, send, supply, transmit. **2** commit, entrust, grant, hand over, present, relinquish, surrender, transfer, yield. **3** declare, proclaim, pronounce, speak, utter. **4** administer, direct, inflict, launch.

delivery *n.* **1** consignment, conveyance, dispatch, distribution, shipment, surrender, transfer, transmission, transport. **2** articulation, elocution, enunciation, intonation, presentation, speech, utterance. **3** childbirth, confinement, labour, travail.

delude *v.* beguile, cheat, deceive, dupe, fool, hoax, hoodwink, impose on, misinform, mislead, take in, trick.

deluge *n.* avalanche, cataclysm, downpour, flood, hail, inundation, rush, spate, torrent.
v. bury, drench, drown, engulf, flood, inundate, overload, overwhelm, soak, submerge, swamp.

delusion *n.* deception, error, fallacy, fancy, hallucination, illusion, mirage, misapprehension, misbelief, misconception, mistake.

demand *v.* **1** ask, call for, challenge, claim, exact, expect, inquire, insist on, interrogate, order, question, request. **2** involve, necessitate, need, require, wait.
n. **1** claim, desire, inquiry, interrogation, order, question, request. **2** call, necessity, need.

demanding *adj.* back-breaking, challenging, difficult, exacting, exhausting, hard, insistent, pressing, taxing, tough, trying, urgent, wearing.
antonyms easy, easy-going, undemanding.

demarcation *n.* bound, boundary, delimitation, differentiation, distinction, division, enclosure, limit, line, margin, separation.

demean *v.* abase, condescend, debase, degrade, deign, descend, humble, lower, stoop.
antonyms enhance, exalt.

demeanour *n.* air, bearing, behaviour, conduct, deportment, manner.

demented *adj.* crazy, deranged, dotty, frenzied, idiotic, insane, lunatic, mad, unbalanced.
antonym sane.

demise *n.* **1** collapse, death, decease, departure, downfall, end, expiration, failure, fall, passing, ruin, termination. **2** alienation, conveyance, inheritance, transfer, transmission.

democracy *n.* autonomy, commonwealth, republic, self-government.

democratic *adj.* autonomous, egalitarian, popular, populist, representative, republican, self-governing.

demolish *v.* annihilate, bulldoze, defeat, delapidate, destroy, dismantle, flatten, knock down, level, overthrow, overturn, pull down, raze, ruin, tear down, wreck.
antonym build up.

demolition *n.* destruction, dismantling, levelling, razing.

demon *n.* devil, evil spirit, fallen angel, fiend, genius, goblin, monster, villain, warlock.

demoniac *adj.* d(a)emonic, devilish, diabolical, fiendish, furious, hellish, infernal, mad, maniacal, possessed, satanic, wild.

demonstrable *adj.* arguable, attestable, certain, clear, evident, obvious, positive, provable, self-evident, verifiable.
antonym unverifiable.

demonstrate *v.* **1** describe, display, establish, exhibit, explain, illustrate, indicate, manifest, prove, show, substantiate, teach, testify to. **2** march, parade, picket, protest, rally, sit in.

demonstration *n.* **1** affirmation, confirmation, description, display, evidence, exhibition, explanation, exposition, expression, illustration, manifestation, presentation, proof, substantiation, test, testimony, trial, validation. **2** demo, march, parade, picket, protest, rally, sit-in, work-in.

demonstrative *adj.* affectionate, emotional, expansive, expressive, loving, open.
antonyms cold, reserved, restrained.

demoralise *v.* crush, deject, depress, disconcert, discourage, dishearten, dispirit, lower, shake, undermine, unnerve, weaken.
antonyms encourage, hearten.

demote *v.* declass, degrade, downgrade, reduce, relegate.
antonyms promote, upgrade.

demur *v.* balk, disagree, dispute, dissent, doubt, hesitate, object, pause, protest, refuse, take exception, waver.
n. compunction, dissent, hesitation, misgiving, objection, protest, qualm, reservation, scruple.

demure *adj.* coy, grave, modest, prim, prissy, prudish, reserved, reticent, retiring, shy, sober, staid, strait-laced.
antonyms forward, wanton.

den *n.* haunt, hide-away, hide-out, hole, lair, retreat, sanctuary, shelter, study.

denial *n.* contradiction, disavowal, disclaimer, dismissal, dissent, negation, prohibition, rebuff, refusal, rejection, renunciation, repudiation, veto.

denigrate *v.* abuse, assail, belittle, besmirch, blacken, criticise, decry, defame, disparage, impugn, malign, revile, run down, slander, vilify, vilipend.
antonyms acclaim, praise.

denomination *n.* belief, body, category, class, classification, communion, creed, group, persuasion, religion, school, sect, style.

denote *v.* designate, express, imply, import, indicate, mark, mean, show, signify, stand for, symbolise, typify.

dénouement *n.* climax, close, conclusion, culmination, finale, finish, outcome, pay-off, resolution, solution, termination, upshot.

denounce *v.* accuse, arraign, attack, censure, condemn, declaim against, decry, fulminate, impugn, revile, vilify.
antonyms acclaim, praise.

dense *adj.* **1** close, close-knit, compact, compressed, condensed, crowded, heavy, impenetrable, opaque, packed, solid, substantial. **2** crass, dull, slow, slow-witted, stupid, thick.
antonyms **1** sparse, thin. **2** clever, intelligent.

density *n.* body, bulk, closeness, compactness, consistency, impenetrability, mass, solidity, thickness, tightness.

dent *n.* bang, crater, depression, dimple, dint, dip, hollow, impression, indentation, pit.
v. depress, gouge, indent, push in.

denude *v.* bare, deforest, divest, expose, strip, uncover.
antonyms clothe, cover.
denunciation *n.* accusation, censure, condemnation, criticism, denouncement, incrimination, invective.
antonyms compliment, praise.
deny *v.* contradict, disaffirm, disagree with, disclaim, disown, disprove, forbid, oppose, rebuff, recant, refuse, refute, reject, renounce, repudiate, revoke, turn down, veto, withhold.
antonyms admit, allow.
deodorant *n.* air-freshener, antiperspirant, deodoriser, disinfectant.
deodorise *v.* aerate, disinfect, freshen, fumigate, purify, refresh, sweeten, ventilate.
depart *v.* absent oneself, decamp, deviate, differ, digress, disappear, diverge, escape, exit, go, leave, make off, migrate, quit, remove, retire, retreat, set forth, swerve, take one's leave, vanish, veer, withdraw.
antonyms arrive, keep to, return.
departed *adj.* dead, deceased, expired, late.
department *n.* area, branch, district, division, domain, field, function, line, office, province, realm, region, responsibility, section, sector, speciality, sphere, station, subdivision, unit.
departure *n.* branching (out), change, deviation, difference, digression, divergence, exit, exodus, going, innovation, leave-taking, removal, retirement, shift, variation, veering, withdrawal.
antonyms arrival, return.
depend on bank on, build upon, calculate on, count on, expect, hang on, hinge on, lean on, reckon on, rely upon, rest on, revolve around, trust in, turn to.
dependable *adj.* certain, conscientious, faithful, honest, reliable, responsible, steady, sure, trustworthy, trusty, unfailing.
antonyms fickle, unreliable.
dependant *n.* child, hanger-on, minor, protégé, relative, subordinate.
dependence *n.* addiction, attachment, confidence, expectation, faith, helplessness, need, reliance, subordination, subservience, trust.
antonym independence.
dependent *adj.* conditional, contingent, determined by, helpless, immature, liable to, relative, relying on, subject, subordinate, tributary, vulnerable, weak.
antonym independent.
depict *v.* characterise, delineate, describe, detail, draw, illustrate, outline, paint, picture, portray, render, reproduce, sketch, trace.
deplete *v.* decrease, drain, empty, evacuate, exhaust, expend, impoverish, lessen, reduce, run down, use up.
deplorable *adj.* appalling, dire, disastrous, disgraceful, dishonourable, disreputable, distressing, grievous, heartbreaking, lamentable, melancholy, miserable, pitiable, regrettable, reprehensible, sad, scandalous, shameful, unfortunate, wretched.
antonyms commendable, excellent, praiseworthy.
deplore *v.* bemoan, censure, condemn, denounce, deprecate, grieve for, lament, mourn, regret, rue.
antonyms extol, praise.
deploy *v.* arrange, dispose, distribute, extend, position, station, use, utilise.
deport *v.* **1** banish, exile, expatriate, expel, extradite, ostracise, oust. **2** acquit, act, bear, behave, carry, conduct, hold, manage.
deportation *n.* banishment, eviction, exile, expatriation, expulsion, extradition, ostracism, transportation.
depose *v.* break, demote, dethrone, disestablish, dismiss, displace, downgrade, oust, topple.
deposit *v.* **1** drop, dump, lay, locate, park, place, precipitate, put, settle, sit. **2** amass, bank, consign, entrust, file, hoard, lodge, save, store.
n. **1** accumulation, dregs, lees, precipitate, sediment, silt. **2** down payment, instalment, money, part payment, pledge, retainer, security, stake.
depot *n.* depository, garage, repository, station, store, storehouse, terminus, warehouse.
deprave *v.* corrupt, debase, debauch, degrade, demoralise, infect, pervert, seduce, subvert.
antonyms improve, reform.
depraved *adj.* base, corrupt, debased, debauched, degenerate, dissolute, evil, immoral, licentious, perverted, shameless, sinful, vile, wicked.
antonyms moral, upright.
depravity *n.* baseness, corruption, criminality, debasement, debauchery, dissoluteness, evil, immorality, lewdness, licence, perversion, profligacy, reprobacy, sinfulness, vice, wickedness.
antonyms morality, uprightness, virtue.
deprecate *v.* condemn, deplore, disapprove of, disparage, object to, protest at, reject.
antonyms approve, commend, praise.
depreciate *v.* decrease, deflate, devalue, downgrade, drop, fall, lessen, lower, minimise, reduce, slump, underestimate, underrate, undervalue.
antonyms appreciate, overrate.
depreciation *n.* deflation, depression, devaluation, fall, slump.
antonym appreciation.
depress *v.* **1** burden, daunt, deject, discourage, dishearten, drain, exhaust, impair, lessen, level, lower, oppress, overburden, press, reduce, sadden, sap, tire, undermine, upset, weaken, weary. **2** bring down, devalue, lower.
antonyms **1** cheer, encourage. **2** increase, raise.
depressed *adj.* **1** cast down, crestfallen, dejected, deprived, despondent, destitute, disadvantaged, discouraged, disheartened, dispirited, distressed, down, downcast, downhearted, fed up, glum, low, low-spirited, melancholy, miserable, moody, morose, pessimistic, sad, unhappy. **2** concave, dented, hollow, indented, recessed, sunken.
antonyms **1** cheerful, encouraged. **2** convex, prominent, protuberant.

depressing *adj.* black, bleak, cheerless, daunting, dejecting, discouraging, disheartening, dismal, distressing, dreary, gloomy, grey, heartbreaking, hopeless, melancholy, sad, saddening, sombre.
antonyms cheerful, encouraging.

depression *n.* **1** dejection, despair, despondency, doldrums, dumps, gloominess, glumness, hopelessness, low spirits, melancholy, sadness. **2** decline, hard times, inactivity, recession, slump, stagnation. **3** basin, bowl, cavity, concavity, dent, dimple, dint, dip, dish, excavation, hollow, impression, indentation, pit, sag, sink, valley.
antonyms **1** cheerfulness. **2** boom, prosperity. **3** convexity, prominence, protuberance.

deprivation *n.* denial, denudation, destitution, disadvantage, dispossession, distress, hardship, need, privation, removal, want, withdrawal, withholding.
antonyms bestowal, endowment.

deprive *v.* bereave, denude, deny, dispossess, divest, expropriate, rob, starve, strip.
antonyms bestow, endow.

deprived *adj.* bereft, destitute, disadvantaged, impoverished, lacking, needy, poor, underprivileged.
antonyms fortunate, prosperous.

depth *n.* abyss, complexity, discernment, drop, exhaustiveness, extent, gulf, insight, intensity, measure, penetration, profoundness, richness, shrewdness, strength, thoroughness, wisdom.
antonyms shallowness, surface.
in depth comprehensively, exhaustively, extensively, in detail, intensively, thoroughly.
antonyms broadly, superficially.

deputation *n.* appointment, commission, delegation, embassy, legation, mission, representatives.

deputise *n.* commission, delegate, double, replace, represent, stand in for, substitute, understudy.

deputy *n.* agent, ambassador, assistant, commissary, commissioner, delegate, lieutenant, proxy, representative, second-in-command, subordinate, substitute, surrogate.

deranged *adj.* berserk, confused, crazy, delirious, demented, disordered, distraught, disturbed, frantic, insane, irrational, lunatic, mad, ordered, unbalanced.
antonyms calm, sane.

derelict *adj.* abandoned, deserted, desolate, dilapidated, discarded, forlorn, forsaken, neglected, ruined.

deride *v.* belittle, disdain, disparage, gibe, insult, jeer, knock, mock, ridicule, satirise, scoff, scorn, sneer, taunt.
antonyms praise, respect.

derision *n.* contempt, disdain, disparagement, disrespect, insult, laughter, mockery, ridicule, satire, scoffing, scorn, sneering.
antonyms praise, respect.

derisive *adj.* contemptuous, disdainful, disrespectful, irreverent, jeering, mocking, scornful, taunting.
antonyms appreciative, flattering, respectful.

derisory *adj.* absurd, contemptible, insulting, laughable, ludicrous, mockable, outrageous, paltry, ridiculous.

derivation *n.* ancestry, basis, beginning, deduction, descent, etymology, extraction, foundation, genealogy, inference, origin, root, source.

derivative *adj.* acquired, borrowed, copied, cribbed, derived, hackneyed, imitative, obtained, plagiarised, secondary, second-hand, transmitted, trite, unoriginal.
n. branch, by-product, derivation, descendant, development, offshoot, outgrowth, product, spin-off.

derive *v.* acquire, arise, borrow, deduce, descend, develop, draw, emanate, extract, flow, follow, gain, gather, get, glean, grow, infer, issue, lift, obtain, originate, proceed, procure, receive, spring, stem, trace.

derogatory *adj.* critical, defamatory, depreciative, destructive, disparaging, injurious, insulting, offensive, pejorative, slighting, snide, uncomplimentary.
antonyms appreciative, favourable, flattering.

descend *v.* **1** alight, arrive, develop, dip, dismount, drop, fall, invade, plummet, plunge, sink, slant, slope, subside, swoop, tumble. **2** degenerate, deteriorate. **3** condescend, deign, stoop. **4** originate, proceed, spring, stem.
antonyms **1** ascend, embark, rise.

descendants *n.* children, family, issue, line, lineage, offspring, posterity, progeny, race, seed, successors.

descent *n.* **1** decline, dip, drop, fall, incline, plunge, slant, slope. **2** comedown, debasement, degradation. **3** ancestry, extraction, family tree, genealogy, heredity, lineage, origin, parentage.
antonyms **1** ascent, rise.

describe *v.* characterise, define, depict, detail, draw, enlarge on, explain, express, illustrate, mark out, narrate, outline, portray, present, recount, relate, report, sketch, specify, tell, trace.

description *n.* account, category, characterisation, class, detail, explanation, exposition, kind, narration, narrative, order, outline, portrayal, presentation, report, representation, sketch, sort, species, specification, type, variety.

descriptive *adj.* colourful, detailed, explanatory, expressive, graphic, illustrative, immediate, pictorial, picturesque, vivid.

desert[1] *n.* void, wasteland, wilderness, wilds.
adj. arid, bare, barren, desolate, dry, infertile, lonely, solitary, sterile, uncultivated, uninhabited, waste, wild.

desert[2] *v.* abandon, abscond, betray, decamp, deceive, defect, forsake, give up, jilt, leave, maroon, quit, relinquish, renounce, resign, strand.
antonyms stand by, support.

desert[3] *n.* come-uppance, deserts, due, merit, payment, recompense, remuneration, requital, retribution, return, reward, right, virtue, worth.

deserted *adj.* abandoned, bereft, betrayed, dere-

lict, desolate, empty, forsaken, friendless, god-forsaken, isolated, lonely, neglected, solitary, stranded, underpopulated, unoccupied, vacant.
antonyms crowded, populous.

deserter *n.* absconder, apostate, backslider, betrayer, defector, delinquent, escapee, fugitive, rat, renegade, runaway, traitor, truant.

desertion *n.* abandonment, betrayal, defection, departure, dereliction, escape, evasion, flight, forsaking, relinquishment, truancy.

deserve *v.* ask for, earn, incur, justify, merit, procure, rate, warrant, win.

deserved *adj.* apposite, appropriate, apt, due, earned, fair, fitting, just, justifiable, legitimate, meet, merited, proper, right, rightful, suitable, warranted, well-earned.
antonyms gratuitous, undeserved.

deserving *adj.* admirable, commendable, estimable, exemplary, laudable, praiseworthy, righteous, worthy.
antonyms undeserving, unworthy.

design *n.* aim, arrangement, blueprint, composition, construction, draft, drawing, end, enterprise, figure, form, goal, guide, intention, manoeuvre, meaning, model, motif, object, objective, organisation, outline, pattern, plan, plot, project, prototype, purpose, scheme, shape, sketch, structure, style, target, undertaking.
v. aim, conceive, construct, create, describe, develop, devise, draft, draw (up), fabricate, fashion, form, intend, invent, make, mean, model, originate, outline, plan, project, propose, purpose, scheme, shape, sketch, structure, tailor.

designate *v.* allot, appoint, assign, call, characterise, choose, deem, define, delegate, denote, depute, describe, dub, earmark, indicate, label, name, nominate, select, show, specify, stipulate, style, term.

designation *n.* category, classification, definition, description, epithet, indication, label, name, nickname, nomination, specification, title.

designer *n.* architect, author, contriver, creator, deviser, fashioner, inventor, maker, originator, stylist.

designing *adj.* artful, conspiring, crafty, cunning, deceitful, devious, guileful, intriguing, plotting, scheming, sharp, shrewd, sly, tricky, underhand, wily.
antonyms artless, naïve.

desirable *adj.* advantageous, advisable, alluring, appropriate, attractive, beneficial, eligible, expedient, fetching, good, pleasing, preferable, profitable, seductive, sensible, tempting, worthwhile.
antonyms disagreeable, undesirable.

desire *v.* ask, covet, crave, fancy, hanker after, hunger for, long for, need, petition, request, want, wish for, yearn for.
n. appeal, appetite, ardour, aspiration, covetousness, craving, greed, hankering, longing, lust, need, passion, petition, request, supplication, want, wish, yearning.

desirous *adj.* ambitious, anxious, aspiring, avid, burning, craving, eager, enthusiastic, hopeful, itching, keen, longing, ready, willing, wishing, yearning.
antonyms reluctant, unenthusiastic.

desist *v.* abstain, break off, cease, discontinue, end, forbear, give up, halt, leave off, pause, peter out, refrain, remit, stop, suspend.
antonyms continue, resume.

desk *n.* bureau, davenport, écritoire, lectern, secretaire, writing-table.

desolate *adj.* abandoned, arid, bare, barren, bereft, bleak, dejected, depressed, depressing, deserted, despondent, disheartened, dismal, dismayed, distressed, downcast, dreary, forlorn, forsaken, friendless, gloomy, god-forsaken, inconsolable, lonely, melancholy, miserable, solitary, unfrequented, uninhabited, waste, wild, wretched.
antonyms cheerful, populous.
v. denude, depopulate, despoil, destroy, devastate, lay waste, pillage, plunder, ravage, ruin, spoil, waste, wreck.

desolation *n.* anguish, barrenness, bleakness, dejection, despair, despondency, destruction, devastation, distress, emptiness, forlornness, gloom, grief, havoc, isolation, loneliness, melancholy, misery, ravages, ruin, sadness, solitude, sorrow, unhappiness, wildness, woe, wretchedness.

despair *v.* collapse, give in, give up, lose heart, lose hope, quit, surrender.
antonym hope.
n. anguish, desperation, despondency, gloom, hopelessness, inconsolableness, melancholy, misery, ordeal, pain, sorrow, trial, tribulation, wretchedness.
antonyms cheerfulness, resilience.

despairing *adj.* anxious, broken-hearted, dejected, desolate, desperate, despondent, disheartened, dismayed, distraught, downcast, grief-stricken, hopeless, inconsolable, miserable, sorrowful, suicidal, wretched.
antonyms cheerful, encouraged.

despatch *see* **dispatch**.

desperado *n.* bandit, brigand, criminal, cutthroat, gangster, gunman, hoodlum, lawbreaker, mugger, outlaw, ruffian, thug.

desperate *adj.* **1** abandoned, audacious, dangerous, daring, despondent, determined, dire, do-or-die, foolhardy, frantic, frenzied, hasty, hazardous, hopeless, impetuous, inconsolable, panic-stricken, precipitate, reckless, risky, violent, wild, wretched. **2** acute, critical, extreme, serious, severe, urgent.
antonyms **1** careful, cautious.

desperately *adv.* appallingly, badly, critically, dangerously, dreadfully, fearfully, frantically, frightfully, gravely, hopelessly, seriously, severely.

desperation *n.* agony, anguish, anxiety, despair, despondency, distress, frenzy, hastiness, hopelessness, madness, misery, pain, rashness, recklessness, sorrow, trouble, worry.

despicable *adj.* contemptible, detestable, disgraceful, disgusting, disreputable, mean, reprobate, shameful, vile, worthless, wretched.
antonyms laudable, noble, principled.

despise *v.* abhor, condemn, deplore, detest, dislike, ignore, loathe, revile, scorn, slight, spurn, undervalue.
antonyms appreciate, prize.

despite *prep.* against, defying, in spite of, in the face of, notwithstanding, regardless of, undeterred by.

despondency *n.* broken-heartedness, dejection, depression, despair, discouragement, downheartedness, gloom, hopelessness, inconsolability, melancholy, misery, sadness, sorrow, wretchedness.
antonyms cheerfulness, hopefulness.

despondent *adj.* broken-hearted, dejected, depressed, despairing, discouraged, disheartened, doleful, down, downcast, gloomy, glum, inconsolable, low, melancholy, miserable, mournful, sad, sorrowful, wretched.
antonyms cheerful, heartened, hopeful.

despot *n.* absolutist, autocrat, boss, dictator, oppressor, tyrant.
antonyms democrat, egalitarian, liberal.

despotic *adj.* absolute, arbitrary, arrogant, authoritarian, autocratic, dictatorial, domineering, imperious, oppressive, overbearing, tyrannical.
antonyms democratic, egalitarian, liberal, tolerant.

despotism *n.* absolutism, autocracy, dictatorship, oppression, repression, totalitarianism, tyranny.
antonyms democracy, egalitarianism, liberalism, tolerance.

dessert *n.* afters, pudding, sweet.

destination *n.* aim, ambition, aspiration, design, end, goal, intention, journey's end, object, objective, purpose, station, stop, target, terminus.

destined *adj.* appointed, assigned, booked, bound, certain, designed, directed, doomed, en route, fated, foreordained, headed, heading, inescapable, inevitable, intended, meant, ordained, predetermined, scheduled, unavoidable.

destiny *n.* doom, fate, fortune, joss, karma, kismet, lot, portion, predestiny.

destitute *adj.* bankrupt, bereft, deficient, depleted, deprived, devoid of, distressed, down and out, impoverished, innocent of, lacking, needy, penniless, poor, poverty-stricken, wanting.
antonyms prosperous, rich, wealthy.

destroy *v.* annihilate, break, crush, demolish, devastate, dismantle, dispatch, eliminate, eradicate, extinguish, gut, kill, level, nullify, overthrow, ravage, raze, ruin, sabotage, shatter, slay, smash, thwart, torpedo, undermine, undo, unshape, waste, wreck.
antonyms build up, create.

destroyer *n.* annihilator, demolisher, despoiler, iconoclast, kiss of death, locust, Luddite, ransacker, ravager, vandal, wrecker.
antonym creator.

destruction *n.* annihilation, crushing, defeat, demolition, desolation, devastation, downfall, elimination, end, eradication, extermination, extinction, havoc, liquidation, massacre, nullification, overthrow, ravagement, ruin, ruination, shattering, slaughter, undoing, wastage, wreckage.
antonym creation.

destructive *adj.* adverse, catastrophic, contrary, damaging, deadly, detrimental, devastating, disastrous, discouraging, disparaging, disruptive, fatal, harmful, hostile, hurtful, lethal, malignant, mischievous, negative, nullifying, ruinous, slaughterous, subversive, undermining, vicious.
antonyms constructive, creative, productive.

desultory *adj.* aimless, capricious, cursory, disconnected, disorderly, erratic, fitful, half-hearted, haphazard, inconsistent, irregular, loose, random, spasmodic, unco-ordinated, undirected.
antonyms concerted, methodical, systematic.

detach *v.* cut off, disconnect, disengage, disentangle, disjoin, dissociate, divide, estrange, free, isolate, loosen, remove, segregate, separate, sever, uncouple, undo, unfasten, unfix, unhitch.
antonym attach.

detached *adj.* **1** disconnected, discrete, dissociated, divided, free, loosened, separate, severed. **2** aloof, disinterested, dispassionate, impartial, impersonal, independent, neutral, objective.
antonyms **2** committed, connected, involved.

detachment *n.* **1** aloofness, coolness, disinterestedness, fairness, impartiality, impassivity, indifference, neutrality, objectivity, remoteness, separation, unconcern. **2** body, brigade, corps, force, party, patrol, squad, task force, unit.

detail *n.* aspect, attribute, complication, component, count, elaboration, element, fact, factor, feature, ingredient, intricacy, item, meticulousness, nicety, particular, point, refinement, respect, specific, technicality, thoroughness, triviality.
v. appoint, assign, charge, commission, delegate, enumerate, individualise, itemise, list, order, recount, relate, specify.

detailed *adj.* complex, complicated, comprehensive, descriptive, elaborate, exact, exhaustive, fine, full, intricate, itemised, meticulous, minute, particular, specific, thorough.
antonyms brief, cursory, summary.

details *n.* complexities, complications, ins and outs, intricacies, minutiae, niceties, particularities, particulars, specifics.

detain *v.* arrest, check, confine, delay, hinder, hold (up), impede, intern, keep, prevent, restrain, retard, slow, stay, stop.
antonym release.

detect *v.* ascertain, catch, discern, disclose, discover, distinguish, expose, find, identify, note, notice, observe, perceive, recognise, reveal, sight, spot, spy, track down, uncover, unmask.

detection *n.* discernment, discovery, exposé, identification, revelation, tracking down, uncovering.

detective *n.* constable, cop, copper, investigator, private eye, private investigator, sleuth, sleuth-hound, thief-catcher.

detention *n.* confinement, constraint, custody, delay, detainment, hindrance, imprisonment, incarceration, quarantine, restraint, withholding.
antonym release.

deter *v.* caution, check, daunt, discourage, disincline, dissuade, frighten, hinder, inhibit, intimidate, prevent, prohibit, put off, restrain, stop, turn off, warn.
antonym encourage.

detergent *n.* cleaner, cleanser, soap.

deteriorate *v.* decay, decline, decompose, degenerate, depreciate, disintegrate, fade, fail, fall off, go downhill, lapse, relapse, slide, slip, weaken, worsen.
antonyms improve, progress.

determination *n.* backbone, conviction, decision, dedication, drive, firmness, fortitude, insistence, intention, judgement, perseverance, persistence, purpose, resolution, resolve, single-mindedness, steadfastness, tenacity, will, will-power.
antonym irresolution.

determine *v.* affect, ascertain, check, choose, conclude, control, decide, detect, direct, discover, establish, finish, fix, govern, guide, identify, influence, intend, ordain, point, purpose, regulate, resolve, rule, settle, undertake, verify.

determined *adj.* convinced, decided, firm, fixed, insistent, intent, persevering, persistent, purposeful, resolute, single-minded, steadfast, strong-minded, strong-willed, unflinching.
antonyms irresolute, wavering.

deterrent *n.* bar, check, curb, difficulty, discouragement, hindrance, impediment, obstacle, obstruction, repellent, restraint.
antonyms encouragement, incentive.

detest *v.* abhor, deplore, despise, dislike, hate, loathe, recoil from.
antonyms adore, love.

detestable *adj.* abhorrent, abominable, accursed, despicable, disgusting, hated, heinous, loathsome, obnoxious, offensive, repellent, repugnant, repulsive, revolting, shocking, sordid, vile.
antonyms admirable, adorable.

dethrone *v.* depose, oust, topple, uncrown, unseat, unthrone.
antonyms crown, enthrone.

detonate *v.* blast, blow up, discharge, explode, ignite, kindle, set off, spark off.

detonation *n.* bang, blast, blow-up, boom, burst, discharge, explosion, ignition.

detour *n.* bypass, bypath, byroad, byway, deviation, digression, diversion.

detract *v.* belittle, diminish, lessen, lower, reduce.
antonyms add to, enhance, praise.

detractor *n.* belittler, defamer, denigrator, disparager, enemy, reviler, scandalmonger, slanderer, vilifier.
antonyms defender, flatterer, supporter.

detriment *n.* damage, disadvantage, disservice, evil, harm, hurt, ill, injury, loss, mischief, prejudice.
antonym advantage.

detrimental *adj.* adverse, damaging, destructive, disadvantageous, harmful, hurtful, injurious, mischievous, prejudicial.
antonyms advantageous, favourable.

devaluation *n.* decrease, deflation, lowering, reduction.

devalue *v.* decrease, deflate, lower, reduce.

devastate *v.* confound, demolish, despoil, destroy, disconcert, floor, lay waste, level, overwhelm, pillage, plunder, ransack, ravage, raze, ruin, sack, spoil, waste, wreck.

devastating *adj.* destructive, disastrous, effective, fatal, overwhelming, stunning.

devastation *n.* annihilation, demolition, desolation, destruction, havoc, pillage, plunder, ravages, ruin, spoliation, wreckage.

develop *v.* **1** advance, branch out, cultivate, evolve, expand, flourish, foster, mature, progress, prosper. **2** amplify, elaborate, enhance, unfold. **3** acquire, begin, break out, create, generate, invent. **4** arise, ensue, follow, form, grow, happen, result.

development *n.* advance, blossoming, change, elaboration, event, evolution, expansion, extension, furtherance, growth, happening, improvement, increase, issue, maturity, occurrence, outcome, phenomenon, progress, promotion, refinement, result, situation, spread, unfolding.

deviant *adj.* aberrant, abnormal, anomalous, bizarre, freakish, heretical, irregular, perverted, twisted, wayward.
antonyms normal, straight.

deviate *v.* depart, differ, digress, diverge, drift, err, go astray, go off the rails, part, stray, swerve, turn (aside), vary, veer, wander, yaw.

deviation *n.* aberration, abnormality, alteration, anomaly, change, deflection, departure, detour, digression, discrepancy, disparity, divergence, eccentricity, fluctuation, freak, irregularity, quirk, shift, variance, variation.
antonyms conformity, regularity.

device *n.* **1** apparatus, appliance, contraption, contrivance, implement, instrument, invention, machine, tool, utensil. **2** dodge, gambit, machination, manoeuvre, plan, plot, ruse, scheme, strategy, trick, wile. **3** badge, colophon, crest, design, emblem, insignia, logo, motif, shield, symbol, token.

devil *n.* Adversary, arch-fiend, Beelzebub, brute, demon, Evil One, fiend, imp, Lucifer, man of

sin, Mephistopheles, monster, ogre, Old Harry, Old Nick, Prince of Darkness, Satan, Slanderer.
devilish *adj.* accursed, damnable, diabolical, fiendish, hellish, impious, infernal, iniquitous, mischievous, monstrous, satanic, wicked.
devious *adj.* calculating, crooked, cunning, deceitful, dishonest, disingenuous, double-dealing, erratic, evasive, indirect, insidious, insincere, misleading, rambling, roundabout, scheming, slippery, sly, subtle, surreptitious, tortuous, treacherous, tricky, underhand, wandering, wily, winding.
antonyms artless, candid, straightforward.
devise *v.* arrange, compose, conceive, concoct, construct, contrive, design, forge, form, formulate, frame, imagine, invent, plan, plot, prepare, project, scheme, shape.
devoid *adj.* barren, bereft, deficient, destitute, empty, free, innocent, lacking, vacant, void, wanting, without.
antonyms blessed, endowed.
devolution *n.* decentralisation, delegation, dispersal, distribution, transference.
antonym centralisation.
devolve *v.* alienate, commission, consign, convey, delegate, deliver, entrust, fall to, hand down, rest with, transfer.
devote *v.* allocate, allot, apply, appropriate, assign, commit, consecrate, dedicate, enshrine, give oneself, pledge, reserve, sacrifice, set apart, set aside, surrender.
devoted *adj.* ardent, attentive, caring, committed, concerned, constant, dedicated, devout, faithful, fond, loving, loyal, staunch, steadfast, tireless, true, unswerving.
antonyms inconstant, indifferent, negligent.
devotee *n.* addict, adherent, admirer, buff, disciple, enthusiast, fan, fanatic, fiend, follower, hound, merchant, supporter, zealot.
antonyms adversary, sceptic.
devotion *n.* adherence, adoration, affection, allegiance, ardour, attachment, commitment, consecration, dedication, devoutness, earnestness, faith, faithfulness, fervour, fondness, godliness, holiness, love, loyalty, passion, piety, prayer, regard, reverence, spirituality, steadfastness, support, worship, zeal.
antonyms inconstancy, negligence.
devour *v.* absorb, bolt, consume, cram, destroy, dispatch, down, eat, engulf, feast on, gluttonise, gobble, gorge, gormandise, gulp, guzzle, polish off, ravage, relish, revel in, spend, stuff, swallow, wolf.
devout *adj.* ardent, constant, deep, devoted, earnest, faithful, fervent, genuine, godly, heartfelt, holy, intense, orthodox, passionate, pious, prayerful, profound, pure, religious, reverent, saintly, serious, sincere, staunch, steadfast, unswerving, whole-hearted, zealous.
antonyms insincere, uncommitted.
dewy *adj.* blooming, innocent, starry-eyed, youthful.
dexterity *n.* ability, adroitness, agility, aptitude, artistry, cleverness, deftness, effortlessness, expertise, facility, finesse, handiness, ingenuity, knack, mastery, nimbleness, proficiency, readiness, skilfulness, skill, smoothness, touch.
antonyms awkwardness, clumsiness, ineptitude.
dexterous *adj.* able, active, adroit, agile, clever, deft, expert, facile, handy, light-handed, masterly, neat-handed, nifty, nimble, nimble-fingered, nippy, proficient, quick, skilful.
antonyms awkward, clumsy, inept.
diabolical *adj.* damnable, devilish, disastrous, dreadful, excruciating, fiendish, hellish, infernal, knavish, nasty, outrageous, shocking, tricky, unpleasant, vile, wicked.
diagnose *v.* analyse, determine, distinguish, explain, identify, interpret, investigate, isolate, pinpoint, recognise.
diagnosis *n.* analysis, answer, conclusion, examination, explanation, identification, interpretation, investigation, opinion, scrutiny, verdict.
diagnostic *adj.* analytical, distinguishing, indicative, interpretive, particular, recognisable, symptomatic.
diagonal *adj.* angled, cornerways, crooked, cross, crosswise, oblique, slanting, sloping.
diagram *n.* chart, drawing, figure, graph, illustration, layout, outline, picture, plan, representation, schema, sketch, table.
diagrammatic *adj.* graphic, illustrative, representational, schematic, tabular.
antonyms imaginative, impressionistic.
dial *n.* circle, clock, control, meter, signal.
v. call (up), phone, ring.
dialect *n.* accent, diction, idiom, jargon, language, lingo, patois, provincialism, regionalism, speech, tongue, vernacular.
dialectic *adj.* analytical, argumentative, deductive, dialectical, inductive, logical, logistic, polemical, rational, rationalistic.
n. analysis, argumentation, contention, debate, deduction, dialectics, discussion, disputation, induction, logic, polemics, rationale, reasoning, sophistry.
dialogue *n.* communication, conference, conversation, converse, debate, discourse, discussion, exchange, interchange, lines, script, talk.
diametric *adj.* antithetical, contrary, contrasting, counter, diametrical, opposed, opposite.
diaphanous *adj.* delicate, filmy, fine, gauzy, gossamer, light, see-through, sheer, thin, translucent, transparent, veily.
antonyms heavy, opaque, thick.
diarrhoea *n.* dysentery, holiday tummy, looseness, the runs, the trots.
antonym constipation.
diary *n.* appointment book, chronicle, day-book, engagement book, journal, logbook, year-book.
diatribe *n.* abuse, attack, criticism, denunciation, harangue, insult, invective, onslaught, reviling, tirade, upbraiding.
antonyms bouquet, praise.
dicey *adj.* chancy, dangerous, difficult, dubious, hairy, iffy, problematic, risky, tricky.
antonyms certain, easy.
dichotomy *n.* difference, distinction, disunion,

isolation, separateness, unlikeness.
antonyms agreement, uniformity.

dictate *v.* announce, command, decree, direct, instruct, order, pronounce, rule, say, speak, transmit, utter.
n. bidding, command, decree, direction, edict, injunction, law, mandate, order, ordinance, precept, principle, requirement, rule, ruling, statute, ultimatum, word.

dictator *n.* autocrat, Big Brother, despot, supremo, tyrant.

dictatorial *adj.* absolute, almighty, arbitrary, authoritarian, autocratic, bossy, despotic, dogmatic, domineering, imperious, oppressive, overbearing, repressive, totalitarian, tyrannical.
antonyms democratic, egalitarian, liberal, tolerant.

dictatorship *n.* absolutism, authoritarianism, autocracy, despotism, fascism, totalitarianism, tyranny.
antonyms democracy, egalitarianism.

diction *n.* articulation, delivery, elocution, enunciation, expression, fluency, inflection, intonation, language, phrasing, pronunciation, speech, style.

dictionary *n.* concordance, encyclopaedia, glossary, lexicon, thesaurus, vocabulary, wordbook.

dictum *n.* axiom, command, decree, dictate, edict, fiat, maxim, order, precept, pronouncement, proverb, ruling, saying, utterance.

didactic *adj.* educational, educative, instructive, moral, moralising, pedagogic, pedantic, prescriptive.

die *v.* **1** breathe one's last, decay, decease, decline, depart, disappear, dwindle, ebb, end, expire, fade, finish, lapse, pass away, perish, peter out, sink, starve, stop, subside, suffer, vanish, wane, wilt, wither. **2** desire, hunger for, long for, pine for, yearn.
antonyms **1** be born, live.

die-hard *n.* blimp, fanatic, hardliner, intransigent, reactionary, rightist, stick-in-the-mud, ultra-conservative, zealot.

diet *n.* abstinence, dietary, fast, food, foodstuffs, nutrition, provisions, rations, subsistence, sustenance.
v. abstain, fast, lose weight, reduce, slim, weight-watch.

differ *v.* argue, be at odds with, clash, conflict, contend, contradict, contrast, debate, depart from, disagree, dispute, dissent, diverge, fall out, oppose, part company with, quarrel, take issue, vary.
antonyms agree, conform.

difference *n.* clash, conflict, contention, contrast, controversy, deviation, differentiation, disagreement, discrepancy, disparity, dispute, dissimilarity, distinction, distinctness, divergence, diversity, exception, remainder, rest, singularity, unlikeness, variation, variety.
antonyms agreement, conformity, uniformity.

different *adj.* altered, anomalous, assorted, at odds, bizarre, clashing, contrasting, deviating, dissimilar, distinct, distinctive, divergent, diverse, extraordinary, inconsistent, individual, many, miscellaneous, numerous, opposed, original, other, peculiar, rare, separate, several, special, strange, sundry, unconventional, unique, unlike, unusual, varied, various.
antonyms conventional, normal, same, similar, uniform.

differentiate *v.* adapt, alter, change, contrast, convert, discriminate, distinguish, individualise, mark off, modify, particularise, separate, tell apart, transform.
antonyms assimilate, associate, confuse, link.

differentiation *n.* contrast, discrimination, distinction, individualisation, modification, separation.
antonyms assimilation, association, confusion, connection.

difficult *adj.* abstract, abstruse, arduous, baffling, complex, complicated, dark, demanding, formidable, hard, intractable, intricate, involved, knotty, laborious, obscure, obstinate, perplexing, perverse, problematical, strenuous, stubborn, thorny, tiresome, tough, troublesome, trying, unco-operative, uphill, wearisome.
antonyms easy, manageable, straightforward.

difficulty *n.* arduousness, awkwardness, block, complication, dilemma, distress, embarrassment, fix, hang-up, hardship, hiccup, hindrance, hurdle, impediment, labour, mess, objection, obstacle, opposition, pain, painfulness, perplexity, pitfall, plight, predicament, problem, protest, quandary, scruple, spot, strain, stumbling-block, trial, tribulation, trouble.
antonyms advantage, ease.

diffidence *n.* backwardness, bashfulness, hesitancy, humility, inhibition, insecurity, meekness, modesty, reluctance, reserve, self-consciousness, self-distrust, self-doubt, self-effacement, sheepishness, shyness, timidity, unassertiveness.
antonym confidence.

diffident *adj.* abashed, backward, bashful, hesitant, inhibited, insecure, meek, modest, reluctant, reserved, self-conscious, self-effacing, shamefaced, sheepish, shrinking, shy, tentative, timid, unsure, withdrawn.
antonyms assertive, confident.

diffuse *adj.* circuitous, copious, diffused, disconnected, discursive, dispersed, imprecise, long-winded, loose, rambling, scattered, unconcentrated, vague, verbose, waffling, wordy.
antonyms concentrated, succinct.
v. circulate, dispense, disperse, disseminate, dissipate, distribute, propagate, scatter, spread.
antonyms concentrate, suppress.

dig *v.* burrow, delve, drive, excavate, go into, gouge, investigate, mine, penetrate, pierce, poke, probe, prod, quarry, research, scoop, search, thrust, till, tunnel.
n. aspersion, crack, gibe, insinuation, insult, jab, jeer, poke, prod, quip, sneer, taunt, wisecrack.
antonym compliment.
dig up discover, disinter, dredge, exhumate, exhume, expose, extricate, find, retrieve, track

down, uncover, unearth.
antonyms bury, obscure.

digest *v.* absorb, assimilate, compress, condense, consider, contemplate, dispose, dissolve, grasp, incorporate, meditate, ponder, process, reduce, shorten, stomach, study, summarise, systematise, tabulate, take in, understand.
n. abbreviation, abridgement, abstract, compendium, compression, précis, reduction, résumé, summary, synopsis.

dignified *adj.* distinguished, exalted, formal, grave, honourable, imposing, impressive, lofty, lordly, majestic, noble, reserved, solemn, stately, upright.
antonyms lowly, undignified.

dignify *v.* adorn, advance, distinguish, elevate, ennoble, exalt, glorify, honour, promote, raise.
antonyms degrade, demean.

dignitary *n.* bigwig, dignity, high-up, personage, VIP, worthy.

dignity *n.* courtliness, eminence, excellence, glory, grandeur, greatness, honour, importance, loftiness, majesty, nobility, poise, pride, propriety, respectability, self-esteem, self-importance, self-respect, solemnity, standing.

dilapidated *adj.* broken-down, crumbling, decayed, decaying, decrepit, neglected, ramshackle, rickety, ruined, ruinous, run-down, shabby, tumble-down, uncared-for, worn-out.

dilate *v.* amplify, broaden, detail, develop, distend, dwell on, elaborate, enlarge, expand, expatiate, expound, extend, increase, puff out, spread, stretch, swell, widen.
antonyms contract, curtail.

dilemma *n.* difficulty, embarrassment, mess, perplexity, pinch, plight, predicament, problem, puzzle, quandary, strait.

diligence *n.* activity, application, attention, attentiveness, care, constancy, earnestness, industry, laboriousness, perseverance.
antonyms carelessness, laziness.

diligent *adj.* active, assiduous, attentive, busy, careful, conscientious, constant, earnest, hard-working, industrious, meticulous, painstaking, persevering, persistent, studious, tireless.
antonyms dilatory, lazy.

dilute *v.* adulterate, decrease, diffuse, diminish, lessen, mitigate, reduce, temper, thin (out), water down, weaken.
antonym concentrate.
adj. adulterated, attenuated, diluted, thin, watered down, weak.
antonym concentrated.

dim *adj.* **1** blurred, cloudy, dark, dingy, dull, dusky, faint, feeble, foggy, fuzzy, gloomy, hazy, ill-defined, imperfect, indistinct, lack-lustre, misty, obscure, pale, shadowy, slow, sombre, sullied, tarnished, unclear, vague, weak. **2** dense, stupid, thick.
antonyms **1** bright, distinct. **2** clever, intelligent.
v. blur, cloud, darken, dull, fade, lower, obscure, tarnish.
antonyms brighten, illuminate.

dimension(s) *n.* angle, extent, greatness, importance, largeness, magnitude, measure, range, scale, scope, side, size.

diminish *v.* abate, contract, curtail, cut, decline, decrease, dwindle, ebb, fade, lessen, lower, recede, reduce, shrink, sink, slacken, subside, taper off, wane, weaken.
antonyms enhance, enlarge, increase.

diminution *n.* contraction, curtailment, cut, cutback, decline, decrease, deduction, ebb, lessening, reduction, shortening.
antonyms enlargement, increase.

diminutive *adj.* dinky, Lilliputian, little, midget, mini, miniature, minute, petite, pint-size(d), pocket(-sized), pygmy, small, tiny, undersized.
antonyms big, great, huge, large.

dimple *n.* concavity, depression, dint, hollow.

din *n.* babble, clamour, clash, clatter, commotion, crash, hubbub, hullabaloo, noise, outcry, pandemonium, racket, row, shout, uproar.
antonyms calm, quiet.

dine *v.* banquet, eat, feast, feed, lunch, sup.
dine on banquet, consume, dine off, eat, feast, feed.

dingy *adj.* colourless, dark, dim, dirty, discoloured, drab, dreary, dull, dusky, faded, gloomy, grimy, murky, obscure, run-down, seedy, shabby, soiled, sombre, worn.
antonyms bright, clean.

dinner *n.* banquet, beanfeast, blow-out, feast, meal, repast, spread, supper, tea.

dip *v.* **1** bathe, douse, dunk, immerse, plunge, rinse, sink. **2** decline, descend, disappear, drop, fall, lower, slump, subside.
n. **1** basin, decline, depression, fall, hole, hollow, incline, lowering, sag, slip, slope, slump. **2** bathe, dive, drenching, ducking, immersion, infusion, plunge, soaking, swim.
dip into browse, dabble, peruse, sample, skim, try.

diplomacy *n.* artfulness, craft, discretion, finesse, manoeuvring, savoir-faire, skill, statesmanship, subtlety, tact, tactfulness.

diplomat *n.* conciliator, go-between, mediator, moderator, negotiator, peacemaker, politician, tactician.

diplomatic *adj.* discreet, judicious, politic, prudent, sensitive, subtle, tactful.
antonyms rude, tactless, thoughtless.

dire *adj.* alarming, appalling, awful, calamitous, catastrophic, crucial, cruel, crying, desperate, disastrous, drastic, dreadful, extreme, grave, ominous, urgent.

direct *v.* **1** control, govern, lead, manage, organise, oversee, regulate, run, superintend, supervise. **2** charge, command, instruct, order. **3** conduct, guide, lead, point, show. **4** aim, focus, point, turn.
adj. **1** straight, through, undeviating, uninterrupted. **2** absolute, blunt, candid, categorical, explicit, frank, honest, outspoken, plain, sincere, straightforward. **3** face-to-face, first-hand, immediate, personal.
antonyms **1** circuitous, devious. **2** equivocal. **3**

indirect.
direction *n.* **1** administration, control, government, guidance, leadership, oversight, supervision. **2** line, path, road, route, way.
directions *n.* briefing, guidance, guidelines, indication, instructions, orders, plan, recipe, recommendations, regulations.
directive *n.* charge, command, decree, dictate, diktat, edict, fiat, imperative, injunction, instruction, mandate, notice, order, ordinance, regulation, ruling.
directly *adv.* **1** exactly, forthwith, immediately, instantaneously, instantly, precisely, presently, promptly, quickly, right away, soon, speedily, straight, straightaway. **2** bluntly, candidly, frankly, honestly.
director *n.* administrator, boss, chairman, chief, conductor, controller, executive, governor, head, leader, manager, organiser, principal, producer, supervisor.
dirge *n.* dead-march, elegy, lament, requiem.
dirt *n.* clay, dust, earth, excrement, filth, grime, impurity, indecency, mire, muck, mud, obscenity, pornography, slime, smudge, soil, stain, tarnish, yuck.
antonyms cleanliness, cleanness.
dirty *adj.* **1** clouded, dark, dull, filthy, foul, grimy, grubby, low, messy, miry, mucky, muddy, nasty, polluted, scruffy, scurvy, shabby, soiled, squalid, sullied. **2** corrupt, filthy, indecent, obscene, pornographic, smutty, sordid, vulgar.
antonyms **1** clean, spotless. **2** clean, decent.
v. blacken, defile, foul, mess up, muddy, pollute, smear, smirch, smudge, soil, spoil, stain, sully.
antonyms clean, cleanse.
disability *n.* affliction, ailment, complaint, defect, disablement, disorder, disqualification, handicap, impairment, inability, incapacity, infirmity, unfitness, weakness.
disable *v.* cripple, damage, debilitate, disqualify, hamstring, handicap, immobilise, impair, incapacitate, invalidate, lame, paralyse, prostrate, unfit, unman, weaken.
disabled *adj.* bedridden, crippled, handicapped, immobilised, incapacitated, infirm, lame, maimed, paralysed, weak, weakened, wrecked.
antonyms able, able-bodied.
disadvantage *n.* drawback, flaw, handicap, hardship, harm, hindrance, hurt, impediment, inconvenience, injury, liability, loss, minus, nuisance, prejudice, privation, snag, trouble, weakness.
antonyms advantage, benefit.
v. hamper, handicap, hinder, inconvenience, wrong-foot.
antonyms aid, help.
disadvantaged *adj.* deprived, handicapped, hindered, impeded, impoverished, struggling, underprivileged.
antonym privileged.
disadvantageous *adj.* adverse, damaging, detrimental, harmful, hurtful, ill-timed, inconvenient, injurious, inopportune, prejudicial, unfavourable.
antonyms advantageous, auspicious, convenient.
disaffected *adj.* alienated, antagonistic, discontented, disgruntled, disloyal, dissatisfied, estranged, hostile, rebellious.
antonyms contented, loyal.
disaffection *n.* alienation, animosity, antagonism, aversion, breach, coolness, disagreement, discontentment, discord, disharmony, dislike, disloyalty, dissatisfaction, hostility, ill-will, resentment, unfriendliness.
antonyms contentment, loyalty.
disagree *v.* argue, bicker, bother, clash, conflict, contend, contest, contradict, counter, depart, deviate, differ, dissent, distress, diverge, fall out, object, oppose, quarrel, run counter to, sicken, squabble, trouble, upset, vary, wrangle.
antonyms agree, correspond.
disagreeable *adj.* bad-tempered, brusque, contrary, cross, difficult, disgusting, irritable, nasty, objectionable, offensive, peevish, repellent, repulsive, rude, surly, unsavoury.
antonyms agreeable, amiable, friendly, pleasant.
disagreement *n.* argument, clash, conflict, difference, discord, discrepancy, disparity, dispute, dissent, dissimilarity, divergence, diversity, division, falling-out, incompatibility, incongruity, misunderstanding, quarrel, squabble, strife, tiff, unlikeness, variance, wrangle.
antonyms agreement, harmony, similarity.
disallow *v.* ban, cancel, debar, dismiss, embargo, forbid, prohibit, proscribe, rebuff, refuse, reject, repudiate, veto.
antonyms allow, permit.
disappear *v.* depart, dissolve, ebb, end, escape, evaporate, expire, fade, flee, fly, go, hide, pass, perish, recede, retire, scarper, vanish, wane, withdraw.
antonyms appear, emerge.
disappearance *n.* departure, desertion, evaporation, fading, flight, going, loss, melting, passing, vanishing.
antonyms appearance, arrival, manifestation.
disappoint *v.* baffle, dash, deceive, defeat, delude, disconcert, disenchant, disgruntle, dishearten, disillusion, dismay, dissatisfy, fail, foil, frustrate, hamper, hinder, let down, sadden, thwart, vex.
antonyms delight, please, satisfy.
disappointed *adj.* depressed, despondent, discouraged, disgruntled, disheartened, disillusioned, dissatisfied, distressed, down-hearted, frustrated, let down, miffed, saddened, thwarted, upset.
antonyms delighted, pleased, satisfied.
disappointing *adj.* anti-climactic, depressing, disagreeable, disconcerting, discouraging, inadequate, inferior, insufficient, sorry, unhappy, unsatisfactory, unworthy.
antonyms encouraging, pleasant, satisfactory.
disappointment *n.* **1** discouragement, disenchantment, disillusionment, displeasure, dissatisfaction, distress, failure, frustration, regret. **2** blow, calamity, comedown, disaster, drop, failure, fiasco, let-down, misfortune, setback,

swiz, swizzle.
antonyms **1** delight, pleasure, satisfaction. **2** boost, success.
disapproval *n.* censure, condemnation, criticism, denunciation, dislike, displeasure, dissatisfaction, objection, reproach.
antonyms approbation, approval.
disapprove of blame, censure, condemn, denounce, deplore, dislike, disparage, object to, reject, spurn, take exception to.
antonym approve of.
disarm *v.* **1** deactivate, demilitarise, demobilise, disable, disband, unarm, unweapon. **2** appease, conciliate, modify, persuade, win over.
antonyms **1** activate, arm.
disarming *adj.* charming, conciliatory, irresistible, likeable, mollifying, persuasive, soothing, winning.
disarrange *v.* confuse, disarray, dislocate, disorder, disorganise, disturb, jumble, mess up, shuffle, unsettle, untidy.
antonyms arrange, order.
disarray *n.* chaos, clutter, confusion, disorder, disorganisation, disunity, indiscipline, jumble, mess, muddle, shambles, tangle, unruliness, untidiness, upset.
antonyms array, order.
disaster *n.* accident, act of God, blow, calamity, cataclysm, catastrophe, debacle, mischance, misfortune, mishap, reverse, ruin, ruination, stroke, tragedy, trouble.
antonyms success, triumph.
disastrous *adj.* calamitous, cataclysmic, catastrophic, destructive, devastating, dire, dreadful, fatal, harmful, ill-fated, miserable, ruinous, terrible, tragic, unfortunate.
antonyms successful, triumphant.
disband *v.* break up, demobilise, dismiss, disperse, dissolve, part company, retire, scatter, separate.
antonyms assemble, band, combine.
disbelief *n.* distrust, doubt, incredulity, mistrust, rejection, scepticism, suspicion, unbelief.
antonym belief.
disbelieve *v.* discount, mistrust, reject, repudiate, suspect, unbelieve.
antonyms believe, trust.
disbursement *n.* disposal, expenditure, outlay, payment, spending.
disc *n.* circle, disk, diskette, face, plate, record, ring.
discard *v.* abandon, cast aside, dispense with, dispose of, ditch, drop, dump, jettison, leave off, reject, relinquish, remove, repudiate, scrap, shed.
antonyms adopt, embrace, espouse.
discern *v.* ascertain, behold, detect, determine, differentiate, discover, discriminate, distinguish, judge, make out, notice, observe, perceive, recognise, see.
discernible *adj.* apparent, appreciable, clear, detectable, discoverable, distinct, manifest, noticeable, observable, obvious, patent, perceptible, plain, recognisable, visible.
antonym invisible.
discerning *adj.* acute, astute, clear-sighted, critical, discriminating, eagle-eyed, penetrating, perceptive, piercing, sagacious, sensitive, sharp, shrewd, subtle, wise.
antonyms dull, obtuse.
discernment *n.* astuteness, awareness, cleverness, discrimination, ingenuity, insight, intelligence, judgement, keenness, penetration, perception, perceptiveness, sharpness, understanding, wisdom.
discharge *v.* **1** absolve, acquit, clear, dismiss, exonerate, free, liberate, pardon, release, relieve. **2** carry out, dispense, execute, fulfil, perform. **3** detonate, explode, fire, let off, set off, shoot. **4** eject, emit, empty, expel, give off, gush, ooze, remove.
antonyms **1** appoint, detain. **2** absorb, neglect, shirk.
n. **1** acquittal, exoneration, liberation, release. **2** ejection, emission, secretion. **3** accomplishment, execution, fulfilment.
antonyms **1** confinement, detention. **2** absorption. **3** disregard, neglect.
disciple *n.* adherent, believer, convert, devotee, follower, learner, proselyte, pupil, student, supporter, votary.
disciplinarian *n.* authoritarian, autocrat, despot, stickler, taskmaster, tyrant.
discipline *n.* chastisement, correction, drill, exercise, orderliness, practice, punishment, regulation, restraint, self-control, strictness, subject, training.
antonyms carelessness, negligence.
v. break in, castigate, chasten, chastise, check, control, correct, drill, educate, exercise, form, govern, instruct, penalise, punish, reprimand, toughen, train.
disclaim *v.* abandon, abjure, decline, deny, disown, reject, renounce, repudiate.
antonyms accept, acknowledge, claim.
disclaimer *n.* denial, rejection, renunciation, retraction.
disclose *v.* communicate, confess, discover, divulge, exhibit, expose, impart, lay bare, leak, let slip, publish, relate, reveal, show, tell, uncover, unfold, unveil, utter.
antonyms conceal, hide.
disclosure *n.* acknowledgement, admission, announcement, declaration, discovery, divulgence, exposé, exposure, leak, publication, revelation, uncovering.
discomfort *n.* ache, annoyance, disquiet, distress, hardship, hurt, irritation, malaise, trouble, uneasiness, vexation.
antonyms comfort, ease.
disconcert *v.* agitate, bewilder, confuse, disturb, fluster, hinder, perplex, perturb, rattle, ruffle, thwart, trouble, unbalance, undo, unnerve, unsettle, upset, worry.
disconcerting *adj.* alarming, awkward, baffling, bewildering, bothersome, confusing, dismaying, distracting, disturbing, embarrassing, off-putting, perplexing, unnerving, upsetting.

disconnect *v.* cut off, detach, disengage, divide, part, separate, sever, uncouple, unhitch, unhook, unlink, unplug.
antonyms attach, connect, engage.
disconnected *adj.* confused, disjointed, free, garbled, illogical, incoherent, irrational, jumbled, loose, rambling, unco-ordinated, unintelligible.
antonyms attached, coherent, connected.
disconsolate *adj.* crushed, dejected, desolate, dispirited, forlorn, gloomy, grief-stricken, heart-broken, heavy-hearted, hopeless, inconsolable, melancholy, miserable, sad, unhappy, wretched.
antonyms cheerful, joyful.
discontent *n.* disquiet, dissatisfaction, fretfulness, impatience, regret, restlessness, uneasiness, unrest, vexation.
antonym happiness.
discontented *adj.* browned off, cheesed off, complaining, disaffected, disgruntled, dissatisfied, exasperated, fed up, impatient, miserable, unhappy.
antonyms contented, happy, satisfied.
discontinue *v.* abandon, break off, cancel, cease, drop, end, finish, halt, interrupt, pause, quit, stop, suspend, terminate.
antonym continue.
discontinuity *n.* breach, disjointedness, disruption, disunion, incoherence, interruption, rupture.
antonym continuity.
discord *n.* clashing, conflict, contention, difference, din, disagreement, discordance, disharmony, dispute, dissension, dissonance, disunity, division, friction, harshness, incompatibility, jarring, opposition, rupture, split, strife, tumult, wrangling.
antonyms agreement, concord, harmony.
discordant *adj.* at odds, cacophonous, clashing, conflicting, contradictory, disagreeing, dissonant, grating, harsh, incompatible, incongruous, inconsistent, jangling, jarring, opposite.
antonyms concordant, harmonious.
discount[1] *v.* disbelieve, disregard, gloss over, ignore, overlook.
discount[2] *n.* abatement, allowance, concession, cut, deduction, mark-down, rebate, rebatement, reduction.
discourage *v.* deject, demoralise, depress, deter, disappoint, disfavour, dishearten, dismay, dispirit, dissuade, hinder, prevent, put off, restrain, scare, unnerve.
antonyms encourage, favour, hearten, inspire.
discouragement *n.* curb, damper, dejection, depression, despair, despondency, deterrent, disappointment, dismay, downheartedness, hindrance, hopelessness, impediment, obstacle, opposition, pessimism, rebuff, restraint, setback.
antonyms encouragement, incentive.
discourse *n.* address, chat, communication, conversation, converse, dialogue, discussion, dissertation, essay, homily, lecture, oration, sermon, speech, talk, treatise.
v. confer, converse, debate, discuss, lecture, talk.
discourteous *adj.* abrupt, bad-mannered, boorish, brusque, curt, disrespectful, ill-bred, ill-mannered, impolite, insolent, offhand, rude, slighting, unceremonious, uncivil.
antonyms courteous, gracious, polite, respectful.
discover *v.* ascertain, detect, determine, devise, dig up, discern, disclose, find, invent, learn, light on, locate, notice, originate, perceive, pioneer, realise, recognise, reveal, see, spot, uncover, unearth.
antonyms conceal, cover (up), hide.
discoverer *n.* author, explorer, finder, founder, initiator, inventor, originator, pioneer.
discovery *n.* breakthrough, detection, disclosure, exploration, find, innovation, introduction, invention, location, origination, revelation.
antonym concealment.
discredit *v.* challenge, defame, degrade, disgrace, dishonour, disparage, dispute, distrust, doubt, explode, mistrust, question, reproach, slander, slur, smear, vilify.
antonyms believe, credit.
n. aspersion, blame, censure, disgrace, dishonour, disrepute, distrust, doubt, ill-repute, mistrust, reproach, scandal, scepticism, shame, slur, smear, stigma, suspicion.
antonym credit.
discreditable *adj.* blameworthy, degrading, dishonourable, disreputable, humiliating, improper, infamous, reprehensible, scandalous, shameful, unprincipled.
antonyms creditable, worthy.
discredited *adj.* debunked, discarded, disgraced, dishonoured, exposed, outworn, refuted, rejected.
discreet *adj.* careful, cautious, delicate, diplomatic, judicious, politic, prudent, reserved, sensible, tactful, wary.
antonyms careless, indiscreet, tactless.
discrepancy *n.* conflict, difference, disagreement, discordance, disparity, dissimilarity, divergence, inconsistency, inequality, variance, variation.
discretion *n.* care, carefulness, caution, choice, circumspection, consideration, diplomacy, discernment, judgement, judiciousness, preference, prudence, responsibility, tact, wariness, will, wisdom, wish.
antonyms indiscretion, rashness.
discriminate *v.* assess, differentiate, discern, distinguish, make a distinction, segregate, separate, sift, tell apart.
antonyms confound, confuse.
discriminate (against) be biased, be prejudiced, victimise.
discriminating *adj.* astute, critical, cultivated, discerning, fastidious, particular, perceptive, selective, sensitive, tasteful.
discrimination *n.* **1** bias, bigotry, favouritism, inequity, intolerance, prejudice, unfairness. **2** acumen, acuteness, discernment, insight, judgement, keenness, penetration, perception, refine-

ment, subtlety, taste.
discursive *adj.* circuitous, erratic, long-winded, loose, meandering, rambling, wide-ranging.
antonyms brief, short.
discuss *v.* argue, confer, consider, consult, converse, debate, deliberate, examine.
discussion *n.* analysis, argument, conference, consideration, consultation, conversation, debate, deliberation, dialogue, discourse, examination, exchange, review, scrutiny, seminar, symposium.
disdain *v.* belittle, deride, despise, disregard, rebuff, reject, scorn, slight, sneer at, spurn, undervalue.
antonyms admire, respect.
n. arrogance, contempt, derision, dislike, haughtiness, scorn, sneering, snobbishness.
antonyms admiration, respect.
disdainful *adj.* aloof, arrogant, contemptuous, derisive, haughty, insolent, proud, scornful, sneering, supercilious, superior.
antonyms admiring, respectful.
disease *n.* affliction, ailment, blight, cancer, canker, complaint, condition, contamination, disorder, epidemic, ill-health, illness, indisposition, infection, infirmity, sickness, upset, virus.
antonym health.
diseased *adj.* ailing, contaminated, infected, poisoned, rotten, sick, tainted, unhealthy, unsound.
antonyms healthy, well.
disembark *v.* alight, arrive, debark, land.
antonym embark.
disembodied *adj.* bodiless, ghostly, immaterial, intangible, phantom, spiritual.
disenchanted *adj.* disappointed, disillusioned, fed up, indifferent, jaundiced, soured.
disenchantment *n.* disappointment, disillusion, disillusionment, revulsion.
disentangle *v.* clarify, detach, disconnect, disengage, extricate, free, loose, ravel out, resolve, separate, sever, simplify, unfold, unravel, untangle, untwist.
antonym entangle.
disfigure *v.* blemish, damage, deface, deform, distort, injure, maim, mar, mutilate, scar, spoil, uglify.
antonyms adorn, embellish.
disfigurement *n.* blemish, defacement, defect, deformity, disgrace, distortion, impairment, injury, mutilation, scar, spot, stain.
antonyms adornment, embellishment.
disgrace *n.* contempt, defamation, discredit, disfavour, dishonour, disrepute, ignominy, reproach, scandal, shame, slur, stain.
antonyms esteem, honour, respect.
v. defame, discredit, disfavour, dishonour, humiliate, reproach, scandalise, shame, slur, stain, stigmatise, sully, taint.
antonyms honour, respect.
disgraceful *adj.* appalling, dishonourable, disreputable, dreadful, mean, scandalous, shameful, shocking, unworthy.
antonyms honourable, respectable.
disgruntled *adj.* annoyed, browned off, cheesed off, discontented, displeased, dissatisfied, irritated, peeved, put out, sulky, sullen, testy, vexed.
antonyms happy, pleased, satisfied.
disguise *v.* camouflage, cloak, conceal, cover, deceive, dress up, explain away, fake, falsify, fudge, hide, mask, misrepresent, screen, shroud, veil.
antonyms expose, reveal, uncover.
n. camouflage, cloak, concealment, costume, cover, deception, façade, front, mask, masquerade, pretence, screen, semblance, travesty, veil, veneer.
disgust *v.* displease, nauseate, offend, outrage, put off, repel, revolt, scandalise, sicken.
antonyms delight, please, tempt.
n. abhorrence, aversion, detestation, dislike, hatred, loathing, nausea, repugnance, repulsion, revulsion.
antonyms admiration, liking.
disgusted *adj.* appalled, offended, outraged, repelled, repulsed, revolted, sick (and tired).
antonyms attracted, delighted.
disgusting *adj.* abominable, detestable, foul, nasty, nauseating, objectionable, obscene, odious, offensive, repellent, repugnant, revolting, shameless, sickening, unappetising, vile, vulgar.
antonyms attractive, delightful, pleasant.
dish *n.* bowl, food, plate, platter, recipe.
dish out allocate, distribute, dole out, give out, hand out, hand round, inflict, mete out.
dish up dispense, ladle, prepare, present, produce, scoop, serve, spoon.
dishearten *v.* cast down, crush, dampen, dash, daunt, deject, depress, deter, disappoint, discourage, dismay, dispirit, frighten, weary.
antonyms encourage, hearten.
dishevelled *adj.* bedraggled, disordered, messy, ruffled, rumpled, slovenly, tousled, uncombed, unkempt, untidy.
antonyms neat, spruce, tidy.
dishonest *adj.* cheating, corrupt, crafty, crooked, deceitful, deceptive, disreputable, double-dealing, false, fraudulent, immoral, lying, shady, snide, swindling, treacherous, unprincipled, untruthful, wrongful.
antonyms fair, honest, scrupulous, trustworthy.
dishonesty *n.* cheating, corruption, criminality, crookedness, deceit, falsehood, falsity, fraud, fraudulence, immorality, insincerity, stealing, treachery, trickery, unscrupulousness, wiliness.
antonyms honesty, truthfulness.
dishonour *v.* debase, debauch, defame, defile, degrade, demean, discredit, disgrace, shame.
antonym honour.
n. abasement, abuse, affront, aspersion, degradation, discourtesy, discredit, disfavour, disgrace, disrepute, ignominy, indignity, insult, outrage, reproach, scandal, shame, slight, slur.
antonyms honour, prestige.
dishonourable *adj.* base, contemptible, corrupt,

despicable, disgraceful, disreputable, scandalous, shameful, shameless, treacherous.
antonyms honourable, principled, worthy.

disillusioned *adj.* disappointed, disenchanted, enlightened, indifferent, undeceived, unenthusiastic.

disinclination *n.* alienation, aversion, dislike, loathness, objection, opposition, reluctance, repugnance, resistance, unwillingness.
antonym inclination.

disinfect *v.* clean, cleanse, decontaminate, deodorise, fumigate, purge, purify, sanitise, sterilise.
antonyms contaminate, infect.

disinfectant *n.* antiseptic, sanitiser, steriliser.

disintegrate *v.* break up, crumble, decompose, disunite, fall apart, moulder, rot, separate, shatter, splinter.
antonyms combine, merge, unite.

disinterest *n.* detachment, disinterestedness, dispassionateness, fairness, impartiality, justice, neutrality, unbiasedness.
antonym interest.

disinterested *adj.* detached, dispassionate, equitable, even-handed, impartial, neutral, open-minded, unbiased, uninvolved, unprejudiced, unselfish.
antonyms biased, concerned, interested, prejudiced.

disjointed *adj.* aimless, bitty, broken, confused, disarticulated, disconnected, dislocated, disordered, displaced, disunited, divided, fitful, incoherent, loose, rambling, separated, spasmodic, split, unconnected.
antonym coherent.

dislike *n.* animosity, antagonism, aversion, detestation, disapprobation, disapproval, disgust, disinclination, displeasure, distaste, enmity, hatred, hostility, loathing, repugnance.
antonyms attachment, liking, predilection.
v. abhor, abominate, despise, detest, disapprove, hate, loathe, scorn, shun.
antonyms favour, like, prefer.

dislocate *v.* disconnect, disengage, disjoint, disorder, displace, disrupt, disturb, disunite, misplace, shift.

dislocation *n.* disorder, disorganisation, disruption, disturbance, misarrangement, misarray, misplacement.
antonym order.

dislodge *v.* displace, disturb, eject, extricate, move, oust, remove, shift, uproot.

disloyal *adj.* apostate, faithless, false, traitorous, treacherous, two-faced, unfaithful, unpatriotic.
antonyms faithful, loyal, trustworthy.

dismal *adj.* bleak, dark, depressing, despondent, discouraging, dreary, forlorn, gloomy, hopeless, incompetent, inept, lonesome, long-faced, low-spirited, melancholy, poor, sad, sombre, sorrowful.
antonyms bright, cheerful.

dismantle *v.* demolish, disassemble, raze, strike, strip, take apart.
antonyms assemble, put together.

dismay *v.* alarm, daunt, depress, disappoint, disconcert, discourage, dishearten, disillusion, dispirit, distress, frighten, horrify, put off, scare, terrify, unnerve, unsettle.
antonyms encourage, hearten.
n. agitation, alarm, anxiety, apprehension, consternation, disappointment, discouragement, distress, dread, fear, fright, horror, panic, terror, trepidation, upset.
antonyms boldness, encouragement.

dismember *v.* amputate, disject, disjoint, dislocate, dissect, divide, mutilate, rend, sever.
antonyms assemble, join.

dismiss *v.* banish, disband, discharge, discount, dispel, disperse, disregard, dissolve, drop, fire, free, lay off, let go, reject, release, relegate, remove, repudiate, sack, send away, set aside, shelve, spurn.
antonyms accept, appoint, employ, retain.

disobey *v.* contravene, defy, disregard, flout, ignore, infringe, overstep, rebel, resist, transgress, violate.
antonyms keep, obey.

disorder *n.* **1** chaos, clutter, confusion, disarray, disorganisation, jumble, mess, muddle, shambles, untidiness. **2** brawl, clamour, commotion, confusion, disturbance, fight, fracas, quarrel, riot, tumult, uproar. **3** affliction, ailment, complaint, disability, disease, illness, malady, sickness.
antonyms **1** neatness, order. **2** law and order, peace.
v. clutter, confound, confuse, discompose, disorganise, disturb, jumble, mess up, misorder, mix up, muddle, scatter, unsettle, upset.
antonyms arrange, organise, tidy.

disorderly *adj.* chaotic, confused, disorganised, lawless, obstreperous, rebellious, rowdy, stormy, tumultuous, turbulent, undisciplined, unmanageable, unruly, untidy.
antonyms neat, orderly, tidy, well-behaved.

disorganise *v.* break up, confuse, destroy, discompose, disorder, disrupt, disturb, jumble, muddle, play havoc with, unsettle, upset.
antonyms organise, regulate, tidy.

disorientate *v.* confuse, disorient, mislead, muddle, perplex, puzzle, unbalance, unsettle, upset.

disown *v.* abandon, cast off, deny, disallow, disclaim, reject, renounce, repudiate.
antonyms accept, acknowledge.

disparaging *adj.* critical, derisive, derogatory, mocking, scornful, snide.
antonyms extolling, flattering, praising.

dispatch, despatch *v.* **1** consign, express, forward, send, transmit. **2** accelerate, conclude, dismiss, dispose of, finish, hasten, hurry, perform, quicken, settle.
antonyms **1** receive. **2** impede.
n. **1** account, bulletin, communication, communiqué, document, item, letter, message, news, piece, report, story. **2** alacrity, celerity, haste, promptness, quickness, rapidity, speed, swiftness.

antonym **2** slowness.
dispel *v.* allay, banish, dismiss, disperse, drive away, eliminate, expel, remove, resolve, scatter.
antonyms create, give rise to.
dispense *v.* **1** allocate, allot, apportion, assign, distribute, give out, mete out, share, supply. **2** administer, apply, discharge, enforce, execute, implement, operate.
dispense with abolish, cancel, discard, dispose of, disregard, forgo, get rid of, ignore, omit, relinquish, waive.
antonyms accept, use.
disperse *v.* break up, circulate, diffuse, disband, dismiss, dispel, dissolve, distribute, drive off, scatter, separate, spread.
antonym gather.
displace *v.* crowd out, depose, discard, discharge, dislocate, dislodge, dismiss, dispossess, disturb, eject, evict, misplace, move, oust, remove, replace, shift, succeed, supersede, supplant, transpose, unsettle.
display *v.* **1** demonstrate, exhibit, manifest, present, show. **2** betray, disclose, expose, reveal, show, unfold, unveil. **3** boast, flaunt, flourish, parade, show off, vaunt.
antonyms **1** conceal, hide. **2** disguise.
n. arrangement, demonstration, exhibition, manifestation, ostentation, parade, presentation, revelation, show, spectacle.
displease *v.* aggravate, anger, annoy, exasperate, incense, infuriate, irritate, offend, provoke, put out, rile, upset.
antonyms calm, please.
displeasure *n.* anger, annoyance, disapproval, discontent, disfavour, dudgeon, indignation, irritation, offence, resentment, wrath.
antonyms gratification, pleasure.
disposal *n.* assignment, clearance, consignment, control, conveyance, discarding, dumping, ejection, jettisoning, removal, riddance, scrapping, settlement, transfer.
dispose of **1** deal with, decide, settle. **2** discard, dump, get rid of, jettison, scrap. **3** destroy, kill.
antonym **2** keep.
disposed *adj.* apt, eager, inclined, liable, likely, minded, moved, predisposed, prone, ready, subject, willing.
antonym disinclined.
disposition *n.* bent, character, constitution, habit, inclination, leaning, make-up, management, nature, predisposition, proneness, readiness, spirit, temperament, tendency.
disproportionate *adj.* excessive, incommensurate, unequal, uneven, unreasonable.
antonyms appropriate, balanced.
disprove *v.* answer, confute, contradict, discredit, explode, expose, invalidate, rebut, refute.
antonyms confirm, prove.
dispute *v.* argue, challenge, clash, contend, contest, contradict, debate, deny, discuss, doubt, quarrel, question, squabble, wrangle.
antonyms agree, settle.
n. argument, conflict, contention, controversy, debate, disagreement, disturbance, feud, friction, quarrel, squabble, strife, wrangle.
antonyms agreement, settlement.
disqualify *v.* debar, disable, eliminate, incapacitate, invalidate, preclude, prohibit, rule out unfit.
antonyms accept, allow, qualify.
disquiet *n.* alarm, anxiety, concern, distress disturbance, fear, fretfulness, nervousness, restlessness, trouble, uneasiness, worry.
antonyms calmness, rest.
v. agitate, annoy, bother, concern, discompose distress, disturb, fret, trouble, upset, vex, worry
antonyms calm, settle.
disregard *v.* brush aside, despise, discount disdain, disobey, disparage, ignore, make ligh of, neglect, overlook, pass over, slight, snub turn a blind eye to.
antonyms note, pay attention to.
n. brush-off, contempt, disdain, disrespect indifference, neglect, negligence, oversight.
antonyms attention, heed.
disrepair *n.* collapse, decay, deterioration dilapidation, ruin, shabbiness.
antonyms good repair, restoration.
disreputable *adj.* base, contemptible, derogatory, disgraceful, dishonourable, disorderly, disrespectable, low, mean, notorious, scandalous seedy, shady, shameful, shocking.
antonyms decent, honourable, principled.
disrespectful *adj.* bad-tempered, cheeky, contemptuous, discourteous, impertinent, impolite impudent, insolent, insulting, irreverent, rude uncivil, unmannerly.
antonyms polite, respectful.
disrupt *v.* break into, break up, confuse, disorganise, disturb, interrupt, intrude, obstruct spoil, unsettle, upset.
dissatisfaction *n.* annoyance, disappointment discomfort, discontent, dislike, dismay, displeasure, distress, exasperation, frustration irritation, regret, resentment.
antonyms fulfilment, happiness, satisfaction.
dissect *v.* analyse, break down, dismember examine, explore, inspect, investigate, pore over, scrutinise, study.
dissension *n.* conflict, contention, disagreement, discord, dispute, dissent, friction, quarrel strife.
antonyms agreement, peace.
dissent *v.* decline, differ, disagree, object, protest, quibble, refuse.
antonyms agree, consent.
n. difference, disagreement, discord, dissension objection, opposition, quibble, refusal, resistance.
antonyms agreement, conformity.
dissenter *n.* dissident, nonconformist, objector protestant, protestor.
disservice *n.* bad turn, disfavour, harm, injury injustice, unkindness, wrong.
antonym favour.
dissident *adj.* differing, disagreeing, discordant dissenting, nonconformist, schismatic.

antonyms acquiescent, agreeing, orthodox.
n. agitator, critic, dissenter, protestor, rebel, recusant, schismatic.
antonym assenter.

dissimilar *adj.* different, divergent, diverse, heterogeneous, incompatible, mismatched, unlike, unrelated, various.
antonyms compatible, like, similar.

dissimilarity *n.* difference, discrepancy, distinction, divergence, diversity, incomparability, incompatibility, unlikeness.
antonyms compatibility, relatedness, similarity.

dissipate *v.* burn up, consume, deplete, disappear, dispel, disperse, dissolve, evaporate, expend, fritter away, lavish, spend, squander, vanish, waste.
antonyms accumulate, appear.

dissociate *v.* break off, detach, disband, disconnect, disrupt, distance, divorce, isolate, leave, quit, segregate, separate.
antonyms associate, attach, share, unite.

dissolute *adj.* abandoned, corrupt, debauched, degenerate, depraved, dissipated, immoral, lewd, licentious, wanton, wild.
antonyms restrained, virtuous.

dissolution *n.* adjournment, break-up, conclusion, decomposition, demise, destruction, disappearance, disbandment, discontinuation, disintegration, dismissal, dispersal, disruption, division, divorce, ending, evaporation, finish, overthrow, parting, resolution, separation, solution, suspension, termination.
antonyms commencement, unification.

dissolve *v.* **1** disintegrate, evaporate, liquefy, melt, thaw. **2** break up, crumble, decompose, destroy, disappear, discontinue, dismiss, disperse, divorce, end, separate, sever, suspend, terminate, wind up.

distance *n.* **1** extent, farness, gap, interval, length, range, reach, space, stretch, width. **2** aloofness, coldness, coolness, isolation, remoteness, reserve, separation.
antonyms **2** closeness, intimacy.

distant *adj.* **1** abroad, dispersed, far, faraway, far-flung, far-off, outlying, out-of-the-way, remote, scattered, separate. **2** aloof, cold, cool, formal, isolated, reserved, restrained, standoffish, stiff.
antonyms **1** close. **2** approachable, friendly.

distil *v.* condense, cull, evaporate, extract, flow, purify, rectify, refine, trickle, vaporise.

distinct *adj.* **1** detached, different, dissimilar, individual, separate, several. **2** apparent, clear, definite, evident, marked, noticeable, obvious, plain, recognisable.
antonyms **2** fuzzy, hazy, indistinct, vague.

distinction *n.* **1** characteristic, contrast, difference, differential, differentiation, discernment, discrimination, dissimilarity, division, feature, individuality, mark, nuance, peculiarity, quality, separation. **2** celebrity, eminence, excellence, fame, glory, greatness, honour, importance, merit, name, note, prestige, prominence, quality, rank, renown, reputation, repute, significance, superiority, worth.
antonyms **2** insignificance, unimportance.

distinctive *adj.* characteristic, different, distinguishing, extraordinary, idiosyncratic, individual, original, peculiar, singular, special, typical, unique.
antonyms common, ordinary.

distinguish *v.* **1** categorise, characterise, classify, decide, determine, differentiate, judge, know. **2** ascertain, discern, discriminate, identify, make out, perceive, pick out, recognise, see, separate, tell apart.

distinguished *adj.* acclaimed, celebrated, conspicuous, eminent, extraordinary, famed, famous, honoured, illustrious, marked, notable, noted, outstanding, renowned, striking, well-known.
antonyms insignificant, ordinary, unimpressive.

distort *v.* bend, colour, deform, disfigure, falsify, garble, misrepresent, misshape, pervert, slant, twist, warp, wrest.

distortion *n.* bend, bias, contortion, crookedness, deformity, falsification, misrepresentation, perversion, skew, slant, twist, warp.

distract *v.* bewilder, confound, confuse, disconcert, disturb, divert, engross, harass, occupy, perplex, puzzle, sidetrack, trouble.

distraught *adj.* agitated, anxious, beside oneself, crazy, distracted, distressed, frantic, hysterical, mad, overwrought, raving, wild, worked up, wrought up.
antonyms calm, unruffled, untroubled.

distress *n.* adversity, affliction, agony, anguish, anxiety, desolation, destitution, difficulties, discomfort, grief, hardship, heartache, misery, misfortune, need, pain, poverty, sadness, sorrow, suffering, torment, trial, trouble, worry, wretchedness.
antonyms comfort, ease, security.
v. afflict, agonise, bother, disturb, grieve, harass, harrow, pain, perplex, sadden, torment, trouble, upset, worry.
antonyms assist, comfort.

distribute *v.* allocate, circulate, convey, deal, deliver, diffuse, dish out, dispense, disperse, dispose, divide, give, group, hand out, scatter, share, spread, supply.
antonyms collect, gather in.

distribution *n.* allocation, apportionment, arrangement, circulation, dealing, delivery, dissemination, division, handling, mailing, marketing, partition, placement, scattering, sharing, spreading, supply, trading, transport.
antonyms collection, gathering.

district *n.* area, canton, community, locale, locality, neighbourhood, parish, precinct, quarter, region, sector, vicinity, ward.

distrust *v.* disbelieve, doubt, mistrust, question, suspect.
antonym trust.
n. disbelief, doubt, misgiving, mistrust, qualm, question, scepticism, suspicion, wariness.
antonym trust.

disturb *v.* **1** disrupt, distract, interrupt. **2** agitate,

annoy, bother, confuse, disorganise, distress, fluster, unsettle, upset, worry.
antonyms **2** calm, quiet, reassure.
disturbance *n.* agitation, annoyance, bother, brawl, bust-up, commotion, confusion, disorder, fracas, fray, hindrance, hubbub, interruption, intrusion, riot, shake-up, trouble, tumult, turmoil, upheaval, uproar, upset.
antonyms peace, quiet, rest.
disturbed *adj.* agitated, anxious, apprehensive, bothered, concerned, confused, flustered, maladjusted, neurotic, troubled, unbalanced, uneasy, upset, worried.
antonyms balanced, calm, sane.
disuse *n.* abandonment, decay, idleness, neglect.
antonym use.
ditch *n.* channel, drain, dyke, furrow, gully, level, moat, trench, watercourse.
dither *v.* hesitate, shilly-shally, vacillate, waver.
antonym decide.
n. bother, flap, fluster, indecision, panic, stew, tizzy.
antonym decision.
dive *v.* descend, dip, drop, fall, jump, leap, nose-dive, pitch, plummet, plunge, rush, sound, submerge, swoop.
n. dash, header, jump, leap, lunge, nose-dive, plunge, rush, spring, swoop.
diverge *v.* branch, conflict, deviate, differ, digress, disagree, dissent, divide, fork, part, separate, split, spread, stray, vary, wander.
antonyms agree, come together, converge, join.
diverse *adj.* assorted, different, differing, discrete, dissimilar, distinct, manifold, many, miscellaneous, numerous, separate, several, some, sundry, varied, various, varying.
antonyms identical, like, similar.
diversify *v.* alter, assort, branch out, change, expand, mix, spread out, vary.
diversion *n.* **1** detour, deviation. **2** amusement, distraction, enjoyment, entertainment, game, pastime, play, pleasure, recreation, relaxation, sport. **3** alteration, change, deflection.
diversity *n.* assortment, difference, dissimilarity, medley, range, variance, variety.
antonyms likeness, sameness, similarity.
divert *v.* avert, deflect, detract, distract, hive off, redirect, reroute, side-track, switch.
divide *v.* **1** bisect, break up, cut, detach, disconnect, part, partition, separate, split. **2** allocate, allot, apportion, deal out, distribute, share. **3** alienate, disunite, estrange, separate. **4** classify, grade, group, segregate, sort, subdivide.
antonyms **1** join. **2** collect, gather. **3** unite.
divine *adj.* angelic, celestial, consecrated, exalted, glorious, godlike, heavenly, holy, mystical, perfect, religious, sacred, sanctified, spiritual, superhuman, supernatural, supreme, transcendent.
antonyms human, mundane.
divinity *n.* deity, god, goddess, godhead, godhood, godliness, holiness, sanctity, spirit.
division *n.* **1** cutting, detaching, dichotomy, disagreement, discord, disunion, estrangement, feud, rupture, schism, separation, split, variance. **2** allotment, apportionment, distribution, sharing. **3** branch, category, class, compartment, department, group, part, section, sector, segment.
antonyms **1** agreement, unification, union. **3** unity, whole.
divorce *n.* annulment, breach, break, break-up, dissolution, disunion, rupture, separation, severance, split-up.
v. annul, cancel, disconnect, dissever, dissociate, dissolve, divide, part, separate, sever, split up.
antonyms marry, unify, unite.
divulge *v.* betray, communicate, confess, declare, disclose, exhibit, expose, impart, leak, let slip, proclaim, promulgate, publish, reveal, tell, uncover.
dizzy *adj.* **1** faint, giddy, reeling, shaky, swimming, wobbly. **2** bewildered, confused, dazed, light-headed, muddled.
do *v.* **1** accomplish, achieve, carry out, complete, conclude, end, execute, finish, fulfil, implement, perform, present, put on, render, undertake, work. **2** act, behave, conduct oneself. **3** arrange, cause, create, deal with, fix, look after, make, manage, organise, prepare, proceed, produce. **4** satisfy, serve, suffice.
n. affair, event, function, gathering, occasion, party.
do away with abolish, destroy, discard, discontinue, do in, eliminate, exterminate, get rid of, kill, murder, remove.
do down belittle, criticise, discredit, humiliate.
do out of balk, cheat, con, deprive, fleece, rook, swindle, trick.
do up 1 fasten, pack, tie. **2** decorate, modernise, redecorate, renovate, repair, restore.
do without abstain from, dispense with, forgo, give up, relinquish, waive.
docile *adj.* amenable, controlled, manageable, obedient, obliging, quiet, submissive, teachable.
antonyms protesting, truculent, unco-operative.
dock[1] *n.* boat-yard, harbour, marina, pier, quay, waterfront, wharf.
v. anchor, berth, drop anchor, land, link up, moor, put in, tie up, unite.
dock[2] *v.* clip, crop, curtail, cut, decrease, deduct, diminish, lessen, reduce, shorten, subtract, withhold.
doctor *n.* clinician, general practitioner, GP, medic, medical officer, medical practitioner, physician.
v. adulterate, alter, change, cobble, cook, cut, dilute, disguise, falsify, fix, misrepresent, pervert, repair, tamper with.
doctrine *n.* belief, canon, concept, conviction, creed, dogma, opinion, precept, principle, teaching, tenet.
document *n.* certificate, deed, form, instrument, paper, parchment, record, report.
v. chronicle, cite, corroborate, detail, instance, list, prove, record, report, support, verify.
documentary *n.* feature, film, programme, video.

dodge *v.* avoid, deceive, elude, evade, shift, shirk, side-step, swerve, trick.
n. machination, manoeuvre, ploy, ruse, scheme, stratagem, trick, wile.

doer *n.* accomplisher, achiever, activist, bustler, dynamo, go-getter, live wire, organiser, powerhouse, wheeler-dealer.

dog *n.* beast, bitch, canine, hound, mongrel, mutt, pup, puppy, yapper.
v. harry, haunt, hound, plague, pursue, shadow, tail, track, trail, trouble, worry.

dogged *adj.* determined, firm, indefatigable, obstinate, persevering, persistent, relentless, resolute, single-minded, staunch, steadfast, steady, stubborn, tenacious, unshakable, unyielding.
antonyms apathetic, flagging, irresolute.

dogma *n.* article (of faith), belief, conviction, credo, creed, doctrine, opinion, precept, principle, teaching, tenet.

dogmatic *adj.* arbitrary, assertive, authoritative, categorical, dictatorial, doctrinal, downright, emphatic, opinionated, overbearing, positive.

doings *n.* actions, activities, acts, adventures, affairs, concerns, dealings, deeds, events, exploits, goings-on, happenings, proceedings.

dole out *v.* administer, allocate, allot, apportion, assign, deal, dispense, distribute, divide, give, hand out, issue, mete out, ration, share.

doll *n.* dolly, figurine, marionette, moppet, plaything, puppet, toy.
doll up deck out, dress up, tart up.

domain *n.* area, authority, business, concern, department, discipline, dominion, empire, field, jurisdiction, kingdom, lands, orbit, power, province, realm, region, scope, speciality, sphere, territory.

domestic *adj.* family, home, home-bred, home-loving, homely, household, house-trained, indigenous, internal, native, pet, private, stay-at-home, tame, trained.
n. au pair, char, charwoman, daily, daily help, help, maid, servant.

domesticate *v.* accustom, break, familiarise, house-train, naturalise, tame, train.

dominant *adj.* assertive, authoritative, chief, commanding, controlling, governing, important, influential, leading, main, outstanding, powerful, predominant, pre-eminent, presiding, prevailing, prevalent, primary, prime, principal, prominent, ruling, superior, supreme.
antonyms submissive, subordinate.

dominate *v.* control, direct, domineer, dwarf, eclipse, govern, lead, master, monopolise, overbear, overrule, overshadow, prevail, rule, tyrannise.

domineering *adj.* arrogant, authoritarian, autocratic, bossy, despotic, dictatorial, harsh, high-handed, imperious, iron-handed, masterful, oppressive, overbearing, severe, tyrannical.
antonyms meek, servile.

dominion *n.* authority, colony, command, control, country, domain, domination, empire, government, jurisdiction, kingdom, lordship, mastery, power, province, realm, region, rule, sovereignty, supremacy, sway, territory.

donate *v.* bequeath, bestow, chip in, confer, contribute, cough up, fork out, give, impart, present, proffer, subscribe.
antonyms receive, take.

donation *n.* alms, benefaction, conferment, contribution, gift, grant, gratuity, largess(e), offering, present, presentation, subscription.

done *adj.* **1** accomplished, completed, concluded, executed, finished, OK, over, perfected, realised, settled. **2** acceptable, conventional, ended, proper. **3** cooked, ready.
done for beaten, broken, dashed, defeated, destroyed, doomed, finished, foiled, lost, ruined, wrecked.
done in all in, bushed, dead, dead beat, dog-tired, exhausted.

donkey *n.* ass, hinny, jackass, jenny, mule.

donor *n.* benefactor, contributor, fairy godmother, giver, granter, philanthropist, provider.
antonym beneficiary.

doom *n.* catastrophe, condemnation, death, death-knell, destiny, destruction, downfall, fate, fortune, judgement, lot, portion, ruin, sentence, verdict.
v. condemn, consign, damn, destine, judge, sentence.

doomed *adj.* condemned, cursed, destined, fated, hopeless, ill-fated, ill-starred, luckless.

door *n.* doorway, entrance, entry, exit, opening, portal, vomitory.

dope *n.* **1** drugs, hallucinogen, narcotic, opiate. **2** blockhead, clot, dimwit, dunce, fool, half-wit, idiot, simpleton.
v. anaesthetise, doctor, drug, inject, load, medicate, sedate.

dormant *adj.* asleep, comatose, fallow, hibernating, inactive, inert, latent, sleeping, sluggish, torpid.
antonyms active, awake, developed, realised.

dose *n.* dosage, measure, portion, potion, prescription, quantity, shot.
v. administer, dispense, medicate, treat.

dot *n.* atom, circle, decimal point, fleck, full stop, iota, jot, mark, pin-point, point, speck, spot.
v. dab, dabble, punctuate, spot, sprinkle, stud.

dote on admire, adore, idolise, indulge, pamper, spoil, treasure.

doting *adj.* adoring, devoted, fond, foolish, indulgent, lovesick, soft.

double *adj.* coupled, doubled, dual, duplicate, paired, twice, twin, twofold.
antonyms half, single.
v. duplicate, enlarge, fold, grow, increase, magnify, multiply, repeat.
n. clone, copy, counterpart, duplicate, fellow, image, impersonator, lookalike, mate, replica, ringer, spitting image, twin.
at the double at once, immediately, quickly, without delay.

double-cross *v.* betray, cheat, con, defraud, hoodwink, mislead, swindle, trick, two-time.

doubly *adv.* again, especially, twice, twofold.

doubt *v.* be dubious, be uncertain, distrust, fear, hesitate, mistrust, query, question, suspect, vacillate, waver.
antonyms believe, trust.
n. **1** apprehension, distrust, incredulity, misgiving, mistrust, reservation, scepticism, suspicion, uncertainty. **2** ambiguity, confusion, difficulty, dilemma, hesitation, indecision, perplexity, problem, quandary.
antonyms **1** faith, trust. **2** belief, certainty.

doubter *n.* agnostic, cynic, disbeliever, doubting Thomas, questioner, sceptic, scoffer, unbeliever.
antonym believer.

doubtful *adj.* debatable, hesitant, obscure, perplexed, precarious, questionable, sceptical, suspicious, tentative, uncertain, unclear, unsure, vacillating, vague, wavering.
antonyms certain, decided, definite, settled.

doubtless *adv.* certainly, clearly, indisputably, most likely, no doubt, of course, precisely, presumably, probably, seemingly, supposedly, surely, truly, undoubtedly, unquestionably, without doubt.

dour *adj.* austere, dismal, dreary, forbidding, gloomy, grim, hard, inflexible, morose, obstinate, rigid, rigorous, severe, sour, strict, sullen, unfriendly, unyielding.
antonyms bright, cheery, easy-going.

douse, dowse *v.* blow out, dip, drench, duck, dunk, extinguish, immerge, immerse, plunge, put out, saturate, smother, snuff, soak, steep, submerge.

dowdy *adj.* dingy, drab, frumpy, ill-dressed, old-fashioned, shabby, slovenly, tacky, tatty, unfashionable.
antonyms fashionable, smart, spruce.

down[1] *n.* bloom, floss, fluff, nap, pile, shag, wool.

down[2] *v.* drink, fell, floor, gulp, knock back, swallow, throw, topple, toss off.
down and out derelict, destitute, impoverished, penniless, ruined.
down at heel dowdy, impoverished, run-down, seedy, shabby, slovenly, worn.
down with away with, exterminate, get rid of.

down-and-out *n.* beggar, derelict, dosser, outcast, pauper, tramp, vagabond, vagrant.

downcast *adj.* crestfallen, dejected, depressed, despondent, disappointed, discouraged, disheartened, dismayed, dispirited, down, miserable, sad, unhappy.
antonyms cheerful, elated, happy.

downfall *n.* collapse, debacle, descent, destruction, disgrace, failure, fall, humiliation, overthrow, ruin, undoing.

downgrade *v.* belittle, decry, degrade, demote, denigrate, detract from, disparage, humble, lower, run down.
antonyms improve, upgrade.

downhearted *adj.* dejected, depressed, despondent, discouraged, disheartened, dismayed, downcast, gloomy, glum, low-spirited, sad, unhappy.
antonyms cheerful, enthusiastic, happy.

downpour *n.* cloudburst, deluge, flood, rainstorm, torrent.

downright *adj., adv.* absolute(ly), clear(ly), complete(ly), explicit(ly), frank(ly), out-and-out, outright, plain(ly), utter(ly).

down-to-earth *adj.* commonsense, hard-headed, matter-of-fact, no-nonsense, practical, realistic, sane, sensible.
antonyms fantastic, impractical, sentimental.

down-trodden *adj.* abused, afflicted, distressed, exploited, helpless, oppressed, subjugated, subservient, trampled on, tyrannised, victimised.

downward *adj.* declining, descending, downhill, sliding, slippery.
antonym upward.

dowry *n.* endowment, gift, inheritance, legacy, property, provision, share.

dowse *see* **douse**.

doze *v.* drop off, kip, nod off, sleep, snooze.
n. catnap, forty winks, kip, nap, shut-eye, siesta, snooze.

drab *adj.* cheerless, dingy, dismal, dreary, dull, flat, gloomy, grey, shabby, sombre.
antonyms bright, cheerful, inspired.

draft[1] *v.* compose, design, draw (up), formulate, outline, plan, sketch.
n. abstract, delineation, outline, plan, protocol, rough, sketch, version.

draft[2] *n.* bill, cheque, order, postal order.

drag *v.* draw, haul, lug, pull, sweep, tow, trail, tug, yank.
n. annoyance, bore, bother, nuisance, pain, pest.
drag on, drag out draw out, extend, hang on, lengthen, persist, prolong, protract, spin out.

drain *v.* **1** bleed, discharge, draw off, dry, empty, evacuate, flow out, leak, milk, ooze, remove, strain, trickle. **2** consume, deplete, drink up, exhaust, sap, swallow, tap, use up.
antonyms **1** fill, flood.
n. channel, conduit, culvert, ditch, duct, outlet, pipe, sap, sewer, sink, strain, trench, watercourse.

drainage *n.* sewage, sewerage, waste.

drama *n.* **1** acting, melodrama, play, scene, show, spectacle, stage-craft, theatre. **2** crisis, excitement, turmoil.

dramatic *adj.* **1** marked, noticeable, significant, striking, sudden, surprising. **2** exciting, expressive, graphic, impressive, stirring, thrilling.
antonyms **1** normal, ordinary.

dramatist *n.* comedian, playwright, play-writer, screen-writer, scriptwriter.

drape *v.* cover, droop, drop, fold, hang, suspend, vest, wrap.

drapery *n.* blind(s), covering(s), curtain(s), hanging(s), tapestry.

drastic *adj.* desperate, dire, extreme, far-reaching, forceful, harsh, radical, severe, strong.
antonyms cautious, mild, moderate.

draught *n.* current, drawing, drink, flow, influx, movement, portion, puff, pulling, quantity, traction.

draw *v.* **1** allure, attract, bring forth, choose,

derive, elicit, engage, evoke, influence, persuade. **2** drag, haul, pull, tow, tug. **3** delineate, depict, design, map out, mark out, paint, pencil, portray, sketch, trace. **4** be equal, be even, tie.
antonyms **2** propel, push.
n. **1** appeal, attraction, bait, enticement, interest, lure. **2** dead-heat, stalemate, tie.
draw on employ, exploit, extract, make use of, rely on, take from, use.
draw out drag out, elongate, extend, lengthen, prolong, protract, spin out, stretch, string out.
antonym curtail.
draw up **1** compose, draft, formulate, frame, halt, prepare, write out. **2** pull up, run in, stop.
drawback *n.* defect, deficiency, detriment, difficulty, disability, disadvantage, fault, flaw, handicap, hindrance, hitch, impediment, imperfection, nuisance, obstacle, snag, stumbling, trouble.
antonyms advantage, benefit.
drawing *n.* cartoon, graphic, illustration, outline, picture, portrait, portrayal, representation, sketch, study.
drawl *v.* drone, protract, twang.
dread *v.* cringe at, fear, flinch, quail, shrink from, shudder, shy, tremble.
n. alarm, apprehension, aversion, awe, dismay, disquiet, fear, fright, horror, misgiving, terror, trepidation, worry.
antonyms confidence, security.
dreadful *adj.* appalling, awful, dire, distressing, frightful, ghastly, grievous, hideous, horrible, shocking, terrible, tragic, tremendous.
antonyms comforting, wonderful.
dream *n.* aspiration, daydream, delight, delusion, design, desire, fantasy, goal, hallucination, hope, illusion, imagination, marvel, notion, pipe-dream, pleasure, reverie, speculation, trance, treasure, vision, wish.
v. conjure, daydream, envisage, fancy, fantasise, hallucinate, imagine, muse, think, visualise.
dream up conceive, concoct, contrive, cook up, create, devise, hatch, imagine, invent, spin, think up.
dreamer *n.* daydreamer, idealist, romancer, star-gazer, theoriser, visionary.
antonyms pragmatist, realist.
dreamlike *adj.* illusory, insubstantial, phantom, strange, trance-like, unreal, visionary.
dreamy *adj.* absent, daydreaming, fanciful, fantastic, faraway, gentle, imaginary, impractical, misty, musing, pensive, romantic, shadowy, speculative, unreal, vague, visionary.
antonyms down-to-earth, practical, realistic.
dreary *adj.* boring, commonplace, depressing, dismal, downcast, drab, dull, gloomy, glum, humdrum, lifeless, lonely, monotonous, mournful, routine, sad, sombre, tedious, trite, uneventful, wearisome.
antonyms bright, cheerful, interesting.
dregs *n.* **1** deposit, dross, fag-end, grounds, lees, residue, sediment, trash, waste. **2** outcasts, riff-raff, scum.
drench *v.* douse, drown, duck, flood, imbue, immerse, inundate, saturate, soak, souse, steep, wet.
dress *n.* clothes, clothing, costume, frock, garb, garment(s), gear, get-up, outfit, robe, suit, togs.
v. adjust, adorn, arrange, change, clothe, deck, decorate, don, drape, fit, garb, garnish, groom, prepare, put on, rig, robe, set, straighten, tend, treat, trim, wear.
antonyms disrobe, strip, undress.
dress up adorn, beautify, deck, disguise, doll up, embellish, gild, improve, tart up.
dressing *n.* bandage, compress, ligature, pad, plaster, poultice, tourniquet.
dressmaker *n.* seamstress, sewing woman, tailor, tailoress.
dribble *v.* drip, drivel, drool, drop, leak, ooze, run, saliva, seep, slaver, slobber, trickle.
n. drip, droplet, gobbet, leak, sprinkling, trickle.
dried *adj.* arid, dehydrated, desiccated, drained, parched, shrivelled, wilted, withered, wizened.
drift *v.* accumulate, coast, drive, float, freewheel, gather, pile up, stray, waft, wander.
n. **1** accumulation, heap, mass, mound, pile, shift. **2** aim, course, current, design, direction, flow, gist, implication, intention, meaning, movement, rush, scope, significance, sweep, tendency, tenor, thrust, trend.
drill *v.* **1** coach, discipline, exercise, instruct, practise, rehearse, teach, train, tutor. **2** bore, penetrate, perforate, pierce, puncture.
n. **1** coaching, discipline, exercise, instruction, practice, preparation, repetition, training, tuition. **2** awl, bit, borer, gimlet.
drink *v.* absorb, booze, carouse, down, drain, gulp, guzzle, imbibe, indulge, knock back, partake of, revel, sip, suck, sup, swallow, swig, swill, tank up, tipple, toss off.
n. alcohol, beverage, booze, glass, gulp, liquid, liquor, noggin, refreshment, sip, spirits, stiffener, swallow, swig, taste, the bottle, tipple, tot.
drinker *n.* alcoholic, boozer, carouser, dipsomaniac, drunk, drunkard, guzzler, inebriate, tippler, wino.
antonyms abstainer, teetotaller.
drip *v.* dribble, drizzle, drop, plop, splash, sprinkle, trickle, weep.
n. **1** dribble, drop, leak, trickle. **2** ninny, softy, weakling, weed, wet.
drive *v.* **1** control, direct, handle, manage, motivate, operate, run. **2** coerce, compel, constrain, force, guide, impel, oblige, press, propel, push, tax, urge. **3** motor, ride, steer, travel.
n. **1** action, ambition, appeal, campaign, crusade, determination, effort, energy, enterprise, get-up-and-go, initiative, motivation, pressure, push. **2** excursion, jaunt, journey, outing, ride, spin, trip.
drive at aim, allude to, get at, imply, indicate, insinuate, intend, intimate, mean, refer to, signify, suggest.
drivel *n.* bunkum, eyewash, gibberish, gobbledegook, mumbo-jumbo, nonsense, slush, twaddle, waffle.
driver *n.* cabbie, cabman, chauffeur, coachman,

motorist, trucker, wag(g)oner.

driving *adj.* compelling, dynamic, energetic, forceful, forthright, heavy, sweeping, vigorous, violent.

drizzle *n.* mist, rain, shower.
v. rain, shower, spit, spot, spray, sprinkle.

drone *v.* buzz, chant, drawl, hum, intone, purr, thrum, vibrate, whirr.
n. buzz, chant, hum, murmuring, purr, vibration, whirring.

droop *v.* bend, dangle, decline, drop, fade, faint, fall down, falter, flag, hang (down), languish, lose heart, sag, sink, slouch, slump, stoop, wilt, wither.
antonyms flourish, rise, straighten.

drop *n.* **1** bead, bubble, dab, dash, drib, drip, droplet, globule, pinch, sip, spot, trace, trickle. **2** decline, decrease, deterioration, downturn, fall, falling-off, lowering, plunge, reduction, slump. **3** abyss, chasm, descent, precipice, slope.
v. **1** decline, depress, descend, diminish, dive, droop, fall, lower, plummet, plunge, sink, tumble. **2** abandon, cease, desert, discontinue, forsake, give up, jilt, leave, quit, reject, relinquish, renounce, repudiate, throw over.
antonyms **1** mount, rise. **2** continue.
drop off **1** doze, have forty winks, nod off, snooze. **2** decline, decrease, diminish, dwindle, fall off, lessen, slacken. **3** deliver, leave, set down.
antonyms **1** wake up. **2** increase. **3** pick up.
drop out abandon, back out, cry off, forsake, leave, quit, stop, withdraw.

drop-out *n.* deviant, dissenter, hippie, loner, non-conformist, rebel, renegade.

droppings *n.* dung, excrement, excreta, faeces, manure, stools.

drought *n.* aridity, dehydration, desiccation, dryness, need, parchedness, shortage, want.

drown *v.* deluge, drench, engulf, extinguish, flood, go under, immerse, inundate, overcome, overpower, overwhelm, sink, stifle, submerge, swallow up, swamp, wipe out.

drowsy *adj.* dazed, dreamy, drugged, heavy, lethargic, lulling, nodding, restful, sleepy, tired.
antonyms alert, awake.

drudge *n.* dogsbody, factotum, galley-slave, hack, lackey, menial, servant, skivvy, slave, toiler, worker.
v. beaver, grind, labour, plod, plug away, slave, toil, work.
antonyms idle, laze.

drudgery *n.* chore, donkey-work, grind, hack-work, labour, skivvying, slavery, slog, sweat, sweated labour, toil.

drug *n.* depressant, medication, medicine, narcotic, opiate, poison, potion, remedy, stimulant.
v. anaesthetise, deaden, dope, dose, drench, knock out, medicate, numb, poison, stupefy, treat.

drum *v.* beat, pulsate, rap, reverberate, tap, tattoo, throb, thrum.
drum into din into, drive home, hammer, instil, reiterate.
drum up attract, canvass, collect, gather, obtain, petition, round up, solicit.

drunk *adj.* blotto, bottled, canned, drunken, inebriated, intoxicated, lit up, loaded, lushy, merry, paralytic, plastered, sloshed, soused, sozzled, stoned, tanked up, tiddly, tight, tipsy, under the influence, well-oiled, wet.
antonyms abstinent, sober, teetotal, temperate.
n. boozer, drunkard, inebriate, lush, soak, wino.

drunkard *n.* alcoholic, carouser, dipsomaniac, drinker, drunk, lush, soak, sot, souse, sponge, tippler, wino.

dry *adj.* **1** arid, barren, dehydrated, desiccated, parched, thirsty, withered. **2** boring, dreary, dull, monotonous, tedious, tiresome. **3** cutting, cynical, deadpan, droll, keen, sarcastic, sharp.
antonyms **1** wet. **2** interesting.
v. dehydrate, desiccate, drain, harden, parch, shrivel, wilt, wither.
antonyms soak, wet.

dual *adj.* binary, combined, coupled, double, duplex, duplicate, matched, paired, twin, two-fold.

dubious *adj.* ambiguous, debatable, doubtful, fishy, hesitant, indefinite, obscure, questionable, sceptical, shady, suspect, suspicious, uncertain, unclear, undecided, unsettled, unsure, wavering.
antonyms certain, reliable, trustworthy.

duck *v.* **1** avoid, bend, crouch, dodge, drop, escape, evade, shirk, shun, sidestep, squat, stoop. **2** dip, dive, douse, dunk, immerse, lower, plunge, souse, submerge, wet.

dud *adj.* broken, bust, duff, failed, inoperative, kaput, valueless, worthless.

due *adj.* **1** in arrears, outstanding, owed, owing, payable, unpaid. **2** appropriate, deserved, fitting, justified, merited, proper, rightful, suitable. **3** adequate, ample, enough, plenty of, sufficient. **4** expected, scheduled.
antonyms **1** paid. **3** inadequate.
adv. dead, direct(ly), exactly, precisely, straight.

duel *n.* affair of honour, clash, combat, competition, contest, encounter, engagement, fight, rivalry, struggle.

dull *adj.* **1** boring, dismal, dreary, flat, heavy, humdrum, lifeless, monotonous, plain, tedious, uneventful, unexciting, unimaginative, uninteresting. **2** cloudy, dark, dim, drab, gloomy, grey, indistinct, insipid, lack-lustre, murky, opaque, overcast. **3** dense, dim, dimwitted, slow, stupid, thick, unintelligent.
antonyms **1** exciting, interesting. **2** bright, clear. **3** clever, intelligent.
v. alleviate, blunt, dampen, discourage, fade, lessen, mitigate, moderate, numb, obscure, paralyse, relieve, sadden, soften, subdue.
antonym stimulate.

duly *adv.* accordingly, appropriately, correctly, properly, rightfully, suitably, sure enough.

dumb *adj.* inarticulate, mum, mute, silent, soundless, speechless, tongue-tied.

dum(b)founded *adj.* amazed, astonished, astounded, bowled over, confounded, confused, dumb, flabbergasted, floored, overcome, overwhelmed, paralysed, speechless, staggered, startled, taken aback, thrown.

dummy *n.* copy, counterfeit, duplicate, figure, form, imitation, lay-figure, manikin, mannequin, model, substitute, teat.
adj. artificial, bogus, fake, false, imitation, mock, phoney, practice, sham, simulated, trial.

dump *v.* deposit, discharge, dispose of, ditch, drop, empty out, get rid of, jettison, let fall, offload, park, scrap, throw away, throw down, tip, unload.
n. hole, hovel, joint, junk-yard, mess, pigsty, rubbish-heap, rubbish-tip, shack, shanty, slum, tip.

dumpy *adj.* chubby, chunky, plump, podgy, pudgy, roly-poly, short, squab, squat, stout, stubby, tubby.
antonyms tall, thin.

dunce *n.* ass, blockhead, dimwit, donkey, halfwit, nincompoop, simpleton.
antonyms brain, intellectual.

dung *n.* excrement, faeces, manure.

dupe *n.* fall guy, flat, gull, instrument, mug, pawn, puppet, push-over, simpleton, stooge, sucker, victim.
v. bamboozle, cheat, con, deceive, defraud, delude, fool, hoax, hoodwink, humbug, outwit, rip off, swindle, trick.

duplicate *adj.* corresponding, identical, matched, matching, twin, twofold.
n. carbon (copy), facsimile, match, photocopy, Photostat®, replica, reproduction, Xerox®.
v. clone, copy, ditto, double, echo, photocopy, Photostat®, repeat, reproduce, Xerox®.

durable *adj.* abiding, constant, dependable, enduring, fast, firm, fixed, hard-wearing, lasting, long-lasting, permanent, persistent, reliable, resistant, sound, stable, strong, sturdy, substantial, tough, unfading.
antonyms fragile, perishable, weak.

duration *n.* continuation, extent, fullness, length, period, span, spell, stretch.

duress *n.* coercion, compulsion, constraint, force, pressure, restraint, threat.

dusk *n.* dark, darkness, evening, gloaming, gloom, nightfall, shade, shadows, sundown, sunset, twilight.
antonyms brightness, dawn.

dust *n.* dirt, earth, grime, grit, ground, particles, powder, soil.
v. clean, cover, polish, powder, sift, spray, spread, wipe.

dusty *adj.* chalky, crumbly, dirty, filthy, granular, grubby, powdery, sandy, sooty.
antonyms clean, hard, polished, solid.

dutiful *adj.* conscientious, devoted, filial, obedient, respectful, reverential, submissive.

duty *n.* **1** assignment, business, calling, charge, chore, function, job, loyalty, obedience, obligation, office, responsibility, role, service, task, work. **2** customs, excise, levy, tariff, tax, toll.
on duty at work, busy, engaged.

dwarf *n.* elf, gnome, goblin, Lilliputian, midget, pygmy, Tom Thumb.
adj. baby, diminutive, Lilliputian, mini, miniature, petite, pocket, small, tiny.
antonym large.
v. check, diminish, dominate, lower, overshadow, tower over.

dwell *v.* abide, inhabit, live, lodge, people, populate, remain, reside, rest, settle, sojourn, stay.
dwell on elaborate, emphasise, harp on (about), linger over, mull over.
antonym pass over.

dwindle *v.* abate, contract, decay, decline, decrease, die, die out, diminish, disappear, ebb, fade, fall, lessen, peter out, shrink, shrivel, sink, subside, tail off, taper off, vanish, wane, waste away, weaken, wither.
antonyms gain, grow, increase.

dye *n.* colour, colouring, grain, pigment, stain, tinge, tint.
v. colour, imbue, pigment, stain, tinge, tint.

dying *adj.* fading, failing, final, going, moribund, mortal, not long for this world, passing, perishing, sinking, vanishing.
antonyms coming, reviving.

dynamic *adj.* active, driving, electric, energetic, forceful, go-ahead, high-powered, lively, powerful, self-starting, spirited, vigorous, vital.
antonyms apathetic, inactive, slow.

E

eager *adj.* earnest, enthusiastic, fervent, impatient, intent, keen, longing, raring, vehement, yearning, zealous.
antonyms apathetic, indifferent, unenthusiastic.

ear *n.* ability, appreciation, attention, consideration, discrimination, hearing, heed, notice, perception, regard, sensitivity, skill.

early *adj.* advanced, forward, prehistoric, premature, primeval, primitive, undeveloped, untimely, young.
adv. ahead of time, beforehand, in advance, in good time, prematurely, too soon.
antonym late.

earn *v.* bring in, collect, deserve, draw, gain, get, gross, make, merit, net, obtain, rate, realise, reap, receive, warrant, win.
antonyms lose, spend.

earnest *adj.* ardent, devoted, eager, enthusiastic, fervent, firm, fixed, grave, heartfelt, impassioned, intent, keen, passionate, resolute, resolved, serious, sincere, solemn, steady, urgent, warm, zealous.
antonyms apathetic, flippant, frivolous.

earnings *n.* emoluments, gain, income, pay, proceeds, profits, receipts, remuneration, return, revenue, reward, salary, stipend, takings, wages.
antonyms expenses, outgoings.

earth *n.* **1** globe, planet, sphere, world. **2** clay, clod, ground, humus, land, loam, mould, sod, soil, topsoil.

earthly *adj.* **1** fleshly, human, material, materialistic, mortal, mundane, physical, profane, secular, sensual, temporal, worldly. **2** conceivable, likely, possible, slight, slightest.
antonyms **1** heavenly, spiritual.

earthquake *n.* earth-tremor, quake, shake, upheaval.

earthy *adj.* bawdy, coarse, crude, down-to-earth, homely, natural, raunchy, ribald, robust, rough, simple, uninhibited, vulgar.
antonyms cultured, modest, refined.

ease *n.* **1** cleverness, deftness, dexterity, effortlessness, facility, naturalness, skilfulness. **2** affluence, comfort, contentment, enjoyment, happiness, leisure, peace, quiet, relaxation, repose, rest.
antonyms **1** difficulty. **2** discomfort.
v. abate, allay, alleviate, assist, assuage, calm, comfort, facilitate, forward, further, inch, lessen, lighten, mitigate, moderate, pacify, quiet, relax, relent, relieve, slide, smooth, soothe, steer, still, tranquillise.
antonyms aggravate, intensify, worsen.
ease off abate, decrease, die away, die down, moderate, relent, slacken, subside, wane.
antonym increase.

easily *adv.* **1** comfortably, effortlessly, readily, simply. **2** by far, certainly, clearly, definitely, doubtlessly, far and away, probably, simply, surely, undeniably, undoubtedly, well.
antonym **1** laboriously.

easy *adj.* **1** cushy, effortless, manageable, painless, simple, straightforward, uncomplicated, undemanding. **2** calm, carefree, comfortable, easy-going, informal, leisurely, natural, relaxed.
antonyms **1** demanding, difficult, exacting. **2** tense, uneasy.

easy-going *adj.* amenable, calm, carefree, even-tempered, happy-go-lucky, laid-back, relaxed, serene, tolerant.
antonyms critical, fussy, intolerant.

eat *v.* **1** chew, consume, devour, dine, feed, munch, scoff, swallow. **2** corrode, crumble, decay, dissolve, erode, rot, wear away.

eatable *adj.* comestible, digestible, edible, good, harmless, palatable, wholesome.
antonym unpalatable.

eavesdrop *v.* bug, listen in, monitor, overhear, snoop, spy, tap.

eavesdropper *n.* listener, monitor, snoop, snooper, spy.
antonyms apathetic, dull, lifeless.

eccentric *adj.* abnormal, bizarre, dotty, erratic, freakish, idiosyncratic, odd, outlandish, peculiar, queer, quirky, screwball, singular, strange, unconventional, way-out, weird.
antonyms normal, orthodox, sane.
n. case, character, crank, freak, nonconformist, oddball, oddity.

eccentricity *n.* aberration, abnormality, anomaly, bizarreness, capriciousness, foible, freakishness, idiosyncrasy, nonconformity, oddity, peculiarity, quirk, singularity, strangeness, weirdness, whimsicality.
antonyms conventionality, normality, ordinariness.

ecclesiastical *adj.* church, churchly, clerical, divine, holy, pastoral, priestly, religious, spiritual.

echo *v.* copy, imitate, mimic, mirror, parallel, recall, reflect, reiterate, repeat, reproduce, resemble, resound, reverberate, ring.
n. copy, image, imitation, memory, mirror image, parallel, reflection, reiteration, reminder, repetition, reproduction, reverberation, suggestion.

eclipse *v.* blot out, cloud, darken, dim, dwarf, exceed, obscure, outdo, outshine, overshadow, surpass, transcend, veil.

n. darkening, decline, dimming, failure, fall, loss, obscuration, overshadowing, shading.
economic *adj.* budgetary, business, commercial, cost-effective, financial, fiscal, industrial, monetary, money-making, productive, profitable, profit-making, trade, viable.
economical *adj.* careful, cheap, cost-effective, efficient, fair, frugal, inexpensive, labour-saving, low, low-priced, modest, prudent, reasonable, saving, sparing, thrifty, time-saving.
antonyms expensive, uneconomical, wasteful.
economise *v.* cut back, cut costs, save, tighten one's belt.
antonyms squander, waste.
economy *n.* frugality, husbandry, parsimony, providence, prudence, restraint, saving, sparingness, thrift.
antonyms extravagance, improvidence.
ecstasy *n.* bliss, delight, elation, euphoria, exaltation, fervour, frenzy, joy, rapture, rhapsody, sublimation, transport.
antonyms misery, torment.
ecstatic *adj.* delirious, elated, entranced, euphoric, fervent, frenzied, joyful, joyous, overjoyed, rapturous, rhapsodic, transported.
antonyms apathetic, downcast.
eddy *n.* counter-current, counterflow, swirl, twist, vortex, well, whirlpool.
v. swirl, whirl.
edge *n.* **1** border, boundary, brim, brink, fringe, limit, line, lip, margin, outline, perimeter, periphery, point, rim, side, threshold, verge. **2** advantage, dominance, effectiveness, force, superiority. **3** acuteness, incisiveness, keenness, pungency, sharpness, zest.
v. creep, ease, inch, sidle, worm.
edgy *adj.* anxious, ill at ease, irritable, keyed-up, nervous, on edge, tense, touchy.
antonym calm.
edible *adj.* digestible, eatable, good, harmless, palatable, safe, wholesome.
antonyms indigestible, inedible.
edict *n.* act, command, decree, injunction, law, mandate, manifesto, order, ordinance, proclamation, pronouncement, regulation, ruling, statute.
edify *v.* educate, enlighten, guide, improve, inform, instruct, nurture, school, teach, train, tutor.
edit *v.* adapt, annotate, assemble, censor, check, compile, compose, correct, emend, polish, rearrange, reorder, rephrase, revise, rewrite, select.
edition *n.* copy, impression, issue, number, printing, version, volume.
educate *v.* coach, cultivate, develop, discipline, drill, edify, exercise, improve, inform, instruct, learn, mature, rear, school, teach, train, tutor.
educated *adj.* civilised, cultured, informed, instructed, knowledgeable, learned, lettered, literary, refined, schooled, taught, trained, tutored, well-bred.
antonyms uncultured, uneducated.
education *n.* coaching, cultivation, culture, development, discipline, enlightenment, guidance, improvement, indoctrination, instruction, knowledge, nurture, scholarship, schooling, teaching, training, tuition, tutoring.
educational *adj.* cultural, didactic, edifying, enlightening, improving, informative, instructive, pedagogic, scholastic.
antonym uninformative.
eerie *adj.* awesome, chilling, creepy, frightening, ghostly, mysterious, scary, spine-chilling, spooky, strange, weird.
antonyms natural, ordinary.
effect *n.* **1** conclusion, consequence, end, fruit, issue, outcome, result, upshot. **2** force, impact, impression, influence, meaning, power, purpose, significance, strength.
antonym **1** cause.
v. accomplish, achieve, cause, complete, consummate, create, execute, fulfil, initiate, make, perform, produce.
in effect actually, effectively, essentially, for all practical purposes, in fact, in reality, in the end, in truth, really, to all intents and purposes, virtually.
take effect be effective, be implemented, become operative, begin, come into force, come into operation, work.
effective *adj.* active, adequate, capable, cogent, compelling, convincing, current, energetic, forceful, impressive, operative, persuasive, powerful, productive, real, serviceable, striking, telling, useful.
antonyms ineffective, powerless, useless.
effects *n.* belongings, chattels, gear, goods, movables, paraphernalia, possessions, property, things, trappings.
effeminate *adj.* delicate, feminine, pansy, sissy, tender, unmanly, weak, womanly.
antonym manly.
effervescent *adj.* animated, bubbly, buoyant, carbonated, ebullient, enthusiastic, excited, exhilarated, exuberant, fermenting, fizzy, foaming, frothy, lively, sparkling, vital, vivacious, zingy.
antonyms apathetic, dull, flat.
efficiency *n.* ability, capability, competence, mastery, power, productivity, proficiency, readiness, skilfulness, skill.
antonyms incompetence, inefficiency.
efficient *adj.* able, businesslike, capable, competent, effective, powerful, proficient, ready, skilful, well-conducted, well-organised.
antonyms incompetent, inefficient.
effigy *n.* carving, dummy, figure, guy, icon, idol, image, likeness, picture, portrait, representation, statue.
effort *n.* **1** application, endeavour, energy, exertion, force, power, strain, stress, striving, struggle, toil, travail, trouble. **2** attempt, go, shot, stab, try. **3** accomplishment, achievement, creation, deed, feat, job, product, production, work.
effortless *adj.* easy, painless, simple, smooth.
antonyms complicated, difficult.

effrontery *n.* arrogance, audacity, boldness, brashness, brazenness, cheek, cheekiness, disrespect, gall, impertinence, impudence, insolence, nerve, presumption, rudeness.
antonym respect.

effusive *adj.* demonstrative, ebullient, enthusiastic, expansive, extravagant, exuberant, fulsome, gushing, lavish, overflowing, profuse, talkative, unrestrained, voluble.
antonyms quiet, reserved, restrained.

egotism *n.* bigheadedness, conceitedness, egoism, egomania, narcissism, self-admiration, self-centredness, self-conceit, self-importance, self-love, self-praise, superiority, vanity.
antonyms altruism, humility.

egotist *n.* bighead, boaster, braggart, egoist, swaggerer.

egotistic *adj.* bigheaded, boasting, bragging, conceited, egocentric, egoistic, self-centred, self-important, superior, swollen-headed, vain.
antonyms altruistic, humble.

ejaculate *v.* **1** discharge, eject, emit, spurt. **2** blurt, call, cry, exclaim, scream, shout, utter, yell.

eject *v.* banish, deport, discharge, dismiss, drive out, emit, evacuate, evict, exile, expel, fire, kick out, oust, remove, sack, spew, spout, throw out, turn out, vomit.

eke out add to, economise on, husband, increase, stretch, supplement.

elaborate *adj.* complex, complicated, decorated, detailed, exact, extensive, fancy, fussy, intricate, involved, laboured, minute, ornamental, ornate, ostentatious, painstaking, perfected, precise, showy, skilful, studied, thorough.
antonyms plain, simple.
v. amplify, develop, devise, enlarge, expand, explain, flesh out, improve, polish, refine.
antonyms précis, simplify.

elapse *v.* go by, lapse, pass, slip away.

elastic *adj.* accommodating, adaptable, adjustable, bouncy, buoyant, flexible, plastic, pliable, pliant, resilient, rubbery, springy, stretchable, supple, tolerant, variable, yielding.
antonym rigid.

elasticity *n.* adaptability, adjustability, bounce, buoyancy, flexibility, give, plasticity, pliability, resilience, springiness, stretch, stretchiness, suppleness, tolerance, variability.
antonym rigidity.

elated *adj.* ecstatic, euphoric, excited, exhilarated, exultant, joyful, joyous, jubilant, overjoyed, proud.
antonyms despondent, downcast.

elbow *v.* bulldoze, bump, crowd, jostle, knock, nudge, plough, push, shoulder, shove.

elbow-room *n.* freedom, latitude, leeway, play, room, scope, space.

elder *adj.* ancient, first-born, older, senior.
antonym younger.

elderly *adj.* aged, aging, hoary, old, senile.
antonyms young, youthful.

eldest *adj.* first, first-begotten, first-born, oldest.
antonym youngest.

elect *v.* adopt, appoint, choose, designate, determine, opt for, pick, prefer, select, vote.
adj. choice, chosen, designate, designated, elite, hand-picked, picked, preferred, prospective, selected, to be.

election *n.* appointment, ballot-box, choice, decision, determination, judgement, preference, selection, voting.

elector *n.* constituent, selector, voter.

electric *adj.* charged, dynamic, electrifying, exciting, rousing, stimulating, stirring, tense, thrilling.
antonyms tedious, unexciting.

electrify *v.* amaze, animate, astonish, astound, excite, fire, invigorate, jolt, rouse, shock, stagger, startle, stimulate, stir, thrill.
antonym bore.

elegant *adj.* appropriate, apt, artistic, beautiful, chic, clever, delicate, effective, exquisite, fashionable, fine, genteel, graceful, handsome, modish, neat, nice, polished, refined, simple, smart, smooth, stylish.
antonyms inelegant, tasteless, unrefined.

elegy *n.* dirge, lament, plaint, requiem.

element *n.* basis, component, constituent, factor, feature, field, fragment, ingredient, medium, member, part, piece, section, subdivision, trace, unit.
antonym whole.

elementary *adj.* basic, clear, easy, fundamental, initial, introductory, original, plain, primary, principal, rudimentary, simple, straightforward, uncomplicated.
antonyms advanced, complex.

elements *n.* basics, essentials, foundations, fundamentals, introduction, principles, rudiments.

elevate *v.* advance, aggrandise, boost, brighten, exalt, heighten, hoist, increase, intensify, lift, magnify, prefer, promote, raise, rouse, swell, upgrade, uplift.
antonyms lessen, lower.

elevated *adj.* dignified, elated, exalted, grand, high, lofty, noble, raised, sublime.
antonyms base, informal, lowly, pedestrian.

elevation *n.* **1** advancement, aggrandisement, eminence, exaltation, grandeur, loftiness, nobility, preferment, promotion, rise, sublimation. **2** altitude, height, hill, hillock, mountain.
antonyms **1** demotion. **2** depth, dip.

eligible *adj.* acceptable, appropriate, available, desirable, fit, proper, qualified, suitable, suited, worthy.
antonyms ineligible, unqualified.

eliminate *v.* annihilate, cut out, delete, dispense with, dispose of, disregard, do away with, drop, eject, eradicate, exclude, expel, exterminate, extinguish, get rid of, ignore, kill, knock out, murder, omit, reject, remove, rub out, stamp out, take out, terminate, waste.
antonyms accept, include.

elite *n.* aristocracy, best, crème de la crème, elect, establishment, gentry, high society, nobility.
adj. aristocratic, best, choice, exclusive, first-

class, noble, pick, selected, top, top-class, upper-class.
antonyms ordinary, run-of-the-mill.
elocution *n.* articulation, delivery, diction, enunciation, oratory, pronunciation, rhetoric, speech, speechmaking, utterance.
elongated *adj.* extended, lengthened, long, prolonged, protracted, stretched.
elope *v.* abscond, bolt, decamp, disappear, do a bunk, escape, leave, run away, run off, slip away, steal away.
eloquent *adj.* articulate, expressive, fluent, forceful, graceful, meaningful, moving, persuasive, plausible, revealing, stirring, suggestive, telling, vivid, vocal, voluble, well-expressed.
antonyms inarticulate, tongue-tied.
elucidate *v.* annotate, clarify, explain, illustrate, interpret, spell out, unfold.
antonyms confuse, obscure.
elude *v.* avoid, baffle, beat, confound, dodge, duck, escape, evade, flee, foil, outrun, puzzle, shirk, shun, stump, thwart.
elusive *adj.* baffling, evasive, illusory, indefinable, intangible, puzzling, shifty, slippery, subtle, transient, .transitory, tricky, unanalysable.
emaciated *adj.* attenuated, gaunt, haggard, lank, lean, meagre, pinched, scrawny, skeletal, thin, wasted.
antonyms plump, well-fed.
emanate *v.* arise, come, derive, discharge, emerge, emit, flow, give off, give out, issue, originate, proceed, radiate, send out, spring, stem.
emancipate *v.* deliver, discharge, enfranchise, free, liberate, release, set free, unbind, unchain, unfetter, unshackle.
antonym enslave.
embalm *v.* conserve, enshrine, immortalise, mummify, preserve, store, treasure.
embankment *n.* causeway, dam, defences, earthwork, levee, rampart.
embargo *n.* ban, bar, barrier, blockage, check, hindrance, impediment, interdiction, prohibition, proscription, restraint, restriction, seizure, stoppage.
v. ban, bar, block, impede, interdict, prohibit, restrict, seize, stop.
antonyms allow, permit.
embark *v.* board (ship), take ship.
antonym disembark.
embark on begin, commence, engage, enter, initiate, launch, set about, start, undertake.
antonyms complete, finish.
embarrass *v.* discompose, disconcert, distress, fluster, shame, show up.
embarrassment *n.* awkwardness, bashfulness, chagrin, confusion, constraint, difficulty, discomfiture, discomfort, discomposure, distress, humiliation, mortification, predicament, self-consciousness, shame.
embassy *n.* consulate, delegation, deputation, legation, mission.
embellish *v.* adorn, beautify, deck, decorate, dress up, elaborate, embroider, enhance, enrich, exaggerate, festoon, garnish, gild, grace, ornament, varnish.
antonyms denude, simplify.
embellishment *n.* adornment, decoration, elaboration, embroidery, enhancement, enrichment, exaggeration, garnish, gilding, ornament, ornamentation, trimming.
embezzle *v.* appropriate, filch, misappropriate, misuse, pilfer, pinch, steal.
embezzlement *n.* appropriation, filching, fraud, larceny, misapplication, misappropriation, misuse, pilfering, stealing, sting, theft, thieving.
embittered *adj.* bitter, disaffected, disillusioned, sour, soured.
antonym pacified.
emblazon *v.* adorn, colour, decorate, depict, embellish, illuminate, ornament, paint, proclaim, publicise, publish.
emblem *n.* badge, crest, device, figure, image, insignia, mark, representation, sign, symbol, token, type.
embodiment *n.* concentration, epitome, example, exemplification, expression, incarnation, incorporation, manifestation, personification, realisation, representation.
embody *v.* contain, exemplify, express, include, incorporate, integrate, manifest, organise, personify, realise, represent, stand for, symbolise.
embrace *v.* **1** clasp, cuddle, grasp, hold, hug, squeeze. **2** accept, comprise, contain, cover, embody, encompass, include, incorporate, involve, take up, welcome.
n. clasp, cuddle, hug, squeeze.
embroidery *n.* needlework, sewing, tapestry.
embryo *n.* beginning, germ, nucleus, root, rudiment.
embryonic *adj.* beginning, early, germinal, immature, primary, rudimentary, underdeveloped.
antonyms advanced, developed.
emend *v.* alter, amend, correct, edit, improve, rectify, revise, rewrite.
emerge *v.* appear, arise, crop up, develop, emanate, issue, materialise, proceed, rise, surface, transpire, turn up.
antonyms disappear, fade.
emergence *n.* advent, appearance, arrival, coming, dawn, development, disclosure, issue, rise.
antonyms decline, disappearance.
emergency *n.* crisis, danger, difficulty, pinch, plight, predicament, quandary, scrape, strait.
adj. alternative, back-up, extra, fall-back, reserve, spare, substitute.
emigration *n.* departure, exodus, journey, migration, moving, removal.
eminence *n.* distinction, esteem, fame, greatness, importance, note, pre-eminence, prestige, prominence, rank, renown, reputation, superiority.
eminent *adj.* celebrated, conspicuous, distinguished, elevated, esteemed, exalted, famous, grand, great, high-ranking, illustrious, impor-

tant, notable, noteworthy, outstanding, pre-eminent, prestigious, prominent, renowned, respected, superior, well-known.
antonyms ordinary, unimportant, unknown.
eminently *adv.* conspicuously, exceedingly, exceptionally, extremely, greatly, highly, notably, par excellence, remarkably, signally, strikingly, strongly, surpassingly.
emissary *n.* agent, ambassador, courier, delegate, deputy, envoy, herald, messenger, representative, scout, spy.
emission *n.* diffusion, discharge, ejaculation, ejection, emanation, exhalation, exudation, issue, radiation, release, transmission, vent.
emit *v.* diffuse, discharge, eject, emanate, exude, give off, give out, issue, radiate, release, shed, vent.
antonym absorb.
emotion *n.* ardour, excitement, feeling, fervour, passion, reaction, sensation, sentiment, vehemence, warmth.
emotional *adj.* ardent, demonstrative, enthusiastic, excitable, exciting, feeling, fervent, fiery, heart-warming, heated, hot-blooded, impassioned, moved, moving, overcharged, passionate, pathetic, poignant, responsive, roused, sensitive, sentimental, stirring, temperamental, tempestuous, tender, thrilling, touching, warm, zealous.
antonyms calm, cold, detached, unemotional.
emotive *adj.* controversial, delicate, heated, impassioned, inflammatory, moving, passionate, pathetic, poignant, sensitive, sentimental, tear-jerking, thrilling, touchy.
emperor *n.* kaiser, ruler, shogun, sovereign, tsar.
emphasis *n.* accent, attention, force, importance, insistence, intensity, mark, moment, positiveness, power, pre-eminence, priority, prominence, significance, strength, stress, underscoring, urgency, weight.
emphasise *v.* accent, accentuate, dwell on, feature, highlight, insist on, intensify, play up, point up, press home, punctuate, spotlight, strengthen, stress, underline, weight.
antonyms depreciate, play down, understate.
emphatic *adj.* absolute, categorical, certain, decided, definite, direct, distinct, earnest, energetic, forceful, forcible, graphic, important, impressive, insistent, marked, momentous, positive, powerful, pronounced, punctuated, significant, striking, strong, telling, unequivocal, vigorous, vivid.
antonyms hesitant, quiet, understated.
empire *n.* authority, command, commonwealth, control, domain, dominion, government, jurisdiction, kingdom, power, realm, rule, sovereignty, supremacy, sway, territory.
employ *v.* apply, bring to bear, commission, engage, enlist, exercise, exert, fill, hire, occupy, ply, retain, spend, take on, take up, use, utilise.
n. employment, hire, pay, service.
employee *n.* hand, job-holder, member of staff, wage-earner, worker.
employer *n.* boss, business, company, establishment, firm, gaffer, management, manager, organisation, owner, proprietor, taskmaster, workmistress.
employment *n.* business, calling, craft, employ, engagement, enlistment, hire, job, line, métier, occupation, profession, pursuit, service, trade, use, utilisation, vocation, work.
antonym unemployment.
emptiness *n.* aimlessness, bareness, barrenness, desire, desolation, futility, hollowness, hunger, idleness, ineffectiveness, meaninglessness, unreality, vacantness, vacuum, vanity, void, waste, worthlessness.
antonym fullness.
empty *adj.* **1** bare, blank, clear, deserted, desolate, hollow, unfilled, uninhabited, unoccupied, vacant, void. **2** aimless, fruitless, futile, ineffective, insincere, insubstantial, meaningless, senseless, trivial, useless, vain, worthless. **3** expressionless, idle, silly, vacant, vacuous.
antonyms **1** full. **2** meaningful.
v. clear, consume, discharge, drain, dump, evacuate, exhaust, gut, lade, pour out, unload, vacate, void.
antonym fill.
empty-headed *adj.* batty, dotty, feather-brained, frivolous, inane, scatter-brained, silly.
emulate *v.* compete with, contend with, copy, echo, follow, imitate, match, mimic, rival, vie with.
enable *v.* allow, authorise, commission, empower, endue, equip, facilitate, fit, license, permit, prepare, qualify, sanction, warrant.
antonyms forbid, inhibit, prevent.
enact *v.* **1** authorise, command, decree, establish, legislate, ordain, order, pass, ratify, sanction. **2** act (out), depict, perform, play, portray, represent.
antonyms **1** repeal, rescind.
enamoured *adj.* captivated, charmed, enchanted, entranced, fascinated, fond, infatuated, keen, smitten, taken..
encapsulate *v.* capture, compress, contain, digest, encompass, epitomise, exemplify, précis, represent, sum up, summarise, typify.
enchant *v.* allure, appeal, attract, captivate, charm, delight, enrapture, enthral, fascinate, hypnotise, mesmerise, spellbind, thrill.
antonyms bore, disenchant, repel.
enclose *v.* bound, circumscribe, comprehend, confine, contain, cover, embrace, encase, encircle, encompass, fence, hedge, hem in, hold, include, incorporate, insert, pen, shut in, wrap.
enclosed *adj.* bound, caged, cocooned, confined, contained, encased, encircled, encompassed, imprisoned, included, sheltered, surrounded.
antonyms open, unenclosed.
enclosure *n.* arena, cloister, compound, corral, court, fold, paddock, pen, pound, ring, stockade, sty.
encompass *v.* admit, circle, circumscribe, comprehend, comprise, contain, cover, embody, embrace, encircle, enclose, envelop, hem in, hold, include, incorporate, involve, surround.

encounter *v.* chance upon, clash with, combat, come upon, confront, contend, cross swords with, engage, experience, face, fight, grapple with, happen on, meet, run across, run into, strive, struggle.
n. action, battle, brush, clash, collision, combat, conflict, confrontation, contest, dispute, engagement, fight, meeting, run-in, set-to, skirmish.

encourage *v.* aid, boost, buoy up, cheer, comfort, console, egg on, exhort, favour, forward, foster, further, hearten, help, incite, inspire, promote, rally, reassure, rouse, spirit, spur, stimulate, strengthen, support, urge.
antonyms depress, discourage, dissuade.

encouragement *n.* aid, boost, cheer, consolation, exhortation, favour, help, incentive, incitement, inspiration, promotion, reassurance, stimulation, stimulus, succour, support, urging.
antonyms disapproval, discouragement.

encouraging *adj.* auspicious, bright, cheerful, cheering, comforting, heartening, hopeful, promising, reassuring, rosy, satisfactory, stimulating, uplifting.
antonym discouraging.

encroach *v.* impinge, infringe, intrude, invade, make inroads, muscle in, overstep, trespass, usurp.

encroachment *n.* incursion, infringement, inroad, intrusion, invasion, trespass, violation.

encumber *v.* burden, cramp, hamper, handicap, hinder, impede, inconvenience, obstruct, oppress, overload, prevent, retard, saddle, slow down, weigh down.

encumbrance *n.* burden, cumbrance, difficulty, handicap, hindrance, impediment, inconvenience, liability, load, obstacle, obstruction, onus.
antonyms aid, support.

encyclopaedic *adj.* all-embracing, all-inclusive, broad, compendious, complete, comprehensive, exhaustive, thorough, universal, vast, wide-ranging.
antonyms incomplete, narrow.

end *n.* **1** cessation, close, completion, conclusion, culmination, dénouement, finish, termination. **2** boundary, edge, extreme, extremity, limit. **3** bit, butt, fragment, left-over, piece, portion, remainder, remnant, scrap, stub, tip. **4** aim, consequence, design, goal, intention, object, objective, outcome, point, purpose, reason, result, upshot. **5** death, demise, destruction, dissolution, doom, downfall, extermination, ruin.
antonyms **1** beginning, start. **5** birth.
v. **1** cease, close, complete, conclude, culminate, finish, stop, terminate, wind up. **2** abolish, annihilate, destroy, dissolve, exterminate, extinguish, ruin.
antonyms **1** begin, start.

endanger *v.* compromise, expose, hazard, imperil, jeopardise, risk, threaten.
antonyms protect, secure, shelter.

endearing *adj.* appealing, attractive, charming, delightful, enchanting, lovable, winsome.

endeavour *n.* aim, attempt, effort, enterprise, essay, go, shot, stab, try, undertaking, venture.
v. aim, aspire, attempt, labour, strive, struggle, take pains, try, undertake, venture.

ending *n.* climax, close, completion, conclusion, consummation, culmination, dénouement, end, epilogue, finale, finish, resolution, termination.
antonyms beginning, start.

endless *adj.* boundless, ceaseless, constant, continual, continuous, eternal, everlasting, immortal, infinite, interminable, monotonous, perpetual, unbroken, undying, unlimited.
antonyms finite, limited, temporary.

endorse *v.* adopt, advocate, affirm, approve, authorise, back, confirm, countersign, favour, ratify, recommend, sanction, sign, subscribe to, support, sustain, vouch for, warrant.
antonyms denounce, disapprove.

endorsement *n.* advocacy, affirmation, approval, authorisation, backing, commendation, comment, confirmation, countersignature, favour, OK, ratification, recommendation, sanction, seal of approval, signature, support, testimonial, warrant.
antonyms denouncement, disapproval.

endow *v.* award, bequeath, bestow, bless, confer, donate, endue, enrich, favour, finance, fund, furnish, give, grant, invest, leave, make over, present, provide, supply, support, will.

endowment *n.* **1** award, benefaction, bequest, bestowal, donation, dowry, fund, gift, grant, income, legacy, property, provision, revenue, settlement. **2** ability, attribute, faculty, flair, genius, qualification, quality, talent.

endurance *n.* fortitude, patience, perseverance, persistence, resolution, stability, stamina, staying power, strength, submission, sustenance, tenacity, toleration.

endure *v.* abide, allow, bear, brave, cope with, experience, face, go through, hold, last, live, permit, persist, prevail, put up with, remain, stand, stay, stick, stomach, submit to, suffer, support, survive, sustain, swallow, tolerate, undergo, weather, withstand.

enemy *n.* adversary, antagonist, competitor, foe, foeman, opponent, opposer, rival, the opposition.
antonyms ally, friend.

energetic *adj.* active, animated, brisk, dynamic, forceful, high-powered, lively, potent, powerful, spirited, strenuous, strong, tireless, vigorous, zippy.
antonyms idle, inactive, lazy, sluggish.

energise *v.* activate, animate, electrify, galvanise, inspire, invigorate, liven, motivate, pep up, quicken, stimulate, vitalise.

energy *n.* activity, animation, ardour, drive, efficiency, exertion, fire, force, forcefulness, get-up-and-go, intensity, life, liveliness, power, spirit, stamina, steam, strength, verve, vigour, vitality, vivacity, zeal, zest, zip.
antonyms inertia, lethargy, weakness.

enervated *adj.* debilitated, done in, drained,

enfeebled, exhausted, fatigued, feeble, incapacitated, limp, paralysed, run-down, spent, tired, washed out, weak, worn out.
antonyms active, energetic.

enforce *v.* administer, apply, carry out, coerce, compel, constrain, discharge, execute, implement, impose, insist on, oblige, prosecute, reinforce, require, urge.

engage *v.* **1** embark, involve, operate, participate, practise, take part, take up. **2** allure, arrest, attract, captivate, catch, charm, draw, fascinate, grip, occupy, win. **3** appoint, commission, contract, employ, enlist, enrol, hire, retain, secure, take on. **4** activate, apply, attach, interact, interconnect, interlock, join, mesh. **5** assail, attack, combat.
antonyms **2** repel. **3** discharge, dismiss. **4** disengage.

engaged *adj.* absorbed, betrothed, busy, committed, employed, engrossed, immersed, involved, occupied, pledged, preoccupied, promised, spoken for, tied up, unavailable.

engagement *n.* **1** appointment, arrangement, booking, date, job, meeting, undertaking. **2** assurance, betrothal, commitment, obligation, pledge, promise, troth, vow. **3** action, battle, combat, conflict, confrontation, contest, encounter, fight.

engaging *adj.* agreeable, appealing, attractive, charming, fascinating, fetching, lik(e)able, lovable, pleasant, pleasing, winsome.
antonyms boring, offensive.

engine *n.* appliance, contraption, device, dynamo, instrument, locomotive, machine, means, mechanism, motor, tool, turbine.

engineer *n.* architect, designer, deviser, driver, inventor, operator, originator, planner.
v. build, cause, contrive, control, create, devise, effect, encompass, manage, manipulate, manoeuvre, mastermind, originate, plan, plot, rig, scheme.

engrave *v.* carve, chisel, cut, etch, fix, grave, impress, imprint, inscribe, lodge, mark, print.

engraving *n.* block, carving, chiselling, cutting, etching, impression, inscription, mark, plate, print, woodcut.

engross *v.* absorb, arrest, captivate, engage, enthral, fascinate, grip, hold, intrigue, involve, occupy, preoccupy, rivet.
antonym bore.

engulf *v.* absorb, bury, consume, cover, deluge, drown, encompass, engross, envelop, flood, hide, immerse, inundate, overwhelm, submerge, swallow up, swamp.

enhance *v.* boost, elevate, embellish, exalt, heighten, improve, increase, intensify, lift, magnify, raise, reinforce, strengthen, swell.
antonyms decrease, minimise, reduce.

enigma *n.* brain-teaser, conundrum, mystery, poser, problem, puzzle, riddle.

enigmatic *adj.* cryptic, mysterious, obscure, perplexing, puzzling, strange.
antonyms obvious, simple, straightforward.

enjoy *v.* appreciate, delight in, have, like, rejoice in, relish, revel in, savour, take pleasure in.
antonyms abhor, detest, dislike, hate.
enjoy oneself have a good time, have fun, make merry.

enjoyable *adj.* agreeable, amusing, delicious, delightful, entertaining, fun, good, gratifying, pleasant, pleasing, satisfying.
antonyms disagreeable, unpleasant.

enjoyment *n.* **1** amusement, comfort, delight, diversion, ease, entertainment, exercise, fun, happiness, indulgence, joy, pleasure, recreation, satisfaction, zest. **2** advantage, benefit, possession, use.
antonyms **1** displeasure, dissatisfaction.

enlarge *v.* add to, amplify, augment, blow up, broaden, develop, elaborate, expand, extend, grow, heighten, increase, inflate, lengthen, magnify, multiply, stretch, swell, wax, widen.
antonyms decrease, diminish, shrink.

enlargement *n.* amplification, augmentation, blow-up, expansion, extension, growth, increase, increment, magnification, swelling.
antonyms contraction, decrease.

enlighten *v.* advise, apprise, counsel, edify, educate, illuminate, inform, instruct, teach.
antonyms confuse, puzzle.

enlightened *adj.* aware, civilised, conversant, cultivated, educated, informed, knowledgeable, liberal, literate, open-minded, reasonable, refined, sophisticated, wise.
antonyms confused, ignorant.

enlist *v.* conscript, employ, engage, enrol, enter, gather, join (up), muster, obtain, procure, recruit, register, secure, sign up, volunteer.

enmity *n.* acrimony, animosity, antagonism, antipathy, aversion, bad blood, bitterness, feud, hate, hatred, hostility, ill-will, malevolence, malice, rancour, spite, venom.
antonym friendship.

enormity *n.* abomination, atrociousness, atrocity, crime, depravity, disgrace, evil, horror, iniquity, monstrosity, outrageousness, viciousness, vileness, wickedness.
antonyms triviality, unimportance.

enormous *adj.* colossal, gigantic, gross, huge, immense, jumbo, mammoth, massive, prodigious, tremendous, vast.
antonyms meagre, small, tiny.

enough *adj.* abundant, adequate, ample, plenty, sufficient.
n. abundance, adequacy, plenty, sufficiency.
adv. adequately, amply, fairly, moderately, passably, reasonably, satisfactorily, sufficiently, tolerably.

enquire, inquire *v.* ask, examine, explore, inspect, investigate, look into, probe, query, question, quiz, scrutinise, search.

enquiry, inquiry *n.* examination, exploration, inquest, inspection, investigation, probe, query, quest, question, research, scrutiny, search, study, survey.

enrage *v.* anger, exasperate, incense, incite, inflame, infuriate, irritate, madden, provoke, rile.

antonyms calm, placate, soothe.
enrich *v.* cultivate, develop, endow, enhance, grace, improve, ornament, refine.
antonym impoverish.
enrol *v.* accept, admit, engage, enlist, inscribe, join up, list, note, record, recruit, register, sign on, sign up, take on.
antonyms leave, reject.
enrolment *n.* acceptance, admission, engagement, enlistment, recruitment, register, registration.
ensconce *v.* establish, install, locate, lodge, nestle, place, protect, put, settle.
ensemble *n.* **1** collection, company, entirety, group, set, sum, total, whole. **2** costume, get-up, outfit, rig-out, suit. **3** band, chorus, group.
ensign *n.* badge, banner, colours, flag, jack, pennant, standard, streamer.
enslave *v.* bind, conquer, dominate, overcome, subject, subjugate, yoke.
antonyms emancipate, free.
ensue *v.* arise, attend, befall, derive, flow, follow, happen, issue, proceed, result, stem, succeed, turn out, turn up.
antonym precede.
ensure *v.* certify, guarantee, guard, protect, safeguard, secure, warrant.
entail *v.* cause, demand, give rise to, impose, involve, lead to, necessitate, occasion, predetermine, require, result in.
entangle *v.* catch, embroil, enlace, enmesh, ensnare, entrap, implicate, involve, jumble, knot, mix up, muddle, perplex, puzzle, ravel, snare, tangle, trap, twist.
antonym disentangle.
enter *v.* **1** arrive, board, come in, go in, insert, introduce, penetrate, pierce. **2** inscribe, list, log, note, record, register, take down. **3** begin, commence, embark upon, enlist, enrol, join, participate, set about, sign up, start.
antonyms **1** depart, leave. **2** delete.
enterprise *n.* **1** effort, endeavour, operation, plan, programme, project, undertaking, venture. **2** adventurousness, boldness, drive, eagerness, energy, enthusiasm, get-up-and-go, initiative, push, resourcefulness, spirit, vigour, zeal. **3** business, company, concern, establishment, firm.
antonyms **2** apathy, inertia.
enterprising *adj.* active, adventurous, ambitious, aspiring, bold, daring, eager, energetic, enthusiastic, go-ahead, imaginative, keen, ready, resourceful, self-reliant, spirited, stirring, venturesome, vigorous, zealous.
antonyms lethargic, unadventurous.
entertain *v.* **1** amuse, charm, cheer, delight, please, put up, recreate, treat. **2** conceive, consider, contemplate, countenance, harbour, hold, imagine.
antonyms **1** bore. **2** reject.
entertainer *n.* acrobat, actor, artiste, comic, conjuror, dancer, musician, performer, singer.
entertaining *adj.* amusing, charming, delightful, fun, funny, humorous, interesting, pleasant, pleasing, recreative, witty.
antonym boring.
entertainment *n.* amusement, cheer, distraction, diversion, enjoyment, extravaganza, fun, pastime, play, pleasure, recreation, satisfaction, show, spectacle, sport, treat.
enthral *v.* beguile, captivate, charm, enchant, engross, fascinate, grip, hypnotise, intrigue, mesmerise, rivet, thrill.
antonyms bore, weary.
enthusiasm *n.* ardour, craze, devotion, eagerness, earnestness, excitement, fervour, frenzy, interest, keenness, mania, passion, rage, relish, spirit, vehemence, warmth, zeal.
antonym apathy.
enthusiast *n.* admirer, buff, bug, devotee, fan, fanatic, fiend, follower, freak, lover, supporter, zealot.
enthusiastic *adj.* ardent, avid, devoted, eager, earnest, excited, exuberant, fervent, forceful, hearty, keen, lively, passionate, spirited, vehement, vigorous, warm, whole-hearted, zealous.
antonyms apathetic, reluctant, unenthusiastic.
entice *v.* attract, coax, draw, induce, lead on, lure, persuade, prevail on, seduce, sweet-talk, tempt.
entire *adj.* complete, full, outright, perfect, total, whole.
antonyms incomplete, partial.
entirely *adv.* absolutely, altogether, completely, every inch, exclusively, fully, in toto, only, perfectly, solely, thoroughly, totally, unreservedly, utterly, wholly.
antonym partially.
entity *n.* being, body, creature, existence, individual, object, organism, presence, quantity, substance, thing.
entourage *n.* associates, attendants, companions, company, cortège, coterie, court, escort, followers, following, retainers, retinue, staff, suite.
entrails *n.* bowels, guts, innards, insides, intestines, offal, viscera.
entrance[1] *n.* access, admission, admittance, appearance, arrival, debut, door, doorway, entrée, entry, gate, initiation, introduction, opening, passage, start, way in.
antonyms departure, exit.
entrance[2] *v.* bewitch, captivate, charm, delight, enchant, enrapture, fascinate, hypnotise, mesmerise, ravish, spellbind, transport.
antonyms bore, repel.
entrant *n.* beginner, candidate, competitor, contender, contestant, convert, entry, initiate, newcomer, novice, participant, player, probationer.
entreat *v.* appeal to, ask, beg, beseech, crave, enjoin, exhort, implore, invoke, petition, plead with, pray, request, supplicate.
entreaty *n.* appeal, entreatment, importunity, invocation, petition, plea, prayer, request, solicitation, suit, supplication.
entrench *v.* anchor, dig in, embed, ensconce, establish, fix, install, lodge, plant, root, seat, set,

settle, trespass.
antonym dislodge.
entrepreneur *n.* businessman, businesswoman, contractor, financier, impresario, industrialist, magnate, tycoon, undertaker.
entrust *v.* assign, authorise, charge, commend, commit, confide, consign, delegate, deliver, depute, invest, trust, turn over.
entry *n.* **1** access, admission, admittance, appearance, door, doorway, entrance, entrée, gate, introduction, opening, passage, threshold, way in. **2** account, item, jotting, listing, memo, memorandum, note, record, statement. **3** candidate, competitor, contestant, entrant, participant, player, registration.
antonym **1** exit.
entwine *v.* braid, embrace, encircle, entwist, knit, plait, splice, surround, twine, twist, weave, wind.
antonym unravel.
enumerate *v.* calculate, cite, count, detail, itemise, list, mention, name, number, quote, recite, reckon, recount, relate, specify, spell out, tell.
enunciate *v.* articulate, declare, express, proclaim, pronounce, propound, publish, say, sound, speak, state, utter, vocalise, voice.
envelop *v.* blanket, cloak, conceal, cover, embrace, encircle, enclose, encompass, enfold, engulf, enwrap, hide, obscure, shroud, surround, swathe, veil, wrap.
envelope *n.* case, casing, coating, cover, covering, jacket, sheath, shell, skin, wrapper, wrapping.
enviable *adj.* advantageous, blessed, desirable, excellent, favoured, fine, fortunate, good, lucky, privileged.
antonym unenviable.
envious *adj.* covetous, dissatisfied, green (with envy), grudging, jaundiced, jealous, malicious, resentful, spiteful.
environment *n.* ambience, atmosphere, background, conditions, context, domain, element, medium, scene, setting, situation, surroundings, territory.
envisage *v.* anticipate, conceive of, contemplate, envision, foresee, image, imagine, picture, preconceive, predict, see, visualise.
envoy *n.* agent, ambassador, courier, delegate, deputy, diplomat, emissary, intermediary, legate, messenger, minister, representative.
envy *n.* covetousness, dissatisfaction, grudge, hatred, ill-will, jealousy, malice, resentfulness, resentment, spite.
v. begrudge, covet, crave, grudge, resent.
epic *adj.* colossal, grand, great, heroic, huge, imposing, impressive, vast.
antonym ordinary.
epidemic *adj.* general, pandemic, prevailing, prevalent, rampant, rife, sweeping, wide-ranging, widespread.
n. growth, outbreak, plague, rash, spread, upsurge, wave.
epilogue *n.* afterword, conclusion, postscript.
antonyms foreword, introduction, preface, prologue.
episode *n.* adventure, business, chapter, circumstance, event, experience, happening, incident, instalment, matter, occasion, occurrence, part, passage, scene, section.
epitome *n.* **1** archetype, embodiment, essence, model, personification, representation, type. **2** abridgement, abstract, summary.
epitomise *v.* **1** embody, exemplify, illustrate, personify, represent, symbolise, typify. **2** abridge, abstract, shorten, summarise.
epoch *n.* age, date, era, period, time.
equable *adj.* calm, composed, consistent, constant, easy-going, even, even-tempered, level-headed, placid, regular, serene, smooth, stable, steady, temperate, tranquil, unexcitable, unflappable, uniform, unvarying.
antonyms excitable, variable.
equal *adj.* **1** alike, commensurate, comparable, corresponding, equivalent, identical, like, the same. **2** balanced, even, matched, regular, uniform, unvarying. **3** able, adequate, capable, competent, fit, sufficient, suitable.
antonyms **1** different. **2** unequal. **3** unsuitable.
n. brother, coequal, counterpart, equivalent, fellow, match, parallel, peer, rival, twin.
v. balance, correspond to, equalise, equate, even, level, match, parallel, rival, square with, tally with.
equalise *v.* balance, compensate, draw level, equal, equate, even up, level, match, smooth, square, standardise.
equality *n.* balance, correspondence, equivalence, evenness, fairness, identity, likeness, par, parity, proportion, sameness, similarity, uniformity.
antonym inequality.
equanimity *n.* calm, composure, coolness, level-headedness, peace, presence of mind, self-possession, serenity, steadiness, tranquillity.
antonyms alarm, anxiety, discomposure.
equate *v.* agree, balance, compare, correspond to, correspond with, equalise, juxtapose, liken, match, offset, pair, parallel, square, tally.
equation *n.* agreement, balancing, comparison, correspondence, equality, equivalence, juxtaposition, likeness, match, pairing, parallel.
equilibrium *n.* balance, calmness, composure, coolness, evenness, poise, rest, self-possession, serenity, stability, steadiness, symmetry.
antonym imbalance.
equip *v.* arm, array, deck out, dress, endow, fit out, fit up, furnish, kit out, prepare, provide, rig, stock, supply.
equipment *n.* accessories, apparatus, baggage, furnishings, furniture, gear, material, outfit, paraphernalia, rig-out, stuff, supplies, tackle, things, tools.
equivalence *n.* agreement, conformity, correspondence, evenness, identity, interchangeability, likeness, match, parallel, sameness, similarity, substitutability.
antonyms dissimilarity, inequality, unlikeness.

equivalent *adj.* alike, comparable, corresponding, equal, even, interchangeable, same, similar, substitutable, tantamount, twin.
antonyms different, dissimilar, unlike.
n. correspondent, counterpart, equal, match, opposite number, parallel, peer, twin.

equivocal *adj.* ambiguous, confusing, dubious, evasive, indefinite, misleading, oblique, obscure, uncertain, vague.
antonyms clear, unequivocal.

equivocate *v.* dodge, evade, fence, hedge, mislead, shuffle, sidestep.

era *n.* aeon, age, century, date, day, days, epoch, period, stage, time.

eradicate *v.* abolish, annihilate, destroy, eliminate, erase, exterminate, extinguish, get rid of, obliterate, remove, root out, stamp out, suppress, uproot, weed out.

erase *v.* blot out, cancel, cleanse, delete, efface, eliminate, eradicate, get rid of, obliterate, remove, rub out.

erect *adj.* elevated, perpendicular, raised, standing, straight, upright, upstanding, vertical.
v. assemble, build, constitute, construct, create, elevate, establish, form, found, initiate, institute, lift, mount, organise, pitch, put up, raise, rear, set up.

erection *n.* assembly, building, construction, creation, edifice, elevation, establishment, fabrication, manufacture, pile, raising, structure.

erode *v.* corrode, denude, destroy, deteriorate, disintegrate, eat away, grind down, spoil, wear away, wear down.

erosion *n.* abrasion, corrosion, denudation, destruction, deterioration, disintegration, fragmentation, undermining, weathering.

erotic *adj.* amorous, aphrodisiac, carnal, lustful, rousing, seductive, sensual, sexy, stimulating, suggestive, titillating, venereal, voluptuous.

err *v.* deviate, fail, go astray, misbehave, misjudge, mistake, misunderstand, offend, sin, slip up, stray, stumble, trespass, trip up, wander.

errand *n.* assignment, charge, commission, duty, job, message, mission, task.

erratic *adj.* aberrant, abnormal, changeable, desultory, eccentric, fitful, fluctuating, inconsistent, inconstant, irregular, meandering, shifting, unstable, variable, wandering, wayward.
antonyms consistent, stable, steady.

erroneous *adj.* amiss, false, faulty, flawed, illogical, inaccurate, incorrect, invalid, mistaken, unfounded, untrue, wrong.
antonyms correct, right.

error *n.* blunder, fault, faux pas, flaw, howler, inaccuracy, lapse, misapprehension, miscalculation, misconception, misprint, mistake, misunderstanding, offence, omission, oversight, slip, slip-up, solecism, wrong, wrongdoing.

erudite *adj.* academic, cultured, educated, highbrow, knowledgeable, learned, lettered, literate, profound, scholarly, scholastic, well-educated, well-read, wise.
antonyms illiterate, unlettered.

erudition *n.* culture, education, knowledge, learnedness, learning, letters, profoundness, scholarship, wisdom.

erupt *v.* belch, break, break out, burst, discharge, explode, flare, gush, rift, spew, spout, vomit.

eruption *n.* discharge, ejection, explosion, inflammation, outbreak, outburst, rash, venting.

escalate *v.* accelerate, amplify, ascend, climb, enlarge, expand, extend, grow, heighten, increase, intensify, magnify, mount, raise, rise, spiral, step up.
antonyms decrease, diminish.

escalator *n.* elevator, lift, moving staircase.

escapade *n.* adventure, antic, caper, doing, exploit, fling, lark, prank, romp, spree, stunt, trick.

escape *v.* **1** abscond, avoid, bolt, break free, break loose, break off, break out, do a bunk, dodge, elude, evade, flee, flit, fly, foil, get away, shake off, shun, skip, slip, slip away. **2** discharge, drain, flow, gush, issue, leak, ooze, pass, pour forth, seep, trickle.
n. **1** avoidance, bolt, break, break-out, evasion, flight, flit, getaway, jail-break. **2** discharge, drain, emanation, emission, gush, leak, leakage, outflow, outlet, outpour, seepage, spurt. **3** distraction, diversion, escapism, pastime, recreation, relaxation, relief, safety-valve.

escapist *n.* daydreamer, dreamer, fantasiser, non-realist, ostrich, wishful thinker.
antonym realist.

escort *n.* aide, attendant, bodyguard, chaperon, companion, company, convoy, cortège, entourage, guard, guardian, guide, partner, pilot, protector, retinue, safeguard, squire, suite, train.
v. accompany, chaperon, conduct, guard, guide, lead, partner, protect, usher.

esoteric *adj.* abstruse, confidential, cryptic, hidden, inner, inscrutable, inside, mysterious, mystic, mystical, obscure, occult, private, recondite, secret.
antonyms familiar, popular, well-known.

especially *adv.* chiefly, expressly, mainly, markedly, notably, particularly, pre-eminently, principally, strikingly, supremely, uniquely, unusually, very.

espionage *n.* counter-intelligence, infiltration, intelligence, investigation, probing, reconnaissance, spying, surveillance, undercover operations.

essay *n.* article, assignment, commentary, composition, critique, discourse, dissertation, leader, paper, piece, review, thesis, tract, treatise.
v. attempt, endeavour, go for, strive, struggle, tackle, take on, test, try, undertake.

essence *n.* attributes, being, centre, character, characteristics, core, crux, entity, heart, kernel, life, lifeblood, marrow, meaning, nature, pith, principle, properties, qualities, quality, significance, soul, spirit, spirits, substance.

essential *adj.* basic, characteristic, constituent, crucial, definitive, fundamental, ideal, important, indispensable, intrinsic, key, main, neces-

sary, needed, perfect, principal, required, requisite, typical, vital.
antonyms incidental, inessential, minor.
n. basic, fundamental, must, necessary, necessity, prerequisite, principle, qualification, quality, requirement, requisite, rudiment, sine qua non.
antonym inessential.

establish *v.* **1** base, create, fix, form, found, inaugurate, install, institute, introduce, lodge, organise, plant, secure, set up, settle, start. **2** accept, affirm, authenticate, certify, confirm, demonstrate, prove, ratify, substantiate, validate, verify.
antonyms **1** unsettle, uproot.

establishment *n.* **1** creation, erection, formation, foundation, founding, inauguration, installation, institution, invention. **2** business, company, concern, enterprise, factory, firm, institute, institution, office, organisation. **3** ruling class, the powers that be, the system, them.

estate *n.* **1** area, assets, belongings, effects, fortune, goods, holdings, lands, lot, manor, possessions, property, ranch, wealth. **2** class, condition, grade, order, place, position, rank, situation, standing, state, status.

estimate *v.* assess, believe, calculate, compute, conjecture, consider, count, evaluate, gauge, guess, judge, number, reckon, think, value.
n. approximation, assessment, belief, computation, conception, estimation, evaluation, guess, judgement, opinion, reckoning, valuation.

estimation *n.* appreciation, assessment, belief, calculation, computation, conception, consideration, credit, esteem, estimate, evaluation, judgement, opinion, reckoning, regard, respect, view.

estranged *adj.* alienated, antagonised, divided, separate.
antonyms reconciled, united.

estuary *n.* arm, creek, firth, fjord, inlet, mouth, sea-loch.

etch *v.* bite, burn, carve, cut, dig, engrave, furrow, groove, impress, imprint, incise, ingrain, inscribe, score, stamp.

etching *n.* carving, cut, engraving, impression, imprint, print, sketch.

eternal *adj.* abiding, ceaseless, constant, endless, enduring, everlasting, immortal, imperishable, incessant, infinite, interminable, lasting, limitless, never-ending, perennial, permanent, perpetual, timeless, undying, unending.
antonyms changeable, ephemeral, temporary.

eternity *n.* aeon, afterlife, age, ages, endlessness, everlasting, everlastingness, heaven, hereafter, immortality, immutability, imperishability, infinity, next world, paradise, perpetuity, timelessness, world to come.

ethereal *adj.* aerial, airy, dainty, delicate, exquisite, fairy, fine, fragile, gossamer, insubstantial, intangible, light, spiritual, subtle.
antonyms earthly, solid.

ethical *adj.* commendable, correct, fair, fitting, good, honest, honourable, just, meet, moral, noble, principled, proper, right, righteous, seemly, upright, virtuous.
antonym unethical.

ethics *n.* beliefs, code, conscience, equity, moral philosophy, moral values, morality, principles, propriety, rules, standards.

ethnic *adj.* aboriginal, cultural, folk, indigenous, national, native, racial, traditional, tribal.

ethos *n.* attitude, beliefs, character, code, disposition, ethic, manners, morality, principles, rationale, spirit, standards, tenor.

etiquette *n.* ceremony, civility, code, conventions, correctness, courtesy, customs, decency, decorum, formalities, manners, politeness, protocol, rules.

etymology *n.* derivation, origin, philology, semantics, source, word history, word-lore.

euphemism *n.* evasion, genteelism, polite term, politeness, substitution, understatement.

euphoria *n.* bliss, cheerfulness, ecstasy, elation, enthusiasm, exaltation, exhilaration, exultation, glee, high, high spirits, intoxication, joy, jubilation, rapture, transport.
antonyms depression, despondency.

euphoric *adj.* blissful, cheerful, ecstatic, elated, enthusiastic, exhilarated, exultant, exulted, gleeful, happy, high, intoxicated, joyful, joyous, jubilant, rapturous.
antonyms depressed, despondent.

evacuate *v.* **1** abandon, clear (out), decamp, depart, desert, forsake, leave, quit, relinquish, remove, retire from, vacate, withdraw. **2** defecate, discharge, eject, eliminate, empty, expel, purge.

evacuation *n.* **1** abandonment, clearance, departure, desertion, exodus, quitting, relinquishment, removal, retiral, retreat, vacation, withdrawal. **2** defecation, discharge, ejection, elimination, emptying, expulsion, urination.

evade *v.* avoid, balk, chicken out of, cop out, decline, dodge, duck, elude, escape, fence, fend off, fudge, hedge, parry, prevaricate, quibble, shirk, shun, sidestep, skive, steer clear of.
antonyms confront, endure, face.

evaluate *v.* assess, calculate, compute, estimate, gauge, judge, rank, rate, reckon, size up, value, weigh.

evaluation *n.* assessment, calculation, computation, estimate, estimation, judgement, opinion, reckoning, valuation.

evangelical *adj.* campaigning, crusading, evangelistic, missionary, propagandising, proselytising, zealous.

evangelise *v.* baptise, campaign, convert, crusade, preach, propagandise, proselytise.

evaporate *v.* condense, dematerialise, disappear, dispel, disperse, dissipate, dissolve, distil, dry, exhale, fade, melt (away), vanish, vaporise.

evasion *n.* avoidance, dodge, escape, excuse, put-off, shift, shirking, subterfuge, trickery.
antonyms directness, frankness.

evasive *adj.* cag(e)y, cunning, deceitful, decep-

tive, devious, equivocating, indirect, misleading, oblique, secretive, shifty, shuffling, slippery, tricky, unforthcoming, vacillating.
antonyms direct, frank.

eve *n.* brink, edge, evening, threshold, verge, vigil.

even *adj.* **1** abreast, balanced, constant, equal, flat, flush, horizontal, level, parallel, plane, proportionate, regular, smooth, stable, steady, symmetrical, uniform, unvarying. **2** identical, like, matching, similar. **3** fifty-fifty, level-pegging, neck and neck, side by side. **4** calm, composed, even-tempered, peaceful, placid, serene, tranquil, unruffled.
antonyms **1** uneven. **2** unequal. **4** upset.
adv. all the more, also, although, as well, at all, indeed, just, much, so much as, still, yet.
v. align, balance, equalise, flatten, flush, level, match, regularise, smooth, square, stabilise, steady, straighten.

even-handed *adj.* balanced, equitable, fair, impartial, just, neutral, reasonable.
antonyms biased, discriminating, prejudiced.

evening *n.* dusk, eve, even, eventide, nightfall, sundown, sunset, twilight.

event *n.* adventure, affair, business, case, circumstance, competition, conclusion, consequence, contest, effect, end, engagement, episode, eventuality, experience, fact, game, happening, incident, issue, match, matter, milestone, occasion, occurrence, outcome, possibility, result, termination, tournament.

even-tempered *adj.* calm, composed, cool, level-headed, peaceable, peaceful, placid, serene, stable, steady, tranquil.
antonyms excitable, quick-tempered.

eventful *adj.* active, busy, exciting, full, interesting, lively, memorable, momentous, notable, noteworthy, remarkable, significant, unforgettable.
antonyms dull, ordinary.

eventual *adj.* concluding, ensuing, final, future, impending, last, later, overall, planned, projected, prospective, resulting, subsequent, ultimate.

eventuality *n.* case, chance, circumstance, contingency, crisis, emergency, event, happening, likelihood, mishap, outcome, possibility, probability.

eventually *adv.* after all, at last, at length, finally, sooner or later, subsequently, ultimately.

ever *adv.* always, at all, at all times, at any time, constantly, continually, endlessly, evermore, for ever, in any case, in any circumstances, on any account, perpetually.
antonym never.

everlasting *adj.* constant, endless, eternal, immortal, imperishable, indestructible, infinite, never-ending, permanent, perpetual, timeless, undying.
antonyms temporary, transient.

everybody *n.* all and sundry, each one, everyone, one and all, the whole world.

everyday *adj.* accustomed, common, common-or-garden, commonplace, conventional, customary, daily, day-to-day, familiar, frequent, habitual, informal, monotonous, normal, ordinary, plain, regular, routine, run-of-the-mill, simple, stock, usual, workaday.
antonyms exceptional, special, unusual.

everyone *n.* all and sundry, each one, everybody, one and all, the whole world.

everything *n.* all, the sum, the total, the (whole) lot.

everywhere *adv.* all around, all over, far and near, far and wide, high and low, left right and centre, ubiquitous.

evict *v.* cast out, chuck out, dislodge, dispossess, eject, expel, expropriate, force out, kick out, oust, put out, remove, turf out.

eviction *n.* clearance, dislodgement, dispossession, ejection, expulsion, removal.

evidence *n.* affirmation, confirmation, data, declaration, demonstration, documentation, grounds, hint, indication, manifestation, mark, pledge, proof, sign, substantiation, suggestion, testimony, token, voucher, witness.

evident *adj.* clear, clear-cut, conspicuous, discernible, distinct, incontestable, incontrovertible, indisputable, manifest, noticeable, obvious, patent, perceptible, plain, tangible, unmistakable, visible.
antonyms obscure, uncertain.

evidently *adv.* apparently, clearly, doubtless(ly), indisputably, manifestly, obviously, outwardly, patently, plainly, seemingly, undoubtedly.

evil *adj.* adverse, bad, base, calamitous, catastrophic, corrupt, cruel, deadly, depraved, destructive, detrimental, devilish, dire, disastrous, foul, ghastly, grim, harmful, heinous, hurtful, immoral, inauspicious, iniquitous, malevolent, malicious, malignant, mischievous, noxious, offensive, painful, pernicious, poisonous, putrid, ruinous, sinful, ugly, vicious, vile, wicked, woeful, wrong.
n. adversity, affliction, badness, baseness, blow, calamity, catastrophe, corruption, curse, demonry, depravity, disaster, distress, harm, heinousness, hurt, ill, immorality, iniquity, injury, malignity, mischief, misery, misfortune, pain, ruin, sin, sinfulness, sorrow, suffering, ulcer, vice, viciousness, wickedness, woe, wrong, wrong-doing.

evoke *v.* arouse, awaken, call, call forth, call up, conjure up, elicit, excite, induce, invoke, produce, provoke, raise, recall, rekindle, stimulate, stir, summon (up).
antonyms quell, suppress.

evolution *n.* Darwinism, derivation, descent, development, expansion, growth, increase, progress, progression, ripening.

evolve *v.* derive, descend, develop, elaborate, emerge, enlarge, expand, grow, increase, mature, progress, result, unravel.

exact *adj.* accurate, blow-by-blow, careful, close, correct, definite, detailed, explicit, express, factual, faithful, faultless, flawless, identical, literal, methodical, meticulous, nice, orderly,

painstaking, particular, precise, right, rigorous, scrupulous, severe, specific, strict, true, unerring, veracious, very, word-perfect.
antonyms ambiguous, imprecise, inexact.
v. claim, command, compel, demand, extort, extract, force, impose, insist on, milk, require, squeeze, wrest, wring.
exacting *adj.* arduous, demanding, difficult, hard, harsh, laborious, painstaking, rigorous, severe, strict, taxing, tough, trying, tyrannical, unsparing.
antonyms easy, simple, tolerant.
exactly *adv.* absolutely, accurately, carefully, correctly, dead, definitely, explicitly, expressly, faithfully, faultlessly, just, literally, methodically, particularly, precisely, quite, rigorously, scrupulously, severely, specifically, strictly, to the letter, truly, truthfully, unambiguously, unequivocally, unerringly, veraciously, verbatim.
antonyms inaccurately, roughly.
exactness *n.* accuracy, carefulness, faithfulness, meticulousness, precision, rigour, strictness, truth, veracity.
antonyms carelessness, inaccuracy.
exaggerate *v.* amplify, embellish, embroider, emphasise, enlarge, magnify, overdo, overemphasise, oversell, overstate, pile it on.
antonyms belittle, understate.
exaggerated *adj.* amplified, excessive, extravagant, inflated, overblown, overcharged, overdone, overstated, pretentious.
antonym understated.
examination *n.* analysis, appraisal, audit, check, check-up, critique, cross-examination, cross-questioning, enquiry, exam, exploration, inquisition, inspection, interrogation, investigation, observation, once-over, perusal, probe, questioning, quiz, research, review, scan, scrutiny, search, study, survey, test, trial, viva.
examine *v.* analyse, appraise, assay, audit, case, catechise, check (out), consider, cross-examine, cross-question, enquire, explore, grill, inspect, interrogate, investigate, peruse, ponder, pore over, probe, question, quiz, review, scan, scrutinise, sift, study, survey, test, vet, visit, weigh.
examiner *n.* adjudicator, analyst, arbiter, assessor, auditor, censor, critic, inspector, interviewer, judge, marker, questioner, reader, reviewer, scrutineer, tester.
example *n.* archetype, case, case in point, citation, exemplification, ideal, illustration, instance, lesson, model, pattern, prototype, sample, specimen, standard, type.
exasperate *v.* anger, annoy, enrage, get on someone's nerves, get to, goad, incense, infuriate, irk, irritate, madden, provoke, rankle, rile, rouse, vex.
antonyms calm, pacify, soothe.
excavate *v.* burrow, cut, delve, dig (out), dig up, disinter, drive, exhume, gouge, hollow, mine, quarry, scoop, tunnel, uncover, undermine, unearth.
excavation *n.* burrow, cavity, cut, cutting, dig, diggings, ditch, dugout, hole, hollow, mine, pit, quarry, shaft, trench, trough.
exceed *v.* beat, better, cap, eclipse, excel, outdo, outreach, outrun, outstrip, overdo, overstep, overtake, pass, surmount, surpass, top, transcend, transgress.
excel *v.* beat, better, cap, eclipse, outclass, outdo, outperform, outrank, outrival, overshadow, pass, predominate, shine, stand out, surmount, surpass, transcend.
excellence *n.* distinction, eminence, fineness, goodness, greatness, merit, perfection, pre-eminence, purity, quality, superiority, supremacy, transcendence, virtue, worth.
antonyms badness, inferiority.
excellent *adj.* A1, admirable, commendable, distinguished, exemplary, exquisite, fine, first-class, first-rate, good, great, notable, noted, noteworthy, outstanding, prime, remarkable, select, splendid, stunning, superb, superior, superlative, surpassing, top-flight, unequalled, wonderful, worthy.
antonyms inferior, poor, seond-rate.
except *prep.* apart from, bar, barring, besides, but, except for, excepting, excluding, exclusive of, leaving out, less, minus, not counting, omitting, other than, save.
v. eliminate, exclude, leave out, omit, pass over, reject, rule out.
exception *n.* abnormality, anomaly, deviation, excepting, exclusion, inconsistency, irregularity, oddity, omission, peculiarity, quirk, rarity, special case.
exceptional *adj.* extraordinary, irregular, marvellous, notable, noteworthy, odd, outstanding, peculiar, phenomenal, prodigious, rare, remarkable, singular, special, strange, superior, uncommon, unequalled, unexpected, unusual.
antonyms average, mediocre, unexceptional.
excerpt *n.* citation, extract, fragment, part, passage, portion, quotation, quote, scrap, section, selection.
v. borrow, cite, crib, cull, extract, lift, mine, quarry, quote, select.
excess *n.* **1** exorbitance, extravagance, glut, left-over, overabundance, overflow, overkill, plethora, remainder, superabundance, superfluity, surfeit, surplus. **2** debauchery, dissipation, immoderateness, intemperance, overindulgence, unrestraint.
antonyms **1** dearth, deficiency.
adj. additional, extra, left-over, redundant, remaining, residual, spare, superfluous, supernumerary, surplus.
antonym inadequate.
excessive *adj.* disproportionate, exorbitant, extravagant, extreme, immoderate, inordinate, steep, superfluous, unasked-for, uncalled-for, undue, unnecessary, unneeded, unreasonable.
antonym insufficient.
exchange *v.* bandy, bargain, barter, change, commute, convert, interchange, reciprocate, replace, substitute, swap, switch, trade.
n. **1** chat, conversation, discussion. **2** bargain,

barter, commerce, dealing, market, trade, traffic. **3** interchange, reciprocity, replacement, substitution, swap, switch.

excitable *adj.* edgy, emotional, fiery, hasty, highly-strung, hot-headed, hot-tempered, irascible, nervous, passionate, quick-tempered, restless, sensitive, susceptible, temperamental, violent, volatile.
antonyms calm, impassive, stable.

excite *v.* affect, agitate, animate, arouse, awaken, disturb, elate, engender, evoke, fire, foment, galvanise, generate, ignite, impress, incite, induce, inflame, initiate, inspire, instigate, kindle, motivate, move, provoke, quicken, rouse, stimulate, stir up, sway, thrill, touch, turn on, upset, waken, warm, whet.
antonyms bore, quell.

excited *adj.* aroused, eager, elated, enthusiastic, frantic, frenzied, high, moved, nervous, overwrought, restless, roused, ruffled, stimulated, stirred, thrilled, wild, worked up, wrought-up.
antonyms apathetic, composed.

excitement *n.* action, activity, ado, adventure, agitation, animation, clamour, commotion, discomposure, eagerness, elation, enthusiasm, ferment, fever, flurry, furore, fuss, heat, hubbub, hue and cry, hurly-burly, passion, restlessness, stimulation, stimulus, thrill, tumult, unrest, urge.
antonyms apathy, calm.

exciting *adj.* cliff-hanging, electrifying, enthralling, exhilarating, impressive, inspiring, interesting, intoxicating, moving, nail-biting, promising, provocative, rousing, sensational, stimulating, stirring, striking, thrilling.
antonyms boring, dull, unexciting.

exclaim *v.* blurt, call, cry, declare, interject, proclaim, shout, utter.

exclamation *n.* call, cry, ejaculation, expletive, interjection, outcry, shout, utterance.

exclude *v.* ban, bar, blacklist, boycott, disallow, eject, eliminate, embargo, evict, excommunicate, expel, forbid, ignore, keep out, leave out, omit, ostracise, oust, prohibit, proscribe, refuse, reject, remove, repudiate, rule out, shut out, veto.
antonyms admit, allow, include.

exclusive *adj.* chic, choice, classy, cliquey, closed, discriminative, elegant, fashionable, limited, narrow, only, peculiar, posh, private, restricted, restrictive, select, selfish, single, snobbish, sole, total, undivided, unshared, whole.

excruciating *adj.* acute, agonising, atrocious, bitter, burning, extreme, harrowing, insufferable, intense, intolerable, painful, piercing, racking, savage, severe, sharp, tormenting, unbearable.

excursion *n.* airing, breather, day trip, detour, deviation, episode, expedition, jaunt, journey, outing, ramble, ride, tour, trip, walk, wandering, wayzgoose.

excusable *adj.* allowable, defensible, explainable, explicable, forgivable, justifiable, minor, pardonable, permissible, slight, understandable.
antonym blameworthy.

excuse *v.* absolve, acquit, apologise for, condone, defend, discharge, exempt, exonerate, explain, forgive, free, ignore, indulge, justify, let off, liberate, overlook, pardon, release, relieve, spare, tolerate, vindicate.
antonyms criticise, punish.
n. alibi, apology, cop-out, defence, evasion, exoneration, explanation, grounds, justification, mockery, plea, pretence, pretext, reason, shift, substitute.

execute *v.* **1** behead, burn, crucify, decapitate, electrocute, guillotine, hang, kill, liquidate, put to death, shoot. **2** accomplish, achieve, administer, carry out, complete, consummate, deliver, discharge, dispatch, do, effect, enact, enforce, expedite, finish, fulfil, implement, perform, realise, render, serve, sign, validate.

execution *n.* **1** beheading, burning, capital punishment, crucifixion, death, death penalty, decapitation, electrocution, firing squad, guillotining, hanging, killing, shooting. **2** accomplishment, achievement, administration, completion, consummation, delivery, discharge, dispatch, effect, enactment, enforcement, implementation, manner, mode, operation, performance, realisation, rendition, style, technique.

executioner *n.* assassin, exterminator, hangman, headsman, hit man, killer, liquidator, murderer, slayer.

executive *n.* administration, administrator, controller, director, government, governor, hierarchy, leader, leadership, management, manager, official, organiser.
adj. administrative, controlling, decision-making, directing, directorial, governing, guiding, leading, managerial, organisational, organising, regulating, supervisory.

exemplary *adj.* admirable, cautionary, commendable, correct, estimable, excellent, faultless, flawless, good, honourable, ideal, laudable, model, perfect, praiseworthy, warning, worthy.
antonyms imperfect, unworthy.

exemplify *v.* demonstrate, depict, display, epitomise, example, exhibit, illustrate, instance, manifest, represent, show, typify.

exempt *v.* absolve, discharge, dismiss, excuse, free, let off, liberate, release, relieve, spare.
adj. absolved, clear, discharged, excluded, excused, favoured, free, immune, liberated, released, spared.
antonym liable.

exemption *n.* absolution, discharge, dispensation, exclusion, exoneration, freedom, immunity, indulgence, privilege, release.
antonym liability.

exercise *v.* **1** apply, discharge, employ, exert, practise, try, use, utilise, wield. **2** discipline, drill, practise, train, work out. **3** afflict, agitate, annoy, burden, distress, disturb, trouble, upset, vex, worry.
n. **1** activity, aerobics, discipline, drill, effort,

exertion, labour, lesson, physical jerks, practice, task, training, work, work-out. **2** accomplishment, application, assignment, discharge, employment, fulfilment, implementation, operation, practice, use, utilisation.

exert *v.* apply, bring to bear, employ, exercise, expend, use, utilise, wield.

exert oneself apply oneself, concentrate, endeavour, labour, strain, strive, struggle, sweat, take pains, toil, work.

exertion *n.* action, application, attempt, diligence, effort, employment, endeavour, exercise, industry, labour, operation, pains, perseverance, strain, stretch, struggle, toil, travail, trial, use, utilisation, work.
antonyms idleness, rest.

exhale *v.* breathe (out), discharge, eject, emanate, emit, evaporate, expel, expire, give off, issue, respire, steam.
antonym inhale.

exhaust *v.* bankrupt, consume, cripple, disable, drain, dry, empty, fatigue, finish, impoverish, overwork, sap, spend, squander, strain, tax, tire (out), use up, waste, weaken, wear out, weary.
antonyms refresh, renew.
n. discharge, emission, exhalation, fumes.

exhausted *adj.* all in, dead tired, dead-beat, disabled, done (in), drained, dry, empty, finished, jaded, jiggered, knackered, spent, tired (out), used up, void, washed-out, weak, whacked, worn out.
antonyms fresh, vigorous.

exhausting *adj.* arduous, backbreaking, crippling, debilitating, difficult, draining, formidable, gruelling, hard, laborious, punishing, severe, strenuous, taxing, testing, tiring, vigorous.
antonym refreshing.

exhaustion *n.* debilitation, emptying, fatigue, feebleness, jet-lag, tiredness, weariness.
antonyms freshness, liveliness.

exhaustive *adj.* all-embracing, all-inclusive, all-out, complete, comprehensive, definitive, detailed, encyclopaedic, extensive, far-reaching, full, full-scale, in-depth, intensive, sweeping, thorough.
antonyms incomplete, restricted.

exhibit *v.* air, demonstrate, disclose, display, expose, express, flaunt, indicate, manifest, offer, parade, present, reveal, show.
antonyms conceal, hide.
n. display, exhibition, illustration, model, show.

exhibition *n.* airing, demonstration, display, exhibit, expo, exposition, fair, manifestation, performance, presentation, representation, show, showcase, showing, spectacle.

exhibitionist *n.* extrovert, pervert, self-advertiser, show-off.

exhilarate *v.* cheer, delight, excite, gladden, hearten, inspire, invigorate, stimulate, thrill, vitalise.
antonyms bore, discourage.

exile *n.* **1** banishment, deportation, expatriation, expulsion, ostracism, separation. **2** deportee, émigré, expatriate, outcast, refugee.
v. banish, deport, drive out, expatriate, expel, ostracise, oust.

exist *v.* abide, be, be available, breathe, continue, endure, happen, have one's being, last, live, occur, prevail, remain, stand, survive.

existence *n.* being, breath, continuance, continuation, creation, creature, endurance, entity, life, reality, subsistence, survival, the world, thing.
antonyms death, non-existence.

existent *adj.* abiding, actual, around, current, enduring, existing, living, present, prevailing, real, remaining, standing, surviving.
antonyms dead, non-existent.

exit *n.* departure, door, doorway, exodus, farewell, gate, going, leave-taking, retirement, retreat, vent, way out, withdrawal.
antonym entrance.
v. arrive, depart, enter, issue, leave, retire, retreat, take one's leave, withdraw.

exonerate *v.* absolve, acquit, clear, discharge, dismiss, excuse, exempt, free, justify, let off, liberate, pardon, release, relieve, vindicate.
antonym incriminate.

exorbitant *adj.* enormous, excessive, extortionate, extravagant, extreme, immoderate, inordinate, outrageous, preposterous, undue, unreasonable, unwarranted.
antonyms fair, moderate, reasonable.

exorcise *v.* cast out, drive out, expel, purify.

exorcism *n.* deliverance, expulsion, purification.

expand *v.* amplify, blow up, branch out, broaden, develop, diversify, elaborate, enlarge, expound, extend, fatten, fill out, grow, increase, inflate, lengthen, magnify, multiply, open, prolong, protract, spread, stretch, swell, thicken, unfold, unroll, wax, widen.
antonyms contract, decrease, shrink.

expanse *n.* area, breadth, extent, field, plain, range, space, stretch, sweep, tract, vastness.

expansion *n.* development, diffusion, diversification, enlargement, expanse, extension, growth, increase, magnification, multiplication, spread, swelling.
antonyms contraction, decrease.

expansive *adj.* **1** affable, communicative, free, friendly, genial, open, outgoing, sociable, talkative, warm. **2** all-embracing, broad, comprehensive, extensive, thorough, wide-ranging.
antonyms **1** cold, reserved. **2** narrow, restricted.

expect *v.* anticipate, assume, await, bank on, bargain for, believe, calculate, contemplate, count on, demand, envisage, forecast, foresee, hope for, imagine, insist on, look for, look forward to, predict, presume, project, reckon, rely on, require, suppose, surmise, think, trust, want, wish.

expectancy *n.* anticipation, belief, curiosity, eagerness, expectation, hope, suspense, waiting.

expectant *adj.* anticipating, anxious, apprehensive, awaiting, curious, eager, hopeful, in suspense, pregnant, ready, watchful.

expecting *adj.* expectant, in the family way, pregnant, with child.

expedition *n.* company, crusade, excursion, exploration, explorers, hike, journey, mission, pilgrimage, quest, raid, ramble, safari, sail, team, tour, travellers, trek, trip, voyage.

expel *v.* ban, banish, bar, cast out, discharge, dislodge, dismiss, drive out, drum out, eject, evict, exclude, exile, expatriate, oust, remove, throw out.
antonyms admit, welcome.

expenditure *n.* charge, cost, disbursement, expense, outgoings, outlay, output, payment, spending.
antonyms profit, savings.

expense *n.* charge, cost, disbursement, expenditure, loss, outlay, payment, spending.

expenses *n.* costs, incidentals, outgoings, outlay, overheads.

expensive *adj.* costly, dear, exorbitant, extortionate, extravagant, high-priced, lavish, steep, stiff.
antonyms cheap, inexpensive, low-priced.

experience *n.* **1** familiarity, involvement, know-how, knowledge, observation, participation, practice, understanding. **2** adventure, affair, encounter, episode, event, happening, incident, occurrence, ordeal, trial.
antonyms **1** ignorance, inexperience.
v. encounter, endure, face, feel, have, know, meet, observe, perceive, sample, sense, suffer, sustain, taste, try, undergo.

experienced *adj.* accomplished, capable, competent, expert, knowledgeable, mature, practised, professional, qualified, seasoned, skilful, skilled, trained, tried, veteran, well-versed, wise.
antonyms inexperienced, unqualified, unskilled, untrained.

experiment *n.* attempt, examination, experimentation, investigation, procedure, proof, research, test, trial, trial and error, trial run, venture.
v. examine, investigate, research, sample, test, try, verify.

experimental *adj.* empirical, exploratory, pilot, preliminary, provisional, speculative, tentative, test, trial, trial-and-error.

expert *n.* authority, connoisseur, dab hand, maestro, pro, professional, specialist, virtuoso.
adj. able, adept, apt, clever, experienced, knowledgeable, masterly, practised, professional, proficient, qualified, skilful, skilled, specialist, trained, virtuoso.
antonyms amateurish, novice.

expertise *n.* cleverness, dexterity, expertness, judgement, know-how, knowledge, mastery, proficiency, skilfulness, skill, virtuosity.
antonym inexperience.

expire *v.* cease, close, conclude, decease, depart, die, discontinue, emit, end, exhale, finish, lapse, perish, run out, stop, terminate.
antonyms begin, continue, start.

expiry *n.* cease, cessation, close, conclusion, death, decease, demise, departure, end, expiration, finish, termination.
antonyms beginning, continuation, start.

explain *v.* account for, clarify, clear up, define, demonstrate, describe, disclose, elucidate, excuse, expound, gloss, illustrate, interpret, justify, resolve, simplify, solve, spell out, teach, translate, unfold, unravel, untangle.
antonyms confound, obscure.

explanation *n.* account, answer, cause, clarification, definition, demonstration, description, elucidation, exegesis, exposition, gloss, illustration, interpretation, justification, meaning, motive, reason, resolution, sense, significance.

explanatory *adj.* demonstrative, descriptive, expository, illuminative, interpretive, justifying.

explicit *adj.* absolute, categorical, certain, clear, declared, definite, detailed, direct, distinct, exact, express, frank, open, outspoken, plain, positive, precise, specific, stated, straightforward, unambiguous, unreserved.
antonyms inexplicit, unspoken, vague.

explode *v.* **1** blow up, burst, detonate, discharge, erupt, go off, set off, shatter. **2** discredit, disprove, give the lie to, invalidate, rebut, refute, repudiate.
antonyms **2** confirm, prove.

exploit *n.* accomplishment, achievement, adventure, attainment, deed, feat, stunt.
v. abuse, capitalise on, cash in on, fleece, impose on, make capital out of, manipulate, misuse, profit by, rip off, skin, soak, take advantage of, turn to account, use, utilise.

exploration *n.* analysis, enquiry, examination, expedition, inspection, investigation, probe, reconnaissance, research, safari, scrutiny, search, study, survey, tour, travel, trip, voyage.

exploratory *adj.* analytical, experimental, fact-finding, investigative, pilot, probing, searching, tentative, trial.

explore *v.* analyse, examine, inspect, investigate, probe, prospect, reconnoitre, research, scout, scrutinise, search, survey, tour, travel.

explosion *n.* bang, blast, burst, clap, crack, detonation, discharge, eruption, fit, outbreak, outburst, report.

explosive *adj.* charged, dangerous, fiery, hazardous, overwrought, perilous, stormy, tense, touchy, ugly, unstable, violent.
antonyms calm, stable.
n. dynamite, gelignite, gun-powder, jelly, nitroglycerine, TNT.

expose *v.* **1** bring to light, detect, disclose, display, exhibit, manifest, present, reveal, show, uncover. **2** denounce, divulge, unmask, unveil. **3** endanger, hazard, jeopardise, risk.
antonyms **1** conceal, cover. **2** cover up.
expose to acquaint with, bring into contact with, familiarise with, introduce to, lay open to, subject to.
antonym protect.

exposed *adj.* bare, exhibited, laid bare, liable, on display, on show, on view, open, revealed, shown, susceptible, unprotected, vulnerable.
antonyms covered, sheltered.

exposure *n.* **1** airing, contact, disclosure, discovery, display, divulgence, exhibition, exposé, familiarity, introduction, knowledge, manifestation, presentation, publicity, revelation, showing, uncovering, unmasking, unveiling. **2** danger, hazard, jeopardy, risk, vulnerability.

express *v.* articulate, assert, communicate, conceive, convey, declare, denote, depict, designate, disclose, divulge, embody, exhibit, formulate, indicate, intimate, manifest, phrase, pronounce, put, put across, represent, reveal, say, show, signify, speak, stand for, state, symbolise, tell, testify, utter, verbalise, voice, word.

adj. **1** categorical, certain, clear, clear-cut, definite, direct, distinct, exact, explicit, manifest, outright, particular, plain, pointed, precise, special, specific, stated, unambiguous. **2** fast, high-speed, non-stop, quick, rapid, speedy.

antonym **1** vague.

expression *n.* **1** air, appearance, aspect, assertion, countenance, demonstration, embodiment, execution, exhibition, face, indication, look, manifestation, mien, representation, show, sign, style. **2** announcement, communication, declaration, delivery, diction, emphasis, enunciation, idiom, intonation, language, mention, phrase, phrasing, pronouncement, remark, set phrase, speaking, speech, statement, symbol, term, turn of phrase, utterance, verbalisation, voicing, word, wording.

expressionless *adj.* blank, dead-pan, dull, empty, glassy, impassive, inscrutable, poker-faced, straight-faced, vacuous.

antonym expressive.

expressive *adj.* communicative, demonstrative, eloquent, emphatic, energetic, indicative, informative, lively, meaningful, moving, poignant, pointed, revealing, significant, striking, strong, suggestive, sympathetic, telling, thoughtful, vivid.

antonym expressionless.

expulsion *n.* banishment, discharge, dismissal, ejection, eviction, exclusion, exile, removal.

exquisite *adj.* attractive, beautiful, charming, dainty, delicate, delicious, delightful, elegant, excellent, fine, flawless, impeccable, incomparable, intense, keen, lovely, matchless, meticulous, outstanding, perfect, pleasing, poignant, polished, precious, rare, refined, sensitive, sharp, splendid, striking, superb, superlative.

antonyms flawed, imperfect, poor, ugly.

extend *v.* **1** continue, reach, spread, stretch. **2** amplify, develop, draw out, elongate, enlarge, expand, increase, lengthen, prolong, protract, spin out, uncoil, unwind, widen. **3** bestow, confer, give, grant, hold out, impart, offer, present.

antonyms **2** contract, shorten. **3** withhold.

extension *n.* addendum, addition, annexe, appendix, branch, broadening, continuation, delay, development, elongation, enhancement, enlargement, expansion, extent, increase, lengthening, postponement, protraction, spread, supplement, widening, wing.

extensive *adj.* all-inclusive, broad, comprehensive, extended, far-reaching, general, great, huge, large, large-scale, lengthy, long, pervasive, prevalent, roomy, spacious, sweeping, thorough, universal, vast, voluminous, wide, widespread.

antonyms narrow, restricted.

extent *n.* amount, area, bounds, breadth, bulk, compass, degree, dimension(s), duration, expanse, length, magnitude, measure, play, proportions, quantity, range, reach, scope, size, sphere, spread, stretch, sweep, term, time, volume, width.

exterior *n.* appearance, aspect, coating, covering, externals, façade, face, finish, outside, shell, skin, surface.

antonyms inside, interior.

adj. alien, exotic, external, extrinsic, foreign, outer, outermost, outside, outward, peripheral, superficial, surface, surrounding.

antonyms inside, interior.

exterminate *v.* abolish, annihilate, destroy, eliminate, eradicate, massacre, wipe out.

extermination *n.* annhilation, destruction, elimination, eradication, genocide, massacre.

external *adj.* alien, apparent, exoteric, exotic, exterior, extramural, extraneous, extrinsic, foreign, independent, outer, outermost, outside, outward, superficial, surface, visible.

antonym internal.

extinct *adj.* abolished, dead, defunct, ended, exterminated, extinguished, gone, inactive, lost, obsolete, out, quenched, terminated, vanished, void.

antonyms alive, living.

extinction *n.* abolition, annihilation, death, destruction, eradication, excision, extermination, obliteration.

extinguish *v.* abolish, annihilate, destroy, eliminate, end, eradicate, erase, expunge, exterminate, kill, obscure, put out, quench, remove, slake, smother, snuff out, stifle, suppress.

extort *v.* blackmail, bleed, bully, coerce, exact, extract, force, milk, squeeze, wring.

extortion *n.* blackmail, coercion, compulsion, demand, exaction, force, oppression, overcharging.

extortionate *adj.* blood-sucking, excessive, exorbitant, extravagant, grasping, hard, harsh, inflated, inordinate, oppressive, outrageous, preposterous, rigorous, severe.

antonyms moderate, reasonable.

extra *adj.* added, additional, ancillary, auxiliary, fresh, further, leftover, more, new, other, redundant, reserve, spare, superfluous, supernumerary, supplemental, supplementary, surplus, unneeded, unused.

antonyms essential, integral.

n. accessory, addendum, addition, adjunct, affix, appendage, attachment, bonus, complement, extension, supplement.

adv. especially, exceptionally, extraordinarily, extremely, particularly, remarkably, unusually.

extract *v.* abstract, choose, cite, cull, deduce,

derive, develop, distil, draw, draw out, elicit, evoke, evolve, exact, express, gather, get, glean, obtain, quote, reap, remove, select, uproot, withdraw, wrest, wring.
antonym insert.
n. abstract, citation, clip, clipping, cutting, distillation, essence, excerpt, juice, passage, quotation, selection.

extraordinary *adj.* amazing, exceptional, fantastic, marvellous, notable, noteworthy, outstanding, particular, peculiar, rare, remarkable, significant, special, strange, striking, surprising, unimaginable, unique, unprecedented, unusual, wonderful.
antonyms commonplace, ordinary.

extravagance *n.* exaggeration, excess, exorbitance, folly, outrageousness, overspending, profusion, recklessness, squandering, waste, wildness.
antonyms moderation, thrift.

extravagant *adj.* costly, excessive, exorbitant, expensive, fanciful, fantastic, flamboyant, flashy, foolish, garish, gaudy, grandiose, lavish, ornate, ostentatious, outrageous, overpriced, preposterous, pretentious, prodigal, profligate, reckless, showy, spendthrift, wasteful, wild.
antonyms moderate, reasonable, thrifty.

extreme *adj.* acute, dire, downright, drastic, exceptional, excessive, extraordinary, extravagant, fanatical, faraway, far-off, farthest, final, great, greatest, harsh, high, highest, immoderate, inordinate, intense, last, maximum, out-and-out, outrageous, radical, red-hot, remarkable, remotest, rigid, severe, sheer, stern, strict, supreme, terminal, ultimate, ultra, uncompromising, unreasonable, unusual, utmost, utter, uttermost, worst, zealous.
antonyms mild, moderate.
n. boundary, climax, consummation, depth, edge, end, excess, extremity, height, limit, maximum, minimum, peak, pinnacle, pole, termination, top, ultimate, utmost.

extremism *n.* fanaticism, radicalism, terrorism, zeal.
antonym moderation.

extremist *n.* die-hard, fanatic, militant, radical, terrorist, ultra, ultraconservative, zealot.
antonym moderate.

extremity *n.* acme, apex, border, bound, boundary, brink, climax, consummation, depth, edge, end, excess, extreme, foot, frontier, hand, hardship, height, limit, margin, maximum, minimum, peak, pinnacle, plight, pole, rim, terminal, termination, terminus, tip, top, ultimate, utmost, verge.

extricate *v.* clear, deliver, disengage, disentangle, free, liberate, release, relieve, remove, rescue, withdraw.
antonym involve.

extrovert *adj.* amiable, amicable, exuberant, friendly, hail-fellow-well-met, hearty, outgoing, social.
antonym introvert.
n. joiner, life and soul of the party, mixer, socialiser.
antonyms introvert, loner.

exult *v.* boast, brag, celebrate, crow, delight, gloat, glory, rejoice, relish, revel, taunt, triumph.

eye *n.* appreciation, belief, discernment, discrimination, eyeball, judgement, mind, opinion, optic, perception, recognition, viewpoint.
v. contemplate, examine, gaze at, glance at, inspect, look at, observe, peruse, regard, scan, scrutinise, stare at, study, survey, view, watch.

eyesight *n.* observation, perception, sight, view, vision.

eyesore *n.* atrocity, blemish, blight, blot, disgrace, horror, mess, monstrosity, sight, ugliness.

eye-witness *n.* bystander, looker-on, observer, onlooker, passer-by, spectator, viewer, watcher, witness.

F

fable *n.* allegory, fabrication, fairy story, falsehood, fantasy, fib, fiction, figment, invention, legend, lie, myth, narrative, old wives' tale, parable, romance, saga, story, tale, tall story, untruth, yarn.

fabled *adj.* fabulous, famed, famous, fictional, legendary, mythical, renowned.

fabric *n.* **1** cloth, material, stuff, textile, texture, web. **2** constitution, construction, foundations, framework, infrastructure, make-up, organisation, structure.

fabricate *v.* **1** concoct, fake, falsify, feign, forge, invent, trump up. **2** assemble, build, construct, create, devise, erect, fashion, form, make, manufacture, shape.
antonyms **2** demolish, destroy.

fabulous *adj.* amazing, astounding, breathtaking, fantastic, immense, inconceivable, incredible, invented, legendary, marvellous, mythical, phenomenal, renowned, spectacular, superb, unbelievable, wonderful.
antonyms moderate, real, small.

face *n.* **1** countenance, features, frown, grimace, physiognomy, scowl, visage. **2** air, appearance, aspect, cover, dial, expression, exterior, façade, front, image, look, outside, surface.
v. **1** be opposite, front, give on to, overlook. **2** confront, cope with, deal with, defy, encounter, experience, face up to, meet, oppose, tackle. **3** clad, coat, cover, dress, overlay.
face to face confronting, eye to eye, eyeball to eyeball, in confrontation, opposite.
face up to accept, acknowledge, come to terms with, confront, cope with, deal with, meet head-on, recognise, stand up to.

face-lift *n.* cosmetic surgery, plastic surgery, redecoration, renovation, restoration.

facet *n.* angle, aspect, characteristic, face, feature, part, plane, point, side, surface.

facetious *adj.* amusing, comical, flippant, frivolous, funny, humorous, jesting, playful, pleasant, tongue-in-cheek, witty.
antonym serious.

facile *adj.* easy, fluent, glib, hasty, light, plausible, quick, ready, shallow, simple, simplistic, slick, smooth, superficial.
antonyms complicated, profound.

facilitate *v.* assist, ease, expedite, forward, further, help, promote, speed up.

facilities *n.* amenities, conveniences, equipment, means, mod cons, opportunities, prerequisites, resources, services.

facility *n.* ability, bent, ease, efficiency, effortlessness, expertness, fluency, gift, knack, proficiency, quickness, readiness, skilfulness, skill, talent.

fact *n.* act, circumstance, deed, detail, event, fait accompli, feature, happening, incident, information, item, occurrence, particular, point, reality, specific, truth.
in fact actually, as a matter of fact, in actual fact, in point of fact, in reality, indeed, really.

faction *n.* **1** camp, clique, coalition, combination, contingent, coterie, crowd, division, gang, ginger group, group, junta, lobby, minority, party, pressure group, section, sector, set, splinter group. **2** conflict, disagreement, discord, dissension, division, fighting, friction, infighting, quarrelling, rebellion, strife, tumult, turbulence.
antonyms **2** agreement, peace, unity.

factor *n.* aspect, cause, circumstance, component, consideration, detail, element, influence, item, parameter, part, point, thing.

factory *n.* manufactory, mill, plant, shop, shop-floor, works.

factual *adj.* accurate, authentic, close, correct, detailed, exact, faithful, genuine, literal, objective, precise, real, straight, sure, true.
antonyms biased, false, imaginary.

faculties *n.* capabilities, functions, intelligence, powers, reason, senses, wits.

faculty *n.* **1** ability, aptitude, bent, brain-power, capability, cleverness, facility, gift, knack, power, readiness, skill, talent. **2** academics, department, discipline, lecturers, profession, school, staff.

fad *n.* affectation, craze, fancy, fashion, mania, mode, rage, trend, vogue, whim.

fade *v.* blanch, bleach, blench, decline, die, dim, diminish, disappear, discolour, disperse, dissolve, droop, dull, dwindle, ebb, fail, fall, flag, languish, pale, perish, shrivel, vanish, wane, wilt, wither, yellow.

fail *v.* **1** come to grief, decline, fall, fall through, flop, flunk, fold, go bankrupt, go wrong, miscarry, misfire, miss, wane, weaken. **2** cease, cut out, die, dwindle, fade, founder, go under, peter out, sink. **3** abandon, desert, disappoint, forget, forsake, give up, leave, let down, neglect.
antonyms **1** succeed. **2** prosper.

failing *n.* blemish, blind spot, defect, deficiency, drawback, error, failure, fault, flaw, frailty, imperfection, lapse, misfortune, shortcoming, weakness.
antonyms advantage, strength.

failure *n.* bankruptcy, breakdown, collapse, crash, decay, decline, defeat, deficiency, deterioration, disappointment, downfall, failing, fiasco, flop, folding, frustration, insolvency, loser, loss, miscarriage, neglect, negligence,

no-hoper, omission, ruin, shortcoming, slip-up, stoppage, wash-out.
antonyms prosperity, success.

faint *adj.* **1** bleached, dim, distant, dull, faded, feeble, hazy, hushed, indistinct, light, low, muffled, remote, slight, soft, subdued, vague, weak. **2** dizzy, exhausted, giddy, lethargic, sick, weak, woozy.
antonyms **1** clear, strong.
v. black out, collapse, drop, flag, flake out, keel over, pass out, swoon.
n. blackout, collapse, swoon, unconsciousness.

fair *adj.* **1** disinterested, dispassionate, equitable, even-handed, honest, honourable, impartial, just, lawful, legitimate, objective, proper, square, trustworthy, unbiased, unprejudiced, upright. **2** blond(e), fair-haired, fair-headed, light. **3** attractive, beautiful, bonny, handsome, lovely, pretty. **4** adequate, all right, average, mediocre, middling, moderate, not bad, OK, passable, reasonable, satisfactory, so-so, tolerable. **5** bright, clear, cloudless, dry, fine, sunny, unclouded.
antonyms **1** unfair. **2** dark. **4** excellent, poor. **5** cloudy, inclement.

fair[2] *n.* bazaar, carnival, expo, exposition, festival, fête, gala, market, show.

fairness *n.* decency, disinterestedness, equity, impartiality, justice, legitimacy, rightfulness, rightness, uprightness.
antonyms prejudice, unfairness.

fairyland *n.* never-never-land, toyland, wonderland.

faith *n.* **1** allegiance, assurance, belief, confidence, conviction, credit, creed, dependence, dogma, faithfulness, fidelity, honesty, honour, loyalty, persuasion, pledge, promise, reliance, sincerity, trust, truth, truthfulness, vow, word, word of honour. **2** church, communion, denomination, religion.
antonyms **1** mistrust, treachery, unfaithfulness.

faithful *adj.* **1** card-carrying, constant, convinced, dependable, devoted, loyal, reliable, staunch, steadfast, true-blue, true-hearted, trusty. **2** accurate, close, exact, precise, strict, true, truthful.
antonyms **1** disloyal, treacherous. **2** inaccurate, vague.
n. adherents, believers, brethren, communicants, congregation, followers, stalwarts, supporters.

fake *v.* affect, assume, copy, counterfeit, fabricate, feign, forge, pretend, put on, sham, simulate.
n. charlatan, copy, forgery, fraud, hoax, imitation, impostor, phon(e)y, reproduction, sham, simulation.
adj. affected, artificial, assumed, bogus, counterfeit, false, forged, hyped up, imitation, mock, phon(e)y, pretended, pseudo, reproduction, sham, simulated, spurious.
antonym genuine.

fall *v.* **1** collapse, crash, decline, decrease, descend, die, diminish, dive, drop (down), dwindle, fall off, flag, go down, incline, keel over, lessen, nose-dive, plummet, plunge, sink, slide, slope, slump, stumble, subside, topple, tumble. **2** be taken, capitulate, give in, give up, give way, resign, submit, surrender, yield.
antonyms **1** increase, rise. **2** beat, succeed, win.
n. **1** death, decline, decrease, descent, dive, drop, dwindling, incline, lessening, lowering, plunge, reduction, slope, slump. **2** capitulation, collapse, defeat, downfall, overthrow, surrender.

fall apart break, crumble, decay, decompose, disband, disintegrate, dissolve, rot, shatter.

fall asleep doze off, drop off, nod off.

fall back on have recourse to, look to, resort to, turn to, use.

fall for accept, be taken in by, swallow.

fall guy dupe, scapegoat, victim.

fall in cave in, collapse, come down, crumble, give way, sink.

fall in with accept, agree with, assent, comply, co-operate with, go along with, meet, support.

fall off decline, decrease, deteriorate, drop, slacken, slow, slump, wane, worsen.

fall on assail, assault, attack, descend on, lay into, pounce on, snatch.

fall out argue, bicker, clash, differ, disagree, fight, quarrel, squabble.
antonym agree.

fall through collapse, come to nothing, fail, fizzle out, founder, miscarry.
antonyms come off, succeed.

fall to apply oneself, begin, commence, get stuck in, set about, start.

fallacy *n.* delusion, error, falsehood, flaw, illusion, inconsistency, misconception, mistake.
antonym truth.

false *adj.* **1** erroneous, faulty, improper, inaccurate, incorrect, inexact, invalid, misleading, mistaken, wrong. **2** artificial, bogus, counterfeit, fake, feigned, forged, hypocritical, imitation, mock, pretended, sham, simulated, synthetic, unreal. **3** deceitful, dishonest, disloyal, double-dealing, double-faced, faithless, fraudulent, insincere, lying, treacherous, two-faced, unreliable.
antonyms **1** right, true. **2** genuine, real. **3** faithful, reliable.

falsehood *n.* deceit, deception, dishonesty, dissimulation, fable, fabrication, fib, fiction, lie, perjury, story, untruthfulness.
antonyms truth, truthfulness.

falsify *v.* adulterate, alter, cook, counterfeit, distort, doctor, fake, forge, misrepresent, misstate, pervert, take liberties with, tamper with.

falter *v.* break, fail, flinch, halt, hesitate, shake, stammer, stumble, stutter, totter, tremble, vacillate, waver.

faltering *adj.* hesitant, stammering, stumbling, tentative, uncertain, weak.
antonyms firm, steady, strong.

fame *n.* celebrity, eminence, esteem, glory, honour, illustriousness, name, prominence, renown, reputation, stardom.

antonyms disgrace, disrepute.

famed *adj.* acclaimed, celebrated, famous, noted, recognised, renowned, well-known.
antonym unknown.

familiar *adj.* **1** common, everyday, household, ordinary, recognisable, routine, well-known. **2** close, confidential, free, free-and-easy, friendly, informal, intimate, relaxed. **3** abreast, acquainted, aware, conversant, knowledgeable, versed.
antonyms **1** strange, unfamiliar. **2** formal, reserved. **3** ignorant, unfamiliar.

familiarise *v.* acclimatise, accustom, brief, coach, instruct, prime, school, train.

familiarity *n.* **1** closeness, friendliness, informality, intimacy, liberty, naturalness, openness, sociability. **2** acquaintance, awareness, experience, grasp, knowledge, understanding.

family *n.* ancestors, ancestry, birth, blood, children, clan, class, classification, descendants, descent, dynasty, extraction, folk, forebears, genealogy, group, house, household, issue, kin, kindred, kinsmen, kith and kin, line, lineage, offspring, parentage, pedigree, people, race, relations, relatives, tribe.
family tree ancestry, extraction, genealogy, line, lineage, pedigree.

famine *n.* destitution, hunger, scarcity, starvation, want.
antonym plenty.

famous *adj.* acclaimed, celebrated, distinguished, eminent, excellent, famed, far-famed, glorious, great, honoured, illustrious, legendary, notable, noted, prominent, remarkable, renowned, signal, well-known.
antonyms obscure, unheard-of, unknown.

fan[1] *v.* agitate, air-condition, air-cool, arouse, blow, cool, excite, increase, provoke, refresh, rouse, stimulate, stir up, ventilate, whip up, winnow, work up.
n. air-conditioner, blower, extractor fan, propeller, vane, ventilator.

fan[2] *n.* adherent, admirer, buff, devotee, enthusiast, fiend, follower, freak, lover, supporter.

fanatic *n.* activist, addict, bigot, devotee, enthusiast, extremist, fiend, freak, militant, visionary, zealot.

fanatical *adj.* bigoted, burning, enthusiastic, extreme, fervent, frenzied, mad, obsessive, overenthusiastic, passionate, rabid, visionary, wild, zealous.
antonyms moderate, unenthusiastic.

fanaticism *n.* bigotry, dedication, enthusiasm, extremism, fervour, infatuation, madness, monomania, obsessiveness, zeal.
antonym moderation.

fanciful *adj.* airy-fairy, curious, extravagant, fabulous, fairy-tale, fantastic, imaginary, imaginative, mythical, romantic, vaporous, visionary, whimsical, wild.
antonyms ordinary, real.

fancy *v.* **1** be attracted to, desire, favour, go for, have an eye for, like, long for, prefer, take a liking to, take to, wish for, yearn for. **2** believe, conceive, conjecture, dream of, guess, imagine, picture, reckon, suppose, think.
antonym **1** dislike.
n. **1** craving, desire, fondness, hankering, inclination, liking, preference, urge. **2** dream, fantasy, imagination, impression, notion, thought.
antonyms **1** aversion, dislike. **2** fact, reality.
adj. baroque, decorated, elaborate, elegant, extravagant, fanciful, fantastic, far-fetched, ornamented, ornate, rococo.
antonym plain.

fantastic *adj.* **1** enormous, excellent, extreme, first-rate, great, incredible, marvellous, overwhelming, ridiculous, sensational, superb, terrific, tremendous, unbelievable, wonderful. **2** exotic, fanciful, grandiose, imaginative, odd, outlandish, strange, visionary, weird.
antonyms **1** ordinary, plain. **2** real.

fantasy *n.* apparition, daydream, delusion, dream, fancy, flight of fancy, hallucination, illusion, imagination, invention, mirage, misconception, nightmare, pipe-dream, reverie, unreality, vision.
antonym reality.

far *adv.* a good way, a long way, considerably, decidedly, deep, extremely, greatly, incomparably, miles, much.
antonyms close, near.
adj. distant, faraway, far-flung, far-off, far-removed, further, god-forsaken, long, opposite, other, outlying, out-of-the-way, remote, removed.
antonyms close, nearby.

faraway *adj.* **1** distant, far, far-flung, far-off, outlying, remote. **2** absent, absent-minded, distant, dreamy.
antonyms **1** nearby. **2** alert.

farce *n.* absurdity, comedy, joke, mockery, nonsense, parody, ridiculousness, satire, sham, slapstick, travesty.

fare[1] *n.* **1** charge, cost, fee, passage, passenger, pick-up, price, traveller. **2** board, diet, eatables, food, meals, menu, provisions, rations, sustenance, table.

fare[2] *v.* be, do, get along, get on, go, go on, happen, manage, proceed, prosper, turn out.

farewell *n.* adieu, departure, good-bye, leave-taking, parting, send-off, valediction.
antonym hello.

far-fetched *adj.* crazy, dubious, fantastic, implausible, improbable, incredible, preposterous, unbelievable, unlikely, unrealistic.
antonym plausible.

farm *n.* acreage, acres, croft, farmstead, grange, holding, homestead, land, plantation, ranch, smallholding, station.
v. cultivate, operate, plant, till, work the land.

farmer *n.* agriculturist, countryman, crofter, husbandman, smallholder, yeoman.

farming *n.* agriculture, crofting, husbandry.

far-reaching *adj.* broad, extensive, important, momentous, significant, sweeping, widespread.
antonym insignificant.

far-sighted *adj.* discerning, far-seeing, judicious,

prudent, shrewd, wise.
antonyms imprudent, short-sighted, unwise.

fascinate *v.* absorb, captivate, charm, delight, engross, enthral, hypnotise, infatuate, intrigue, mesmerise, rivet, spellbind, transfix.
antonyms bore, repel.

fascination *n.* attraction, charm, enchantment, glamour, interest, lure, magic, magnetism, pull, sorcery, spell, witchery.
antonyms boredom, repulsion.

fascism *n.* absolutism, authoritarianism, autocracy, dictatorship, Hitlerism, totalitarianism.

fascist *n.* absolutist, authoritarian, autocrat, Blackshirt, Hitlerite, totalitarian.
adj. absolutist, authoritarian, autocratic, fascistic, Hitlerite, totalitarian.

fashion *n.* **1** attitude, form, kind, manner, method, mould, pattern, shape, sort, style, trend, type, way. **2** appearance, clothing, cut, line, look, mode, style, vogue. **3** craze, custom, fad, latest, rage.
v. adapt, adjust, alter, create, design, fit, forge, form, model, mould, shape, suit, tailor.

fashionable *adj.* à la mode, all the rage, chic, contemporary, current, customary, in, in vogue, latest, modern, modish, popular, prevailing, smart, stylish, trendsetting, trendy, up-to-date, up-to-the-minute, with it.
antonym unfashionable.

fast[1] *adj.* **1** accelerated, brisk, flying, hasty, hurried, nippy, quick, rapid, speedy, swift, winged. **2** fastened, firm, fixed, immovable, permanent. **3** extravagant, immoral, intemperate, licentious, loose, promiscuous, reckless, self-indulgent, wanton, wild.
antonyms **1** slow, unhurried. **2** impermanent. **3** chaste, moral.
adv. apace, hastily, hurriedly, like a flash, like a shot, presto, quickly, rapidly, speedily, swiftly.
antonyms gradually, slowly.

fast[2] *v.* abstain, diet, go hungry, starve.
n. abstinence, diet, fasting, starvation.
antonyms gluttony, self-indulgence.

fasten *v.* aim, anchor, attach, bend, bind, bolt, chain, clamp, close, connect, direct, fix, focus, grip, interlock, join, lace, link, lock, nail, rivet, seal, secure, shut, tie, unite.
antonyms unfasten, untie.

fat *adj.* **1** beefy, corpulent, fatty, fleshy, gross, heavy, obese, overweight, paunchy, plump, podgy, portly, pot-bellied, round, solid, squab, stout, tubby. **2** lucrative, profitable, remunerative, rich.
antonyms **1** thin. **2** poor.
n. blubber, corpulence, fatness, flab, obesity, overweight, paunch, pot (belly).

fatal *adj.* calamitous, catastrophic, deadly, destructive, disastrous, final, incurable, killing, lethal, malignant, mortal, terminal, vital.
antonym harmless.

fatality *n.* casualty, deadliness, death, disaster, lethalness, loss, mortality.

fate *n.* chance, death, destiny, destruction, divine will, doom, end, fortune, future, horoscope, lot, outcome, providence, ruin, stars.

fated *adj.* destined, doomed, foreordained, inescapable, inevitable, predestined, pre-elected, preordained, sure, unavoidable.
antonym avoidable.

fateful *adj.* critical, crucial, decisive, disastrous, fatal, important, lethal, momentous, ominous, significant.
antonym unimportant.

father *n.* **1** ancestor, dad, daddy, elder, forebear, forefather, old boy, old man, papa, parent, patriarch, predecessor, procreator, progenitor, sire. **2** architect, author, begetter, creator, founder, inventor, leader, maker, originator, patron, prime mover. **3** abbé, confessor, curé, padre, pastor, priest.
v. beget, conceive, create, dream up, establish, found, get, institute, invent, originate, procreate, produce, sire.

fatherly *adj.* affectionate, avuncular, benevolent, benign, forbearing, indulgent, kind, kindly, paternal, protective, supportive, tender.
antonyms cold, harsh, unkind.

fathom *v.* comprehend, gauge, get to the bottom of, grasp, interpret, measure, penetrate, plumb, plummet, probe, see, sound, understand, work out.

fatigue *n.* debility, decay, degeneration, failure, heaviness, lethargy, listlessness, tiredness.
antonyms energy, freshness.

fatigued *adj.* all in, beat, dead-beat, exhausted, tired (out), weary.
antonym refreshed.

fatten *v.* bloat, build up, cram, expand, feed, fertilise, nourish, overfeed, spread, stuff, swell, thicken, thrive.

fatty *adj.* fat, greasy, oily, suet(t)y.

fault *n.* **1** blemish, defect, deficiency, failing, flaw, imperfection, inaccuracy, indiscretion, negligence, omission, shortcoming, weakness. **2** blunder, error, lapse, misdeed, mistake, offence, sin, slip, slip-up, wrong. **3** accountability, culpability, liability, responsibility.
v. blame, call to account, censure, complain, criticise, find fault with, impugn, knock, pick at, pick holes in.
antonym praise.
at fault blameworthy, guilty, (in the) wrong, responsible.

faulty *adj.* blemished, broken, damaged, defective, flawed, impaired, imperfect, out of order, wrong.

favour *n.* **1** approval, backing, esteem, favouritism, friendliness, goodwill, partiality, support, sympathy. **2** courtesy, good turn, kindness, service.
antonym **1** disapproval.
v. **1** advocate, approve, back, champion, choose, like, opt for, prefer, support. **2** aid, assist, benefit, encourage, help, pamper, promote, spoil, take kindly to.
antonyms **1** dislike. **2** mistreat.
in favour of on the side of, supporting.
antonym against.

favourable *adj.* advantageous, agreeable, amicable, beneficial, convenient, encouraging, enthusiastic, fair, fit, friendly, good, helpful, hopeful, kind, opportune, positive, promising, reassuring, suitable, sympathetic, timely, understanding, welcoming, well-disposed.
antonyms negative, unfavourable, unhelpful.

favourite *adj.* best-loved, choice, dearest, esteemed, favoured, pet, preferred.
antonym hated.
n. beloved, blue-eyed boy, choice, darling, dear, idol, pet, pick, preference, teacher's pet, the apple of one's eye.
antonyms bête noire, pet hate.

favouritism *n.* bias, injustice, nepotism, one-sidedness, partiality, partisanship, preference, preferential treatment.
antonym impartiality.

fawn[1] *v.* bow and scrape, crawl, creep, cringe, curry favour, flatter, grovel, ingratiate oneself, kneel, kowtow, pay court, smarm, toady.

fawn[2] *adj.* beige, buff, khaki, sand-coloured, sandy.

fear *n.* agitation, alarm, anxiety, apprehension, awe, consternation, danger, dismay, distress, doubt, dread, foreboding, fright, horror, misgivings, nightmare, panic, phobia, qualms, terror, trepidation, uneasiness, worry.
antonyms bravery, confidence, courage.
v. anticipate, apprehend, dread, expect, foresee, respect, reverence, shudder at, suspect, take fright, tremble, venerate, worry.

fearful *adj.* **1** afraid, alarmed, anxious, apprehensive, frightened, hesitant, nervous, nervy, panicky, scared, tense, uneasy. **2** appalling, atrocious, awful, distressing, dreadful, frightful, ghastly, gruesome, hideous, horrible, monstrous, shocking, terrible.
antonyms **1** brave, courageous. **2** delightful, wonderful.

feasible *adj.* achievable, attainable, likely, possible, practicable, practical, realisable, reasonable, viable, workable.
antonym impossible.

feast *n.* banquet, barbecue, beano, binge, blow-out, carousal, celebration, delight, dinner, enjoyment, entertainment, festival, fête, gala, gratification, holiday, pleasure, revels, spread, treat.
v. delight, eat one's fill, entertain, gratify, indulge, rejoice, treat, wine and dine.

feat *n.* accomplishment, achievement, act, attainment, deed, exploit, performance.

feather *n.* pinion, plume, quill.

feature *n.* **1** aspect, attribute, character, characteristic, facet, factor, hallmark, highlight, item, lineament, mark, peculiarity, point, property, quality, speciality, trait. **2** article, column, comment, piece, report, story.
v. emphasise, highlight, play up, present, promote, show, spotlight, star.

fed up bored, depressed, discontented, dismal, dissatisfied, gloomy, glum, tired, weary.
antonyms contented, happy.

federation *n.* alliance, amalgamation, association, coalition, combination, confederacy, confederation, entente, league, partnership, syndicate, union.

fee *n.* account, bill, charge, compensation, hire, pay, payment, recompense, remuneration, retainer, reward, terms, toll.

feeble *adj.* exhausted, failing, faint, flat, frail, inadequate, incompetent, indecisive, ineffective, infirm, lame, poor, powerless, puny, sickly, tame, thin, weak.
antonyms powerful, strong.

feed *v.* cater for, dine, eat, foster, fuel, graze, grub, nourish, nurture, pasture, provide for, strengthen, supply, sustain.
n. fodder, food, forage, pasture, silage.
feed on consume, devour, eat, exist on, live on, partake of.

feel *v.* **1** endure, enjoy, experience, go through, suffer, undergo. **2** caress, finger, fondle, fumble, grope, handle, hold, manipulate, paw, stroke, touch. **3** appear, seem. **4** believe, consider, judge, know, notice, observe, perceive, reckon, sense, think.
n. bent, feeling, finish, impression, knack, quality, sense, surface, texture, touch, vibes.
feel for be sorry for, bleed for, commiserate (with), pity, sympathise with.
feel like desire, fancy, want.

feeler *n.* **1** antenna, horn, tentacle. **2** advance, approach, overture, probe.

feeling *n.* affection, air, appreciation, apprehension, atmosphere, compassion, concern, emotion, fondness, hunch, idea, impression, inclination, inkling, instinct, intensity, mood, notion, opinion, passion, perception, pity, point of view, quality, sensation, sense, sensitivity, sentiment, sentimentality, suspicion, sympathy, understanding, view, warmth.

feelings *n.* affections, ego, emotions, passions, self-esteem, susceptibilities.

fell *v.* cut down, demolish, flatten, floor, hew down, knock down, lay level, level, raze, strike down.

fellow *n.* **1** bloke, boy, chap, character, customer, guy, individual, man, person. **2** associate, colleague, companion, compeer, comrade, counterpart, co-worker, double, equal, fellow-member, friend, like, match, mate, member, partner, peer, twin.
adj. associate, associated, co-, like, related, similar.

fellow-feeling *n.* commiseration, compassion, sympathy, understanding.

fellowship *n.* association, brotherhood, camaraderie, club, communion, companionship, familiarity, fraternity, guild, intimacy, league, order, sisterhood, sociability, society.

female *adj.* feminine, womanish, womanly.
antonym male.

feminine *adj.* delicate, effeminate, gentle, girlish, graceful, ladylike, modest, sissy, soft, tender, unmanly, unmasculine, weak, womanish, womanly.

antonym masculine.

femininity *n.* delicacy, effeminacy, feminineness, gentleness, softness, unmanliness, womanhood, womanishness, womanliness.
antonym masculinity.

feminism *n.* female emancipation, women's emancipation, women's lib(eration), women's movement, women's rights.

fence *n.* barricade, barrier, defence, guard, hedge, paling, railings, rampart, stockade, wall, windbreak.
v. **1** bound, confine, coop, defend, encircle, enclose, fortify, guard, hedge, pen, protect, restrict, secure, separate, surround. **2** dodge, equivocate, evade, hedge, parry, pussyfoot, quibble, shift, stonewall.

fend for look after, maintain, provide for, shift for, support, sustain.

fend off avert, beat off, defend, deflect, hold at bay, keep off, repel, repulse, resist, shut out, ward off.

ferment *v.* agitate, boil, brew, bubble, effervesce, excite, fester, foam, foment, froth, heat, incite, inflame, leaven, provoke, rise, rouse, seethe, smoulder, stir up, work, work up.
n. agitation, commotion, disruption, excitement, fever, frenzy, furore, glow, hubbub, stew, stir, tumult, turbulence, turmoil, unrest, uproar, yeast.
antonym calm.

ferocious *adj.* barbaric, barbarous, brutal, cruel, fiendish, fierce, inhuman, merciless, murderous, pitiless, ruthless, sadistic, savage, vicious, violent, wild.
antonyms gentle, mild, tame.

ferocity *n.* barbarity, bloodthirstiness, brutality, cruelty, fierceness, inhumanity, ruthlessness, sadism, savageness, viciousness, wildness.
antonyms gentleness, mildness.

ferry *n.* boat, ferryboat, ship, vessel.
v. carry, convey, drive, move, remove, run, shift, ship, shuttle, taxi, transport.

fertile *adj.* abundant, fat, flowering, fruit-bearing, fruitful, generative, lush, luxuriant, plenteous, plentiful, productive, prolific, rich, teeming, yielding.
antonyms arid, barren, unproductive.

fertilise *v.* compost, dress, dung, enrich, feed, impregnate, inseminate, manure, pollinate.

fertiliser *n.* compost, dressing, dung, manure, plant-food.

fervent *adj.* ardent, devout, eager, earnest, emotional, energetic, enthusiastic, excited, fiery, full-blooded, heartfelt, impassioned, intense, passionate, spirited, vehement, vigorous, warm, whole-hearted, zealous.

fervour *n.* animation, ardour, eagerness, energy, enthusiasm, excitement, intensity, passion, spirit, unction, vehemence, verve, vigour, warmth, zeal.
antonym apathy.

fester *v.* decay, discharge, gall, gather, putrefy, rankle, smoulder, suppurate, ulcerate.
antonyms dissipate, heal.

festival *n.* anniversary, carnival, celebration, commemoration, eisteddfod, entertainment, feast, festa, festivities, fête, field day, fiesta, gala, holiday, jubilee, merrymaking, treat.

festive *adj.* carnival, cheery, convivial, cordial, festal, gala, gleeful, happy, hearty, holiday, jovial, joyful, jubilant, merry.
antonyms gloomy, sober, sombre.

festivities *n.* banqueting, carousal, celebration, entertainment, feasting, festival, fun and games, glorification, party, rejoicings.

festivity *n.* amusement, enjoyment, feasting, fun, jollity, joviality, joyfulness, merriment, merrymaking, pleasure, revelry, sport.

festoon *v.* adorn, bedeck, deck, decorate, drape, garland, garnish, hang, swathe, wreath.

fetch *v.* **1** carry, collect, deliver, escort, get, lead, transport. **2** bring, bring in, earn, get, go for, make, realise, sell for, yield.
fetch up arrive, come, end up, finish, finish up, halt, land (up), reach, stop, turn up.

fetching *adj.* attractive, captivating, charming, cute, enchanting, fascinating, pretty, sweet, taking, winning, winsome.
antonym repellent.

fête *n.* bazaar, carnival, fair, festival, gala, garden party, sale of work.
v. entertain, fuss over, honour, lionise, regale, treat, welcome.

fetter *v.* bind, chain, confine, curb, hamper, hamstring, hobble, manacle, pinion, restrain, restrict, shackle, tie (up), trammel, truss.
antonym free.

feud *n.* animosity, antagonism, argument, bitterness, conflict, disagreement, discord, dispute, enmity, faction, feuding, hostility, ill will, quarrel, rivalry, row, strife, vendetta.
antonyms agreement, peace.

fever *n.* **1** delirium, heat, intensity, restlessness, temperature. **2** agitation, ecstasy, excitement, turmoil, unrest.

feverish *adj.* agitated, delirious, excited, flurried, flushed, frantic, frenzied, hasty, hectic, hot, hurried, impatient, nervous, obsessive, overwrought, restless.
antonyms calm, cool.

few *adj.* few and far between, hard to come by, in short supply, inadequate, inconsiderable, insufficient, meagre, negligible, rare, scant, scanty, scarce, sparse, sporadic, thin, uncommon.
pron. a couple, handful, not many, oddments, one or two, scarcely any, scattering, small number, small quantity, some, sprinkling.

fiancé(e) *n.* betrothed, bridegroom-to-be, bride-to-be, husband-to-be, intended, wife-to-be.

fibre *n.* **1** filament, nerve, pile, sinew, strand, texture, thread. **2** backbone, calibre, character, courage, determination, resolution, stamina, strength, toughness.

fickle *adj.* capricious, changeable, disloyal, faithless, inconstant, irresolute, treacherous, unpredictable, unreliable, vacillating.
antonyms constant, stable, steady.

fiction *n.* concoction, fable, fabrication, fancy,

fantasy, figment, imagination, improvisation, invention, legend, lie, myth, novel, parable, romance, story, story-telling, tale, yarn.
antonyms fact, non-fiction, truth.

fictional *adj.* imaginary, invented, legendary, literary, made-up, mythical, non-existent, unreal.
antonyms real, true.

fictitious *adj.* artificial, bogus, counterfeit, fabricated, false, imaginary, improvised, invented, made-up, make-believe, mythical, non-existent, spurious, supposed.
antonyms genuine, real.

fiddle *v.* cheat, cook the books, diddle, fidget, fix, gerrymander, graft, interfere, juggle, manoeuvre, meddle, mess around, play, racketeer, swindle, tamper, tinker, toy, trifle.
n. con, fraud, graft, monkey-business, racket, rip-off, sharp practice, swindle, violin.

fiddling *adj.* insignificant, negligible, paltry, petty, trifling, trivial.
antonyms important, significant.

fidelity *n.* **1** adherence, allegiance, constancy, devotion, faithfulness, loyalty. **2** accuracy, closeness, exactness, precision, reliability.
antonyms **1** inconstancy, treachery. **2** inaccuracy.

fidget *v.* bustle, fiddle, fret, jerk, jiggle, jitter, jump, mess about, play around, shuffle, squirm, twitch.

fidgety *adj.* agitated, impatient, jittery, jumpy, nervous, on edge, restless, twitchy, uneasy.
antonym still.

field *n.* **1** grassland, green, lawn, meadow, paddock, pasture, playing-field. **2** area, bounds, confines, department, discipline, domain, environment, forte, limits, line, period, province, range, scope, speciality, territory. **3** applicants, candidates, competition, competitors, contenders, contestants, entrants, opponents, opposition, possibilities, runners.
v. answer, catch, cope with, deal with, deflect, handle, parry, pick up, receive, retrieve, return, stop.

fiend *n.* **1** demon, devil, evil spirit, monster. **2** addict, devotee, enthusiast, fanatic, freak, nut.

fiendish *adj.* cruel, cunning, devilish, diabolical, infernal, inhuman, malevolent, monstrous, savage, unspeakable, wicked.

fierce *adj.* aggressive, brutal, cruel, dangerous, ferocious, frightening, grim, howling, intense, menacing, merciless, murderous, passionate, powerful, raging, relentless, savage, stern, stormy, strong, tempestuous, threatening, tumultuous, wild.
antonyms calm, gentle, kind.

fiery *adj.* ablaze, afire, aflame, aglow, ardent, blazing, burning, excitable, fervent, fierce, flaming, flushed, glowing, heated, hot, hot-headed, impatient, impetuous, impulsive, inflamed, passionate, red-hot, sultry, torrid, violent, volcanic.
antonyms cold, impassive.

fight *v.* argue, assault, battle, bicker, box, brawl, clash, close, combat, contend, cross swords, defy, dispute, do battle, engage, exchange blows, fence, grapple, joust, oppose, prosecute, quarrel, resist, scrap, scuffle, skirmish, squabble, stand up to, strive, struggle, tussle, wage war, war, withstand, wrangle, wrestle.
n. action, argument, battle, bout, brawl, brush, clash, combat, conflict, contest, dispute, dissension, duel, encounter, engagement, fracas, fray, free-for-all, hostilities, joust, militancy, quarrel, riot, row, scrap, scuffle, set-to, skirmish, strength, struggle, tussle, war.

fight back 1 defend oneself, put up a fight, reply, resist, retaliate, retort. **2** bottle up, contain, control, curb, hold back, repress, resist, restrain, suppress.

fight off beat off, hold off, keep at bay, put to flight, rebuff, repel, repress, resist, rout, stave off, ward off.

fight shy of avoid, disdain, eschew, keep at arm's length, shun, spurn, steer clear of.

fighter *n.* boxer, champion, combatant, contender, contestant, disputant, fighting man, gladiator, man-at-arms, mercenary, militant, prize-fighter, pugilist, soldier, swordsman, trouper, warrior, wrestler.

figment *n.* concoction, creation, fable, fabrication, fancy, fiction, illusion, improvisation, invention, product, production, work.

figurative *adj.* allegorical, descriptive, metaphorical, ornate, parabolic, pictorial, poetical, representative, symbolic, typical.
antonym literal.

figure *n.* **1** digit, number, numeral, symbol. **2** body, build, configuration, form, frame, outline, shape, silhouette. **3** celebrity, character, dignitary, person, personality, somebody. **4** design, diagram, drawing, illustration, image, picture, representation, sketch.
v. **1** believe, estimate, guess, judge, reckon, think. **2** appear, feature.

figure of speech figure, image, imagery, rhetorical device, turn of phrase.

figure out calculate, compute, decipher, explain, fathom, make out, puzzle out, reason out, reckon, resolve, see, understand, work out.

figurehead *n.* **1** bust, carving. **2** dummy, front man, image, leader, mouthpiece, name, nominal head, titular head.

filament *n.* fibre, hair, pile, staple, strand, string, thread, whisker, wire.

file[1] *v.* abrade, grate, hone, pare, plane, polish, refine, rub (down), sand, scour, scrape, shape, shave, smooth, trim, whet.

file[2] *n.* binder, case, date, documents, dossier, folder, information, portfolio, record.
v. capture, document, enter, memorise, note, pigeonhole, process, record, register, slot in, store.

file[3] *n.* column, cortège, line, list, procession, queue, row, stream, string, trail, train.
v. defile, march, parade, stream, trail, troop.

filial *adj.* daughterly, dutiful, fond, loving, loyal, respectful, sonly.

antonym disloyal.
fill *v.* **1** block, bung, clog, close, congest, cork, cram, crowd, furnish, pack, plug, replenish, satisfy, seal, soak, stock, stop, stuff, supply. **2** imbue, impregnate, permeate, pervade. **3** discharge, fulfil, hold, occupy, take up.
antonyms **1** drain, empty. **3** give up.
n. abundance, ample, enough, plenty, sufficiency, sufficient.
fill in 1 answer, complete, fill out. **2** act for, deputise, replace, represent, stand in, substitute, understudy. **3** acquaint, advise, brief, bring up to date, inform.
filling *n.* contents, filler, grouting, inside, padding, rubble, stuffing, wadding.
adj. ample, big, generous, heavy, large, nutritious, satisfying, solid, square, substantial, sustaining.
antonym insubstantial.
fillip *n.* boost, impetus, incentive, prod, push, shove, spur, stimulus, zest.
antonym damper.
film *n.* **1** documentary, epic, feature film, motion picture, movie, picture, short, video, western. **2** cloud, coat, coating, covering, dusting, glaze, layer, membrane, mist, screen, sheet, skin, tissue, veil, web.
v. photograph, shoot, take, video, videotape.
filmy *adj.* delicate, fine, flimsy, gauzy, gossamer, insubstantial, light, see-through, sheer, shimmering, thin, transparent.
filter *v.* dribble, escape, exude, leak, ooze, penetrate, percolate, screen, seep, sieve, sift, strain, transpire, trickle, well.
n. colander, gauze, membrane, mesh, sieve, sifter, strainer.
filth *n.* coarseness, contamination, corruption, defilement, dirt, dung, excrement, faeces, foulness, garbage, grime, impurity, indecency, muck, nastiness, obscenity, pollution, pornography, refuse, sewage, slime, sludge, smut, soil, sordidness, squalor, uncleanness, vileness, vulgarity.
antonyms cleanliness, decency, purity.
filthy *adj.* base, bawdy, coarse, contemptible, corrupt, depraved, despicable, dirty, foul, foul-mouthed, grimy, gross, grubby, impure, indecent, low, mean, miry, mucky, muddy, nasty, obscene, offensive, pornographic, slimy, smoky, smutty, sooty, sordid, squalid, suggestive, unclean, vicious, vile, vulgar.
antonyms clean, decent, pure.
final *adj.* closing, concluding, conclusive, decisive, definite, definitive, dying, eventual, finished, incontrovertible, last, last-minute, latest, terminal, ultimate.
antonyms first, initial.
finale *n.* climax, close, conclusion, crescendo, crowning glory, culmination, curtain, dénouement, epilogue, finis.
finalise *v.* agree, clinch, complete, conclude, decide, finish, resolve, round off, seal, settle, sew up, tie up, work out, wrap up.
finality *n.* certainty, conclusiveness, definiteness, firmness, inevitability, irreversibility, resolution, unavoidability.
finally *adv.* at last, at length, conclusively, definitely, eventually, for ever, in conclusion, in the end, inexorably, irreversibly, irrevocably, lastly, once and for all, ultimately.
finance *n.* accounting, accounts, banking, business, commerce, economics, investment, money, money management, stock market, trade.
v. back, bail out, capitalise, float, fund, guarantee, pay for, set up, subsidise, support, underwrite.
finances *n.* affairs, assets, bank account, budget, capital, cash, coffers, funds, income, liquidity, money, resources, revenue, wealth, wherewithal.
financial *adj.* budgetary, commercial, economic, fiscal, monetary, money.
financier *n.* banker, broker, financialist, gnome, investor, money-maker, speculator, stockbroker.
find *v.* **1** catch, chance on, come across, detect, discover, encounter, experience, get, learn, locate, meet, note, notice, observe, obtain, perceive, realise, recognise, retrieve, stumble on, track down, uncover, unearth. **2** achieve, attain, gain, provide, reach, win. **3** consider, declare, judge, think.
n. acquisition, asset, bargain, catch, coup, discovery, good buy.
find out ascertain, catch, detect, dig up, disclose, discover, establish, expose, learn, note, observe, perceive, realise, reveal, rumble, show up, sus out, tumble to, uncover, unmask.
finding *n.* award, breakthrough, conclusion, decision, decree, discovery, evidence, judgement, pronouncement, recommendation, verdict.
fine[1] *adj.* **1** acceptable, all right, attractive, beautiful, brilliant, elegant, excellent, exceptional, good, handsome, lovely, magnificent, nice, OK, outstanding, satisfactory, splendid, superior. **2** dainty, delicate, exquisite, flimsy, fragile, gauzy, powdery, sheer, slender, thin. **3** hair-splitting, minute, nice, precise, refined, subtle. **4** bright, clear, cloudless, dry, fair, pleasant, sunny.
antonyms **1** mediocre. **2** coarse, thick. **4** cloudy.
fine[2] *v.* penalise, punish, sting.
n. damages, forfeit, forfeiture, penalty, punishment.
finery *n.* decorations, frills and furbelows, frippery, gear, jewellery, ornaments, splendour, Sunday best, trappings.
finger *v.* caress, feel, fiddle with, fondle, handle, manipulate, meddle with, paw, play about with, stroke, touch, toy with.
n. claw, digit, digital, index, talon.
finicky *adj.* choosy, critical, delicate, difficult, fastidious, fussy, hypercritical, meticulous, nit-picking, particular, pernickety, scrupulous.
antonyms easy, easy-going.
finish *v.* **1** accomplish, achieve, cease, close,

complete, conclude, culminate, deal with, discharge, do, end, fulfil, perfect, round off, settle, stop, terminate, wind up. **2** annihilate, defeat, destroy, exterminate, get rid of, kill, overcome, overthrow, rout, ruin. **3** consume, devour, dispose of, drain, drink, eat, empty, exhaust, use (up).
antonyms **1** begin, start.
n. **1** close, closing, completion, conclusion, culmination, death, defeat, end, ending, finale, ruin, termination. **2** appearance, gloss, grain, lustre, polish, refinement, shine, smoothness, surface, texture.
antonyms **1** beginning, commencement, start.

fire *n.* **1** blaze, bonfire, burning, combustion, conflagration, flames, heat, inferno. **2** enthusiasm, excitement, feeling, inspiration, intensity, passion, radiance, sparkle, spirit.
v. **1** detonate, electrify, explode, ignite, kindle, let off, light, set alight, set fire to, set off, set on fire, shoot, touch off. **2** arouse, enliven, excite, galvanise, incite, inspire, quicken, rouse, stimulate, stir, trigger off, whet. **3** depose, discharge, dismiss, eject, sack.
on fire ablaze, aflame, alight, blazing, burning, fiery, fired, flaming, ignited, in flames.

firm[1] *adj.* **1** compact, compressed, concentrated, dense, hard, inflexible, rigid, set, solid, stiff, unyielding. **2** anchored, embedded, fast, fastened, fixed, grounded, immovable, motionless, secure, settled, stable, stationary, steady, strong, sturdy. **3** adamant, committed, constant, convinced, definite, dependable, determined, dogged, resolute, staunch, steadfast, strict, sure, true, unshakable, unwavering.
antonyms **1** flabby, soft. **2** unsteady. **3** hesitant.

firm[2] *n.* association, business, company, concern, conglomerate, corporation, enterprise, establishment, house, institution, organisation, partnership, set-up, syndicate.

first *adj.* basic, chief, earliest, eldest, elementary, fundamental, head, highest, initial, introductory, key, leading, main, oldest, opening, original, paramount, predominant, preeminent, primary, prime, primeval, primitive, principal, prior, ruling, senior, sovereign, uppermost.
antonyms final, last.
adv. at the outset, before all else, beforehand, early on, in preference, in the beginning, initially, originally, rather, sooner, to begin with, to start with.
first name baptismal name, Christian name, forename, given name.

firsthand *adj.* direct, immediate, personal, straight from the horse's mouth.
antonym indirect.

first-rate *adj.* A1, admirable, excellent, exceptional, exclusive, fine, first-class, leading, matchless, outstanding, peerless, prime, second-to-none, splendid, superb, superior, superlative, top, top-flight, top-notch.
antonym inferior.

fiscal *adj.* budgetary, economic, financial, monetary, money, pecuniary, treasury.

fish *v.* angle, cast, delve, hunt, invite, seek, solicit, trawl.
fish out come up with, dredge up, extract, extricate, find, haul up, produce.

fishing *n.* angling, fishery, trawling.

fission *n.* breaking, cleavage, division, parting, rending, rupture, schism, severance, splitting.

fit[1] *adj.* **1** able, appropriate, apt, capable, competent, correct, eligible, fitting, prepared, proper, qualified, ready, right, suitable, well-suited, worthy. **2** able-bodied, hale and hearty, healthy, in good form, in good shape, robust, sound, strong, sturdy, trained, well.
antonyms **1** unsuitable, unworthy. **2** unfit.
v. accommodate, adapt, adjust, agree, alter, arrange, belong, change, concur, conform, correspond, dovetail, fashion, fay, figure, follow, go, harmonise, interlock, join, match, meet, modify, place, position, reconcile, shape, suit, tally.
fit out accommodate, arm, equip, kit out, outfit, prepare, provide, rig out, supply.

fit[2] *n.* attack, bout, burst, convulsion, eruption, explosion, outbreak, outburst, paroxysm, seizure, spasm, spell, storm, surge.

fitful *adj.* broken, disturbed, erratic, intermittent, irregular, occasional, spasmodic, sporadic, uneven.
antonyms regular, steady.

fitted *adj.* adapted, appointed, armed, built-in, equipped, fit, furnished, permanent, prepared, provided, qualified, rigged out, right, suitable, suited, tailor-made.

fitting *adj.* appropriate, apt, correct, deserved, desirable, harmonious, meet, proper, right, suitable.
antonyms improper, unsuitable.
n. accessory, attachment, component, connection, fitment, fixture, part, piece, unit.

fittings *n.* accessories, appointments, conveniences, equipment, extras, fitments, fixtures, furnishings, furniture, installations.

fix *v.* **1** anchor, attach, bind, cement, congeal, connect, couple, embed, establish, fasten, freeze, glue, harden, implant, install, link, locate, nail, pin, place, plant, position, rivet, root, seal, secure, solidify, stabilise, stick, stiffen, thicken, tie. **2** agree on, arrange, confirm, decide, define, determine, finalise, resolve, see to, set, settle, specify. **3** adjust, correct, mend, repair, restore.
antonyms **1** change, move, shift. **3** damage, harm.
n. corner, difficulty, dilemma, embarrassment, hole, mess, muddle, plight, predicament, quandary, spot.
fix up arrange (for), bring about, equip, fix, furnish, lay on, organise, plan, produce, provide, settle, sort out, supply.

fixation *n.* complex, compulsion, fetish, hang-up, infatuation, mania, obsession, preoccupation, thing.

fixed *adj.* arranged, decided, definite, estab-

lished, fast, firm, inflexible, permanent, planned, rigid, rooted, secure, set, settled, steadfast, steady.
antonyms alterable, variable.

fixity *n.* determination, doggedness, fixedness, intentness, perseverance, persistence, stability, steadiness, strength.

fizz *v.* bubble, effervesce, fizzle, froth, hiss, sizzle, sparkle, spit, sputter.

fizzle out collapse, come to nothing, die away, die down, disappear, evaporate, fail, fall through, fold, peter out, stop, subside.

fizzy *adj.* aerated, bubbling, bubbly, carbonated, effervescent, frothy, gassy, sparkling.

flabbergasted *adj.* amazed, astonished, astounded, bowled over, confounded, dazed, dumbfounded, overcome, overwhelmed, speechless, staggered, stunned.

flabby *adj.* drooping, feeble, fleshy, floppy, hanging, lax, limp, loose, sagging, slack, unfit, weak, yielding.
antonyms firm, strong.

flag[1] *v.* abate, decline, degenerate, deteriorate, die, diminish, droop, dwindle, fade, fail, faint, fall (off), falter, flop, lessen, peter out, sag, sink, slow, slump, subside, tire, weaken, weary, wilt.
antonym revive.

flag[2] *n.* banner, colours, ensign, jack, pennant, standard, streamer.
v. indicate, label, mark, motion, note, salute, signal, tab, tag, warn, wave.

flail *v.* beat, thrash, thresh, whip.

flair *n.* ability, accomplishment, acumen, aptitude, discernment, elegance, facility, faculty, feel, genius, gift, knack, mastery, panache, skill, style, stylishness, talent, taste.
antonyms inability, ineptitude.

flak *n.* abuse, brickbats, censure, complaints, condemnation, criticism, disapproval, fault-finding, hostility, opposition.

flake *n.* chip, disc, layer, paring, peeling, scale, shaving, sliver, wafer.
v. blister, chip, peel, scale.

flaky *adj.* dry, layered, scaly, scurfy.

flamboyant *adj.* brilliant, colourful, dazzling, elaborate, exciting, extravagant, flashy, florid, gaudy, ostentatious, rich, showy, striking, stylish.
antonyms modest, restrained.

flame *v.* beam, blaze, burn, flare, flash, glare, glow, radiate, shine.
n. **1** blaze, brightness, fire, light, warmth. **2** affection, ardour, enthusiasm, fervour, intensity, passion, radiance, zeal. **3** heart-throb, lover, sweetheart.

flaming *adj.* alight, aroused, blazing, brilliant, burning, fiery, frenzied, glowing, hot, impassioned, intense, raging, red, red-hot, scintillating, smouldering, vivid.

flammable *adj.* combustible, ignitable, inflammable.
antonyms fire-resistant, flameproof, incombustible, non-flammable, non-inflammable.

flange *n.* flare, lip, rim, skirt, splay.

flank *n.* edge, hip, loin, quarter, side, thigh, wing.
v. accompany, border, bound, confine, edge, fringe, line, screen, skirt, wall.

flap *v.* agitate, beat, flutter, fuss, panic, shake, swing, swish, thrash, vibrate, wag, wave.
n. **1** agitation, commotion, dither, fluster, flutter, fuss, state, tizzy. **2** aileron, cover, fly, fold, lapel, lug, skirt, tab, tag, tail.

flare *v.* blaze, burn (up), burst, dazzle, erupt, explode, flame, flash, flicker, flutter, glare, waver.
n. **1** blaze, burst, dazzle, flame, flash, flicker, glare. **2** bell-bottom, broadening, flange, splay, widening.
flare out broaden, splay, spread out, widen.
flare up blaze, blow up, erupt, explode.

flash *v.* **1** beam, blaze, flare, flicker, glare, gleam, glint, glitter, light, shimmer, sparkle, twinkle. **2** dart, dash, fly, race, streak.
n. blaze, burst, dazzle, flare, flicker, gleam, glint, outburst, ray, shaft, shake, shimmer, spark, sparkle, streak, touch, twinkle, twinkling.

flashy *adj.* bold, cheap, flamboyant, flash, garish, gaudy, glamorous, jazzy, loud, ostentatious, showy, tasteless, tawdry, vulgar.
antonyms plain, simple, tasteful.

flat[1] *adj.* **1** even, horizontal, level, low, outstretched, plane, prone, prostrate, reclining, recumbent, smooth, unbroken, uniform. **2** bored, boring, burst, collapsed, dead, deflated, depressed, dull, empty, insipid, lacklustre, lifeless, monotonous, pointless, punctured, spiritless, stale, tedious, unexciting, uninteresting, vapid, watery, weak. **3** absolute, categorical, direct, explicit, final, fixed, plain, point-blank, positive, straight, total, uncompromising, unconditional, unequivocal, unqualified.
antonyms **1** bumpy. **2** exciting, full. **3** equivocal.
n. lowland, marsh, morass, moss, mud flat, plain, shallow, shoal, strand, swamp.
flat out all out, at full speed, at top speed, double-quick, for all one is worth.

flat[2] *n.* apartment, bed-sit, bed-sitter, maison(n)-ette, pad, penthouse, rooms, tenement.

flatly *adv.* absolutely, categorically, completely, point-blank, positively, unconditionally.

flatten *v.* compress, crush, demolish, even out, fell, floor, iron out, knock down, level, overwhelm, plaster, prostrate, raze, roll, slight, smooth, squash, subdue.

flatter *v.* adulate, butter up, compliment, court, enhance, fawn, humour, play up to, praise, sweet-talk, wheedle.
antonyms criticise, oppose.

flattery *n.* adulation, butter, cajolery, eulogy, fawning, flannel, ingratiation, servility, soft soap, sweet talk, sycophancy, toadyism.
antonym criticism.

flatulence *n.* flatus, gas, pomposity, wind, windiness.

flavour *n.* aroma, aspect, character, essence, extract, feel, feeling, flavouring, hint, odour, property, quality, relish, savour, seasoning, smack, style, suggestion, tang, taste, tinge, tone,

touch, zest, zing.
v. contaminate, ginger up, imbue, infuse, season, spice.
flavouring *n.* essence, extract, seasoning, spirit, zest.
flaw *n.* blemish, breach, break, cleft, crack, craze, crevice, defect, disfigurement, failing, fallacy, fault, fissure, fracture, imperfection, lapse, mark, mistake, rent, rift, shortcoming, slip, speck, split, spot, tear, weakness, wreath.
flawed *adj.* blemished, broken, chipped, cracked, damaged, defective, disfigured, erroneous, faulty, imperfect, marked, marred, spoilt, unsound, vicious.
antonyms flawless, perfect.
fleck *v.* dapple, dot, dust, mark, mottle, speckle, spinkle, spot, stipple, streak.
n. dot, freak, mark, point, speck, speckle, spot, streak.
fledgling *n.* apprentice, beginner, greenhorn, learner, nestling, newcomer, novice, recruit, tenderfoot, trainee, tyro.
flee *v.* abscond, avoid, bolt, bunk (off), cut and run, decamp, depart, escape, fly, get away, leave, make off, retreat, shun, take flight, take off, vanish, withdraw.
antonyms stand, stay.
fleet[1] *n.* argosy, armada, flotilla, navy, squadron, task force.
fleet[2] *adj.* fast, flying, light-footed, meteoric, nimble, quick, rapid, speedy, swift, winged.
antonyms slow, unhurried.
fleeting *adj.* brief, ephemeral, flitting, flying, momentary, passing, short, short-lived, temporary, transient, transitory, vanishing.
antonyms lasting, permanent.
flesh *n.* blood, body, brawn, fat, fatness, food, matter, meat, physicality, pulp, substance, tissue.
fleshy *adj.* beefy, brawny, chubby, chunky, corpulent, fat, flabby, meaty, obese, overweight, paunchy, plump, podgy, portly, stout, tubby.
antonym thin.
flex *v.* angle, bend, bow, contract, curve, double up, ply, tighten.
antonyms extend, straighten.
flexible *adj.* accommodating, adaptable, adjustable, agreeable, amenable, bendable, double-jointed, elastic, limber, lithe, manageable, mobile, mouldable, open, plastic, pliable, pliant, responsive, springy, stretchy, supple, variable, yielding.
antonyms inflexible, rigid.
flick *v.* dab, flap, flicker, hit, jab, jerk, rap, strike, tap, touch, whip.
n. click, flap, flip, jab, jerk, rap, tap, touch.
flick through flip through, glance at, scan, skim, thumb through.
flicker *v.* flare, flash, flutter, glimmer, gutter, quiver, shimmer, sparkle, twinkle, vibrate, waver.
n. atom, breath, drop, flare, flash, gleam, glimmer, glint, indication, inkling, iota, spark, trace.
flight[1] *n.* aeronautics, air transport, air travel, aviation, flying, formation, journey, soaring, squadron, trip, voyage, winging.
flight[2] *n.* breakaway, departure, escape, exit, exodus, fleeing, getaway, retreat, running away.
flighty *adj.* capricious, changeable, fickle, hare-brained, impulsive, irresponsible, scatter-brained, skittish, thoughtless.
antonyms constant, steady.
flimsy *adj.* cardboard, delicate, ethereal, feeble, fragile, implausible, inadequate, insubstantial, light, makeshift, meagre, poor, rickety, shaky, shallow, slight, superficial, thin, transparent, trivial, unconvincing, weak.
antonym sturdy.
fling *v.* cast, catapult, heave, hurl, jerk, let fly, lob, pitch, propel, send, shoot, sling, slug, throw, toss.
n. **1** heave, lob, pitch, shot, throw, toss, whirl. **2** binge, indulgence, spree.
flip *v.* cast, flap, flick, jerk, pitch, spin, throw, toss, turn, twirl, twist.
n. flap, flick, jerk, toss, turn, twirl, twist.
flippant *adj.* brash, cheeky, disrespectful, flip, frivolous, glib, impertinent, impudent, irreverent, offhand, rude, saucy, superficial.
antonyms earnest, respectful, serious.
flirt *v.* chat up, dally, ogle.
flirt with consider, dabble in, entertain, make up to, play with, toy with, trifle with, try.
flit *v.* bob, dance, dart, flash, flutter, fly, pass, skim, slip, speed, whisk, wing.
float *v.* **1** bob, drift, glide, hover, poise, ride, sail, slide, swim, waft. **2** initiate, launch, promote, set up.
antonym **1** sink.
floating *adj.* **1** afloat, bobbing, buoyant, buoyed up, sailing, swimming, unsinkable. **2** fluctuating, free, migratory, movable, transitory, unattached, uncommitted, variable, wandering.
antonyms **1** sinking. **2** fixed, loyal.
flock *v.* bunch, cluster, collect, congregate, converge, crowd, gather, group, herd, huddle, mass, swarm, throng, troop.
n. assembly, collection, congregation, convoy, crowd, gathering, group, herd, mass, multitude, pack, throng.
flog *v.* beat, birch, chastise, drive, drub, flay, hide, lash, punish, push, scourge, strain, swish, thrash, whack, whip.
flogging *n.* beating, caning, flaying, hiding, lashing, scourging, thrashing, whipping.
flood *v.* deluge, drench, drown, engulf, fill, flow, gush, immerse, inundate, overflow, overwhelm, pour, rush, saturate, soak, submerge, surge, swamp, sweep.
n. abundance, deluge, downpour, flow, glut, inundation, multitude, outpouring, overflow, profusion, rush, spate, stream, tide, torrent.
antonyms dearth, drought, trickle.
floor *n.* base, basis, deck, landing, level, stage, storey, tier.
v. baffle, beat, bewilder, confound, defeat,

disconcert, dumbfound, frustrate, overthrow, overwhelm, perplex, puzzle, stump, throw.

flop *v.* collapse, dangle, droop, drop, fail, fall, fall flat, fold, founder, hang, misfire, plump, sag, slump, topple, tumble.
n. debacle, disaster, failure, fiasco, no go, non-starter, wash-out.

floppy *adj.* baggy, dangling, droopy, hanging, limp, loose, sagging, soft.
antonym firm.

flora *n.* botany, plant-life, plants, vegetable kingdom, vegetation.

florid *adj.* baroque, elaborate, embellished, flamboyant, flowery, fussy, grandiloquent, ornate, overelaborate, purple, red, rococo, ruddy.
antonyms pale, plain, simple.

flotsam *n.* debris, jetsam, junk, oddments, rubbish, scum, sweepings, wreckage.

flounce *v.* fling, spring, stamp, storm, throw, toss, twist.
n. frill, fringe, ruffle, trimming, valance.

flounder *v.* blunder, falter, fumble, grope, muddle, plunge, stagger, struggle, stumble, wallop, wallow.

flourish *v.* **1** bloom, blossom, boom, develop, do well, flower, get on, grow, increase, progress, prosper, succeed, thrive, wax. **2** brandish, display, flaunt, parade, shake, swing, swish, twirl, vaunt, wave, wield.
antonyms **1** decline, fail, languish.
n. brandishing, dash, decoration, display, fanfare, gesture, ornament, panache, parade, pizzazz, shaking, show, sweep, twirling, wave.

flout *v.* defy, disregard, insult, jeer at, mock, outrage, reject, ridicule, scoff at, scorn, spurn.
antonyms regard, respect.

flow *v.* **1** bubble, circulate, deluge, drift, flood, glide, gush, inundate, move, overflow, pour, ripple, roll, run, rush, slide, slip, spill, spurt, squirt, stream, surge, sweep, swirl, teem, well, whirl. **2** arise, derive, emanate, emerge, issue, originate, proceed, result, spring.
n. abundance, cascade, course, current, deluge, drift, flood, flux, gush, outpouring, plenty, spate, spurt, stream, tide, wash.

flower *n.* best, bloom, blossom, choice, cream, élite, freshness, height, pick, prime, vigour.

flowering *adj.* blooming, blossoming, maturing.
n. blooming, blossoming, burgeoning, development, flourishing, flowerage, maturing.

flowery *adj.* baroque, elaborate, fancy, floral, ornate, rhetorical.
antonyms plain, simple.

fluctuate *v.* alter, alternate, change, ebb and flow, float, hesitate, oscillate, rise and fall, seesaw, shift, shuffle, sway, swing, vacillate, vary, waver.

fluency *n.* articulateness, assurance, command, control, ease, eloquence, facility, readiness, slickness, smoothness.
antonyms brokenness, incoherence.

fluent *adj.* articulate, easy, effortless, eloquent, flowing, natural, ready, smooth, voluble, well-versed.
antonyms broken, incoherent, tongue-tied.

fluff *n.* down, dust, floss, fuzz, lint, nap, pile.

fluffy *adj.* downy, feathery, fleecy, fuzzy, gossamer, hairy, oozy, shaggy, silky, soft, velvety, woolly.

fluid *adj.* **1** aqueous, liquefied, liquid, melted, molten, running, runny, watery. **2** adaptable, adjustable, changeable, flexible, inconstant, indefinite, mobile, shifting, unstable, variable. **3** graceful, smooth.
antonyms **1** solid. **2** stable.
n. juice, liquid, liquor, sap, solution.

flummox *v.* baffle, bewilder, confuse, defeat, fox, mystify, perplex, puzzle, stump.

flurry *n.* burst, bustle, commotion, disturbance, excitement, flap, fluster, flutter, fuss, gust, hurry, outbreak, spell, spurt, squall, stir, to-do, tumult, whirl.

flush[1] *v.* **1** blush, burn, colour, crimson, flame, glow, go red, redden, suffuse. **2** cleanse, drench, eject, empty, evacuate, expel, hose, rinse, swab, syringe, wash.
n. bloom, blush, colour, freshness, glow, redness, rosiness, vigour.
adj. **1** abundant, full, generous, in funds, lavish, moneyed, overflowing, prosperous, rich, rolling, wealthy, well-heeled, well-off, well-supplied, well-to-do. **2** even, flat, level, plane, smooth, square, true.

flush[2] *v.* discover, disturb, drive out, force out, rouse, run to earth, start, uncover.

fluster *v.* agitate, bother, bustle, confound, confuse, disconcert, discountenance, disturb, embarrass, excite, flurry, heat, hurry, perturb, rattle, ruffle, unnerve, unsettle, upset.
antonym calm.
n. agitation, bustle, commotion, discomposure, disturbance, dither, embarrassment, flap, flurry, flutter, kerfuffle, ruffle, state, tizzy, turmoil.
antonym calm.

fluted *adj.* channelled, corrugated, furrowed, gouged, grooved, ribbed, ridged, valleculate.

flutter *v.* agitate, bat, beat, dance, flap, flicker, flit, fluctuate, hover, palpitate, quiver, ripple, ruffle, shiver, toss, tremble, vibrate, wave, waver.
n. agitation, commotion, confusion, dither, excitement, flurry, fluster, nervousness, palpitation, quivering, shiver, shudder, state, tremble, tremor, tumult, twitching, upset, vibration.

flux *n.* alteration, change, chaos, development, flow, fluctuation, fluidity, instability, modification, motion, movement, transition.
antonyms rest, stability.

fly[1] *v.* **1** career, float, glide, hover, mount, pilot, raise, soar, take off, wing, zoom. **2** dart, dash, hurry, race, rush, shoot, speed, sprint, tear. **3** elapse, pass, roll by.
fly at attack, fall upon, go for, rush at.

fly[2] *adj.* alert, artful, astute, canny, cunning, knowing, sharp, shrewd, smart, wide-awake.

foam *n.* bubbles, effervescence, froth, head, lather, scum, suds.

v. boil, bubble, effervesce, fizz, froth, lather.

fob off deceive, dump, foist, get rid of, impose, inflict, palm off, pass off, put off, unload.

focus *n.* axis, centre, centre of attraction, core, crux, focal point, headquarters, heart, hinge, hub, kernel, linchpin, nucleus, pivot, target.
v. aim, centre, concentrate, converge, direct, fix, home in, join, meet, rivet, spotlight, zero in, zoom in.

fodder *n.* feed, food, foodstuff, forage, fuel, nourishment, silage.

fog *n.* **1** blanket, cloud, gloom, haze, mist, murkiness, pea-souper, smog. **2** bewilderment, confusion, daze, obscurity, perplexity, puzzlement, trance, vagueness.
v. blind, cloud, confuse, darken, daze, dim, dull, mist, muddle, obscure, shroud, steam up.

foggy *adj.* cloudy, dark, dim, grey, hazy, misty, murky, shadowy, smoggy.
antonym clear.

foil[1] *v.* baffle, check, circumvent, counter, defeat, disappoint, elude, frustrate, nullify, obstruct, stop, stump, thwart.
antonym abet.

foil[2] *n.* background, balance, complement, contrast, relief, setting.

fold *v.* **1** bend, clasp, close, crease, crimp, crumple, double, embrace, enclose, entwine, envelop, gather, hug, intertwine, overlap, pleat, tuck, wrap (up). **2** collapse, crash, fail, go bust, shut down.
antonyms **1** open up. **2** start.
n. bend, corrugation, crease, crimp, furrow, knife-edge, layer, overlap, pleat, ply, turn, wrinkle.

folder *n.* binder, envelope, file, folio, holder, portfolio.

folk *n.* clan, family, kin, kindred, kinfolk, kinsmen, nation, people, race, society, tribe.
adj. ancestral, ethnic, indigenous, national, native, traditional, tribal.

follow *v.* **1** accompany, attend, escort, go (along) with. **2** catch, chase, hound, hunt, pursue, shadow, tail, track, trail. **3** come after, come next, succeed, supersede. **4** arise, develop, emanate, ensue, result. **5** act according to, adhere to, carry out, comply, conform, heed, mind, obey, observe, practise. **6** comprehend, fathom, grasp, understand.
antonyms **1** abandon, desert. **3** go before, precede. **5** disobey.
follow through complete, conclude, consummate, continue, finish, fulfil, implement, pursue, see through.
follow up check out, consolidate, continue, investigate, pursue, reinforce.

follower *n.* adherent, admirer, apostle, attendant, backer, believer, buff, companion, convert, devotee, disciple, emulator, fan, freak, hanger-on, helper, imitator, pupil, representative, retainer, sidekick, supporter.
antonyms leader, opponent.

following *adj.* coming, consequent, ensuing, later, next, resulting, subsequent, succeeding, successive.
antonym previous.
n. audience, backing, circle, clientèle, entourage, fans, followers, patronage, public, retinue, suite, support, supporters.

folly *n.* **1** absurdity, craziness, idiocy, imbecility, indiscretion, insanity, irresponsibility, lunacy, madness, nonsense, rashness, recklessness, senselessness, silliness, stupidity. **2** belvedere, monument, tower.
antonyms **1** prudence, wisdom.

foment *v.* activate, agitate, arouse, encourage, excite, foster, incite, instigate, kindle, promote, prompt, provoke, quicken, raise, rouse, spur, stimulate, stir up, whip up, work up.
antonyms quell, subdue.

fond *adj.* **1** adoring, affectionate, caring, devoted, doting, indulgent, loving, tender, warm. **2** absurd, deluded, empty, foolish, naïve, over-optimistic, silly, vain.
antonyms **1** hostile. **2** realistic, sensible.
fond of addicted to, attached to, enamoured of, hooked on, keen on, partial to, predisposed towards, sweet on.

fondle *v.* caress, cuddle, dandle, pat, pet, stroke.

food *n.* bread, comestibles, cooking, cuisine, diet, eatables, eats, fare, feed, foodstuffs, grub, larder, menu, nourishment, nutriment, nutrition, provisions, rations, refreshment, stores, subsistence, sustenance, table, tuck.

fool *n.* ass, blockhead, buffoon, chump, clot, clown, dimwit, dope, dunce, dupe, halfwit, idiot, imbecile, moron, mug, nincompoop, ninny, nit, nitwit, numskull, silly-billy, simpleton, softie, softy, stooge, sucker, twit, wally.
v. cheat, con, deceive, delude, diddle, dupe, feign, fiddle, gull, have on, hoax, hoodwink, jest, joke, kid, mislead, pretend, put one over on, string along, swindle, take in, tease, toy, trick.
fool about horse around, lark about, mess about, mess around, play about.

foolhardy *adj.* adventurous, ill-advised, imprudent, irresponsible, rash, reckless.
antonyms cautious, prudent, responsible.

foolish *adj.* absurd, crazy, daft, dotish, half-baked, half-witted, hare-brained, idiotic, ill-advised, ill-considered, inept, ludicrous, mad, moronic, nonsensical, ridiculous, senseless, short-sighted, silly, simple, simple-minded, stupid, unintelligent, unreasonable, weak.
antonyms cautious, prudent, wise.

foolproof *adj.* certain, fail-safe, guaranteed, idiot-proof, infallible, safe, sure-fire, unbreakable.
antonym unreliable.

footing *n.* balance, base, basis, conditions, establishment, foot-hold, foundation, grade, ground, groundwork, installation, level, position, purchase, rank, relations, relationship, settlement, standing, state, status, terms.

footnote *n.* annotation, commentary, note.

footprint *n.* footmark, trace, track, trail, vestige.

footstep *n.* plod, step, tramp, tread, trudge.

forage *n.* feed, fodder, food, foodstuffs, pasturage.
v. cast about, explore, hunt, plunder, raid, ransack, rummage, scavenge, scour, scrounge, search, seek.

forbid *v.* ban, block, debar, deny, exclude, hinder, inhibit, interdict, outlaw, preclude, prevent, prohibit, proscribe, refuse, rule out, veto.
antonyms allow, approve, permit.

forbidden *adj.* banned, barred, out of bounds, outlawed, prohibited, proscribed, taboo, vetoed.

forbidding *adj.* awesome, daunting, formidable, frightening, menacing, off-putting, ominous, repellent, sinister, stern, threatening.
antonyms approachable, congenial, friendly.

force *n.* **1** aggression, coercion, compulsion, duress, fierceness, pressure, punch, violence. **2** drive, dynamism, emphasis, energy, impulse, influence, intensity, motivation, power, strength, stress. **3** army, battalion, body, corps, detachment, detail, division, host, legion, patrol, regiment, squad, squadron, troop, unit.
antonyms **1** compassion. **2** weakness.
v. bulldoze, coerce, compel, constrain, drive, exact, extort, impose, lean on, make, necessitate, obligate, press, press-gang, pressurise, prise, propel, push, strong-arm, thrust, urge, wrench, wrest, wring.

forced *adj.* affected, artificial, contrived, false, feigned, insincere, involuntary, laboured, stiff, stilted, strained, unnatural, wooden.
antonyms sincere, spontaneous, voluntary.

forceful *adj.* cogent, compelling, convincing, dynamic, effective, emphatic, energetic, persuasive, potent, powerful, strong, urgent, vigorous, weighty.
antonyms feeble, weak.

forcible *adj.* compelling, effective, energetic, forceful, mighty, potent, powerful, strong, telling, urgent, vehement, violent, weighty.
antonym feeble.

forebear *n.* ancestor, antecedent, father, forefather, forerunner, predecessor.
antonym descendant.

foreboding *n.* anticipation, anxiety, apprehension, dread, fear, intuition, misgiving, omen, prediction, premonition, prognostication, sign, token, warning, worry.

forecast *v.* anticipate, calculate, estimate, expect, foresee, foretell, plan, predict, prophesy.
n. forethought, guess, guesstimate, outlook, planning, prediction, prognosis, projection, prophecy.

forefather *n.* ancestor, antecedent, father, forebear, forerunner, predecessor, procreator.
antonym descendant.

forefront *n.* avant-garde, centre, firing line, fore, foreground, front, front line, lead, prominence, van, vanguard.
antonym rear.

foregoing *adj.* above, antecedent, anterior, earlier, former, preceding, previous, prior.

foregone *adj.* anticipated, cut-and-dried, inevitable, open and shut.
antonym unpredictable.

foreground *n.* centre, fore, forefront, front, limelight, prominence.
antonym background.

forehead *n.* brow, front, temples.

foreign *adj.* alien, borrowed, distant, exotic, external, extraneous, extrinsic, imported, incongruous, outside, overseas, remote, strange, uncharacteristic, unfamiliar, unknown.
antonym native.

foreigner *n.* alien, barbarian, immigrant, incomer, newcomer, stranger.
antonym native.

foremost *adj.* cardinal, central, chief, first, front, highest, leading, main, paramount, preeminent, primary, prime, principal, supreme, uppermost.

forerunner *n.* ancestor, announcer, antecedent, envoy, harbinger, herald, precursor, predecessor, sign, token.
antonyms follower, successor.

foresee *v.* anticipate, divine, envisage, expect, forebode, forecast, foretell, predict, prognosticate, prophesy.

foreshadow *v.* anticipate, augur, imply, indicate, predict, prefigure, presage, promise, prophesy, signal.

foresight *n.* anticipation, care, caution, circumspection, far-sightedness, forethought, precaution, preparedness, providence, provision, prudence, readiness, vision.
antonym improvidence.

forestall *v.* anticipate, avert, balk, circumvent, frustrate, head off, hinder, obviate, parry, preclude, pre-empt, prevent, thwart, ward off.
antonyms encourage, facilitate.

foretaste *n.* example, indication, prelude, preview, sample, specimen, trailer, warning, whiff.

foretell *v.* forecast, forewarn, predict, presage, prophesy, signify.

forethought *n.* anticipation, circumspection, far-sightedness, foresight, forward planning, planning, precaution, preparation, providence, provision, prudence.
antonyms carelessness, improvidence.

forever *adv.* always, constantly, continually, endlessly, eternally, evermore, for all time, incessantly, permanently, perpetually, persistently, world without end.

forewarn *v.* admonish, advise, alert, apprise, caution, dissuade, tip off.

foreword *n.* introduction, preface, preliminary, prologue.
antonyms appendix, epilogue, postscript.

forfeit *n.* damages, fine, loss, penalisation, penalty, surrender.
v. abandon, forgo, give up, lose, relinquish, renounce, sacrifice, surrender.

forger *n.* contriver, counterfeiter, creator, deviser, fabricator, faker, falsifier.

forgery *n.* coining, counterfeit, counterfeiting, dud, fake, fraud, fraudulence, imitation,

phoney, sham.
antonym original.
forget *v.* discount, dismiss, disregard, fail, ignore, let slip, lose sight of, neglect, omit, overlook, think no more of, unlearn.
antonyms recall, recollect, remember.
forgetful *adj.* absent-minded, dreamy, heedless, lax, negligent, oblivious.
antonyms attentive, heedful.
forgive *v.* absolve, acquit, condone, exculpate, excuse, exonerate, let off, overlook, pardon, remit.
antonyms censure, punish.
forgiveness *n.* absolution, acquittal, amnesty, exoneration, mercy, pardon, remission.
antonyms blame, censure, punishment.
forgiving *adj.* compassionate, forbearing, humane, indulgent, lenient, merciful, mild, remissive, soft-hearted, sparing, tolerant.
antonyms censorious, harsh, merciless.
forgo *v.* abandon, abstain from, do without, forfeit, give up, pass up, refrain from, relinquish, renounce, resign, sacrifice, surrender, waive, yield.
antonyms claim, indulge in, insist on.
fork *v.* branch (off), diverge, divide, part, separate, split.
n. branching, divergence, division, intersection, junction, separation, split.
forlorn *adj.* abandoned, bereft, deserted, desolate, destitute, forgotten, forsaken, friendless, helpless, homeless, hopeless, lonely, lost, miserable, pathetic, pitiable, unhappy, wretched.
antonyms cheerful, hopeful.
form *v.* **1** assemble, build, combine, construct, create, fashion, make, manufacture, model, mould, produce, shape. **2** compose, comprise, constitute, make up. **3** arrange, concoct, design, devise, draw up, formulate, found, invent, organise, plan, put together. **4** appear, crystallise, develop, grow, materialise, take shape.
n. **1** appearance, build, cast, cut, figure, format, frame, model, mould, outline, pattern, shape, silhouette, structure. **2** arrangement, character, description, design, genre, kind, manner, nature, order, organisation, sort, species, style, system, type, variety, way. **3** class, grade. **4** condition, fitness, health. **5** behaviour, convention, custom, etiquette, manners, protocol, ritual. **6** document, paper, questionnaire, sheet.
formal *adj.* **1** conventional, correct, exact, fixed, methodical, official, precise, regular. **2** ceremonious, prim, punctilious, reserved, rigid, solemn, starchy, stiff, stilted, strict.
antonyms **2** casual, informal.
formality *n.* ceremoniousness, ceremony, convention, correctness, custom, decorum, etiquette, form, formalism, gesture, matter of form, politeness, politesse, procedure, propriety, protocol, red tape, ritual.
antonym informality.
formation *n.* accumulation, appearance, arrangement, compilation, composition, configuration, constitution, construction, creation, design, development, establishment, figure, format, forming, generation, grouping, manufacture, organisation, pattern, production, rank, shaping, structure.
formative *adj.* controlling, determining, developing, dominant, guiding, impressionable, influential, mouldable, moulding, pliant, sensitive, shaping, susceptible.
former *adj.* above, ancient, antecedent, anterior, bygone, departed, earlier, ex-, first mentioned, foregoing, late, long ago, old, old-time, onetime, past, preceding, previous, prior, sometime.
antonyms current, future, later, present.
formerly *adv.* already, at one time, before, earlier, lately, once, previously.
antonyms currently, later, now.
formidable *adj.* challenging, daunting, fearful, frightening, frightful, great, huge, impressive, intimidating, overwhelming, powerful, prodigious, staggering, terrific, terrifying, threatening, toilsome, tremendous.
formless *adj.* amorphous, chaotic, confused, indefinite, nebulous, shapeless, unformed, unshaped, vague.
antonyms definite, orderly, organised.
formula *n.* blueprint, code, form, method, prescription, principle, procedure, proposal, recipe, rule, rule of thumb, solution, way, wording.
formulate *v.* block out, create, define, detail, develop, devise, evolve, express, form, frame, invent, originate, plan, specify, work out.
forsake *v.* abandon, desert, discard, disown, forgo, give up, jettison, jilt, leave, quit, reject, relinquish, renounce, surrender, throw over, turn one's back on.
antonyms return, revert to.
fort *n.* camp, castle, citadel, fortification, fortress, garrison, hill-fort, station, stronghold, tower.
forthcoming *adj.* **1** accessible, approaching, at hand, available, coming, expected, future, imminent, impending, obtainable, projected, prospective, ready. **2** chatty, communicative, conversational, direct, frank, free, informative, open, sociable, talkative.
antonyms quiet, reserved.
forthright *adj.* blunt, bold, candid, direct, frank, open, outspoken, plain, straightforward.
antonyms devious, secretive.
fortify *v.* boost, brace, buttress, confirm, encourage, enrich, garrison, invigorate, load, protect, reassure, reinforce, secure, shore up, stiffen, strengthen, support, sustain.
antonym weaken.
fortitude *n.* bravery, courage, determination, endurance, firmness, grit, hardihood, intrepidity, perseverance, pluck, resolution, strength, strength of mind, valour.
antonyms cowardice, fear, weakness.
fortuitous *adj.* accidental, arbitrary, casual, chance, coincidental, fortunate, incidental, lucky, providential, random, unforeseen.
antonyms expected, intentional, planned.
fortunate *adj.* advantageous, auspicious, blessed,

bright, convenient, encouraging, favourable, felicitous, happy, lucky, opportune, profitable, promising, prosperous, rosy, successful, timely, well-off, well-timed.
antonyms disastrous, unfortunate, unhappy.

fortunately *adv.* happily, luckily, providentially.
antonym unfortunately.

fortune *n.* **1** affluence, assets, estate, income, means, mint, pile, possessions, property, prosperity, riches, treasure, wealth. **2** accident, chance, circumstances, destiny, doom, experience, fate, history, life, lot, luck, portion, providence, star, success.

fortune-telling *n.* augury, crystal-gazing, divination, palmistry, prediction, prophecy, second sight.

forward *adj.* **1** advance, advanced, early, enterprising, first, fore, foremost, forward-looking, front, go-ahead, head, leading, onward, precocious, premature, progressive, well-advanced, well-developed. **2** assertive, audacious, barefaced, bold, brash, brazen, cheeky, confident, familiar, fresh, impertinent, impudent, presumptuous, pushy.
antonyms **1** backward, retrograde. **2** modest, shy.
adv. ahead, forwards, into view, on, onward, out, outward, to light, to the fore, to the surface.
v. accelerate, advance, aid, assist, back, dispatch, encourage, expedite, facilitate, favour, foster, further, hasten, help, hurry, post, promote, route, send (on), ship, speed, support, transmit.
antonyms hinder, impede, obstruct.

forward-looking *adj.* dynamic, enlightened, enterprising, far-sighted, go-ahead, go-getting, innovative, modern, progressive, reforming.
antonym backward-looking.

foster *v.* accommodate, bring up, care for, cherish, cultivate, encourage, entertain, feed, make much of, nourish, nurse, nurture, promote, raise, rear, stimulate, support, sustain, take care of.
antonyms discourage, neglect.

foul *adj.* **1** contaminated, dirty, disgusting, fetid, filthy, nauseating, offensive, polluted, putrid, rank, repulsive, revolting, rotten, squalid, stinking, sullied, tainted, unclean. **2** abhorrent, abusive, base, blasphemous, coarse, disagreeable, disgraceful, gross, impure, indecent, lewd, nasty, obscene, shameful, smutty, vicious, vile, wicked. **3** bad, rainy, rough, stormy, unpleasant, wet.
antonyms **1** clean. **2** noble, pure. **3** fine.
v. block, catch, choke, clog, contaminate, defile, dirty, ensnare, entangle, foul up, pollute, snarl, soil, stain, sully, taint, twist.
antonyms clean, clear, disentangle.
foul play corruption, crime, deception, dirty work, double-dealing, fraud, funny business, jiggery-pokery, sharp practice, treachery.
antonyms fair play, justice.

found *v.* base, bottom, build, constitute, construct, create, endow, erect, establish, fix, ground, inaugurate, initiate, institute, organise, originate, plant, raise, rest, set up, settle, start, sustain.

foundation *n.* base, basis, bedrock, bottom, endowment, establishment, fond, footing, ground, groundwork, inauguration, institution, organisation, setting up, settlement, substance.

founder[1] *n.* architect, author, benefactor, builder, constructor, designer, establisher, father, generator, initiator, institutor, inventor, maker, mother, organiser, originator, patriarch.

founder[2] *v.* abort, break down, collapse, come to grief, come to nothing, fail, fall, fall through, go lame, misfire, sink, stagger, stumble, submerge, subside, trip.

foundling *n.* orphan, outcast, stray, urchin, waif.

fountain *n.* font, fount, fountain-head, inspiration, jet, origin, reservoir, source, spout, spray, spring, waterworks, well, well-head, well-spring.

four-square *adv.* firmly, frankly, honestly, resolutely, squarely.
adj. firm, forthright, frank, honest, immovable, resolute, solid, steady, strong, unyielding.
antonyms uncertain, wavering.

fox *n.* cunning devil, reynard, sly one, slyboots.

foxy *adj.* artful, astute, canny, crafty, cunning, devious, fly, knowing, sharp, shrewd, sly, tricky, wily.
antonyms naïve, open.

fractious *adj.* awkward, cross, crotchety, irritable, peevish, quarrelsome, touchy, unruly.
antonyms agreeable, quiet.

fracture *n.* breach, break, cleft, crack, fissure, gap, opening, rent, rift, rupture, schism, split.
v. break, crack, rupture, splinter, split.
antonym join.

fragile *adj.* breakable, brittle, dainty, delicate, feeble, fine, flimsy, frail, infirm, insubstantial, slight, weak.
antonyms durable, robust, tough.

fragment *n.* bit, chip, fraction, fritter, morsel, part, particle, piece, portion, remnant, scrap, shatter, shred, sliver, splinter.
v. break, break up, come apart, come to pieces, crumble, disintegrate, disunite, divide, shatter, shiver, splinter, split (up).
antonyms hold together, join.

fragmentary *adj.* bitty, broken, disconnected, disjointed, incomplete, partial, piecemeal, scattered, scrappy, separate, sketchy.
antonyms complete, whole.

fragrance *n.* aroma, balm, bouquet, odour, perfume, scent, smell.

fragrant *adj.* aromatic, balmy, odorous, perfumed, sweet, sweet-scented, sweet-smelling.
antonym unscented.

frail *adj.* breakable, brittle, delicate, feeble, flimsy, fragile, infirm, insubstantial, puny, slight, tender, unchaste, unsound, vulnerable, weak.
antonyms firm, robust, strong, tough.

frailty *n.* blemish, defect, deficiency, failing, fallibility, fault, flaw, foible, imperfection, shortcoming, susceptibility, weakness.

antonyms firmness, robustness, strength, toughness.

frame *v.* **1** assemble, block out, build, case, compose, conceive, concoct, constitute, construct, contrive, cook up, devise, draft, draw up, enclose, fabricate, fashion, forge, form, formulate, institute, invent, make, manufacture, map out, model, mould, mount, plan, put together, shape, sketch, surround. **2** set up, trap, victimise.

n. body, bodywork, build, carcass, casing, chassis, construction, fabric, form, framework, mount, mounting, scaffolding, scheme, setting, shell, skeleton, structure, system.

frame of mind attitude, disposition, humour, mood, morale, outlook, spirit, state, temper, vein.

framework *n.* bare bones, core, fabric, foundation, frame, gantry, groundwork, plan, shell, skeleton, structure.

franchise *n.* authorisation, charter, exemption, freedom, immunity, liberty, prerogative, privilege, right, suffrage, vote.

frank *adj.* blunt, candid, direct, downright, forthright, free, honest, open, outspoken, plain, sincere, straight, straightforward, truthful.

antonyms evasive, insincere.

frankly *adv.* bluntly, candidly, directly, freely, honestly, in truth, openly, plainly, straight, to be frank, to be honest, unreservedly.

antonyms evasively, insincerely.

frantic *adj.* berserk, beside oneself, desperate, fraught, frenzied, furious, hectic, mad, overwrought, raging, raving, wild.

antonyms calm, composed.

fraternise *v.* affiliate, associate, concur, consort, cooperate, mingle, mix, socialise, sympathise, unite.

antonyms ignore, shun.

fraternity *n.* association, brotherhood, camaraderie, circle, clan, club, companionship, company, comradeship, crowd, fellowship, guild, kinship, league, set, society, union.

fraud *n.* **1** deceit, deception, double-dealing, fake, forgery, guile, hoax, sham, sharp practice, swindling, treachery. **2** bluffer, charlatan, cheat, counterfeit, double-dealer, hoaxer, impostor, phoney, pretender, swindler.

fraudulent *adj.* bogus, counterfeit, crafty, criminal, crooked, deceitful, deceptive, dishonest, double-dealing, false, phoney, sham, swindling, treacherous.

antonyms genuine, honest.

fray *n.* battle, brawl, clash, combat, conflict, disturbance, dust-up, fight, free-for-all, quarrel, riot, row, rumpus, scuffle, set-to.

frayed *adj.* edgy, frazzled, on edge, ragged, shreddy, tattered, threadbare, worn.

antonyms calm, tidy.

freak *n.* **1** aberration, abnormality, anomaly, caprice, folly, irregularity, malformation, misgrowth, monster, monstrosity, mutant, oddity, quirk, sport, turn, twist, vagary. **2** addict, buff, devotee, enthusiast, fan, fanatic, fiend, nut.

adj. aberrant, abnormal, atypical, bizarre, capricious, chance, erratic, exceptional, fluky, fortuitous, odd, queer, surprise, unexpected, unpredicted, unusual.

antonyms common, expected.

free *adj.* **1** at large, at liberty, democratic, emancipated, independent, liberated, loose, self-governing, unattached, unrestrained. **2** available, empty, idle, leisured, spare, unemployed, unoccupied, vacant. **3** complimentary, cost-free, for nothing, free of charge, gratis, on the house, without charge. **4** clear, open, unimpeded, unobstructed. **5** charitable, free and easy, generous, hospitable, lavish, liberal, openhanded.

antonyms **1** confined, limited, restricted. **2** busy, occupied. **3** costly.

v. absolve, clear, deliver, disengage, disentangle, emancipate, exempt, extricate, let go, liberate, loose, ransom, release, relieve, rescue, rid, set free, turn loose, unbind, unburden, unchain, unleash, unlock, untie.

antonyms confine, enslave, imprison.

free hand authority, carte-blanche, discretion, freedom, latitude, liberty, permission, power, scope.

free of devoid of, exempt from, immune to, innocent of, lacking, not liable to, safe from, unaffected by, untouched by, without.

freedom *n.* autonomy, deliverance, emancipation, exemption, free rein, home rule, immunity, impunity, independence, informality, leeway, liberty, licence, openness, opportunity, play, power, presumption, privilege, range, release, scope, self-government.

antonyms captivity, confinement, restriction.

freely *adv.* abundantly, amply, bountifully, candidly, cleanly, easily, extravagantly, frankly, generously, lavishly, liberally, openly, plainly, readily, spontaneously, sponte sua, unreservedly, voluntarily, willingly.

antonyms cautiously, evasively, grudgingly.

free-thinker *n.* agnostic, doubter, independent, rationalist, sceptic.

free-will *n.* autonomy, election, freedom, independence, liberty, self-determination, self-sufficiency, spontaneity, volition.

freeze *v.* chill, congeal, fix, glaciate, harden, hold, ice (over), inhibit, solidify, stiffen, stop, suspend.

n. embargo, freeze-up, halt, interruption, moratorium, postponement, shut-down, standstill, stay, stoppage, suspension.

freezing *adj.* arctic, biting, bitter, chilly, cutting, frosty, glacial, icy, numbing, penetrating, polar, raw, Siberian, wintry.

antonyms hot, warm.

frenetic *adj.* excited, frantic, frenzied, hyperactive, unbalanced, wild.

antonym calm.

frenzied *adj.* convulsive, demented, desperate, feverish, frantic, frenetic, furious, hysterical, mad, uncontrolled, wild.

antonyms calm, composed.

frenzy *n.* agitation, burst, convulsion, delirium, derangement, distraction, fit, fury, hysteria, lunacy, madness, mania, must, outburst, paroxysm, passion, rage, seizure, spasm, transport, turmoil.
antonyms calm, composure, placidness.

frequency *n.* constancy, periodicity, prevalence, recurrence, repetition.
antonym infrequency.

frequent *adj.* common, commonplace, constant, continual, customary, everyday, familiar, incessant, numerous, persistent, recurring, regular, repeated, usual.
antonym infrequent.
v. associate with, attend, crowd, hang about, hang out at, haunt, patronise, visit.

frequently *adv.* commonly, continually, customarily, habitually, many a time, many times, much, often, over and over (again), persistently, repeatedly.
antonyms infrequently, rarely.

fresh *adj.* **1** additional, extra, further, more, other, supplementary. **2** different, latest, modern, new, novel, original, recent, unconventional, up-to-date. **3** bracing, bright, brisk, clear, cool, crisp, dewy, fair, invigorating, keen, pure, refreshing. **4** crude, natural, raw. **5** alert, energetic, invigorated, lively, refreshed, renewed, rested, restored, revived, vital. **6** bold, brazen, cheeky, disrespectful, familiar, forward, impudent, insolent, pert, presumptuous, saucy.
antonyms **2** hackneyed, old. **3** stale. **4** processed. **5** tired.

freshen *v.* air, enliven, liven, purify, refresh, reinvigorate, restore, revitalise, spruce up, tart up, ventilate.
antonym tire.

fret *v.* agonise, bother, brood, nag, nettle, pine, torment, trouble, vex, worry.
antonym calm.

friction *n.* **1** animosity, antagonism, bad blood, bad feeling, bickering, conflict, disagreement, disharmony, dispute, dissension, hostility, ill-feeling, opposition, quarrelling, resentment, resistance, rivalry. **2** abrasion, chafing, erosion, grating, irritation, rasping, rubbing, scraping, wearing away.

friend *n.* acquaintance, adherent, advocate, ally, associate, backer, bosom friend, buddy, chum, companion, comrade, confidant, crony, familiar, intimate, mate, pal, partner, patron, playmate, soul mate, supporter, well-wisher.
antonyms enemy, foe, opponent.

friendless *adj.* abandoned, alone, deserted, forsaken, isolated, lonely, ostracised, shunned, unattached, unloved.

friendly *adj.* **1** affable, affectionate, amiable, amicable, approachable, chummy, close, clubby, companionable, comradely, familiar, fond, genial, good, helpful, intimate, kind, kindly, maty, neighbourly, outgoing, peaceable, receptive, sociable, sympathetic, well-disposed. **2** auspicious, convivial, cordial, favourable, welcoming.
antonyms **1** cold, unsociable. **2** hostile.

friendship *n.* affection, affinity, alliance, attachment, closeness, concord, familiarity, fellowship, fondness, friendliness, goodwill, harmony, intimacy, love, rapport, regard.
antonyms animosity, enmity.

fright *n.* alarm, apprehension, consternation, dismay, dread, fear, horror, panic, quaking, scare, shock, terror, the shivers, trepidation.

frighten *v.* alarm, appal, daunt, dismay, intimidate, petrify, scare, scare stiff, shock, startle, terrify, terrorise, unnerve.
antonyms calm, reassure.

frightful *adj.* alarming, appalling, awful, dire, disagreeable, dread, dreadful, fearful, ghastly, great, grim, grisly, gruesome, harrowing, hideous, horrible, horrid, macabre, petrifying, shocking, terrible, terrifying, traumatic, unpleasant, unspeakable.
antonyms agreeable, pleasant.

frigid *adj.* **1** aloof, cool, lifeless, passionless, passive, unfeeling, unloving, unresponsive. **2** arctic, chill, chilly, cold, frosty, frozen, glacial, icy, wintry.
antonyms **1** responsive. **2** hot.

frills *n.* accessories, additions, decoration, embellishment, extras, finery, frilliness, frippery, ornamentation, superfluities, trimmings.

frilly *adj.* fancy, frothy, lacy, ornate, ruffled.
antonyms plain, unadorned.

fringe *n.* borderline, edge, limits, margin, outskirts, perimeter, periphery.
adj. alternative, avant-garde, unconventional, unofficial, unorthodox.
antonyms conventional, mainstream.

fringed *adj.* bordered, edged, tasselled, tasselly, trimmed.

frisk *v.* **1** bounce, caper, dance, frolic, gambol, hop, jump, leap, play, rollick, romp, skip, sport, trip. **2** check, inspect, search, shake down.

frisky *adj.* bouncy, frolicsome, high-spirited, lively, playful, rollicking, romping, spirited.
antonym quiet.

fritter *v.* blow, dissipate, idle, misspend, run through, squander, waste.

frivolity *n.* childishness, flippancy, folly, fun, gaiety, jest, light-heartedness, nonsense, silliness, superficiality, trifling, triviality.
antonym seriousness.

frizzy *adj.* crimped, crisp, curled, curly, frizzed, wiry.
antonym straight.

frolic *v.* caper, frisk, gambol, lark, make merry, play, rollick, romp.
n. amusement, antic, fun, gaiety, high jinks, lark, merriment, prank, revel, rig, romp, sport, spree.

front *n.* **1** aspect, countenance, cover, exterior, façade, face, facing, forefront, foreground, forepart, front line, frontage, head, lead, obverse, top, vanguard. **2** air, appearance, cover-up, disguise, expression, manner, mask, pretence, pretext, show.
antonyms **1** back, rear.
adj. first, fore, foremost, head, lead, leading.

antonyms back, last, least.
v. confront, face, look over, meet, oppose, overlook.
in front ahead, before, first, in advance, leading, preceding.
antonym behind.
frontier *n.* border, borderline, boundary, confines, edge, limit, march, marches, perimeter, verge.
frosty *adj.* chilly, cold, discouraging, frigid, frozen, icy, off-putting, stand-offish, stiff, unfriendly, unwelcoming, wintry.
antonym warm.
froth *n.* bubbles, effervescence, foam, frivolity, head, lather, scum, suds, triviality.
v. bubble, effervesce, ferment, fizz, foam.
frown *v.* glare, glower, grimace, lower, scowl.
n. dirty look, glare, glower, grimace, scowl.
frown on disapprove of, discourage, dislike, object to.
antonym approve of.
frozen *adj.* arctic, chilled, fixed, frigid, icebound, ice-cold, ice-covered, icy, numb, rigid, solidified, stiff.
antonym warm.
frugal *adj.* careful, economical, meagre, parsimonious, penny-wise, provident, prudent, saving, sparing, thrifty.
antonyms generous, wasteful.
fruit *n.* advantage, benefit, consequence, crop, effect, harvest, outcome, produce, product, profit, result, return, reward, yield.
fruitful *adj.* abundant, advantageous, beneficial, fertile, plentiful, productive, profitable, prolific, rewarding, rich, successful, teeming, useful, well-spent, worthwhile.
antonyms barren, fruitless.
fruition *n.* attainment, completion, consummation, enjoyment, fulfilment, maturity, perfection, realisation, ripeness, success.
fruitless *adj.* abortive, barren, futile, hopeless, idle, pointless, useless, vain.
antonyms fruitful, profitable, successful.
fruity *adj.* **1** juicy, ripe. **2** full, mellow, resonant, rich. **3** bawdy, indecent, lewd, racy, risqué, saucy, smutty, spicy, suggestive, vulgar.
antonyms **2** light. **3** decent.
frustrate *v.* baffle, balk, block, check, circumvent, confront, counter, defeat, depress, disappoint, discourage, dishearten, foil, forestall, inhibit, neutralise, nullify, spike, thwart.
antonyms fulfil, further, promote.
fudge *v.* avoid, cook, dodge, equivocate, evade, fake, falsify, fiddle, fix, hedge, misrepresent, shuffle, stall.
fuel *n.* **1** coal, combustible, energy source, gas, oil, petrol, propellant, wood. **2** ammunition, encouragement, incitement, material, means, provocation.
v. charge, encourage, fan, feed, fire, incite, inflame, nourish, stoke up, sustain.
antonyms damp down, discourage.
fugitive *n.* deserter, escapee, refugee, runaway.
adj. brief, elusive, escaping, fleeing, flying, passing, short, temporary.
antonym permanent.
fulfil *v.* accomplish, achieve, answer, carry out, complete, comply with, conclude, conform to, consummate, discharge, execute, fill, finish, implement, keep, obey, observe, perfect, perform, realise, satisfy.
antonyms break, fail, frustrate.
fulfilment *n.* accomplishment, achievement, bringing about, carrying out, completion, consummation, crowning, discharge, implementation, observance, perfection, performance, realisation, success.
antonyms failure, frustration.
full *adj.* **1** crammed, crowded, filled, jammed, loaded, packed, saturated. **2** complete, entire, intact, maximum, unabridged, unexpurgated. **3** abundant, adequate, all-inclusive, ample, comprehensive, copious, exhaustive, extensive, generous, thorough. **4** clear, deep, distinct, loud, resonant, rich.
antonyms **1** empty. **2** incomplete, partial. **3** superficial.
in full completely, entirely, in total, unabridged.
full-blooded *adj.* hearty, lusty, thoroughbred, vigorous, whole-hearted.
full-grown *adj.* adult, developed, full-blown, full-scale, grown-up, marriageable, mature, of age, ripe.
antonyms undeveloped, young.
fullness *n.* **1** abundance, adequateness, ampleness, broadness, completeness, comprehensiveness, entirety, extensiveness, fill, glut, plenty, profusion, strength, sufficiency, totality, vastness, wholeness. **2** enlargement, roundness, swelling. **3** clearness, loudness, resonance, richness.
antonyms **1** emptiness, incompleteness.
fully *adv.* altogether, completely, comprehensively, enough, entirely, in all respects, perfectly, positively, quite, sufficiently, thoroughly, totally, utterly, wholly, without reserve.
antonym partly.
fully-fledged *adj.* developed, experienced, mature, professional, proficient, qualified, trained.
antonym inexperienced.
fulminate *v.* condemn, criticise, curse, denounce, protest, rage, rail, thunder.
antonym praise.
fumble *v.* botch, bumble, bungle, grope, mishandle, mismanage, spoil.
fume *v.* **1** boil, give off, smoke, smoulder. **2** rage, rant, seethe.
fumes *n.* exhaust, gas, haze, pollution, smog, smoke, stench, vapour.
fumigate *v.* cleanse, deodorise, disinfect, purify, sterilise.
fun *n.* amusement, distraction, diversion, enjoyment, entertainment, foolery, game, horseplay, jesting, jocularity, joking, joy, merrymaking, mirth, play, playfulness, pleasure, recreation, romp, sport, teasing, treat.
make fun of laugh at, mock, rag, rib, ridicule,

taunt.

function *n.* **1** activity, business, charge, concern, duty, employment, job, occupation, office, operation, part, purpose, responsibility, role, situation, task. **2** affair, dinner, do, gathering, luncheon, party, reception.
v. act, behave, go, operate, perform, run, serve, work.

functional *adj.* hard-wearing, operational, plain, practical, useful, utilitarian, utility, working.
antonyms decorative, useless.

fund *n.* cache, foundation, hoard, kitty, mine, pool, repository, reserve, source, stack, stock, store, storehouse, supply, treasury, well.
v. back, capitalise, endow, finance, float, promote, subsidise, support, underwrite.

fundamental *adj.* basic, central, crucial, elementary, essential, first, important, indispensable, integral, key, keynote, necessary, organic, primary, prime, principal, rudimentary, underlying, vital.
antonym advanced.

funds *n.* backing, capital, cash, finance, hard cash, money, resources, savings.

funeral *n.* burial, interment.

funereal *adj.* deathlike, depressing, dirgelike, dismal, dreary, gloomy, grave, lamenting, mournful, sad, sepulchral, solemn, sombre.
antonyms happy, lively.

funnel *v.* channel, convey, direct, filter, move, pass, pour, siphon, transfer.

funny *adj.* **1** absurd, amusing, comic, comical, droll, entertaining, facetious, farcical, hilarious, humorous, laughable, ridiculous, silly, witty. **2** curious, dubious, mysterious, odd, peculiar, perplexing, puzzling, queer, remarkable, strange, unusual, weird.
antonyms **1** sad, serious, solemn. **2** normal, ordinary, usual.

furious *adj.* **1** angry, boiling, enraged, fierce, fuming, incensed, infuriated, livid, mad, raging, up in arms. **2** boisterous, frantic, impetuous, intense, stormy, vigorous, violent.
antonyms **1** calm, pleased.

furnish *v.* afford, appoint, decorate, equip, fit out, fit up, give, grant, offer, present, provide, reveal, rig, stock, store, suit, supply.
antonym divest.

furniture *n.* appliances, appointments, effects, equipment, fittings, furnishings, goods, household goods, movables, possessions, things.

furrow *n.* channel, crease, groove, hollow, line, rut, seam, trench, wrinkle.
v. corrugate, crease, draw together, flute, knit, line, seam, wrinkle.

further *adj.* additional, extra, fresh, more, new, opposite, other, supplementary.
v. accelerate, advance, aid, assist, champion, contribute to, ease, encourage, facilitate, forward, foster, hasten, help, patronise, promote, push, speed.
antonyms frustrate, stop.

furthest *adj.* extreme, farthest, furthermost, most distant, outermost, outmost, remotest, ultimate, uttermost.
antonym nearest.

furtive *adj.* hidden, secret, secretive, sly, stealthy, surreptitious, underhand.
antonym open.

fury *n.* anger, desperation, ferocity, fierceness, frenzy, madness, passion, power, rage, turbulence, vehemence, violence, wrath.
antonyms calm, peacefulness.

fusion *n.* alloy, amalgam, amalgamation, blend, blending, coalescence, federation, integration, melting, merger, merging, mixture, smelting, synthesis, union, welding.

fuss *n.* agitation, bother, bustle, commotion, confusion, difficulty, display, excitement, flap, flurry, fluster, furore, hassle, hoo-ha, hurry, kerfuffle, palaver, row, squabble, stir, to-do, trouble, unrest, upset, worry.
antonym calm.
v. bustle, complain, fidget, flap, fret, fume, niggle, take pains, worry.

fussy *adj.* **1** choosy, discriminating, fastidious, finicky, hard to please, particular, pernickety. **2** cluttered, dainty, elaborate.
antonyms **1** casual, uncritical. **2** plain.

fusty *adj.* **1** antiquated, archaic, old-fashioned, outdated, out-of-date, passé. **2** airless, close, damp, dank, mouldering, mouldy, musty, stale, stuffy.
antonyms **1** up-to-date. **2** airy.

futile *adj.* abortive, barren, empty, forlorn, fruitless, hollow, idle, pointless, profitless, trifling, trivial, unavailing, unproductive, unprofitable, unsuccessful, useless, vain.
antonyms fruitful, profitable.

futility *n.* aimlessness, emptiness, hollowness, ineffectiveness, pointlessness, unimportance, uselessness.
antonyms fruitfulness, profitability.

future *n.* expectation, hereafter, outlook, prospects.
antonym past.
adj. approaching, coming, designate, destined, eventual, expected, fated, forthcoming, impending, in the offing, later, prospective, rising, subsequent, to be, to come, ultimate, unborn.
antonym past.

fuzz *n.* down, fibre, flock, floss, fluff, hair, lint, nap, ooze, pile.

fuzzy *adj.* **1** downy, fluffy, frizzy, linty, napped. **2** blurred, distorted, faint, hazy, ill-defined, muffled, shadowy, unclear, unfocused, vague, woolly.
antonyms **2** clear, distinct.

G

gadget *n.* appliance, contraption, contrivance, device, gimmick, invention, novelty, thing, thingumajig, tool.

gag[1] *v.* **1** curb, muffle, muzzle, quiet, silence, stifle, still, stop up, suppress, throttle. **2** choke (up), gasp, heave, retch, vomit.

gag[2] *n.* funny, hoax, jest, joke, one-liner, pun, quip, wisecrack, witticism.

gaiety *n.* brightness, brilliance, celebration, cheerfulness, colour, colourfulness, exhilaration, festivity, fun, glee, glitter, good humour, high spirits, hilarity, joie de vivre, jollity, joviality, light-heartedness, liveliness, merriment, merrymaking, mirth, revelry, show, showiness, sparkle.
antonyms drabness, dreariness, sadness.

gaily *adv.* blithely, brightly, brilliantly, cheerfully, colourfully, fancily, flamboyantly, happily, joyfully, light-heartedly, merrily.
antonyms dully, sadly.

gain *v.* achieve, acquire, advance, arrive at, attain, bring in, capture, clear, collect, come to, earn, gather, get, get to, harvest, improve, increase, make, net, obtain, pick up, procure, produce, profit, progress, reach, realise, reap, secure, win, win over, yield.
antonym lose.
n. achievement, acquisition, advance, advantage, attainment, benefit, dividend, earnings, growth, headway, improvement, income, increase, increment, lucre, proceeds, produce, profit, progress, return, rise, winnings, yield.
antonyms loss, losses.
gain on approach, catch up with, close with, come up with, encroach on, leave behind, level with, narrow the gap, outdistance, overtake.
gain time delay, drag one's feet, procrastinate, stall, temporise.

gala *n.* carnival, celebration, festival, festivity, fête, jamboree, jubilee, pageant, party, procession.

gale *n.* blast, burst, cyclone, eruption, explosion, fit, hurricane, outbreak, outburst, shout, squall, storm, tornado, typhoon.

gallant *adj.* bold, brave, chivalrous, courageous, courteous, courtly, daring, dashing, dauntless, fearless, gentlemanly, heroic, honourable, noble, valiant.
antonyms cowardly, ungentlemanly.

gallantry *n.* boldness, bravery, chivalry, courage, courteousness, courtesy, courtliness, fearlessness, gentlemanliness, graciousness, heroism, nobility, politeness, valour.
antonyms cowardice, ungentlemanliness.

gallery *n.* arcade, art-gallery, balcony, circle, gods, grandstand, museum, passage, spectators, walk.

gallop *v.* bolt, career, dart, dash, fly, hasten, hie, hurry, race, run, rush, scud, shoot, speed, sprint, tear, zoom.

gallows *n.* gibbet, scaffold, the rope.

galvanise *v.* arouse, electrify, excite, fire, inspire, invigorate, jolt, move, prod, provoke, quicken, shock, spur, stimulate, stir, vitalise.
antonyms hinder, retard.

gamble *v.* back, bet, chance, have a flutter, hazard, play, punt, risk, speculate, stake, take a chance, try one's luck, venture, wager.
n. bet, chance, flutter, lottery, punt, risk, speculation, venture, wager.

gambler *n.* better, punter.

gambol *v.* bounce, bound, caper, cut a caper, frisk, frolic, hop, jump, rollick, skip.

game[1] *n.* **1** amusement, competition, contest, distraction, diversion, entertainment, event, frolic, fun, jest, joke, match, meeting, pastime, play, ploy, recreation, romp, round, sport, tactic, tournament. **2** animals, bag, flesh, game-birds, meat, prey, quarry, spoils.

game[2] *adj.* bold, brave, courageous, eager, fearless, gallant, inclined, intrepid, persevering, persistent, prepared, ready, resolute, spirited, valiant.
antonyms cowardly, unwilling.

gamekeeper *n.* keeper, warden.

gamut *n.* area, compass, field, range, scale, scope, series, spectrum, sweep.

gang *n.* band, circle, clique, club, company, core, coterie, crew, crowd, group, herd, horde, lot, mob, pack, party, ring, set, shift, squad, team, troupe.

gangster *n.* bandit, brigand, criminal, crook, desperado, heavy, hoodlum, mobster, racketeer, robber, rough, ruffian, thug, tough.

gaol *see* **jail**.

gaoler *see* **jailer**.

gap *n.* blank, breach, break, chink, cleft, crack, crevice, difference, divergence, divide, hole, interlude, intermission, interruption, interval, lull, opening, pause, recess, rift, space, void.

gape *v.* **1** gawk, gawp, goggle, stare, wonder. **2** crack, open, split.

gaping *adj.* broad, cavernous, great, open, vast, wide, yawning.
antonym tiny.

garage *n.* lock-up, petrol station, service station.

garble *v.* confuse, distort, jumble, mix up, muddle, pervert, slant, twist.
antonyms decipher, make clear.

garden *n.* backyard, orchard, park, plot, yard.

garish *adj.* flashy, flaunting, gaudy, glaring, glittering, loud, showy, tasteless, tawdry, vulgar.
antonyms modest, plain, quiet.

garland *n.* bays, crown, decoration, festoon, flowers, honours, laurels, wreath.
v. adorn, crown, deck, festoon, wreathe.

garments *n.* attire, clothes, clothing, costume, dress, gear, get-up, outfit, robes, uniform, vestments, wear.

garnish *v.* adorn, decorate, embellish, enhance, furnish, grace, ornament, set off, trim.
antonym divest.
n. decoration, embellishment, enhancement, ornament, relish, trimming.

garrison *n.* armed force, barracks, base, camp, command, detachment, fort, fortification, fortress, post, station, stronghold, troops, unit.
v. defend, guard, man, mount, occupy, place, position, post, protect, station.

gash *v.* cut, gouge, incise, lacerate, notch, rend, score, slash, slit, split, tear, wound.
n. cut, gouge, incision, laceration, notch, rent, score, slash, slit, split, tear, wound.

gasp *v.* blow, breathe, choke, gulp, pant, puff, utter.
n. blow, breath, exclamation, gulp, pant, puff.

gate *n.* barrier, door, doorway, entrance, exit, gateway, opening, passage.

gather *v.* **1** accumulate, amass, assemble, build, collect, congregate, convene, fold, glean, group, harvest, heap, hoard, muster, pile up, pleat, pluck, rake up, reap, round up, select, stockpile, swell, thicken, tuck. **2** assume, conclude, deduce, hear, infer, learn, surmise, understand. **3** gain, increase.
antonyms **1** dissipate, scatter. **3** decrease.

gathering *n.* assembly, collection, company, congregation, congress, convention, convocation, crowd, get-together, group, jamboree, mass, meeting, party, rally, round-up, throng, turn-out.

gaudy *adj.* bright, brilliant, flash, flashy, garish, glaring, glitzy, loud, ostentatious, showy, tasteless, tawdry, tinsel(ly), vulgar.
antonyms drab, plain, quiet.

gauge *v.* adjust, ascertain, assess, calculate, check, compute, count, determine, estimate, evaluate, figure, guess, judge, measure, rate, reckon, value, weigh.
n. **1** basis, criterion, example, guide, guideline, indicator, measure, meter, micrometer, model, pattern, rule, sample, standard, test, yardstick. **2** bore, calibre, capacity, degree, depth, extent, height, magnitude, measure, scope, size, span, thickness, width.

gaunt *adj.* **1** angular, bony, emaciated, haggard, hollow-eyed, lank, lean, scraggy, scrawny, skeletal, skinny, thin, wasted. **2** bare, bleak, desolate, dismal, dreary, forlorn, grim, harsh, stark.
antonyms **1** hale, plump.

gawky *adj.* awkward, clumsy, gauche, oafish, ungainly.
antonym graceful.

gay *adj.* **1** animated, blithe, bright, brilliant, carefree, cheerful, colourful, convivial, debonair, festive, flamboyant, flashy, fresh, fun-loving, garish, gaudy, glad, happy, hilarious, jolly, joyful, light-hearted, lively, merry, playful, pleasure-seeking, rich, rollicking, showy, sparkish, sparkling, sunny, vivid. **2** homosexual, lesbian, queer.
antonyms **1** gloomy, sad. **2** heterosexual, straight.
n. homosexual, lesbian, poof, queer.
antonym heterosexual.

gaze *v.* contemplate, gape, look, regard, stare, view, watch.
n. look, stare.

gear *n.* **1** accessories, affair, apparatus, apparel, array, attire, baggage, belongings, clothes, clothing, costume, doings, dress, equipment, garb, garments, get-up, habit, instruments, kit, luggage, outfit, paraphernalia, possessions, stuff, supplies, tackle, things, togs, tools, trappings, traps, wear. **2** cam, cam-wheel, cog, cogwheel, gearing, gear-wheel, machinery, mechanism, workings, works.
v. adapt, adjust, equip, fit, harness, rig, suit, tailor.

gel *see* **jell**.

gelatinous *adj.* congealed, gluey, glutinous, gooey, gummy, jellied, jelly, jelly-like, rubbery, sticky, viscous.

gem *n.* jewel, masterpiece, pearl, pick, pièce de résistance, precious stone, prize, stone, treasure.

gen *n.* background, data, details, facts, info, information, low-down.

genealogy *n.* ancestry, background, derivation, descent, extraction, family, family tree, line, lineage, pedigree, stock, strain.

general *adj.* **1** across-the-board, all-inclusive, blanket, broad, common, comprehensive, extensive, overall, panoramic, prevalent, public, sweeping, total, universal, widespread. **2** approximate, ill-defined, imprecise, indefinite, inexact, loose, miscellaneous, unspecific, vague. **3** conventional, customary, everyday, normal, ordinary, regular, typical, usual.
antonyms **1** limited, particular. **2** specific. **3** rare.
n. chief, commander, commander in chief, head, leader, marshal, officer.

generality *n.* approximateness, breadth, commonness, comprehensiveness, extensiveness, generalisation, impreciseness, indefiniteness, looseness, sweeping statement, universality, vagueness.
antonyms exactness, particular, uncommonness.

generate *v.* breed, bring about, cause, create, engender, father, form, give rise to, initiate, make, originate, produce, propagate, whip up.
antonym prevent.

generation *n.* **1** age, age group, epoch, era, period, time, times. **2** breed, breeding, creation, crop, formation, genesis, origination, procreation, production, propagation, reproduction.

generosity *n.* benevolence, big-heartedness, bounty, charity, goodness, kindness, liberality,

magnanimity, open-handedness, soft-heartedness, unsparingness.
antonyms meanness, selfishness.
generous *adj.* benevolent, big-hearted, bountiful, charitable, copious, free, full, good, high-minded, hospitable, kind, large-hearted, large-minded, lavish, liberal, lofty, magnanimous, noble, open-handed, overflowing, plentiful, princely, rich, soft-hearted, unstinted, unstinting.
antonyms mean, miserly, selfish.
genial *adj.* affable, agreeable, amiable, cheerful, convivial, cordial, easy-going, friendly, glad, good-natured, happy, hearty, jolly, jovial, joyous, kind, kindly, pleasant, warm, warm-hearted.
antonym cold.
genius *n.* **1** adept, brain, expert, intellect, maestro, master, master-hand, mastermind, pastmaster, virtuoso. **2** ability, aptitude, bent, brightness, brilliance, capacity, endowment, faculty, flair, gift, inclination, intellect, knack, propensity, talent, turn. **3** daemon, double, genie, spirit.
gentle *adj.* **1** amiable, calm, compassionate, kind, merciful, mild, placid, quiet, refined, soft, tender, tranquil. **2** easy, gradual, imperceptible, light, moderate, slight, slow, smooth. **3** balmy, peaceful, quiet, serene, soft, soothing.
antonyms **1** rough, spiteful, tough, unkind, wild. **2** sudden. **3** troubled.
genuine *adj.* actual, authentic, bona fide, candid, earnest, frank, honest, legitimate, natural, original, pure, real, sincere, sound, true, veritable.
antonyms artificial, false, insincere.
germ *n.* bacterium, beginning, bud, bug, cause, egg, embryo, microbe, micro-organism, nucleus, origin, ovule, ovum, root, rudiment, seed, source, spark, spore, sprout, virus.
germinate *v.* bud, develop, generate, grow, originate, shoot, sprout, swell.
gestation *n.* conception, development, drafting, evolution, incubation, maturation, planning, pregnancy, ripening.
gesticulate *v.* gesture, indicate, motion, point, sign, signal, wave.
gesticulation *n.* motion, sign, signal, wave.
gesture *n.* act, action, gesticulation, indication, motion, sign, signal, wave.
v. gesticulate, indicate, motion, point, sign, signal, wave.
get *v.* **1** achieve, acquire, come by, contact, earn, gain, inherit, obtain, realise, receive, secure, win. **2** become, develop, grow, turn. **3** coax, induce, influence, persuade, sway, urge. **4** arrive, come, move, reach. **5** bring, carry, catch, collect, fetch, grab, pick up, seize, take. **6** come down with, contract.
antonyms **1** lose. **4** leave.
get across bring home to, communicate, convey, cross, impart, negotiate, put over, transmit.
get ahead advance, flourish, get there, go places, make good, make it, progress, prosper, succeed, thrive.
antonyms fail, fall behind.
get along cope, develop, fare, get by, get on, harmonise, hit it off, manage, progress, succeed, survive.
get at 1 attain, find, reach. **2** discover, find (out). **3** hint, imply, insinuate, intend, mean, suggest. **4** annoy, attack, criticise, find fault with, make fun of, nag, pick on. **5** bribe, buy off, corrupt, influence.
get away break out, depart, disappear, escape, flee, get out, leave, run away.
get back 1 recoup, recover, regain, repossess, retrieve, return, revert, revisit. **2** get even, get one's own back (on), retaliate.
get by cope, exist, get along, make both ends meet, manage, survive.
get down 1 depress, dishearten, dispirit, sadden. **2** alight, descend, disembark, dismount.
antonyms **1** encourage. **2** board, get on.
get in 1 collect, gather (in). **2** arrive, come, embark, enter, land. **3** include, infiltrate, insert, interpose, penetrate.
get off 1 alight, depart, descend, disembark, dismount, escape, leave, shed. **2** detach, remove, separate.
antonyms **1** arrive, get on. **2** put on.
get out alight, break out, clear out, deliver, escape, extricate oneself, flee, flit, free oneself, leave, produce, publish, quit, scarper, vacate, withdraw.
antonym board.
get out of avoid, dodge, escape, evade, shirk, skive.
get over 1 recover from, shake off, survive. **2** deal with, defeat, overcome, surmount. **3** communicate, convey, explain, get across, impart, put across.
get round 1 bypass, circumvent, evade, overcome. **2** coax, persuade, prevail upon, talk round, win over.
get together accumulate, assemble, collaborate, collect, congregate, converge, gather, join, meet, rally, unite.
get up arise, ascend, climb, increase, mount, rise, scale, stand (up).
ghastly *adj.* awful, deathly, dreadful, frightful, ghostly, grim, gruesome, hideous, horrible, horrid, loathsome, lurid, pale, repellent, shocking, terrible, terrifying.
antonyms attractive, delightful.
ghost *n.* apparition, larva, phantom, shadow, soul, spectre, spirit, spook, visitant.
ghostly *adj.* eerie, faint, ghostlike, illusory, phantom, spectral, spooky, supernatural, unearthly, weird, wraith-like.
ghoulish *adj.* grisly, gruesome, macabre, morbid, revolting, sick, unhealthy, unwholesome.
giant *n.* Goliath, Hercules, monster, titan.
adj. colossal, enormous, gigantic, huge, immense, jumbo, king-size, large, mammoth, monstrous, titanic, vast.
gibber *v.* babble, blab, cackle, chatter, gabble,

jabber, prattle.
gibe *see* **jibe**.
giddy *adj.* **1** dizzy, faint. **2** careless, intoxicating, light-headed, silly, wild.
gift *n.* **1** bequest, bonus, bounty, contribution, donation, freebie, grant, gratuity, largess(e), legacy, offering, present. **2** ability, aptitude, attribute, bent, capability, capacity, endowment, faculty, flair, genius, knack, power, talent.
gifted *adj.* able, accomplished, ace, adroit, bright, brilliant, capable, clever, expert, intelligent, masterly, skilful, skilled, talented.
antonym dull.
gigantic *adj.* colossal, enormous, giant, huge, immense, mammoth, stupendous, tremendous, vast.
antonyms small, tiny.
giggle *v.* chortle, chuckle, laugh, snigger, titter.
n. chortle, chuckle, laugh, snigger, titter.
gild *v.* adorn, array, beautify, brighten, coat, deck, dress up, embellish, embroider, enhance, enrich, festoon, garnish, grace, ornament, paint, trim.
gilded *adj.* gilt, gold, golden.
gimmick *n.* attraction, contrivance, device, dodge, gadget, manoeuvre, ploy, scheme, stratagem, stunt, trick.
gingerly *adv.* carefully, cautiously, delicately, hesitantly, tentatively, timidly, warily.
antonyms carelessly, roughly.
gipsy *see* **gypsy**.
girdle *n.* band, belt, corset, sash, waistband, zone.
girl *n.* damsel, daughter, girl-friend, lass, maiden, sweetheart.
girth *n.* band, belly-band, bulk, circumference, measure, saddle-band, size, strap.
gist *n.* core, direction, drift, essence, force, idea, import, marrow, matter, meaning, nub, pith, point, quintessence, sense, significance, substance.
give *v.* **1** award, bestow, commit, confer, contribute, deliver, devote, donate, entrust, furnish, grant, hand over, lend, make over, offer, present, provide, supply. **2** announce, communicate, impart, pronounce, publish, set forth, transmit, utter. **3** allow, concede, surrender, yield. **4** cause, do, make, occasion, perform, produce. **5** bend, break, collapse, fall, sink, yield.
antonyms **1** take, withhold. **5** withstand.
give away betray, disclose, divulge, expose, inform on, leak, let out, let slip, reveal, uncover.
antonym keep (in).
give in capitulate, collapse, comply, concede, give way, quit, submit, surrender, yield.
antonym hold out.
give off discharge, emit, exhale, exude, pour out, produce, release, send out, throw out, vent.
give on to lead to, open on to, overlook.
give out 1 deal, distribute, dole out, hand out. **2** advertise, announce, broadcast, communicate, disseminate, impart, notify, publish, transmit, utter. **3** discharge, emit, exhale, exude, give off, pour out, produce, release, send out. **4** break down, stop.
antonym **3** take in.
give up 1 cease, renounce, stop. **2** abandon, quit, relinquish, resign. **3** capitulate, surrender, waive.
antonyms **1** start. **3** hold out.
give-and-take *n.* adaptability, flexibility, goodwill, willingness.
given *adj.* **1** definite, particular, specified. **2** disposed, inclined, liable, likely, prone.
glad *adj.* bright, cheerful, cheery, contented, delighted, gratified, happy, joyful, merry, pleased, willing.
antonyms sad, unhappy.
gladden *v.* brighten, cheer, delight, enliven, exhilarate, gratify, hearten, please, rejoice.
antonym sadden.
glamorous *adj.* alluring, attractive, beautiful, captivating, charming, dazzling, elegant, enchanting, exciting, fascinating, glossy, gorgeous, lovely, smart.
antonyms boring, drab, plain.
glamour *n.* allure, appeal, attraction, beauty, charm, fascination, magic, prestige.
glance *v.* browse, dip, flip, gaze, glimpse, leaf, look, peek, peep, scan, skim, thumb, view.
n. glimpse, look, mention, peek, peep, squint, view.
glare *v.* **1** frown, glower, look daggers, scowl. **2** blaze, dazzle, flame, flare, shine.
n. **1** black look, dirty look, frown, look, scowl, stare. **2** blaze, brilliance, dazzle, flame, glow, light, spotlight.
glaring *adj.* blatant, conspicuous, flagrant, gross, manifest, obvious, open, outrageous, patent.
antonyms concealed, hidden, minor.
glassware *n.* crystal, glass.
glassy *adj.* blank, clear, cold, dazed, dull, empty, expressionless, fixed, glasslike, glazed, glossy, icy, lifeless, shiny, slippery, smooth, transparent, vacant.
glaze *v.* burnish, coat, enamel, gloss, lacquer, polish, varnish.
n. coat, coating, enamel, finish, gloss, lacquer, lustre, polish, shine, varnish.
gleam *n.* beam, brightness, brilliance, flash, flicker, glimmer, glint, gloss, glow, lustre, ray, sheen, shimmer, sparkle, splendour.
v. flare, flash, glance, glimmer, glint, glisten, glister, glitter, glow, shimmer, shine, sparkle.
glee *n.* delight, excitement, exhilaration, gladness, joy, joyfulness, liveliness, pleasure, triumph.
glib *adj.* easy, facile, fluent, insincere, plausible, quick, ready, slick, slippery, smooth, smooth-tongued, suave, talkative.
antonyms implausible, tongue-tied.
glide *v.* coast, drift, float, flow, fly, roll, run, sail, skim, slide, slip, soar.
glimmer *v.* blink, flicker, gleam, glisten, glitter, glow, shimmer, shine, sparkle, twinkle.
n. blink, flicker, gleam, glint, glow, grain, hint,

ray, shimmer, sparkle, suggestion, trace, twinkle.

glimpse *n.* glance, look, peek, peep, sight, sighting, squint.
v. catch sight of, espy, sight, spot, spy, view.

glint *v.* flash, gleam, glimmer, glitter, reflect, shine, sparkle, twinkle.
n. flash, gleam, glimmer, glitter, shine, sparkle, twinkle, twinkling.

glisten *v.* flash, glance, glare, gleam, glimmer, glint, glister, glitter, shimmer, shine, sparkle, twinkle.

glitter *v.* flare, flash, glare, gleam, glimmer, glint, glisten, shimmer, shine, spangle, sparkle, twinkle.
n. beam, brightness, brilliance, display, flash, gaudiness, glamour, glare, gleam, lustre, radiance, scintillation, sheen, shimmer, shine, show, showiness, sparkle, splendour, tinsel.

gloat *v.* crow, exult, glory, rejoice, relish, revel in, rub it in, triumph, vaunt.

global *adj.* all-encompassing, all-inclusive, comprehensive, encylopaedic, exhaustive, general, international, thorough, total, universal, unlimited, world, world-wide.
antonyms limited, parochial.

globe *n.* ball, earth, orb, planet, round, sphere, world.

gloom *n.* cloud, cloudiness, damp, dark, darkness, dejection, depression, desolation, despair, despondency, dimness, downheartedness, dullness, dusk, glumness, low spirits, melancholy, misery, obscurity, sadness, shade, shadow, sorrow, twilight, unhappiness, woe.
antonyms brightness, cheerfulness, happiness.

gloomy *adj.* **1** cheerless, comfortless, dejected, depressing, despondent, dismal, dispirited, down, downcast, downhearted, glum, long-faced, low-spirited, miserable, moody, morose, pessimistic, sad. **2** dark, dim, dreary, dull, obscure, overcast, shadowy.
antonyms **1** cheerful. **2** bright.

glorify *v.* bless, celebrate, eulogise, exalt, extol, honour, idolise, magnify, praise, revere, venerate, worship.
antonyms denounce, vilify.

glorious *adj.* beautiful, bright, brilliant, dazzling, delightful, distinguished, divine, eminent, enjoyable, excellent, famous, fine, gorgeous, grand, great, heavenly, honoured, illustrious, magnificent, majestic, marvellous, noble, noted, pleasurable, radiant, renowned, shining, splendid, superb, triumphant, wonderful.
antonyms plain, unknown.

glory *n.* **1** celebrity, dignity, distinction, eminence, fame, honour, illustriousness, kudos, prestige, renown. **2** heaven, immortality, majesty. **3** beauty, brightness, brilliance, grandeur, greatness, magnificence, radiance, resplendence, splendour, triumph. **4** adoration, blessing, exaltation, gratitude, homage, praise, thanksgiving, veneration, worship.
v. boast, delight, exult, gloat, pride oneself, rejoice, relish, revel, triumph.

gloss[1] *n.* appearance, brightness, brilliance, façade, front, gleam, lustre, mask, polish, semblance, sheen, shine, show, surface, varnish, veneer, window-dressing.
gloss over camouflage, conceal, disguise, explain away, hide, mask, smooth over, veil, whitewash.

gloss[2] *n.* annotation, comment, commentary, elucidation, explanation, footnote, interpretation, note, translation.
v. annotate, comment, construe, elucidate, explain, interpret, postil, postillate, translate.

glossy *adj.* bright, brilliant, burnished, enamelled, glacé, glassy, glazed, lustrous, polished, sheeny, shining, shiny, silky, sleek, smooth.
antonym mat(t).

glow *n.* ardour, bloom, blush, brightness, brilliance, burning, earnestness, enthusiasm, excitement, fervour, flush, gleam, glimmer, gusto, intensity, light, passion, radiance, redness, rosiness, splendour, vividness, warmth.
v. blush, brighten, burn, colour, fill, flush, gleam, glimmer, glowing, radiate, redden, shine, smoulder, thrill, tingle.

glower *v.* frown, glare, look daggers, scowl.
n. black look, dirty look, frown, glare, look, scowl, stare.

glowing *adj.* complimentary, ecstatic, enthusiastic, flaming, flushed, rave, red, rhapsodic, rich, suffused, vibrant, vivid, warm.
antonyms colourless, dull, restrained.

glue *n.* adhesive, cement, gum, paste, size.
v. affix, cement, fix, gum, paste, seal, stick.

glut *n.* excess, overabundance, pleroma, saturation, superabundance, superfluity, surfeit, surplus.
antonyms lack, scarcity.
v. choke, deluge, fill, flesh, flood, gorge, inundate, sate, satiate, saturate, stuff, swamp.

glutinous *adj.* adhesive, cohesive, gluey, gummy, sticky, viscous.

glutton *n.* gobbler, gorger, gormandiser, gourmand, guzzler, pig, whale.
antonym ascetic.

gluttony *n.* gormandising, go(u)rmandise, go(u)rmandism, greed, greediness, insatiability, piggishness, voracity.
antonyms abstinence, asceticism.

gnarled *adj.* contorted, distorted, gnarly, knotted, knurled, rough, rugged, twisted, weather-beaten, wrinkled.

gnaw *v.* bite, chew, consume, devour, eat, erode, fret, haunt, munch, nag, nibble, niggle, plague, prey, trouble, wear, worry.

go *v.* **1** advance, depart, disappear, journey, leave, make for, move, pass, proceed, progress, retreat, take one's leave, travel, vanish, walk, wend, withdraw. **2** act, function, operate, perform, run, work. **3** continue, extend, reach, span, spread, stretch, unfold. **4** elapse, lapse, pass, roll on.
antonyms **2** break down, fail.
n. **1** attempt, stab, try, turn. **2** dynamism, effort,

energy, get-up-and-go, life, spirit, vitality.
go about address, approach, begin, engage in, perform, set about, tackle, undertake, work.
go ahead advance, begin, continue, march on, move, proceed, progress.
go at argue, attack, blame, criticise, set about, turn on.
go away depart, disappear, leave, recede, retreat, vanish, withdraw.
go back backslide, desert, forsake, repudiate, retract, retreat, return, revert.
go by 1 elapse, flow, pass, proceed. **2** follow, heed, observe, trust.
go down collapse, decline, decrease, degenerate, deteriorate, disappear, drop, fail, fall, founder, go under, lose, set, sink, submerge, submit, succumb, vanish.
go for 1 admire, be into, choose, enjoy, favour, fetch, like, obtain, prefer, reach, seek. **2** attack, lunge at, set about.
go in for adopt, choose, embrace, engage in, enter, enter (for), follow, participate in, practise, pursue, take part in, take up, undertake.
go into analyse, begin, check out, consider, delve into, discuss, dissect, enquire into, enter, examine, investigate, make a study of, participate in, probe, pursue, review, scrutinise, study, sus out, undertake.
go off 1 abscond, depart, leave, part, quit, vanish. **2** dislike, loathe, object to. **3** blow up, detonate, explode. **4** deteriorate, go bad, rot, turn. **5** happen, occur, proceed.
go on 1 carry on, continue, endure, happen, last (out), occur, persist, proceed, stay, take place. **2** chatter, ramble on, waffle.
go out depart, die out, exit, expire, fade out, leave.
go over check, detail, examine, inspect, list, peruse, read, recall, rehearse, repeat, review, revise, scan, skim, study.
go through bear, brave, check, consume, endure, examine, exhaust, experience, explore, face, hunt, investigate, look, rehearse, search, squander, suffer, tolerate, undergo, use, withstand.
go together accord, agree, fit, harmonise, match.
go under close down, collapse, die, drown, fail, fold, founder, go down, sink, submerge, succumb.
go with accompany, agree, blend, complement, correspond, fit, harmonise, match, suit.
antonym clash.
go without do without, fall short, manage without, spare, want.

goad *v.* annoy, arouse, drive, harass, hassle, hound, incite, instigate, irritate, nag, prod, prompt, propel, push, spur, stimulate, sting, urge, vex.

go-ahead *n.* agreement, assent, authorisation, clearance, consent, green light, OK, permission, sanction.
antonyms ban, embargo, veto.
adj. ambitious, enterprising, pioneering, progressive, up-and-coming.
antonyms sluggish, unenterprising.

goal *n.* aim, ambition, aspiration, destination, destiny, end, intention, limit, mark, object, objective, purpose, target.

gobble *v.* bolt, consume, cram, devour, gorge, gulp, guzzle, put away, stuff, swallow.

go-between *n.* agent, broker, contact, dealer, informer, intermediary, liaison, mediator, medium, messenger, middleman.

goblet *n.* chalice, drinking-cup, glass, wine-glass.

goblin *n.* bogey, brownie, demon, fiend, gremlin, hobgoblin, imp, red-cap, spirit, sprite.

God, god *n.* Allah, Almighty, Brahma, Creator, deity, divinity, Godhead, Holy One, idol, Jehovah, Jupiter, Lord, Lord God, power, Providence, spirit, Trinity, Yahweh, Zeus.

god-forsaken *adj.* abandoned, bleak, deserted, desolate, dismal, dreary, forlorn, gloomy, isolated, lonely, miserable, neglected, remote, wretched.
antonyms congenial, friendly.

godless *adj.* atheistic, depraved, evil, heathen, impious, irreligious, irreverent, pagan, profane, sacrilegious, ungodly, unholy, unrighteous, wicked.
antonyms godly, pious.

godly *adj.* blameless, devout, god-fearing, good, holy, innocent, pious, pure, religious, righteous, virtuous.
antonyms godless, impious.

godsend *n.* blessing, boon, lucky break, manna, miracle, stroke of luck, windfall.
antonyms blow, bombshell, setback.

golden *adj.* **1** blond(e), bright, fair, lustrous, resplendent, rich, rosy, shining, yellow. **2** advantageous, best, brilliant, excellent, favourable, glorious, happy, invaluable, joyful, precious, priceless, promising, prosperous, successful, timely, valuable.
antonym unfavourable.

good *adj.* **1** acceptable, advantageous, agreeable, auspicious, beneficial, cheerful, commendable, congenial, convivial, enjoyable, excellent, favourable, first-class, first-rate, friendly, great, happy, helpful, pleasant, pleasing, profitable, satisfactory, satisfying, splendid, super, superior, useful, worthwhile. **2** able, accomplished, appropriate, capable, clever, competent, dependable, expert, fit, fitting, professional, proficient, reliable, skilful, skilled, suitable, talented, trustworthy. **3** benevolent, charitable, considerate, gracious, kind. **4** exemplary, moral, righteous, upright, virtuous, worthy. **5** obedient, well-behaved, well-mannered. **6** complete, thorough, whole.
antonyms **1** bad. **2** incompetent, poor. **3** inconsiderate, unkind. **4** immoral, wicked. **5** disobedient.
n. advantage, avail, behalf, benefit, boon, convenience, excellence, gain, goodness, interest, merit, morality, probity, profit, rectitude, right, righteousness, service, uprightness, use, usefulness, virtue, weal, welfare, well-being,

worth, worthiness.

good-bye *n.*. adieu, au revoir, farewell, leave-taking, parting, valediction.

good-for-nothing *n.* idler, layabout, lazy-bones, loafer, rapscallion, reprobate, wastrel.
antonyms achiever, success, winner.

good-humoured *adj.* affable, amiable, approachable, cheerful, congenial, expansive, genial, good-tempered, happy, jovial, pleasant.
antonym ill-humoured.

good-looking *adj.* attractive, beautiful, fair, handsome, personable, presentable, pretty.
antonyms plain, ugly.

good-natured *adj.* agreeable, approachable, benevolent, friendly, gentle, good-hearted, helpful, kind, kind-hearted, kindly, neighbourly, open-minded, sympathetic, tolerant, warm-hearted.
antonym ill-natured.

goodness *n.* benevolence, compassion, friendliness, generosity, goodwill, graciousness, helpfulness, honesty, kindness, unselfishness, virtue.
antonyms badness, wickedness.

goods *n.* bags and baggage, belongings, chattels, commodities, effects, furnishings, furniture, gear, merchandise, movables, paraphernalia, possessions, property, stock, stuff, wares.

goodwill *n.* benevolence, compassion, favour, friendliness, friendship, generosity, kindliness, loving-kindness, sincerity, sympathy, zeal.
antonym ill-will.

goody-goody *adj.* pious, priggish, sanctimonious, self-righteous.

gore[1] *n.* blood, bloodiness, bloodshed, butchery, carnage, slaughter.

gore[2] *v.* impale, penetrate, pierce, rend, spear, stab, stick, wound.

gorge *n.* abyss, canyon, chasm, cleft, clough, defile, fissure, gap, gully, pass, ravine.
v. bolt, cram, devour, feed, fill, glut, gobble, gulp, guzzle, hog, overeat, sate, stuff, surfeit, swallow, wolf.
antonyms abstain, fast.

gorgeous *adj.* attractive, beautiful, brilliant, dazzling, delightful, enjoyable, fine, glamorous, glorious, good, good-looking, grand, lovely, luxurious, magnificent, pleasing, ravishing, rich, showy, splendid, stunning, sumptuous, superb.
antonyms dull, plain, shabby.

gory *adj.* blood-soaked, bloodstained, bloody, brutal, murderous, savage.

gospel *n.* certainty, creed, doctrine, fact, message, news, revelation, teaching, testament, truth.

gossamer *adj.* airy, cobwebby, delicate, fine, flimsy, gauzy, insubstantial, light, sheer, shimmering, silky, thin.
antonyms heavy, thick.

gossip *n.* **1** chitchat, hearsay, idle talk, jaw, prattle, report, rumour, scandal, tittle-tattle. **2** babbler, busybody, chatterbox, gossip-monger, nosy parker, prattler, scandalmonger, tale-bearer, tattler, telltale, whisperer.
v. blather, chat, clash, gabble, jaw, prattle, rumour, tattle, tell tales, whisper.

gouge *v.* chisel, claw, cut, dig, extract, force, gash, groove, hack, hollow, incise, scoop, score, scratch, slash.
n. cut, furrow, gash, groove, hack, hollow, incision, notch, scoop, score, scratch, slash, trench.

gourmand *n.* glutton, gorger, guzzler, hog, pig.
antonym ascetic.

gourmet *n.* bon vivant, connoisseur, epicure, epicurean, gastronome.

govern *v.* command, conduct, contain, control, decide, determine, direct, discipline, dominate, guide, influence, lead, manage, master, order, oversee, pilot, preside, quell, regulate, reign, restrain, rule, steer, subdue, superintend, supervise, sway, tame.

governess *n.* companion, guide, instructress, mentor, teacher, tutoress, tutress.

government *n.* administration, authority, charge, command, conduct, control, direction, domination, dominion, Establishment, executive, guidance, law, management, ministry, powers-that-be, régime, regulation, restraint, rule, sovereignty, state, superintendence, supervision, surveillance, sway.

governor *n.* administrator, alderman, boss, chief, commander, commissioner, controller, director, executive, head, leader, manager, overseer, ruler, superintendent, supervisor.

gown *n.* costume, creation, dress, dressing-gown, frock, garb, garment, habit, robe.

grab *v.* annex, appropriate, bag, capture, catch, catch hold of, clutch, collar, commandeer, grasp, grip, impress, latch on to, nab, pluck, rap, seize, snap up, snatch, strike.

grace *n.* **1** attractiveness, beauty, breeding, charity, charm, compassion, consideration, courtesy, decency, decorum, elegance, etiquette, favour, forgiveness, generosity, goodness, goodwill, gracefulness, indulgence, kindliness, kindness, leniency, love, loveliness, manners, mercy, merit, pardon, pleasantness, poise, polish, quarter, refinement, reprieve, shapeliness, tact, tastefulness, virtue. **2** benediction, blessing, consecration, prayer, thanks, thanksgiving.
antonyms **1** cruelty, harshness.
v. adorn, decorate, dignify, distinguish, dress, elevate, embellish, enhance, enrich, favour, garnish, glorify, honour, ornament, prettify, set off, trim.
antonyms deface, detract from, spoil.

graceful *adj.* beautiful, becoming, charming, deft, easy, elegant, fine, flowing, natural, pleasing, slender, smooth, suave, supple, tasteful.
antonyms awkward, clumsy, graceless.

gracious *adj.* accommodating, benevolent, charitable, compassionate, condescending, considerate, courteous, elegant, friendly, hospitable, indulgent, kind, kindly, lenient, loving, luxurious, merciful, mild, obliging, pleasant, pleasing, polite, refined, sweet, well-mannered.
antonym ungracious.

grade *n.* brand, category, class, condition, degree, group, level, mark, notch, order, place, position, quality, rank, rung, size, stage, station, step, upgrade.
v. arrange, blend, brand, categorise, class, classify, evaluate, group, label, mark, order, pigeonhole, range, rank, rate, shade, size, sort, type, value.

gradient *n.* bank, decline, hill, incline, rise, slope.

gradual *adj.* cautious, continuous, deliberate, even, gentle, leisurely, measured, moderate, progressive, regular, slow, steady, step-by-step, successive, unhurried.
antonyms immediate, precipitate, sudden.

gradually *adv.* bit by bit, by degrees, cautiously, evenly, gently, gingerly, imperceptibly, inch by inch, little by little, moderately, piecemeal, progressively, slowly, steadily, step by step.

graduate *v.* arrange, calibrate, classify, grade, group, mark off, measure out, order, pass, proportion, qualify, range, rank, regulate, sort.

graft *n.* bud, implant, implantation, scion, shoot, splice, sprout, transplant.
v. engraft, implant, insert, join, splice, transplant.

grain *n.* **1** atom, bit, crumb, fibre, fragment, iota, jot, mite, modicum, molecule, morsel, particle, piece, scrap, speck, trace. **2** cereals, corn, granule, kernel, seed. **3** marking, pattern, surface, texture, weave.

grand *adj.* admirable, ambitious, excellent, fine, first-rate, glorious, great, head, highest, illustrious, impressive, large, leading, lofty, lordly, magnificent, majestic, marvellous, monumental, noble, outstanding, pompous, pre-eminent, pretentious, princely, regal, senior, splendid, stately, striking, sublime, super, superb, supreme, wonderful.
antonyms common, poor, unimportant.

grandeur *n.* dignity, greatness, importance, loftiness, magnificence, majesty, nobility, pomp, splendour, state, stateliness, sublimity.
antonyms humbleness, lowliness, simplicity.

grandiloquent *adj.* bombastic, flowery, high-flown, high-sounding, magniloquent, pompous, pretentious, rhetorical, swollen.
antonyms plain, restrained, simple.

grandiose *adj.* affected, ambitious, extravagant, flamboyant, grand, high-flown, imposing, impressive, lofty, magnificent, majestic, monumental, ostentatious, pompous, pretentious, showy, stately, weighty.
antonym unpretentious.

grant *v.* **1** allocate, allot, apportion, assign, award, bestow, confer, convey, dispense, donate, give, impart, present, provide, transfer, transmit. **2** accede to, acknowledge, admit, agree to, allow, concede, consent to, permit.
antonym **1** withhold.
n. allocation, allowance, annuity, award, bequest, bursary, concession, donation, endowment, gift, honorarium, scholarship, subsidy.

granular *adj.* crumbly, grainy, granulated, gritty, rough, sandy.

granule *n.* atom, crumb, fragment, grain, iota, jot, molecule, particle, scrap, seed, speck.

graph *n.* chart, diagram, grid, table.

graphic *adj.* blow-by-blow, clear, descriptive, detailed, diagrammatic, drawn, explicit, expressive, illustrative, lively, lucid, pictorial, specific, striking, telling, visible, visual, vivid.
antonyms impressionistic, vague.

grapple *v.* attack, clash, clasp, clinch, clutch, combat, confront, contend, cope, deal with, encounter, engage, face, fasten, fight, grab, grasp, grip, hold, hug, lay hold, seize, snatch, struggle, tackle, tussle, wrestle.
antonyms avoid, evade, release.

grasp *v.* catch (on), clasp, clutch, comprehend, follow, get, grab, grapple, grip, gripe, hold, lay hold of, realise, see, seize, snatch, understand.
n. **1** clasp, clutches, control, embrace, grip, hold, possession, power. **2** apprehension, comprehension, familiarity, knowledge, mastery, understanding.

grasping *adj.* acquisitive, close-fisted, grabbing, greedy, mean, miserly, parsimonious, penny-pinching, selfish, stingy, tight-fisted.
antonym generous.

grass *n.* grassland, green, lawn, pasture, turf.

grassland *n.* downs, meadow, pampas, pasture, prairie, savanna, steppe.

grate *v.* **1** grind, mince, pulverise, rub, scrape, scratch, shred. **2** aggravate, annoy, exasperate, get on one's nerves, irk, irritate, jar, set one's teeth on edge, vex.

grateful *adj.* appreciative, indebted, mindful, obligated, obliged, sensible, thankful.
antonym ungrateful.

gratify *v.* delight, favour, fulfil, gladden, humour, indulge, pander to, please, recompense, satisfy, thrill.
antonyms frustrate, thwart.

grating[1] *adj.* annoying, disagreeable, discordant, displeasing, harsh, irritating, jarring, rasping, scraping, squeaky, strident, unpleasant.
antonyms harmonious, pleasing.

grating[2] *n.* grid, grill, grille, lattice, lattice-work, trellis.

gratitude *n.* acknowledgement, appreciation, gratefulness, indebtedness, mindfulness, obligation, recognition, thankfulness, thanks.
antonyms ingratitude, ungratefulness.

gratuitous *adj.* complimentary, free, gratis, groundless, irrelevant, needless, superfluous, unasked-for, uncalled-for, unjustified, unnecessary, unprovoked, unsolicited, unwarranted, voluntary, wanton.
antonyms justified, provoked, reasonable.

gratuity *n.* bonus, boon, bounty, donation, gift, largess, perk, present, recompense, reward, tip.

grave[1] *n.* barrow, burial-place, burying-place, cairn, crypt, mausoleum, pit, sepulchre, tomb, vault.

grave[2] *adj.* **1** acute, critical, crucial, dangerous, hazardous, important, momentous, serious, significant, urgent, vital, weighty. **2** dignified, dull, earnest, long-faced, quiet, reserved,

restrained, sedate, serious, severe, sober, solemn, subdued, thoughtful.
antonyms **1** light, slight, trivial. **2** cheerful.

gravelly *adj.* **1** grainy, gritty, pebbly, shingly, stony. **2** guttural, harsh, hoarse, throaty.

graveyard *n.* burial-ground, burial-place, cemetery, churchyard.

gravitate *v.* descend, drop, fall, head for, incline, lean, move, precipitate, settle, sink, tend.

gravity *n.* **1** acuteness, consequence, danger, importance, seriousness, significance, urgency. **2** demureness, dignity, reserve, restraint, seriousness, severity, sobriety, solemnity, sombreness, thoughtfulness.
antonyms **1** triviality. **2** gaiety, levity.

graze *v.* abrade, brush, chafe, rub, score, scrape, scratch, shave, skim, skin, touch.
n. abrasion, score, scrape, scratch.

grease *n.* dripping, fat, lard, oil, ointment, tallow, wax.

greasy *adj.* fatty, lardy, oily, slimy, slippery, smeary, smooth, waxy.

great *adj.* **1** big, colossal, enormous, gigantic, huge, immense, impressive, large, mammoth, massive, vast. **2** considerable, excessive, extreme, inordinate, pronounced. **3** celebrated, distinguished, eminent, famous, fine, glorious, grand, illustrious, notable, noteworthy, outstanding, prominent, remarkable, renowned. **4** chief, important, leading, main, major, primary, principal, serious, significant. **5** excellent, fabulous, fantastic, first-rate, marvellous, superb, terrific, tremendous, wonderful.
antonyms **1** small. **2** slight. **3** unknown. **4** insignificant, unimportant.

greed *n.* acquisitiveness, avarice, covetousness, craving, desire, eagerness, gluttony, hunger, insatiability, longing, ravenousness, selfishness, voracity.
antonyms abstemiousness, self-restraint.

greedy *adj.* avaricious, covetous, craving, desirous, eager, gluttonous, gormandising, grasping, hungry, impatient, insatiable, ravenous, voracious.
antonym abstemious.

green *adj.* **1** blooming, budding, flourishing, fresh, grassy, leafy, tender, unripe, unseasoned, verdant. **2** covetous, envious, jealous, resentful. **3** ignorant, immature, inexperienced, naïve, new, raw, recent, unsophisticated, untrained, young.
n. common, grass, lawn, turf.

greenery *n.* foliage, greenness, vegetation, verdure.

greenhouse *n.* conservatory, glasshouse, hothouse, nursery, pavilion, vinery.

greet *v.* accost, acknowledge, address, compliment, hail, hallo, meet, receive, salute, wave to, welcome.
antonym ignore.

greeting *n.* accost, acknowledgement, address, reception, salutation, the time of day, welcome.

greetings *n.* best wishes, compliments, formalities, good wishes, love, regards, respects, salutations.

gregarious *adj.* affable, chummy, convivial, cordial, extrovert, friendly, outgoing, sociable, social, warm.
antonym unsociable.

grey *adj.* **1** ashen, cheerless, cloudy, colourless, dark, dim, dull, leaden, murky, neutral, overcast, pale, sunless, unclear, unidentifiable. **2** bleak, depressing, dismal, dreary, gloomy.

grief *n.* affliction, agony, anguish, bereavement, blow, burden, dejection, desolation, distress, grievance, heartache, heartbreak, misery, mourning, pain, regret, remorse, sadness, sorrow, suffering, tragedy, trial, tribulation, trouble, woe.
antonyms delight, happiness.

grievance *n.* affliction, charge, complaint, damage, distress, grief, hardship, injury, injustice, moan, resentment, sorrow, trial, tribulation, trouble, unhappiness, wrong.

grim *adj.* **1** cruel, fearsome, frightening, ghastly, gruesome, harsh, horrible, horrid, shocking, sinister, terrible, unpleasant. **2** depressing, dour, forbidding, gloomy, morose, resolute, severe, stern, sullen, surly, unattractive.
antonyms **1** pleasant. **2** attractive.

grimace *n.* face, frown, pout, scowl, smirk, sneer, wry face.
v. frown, make a face, pout, pull a face, scowl, smirk, sneer.

grime *n.* dirt, filth, muck, soot, squalor.

grimy *adj.* contaminated, dirty, filthy, foul, grubby, murky, smudgy, smutty, soiled, sooty, squalid.
antonyms clean, pure.

grind *v.* abrade, crush, file, gnash, grate, grit, mill, polish, pound, powder, pulverise, sand, scrape, sharpen, smooth, whet.
n. chore, drudgery, exertion, labour, round, routine, slavery, sweat, task, toil.

grind down afflict, crush, harass, hound, oppress, persecute, plague, trouble.

grip *n.* **1** clasp, clutches, control, embrace, grasp, hold, power, sway. **2** acquaintance, comprehension, grasp, mastery, understanding.
v. absorb, catch, clasp, clutch, compel, divert, engross, enthral, fascinate, grasp, hold, involve, latch on to, mesmerise, rivet, seize, spellbind, thrill.

grisly *adj.* abominable, appalling, awful, dreadful, frightful, ghastly, grim, gruesome, horrible, horrid, shocking, terrible, terrifying.
antonym delightful.

grit *n.* **1** dust, grail, gravel, pebbles, sand, shingle. **2** bravery, courage, determination, doggedness, guts, nerve, perseverance, resolution, spirit, stamina, staying power, tenacity, toughness.
v. clench, gnash, grate, grind, lock.

grizzle *v.* cry, fret, sniffle, snivel, snuffle, whimper, whine, whinge.

grizzled *adj.* grey, grey-haired, grey-headed, greying, grizzly.

groan *n.* complaint, cry, moan, objection, outcry, protest, sigh, wail.

antonyms cheer, praise.
v. complain, cry, lament, moan, object, protest, sigh, wail.
antonyms cheer, praise.

groom *v.* **1** brush, clean, curry, dress, neaten, preen, smarten, spruce up, tend, tidy. **2** drill, educate, nurture, prepare, school, train.

groove *n.* canal, channel, cutting, furrow, gutter, hollow, indentation, rut, score, trench.
antonym ridge.

grope *v.* cast about, feel, feel about, finger, fish, flounder, fumble, grabble, probe, scrabble, search.

gross *adj.* **1** blatant, flagrant, glaring, grievous, obvious, outright, plain, serious, shameful, sheer, shocking, utter. **2** coarse, crude, foul, improper, impure, indecent, lewd, obscene, offensive, rude, tasteless, vulgar. **3** big, bulky, colossal, fat, heavy, huge, hulking, large, overweight. **4** aggregate, all-inclusive, complete, entire, inclusive, total, whole.
antonyms **3** slight. **4** net.
n. aggregate, bulk, entirety, sum, total, totality, whole.
v. accumulate, aggregate, bring, earn, make, rake in, take, total.

grotesque *adj.* absurd, bizarre, deformed, distorted, extravagant, fanciful, fantastic, freakish, hideous, macabre, monstrous, odd, ugly, unnatural, unsightly, weird.
antonyms graceful, normal.

grotto *n.* catacomb, cave, cavern, chamber, subterranean (chamber), underground chamber.

ground *n.* **1** bottom, clay, clod, dirt, dry land, dust, earth, field, foundation, land, loam, mould, soil, surface, terra firma, terrain, turf. **2** arena, ball-park, park, pitch, stadium.
v. acquaint with, base, build up, coach, drill, establish, familiarise with, fix, found, inform, initiate, instruct, introduce, prepare, set, settle, teach, train, tutor.

groundless *adj.* baseless, empty, false, imaginary, uncalled-for, unfounded, unjustified, unprovoked, unsubstantiated, unsupported, unwarranted.
antonyms justified, reasonable, well-founded.

grounds[1] *n.* acres, area, country, district, domain, estate, fields, gardens, holding, land, park, property, realm, surroundings, terrain, territory, tract.

grounds[2] *n.* account, argument, base, basis, call, cause, excuse, factor, foundation, inducement, justification, motive, occasion, principle, reason, score, vindication.

grounds[3] *n.* deposit, dregs, lees, sediment.

group *n.* association, band, batch, bunch, category, circle, class, classification, clique, clump, cluster, clutch, collection, combination, company, conglomeration, congregation, constellation, core, crowd, detachment, faction, formation, front, gang, gathering, genus, grouping, lot, organisation, pack, party, set, species, team, troop.
v. arrange, assemble, associate, assort, band, categorise, class, classify, cluster, collect, congregate, gather, get together, link, marshal, mass, order, organise, range, sort.

grovel *v.* cower, crawl, creep, cringe, crouch, defer, demean oneself, fawn, flatter, ingratiate oneself, kowtow, sneak.

grow *v.* **1** develop, enlarge, expand, extend, increase, proliferate, rise, spread, stretch, swell. **2** arise, flourish, flower, germinate, improve, issue, originate, progress, prosper, shoot, spring, sprout. **3** breed, cultivate, farm, produce, propagate, raise. **4** become, evolve, turn.
antonyms **1** decrease, diminish. **4** fail.

growl *v.* gnar, gnarl, gnarr, knar, snap, snarl, yap.

grown-up *adj.* adult, full-grown, fully-fledged, fully-grown, mature, of age.
antonyms childish, immature.
n. adult, gentleman, lady, man, woman.
antonym child.

growth *n.* **1** advance, development, enlargement, evolution, expansion, extension, improvement, increase, production, progress, proliferation, rise, success, transformation. **2** lump, outgrowth, protuberance, swelling, tumour.
antonyms **1** decline, decrease, failure, stagnation.

grub *v.* burrow, delve, dig, explore, ferret, forage, hunt, investigate, probe, pull up, root, rummage, scour, uproot.
n. caterpillar, chrysalis, larva, maggot, nymph, pupa, worm.

grubby *adj.* dirty, filthy, mucky, scruffy, seedy, shabby, slovenly, soiled, squalid, untidy, unwashed.
antonyms clean, smart.

grudge *n.* animosity, antagonism, aversion, bitterness, dislike, enmity, envy, grievance, hard feelings, hate, ill-will, jealousy, malice, resentment, spite.
antonyms favour, regard.
v. begrudge, covet, dislike, envy, mind, object to, regret, resent, stint, take exception to.
antonyms applaud, approve, celebrate.

grudging *adj.* cautious, guarded, half-hearted, hesitant, reluctant, secret, unenthusiastic, unwilling.

gruelling *adj.* arduous, backbreaking, brutal, crushing, demanding, difficult, exhausting, hard, hard-going, harsh, laborious, punishing, severe, stern, strenuous, taxing, tiring, tough, trying.
antonym easy.

gruesome *adj.* abominable, awful, fearful, ghastly, grim, grisly, hideous, horrific, horrifying, macabre, monstrous, repellent, repugnant, repulsive, shocking, spine-chilling, terrible.
antonyms charming, pleasant.

grumble *v.* bleat, carp, complain, find fault, gripe, grouch, growl, moan, murmur, mutter, rumble, whine.
n. complaint, grievance, gripe, grouse, moan, objection, rumble.

grumpy *adj.* bad-tempered, cantankerous, crabbed, cross, crotchety, discontented, grouchy, ill-tempered, irritable, sulky, sullen, surly.
antonyms contented, happy.

guarantee *n.* assurance, bond, certainty, collateral, covenant, endorsement, insurance, oath, pledge, promise, security, surety, testimonial, undertaking, voucher, warranty, word, word of honour.
v. answer for, assure, certify, ensure, insure, maintain, make certain, make sure of, pledge, promise, protect, secure, swear, underwrite, vouch for, warrant.

guard *v.* beware, cover, defend, escort, keep, look out, mind, oversee, patrol, police, preserve, protect, safeguard, save, screen, secure, shelter, shield, supervise, tend, watch.
n. **1** attention, care, caution, defence, guarantee, heed, precaution, protection, safeguard, security, vigilance, wariness, watch, watchfulness. **2** barrier, buffer, bumper, pad, screen, shield, wall. **3** custodian, defender, escort, lookout, minder, patrol, picket, protector, sentry, warder, watchman.

guarded *adj.* cagey, careful, cautious, discreet, non-committal, reserved, restrained, reticent, secretive, suspicious, wary, watchful.
antonyms communicative, frank.

guardian *n.* attendant, champion, conserver, curator, custodian, defender, escort, guard, keeper, minder, preserver, protector, trustee, warden, warder.

guerrilla *n.* freedom-fighter, irregular, partisan, resistance fighter, sniper.

guess *v.* assume, believe, conjecture, dare say, deem, estimate, fancy, fathom, feel, imagine, judge, predict, reckon, solve, speculate, suppose, surmise, suspect, think, work out.
n. assumption, belief, fancy, feeling, hypothesis, intuition, judgement, notion, opinion, prediction, reckoning, speculation, suspicion, theory.

guesswork *n.* assumption, conjecture, estimation, intuition, presumption, presupposition, reckoning, speculation, supposition, surmise, suspicion, theory.

guidance *n.* advice, control, counsel, counselling, direction, guidelines, help, illumination, indications, instruction, leadership, management, pointers, recommendation, regulation, steering, teaching.

guide *v.* accompany, advise, attend, command, conduct, control, convoy, counsel, direct, educate, escort, govern, handle, head, influence, instruct, lead, manage, manoeuvre, oversee, pilot, point, rule, shape, steer, superintend, supervise, sway, teach, train, usher.
n. **1** adviser, attendant, chaperon, companion, conductor, counsellor, courier, escort, informant, leader, master, mentor, pilot, steersman, teacher, usher. **2** catalogue, directory, guidebook, handbook, instructions, manual. **3** criterion, example, guideline, ideal, indication, key, marker, model, pointer, sign, signal, signpost, standard.

guild *n.* association, chapel, club, company, corporation, fellowship, incorporation, league, lodge, order, organisation, society, union.

guilt *n.* blame, conscience, contrition, culpability, disgrace, dishonour, guilty conscience, regret, remorse, responsibility, self-condemnation, self-reproach, shame.
antonyms innocence, righteousness, shamelessness.

guiltless *adj.* blameless, clean, clear, immaculate, innocent, irreproachable, pure, sinless, spotless, unimpeachable, unspotted.
antonyms guilty, tainted.

guilty *adj.* ashamed, blamable, blameworthy, conscience-stricken, contrite, convicted, criminal, culpable, offending, penitent, regretful, remorseful, repentant, responsible, shamefaced, sheepish, sinful, sorry, wicked, wrong.
antonyms blameless, guiltless, innocent.

guise *n.* air, appearance, aspect, custom, disguise, dress, façade, face, fashion, features, form, front, manner, mask, mode, pretence, show.

gulf *n.* abyss, basin, bay, bight, breach, chasm, cleft, gap, gorge, opening, rift, separation, split, void.

gullible *adj.* credulous, foolish, innocent, naïve, trusting, unsuspecting.
antonym astute.

gully *n.* channel, ditch, gutter, ravine, watercourse.

gulp *v.* bolt, choke, devour, gasp, gobble, guzzle, knock back, stuff, swallow, swig, swill, wolf.
antonyms nibble, sip.
n. draught, mouthful, slug, swallow, swig.

gum *n.* adhesive, cement, glue, paste.
v. cement, clog, fix, glue, paste, seal, stick.

gun *n.* bazooka, cannon, howitzer, pistol, shooter, shooting-iron.

gunman *n.* assassin, bandit, desperado, gangster, hatchet man, hit man, killer, murderer, sniper, terrorist, thug.

gurgle *v.* babble, bubble, burble, crow, lap, murmur, ripple, splash.
n. babble, murmur, ripple.

gush *v.* babble, burst, cascade, chatter, drivel, enthuse, flood, flow, jabber, jet, pour, run, rush, spout, spurt, stream, yatter.
n. babble, burst, cascade, chatter, exuberance, flood, flow, jet, outburst, outflow, rush, spout, spurt, stream, tide, torrent.

gust *n.* blast, blow, breeze, burst, flurry, gale, puff, rush, squall.
v. blast, blow, bluster, breeze, flurry, puff, squall.

gusto *n.* appreciation, delight, élan, enjoyment, enthusiasm, exhilaration, exuberance, relish, verve, zeal, zest.
antonyms apathy, distaste.

gusty *adj.* blowy, blustering, blustery, breezy, gustful, squally, stormy, tempestuous, windy.
antonym calm.

gut *v.* **1** clean (out), disembowel, empty. **2** plunder, ransack, ravage, rifle, sack.

adj. basic, deep-seated, emotional, heartfelt, innate, instinctive, intuitive, natural, spontaneous, strong.

gutter *n.* channel, conduit, ditch, drain, duct, passage, pipe, sluice, trench, trough, tube.

guttural *adj.* deep, grating, gravelly, gruff, harsh, hoarse, husky, low, rasping, rough, thick, throaty.

guy *n.* bloke, boy, chap, fellow, individual, man, person, youth.

guzzle *v.* bolt, cram, devour, gobble, gormandise, stuff, wolf.

gypsy, gipsy *n.* nomad, rambler, roamer, Romany, tinker, traveller, wanderer.

gyrate *v.* circle, gyre, pirouette, revolve, rotate, spin, spiral, twirl, whirl.

H

habit *n.* **1** addiction, bent, custom, fixation, frame of mind, inclination, make-up, manner, mannerism, mode, nature, obsession, practice, routine, rule, second nature, tendency, usage, way, weakness, wont. **2** apparel, attire, clothes, clothing, dress, garb, garment.
habitat *n.* abode, domain, element, environment, home, locality, surroundings, terrain, territory.
habitual *adj.* common, customary, established, familiar, fixed, natural, normal, ordinary, persistent, recurrent, regular, routine, standard, traditional, usual, wonted.
antonyms infrequent, occasional.
hack[1] *v.* chop, cut, gash, haggle, kick, mutilate, notch, rasp, slash.
n. bark, chop, cough, cut, gash, notch, rasp, slash.
hack[2] *adj.* hackneyed, mediocre, pedestrian, poor, stereotyped, tired, undistinguished, uninspired, unoriginal.
n. drudge, journalist, scribbler, slave.
hackneyed *adj.* clichéd, common, commonplace, corny, overworked, stale, stereotyped, stock, threadbare, time-worn, tired, trite, worn-out.
antonyms fresh, new, original.
hag *n.* battle-axe, fury, shrew, vixen, witch.
haggard *adj.* careworn, drawn, gaunt, ghastly, pinched, shrunken, thin, wan, wasted, wrinkled.
antonym hale.
haggle *v.* bargain, barter, bicker, dispute, quarrel, squabble, wrangle.
hail[1] *n.* barrage, bombardment, rain, shower, storm, torrent, volley.
v. assail, barrage, batter, bombard, pelt, rain, shower, storm.
hail[2] *v.* acknowledge, address, applaud, call, cheer, exalt, flag down, greet, honour, salute, shout, signal to, wave, welcome.
n. call, cry, holla, shout.
hair *n.* locks, mane, mop, shock, tresses.
hair-do *n.* coiffure, cut, haircut, hairstyle, perm, set, style.
hairdresser *n.* barber, coiffeur, coiffeuse, friseur, hair-stylist, stylist.
hairless *adj.* bald, bald-headed, beardless, clean-shaven, shorn, tonsured.
antonyms hairy, hirsute.
hair-raising *adj.* alarming, bloodcurdling, eerie, frightening, horrifying, scary, shocking, spine-chilling, startling, terrifying, thrilling.
antonym calming.
hairy *adj.* **1** bearded, bushy, furry, hirsute, shaggy, stubbly, woolly. **2** dangerous, difficult, frightening, nerve-racking, risky, scaring.
antonyms **1** bald, clean-shaven.
half *n.* bisection, division, fifty per cent, fraction, half-share, hemisphere, portion, section, segment, share.
adj. divided, fractional, halved, incomplete, limited, moderate, part, partial, semi-.
antonym whole.
adv. imperfectly, in part, incompletely, partially, partly, slightly.
antonym completely.
half-baked *adj.* crazy, foolish, ill-conceived, impractical, short-sighted, stupid.
antonyms planned, sensible.
half-hearted *adj.* apathetic, cool, feeble, lukewarm, neutral, passive, uninterested.
antonyms energetic, enthusiastic.
halfway *adv.* imperfectly, in the middle, incompletely, midway, moderately, nearly, partially, partly, rather.
antonym completely.
adj. central, equidistant, incomplete, intermediate, mid, middle, midway, partial.
antonym complete.
hall *n.* assembly-room, auditorium, chamber, concert-hall, concourse, corridor, entrance-hall, entry, foyer, hallway, lobby, vestibule.
hallmark *n.* badge, brand-name, device, emblem, endorsement, indication, mark, seal, sign, stamp, symbol, trademark.
hallucinate *v.* daydream, dream, fantasise, freak out, imagine.
hallucination *n.* apparition, delusion, dream, fantasy, figment, illusion, mirage, vision.
halo *n.* aureola, corona, glory, radiance.
halt *v.* break off, call it a day, cease, check, curb, desist, draw up, end, impede, obstruct, quit, rest, stem, stop, terminate, wait.
antonyms assist, continue, start.
n. arrest, break, close, end, interruption, pause, stand, standstill, stop, stoppage, termination.
antonyms continuation, start.
halting *adj.* awkward, broken, faltering, hesitant, imperfect, laboured, stammering, stumbling, stuttering.
antonym fluent.
halve *v.* bisect, cut down, divide, lessen, reduce, share, split.
hammer *v.* **1** bang, beat, form, hit, knock, make, shape. **2** din, drive, drive home, drum, impress upon, instruct, repeat. **3** beat, defeat, slate, thrash, trounce.
n. gavel, mallet.
hammer out accomplish, bring about, complete, fashion, finish, negotiate, produce, settle, sort out, thrash out.
hamper *v.* cramp, curb, curtail, frustrate, ham-

string, handicap, hinder, hold up, impede, interfere with, obstruct, prevent, restrain, restrict, shackle, slow down, thwart.
antonyms aid, encourage, facilitate.

hand *n.* **1** fist, mitt, palm, paw. **2** ability, agency, aid, assistance, direction, help, influence, part, participation, skill, support. **3** calligraphy, handwriting, script. **4** artisan, craftsman, employee, farm-hand, hireling, labourer, operative, worker, workman. **5** applause, clap, ovation.
v. aid, assist, conduct, convey, deliver, give, guide, help, lead, offer, pass, present, provide, transmit, yield.
at hand available, close, handy, immediate, imminent, near, ready.
hand down bequeath, give, grant, pass on, transfer, will.
hand out deal out, dish out, dispense, disseminate, distribute, give out, mete out, share out.
hand over deliver, donate, present, release, relinquish, surrender, turn over, yield.
antonyms keep, retain.

handbook *n.* companion, guide, guidebook, instruction book, manual.

handcuff *v.* fasten, fetter, manacle, secure, shackle, tie.

handcuffs *n.* bracelets, cuffs, fetters, manacles, shackles.

handful *n.* few, scattering, smattering, sprinkling.
antonyms lot, many.

handicap *n.* barrier, block, defect, disability, disadvantage, drawback, hindrance, impairment, impediment, limitation, obstacle, penalty, restriction, shortcoming, stumbling-block.
antonyms assistance, benefit.
v. burden, disadvantage, hamper, hinder, impede, limit, restrict, retard.
antonyms assist, further.

handicraft *n.* art, artisanship, craft, craftsmanship, handiwork, skill, workmanship.

handiwork *n.* achievement, craft, creation, design, doing, handicraft, handwork, invention, product, production, result, work.

handle *n.* grip, handgrip, knob, lug, stock.
v. **1** feel, finger, fondle, grasp, hold, pick up, touch. **2** control, cope with, deal with, manage, supervise, tackle, treat.

hand-out *n.* **1** alms, charity, dole, freebie, issue, largess(e), share, share-out. **2** bulletin, circular, free sample, leaflet, literature, press release, statement.

hand-picked *adj.* chosen, elite, picked, select, selected.

hands *n.* authority, care, charge, command, control, custody, guidance, possession, power, supervision.
hands down easily, effortlessly, with ease.
antonym with difficulty.

handsome *adj.* **1** attractive, elegant, good-looking, graceful, majestic. **2** abundant, considerable, generous, large, liberal.
antonyms **1** ugly, unattractive. **2** mean.

handwriting *n.* calligraphy, fist, hand, longhand, penmanship, script.

handy *adj.* **1** accessible, at hand, available, convenient, helpful, manageable, near, ready, useful. **2** clever, expert, practical, proficient, skilful, skilled.
antonyms **1** inconvenient. **2** clumsy.

handyman *n.* DIYer, Jack-of-all-trades, odd-job man.

hang *v.* **1** dangle, drape, droop, drop, incline, lean, sag, suspend, swing, trail. **2** attach, fasten, fix, stick. **3** cling, drift, float, hover, linger, remain. **4** execute, gibbet, string up.
hang about/around associate with, frequent, haunt, linger, loiter, roam, waste time.
hang back hesitate, hold back, shy away.
hang on 1 carry on, continue, endure, hold on, hold out, persevere, persist, remain, rest, wait. **2** grasp, grip, hold fast. **3** depend on, hinge on, turn on.
antonym **1** give up.

hanger-on *n.* dependant, follower, lackey, minion, parasite, sponger, sycophant, toady.

hang-up *n.* block, difficulty, inhibition, mental block, obsession, preoccupation, problem, thing.

hanker for/after covet, crave, desire, hunger for, itch for, long for, pine for, thirst for, want, wish, yearn for.
antonyms dislike, hate.

hankering *n.* craving, desire, hunger, itch, longing, thirst, urge, wish, yearning.
antonyms dislike, hatred.

haphazard *adj.* careless, casual, chance, disorderly, disorganised, hit-or-miss, random, slapdash, slipshod, unsystematic.
antonyms methodical, planned.

happen *v.* arise, chance, come about, crop up, develop, ensue, follow, materialise, occur, result, take place, transpire, turn out.

happening *n.* accident, adventure, affair, case, chance, circumstance, episode, event, experience, incident, occasion, occurrence, phenomenon, proceeding, scene.

happy *adj.* **1** cheerful, content, contented, delighted, glad, jolly, joyful, pleased, thrilled. **2** appropriate, apt, favourable, felicitous, fitting, fortunate, lucky, satisfactory.
antonyms **1** discontented, unhappy. **2** inappropriate, unfortunate.

happy-go-lucky *adj.* carefree, casual, devil-may-care, easy-going, irresponsible, reckless.
antonyms anxious, wary.

harangue *n.* diatribe, lecture, speech, spiel, tirade.
v. address, declaim, hold forth, lecture, preach, rant, spout.

harass *v.* annoy, bother, distress, disturb, exasperate, exhaust, fatigue, harry, hassle, perplex, persecute, pester, plague, tease, tire, torment, trouble, vex, wear out, worry.
antonyms assist, help.

harbour *n.* anchorage, marina, port.
v. believe, cherish, cling to, conceal, entertain, foster, hide, hold, imagine, nurse, nurture, protect, retain.

hard *adj.* **1** compact, dense, firm, impenetrable, rigid, solid, stiff, strong, tough, unyielding. **2** arduous, backbreaking, baffling, complex, complicated, difficult, exhausting, involved, laborious, perplexing, puzzling, strenuous. **3** callous, cruel, difficult, distressing, harsh, inflexible, painful, pitiless, ruthless, severe, strict, stubborn, unfeeling, unrelenting, unsympathetic.
antonyms **1** soft, yielding. **2** easy, simple. **3** kind, pleasant.
adv. assiduously, diligently, doggedly, earnestly, energetically, industriously, intensely, intently, keenly, laboriously, sorely, steadily, strenuously, strongly, vigorously, violently, with difficulty.
antonym unenthusiastically.
hard and fast binding, fixed, rigid, set, strict, stringent, unchangeable.
antonym flexible.
hard up bankrupt, broke, bust, impoverished, in the red, penniless, poor, short.
antonym rich.

hard-bitten *adj.* callous, hard-boiled, hard-headed, hard-nosed, matter-of-fact, practical, realistic, ruthless, shrewd, tough.
antonym sentimental.

hard-core *adj.* dedicated, die-hard, dyed-in-the-wool, extreme, rigid, staunch, steadfast.
antonym moderate.

harden *v.* accustom, bake, brace, buttress, fortify, freeze, gird, nerve, reinforce, season, set, solidify, steel, stiffen, strengthen, toughen, train.
antonyms soften, weaken.

hard-headed *adj.* clear-thinking, hard-boiled, level-headed, practical, pragmatic, realistic, sensible, shrewd, tough, unsentimental.
antonym unrealistic.

hard-hearted *adj.* callous, cold, cruel, hard, heartless, inhuman, intolerant, merciless, pitiless, stony, unfeeling, unsympathetic.
antonyms kind, merciful, sensitive.

hard-hitting *adj.* condemnatory, critical, forceful, no-holds-barred, strongly-worded, tough, unsparing, vigorous.
antonym mild.

hardline *adj.* definite, extreme, immoderate, intransigent, militant, tough, uncompromising.
antonyms flexible, moderate.

hardly *adv.* barely, by no means, just, no sooner, no way, not at all, not quite, only, only just, scarcely.

hardness *n.* coldness, difficulty, firmness, harshness, inhumanity, insensitivity, pitilessness, rigidity, severity, solidity, sternness, toughness.
antonyms ease, mildness, softness.

hard-pressed *adj.* hard-pushed, under pressure, up against it, with one's back to the wall.
antonym untroubled.

hardship *n.* adversity, affliction, calamity, destitution, difficulty, labour, misery, misfortune, need, oppression, persecution, privation, suffering, toil, torment, trial, tribulation, trouble, want.
antonyms comfort, ease, prosperity.

hard-wearing *adj.* durable, resilient, rugged, stout, strong, sturdy, tough.
antonym delicate.

hard-working *adj.* busy, conscientious, diligent, energetic, industrious, zealous.
antonyms idle, lazy.

hardy *adj.* firm, healthy, robust, sound, strong, sturdy, tough, vigorous.
antonyms unhealthy, weak.

hare-brained *adj.* careless, crackpot, daft, foolish, half-baked, inane, rash, reckless, scatter-brained, wild.
antonym sensible.

hark back go back, recall, recollect, remember, revert.

harm *n.* abuse, damage, hurt, ill, injury, loss, misfortune, wrong.
antonyms benefit, service.
v. abuse, blemish, damage, hurt, ill-treat, impair, injure, mar, ruin, scathe, spoil, wound.
antonyms benefit, improve.

harmful *adj.* damaging, destructive, detrimental, injurious, pernicious.
antonym harmless.

harmless *adj.* gentle, innocent, innocuous, inoffensive, non-toxic, safe, uninjured.
antonyms dangerous, destructive, harmful.

harmonious *adj.* agreeable, amicable, balanced, compatible, co-ordinated, cordial, friendly, matching, melodious, musical, sweet-sounding, sympathetic, tuneful.
antonym discordant.

harmonise *v.* accommodate, adapt, agree, arrange, blend, compose, co-ordinate, correspond, fit in, match, reconcile, suit, tone.
antonym clash.

harmony *n.* accord, agreement, amicability, balance, compatibility, concord, conformity, co-operation, co-ordination, correspondence, like-mindedness, parallelism, peace, rapport, suitability, symmetry, sympathy, tune, tunefulness, unanimity, understanding, unity.
antonyms conflict, discord.

harness *n.* equipment, gear, reins, straps, tack, tackle, trappings.
v. apply, channel, control, couple, employ, exploit, make use of, mobilise, saddle, use, utilise.

harp on (about) dwell on, labour, press, reiterate, renew, repeat.

harpoon *n.* arrow, barb, dart, spear.

harrowing *adj.* agonising, alarming, distressing, disturbing, excruciating, frightening, heart-rending, nerve-racking, terrifying, tormenting, traumatic.
antonyms calming, heartening.

harry *v.* annoy, chivvy, devastate, disturb, fret, harass, hassle, molest, persecute, pester, plague, plunder, raid, tease, torment, trouble, vex, worry.
antonyms calm, help.

harsh *adj.* **1** austere, bleak, comfortless, cruel, Draconian, grim, hard, pitiless, ruthless, severe,

Spartan, unfeeling. **2** coarse, croaking, discordant, grating, guttural, jarring, rasping, rough, sharp, strident, unpleasant.
antonyms **1** lenient. **2** soft.

harvest *n.* collection, consequence, crop, harvesting, harvest-time, ingathering, produce, product, reaping, result, return, yield.
v. accumulate, amass, collect, gather, mow, pick, pluck, reap.

hash *n.* **1** botch, confusion, hotchpotch, jumble, mess, mishmash, mix-up, muddle, shambles. **2** goulash, hotpot, stew.

hashish *n.* cannabis, dope, grass, hash, hemp, marijuana, pot.

haste *n.* briskness, bustle, hurry, hustle, quickness, rapidity, rashness, rush, speed, urgency, velocity.
antonym slowness.

hasten *v.* accelerate, advance, bolt, dash, dispatch, expedite, fly, hurry, make haste, precipitate, press, quicken, race, run, rush, scurry, scuttle, speed (up), sprint, step on it, step up, tear, trot, urge.
antonyms dawdle, delay.

hasty *adj.* brisk, fast, headlong, heedless, hotheaded, hurried, impatient, impetuous, impulsive, prompt, quick, rapid, rash, reckless, rushed, short, speedy, swift, thoughtless, urgent.
antonyms careful, deliberate, slow.

hat *n.* beret, biretta, boater, bonnet, bowler, cap, deerstalker, night-cap, skull-cap, sombrero, sou'wester, tam-o'-shanter, top-hat, trilby, yarmulka.

hatch *v.* **1** breed, brood, incubate. **2** conceive, concoct, contrive, design, develop, devise, dream up, originate, plan, plot, project, think up.

hate *v.* abhor, abominate, despise, detest, dislike, loathe.
antonyms like, love.
n. abhorrence, abomination, animosity, antagonism, aversion, dislike, enmity, hatred, hostility, loathing.
antonyms like, love.

hatred *n.* abomination, animosity, antagonism, aversion, dislike, enmity, hate, ill-will, repugnance, revulsion.
antonyms like, love.

haughty *adj.* arrogant, assuming, cavalier, conceited, contemptuous, disdainful, high and mighty, imperious, lofty, proud, scornful, snobbish, snooty, stuck-up, supercilious, superior.
antonyms friendly, humble.

haul *v.* carry, cart, convey, drag, draw, heave, hump, lug, move, pull, tow, trail, transport, tug.
antonym push.
n. **1** catch, drag, heave, pull, tug. **2** booty, find, gain, loot, spoils, swag, takings, yield.
antonym **1** push.

haunches *n.* buttocks, thighs.

haunt *v.* **1** frequent, visit. **2** beset, disturb, obsess, plague, possess, prey on, recur, torment, trouble.
n. den, gathering-place, hangout, meeting place, rendezvous, resort, stamping ground.

haunted *adj.* cursed, eerie, ghostly, jinxed, plagued, possessed, spooky, tormented, troubled, worried.

haunting *adj.* evocative, memorable, nostalgic, persistent, poignant, recurrent, recurring, unforgettable.
antonym unmemorable.

have *v.* **1** accept, acquire, endure, enjoy, experience, feel, gain, get, hold, keep, obtain, own, possess, procure, put up with, receive, secure, suffer, undergo. **2** bear, give birth to. **3** comprehend, contain, include, incorporate.
antonym **1** lack.
have done with be through with, cease, finish with, give up, stop.
have to be compelled, be forced, be obliged, be required, have got to, must, ought, should.

haven *n.* anchorage, asylum, harbour, port, refuge, retreat, sanctuary, shelter.

havoc *n.* chaos, confusion, damage, desolation, destruction, devastation, disorder, disruption, rack and ruin, ravages, ruin, slaughter, waste, wreck.

hawk *v.* offer, peddle, sell, tout, vend.

haywire *adj.* chaotic, confused, crazy, disordered, disorganised, mad, out of control, tangled, topsy-turvy, wild, wrong.
antonyms correct, in order.

hazard *n.* accident, chance, danger, death-trap, misfortune, peril, risk, threat.
antonym safety.
v. **1** endanger, expose, jeopardise. **2** chance, gamble, risk, speculate, suggest, suppose.

hazardous *adj.* chancy, dangerous, difficult, haphazard, insecure, precarious, risky.
antonyms safe, secure, sure.

haze *n.* cloud, dimness, film, fog, mist, obscurity, smog, smokiness, steam, unclearness, vapour.

hazy *adj.* blurred, clouded, cloudy, dull, faint, foggy, fuzzy, ill-defined, indefinite, indistinct, loose, milky, misty, obscure, overcast, smoky, uncertain, unclear, vague, veiled.
antonyms bright, clear, definite.

head *n.* **1** brain, brains, cranium, intellect, intelligence, mentality, mind, skull, thought, understanding. **2** climax, crown, fore, front, height, peak, summit, tip, top. **3** boss, captain, chief, commander, director, head teacher, leader, manager, master, principal, superintendent, supervisor.
antonyms **1** foot, tail. **2** base. **3** subordinate.
adj. chief, dominant, first, foremost, front, highest, leading, main, pre-eminent, premier, prime, principal, supreme, top.
v. command, control, direct, govern, guide, lead, manage, oversee, rule, run, steer, superintend, supervise.
head for aim for, direct towards, gravitate towards, make for, point to, steer for, turn for, zero in on.
head off avert, deflect, distract, divert, fend off, forestall, intercept, interpose, intervene, pre-

vent, stop, ward off.
headache *n.* **1** migraine, neuralgia. **2** bother, hassle, inconvenience, nuisance, problem, trouble, vexation, worry.
heading *n.* caption, category, class, division, headline, name, rubric, section, title.
headland *n.* cape, cliff, foreland, head, point, promontory.
headlong *adj.* breakneck, dangerous, hasty, head-first, impetuous, impulsive.
adv. hastily, head first, heedlessly, hurriedly, precipitately, rashly, thoughtlessly, wildly.
head-man *n.* captain, chief, leader, ruler.
headquarters *n.* base (camp), head office, high command, HQ, nerve centre.
headstrong *adj.* intractable, obstinate, perverse, pig-headed, self-willed, stubborn, wilful.
antonyms docile, obedient.
headway *n.* advance, improvement, inroad(s), progress, way.
heady *adj.* exciting, exhilarating, hasty, impulsive, inconsiderate, intoxicating, rash, reckless, spirituous, stimulating, strong, thoughtless, thrilling.
heal *v.* cure, mend, patch up, reconcile, remedy, restore, salve, settle, soothe, treat.
health *n.* condition, constitution, fitness, form, good condition, haleness, heal, healthiness, robustness, shape, soundness, state, strength, tone, vigour, welfare, well-being.
antonyms disease, infirmity.
healthy *adj.* **1** blooming, fine, fit, flourishing, good, hale (and hearty), in fine fettle, in fine form, in good condition, physically fit, robust, sound, strong, sturdy, thriving, vigorous, well, wholesome. **2** bracing, invigorating, nourishing, nutritious.
antonyms **1** ill, infirm, sick.
heap *n.* accumulation, collection, hoard, lot, mass, mound, mountain, pile, stack, stockpile, store.
v. accumulate, amass, bank, build, burden, collect, confer, gather, hoard, increase, lavish, load, mound, pile, shower, stack, stockpile, store.
heaps *n.* a lot, abundance, great deal, load(s), lots, mass, millions, plenty, quantities, scores, stack(s), tons.
hear *v.* **1** catch, eavesdrop, hearken, listen, overhear, pick up. **2** acknowledge, ascertain, discover, examine, find, gather, heed, investigate, judge, learn, try, understand.
hearing *n.* **1** ear, ear-shot, perception, range, reach, sound. **2** audience, enquiry, interview, investigation, trial.
hearsay *n.* buzz, gossip, grapevine, report, rumour, talk, talk of the town, tittle-tattle, word of mouth.
heart *n.* **1** character, compassion, disposition, emotion, feeling, love, mind, nature, pity, sentiment, soul, sympathy, temperament, tenderness. **2** boldness, bravery, courage, resolution, spirit. **3** centre, core, crux, essence, middle, nerve centre, nub, nucleus.
antonyms **2** cowardice. **3** periphery.
by heart by rote, off pat, parrot-fashion, pat, word for word.
heart and soul absolutely, completely, eagerly, entirely, gladly, unreservedly, whole-heartedly.
heartache *n.* affliction, agony, anguish, dejection, despair, distress, grief, heartbreak, pain, sorrow, suffering, torment, torture.
heartbreaking *adj.* agonising, bitter, disappointing, distressing, grievous, harrowing, heart-rending, pitiful, sad, tragic.
antonyms heartening, heartwarming, joyful.
heartbroken *adj.* broken-hearted, crestfallen, crushed, dejected, desolate, despondent, disappointed, dispirited, downcast, grieved, miserable.
antonyms delighted, elated.
hearten *v.* cheer, comfort, console, encourage, incite, inspire, pep up, reassure, rouse, stimulate.
antonym dishearten.
heart-felt *adj.* deep, devout, earnest, fervent, genuine, honest, profound, sincere, warm, whole-hearted.
antonyms false, insincere.
heartless *adj.* brutal, callous, cold, cruel, hard, hard-hearted, harsh, merciless, pitiless, uncaring, unfeeling, unkind.
antonyms considerate, kind, merciful, sympathetic.
heart-rending *adj.* affecting, distressing, harrowing, heartbreaking, moving, pathetic, piteous, pitiful, poignant, sad, tragic.
heart-throb *n.* idol, pin-up, star.
heartwarming *adj.* affecting, cheering, encouraging, heartening, moving, pleasing, rewarding, satisfying, touching, warming.
antonym heart-breaking.
hearty *adj.* **1** boisterous, cheerful, ebullient, energetic, enthusiastic, exuberant, friendly, generous, jovial, unreserved, vigorous, warm, whole-hearted. **2** active, real, strong, thorough. **3** ample, filling, sizeable, substantial.
antonyms **1** cold, cool, emotionless.
heat *n.* **1** fever, sizzle, sultriness, swelter, warmth. **2** ardour, earnestness, excitement, fervour, fieriness, fury, impetuosity, intensity, passion, vehemence, zeal.
antonyms **1** cold(ness). **2** coolness.
v. animate, excite, flush, glow, inflame, reheat, rouse, stimulate, stir, toast, warm up.
antonyms chill, cool.
heated *adj.* acrimonious, angry, bitter, excited, fierce, fiery, frenzied, furious, intense, passionate, raging, stormy, tempestuous, vehement, violent.
antonyms calm, dispassionate.
heave *v.* **1** drag, haul, hitch, hoist, lever, lift, pull, raise, rise, surge, tug. **2** cast, chuck, fling, hurl, let fly, send, throw, toss. **3** breathe, exhale, groan, palpitate, pant, puff, sigh, sob. **4** retch, spew, throw up, vomit.
heaven *n.* bliss, ecstasy, firmament, happiness, hereafter, next world, paradise, rapture, sky,

utopia.
antonym hell.

heavenly *adj.* **1** beautiful, blissful, delightful, glorious, lovely, ravishing, wonderful. **2** angelic, blessed, celestial, divine, godlike, holy, immortal, sublime, superhuman, supernatural.
antonym **2** hellish.

heavy *adj.* **1** bulky, hefty, large, massive, solid, stodgy, weighty. **2** burdensome, hard, harsh, intense, oppressive, serious, severe, tedious, violent. **3** crestfallen, dejected, depressed, despondent, downcast, gloomy, oppressed, sad, sorrowful.
antonyms **1** airy, light. **2** slight. **3** happy.

heavy-handed *adj.* autocratic, awkward, domineering, graceless, harsh, insensitive, oppressive, overbearing, tactless, thoughtless, unsubtle.

heckle *v.* bait, barrack, disrupt, gibe, interrupt, jeer, pester, shout down, taunt.

hectic *adj.* busy, chaotic, excited, fast, feverish, frantic, frenetic, furious, heated, wild.
antonyms leisurely, quiet.

hedge *n.* **1** barrier, boundary, dike, dyke, guard, hedgerow, screen, wind-break. **2** compensation, counterbalance, insurance, protection.
v. **1** block, confine, cover, fortify, guard, hem in, hinder, obstruct, protect, restrict, safeguard, shield. **2** dodge, duck, equivocate, sidestep, stall.

heedless *adj.* careless, inattentive, negligent, oblivious, rash, reckless, thoughtless, unconcerned, unobservant, unthinking.
antonyms attentive, heedful, mindful.

hefty *adj.* ample, beefy, big, brawny, bulky, burly, colossal, forceful, heavy, hulking, large, massive, powerful, robust, solid, strapping, strong, substantial, thumping, tremendous, unwieldy, vigorous, weighty.
antonyms slight, small.

height *n.* **1** altitude, elevation, highness, loftiness, stature, tallness. **2** apex, ceiling, climax, crest, crown, culmination, degree, dignity, exaltation, extremity, grandeur, limit, maximum, mountain, peak, pinnacle, prominence, summit, top, ultimate, utmost.
antonym **1** depth.

heighten *v.* add to, elevate, enhance, improve, increase, intensify, magnify, raise, sharpen, strengthen.
antonyms decrease, diminish.

heir *n.* beneficiary, co-heir, heiress, inheritor, successor.

hell *n.* abyss, affliction, agony, anguish, inferno, lower regions, misery, nether world, nightmare, ordeal, suffering, torment, trial, underworld.
antonym heaven.

hell-bent *adj.* determined, fixed, intent, resolved, set, settled.

hellish *adj.* **1** abominable, atrocious, cruel, detestable, dreadful, fiendish, infernal, monstrous, vicious, wicked. **2** accursed, damnable, devilish, diabolical.
antonym **2** heavenly.

helm *n.* command, control, direction, driving seat, leadership, reins, rudder, rule, saddle, wheel.

help *v.* **1** aid, assist, back, be of use, co-operate, stand by, support. **2** alleviate, ameliorate, ease, facilitate, improve, mitigate, relieve.
antonyms **1** hinder. **2** worsen.
n. **1** advice, aid, assistance, avail, benefit, co-operation, guidance, service, support, use, utility. **2** assistant, daily, employee, hand, helper, worker.
antonym **1** hindrance.

helper *n.* ally, assistant, attendant, auxiliary, collaborator, colleague, deputy, girl Friday, man Friday, mate, PA, partner, right-hand man, second, subsidiary, supporter.

helpful *adj.* caring, considerate, constructive, co-operative, fortunate, friendly, kind, neighbourly, practical, supportive, sympathetic, useful.
antonyms futile, useless.

helping *n.* amount, dollop, piece, plateful, portion, ration, serving, share.

helpless *adj.* abandoned, defenceless, dependent, destitute, disabled, exposed, feeble, forlorn, friendless, incapable, incompetent, infirm, paralysed, powerless, unprotected, vulnerable, weak.
antonyms competent, independent, resourceful, strong.

helter-skelter *adv.* carelessly, confusedly, hastily, headlong, hurriedly, impulsively, pell-mell, rashly, recklessly, wildly.
adj. confused, disordered, disorganised, haphazard, higgledy-piggledy, hit-or-miss, jumbled, muddled, random, rushed, topsy-turvy, unsystematic.

hem *n.* border, edge, fringe, margin, skirt, trimming.
hem in box in, confine, enclose, restrict, surround.

henchman *n.* aide, associate, attendant, bodyguard, cohort, crony, follower, heavy, minder, minion, right-hand man, sidekick, subordinate, supporter.

henpecked *adj.* browbeaten, bullied, cringing, dominated, intimidated, meek, subject, subjugated, timid.
antonym dominant.

herald *n.* courier, crier, forerunner, harbinger, indication, messenger, omen, precursor, sign, signal, token.
v. advertise, announce, broadcast, indicate, pave the way, precede, proclaim, promise, publicise, publish, show, trumpet, usher in.

heraldry *n.* arms, badge, blazonry, crest, emblem, ensign, insignia, regalia.

herd *n.* crowd, crush, drove, flock, horde, mass, mob, multitude, pack, press, rabble, swarm, the masses, throng.
v. assemble, associate, collect, congregate, drive, flock, force, gather, guide, lead, protect, rally, shepherd.

hereditary *adj.* ancestral, bequeathed, congenital, family, genetic, handed down, inborn,

inbred, inherited, traditional, willed.
heresy *n.* apostasy, dissidence, error, free-thinking, heterodoxy, schism, unorthodoxy.
antonym orthodoxy.
heretic *n.* apostate, dissenter, dissident, free-thinker, nonconformist, renegade, revisionist, schismatic, sectarian, separatist.
antonym conformist.
heretical *adj.* free-thinking, heterodox, impious, irreverent, rationalistic, schismatic.
antonyms conformist, conventional, orthodox.
heritage *n.* bequest, birthright, due, endowment, estate, history, inheritance, legacy, lot, past, portion, record, share, tradition.
hermetic *adj.* airtight, sealed, shut, watertight.
hermit *n.* ascetic, monk, recluse, solitaire, solitarian.
hero *n.* celebrity, champion, conqueror, goody, heart-throb, idol, paragon, protagonist, star, superstar.
heroic *adj.* bold, brave, courageous, daring, dauntless, fearless, intrepid, legendary, lion-hearted, mythological, stout-hearted, undaunted, valiant.
antonyms cowardly, timid.
heroine *n.* celebrity, champion, conquerer, goddess, goody, ideal, idol, paragon, protagonist, star, superstar.
heroism *n.* boldness, bravery, courage, daring, gallantry, intrepidity, prowess, spirit, valour.
antonyms cowardice, timidity.
hesitancy *n.* indecision, irresolution, reluctance, reservation, wavering.
antonyms certainty, willingness.
hesitant *adj.* half-hearted, halting, hesitating, irresolute, reluctant, shy, timid, uncertain, unsure, vacillating, wavering.
antonyms resolute, staunch.
hesitate *v.* be reluctant, be uncertain, be unwilling, boggle, delay, demur, dither, doubt, falter, fumble, halt, pause, scruple, shillyshally, shrink from, stammer, stumble, stutter, think twice, vacillate, wait, waver.
antonyms be confident, decide.
hesitation *n.* delay, doubt, faltering, fumbling, indecision, irresolution, misdoubt, misgiving(s), pause, qualm(s), reluctance, scruple(s), second thought(s), stammering, stumbling, stuttering, uncertainty, unwillingness, vacillation.
antonyms assurance, eagerness.
hew *v.* axe, carve, chop, cut, fashion, fell, form, hack, lop, make, model, sculpt, sculpture, sever, shape, split.
heyday *n.* bloom, boom time, flowering, golden age, peak, prime, vigour.
hidden *adj.* abstruse, close, concealed, covered, covert, cryptic, dark, latent, mysterious, mystical, obscure, occult, secret, shrouded, ulterior, unseen, veiled.
antonyms apparent, open, showing.
hide[1] *v.* bury, camouflage, cloak, conceal, cover, disguise, earth, eclipse, go to ground, go underground, hole up, keep dark, lie low, mask, obscure, screen, secrete, shadow, shelter, shroud, stash, suppress, take cover, veil, withhold.
antonyms display, reveal, show.
hide[2] *n.* fell, pelt, skin.
hide-away *n.* cloister, haven, hideout, hiding-place, nest, refuge, retreat, sanctuary.
hidebound *adj.* conventional, entrenched, narrow, narrow-minded, rigid, set, strait-laced, ultra-conservative.
antonyms liberal, progressive, unconventional.
hideous *adj.* appalling, awful, disgusting, dreadful, frightful, ghastly, grim, grotesque, gruesome, horrible, horrid, macabre, monstrous, repulsive, revolting, shocking, terrible, terrifying, ugly.
antonyms attractive, beautiful.
hideout *n.* den, hide-away, hiding-place, hole, lair, retreat, shelter.
hiding[1] *n.* beating, caning, flogging, spanking, tanning, thrashing, walloping, whipping.
hiding[2] *n.* camouflage, concealment, disguise, screening, veiling.
hiding-place *n.* den, haven, hide-away, hideout, hole, lair, lurking-place, priest hole, refuge, retreat, sanctuary, starting-hole.
hierarchy *n.* echelons, grading, pecking order, ranking, scale, strata.
higgledy-piggledy *adv.* any old how, anyhow, confusedly, haphazardly, helter-skelter, indiscriminately, pell-mell, topsy-turvy.
adj. confused, disorderly, disorganised, haphazard, indiscriminate, jumbled, muddled, topsy-turvy.
high *adj.* **1** elevated, lofty, soaring, tall, towering. **2** excessive, extreme, great, intense, sharp, strong. **3** chief, distinguished, eminent, experienced, important, influential, leading, powerful, prominent. **4** altissimo, high-pitched, piercing, shrill, soprano, treble. **5** costly, dear, exorbitant, expensive.
antonyms **1** low, short. **3** lowly. **4** deep. **5** cheap.
n. height, level, peak, record, summit, top.
antonym low.
high-born *adj.* aristocratic, blue-blooded, noble, thoroughbred, well-born.
highbrow *n.* brain, egghead, intellectual, mastermind, scholar.
adj. bookish, brainy, cultivated, cultured, deep, intellectual, serious, sophisticated.
high-class *adj.* choice, classy, de luxe, exclusive, first-rate, high-quality, posh, quality, select, superior, top-flight, upper-class.
antonyms mediocre, ordinary.
high-falutin(g) *adj.* affected, big, grandiose, high-flown, high-sounding, la(h)-di-da(h), lofty, pompous, pretentious, supercilious, swanky.
high-flown *adj.* elaborate, exaggerated, extravagant, florid, grandiose, high-falutin(g), la(h)-di-da(h), pretentious.
high-handed *adj.* arbitrary, autocratic, bossy, despotic, dictatorial, domineering, imperious, inconsiderate, oppressive, overbearing, self-willed, tyrannical.
highlight *n.* best, climax, cream, feature, focal

point, focus, high point, high spot, peak.
v. accentuate, emphasise, feature, focus on, illuminate, play up, point up, set off, show up, spotlight, stress, underline.
highly *adv.* **1** considerably, decidedly, exceptionally, extraordinarily, extremely, greatly, immensely, tremendously, very. **2** appreciatively, approvingly, enthusiastically, favourably, warmly, well.
highly-strung *adj.* edgy, excitable, jittery, nervous, nervy, neurotic, restless, sensitive, temperamental, tense.
antonyms calm, relaxed.
high-minded *adj.* ethical, fair, honourable, idealistic, lofty, moral, noble, principled, pure, righteous, scrupulous, upright, virtuous, worthy.
antonyms immoral, unscrupulous.
high-powered *adj.* aggressive, driving, dynamic, effective, energetic, enterprising, forceful, go-ahead, vigorous.
high-sounding *adj.* affected, artificial, extravagant, flamboyant, grandiose, high-flown, ostentatious, pompous, pretentious, stilted, strained.
high-spirited *adj.* boisterous, bold, bouncy, daring, dashing, ebullient, effervescent, energetic, exuberant, frolicsome, lively, peppy, sparkling, spirited, vibrant, vivacious.
antonyms downcast, glum.
highwayman *n.* bandit, knight of the road, land-pirate, robber.
hijack *v.* commandeer, expropriate, kidnap, seize, skyjack, snatch, steal.
hike *v.* back-pack, leg it, plod, ramble, tramp, treck, trudge, walk.
n. march, plod, ramble, tramp, trek, trudge, walk.
hilarious *adj.* amusing, comical, entertaining, funny, humorous, hysterical, jolly, jovial, noisy, rollicking, side-splitting, uproarious.
antonyms grave, sad, serious.
hilarity *n.* amusement, boisterousness, conviviality, entertainment, exhilaration, exuberance, frivolity, high spirits, jollity, laughter, levity, merriment, mirth.
antonyms gravity, seriousness.
hill *n.* climb, down, drift, elevation, eminence, fell, gradient, height, hillock, hilltop, incline, knoll, mound, mount, prominence, rise, slope.
hilt *n.* grip, haft, handgrip, handle.
hind *adj.* after, back, hinder, rear, tail.
antonym fore.
hinder *v.* check, counteract, delay, deter, encumber, frustrate, hamper, hamstring, handicap, hold back, hold up, impede, interrupt, obstruct, oppose, prevent, retard, slow down, stop, thwart.
antonyms aid, assist, help.
hindrance *n.* bar, barrier, check, deterrent, difficulty, drag, drawback, encumbrance, handicap, hitch, impediment, interruption, limitation, obstacle, obstruction, restraint, restriction, stoppage, stumbling-block.
antonyms aid, assistance, help.
hinge *v.* be contingent, centre, depend, hang, pivot, rest, revolve around, turn.
hint *n.* **1** advice, allusion, clue, help, implication, indication, insinuation, intimation, mention, pointer, reminder, sign, signal, suggestion. **2** dash, inkling, soupçon, speck, suspicion, taste, tinge, tip, tip-off, touch, trace.
v. allude, imply, indicate, insinuate, intimate, mention, prompt, suggest, tip off.
hippy *n.* beatnik, bohemian, drop-out, flower child, hippie.
hire *v.* appoint, book, charter, commission, employ, engage, lease, let, rent, reserve, retain, sign up, take on.
antonyms dismiss, fire.
n. charge, cost, fare, fee, price, rent, rental, toll.
hiss *n.* boo, buzz, catcall, contempt, derision, hissing, hoot, jeer, mockery, whistle.
v. boo, hoot, jeer, mock, ridicule, shrill, whistle.
historic *adj.* celebrated, consequential, epoch-making, extraordinary, famed, famous, momentous, notable, outstanding, remarkable, renowned, significant.
antonyms ordinary, unknown.
historical *adj.* actual, attested, authentic, documented, factual, real, traditional, verifiable.
antonyms contemporary, fictional, legendary.
history *n.* account, annals, antiquity, autobiography, biography, chronicle, chronology, days of old, genealogy, memoirs, narration, narrative, olden days, recital, record, relation, saga, story, tale, the past.
hit *v.* **1** bash, batter, beat, belt, clobber, flog, knock, punch, slap, smack, strike, thump, wallop, whack. **2** bang, bump, collide with, crash, damage, smash.
n. **1** blow, bump, clash, collision, impact, knock, rap, shot, slap, smack, smash, stroke, wallop. **2** success, triumph, winner.
antonym **2** failure.
hit back reciprocate, retaliate.
hit on chance on, discover, guess, invent, light on, realise, stumble on.
hit out assail, attack, condemn, criticise, denounce, lash, lay about one, rail.
hitch *v.* attach, connect, couple, fasten, harness, heave, hike (up), hitch-hike, hoist, jerk, join, pull, tie, tug, unite, yank, yoke.
antonyms unfasten, unhitch.
n. catch, check, delay, difficulty, drawback, hiccup, hindrance, hold-up, impediment, mishap, problem, snag, trouble.
hoard *n.* accumulation, cache, fund, heap, mass, pile, reserve, reservoir, stockpile, store, supply, treasure-trove.
v. accumulate, amass, collect, deposit, gather, husband, lay up, put by, save, stash away, stockpile, store, treasure.
antonyms spend, squander, use.
hoarder *n.* collector, gatherer, magpie, miser, squirrel.
hoarse *adj.* croaky, discordant, grating, gravelly, growling, gruff, guttural, harsh, husky, rasping, raspy, raucous, rough, throaty.

antonyms clear, smooth.
hoary *adj.* aged, ancient, frosty, grey, grey-haired, grizzled, old, silvery, venerable, white, white-haired.
hoax *n.* cheat, con, deception, fast one, fraud, hum, joke, leg-pull, practical joke, prank, put-on, ruse, spoof, string, swindle, trick.
v. bamboozle, bluff, cod, con, deceive, delude, dupe, fool, gull, have on, hoodwink, lead on, pull someone's leg, spoof, swindle, take for a ride, trick.
hobble *v.* clog, dodder, falter, fasten, fetter, halt, limp, shuffle, stagger, stumble, totter.
hobby *n.* diversion, pastime, pursuit, recreation, relaxation, sideline.
hoist *v.* elevate, erect, heave, jack up, lift, raise, rear, uplift.
n. crane, elevator, jack, lift, tackle, winch.
hold *v.* **1** clasp, clutch, embrace, grasp, grip, have, keep, own, possess, retain. **2** assemble, call, carry on, conduct, continue, convene, summon. **3** believe, consider, deem, judge, maintain, reckon, regard, think. **4** accommodate, bear, carry, comprise, contain, support, sustain. **5** arrest, check, curb, detain, imprison, restrain, stop. **6** adhere, cling, stay, stick.
antonyms **1** drop. **5** free, liberate, release. **6** give way, loosen.
n. **1** clasp, grasp, grip, stay, support. **2** authority, control, dominance, dominion, influence, leverage, mastery, sway.
hold back check, control, curb, delay, desist, inhibit, refuse, repress, restrain, retain, stifle, suppress, withhold.
antonym release.
hold off **1** avoid, fend off, keep off, rebuff, refrain, repel, stave off. **2** defer, delay, postpone, put off, wait.
hold out **1** extend, give, offer, present. **2** continue, endure, hang on, last, persevere, persist, stand fast.
antonyms **2** give in, yield.
hold up **1** brace, lift, raise, support, sustain. **2** delay, detain, hinder, impede, retard, slow.
hold with accept, agree to, approve of, countenance, go along with, subscribe to, support.
holder *n.* bearer, case, container, cover, custodian, housing, incumbent, keeper, occupant, owner, possessor, proprietor, purchaser, receptacle, rest, sheath, stand.
holdings *n.* assets, bonds, estate, investments, land, possessions, property, real estate, resources, securities, shares, stocks.
hold-up *n.* **1** bottle-neck, delay, difficulty, hitch, obstruction, setback, snag, stoppage, (traffic) jam, trouble, wait. **2** heist, robbery, stick-up.
hole *n.* aperture, breach, break, burrow, cave, cavern, cavity, chamber, crack, defect, depression, dimple, excavation, fault, fissure, fix, flaw, gap, hollow, hovel, joint, lair, loophole, mess, nest, opening, orifice, outlet, perforation, pit, pocket, pore, puncture, retreat, scrape, shaft, split, spot, tear, tight spot, vent.
holiday *n.* anniversary, break, celebration, feast, festival, festivity, fête, gala, hols, leave, recess, rest, time off, vacation.
holiness *n.* devoutness, godliness, piety, purity, righteousness, sacredness, saintliness, sanctity, spirituality, virtuousness.
antonyms impiety, wickedness.
holler *n.*, *v.* bawl, call, cheer, clamour, cry, hail, halloo, hollo, howl, roar, shout, shriek, whoop, yell, yelp.
hollow *adj.* **1** cavernous, concave, deep, depressed, indented, sunken, unfilled. **2** artificial, deceptive, empty, false, flimsy, fruitless, futile, insincere, meaningless, worthless.
antonyms **1** solid. **2** real.
n. basin, bottom, bowl, cave, cavern, cavity, channel, concavity, crater, cup, dent, depression, dimple, excavation, groove, hole, hope, indentation, pit, trough, valley, well.
v. burrow, channel, dent, dig, dint, excavate, furrow, gouge, groove, indent, pit, scoop.
holocaust *n.* annihilation, carnage, destruction, devastation, extermination, extinction, flames, genocide, inferno, mass murder, massacre, sacrifice, slaughter.
holy *adj.* blessed, consecrated, dedicated, devout, divine, evangelical, faithful, god-fearing, godly, good, hallowed, perfect, pious, pure, religious, righteous, sacred, sacrosanct, saintly, sanctified, spiritual, venerated, virtuous.
antonyms impious, unsanctified, wicked.
homage *n.* acknowledgement, admiration, adoration, adulation, allegiance, awe, deference, devotion, duty, esteem, faithfulness, fidelity, honour, loyalty, praise, recognition, regard, respect, reverence, service, tribute, veneration, worship.
home *n.* abode, birthplace, dwelling, dwelling-place, family, fireside, hearth, home ground, home town, homestead, house, nest, pied-à-terre, residence, roof, territory.
adj. **1** central, direct, domestic, familiar, family, household, inland, internal, intimate, local, national, native. **2** candid, penetrating, plain, pointed, uncomfortable.
antonym **1** foreign.
at home **1** at ease, comfortable, relaxed. **2** experienced, knowledgeable, skilled.
homeland *n.* fatherland, mother country, motherland, native country, native land, native soil.
homeless *adj.* abandoned, destitute, disinherited, displaced, dispossessed, down-and-out, exiled, forlorn, forsaken, houseless, itinerant, outcast, unsettled, vagabond, wandering.
n. derelicts, dossers, down-and-outs, squatters, tramps, travellers, vagrants.
homely *adj.* comfortable, cosy, domestic, everyday, familiar, folksy, friendly, homelike, homespun, informal, intimate, modest, natural, ordinary, plain, relaxed, simple, snug, unassuming, unpretentious.
antonyms formal, grand.
homespun *adj.* amateurish, artless, crude, folksy, homely, home-made, plain, rough, rude,

rustic, unpolished, unrefined, unsophisticated.
antonym sophisticated.

homicidal *adj.* blood-thirsty, deadly, lethal, murderous, violent.

homicide *n.* assassination, bloodshed, killing, manslaughter, murder, slaying.

homogeneous *adj.* alike, analogous, comparable, consistent, consonant, harmonious, identical, kindred, similar, uniform, unvarying.
antonym different.

homosexual *n.* lesbian, poof, queer.
antonyms heterosexual, straight.

hone *v.* edge, file, grind, point, polish, rasp, sharpen, whet.

honest *adj.* above-board, candid, direct, ethical, fair, forthright, frank, genuine, high-minded, honourable, impartial, just, law-abiding, legitimate, modest, objective, on the level, open, outright, outspoken, plain, real, reliable, reputable, respectable, scrupulous, simple, sincere, straight, straightforward, true, trustworthy, truthful, upright, virtuous.
antonyms devious, dishonest, dishonourable.

honestly *adv.* conscientiously, directly, fairly, frankly, honourably, in all sincerity, in good faith, justly, lawfully, legally, legitimately, objectively, on the level, openly, outright, plainly, really, sincerely, truly, truthfully, unreservedly.
antonyms dishonestly, dishonourably.

honesty *n.* candour, equity, even-handedness, explicitness, fairness, faithfulness, fidelity, frankness, genuineness, honour, integrity, justness, morality, objectivity, openness, outspokenness, plain-speaking, scrupulousness, sincerity, straightforwardness, trustworthiness, truthfulness, uprightness, veracity, virtue.
antonyms deviousness, dishonesty.

honorary *adj.* complimentary, ex officio, formal, honorific, in name only, nominal, titular, unofficial, unpaid.
antonyms paid, salaried, waged.

honour *n.* **1** credit, dignity, distinction, esteem, good name, pride, privilege, regard, renown, reputation, repute, respect, self-respect. **2** accolade, acknowledgement, award, commendation, recognition, tribute. **3** acclaim, admiration, adoration, homage, praise, reverence, worship.
antonyms **1** disgrace, dishonour.
v. **1** acclaim, admire, adore, commemorate, crown, decorate, esteem, exalt, glorify, hallow, pay homage, praise, prize, respect, revere, value, worship. **2** accept, acknowledge, carry out, celebrate, discharge, execute, fulfil, keep, observe, perform, remember, respect.
antonyms **1** disgrace, dishonour.

honourable *adj.* distinguished, eminent, ethical, fair, great, high-minded, honest, just, moral, noble, prestigious, principled, proper, renowned, reputable, respectable, respected, right, righteous, sincere, straight, true, trustworthy, trusty, upright, upstanding, virtuous, worthy.
antonyms dishonest, dishonourable, unworthy.

hoodwink *v.* bamboozle, cheat, con, deceive, delude, dupe, fool, gull, have on, hoax, mislead, rook, swindle, take in, trick.

hook *n.* barb, catch, clasp, fastener, hasp, holder, link, lock, peg, sickle, snare, trap.
v. bag, catch, clasp, collar, ensnare, entangle, fasten, fix, grab, hitch, secure, snare, trap.

hooked *adj.* **1** barbed, beaked, bent, curled, curved, sickle-shaped. **2** addicted, devoted, enamoured, obsessed.

hooligan *n.* bovver boy, delinquent, hoodlum, lout, mobster, rough, rowdy, ruffian, thug, tough, vandal, yob.

hoop *n.* bail, band, circle, circlet, girdle, loop, ring, round, wheel.

hoot *n.* beep, boo, call, catcall, cry, hiss, howl, jeer, laugh, scream, shout, shriek, toot, whistle, whoop, yell.
v. beep, boo, cry, explode, hiss, howl down, jeer, ridicule, scream, shout, shriek, toot, ululate, whistle, whoop, yell.

hop *v.* bound, dance, fly, frisk, hobble, jump, leap, limp, prance, skip, spring, vault.
n. ball, barn-dance, bounce, crossing, dance, jump, leap, skip, spring, step, trip, vault.

hope *n.* ambition, anticipation, aspiration, assurance, belief, confidence, conviction, desire, dream, expectation, faith, hopefulness, longing, optimism, promise, prospect, wish.
antonyms apathy, despair, pessimism.
v. anticipate, aspire, assume, await, believe, contemplate, desire, expect, foresee, long, reckon on, rely, trust, wish.
antonym despair.

hopeful *adj.* assured, auspicious, bright, bullish, buoyant, cheerful, confident, encouraging, expectant, favourable, heartening, optimistic, promising, reassuring, rosy, sanguine.
antonyms despairing, discouraging, pessimistic.

hopeless *adj.* defeatist, dejected, demoralised, despairing, despondent, downhearted, foolish, forlorn, futile, helpless, impossible, impracticable, lost, pessimistic, pointless, poor, reckless, unachievable, unattainable, useless, vain, worthless, wretched.
antonyms curable, hopeful, optimistic.

horde *n.* band, bevy, concourse, crew, crowd, drove, flock, gang, herd, host, mob, multitude, pack, press, swarm, throng.

horizon *n.* compass, perspective, prospect, range, realm, scope, skyline, sphere, stretch, verge, vista.

horrible *adj.* abominable, appalling, awful, disagreeable, dreadful, fearful, frightful, ghastly, grim, hideous, horrid, nasty, repulsive, revolting, shocking, terrible, terrifying, unkind, unpleasant, weird.
antonyms agreeable, attractive, pleasant.

horrid *adj.* awful, disagreeable, disgusting, dreadful, horrible, nasty, offensive, repulsive, revolting, shocking, terrible, terrifying.
antonyms agreeable, lovely, pleasant.

horrific *adj.* appalling, awful, dreadful, frightening, ghastly, grim, harrowing, scaring, shocking, terrifying.

horrify *v.* alarm, appal, disgust, dismay, frighten, harrow, intimidate, outrage, scandalise, scare, shock, sicken, startle, terrify.
antonyms delight, gratify, please.

horror *n.* abhorrence, alarm, apprehension, awfulness, consternation, disgust, dismay, dread, fear, fright, frightfulness, ghastliness, hideousness, loathing, outrage, panic, repugnance, revulsion, shock, terror.
antonyms approval, delight.

horror-struck *adj.* appalled, frightened, petrified, shocked, stunned.
antonyms delighted, pleased.

horseman *n.* buckaroo, cavalier, cavalryman, cowboy, equestrian, hussar, jockey, rider.

horsemanship *n.* equestrianism, equitation, manège.

horseplay *n.* capers, clowning, fooling, fooling around, fun and games, high jinks, pranks, romping, rough-and-tumble, rumpus, skylarking.

hospitable *adj.* **1** amicable, congenial, convivial, cordial, friendly, generous, genial, gracious, kind, liberal, receptive, sociable, welcoming. **2** accessible, amenable.
antonyms **1** unfriendly. **2** hostile.

hospital *n.* clinic, lazaret, sanatorium.

hospitality *n.* cheer, conviviality, friendliness, generosity, open-handedness, sociability, warmth, welcome.
antonym unfriendliness.

host[1] *n.* anchor-man, announcer, compère, entertainer, innkeeper, landlord, link man, master of ceremonies, presenter, proprietor.
v. compère, introduce, present.

host[2] *n.* army, array, band, company, horde, legion, multitude, myriad, pack, swarm, throng.

hostel *n.* boarding-house, doss-house, guest-house, hostelry, hotel, inn, residence, youth hostel.

hostile *adj.* adverse, antagonistic, belligerent, contrary, ill-disposed, inhospitable, inimical, malevolent, opposed, opposite, unfriendly, unkind, unsympathetic, warlike.
antonyms friendly, sympathetic, welcoming.

hostilities *n.* battle, bloodshed, conflict, encounter, fighting, strife, war, warfare.

hostility *n.* abhorrence, animosity, antagonism, aversion, dislike, enmity, estrangement, hate, hatred, ill-will, malice, opposition, resentment.
antonyms friendliness, sympathy.

hot *adj.* **1** blistering, boiling, burning, feverish, fiery, heated, roasting, scalding, scorching, sizzling, steaming, sultry, sweltering, torrid, tropical, warm. **2** peppery, piquant, pungent, sharp, spicy, strong.
antonyms **1** cold, cool. **2** mild.

hotbed *n.* breeding-ground, den, hive, nest, nursery, school, seedbed.

hot-blooded *adj.* ardent, bold, eager, excitable, fervent, fiery, heated, high-spirited, impetuous, impulsive, lustful, passionate, rash, sensual, spirited, temperamental, warm-blooded, wild.
antonym cool.

hotchpotch *n.* collection, confusion, jumble, medley, mess, miscellany, mishmash, mix, mixture.

hotel *n.* boarding-house, doss-house, guest-house, inn, motel, pension, pub, public house, tavern.

hothead *n.* daredevil, desperado, hotspur, madcap, madman, tearaway, terror.

hotheaded *adj.* fiery, hasty, headstrong, hot-tempered, impetuous, impulsive, quick-tempered, rash, reckless, volatile.
antonyms calm, cool.

hothouse *n.* conservatory, glasshouse, greenhouse, nursery, plant-house, vinery.

hound *v.* badger, chase, chivvy, drive, goad, harass, hunt (down), impel, persecute, pester, prod, provoke, pursue.

house *n.* **1** building, bungalow, chalet, cottage, dwelling, home, lodgings, maison(n)ette, pied-à-terre, residence, roof, villa. **2** ancestry, blood, clan, dynasty, family, family tree, kindred, line, lineage, race, tribe.
v. **1** accommodate, bed, billet, board, harbour, lodge, put up, quarter, shelter, store, take in. **2** contain, cover, hold, keep, place, protect, sheathe.

household *n.* establishment, family, family circle, home, house, set-up.
adj. common, domestic, established, everyday, familiar, family, home, ordinary, plain, well-known.

householder *n.* freeholder, head of the household, home-owner, landlady, landlord, occupant, occupier, owner, property owner, proprietor, resident, tenant.

housing *n.* **1** accommodation, dwellings, habitation, homes, houses, living quarters, roof, shelter. **2** case, casing, container, cover, covering, enclosure, holder, protection, sheath.

hovel *n.* cabin, croft, den, dump, hole, hut, shack, shanty, shed.

hover *v.* drift, flap, float, fluctuate, flutter, fly, hang, hang about, hesitate, linger, loom, pause, poise, seesaw, waver.

however *conj.* anyhow, but, even so, in spite of that, nevertheless, nonetheless, notwithstanding, still, though, yet.

howl *n.* bay, bellow, clamour, cry, groan, holler, hoot, outcry, roar, scream, shriek, wail, yell, yelp.
v. bellow, cry, holler, hoot, lament, roar, scream, shout, shriek, wail, weep, yell, yelp.

hub *n.* axis, centre, core, focal point, focus, heart, linchpin, middle, nerve centre, pivot.

hubbub *n.* chaos, confusion, din, disorder, disturbance, hue and cry, hullabaloo, hurly-burly, noise, palaver, pandemonium, racket, riot, rumpus, tumult, uproar, upset.
antonyms calm, peace.

huddle *n.* clump, clutch, conclave, crowd, disorder, heap, jumble, knot, mass, muddle.
v. cluster, congregate, converge, crouch, crowd,

cuddle, curl up, flock, gather, gravitate, hunch, meet, nestle, press, snuggle, throng.
antonym disperse.
hue *n.* aspect, colour, complexion, dye, light, nuance, shade, tinge, tint, tone.
hue and cry clamour, furore, hullabaloo, outcry, rumpus, uproar.
huff *n.* anger, bad mood, mood, passion, pique, sulks, tiff.
hug *v.* clasp, cling to, clutch, cuddle, embrace, enclose, enfold, follow, grip, hold, lock, skirt, squeeze.
n. clasp, clinch, cuddle, embrace, squeeze.
huge *adj.* bulky, colossal, enormous, giant, gigantic, great, immense, large, mammoth, massive, monumental, tremendous, unwieldy, vast, walloping, whacking.
antonyms minute, tiny.
hulking *adj.* awkward, bulky, massive, overgrown, ungainly, unwieldy.
antonyms delicate, small.
hull[1] *n.* body, casing, covering, frame, framework, structure.
hull[2] *n.* capsule, husk, legume, peel, pod, rind, shell, skin.
v. husk, pare, peel, shell, skin, strip, trim.
hullabaloo *n.* chaos, clamour, commotion, confusion, din, disturbance, furore, fuss, hue and cry, noise, outcry, pandemonium, panic, racket, rumpus, to-do, uproar.
hum *v.* buzz, croon, drone, move, mumble, murmur, pulse, purr, sing, stir, throb, thrum, vibrate, whirr, zoom.
n. buzz, drone, mumble, murmur, noise, pulsation, purring, stir, throb, vibration, whirr.
human *adj.* compassionate, considerate, fallible, humane, kind, kindly, mortal, natural, reasonable, susceptible, understandable, understanding.
antonym inhuman.
n. body, child, creature, homo sapiens, human being, individual, living soul, man, mortal, person, soul, woman.
humane *adj.* benevolent, charitable, compassionate, forbearing, forgiving, gentle, good, good-natured, kind, kind-hearted, kindly, lenient, loving, merciful, mild, sympathetic, tender, understanding.
antonyms cruel, inhumane.
humanise *v.* better, civilise, domesticate, edify, educate, enlighten, improve, polish, reclaim, refine, soften, tame, temper.
humanitarian *adj.* altruistic, benevolent, charitable, compassionate, humane, philanthropic, public-spirited.
n. altruist, benefactor, do-gooder, Good Samaritan, philanthropist.
antonyms egoist, self-seeker.
humanitarianism *n.* benevolence, charitableness, charity, compassionateness, generosity, goodwill, humanism, loving-kindness, philanthropy.
antonyms egoism, self-seeking.
humanity *n.* **1** human race, humankind, mankind, mortality, people. **2** benevolence, compassion, fellow-feeling, generosity, goodwill, human nature, humaneness, kindness, tenderness, understanding.
humble *adj.* **1** deferential, lowly, modest, obedient, polite, respectful, self-effacing, servile, submissive, subservient, unassertive, unassuming. **2** common, commonplace, insignificant, ordinary, simple, unimportant, unostentatious, unpretentious.
antonyms **1** assertive, proud. **2** important, pretentious.
v. abase, break, bring down, bring low, chasten, confound, crush, deflate, demean, discredit, disgrace, humiliate, lower, mortify, reduce, shame, sink, subdue.
antonyms exalt, raise.
humbug *n.* **1** baloney, bluff, bunkum, cant, claptrap, deceit, deception, dodge, eyewash, hoax, hype, hypocrisy, nonsense, pretence, rubbish, ruse, sham, swindle, trick, trickery, wile. **2** cheat, con man, fraud, impostor, swindler, trickster.
humdrum *adj.* boring, commonplace, dreary, dull, everyday, monotonous, mundane, ordinary, routine, tedious, tiresome, uneventful, uninteresting.
antonyms exceptional, lively, unusual.
humid *adj.* clammy, damp, moist, muggy, steamy, sticky, sultry, wet.
antonym dry.
humiliate *v.* bring low, chasten, confound, crush, deflate, discredit, disgrace, embarrass, humble, mortify, shame, subdue.
antonyms dignify, exalt, vindicate.
humiliation *n.* abasement, affront, condescension, deflation, disgrace, dishonour, embarrassment, mortification, put-down, rebuff, shame, snub.
antonyms gratification, triumph.
humility *n.* deference, lowliness, meekness, modesty, obedience, self-abasement, servility, submissiveness, unpretentiousness.
antonyms arrogance, assertiveness, pride.
humorist *n.* clown, comedian, comédienne, comic, entertainer, funny man, jester, joker, satirist, wag, wisecracker, wit.
humorous *adj.* amusing, comic, comical, entertaining, facetious, farcical, funny, hilarious, jocular, ludicrous, merry, playful, pleasant, satirical, side-splitting, waggish, whimsical, witty, zany.
antonyms earnest, serious.
humour *n.* **1** amusement, comedy, disposition, drollery, facetiousness, fancy, farce, fun, funniness, gags, jesting, jests, jokes, repartee, spirits, wit. **2** frame of mind, mood, temper, temperament.
v. accommodate, comply with, favour, flatter, go along with, gratify, indulge, mollify, pamper, play up to, spoil.
humourless *adj.* austere, boring, dry, dull, glum, heavy-going, morose, solemn, tedious, thick.
antonyms humorous, witty.

hump *n.* bulge, bump, knob, lump, mound, projection, prominence, protuberance, swelling.

hump-backed *adj.* crookbacked, crooked, deformed, humped, hunchbacked, hunched, misshapen, stooped.
antonyms straight, upright.

hunch *n.* feeling, guess, guesswork, idea, impression, intuition, premonition, suspicion.
v. arch, bend, crouch, curl up, curve, draw in, huddle, hump, shrug, squat, stoop, tense.

hunger *n.* appetite, craving, desire, emptiness, famine, greediness, hungriness, itch, ravenousness, starvation, voracity, yearning.
antonym satisfaction.
v. ache, crave, desire, hanker, itch, long, pine, starve, thirst, want, wish, yearn.

hungry *adj.* aching, craving, desirous, eager, empty, famished, greedy, hollow, longing, peckish, ravenous, starving, underfed, undernourished.
antonym satisfied.

hunk *n.* block, chunk, clod, dollop, lump, mass, piece, slab, wedge.

hunt *v.* chase, dog, forage, gun for, hound, investigate, look for, pursue, rummage, scour, search, seek, track, trail.
n. chase, investigation, pursuit, quest, search.

hurdle *n.* barricade, barrier, complication, difficulty, fence, handicap, hedge, hindrance, impediment, jump, obstacle, obstruction, problem, snag, stumbling-block, wall.

hurl *v.* catapult, fire, fling, launch, project, propel, send, sling, throw, toss.

hurly-burly *n.* bustle, chaos, commotion, confusion, disorder, furore, hubbub, hustle.

hurricane *n.* cyclone, gale, squall, storm, tempest, tornado, typhoon, whirlwind.

hurried *adj.* breakneck, brief, careless, hasty, hectic, passing, precipitate, quick, rushed, shallow, short, slapdash, speedy, superficial, swift.
antonym leisurely.

hurry *v.* dash, fly, get a move on, hasten, hustle, move, quicken, rush, speed up.
antonyms dally, delay, slow down.
n. bustle, commotion, flurry, quickness, rush, scurry, speed, urgency.
antonyms calm, leisureliness.

hurt *v.* ache, afflict, annoy, bruise, burn, damage, disable, distress, grieve, harm, impair, injure, maim, maltreat, mar, pain, sadden, spoil, sting, throb, torture, upset, wound.
n. abuse, discomfort, distress, harm, injury, pain, sore, soreness, suffering, wound.
adj. aggrieved, annoyed, bruised, crushed, cut up, damaged, grazed, harmed, huffed, injured, maimed, offended, sad, saddened, scarred, wounded.

hurtful *adj.* catty, cruel, cutting, damaging, derogatory, destructive, harmful, humiliating, injurious, malicious, mean, nasty, pernicious, scathing, spiteful, unkind, upsetting, vicious, wounding.
antonyms helpful, kind.

hurtle *v.* charge, chase, crash, dash, fly, plunge, race, rattle, rush, scoot, scramble, shoot, speed, spin, spurt, tear.

husband *n.* better half, groom, hubby, man, married man, mate, partner, spouse.
v. budget, conserve, economise, eke out, hoard, ration, save, save up, store, use sparingly.
antonyms squander, waste.

husbandry *n.* agriculture, conservation, cultivation, farming, good housekeeping, land management, management, thrift.
antonym wastefulness.

hush *v.* calm, compose, quieten, settle, silence, soothe, still, subdue.
antonyms disturb, rouse.
n. calm, calmness, peace, quietness, repose, serenity, silence, stillness, tranquillity.
antonyms clamour, uproar.
interj. hold your tongue, not another word, quiet, shut up.
hush up conceal, cover up, gag, keep dark, squash, stifle, suppress.
antonym publicise.

hush-hush *adj.* classified, confidential, restricted, secret, top-secret, under wraps, unpublished.
antonyms open, public.

husk *n.* bark, bran, case, chaff, covering, hull, pod, rind, shell.

husky[1] *adj.* croaking, croaky, gruff, guttural, harsh, hoarse, low, rasping, rough, throaty.

husky[2] *adj.* beefy, brawny, burly, hefty, muscular, powerful, rugged, stocky, strapping, strong, sturdy, thickset, tough.

hustle *v.* bundle, elbow, force, hasten, hurry, jog, jostle, push, rush, shove, thrust.

hut *n.* booth, cabin, den, lean-to, shack, shanty, shed, shelter.

hybrid *n.* amalgam, combination, composite, compound, conglomerate, cross, crossbreed, half-breed, heterogeny, mixture, mongrel.
adj. combined, composite, compound, cross, heterogeneous, mixed, mongrel, mule.
antonyms pure, pure-bred.

hygiene *n.* cleanliness, disinfection, purity, sanitation, sterility, wholesomeness.
antonyms filth, insanitariness.

hygienic *adj.* clean, disinfected, germ-free, healthy, pure, salubrious, sanitary, sterile, wholesome.
antonym unhygenic.

hyperbole *n.* exaggeration, extravagance, magnification, overstatement.
antonym understatement.

hypnotic *adj.* compelling, irresistible, magnetic, mesmerising, sleep-inducing, soporific, spellbinding.

hypnotise *v.* captivate, entrance, fascinate, magnetise, mesmerise, spellbind.

hypnotism *n.* hypnosis, mesmerism, suggestion.

hypocrisy *n.* deceit, deception, double-talk, falsity, insincerity, pretence, two-facedness.
antonym sincerity.

hypocrite *n.* charlatan, deceiver, fraud, impostor, phon(e)y, pretender.

hypocritical *adj.* deceitful, deceptive, dissembling, double-faced, false, fraudulent, hollow, insincere, pharisaic(al), phoney, self-righteous, specious, spurious, two-faced.
antonyms genuine, humble, sincere.

hypothetical *adj.* imaginary, proposed, speculative, supposed, theoretical.
antonyms actual, real.

hysteria *n.* agitation, frenzy, hysterics, madness, neurosis, panic.
antonyms calm, composure, reason.

hysterical *adj.* **1** berserk, crazed, demented, frantic, frenzied, mad, neurotic, overwrought, raving, uncontrollable. **2** comical, farcical, hilarious, priceless, side-splitting, uproarious.
antonyms **1** calm, composed, self-possessed.

I

ice *n.* **1** chill, coldness, frost, frostiness, ice-cream, iciness, icing, rime. **2** coldness, distance, formality, reserve, stiffness.
v. freeze, frost, glaze.

ice-cold *adj.* arctic, biting, bitter, chilled to the bone, freezing, frozen, frozen to the marrow, glacial, icy, raw, refrigerated.

icon *n.* figure, idol, image, portrait, portrayal, representation, symbol.

icy *adj.* **1** arctic, biting, bitter, chill, chilling, chilly, cold, freezing, frost-bound, frosty, frozen over, glacial, glassy, hoar, ice-cold, raw, slippery. **2** aloof, cool, distant, forbidding, formal, hostile, indifferent, reserved, stiff, stony.
antonyms **1** hot. **2** friendly, warm.

idea *n.* aim, belief, clue, concept, conception, conjecture, design, end, guess, hypothesis, image, impression, inkling, intention, interpretation, judgement, meaning, notion, object, opinion, pattern, perception, plan, purpose, reason, recommendation, scheme, sense, significance, suggestion, suspicion, theory, type, understanding, view, viewpoint, vision.

ideal *n.* archetype, criterion, epitome, example, image, last word, model, paragon, pattern, perfection, principle, prototype, standard, type.
adj. archetypal, best, complete, highest, hypothetical, imaginary, impractical, model, optimal, optimum, perfect, supreme, theoretical, unattainable, unreal.

idealise *v.* exalt, glorify, romanticise, utopianise, worship.
antonym caricature.

idealism *n.* impracticality, perfectionism, romanticism, utopianism.
antonyms pragmatism, realism.

idealist *n.* dreamer, perfectionist, romantic, visionary.
antonyms pragmatist, realist.

idealistic *adj.* impracticable, impractical, optimistic, perfectionist, quixotic, romantic, starry-eyed, unrealistic, utopian, visionary.
antonyms pragmatic, realistic.

identical *adj.* alike, corresponding, duplicate, equal, equivalent, indistinguishable, interchangeable, like, matching, same, self-same, twin.
antonyms different, separate.

identifiable *adj.* ascertainable, detectable, discernible, distinguishable, known, noticeable, perceptible, recognisable, unmistakable.
antonyms indefinable, unfamiliar, unknown.

identification *n.* **1** detection, diagnosis, labelling, naming, pinpointing, recognition, relationship. **2** association, empathy, fellow-feeling, involvement, rapport, sympathy. **3** credentials, documents, identity card, papers.

identify *v.* catalogue, classify, detect, diagnose, distinguish, know, label, make out, name, notice, pick out, pinpoint, place, recognise, single out, specify, tag.
identify with ally with, associate with, empathise with, equate with, feel for, relate to, respond to, sympathise with.

identity *n.* existence, individuality, likeness, oneness, particularity, personality, sameness, self, uniqueness, unity.

ideology *n.* belief(s), convictions, creed, doctrine(s), dogma, faith, ideas, philosophy, principles, tenets, world view.

idiocy *n.* folly, lunacy, senselessness, silliness, stupidity.
antonyms sanity, wisdom.

idiom *n.* colloquialism, expression, jargon, language, phrase, style, turn of phrase, usage, vernacular.

idiomatic *adj.* colloquial, dialectal, grammatical, vernacular.

idiosyncrasy *n.* characteristic, eccentricity, feature, freak, habit, mannerism, oddity, peculiarity, quirk, singularity, trait.

idiosyncratic *adj.* characteristic, distinctive, eccentric, individual, odd, peculiar, quirky, typical.
antonyms common, general.

idiot *n.* ass, blockhead, dimwit, fool, imbecile, mental defective, moron, nitwit.

idiotic *adj.* crazy, daft, foolhardy, foolish, half-witted, harebrained, inane, insane, lunatic, moronic, senseless, simple, stupid.
antonyms sane, sensible.

idle *adj.* **1** inactive, inoperative, jobless, redundant, unemployed, unused. **2** indolent, lazy, work-shy. **3** casual, empty, foolish, futile, pointless, trivial, unproductive, vain.
antonyms **1** active. **2** busy.
v. dally, dawdle, fritter, kill time, laze, loiter, lounge, potter, skive, slack, take it easy, tick over, waste.
antonyms act, work.

idler *n.* clock-watcher, dawdler, do-nothing, good-for-nothing, layabout, lazybones, loafer, shirker, skiver, slacker.

idol *n.* beloved, darling, deity, favourite, fetish, god, graven image, hero, icon, image, pin-up, superstar.

idolise *v.* admire, adore, dote on, exalt, glorify, hero-worship, lionise, love, revere, venerate, worship.
antonym despise.

idyllic *adj.* charming, delightful, happy, heavenly, idealised, pastoral, peaceful, perfect, picturesque, rustic, unspoiled.
antonym unpleasant.

ignite *v.* burn, catch fire, conflagrate, fire, flare up, kindle, set alight, set fire to, spark off, touch off.
antonym quench.

ignoble *adj.* base, contemptible, despicable, disgraceful, dishonourable, heinous, infamous, low, mean, petty, shameless, vile, vulgar, wretched.
antonyms honourable, noble, worthy.

ignominious *adj.* degrading, despicable, discreditable, disgraceful, dishonourable, disreputable, humiliating, mortifying, scandalous, shameful, undignified.
antonyms honourable, triumphant.

ignorance *n.* blindness, inexperience, innocence, naïvety, oblivion, unawareness, unconsciousness, unfamiliarity.
antonyms knowledge, wisdom.

ignorant *adj.* clueless, ill-informed, inexperienced, naïve, oblivious, stupid, unaware, unconscious, uneducated, unenlightened, uninformed, uninitiated, unread, untaught, untrained, unwitting.
antonyms educated, knowlegeable, wise.

ignore *v.* disregard, neglect, omit, overlook, pass over, pay no attention to, reject, set aside, shut one's eyes to, take no notice of.
antonyms notice, observe.

ilk *n.* character, class, description, kind, make, sort, stamp, style, type, variety.

ill *adj.* **1** ailing, diseased, frail, indisposed, infirm, laid up, off-colour, out of sorts, poorly, queasy, seedy, sick, under the weather, unhealthy, unwell. **2** adverse, antagonistic, bad, cross, damaging, detrimental, difficult, disturbing, harmful, harsh, inauspicious, incorrect, injurious, malicious, ominous, sinister, sullen, surly, threatening, unfavourable, unfortunate, unfriendly, unhealthy, unkind, unlucky, unpromising, unwholesome, vile, wicked, wrong.
antonyms **1** well. **2** fortunate, good, kind.

ill-advised *adj.* daft, foolish, hasty, ill-considered, imprudent, inappropriate, indiscreet, injudicious, rash, short-sighted, thoughtless.
antonyms sensible, wise.

ill-assorted *adj.* discordant, incompatible, inharmonious, mismatched, unsuited.
antonym harmonious.

ill-bred *adj.* bad-mannered, coarse, discourteous, ill-mannered, impolite, indelicate, rude.
antonym well-behaved.

ill-disposed *adj.* against, antagonistic, averse, opposed, unco-operative, unfriendly, unsympathetic, unwelcoming.
antonym well-disposed.

illegal *adj.* banned, criminal, forbidden, illicit, outlawed, prohibited, unauthorised, unconstitutional, under-the-counter, unlawful, wrongful.
antonyms legal, permissible.

illegible *adj.* faint, indecipherable, indistinct, obscure, scrawled, unreadable.
antonym legible.

illegitimate *adj.* **1** bastard, born on the wrong side of the blanket, born out of wedlock. **2** illegal, illicit, illogical, improper, incorrect, invalid, spurious, unauthorised, unlawful, unsound, unwarranted.

ill-fated *adj.* doomed, ill-starred, luckless, star-crossed, unfortunate, unhappy, unlucky.
antonym lucky.

illiberal *adj.* bigoted, hidebound, intolerant, mean, miserly, narrow-minded, niggardly, parsimonious, petty, prejudiced, reactionary, repressive, small-minded, tight, tightfisted.
antonym liberal.

illicit *adj.* black, black-market, clandestine, contraband, criminal, forbidden, furtive, guilty, illegal, illegitimate, ill-gotten, immoral, improper, prohibited, unauthorised, unlawful, unlicensed, unsanctioned, wrong.
antonyms legal, permissible.

ill-mannered *adj.* badly-behaved, coarse, crude, discourteous, impolite, rude.
antonym polite.

illness *n.* affliction, ailment, attack, complaint, disability, disease, disorder, distemper, ill-being, ill-health, indisposition, infirmity, sickness.

illogical *adj.* absurd, fallacious, faulty, inconsistent, invalid, irrational, meaningless, senseless, sophistical, specious, spurious, unreasonable, unscientific, unsound.
antonym logical.

ill-omened *adj.* doomed, ill-fated, inauspicious, unfortunate, unhappy, unlucky.
antonym fortunate.

ill-tempered *adj.* bad-tempered, cross, curt, grumpy, ill-humoured, ill-natured, impatient, irritable, sharp, spiteful, touchy, vicious.
antonym good-tempered.

ill-timed *adj.* awkward, inappropriate, inconvenient, inopportune, unseasonable, untimely, unwelcome.
antonym well-timed.

ill-treat *v.* abuse, damage, harass, harm, injure, maltreat, mishandle, mistreat, misuse, neglect, oppress, wrong.
antonym care for.

ill-treatment *n.* abuse, damage, harm, injury, mishandling, mistreatment, misuse, neglect.
antonym care.

illuminate *v.* brighten, clarify, clear up, decorate, edify, elucidate, enlighten, explain, illumine, illustrate, instruct, light, light up.
antonyms darken, mystify.

illumination *n.* beam, brightening, brightness, decoration, light, lighting, lights, ornamentation, radiance, ray, splendour.
antonym darkness.

illusion *n.* apparition, delusion, error, fallacy, fancy, fantasy, figment, hallucination, mirage, misapprehension, misconception.

antonyms reality, truth.

illusory *adj.* apparent, deceitful, deceptive, deluding, delusive, fallacious, false, illusive, misleading, mistaken, seeming, sham, unreal, unsubstantial, untrue, vain.
antonym real.

illustrate *v.* adorn, clarify, decorate, demonstrate, depict, draw, elucidate, emphasise, exemplify, exhibit, explain, illuminate, interpret, ornament, picture, show, sketch.

illustration *n.* **1** decoration, drawing, figure, half-tone, photograph, picture, plate, representation, sketch, specimen. **2** analogy, case, demonstration, example, explanation, instance, interpretation.

illustrative *adj.* descriptive, diagrammatic, explanatory, graphic, pictorial, representative, sample, specimen, typical.

illustrious *adj.* brilliant, celebrated, distinguished, eminent, exalted, excellent, famed, famous, glorious, great, magnificent, noble, notable, noted, outstanding, prominent, remarkable, renowned, splendid.
antonyms inglorious, shameful.

ill-will *n.* antagonism, aversion, bad blood, dislike, enmity, envy, grudge, hard feelings, hatred, hostility, malevolence, malice, resentment, spite, unfriendliness.
antonyms friendship, good-will.

image *n.* **1** appearance, concept, conception, idea, impression, notion, perception. **2** effigy, figure, icon, idol, likeness, picture, portrait, reflection, replica, representation, statue.

imaginable *adj.* believable, comprehensible, conceivable, likely, plausible, possible, thinkable.
antonym unimaginable.

imaginary *adj.* assumed, dreamlike, fanciful, fictional, fictitious, hallucinatory, hypothetical, ideal, illusory, imagined, invented, legendary, made-up, mythological, non-existent, shadowy, supposed, visionary.
antonym real.

imagination *n.* **1** creativity, enterprise, imaginativeness, ingenuity, insight, inspiration, inventiveness, mind's eye, originality, resourcefulness, vision. **2** conception, fancy, idea, illusion, image, notion, supposition, wit.
antonyms **1** unimaginativeness. **2** reality.

imaginative *adj.* clever, creative, dreamy, enterprising, fanciful, fantastic, fertile, ingenious, innovative, inspired, inventive, original, resourceful, visionary, vivid.
antonyms uncreative, unimaginative.

imagine *v.* assume, believe, conceive, conjecture, conjure up, create, deem, devise, dream up, envisage, fancy, fantasise, frame, gather, guess, invent, judge, picture, plan, project, realise, suppose, suspect, take it, think, think of, think up, visualise.

imbalance *n.* bias, disparity, disproportion, imparity, inequality, partiality, unevenness, unfairness.
antonym parity.

imbecile *n.* blockhead, bungler, cretin, fool, half-wit, idiot, moron, thickhead.
adj. fatuous, feeble-minded, foolish, idiotic, inane, moronic, simple, stupid, thick, witless.
antonyms intelligent, sensible.

imbue *v.* fill, impregnate, inculcate, infuse, ingrain, instil, permeate, pervade, saturate, stain, steep, suffuse, tinge, tint.

imitate *v.* ape, caricature, copy, counterfeit, duplicate, echo, emulate, follow, follow suit, forge, impersonate, mimic, mirror, mock, parody, parrot, repeat, reproduce, send up, simulate, spoof, take off.

imitation *n.* aping, copy, counterfeit, counterfeiting, duplication, fake, forgery, impersonation, impression, likeness, mimicry, mockery, parody, reflection, replica, reproduction, resemblance, sham, simulation, substitution, take-off, travesty.
adj. artificial, dummy, ersatz, fake, man-made, mock, phoney, pseudo, reproduction, sham, simulated, synthetic.
antonym genuine.

imitative *adj.* copying, derivative, mimicking, mock, parrot-like, pseudo, put-on, second-hand, simulated, unoriginal.

imitator *n.* copier, copy-cat, follower, impersonator, impressionist, mimic, parrot.

immaculate *adj.* blameless, clean, faultless, flawless, impeccable, incorrupt, innocent, neat, perfect, pure, sinless, spick-and-span, spotless, spruce, stainless, unblemished, undefiled, unsullied, untainted.
antonyms contaminated, spoiled, stained.

immaterial *adj.* insignificant, irrelevant, minor, trifling, trivial, unimportant, unnecessary.
antonyms important, material.

immature *adj.* adolescent, babyish, childish, crude, inexperienced, infantile, juvenile, puerile, raw, under-age, unripe, unseasonable, untimely, young.
antonym mature.

immeasurable *adj.* bottomless, boundless, endless, immense, incalculable, inestimable, inexhaustible, infinite, limitless, unbounded, unlimited, vast.
antonym limited.

immediacy *n.* directness, imminence, instantaneity, simultaneity, swiftness.
antonym remoteness.

immediate *adj.* actual, adjacent, close, current, direct, existing, instant, near, nearest, next, on hand, present, pressing, primary, prompt, recent, up-to-date, urgent.
antonyms delayed, distant.

immediately *adv.* at once, closely, directly, forthwith, instantly, nearly, now, promptly, right away, straight away, unhesitatingly, without delay.
antonyms eventually, never.

immemorial *adj.* age-old, ancient, archaic, fixed, long-standing, time-honoured, traditional.
antonym recent.

immense *adj.* enormous, gigantic, great, huge,

large, massive, monumental, tremendous, vast.
antonyms minute, tiny.
immensity *n.* bulk, enormousness, expanse, greatness, hugeness, infinity, magnitude, massiveness, vastness.
antonym minuteness.
immerse *v.* bathe, dip, douse, duck, plunge, sink, submerge, submerse.
immigrant *n.* incomer, newcomer, settler.
antonym emigrant.
imminence *n.* approach, immediacy, instancy, menace, threat.
antonym remoteness.
imminent *adj.* approaching, brewing, close, coming, forthcoming, impending, in the air, in the offing, looming, menacing, near, threatening.
antonyms far-off, remote.
immobilise *v.* cripple, disable, fix, freeze, halt, paralyse, stop, transfix.
antonym mobilise.
immoderate *adj.* exaggerated, excessive, exorbitant, extravagant, extreme, inordinate, over the top, uncalled-for, uncontrolled, unreasonable, unrestrained, unwarranted.
antonym moderate.
immodest *adj.* **1** coarse, immoral, improper, impure, indecent, lewd, obscene, revealing, risqué, shameless. **2** forward, impudent, pushy.
immoral *adj.* bad, corrupt, degenerate, depraved, dishonest, dissolute, evil, foul, impure, indecent, lewd, obscene, pornographic, sinful, unethical, vile, wanton, wicked, wrong.
antonyms good, moral, right.
immortal *adj.* abiding, endless, enduring, eternal, everlasting, imperishable, incorruptible, lasting, perennial, perpetual, timeless, undying.
antonym mortal.
n. deity, divinity, god, goddess, great, hero.
immortalise *v.* celebrate, commemorate, enshrine, memorialise, perpetuate.
immovable *adj.* adamant, constant, determined, fast, firm, fixed, obstinate, resolute, rooted, secure, set, stable, steadfast, stuck, unshakable, unyielding.
antonym movable.
immune *adj.* clear, exempt, free, insusceptible, invulnerable, proof, protected, resistant, safe, unsusceptible.
antonym susceptible.
immunise *v.* inject, inoculate, protect, safeguard, vaccinate.
immunity *n.* exemption, exoneration, franchise, freedom, indemnity, liberty, licence, privilege, protection, release, resistance, right.
antonym susceptibility.
impact *n.* **1** consequences, effect, impression, influence, meaning, power, repercussions, significance. **2** bang, blow, brunt, bump, collision, contact, crash, jolt, knock, shock, smash.
v. collide, crash, crush, drive, embed, fix, press together, strike, wedge.
impair *v.* blunt, damage, devalue, diminish, harm, hinder, injure, lessen, mar, reduce, spoil, undermine, weaken, worsen.
antonyms enhance, improve.
impale *v.* lance, perforate, pierce, puncture, run through, skewer, spear, spike, spit, stick, transfix.
impart *v.* communicate, confer, contribute, convey, disclose, discover, divulge, give, grant, hand over, lend, make known, offer, pass on, relate, reveal, tell, yield.
impartial *adj.* detached, disinterested, dispassionate, equal, equitable, even-handed, fair, just, neutral, non-partisan, objective, open-minded, unbiased, unprejudiced.
antonyms biased, prejudiced.
impassable *adj.* blocked, closed, impenetrable, obstructed, unnavigable, unpassable.
antonym passable.
impasse *n.* blind alley, cul-de-sac, dead end, deadlock, halt, stalemate, standstill.
impassive *adj.* calm, composed, cool, dispassionate, expressionless, indifferent, reserved, stoical, stolid, unconcerned, unemotional, unexcitable, unfeeling, unmoved, unruffled.
antonyms moved, responsive.
impatience *n.* agitation, eagerness, haste, intolerance, irritability, nervousness, rashness, restlessness, shortness, snappishness, uneasiness, vehemence.
antonym patience.
impatient *adj.* abrupt, brusque, demanding, eager, edgy, fretful, hasty, headlong, hot-tempered, impetuous, intolerant, irritable, precipitate, quick-tempered, restless, snappy.
antonym patient.
impeach *v.* accuse, arraign, blame, cast doubt on, censure, challenge, charge, denounce, disparage, impugn, indict.
impeachment *n.* accusation, arraignment, charge, disparagement, indictment.
impeccable *adj.* blameless, exact, exquisite, flawless, immaculate, innocent, irreproachable, perfect, pure, scrupulous, sinless, stainless, unblemished.
antonyms corrupt, faulty, flawed.
impede *v.* bar, block, brake, check, clog, curb, delay, disrupt, hamper, hinder, hold up, let, obstruct, restrain, retard, slow, stop, thwart, trammel.
antonyms aid, further, promote.
impediment *n.* bar, barrier, block, check, curb, defect, difficulty, hindrance, obstacle, obstruction, snag, stammer, stumbling-block, stutter.
antonym aid.
impel *v.* compel, constrain, drive, excite, force, goad, incite, induce, influence, inspire, instigate, motivate, move, oblige, prompt, propel, push, spur, stimulate, urge.
antonyms deter, dissuade.
impending *adj.* approaching, close, coming, forthcoming, imminent, looming, menacing, near, nearing, threatening.
antonym remote.
impenetrable *adj.* baffling, cryptic, dark, dense, enigmatic, fathomless, hidden, impassable,

incomprehensible, indiscernible, inscrutable, mysterious, obscure, solid, thick, unfathomable, unintelligible.
antonyms accessible, understandable.

imperative *adj.* **1** compulsory, crucial, essential, pressing, urgent, vital. **2** authoritative, autocratic, bossy, commanding, dictatorial, domineering, high-handed, imperious, insistent, lordly, magisterial, tyrannical.
antonyms **1** optional, unimportant. **2** humble.

imperceptible *adj.* faint, fine, gradual, inappreciable, inaudible, indiscernible, infinitesimal, microscopic, minute, shadowy, slight, small, subtle, tiny.
antonym perceptible.

imperfect *adj.* broken, damaged, defective, deficient, faulty, flawed, inexact, unideal.
antonym perfect.

imperfection *n.* blemish, blotch, defect, deficiency, failing, fault, flaw, shortcoming, weakness.
antonyms asset, perfection.

imperial *adj.* grand, great, kingly, lofty, magnificent, majestic, noble, princely, queenly, regal, royal, sovereign, superior, supreme.

imperialism *n.* acquisitiveness, adventurism, colonialism, empire-building, expansionism.

imperil *v.* compromise, endanger, expose, hazard, jeopardise, risk, threaten.

imperious *adj.* arrogant, authoritarian, autocratic, commanding, demanding, despotic, dictatorial, domineering, high-handed, overbearing.
antonym humble.

imperishable *adj.* abiding, enduring, eternal, everlasting, immortal, incorruptible, indestructible, permanent, perpetual, undying, unfading.
antonyms corruptible, perishable.

impersonal *adj.* aloof, bureaucratic, businesslike, cold, detached, dispassionate, distant, faceless, formal, frosty, glassy, inhuman, neutral, objective, remote.
antonyms friendly, sympathetic.

impersonate *v.* act, caricature, imitate, masquerade as, mimic, mock, parody, pose as, take off.

impertinence *n.* boldness, brass, brazenness, cheek, disrespect, forwardness, impoliteness, impudence, insolence, nerve, politeness, presumption, rudeness, sauciness.

impertinent *adj.* bold, brazen, cheeky, discourteous, disrespectful, forward, fresh, ill-mannered, impolite, impudent, insolent, interfering, pert, presumptuous, rude, saucy.
antonyms civil, polite, respectful.

imperturbable *adj.* calm, collected, composed, cool, equanimous, optimistic, self-possessed, tranquil, unexcitable, unflappable.
antonyms jittery, touchy.

impervious *adj.* closed, damp-proof, hermetic, immune, impenetrable, impermeable, invulnerable, resistant, sealed, unaffected, unmoved, untouched.
antonyms pervious, responsive.

impetuous *adj.* hasty, impulsive, precipitate, rash, unplanned, unpremeditated, unthinking.
antonyms cautious, circumspect, wary.

impetus *n.* drive, energy, force, impulse, incentive, momentum, motivation, motive, power, push, spur, stimulus.

impinge *v.* affect, clash, encroach, enter, hit, influence, infringe, intrude, invade, touch (on), trespass, violate.

impious *adj.* blasphemous, godless, irreligious, irreverent, profane, sacrilegious, sinful, ungodly, unholy, unrighteous, wicked.
antonyms pious, religious.

impish *adj.* cheeky, mischievous, naughty, rascally, roguish.

implacable *adj.* cruel, inexorable, inflexible, intransigent, merciless, pitiless, relentless, remorseless, ruthless.
antonyms compassionate, compromising.

implant *v.* embed, fix, graft, inculcate, infuse, ingraft, inoculate, inseminate, insert, instil, place, plant, root, sow.

implausible *adj.* dubious, far-fetched, flimsy, improbable, suspect, thin, transparent, unconvincing, unlikely, weak.
antonyms likely, plausible, reasonable.

implement *n.* apparatus, appliance, device, gadget, instrument, tool, utensil.
v. accomplish, bring about, carry out, complete, discharge, do, effect, enforce, execute, fulfil, perfect, perform, realise.

implicate *v.* associate, compromise, connect, embroil, entangle, include, incriminate, involve, throw suspicion on.
antonyms absolve, exonerate.

implication *n.* **1** conclusion, connection, inference, insinuation, meaning, ramification, repercusssion, significance, suggestion. **2** association, incrimination, involvement.

implicit *adj.* **1** implied, tacit, understood, unspoken. **2** absolute, complete, full, total, unqualified, unquestioning, unreserved, utter, wholehearted.
antonyms **1** explicit. **2** half-hearted.

implore *v.* ask, beg, crave, entreat, plead, pray, solicit.

imply *v.* denote, hint, indicate, insinuate, intimate, involve, mean, point to, require, signify, suggest.
antonym state.

impolite *adj.* abrupt, bad-mannered, coarse, cross, discourteous, disrespectful, ill-bred, ill-mannered, insolent, rough, rude.
antonyms courteous, polite.

import *v.* bring in, introduce, receive.
antonyms export, send.

importance *n.* concern, consequence, consideration, distinction, eminence, esteem, influence, interest, mark, momentousness, prestige, prominence, significance, standing, status, substance, usefulness, value, weight, worth.
antonym unimportance.

important *adj.* essential, far-reaching, foremost, heavy, high-level, high-ranking, influential, key,

keynote, leading, material, meaningful, momentous, notable, noteworthy, outstanding, powerful, pre-eminent, primary, prominent, relevant, salient, seminal, serious, significant, substantial, urgent, valuable, valued, vital, weighty.
antonyms insignificant, secondary, trivial, unimportant.

impose *v.* **1** appoint, burden, charge (with), dictate, enforce, exact, fix, inflict, institute, introduce, lay, levy, ordain, place, prescribe, promulgate, put, saddle, set. **2** butt in, encroach, foist, force oneself, interpose, intrude, obtrude, presume, take liberties, trespass.

imposing *adj.* distinguished, grand, impressive, majestic, stately, striking.
antonyms modest, unimposing.

imposition *n.* **1** application, decree, exaction, infliction, introduction, levying. **2** burden, charge, constraint, duty, encroachment, intrusion, liberty, lines, punishment, task, tax.

impossible *adj.* absurd, hopeless, impracticable, inadmissible, inconceivable, insoluble, ludicrous, outrageous, preposterous, ridiculous, unacceptable, unachievable, unobtainable, unreasonable, unthinkable, unworkable.
antonym possible.

impostor *n.* charlatan, cheat, con man, deceiver, fake, fraud, hypocrite, impersonator, phoney, pretender, quack, rogue, sham, swindler.

impotent *adj.* disabled, feeble, frail, helpless, inadequate, incapable, incapacitated, incompetent, ineffective, infirm, paralysed, powerless, unable, weak.
antonyms potent, strong.

impoverish *v.* bankrupt, beggar, break, denude, deplete, diminish, drain, exhaust, reduce, ruin, weaken.
antonym enrich.

impracticable *adj.* awkward, impossible, impractical, inconvenient, unachievable, unattainable, unfeasible, unserviceable, unsuitable, unworkable, useless.
antonym practicable.

impractical *adj.* academic, idealistic, impossible, impracticable, inoperable, ivory-tower, romantic, starry-eyed, unbusinesslike, unrealistic, unserviceable, unworkable.
antonyms practical, realistic, sensible.

imprecise *adj.* ambiguous, equivocal, estimated, ill-defined, inaccurate, indefinite, inexact, loose, rough, sloppy, vague, woolly.
antonyms exact, precise.

impregnable *adj.* fortified, impenetrable, indestructible, invincible, secure, solid, strong, unassailable, unbeatable, unconquerable.
antonym vulnerable.

impregnate *v.* fertilise, fill, fructify, imbue, infuse, inseminate, permeate, pervade, saturate, soak, steep, suffuse.

impress *v.* emphasise, excite, fix, grab, imprint, inculcate, indent, influence, inspire, instil, mark, move, stamp, stand out, stir, strike, touch.

impression *n.* **1** awareness, belief, concept, consciousness, conviction, effect, feeling, hunch, idea, illusion, impact, influence, memory, notion, opinion, reaction, recollection, sense, suspicion. **2** appearance, issue, mark, outline, stamp, stamping. **3** imitation, impersonation, parody, send-up, take-off.

impressionable *adj.* gullible, naïve, open, receptive, responsive, sensitive, susceptible, vulnerable.

impressive *adj.* effective, exciting, grand, imposing, moving, powerful, stirring, striking, touching.
antonyms unimposing, unimpressive, uninspiring.

imprint *n.* badge, brand mark, impression, logo. mark, print, sign, stamp.
v. brand, engrave, etch, fix, impress, mark, print, stamp.

imprison *v.* cage, confine, constrain, detain, encage, enchain, incarcerate, intern, jail, lock up, put away, send down.
antonyms free, release.

imprisonment *n.* confinement, custody, detention, incarceration, internment.
antonyms freedom, liberty.

improbable *adj.* doubtful, dubious, far-fetched, implausible, preposterous, questionable, unbelievable, uncertain.
antonyms convincing, likely, probable.

impromptu *adj.* ad-lib, extempore, improvised, off the cuff, spontaneous, unprepared, unrehearsed, unscripted.
antonyms considered, planned, rehearsed.
adv. ad lib, extempore, off the cuff, off the top of one's head, on the spur of the moment, spontaneously.

improper *adj.* dishonest, inappropriate, incongruous, incorrect, indecent, inopportune, irregular, out of place, rude, shocking, unbecoming, unseemly, unsuitable, vulgar, wrong.
antonyms appropriate, decent, proper.

improve *v.* advance, amend, better, correct, develop, enhance, help, increase, look up, mend, mend one's ways, perk up, pick up, polish, progress, rally, recover, rectify, recuperate, reform, rise, touch up, turn over a new leaf, up, upgrade.
antonyms decline, diminish, worsen.

improvement *n.* advance, amendment, correction, development, enhancement, furtherance, gain, increase, progress, rally, recovery, rectification, reformation, rise, upswing.
antonyms decline, retrogression.

improvise *v.* ad-lib, concoct, contrive, devise, invent, make do, play it by ear, throw together.

imprudent *adj.* careless, foolish, hasty, heedless, ill-advised, impolitic, indiscreet, irresponsible, rash, reckless, short-sighted, unwise.
antonyms cautious, prudent, wise.

impudence *n.* boldness, cheek, effrontery, face, impertinence, insolence, nerve, presumption, rudeness.
antonym politeness.

impudent *adj.* bold, cheeky, cocky, forward, fresh, immodest, impertinent, insolent, presumptuous, rude, saucy, shameless.
antonym polite.

impulse *n.* desire, drive, feeling, force, impetus, incitement, inclination, influence, instinct, momentum, motive, movement, notion, passion, pressure, push, stimulus, surge, thrust, urge, wish.

impulsive *adj.* hasty, impetuous, instinctive, intuitive, passionate, quick, rash, reckless, spontaneous.
antonyms cautious, considered, premeditated.

impunity *n.* amnesty, dispensation, exemption, freedom, immunity, liberty, licence, permission, security.
antonym liability.

impure *adj.* **1** adulterated, alloyed, contaminated, corrupt, debased, diluted, infected, polluted, tainted, unclean, unrefined. **2** dirty, foul, immodest, indecent, obscene.
antonyms **1** pure. **2** chaste, decent.

impurity *n.* **1** adulteration, contaminant, contamination, corruption, defilement, dirt, dirtiness, filth, foreign body, foreign matter, foulness, grime, infection, mark, mixture, pollution, scum, spot, stain. **2** immodesty, immorality, indecency, licentiousness, obscenity, unchastity, vulgarity.
antonyms **1** purity. **2** chasteness.

impute *v.* ascribe, assign, attribute, charge, credit, put down to, refer.

inability *n.* disability, handicap, impotence, inadequacy, incapability, powerlessness, weakness.
antonym ability.

inaccessible *adj.* isolated, obscure, remote, unapproachable, unattainable, unfrequented, unget-at-able.
antonym accessible.

inaccuracy *n.* blunder, carelessness, defect, error, fault, faultiness, imprecision, inexactness, miscalculation, mistake, slip, unreliability.
antonym accuracy.

inaccurate *adj.* careless, defective, erroneous, faulty, imprecise, in error, incorrect, inexact, loose, mistaken, unfaithful, unreliable, wild, wrong.
antonyms accurate, correct.

inaction *n.* idleness, immobility, inactivity, inertia, rest, stagnation, torpor.
antonym activeness.

inactive *adj.* dormant, idle, immobile, inert, inoperative, lazy, lethargic, passive, quiet, sedentary, sleepy, sluggish, stagnating, torpid, unused.
antonyms active, busy, working.

inadequacy *n.* **1** dearth, defectiveness, deficiency, inability, incompetence, ineffectiveness, insufficiency, lack, meagreness, poverty, scantiness, shortage, unsuitableness, want. **2** defect, failing, fault, imperfection, shortcoming, weakness.
antonym **1** adequacy.

inadequate *adj.* **1** deficient, insufficient, leaving a little/a lot/much to be desired, meagre, niggardly, scanty, short, sparse, unequal, wanting. **2** defective, faulty, imperfect, incapable, incompetent, ineffective, unfitted, unqualified.
antonyms **1** adequate. **2** satisfactory.

inadmissible *adj.* disallowed, immaterial, inappropriate, irrelevant, prohibited, unacceptable.
antonym admissible.

inadvertent *adj.* accidental, careless, chance, heedless, unintended, unintentional, unplanned, unpremeditated, unthinking.
antonyms careful, conscious, deliberate.

inadvisable *adj.* daft, foolish, ill-advised, imprudent, indiscreet, injudicious, misguided.
antonyms advisable, wise.

inalienable *adj.* absolute, inherent, inviolable, non-negotiable, non-transferable, permanent, sacrosanct, unassailable.

inane *adj.* daft, empty, fatuous, foolish, frivolous, futile, idiotic, mindless, nutty, puerile, senseless, silly, stupid, trifling, unintelligent, vacuous, vain, vapid, worthless.
antonym sensible.

inanimate *adj.* dead, defunct, dormant, dull, extinct, inactive, inert, inorganic, lifeless, spiritless, stagnant.
antonyms alive, animate, living.

inapplicable *adj.* inapposite, inappropriate, irrelevant, unsuitable, unsuited.
antonyms applicable, relevant.

inappropriate *adj.* ill-suited, ill-timed, improper, incongruous, out of place, tactless, unbecoming, unfitting, unseemly, unsuitable, untimely.
antonyms appropriate, suitable.

inapt *adj.* awkward, clumsy, ill-fitted, ill-suited, ill-timed, inappropriate, tactless, unfortunate, unhappy, unsuitable, unsuited.
antonyms appropriate, apt.

inarticulate *adj.* faltering, halting, hesitant, incoherent, incomprehensible, indistinct, tongue-tied, unclear, unintelligible, unuttered, unvoiced, wordless.
antonym articulate.

inattention *n.* absence of mind, absent-mindedness, carelessness, daydreaming, disregard, forgetfulness, neglect, preoccupation.
antonym attentiveness.

inattentive *adj.* absent-minded, careless, distracted, dreamy, negligent, preoccupied, regardless, unheeding, unmindful.
antonym attentive.

inaudible *adj.* faint, imperceptible, indistinct, low, muffled, mumbled, muted, noiseless, out of earshot, silent.
antonym audible.

inaugural *adj.* first, initial, introductory, launching, opening.

inaugurate *v.* begin, commence, commission, consecrate, dedicate, enthrone, induct, initiate, install, institute, introduce, invest, launch, open, ordain, originate, set up, start, start off, usher in.

inauspicious *adj.* bad, black, discouraging, ominous, threatening, unfavourable, unfor-

tunate, unlucky, unpromising.
antonyms auspicious, promising.

inborn *adj.* congenital, hereditary, inbred, ingrained, inherited, innate, intuitive, native, natural.
antonym learned.

inbred *adj.* ingrained, inherent, innate, native, natural.
antonym learned.

incalculable *adj.* countless, immense, inestimable, limitless, unlimited, untold, vast.
antonyms limited, restricted.

incantation *n.* chant, charm, formula, invocation, spell.

incapable *adj.* disqualified, feeble, helpless, inadequate, incompetent, ineffective, insufficient, powerless, unable, unfit, unqualified, unsuited, weak.
antonym capable.

incapacitate *v.* cripple, disable, disqualify, immobilise, lay up, paralyse, put out of action, scupper, unfit.
antonyms facilitate, set up.

incapacity *n.* disability, feebleness, impotence, inability, inadequacy, incapability, incompetency, ineffectiveness, powerlessness, weakness.
antonym capability.

incarnate *adj.* embodied, made flesh, personified, typified.

incarnation *n.* embodiment, impersonation, manifestation, personification, type.

incautious *adj.* careless, hasty, ill-judged, imprudent, impulsive, inconsiderate, rash, reckless, thoughtless, unthinking.
antonyms cautious, guarded.

incendiary *n.* **1** arsonist, firebug, fire-raiser, pyromaniac. **2** agitator, demagogue, firebrand, insurgent, rabble-rouser, revolutionary.
adj. inciting, inflammatory, provocative, rabble-rousing, seditious, subversive.
antonym calming.

incense¹ *n.* aroma, balm, bouquet, fragrance, joss-stick, perfume, scent, worship.

incense² *v.* anger, enrage, exasperate, excite, infuriate, irritate, madden, make one see red, provoke, raise one's hackles, rile.
antonym calm.

incentive *n.* bait, encouragement, enticement, impetus, impulse, inducement, lure, motivation, motive, reason, reward, spur, stimulant, stimulus.
antonyms deterrent, discouragement, disincentive.

incessant *adj.* ceaseless, constant, continual, continuous, endless, eternal, everlasting, interminable, never-ending, non-stop, perpetual, persistent, unbroken, unceasing.
antonyms intermittent, periodic.

incidence *n.* amount, commonness, degree, extent, frequency, occurrence, prevalence, range, rate.

incident *n.* **1** adventure, affair, episode, event, happening, instance, occasion, occurrence, scene. **2** clash, commotion, confrontation, disturbance, fight, mishap, skirmish.

incidental *adj.* accidental, accompanying, ancillary, attendant, contributory, minor, non-essential, random, related, secondary, subordinate, subsidiary, supplementary.
antonyms essential, important.

incinerate *v.* burn, cremate, reduce to ashes.

incision *n.* cut, gash, notch, opening, slit.

incisive *adj.* acid, acute, astute, biting, caustic, cutting, keen, penetrating, perceptive, piercing, sharp, trenchant.
antonyms vague, woolly.

incite *v.* abet, animate, drive, egg on, encourage, excite, goad, impel, instigate, prompt, provoke, put up to, rouse, set on, solicit, spur, stimulate, stir up, urge, whip up.
antonym restrain.

incitement *n.* agitation, encouragement, goad, impetus, impulse, inducement, instigation, motivation, motive, prompting, provocation, spur, stimulus.
antonyms check, discouragement.

inclement *adj.* bitter, harsh, intemperate, rough, severe, stormy, tempestuous.
antonym fine.

inclination *n.* **1** bias, disposition, fancy, fondness, leaning, liking, taste, tendency, wish. **2** angle, bend, bending, bow, bowing, deviation, gradient, incline, leaning, nod, pitch, slant, slope, tilt.
antonyms **1** disinclination, dislike.

incline *v.* **1** affect, bias, dispose, influence, persuade, prejudice. **2** lean, slant, slope, tend, tilt, tip, veer.
n. acclivity, ascent, declivity, descent, dip, grade, gradient, hill, ramp, rise, slope.

inclined *adj.* apt, disposed, given, liable, likely, of a mind, willing.

include *v.* add, allow for, comprehend, comprise, contain, cover, embody, embrace, enclose, encompass, incorporate, involve, number among, rope in, subsume, take in, take into account.
antonyms eliminate, exclude, ignore, omit.

inclusion *n.* addition, incorporation, insertion, involvement.
antonym exclusion.

inclusive *adj.* across-the-board, all in, all-embracing, blanket, catch-all, comprehensive, full, general, overall, sweeping.
antonyms exclusive, narrow.

incognito *adj.* disguised, in disguise, masked, unknown, unmarked, unrecognisable, unrecognised, veiled.
antonyms openly, undisguised.

incoherence *n.* confusion, disjointedness, illogicality, inarticulateness, inconsistency, unintelligibility.
antonym coherence.

incoherent *adj.* confused, disconnected, disordered, inarticulate, jumbled, muddled, rambling, stammering, stuttering, unconnected, unco-ordinated, unintelligible, wandering.
antonyms coherent, intelligible.

income *n.* earnings, gains, interest, means, pay, proceeds, profits, receipts, returns, revenue, salary, takings, wages.
antonyms expenditure, expenses.

incoming *adj.* approaching, arriving, coming, ensuing, entering, homeward, new, next, returning, succeeding.
antonym outgoing.

incomparable *adj.* brilliant, matchless, peerless, superb, superlative, supreme, unequalled, unmatched, unparalleled, unrivalled.
antonyms ordinary, poor, run-of-the-mill.

incompatible *adj.* clashing, conflicting, contradictory, inconsistent, irreconcilable, mismatched, uncongenial, unsuited.
antonym compatible.

incompetence *n.* bungling, inability, incapability, inefficiency, ineptness, stupidity, uselessness.
antonyms ability, competence.

incompetent *adj.* bungling, incapable, ineffective, inexpert, stupid, unable, unfit, unfitted, unskilful, useless.
antonyms able, competent.

incomplete *adj.* broken, defective, deficient, fragmentary, imperfect, lacking, part, partial, short, unfinished.
antonyms complete, exhaustive.

incomprehensible *adj.* above one's head, baffling, impenetrable, inscrutable, mysterious, obscure, opaque, perplexing, puzzling, unintelligible.
antonyms comprehensible, intelligible.

inconceivable *adj.* implausible, incredible, mind-boggling, staggering, unbelievable, unheard-of, unimaginable, unthinkable.
antonym conceivable.

inconclusive *adj.* ambiguous, indecisive, open, uncertain, unconvincing, undecided, unsatisfying, unsettled, vague.
antonym conclusive.

incongruity *n.* conflict, inappropriateness, incompatibility, inconsistency, unsuitability.
antonyms consistency, harmoniousness.

incongruous *adj.* conflicting, contradictory, contrary, inappropriate, inconsistent, out of keeping, out of place, unbecoming, unsuitable.
antonyms consistent, harmonious.

inconsequential *adj.* immaterial, insignificant, minor, trifling, trivial, unimportant.
antonym important.

inconsiderable *adj.* insignificant, minor, negligible, petty, slight, small, trivial, unimportant.
antonyms considerable, large.

inconsiderate *adj.* careless, insensitive, intolerant, rash, rude, self-centred, selfish, tactless, thoughtless, unconcerned, unkind, unthinking.
antonym considerate.

inconsistency *n.* contrariety, disagreement, discrepancy, divergence, incompatibility, incongruity, instability, unreliability, unsteadiness, variance.
antonym consistency.

inconsistent *adj.* at odds, at variance, changeable, conflicting, contradictory, contrary, discordant, fickle, incompatible, incongruous, inconstant, irregular, unpredictable, unstable, unsteady, variable, varying.
antonym constant.

inconsolable *adj.* brokenhearted, desolate, desolated, despairing, devastated, heartbroken, wretched.
antonym consolable.

inconspicuous *adj.* camouflaged, hidden, insignificant, low-key, modest, ordinary, plain, quiet, retiring, unassuming.
antonyms conspicuous, noticeable, obtrusive.

incontrovertible *adj.* certain, clear, indisputable, irrefutable, self-evident, undeniable, unshakable.
antonyms questionable, uncertain.

inconvenience *n.* annoyance, awkwardness, bother, difficulty, disruption, disturbance, drawback, fuss, hindrance, nuisance, trouble, uneasiness, upset.
antonym convenience.
v. bother, disrupt, disturb, irk, put out, put to trouble, trouble, upset.
antonym convenience.

inconvenient *adj.* annoying, awkward, difficult, disturbing, embarrassing, troublesome, unmanageable, unsuitable, unwieldy.
antonym convenient.

incorporate *v.* absorb, assimilate, blend, coalesce, combine, consolidate, contain, embody, fuse, include, integrate, merge, mix, subsume, unite.
antonyms separate, split off.

incorporation *n.* absorption, amalgamation, assimilation, association, blend, company, federation, fusion, inclusion, integration, merger, society, unification, unifying.
antonyms separation, splitting off.

incorrect *adj.* erroneous, false, faulty, illegitimate, imprecise, improper, inaccurate, inappropriate, inexact, mistaken, ungrammatical, unsuitable, untrue, wrong.
antonym correct.

incorrigible *adj.* hardened, hopeless, incurable, inveterate, irredeemable, unteachable.
antonym reformable.

incorruptible *adj.* everlasting, honest, honourable, imperishable, just, straight, trustworthy, unbribable, undecaying, upright.
antonym corruptible.

increase *v.* add to, advance, boost, build up, develop, eke out, enhance, enlarge, escalate, expand, extend, grow, heighten, intensify, magnify, multiply, proliferate, prolong, raise, soar, spread, step up, strengthen, swell, wax.
antonyms decline, decrease, reduce.
n. addition, boost, development, enlargement, escalation, expansion, extension, gain, growth, increment, intensification, proliferation, rise, step-up, surge, upsurge, upturn.
antonyms decline, decrease, reduction.

incredible *adj.* absurd, amazing, astonishing,

astounding, extraordinary, far-fetched, great, implausible, impossible, improbable, inconceivable, preposterous, superb, unbelievable, unimaginable, unthinkable, wonderful.
antonyms believable, run-of-the-mill.

incredulity *n.* disbelief, distrust, doubt, doubting, scepticism, unbelief.
antonym credulity.

incredulous *adj.* disbelieving, distrustful, doubtful, doubting, sceptical, suspicious, unbelieving, uncertain, unconvinced.
antonym credulous.

increment *n.* addition, advancement, extension, gain, growth, increase, step up, supplement.
antonym decrease.

incriminate *v.* accuse, blame, charge, impeach, implicate, indict, involve, point the finger at, recriminate.
antonym exonerate.

incur *v.* bring upon, contract, expose oneself to, gain, meet with, provoke, run up, suffer, sustain.

incurable *adj.* **1** fatal, hopeless, inoperable, terminal, untreatable. **2** dyed-in-the-wool, incorrigible, inveterate.
antonym **1** curable.

incursion *n.* attack, foray, infiltration, inroads, invasion, penetration, raid.

indebted *adj.* grateful, in debt, obliged, thankful.

indecency *n.* coarseness, crudity, foulness, grossness, immodesty, impurity, indecorum, lewdness, obscenity, pornography, vulgarity.
antonyms decency, modesty.

indecent *adj.* coarse, crude, dirty, filthy, foul, gross, immodest, improper, impure, indelicate, licentious, offensive, outrageous, pornographic, shocking, vulgar.
antonyms decent, modest.

indecipherable *adj.* cramped, illegible, indistinct, tiny, unclear, unintelligible, unreadable.
antonym readable.

indecision *n.* ambivalence, doubt, hesitancy, hesitation, indecisiveness, irresolution, uncertainty, vacillation, wavering.
antonym decisiveness.

indecisive *adj.* doubtful, faltering, hesitating, in two minds, inconclusive, indefinite, indeterminate, irresolute, tentative, uncertain, unclear, undecided, undetermined, unsure, vacillating, wavering.
antonym decisive.

indeed *adv.* actually, certainly, in fact, positively, really, to be sure, truly, undeniably, undoubtedly.

indefensible *adj.* faulty, inexcusable, insupportable, unforgivable, unjustifiable, unpardonable, untenable, wrong.
antonyms defensible, excusable.

indefinite *adj.* ambiguous, confused, doubtful, evasive, general, ill-defined, imprecise, indistinct, inexact, loose, obscure, uncertain, unclear, undecided, undefined, undetermined, unfixed, unknown, unlimited, unresolved, unsettled, vague.
antonyms clear, limited.

indefinitely *adv.* ad infinitum, continually, endlessly, eternally, for ever, for life, time without end.

indelible *adj.* enduring, indestructible, ingrained, lasting, permanent.
antonyms erasable, impermanent.

indelicate *adj.* coarse, crude, embarrassing, immodest, improper, indecent, obscene, offensive, risqué, rude, shocking, suggestive, tasteless, unseemly, vulgar.
antonym delicate.

indemnity *n.* amnesty, compensation, guarantee, immunity, insurance, protection, reimbursement, remuneration, reparation, security.

independence *n.* autonomy, freedom, home rule, individualism, liberty, self-determination, self-government, self-rule, separation, sovereignty.
antonyms conventionality, dependence.

independent *adj.* absolute, autonomous, decontrolled, free, impartial, individual, individualistic, liberated, non-aligned, one's own man, self-contained, self-determining, self-governing, self-reliant, self-sufficient, self-supporting, separate, separated, sovereign, unaided, unbiased, unconnected, unconstrained, uncontrolled, unconventional, unrelated.
antonyms clinging, dependent.

indescribable *adj.* indefinable, inexpressible, unutterable.
antonym describable.

indestructible *adj.* abiding, durable, enduring, eternal, everlasting, immortal, imperishable, incorruptible, lasting, permanent, unbreakable, unfading.
antonyms breakable, mortal.

indeterminate *adj.* imprecise, indefinite, inexact, open-ended, uncertain, undecided, undefined, undetermined, unfixed, unspecified, unstated, vague.
antonyms exact, known, limited.

index *n.* clue, guide, hand, indication, indicator, mark, needle, pointer, sign, symptom, table, token.

indicate *v.* add up to, denote, designate, display, express, imply, manifest, mark, point out, point to, read, record, register, reveal, show, signify, specify, suggest.

indication *n.* clue, evidence, explanation, hint, intimation, manifestation, mark, note, omen, sign, signal, suggestion, symptom, warning.

indicative *adj.* suggestive, symptomatic.

indicator *n.* display, gauge, guide, index, mark, marker, meter, pointer, sign, signal, signpost, symbol, winker.

indict *v.* accuse, arraign, charge, impeach, incriminate, prosecute, summon, summons.
antonym exonerate.

indictment *n.* accusation, allegation, charge, impeachment, incrimination, prosecution, summons.
antonym exoneration.

indifference *n.* apathy, coldness, coolness, disinterestedness, disregard, inattention, negligence,

unconcern, unimportance.
antonyms concern, interest.

indifferent *adj.* **1** apathetic, careless, cold, cool, detached, distant, heedless, inattentive, uncaring, unconcerned, unenthusiastic, unexcited, uninterested, uninvolved, unmoved, unresponsive, unsympathetic. **2** average, mediocre, middling, moderate, ordinary, passable.
antonyms **1** caring, interested. **2** excellent.

indigenous *adj.* aboriginal, home-grown, local, native, original.
antonym foreign.

indignant *adj.* angry, annoyed, exasperated, fuming, furious, heated, incensed, irate, livid, mad, outraged.
antonyms delighted, pleased.

indignation *n.* anger, exasperation, fury, ire, outrage, rage, resentment, scorn, wax, wrath.
antonyms joy, pleasure.

indignity *n.* abuse, contempt, disgrace, dishonour, disrespect, humiliation, injury, insult, outrage, reproach, slight, snub.
antonym honour.

indirect *adj.* ancillary, circuitous, incidental, meandering, rambling, roundabout, secondary, subsidiary, tortuous, unintended, wandering, winding, zigzag.
antonym direct.

indiscernible *adj.* hidden, imperceptible, indistinct, invisible, minute, tiny, unapparent, undiscernible, unfathomable.
antonyms clear, obvious.

indiscreet *adj.* careless, foolish, hasty, heedless, imprudent, naïve, rash, reckless, tactless, undiplomatic, unthinking.
antonyms cautious, discreet.

indiscretion *n.* boob, brick, error, faux pas, folly, foolishness, gaffe, mistake, rashness, recklessness, slip, tactlessness.

indiscriminate *adj.* aimless, general, haphazard, hit or miss, indiscriminating, miscellaneous, mixed, motley, random, sweeping, uncritical, unmethodical, unsystematic, wholesale.
antonyms precise, selective, specific.

indispensable *adj.* basic, crucial, essential, imperative, key, necessary, needed, required, requisite, vital.
antonym unnecessary.

indisposed *adj.* ailing, ill, laid up, poorly, sick, unwell.
antonym well.

indisposition *n.* ailment, illness, sickness.
antonym health.

indisputable *adj.* absolute, certain, incontrovertible, irrefutable, positive, sure, unanswerable, undeniable, unquestionable.
antonym doubtful.

indistinct *adj.* ambiguous, blurred, confused, dim, distant, doubtful, faint, fuzzy, hazy, ill-defined, indefinite, misty, obscure, shadowy, unclear, undefined, unintelligible, vague.
antonym distinct.

individual *n.* being, bloke, body, chap, character, creature, fellow, party, person, soul.
adj. characteristic, distinct, distinctive, exclusive, identical, idiosyncratic, own, particular, peculiar, personal, personalised, proper, respective, separate, several, single, singular, special, specific, unique.
antonyms collective, general, shared.

individualist *n.* free-thinker, independent, libertarian, lone wolf, loner, maverick, nonconformist.
antonym conventionalist.

individuality *n.* character, distinction, distinctiveness, originality, peculiarity, personality, separateness, uniqueness.
antonym sameness.

indoctrinate *v.* brainwash, drill, ground, imbue, initiate, instruct, school, teach, train.

induce *v.* bring about, cause, draw, effect, encourage, generate, get, give rise to, impel, incite, influence, instigate, lead to, move, occasion, persuade, press, prevail upon, produce, prompt, talk into.
antonyms deter, discourage.

inducement *n.* attraction, bait, consideration, encouragement, impulse, incentive, incitement, influence, lure, reason, reward, spur, stimulus.
antonym disincentive.

induction *n.* **1** conclusion, deduction, generalisation, inference. **2** consecration, enthronement, inauguration, initiation, installation, institution, introduction, investiture, ordination..

indulge *v.* coddle, cosset, favour, foster, give in to, go along with, gratify, humour, mollycoddle, pamper, pander to, pet, regale, satisfy, spoil, treat (oneself), yield to.
indulge in give free rein to, give oneself up to, give way to, revel in, wallow in.

indulgence *n.* excess, extravagance, favour, immoderation, intemperance, luxury.

indulgent *adj.* easy-going, favourable, fond, generous, gratifying, kind, liberal, mild, permissive, tender, tolerant, understanding.
antonyms harsh, moderate, strict.

industrious *adj.* active, busy, conscientious, diligent, energetic, hard-working, persevering, persistent, productive, steady, tireless, zealous.
antonyms idle, lazy.

industry *n.* **1** business, commerce, manufacturing, production, trade. **2** application, determination, diligence, effort, labour, perseverance, persistence, toil.

inebriated *adj.* drunk, intoxicated, merry, tipsy, under the influence.
antonym sober.

inedible *adj.* deadly, harmful, noxious, poisonous, uneatable.
antonym edible.

ineffective *adj.* feeble, fruitless, futile, idle, impotent, inadequate, ineffectual, inept, lame, powerless, unavailing, unproductive, unsuccessful, useless, vain, void, weak, worthless.
antonyms effective, effectual.

inefficiency *n.* carelessness, disorganisation, incompetence, muddle, negligence, slackness, sloppiness, waste, wastefulness.

antonym efficiency.

inefficient *adj.* incompetent, inept, inexpert, money-wasting, negligent, slipshod, sloppy, time-wasting, unworkmanlike, wasteful.
antonym efficient.

inelegant *adj.* awkward, clumsy, crass, crude, graceless, laboured, rough, ugly, uncouth, uncultivated, ungraceful, unpolished, unrefined, unsophisticated.
antonym elegant.

ineligible *adj.* disqualified, improper, incompetent, unacceptable, unequipped, unfit, unqualified, unsuitable, unworthy.
antonym eligible.

inept *adj.* awkward, bungling, clumsy, incompetent, unskilful.
antonyms competent, skilful.

inequality *n.* bias, difference, disparity, disproportion, dissimilarity, diversity, imparity, unequalness, unevenness.
antonym equality.

inert *adj.* apathetic, dead, dormant, dull, idle, immobile, inactive, inanimate, lazy, lifeless, motionless, passive, senseless, sleepy, sluggish, still, torpid, unmoving, unresponsive.
antonyms alive, animated.

inertia *n.* apathy, dullness, idleness, immobility, inactivity, laziness, lethargy, passivity, stillness, torpor, unresponsiveness.
antonyms activity, liveliness.

inescapable *adj.* certain, destined, fated, inevitable, irrevocable, sure, unalterable, unavoidable.
antonym escapable.

inessential *adj.* accidental, dispensable, extra, extraneous, irrelevant, optional, redundant, secondary, spare, superfluous, surplus, unasked-for, uncalled-for, unimportant, unnecessary.
antonyms essential, necessary.
n. accessory, appendage, expendable, extra, extravagance, luxury, non-essential, superfluity, trimming.
antonym essential.

inevitable *adj.* assured, automatic, certain, decreed, definite, destined, fated, fixed, inescapable, inexorable, irrevocable, necessary, settled, sure, unalterable, unavoidable.
antonyms alterable, avoidable, uncertain.

inevitably *adv.* automatically, certainly, inescapably, necessarily, of necessity, surely, unavoidably, undoubtedly.

inexact *adj.* erroneous, fuzzy, imprecise, inaccurate, incorrect, indefinite, indistinct, loose, muddled, woolly.
antonyms exact, precise.

inexcusable *adj.* blameworthy, indefensible, intolerable, outrageous, reprehensible, shameful, unacceptable, unforgivable.
antonyms excusable, justifiable.

inexhaustible *adj.* abundant, boundless, endless, indefatigable, infinite, limitless, never-ending, never-failing, unbounded, undaunted, unfailing, unflagging, unlimited, untiring, unwearied, unwearying.
antonym limited.

inexorable *adj.* cruel, hard, harsh, immovable, inescapable, inflexible, irresistible, irrevocable, relentless, remorseless, unalterable, unrelenting.
antonyms flexible, lenient, yielding.

inexpensive *adj.* bargain, budget, cheap, economical, low-cost, low-priced, modest, reasonable.
antonyms dear, expensive.

inexperience *n.* ignorance, inexpertness, innocence, naïvety, newness, rawness, strangeness, unfamiliarity.
antonym experience.

inexperienced *adj.* amateur, callow, fresh, immature, inexpert, innocent, new, raw, unaccustomed, unacquainted, unfamiliar, unseasoned, unskilled, unsophisticated, untrained.
antonyms experienced, mature.

inexplicable *adj.* baffling, enigmatic, incomprehensible, incredible, miraculous, mysterious, mystifying, puzzling, strange, unaccountable, unfathomable.
antonym explicable.

inexpressible *adj.* indefinable, indescribable, nameless, unspeakable, unutterable.

inexpressive *adj.* bland, blank, dead-pan, emotionless, empty, expressionless, impassive, inanimate, inscrutable, lifeless, unexpressive, vacant.
antonym expressive.

inextricably *adv.* indissolubly, indistinguishably, inseparably, intricately.

infallible *adj.* accurate, certain, dependable, fail-safe, faultless, foolproof, impeccable, inerrant, omniscient, perfect, reliable, sound, sure, sure-fire, trustworthy, unerring, unfailing, unfaltering, unimpeachable.
antonym fallible.

infamous *adj.* disreputable, ill-famed, iniquitous, knavish, loathsome, notorious, outrageous, scandalous, shameful, shocking, wicked.
antonyms glorious, illustrious.

infamy *n.* discredit, disgrace, dishonour, disrepute, ignominy, notoriety, shame, wickedness.
antonym glory.

infancy *n.* **1** babyhood, birth, childhood, cradle, youth. **2** beginnings, commencement, dawn, embryonic stage, emergence, genesis, inception, origins, outset, start.
antonym **1** adulthood.

infant *n.* babe, babe in arms, baby, child, suckling, toddler, tot.
antonym adult.
adj. baby, childish, dawning, developing, early, emergent, growing, immature, initial, juvenile, new, newborn, rudimentary, young, youthful.
antonyms adult, mature.

infantile *adj.* adolescent, babyish, childish, immature, juvenile, puerile, undeveloped, young, youthful.
antonyms adult, mature.

infatuated *adj.* besotted, captivated, crazy, enamoured, enraptured, fascinated, mesmerised, obsessed, ravished, smitten, spellbound.
antonyms disenchanted, indifferent.

infatuation *n.* besottedness, crush, dotage, fascination, fixation, folly, fondness, obsession, passion.
antonyms disenchantment, indifference.

infect *v.* affect, blight, contaminate, corrupt, defile, enthuse, influence, inspire, pervert, poison, pollute, taint, touch.

infection *n.* contagion, contamination, corruption, defilement, disease, epidemic, illness, inflammation, influence, pestilence, poison, pollution, taint, virus.

infectious *adj.* catching, communicable, contagious, contaminating, corrupting, deadly, defiling, epidemic, infective, polluting, spreading, transmissible, virulent.

infer *v.* assume, conclude, deduce, derive, extrapolate, gather, presume, surmise, understand.

inference *n.* assumption, conclusion, conjecture, consequence, construction, corollary, deduction, extrapolation, interpretation, presumption, reading, surmise.

inferior *adj.* **1** humble, junior, lesser, low, lower, menial, minor, secondary, second-class, subordinate, subsidiary. **2** bad, mediocre, poor, second-rate, shoddy, slipshod, substandard, unsatisfactory.
antonyms **1** superior. **2** excellent.
n. junior, menial, minion, subordinate, underling, vassal.
antonym superior.

inferiority *n.* **1** humbleness, lowliness, subordination, subservience. **2** imperfection, inadequacy, insignificance, meanness, mediocrity, shoddiness, slovenliness.
antonyms **1** superiority. **2** excellence.

infernal *adj.* accursed, damnable, damned, devilish, diabolical, fiendish, hellish, malevolent, malicious, satanic, underworld.
antonym heavenly.

infertile *adj.* arid, barren, dried-up, nonproductive, parched, sterile, unbearing, unfruitful, unproductive.
antonym fertile.

infest *v.* flood, infiltrate, invade, overrun, overspread, penetrate, permeate, pervade, ravage, swarm, throng.

infidelity *n.* adultery, bad faith, betrayal, cheating, disbelief, disloyalty, duplicity, faithlessness, falseness, treachery, unbelief, unfaithfulness.
antonym fidelity.

infiltrate *v.* creep into, filter, insinuate, intrude, penetrate, percolate, permeate, pervade, sift.

infiltration *n.* intrusion, penetration, permeation, pervasion.

infiltrator *n.* intruder, penetrator, spy, subversive, subverter.

infinite *adj.* absolute, bottomless, boundless, countless, enormous, fathomless, immeasurable, immense, incomputable, inestimable, inexhaustible, limitless, never-ending, stupendous, total, unbounded, uncountable, unfathomable, untold, vast, wide.
antonym finite.

infinitesimal *adj.* atomic, imperceptible, inappreciable, inconsiderable, insignificant, microscopic, minuscule, minute, negligible, teeny, tiny.
antonyms large, significant, substantial.

infinity *n.* boundlessness, countlessness, endlessness, eternity, everlasting, immeasurableness, immensity, inexhaustibility, interminableness, limitlessness, perpetuity, vastness.
antonyms finiteness, limitation.

infirm *adj.* ailing, dicky, doddery, failing, faltering, feeble, frail, ill, lame, poorly, sickly, weak, wobbly.
antonyms healthy, strong.

inflame *v.* aggravate, agitate, anger, arouse, enrage, exasperate, excite, fan, fire, foment, fuel, heat, ignite, impassion, incense, increase, infuriate, intensify, kindle, madden, provoke, rouse, stimulate, worsen.
antonyms cool, quench.

inflamed *adj.* angry, chafing, enraged, excited, fevered, heated, hot, impassioned, incensed, infected, poisoned, red, septic, sore, swollen.

inflammable *adj.* burnable, combustible, flammable.
antonyms flameproof, incombustible, nonflammable, non-inflammable.

inflammation *n.* abscess, burning, heat, infection, painfulness, rash, redness, sore, soreness, swelling, tenderness.

inflammatory *adj.* explosive, fiery, provocative, rabble-rousing, riotous, seditious.
antonyms calming, pacific.

inflate *v.* bloat, blow out, blow up, boost, enlarge, escalate, exaggerate, expand, increase, puff out, puff up, pump up, swell.
antonym deflate.

inflation *n.* escalation, expansion, hyperinflation, increase, rise.
antonym deflation.

inflexible *adj.* adamant, dyed-in-the-wool, entrenched, fast, firm, fixed, hard, immovable, implacable, intransigent, iron, obstinate, relentless, resolute, rigid, set, stiff, strict, stringent, stubborn, taut, unaccommodating, uncompromising.
antonyms adaptable, flexible, yielding.

inflict *v.* administer, afflict, apply, burden, deal, deliver, enforce, exact, force, impose, lay, levy, mete out, perpetrate, visit, wreak.

influence *n.* agency, authority, bias, control, direction, domination, effect, guidance, hold, importance, mastery, power, pressure, prestige, pull, reach, rule, standing, strength, sway.
v. affect, alter, arouse, bias, change, control, direct, dispose, dominate, edge, guide, head, impel, impress, incite, incline, induce, instigate, manipulate, manoeuvre, modify, motivate, move, persuade, point, predispose, prompt, rouse, sway, teach, train, weigh with.

influential *adj.* authoritative, charismatic, compelling, controlling, dominant, dominating, effective, guiding, important, instrumental, leading, momentous, moving, persuasive, potent, powerful, significant, strong, telling, weighty, well-placed.
antonyms ineffective, unimportant.

inform *v.* acquaint, advise, brief, clue up, communicate, enlighten, fill in, illuminate, impart, instruct, intimate, leak, notify, tell (on), tip off.
inform on accuse, betray, blab, denounce, grass, incriminate, spy, squeal, tell on.

informal *adj.* casual, colloquial, cosy, easy, familiar, free, natural, relaxed, simple, unceremonious, unofficial, unpretentious.
antonyms formal, solemn.

information *n.* advice, blurb, briefing, bulletin, bumf, clues, communiqué, data, databank, database, dossier, facts, gen, illumination, input, instruction, intelligence, knowledge, message, news, notice, report, word.

informative *adj.* chatty, communicative, constructive, educational, enlightening, forthcoming, gossipy, illuminating, instructive, newsy, revealing, useful, valuable.
antonym uninformative.

informed *adj.* abreast, acquainted, au fait, authoritative, briefed, clued up, conversant, enlightened, erudite, expert, familiar, filled in, genned up, in the know, knowledgeable, learned, posted, primed, trained, up to date, versed, well-informed, well-read, well-researched.
antonyms ignorant, unaware.

informer *n.* betrayer, grass, Judas, mole, sneak, spy, squealer, supergrass.

infringe *v.* break, contravene, defy, disobey, encroach, flout, ignore, intrude, invade, overstep, transgress, trespass, violate.

infringement *n.* breach, contravention, defiance, encroachment, evasion, intrusion, invasion, transgression, trespass, violation.

infuriate *v.* anger, annoy, antagonise, enrage, exasperate, incense, irritate, madden, provoke, rile, rouse, vex.
antonyms calm, pacify.

infuse *v.* breathe into, brew, draw, imbue, impart to, implant, inculcate, inject, inspire, instil, introduce, saturate, soak, steep.

ingenious *adj.* clever, crafty, creative, imaginative, innovative, intricate, inventive, masterly, original.
antonyms clumsy, unimaginative.

ingenuity *n.* cleverness, cunning, faculty, flair, genius, gift, innovativeness, inventiveness, knack, originality, resourcefulness, shrewdness, skill.
antonyms awkwardness, clumsiness.

ingenuous *adj.* guileless, honest, innocent, naïve, open, plain, simple, sincere, trustful, trusting, unsophisticated.
antonyms artful, sly.

ingrained *adj.* deep-rooted, deep-seated, entrenched, fixed, immovable, inborn, inbred, inbuilt, ineradicable, permanent, rooted.

ingratiate *v.* crawl, curry favour, fawn, flatter, get in with, grovel, insinuate, suck up.

ingratiating *adj.* bootlicking, crawling, fawning, flattering, servile, smooth-tongued.

ingratitude *n.* thanklessness, unappreciativeness, ungraciousness, ungratefulness.
antonyms gratitude, thankfulness.

ingredient *n.* component, constituent, element, factor, part.

inhabit *v.* dwell, live, make one's home, occupy, people, populate, possess, reside, settle in, stay.

inhabitant *n.* citizen, dweller, lodger, native, occupant, occupier, resident, tenant.

inhale *v.* breathe in, draw, draw in, respire, suck in, whiff.

inherent *adj.* basic, characteristic, essential, fundamental, hereditary, inbred, inbuilt, ingrained, inherited, instinctive, intrinsic, native, natural.

inherit *v.* accede to, assume, be bequeathed, be heir to, be left, come in for, come into, receive, succeed to.

inheritance *n.* accession, bequest, birthright, descent, heredity, heritage, legacy, succession.

inheritor *n.* beneficiary, heir, heiress, recipient, successor.

inhibit *v.* curb, debar, discourage, forbid, frustrate, hinder, hold, impede, interfere with, obstruct, prevent, prohibit, repress, restrain, stanch, stem, stop, suppress, thwart.
antonyms encourage, support.

inhibited *adj.* frustrated, guarded, repressed, reserved, reticent, self-conscious, shamefaced, shy, strained, subdued, tense, withdrawn.
antonyms open, relaxed, uninhibited.

inhibition *n.* bar, check, hang-up, hindrance, impediment, obstruction, repression, reserve, restraint, restriction, reticence, self-consciousness, shyness.
antonym freedom.

inhuman *adj.* animal, barbaric, barbarous, brutal, callous, cold-blooded, cruel, heartless, inhumane, ruthless, savage, sublime, unfeeling, vicious.
antonyms compassionate, human.

inhumane *adj.* brutal, callous, cold-hearted, cruel, heartless, inhuman, insensitive, pitiless, unfeeling, unkind.
antonyms compassionate, humane, sympathetic.

inhumanity *n.* barbarity, brutality, callousness, cold-bloodedness, cruelty, hard-heartedness, heartlessness, ruthlessness, sadism, unkindness, viciousness.
antonyms humanity, love.

inimitable *adj.* distinctive, exceptional, incomparable, matchless, peerless, superlative, supreme, unequalled, unique, unmatched, unparalleled, unrivalled.

initial *adj.* beginning, commencing, early, first, formative, inaugural, infant, introductory, opening, original, primary.
antonyms final, last.

initially *adv.* at first, at the outset, first, first of all, firstly, in the beginning, introductorily, origin-

ally, to begin with, to start with.
antonyms finally, in the end.

initiate *v.* **1** begin, cause, commence, inaugurate, induce, institute, introduce, launch, open, originate, prompt, start, stimulate. **2** coach, indoctrinate, instruct, teach, train.

initiation *n.* admission, commencement, début, enrolment, entrance, entry, inauguration, inception, induction, installation, instruction, introduction, investiture, reception.

initiative *n.* **1** ambition, drive, dynamism, energy, enterprise, get-up-and-go, innovativeness, inventiveness, originality, resourcefulness. **2** action, recommendation, statement, step, suggestion.

inject *v.* add, bring, fix, infuse, inoculate, insert, instil, interject, introduce, jab, shoot, vaccinate.

injection *n.* dose, fix, infusion, inoculation, insertion, introduction, jab, shot, vaccination, vaccine.

injunction *n.* command, direction, directive, instruction, interdict, mandate, order, ruling.

injure *v.* abuse, blight, cripple, damage, deface, disable, disfigure, harm, hurt, ill-treat, impair, maim, maltreat, mar, offend, put out, ruin, scathe, spoil, tarnish, upset, vandalise, weaken, wound, wrong.

injury *n.* abuse, annoyance, damage, harm, hurt, ill, impairment, injustice, insult, lesion, loss, ruin, scathe, trauma, wound, wrong.

injustice *n.* bias, discrimination, disparity, favouritism, inequality, iniquity, one-sidedness, oppression, partiality, partisanship, prejudice, unfairness, wrong.
antonyms fairness, justice.

inkling *n.* allusion, clue, faintest, glimmering, hint, idea, indication, intimation, notion, pointer, sign, suggestion, suspicion, whisper.

inlaid *adj.* enchased, set, studded.

inlet *n.* bay, cove, creek, entrance, fjord, fleet, hope, opening, passage.

inn *n.* hostelry, hotel, local, pub, public house, saloon, tavern.

innate *adj.* essential, inborn, inbred, ingrained, inherent, inherited, instinctive, intrinsic, intuitive, native, natural.
antonyms acquired, learnt.

inner *adj.* central, concealed, emotional, essential, hidden, inside, interior, internal, intimate, inward, mental, middle, personal, private, psychological, secret, spiritual.
antonyms expressed, outer, outward.

innocence *n.* artlessness, blamelessness, chastity, freshness, guilelessness, guiltlessness, gullibility, harmlessness, honesty, ignorance, incorruptibility, inexperience, innocuousness, naïvety, naturalness, righteousness, simplicity, trustfulness, unfamiliarity, unsophistication, unworldliness, virginity, virtue.
antonyms experience, guilt, knowledge.

innocent *adj.* artless, bereft of, blameless, chaste, childlike, clear, credulous, dewy-eyed, faultless, frank, free of, fresh, green, guileless, guiltless, gullible, harmless, honest, immaculate, impeccable, incorrupt, ingenuous, innocuous, inoffensive, irreproachable, naïve, natural, open, pure, righteous, simple, sinless, spotless, stainless, trustful, trusting, uncontaminated, unimpeachable, unsullied, untainted, untouched, unworldly.
antonyms experienced, guilty, knowing.
n. babe, babe in arms, beginner, child, ignoramus, infant, tenderfoot.
antonyms connoisseur, expert.

innocuous *adj.* bland, harmless, innocent, inoffensive, safe, unobjectionable.
antonym harmful.

innovation *n.* alteration, change, departure, introduction, modernisation, neologism, newness, progress, reform, variation.

innovative *adj.* adventurous, bold, daring, enterprising, fresh, go-ahead, imaginative, inventive, modernising, new, original, progressive, reforming, resourceful.
antonyms conservative, unimaginative.

innuendo *n.* aspersion, hint, implication, imputation, insinuation, intimation, slant, slur, suggestion, whisper.

innumerable *adj.* countless, incalculable, infinite, many, numberless, numerous, uncountable, unnumbered.

inoculation *n.* immunisation, injection, protection, shot, vaccination.

inoffensive *adj.* harmless, innocuous, mild, peaceable, quiet, retiring, unassertive, unobtrusive.
antonyms malicious, offensive, provocative.

inoperative *adj.* defective, ineffective, non-functioning, out of action, out of order, out of service, unserviceable, unworkable, useless.
antonym operative.

inordinate *adj.* disproportionate, excessive, extravagant, great, immense, unreasonable, unwarranted.
antonyms moderate, reasonable.

input *v.* capture, code, feed in, insert, key in, process, store.
antonyms output, produce.

inquire *see* **enquire**.

inquiry *see* **enquiry**.

inquisition *n.* cross-examination, cross-questioning, examination, grilling, inquest, interrogation, investigation, questioning, quizzing, witch-hunt.

inquisitive *adj.* curious, intrusive, nosy, peeping, peering, probing, prying, questioning, snooping, snoopy.

insane *adj.* **1** crazy, demented, deranged, disturbed, lunatic, mad, mental, mentally ill. **2** foolish, impractical, senseless, stupid.
antonyms **1** sane. **2** sensible.

insanity *n.* aberration, craziness, delirium, derangement, folly, frenzy, irresponsibility, lunacy, madness, mania, mental illness, neurosis, senselessness, stupidity.
antonym sanity.

insatiable *adj.* immoderate, incontrollable, inordinate, persistent, ravenous, unquenchable, unsatisfiable.

inscribe *v.* **1** carve, cut, engrave, etch, impress, imprint, incise, stamp. **2** address, autograph, dedicate, enlist, enrol, enter, record, register, sign, write.

inscription *n.* autograph, caption, dedication, engraving, epitaph, label, legend, lettering, saying, signature, words.

inscrutable *adj.* baffling, cryptic, deep, enigmatic, hidden, impenetrable, incomprehensible, inexplicable, mysterious, unexplainable, unfathomable, unintelligible, unsearchable.
antonyms clear, comprehensible, expressive.

insecure *adj.* **1** afraid, anxious, nervous, uncertain, unsure, worried. **2** dangerous, defenceless, exposed, hazardous, loose, perilous, precarious, shaky, unprotected, unsafe, unsteady, vulnerable.
antonyms **1** confident, self-assured. **2** safe, secure.

insensitive *adj.* blunted, callous, dead, hardened, immune, impenetrable, impervious, indifferent, obtuse, resistant, thick-skinned, tough, unaffected, uncaring, unconcerned, unfeeling, unimpressionable, unmoved, unresponsive, unsusceptible.
antonym sensitive.

inseparable *adj.* bosom, close, devoted, indissoluble, indivisible, inextricable, intimate.
antonym separable.

insert *v.* embed, engraft, enter, implant, infix, inset, interleave, introduce, let in, place, put, put in, set, stick in.
n. advertisement, enclosure, insertion, inset, notice.

insertion *n.* addition, entry, implant, inclusion, insert, inset, introduction, intrusion, supplement.

inside *n.* content, contents, interior.
antonym outside.
adv. indoors, internally, inwardly, privately, secretly, within.
antonym outside.
adj. classified, confidential, exclusive, hush-hush, inner, innermost, interior, internal, inward, private, restricted, secret.

insides *n.* belly, bowels, entrails, gut, innards, organs, stomach, viscera.

insidious *adj.* crafty, crooked, cunning, deceitful, deceptive, devious, sly, sneaking, stealthy, subtle, surreptitious, treacherous, tricky, wily.
antonyms direct, straightforward.

insight *n.* acumen, acuteness, apprehension, awareness, comprehension, discernment, grasp, intelligence, intuition, judgement, knowledge, observation, penetration, perception, sensitivity, understanding, vision, wisdom.

insignia *n.* badge, brand, crest, decoration, emblem, mark, regalia, signs, symbol.

insignificant *adj.* inconsequential, inconsiderable, insubstantial, irrelevant, meaningless, minor, nonessential, paltry, petty, scanty, tiny, trifling, trivial, unimportant, unsubstantial.
antonyms important, significant.

insincere *adj.* deceitful, devious, dishonest, double-dealing, faithless, false, hollow, hypocritical, lying, phoney, pretended, two-faced, unfaithful, ungenuine, untrue, untruthful.
antonym sincere.

insinuate *v.* allude, get at, hint, imply, indicate, intimate, suggest.
insinuate oneself curry favour, get in with, ingratiate, sidle, work, worm.

insipid *adj.* bland, characterless, colourless, drab, dry, dull, flat, flavourless, lifeless, monotonous, pointless, savourless, spiritless, stale, tame, tasteless, trite, unappetising, unimaginative, uninteresting, unsavoury, watery, weak, weedy, wishy-washy.
antonyms appetising, piquant, punchy, tasty.

insist *v.* assert, claim, contend, demand, dwell on, emphasise, harp on, hold, maintain, persist, reiterate, repeat, request, require, stand firm, stress, swear, urge, vow.

insistence *n.* advice, certainty, contention, demand, determination, emphasis, encouragement, entreaty, exhortation, firmness, importunity, instance, persistence, persuasion, pressing, reiteration, stress, urgency, urging.

insistent *adj.* demanding, dogged, emphatic, forceful, importunate, incessant, persevering, persistent, pressing, relentless, tenacious, unrelenting, unremitting, urgent.

insolent *adj.* abusive, arrogant, bold, cheeky, contemptuous, defiant, disrespectful, forward, fresh, impertinent, impudent, insubordinate, insulting, presumptuous, rude, saucy.
antonyms polite, respectful.

insoluble *adj.* baffling, impenetrable, indecipherable, inexplicable, mysterious, mystifying, obscure, perplexing, unexplainable, unfathomable, unsolvable.
antonym explicable.

insolvency *n.* bankruptcy, default, failure, liquidation, ruin.
antonym solvency.

insolvent *adj.* bankrupt, broke, bust, defaulting, destitute, failed, flat broke, ruined.
antonym solvent.

inspect *v.* check, examine, investigate, look over, oversee, scan, scrutinise, search, study, superintend, supervise, survey, visit.

inspection *n.* check, check-up, examination, investigation, post-mortem, review, scan, scrutiny, search, supervision, survey.

inspector *n.* checker, controller, critic, examiner, investigator, overseer, reviewer, scrutiniser, superintendent, supervisor, surveyor, tester, viewer.

inspiration *n.* awakening, brain-wave, creativity, encouragement, enthusiasm, genius, illumination, influence, insight, revelation, spur, stimulation, stimulus.

inspire *v.* animate, arouse, encourage, enliven, enthuse, excite, fill, fire, galvanise, hearten, imbue, influence, infuse, inhale, instil, kindle, motivate, quicken, spark off, spur, stimulate, stir, trigger.

inspired *adj.* aroused, brilliant, dazzling, elated, enthralling, enthusiastic, exciting, exhilarated, fired, impressive, invigorated, memorable, outstanding, reanimated, stimulated, superlative, thrilled, thrilling, uplifted, wonderful.
antonyms dull, uninspired.

inspiring *adj.* affecting, encouraging, exciting, exhilarating, heartening, invigorating, moving, rousing, stimulating, stirring, uplifting.
antonyms dull, uninspiring.

instability *n.* changeableness, frailty, inconstancy, insecurity, irresolution, restlessness, shakiness, uncertainty, unpredictability, unreliability, unsafeness, unsoundness, unsteadiness, vacillation, variability, volatility, wavering, weakness.
antonym stability.

instal(l) *v.* **1** establish, fix, introduce, lay, locate, place, plant, position, put, set (up), settle, site, situate, station. **2** inaugurate, induct, institute, invest, ordain.

installation *n.* **1** base, depot, equipment, establishment, fitting, location, machinery, placing, plant, positioning, post, siting, station, system. **2** consecration, inauguration, induction, investiture, ordination.

instalment *n.* **1** payment, repayment. **2** chapter, division, episode, part, portion, section.

instant *n.* flash, minute, moment, occasion, point, second, split second, tick, time, twinkling.
adj. direct, fast, immediate, instantaneous, on-the-spot, prompt, quick, rapid, ready-mixed, urgent.
antonym slow.

instead *adv.* alternatively, as a substitute, as an alternative, in preference, preferably, rather.
instead of in lieu of, in place of, in preference to, on behalf of, rather than.

instigation *n.* incitement, initiative, insistence, prompting, urging.

instigator *n.* agent, author, inciter, leader, motivator, prime mover, provoker, ringleader, spur, troublemaker.

instil *v.* din into, engender, imbue, implant, impress, inculcate, infuse, inject, insinuate, introduce.

instinct *n.* ability, aptitude, faculty, feel, feeling, flair, gift, gut reaction, impulse, intuition, knack, predisposition, sixth sense, talent, tendency, urge.

instinctive *adj.* automatic, gut, immediate, impulsive, inborn, inherent, innate, intuitional, intuitive, involuntary, mechanical, native, natural, reflex, spontaneous, unpremeditated, unthinking.
antonyms conscious, deliberate, voluntary.

institute *v.* appoint, begin, commence, create, enact, establish, fix, found, inaugurate, induct, initiate, install, introduce, invest, launch, open, ordain, organise, originate, set up, settle, start, take up.
antonyms abolish, cancel, discontinue.
n. academy, association, college, conservatory, foundation, guild, institution, organisation, poly, polytechnic, school, seminary, society.

institution *n.* **1** convention, custom, law, practice, ritual, rule, tradition, usage. **2** academy, college, concern, corporation, establishment, foundation, hospital, institute, organisation, school, seminary, society, university. **3** creation, enactment, establishment, formation, foundation, founding, inception, initiation, installation, introduction.

institutional *adj.* accepted, bureaucratic, clinical, cold, customary, dreary, established, forbidding, formal, impersonal, monotonous, orthodox, regimented, routine, set, uniform, unwelcoming.
antonyms individualistic, unconventional.

instruct *v.* advise, coach, command, counsel, direct, discipline, drill, educate, enlighten, ground, guide, inform, mandate, notify, order, school, teach, tell, train, tutor.

instruction *n.* command, direction, directive, discipline, drilling, education, grounding, guidance, information, injunction, lesson(s), mandate, order, preparation, ruling, schooling, teaching, training, tuition.

instructive *adj.* educational, enlightening, helpful, illuminating, informative, useful.
antonym unenlightening.

instructor *n.* adviser, coach, demonstrator, exponent, guide, guru, master, mentor, mistress, teacher, trainer, tutor.

instrument *n.* agency, agent, apparatus, appliance, channel, contraption, contrivance, device, factor, force, gadget, implement, means, mechanism, medium, organ, tool, utensil, vehicle, way.

instrumental *adj.* active, assisting, auxiliary, conducive, contributory, helpful, influential, involved, subsidiary, useful.
antonyms obstructive, unhelpful.

insufferable *adj.* detestable, dreadful, impossible, intolerable, loathesome, unbearable.
antonyms pleasant, tolerable.

insufficiency *n.* dearth, deficiency, inadequacy, lack, need, poverty, scarcity, shortage, want.
antonyms excess, sufficiency.

insufficient *adj.* deficient, inadequate, lacking, short, sparse.
antonyms excessive, sufficient.

insular *adj.* blinkered, closed, cut off, detached, illiberal, inward-looking, isolated, limited, narrow, narrow-minded, parochial, petty, prejudiced, provincial, withdrawn.
antonym cosmopolitan.

insulate *v.* cocoon, cushion, cut off, isolate, protect, separate off, shelter, shield.

insulation *n.* cushioning, deadening, padding, protection, stuffing.

insult *v.* abuse, affront, call names, fling/throw mud at, give offence to, injure, libel, offend, outrage, revile, slander, slight, snub.
antonyms compliment, honour, praise.
n. abuse, affront, indignity, insolence, libel, offence, outrage, rudeness, slander, slap in the face, slight, snub.

antonyms compliment, honour, praise.

insurance *n.* assurance, cover, coverage, guarantee, indemnity, policy, premium, protection, provision, safeguard, security, warranty.

insure *v.* assure, cover, guarantee, indemnify, protect, underwrite, warrant.

insurer *n.* assurer, underwriter.

insurgent *n.* insurrectionist, mutineer, partisan, rebel, resister, revolutionary, rioter.
adj. disobedient, insubordinate, mutinous, partisan, rebellious, revolting, revolutionary, riotous.

insurmountable *adj.* hopeless, impossible, insuperable, invincible, overwhelming, unconquerable, unsurmountable.
antonym surmountable.

insurrection *n.* coup, insurgence, mutiny, putsch, rebellion, revolt, revolution, riot, rising, uprising.

intact *adj.* all in one piece, complete, entire, perfect, sound, together, unbroken, undamaged, unhurt, uninjured, whole.
antonyms broken, damaged, harmed.

intangible *adj.* airy, bodiless, elusive, imponderable, indefinite, invisible, shadowy, unreal, vague.
antonyms real, tangible.

integral *adj.* basic, complete, constituent, elemental, entire, essential, full, fundamental, indispensable, intrinsic, necessary, undivided, whole.
antonyms additional, extra, unnecessary.

integrate *v.* accommodate, amalgamate, assimilate, blend, coalesce, combine, fuse, harmonise, incorporate, join, knit, merge, mesh, mix, unite.
antonyms divide, separate.

integrity *n.* **1** goodness, honesty, incorruptibility, principle, probity, purity, righteousness, soundness, uprightness, virtue. **2** coherence, cohesion, completeness, unity, wholeness.
antonyms **1** dishonesty. **2** incompleteness.

intellect *n.* brain, brain power, brains, genius, highbrow, intellectual, intelligence, judgement, mind, reason, sense, understanding.
antonym stupidity.

intellectual *adj.* academic, intelligent, mental, rational, scholarly, studious, thoughtful.
antonym low-brow.
n. academic, highbrow, mastermind, thinker.
antonym low-brow.

intelligence *n.* **1** alertness, aptitude, brain power, brains, brightness, cleverness, comprehension, discernment, intellect, perception, quickness, reason, understanding. **2** advice, data, disclosure, facts, findings, gen, information, knowledge, low-down, news, tip-off.
antonyms **1** foolishness, stupidity.

intelligent *adj.* acute, alert, brainy, bright, clever, instructed, knowing, quick, quick-witted, rational, sharp, smart, thinking, well-informed.
antonyms foolish, stupid, unintelligent.

intend *v.* aim, contemplate, design, destine, determine, earmark, have a mind, mark out, mean, meditate, plan, project, propose, purpose, scheme, set apart.

intended *adj.* designated, desired, destined, future, intentional, planned, proposed, prospective.
antonym accidental.

intense *adj.* acute, close, concentrated, deep, eager, earnest, energetic, fervent, fervid, fierce, forceful, forcible, great, harsh, heightened, intensive, keen, passionate, powerful, profound, severe, strained, strong, vehement.
antonyms mild, moderate, weak.

intensify *v.* add to, aggravate, boost, concentrate, deepen, emphasise, enhance, escalate, fire, fuel, heighten, hot up, increase, quicken, reinforce, sharpen, step up, strengthen, whip up.
antonyms damp down, die down.

intensive *adj.* all-out, comprehensive, concentrated, demanding, detailed, exhaustive, in detail, in-depth, thorough, thoroughgoing.
antonym superficial.

intent *adj.* absorbed, alert, attentive, bent, committed, concentrated, determined, eager, earnest, engrossed, fixed, occupied, preoccupied, resolute, resolved, set, steadfast, steady, wrapped up.
antonyms absent-minded, distracted.

intention *n.* aim, design, end, goal, idea, meaning, object, objective, plan, point, purpose, scope, target, view.

intentional *adj.* calculated, deliberate, designed, intended, meant, planned, prearranged, premeditated, purposed, studied, wilful.
antonym accidental.

interbreeding *n.* cross-breeding, crossing, hybridisation, miscegenation.

intercede *v.* arbitrate, intervene, mediate, plead, speak.

intercept *v.* arrest, block, catch, check, cut off, delay, frustrate, head off, interrupt, obstruct, seize, stop, take, thwart.

intercession *n.* advocacy, agency, beseeching, entreaty, good offices, intervention, mediation, pleading, prayer, supplication.

interchangeable *adj.* equivalent, identical, reciprocal, similar, standard, synonymous, the same.
antonym different.

interest *n.* **1** attention, care, concern, curiosity, importance, involvement, note, notice, participation, significance. **2** activity, hobby, pastime, pursuit. **3** advantage, benefit, gain, influence, profit.
antonyms **1** boredom, irrelevance.
v. absorb, amuse, attract, concern, engage, engross, fascinate, intrigue, involve, move, touch, warm.
antonym bore.

interested *adj.* affected, attentive, attracted, concerned, curious, engrossed, fascinated, involved, keen, responsive.
antonyms apathetic, indifferent, unaffected.

interesting *adj.* absorbing, appealing, attractive, compelling, curious, engaging, engrossing, entertaining, gripping, intriguing, provocative,

stimulating, thought-provoking, unusual.
antonyms boring, dull, monotonous, tedious.

interfere *v.* block, butt in, clash, collide, conflict, cramp, frustrate, hamper, handicap, hinder, impede, inhibit, intervene, intrude, meddle, obstruct, poke one's nose in.
antonym assist.

interference *n.* clashing, collision, conflict, intervention, intrusion, meddling, obstruction, opposition, prying.
antonym assistance.

interim *adj.* acting, caretaker, improvised, intervening, makeshift, permanent, pro tem, provisional, stand-in, stop-gap, temporary.
n. interval, meantime, meanwhile.

interior *adj.* central, domestic, hidden, home, inland, inner, inside, internal, inward, mental, private, remote, secret, spiritual, up-country.
antonyms exterior, external.
n. centre, core, heart, heartland, inside.
antonyms exterior, outside.

interjection *n.* call, cry, ejaculation, exclamation, interpolation, shout.

interlink *v.* clasp together, interconnect, interlock, intertwine, interweave, knit, link, link together, lock together, mesh.
antonyms divide, separate.

interloper *n.* gate-crasher, intruder, trespasser, uninvited guest.

interlude *n.* break, breathing-space, delay, halt, intermission, interval, pause, rest, spell, stop, stoppage, wait.

intermediary *n.* agent, broker, go-between, in-between, mediator, middleman, ombudsman.

intermediate *adj.* halfway, in-between, intermediary, intervening, mean, median, mid, middle, midway, transitional.
antonym extreme.

interminable *adj.* dragging, endless, limitless, long, long-drawn-out, long-winded, never-ending, perpetual, unlimited, wearisome.
antonyms brief, limited.

intermingle *v.* amalgamate, blend, combine, fuse, intermix, merge, mix (together).
antonyms divide, separate.

intermission *n.* break, breather, breathing-space, cessation, interlude, interruption, interval, let-up, lull, pause, recess, remission, respite, rest, stop, stoppage, suspense, suspension.

intermittent *adj.* broken, irregular, occasional, periodical, spasmodic, sporadic, stop-go.
antonyms constant, continuous.

internal *adj.* domestic, in-house, inner, inside, interior, intimate, inward, private, subjective.
antonym external.

international *adj.* cosmopolitan, general, global, intercontinental, universal, worldwide.
antonyms local, national, parochial.

interplay *n.* exchange, give-and-take, interaction, interchange, meshing, reciprocation.

interpose *v.* come between, insert, interfere, interrupt, intervene, introduce, intrude, mediate, offer, place between, put in, step in, thrust in.

interpret *v.* clarify, decipher, decode, define, elucidate, explain, expound, make sense of, paraphrase, read, render, solve, take, throw light on, translate, understand.

interpretation *n.* analysis, clarification, explanation, meaning, performance, reading, rendering, sense, signification, translation, understanding, version.

interpreter *n.* annotator, commentator, exponent, expositor, linguist, translator.

interrogate *v.* ask, cross-examine, cross-question, debrief, enquire, examine, give (someone) the third degree, grill, investigate, pump, question, quiz.

interrogation *n.* cross-examination, cross-questioning, enquiry, examination, grilling, inquisition, probing, questioning, third degree.

interrupt *v.* barge in, break, break in, butt in, check, cut, cut off, cut short, disturb, divide, heckle, hinder, hold up, interfere, interject, intrude, obstruct, punctuate, separate, stay, stop, suspend.
antonym forbear.

interruption *n.* break, disconnection, discontinuance, disruption, disturbance, division, halt, hindrance, hitch, impediment, intrusion, obstacle, obstruction, pause, separation, stop, stoppage, suspension.

intersect *v.* bisect, criss-cross, cross, cut, cut across, divide, meet.

intersection *n.* crossing, crossroads, division, interchange, junction.

intersperse *v.* dot, pepper, scatter, sprinkle.

intertwine *v.* cross, entwine, interweave, link, twist.

interval *n.* break, delay, distance, gap, in-between, interim, interlude, intermission, meantime, meanwhile, opening, pause, period, playtime, rest, season, space, spell, term, time, wait.

intervene *v.* arbitrate, happen, interfere, interrupt, intrude, involve, mediate, occur, step in, succeed.

intervention *n.* agency, intercession, interference, intrusion, mediation.

interview *n.* audience, conference, consultation, dialogue, enquiry, inquisition, meeting, oral examination, press conference, talk, viva.
v. examine, interrogate, question, viva.

intestines *n.* bowels, entrails, guts, innards, insides, offal, viscera, vitals.

intimacy *n.* brotherliness, closeness, confidence, familiarity, friendship, sisterliness, understanding.
antonym distance.

intimate[1] *v.* allude, announce, communicate, declare, hint, impart, imply, indicate, insinuate, state, suggest, tell.

intimate[2] *adj.* bosom, cherished, close, confidential, cosy, dear, deep, deep-seated, detailed, exhaustive, friendly, informal, innermost, internal, near, penetrating, personal, private, secret, warm.
antonyms cold, distant, unfriendly.
n. associate, bosom friend, buddy, chum, com-

rade, confidant, confidante, friend, mate, pal.
antonym stranger.

intimidate *v.* alarm, appal, browbeat, bulldoze, bully, coerce, dismay, frighten, lean on, overawe, scare, terrify, terrorise, threaten.

intimidation *n.* arm-twisting, browbeating, bullying, coercion, fear, menacing, pressure, terrorisation, terrorising, threats.

intolerable *adj.* impossible, insufferable, insupportable, painful, unbearable, unendurable.
antonym tolerable.

intolerant *adj.* bigoted, dogmatic, fanatical, illiberal, impatient, narrow-minded, opinionated, prejudiced, racialist, racist, small-minded, uncharitable.
antonym tolerant.

intonation *n.* accentuation, inflection, modulation, tone.

intoxicated *adj.* drunk, drunken, inebriated, tipsy, under the influence.
antonym sober.

intoxicating *adj.* **1** alcoholic, strong. **2** exciting, exhilarating, heady, stimulating, thrilling.
antonym **1** sobering.

intoxication *n.* **1** drunkenness, inebriation, tipsiness. **2** elation, euphoria, excitement, exhilaration.
antonym **1** sobriety.

intrepid *adj.* bold, brave, courageous, daring, dauntless, fearless, gallant, gutsy, heroic, lion-hearted, plucky, resolute, stalwart, stout-hearted, undaunted, valiant.
antonyms afraid, cowardly, timid.

intricacy *n.* complexity, complication, elaborateness, entanglement, intricateness, involvement, knottiness, obscurity.
antonym simplicity.

intricate *adj.* complex, complicated, convoluted, difficult, elaborate, fancy, involved, knotty, perplexing, rococo, sophisticated, tangled, tortuous.
antonyms plain, simple, straightforward.

intrigue *n.* affair, amour, collusion, conspiracy, double-dealing, intimacy, liaison, machination, manipulation, manoeuvre, plot, romance, ruse, scheme, sharp practice, stratagem, trickery, wile.
v. **1** attract, charm, excite, fascinate, puzzle, rivet, tantalise. **2** connive, conspire, machinate, manoeuvre, plot, scheme.
antonym **1** bore.

introduce *v.* **1** acquaint, announce, begin, bring in, commence, establish, familiarise, found, inaugurate, initiate, institute, launch, open, present, start. **2** advance, offer, propose, put forward, submit, suggest.
antonyms **1** conclude, end. **2** remove, take away.

introduction *n.* **1** commencement, debut, establishment, inauguration, induction, initiation, institution, launch, pioneering, presentation. **2** foreword, lead-in, opening, overture, preamble, preface, preliminaries, prelude, prologue.
antonyms **1** removal, withdrawal. **2** appendix, conclusion.

introductory *adj.* early, elementary, first, inaugural, initial, opening, preliminary, preparatory, starting.

introspection *n.* brooding, heart-searching, self-analysis, self-examination, soul-searching.

introspective *adj.* brooding, contemplative, introverted, inward-looking, meditative, pensive, subjective, thoughtful.
antonym outward-looking.

introverted *adj.* introspective, inward-looking, self-centred, withdrawn.
antonym extroverted.

intrude *v.* butt in, encroach, infringe, interfere, interrupt, meddle, trespass, violate.
antonyms stand back, withdraw.

intruder *n.* burglar, gate-crasher, infiltrator, interloper, invader, prowler, raider, trespasser.

intrusion *n.* encroachment, incursion, infringement, interference, invasion, trespass, violation.
antonym withdrawal.

intrusive *adj.* disturbing, interfering, obtrusive, uncalled-for, unwanted, unwelcome.
antonyms unintrusive, welcome.

intuition *n.* discernment, feeling, gut feeling, hunch, insight, instinct, perception, sixth sense.
antonym reasoning.

intuitive *adj.* innate, instinctive, involuntary, spontaneous, unreflecting, untaught.
antonym reasoned.

inundate *v.* bury, deluge, drown, engulf, fill, flood, immerse, overflow, overrun, overwhelm, submerge, swamp.

invade *v.* attack, burst in, come upon, descend upon, enter, infest, infringe, occupy, overrun, overspread, penetrate, pervade, raid, rush into, seize, swarm over, violate.
antonyms evacuate, withdraw.

invader *n.* aggressor, attacker, intruder, raider, trespasser.

invalid[1] *adj.* ailing, bedridden, disabled, feeble, frail, ill, infirm, poorly, sick, sickly, weak.
antonym healthy.
n. convalescent, patient, sufferer.

invalid[2] *adj.* baseless, false, illegal, ill-founded, illogical, incorrect, irrational, unfounded, unscientific, unsound, worthless.
antonyms legal, valid.

invalidate *v.* abrogate, annul, cancel, negate, nullify, quash, rescind, undo.
antonym validate.

invaluable *adj.* costly, exquisite, inestimable, precious, priceless, valuable.
antonyms cheap, worthless.

invariable *adj.* constant, fixed, habitual, inflexible, permanent, regular, rigid, set, static, unchangeable, unchanging, uniform, unwavering.
antonym variable.

invariably *adv.* always, consistently, habitually, inevitably, perpetually, regularly, unfailingly, without exception, without fail.
antonym never.

invasion *n.* aggression, attack, breach, encroachment, foray, incursion, infiltration,

infringement, intrusion, offensive, onslaught, raid, seizure, violation.
antonyms evacuation, withdrawal.
invent *v.* conceive, concoct, contrive, cook up, create, design, devise, discover, dream up, fabricate, formulate, frame, imagine, improvise, make up, originate, think up, trump up.
invention *n.* **1** brainchild, creation, creativity, design, development, device, discovery, gadget, genius. **2** deceit, fabrication, fake, falsehood, fantasy, fib, fiction, figment of (someone's) imagination, forgery, lie, sham, tall story.
antonym **2** truth.
inventive *adj.* creative, fertile, gifted, imaginative, ingenious, innovative, inspired, original, resourceful.
antonym uninventive.
inventor *n.* architect, author, builder, coiner, creator, designer, father, framer, maker, originator.
inverse *adj.* contrary, converse, inverted, opposite, reverse, reversed, transposed, upside down.
antonym direct.
invert *v.* capsize, overturn, reverse, transpose, turn upside down, upset, upturn.
antonym right.
invest *v.* **1** charge, devote, lay out, put in, sink, spend. **2** authorise, consecrate, empower, endow, endue, establish, provide, sanction, supply, vest.
investigate *v.* consider, enquire into, examine, explore, go into, inspect, look into, probe, scrutinise, search, sift, study.
investigation *n.* analysis, enquiry, examination, exploration, fact finding, hearing, inquest, inspection, probe, research, review, scrutiny, search, study, survey.
investigator *n.* detective, enquirer, examiner, inquisitor, private detective, private eye, researcher, sleuth.
investiture *n.* coronation, enthronement, inauguration, installation, investing, investment, ordination.
investment *n.* asset, contribution, investing, outlay, speculation, stake, transaction, venture.
invidious *adj.* discriminating, discriminatory, impossible, objectionable, odious, offensive, slighting, undesirable, unfair, unpleasant.
antonyms desirable, fair.
invigorate *v.* animate, brace, energise, enliven, exhilarate, fortify, freshen, harden, inspire, liven up, nerve, perk up, quicken, refresh, revitalise, stimulate, strengthen, vitalise.
antonyms dishearten, tire, weary.
invincible *adj.* impenetrable, impregnable, indestructible, indomitable, insuperable, invulnerable, unassailable, unsurmountable, unyielding.
antonym beatable.
invisible *adj.* concealed, disguised, hidden, imaginary, imperceptible, inconspicuous, indiscernible, infinitesimal, microscopic, nonexistent, out of sight, unseeable, unseen.
antonym visible.
invitation *n.* allurement, asking, begging, call, challenge, come-on, enticement, incitement, inducement, overture, provocation, request, solicitation, summons, temptation.
invite *v.* allure, ask, ask for, attract, bring on, call, draw, encourage, entice, inspire, lead, provoke, request, seek, solicit, summon, tempt, welcome.
antonyms force, order.
inviting *adj.* appealing, attractive, captivating, delightful, enticing, fascinating, intriguing, mouthwatering, pleasing, seductive, tantalising, tempting, warm, welcoming, winning.
antonyms unappealing, uninviting.
invoke *v.* adjure, appeal to, apply, base on, beg, beseech, call upon, conjure, entreat, implore, initiate, petition, pray, quote, refer to, resort to, solicit, supplicate, use.
involuntary *adj.* automatic, blind, conditioned, forced, instinctive, reflex, spontaneous, unconscious, uncontrolled, unintentional, unthinking, unwilled, unwilling.
antonyms deliberate, intentional.
involve *v.* **1** affect, concern, contain, cover, draw in, embrace, entail, imply, include, incorporate, incriminate, mean, necessitate, require, take in. **2** associate, commit, implicate, mix up. **3** absorb, engage, engross, grip, hold, preoccupy, rivet.
antonym **1** exclude.
involved *adj.* **1** caught up, concerned, in on, mixed up, occupied, participating. **2** complex, complicated, confusing, difficult, elaborate, intricate, knotty, tangled, tortuous.
antonyms **1** uninvolved. **2** simple.
involvement *n.* association, commitment, concern, connection, entanglement, implication, participation, responsibility.
invulnerable *adj.* impenetrable, indestructible, insusceptible, invincible, proof against, safe, secure, unassailable, unwoundable.
antonym vulnerable.
inward *adj.* confidential, entering, hidden, incoming, inmost, inner, innermost, inside, interior, internal, penetrating, personal, private, secret.
antonyms external, outward.
iota *n.* atom, bit, drop, grain, hint, jot, mite, particle, scrap, speck, trace.
irate *adj.* angered, angry, annoyed, exasperated, fuming, furious, incensed, indignant, infuriated, irritated, livid, mad, provoked, riled, up in arms, worked up.
antonyms calm, composed.
irk *v.* aggravate, annoy, distress, gall, get to, irritate, provoke, put out, ruffle, vex, weary.
antonyms delight, please.
iron *adj.* adamant, cruel, determined, fixed, grating, hard, harsh, heavy, immovable, inflexible, insensitive, rigid, robust, steel, steely, strong, tough, unbending, unyielding.
antonyms pliable, weak.
v. flatten, press, smooth, uncrease.
iron out clear up, deal with, eliminate, eradicate, erase, fix, get rid of, put right, reconcile, resolve, settle, smooth over, solve, sort out,

straighten out.

ironic *adj.* contemptuous, derisive, incongruous, ironical, mocking, paradoxical, sarcastic, sardonic, satirical, scoffing, scornful, sneering, wry.

irony *n.* contrariness, incongruity, mockery, paradox, sarcasm, satire.

irrational *adj.* absurd, crazy, foolish, illogical, mindless, senseless, silly, unreasonable, unsound, unwise, wild.
antonym rational.

irreconcilable *adj.* clashing, conflicting, incompatible, incongruous, inconsistent, opposed.
antonym reconcilable.

irrefutable *adj.* certain, incontestable, incontrovertible, indisputable, invincible, sure, unanswerable, undeniable, unquestionable.

irregular *adj.* **1** bumpy, crooked, rough, uneven. **2** disorderly, erratic, fitful, fluctuating, haphazard, intermittent, occasional, random, spasmodic, sporadic, unsystematic, variable, wavering. **3** abnormal, anomalous, exceptional, unconventional, unorthodox, unusual.
antonyms **1** level, smooth. **2** regular. **3** conventional.

irrelevant *adj.* inapplicable, inappropriate, inconsequent, peripheral, tangential, unconnected, unnecessary, unrelated.
antonym relevant.

irreplaceable *adj.* indispensable, matchless, peerless, priceless, sublime, unique, unmatched, vital.
antonym replaceable.

irrepressible *adj.* boisterous, bubbling over, buoyant, ebullient, resilient, uncontrollable, uninhibited, unstoppable.
antonyms depressed, despondent, resistible.

irreproachable *adj.* blameless, faultless, immaculate, impeccable, irreprehensible, perfect, pure, reproachless, stainless, taintless, unblemished, unimpeachable.
antonyms blameworthy, culpable.

irresistible *adj.* charming, compelling, enchanting, fascinating, imperative, inescapable, inevitable, overpowering, overwhelming, potent, pressing, ravishing, resistless, seductive, tempting, unavoidable, uncontrollable, urgent.
antonyms avoidable, resistible.

irresponsible *adj.* carefree, careless, foot-loose, heedless, ill-considered, immature, lighthearted, negligent, rash, reckless, thoughtless, unreliable, untrustworthy, wild.
antonyms cautious, responsible.

irreverent *adj.* discourteous, disrespectful, flippant, godless, impertinent, impious, impudent, mocking, profane, rude, sacrilegious.
antonyms respectful, reverent.

irreversible *adj.* final, hopeless, incurable, irreparable, irretrievable, irrevocable, lasting, lost, permanent, unalterable.
antonyms curable, remediable, reversible.

irrevocable *adj.* changeless, fixed, hopeless, immutable, inexorable, invariable, irretrievable, predetermined, settled, unalterable, unchangeable.
antonyms alterable, flexible, reversible.

irrigate *v.* dampen, flood, inundate, moisten, water, wet.

irritable *adj.* bad-tempered, cantankerous, crabby, cross, crotchety, crusty, edgy, fractious, fretful, hasty, hypersensitive, ill-humoured, ill-tempered, impatient, peevish, prickly, short, short-tempered, snappish, snappy, tense, testy, thin-skinned, touchy.
antonyms cheerful, complacent.

irritate *v.* **1** aggravate, anger, annoy, bother, enrage, exasperate, get on one's nerves, get to, harass, incense, infuriate, irk, offend, peeve, provoke, put out, rile, rouse. **2** chafe, inflame, rub.
antonyms **1** gratify, please.

irritation *n.* aggravation, anger, annoyance, crossness, displeasure, dissatisfaction, exasperation, fury, impatience, indignation, irritability, irritant, nuisance, pain, provocation, resentment, snappiness, testiness, vexation.
antonyms delight, pleasure, satisfaction.

isolate *v.* abstract, alienate, boycott, cut off, detach, disconnect, divorce, exclude, identify, insulate, keep apart, ostracise, quarantine, remove, seclude, segregate, separate, sequester, set apart.
antonyms assimilate, incorporate.

isolated *adj.* **1** cut off, deserted, detached, godforsaken, lonely, outlying, out-of-the-way, remote, retired, secluded, single, solitary, unfrequented, unvisited. **2** abnormal, anomalous, atypical, exceptional, freak, special, unique, unusual.
antonyms **1** populous. **2** typical.

isolation *n.* alienation, detachment, disconnection, dissociation, exile, insulation, loneliness, quarantine, remoteness, retirement, seclusion, segregation, self-sufficiency, separation, solitariness, solitude, withdrawal.

issue *n.* **1** affair, argument, concern, controversy, crux, debate, matter, point, problem, question, subject, topic. **2** announcement, broadcast, circulation, copy, delivery, dispersal, distribution, edition, flow, granting, handout, impression, instalment, number, printing, promulgation, propagation, publication, release, supply, supplying.
v. **1** announce, broadcast, circulate, deal out, deliver, distribute, emit, give out, produce, promulgate, publicise, publish, put out, release, supply. **2** arise, burst forth, emanate, emerge, flow, leak, originate, proceed, rise, spring, stem.

itch *v.* crawl, prickle, tickle, tingle.
n. **1** irritation, itchiness, prickling, scabies. **2** craving, desire, eagerness, hankering, keenness, longing, yearning.

itchy *adj.* fidgety, impatient, restless, roving, unsettled.

item *n.* account, article, aspect, component, consideration, detail, element, entry, factor, feature, ingredient, matter, note, notice, object, paragraph, particular, piece, point, report, thing.

itinerant *adj.* journeying, migratory, nomadic, peripatetic, rambling, roaming, rootless, roving, travelling, wandering, wayfaring.
antonyms settled, stationary.
n. gypsy, nomad, peripatetic, pilgrim, Romany, tinker, tramp, traveller, vagrant, wanderer, wayfarer.

itinerary *n.* circuit, course, journey, plan, programme, route, schedule, tour.

J

jab *v.* dig, elbow, lunge, nudge, poke, prod, punch, push, stab, tap, thrust.
jabber *v.* babble, blather, chatter, gab, jaw, mumble, prate, rabbit, ramble, witter, yap.
jackpot *n.* award, big time, bonanza, kitty, pool, pot, prize, reward, stakes, winnings.
jaded *adj.* bored, dulled, exhausted, fagged, fatigued, played-out, spent, tired, tired out, weary.
antonyms fresh, refreshed.
jagged *adj.* barbed, broken, craggy, indented, irregular, notched, pointed, ragged, ridged, rough, saw-edged, serrated, toothed, uneven.
antonyms even, smooth.
jail, gaol *n.* custody, guardhouse, inside, jailhouse, jankers, lock-up, nick, penitentiary, prison.
v. confine, detain, immure, impound, imprison, incarcerate, intern, lock up, put away, send down.
jailer, gaoler *n.* captor, guard, keeper, prison officer, screw, warden, warder.
jam[1] *v.* block, clog, confine, congest, cram, crowd, crush, force, obstruct, pack, press, ram, sandwich, squash, squeeze, stall, stick, stuff, wedge.
n. bottle-neck, concourse, crowd, crush, herd, horde, mass, mob, multitude, pack, press, swarm, throng, traffic jam.
jam[2] *n.* confiture, conserve, jelly, marmalade, preserve, spread.
jangle *v.* chime, clank, clash, clatter, jar, jingle, rattle, upset, vibrate.
n. cacophony, clang, clash, din, dissonance, jar, racket, rattle, reverberation, stridence.
antonyms euphony, harmony.
janitor *n.* caretaker, custodian, doorkeeper, doorman, porter.
jar[1] *n.* can, carafe, container, crock, cruse, flagon, jug, mug, pitcher, pot, receptacle, urn, vase, vessel.
jar[2] *v.* agitate, annoy, clash, disagree, discompose, disturb, grate, grind, interfere, irk, irritate, jangle, jolt, nettle, offend, quarrel, rasp, rattle, rock, shake, upset, vibrate.
jargon *n.* gobbledegook, mumbo-jumbo, nonsense, parlance, tongue, twaddle, vernacular.
jarring *adj.* cacophonous, discordant, dissonant, disturbing, grating, irritating, jangling, jolting, rasping, strident, upsetting.
jaunty *adj.* airy, breezy, buoyant, carefree, cheeky, dapper, debonair, high-spirited, lively, perky, self-confident, showy, smart, sparkish, sprightly.
antonyms anxious, depressed, dowdy.
jaw[1] *n.* jaws, masticator, mouth, muzzle.
jaw[2] *v.* babble, chat, chatter, gab, gabble, gossip, natter, talk.
n. chat, chinwag, conversation, discussion, gab, gossip, natter, talk.
jazz *n.* blues, boogie, boogie-woogie, guff, hard rock, heavy metal, ragtime, rhythm, rock, swing, talk.
jazzy *adj.* avant-garde, bold, fancy, flashy, gaudy, lively, smart, snazzy, swinging, wild.
antonym dull.
jealous *adj.* covetous, desirous, envious, green, green-eyed, grudging, possessive, protective, resentful, rival, suspicious, wary.
antonyms contented, satisfied.
jealousy *n.* covetousness, distrust, envy, grudge, ill-will, mistrust, possessiveness, resentment, spite, suspicion.
jeer *v.* banter, barrack, chaff, explode, heckle, hector, jibe, knock, mock, ridicule, scoff, sneer, taunt, twit.
n. abuse, catcall, derision, dig, hiss, hoot, jibe, mockery, ridicule, scoff, sneer, taunt.
jell, gel *v.* coagulate, congeal, crystallise, finalise, form, harden, materialise, set, solidify, take form, take shape, thicken.
antonym disintegrate.
jeopardise *v.* chance, endanger, expose, gamble, hazard, imperil, menace, risk, stake, threaten, venture.
antonyms protect, safeguard.
jeopardy *n.* danger, endangerment, exposure, hazard, insecurity, liability, peril, precariousness, risk, venture, vulnerability.
antonyms safety, security.
jerk *n.* bounce, jog, jolt, lurch, pluck, pull, shrug, throw, thrust, tug, twitch, wrench, yank.
v. bounce, flirt, jigger, jog, jolt, lurch, pluck, pull, shrug, throw, thrust, tug, twitch, wrench, yank.
jerky *adj.* bouncy, bumpy, convulsive, disconnected, fitful, incoherent, jolting, jumpy, rough, shaky, spasmodic, twitchy, uncontrolled, uncoordinated.
antonym smooth.
jerry-built *adj.* cheap, defective, faulty, flimsy, insubstantial, ramshackle, rickety, shoddy, slipshod.
antonyms firm, stable, substantial.
jersey *n.* jumper, pullover, sweater, sweat-shirt, woolly.
jet[1] *n.* flow, fountain, gush, issue, nose, nozzle, rose, rush, spout, spray, sprayer, spring, sprinkler, spurt, squirt, stream, surge.
jet[2] *adj.* black, coal-black, ebony, inky, jetty,

pitch-black, pitchy, sooty.
jetty *n.* breakwater, dock, groyne, pier, quay, wharf.
jewel *n.* charm, find, gem, gemstone, locket, masterpiece, ornament, paragon, pearl, precious stone, prize, rarity, rock, stone, treasure, wonder.
jewellery *n.* finery, gems, jewels, ornaments, regalia, treasure.
jibe, gibe *n.* crack, dig, jeer, mockery, poke, quip, raillery, ridicule, sarcasm, scoff, slant, sneer, taunt, thrust.
jig *v.* bob, bounce, caper, hop, jerk, jump, prance, shake, skip, twitch, wiggle, wobble.
jiggle *v.* fidget, jerk, jig, jog, joggle, shake, shift, twitch, wiggle, wobble.
jilt *v.* abandon, betray, brush off, desert, discard, ditch, drop, reject, spurn.
jingle *v.* chime, chink, clatter, clink, jangle, rattle, ring.
n. **1** clang, clangour, clink, rattle, ringing. **2** chant, chorus, couplet, ditty, melody, poem, rhyme, song, tune, verse.
jingoism *n.* chauvinism, flag-waving, imperialism, insularity, nationalism, parochialism, patriotism.
jinx *n.* black magic, charm, curse, evil eye, gremlin, hex, hoodoo, plague, spell, voodoo.
v. bedevil, bewitch, curse, doom, plague.
jitters *n.* anxiety, fidgets, nerves, nervousness, tenseness, the shakes.
jittery *adj.* agitated, anxious, edgy, fidgety, jumpy, nervous, quaking, quivering, shaky, shivery, trembling, uneasy.
antonyms calm, composed, confident.
job *n.* activity, affair, assignment, batch, business, calling, capacity, career, charge, chore, commission, concern, consignment, contract, contribution, duty, employment, enterprise, errand, function, livelihood, message, mission, occupation, office, part, place, position, post, proceeding, product, profession, project, province, pursuit, responsibility, role, share, situation, stint, task, trade, undertaking, venture, vocation, work.
jobless *adj.* idle, inactive, laid off, on the dole, out of work, unemployed.
antonym employed.
jocular *adj.* amusing, comical, droll, entertaining, facetious, funny, humorous, jesting, jocose, joking, jovial, teasing, whimsical, witty.
antonym serious.
jog *v.* **1** activate, arouse, bounce, bump, jar, jerk, joggle, jolt, jostle, nudge, poke, prod, prompt, push, remind, rock, shake, stimulate, stir. **2** run, trot.
n. **1** bump, jerk, jolt, nudge, poke, prod, push, reminder, shake, shove. **2** run, trot.
join *v.* abut, accompany, add, adhere, affiliate, amalgamate, annex, associate, attach, border (on), butt, cement, coincide, combine, connect, couple, dock, enlist, enrol, enter, fasten, knit, link, march with, marry, meet, merge, reach, sign up, splice, team, tie, touch, unite, verge on, yoke.
antonyms divide, leave, separate.
join in chip in, contribute, co-operate, help, lend a hand, muck in, partake, participate, pitch in, take part in.
join up enlist, enroll, enter, sign up.
joint *n.* articulation, connection, hinge, intersection, junction, juncture, knot, seam, union.
adj. adjunct, amalgamated, collective, combined, communal, concerted, consolidated, co-operative, co-ordinated, joined, mutual, shared, united.
joke *n.* frolic, fun, gag, hoot, jest, lark, play, pun, quip, quirk, spoof, target, whimsy, wisecrack, witticism, yarn, yell.
v. banter, clown, fool, frolic, gambol, jest, kid, laugh, mock, quip, ridicule, taunt, tease.
joker *n.* buffoon, card, character, clown, comedian, comic, droll, humorist, jester, kidder, sport, trickster, wag, wit.
jolly *adj.* cheerful, exuberant, happy, hearty, jovial, merry, playful.
antonym sad.
jolt *v.* bounce, bump, discompose, disconcert, dismay, disturb, jar, jerk, jog, jostle, knock, push, shake, shock, startle, stun, surprise, upset.
n. blow, bump, hit, impact, jar, jerk, jog, jump, lurch, quiver, reversal, setback, shake, shock, start, surprise.
jostle *v.* bump, crowd, elbow, force, jog, joggle, jolt, press, push, rough up, scramble, shake, shoulder, shove, squeeze, throng, thrust.
journal *n.* book, chronicle, daybook, diary, gazette, log, magazine, monthly, newspaper, paper, periodical, publication, record, register, review, tabloid, weekly.
journalism *n.* copy-writing, correspondence, feature-writing, Fleet Street, fourth estate, news, press, reportage, reporting, writing.
journalist *n.* broadcaster, columnist, commentator, contributor, correspondent, diarist, editor, feature-writer, hack, newsman, newspaperman, news-writer, reporter, scribe, writer.
journey *n.* course, expedition, itinerary, outing, passage, progress, ramble, route, safari, tour, travel, trek, trip, voyage, wanderings.
v. fare, fly, gallivant, go, jaunt, proceed, ramble, range, roam, rove, safari, tour, tramp, travel, traverse, trek, voyage, wander, wend.
jovial *adj.* affable, cheery, cordial, happy, jolly, merry.
antonyms gloomy, sad.
joy *n.* blessedness, bliss, charm, delight, ecstasy, elation, exultation, gladness, gratification, happiness, joyfulness, pleasure, rapture, ravishment, treasure, wonder.
antonyms despair, grief, mourning, sorrow.
joyful *adj.* delighted, ecstatic, elated, glad, happy, pleased, triumphant.
antonyms mournful, sorrowful.
jubilation *n.* celebration, ecstasy, elation, euphoria, excitement, exultation, festivity, triumph.

antonyms depression, lamentation.

jubilee *n.* anniversary, carnival, celebration, commemoration, festival, festivity, fête, gala, holiday.

judge *n.* adjudicator, arbiter, arbitrator, assessor, authority, connoisseur, critic, evaluator, expert, justice, Law Lord, magistrate, mediator, moderator, referee, umpire.
v. **1** adjudicate, arbitrate, ascertain, assess, conclude, consider, decide, decree, determine, discern, distinguish, esteem, estimate, evaluate, examine, find, gauge, mediate, rate, reckon, referee, review, rule, sentence, sit, try, umpire, value. **2** condemn, criticise, doom.

judgement *n.* **1** appraisal, arbitration, assessment, belief, common sense, conclusion, decision, decree, diagnosis, discernment, discrimination, enlightenment, estimate, finding, intelligence, mediation, opinion, order, penetration, prudence, result, ruling, sense, sentence, shrewdness, taste, understanding, valuation, verdict, view, wisdom. **2** conviction, damnation, doom, fate, misfortune, punishment, retribution.

judicial *adj.* critical, discriminating, distinguished, forensic, impartial, judiciary, legal, magistral, official.

judicious *adj.* astute, careful, cautious, considered, discerning, informed, prudent, reasonable, sensible, shrewd, skilful, sound, thoughtful, well-advised, well-judged, well-judging, wise.
antonym injudicious.

jug *n.* carafe, churn, container, crock, flagon, jar, pitcher, urn, vessel.

juggle *v.* alter, change, disguise, doctor, manipulate, manoeuvre, modify, rearrange, rig.

juice *n.* essence, extract, fluid, liquid, liquor, nectar, sap, secretion, serum.

juicy *adj.* **1** lush, moist, succulent, watery. **2** colourful, interesting. **3** naughty, racy, risqué, sensational, spicy, suggestive.
antonyms **1** dry. **2** boring.

jumble *v.* confuse, disarray, disorganise, mix (up), muddle, shuffle, tangle.
antonym order.
n. chaos, clutter, collection, confusion, conglomeration, disarray, disorder, hotch-potch, medley, mess, mishmass, mixture, mix-up, muddle.

jump *v.* **1** bounce, bound, clear, frisk, frolic, gambol, hop, hurdle, jig, leap, pounce, prance, skip, spring, vault. **2** flinch, jerk, jump out of one's skin, leap in the air, quail, recoil, start, wince. **3** avoid, bypass, digress, disregard, evade, ignore, leave out, miss, omit, pass over, skip, switch. **4** advance, appreciate, ascend, boost, escalate, gain, increase, mount, rise, spiral, surge.
n. **1** bounce, dance, frisk, frolic, hop, leap, pounce, prance, skip, spring, vault. **2** jar, jerk, jolt, quiver, shiver, shock, spasm, start, swerve, twitch. **3** breach, break, gap, interruption, interval, lapse, omission, switch. **4** advance, boost, escalation, increase, increment, mounting, rise, upsurge, upturn. **5** barricade, barrier, fence, gate, hedge, hurdle, impediment, obstacle.

jumper *n.* jersey, pullover, sweater, sweat-shirt, woolly.

jumpy *adj.* agitated, anxious, apprehensive, edgy, fidgety, nervous, nervy, shaky, tense.
antonyms calm, composed.

junction *n.* confluence, connection, coupling, intersection, join, joining, joint, juncture, linking, meeting-point, union.

juncture *n.* minute, moment, occasion, period, point, stage, time.

junior *adj.* inferior, lesser, lower, minor, secondary, subordinate, subsidiary, younger.
antonym senior.

junk *n.* clutter, debris, dregs, garbage, litter, oddments, refuse, rubbish, rummage, scrap, trash, waste, wreckage.

jurisdiction *n.* area, authority, bounds, command, control, domination, dominion, field, influence, orbit, power, prerogative, province, range, reach, rule, scope, sovereignty, sphere, sway, zone.

jury *n.* jurors, jurymen, jurywomen, panel.

just *adj.* blameless, conscientious, correct, deserved, due, equitable, even-handed, exact, fair, fair-minded, fitting, good, honest, honourable, impartial, irreproachable, lawful, legitimate, merited, normal, precise, proper, pure, reasonable, regular, right, righteous, rightful, true, unbiased, unprejudiced, upright, virtuous, well-deserved.
antonyms corrupt, undeserved, unjust.
adv. **1** directly, exactly, recently, soon. **2** merely, only, simply.

justice *n.* **1** appropriateness, equitableness, equity, fairness, honesty, impartiality, justifiableness, justness, law, legality, legitimacy, penalty, reasonableness, recompense, rectitude, reparation, right, rightfulness, rightness, satisfaction. **2** JP, judge, Justice of the Peace, magistrate.
antonyms **1** injustice, unfairness.

justifiable *adj.* acceptable, defensible, excusable, explainable, explicable, fit, forgivable, justified, lawful, legitimate, pardonable, proper, reasonable, right, sound, tenable, understandable, valid, warrantable, warranted, well-founded.
antonyms illicit, unjustifiable.

justification *n.* apology, basis, defence, excuse, explanation, foundation, grounds, mitigation, plea, rationalisation, reason, substance, vindication, warrant.

justify *v.* absolve, acquit, defend, establish, excuse, exonerate, explain, forgive, maintain, pardon, substantiate, support, sustain, uphold, validate, vindicate, warrant.

jut out *v.* bulge, extend, overhang, poke, project, protrude, stick out.
antonym recede.

juvenile *n.* adolescent, boy, child, girl, infant, minor, young person, youngster, youth.
antonym adult.
adj. adolescent, babyish, childish, immature, infantile, puerile, tender, unsophisticated, young, youthful.
antonym mature.

juxtaposition *n.* closeness, contact, contiguity, immediacy, nearness, proximity, vicinity.
antonyms dissociation, separation.

K

kaleidoscopic *adj.* changeable, ever-changing, fluctuating, manifold, many-coloured, mobile, multicoloured, patterned, variegated.
antonyms dull, monochrome, monotonous.

keel over capsize, collapse, drop, faint, fall, founder, overturn, pass out, stagger, swoon, topple over, upset.

keen *adj.* **1** anxious, devoted, eager, earnest, enthusiastic, fond. **2** astute, avid, clever, deep, diligent, discerning, industrious, intense, perceptive, wise. **3** acute, incisive, penetrating, piercing, pointed, pungent, sensitive, sharp, shrewd, trenchant.
antonyms **1** apathetic. **2** superficial. **3** dull.

keep *v.* **1** accumulate, amass, carry, collect, conserve, control, deal in, deposit, furnish, hang on to, heap, hold, hold on to, maintain, pile, place, possess, preserve, retain, stack, stock, store. **2** be responsible for, care for, defend, feed, foster, guard, have charge of, have custody of, look after, maintain, manage, mind, nourish, nurture, operate, protect, provide for, safeguard, shelter, shield, subsidise, support, sustain, tend, watch (over). **3** arrest, block, check, constrain, control, curb, delay, detain, deter, hamper, hinder, hold (up), impede, inhibit, interfere with, keep back, limit, obstruct, prevent, restrain, retard, withhold. **4** adhere to, celebrate, commemorate, comply with, fulfil, hold, honour, keep faith with, keep up, maintain, mark, obey, observe, perform, perpetuate, recognise, respect.
n. **1** board, food, livelihood, living, maintenance, means, nourishment, nurture, subsistence, support, upkeep. **2** castle, citadel, fort, fortress, stronghold, tower.
keep at be steadfast, carry on, complete, continue, endure, finish, labour, persevere, persist, plug away at, remain, slave, slog at, stay, stick at, toil.
antonyms abandon, neglect.
keep back censor, check, conceal, constrain, control, curb, delay, hide, hold back, hush up, impede, limit, prohibit, reserve, restrain, restrict, retain, retard, stifle, stop, suppress, withhold.
keep in bottle up, conceal, confine, control, detain, hide, inhibit, keep back, quell, restrain, retain, stifle, stop up, suppress.
antonyms declare, release.
keep on carry on, continue, endure, hold on, keep at it, last, maintain, persevere, persist, remain, retain, soldier on, stay, stay the course.
keep on at badger, go on at, harass, harry, importune, nag, pester, pursue.
keep up compete, contend, continue, emulate, equal, keep pace, maintain, match, persevere, preserve, rival, support, sustain, vie.

keeper *n.* attendant, caretaker, conservator, curator, custodian, defender, gaoler, governor, guard, guardian, inspector, jailer, nab, overseer, steward, superintendent, supervisor, surveyor, warden, warder.

keepsake *n.* emblem, memento, pledge, relic, remembrance, reminder, souvenir, token.

keg *n.* barrel, butt, cask, drum, tun, vat.

kernel *n.* core, essence, germ, gist, grain, heart, marrow, nitty-gritty, nub, pith, seed, substance.

key *n.* answer, clue, code, cue, digital, explanation, glossary, guide, index, indicator, interpretation, means, pointer, secret, sign, solution, table, translation.
adj. basic, central, chief, crucial, decisive, essential, fundamental, important, leading, main, major, principal, salient, vital.
key in capture, enter, input, load, process, store, type in.

keynote *n.* accent, centre, core, emphasis, essence, gist, heart, stress, substance, theme.

keystone *n.* base, basis, core, cornerstone, crux, foundation, ground, linchpin, mainspring, motive, principle, root, source, spring.

kick *v.* **1** boot, hit, jolt, strike. **2** abandon, break, desist from, give up, leave off, quit, stop.
n. blow, jolt, recoil, striking.
kick off begin, commence, get under way, inaugurate, initiate, introduce, open, open the proceedings, set the ball rolling, start.
kick out chuck out, discharge, dismiss, eject, evict, expel, get rid of, oust, reject, remove, sack, throw out, toss out.

kid[1] *n.* boy, child, girl, halfling, infant, juvenile, lad, nipper, teenager, tot, youngster, youth.

kid[2] *v.* bamboozle, con, delude, dupe, fool, have on, hoax, hoodwink, humbug, jest, joke, mock, pretend, pull someone's leg, rag, ridicule, tease, trick.

kidnap *v.* abduct, capture, hijack, seize, skyjack, snatch, steal.

kill *v.* annihilate, assassinate, bump off, butcher, deaden, defeat, destroy, do away with, do in, do to death, eliminate, execute, exterminate, extinguish, finish off, liquidate, massacre, murder, obliterate, occupy, pass, put to death, quash, quell, rub out, slaughter, slay, smite, spoil, suppress, veto.
n. climax, conclusion, death, death-blow, dénouement, dispatch, end, finish, shoot-out.

killer *n.* assassin, butcher, cut-throat, destroyer, executioner, gunman, hatchet man, hit-man, matricide, murderer, slaughterer.

killing *n.* **1** assassination, bloodshed, carnage, elimination, execution, extermination, fatality, homicide, liquidation, manslaughter, massacre, murder, slaughter, slaying. **2** big hit, bonanza, clean-up, coup, fortune, gain, hit, lucky break, profit, success, windfall, winner.
adj. absurd, amusing, comical, funny, hilarious, ludicrous, side-splitting.

killjoy *n.* complainer, dampener, damper, misery, pessimist, spoil-sport, wet blanket.
antonyms enthusiast, optimist, sport.

kind *n.* brand, breed, category, character, class, description, essence, family, manner, mould, nature, persuasion, race, set, sort, species, stamp, style, temperament, type, variety.
adj. affectionate, amiable, benevolent, compassionate, congenial, considerate, courteous, friendly, generous, gentle, giving, good, gracious, hospitable, humane, indulgent, kind-hearted, kindly, lenient, loving, mild, neighbourly, soft-hearted, sympathetic, tactful, tender-hearted, thoughtful, understanding.
antonyms cruel, inconsiderate, unhelpful.

kind-hearted *adj.* amicable, compassionate, considerate, generous, good-hearted, good-natured, gracious, helpful, humane, humanitarian, kind, obliging, sympathetic, tender-hearted, warm, warm-hearted.
antonym ill-natured.

kindle *v.* arouse, awaken, excite, fan, fire, ignite, incite, induce, inflame, inspire, light, provoke, rouse, set alight, sharpen, stimulate, stir, thrill.

kindly *adj.* benevolent, charitable, compassionate, cordial, favourable, generous, gentle, giving, good-natured, helpful, indulgent, kind, mild, patient, pleasant, polite, sympathetic, tender, warm.
antonyms cruel, inconsiderate, uncharitable.

kindness *n.* affection, assistance, benevolence, compassion, courtesy, favour, friendliness, generosity, gentleness, good will, goodness, grace, help, hospitality, humanity, indulgence, loving-kindness, magnanimity, mildness, patience, service, tenderness, tolerance, understanding.
antonyms cruelty, illiberality, inhumanity.

king *n.* boss, chief, chieftain, emperor, leading light, majesty, monarch, prince, ruler, sovereign, supremo.

kingdom *n.* area, commonwealth, country, division, domain, dominion, dynasty, empire, field, land, monarchy, nation, principality, province, realm, reign, royalty, sovereignty, sphere, state, territory.

kink *n.* bend, coil, complication, crick, crimp, defect, dent, difficulty, entanglement, flaw, hitch, imperfection, indentation, knot, loop, tangle, twist, wrinkle.
v. bend, coil, crimp, curl, tangle, twist, wrinkle.

kinky *adj.* coiled, crimped, crumpled, curled, curly, frizzy, tangled, twisted, wrinkled.

kinship *n.* affinity, alliance, association, bearing, blood, community, conformity, connection, correspondence, kin, relation, relationship, similarity, tie.

kiosk *n.* bookstall, booth, box, cabin, counter, news-stand, stall, stand.

kiss *v.* **1** caress, neck, peck, smooch, snog. **2** brush, fan, glance, graze, lick, scrape, touch.
n. peck, smack, snog.

kit *n.* apparatus, baggage, effects, equipment, gear, implements, instruments, luggage, outfit, paraphernalia, provisions, set, supplies, tackle, tools, trappings, traps, utensils.
kit out arm, deck out, dress, equip, fit out, fix up, furnish, outfit, prepare, supply.

knack *n.* ability, bent, capacity, dexterity, expertise, facility, faculty, flair, forte, genius, gift, handiness, hang, propensity, quickness, skilfulness, skill, talent, trick, turn.

knapsack *n.* backpack, bag, haversack, pack, rucksack.

knead *v.* form, knuckle, manipulate, massage, mould, ply, press, rub, shape, squeeze, work.

knell *n.* chime, knoll, peel, ringing, sound, toll.

knick-knack *n.* bauble, bric-à-brac, gimcrack, plaything, pretty, trifle, trinket.

knife *n.* blade, carver, cutter, dagger, flick-knife, jack-knife, machete, pen-knife, pocket-knife, switchblade.
v. cut, pierce, rip, slash, stab, wound.

knight *n.* cavalier, champion, free-lance, gallant, horseman, soldier, warrior.

knit *v.* connect, crotchet, fasten, furrow, interlace, intertwine, join, knot, link, loop, mend, secure, tie, unite, weave, wrinkle.

knock *v.* hit, rap, slap, smack, strike, thump, thwack.
n. blow, box, clip, con, cuff, hammering, rap, slap, smack, thump.
knock about 1 associate, go around, ramble, range, roam, rove, saunter, traipse, travel, wander. **2** abuse, bash, batter, beat up, bruise, buffet, damage, hit, hurt, maltreat, manhandle, mistreat.
knock down batter, clout, demolish, destroy, fell, floor, level, pound, prop, raze, smash, wallop, wreck.
knock off 1 cease, clock off, clock out, finish, pack (it) in, stop, terminate. **2** deduct, filch, nick, pilfer, pinch, rob, steal, take away. **3** assassinate, bump off, do away with, do in, kill, murder, slay, waste.

knockout *n.* bestseller, hit, KO, sensation, smash, smash-hit, stunner, success, triumph, winner.
antonyms flop, loser.

knot *v.* bind, entangle, entwine, knit, secure, tangle, tether, tie, weave.
n. bond, bunch, cluster, hitch, joint, loop, splice, tie, tuft.

knotty *adj.* baffling, bumpy, complex, complicated, difficult, gnarled, hard, intricate, knobby, knotted, mystifying, perplexing, problematical, puzzling, rough, rugged, thorny, tricky, troublesome.

know *v.* apprehend, comprehend, discern, distinguish, experience, fathom, identify, learn, make out, notice, perceive, realise, recognise, see, tell, undergo, understand.

knowledge *n.* ability, acquaintance, apprehension, cognition, comprehension, consciousness, discernment, education, enlightenment, familiarity, grasp, information, instruction, intelligence, intimacy, judgement, know-how, learning, notice, recognition, scholarship, schooling, science, tuition, understanding, wisdom.
antonyms ignorance, unawareness.

knowledgeable *adj.* acquainted, aware, conscious, conversant, educated, experienced, familiar, in the know, intelligent, learned, lettered, scholarly, well-informed.
antonym ignorant.

known *adj.* acknowledged, admitted, avowed, celebrated, commonplace, confessed, familiar, famous, noted, obvious, patent, plain, published, recognised, well-known.

knuckle under accede, acquiesce, capitulate, defer, give in, give way, submit, succumb, surrender, yield.

kowtow *v.* cringe, defer, fawn, flatter, kneel, pander, suck up, toady.

L

label *n.* badge, brand, categorisation, characterisation, classification, description, docket, mark, marker, sticker, tag, tally, ticket, trademark.
v. brand, call, categorise, characterise, class, classify, define, describe, designate, dub, identify, mark, name, stamp, tag.

laborious *adj.* arduous, backbreaking, difficult, hard, hard-working, heavy, indefatigable, industrious, laboured, onerous, painstaking, persevering, strenuous, tiresome, toilsome, tough, uphill, wearisome.
antonyms easy, effortless, simple.

labour *n.* **1** chore, drudgery, effort, exertion, grind, job, slog, sweat, task, toil, work. **2** employees, labourers, workers, workforce. **3** birth, childbirth, contractions, delivery, labour pains, pains.
antonyms **1** ease, leisure, relaxation, rest. **2** management, managers.
v. **1** drudge, endeavour, grind, pitch, plod, roll, slave, strive, struggle, suffer, sweat, toil, toss, travail, work. **2** dwell on, elaborate, overdo, overemphasise, overstress, strain.
antonyms **1** idle, laze, lounge.

labourer *n.* drudge, farm-hand, hand, hireling, manual worker, navvy, worker.

labyrinth *n.* complexity, complication, intricacy, jungle, maze, perplexity, puzzle, riddle, tangle, windings.

lace *n.* **1** crochet, mesh-work, netting, openwork. **2** bootlace, cord, shoe-lace, string.
v. **1** attach, bind, close, do up, fasten, intertwine, interweave, string, thread, tie. **2** add to, fortify, intermix, mix in.

lacerate *v.* afflict, claw, cut, distress, gash, maim, mangle, rend, rip, slash, tear, torment, torture, wound.

laceration *n.* cut, gash, injury, mutilation, rent, rip, slash, tear, wound.

lack *n.* absence, dearth, deficiency, deprivation, destitution, emptiness, insufficiency, need, privation, scantiness, scarcity, shortage, vacancy, void, want.
antonyms abundance, profusion.
v. miss, need, require, want.

lackadaisical *adj.* dreamy, half-hearted, idle, indifferent, lazy, lethargic, limp, listless, spiritless, supine.
antonyms active, dynamic, energetic, vigorous.

lackey *n.* attendant, creature, fawner, footman, hanger-on, instrument, manservant, menial, minion, parasite, pawn, valet, yes-man.

lacking *adj.* defective, deficient, flawed, inadequate, minus, missing, needing, short of, wanting, without.

laconic *adj.* brief, close-mouthed, concise, crisp, curt, pithy, short, succinct, taciturn, terse.
antonyms verbose, wordy.

lad *n.* boy, chap, fellow, guy, kid, schoolboy, youngster, youth.

ladle *v.* bail, dip, dish, scoop, spoon.
ladle out disburse, dish out, distribute, dole out, hand out.

laid up bedridden, disabled, housebound, ill, immobilised, incapacitated, injured, on the sick list, out of action, sick.

laid-back *adj.* at ease, calm, casual, cool, easy-going, free and easy, relaxed, unflappable, unhurried, untroubled, unworried.
antonyms tense, uptight.

lair *n.* burrow, den, earth, form, hideout, hole, nest, refuge, retreat, roost, sanctuary, stronghold.

lake *n.* lagoon, loch, mere, reservoir, tarn.

lame *adj.* **1** crippled, disabled, handicapped, hobbling, limping. **2** feeble, flimsy, inadequate, poor, unsatisfactory, weak.
antonyms **1** able-bodied. **2** convincing.

lament *v.* bemoan, bewail, complain, deplore, grieve, mourn, regret, sorrow, wail, weep, yammer.
antonyms celebrate, rejoice.
n. dirge, elegy, lamentation, moan, moaning, requiem, wail, wailing.

lamentable *adj.* deplorable, disappointing, distressing, inadequate, insufficient, low, meagre, mean, miserable, mournful, pitiful, poor, regrettable, sorrowful, tragic, unfortunate, unsatisfactory.

lamp *n.* beacon, flare, floodlight, lantern, light, limelight, searchlight, torch.

lampoon *n.* burlesque, caricature, parody, satire, send-up, skit, spoof, take-off.
v. burlesque, caricature, make fun of, mock, parody, ridicule, satirise, send up, spoof, take off, take the mickey out of.

land *n.* **1** country, countryside, earth, estate, farmland, ground, grounds, property, real estate, soil, terra firma, tract. **2** country, nation, province, region, territory.
v. **1** alight, arrive, berth, bring, carry, cause, come to rest, deposit, disembark, dock, drop, end up, plant, touch down, turn up, wind up. **2** achieve, acquire, capture, gain, get, net, obtain, secure, win.

landlord *n.* freeholder, host, hotelier, hotel-keeper, innkeeper, letter, owner, proprietor, publican.
antonym tenant.

landmark *n.* beacon, boundary, cairn, feature,

milestone, monument, signpost, turning-point, watershed.

lands *n.* acreage, acres, estate(s), grounds, manor, policies, spread.

landscape *n.* aspect, countryside, outlook, panorama, prospect, scene, scenery, view, vista.

landslide *n.* avalanche, earthfall, landslip, rockfall.
adj. decisive, emphatic, overwhelming, runaway.

lane *n.* alley(way), avenue, byroad, byway, channel, driveway, footpath, footway, passage(way), path(way), towpath, way.

language *n.* conversation, dialect, diction, discourse, expression, idiom, jargon, parlance, phraseology, phrasing, speech, style, talk, terminology, tongue, utterance, vernacular, vocabulary, wording.

languish *v.* brood, decline, desire, droop, fade, fail, faint, flag, grieve, hanker, hunger, long, pine, sicken, sigh, sink, sorrow, suffer, sulk, want, waste, waste away, weaken, wilt, wither, yearn.
antonym flourish.

lank *adj.* drooping, flabby, lifeless, limp, long, straggling.

lanky *adj.* gangling, gaunt, scraggy, scrawny, tall, thin, weedy.
antonyms brawny, short, squat.

lap¹ *v.* **1** drink, lick, sip, sup, tongue. **2** gurgle, ripple, slap, slosh, splash, swish, wash.

lap² *n.* circle, circuit, course, distance, loop, orbit, round, tour.
v. cover, enfold, envelop, fold, surround, swaddle, swathe, turn, twist, wrap.

lapse *n.* aberration, backsliding, break, decline, descent, deterioration, drop, error, failing, fall, fault, gap, indiscretion, intermission, interruption, interval, lull, mistake, negligence, omission, oversight, passage, pause, relapse, slip.
v. backslide, decline, degenerate, deteriorate, drop, end, expire, fail, fall, run out, sink, slide, slip, stop, terminate, worsen.

large *adj.* big, broad, bulky, considerable, enormous, extensive, full, generous, giant, gigantic, grand, grandiose, great, huge, immense, king-sized, liberal, massive, monumental, plentiful, roomy, sizeable, spacious, substantial, sweeping, vast, wide.
antonyms diminutive, little, slight, small, tiny.
at large at liberty, free, independent, on the loose, on the run.

large-scale *adj.* extensive, far-reaching, global, nation-wide, sweeping, vast, wide-ranging.
antonyms minor, small-scale.

lark *n.* antic, caper, escapade, fling, frolic, fun, gambol, game, mischief, prank, revel, rollick, romp, skylark.
lark about muck about, play, romp, skylark, sport.

lash¹ *n.* blow, cat-o'-nine-tails, hit, stripe, stroke, swipe, whip.
v. **1** beat, flog, hit, scourge, strike, thrash, whip. **2** attack, criticise, lay into, scold.

lash² *v.* affix, bind, fasten, join, make fast, rope, secure, strap, tether, tie.

last¹ *adj.* closing, concluding, conclusive, definitive, extreme, final, furthest, latest, rearmost, remotest, terminal, ultimate, utmost.
antonyms first, initial.
adv. after, behind, finally, ultimately.
antonyms first, firstly.
at last at length, eventually, finally, in due course, in the end.

last² *v.* abide, carry on, continue, endure, hold on, hold out, keep (on), persist, remain, stand up, stay, survive, wear.
antonyms cease, fade, stop.

lasting *adj.* continuing, enduring, lifelong, long-standing, long-term, permanent, perpetual, unceasing, unchanging, unending.
antonyms brief, fleeting, short-lived.

lastly *adv.* finally, in conclusion, in the end, to sum up, ultimately.
antonym firstly.

latch *n.* bar, bolt, catch, fastening, hasp, hook, lock.
latch on to apprehend, attach oneself to, comprehend, understand.

late *adj.* **1** behind, behind-hand, delayed, last-minute, overdue, slow, unpunctual. **2** dead, deceased, departed, ex-, former, old, past, preceding, previous.
antonyms **1** early, punctual.
adv. behind-hand, belatedly, formerly, recently, slowly, unpunctually.
antonyms early, punctually.

lately *adv.* formerly, of late, recently.

latent *adj.* concealed, hidden, inherent, invisible, lurking, potential, secret, underlying, undeveloped, unexpressed, unrealised, unseen, veiled.
antonyms active, patent.

later *adv.* after, afterwards, next, subsequently, successively.
antonym earlier.

lateral *adj.* edgeways, flanking, marginal, oblique, side, sideward, sideways.
antonym central.

latest *adj.* current, fashionable, modern, newest, now, ultimate, up-to-date, up-to-the-minute.
antonym earliest.

lather *n.* **1** bubbles, foam, froth, shampoo, soap, soap-suds, suds. **2** agitation, dither, fever, flap, fluster, flutter, fuss, state.
v. foam, froth, shampoo, soap, whip up.

latitude *n.* breadth, clearance, elbow-room, extent, field, freedom, leeway, liberty, licence, play, range, reach, room, scope, space, span, spread, sweep, width.

latter *adj.* closing, concluding, ensuing, last, last-mentioned, later, second, succeeding, successive.
antonym former.

laugh *v.* chortle, chuckle, crease up, fall about, giggle, guffaw, snigger, split one's sides, titter.
antonym cry.
n. chortle, chuckle, giggle, guffaw, hoot, joke,

lark, scream, snigger, titter.
laugh at deride, jeer, make fun of, mock, ridicule, scoff at, scorn, taunt.
laugh off brush aside, dismiss, disregard, ignore, make little of, minimise, pooh-pooh, shrug off.
laughable *adj.* absurd, amusing, comical, derisive, derisory, diverting, droll, farcical, funny, hilarious, humorous, ludicrous, nonsensical, preposterous, ridiculous.
antonyms impressive, serious, solemn.
laughing-stock *n.* butt, derision, fair game, figure of fun, target, victim.
laughter *n.* amusement, chortling, chuckling, convulsions, giggling, glee, guffawing, hilarity, laughing, merriment, mirth, tittering.
launch *v.* begin, commence, discharge, dispatch, embark on, establish, fire, float, found, inaugurate, initiate, instigate, introduce, open, project, propel, send off, set in motion, start, throw.
lavatory *n.* bathroom, cloakroom, convenience, loo, powder-room, public convenience, restroom, toilet, urinal, washroom, water-closet, WC.
lavish *adj.* abundant, exaggerated, excessive, extravagant, generous, immoderate, intemperate, liberal, lush, luxuriant, open-handed, plentiful, profuse, prolific, unlimited, unstinting, wild.
antonyms economical, frugal, parsimonious, scanty, sparing, thrifty.
v. deluge, dissipate, expend, heap, pour, shower, spend, squander, waste.
law *n.* act, axiom, canon, charter, code, command, commandment, constitution, covenant, criterion, decree, edict, enactment, formula, institute, jurisprudence, order, ordinance, precept, principle, regulation, rule, standard, statute.
law-abiding *adj.* decent, good, honest, honourable, lawful, obedient, orderly, upright.
antonym lawless.
lawful *adj.* allowable, authorised, legal, legalised, legitimate, permissible, proper, rightful, valid, warranted.
antonyms illegal, illicit, lawless, unlawful.
lawless *adj.* anarchic(al), chaotic, disorderly, rebellious, reckless, riotous, ruleless, unrestrained, unruly, wild.
antonyms civilised, lawful.
lawsuit *n.* action, argument, case, cause, contest, dispute, litigation, proceedings, process, prosecution, suit, trial.
lawyer *n.* advocate, attorney, barrister, counsel, counsellor, solicitor.
lax *adj.* careless, casual, easy-going, indefinite, lenient, loose, negligent, remiss, slack, slipshod.
antonyms rigid, strict, stringent.
lay *v.* **1** deposit, establish, leave, lodge, place, plant, put, set, set down, settle. **2** arrange, devise, locate, position, prepare, present, set out, submit, work out. **3** ascribe, assign, attribute, charge.
lay aside abandon, cast aside, discard, dismiss, postpone, put aside, put off, reject, shelve, store.
lay down affirm, assert, assume, discard, drop, establish, formulate, give, give up, ordain, prescribe, relinquish, state, stipulate, surrender, yield.
lay in accumulate, amass, build up, collect, gather, glean, hoard, stock up, stockpile, store (up).
lay into assail, attack, let fly at, pitch into, set about, tear into, turn on.
lay off axe, cease, desist, discharge, dismiss, drop, give up, leave alone, leave off, let go, let up, make redundant, oust, pay off, quit, stop, withhold.
lay on contribute, furnish, give, provide, set up, supply.
lay out **1** arrange, design, display, exhibit, plan, set out, spread out. **2** demolish, fell, flatten, knock out. **3** expend, fork out, give, invest, pay, shell out, spend.
lay up **1** hospitalise, incapacitate. **2** accumulate, amass, hoard, keep, put away, salt away, save, store up.
layer *n.* bed, blanket, coat, coating, cover, covering, film, lame, lamina, mantle, plate, ply, row, seam, sheet, stratum, table, thickness, tier, touch.
layman *n.* amateur, layperson, outsider, parishioner.
antonyms clergyman, expert.
layout *n.* arrangement, design, draft, formation, geography, map, outline, plan, sketch.
lazy *adj.* idle, inactive, lethargic, slack, slothful, work-shy.
antonyms diligent, industrious.
lazy-bones *n.* idler, loafer, lounger, shirker, skiver, sluggard.
lead *v.* conduct, direct, escort, govern, guide, head, incline, influence, outdo, outstrip, pass, persuade, pilot, precede, preside over, prevail, steer, supervise, surpass, transcend, undergo, usher.
antonym follow.
n. advance, advantage, clue, direction, edge, example, first place, guidance, guide, hint, indication, leadership, margin, model, precedence, principal, priority, start, suggestion, tip, title role, trace, van, vanguard.
adj. chief, first, foremost, head, leading, main, premier, primary, prime, principal, star.
lead off begin, commence, get going, inaugurate, initiate, kick off, open, start (off), start the ball rolling.
lead on beguile, deceive, draw on, entice, lure, persuade, seduce, string along, tempt, trick.
lead to bring about, bring on, cause, contribute to, produce, result in, tend towards.
lead up to approach, introduce, make overtures, overture, pave the way, prepare (the way) for.
leader *n.* boss, captain, chief, chieftain, commander, conductor, counsellor, director, guide, head, principal, ringleader, ruler, skipper, superior.
antonym follower.
leadership *n.* administration, authority, com-

mand, control, direction, directorship, domination, guidance, influence, initiative, management, pre-eminence, premiership, superintendency, sway.

leading *adj.* chief, dominant, first, foremost, governing, greatest, highest, main, number one, outstanding, pre-eminent, primary, principal, ruling, superior, supreme.
antonyms following, minor, subordinate.

leaflet *n.* advert, bill, booklet, brochure, circular, handbill, handout, pamphlet.

league *n.* alliance, association, band, cartel, category, class, coalition, combination, combine, compact, confederacy, confederation, consortium, federation, fellowship, fraternity, group, guild, level, partnership, syndicate, union.
in league allied, collaborating, conspiring.

leak *n.* aperture, chink, crack, crevice, disclosure, divulgence, drip, hole, leakage, leaking, oozing, opening, percolation, perforation, puncture, seepage.
v. **1** discharge, drip, escape, exude, ooze, pass, percolate, seep, spill, trickle. **2** disclose, divulge, give away, let slip, make known, make public, pass on, reveal, tell.

leaky *adj.* cracked, holey, leaking, perforated, permeable, porous, punctured, split, waterlogged.

lean[1] *v.* bend, confide, count on, depend, favour, incline, list, prefer, prop, recline, rely, rest, slant, slope, tend, tilt, trust.
lean on force, persuade, pressurise, put pressure on.

lean[2] *adj.* angular, bare, barren, bony, emaciated, gaunt, inadequate, lank, scanty, scraggy, scrawny, skinny, slender, slim, thin.
antonyms fat, fleshy.

leaning *n.* aptitude, bent, bias, disposition, inclination, liking, partiality, susceptibility, taste, tendency.

leap *v.* advance, bounce, bound, caper, clear, escalate, frisk, gambol, hasten, hop, hurry, increase, jump (over), reach, rocket, rush, skip, soar, spring, surge, vault.
antonyms drop, fall, sink.
n. bound, caper, escalation, frisk, hop, increase, jump, rise, skip, spring, surge, upsurge, upswing, vault.

learn *v.* acquire, ascertain, assimilate, attain, detect, determine, discern, discover, find out, gather, grasp, hear, learn by heart, master, memorise, pick up, see, understand.

learning *n.* culture, edification, education, enlightenment, erudition, information, knowledge, letters, literature, research, scholarship, schooling, study, tuition, wisdom.

lease *v.* charter, farm out, hire, let, loan, rent, sublet.

leash *n.* check, control, curb, discipline, hold, lead, rein, restraint, tether.

least *adj.* fewest, last, lowest, meanest, merest, minimum, minutest, poorest, slightest, smallest, tiniest.
antonym most.

leave[1] *v.* **1** abandon, cease, cede, decamp, depart, desert, desist, disappear, do a bunk, drop, exit, flit, forsake, give up, go, go away, move, produce, pull out, quit, relinquish, renounce, retire, set out, stop, surrender, take off, withdraw. **2** allot, assign, bequeath, commit, consign, deposit, entrust, give over, hand down, leave behind, transmit.
antonyms **1** arrive. **2** inherit, receive.
leave off abstain, break off, cease, desist, discontinue, end, give over, halt, lay off, quit, refrain, stop, terminate.
leave out bar, cast aside, count out, cut (out), disregard, eliminate, except, exclude, ignore, neglect, omit, overlook, pass over, reject.

leave[2] *n.* allowance, authorisation, concession, consent, dispensation, freedom, furlough, holiday, indulgence, liberty, permission, sabbatical, sanction, time off, vacation.
antonyms refusal, rejection.

lecture *n.* **1** address, discourse, instruction, lesson, speech, talk. **2** censure, chiding, dressing-down, harangue, rebuke, reprimand, reproof, scolding, talking-to, telling-off.
v. **1** address, expound, hold forth, speak, talk, teach. **2** admonish, censure, chide, harangue, reprimand, reprove, scold, tell off.

ledge *n.* mantle, projection, ridge, shelf, shelve, sill, step.

leech *n.* bloodsucker, freeloader, hanger-on, parasite, sponger, sycophant, usurer.

leer *v.* eye, fleer, gloat, goggle, grin, ogle, smirk, squint, stare, wink.
n. grin, ogle, smirk, squint, stare, wink.

leeway *n.* elbow-room, latitude, play, room, scope, space.

left *adj.* communist, left-wing, liberal, progressive, radical, socialist.
antonym right.

left-overs *n.* dregs, leavings, oddments, odds and ends, refuse, remainder, remains, remnants, residue, scraps, surplus, sweepings.

leg *n.* **1** limb, member, shank, stump. **2** prop, support, upright. **3** part, portion, section, segment, stage, stretch.

legacy *n.* bequest, birthright, endowment, estate, gift, heirloom, heritage, heritance, inheritance.

legal *adj.* above-board, allowable, allowed, authorised, constitutional, forensic, judicial, lawful, legalised, legitimate, permissible, proper, rightful, sanctioned, valid, warrantable.
antonym illegal.

legalise *v.* allow, approve, authorise, legitimise, license, permit, sanction, validate, warrant.

legality *n.* admissibleness, constitutionality, lawfulness, legitimacy, permissibility, rightfulness, validity.
antonym illegality.

legation *n.* commission, consulate, delegation, deputation, embassy, ministry, mission, representation.

legend *n.* **1** fable, fiction, folk-tale, myth, narrative, story, tale, tradition. **2** caption,

inscription, key, motto. **3** celebrity, household name, luminary, wonder.
legendary *adj.* celebrated, famed, famous, illustrious, immortal, mythical, renowned, romantic, storied, story-book, traditional, well-known.
legible *adj.* clear, decipherable, discernible, distinct, intelligible, neat, readable.
antonym illegible.
legislate *v.* authorise, codify, constitutionalise, enact, establish, ordain, prescribe.
legislation *n.* act, authorisation, bill, charter, codification, enactment, law, law-making, measure, prescription, regulation, ruling, statute.
legislative *adj.* congressional, judicial, law-giving, law-making, ordaining, parliamentary, senatorial.
legislator *n.* law-giver, law-maker, member of parliament, parliamentarian.
legislature *n.* assembly, chamber, congress, governing body, house, parliament, senate.
legitimate *adj.* acceptable, acknowledged, admissible, authorised, correct, genuine, just, justifiable, lawful, legal, proper, real, reasonable, rightful, sensible, statutory, true, valid, warranted, well-founded.
antonyms false, illegitimate.
leisure *n.* ease, freedom, holiday, liberty, opportunity, pause, quiet, recreation, relaxation, rest, retirement, spare time, time off, vacation.
antonyms toil, work.
leisurely *adj.* carefree, comfortable, deliberate, easy, gentle, laid-back, lazy, loose, relaxed, restful, slow, tranquil, unhasty, unhurried.
antonyms hectic, hurried, rushed.
lend *v.* add, advance, afford, bestow, confer, contribute, furnish, give, grant, impart, lease, loan, present, provide, supply.
antonym borrow.
length *n.* distance, extent, measure, period, piece, portion, reach, section, segment, space, span, stretch, term.
lengthen *v.* continue, draw out, eke (out), elongate, expand, extend, increase, pad out, prolong, protract, spin out, stretch.
antonyms curtail, reduce, shorten.
lengthy *adj.* diffuse, drawn-out, extended, interminable, lengthened, long, long-drawn-out, long-winded, overlong, prolonged, protracted, rambling, tedious, verbose.
antonyms brief, concise, short.
lenient *adj.* compassionate, forbearing, forgiving, gentle, kind, merciful, mild, soft-hearted, sparing, tender, tolerant.
antonyms harsh, severe, strict.
lessen *v.* abate, abridge, contract, curtail, deaden, decrease, de-escalate, die down, diminish, dwindle, ease, erode, fail, flag, impair, lighten, lower, minimise, moderate, narrow, reduce, shrink, slack, slow down, weaken.
antonyms grow, increase, swell.
lesser *adj.* inferior, lower, minor, secondary, slighter, smaller, subordinate.
antonym greater.
lesson *n.* assignment, class, coaching, drill, example, exercise, homework, instruction, lecture, period, practice, reading, schooling, task, teaching, tutorial.
let[1] *v.* **1** agree to, allow, authorise, consent to, give leave, give permission, grant, make, OK, permit, sanction, tolerate. **2** hire, lease, rent.
antonyms **1** forbid, prohibit.
let down abandon, betray, desert, disappoint, disenchant, disillusion, dissatisfy, fail, fall short.
let in accept, admit, include, incorporate, receive, take in, welcome.
antonyms bar, forbid, prohibit.
let off **1** absolve, acquit, excuse, exempt, exonerate, forgive, ignore, leak, liberate, pardon, release, spare. **2** detonate, discharge, emit, explode, fire.
antonym **1** punish.
let out betray, disclose, emit, free, give, give vent to, leak, let fall, let go, let slip, make known, produce, release, reveal, utter.
antonym keep in.
let up abate, cease, decrease, diminish, ease (up), end, halt, moderate, slacken, stop, subside.
antonym continue.
let[2] *n.* check, constraint, hindrance, impediment, interference, obstacle, obstruction, prohibition, restraint, restriction.
antonyms aid, assistance, help.
lethal *adj.* dangerous, deadly, deathly, destructive, devastating, fatal, mortal, noxious, poisonous.
antonyms harmless, innocuous, safe.
lethargy *n.* apathy, drowsiness, dullness, inaction, indifference, inertia, lassitude, listlessness, sleepiness, slowness, sluggishness, stupor, torpor.
antonyms agility, liveliness, spirit.
letter *n.* **1** acknowledgement, answer, chit, communication, dispatch, epistle, line, message, missive, note, reply. **2** character, grapheme, sign, symbol.
letters *n.* belles-lettres, books, culture, erudition, humanities, learning, literature, scholarship, writing.
level *adj.* aligned, balanced, equal, even, flat, flush, horizontal, neck and neck, plain, smooth, stable, steady, uniform.
antonyms bumpy, rough, uneven, unstable.
v. bulldoze, demolish, destroy, devastate, direct, equalise, even out, flatten, flush, knock down, lay low, plane, point, pull down, raze, smooth, tear down.
n. class, degree, echelon, elevation, grade, height, horizontal, layer, plane, position, rank, stage, standard, standing, status, storey, stratum, zone.
level-headed *adj.* balanced, calm, composed, cool, dependable, even-tempered, reasonable, sane, self-possessed, sensible, steady, unflappable.
lever *n.* bar, crowbar, handle, jemmy, joy-stick.
v. dislodge, force, heave, jemmy, move, prise,

pry, raise, shift.

levity *n.* facetiousness, flippancy, frivolity, irreverence, light-heartedness, silliness, triviality. *antonyms* seriousness, sobriety, solemnity.

levy *v.* charge, collect, demand, exact, impose, raise, tax.
n. assessment, collection, contribution, duty, excise, fee, imposition, subscription, tariff, tax, toll.

lewd *adj.* bawdy, dirty, impure, indecent, lascivious, licentious, loose, lustful, obscene, pornographic, profligate, salacious, smutty, unchaste, vile, vulgar, wanton, wicked.
antonyms chaste, decent, polite, pure.

liability *n.* accountability, arrears, burden, debt, disadvantage, drag, drawback, duty, encumbrance, hindrance, impediment, indebtedness, obligation, onus, responsibility.
antonyms asset(s), unaccountability.

liable *adj.* **1** apt, disposed, inclined, likely, prone, susceptible, tending. **2** accountable, amenable, answerable, responsible, subject.

liar *n.* deceiver, falsifier, fibber, perjurer, storyteller.

libel *n.* aspersion, calumny, defamation, slander, slur, smear, vilification.
v. defame, malign, revile, slander, slur, smear, vilify.

libellous *adj.* defamatory, derogatory, false, injurious, malicious, maligning, scurrilous, slanderous, untrue, vilifying.
antonyms complimentary, flattering, praising.

liberal *adj.* **1** broad-minded, lenient, open-minded, tolerant. **2** moderate, progressive, reformist. **3** ample, bountiful, generous, handsome, lavish, plentiful.
antonyms **1** bigoted, narrow-minded. **2** conservative, old-fashioned, traditional. **3** mean, miserly, stingy.

liberate *v.* deliver, discharge, emancipate, free, let go, let loose, let out, ransom, redeem, release, rescue, set free, unchain, unshackle.
antonyms enslave, imprison, restrict.

liberties *n.* audacity, disrespect, familiarity, forwardness, impertinence, impudence, insolence, overfamiliarity, presumption.
antonyms deference, honour, politeness, respect.

liberty *n.* **1** autonomy, emancipation, freedom, independence, release. **2** authorisation, dispensation, franchise, licence, permission, right, sanction, self-determination, sovereignty.
antonyms **1** imprisonment, restriction, slavery.
at liberty free, not confined, unconstrained, unrestricted.

library *n.* archives, reading-room, reference-room, stack, study.

licence *n.* **1** authorisation, authority, carte blanche, certificate, charter, dispensation, entitlement, exemption, freedom, imprimatur, independence, leave, liberty, permission, permit, privilege, right, warrant. **2** abandon, anarchy, debauchery, disorder, dissipation, dissoluteness, excess, immoderation, impropriety, indulgence, irresponsibility, lawlessness, unruliness.
antonyms **1** prohibition, restriction, veto. **2** decorum, moderation, temperance.

license *v.* accredit, allow, authorise, certify, commission, empower, entitle, permit, sanction, warrant.
antonyms ban, prohibit, veto.

licentious *adj.* abandoned, debauched, disorderly, dissolute, immoral, impure, lascivious, lax, lewd, libertine, lustful, profligate, promiscuous, sensual, uncontrollable, unruly, wanton.
antonyms chaste, modest, pure, temperate.

lick *v.* brush, dart, flick, flicker, lap, play over, smear, taste, tongue, touch, wash.

lie[1] *v.* equivocate, fabricate, falsify, fib, forswear oneself, invent, misrepresent, perjure, prevaricate.
n. deceit, fabrication, falsehood, falsification, falsity, fib, fiction, invention, prevarication, stretcher, untruth, white lie.
antonym truth.

lie[2] *v.* be, belong, dwell, exist, extend, remain, stretch out.
lie down couch, laze, lounge, recline, repose, rest.

life *n.* activity, animation, behaviour, being, breath, career, conduct, continuance, course, duration, élan, energy, entity, essence, existence, growth, liveliness, soul, span, sparkle, spirit, verve, viability, vigour, vitality, vivacity, zest.

lifeless *adj.* apathetic, bare, barren, cold, colourless, dead, deceased, defunct, dull, empty, heavy, hollow, inanimate, insensible, insipid, lethargic, listless, passive, slow, sluggish, static, stiff, unconscious, unproductive.
antonyms alive, lively, vigorous.

lifelike *adj.* authentic, exact, faithful, graphic, natural, photographic, picturesque, real, realistic, true, true-to-life, vivid.
antonyms inexact, unnatural, unrealistic.

lifelong *adj.* abiding, constant, enduring, lasting, lifetime, long-lasting, long-standing, permanent, persistent.
antonyms impermanent, passing, temporary.

lift *v.* ascend, buoy up, cancel, draw up, elevate, exalt, hoist, mount, pick up, raise, rise, uplift, upraise.
antonyms drop, fall, lower.
n. elevator, escalator, hoist, paternoster.

light[1] *n.* beacon, blaze, brightness, brilliance, bulb, candle, dawn, day, daybreak, daylight, daytime, flame, flare, flash, glare, gleam, glim, glint, glow, illumination, lamp, lantern, lighter, lighthouse, luminescence, lustre, match, morning, radiance, ray, shine, sparkle, sunrise, sunshine, torch.
antonyms blackness, darkness, night, obscurity.
v. animate, brighten, cheer, fire, ignite, illuminate, kindle, light up, lighten, put on, set alight, set fire to, switch on, turn on.
antonyms darken, extinguish, obscure.

adj. bleached, blond, blonde, bright, brilliant, faded, faint, fair, glowing, illuminated, luminous, pale, pastel, shining, sunny, well-lit.
antonyms black, dark, shadowy.
in the light of bearing/keeping in mind, because of, considering, in view if, taking into account.
light[2] *adj.* **1** airy, buoyant, delicate, feathery, flimsy, insubstantial, slight, weightless. **2** inconsequential, inconsiderable, trifling, trivial, worthless. **3** amusing, blithe, carefree, cheerful, cheery, entertaining, frivolous, funny, humorous, lively, merry, pleasing, witty.
antonyms **1** bulky, heavy, weighty. **2** important, serious, weighty. **3** serious, solemn.
lighten[1] *v.* brighten, illume, illuminate, illumine, light up, shine.
antonyms darken, obscure, overshadow.
lighten[2] *v.* alleviate, brighten, buoy up, cheer, ease, elate, encourage, gladden, hearten, inspire, inspirit, lessen, lift, mitigate, perk up, reduce, relieve, revive, unload, uplift.
antonyms burden, depress, oppress.
light-headed *adj.* bird-brained, delirious, dizzy, faint, feather-brained, fickle, flighty, flippant, foolish, frivolous, giddy, hazy, shallow, silly, superficial, thoughtless, trifling, unsteady, vacuous.
antonyms level-headed, sober, solemn.
light-hearted *adj.* bright, carefree, cheerful, elated, glad, happy-go-lucky, jolly, jovial, joyful, merry, playful, sunny, untroubled.
antonyms sad, serious, sober, unhappy.
like[1] *adj.* akin, alike, allied, analogous, approximating, corresponding, equivalent, identical, parallel, related, relating, resembling, same, similar.
antonyms dissimilar, unlike.
prep. in the same manner as, on the lines of, similar to.
like[2] *v.* admire, adore, appreciate, approve, care for, cherish, choose, delight in, desire, enjoy, esteem, feel inclined, go for, hold dear, love, prefer, prize, relish, revel in, select, take (kindly) to, want, wish.
antonyms dislike, hate, reject.
likeable *adj.* agreeable, amiable, appealing, attractive, charming, congenial, engaging, friendly, genial, loveable, nice, pleasant, pleasing, sympathetic, winsome.
antonyms disagreeable, unfriendly, unpleasant.
likelihood *n.* chance, liability, likeliness, possibility, probability, prospect, reasonableness.
antonyms improbability, unlikeliness.
likely *adj.* anticipated, appropriate, believable, credible, expected, favourite, feasible, fit, foreseeable, hopeful, inclined, liable, odds-on, plausible, pleasing, possible, predictable, probable, promising, prone, proper, qualified, reasonable, suitable, tending.
antonyms unlikely, unsuitable.
adv. doubtlessly, in all probability, like as not, no doubt, odds on, presumably, probably.
liken *v.* associate, compare, equate, juxtapose, match, parallel, relate, set beside.
likeness *n.* affinity, appearance, copy, correspondence, counterpart, facsimile, form, guise, image, model, photograph, picture, portrait, replica, representation, reproduction, resemblance, semblance, similarity.
antonyms dissimilarity, unlikeness.
likewise *adv.* also, besides, by the same token, further, furthermore, in addition, moreover, similarly, too.
liking *n.* affection, affinity, appreciation, attraction, bias, desire, favour, fondness, inclination, love, partiality, penchant, predilection, preference, proneness, propensity, satisfaction, taste, tendency, weakness.
antonyms aversion, dislike, hate.
lilt *n.* air, beat, cadence, flow, measure, rhythm, song, sway, swing.
limb *n.* appendage, arm, bough, branch, extension, extremity, fork, leg, member, offshoot, part, projection, spur, wing.
limber *adj.* agile, flexible, graceful, lithe, pliable, pliant, supple.
antonym stiff.
limber up exercise, loosen up, prepare, warm up, work out.
antonym stiffen up.
limelight *n.* attention, celebrity, fame, prominence, public eye, public notice, publicity, recognition, renown, spotlight, stardom.
limit *n.* border, bound, boundary, brim, brink, ceiling, check, compass, confines, curb, cut-off point, deadline, edge, end, extent, frontier, limitation, maximum, obstruction, perimeter, restraint, restriction, rim, saturation point, termination, terminus, threshold, ultimate, utmost, verge.
v. bound, check, condition, confine, constrain, curb, delimit, demarcate, fix, hem in, hinder, ration, restrain, restrict, specify.
antonyms extend, free.
limitation *n.* block, check, condition, constraint, control, curb, delimitation, demarcation, disadvantage, drawback, impediment, obstruction, qualification, reservation, restraint, restriction.
antonyms extension, furtherance.
limited *adj.* checked, confined, constrained, controlled, cramped, defined, finite, fixed, hemmed in, inadequate, insufficient, minimal, narrow, reduced, restricted.
antonym limitless.
limitless *adj.* boundless, countless, endless, illimited, immeasurable, immense, incalculable, inexhaustible, infinite, never-ending, unbounded, undefined, unending, unlimited, untold, vast.
antonym limited.
limp[1] *v.* falter, halt, hitch, hobble, hop, shamble, shuffle.
n. hitch, hobble, lameness.
limp[2] *adj.* debilitated, drooping, enervated, exhausted, flabby, flaccid, flexible, flexile, floppy, lax, lethargic, limber, loose, pliable, relaxed, slack, soft, spent, tired, weak, worn out.
antonyms stiff, strong.

limpid *adj.* bright, clear, comprehensible, crystal-clear, glassy, intelligible, lucid, pure, still, translucent, transparent.
antonyms muddy, ripply, turbid, unintelligible.

line[1] *n.* **1** band, bar, border, borderline, boundary, cable, chain, channel, column, configuration, contour, cord, crease, dash, demarcation, disposition, edge, figure, filament, file, formation, front, frontier, furrow, groove, limit, mark, outline, position, procession, profile, queue, rank, rope, row, rule, score, scratch, sequence, series, silhouette, strand, streak, string, stroke, tail, thread, trail, trenches, underline, wire, wrinkle. **2** activity, approach, area, avenue, axis, belief, business, calling, course (of action), department, direction, employment, field, forte, interest, job, method, occupation, path, policy, position, practice, procedure, profession, province, pursuit, route, scheme, specialisation, specialism, speciality, specialty, system, track, trade, vocation. **3** ancestry, breed, family, lineage, pedigree, race, stock, strain, succession.
line up align, arrange, array, assemble, dispose, engage, fall in, form ranks, hire, lay on, marshal, obtain, order, organise, prepare, procure, produce, queue up, range, regiment, secure, straighten.

line[2] *v.* cover, encase, face, fill, reinforce, strengthen, stuff.

lineage *n.* ancestors, ancestry, birth, breed, descendants, descent, extraction, family, forebears, forefathers, genealogy, heredity, house, line, offspring, pedigree, race, stock, succession.

lined *adj.* feint, furrowed, ruled, wizened, worn, wrinkled.
antonyms smooth, unlined.

line-up *n.* arrangement, array, bill, cast, queue, row, selection, team.

linger *v.* abide, continue, dally, dawdle, delay, dilly-dally, endure, hang on, hold out, idle, lag, last, loiter, persist, procrastinate, remain, stay, stop, survive, tarry, wait.
antonyms leave, rush.

lingerie *n.* frillies, linen, smalls, underclothes, underclothing, undergarments, underlinen, unmentionables.

lining *n.* backing, encasement, inlay, interfacing, padding, stiffening.

link *n.* association, attachment, bond, communication, component, connection, constituent, division, element, joint, knot, liaison, member, part, piece, relationship, tie, tie-up, union.
v. associate, attach, bind, bracket, connect, couple, fasten, identify, join, relate, tie, unite, yoke.
antonyms separate, unfasten.
link up ally, amalgamate, connect, dock, hook up, join, join forces, merge, team up, unify.
antonym separate

lip *n.* border, brim, brink, edge, margin, rim, verge.

liquid *n.* drink, fluid, juice, liquor, lotion, sap, solution.
adj. clear, flowing, fluid, limpid, liquefied, melted, molten, runny, shining, smooth, soft, sweet, thawed, transparent, watery, wet.
antonym solid.

liquidate *v.* **1** abolish, annihilate, annul, assassinate, clear, destroy, discharge, dispatch, dissolve, do away with, eliminate, exterminate, finish off, honour, kill, massacre, murder, remove, rub out, silence, square, terminate. **2** close down, pay (off), sell, wind up.

liquor *n.* alcohol, drink, grog, hard stuff, intoxicant, spirits, strong drink.

list[1] *n.* catalogue, directory, enumeration, file, index, inventory, invoice, listing, record, register, roll, schedule, series, syllabus, table, tabulation, tally.
v. alphabeticise, bill, book, catalogue, enrol, enter, enumerate, file, index, itemise, note, record, register, schedule, set down, tabulate, write down.

list[2] *v.* heel (over), incline, lean, slope, tilt, tip.

listen *v.* attend, give ear, give heed, hang on (someone's) words, hark, hear, hearken, heed, lend an ear, mind, obey, observe, pay attention, prick up one's ears, take notice.

listless *adj.* apathetic, bored, depressed, enervated, heavy, impassive, inattentive, indifferent, indolent, inert, lethargic, lifeless, limp, mopish, sluggish, spiritless, torpid, uninterested, vacant.
antonyms attentive, excited, lively.

literacy *n.* ability, articulateness, culture, education, erudition, intelligence, knowledge, learning, proficiency, scholarship.
antonym illiteracy.

literal *adj.* accurate, actual, close, down-to-earth, exact, factual, faithful, genuine, plain, prosaic, real, simple, strict, true, unexaggerated, unimaginative, uninspired, verbatim, word-for-word.
antonyms imprecise, loose, vague.

literary *adj.* bookish, cultivated, cultured, educated, erudite, formal, learned, lettered, literate, refined, scholarly, well-read.
antonyms ignorant, illiterate.

literature *n.* belles-lettres, brochure(s), bumf, circular(s), hand-out(s), information, leaflet(s), letters, pamphlet(s), paper(s), writings.

lithe *adj.* double-jointed, flexible, limber, loose-jointed, loose-limbed, pliant, supple.
antonym stiff.

litigation *n.* action, case, contention, lawsuit, process, prosecution, suit.

litter *n.* **1** clutter, confusion, debris, disarray, disorder, fragments, jumble, mess, muck, refuse, rubbish, scatter, shreds, untidiness, wastage. **2** brood, family, offspring, progeny, young.
v. clutter, disorder, mess up, scatter, strew.
antonym tidy.

little *adj.* babyish, brief, fleeting, inconsiderable, infant, insignificant, insufficient, junior, meagre, microscopic, miniature, minor, minute, negligible, paltry, passing, petite, petty, pint-size(d), scant, short, short-lived, skimpy, slender, small,

sparse, tiny, transient, trifling, trivial, undeveloped, unimportant, wee, young.
antonyms big, great, large, long.
adv. barely, hardly, infrequently, rarely, scarcely, seldom.
antonyms frequently, greatly.
n. bit, dab, dash, drib, fragment, hint, modicum, particle, pinch, speck, spot, taste, touch, trace, trifle.
antonym lot.

liturgy *n.* celebration, ceremony, form, formula, office, rite, ritual, sacrament, service, worship.

live¹ *v.* abide, breathe, continue, draw breath, dwell, endure, exist, get along, inhabit, last, lead, lodge, pass, persist, remain, reside, settle, stay, subsist, survive.
antonyms cease, die.

live² *adj.* active, alert, alive, blazing, brisk, burning, controversial, current, dynamic, earnest, energetic, existent, glowing, hot, ignited, lively, living, pertinent, pressing, relevant, topical, vigorous, vital, vivid, wide-awake.
antonyms apathetic, dead.

livelihood *n.* employment, income, job, living, maintenance, means, occupation, subsistence, support, sustenance, work.

lively *adj.* active, agile, alert, animated, blithe, breezy, bright, brisk, bustling, busy, buzzing, cheerful, chirpy, colourful, crowded, energetic, eventful, exciting, forceful, frisky, frolicsome, invigorating, keen, merry, moving, nimble, perky, quick, racy, refreshing, sparkling, spirited, sprightly, spry, stimulating, stirring, swinging, vigorous, vivacious, vivid.
antonyms apathetic, inactive, moribund.

liven up animate, brighten, buck up, energise, enliven, hot up, invigorate, pep up, perk up, put life into, rouse, stir (up), vitalise.
antonyms deaden, dishearten.

liverish *adj.* bilious, crabby, crotchety, disagreeable, grumpy, ill-humoured, irascible, irritable, peevish, snappy, testy, tetchy.
antonyms calm, easy-going.

livery *n.* apparel, attire, clothes, clothing, costume, dress, garb, habit, raiment, regalia, suit, uniform, vestments.

livid *adj.* **1** angry, boiling, enraged, exasperated, fuming, furious, incensed, indignant, infuriated, irate, mad, outraged. **2** ashen, black-and-blue, blanched, bloodless, bruised, discoloured, greyish, leaden, pale, pallid, pasty, purple, wan, waxy.
antonyms **1** calm, composed, undisturbed. **2** healthy, rosy.

living *adj.* active, alive, animated, breathing, existing, live, lively, strong, vigorous, vital.
antonyms dead, sluggish.
n. being, benefice, existence, income, job, life, livelihood, maintenance, occupation, profession, property, subsistence, support, sustenance, way of life, work.

load *n.* burden, cargo, consignment, encumbrance, freight, goods, lading, millstone, onus, oppression, pressure, shipment, weight.
v. burden, charge, encumber, fill, fortify, freight, heap, lade, oppress, overburden, pack, pile, saddle with, stack, trouble, weigh down, weight.

loaded *adj.* burdened, charged, flush, full, laden, weighted.

loan *n.* advance, allowance, credit, mortgage.
v. advance, allow, credit, lend, let out, oblige.
antonyms borrow, give.

lo(a)th *adj.* against, averse, counter, disinclined, grudging, hesitant, indisposed, opposed, reluctant, resisting, unwilling.
antonyms eager, keen, willing.

loathe *v.* abhor, abominate, despise, detest, dislike, hate.
antonyms adore, like, love.

loathing *n.* abhorrence, abomination, aversion, disgust, dislike, hatred, horror, nausea, repugnance, repulsion, revulsion.
antonyms affection, liking, love.

loathsome *adj.* abhorrent, abominable, detestable, disgusting, hateful, horrible, nasty, odious, offensive, repellent, repugnant, repulsive, revolting, vile.

lobby *v.* call for, campaign for, demand, influence, persuade, press for, pressure, promote, pull strings, push for, solicit, urge.
n. **1** anteroom, corridor, entrance hall, foyer, hall, hallway, passage, passageway, porch, vestibule, waiting-room. **2** ginger group, pressure group.

local *adj.* community, district, limited, narrow, neighbourhood, parish(-pump), parochial, provincial, regional, restricted, small-town, vernacular.
antonyms national, regional.
n. citizen, inhabitant, native, resident, yokel.

localise *v.* concentrate, confine, contain, delimit, limit, locate, narrow down, pin-point, restrain, restrict, specify.

locality *n.* area, district, locale, neighbourhood, place, position, region, scene, setting, site, spot, vicinity.

locate *v.* detect, discover, establish, find, fix, identify, lay one's hands on, pin-point, place, put, run to earth, seat, set, settle, situate, track down, unearth.

location *n.* bearings, locale, locus, place, point, position, site, situation, spot, venue, whereabouts.

lock¹ *n.* bolt, clasp, fastening, padlock.
v. bolt, clasp, clench, close, clutch, disengage, embrace, encircle, enclose, engage, entangle, entwine, fasten, grapple, grasp, hug, join, latch, link, mesh, press, seal, secure, shut, unite, unlock.
lock out ban, bar, debar, exclude, keep out, ostracise, refuse admittance to, shut out.
lock up cage, close up, confine, detain, imprison, incarcerate, jail, pen, secure, shut, shut in, shut up.
antonym free.

lock² *n.* curl, plait, ringlet, strand, tress, tuft.

lodge *n.* cabin, chalet, club, cottage, den,

gatehouse, haunt, house, hunting-lodge, hut, meeting-place, retreat, shelter.
v. **1** accommodate, billet, board, put up, quarter, room, shelter, stay, stick. **2** deposit, get stuck, harbour, imbed, implant, place, put, register, submit.

lodger *n.* boarder, guest, inmate, paying guest, renter, resident, roomer, tenant.

lodgings *n.* abode, accommodation, apartments, billet, boarding, digs, dwelling, pad, quarters, residence, rooms, shelter.

log *n.* **1** block, chunk, stump, timber, trunk. **2** account, chart, daybook, diary, journal, listing, logbook, record, tally.
v. book, chart, note, record, register, report, tally, write down, write in, write up.

logic *n.* argumentation, deduction, rationale, reason, reasoning, sense.

logical *adj.* clear, coherent, consistent, deducible, methodical, necessary, obvious, rational, reasonable, reasoned, relevant, sensible, sound, valid, well-founded, well-organised, wise.
antonyms illogical, irrational, unorganised.

loiter *v.* dally, dawdle, delay, dilly-dally, hang about, idle, linger, mooch, saunter, stroll.

lone *adj.* isolated, one, only, separate, separated, single, sole, solitary, unaccompanied, unattached, unattended.
antonym accompanied.

loneliness *n.* aloneness, desolation, isolation, lonesomeness, seclusion, solitariness, solitude.

lonely *adj.* **1** alone, companionless, destitute, friendless, lonely-heart, lonesome, solitary. **2** abandoned, deserted, forsaken, isolated, out-of-the-way, remote, secluded, unfrequented, uninhabited.
antonyms **1** popular. **2** crowded, populous.

loner *n.* hermit, individualist, lone wolf, outsider, recluse, solitary.

lonesome *adj.* cheerless, companionless, deserted, desolate, dreary, forlorn, forsaken, friendless, isolated, lone, lonely, solitary.

long *adj.* expanded, expansive, extended, extensive, far-reaching, late, lengthy, long-drawn-out, prolonged, protracted, slow, spread out, stretched, sustained.
antonyms abbreviated, brief, fleeting, short.
long for covet, crave, desire, dream of, hanker for, hunger after, itch for, lust after, pine, thirst for, want, wish, yearn for, yen for.

longing *n.* ambition, aspiration, coveting, craving, desire, hankering, hungering, itch, thirst, urge, wish, yearning.
antonyms abhorrence, hate.

long-lasting *adj.* abiding, continuing, enduring, imperishable, long-standing, permanent, prolonged, protracted, unchanging, unfading.
antonyms ephemeral, short-lived, transient.

long-lived *adj.* durable, enduring, lasting, long-lasting, long-standing.
antonyms brief, ephemeral, short-lived.

long-standing *adj.* abiding, enduring, established, long-established, long-lasting, long-lived, time-honoured, traditional.

long-suffering *adj.* easy-going, forbearing, forgiving, patient, stoical, tolerant, uncomplaining.

long-winded *adj.* diffuse, discursive, lengthy, long-drawn-out, overlong, prolonged, rambling, repetitious, tedious, verbose, voluble, wordy.
antonyms brief, compact, terse.

look *v.* **1** consider, contemplate, examine, gawp, gaze, glance, inspect, observe, peep, regard, scan, scrutinise, see, stare, study, survey, view, watch. **2** appear, display, exhibit, seem, show.
n. **1** examination, gaze, glance, glimpse, inspection, observation, once-over, peek, review, sight, squint, survey, view. **2** appearance, aspect, bearing, complexion, expression, face, manner, mien, semblance.

look after attend to, care for, guard, keep an eye on, mind, protect, supervise, take care of, take charge of, tend, watch.
antonym neglect.

look down on despise, hold in contempt, look down one's nose at, scorn, sneer at, spurn, turn one's nose up at.
antonyms approve, esteem.

look forward to anticipate, await, count on, envisage, envision, expect, hope for, long for, look for, wait for.

look into check out, enquire about, examine, explore, fathom, follow up, go into, inspect, investigate, look over, plumb, probe, research, scrutinise, study.

look out be careful, beware, keep an eye out, pay attention, watch out.

look out on face, front, front on, give on (to), overlook.

look over cast an eye over, check, examine, flick through, give a once-over, inspect, look through, monitor, scan, view.

look up **1** call on, drop by, drop in on, find, hunt for, look in on, pay a visit to, research, search for, seek out, stop by, track down, visit. **2** come on, get better, improve, pick up, progress, shape up.

look up to admire, esteem, have a high opinion of, honour, respect, revere.

look-alike *n.* clone, doppel-gänger, double, living image, replica, ringer, spit, spitting image, twin.

look-out *n.* **1** guard, post, sentinal, sentry, tower, vigil, watch, watchman, watch-tower. **2** affair, business, concern, problem, worry.

loom *v.* appear, dominate, emerge, hang over, impend, menace, mount, overhang, overshadow, overtop, rise, soar, take shape, threaten, tower.

loop *n.* bend, circle, coil, curl, curve, eyelet, hoop, kink, loophole, noose, ring, spiral, turn, twirl, twist, whorl.
v. bend, braid, circle, coil, connect, curve round, encircle, fold, gird, join, knot, roll, spiral, turn, twist.

loophole *n.* escape, evasion, excuse, let-out, plea, pretence, pretext.

loose *adj.* **1** free, insecure, movable, shaky, unattached, unfastened, untied, wobbly. **2**

baggy, hanging, slack. **3** ill-defined, imprecise, inaccurate, indefinite, indistinct, inexact, vague.
antonyms **1** firm, secure. **2** tight. **3** precise.
loosen *v.* deliver, detach, free, let go, let out, release, separate, set free, slacken, unbind, undo, unfasten, unloosen, unstick, untie.
antonym tighten.
loosen up ease up, go easy, lessen, let up, moderate, relax, soften, unbend, weaken.
loot *n.* boodle, booty, goods, haul, plunder, prize, riches, spoils, swag.
v. maraud, pillage, plunder, raid, ransack, ravage, rifle, rob, sack.
lop-sided *adj.* askew, crooked, disproportionate, ill-balanced, off balance, one-sided, out of true, squint, tilting, uneven.
antonyms balanced, symmetrical.
lord *n.* baron, commander, count, duke, earl, governor, king, leader, master, monarch, noble, nobleman, overlord, peer, prince, ruler, sovereign, superior.
lord it over act big, boss around, domineer, order around, repress, tyrannise.
lordly *adj.* aristocratic, arrogant, authoritarian, condescending, despotic, dictatorial, disdainful, domineering, haughty, high-handed, imperious, lofty, overbearing, proud, tyrannical.
antonyms humble, low(ly), mean.
lose *v.* **1** displace, forfeit, forget, mislay, misplace, miss. **2** consume, dissipate, drain, exhaust, expend, misspend, squander, use up, waste. **3** fail, fall short, suffer defeat.
antonyms **1** gain. **2** make. **3** win.
loser *n.* also-ran, dud, failure, flop, no-hoper, runner-up, sucker, underdog, wash-out.
antonym winner.
loss *n.* bereavement, cost, damage, debt, defeat, deficiency, deficit, depletion, deprivation, destruction, disadvantage, disappearance, failure, harm, hurt, injury, losing, misfortune, squandering, waste, write-off.
antonyms acquisition, benefit, gain.
losses *n.* casualties, dead, death toll, fatalities, missing, wounded.
lost *adj.* **1** abandoned, astray, disappeared, mislaid, misplaced, missing, vanished. **2** baffled, bewildered, confused, disoriented, mystified, overwhelmed, perplexed, preoccupied, puzzled, strayed.
antonym **1** found.
lot *n.* assortment, batch, collection, consignment, crowd, cut, group, parcel, part, piece, portion, quantity, quota, set, share.
loth *see* **loath**.
lotion *n.* balm, cream, liniment, salve, solution.
loud *adj.* **1** blaring, booming, clamorous, deafening, ear-piercing, ear-splitting, noisy, piercing, resounding, rowdy, strong, thundering, tumultuous, vociferous. **2** brash, flashy, garish, gaudy, glaring, ostentatious, showy, tasteless.
antonyms **1** quiet. **2** soft.
loudmouth *n.* big mouth, boaster, brag, braggart, gasbag, swaggerer, windbag.
lounge *v.* idle, kill time, laze, lie about, lie back, loll, recline, relax, slump, sprawl, take it easy, waste time.
n. day-room, drawing-room, living-room, parlour, sitting-room.
lousy *adj.* awful, bad, despicable, inferior, low, mean, miserable, poor, rotten, second-rate, slovenly, terrible.
antonyms excellent, superb.
lovable *adj.* adorable, attractive, captivating, charming, cuddly, delightful, endearing, engaging, fetching, lovely, pleasing, sweet, winsome.
antonyms detestable, hateful.
love *v.* adore, appreciate, cherish, delight in, desire, dote on, enjoy, fancy, hold dear, idolise, like, take pleasure in, treasure, worship.
antonyms detest, hate, loathe.
n. adoration, adulation, affection, amorousness, ardour, attachment, delight, devotion, enjoyment, fondness, friendship, inclination, infatuation, liking, passion, rapture, regard, soft spot, taste, tenderness, warmth, weakness.
antonyms detestation, hate, loathing.
love-affair *n.* affair, liaison, love, passion, relationship, romance.
lovely *adj.* adorable, agreeable, attractive, beautiful, charming, delightful, enchanting, enjoyable, exquisite, graceful, gratifying, handsome, marvellous, nice, pleasant, pleasing, pretty, sweet, winning, wonderful.
antonyms hideous, ugly.
love-making *n.* courtship, foreplay, intimacy, romance, sexual intercourse, sexual relations, sexual union.
lover *n.* admirer, beloved, boyfriend, fiancé(e), flame, girlfriend, mistress, philanderer, suitor, sweetheart.
loving *adj.* affectionate, amorous, ardent, dear, devoted, doting, fond, friendly, kind, passionate, solicitous, tender, warm, warm-hearted.
antonyms cruel, unconcerned.
low[1] *adj.* **1** deep, depressed, little, shallow, short, small, squat, stunted, sunken. **2** deficient, inadequate, insignificant, meagre, paltry, poor, scant, sparse. **3** depressed, downcast, gloomy, unhappy.
antonyms **1** high. **2** high. **3** cheerful.
low[2] *v.* bellow, moo.
lower *adj.* inferior, insignificant, junior, lesser, low-level, lowly, minor, secondary, second-class, subordinate, under.
antonyms higher, upper.
v. cut, decrease, depress, devalue, diminish, drop, lessen, minimise, reduce.
antonyms increase, raise, rise.
low-key *adj.* low-pitched, muffled, muted, quiet, restrained, slight, soft, subdued.
lowly *adj.* humble, inferior, low-born, mean, mean-born, meek, mild, modest, obscure, ordinary, plain, poor, simple, submissive, subordinate.
antonyms lofty, noble.
low-spirited *adj.* depressed, despondent, down, down-hearted, fed up, gloomy, heavy-hearted, low, miserable, moody, sad, unhappy.

antonyms cheerful, high-spirited.
loyal *adj.* devoted, faithful, patriotic, sincere, staunch, steadfast, true, trustworthy.
antonyms disloyal, fickle, traitorous.
loyalty *n.* allegiance, devotion, faithfulness, patriotism, reliability, steadfastness, true-heartedness, trueness, trustworthiness.
antonyms disloyalty, treachery.
lubricate *v.* grease, lard, oil, smear, wax.
luck *n.* accident, break, chance, destiny, fate, fluke, fortuity, fortune, godsend, good fortune, stroke, success, windfall.
antonyms misfortune, trouble.
luckily *adv.* fortunately, happily, providentially.
antonym unfortunately.
lucky *adj.* advantageous, auspicious, favoured, fortunate, prosperous, successful, timely.
antonyms unfortunate, unlucky.
lucky dip bran tub, grab-bag.
lucrative *adj.* advantageous, profitable, remunerative, well-paid.
antonym unprofitable.
ludicrous *adj.* absurd, comical, crazy, farcical, funny, laughable, nonsensical, odd, outlandish, preposterous, ridiculous, silly.
antonyms serious, solemn.
lug *v.* carry, cart, drag, haul, heave, hump, pull, tow.
luggage *n.* baggage, bags, cases, gear, paraphernalia, suitcases, things.
lukewarm *adj.* apathetic, cold, cool, half-hearted, indifferent, tepid, unconcerned, unenthusiastic, uninterested, unresponsive.
lull *v.* calm, compose, hush, let up, pacify, quell, quiet, quieten down, slacken, soothe, subdue.
antonym agitate.
n. calm, hush, let-up, pause, peace, quiet, silence, stillness, tranquillity.
antonym agitation.
lumber¹ *n.* bits and pieces, clutter, jumble, junk, odds and ends, refuse, rubbish, trash.
lumber² *v.* clump, plod, shuffle, stump, trudge, trundle, waddle.
luminous *adj.* bright, brilliant, glowing, illuminated, lighted, lit, lustrous, radiant, shining, vivid.
lump *n.* ball, bulge, bump, bunch, cake, chunk, clod, cluster, dab, group, growth, hunk, mass, nugget, piece, protrusion, protuberance, spot, swelling, tuber, tumour, wedge.
v. coalesce, collect, combine, consolidate, group, mass, unite.
lumpy *adj.* bumpy, cloggy, clotted, curdled, grainy, granular, knobbly.
antonyms even, smooth.
lunacy *n.* aberration, absurdity, craziness, derangement, folly, foolishness, idiocy, imbecility, insanity, madness, mania, stupidity.
antonym sanity.
lunatic *n.* loony, madman, maniac, nutcase, nutter.
adj. crazy, daft, deranged, insane, irrational, mad.
antonyms sane, sensible.
lunge *v.* charge, dart, dash, dive, fall upon, grab (at), hit (at), jab, leap, pitch into, plunge, poke, pounce, set upon, stab, strike (at), thrust.
n. charge, cut, jab, pass, pounce, spring, stab, thrust.
lurch *v.* flounder, heave, lean, list, pitch, reel, rock, roll, stagger, stumble, sway, tilt, totter.
lure *v.* allure, attract, draw, ensnare, entice, inveigle, invite, lead on, seduce, tempt.
n. attraction, bait, enticement, inducement, temptation.
lurid *adj.* **1** bloody, disgusting, exaggerated, ghastly, gory, graphic, grisly, gruesome, macabre, sensational, shocking, startling. **2** fiery, flaming, garish, glaring, intense, loud, vivid.
lurk *v.* crouch, hide, lie in wait, lie low, prowl, skulk, snoop.
luscious *adj.* appetising, delicious, desirable, juicy, mouth-watering, savoury, succulent, sweet, tasty.
lush *adj.* elaborate, flourishing, green, juicy, luxuriant, ornate, overgrown, plush, rich, succulent, sumptuous, tender, verdant.
lust *n.* appetite, covetousness, craving, desire, greed, lechery, lewdness, licentiousness, longing, passion, sensuality, thirst.
lust after crave, desire, hunger for, need, thirst for, want, yearn for.
lustre *n.* brightness, brilliance, burnish, gleam, glint, glitter, glory, gloss, glow, honour, illustriousness, prestige, radiance, resplendence, sheen, shimmer, shine, sparkle.
luxurious *adj.* comfortable, costly, deluxe, expensive, lavish, magnificent, opulent, pampered, plush, rich, self-indulgent, sensual, splendid, sumptuous.
antonyms austere, frugal, spartan.
luxury *n.* affluence, bliss, comfort, delight, enjoyment, extravagance, gratification, hedonism, indulgence, opulence, pleasure, richness, satisfaction, splendour, sumptuousness, treat, well-being.
antonyms austerity, essential, poverty.
lying *adj.* deceitful, dishonest, double-dealing, false, guileful, treacherous, two-faced, untruthful.
antonyms honest, truthful.
n. deceit, dishonesty, double-dealing, duplicity, fabrication, falsity, fibbing, guile, perjury, untruthfulness.
antonyms honesty, truthfulness.
lyrical *adj.* carried away, ecstatic, emotional, enthusiastic, expressive, inspired, passionate, rapturous, rhapsodic.

M

macabre *adj.* dreadful, eerie, frightening, frightful, ghostly, grim, grisly, gruesome, horrible, horrific, morbid, weird.
antonyms delightful, pleasant.

machine *n.* **1** apparatus, appliance, automaton, contraption, contrivance, device, engine, gadget, instrument, machinery, mechanism, robot, tool. **2** agency, agent, organisation, party, set-up, structure, system.

machinery *n.* **1** apparatus, equipment, gear, instruments, kit, machine, mechanism, tackle, tools, works. **2** channels, organisation, procedure, structure, system.

mad *adj.* **1** barmy, berserk, crazy, demented, deranged, insane, lunatic, out of one's mind, unbalanced, unhinged, wild. **2** angry, enraged, exasperated, fuming, furious, incensed, infuriated, livid. **3** absurd, foolish, irrational, ludicrous, nonsensical, preposterous, unreasonable. **4** ardent, avid, devoted, enamoured, enthusiastic, fanatical, infatuated, keen.
antonyms **1** sane. **2** calm. **3** sensible. **4** apathetic.

madden *v.* annoy, craze, derange, enrage, exasperate, incense, inflame, infuriate, irritate, provoke, upset, vex.
antonyms calm, pacify, please.

made-up *adj.* fabricated, fairy-tale, false, fictional, imaginary, invented, make-believe, mythical, unreal, untrue.

madly *adv.* crazily, deliriously, devotedly, energetically, exceedingly, excitedly, extremely, fanatically, frantically, furiously, hastily, hurriedly, hysterically, intensely, rapidly, recklessly, violently, wildly.

madman *n.* lunatic, maniac, psychopath, psychotic.

magazine *n.* **1** journal, monthly, paper, periodical, quarterly, weekly. **2** ammunition dump, arsenal, depot, ordnance, powder-room, store, storehouse.

magic *n.* black art, conjuring, hocus-pocus, illusion, jiggery-pokery, occultism, sleight of hand, sorcery, spell, trickery, voodoo, witchcraft.
adj. bewitching, charming, enchanting, fascinating, marvellous, spellbinding.

magician *n.* conjuror, miracle-worker, sorcerer, spellbinder, warlock, witch, witch-doctor, wizard, wonder-worker.

magisterial *adj.* arrogant, assertive, authoritarian, authoritative, commanding, domineering, lordly, masterful, overbearing.

magistrate *n.* bailiff, JP, judge, justice, justice of the peace, tribune.

magnanimous *adj.* beneficent, big, big-hearted, generous, great-hearted, kind, noble, open-handed, selfless, ungrudging, unselfish.
antonyms mean, miserly.

magnate *n.* baron, captain of industry, chief, leader, merchant, mogul, notable, personage, tycoon.

magnetic *adj.* absorbing, alluring, attractive, captivating, charismatic, charming, entrancing, fascinating, gripping, irresistible, mesmerising, seductive.
antonyms repellent, repugnant, repulsive.

magnetism *n.* allure, appeal, attraction, charisma, charm, draw, drawing power, fascination, grip, hypnotism, lure, magic, mesmerism, power, pull, spell.

magnification *n.* amplification, blow-up, boost, build-up, enhancement, enlargement, expansion, increase, inflation, intensification.
antonyms diminution, reduction.

magnificent *adj.* brilliant, elegant, excellent, fine, glorious, gorgeous, grand, imposing, impressive, majestic, outstanding, plush, posh, rich, splendid, superb.
antonyms humble, modest, plain, simple.

magnify *v.* amplify, blow up, boost, build up, deepen, dramatise, enhance, enlarge, exaggerate, expand, greaten, heighten, increase, intensify, overdo, overemphasise, overplay, overstate, praise.
antonyms belittle, play down.

magnitude *n.* amount, amplitude, bulk, dimensions, expanse, extent, greatness, immensity, importance, intensity, largeness, mark, mass, measure, proportions, quantity, significance, size, space, strength, vastness, volume, weight.

maiden *n.* damsel, girl, lass, lassie, maid, miss.

mail *n.* correspondence, delivery, letters, packages, parcels, post.
v. air-mail, dispatch, forward, post, send.

maim *v.* cripple, disable, hurt, impair, incapacitate, injure, lame, mangle, mar, mutilate, savage, wound.
antonyms heal, repair.

main *adj.* central, chief, critical, crucial, direct, downright, entire, essential, extensive, first, foremost, general, great, head, leading, necessary, outstanding, paramount, particular, predominant, pre-eminent, primary, prime, principal, pure, special, supreme, vital.
antonyms insignificant, minor, unimportant.
n. cable, channel, conduit, duct, line, pipe.

mainly *adv.* above all, as a rule, chiefly, especially, for the most part, generally, in general, in the main, largely, mostly, on the whole, overall, primarily, principally.

mainspring *n.* cause, driving force, fountainhead, incentive, inspiration, motivation, motive, origin, prime mover, source.

mainstay *n.* backbone, bulwark, buttress, foundation, linchpin, pillar, prop, support.

mainstream *adj.* accepted, conventional, established, general, normal, orthodox, received, regular, standard.
antonyms heterodox, peripheral.

maintain *v.* **1** care for, carry on, conserve, continue, finance, keep (up), look after, preserve, retain, supply, support, sustain, take care of. **2** affirm, assert, believe, claim, contend, declare, fight for, hold, insist, state.
antonyms **1** neglect. **2** deny.

maintenance *n.* **1** care, conservation, continuation, defence, keeping, preservation, protection, repairs, running, support, upkeep. **2** alimony, allowance, food, keep, livelihood, living.
antonym **1** neglect.

majestic *adj.* dignified, exalted, grand, imperial, imposing, impressive, lofty, magnificent, monumental, noble, pompous, regal, royal, splendid, stately, sublime, superb.
antonyms unimportant, unimposing, unimpressive.

majesty *n.* dignity, exaltedness, glory, grandeur, impressiveness, loftiness, magnificence, nobility, pomp, resplendence, royalty, splendour, stateliness.
antonyms unimportance, unimpressiveness.

major *adj.* better, bigger, chief, crucial, great, greater, higher, important, key, keynote, larger, leading, main, most, notable, older, outstanding, pre-eminent, radical, senior, significant, superior, supreme, uppermost, vital, weighty.
antonyms minor, trivial, unimportant.

majority *n.* **1** bulk, mass, preponderance, the many. **2** adulthood, manhood, maturity, womanhood, years of discretion.
antonyms **1** minority. **2** childhood.

make *v.* **1** build, compose, construct, create, form, manufacture, mould, originate, produce, put together, shape. **2** accomplish, bring about, cause, generate, give rise to, lead to, occasion, perform, render. **3** coerce, compel, constrain, force, oblige, press, pressurise, prevail upon, require. **4** appoint, designate, elect, install, nominate, ordain. **5** acquire, earn, gain, net, obtain.
antonyms **1** dismantle. **3** persuade. **5** lose.
n. brand, form, kind, manufacture, mark, model, sort, structure, style, type, variety.
make for 1 aim for, head for, move towards. **2** contribute to, ensure, facilitate, forward, further, promote.
make off beat a hasty retreat, bolt, clear off, cut and run, depart, fly, leave, run away, run off.
make off with appropriate, carry off, pilfer, pinch, run away with, run off with, steal, walk off with.
antonym bring.
make out 1 decipher, detect, discern, discover, distinguish, fathom, follow, grasp, perceive, read, realise, recognise, see, understand, work out. **2** complete, fill in, fill out, write out. **3** assert, claim, demonstrate, describe, imply, infer, maintain, prove. **4** fare, get on, manage, progress, succeed.
make up 1 arrange, collect, complete, compose, construct, create, devise, dream up, fabricate, fill, formulate, invent, meet, originate, prepare, put together, repair, supplement, supply. **2** comprise, constitute, form. **3** bury the hatchet, call it quits, forgive and forget, make peace, settle differences, shake hands.
make up for atone for, compensate for, make amends for, make good, recompense, redeem, redress.
make up to butter up, curry favour with, fawn on, flatter, make overtures to.

make-believe *n.* charade, dream, fantasy, imagination, play-acting, pretence, role-play, unreality.
antonym reality.

maker *n.* architect, author, builder, constructor, creator, director, manufacturer, producer.
antonym dismantler.

makeshift *adj.* expedient, improvised, make-do, provisional, rough and ready, stop-gap, substitute, temporary.
antonyms finished, permanent.

make-up *n.* **1** cosmetics, paint, powder. **2** arrangement, assembly, character, composition, constitution, construction, figure, form, format, formation, nature, organisation, stamp, structure, style.

making *n.* assembly, building, composition, construction, creation, fabrication, forging, manufacture, modelling, moulding, production.
antonym dismantling.

makings *n.* beginnings, capacity, ingredients, possibilities, potential, promise, qualities.

maladjusted *adj.* alienated, confused, disturbed, estranged, neurotic, unstable.
antonym well-adjusted.

male *adj.* bull, manlike, manly, masculine, virile.
antonym female.

malevolent *adj.* evil-minded, hostile, ill-natured, malicious, spiteful, venomous, vicious, vindictive.
antonyms benevolent, kind.

malformation *n.* deformity, distortion, irregularity, warp.

malformed *adj.* abnormal, bent, crooked, deformed, distorted, irregular, misshapen, twisted, warped.
antonym perfect.

malfunction *n.* breakdown, defect, failure, fault.
v. break down, fail, go wrong.

malice *n.* animosity, bitterness, enmity, hate, hatred, ill-will, malevolence, spite, vindictiveness.
antonyms kindness, love.

malicious *adj.* bitchy, bitter, catty, evil-minded, ill-natured, malevolent, resentful, spiteful, vengeful, venomous, vicious.

antonyms friendly, kind, thoughtful.
malign *adj.* bad, destructive, evil, harmful, hostile, hurtful.
antonyms benign, good.
v. abuse, defame, harm, injure, libel, run down, slander.
antonym praise.
malignant *adj.* **1** destructive, evil, harmful, hostile, hurtful, malevolent, malicious, pernicious, spiteful, venomous, vicious. **2** cancerous, dangerous, deadly, fatal, incurable, uncontrollable, virulent.
antonyms **1** kind. **2** benign.
malleable *adj.* adaptable, compliant, governable, impressionable, manageable, plastic, pliable, soft, tractable, workable.
antonyms intractable, unworkable.
malnutrition *n.* anorexia (nervosa), hunger, starvation, undernourishment.
antonym nourishment.
malpractice *n.* abuse, dereliction, impropriety, misconduct, misdeed, mismanagement, negligence.
maltreat *v.* abuse, damage, harm, hurt, ill-treat, injure, mistreat, misuse.
antonym care for.
mammoth *adj.* colossal, enormous, giant, gigantic, huge, immense, massive, mighty, monumental, vast.
antonyms minute, tiny.
man *n.* **1** bloke, chap, fellow, gentleman, male. **2** adult, human, human being, individual, person. **3** Homo sapiens, human race, humanity, humankind, mankind, mortals, people. **4** boyfriend, fellow, guy, husband, lover, partner, spouse.
v. crew, fill, occupy, operate, staff, take charge of.
manacle *v.* bind, chain, check, curb, fetter, hamper, hamstring, handcuff, inhibit, put in chains, restrain, shackle.
antonyms free, unshackle.
manacles *n.* bonds, bracelets, chains, fetters, handcuffs, irons, shackles.
manage *v.* **1** accomplish, bring about, bring off, succeed. **2** administer, arrange, command, conduct, direct, dominate, govern, oversee, preside over, rule, run, superintend, supervise. **3** control, deal with, guide, handle, influence, operate. **4** find, make, spare. **5** cope, fare, get along, get by, get on, make do, make out.
antonyms **1** fail. **2** mismanage.
manageable *adj.* controllable, convenient, easy, governable, handy, submissive.
antonym unmanageable.
management *n.* **1** administration, care, charge, command, control, direction, government, handling, operation, oversight, running, superintendence, supervision. **2** board, bosses, directorate, directors, executive, executives, governors, managers, supervisors.
antonyms **1** mismanagement. **2** workers.
manager *n.* administrator, boss, controller, director, executive, governor, head, organiser, overseer, superintendent, supervisor.
mandate *n.* authorisation, authority, charge, command, commission, decree, directive, injunction, instruction, order, sanction, warrant.
mandatory *adj.* binding, compulsory, necessary, obligatory, required.
antonym optional.
manfully *adv.* boldly, bravely, courageously, determinedly, gallantly, heroically, pluckily, resolutely, valiantly, vigorously.
antonyms half-heartedly, timidly.
mangle *v.* butcher, crush, cut, deform, destroy, disfigure, distort, hack, maim, mar, maul, mutilate, rend, spoil, tear, twist, wreck.
mangy *adj.* dirty, mean, moth-eaten, scabby, scruffy, seedy, shabby, shoddy, tatty.
antonyms clean, neat, spruce.
manhandle *v.* carry, haul, heave, hump, knock about, maltreat, mistreat, misuse, pull, push, rough up, shove, tug.
manhood *n.* adulthood, machismo, manfulness, manliness, masculinity, maturity, mettle, virility.
mania *n.* aberration, compulsion, craving, craze, craziness, derangement, desire, disorder, enthusiasm, fad, fixation, frenzy, infatuation, itch, lunacy, madness, obsession, passion, rage.
maniac *n.* **1** lunatic, madman, madwoman, psychopath. **2** enthusiast, fan, fanatic, fiend, freak.
manic *adj.* crazy, demented, deranged, frenzied, insane, lunatic, mad, psychotic, raving, wild.
antonym sane.
manifest *adj.* apparent, clear, conspicuous, evident, noticeable, obvious, open, patent, plain, unconcealed, unmistakable, visible.
antonyms hidden, unclear.
v. demonstrate, display, establish, exhibit, expose, illustrate, prove, reveal, set forth, show.
antonyms conceal, hide.
manifestation *n.* appearance, demonstration, disclosure, display, exhibition, exposure, expression, indication, mark, revelation, show, sign.
manifesto *n.* declaration, platform, policies, policy.
manifold *adj.* abundant, copious, diverse, kaleidoscopic, many, multiple, numerous, varied, various.
manipulate *v.* conduct, control, cook, direct, employ, engineer, gerrymander, guide, handle, influence, juggle with, manoeuvre, negotiate, operate, shuffle, steer, use, wield, work.
mankind *n.* Homo sapiens, human race, humanity, humankind, man, people.
manly *adj.* fatherly, macho, male, manful, masculine, paternal, virile.
man-made *adj.* artificial, imitation, manufactured, simulated, synthetic.
antonym natural.
manner *n.* **1** fashion, form, means, method, procedure, process, style, way. **2** air, appearance, bearing, behaviour, character, conduct, demeanour, look, tenor, tone.
mannered *adj.* affected, artificial, posed, pre-

cious, pretentious, put-on, stilted.
antonym natural.

mannerism *n.* characteristic, feature, foible, habit, idiosyncrasy, peculiarity, quirk, trait.

manners *n.* bearing, behaviour, conduct, demeanour, formalities, politeness, p's and q's, social graces.
antonyms impoliteness, indecorousness.

manoeuvre *n.* action, dodge, exercise, gambit, intrigue, machination, move, movement, operation, plan, plot, ploy, ruse, scheme, tactic, trick.
v. contrive, deploy, devise, direct, drive, engineer, exercise, guide, handle, jockey, manage, manipulate, move, navigate, negotiate, pilot, plan, plot, pull strings, scheme, steer, wangle.

mantle *n.* blanket, canopy, cape, cloak, cloud, cover, covering, curtain, hood, screen, shawl, shroud, veil, wrap.

manual *n.* bible, book of words, companion, guide, guide-book, handbook, instructions.
adj. hand, hand-operated, human, physical.

manufacture *v.* assemble, build, concoct, construct, create, devise, fabricate, forge, form, hatch, invent, make, make up, mass-produce, mould, process, produce, shape, think up, turn out.
n. assembly, construction, creation, fabrication, facture, formation, making, mass-production, production.

manufacturer *n.* builder, constructor, creator, factory-owner, industrialist, maker, producer.

manure *n.* compost, dung, fertiliser, muck.

manuscript *n.* deed, document, handwriting, parchment, scroll, text, vellum.

many *adj.* countless, diverse, lots of, manifold, numerous, sundry, umpteen, varied, various.
antonym few.

map *n.* atlas, chart, graph, plan, plot, street plan.

mar *v.* damage, deface, detract from, disfigure, harm, hurt, impair, injure, maim, mangle, mutilate, ruin, scar, spoil, tarnish, temper, wreck.
antonym enhance.

marauder *n.* bandit, brigand, buccaneer, outlaw, pillager, pirate, plunderer, predator, raider, ravager, robber.

march *v.* file, pace, parade, stalk, stride, tread, walk.
n. **1** demo, demonstration, footslog, hike, pace, parade, procession, step, stride, trek, walk. **2** advance, development, evolution, passage, progress.

margin *n.* allowance, border, bound, boundary, brink, confine, edge, extra, latitude, leeway, limit, perimeter, periphery, play, rim, room, scope, side, skirt, space, surplus, verge.
antonyms centre, core.

marginal *adj.* borderline, doubtful, insignificant, low, minimal, minor, negligible, peripheral, slight, small.
antonyms central, core.

marijuana *n.* cannabis, dope, grass, hash, hashish, hemp, pot, weed.

marina *n.* dock, harbour, mooring, port, yacht station.

marine *adj.* maritime, nautical, naval, ocean-going, salt-water, sea, seafaring, sea-going.

mariner *n.* deckhand, hand, navigator, sailor, sea-dog, seafarer, seaman.

marital *adj.* conjugal, married, matrimonial, nuptial, spousal, wedded.

maritime *adj.* coastal, marine, nautical, naval, oceanic, sea, seafaring, seaside.

mark *n.* **1** blemish, blot, blotch, bruise, dent, impression, line, scar, scratch, smudge, spot, stain. **2** badge, brand, characteristic, emblem, evidence, feature, indication, proof, sign, stamp, symbol, token. **3** assessment, grade.
v. **1** blemish, blot, bruise, dent, scar, scratch, smudge, splotch, stain. **2** brand, characterise, distinguish, identify, label, stamp. **3** assess, correct, evaluate, grade. **4** heed, listen, mind, note, notice, observe, regard, take to heart.

marked *adj.* **1** apparent, clear, considerable, conspicuous, decided, distinct, emphatic, glaring, noticeable, obvious, pronounced, remarkable. **2** doomed, suspected, watched.
antonyms **1** slight, unnoticeable.

market *n.* bazaar, fair, market-place, mart, outlet, shop.
v. hawk, peddle, retail, sell.
antonym buy.

marketable *adj.* in demand, merchantable, salable, sellable, sought after, wanted.
antonym unsalable.

maroon *v.* abandon, cast away, desert, isolate, leave, put ashore, strand.
antonyms rescue, save.

marriage *n.* alliance, amalgamation, association, confederation, coupling, link, matrimony, merger, nuptials, union, wedding, wedlock.
antonyms divorce, separation.

married *adj.* conjugal, marital, matrimonial, nuptial, united, wed, wedded, yoked.
antonyms divorced, single.

marrow *n.* core, essence, gist, heart, kernel, nub, quick, soul, spirit, stuff, substance.

marry *v.* ally, join, knit, link, match, merge, tie the knot, unify, unite, wed, yoke.
antonyms divorce, separate.

marsh *n.* bog, fen, marshland, morass, moss, quagmire, slump, swamp.

marshal *v.* align, arrange, assemble, collect, conduct, convoy, deploy, dispose, draw up, escort, gather, group, guide, lead, line up, muster, order, organise, rank, take.

marshy *adj.* boggy, miry, quaggy, swampy, waterlogged, wet.
antonyms firm, solid.

martial *adj.* belligerent, brave, heroic, militant, military, soldierly, warlike.
antonym pacific.

martyrdom *n.* death, ordeal, persecution, suffering, torment, torture.

marvel *n.* genius, glory, miracle, phenomenon, prodigy, sensation, spectacle, wonder.
v. gape, gaze, wonder.

marvellous *adj.* amazing, astonishing, astounding, excellent, extraordinary, fantastic, glorious, incredible, magnificent, remarkable, sensational, spectacular, splendid, superb, surprising, terrific, unbelievable, wonderful.
antonyms awful, ordinary, run-of-the-mill, terrible.

masculine *adj.* bold, brave, gallant, macho, male, manlike, manly, mannish, muscular, powerful, red-blooded, resolute, robust, stout-hearted, strapping, strong, vigorous, virile.
antonym feminine.

masculinity *n.* maleness, manhood, manliness, mannishness, virileness, virility.
antonym femininity.

mash *v.* beat, champ, crush, grind, pound, pulverise, pummel, smash.

mask *n.* blind, camouflage, cloak, concealment, cover, cover-up, disguise, façade, front, guise, pretence, semblance, show, veil, veneer, visor..
v. camouflage, cloak, conceal, cover, disguise, hide, obscure, screen, shield, veil.
antonyms expose, uncover.

masked *adj.* cloaked, concealed, covered, disguised, screened, shielded, shrouded.
antonyms uncovered, unshielded.

masquerade *n.* **1** costume ball, fancy dress party, masked ball. **2** cloak, counterfeit, cover, cover-up, deception, disguise, front, pose, pretence, put-on.
v. disguise, dissimulate, impersonate, mask, pass oneself off, play, pose, pretend, profess.

mass[1] *n.* accumulation, aggregate, band, batch, block, body, bulk, bunch, chunk, collection, combination, conglomeration, crowd, dimension, entirety, extensity, group, heap, horde, hunk, load, lot, lump, majority, mob, piece, pile, quantity, size, sum, throng, totality, troop, whole.
adj. across-the-board, blanket, comprehensive, extensive, general, indiscriminate, large-scale, popular, sweeping, wholesale, widespread.
antonyms limited, modest, small-scale.
v. assemble, cluster, collect, congregate, crowd, gather, rally.
antonym separate.
the masses hoi polloi, the common people, the crowd, the majority, the many, the multitude, the people, the plebs, the rank and file.

mass[2] *n.* communion, eucharist, holy communion, Lord's Supper, Lord's Table.

massacre *n.* annihilation, blood bath, butchery, carnage, extermination, holocaust, killing, murder, slaughter.
v. annihilate, butcher, decimate, exterminate, kill, mow down, murder, slaughter, wipe out.

massage *n.* kneading, manipulation, rubbing, rub-down.
v. knead, manipulate, rub (down).

massive *adj.* big, bulky, colossal, enormous, extensive, great, heavy, huge, immense, large-scale, monumental, solid, substantial, vast.
antonyms slight, small.

master *n.* ace, boss, captain, chief, commander, controller, dab hand, director, employer, expert, genius, governor, guide, guru, head, instructor, lord, maestro, manager, overlord, overseer, owner, past master, preceptor, principal, pro, ruler, schoolmaster, skipper, superintendent, teacher, tutor, virtuoso.
antonyms amateur, learner, pupil, servant, slave.
adj. chief, controlling, expert, foremost, grand, great, leading, main, masterly, predominant, prime, principal, proficient, skilful, skilled.
antonyms subordinate, unskilled.
v. **1** conquer, control, defeat, overcome, quell, rule, subdue, suppress, tame, triumph over. **2** acquire, get the hang of, grasp, learn, manage.

masterful *adj.* **1** arrogant, authoritative, autocratic, bossy, despotic, dictatorial, domineering, high-handed, overbearing, powerful, superior, tyrannical. **2** dexterous, expert, first-rate, masterly, professional, skilful, skilled.
antonyms **1** humble. **2** clumsy, unskilful.

mastermind *v.* conceive, design, devise, direct, dream up, forge, manage, organise, originate, plan.
n. architect, authority, brain(s), creator, director, engineer, genius, intellect, manager, organiser, originator, planner, prime mover, virtuoso.

masterpiece *n.* chef d'oeuvre, jewel, magnum opus, master-work, pièce de résistance.

mastery *n.* **1** ability, cleverness, command, conversancy, dexterity, expertise, familiarity, grasp, know-how, knowledge, proficiency, skill, understanding, virtuosity. **2** authority, conquest, control, domination, dominion, superiority, supremacy, upper hand, victory.
antonyms **1** clumsiness, unfamiliarity.

match *n.* **1** bout, competition, contest, game, test, trial, venue. **2** affiliation, alliance, combination, companion, complement, copy, counterpart, couple, double, duet, duplicate, equal, equivalent, fellow, like, look-alike, marriage, mate, pair, partnership, peer, replica, rival, twin, union.
v. **1** compete, contend, oppose, pit against, rival, vie. **2** accompany, accord, adapt, agree, ally, blend, combine, compare, co-ordinate, correspond, couple, equal, fit, gee, go together, go with, harmonise, join, link, marry, mate, measure up to, pair, relate, rival, suit, tally, team, tone with, unite, yoke.
antonyms **2** clash, separate.

matching *adj.* comparable, co-ordinating, corresponding, double, duplicate, equal, equivalent, identical, like, paired, parallel, same, similar, twin.
antonyms clashing, different.

matchless *adj.* excellent, incomparable, inimitable, perfect, supreme, unequalled, unique, unmatched, unparalleled, unrivalled, unsurpassed.
antonyms inferior, mediocre.

mate *n.* assistant, associate, better half, buddy, chum, colleague, companion, comrade, confidant(e), co-worker, fellow, fellow-worker,

friend, helper, husband, match, pal, partner, side-kick, spouse, subordinate, twin, wife.
v. breed, copulate, couple, join, marry, match, pair, wed, yoke.

material *n.* **1** body, matter, stuff, substance. **2** cloth, fabric, textile. **3** constituents, data, evidence, facts, information, literature, notes, work.
adj. **1** concrete, physical, substantial, tangible. **2** essential, important, indispensable, meaningful, pertinent, relevant, serious, significant, vital.
antonyms **1** abstract, spiritual. **2** irrelevant, unimportant.

maternal *adj.* loving, matronal, motherly, protective.
antonym paternal.

matrimonial *adj.* conjugal, marital, marriage, married, nuptial, wedded, wedding.

matrimony *n.* marriage, nuptials, wedlock.

matted *adj.* knotted, tangled, tousled, twisted, uncombed.
antonyms tidy, untangled.

matter *n.* **1** affair, business, complication, concern, difficulty, episode, event, incident, issue, problem, proceeding, situation, subject, thing, trouble, worry. **2** body, content, material, stuff, substance.
v. **1** be important, count, make a difference, mean something. **2** be wrong, upset, worry.

matter-of-fact *adj.* deadpan, down-to-earth, emotionless, flat, lifeless, plain, sober, unimaginative, unsentimental.
antonym emotional.

mature *adj.* adult, complete, full-grown, fully fledged, grown, grown-up, mellow, perfect, perfected, ready, ripe, ripened, seasoned, well-thought-out.
antonyms childish, immature.
v. age, bloom, come of age, develop, fall due, grow up, mellow, perfect, ripen.

maturity *n.* adulthood, experience, fullness, majority, manhood, perfection, readiness, ripeness, wisdom, womanhood.
antonyms childishness, immaturity.

maudlin *adj.* drunk, emotional, half-drunk, mawkish, sentimental, sickly, slushy, soppy, tearful, weepy.

maul *v.* abuse, batter, beat (up), claw, ill-treat, knock about, maltreat, manhandle, molest, paw, rough up, thrash.

mawkish *adj.* emotional, gushy, insipid, maudlin, mushy, nauseous, offensive, sentimental, sickly, slushy, soppy.

maxim *n.* adage, aphorism, axiom, byword, epigram, motto, precept, proverb, rule, saying.

maximum *adj.* biggest, greatest, highest, largest, most, supreme, utmost.
antonym minimum.
n. ceiling, extremity, height, most, peak, pinnacle, summit, top (point), upper limit, utmost, zenith.
antonym mimimum.

maybe *adv.* perhaps, possibly.
antonyms certainly, definitely.

maze *n.* confusion, intricacy, labyrinth, puzzle, tangle, web.

meadow *n.* field, grassland, lea, pasture.

meagre *adj.* deficient, inadequate, insubstantial, little, negligible, paltry, poor, puny, scanty, slender, slight, small, sparse, thin, weak.
antonyms ample, substantial.

meal[1] *n.* banquet, barbecue, blow-out, breakfast, dinner, feast, lunch, luncheon, picnic, snack, supper, tea, tuck-in.

meal[2] *n.* flour, grits, oatmeal.

mealy-mouthed *adj.* equivocal, evasive, flattering, glib, indirect, over-squeamish, plausible, prim, reticent, smooth-tongued.

mean[1] *adj.* **1** cheese-paring, miserly, niggardly, parsimonious, penny-pinching, selfish, stingy, tight, tight-fisted. **2** bad-tempered, callous, contemptible, cruel, despicable, disgraceful, nasty, unfriendly, unpleasant.
antonyms **1** generous. **2** kind.

mean[2] *v.* **1** denote, express, get at, imply, indicate, represent, signify, stand for, suggest, symbolise. **2** aim, cause, design, give rise to, intend, propose.

mean[3] *adj.* average, half-way, intermediate, median, medium, middle, moderate, normal, standard.
antonym extreme.
n. average, balance, compromise, golden mean, happy medium, median, middle, middle course, middle way, mid-point, norm.
antonym extreme.

meander *v.* amble, curve, ramble, snake, stray, stroll, turn, twist, wander, wind, zigzag.

meandering *adj.* circuitous, indirect, roundabout, tortuous, twisting, wandering, winding.
antonyms direct, straight.

meaning *n.* explanation, force, gist, idea, intention, interpretation, message, point, purpose, sense, significance, thrust, trend, upshot, value, worth.

meaningful *adj.* expressive, important, material, pointed, purposeful, relevant, serious, significant, speaking, suggestive, useful, valid, warning, worthwhile.
antonyms useless, worthless.

meaningless *adj.* absurd, aimless, empty, expressionless, futile, hollow, insignificant, insubstantial, nonsensical, pointless, purposeless, senseless, trifling, trivial, useless, vain, worthless.
antonyms important, meaningful, worthwhile.

means *n.* **1** agency, capacity, channel, course, instrument, medium, method, mode, process, way. **2** affluence, fortune, funds, income, money, resources, riches, substance, wealth, wherewithal.

meanwhile *adv.* at the same time, for now, for the moment, in the meantime, in the meanwhile.

measure *n.* **1** portion, ration, share. **2** amount, degree, extent, magnitude, proportion, quantity, range, scope, size. **3** criterion, gauge, norm, rule, scale, standard, system, test, touchstone, yardstick. **4** act, action, bill, course, deed, law,

means, method, procedure, resolution, statute, step.
v. assess, calculate, calibrate, choose, compute, determine, estimate, evaluate, fathom, gauge, judge, mark out, measure off, measure out, plumb, quantify, size, sound, step, survey, value, weigh.
measure out allot, apportion, assign, deal out, dispense, distribute, divide, dole out, hand out, issue, mete out, parcel out, pour out, share out.
measure up to compare with, equal, make the grade, match, meet, rival, touch.
measured *adj.* calculated, careful, considered, deliberate, planned, precise, reasoned, slow, steady, studied, unhurried, well-thought-out.
measurement *n.* amount, appraisal, appreciation, area, assessment, calculation, calibration, capacity, computation, depth, dimension, estimation, evaluation, extent, gauging, height, judgement, length, magnitude, size, survey, volume, weight, width.
meat *n.* eats, flesh, food, nourishment, provisions, rations, subsistence, sustenance.
meaty *adj.* **1** beefy, brawny, fleshy, heavy, husky, muscular. **2** interesting, profound, significant, solid, substantial.
mechanic *n.* engineer, machinist, operative, operator, repairman, technician, worker.
mechanical *adj.* automatic, cold, dead, dull, emotionless, habitual, impersonal, instinctive, involuntary, lifeless, matter-of-fact, routine, unfeeling.
antonyms conscious, thinking.
mechanism *n.* action, agency, apparatus, appliance, components, contrivance, device, functioning, gadget, gears, instrument, machine, machinery, means, medium, method, motor, operation, performance, procedure, process, structure, system, technique, tool, workings, works.
medal *n.* award, decoration, honour, medallion, prize, reward, trophy.
meddle *v.* interfere, interpose, intervene, intrude, pry, tamper.
meddlesome *adj.* interfering, intruding, intrusive, meddling, mischievous, prying.
medi(a)eval *adj.* antiquated, archaic, old-fashioned, outmoded, primitive.
mediate *v.* arbitrate, conciliate, intercede, intervene, moderate, negotiate, reconcile, referee, resolve, settle, step in, umpire.
mediator *n.* advocate, arbitrator, go-between, interceder, intermediary, judge, middleman, moderator, negotiator, ombudsman, ombudswoman, peacemaker, referee, umpire.
medicinal *adj.* curative, healing, homeopathic, medical, remedial, restorative, therapeutic.
medicine *n.* **1** cure, drug, medication, panacea, remedy. **2** acupuncture, homeopathy, surgery, therapeutics.
medieval *see* **mediaeval**.
mediocre *adj.* average, commonplace, indifferent, inferior, insignificant, medium, middling, ordinary, run-of-the-mill, second-rate, so-so, undistinguished, unexceptional, uninspired.
antonyms distinctive, exceptional, extraordinary.
mediocrity *n.* **1** indifference, inferiority, ordinariness, poorness, unimportance. **2** insignificance, nobody, nonentity.
meditate *v.* consider, contemplate, deliberate, devise, intend, mull over, plan, ponder, reflect, ruminate, scheme, speculate, study, think, think over.
meditation *n.* concentration, contemplation, musing, pondering, reflection, speculation, study, thought.
meditative *adj.* contemplative, deliberative, pensive, reflective, studious, thoughtful.
medium *adj.* average, fair, intermediate, medial, median, middle, middling, midway, standard.
n. **1** average, centre, compromise, golden mean, happy medium, middle, middle ground, midpoint. **2** agency, base, channel, form, instrument, means, mode, organ, vehicle, way. **3** clairvoyant, psychic, spiritist, spiritualist.
medley *n.* assortment, collection, hodge-podge, hotchpotch, jumble, miscellany, mixture, potpourri.
meek *adj.* docile, forbearing, humble, long-suffering, modest, patient, peaceful, resigned, soft, spiritless, submissive, tame, timid, unassuming, unpretentious.
antonyms arrogant, assertive, rebellious.
meet *v.* **1** bump into, chance on, come across, contact, encounter, endure, experience, face, go through, run across, run into, undergo. **2** assemble, collect, congregate, convene, gather. **3** answer, discharge, equal, fulfil, match, measure up to, perform, satisfy. **4** abut, come together, connect, converge, cross, intersect, join, touch, unite.
antonyms **2** scatter. **4** diverge.
meeting *n.* **1** assembly, audience, company, conclave, conference, confrontation, congregation, convention, convocation, encounter, engagement, forum, gathering, get-together, rally, rendezvous, reunion, session. **2** confluence, convergence, intersection, junction, union.
melancholy *adj.* dejected, depressed, despondent, dismal, dispirited, down, downcast, downhearted, gloomy, heavy-hearted, low, low-spirited, miserable, moody, mournful, sad, sorrowful, unhappy.
antonyms cheerful, happy, joyful.
n. dejection, depression, despondency, gloom, low spirits, sadness, sorrow, unhappiness, woe.
antonyms exhilaration, joy.
mélange *n.* assortment, jumble, medley, miscellany, mix, mixture.
mêlée *n.* affray, brawl, fracas, fray, free-for-all, scrimmage, scrum, scuffle, set-to.
mellow *adj.* **1** full-flavoured, juicy, mature, mild, ripe, sweet, tender. **2** cheerful, cordial, genial, happy, jolly, jovial, melodious, placid, pleasant, relaxed, rich, rounded, serene, smooth, soft,

tranquil.
antonyms **1** green, immature, unripe.
v. improve, mature, perfect, ripen, season, soften, sweeten, temper.

melodious *adj.* dulcet, euphonious, harmonious, musical, sonorous, sweet-sounding, tuneful.
antonyms discordant, grating, harsh.

melodramatic *adj.* blood-and-thunder, exaggerated, overdramatic, overemotional, sensational, theatrical.

melody *n.* air, aria, harmony, music, refrain, song, theme, tune.

melt *v.* dissolve, fuse, liquefy, thaw.
antonyms freeze, harden, solidify.
melt away disappear, disperse, dissolve, evaporate, fade, vanish.

member *n.* adherent, associate, comrade, fellow, representative, subscriber.

membership *n.* adherence, allegiance, associates, body, fellows, fellowship, members.

membrane *n.* diaphragm, film, skin, tissue, veil.

memento *n.* keepsake, memorial, record, relic, remembrance, reminder, souvenir, token.

memoirs *n.* annals, autobiography, chronicles, confessions, diary, experiences, journals, life story, recollections, records, reminiscences.

memorable *adj.* catchy, extraordinary, important, impressive, notable, noteworthy, outstanding, remarkable, significant, unforgettable.
antonyms forgettable, trivial, unimportant.

memorial *n.* mausoleum, memento, monument, plaque, record, remembrance, souvenir, stone.
adj. celebratory, commemorative.

memorise *v.* learn, learn by heart, remember, swot up.
antonym forget.

memory *n.* commemoration, recall, recollection, remembrance, reminiscence, retention.
antonym forgetfulness.

menace *v.* alarm, bully, frighten, impend, intimidate, loom, terrorise, threaten.
n. annoyance, danger, hazard, intimidation, jeopardy, nuisance, peril, plague, scare, terror, threat, troublemaker, warning.

mend *v.* better, cobble, correct, darn, fix, heal, improve, patch, recover, rectify, refit, reform, remedy, renew, renovate, repair, restore, revise.
antonyms break, destroy, deteriorate.

menial *adj.* boring, degrading, demeaning, dull, helping, humble, humdrum, ignominious, low, lowly, routine, servile, slavish, subservient, unskilled.
n. attendant, creature, dog's-body, domestic, drudge, labourer, minion, servant, skivvy, slave, underling.

mental *adj.* **1** abstract, cerebral, cognitive, conceptual, intellectual, rational, theoretical. **2** crazy, deranged, disturbed, insane, lunatic, mad, psychiatric, psychotic, unbalanced, unstable.
antonyms **1** physical. **2** balanced, sane.

mentality *n.* brains, character, disposition, endowment, faculty, frame of mind, intellect, IQ, make-up, mind, outlook, personality, psychology, rationality, understanding.

mention *v.* acknowledge, allude to, bring up, broach, cite, communicate, declare, disclose, divulge, hint at, impart, intimate, make known, name, point out, quote, refer to, report, reveal, speak of, state, tell, touch on.
n. acknowledgement, allusion, announcement, citation, indication, notification, observation, recognition, reference, remark, tribute.

mercenary *adj.* acquisitive, avaricious, covetous, grasping, greedy, hired, materialistic, paid, venal.
n. hireling, soldier of fortune.

merchandise *n.* cargo, commodities, freight, goods, produce, products, shipment, stock, stock in trade, wares.

merchant *n.* broker, dealer, jobber, retailer, salesman, seller, shopkeeper, trader, tradesman, trafficker, vendor, wholesaler.

merciful *adj.* compassionate, forbearing, forgiving, generous, gracious, humane, humanitarian, kind, lenient, liberal, mild, pitying, soft, sparing, sympathetic, tender-hearted.
antonyms cruel, hard-hearted, merciless.

merciless *adj.* barbarous, callous, cruel, hard, hard-hearted, harsh, heartless, implacable, inhuman, inhumane, pitiless, relentless, remorseless, ruthless, severe, unforgiving, unmerciful, unpitying, unsparing.
antonyms compassionate, merciful.

mercy *n.* **1** clemency, compassion, favour, forbearance, forgiveness, grace, humanitarianism, kindness, leniency, pity, relief. **2** blessing, godsend.
antonyms **1** cruelty, harshness, revenge.

mere *adj.* absolute, bare, common, complete, paltry, petty, plain, pure, sheer, simple, stark, utter, very.

merge *v.* amalgamate, blend, coalesce, combine, consolidate, converge, fuse, incorporate, intermix, join, meet, meld, melt into, mingle, mix, unite.

merger *n.* amalgamation, coalition, combination, confederation, consolidation, fusion, incorporation, union.

merit *n.* advantage, asset, claim, credit, due, excellence, good, goodness, integrity, justification, quality, strong point, talent, value, virtue, worth.
antonym fault.
v. deserve, earn, justify, warrant.

merriment *n.* amusement, conviviality, festivity, frolic, fun, hilarity, jollity, joviality, laughter, liveliness, mirth, revelry, waggery.
antonyms gloom, sadness, seriousness.

merry *adj.* cheerful, convivial, festive, glad, happy, jolly, joyful, light-hearted, mirthful.
antonyms gloomy, glum, melancholy, serious, sober.

merry-go-round *n.* carousel, roundabout, whirligig.

merrymaking *n.* carousing, celebration, festivity, fun, jollification, merriment, party, revelry.

mesh *n.* entanglement, lattice, net, netting,

network, snare, tangle, trap, web.
v. combine, come together, connect, co-ordinate, dovetail, engage, fit, harmonise, interlock.
mesmerise *v.* captivate, enthral, entrance, fascinate, grip, hypnotise, magnetise, spellbind, stupefy.
mess *n.* botch, chaos, clutter, confusion, dilemma, disarray, disorder, disorganisation, fix, jumble, mix-up, muddle, shambles, turmoil, untidiness.
antonyms order, tidiness.
mess about fool around, interfere, mess around, muck about, play, play about, play around, tamper, trifle.
mess up botch, bungle, disrupt, jumble, muck up, muddle, spoil, tangle.
message *n.* **1** bulletin, cable, communication, communiqué, dispatch, errand, letter, memorandum, mission, missive, note, notice. **2** idea, meaning, moral, point, theme.
messenger *n.* agent, ambassador, bearer, carrier, courier, delivery boy, emissary, envoy, errand-boy, go-between, harbinger, herald, runner.
messy *adj.* chaotic, cluttered, confused, dirty, dishevelled, disorganised, grubby, muddled, sloppy, slovenly, unkempt, untidy.
antonyms neat, ordered, tidy.
metamorphosis *n.* alteration, change, changeover, conversion, modification, rebirth, transformation.
metaphor *n.* allegory, analogy, figure of speech, image, picture, symbol.
metaphorical *adj.* allegorical, figurative, symbolic.
metaphysical *adj.* abstract, basic, deep, esoteric, essential, eternal, fundamental, general, philosophical, profound, theoretical, transcendental.
mete out administer, allot, apportion, assign, deal out, dispense, distribute, divide out, dole out, hand out, measure out, portion, ration out, share out.
meteor *n.* comet, fire-ball, meteorite, meteoroid, shooting-star.
meteoric *adj.* brief, brilliant, dazzling, instantaneous, momentary, overnight, rapid, spectacular, speedy, sudden, swift.
method *n.* approach, course, fashion, form, manner, mode, order, organisation, pattern, plan, planning, procedure, process, programme, purpose, regularity, routine, rule, scheme, structure, style, system, technique, way.
methodical *adj.* business-like, deliberate, disciplined, efficient, meticulous, neat, ordered, orderly, organised, painstaking, planned, precise, regular, scrupulous, structured, systematic, tidy.
antonyms chaotic, confused, irregular.
meticulous *adj.* accurate, detailed, exact, fastidious, fussy, painstaking, precise, punctilious, scrupulous, strict, thorough.
antonyms careless, slapdash.
métier *n.* calling, field, forte, line, occupation, profession, pursuit, speciality, specialty, sphere, vocation.
metropolis *n.* capital, city, megalopolis.
mettle *n.* boldness, bravery, character, courage, daring, fortitude, indomitability, life, nerve, pluck, resolve, spirit, valour, vigour.
microbe *n.* bacillus, bacterium, bug, germ, micro-organism, pathogen, virus.
microscopic *adj.* imperceptible, indiscernible, infinitesimal, invisible, minuscule, minute, tiny.
antonyms huge, vast.
middle *adj.* central, halfway, inner, inside, intermediate, intervening, mean, median.
n. centre, focus, halfway point, heart, inside, mean, midpoint.
antonyms beginning, border, edge, end, extreme.
middle-class *adj.* bourgeois, conventional, suburban.
middleman *n.* broker, distributor, entrepreneur, go-between, intermediary, negotiator, retailer.
middling *adj.* average, indifferent, mediocre, medium, moderate, modest, OK, ordinary, passable, run-of-the-mill, so-so, tolerable, unexceptional, unremarkable.
midget *n.* dwarf, gnome, pygmy, Tom Thumb.
antonym giant.
adj. little, miniature, pocket, pocket-sized, small, tiny.
antonym giant.
midst *n.* centre, heart, hub, interior, middle, mid-point.
migrant *n.* drifter, emigrant, globe-trotter, gypsy, immigrant, itinerant, nomad, rover, tinker, traveller, vagrant, wanderer.
migrate *v.* drift, emigrate, journey, move, roam, rove, shift, travel, trek, voyage, wander.
migration *n.* emigration, journey, movement, roving, shift, travel, trek, voyage, wandering.
mild *adj.* **1** amiable, calm, compassionate, forbearing, forgiving, gentle, kind, lenient, mellow, merciful, moderate, peaceable, placid, smooth, soft, tender. **2** calm, fair, pleasant, temperate, warm.
antonyms **1** fierce, harsh. **2** stormy.
milieu *n.* arena, environment, scene, setting, sphere, surroundings.
militant *adj.* aggressive, belligerent, fighting, vigorous, warring.
antonyms pacifist, peaceful.
n. activist, aggressor, belligerent, combatant, fighter, struggler, warrior.
military *adj.* armed, martial, service, soldierly, warlike.
n. armed forces, army, forces, services, soldiers.
militate against contend, count against, counter, counteract, oppose, resist, tell against, weigh against.
milk *v.* bleed, drain, draw off, exploit, express, extract, press, pump, siphon, squeeze, tap, use, wring.
milky *adj.* chalky, clouded, cloudy, milk-white, opaque, white.
mill *n.* **1** factory, foundry, plant, shop, works. **2**

crusher, grinder.
v. crush, grate, grind, pound, powder, press, pulverise, roll.
millstone *n.* affliction, burden, encumbrance, grindstone, load, weight.
mime *n.* dumb show, gesture, mimicry, pantomime.
v. act out, gesture, impersonate, mimic, represent, signal, simulate.
mimic *v.* ape, caricature, echo, imitate, impersonate, look like, mirror, parody, parrot, simulate, take off.
n. caricaturist, copy, copy-cat, imitator, impersonator, impressionist.
mimicry *n.* burlesque, caricature, copying, imitating, imitation, impersonation, impression, parody, take-off.
mince *v.* **1** chop, crumble, cut, dice, grind, hash. **2** diminish, hold back, moderate, play down, soften, spare, suppress, tone down, weaken.
mincing *adj.* affected, dainty, effeminate, foppish, lah-di-dah, nice, pretentious, sissy.
mind *n.* **1** attention, brains, concentration, genius, grey matter, head, intellect, intelligence, mentality, psyche, reason, sense, spirit, thinking, thoughts, understanding, wits. **2** memory, recollection, remembrance. **3** attitude, belief, feeling, judgement, opinion, point of view, sentiment, view. **4** desire, disposition, inclination, intention, tendency, will, wish.
v. **1** care, disapprove, dislike, object, resent, take offence. **2** be careful, comply with, follow, heed, listen to, note, obey, observe, pay attention, pay heed to, regard, watch. **3** guard, have charge of, keep an eye on, look after, take care of, watch over.
bear in mind consider, note, remember.
make up one's mind choose, decide, determine, resolve, settle.
mind out be careful, be on one's guard, beware, keep one's eyes open, look out, pay attention, take care, watch (out).
mindful *adj.* alert, alive (to), attentive, aware, careful, conscious, obedient, wary, watchful.
antonyms heedless, inattentive, mindless.
mindless *adj.* **1** foolish, gratuitous, idiotic, illogical, irrational, negligent, senseless, stupid, thoughtless. **2** automatic, mechanical, tedious.
antonyms **1** intelligent, thoughtful.
mine *n.* **1** coalfield, colliery, deposit, excavation, pit, reserve, shaft, trench, tunnel, vein. **2** fund, hoard, source, stock, store, supply, treasury, wealth. **3** bomb, depth charge, explosive, landmine.
v. delve, dig for, dig up, excavate, extract, quarry, remove, tunnel, undermine, unearth, weaken.
miner *n.* coal-miner, collier, pitman.
mingle *v.* alloy, associate, blend, circulate, coalesce, combine, compound, hobnob, intermingle, intermix, interweave, join, marry, merge, mix, rub shoulders, socialise, unite.
miniature *adj.* baby, diminutive, little, mini, minute, pint-size(d), pocket-sized, scaled-down, small, tiny.
antonym giant.
minimal *adj.* least, littlest, minimum, minute, negligible, slightest, smallest, token.
minimise *v.* belittle, decrease, decry, deprecate, diminish, discount, disparage, make light of, make little of, play down, reduce, underestimate, underrate.
antonym maximise.
minimum *n.* bottom, least, lowest point, slightest.
antonym maximum.
adj. least, littlest, lowest, minimal, slightest, smallest, tiniest.
antonym maximum.
minion *n.* bootlicker, creature, darling, dependant, follower, hanger-on, henchman, hireling, lackey, parasite, underling, yes-man.
minister *n.* **1** administrator, agent, aide, ambassador, assistant, delegate, diplomat, envoy, executive, office-holder, official, politician, servant, subordinate, underling. **2** churchman, clergyman, cleric, divine, ecclesiastic, parson, pastor, preacher, priest, vicar.
v. accommodate, attend, cater to, nurse, pander to, serve, take care of, tend.
ministry *n.* **1** administration, bureau, cabinet, council, department, office. **2** holy orders, the church, the priesthood.
minor *adj.* inconsiderable, inferior, insignificant, junior, lesser, light, negligible, petty, secondary, second-class, slight, small, smaller, subordinate, trifling, trivial, unclassified, younger.
antonyms important, major, significant.
mint *v.* cast, coin, construct, devise, fashion, forge, invent, make, make up, manufacture, produce, punch, stamp, strike.
adj. brand-new, excellent, first-class, fresh, immaculate, perfect, unblemished.
minuscule *adj.* diminutive, fine, infinitesimal, little, microscopic, miniature, minute, tiny.
antonyms gigantic, huge.
minute[1] *n.* flash, instant, jiffy, moment, second, tick.
minute[2] *adj.* **1** inconsiderable, infinitesimal, microscopic, miniature, minuscule, negligible, small, tiny. **2** close, critical, detailed, exhaustive, meticulous, painstaking, precise.
antonyms **1** gigantic, huge, immense. **2** superficial.
minutes *n.* details, memorandum, notes, proceedings, record(s), tapes, transactions, transcript.
minutiae *n.* details, niceties, particulars, subtleties, trifles.
miracle *n.* marvel, phenomenon, prodigy, wonder.
miraculous *adj.* amazing, astonishing, astounding, extraordinary, incredible, inexplicable, marvellous, phenomenal, stupendous, supernatural, unaccountable, unbelievable, wonderful.
antonyms natural, normal.
mirage *n.* fantasy, hallucination, illusion, optical

illusion, phantasm.

mirror *n.* glass, looking-glass, pocket-glass, reflection, reflector.
v. copy, depict, echo, imitate, mimic, reflect, represent, show.

mirth *n.* amusement, cheerfulness, fun, glee, hilarity, jocularity, jollity, joviality, laughter, merriment, revelry.
antonyms gloom, glumness, melancholy.

miry *adj.* boggy, dirty, fenny, marshy, muddy, oozy, slimy, swampy.

misapply *v.* abuse, exploit, misappropriate, misuse, pervert.

misapprehension *n.* delusion, error, fallacy, misconception, misinterpretation, misreading, mistake, misunderstanding.
antonym apprehension.

misappropriate *v.* abuse, embezzle, misapply, misspend, misuse, pervert, pocket, steal, swindle.

misbehave *v.* act up, carry on, get up to mischief, mess about, muck about, offend, play up, transgress, trespass.

misbehaviour *n.* disobedience, insubordination, misconduct, misdemeanour, monkey business, naughtiness, rudeness.

miscalculate *v.* blunder, boob, get wrong, misjudge, overestimate, overvalue, slip up, underestimate, underrate, undervalue.

miscarriage *n.* abortion, breakdown, disappointment, error, failure, mishap, mismanagement.
antonym success.

miscarry *v.* abort, bite the dust, come to grief, come to nothing, fail, fall through, flounder, misfire.
antonym succeed.

miscellaneous *adj.* assorted, diverse, diversified, indiscriminate, jumbled, many, mixed, motley, sundry, varied, various.

miscellany *n.* anthology, assortment, collection, diversity, hotch-potch, jumble, medley, mixed bag, mixture, pot-pourri, variety.

mischief *n.* damage, disruption, evil, harm, impishness, injury, misbehaviour, monkey business, naughtiness, pranks, trouble.

mischievous *adj.* **1** bad, destructive, evil, malicious, pernicious, spiteful, vicious, wicked. **2** impish, naughty, playful, rascally, roguish, teasing.
antonyms **1** kind. **2** good, serious, well-behaved.

misconceived *adj.* misconstrued, misjudged, misread, mistaken, wrong.

misconception *n.* delusion, error, fallacy, misapprehension, misreading, misunderstanding, the wrong end of the stick.

misconduct *n.* dereliction, impropriety, malpractice, misbehaviour, misdemeanour, mismanagement, wrong-doing.

miser *n.* meanie, niggard, penny-pincher, scrimp, Scrooge, skinflint.
antonym spendthrift.

miserable *adj.* **1** crushed, dejected, despondent, distressed, downcast, heartbroken, sad, unhappy, wretched. **2** cheerless, depressing, dismal, dreary, forlorn, gloomy, ignominious, impoverished, joyless, poor, shabby, sorry, squalid. **3** contemptible, despicable, detestable. **4** deplorable, disgraceful, meagre, niggardly, paltry, pathetic, pitiful, shameful, worthless.
antonyms **1** cheerful, happy. **2** pleasant. **4** generous, respectable.

miserly *adj.* beggarly, cheese-paring, covetous, grasping, mean, mercenary, mingy, niggardly, parsimonious, penny-pinching, sparing, stingy, tight-fisted.
antonyms generous, lavish, spendthrift.

misery *n.* **1** affliction, depression, despair, distress, gloom, grief, sadness, suffering, unhappiness, wretchedness. **2** deprivation, hardship, oppression, poverty, privation, squalor, want. **3** grouch, killjoy, moaner, pessimist, spoil-sport, wet blanket.
antonyms **1** contentment, pleasure. **2** comfort, ease, luxury.

misfit *n.* drop-out, eccentric, fish out of water, individualist, lone wolf, loner, nonconformist, odd man out, oddball, weirdo.
antonym conformist.

misfortune *n.* accident, bad luck, blow, calamity, catastrophe, disaster, failure, grief, hardship, harm, ill-luck, misery, setback, sorrow, tragedy, trial, tribulation, trouble.
antonyms fortune, luck, success.

misgiving *n.* anxiety, apprehension, doubt, fear, hesitation, niggle, qualm, reservation, scruple, second thoughts, suspicion, uncertainty, worry.
antonym confidence.

misguided *adj.* deluded, erroneous, foolish, ill-advised, ill-considered, ill-judged, imprudent, misconceived, misled, misplaced, mistaken, rash.
antonyms reasonable, sensible, wise.

mishandle *v.* botch, bungle, fumble, make a mess of, mess up, misjudge, mismanage, muff.
antonyms cope, manage.

mishap *n.* accident, adversity, calamity, disaster, hiccup, ill-fortune, misadventure, misfortune, setback.

misinterpret *v.* distort, garble, misconstrue, misread, mistake, misunderstand, pervert.

misjudge *v.* miscalculate, misinterpret, mistake, overestimate, overrate, underestimate, underrate, undervalue.

mislay *v.* lose, lose sight of, misplace, miss.

mislead *v.* deceive, delude, fool, hoodwink, misinform, take in.

misleading *adj.* ambiguous, biased, confusing, deceptive, evasive, loaded, tricky, unreliable.
antonyms authentic, authoritative, informative, plain, unequivocal.

mismanage *v.* botch, bungle, foul up, make a mess of, mar, mess up, mishandle, misjudge, misrule, misspend, waste.

misogynist *n.* anti-feminist, male chauvinist, sexist, woman-hater.
antonym feminist.

misplace *v.* lose, misapply, mislay, miss.

misprint *n.* error, mistake.

misquote *v.* distort, falsify, garble, misreport, misrepresent, muddle, pervert, twist.

misrepresent *v.* distort, exaggerate, falsify, garble, minimise, misconstrue, misinterpret, misquote, pervert, slant, twist.

miss *v.* **1** avoid, bypass, circumvent, err, escape, evade, fail, forego, jump, lack, leave out, let go, let slip, lose, miscarry, mistake, omit, overlook, pass over, skip, slip, trip. **2** grieve for, lament, long for, mourn, need, pine for, regret, sorrow for, want, wish, yearn for.
n. blunder, error, failure, fault, fiasco, flop, lack, loss, mistake, need, omission, oversight, want.
miss out 1 bypass, dispense with, disregard, ignore, jump, leave out, omit, pass over, skip. **2** lose out.
antonyms **1** include. **2** take part in.

misshapen *adj.* contorted, crippled, crooked, deformed, distorted, grotesque, malformed, monstrous, twisted, ugly, warped.
antonyms regular, shapely.

missile *n.* arrow, ball, bomb, dart, flying bomb, grenade, projectile, rocket, shaft, shell, shot, torpedo, weapon.

missing *adj.* absent, astray, disappeared, gone, lacking, lost, mislaid, misplaced, strayed, unaccounted-for, wanting.
antonyms found, present.

mission *n.* **1** assignment, business, campaign, crusade, errand, operation, task, undertaking. **2** aim, calling, charge, duty, job, office, purpose, raison d'être, vocation, work. **3** commission, delegation, deputation, embassy, legation, ministry.

missionary *n.* ambassador, apostle, campaigner, champion, crusader, emissary, envoy, evangelist, preacher, promoter, propagandist, teacher.

misspent *adj.* dissipated, frittered away, idle, misused, squandered, thrown away, wasted.
antonym profitable.

mist *n.* cloud, condensation, dew, dimness, drizzle, film, fog, haze, smog, spray, steam, vapour, veil.
mist over blur, cloud over, dim, fog, obscure, steam up, veil.
antonym clear.

mistake *n.* aberration, bloomer, blunder, clanger, error, fault, faux pas, folly, gaffe, inaccuracy, indiscretion, lapse, miscalculation, misjudgement, misprint, mispronunciation, misreading, misspelling, misunderstanding, oversight, slip, slip-up, solecism, trespass.
v. blunder, confound, confuse, err, misapprehend, miscalculate, misconstrue, misjudge, misread, misunderstand, slip up.

mistaken *adj.* deceived, deluded, erroneous, false, faulty, ill-judged, inaccurate, inappropriate, inauthentic, incorrect, inexact, misinformed, mislead, untrue, wrong.
antonyms correct, justified, right.

mistreat *v.* abuse, batter, harm, hurt, ill-treat, ill-use, injure, knock about, maltreat, molest.
antonyms pamper, spoil.

mistress *n.* **1** concubine, courtesan, girlfriend, kept woman, lady, lady-love, lover, paramour, woman. **2** governess, matron, teacher.

mistrust *n.* apprehension, caution, chariness, distrust, doubt, fear, hesitancy, misgiving, reservations, scepticism, suspicion, uncertainty, wariness.
antonym trust.
v. be wary of, beware, distrust, doubt, fear, fight shy of, suspect.
antonym trust.

misty *adj.* blurred, cloudy, dark, dim, faint, foggy, fuzzy, hazy, indistinct, murky, obscure, opaque, smoky, unclear, vague, veiled.
antonyms bright, clear.

misunderstand *v.* get hold of the wrong end of the stick, get wrong, misapprehend, misconstrue, mishear, misinterpret, misjudge, miss the point, mistake.
antonyms grasp, understand.

misunderstanding *n.* **1** error, misapprehension, misconception, misinterpretation, misjudgement, misreading, mistake, mix-up. **2** argument, breach, clash, conflict, difference, disagreement, discord, disharmony, dispute, quarrel, rift, squabble.
antonyms **1** understanding. **2** agreement, reconciliation.

misuse *n.* abuse, corruption, desecration, distortion, exploitation, harm, ill-treatment, injury, maltreatment, misapplication, misappropriation, mistreatment, perversion, waste.
v. abuse, corrupt, desecrate, dissipate, distort, exploit, harm, ill-treat, ill-use, injure, misapply, misappropriate, mistreat, pervert, squander, waste, wrong.

mitigating *adj.* extenuating, justifying, modifying, qualifying, vindicating.

mix *v.* **1** amalgamate, associate, blend, coalesce, combine, compound, cross, dash, fold in, fuse, homogenise, incorporate, intermingle, intermix, interweave, join, jumble, merge, synthesise, unite. **2** fraternise, hobnob, join, mingle, socialise.
antonyms **1** divide, separate.
n. amalgam, assortment, blend, combination, composite, compound, conglomerate, fusion, medley, mishmash, mixture, synthesis.
mix up bewilder, complicate, confound, confuse, disturb, garble, implicate, involve, jumble, mix, muddle, perplex, puzzle, snarl up, upset.

mixed *adj.* **1** alloyed, amalgamated, assorted, blended, combined, composite, compound, crossbred, diverse, diversified, fused, hybrid, incorporated, joint, mingled, miscellaneous, mongrel, motley, united, varied. **2** cosmopolitan, heterogeneous, integrated, international, unsegregated.
mixed up bewildered, complicated, confused, disoriented, distracted, distraught, disturbed, muddled, perplexed, puzzled, upset.

mixture *n.* alloy, amalgam, amalgamation, association, assortment, blend, brew, coalescence, combination, combine, composite, compost, compound, concoction, conglomeration, cross, fusion, half-breed, hotchpotch, hybrid, jumble, medley, mélange, miscellany, mix, mixed bag, mongrel, pot-pourri, salad, synthesis, union, variety.

moan *n.* complaint, gripe, groan, grouch, grouse, grumble, howl, keen, lament, lamentation, sigh, snivel, sob, wail, whimper, whine.
v. carp, complain, deplore, grieve, gripe, groan, grouch, grumble, howl, lament, mourn, sigh, snivel, sob, wail, weep, whimper, whine.
antonym rejoice.

mob *n.* class, collection, company, crew, crowd, flock, gang, gathering, group, herd, horde, host, lot, mass, masses, multitude, pack, plebs, populace, rabble, riff-raff, scum, set, swarm, throng, tribe, troop.
v. besiege, charge, cram, crowd round, descend on, fill, jostle, overrun, pack, pester, set upon, surround, swarm round.
antonyms avoid, shun.

mobile *adj.* active, agile, changeable, changing, energetic, ever-changing, expressive, flexible, itinerant, lively, migrant, movable, moving, nimble, peripatetic, portable, roaming, roving, travelling, wandering.
antonym immobile.

mobilise *v.* activate, animate, assemble, call up, enlist, galvanise, marshal, muster, organise, prepare, rally, ready, shift, stir, summon.

mobility *n.* agility, animation, flexibility, motion, movability, portability.
antonyms immobility, inflexibility, rigidity.

mock *v.* ape, caricature, deride, disparage, fool, insult, jeer, laugh at, laugh in (someone's) face, make fun of, poke fun at, ridicule, satirise, scoff, scorn, sneer, taunt, tease.
antonyms flatter, praise.
adj. artificial, bogus, counterfeit, dummy, fake, faked, false, feigned, forged, fraudulent, imitation, phoney, pretended, pseudo, sham, simulated, spurious, synthetic.

mockery *n.* contempt, derision, disdain, disrespect, insults, jeering, ridicule, sarcasm, satire, scoffing, scorn, sham, travesty.

mocking *adj.* contemptuous, cynical, derisive, disdainful, disrespectful, impudent, insulting, irreverent, sarcastic, sardonic, satirical, scoffing, scornful, snide, taunting.

model *n.* **1** copy, facsimile, imitation, miniature, mock-up, replica, representation. **2** example, ideal, mould, pattern, standard, template. **3** design, kind, mark, style, type, version. **4** dummy, manikin, mannequin, poser, sitter, subject.
adj. archetypal, complete, consummate, exemplary, ideal, perfect.
v. base, carve, cast, create, design, display, fashion, form, illustrate, make, mould, pattern, plan, sculpt, shape, show off, sport, wear, work.

moderate *adj.* average, calm, controlled, cool, deliberate, disciplined, fair, indifferent, judicious, limited, mediocre, medium, middle-of-the-road, mild, modest, ordinary, reasonable, restrained, sensible, well-regulated.
antonyms exceptional, extreme, immoderate.
v. abate, allay, alleviate, calm, check, control, curb, cushion, decrease, diminish, dwindle, ease, lessen, mitigate, modify, modulate, pacify, play down, quiet, regulate, repress, restrain, soften, soft-pedal, subdue, subside, tame, temper, tone down.

moderation *n.* abstemiousness, alleviation, caution, composure, control, decrease, discretion, easing, reasonableness, reduction, restraint, self-control, sobriety, temperance.
antonyms increase, intemperance.

modern *adj.* advanced, avant-garde, contemporary, current, fashionable, fresh, go-ahead, innovative, inventive, jazzy, late, latest, mod, modernistic, modish, new, newfangled, novel, present, present-day, progressive, recent, stylish, trendy, up-to-date, up-to-the-minute, with-it.
antonyms antiquated, old, old-fashioned, out-of-date.

modernise *v.* do up, improve, modify, progress, redesign, reform, refresh, refurbish, regenerate, rejuvenate, remake, remodel, renew, renovate, revamp, streamline, transform, update.
antonym regress.

modest *adj.* **1** bashful, discreet, humble, quiet, reserved, retiring, self-effacing, shy, timid, unassuming. **2** fair, limited, moderate, ordinary, reasonable, small, unexceptional.
antonyms **1** conceited, immodest, pretentious, vain. **2** excessive.

modesty *n.* bashfulness, coyness, decency, demureness, humbleness, humility, propriety, quietness, reserve, reticence, self-effacement, shyness.
antonyms conceit, immodesty, vanity.

modification *n.* adjustment, alteration, change, limitation, moderation, modulation, qualification, refinement, reformation, revision, variation.

modify *v.* adapt, adjust, alter, change, convert, improve, limit, moderate, qualify, redesign, reduce, reform, reorganise, revise, soften, temper, tone down, transform, vary.

moist *adj.* damp, dewy, dripping, drizzly, humid, marshy, muggy, rainy, soggy, swampy, watery, wet.
antonyms arid, dry.

moisten *v.* damp, dampen, irrigate, lick, moisturise, soak, water, wet.
antonym dry.

moisture *n.* damp, dampness, dankness, dew, humidity, liquid, mugginess, perspiration, sweat, tears, vapour, water, wateriness, wetness.
antonym dryness.

molest *v.* abuse, accost, afflict, annoy, assail, attack, bother, disturb, harass, harm, hound, hurt, ill-treat, injure, irritate, maltreat, mistreat, persecute, pester, plague, tease, torment, trouble, upset, vex, worry.

mollify *v.* allay, appease, assuage, calm, compose, conciliate, cushion, ease, lessen, lull,

mitigate, moderate, modify, pacify, placate, quell, quiet, relieve, soften, soothe, temper.
antonyms aggravate, anger.
mollycoddle *v.* baby, coddle, cosset, indulge, mother, overprotect, pamper, pander to, pet, spoil, spoon-feed.
antonyms ignore, ill-treat, neglect.
moment *n.* instant, jiffy, minute, second, split second, tick, time.
momentary *adj.* brief, fleeting, fugitive, hasty, passing, quick, short, short-lived, temporary, transient, transitory.
antonyms lasting, permanent.
momentous *adj.* critical, crucial, decisive, earth-shaking, epoch-making, eventful, fateful, grave, historic, important, major, serious, significant, tremendous, vital, weighty.
antonyms insignificant, trivial, unimportant.
momentum *n.* drive, energy, force, impact, impetus, impulse, incentive, power, push, speed, stimulus, strength, thrust, urge, velocity.
monarch *n.* despot, emperor, empress, king, potentate, prince, princess, queen, ruler, sovereign, tyrant.
monarchy *n.* absolutism, autocracy, despotism, empire, kingdom, majesty, principality, realm, royalism, royalty, rule, sovereignty, tyranny.
monastic *adj.* ascetic, austere, celibate, cloistered, contemplative, recluse, secluded, withdrawn.
antonyms gregarious, materialistic, worldly.
monetary *adj.* budgetary, capital, cash, economic, financial, fiscal, money.
money *n.* banknotes, capital, cash, coin, currency, funds, gold, legal tender, riches, silver, wealth.
mongrel *n.* cross, crossbreed, half-breed, hybrid, mule.
adj. bastard, crossbred, half-breed, hybrid, ill-defined, mixed.
antonyms pedigree, pure-bred.
monitor *n.* **1** detector, guide, recorder, scanner, screen. **2** adviser, invigilator, overseer, prefect, supervisor, watchdog.
v. check, detect, follow, keep an eye on, keep track of, keep under surveillance, note, observe, plot, record, scan, supervise, survey, trace, track, watch.
monkey *n.* **1** ape, primate. **2** ass, fool, imp, rascal, rogue, scallywag, scamp.
v. fiddle, fidget, fool, interfere, meddle, mess, play, tamper, tinker, trifle.
monochrome *adj.* black-and-white, monotone, monotonous, sepia.
antonym kaleidoscopic.
monologue *n.* homily, lecture, oration, sermon, soliloquy, speech.
antonyms conversation, dialogue, discussion.
monopolise *v.* control, corner, dominate, engross, hog, occupy, preoccupy, take over, take up, tie up.
antonym share.
monotonous *adj.* boring, colourless, dull, flat, humdrum, monochrome, plodding, repetitive, routine, soul-destroying, tedious, tiresome, toneless, unchanging, uneventful, uniform, unvaried, wearisome.
antonyms colourful, lively, varied.
monotony *n.* boredom, colourlessness, dullness, flatness, repetitiveness, routine, sameness, tedium, tiresomeness, uneventfulness, uniformity, wearisomeness.
antonyms colour, liveliness.
monster *n.* beast, brute, freak, giant, mammoth, monstrosity, ogre, ogress, prodigy, savage, villain.
adj. colossal, enormous, giant, gigantic, huge, immense, jumbo, mammoth, massive, monstrous, tremendous, vast.
antonyms minute, tiny.
monstrosity *n.* atrocity, eyesore, freak, horror, miscreation, monster, obscenity, ogre.
monstrous *adj.* **1** abhorrent, atrocious, criminal, cruel, deformed, disgraceful, dreadful, evil, freakish, frightful, grotesque, hideous, horrible, horrifying, inhuman, intolerable, malformed, obscene, outrageous, scandalous, terrible, unnatural, vicious, wicked. **2** colossal, enormous, gigantic, great, huge, immense, mammoth, massive, towering, vast.
monument *n.* antiquity, barrow, cairn, cenotaph, commemoration, cross, evidence, gravestone, headstone, marker, mausoleum, memento, memorial, obelisk, pillar, record, relic, remembrance, reminder, shrine, statue, testament, token, tombstone.
monumental *adj.* abiding, awe-inspiring, awesome, classic, colossal, commemorative, enormous, epoch-making, great, historic, huge, immense, immortal, important, imposing, impressive, lasting, magnificent, majestic, massive, memorable, memorial, notable, outstanding, overwhelming, significant, terrible, tremendous, vast.
antonyms insignificant, unimportant.
mood *n.* **1** disposition, frame of mind, humour, spirit, state of mind, temper, tenor, whim. **2** blues, depression, doldrums, dumps, fit, melancholy, pique, sulk, temper, the sulks.
moody *adj.* angry, broody, capricious, changeable, crabby, crotchety, crusty, doleful, downcast, fickle, flighty, gloomy, glum, impulsive, irritable, melancholy, miserable, mopy, morose, short-tempered, sulky, sullen, temperamental, testy, touchy, unpredictable.
antonyms cheerful, equable, happy.
moon *v.* brood, daydream, dream, fantasise, idle, languish, loaf, mooch, mope, pine, potter.
n. crescent, full moon, half-moon.
moor[1] *v.* anchor, berth, bind, dock, drop anchor, fasten, fix, hitch, lash, secure, tie up.
antonym loose.
moor[2] *n.* fell, heath, moorland, upland.
mop *n.* **1** sponge, squeegee, swab. **2** head of hair, mass, shock, tangle, thatch.
v. absorb, clean, soak, sponge, wash, wipe.
mop up 1 absorb, clean up, soak up, sponge, swab, tidy up, wash, wipe. **2** account for,

eliminate, finish off, neutralise, round up, take care of.

mope *v.* brood, despair, droop, fret, grieve, idle, languish, pine, sulk.

moral *adj.* blameless, chaste, clean-living, decent, ethical, good, high-minded, honest, honourable, incorruptible, innocent, just, noble, principled, proper, pure, responsible, right, righteous, straight, temperate, upright, upstanding, virtuous.
antonym immoral.
n. adage, aphorism, dictum, epigram, lesson, maxim, meaning, message, motto, point, precept, proverb, saying, teaching.

morale *n.* confidence, esprit de corps, heart, mettle, mood, resolve, self-esteem, spirits, state of mind.

morality *n.* chastity, conduct, decency, ethics, goodness, honesty, ideals, integrity, justice, manners, morals, philosophy, principles, propriety, rationale, rectitude, righteousness, standards, uprightness, virtue.
antonym immorality.

morals *n.* behaviour, conduct, ethics, ethos, habits, ideals, integrity, manners, morality, principles, scruples, standards.

morbid *adj.* deadly, ghastly, ghoulish, gloomy, grim, gruesome, hideous, horrid, macabre, melancholy, pessimistic, sombre, unhealthy, unsalubrious, unwholesome.

more *adj.* added, additional, alternative, extra, fresh, further, increased, new, other, repeated, spare, supplementary.
antonym less.
adv. again, better, further, longer.
antonym less.

moreover *adv.* additionally, also, as well, besides, further, furthermore, in addition, what is more.

morning *n.* before lunch, before noon, break of day, cock-crow, dawn, daybreak, daylight, first thing, sunrise.

moronic *adj.* brainless, daft, dimwitted, foolish, gormless, halfwitted, idiotic, mindless, simple, simple-minded, stupid, thick.

morose *adj.* depressed, down, gloomy, glum, grim, grouchy, gruff, grum, low, melancholy, moody, mournful, sulky, sullen, surly.
antonyms cheerful, communicative.

morsel *n.* atom, bit, bite, crumb, fraction, fragment, grain, modicum, mouthful, nibble, part, piece, scrap, slice, snack, soupçon, taste, titbit.

mortal *adj.* **1** bodily, earthly, human, perishable, temporal, worldly. **2** deadly, fatal, lethal. **3** awful, extreme, great, intense, severe, terrible.
antonym **1** immortal.
n. being, body, creature, human, human being, individual, man, person, woman.
antonyms god, immortal.

mortality *n.* corruptibility, death, fatality, impermanence, perishability.
antonym immortality.

mortified *adj.* ashamed, crushed, dead, deflated, embarrassed, horrified, humbled, humiliated, put to shame, shamed.
antonyms elated, jubilant.

mostly *adv.* as a rule, chiefly, commonly, for the most part, generally, largely, mainly, normally, on the whole, principally, typically, usually.

mother *n.* dam, mamma, mom, mommy, mum, mummy, old woman.
v. baby, bear, care for, cherish, cosset, foster, fuss over, indulge, nurse, nurture, overprotect, pamper, produce, protect, raise, rear, spoil, tend.
antonyms ignore, neglect.

motherly *adj.* affectionate, caring, comforting, fond, gentle, kind, kindly, loving, maternal, protective, tender, warm.
antonyms indifferent, neglectful, uncaring.

motif *n.* concept, decoration, design, device, figure, form, idea, logo, notion, ornament, pattern, shape, theme.

motion *n.* **1** action, change, dynamics, flow, flux, inclination, mechanics, mobility, movement, passage, passing, progress, transit, travel. **2** gesture, sign, signal, wave. **3** proposal, proposition, recommendation, suggestion.
v. beckon, direct, gesticulate, gesture, nod, sign, signal, usher, wave.

motionless *adj.* at a standstill, at rest, fixed, frozen, halted, immobile, lifeless, moveless, paralysed, resting, rigid, stagnant, standing, static, stationary, still, unmoved.
antonym active.

motivate *v.* arouse, bring, cause, draw, drive, encourage, impel, incite, induce, inspire, kindle, lead, move, persuade, prompt, propel, provoke, push, spur, stimulate, stir, trigger, urge.
antonyms deter, prevent.

motivation *n.* ambition, desire, drive, hunger, impulse, incentive, incitement, inducement, inspiration, interest, motive, persuasion, provocation, push, reason, spur, stimulus, urge, wish.
antonyms discouragement, prevention.

motive *n.* cause, consideration, design, desire, encouragement, ground(s), impulse, incentive, incitement, influence, inspiration, intention, motivation, object, purpose, rationale, reason, stimulus, thinking, urge.
antonyms deterrent, discouragement, disincentive.
adj. activating, driving, impelling, motivating, moving, operative, prompting.
antonyms deterrent, preventive.

mottled *adj.* blotchy, chequered, dappled, flecked, freckled, piebald, pied, speckled, spotted, stippled, streaked.
antonyms monochrome, plain, uniform.

motto *n.* adage, byword, catchword, dictum, formula, golden rule, maxim, precept, proverb, rule, saying, slogan, watchword.

mould[1] *n.* arrangement, brand, build, cast, character, construction, cut, design, form, format, frame, framework, kind, line, make, matrix, model, nature, pattern, quality, shape, sort, stamp, structure, style, template, type.

v. cast, construct, control, create, design, direct, fashion, fit, forge, form, influence, make, model, sculpt, shape, stamp, work.

mould[2] *n.* blight, fungus, mildew, mouldiness, mustiness.

mould[3] *n.* dirt, dust, earth, ground, humus, loam, soil.

moulder *v.* crumble, decay, decompose, disintegrate, perish, rot, turn to dust, waste.

mouldy *adj.* bad, blighted, corrupt, decaying, fusty, mildewed, musty, putrid, rotten, spoiled, stale.
antonyms fresh, wholesome.

mound *n.* bank, barrow, dune, earthwork, elevation, embankment, heap, hill, hillock, knoll, rampart, ridge, rise, tumulus.

mount *v.* **1** display, exhibit, launch, prepare, produce, put on, set up, stage. **2** accumulate, grow, increase, intensify, multiply, rise, soar, swell. **3** ascend, clamber up, climb, get astride, get on, get up, go up, scale.
antonyms **2** decrease, descend. **3** descend, get off, go down.
n. horse, mounting, steed, support.

mountain *n.* **1** alp, elevation, fell, height, massif, mound, mount, peak. **2** abundance, backlog, heap, mass, pile, stack.

mountainous *adj.* alpine, high, highland, hilly, rocky, rugged, soaring, steep, towering, upland.
antonym flat.

mourn *v.* bemoan, deplore, grieve, lament, miss, regret, sorrow, wail, weep.
antonyms bless, rejoice.

mourner *n.* bereaved, griever.

mournful *adj.* broken-hearted, cast-down, dejected, depressed, desolate, dismal, downcast, gloomy, grief-stricken, heartbroken, heavy-hearted, long-faced, melancholy, miserable, painful, plaintive, rueful, sad, sombre, sorrowful, tragic, unhappy, woeful.
antonyms cheerful, joyful.

mourning *n.* bereavement, desolation, grief, grieving, lamentation, sadness, sorrow, wailing, weeping, woe.
antonym rejoicing.

mouth *n.* **1** cavity, embouchure, jaws, lips, opening, orifice. **2** entrance, estuary, gateway, inlet, outlet.
v. articulate, enunciate, form, pronounce, shape, utter, whisper.

movable *adj.* adjustable, alterable, changeable, detachable, flexible, mobile, portable, transferable, transportable.
antonyms fixed, immovable.

move *v.* **1** advance, budge, change, go, make strides, march, proceed, progress, stir, transfer, transport. **2** decamp, depart, go away, leave, migrate, move house, quit, relocate, remove. **3** impel, incite, induce, inspire, motivate, persuade, prompt, stimulate, urge. **4** drive, propel, pull, push. **5** affect, excite, impress, touch.
n. migration, motion, movement, relocation, removal, step, transfer.

movement *n.* **1** act, action, activity, advance, agitation, change, current, development, drift, evolution, exercise, flow, front, manoeuvre, motion, operation, passage, progress, progression, shift, stirring, swing, tempo, tendency, transfer, trend. **2** campaign, crusade, drive, faction, group, grouping, organisation, party.

movie *n.* feature, film, motion picture, silent picture, talkie, video.

moving *adj.* affecting, arousing, dynamic, emotional, exciting, impressive, inspirational, inspiring, persuasive, poignant, stimulating, stirring, touching.
antonym unemotional.

mow *v.* clip, crop, cut, scythe, shear, trim.
mow down butcher, cut down, cut to pieces, decimate, massacre, shoot down, slaughter.

much *adv.* considerably, exceedingly, frequently, greatly, often.
adj. a lot of, ample, considerable, copious, great, plenteous, plenty of, substantial.
n. heaps, lashings, loads, lots, plenty.
antonym little.

muck *n.* dirt, droppings, dung, faeces, filth, gunge, manure, mire, mud, scum, sewage, slime, sludge.
muck up botch, bungle, make a mess of, mess up, ruin, spoil, waste.

mud *n.* clay, dirt, mire, ooze, silt, sludge.

muddle *v.* confuse, disorder, disorganise, disorient(ate), fuddle, fuzzle, jumble, mix up, scramble, spoil, tangle.
n. chaos, clutter, confusion, disorder, jumble, mess, mix-up, predicament, tangle.
muddle through cope, get along, get by, make it, manage, muddle along, scrape by.

muddy *adj.* blurred, boggy, cloudy, dirty, dull, foul, fuzzy, grimy, hazy, impure, indistinct, marshy, miry, mucky, muddled, murky, quaggy, swampy.
antonyms clean, clear.
v. cloud, dirty, smear, soil.
antonym clean.

muffle *v.* cloak, dampen, deaden, dull, hush, mute, muzzle, quieten, silence, soften, stifle, suppress.
antonym amplify.

mug[1] *n.* beaker, cup, jug, pot, stoup, tankard.

mug[2] *v.* attack, bash, beat up, jump (on), rob, set upon, steal from, waylay.

muggy *adj.* clammy, close, damp, humid, moist, oppressive, sticky, stuffy, sultry, sweltering.
antonym dry.

mull *v.* chew, consider, contemplate, deliberate, examine, meditate, ponder, reflect on, ruminate, study, think about, think over, weigh up.

multiple *adj.* collective, manifold, many, numerous, several, sundry, various.

multiplicity *n.* abundance, array, diversity, host, loads, lot, lots, mass, myriad, number, numerousness, piles, profusion, scores, stacks, tons, variety.

multiply *v.* accumulate, augment, boost, breed, build up, expand, extend, increase, intensify, proliferate, propagate, reproduce, spread.

antonyms decrease, lessen.

multitude *n.* congregation, crowd, herd, horde, host, legion, lot, lots, mass, mob, people, populace, public, swarm, throng.
antonyms handful, scattering.

munch *v.* champ, chew, crunch, eat, masticate.

mundane *adj.* banal, commonplace, day-to-day, everyday, humdrum, ordinary, prosaic, routine, workaday.
antonyms extraordinary, remarkable.

municipal *adj.* borough, city, civic, community, public, town, urban.

murder *n.* assassination, bloodshed, carnage, danger, homicide, killing, manslaughter, massacre, slaying.
v. assassinate, butcher, destroy, eliminate, kill, massacre, slaughter, slay.

murderer *n.* assassin, butcher, cut-throat, hit-man, homicide, killer, slaughterer, slayer.

murderous *adj.* **1** barbarous, bloodthirsty, bloody, brutal, cruel, cut-throat, deadly, destructive, fatal, ferocious, homicidal, killing, lethal, savage, slaughterous. **2** dangerous, difficult, exhausting, strenuous, unpleasant.

murky *adj.* cloudy, dark, dim, dismal, dull, dusky, foggy, gloomy, grey, misty, mysterious, obscure, overcast, veiled.
antonyms bright, clear.

murmur *n.* drone, grumble, humming, moan, mumble, muttering, rumble, undertone, whisper.
v. burble, buzz, hum, mumble, mutter, purr, rumble, whisper.

muscle *n.* brawn, force, forcefulness, might, power, sinew, stamina, strength, tendon, weight.
muscle in elbow one's way in, force one's way in, impose oneself, jostle, push in, shove.

muscular *adj.* athletic, beefy, brawny, hefty, husky, powerful, powerfully-built, robust, sinewy, stalwart, strapping, strong, vigorous.
antonyms feeble, flabby, puny, weak.

musical *adj.* dulcet, euphonious, harmonious, lyrical, melodious, sweet-sounding, tuneful.
antonyms discordant, unmusical.

musician *n.* accompanist, composer, conductor, instrumentalist, performer, player, singer, vocalist.

muster *v.* assemble, call together, call up, collect, come together, congregate, convene, enrol, gather, group, marshal, mass, meet, mobilise, rally, round up, summon, throng.

musty *adj.* airless, dank, decayed, fusty, mildewy, mouldy, smelly, stale, stuffy.

mute *adj.* dumb, mum, noiseless, silent, speechless, unexpressed, unpronounced, unspoken, voiceless, wordless.
antonyms articulate, vocal.
v. dampen, deaden, lower, moderate, muffle, silence, soften, subdue, tone down.

mutilate *v.* butcher, censor, cut, cut to pieces, cut up, damage, disable, disfigure, dismember, injure, lame, maim, mangle, mar, spoil.

mutilation *n.* amputation, damage, disfigurement, dismembering, maiming.

mutinous *adj.* bolshie, disobedient, insubordinate, insurgent, rebellious, revolutionary, riotous, subversive, unruly.
antonyms compliant, dutiful, obedient.

mutiny *n.* defiance, disobedience, insubordination, insurrection, putsch, rebellion, resistance, revolt, revolution, riot, rising, strike, uprising.
v. disobey, protest, rebel, resist, revolt, rise up, strike.

mutter *v.* complain, grouse, grumble, mumble, murmur, rumble.

mutual *adj.* common, complementary, exchanged, interchangeable, interchanged, joint, reciprocal, shared.

muzzle *n.* bit, curb, gag, guard, jaws, mouth, nose, snout.
v. censor, choke, gag, mute, restrain, silence, stifle, suppress.

myopic *adj.* half-blind, near-sighted, short-sighted.
antonym long-sighted.

mysterious *adj.* baffling, cryptic, curious, dark, enigmatic, furtive, hidden, incomprehensible, inexplicable, insoluble, mystical, mystifying, obscure, perplexing, puzzling, secret, secretive, strange, unfathomable, unsearchable, veiled, weird.
antonyms comprehensible, frank, straightforward.

mystery *n.* conundrum, enigma, problem, puzzle, question, riddle, secrecy, secret.

mystical *adj.* hidden, metaphysical, mysterious, mystic, occult, otherworldly, paranormal, supernatural, transcendental.

mystify *v.* baffle, bewilder, confound, confuse, escape, perplex, puzzle.

mystique *n.* appeal, awe, charisma, charm, fascination, glamour, magic, spell.

myth *n.* allegory, fable, fairy tale, fancy, fantasy, fiction, figment, illusion, legend, old wives' tale, parable, saga, story, superstition, tradition.

mythical *adj.* fabled, fairy-tale, fanciful, fictitious imaginary, invented, legendary, made-up, make-believe, mythological, non-existent, pretended, unreal.
antonyms actual, historical, real, true.

mythology *n.* folklore, folk-tales, legend, lore, myths, tales, tradition(s).

N

nag *v.* annoy, badger, berate, goad, harass, harry, henpeck, irritate, pester, plague, scold, torment, upbraid, vex.

nagging *adj.* continuous, distressing, irritating, niggling, painful, persistent, scolding, upsetting, worrying.

nail *v.* attach, fasten, fix, hammer, join, pin, secure, tack.
n. brad, pin, rivet, screw, skewer, spike, staple, tack.

naïve *adj.* childlike, credulous, green, guileless, gullible, ingenuous, innocent, natural, open, simple, trusting, unaffected, unsophisticated, unsuspecting, wide-eyed.
antonyms experienced, sly, sophisticated.

naïvety *n.* credulity, frankness, gullibility, inexperience, ingenuousness, innocence, naturalness, openness, simplicity.
antonyms experience, sophistication.

naked *adj.* **1** bare, denuded, disrobed, divested, in the altogether, nude, stark-naked, stripped, unclothed, uncovered. **2** blatant, evident, exposed, open, overt, patent, plain, stark, unqualified.
antonyms **1** clothed, covered. **2** concealed.

name *n.* **1** designation, epithet, handle, nickname, stage name, term, title. **2** character, distinction, eminence, esteem, fame, honour, note, praise, renown, reputation, repute.
v. appoint, baptise, call, choose, christen, cite, classify, commission, designate, dub, entitle, identify, label, nominate, select, specify, style, term, title.

nameless *adj.* anonymous, indescribable, inexpressible, obscure, shapeless, unheard-of, unknown, unmentionable, unnamed, unspeakable, unutterable.
antonym named.

namely *adv.* ie, specifically, that is, that is to say, viz.

nap[1] *v.* doze, drop off, kip, nod (off), rest, sleep, snooze.
n. catnap, forty winks, kip, rest, siesta, sleep.

nap[2] *n.* down, fibre, fuzz, pile, shag, weave.

nappy *n.* diaper, napkin, towel.

narcotic *n.* drug, opiate, pain-killer, sedative, tranquilliser.
adj. analgesic, calming, dulling, hypnotic, numbing, pain-killing, sedative, soporific, stupefying.

narrate *v.* describe, detail, recite, recount, relate, report, state, tell, unfold.

narration *n.* description, explanation, reading, recital, story-telling, telling, voice-over.

narrative *n.* account, chronicle, detail, history, report, statement, story, tale.

narrator *n.* author, chronicler, commentator, reciter, reporter, story-teller, writer.

narrow *adj.* **1** close, confined, cramped, fine, limited, marginal, near, slender, slim, tapering, thin, tight. **2** biased, bigoted, dogmatic, exclusive, narrow-minded, restricted.
antonyms **1** broad, wide. **2** broad-minded, tolerant.
v. constrict, diminish, limit, reduce, simplify, tighten.
antonyms broaden, increase, loosen, widen.

narrowly *adv.* barely, carefully, closely, just, only just, precisely, scarcely, strictly.

narrow-minded *adj.* biased, conservative, insular, opinionated, petty, prejudiced, provincial, reactionary, short-sighted, small-minded.
antonym broad-minded.

nasty *adj.* **1** annoying, disgusting, filthy, foul, horrible, objectionable, offensive, polluted, pornographic, repellent, repugnant, sickening, unpleasant. **2** disagreeable, malicious, mean, spiteful, vicious.
antonyms **1** agreeable, clean, decent, pleasant. **2** kind, loving.

nation *n.* community, country, people, population, race, realm, society, state.

national *adj.* civil, countrywide, domestic, general, governmental, internal, nationwide, public, social, state, widespread.
n. citizen, inhabitant, native, resident, subject.

nationalism *n.* allegiance, chauvinism, jingoism, loyalty, nationality, patriotism.

nationalistic *adj.* chauvinistic, loyal, patriotic.

nationality *n.* birth, clan, ethnic group, nation, race, tribe.

native *adj.* aboriginal, domestic, hereditary, home, home-bred, inborn, inbred, indigenous, inherent, inherited, innate, instinctive, intrinsic, local, mother, natal, natural, original, real, vernacular.
n. aborigine, citizen, countryman, dweller, inhabitant, national, resident.
antonyms foreigner, outsider, stranger.

nativity *n.* birth, childbirth, delivery.

natter *v.* blather, chatter, gab, gabble, gossip, jaw, prattle, talk.
n. blather, chat, chinwag, chitchat, conversation, gossip, jabber, jaw, talk.

natural *adj.* **1** normal, ordinary, regular, typical, usual. **2** congenital, inborn, indigenous, inherent, innate, instinctive, intuitive, native. **3** genuine, pure, real, unmixed, unrefined. **4** genuine, open, sincere, spontaneous, unaffected, unsophisticated.
antonyms **1** unnatural. **3** artificial, man-made. **4**

affected, contrived.
naturalistic *adj.* graphic, lifelike, natural, photographic, realistic, real-life, representational, true-to-life.
naturally *adj.* absolutely, as a matter of course, certainly, genuinely, logically, normally, obviously, of course, simply, spontaneously, typically.
nature *n.* **1** attributes, category, character, constitution, description, disposition, essence, features, inbeing, kind, make-up, mood, outlook, quality, sort, species, style, temper, temperament, type, variety. **2** creation, earth, environment, universe, world. **3** country, countryside, landscape, natural history, scenery.
naught *n.* nil, nothing, nothingness, nought, zero.
naughty *adj.* annoying, bad, disobedient, exasperating, misbehaved, mischievous, playful, roguish, wayward.
antonyms good, polite, well-behaved.
nausea *n.* biliousness, loathing, motion sickness, queasiness, retching, sickness, travel sickness, vomiting.
nauseate *v.* disgust, horrify, offend, repel, revolt, sicken, turn one's stomach.
nautical *adj.* marine, maritime, naval, oceanic, sailing, seafaring, sea-going, yachting.
naval *adj.* marine, maritime, nautical, sea.
navigate *v.* cross, cruise, direct, drive, guide, handle, helm, journey, manoeuvre, pilot, plan, plot, sail, skipper, steer, voyage.
navigation *n.* cruising, helmsmanship, sailing, seamanship, steering, voyaging.
navigator *n.* helmsman, mariner, pilot, seaman.
navvy *n.* digger, labourer, worker, workman.
navy *n.* armada, fleet, flotilla, ships, warships.
near *adj.* accessible, adjacent, adjoining, alongside, approaching, at close quarters, attached, beside, bordering, close, connected, handy, imminent, nearby, neighbouring, related, touching.
antonyms distant, far, remote.
nearby *adj.* accessible, adjacent, adjoining, convenient, handy, near, neighbouring.
antonym faraway.
adv. at close quarters, close at hand, near, not far away, within reach.
nearly *adv.* almost, approximately, as good as, closely, just about, not quite, practically, roughly, virtually, well-nigh.
antonyms completely, totally.
neat *adj.* **1** clean, efficient, orderly, precise, shipshape, smart, spick-and-span, spruce, tidy. **2** clever, skilful. **3** pure, straight, undiluted, unmixed.
antonyms **1** cluttered, disorderly, scruffy, shabby, untidy. **3** diluted.
nebulous *adj.* ambiguous, amorphous, cloudy, confused, dim, fuzzy, hazy, imprecise, indefinite, indistinct, misty, obscure, shapeless, uncertain, unclear, vague.
antonym clear.
necessarily *adv.* automatically, certainly, consequently, incontrovertibly, inevitably, naturally, of course, of necessity, therefore.
necessary *adj.* certain, compulsory, essential, imperative, indispensable, inescapable, inevitable, inexorable, mandatory, needed, needful, obligatory, required, unavoidable, vital.
antonyms inessential, unimportant, unnecessary.
necessitate *v.* call for, compel, constrain, demand, entail, force, involve, oblige, require.
necessities *n.* essentials, fundamentals, indispensables, needs, requirements.
antonym luxuries.
necessity *n.* compulsion, demand, destiny, essential, extremity, fate, fundamental, inevitability, necessary, need, obligation, poverty, prerequisite, requirement, want.
neck *n.* nape, scrag, scruff.
necklace *n.* chain, choker, locket, pendant.
need *v.* call for, could do with, crave, demand, have to, lack, miss, necessitate, require, want.
n. demand, essential, inadequacy, insufficiency, lack, longing, necessity, neediness, obligation, requirement, requisite, shortage, urgency, want, wish.
needless *adj.* gratuitous, groundless, pointless, purposeless, redundant, superfluous, uncalled-for, unnecessary, unwanted, useless.
antonyms essential, necessary, needful.
needy *adj.* deprived, destitute, disadvantaged, impoverished, penniless, poor, poverty-stricken, underprivileged.
antonyms affluent, wealthy, well-off.
negate *v.* abrogate, annul, cancel, contradict, countermand, deny, disprove, invalidate, neutralise, nullify, oppose, quash, refute, repeal, repudiate, rescind, retract, reverse, revoke, undo, void, wipe out.
antonym affirm.
negation *n.* cancellation, contradiction, contrary, converse, denial, disclaimer, neutralisation, opposite, rejection, renunciation, reverse, veto.
antonym affirmation.
negative *adj.* **1** annulling, contradictory, contrary, invalidating, neutralising, nullifying, opposing, rejecting. **2** cynical, unco-operative, unenthusiastic, uninterested, unwilling.
antonyms **1** affirmative, positive. **2** constructive, positive.
n. contradiction, denial, opposite, refusal.
neglect *v.* disdain, disregard, forget, ignore, leave alone, let slide, omit, overlook, pass by, pigeon-hole, rebuff, scorn, shirk, skimp, slight, spurn.
antonyms appreciate, cherish, nurture, treasure.
n. carelessness, disregard, disrespect, failure, forgetfulness, heedlessness, inattention, indifference, negligence, oversight, slackness, slight, slovenliness.
antonyms attention, care, concern.
negligence *n.* carelessness, default, disregard, failure, forgetfulness, inattentiveness, indifference, laxity, neglect, omission, oversight, slackness, thoughtlessness.

antonyms attentiveness, care, regard.
negligent *adj.* careless, casual, forgetful, inattentive, indifferent, lax, neglectful, nonchalant, offhand, remiss, slack, thoughtless, uncaring.
antonyms attentive, careful, scrupulous.
negligible *adj.* imperceptible, insignificant, minor, minute, small, trifling, trivial, unimportant.
antonym significant.
negotiate *v.* arbitrate, arrange, bargain, confer, consult, contract, deal, debate, discuss, manage, mediate, pass, settle, surmount, transact, traverse, work out.
negotiation *n.* arbitration, bargaining, debate, diplomacy, discussion, mediation, transaction.
negotiator *n.* adjudicator, ambassador, arbitrator, broker, delegate, diplomat, go-between, intermediary, mediator, moderator.
neigh *v.* bray, hinny, whinny.
neighbourhood *n.* community, confines, district, environs, locale, locality, proximity, region, surroundings, vicinity.
neighbouring *adj.* adjacent, bordering, connecting, near, nearby, nearest, next, surrounding.
antonyms distant, faraway, remote.
neighbourly *adj.* amiable, companionable, considerate, friendly, genial, helpful, hospitable, kind, obliging, sociable.
nemesis *n.* destiny, destruction, fate, punishment, retribution, vengeance.
nerve *n.* **1** bravery, courage, daring, determination, endurance, energy, fearlessness, firmness, force, fortitude, guts, intrepidity, mettle, pluck, resolution, spirit, steadfastness, vigour, will. **2** audacity, boldness, brazenness, cheek, chutzpah, effrontery, impertinence, impudence, insolence.
antonyms **1** weakness. **2** cowardice.
v. bolster, brace, encourage, fortify, hearten, invigorate, steel, strengthen.
antonym unnerve.
nerveless *adj.* afraid, cowardly, debilitated, enervated, feeble, flabby, nervous, spineless, timid, weak.
antonyms bold, strong.
nerve-racking *adj.* annoying, difficult, distressing, frightening, harrowing, maddening, stressful, tense, trying, worrying.
nerves *n.* anxiety, fretfulness, nervousness, strain, stress, tension, worry.
nervous *adj.* agitated, anxious, apprehensive, edgy, excitable, fearful, fidgety, flustered, highly-strung, jittery, jumpy, neurotic, on edge, shaky, tense, uneasy, uptight, worried.
antonyms calm, confident, cool, relaxed.
nervy *adj.* agitated, anxious, excitable, fidgety, jittery, jumpy, nervous, on edge, restless, tense, unquiet.
antonyms calm, relaxed.
nest *n.* breeding-ground, burrow, den, earth, form, haunt, hideaway, hotbed, refuge, retreat.
nestle *v.* cuddle, curl up, huddle, snuggle.
nestling *adj.* baby, chick, fledgling, suckling.
net¹ *n.* drag, drag-net, drop-net, lattice, mesh, netting, network, open-work, tracery, web.
v. bag, capture, catch, ensnare, entangle, nab, trap.
net² *adj.* after tax, clear, final, lowest, nett.
v. accumulate, bring in, clear, earn, gain, make, obtain, realise, receive.
nettled *adj.* aggrieved, angry, annoyed, cross, exasperated, incensed, irritated, peeved, piqued, riled, ruffled, vexed.
network *n.* arrangement, channels, circuitry, complex, convolution, grid, grill, interconnections, labyrinth, maze, mesh, meshwork, net, organisation, structure, system, tracks.
neurosis *n.* abnormality, affliction, derangement, deviation, disorder, disturbance, obsession, phobia.
neurotic *adj.* abnormal, anxious, compulsive, deviant, disturbed, maladjusted, manic, nervous, obsessive, overwrought, paranoid, unhealthy, unstable, wearisome.
antonyms normal, stable.
neuter *v.* castrate, doctor, emasculate, geld, spay.
neutral *adj.* **1** disinterested, dispassionate, even-handed, impartial, indifferent, intermediate, non-aligned, non-committal, non-partisan, unbia(s)sed, uncommitted, undecided, unprejudiced. **2** colourless, dull, expressionless, indistinct, indistinguishable, nondescript.
antonyms **1** biased, prejudiced. **2** coloured.
neutralise *v.* cancel, counteract, counterbalance, frustrate, invalidate, negate, nullify, offset, undo.
neutrality *n.* disinterestedness, impartiality, non-alignment, non-intervention, non-involvement, unbiasedness.
never *adv.* at no time, not at all, on no account, under no circumstances.
antonym always.
never-ending *adj.* eternal, everlasting, incessant, interminable, non-stop, permanent, perpetual, persistent, relentless, unbroken, unceasing, unchanging, uninterrupted, unremitting.
antonyms fleeting, transitory.
nevertheless *adv.* anyhow, anyway, but, even so, however, nonetheless, regardless, still, yet.
new *adj.* added, advanced, altered, changed, contemporary, current, different, extra, fresh, improved, latest, modern, modernised, more, newborn, newfangled, novel, original, recent, redesigned, renewed, restored, supplementary, topical, trendy, ultra-modern, unfamiliar, unknown, unused, unusual, up-to-date, up-to-the-minute, virgin.
antonyms hackneyed, old, outdated, out-of-date, usual.
newcomer *n.* alien, arrival, beginner, colonist, foreigner, immigrant, incomer, novice, outsider, settler, stranger.
newly *adv.* anew, freshly, just, lately, recently.
news *n.* account, advice, bulletin, communiqué, disclosure, dispatch, exposé, gen, gossip, hearsay, information, intelligence, latest, release, report, revelation, rumour, scandal, statement, story, word.

newspaper *n.* daily, journal, organ, paper, periodical, publication, tabloid.

newsworthy *adj.* arresting, important, interesting, notable, noteworthy, remarkable, significant, stimulating, unusual.

next *adj.* adjacent, adjoining, closest, ensuing, following, later, nearest, neighbouring, subsequent, succeeding.
antonyms preceding, previous.
adv. afterwards, later, subsequently, then.

nibble *n.* bit, bite, crumb, morsel, peck, piece, snack, taste.
v. bite, eat, gnaw, munch, peck, pick at.

nice *adj.* **1** attractive, charming, delightful, friendly, good, kind, lik(e)able, pleasant, polite, respectable, tidy, well-mannered. **2** accurate, careful, exact, fine, precise, scrupulous, strict, subtle.
antonyms **1** disagreeable, nasty, unpleasant. **2** careless.

nicety *n.* delicacy, distinction, finesse, meticulousness, minuteness, nuance, precision, refinement, subtlety.

niche *n.* **1** alcove, corner, cubby, cubby-hole, hollow, nook, opening, recess. **2** calling, métier, place, position, slot, vocation.

nick *n.* chip, cut, dent, indentation, mark, notch, scar, scratch, snick.
v. **1** chip, cut, damage, dent, indent, mark, notch, scar, score, scratch, snick. **2** knock off, pilfer, pinch, steal.

nickname *n.* epithet, label, pet name, sobriquet.

niggardly *adj.* beggarly, cheese-paring, close, grudging, hard-fisted, meagre, mean, miserable, miserly, parsimonious, skimpy, stingy, tight-fisted.
antonyms generous, lavish.

night *n.* dark, darkness, dead of night, night-time.
antonyms day, daytime.

nightclub *n.* cabaret, club, disco, discotheque, nightspot.

nightfall *n.* dusk, eve, evening, gloaming, sunset, twilight.
antonyms dawn, sunrise.

nightmare *n.* bad dream, hallucination, horror, ordeal, torment, trial.

nightmarish *adj.* agonising, alarming, disturbing, dreadful, frightening, harrowing, horrible, horrific, scaring, terrifying.

nil *n.* duck, love, naught, none, nothing, zero.

nimble *adj.* active, agile, alert, brisk, deft, light-footed, lively, nippy, proficient, prompt, quick, quick-witted, ready, smart, sprightly, spry, swift.
antonyms awkward, clumsy, slow.

nip[1] *v.* bite, catch, check, clip, grip, nibble, pinch, snip, squeeze.

nip[2] *n.* dram, draught, drop, mouthful, portion, shot, sip, swallow, taste.

nipple *n.* breast, mamilla, pap, teat, udder.

nippy *adj.* **1** biting, chilly, sharp, stinging. **2** active, agile, fast, nimble, quick, speedy, sprightly, spry.
antonyms **1** warm. **2** slow.

nit-picking *adj.* carping, cavilling, finicky, fussy, hair-splitting, hypercritical, pedantic, quibbling.

nobility *n.* **1** dignity, eminence, excellence, generosity, grandeur, honour, illustriousness, magnificence, majesty, stateliness, superiority, uprightness, virtue, worthiness. **2** aristocracy, élite, gentry, high society, lords, nobles, peerage.
antonyms **1** baseness. **2** proletariat.

noble *n.* aristocrat, baron, lord, nobleman, peer.
antonyms commoner, pleb, prole.
adj. aristocratic, august, blue-blooded, dignified, distinguished, elevated, eminent, excellent, fine, generous, gentle, grand, great, high-born, honourable, honoured, imposing, impressive, magnificent, majestic, splendid, stately, upright, virtuous, worthy.
antonyms base, contemptible, ignoble, low-born.

nobody *n.* also-ran, menial, nonentity, no-one, nothing.
antonym somebody.

nod *v.* **1** acknowledge, agree, assent, bow, gesture, indicate, salute, sign, signal. **2** doze, sleep.
n. acknowledgement, beck, cue, gesture, greeting, indication, salute, sign, signal.

node *n.* bud, bump, burl, growth, knob, knot, lump, nodule, protuberance, swelling.

noise *n.* babble, blare, clamour, clash, clatter, commotion, cry, din, hubbub, outcry, pandemonium, racket, row, sound, talk, tumult, uproar.
antonyms quiet, silence.
v. announce, circulate, publicise, report, rumour.

noiseless *adj.* hushed, inaudible, mute, quiet, silent, soundless, still.
antonyms loud, noisy.

noisy *adj.* boisterous, chattering, deafening, ear-splitting, loud, piercing, tumultuous, turbulent, vocal, vociferous.
antonyms peaceful, quiet, silent.

nom de plume alias, assumed name, pen name, pseudonym.

nomad *n.* itinerant, migrant, rambler, roamer, rover, traveller, wanderer.

nominal *adj.* **1** ostensible, professed, puppet, purported, self-styled, so-called, supposed, symbolic, theoretical, titular. **2** insignificant, minimal, small, token, trifling, trivial.
antonyms **1** actual, genuine, real, true.

nominate *v.* appoint, assign, choose, commission, designate, elect, elevate, name, present, propose, put up, recommend, select, submit, suggest, term.

nomination *n.* appointment, choice, designation, election, proposal, recommendation, selection, submission, suggestion.

nominee *n.* appointee, assignee, candidate, contestant, entrant, runner.

nonchalant *adj.* apathetic, blasé, carefree, careless, casual, collected, cool, detached, indifferent, offhand, unconcerned.

antonyms careful, concerned, worried.
non-committal *adj.* ambiguous, careful, cautious, circumspect, discreet, equivocal, evasive, guarded, indefinite, neutral, politic, reserved, tactful, tentative, unrevealing, vague, wary.
nonconformist *n.* dissenter, eccentric, heretic, iconoclast, individualist, maverick, oddball, protester, radical, rebel, secessionist.
antonym conformist.
nondescript *adj.* commonplace, dull, featureless, ordinary, plain, unclassified, undistinctive, undistinguished, unexceptional, uninspiring, uninteresting, vague.
antonyms distinctive, memorable, remarkable.
none *pron.* nil, nobody, no-one, not any, not one, zero.
nonentity *n.* cipher, nobody.
antonyms somebody, VIP.
non-essential *adj.* peripheral, superfluous, supplementary, unimportant, unnecessary.
antonyms essential, indispensable.
non-existent *adj.* fancied, fictional, hallucinatory, hypothetical, illusory, imaginary, imagined, immaterial, legendary, missing, mythical, unreal.
antonyms actual, existing, real.
non-flammable *adj.* fire-proof, fire-resistant, flame-resistant, incombustible.
antonym flammable.
nonplussed *adj.* astonished, astounded, baffled, bewildered, confounded, disconcerted, dismayed, dumbfounded, embarrassed, flabbergasted, flummoxed, perplexed, puzzled, stumped, stunned, taken aback.
nonsense *n.* balderdash, drivel, fiddlesticks, folly, foolishness, gibberish, gobbledygook, moonshine, ridiculousness, rot, rubbish, senselessness, silliness, stupidity, trash, twaddle, waffle.
antonyms sense, wisdom.
nonsensical *adj.* absurd, crazy, daft, fatuous, foolish, inane, incomprehensible, irrational, ludicrous, meaningless, ridiculous, silly.
antonyms logical, reasonable, sensible.
non-stop *adj.* constant, continuous, direct, endless, interminable, never-ending, on-going, round-the-clock, unbroken, unending, uninterrupted.
antonyms intermittent, occasional.
non-violent *adj.* dov(e)ish, irenic, pacifist, passive, peaceable, peaceful.
antonym violent.
norm *n.* average, bench-mark, criterion, measure, model, pattern, reference, rule, standard, type, yardstick.
normal *adj.* accustomed, average, common, conventional, mainstream, natural, ordinary, popular, rational, reasonable, regular, routine, standard, straight, typical, usual, well-adjusted.
antonyms abnormal, irregular, odd, peculiar.
normality *n.* adjustment, balance, commonness, conventionality, naturalness, ordinariness, popularity, rationality, reason, regularity, routine, typicality, usualness.
antonyms abnormality, irregularity, oddity, peculiarity.
normally *adv.* as a rule, characteristically, commonly, ordinarily, typically, usually.
antonyms abnormally, exceptionally, oddly.
nose *n.* beak, bill, snout.
v. **1** intrude, nudge, nuzzle, push. **2** detect, scent, search, smell, sniff, snoop.
nose-dive *n.* dive, drop, plummet, plunge.
v. dive, drop, plummet, plunge, submerge.
nosegay *n.* bouquet, posy, spray.
nos(e)y *adj.* curious, eavesdropping, inquisitive, interfering, meddlesome, prying, snooping.
nostalgia *n.* homesickness, longing, pining, regretfulness, remembrance, reminiscence, yearning.
nostalgic *adj.* emotional, homesick, longing, regretful, romantic, sentimental.
notability *n.* celebrity, dignitary, luminary, magnate, notable, personage, somebody, VIP, worthy.
antonym nonentity.
notable *adj.* celebrated, distinguished, eminent, extraordinary, famous, impressive, marked, noteworthy, noticeable, notorious, outstanding, rare, remarkable, renowned, striking, unusual, well-known.
antonyms commonplace, ordinary, usual.
n. celebrity, dignitary, luminary, notability, personage, somebody, VIP, worthy.
antonyms nobody, nonentity.
notably *adv.* conspicuously, distinctly, eminently, especially, impressively, markedly, noticeably, outstandingly, particularly, remarkably, strikingly.
notation *n.* alphabet, characters, code, noting, record, script, shorthand, signs, symbols, system.
notch *n.* cleft, cut, degree, grade, incision, indentation, mark, nick, score, sinus, snip, step.
v. cut, indent, mark, nick, score, scratch.
notch up achieve, gain, make, record, register, score.
notched *adj.* jagged, jaggy, pinked, serrate(d).
note *n.* **1** annotation, comment, communication, gloss, indication, jotting, letter, line, mark, memo, memorandum, message, record, remark, reminder, signal, symbol, token. **2** consequence, distinction, eminence, fame, renown, reputation. **3** heed, notice, observation, regard.
v. denote, designate, detect, enter, indicate, mark, mention, notice, observe, record, register, remark, see, witness.
noted *adj.* acclaimed, celebrated, distinguished, eminent, famous, great, illustrious, notable, prominent, recognised, renowned, respected, well-known.
antonyms obscure, unknown.
notes *n.* draft, impressions, jottings, outline, record, report, sketch, synopsis.
noteworthy *adj.* exceptional, extraordinary, important, notable, on the map, outstanding, remarkable, significant, unusual.
antonyms commonplace, ordinary, unexcep-

tional, usual.

nothing *n.* emptiness, naught, nobody, non-entity, non-existence, nothingness, nought, nullity, void, zero.
antonyms everything, something.

nothingness *n.* nihilism, non-existence, vacuum.

notice *v.* detect, discern, distinguish, heed, mark, mind, note, observe, perceive, remark, see, spot.
antonyms disregard, ignore, overlook.
n. **1** advertisement, announcement, bill, comment, communication, instruction, intelligence, news, note, notification, poster, review, sign. **2** attention, consideration, heed, note, observation, regard.

noticeable *adj.* appreciable, clear, conspicuous, distinct, evident, manifest, measurable, observable, obvious, perceptible, plain, significant, striking, unmistakable.
antonyms hidden, insignificant, obscure.

notification *n.* advice, announcement, declaration, disclosure, information, intelligence, message, notice, publication, revelation, statement, telling, warning.

notify *v.* acquaint, advise, alert, announce, declare, disclose, inform, publish, reveal, tell, warn.

notion *n.* apprehension, belief, concept, conception, fancy, idea, image, impression, inclination, judgement, knowledge, opinion, understanding, view, wish.

notional *adj.* abstract, conceptual, hypothetical, imaginary, speculative, theoretical, unfounded, unreal.
antonym real.

notoriety *n.* disfame, dishonour, disrepute, infamy, scandal.

notorious *adj.* blatant, dishonourable, disreputable, flagrant, glaring, infamous, open, overt, patent, scandalous, undisputed.

nought *n.* naught, nil, nothing, nothingness, zero.

nourish *v.* attend, cherish, comfort, cultivate, encourage, feed, foster, furnish, maintain, nurse, nurture, promote, supply, support, sustain, tend.

nourishment *n.* diet, food, nutrition, sustenance.

novel *adj.* different, fresh, imaginative, innovative, new, original, rare, strange, surprising, uncommon, unconventional, unfamiliar, unusual.
antonyms familiar, old-fashioned, ordinary, usual.
n. fiction, narrative, romance, story, tale, yarn.

novelty *n.* **1** freshness, innovation, newness, originality, peculiarity, strangeness, unfamiliarity, uniqueness. **2** bauble, curiosity, gadget, gimcrack, gimmick, knick-knack, memento, souvenir, trifle, trinket.

novice *n.* amateur, apprentice, beginner, convert, learner, newcomer, probationer, pupil.
antonyms expert, master, professional.

now *adv.* at once, at present, directly, immediately, instantly, next, nowadays, promptly, straightaway, these days.

now and then at times, from time to time, infrequently, intermittently, now and again, occasionally, on and off, on occasion, once in a while, periodically, sometimes.

nowadays *adv.* any more, as things are, at the moment, now, these days, today.

noxious *adj.* baneful, corrupting, deadly, destructive, foul, harmful, injurious, pernicious, poisonous, unhealthy.
antonyms healthy, innocuous, wholesome.

nuance *n.* degree, distinction, gradation, hint, nicety, overtone, refinement, shade, subtlety, suggestion, suspicion, tinge, touch, trace.

nub *n.* centre, core, crux, essence, gist, heart, kernel, nucleus, pith, point.

nucleus *n.* basis, centre, core, crux, focus, heart, kernel, nub, pivot.

nude *adj.* bare, in one's birthday suit, naked, stark-naked, stripped, unclothed, uncovered, undressed.
antonyms clothed, covered, dressed.

nudge *v., n.* bump, dig, jog, poke, prod, prompt, push, shove, touch.

nudity *n.* bareness, nakedness, nudism, undress.

nuisance *n.* annoyance, bore, bother, drag, drawback, inconvenience, infliction, irritation, offence, pain, problem, trouble.

null *adj.* ineffectual, inoperative, invalid, powerless, useless, vain, void, worthless.
antonym valid.

nullify *v.* abolish, abrogate, annul, cancel, counteract, invalidate, negate, neutralise, quash, repeal, rescind, revoke, undermine, veto.
antonym validate.

numb *adj.* dead, frozen, immobilised, insensitive, paralysed, stunned, stupefied, unfeeling.
antonym sensitive.
v. anaesthetise, deaden, dull, freeze, immobilise, paralyse, stun, stupefy.
antonym sensitise.

number *n.* **1** character, digit, figure, integer, numeral, unit. **2** aggregate, amount, collection, company, crowd, horde, many, multitude, quantity, several, sum, throng, total. **3** copy, edition, impression, issue, printing, volume.
v. account, add, calculate, compute, count, enumerate, include, reckon, total.

numeral *n.* character, cipher, digit, figure, integer, number.

numerous *adj.* abundant, copious, many, plentiful, profuse, several, sundry.
antonyms few, scanty.

nun *n.* abbess, mother superior, prioress, sister.

nurse *v.* breast-feed, care for, cherish, encourage, feed, foster, keep, nourish, nurture, preserve, promote, succour, suckle, support, sustain, tend, treat.
n. district-nurse, home-nurse, nanny, nursemaid.

nurture *n.* care, cultivation, development, discipline, education, food, nourishment, rearing, training, upbringing.
v. bring up, care for, cultivate, develop, disci-

pline, educate, feed, instruct, nourish, nurse, protect, rear, school, support, sustain, tend, train.

nut *n.* kernel, pip, seed, stone.

nutriment *n.* food, foodstuff, nourishment, nutrition, sustenance.

nutrition *n.* food, nourishment, sustenance.

nutritious *adj.* beneficial, good, healthful, health-giving, invigorating, nourishing, nutritive, strengthening, substantial, wholesome.
antonyms bad, unwholesome.

nuzzle *v.* cuddle, fondle, nestle, nudge, pet, snuggle.

O

oasis *n.* haven, island, refuge, resting-place, retreat, sanctuary, watering-hole.
oath *n.* **1** affirmation, assurance, pledge, promise, vow, word, word of honour. **2** blasphemy, curse, expletive, imprecation, profanity, swear-word.
obedience *n.* agreement, allegiance, conformability, deference, docility, duty, observance, passivity, respect, reverence, submission, subservience.
antonym disobedience.
obedient *adj.* amenable, deferential, docile, dutiful, law-abiding, observant, respectful, submissive, subservient, unquestioning, well-trained, yielding.
antonyms disobedient, rebellious, unruly, wilful.
obesity *n.* bulk, corpulence, fatness, grossness, middle-age(d) spread, overweight, portliness, stoutness.
antonyms skinniness, slenderness, thinness.
obey *v.* abide by, act upon, adhere to, be ruled by, bow to, carry out, comply, conform, defer (to), discharge, execute, follow, fulfil, give way, heed, keep, mind, observe, perform, respond, submit, surrender, take orders from, yield.
antonym disobey.
object[1] *n.* **1** article, body, entity, thing. **2** aim, design, focus, goal, intention, motive, objective, point, purpose, reason, target. **3** butt, recipient, target, victim.
object[2] *v.* argue, complain, demur, oppose, protest, rebut, refuse, repudiate, take exception.
antonyms accept, acquiesce, agree, approve.
objection *n.* censure, challenge, complaint, doubt, niggle, opposition, protest, scruple.
antonyms agreement, approval, assent.
objectionable *adj.* abhorrent, deplorable, despicable, detestable, disagreeable, obnoxious, offensive, repugnant, unacceptable, unpleasant.
antonyms acceptable, pleasant, welcome.
objective *adj.* detached, disinterested, dispassionate, equitable, even-handed, factual, fair, impartial, impersonal, just, open-minded, sensible, unbiased.
antonyms biased, subjective.
n. aim, ambition, design, end, goal, intention, mark, object, purpose, target.
obligation *n.* bond, burden, charge, commitment, contract, debt, duty, liability, onus, promise, requirement, responsibility, stipulation, trust, understanding.
obligatory *adj.* binding, compulsory, enforced, essential, mandatory, necessary, required, statutory.
antonyms optional, avoidable.
oblige *v.* **1** bind, coerce, compel, constrain, force, make, necessitate, require. **2** accommodate, assist, benefit, do a favour, favour, gratify, help, please, serve.
obliterate *v.* annihilate, blot out, cancel, delete, destroy, eradicate, erase, rub out, wipe out.
oblivion *n.* limbo, nothingness, obscurity, unawareness, unconsciousness, void.
antonyms awareness, consciousness.
oblivious *adj.* blind, careless, forgetful, heedless, ignorant, inattentive, insensible, negligent, unaware, unconscious.
antonyms aware, conscious, mindful.
obnoxious *adj.* abhorrent, abominable, detestable, disagreeable, disgusting, dislik(e)able, horrid, loathsome, nasty, nauseating, nauseous, objectionable, odious, repellent, repugnant, repulsive, revolting, sickening, unpleasant.
antonyms agreeable, lik(e)able, pleasant.
obscene *adj.* atrocious, bawdy, blue, coarse, dirty, disgusting, evil, filthy, foul, gross, immoral, improper, impure, indecent, lewd, licentious, loathsome, offensive, outrageous, pornographic, scurrilous, shameless, shocking, sickening, suggestive, wicked.
antonyms clean, decent, decorous, wholesome.
obscenity *n.* **1** atrocity, coarseness, dirtiness, evil, filthiness, foulness, grossness, immodesty, impropriety, impurity, indecency, indelicacy, lewdness, licentiousness, offence, outrage, pornography, suggestiveness. **2** expletive, four-letter word, profanity, swear-word.
obscure *adj.* **1** humble, inconspicuous, little-known, minor, nameless, unheard-of, unimportant, unknown, unseen, unsung. **2** abstruse, confusing, cryptic, deep, enigmatic, incomprehensible, intricate. **3** blurred, cloudy, dim, dusky, faint, gloomy, hazy, indefinite, indistinct, misty, murky, shadowy, shady, unclear, vague.
antonyms **1** famous, renowned. **2** intelligible, straightforward. **3** clear, definite.
v. block out, blur, cloak, cloud, conceal, cover, darken, dim, disguise, dull, eclipse, hide, mask, overshadow, screen, shade, shadow, shroud, veil.
antonyms clarify, illuminate.
obscurity *n.* **1** abstruseness, complexity, impenetrability, incomprehensibility, inconspicuousness, insignificance, intricacy, unimportance. **2** darkness, dimness, dusk, fogginess, gloom, haze, haziness, indistinctness, mirkiness, murkiness, shadows.
antonyms **1** fame. **2** clarity.
obsequious *adj.* cringing, deferential, fawning, flattering, grovelling, ingratiating, menial, oily, servile, slavish, smarmy, submissive, subser-

vient, sycophantic, toadying, unctuous.
antonym assertive.

observance *n.* adherence, attention, celebration, ceremony, compliance, custom, formality, fulfilment, honouring, notice, obedience, observation, performance, practice.

observant *adj.* alert, attentive, eagle-eyed, perceptive, quick, vigilant, watchful, wide-awake.
antonyms inattentive, unobservant.

observation *n.* attention, consideration, discernment, examination, experience, finding, information, inspection, knowledge, monitoring, note, notice, opinion, perception, pronouncement, reading, reflection, remark, review, study, thought, utterance, watching.

observe *v.* **1** contemplate, discover, keep an eye on, note, notice, perceive, see, study, view, watch. **2** abide by, celebrate, commemorate, comply, follow, fulfil, honour, keep, obey, perform, remember.
antonyms **1** miss. **2** break, violate.

observer *n.* bystander, commentator, eyewitness, looker-on, onlooker, spectator, spotter, viewer, watcher, witness.

obsess *v.* consume, dominate, engross, grip, haunt, hold, monopolise, plague, possess, preoccupy, prey on, rule, torment.

obsession *n.* complex, enthusiasm, fetish, fixation, hang-up, infatuation, mania, phobia, preoccupation, ruling passion, thing.

obsessive *adj.* compulsive, consuming, fixed, gripping, haunting, maddening, tormenting.

obsolescent *adj.* ag(e)ing, declining, disappearing, dying out, fading, on the decline, past its prime, waning.

obsolete *adj.* antiquated, antique, dated, dead, disused, extinct, old, old-fashioned, out of date, outmoded, outworn, passé.
antonyms contemporary, current, modern, new, up-to-date.

obstacle *n.* bar, barrier, catch, check, difficulty, drawback, hindrance, hitch, hurdle, impediment, interference, interruption, obstruction, snag, stop, stumbling-block.
antonyms advantage, help.

obstinacy *n.* doggedness, firmness, inflexibility, intransigence, persistence, perversity, pigheadedness, stubbornness, wilfulness.
antonyms co-operativeness, flexibility, submissiveness.

obstinate *adj.* determined, dogged, firm, headstrong, immovable, inflexible, intractable, intransigent, persistent, self-willed, steadfast, strong-minded, stubborn, unyielding, wilful.
antonyms co-operative, flexible, submissive.

obstreperous *adj.* boisterous, disorderly, noisy, raucous, riotous, rip-roaring, rough, rowdy, stroppy, tempestuous, uncontrolled, unruly, wild.
antonyms calm, disciplined, manageable, quiet.

obstruct *v.* arrest, bar, barricade, block, check, choke, clog, curb, cut off, frustrate, hamper, hide, hinder, hold up, impede, inhibit, interfere with, interrupt, obscure, prevent, restrict, retard, shield, shut off, slow down, stall, stop, stuff, thwart.
antonyms aid, assist, further, help.

obstruction *n.* bar, barricade, barrier, blockage, check, difficulty, hindrance, impediment, stop, stoppage.
antonym help.

obstructive *adj.* awkward, blocking, delaying, difficult, hindering, inhibiting, restrictive, stalling, unhelpful.
antonyms accommodating, co-operative, helpful.

obtain *v.* **1** achieve, acquire, attain, come by, earn, gain, get, secure. **2** be in force, be prevalent, be the case, exist, hold, prevail, reign, rule, stand.

obtainable *adj.* achievable, at hand, attainable, available, on call, ready.
antonym unobtainable.

obtrusive *adj.* blatant, forward, interfering, intrusive, meddling, nosy, noticeable, obvious, prominent, protruding, prying, pushy.
antonym unobtrusive.

obtuse *adj.* blunt, crass, dense, dull, dull-witted, dumb, slow, stolid, stupid, thick, thick-skinned.
antonyms bright, intelligent, sharp.

obvious *adj.* apparent, clear, conspicuous, distinct, evident, glaring, manifest, noticeable, open, patent, perceptible, plain, prominent, pronounced, recognisable, self-evident, self-explanatory, straightforward, transparent, unconcealed, undeniable, unmistakable, visible.
antonyms indistinct, obscure, unclear.

obviously *adv.* certainly, clearly, distinctly, evidently, manifestly, of course, plainly, undeniably, unmistakably, without doubt.

occasion *n.* **1** case, cause, chance, event, excuse, ground(s), incident, instance, justification, occurrence, opportunity, reason, time. **2** celebration, function, party.
v. bring about, cause, create, evoke, generate, give rise to, induce, influence, inspire, lead to, make, originate, persuade, produce, prompt, provoke.

occasional *adj.* casual, incidental, infrequent, intermittent, irregular, odd, periodic, rare, sporadic, uncommon.
antonyms constant, frequent, regular.

occasionally *adv.* at intervals, at times, every so often, from time to time, infrequently, irregularly, now and again, now and then, off and on, on occasion, once in a while, periodically, sometimes.
antonyms always, frequently, often.

occult *adj.* concealed, esoteric, hidden, magical, mysterious, mystical, obscure, secret, supernatural, veiled.

occultism *n.* black magic, magic, mysticism, sorcery, spiritualism, supernaturalism, the black arts, witchcraft.

occupant *n.* holder, householder, inhabitant, lessee, occupier, resident, squatter, tenant, user.

occupation *n.* **1** activity, business, calling, craft, employment, job, line, post, profession, pursuit, trade, vocation, walk of life, work. **2** conquest, control, invasion, possession, seizure, takeover. **3** habitation, holding, occupancy, residence, tenancy, tenure, use.

occupy *v.* **1** inhabit, live in, own, possess, reside in, stay in, take possession of. **2** absorb, amuse, busy, engage, engross, hold, interest, involve, keep, preoccupy, take up. **3** capture, invade, overrun, seize, take over.

occur *v.* appear, arise, be found, be present, come about, come to pass, crop up, develop, exist, happen, manifest itself, materialise, obtain, result, show itself, take place, transpire, turn up.

occur to come to mind, come to one, cross one's mind, dawn on, enter one's head, present itself, spring to mind, strike one, suggest itself.

occurrence *n.* **1** action, adventure, affair, case, circumstance, development, episode, event, incident, instance. **2** appearance, existence, incidence, manifestation.

odd *adj.* **1** abnormal, atypical, bizarre, curious, different, eccentric, exceptional, extraordinary, fantastic, funny, irregular, outlandish, peculiar, queer, rare, remarkable, strange, uncommon, unconventional, unusual, weird. **2** incidental, irregular, occasional, random. **3** left-over, miscellaneous, remaining, single, spare, sundry, surplus, unmatched, unpaired, various.

antonyms **1** normal, usual. **2** regular.

oddity *n.* abnormality, character, curiosity, eccentricity, freak, idiosyncrasy, misfit, peculiarity, phenomenon, quirk, rarity.

oddment *n.* bit, end, fragment, left-over, offcut, patch, remnant, scrap, shred, snippet.

odds *n.* chances, likelihood, probability.

at odds at loggerheads, opposed, quarrelling.

odds and ends bits and pieces, debris, junk, oddments, remnants, rubbish, scraps.

odious *adj.* abhorrent, abominable, annoying, detestable, disgusting, execrable, foul, hateful, horrible, horrid, loathsome, offensive, repugnant, repulsive, revolting, unpleasant.

antonym pleasant.

odour *n.* air, aroma, atmosphere, aura, bouquet, breath, fragrance, perfume, scent, smell.

odyssey *n.* journey, travels, wandering.

off *adj.* **1** bad, decomposed, mouldy, rancid, rotten, sour, turned. **2** cancelled, postponed. **3** absent, gone. **4** below par, disappointing, substandard, unsatisfactory, wrong.

adv. apart, aside, at a distance, away, elsewhere, out.

off and on from time to time, intermittently, now and again, now and then, occasionally, on and off, periodically, sometimes.

off-colour *adj.* faded, ill, indisposed, off form, out of sorts, poorly, queasy, sick, under the weather, unwell.

off-duty *adj.* at leisure, free, off, off work, on holiday.

offence *n.* **1** crime, misdeed, misdemeanour, transgression, trespass, violation, wrong, wrongdoing. **2** hard feelings, hurt, indignation, resentment.

offend *v.* annoy, disgust, displease, fret, hurt, insult, irritate, miff, outrage, pain, provoke, repel, rile, snub, transgress, turn off, upset, violate, wound, wrong.

antonym please.

offender *n.* criminal, culprit, delinquent, guilty party, law-breaker, miscreant, transgressor, wrong-doer.

offensive *adj.* abominable, annoying, detestable, disagreeable, disgusting, displeasing, embarrassing, impertinent, insolent, insulting, intolerable, irritating, loathsome, nasty, nauseating, objectionable, obnoxious, odious, repellent, repugnant, revolting, rude, vile.

antonyms delightful, pleasant, pleasing, polite.

n. attack, drive, onslaught, push, raid, sortie, thrust.

offer *v.* advance, afford, extend, give, hold out, make available, move, present, propose, provide, put forth, put forward, show, submit, suggest, tender, volunteer.

n. approach, attempt, bid, overture, presentation, proposal, proposition, submission, suggestion, tender.

offering *n.* contribution, donation, gift, present, subscription.

offhand *adj.* abrupt, brusque, careless, casual, cavalier, informal, perfunctory, take-it-or-leave-it, unconcerned, uninterested.

antonyms calculated, planned, thoughtful.

adv. extempore, immediately, off the cuff, off the top of one's head.

office *n.* appointment, business, capacity, charge, commission, duty, employment, function, obligation, occupation, post, responsibility, role, room, service, situation, work.

officer *n.* administrator, agent, appointee, bureaucrat, dignitary, executive, functionary, office-holder, official, public servant, representative.

offices *n.* aegis, aid, auspices, backing, back-up, favour, help, intervention, mediation, patronage, recommendation, referral, support.

official *adj.* accredited, approved, authentic, authenticated, authorised, authoritative, bona fide, certified, formal, legitimate, licensed, proper.

antonym unofficial.

n. agent, bureaucrat, executive, functionary, office-bearer, officer, representative.

officiate *v.* adjudicate, chair, conduct, manage, oversee, preside, referee, serve, superintend, umpire.

officious *adj.* bossy, bustling, dictatorial, forward, impertinent, inquisitive, interfering, meddlesome, mischievous, obtrusive, overzealous, pushy, self-important.

off-key *adj.* discordant, dissonant, jarring, out of tune.

offload *v.* deposit, discharge, drop, dump, get rid of, jettison, shift, transfer, unburden, unload, unship.

off-putting *adj.* daunting, demoralising, disconcerting, discouraging, disheartening, disturbing, formidable, intimidating, unnerving, unsettling, upsetting.

offset *v.* balance out, cancel out, compensate for, counteract, counterbalance, juxtapose, make up for, neutralise.

offshoot *n.* adjunct, appendage, arm, branch, by-product, development, limb, outgrowth, spin-off, spur.

offspring *n.* brood, child, children, creation, descendants, family, heirs, issue, successors, young.
antonym parent(s).

often *adv.* again and again, frequently, generally, much, regularly, repeatedly, time after time, time and again.
antonyms never, rarely, seldom.

ogle *v.* eye (up), leer, look, make eyes at, stare.

ogre *n.* bogey, bogeyman, demon, devil, giant, monster, spectre.

oil *v.* anoint, grease, lubricate.
n. balm, cream, grease, liniment, lotion, lubricant, ointment.

oily *adj.* **1** fatty, greasy. **2** flattering, hypocritical, servile, slippery, smarmy, smooth, unctuous.

ointment *n.* balm, balsam, cream, embrocation, liniment, lotion, salve.

okay *adj.* acceptable, accurate, adequate, all right, convenient, correct, fair, fine, good, in order, not bad, OK, passable, permitted, reasonable, right as rain, satisfactory, tolerable.
n. agreement, approval, authorisation, consent, endorsement, go-ahead, green light, OK, permission, say-so, seal of approval, support.
v. agree to, approve, authorise, back, give the go-ahead to, give the green light to, OK, pass, rubber-stamp.
interj. agreed, all right, fine, OK, right, very good, very well, yes.

old *adj.* **1** aged, elderly, grey, grey-haired, senile. **2** ancient, antiquated, decayed, decrepit, long-established, long-standing, mature, obsolete, old-fashioned, original, out of date, primitive, time-honoured, traditional, worn-out. **3** earlier, ex-, former, one-time, previous.
antonyms **1** young. **2** new. **3** current, modern.

old-fashioned *adj.* ancient, antiquated, archaic, behind the times, dated, dead, obsolescent, obsolete, out of date, outmoded, past, unfashionable.
antonyms contemporary, modern, up-to-date.

omen *n.* auspice, foreboding, indication, portent, premonition, sign, warning.

ominous *adj.* fateful, inauspicious, menacing, portentous, sinister, threatening, unpromising.
antonyms auspicious, favourable, promising.

omission *n.* avoidance, default, exclusion, failure, gap, lack, neglect, oversight.
antonyms addition, inclusion.

omit *v.* disregard, drop, edit out, eliminate, exclude, fail, forget, leave out, leave undone, miss out, neglect, overlook, pass over, skip.
antonyms add, include.

on and off from time to time, intermittently, now and again, now and then, off and on, on occasion, periodically, sometimes.

once *adv.* at one time, formerly, in the old days, in the past, in times gone by, in times past, long ago, once upon a time, previously.
at once **1** directly, forthwith, immediately, instantly, now, promptly, right away, straightaway, without delay. **2** at the same time, simultaneously, together.
once and for all conclusively, decisively, definitively, finally, for good, for the last time, permanently, positively.

oncoming *adj.* advancing, approaching, gathering, looming, onrushing, upcoming.

one *adj.* alike, compatible, complete, entire, equal, harmonious, identical, like-minded, united, whole.

onerous *adj.* burdensome, demanding, difficult, exacting, exhausting, formidable, hard, heavy, laborious, oppressive, responsible, taxing, troublesome, weighty.
antonyms easy, light.

one-sided *adj.* biased, coloured, lopsided, partial, partisan, prejudiced, unequal, unfair, unilateral, unjust.
antonyms balanced, impartial.

one-time *adj.* ex-, former, late, previous, sometime.

ongoing *adj.* advancing, continuing, continuous, current, developing, evolving, growing, in progress, lasting, progressing, successful, unfinished, unfolding.

onlooker *n.* bystander, eye-witness, looker-on, observer, spectator, viewer, watcher, witness.

only *adv.* at most, barely, exclusively, just, merely, purely, simply, solely.
adj. exclusive, individual, lone, single, sole, solitary, unique.

onrush *n.* cascade, charge, flood, flow, onset, onslaught, push, rush, stampede, stream, surge.

onset *n.* assault, attack, beginning, commencement, inception, onrush, onslaught, outbreak, outset, start.
antonyms end, finish.

onslaught *n.* assault, attack, blitz, bombardment, charge, offensive.

onus *n.* burden, duty, liability, load, obligation, responsibility, task.

onward(s) *adv.* ahead, beyond, forth, forward, in front, on.
antonym backward(s).

ooze *v.* bleed, discharge, drain, dribble, drip, drop, emit, escape, filter, leak, overflow with, percolate, seep, strain, sweat.
n. deposit, mire, muck, mud, sediment, silt, slime, sludge.

opacity *n.* cloudiness, density, dullness, impermeability, obscurity, opaqueness, unclearness.
antonym transparency.

opaque *adj.* **1** clouded, cloudy, dim, dull, hazy, muddied, muddy, murky, turbid. **2** difficult, enigmatic, impenetrable, incomprehensible, obscure, unclear, unintelligible.
antonyms **1** transparent. **2** clear, obvious.

open *adj.* **1** ajar, gaping, lidless, unclosed, uncovered, unfastened, unlocked, unsealed, yawning. **2** accessible, clear, exposed, free, porous, unobstructed, unprotected, unrestricted, unsheltered, vacant, wide. **3** conspicuous, evident, flagrant, manifest, noticeable, obvious, plain. **4** undecided, unresolved, unsettled. **5** candid, frank, guileless, honest, natural.
antonyms **1** closed, shut. **3** hidden. **4** decided. **5** reticent, withdrawn.
v. **1** clear, expose, unblock, uncork, uncover, undo, unfasten, unfold, unlock, unseal. **2** disclose, divulge, explain, lay bare, separate, split, spread (out). **3** begin, commence, inaugurate, initiate, launch, set in motion, start.
antonyms **1** close, shut. **3** end, finish.
open to accessible, disposed, exposed, liable, receptive, susceptible, vulnerable.

open-air *adj.* alfresco, outdoor.
antonym indoor.

open-and-shut *adj.* obvious, simple, straightforward.

open-handed *adj.* bountiful, free, generous, large-hearted, lavish, liberal.
antonym tight-fisted.

opening *n.* **1** aperture, break, chasm, chink, cleft, crack, fissure, gap, hole, perforation, rupture, space, split, vent. **2** beginning, birth, dawn, inauguration, inception, launch, onset, start. **3** chance, occasion, opportunity, place, vacancy.
antonyms **1** closing, closure. **2** end.
adj. beginning, commencing, early, first, inaugural, initial, initiatory, introductory, primary.
antonym closing.

openly *adv.* blatantly, candidly, face to face, flagrantly, frankly, glaringly, in full view, in public, overtly, plainly, shamelessly, unashamedly, unreservedly.
antonyms secretly, slyly.

open-minded *adj.* broad-minded, impartial, liberal, objective, receptive, tolerant, unbiased, unprejudiced.
antonyms bigoted, intolerant, prejudiced.

open-mouthed *adj.* amazed, astounded, dumbfounded, flabbergasted, greedy, spellbound, thunderstruck.

operate *v.* act, function, go, handle, manage, manoeuvre, perform, run, serve, use, utilise, work.

operation *n.* action, activity, affair, agency, business, campaign, course, deal, effort, employment, enterprise, exercise, force, influence, instrumentality, manipulation, manoeuvre, motion, movement, performance, procedure, proceeding, process, transaction, undertaking, use, utilisation, working.

operational *adj.* functional, going, in service, in working order, on duty, prepared, ready, usable, workable, working.
antonym out of order.

operative *adj.* **1** active, effective, efficient, engaged, functional, functioning, in action, in force, in operation, serviceable, standing, workable. **2** crucial, important, key, relevant, significant.
antonyms **1** inoperative, out of service.

operator *n.* administrator, conductor, contractor, dealer, director, driver, handler, machinist, manager, mechanic, operative, practitioner, punter, technician, trader, wheeler-dealer, worker.

opinion *n.* assessment, belief, conception, estimation, feeling, idea, impression, judgement, mind, notion, perception, persuasion, point of view, sentiment, stance, tenet, theory, view, voice.

opinionated *adj.* biased, bigoted, cocksure, dictatorial, dogmatic, obstinate, partisan, prejudiced, self-assertive, single-minded, stubborn, uncompromising.
antonym open-minded.

opponent *n.* adversary, antagonist, challenger, competitor, contestant, dissident, enemy, foe, objector, opposer, opposition, rival.
antonyms ally, helper.

opportunity *n.* break, chance, convenience, hour, moment, occasion, opening.

oppose *v.* bar, check, combat, compare, confront, contradict, contrast, contravene, counter, counterattack, defy, face, fight, fly in the face of, hinder, obstruct, play off, prevent, resist, stand up to, take a stand against, take issue with, thwart, withstand.
antonyms defend, favour, support.

opposed *adj.* against, antagonistic, anti, clashing, conflicting, contrary, hostile, in opposition, incompatible, opposing, opposite.
antonym in favour.

opposing *adj.* antagonistic, clashing, combatant, conflicting, contentious, contrary, enemy, hostile, incompatible, irreconcilable, opposed, opposite, rival, warring.

opposite *adj.* adverse, antagonistic, conflicting, contradictory, contrary, contrasted, corresponding, different, differing, diverse, facing, fronting, hostile, inconsistent, irreconcilable, opposed, reverse, unlike.
antonym same.
n. antithesis, contradiction, contrary, converse, inverse, reverse.
antonym same.

opposition *n.* **1** antagonism, disapproval, hostility, obstructiveness, resistance, unfriendliness. **2** antagonist, foe, opponent, other side, rival.
antonyms **1** co-operation, support. **2** ally, helper, supporter.

oppress *v.* abuse, afflict, burden, crush, depress, harass, lie heavy on, maltreat, overpower, overwhelm, persecute, sadden, subdue, subjugate, suppress, torment, trample, tyrannise, vex.

oppressed *adj.* abused, disadvantaged, downtrodden, harassed, henpecked, maltreated, misused, persecuted, prostrate, slave, subject, subjugated, troubled, tyrannised, underprivileged.
antonym free.

oppression *n.* abuse, brutality, cruelty, hardship, harshness, injustice, maltreatment, misery, persecution, subjection, suffering.

oppressive *adj.* **1** airless, close, heavy, muggy, stifling, stuffy, suffocating, sultry. **2** brutal, burdensome, cruel, despotic, harsh, inhuman, intolerable, onerous, overbearing, overwhelming, repressive, tyrannical, unjust.
antonyms **1** airy. **2** gentle, just.

oppressor *n.* autocrat, bully, despot, dictator, intimidator, persecutor, slave-driver, taskmaster, tormentor, tyrant.

optimistic *adj.* assured, bright, buoyant, cheerful, confident, encouraged, expectant, heartened, hopeful, idealistic, positive.
antonym pessimistic.
n. best, peak, zenith.

option *n.* alternative, choice, possibility, preference, selection.

optional *adj.* discretionary, elective, extra, open, possible, voluntary.
antonyms compulsory, forced, obligatory.

oral *adj.* spoken, unwritten, verbal, vocal.
antonym written.

orator *n.* lecturer, preacher, public speaker, speaker, spellbinder.

orbit *n.* circle, compass, course, domain, ellipse, influence, path, range, reach, revolution, rotation, scope, sphere of influence, sweep, track, trajectory.
v. circle, circumnavigate, encircle, revolve.

ordain *v.* **1** appoint, call, consecrate, elect, invest. **2** decree, destine, fix, intend, lay down, legislate, order, predestine, predetermine, require, rule, set, will.

ordeal *n.* affliction, agony, anguish, nightmare, pain, persecution, suffering, test, torture, trial, tribulation(s), trouble(s).

order *n.* **1** command, commission, decree, direction, directive, injunction, instruction, law, mandate, ordinance, precept, regulation, rule, stipulation. **2** application, booking, chit, request, requisition, reservation. **3** arrangement, array, categorisation, classification, disposition, grouping, layout, line-up, method, organisation, pattern, plan, structure, symmetry, system. **4** calm, discipline, harmony, law and order, peace, quiet, tranquillity. **5** association, brotherhood, class, community, company, family, fraternity, guild, hierarchy, lodge, organisation, position, rank, sect, sisterhood, society, tribe, union.
antonyms **3** confusion, disorder. **4** anarchy.
v. **1** authorise, bid, command, decree, direct, instruct, require. **2** book, request, reserve. **3** arrange, catalogue, classify, control, dispose, group, lay out, manage, marshal, organise, sort out.
in order acceptable, all right, allowed, appropriate, arranged, called for, correct, done, fitting, in sequence, neat, OK, orderly, permitted, right, suitable, tidy.
in order to intending to, so that, to, with a view to, with the intention of, with the purpose of.
out of order broken, broken down, burst, haywire, inoperative.

orderly *adj.* businesslike, controlled, disciplined, in order, methodical, neat, ordered, regular, ruly, scientific, systematic, tidy, trim, well-behaved, well-organised, well-regulated.
antonyms chaotic, disorderly, disorganised.

ordinary *adj.* average, common, common-or-garden, commonplace, conventional, customary, established, everyday, familiar, habitual, indifferent, mediocre, modest, normal, pedestrian, plain, prevailing, prosaic, regular, routine, run-of-the-mill, settled, simple, standard, stock, typical, undistinguished, unexceptional, unremarkable, usual.
antonyms extraordinary, special, unusual.

organ *n.* **1** agency, channel, device, element, forum, implement, instrument, journal, means, medium, mouthpiece, newspaper, periodical, process, publication, structure, unit, vehicle, voice. **2** harmonium, hurdy-gurdy.

organic *adj.* anatomical, animate, biological, live, living, natural.

organisation *n.* **1** association, business, club, company, concern, confederation, consortium, corporation, federation, firm, group, institution, league, society, syndicate. **2** arrangement, composition, configuration, constitution, construction, co-ordination, design, formation, formulation, framework, grouping, make-up, management, method, methodology, pattern, plan, running, standardisation, structure, system.

organise *v.* arrange, catalogue, classify, constitute, construct, co-ordinate, establish, form, frame, group, marshal, regiment, run, see to, set up, shape, structure, systematise, tabulate.
antonym disorganise.

organism *n.* animal, being, body, cell, creature, entity, living thing, structure.

orgy *n.* bout, carousal, excess, indulgence, revelry, spree.

orient *v.* acclimatise, accommodate, adapt, adjust, align, familiarise, get one's bearings, orientate.

orientation *n.* acclimatisation, adaptation, adjustment, assimilation, bearings, direction, familiarisation, location, position, sense of direction, settling in.

origin *n.* ancestry, base, basis, beginning, birth, commencement, creation, dawning, derivation, descent, emergence, extraction, family, foundation, fountain, heritage, inauguration, launch, lineage, parentage, paternity, pedigree, provenance, roots, source, spring, start, stock, wellspring.
antonyms end, termination.

original *adj.* **1** archetypal, commencing, earliest, early, embryonic, first, first-hand, infant, initial, introductory, new, novel, opening, primary, rudimentary, starting. **2** creative, fertile, fresh, genuine, imaginative, innovative, inventive, resourceful.
antonyms **1** latest. **2** hackneyed, unoriginal.
n. archetype, master, model, paradigm, pattern, prototype, standard, type.

originate *v.* arise, be born, begin, come, commence, conceive, create, derive, develop, discover, emerge, establish, evolve, flow, form, generate, give birth to, inaugurate, introduce, invent, issue, launch, pioneer, proceed, produce, result, rise, set up, spring, start, stem.
antonyms end, terminate.

ornament *n.* accessory, adornment, bauble, decoration, embellishment, flower, frill, garnish, jewel, treasure, trimming, trinket.
v. adorn, beautify, brighten, deck, decorate, dress up, embellish, garnish, gild, grace, trim.

ornamental *adj.* attractive, decorative, embellishing, flashy, for show, showy.

ornate *adj.* baroque, busy, decorated, elaborate, fancy, florid, flowery, fussy, ornamented, rococo, sumptuous.
antonyms austere, plain.

orthodox *adj.* accepted, conformist, conventional, correct, customary, established, official, received, sound, traditional, true, usual, well-established.
antonyms nonconformist, unorthodox.

orthodoxy *n.* authenticity, conformity, conventionality, faithfulness, inflexibility, properness, received wisdom, soundness, traditionalism.

oscillate *v.* fluctuate, seesaw, sway, swing, vacillate, vary, waver.

ostensible *adj.* alleged, apparent, outward, plausible, presumed, pretended, professed, put-on, seeming, so-called, supposed.
antonyms actual, real, true.

ostentatious *adj.* conspicuous, extravagant, flamboyant, flashy, garish, gaudy, loud, pretentious, showy, vulgar.
antonyms modest, plain, restrained.

ostracise *v.* avoid, banish, boycott, cold-shoulder, cut, debar, exclude, excommunicate, exile, expel, reject, segregate, send to Coventry, shun, snub.
antonyms accept, receive, reinstate, welcome.

other *adj.* added, additional, alternative, auxiliary, contrasting, different, dissimilar, distinct, extra, fresh, further, more, new, remaining, separate, spare, supplementary, unrelated.

ounce *n.* atom, crumb, drop, grain, iota, jot, modicum, morsel, particle, scrap, shred, speck, spot, trace.

oust *v.* depose, disinherit, displace, dispossess, drive out, eject, evict, expel, overthrow, replace, throw out, topple, turn out, unseat, upstage.
antonyms install, reinstate, settle.

out *adj.* **1** abroad, absent, away, elsewhere, gone, not at home, outside. **2** disclosed, evident, exposed, manifest, public, revealed. **3** disallowed, excluded, forbidden, impossible, unacceptable. **4** antiquated, dated, dead, expired, old-fashioned, out of date, passé, unfashionable, used up.
antonyms **1** in, inside. **2** concealed. **3** allowed. **4** modern, up to date.

out-and-out *adj.* absolute, complete, downright, outright, perfect, total, uncompromising, unmitigated, unqualified, utter.

outbreak *n.* burst, epidemic, eruption, explosion, flare-up, flash, outburst, rash, spasm.

outburst *n.* access, attack, discharge, explosion, fit, fit of temper, flare-up, gale, gush, outbreak, outpouring, seizure, spasm, storm, surge.

outcast *n.* castaway, exile, leper, outsider, pariah, refugee, reject, reprobate, untouchable.
antonyms favourite, idol.

outcome *n.* conclusion, consequence, effect, end result, result, upshot.

outcry *n.* clamour, commotion, complaint, cry, exclamation, flap, howl, hue and cry, hullaballoo, noise, outburst, protest, row, scream, uproar, yell.

outdated *adj.* antiquated, archaic, behind the times, dated, obsolescent, obsolete, old-fashioned, out of date, outmoded, unfashionable.
antonyms fashionable, modern, modish.

outdistance *v.* leave behind, leave standing, outpace, outrun, outstrip, overtake, pass, pull ahead of, shake off.

outdo *v.* beat, get the better of, outclass, outdistance, outshine, outstrip, overcome, surpass.

outdoor *adj.* open-air, out-of-door(s), outside.
antonym indoor.

outer *adj.* distant, exterior, external, further, outlying, outside, outward, peripheral, remote, superficial, surface.
antonyms central, inner.

outfit *n.* **1** clothes, costume, ensemble, equipment, garb, gear, get-up, kit, paraphernalia, rig, togs, trappings. **2** business, clan, clique, company, coterie, crew, firm, gang, group, organisation, set, set-up, squad, team, unit.

outfitter *n.* costumer, dressmaker, haberdasher, tailor.

outflow *n.* discharge, drainage, ebb, effluent, emanation, emergence, gush, jet, outfall, outpouring, rush, spout.

outgoing *adj.* **1** affable, approachable, chatty, communicative, cordial, demonstrative, easy, expansive, extrovert, friendly, open, sociable, sympathetic, unreserved, warm. **2** departing, ex-, former, last, past, retiring.
antonyms **1** introvert, unsociable. **2** incoming, new.

outgrowth *n.* **1** consequence, effect, product. **2** offshoot, protuberance, shoot, sprout, swelling.

outing *n.* excursion, expedition, jaunt, picnic, pleasure trip, ramble, spin, trip.

outlast *v.* come through, outlive, survive, weather.

outlaw *n.* bandit, brigand, desperado, fugitive, highwayman, marauder, outcast, outsider, robber.
v. ban, banish, bar, condemn, debar, disallow, embargo, exclude, forbid, prohibit.
antonyms allow, legalise.

outlay *n.* cost, disbursement, expenditure, expenses, investment, outgoings, payment, price.
antonym income.

outlet *n.* **1** avenue, channel, duct, exit, opening, release, safety valve, vent, way out. **2** market, shop, store.
antonyms **1** entry, inlet.

outline *n.* **1** bare facts, delineation, explanation, rough, sketch, summary, synopsis, thumbnail sketch. **2** contour, form, profile, shape, silhouette.
v. draft, plan, rough out, sketch, summarise.

outlive *v.* come through, live through, outlast, survive, weather.

outlook *n.* **1** angle, aspect, attitude, frame of mind, look-out, panorama, perspective, point of view, scene, slant, standpoint, vantage-point, view, viewpoint, vista. **2** expectations, forecast, future, prognosis, prospect.

outlying *adj.* distant, far-away, far-flung, far-off, further, outer, provincial, remote.
antonyms central, inner.

out-of-the-way *adj.* distant, far-away, far-flung, far-off, inaccessible, isolated, little-known, obscure, remote, unfrequented.

outpouring *n.* cascade, deluge, flow, flux, outflow, spate, spurt, stream, torrent.

output *n.* achievement, manufacture, product, production, productivity, yield.
antonyms input, outlay.

outrage *n.* **1** anger, fury, horror, indignation, shock. **2** atrocity, barbarism, crime, evil, injury, offence, scandal, violation, violence.
v. disgust, incense, infuriate, injure, madden, offend, scandalise, shock.

outrageous *adj.* **1** abominable, atrocious, disgraceful, flagrant, horrible, monstrous, offensive, scandalous, shocking, violent. **2** excessive, exorbitant, extortionate, inordinate, preposterous, steep, unreasonable.
antonyms **1** fair, irreproachable. **2** acceptable, reasonable.

outrider *n.* advance guard, attendant, bodyguard, escort, guard, herald, scout, vanguard.

outright *adj.* absolute, categorical, complete, definite, direct, downright, out-and-out, perfect, pure, straightforward, thorough, total, unconditional, unqualified, utter.
antonyms ambiguous, indefinite, provisional.
adv. **1** absolutely, completely, directly, explicitly, openly, positively, straightforwardly, thoroughly, without restraint. **2** at once, immediately, instantaneously, instantly, there and then.

outset *n.* beginning, commencement, early days, inauguration, inception, kick-off, opening, start.
antonyms conclusion, end, finish.

outshine *v.* beat, eclipse, excel, outclass, outdo, outstrip, overshadow, surpass, top.

outside *adj.* **1** exterior, external, extraneous, extreme, outdoor, outer, outermost, outward, superficial, surface. **2** distant, faint, infinitesimal, marginal, negligible, remote, slight, slim, small.
antonyms **1** inside. **2** likely, real, substantial.
n. cover, exterior, façade, face, front, skin, surface.
antonym inside.

outsider *n.* alien, foreigner, immigrant, intruder, misfit, newcomer, non-member, non-resident, observer, odd man out, settler, stranger.
antonyms inhabitant, insider, local, member, native, resident, specialist.

outskirts *n.* borders, boundary, edge, fringes, margin, periphery, suburbs, vicinity.
antonyms centre, city-centre.

outspoken *adj.* candid, direct, explicit, forthright, frank, plain-spoken, pointed, sharp.
antonyms diplomatic, tactful.

outspread *adj.* expanded, extended, fanned out, flared, open, outstretched, spread out, stretched, unfolded, wide-open.

outstanding *adj.* **1** celebrated, distinguished, eminent, excellent, exceptional, extraordinary, great, important, impressive, marked, memorable, notable, noteworthy, pre-eminent, prominent, remarkable, special, striking, superior, superlative, surpassing. **2** due, left, ongoing, open, over, owing, payable, pending, remaining, uncollected, undone, unpaid, unresolved, unsettled.
antonyms **1** ordinary, unexceptional. **2** paid, processed, settled.

outstrip *v.* beat, better, eclipse, exceed, gain on, leave behind, leave standing, outdistance, outdo, outrun, outshine, overtake, pass, surpass, top, transcend.

outward *adj.* apparent, evident, exterior, external, noticeable, observable, obvious, outer, outside, professed, public, superficial, supposed, surface, visible.
antonyms inner, private.

outwardly *adv.* apparently, at first sight, externally, on the surface, seemingly, superficially, supposedly, to all appearances, to the eye.

outweigh *v.* cancel out, compensate for, make up for, override, overrule, predominate, prevail over, take precedence over.

outwit *v.* beat, better, cheat, deceive, defraud, dupe, get the better of, outsmart, outthink, swindle, trick.

outworn *adj.* antiquated, defunct, discredited, disused, exhausted, hackneyed, obsolete, out of date, outdated, outmoded, rejected, stale.
antonyms fresh, new.

oval *adj.* egg-shaped, elliptical.

ovation *n.* acclaim, acclamation, applause, bravos, cheering, cheers, clapping, praises, tribute.
antonyms abuse, catcalls, mockery.

over *adj.* accomplished, closed, completed, concluded, done with, ended, finished, forgotten, gone, in the past, past, settled, up.
adv. above, beyond, extra, in addition, in excess, left, on high, overhead, remaining, superfluous, surplus, unclaimed, unused, unwanted.
prep. above, exceeding, in charge of, in command of, in excess of, more than, on, on top of, upon.
over and above added to, along with, as well as, besides, in addition to, let alone, not to mention, on top of, plus, together with.

over and over (again) again and again, continually, endlessly, frequently, often, repeatedly, time and (time) again.
overact *v.* exaggerate, overdo, overplay.
antonyms underact, underplay.
overall *adj.* all-embracing, all-inclusive, all-over, blanket, broad, complete, comprehensive, general, global, inclusive, total, umbrella.
antonyms narrow, specific.
adv. broadly, by and large, generally speaking, in general, on the whole.
overawe *v.* awe, daunt, disconcert, dismay, frighten, intimidate, scare, terrify, unnerve.
antonym reassure.
overbalance *v.* capsize, fall over, keel over, lose (one's) balance, lose one's footing, overturn, slip, tip over, topple over, tumble, turn turtle.
overbearing *adj.* arrogant, bossy, cavalier, dictatorial, domineering, haughty, high-handed, imperious, officious, pompous, supercilious, superior, tyrannical.
antonyms modest, unassertive, unassuming.
overcharge *v.* cheat, diddle, do, extort, rip off, short-change, sting, surcharge.
antonym undercharge.
overcome *v.* beat, conquer, defeat, master, overpower, overthrow, overwhelm, rise above, subdue, surmount, survive, triumph over, vanquish, weather.
overcrowded *adj.* chock-full, congested, crammed full, jam-packed, overloaded, overpopulated, packed (out), swarming.
antonyms deserted, empty.
overdo *v.* exaggerate, go too far, lay it on thick, overact, overplay, overstate, overwork.
antonyms neglect, underuse.
overdue *adj.* behind schedule, behindhand, delayed, late, owing, slow, unpunctual.
antonym early.
overeat *v.* eat like a horse, guzzle, make a pig of oneself, overindulge, stuff oneself.
antonyms abstain, starve.
overflow *v.* brim over, bubble over, cover, deluge, discharge, drown, flood, inundate, pour over, shower, soak, spill, submerge, surge, swamp, well over.
n. flood, inundation, overabundance, overspill, spill, surplus.
overhang *v.* bulge, extend, impend, jut, project, protrude, stick out.
overhaul *v.* **1** check, do up, examine, fix, inspect, mend, recondition, re-examine, repair, service, survey. **2** gain on, outpace, outstrip, overtake, pass, pull ahead of.
n. check, check-up, examination, going-over, inspection, reconditioning, repair, service.
overhead *adv.* above, on high, up above, upward.
antonyms below, underfoot.
adj. aerial, elevated, overhanging, upper.
overheads *n.* expenses, operating costs, outgoings, running costs.
antonyms income, profit.
overheated *adj.* agitated, excited, fiery, impassioned, inflamed, overexcited, overwrought, passionate, roused.
antonyms calm, cool, impassive.
overjoyed *adj.* delighted, ecstatic, elated, enraptured, euphoric, in raptures, jubilant, over the moon, thrilled.
antonyms disappointed, sad.
overlap *v.* coincide, cover, flap over, overlay.
overlook *v.* **1** command a view of, face, front on to, look on to, look over. **2** disregard, ignore, let pass, let ride, miss, neglect, omit, pass, pass over, slight, turn a blind eye to. **3** excuse, forgive, pardon.
antonyms **2** note, notice, remember. **3** penalise.
overpowering *adj.* compelling, extreme, forceful, irresistible, nauseating, oppressive, overwhelming, powerful, sickening, strong, suffocating, telling, unbearable, uncontrollable.
overrate *v.* blow up, magnify, make too much of, overestimate, overpraise, overvalue.
antonym underrate.
override *v.* cancel, disregard, nullify, outweigh, overrule, quash, rescind, reverse, ride roughshod over, set aside, supersede.
overriding *adj.* final, first, major, number one, paramount, predominant, prevailing, primary, prime, prior, ruling, supreme, ultimate.
antonyms insignificant, unimportant.
overrule *v.* cancel, countermand, invalidate, outvote, override, overturn, recall, repeal, rescind, reverse, revoke, set aside, veto, vote down.
antonyms allow, approve.
overrun *v.* **1** infest, inundate, invade, occupy, overgrow, overwhelm, ravage, run riot, spread over, surge over, swamp, swarm over. **2** exceed, overdo, overshoot, overstep.
antonyms **1** desert, evacuate.
overseas *adj.* exotic, foreign.
antonyms domestic, home.
adv. abroad, in/to foreign parts.
overseer *n.* boss, chief, foreman, forewoman, manager, master, superintendent, supervisor.
overshadow *v.* cloud, darken, dim, dominate, dwarf, eclipse, excel, mar, obscure, outshine, outweigh, protect, put in the shade, rise above, ruin, shelter, spoil, surpass, tower above, veil.
oversight *n.* **1** blunder, carelessness, error, fault, lapse, mistake, neglect, omission, slip-up. **2** administration, care, charge, control, custody, direction, guidance, handling, inspection, keeping, management, responsibility, supervision.
overtake *v.* **1** catch up with, draw level with, outdistance, outstrip, overhaul, pass, pull ahead of. **2** befall, come upon, engulf, happen, strike.
overthrow *v.* abolish, beat, bring down, conquer, crush, defeat, demolish, depose, destroy, displace, knock down, level, master, oust, overcome, overpower, overturn, overwhelm, raze, ruin, subdue, topple, unseat, upset.
antonyms guard, install, protect, reinstate.
n. defeat, destruction, downfall, end, fall, humiliation, ousting, rout, ruin, suppression, undoing, unseating.

overtone *n.* association, connotation, feeling, flavour, hint, implication, intimation, nuance, sense, suggestion, undercurrent.

overture *n.* advance, approach, introduction, invitation, motion, move, offer, opening, (opening) gambit, opening move, prelude, proposal, proposition, signal, suggestion.

overturn *v.* **1** capsize, keel over, knock over, overbalance, spill, tip over, topple, upset, upturn. **2** abolish, annul, destroy, overthrow, quash, repeal, rescind, reverse, set aside.

overweight *adj.* bulky, buxom, chubby, chunky, fat, flabby, gross, heavy, obese, plump, podgy, portly, stout, tubby.
antonyms skinny, thin, underweight.

overwhelm *v.* bowl over, confuse, crush, defeat, destroy, devastate, engulf, floor, inundate, massacre, overcome, overpower, overrun, rout, snow under, stagger, submerge, swamp.

overwhelming *adj.* breathtaking, crushing, devastating, invincible, irrepressible, irresistible, overpowering, shattering, stunning, towering, uncontrollable, vast.
antonyms insignificant, negligible, resistible.

overwork *v.* burden, exhaust, exploit, oppress, overload, overstrain, overtax, overuse, strain, sweat, wear out, weary.

owing *adj.* due, in arrears, outstanding, overdue, owed, payable, unpaid, unsettled.
owing to as a result of, because of, on account of, thanks to.

own *adj.* idiosyncratic, individual, particular, personal, private.
v. enjoy, grant, have, hold, keep, possess, retain.
own up admit, come clean, confess, make a clean breast of it, spill the beans, tell the truth.

owner *n.* freeholder, holder, landlady, landlord, lord, master, mistress, possessor, proprietor, proprietress.

ownership *n.* dominion, freehold, possession, proprietary rights, right of possession, title.

ox *n.* bison, buffalo, bullock, steer.

P

pace *n.* celerity, gait, measure, momentum, motion, movement, progress, quickness, rapidity, rate, speed, step, stride, tempo, tread, velocity, walk.
v. march, mark out, measure, pad, patrol, pound, step, stride, tramp, tread, walk.

pacifism *n.* non-violence, pacificism, passive resistance.

pacifist *n.* conscientious objector, dove, pacificist, passive resister, peace-lover, peacemonger.
antonyms hawk, warmonger.

pacify *v.* allay, appease, assuage, calm, chasten, compose, conciliate, crush, lull, moderate, mollify, placate, put down, quell, quiet, repress, silence, smooth down, soften, soothe, still, subdue, tame.
antonyms aggravate, anger.

pack *n.* **1** back-pack, bundle, burden, haversack, kit, kitbag, knapsack, load, package, packet, parcel, rucksack. **2** band, collection, company, crowd, flock, gang, group, herd, lot, mob, troop.
v. batch, bundle, charge, compact, compress, cram, crowd, fill, load, mob, package, packet, press, ram, store, stow, stuff, throng, wedge.

package *n.* bale, box, carton, consignment, container, kit, pack, packet, parcel.
v. batch, box, pack (up), parcel (up), wrap (up).

packed *adj.* brimful, chock-a-block, chock-full, congested, crammed, crowded, filled, full, jam-packed.
antonyms deserted, empty.

packet *n.* bag, carton, case, container, pack, package, packing, parcel, wrapper, wrapping.

pact *n.* agreement, alliance, arrangement, bargain, bond, cartel, compact, contract, convention, covenant, deal, treaty, understanding.
antonyms breach, disagreement, quarrel.

pad *n.* **1** buffer, cushion, pillow, protection. **2** block, jotter, notepad, wad, writing-pad. **3** foot, footprint, paw, print, sole.
v. **1** cushion, fill, line, pack, protect, shape, stuff, wrap. **2** move, run, step, tiptoe, tramp, tread, walk.
pad out amplify, augment, elaborate, expand, fill out, flesh out, inflate, lengthen, spin out, stretch.

padding *n.* **1** filling, packing, stuffing, wadding. **2** bombast, hot air, verbosity, waffle, wordiness.

paddle[1] *n.* oar, scull.
v. oar, ply, propel, pull, row, steer.

paddle[2] *v.* dabble, slop, splash, trail, wade.

pagan *n.* atheist, heathen, idolater, infidel, unbeliever.
antonym believer.
adj. atheistic, godless, heathen, idolatrous, infidel, irreligious.

page[1] *n.* **1** folio, leaf, sheet, side. **2** chapter, episode, epoch, era, event, incident, period, phase, point, stage, time.

page[2] *n.* attendant, bell-boy, boy, footboy, footman, page-boy, servant.
v. announce, bid, call, call out, send for, summon.

pageant *n.* display, extravaganza, parade, play, procession, representation, scene, show, spectacle.

pageantry *n.* ceremony, display, drama, extravagance, glamour, glitter, grandeur, magnificence, melodrama, parade, pomp, show, spectacle, splendour, theatricality.

pail *n.* bucket, churn, tub.

pain *n.* ache, affliction, aggravation, agony, anguish, annoyance, bitterness, bore, bother, burden, cramp, discomfort, distress, grief, headache, heartache, heartbreak, hurt, irritation, misery, nuisance, soreness, spasm, suffering, tenderness, throb, torment, torture, tribulation, trouble, twinge, vexation, woe, wretchedness.
v. afflict, agonise, annoy, distress, harass, hurt, irritate, sadden, torment, torture, vex, worry, wound.
antonyms delight, gratify, please.

pained *adj.* aggrieved, cut up, disappointed, distressed, grieved, hurt, injured, offended, reproachful, saddened, stung, upset, wounded.
antonyms gratified, pleased.

painful *adj.* **1** aching, achy, agonising, distasteful, excruciating, smarting, sore, tender. **2** disagreeable, distressing, harrowing, saddening, traumatic, unpleasant. **3** difficult, hard, laborious, tedious.
antonyms **1** painless, soothing. **2** agreeable, pleasant. **3** easy.

painfully *adv.* acutely, alarmingly, distressingly, dreadfully, excessively, markedly, pitiably, pitifully.

painkiller *n.* anaesthetic, analgesic, anodyne, drug, palliative, remedy, sedative.
antonym irritant.

painless *adj.* **1** pain-free. **2** easy, effortless, simple, trouble-free, undemanding.
antonyms **1** painful. **2** difficult.

pains *n.* bother, care, diligence, effort, trouble.

painstaking *adj.* careful, conscientious, dedicated, devoted, diligent, earnest, hardworking, industrious, meticulous, persevering, scrupulous, thorough.
antonyms careless, negligent.

paint *n.* colour, colouring, cosmetics, distemper,

dye, emulsion, enamel, glaze, greasepaint, lacquer, lake, make-up, oils, pigment, primer, stain, tint, undercoat, wash, water-colour, whitewash.
v. **1** apply, coat, colour, cover, daub, decorate, glaze, lacquer. **2** describe, picture, portray, recount, represent.

painter *n.* artist, colourist, oil-painter, water-colourist.

painting *n.* fresco, illustration, landscape, miniature, mural, oil, oil-painting, picture, portrait, representation, scene, still life, water-colour.

pair *n.* brace, combination, couple, match, twins, two of a kind, twosome.
v. bracket, couple, join, link, marry, match, match up, mate, pair off, put together, splice, team, twin, wed.
antonyms separate, sever.

palace *n.* basilica, château, dome, schloss.

palatable *adj.* acceptable, agreeable, appetising, attractive, enjoyable, fair, pleasant, satisfactory, savoury, tasty, toothsome.
antonyms disagreeable, unacceptable, unpleasant.

palate *n.* appetite, appreciation, enjoyment, heart, liking, relish, stomach, taste, zest.

palatial *adj.* de luxe, grand, grandiose, imposing, luxurious, magnificent, majestic, plush, posh, regal, spacious, splendid, stately, sumptuous.
antonyms cramped, poky.

pale *adj.* anaemic, ashen, bleached, chalky, colourless, dim, faded, faint, feeble, light, lily-livered, pallid, pasty, poor, sallow, thin, wan, washed-out, weak, white, white-livered.
antonym ruddy.
v. blanch, dim, dull, fade, whiten.
antonyms blush, colour.

palisade *n.* barricade, bulwark, defence, enclosure, fence, fortification, paling, stockade.

pall[1] *n.* cloud, damper, dismay, gloom, mantle, shadow, shroud, veil.

pall[2] *v.* cloy, jade, satiate, sicken, tire, weary.

palliative *adj.* alleviative, calmative, calming, mitigatory, mollifying, sedative, soothing.
antonym irritant.
n. analgesic, calmative, painkiller, sedative, tranquilliser.

pallid *adj.* anaemic, ashen, ashy, colourless, insipid, lifeless, livid, pale, pasty, pasty-faced, sallow, spiritless, sterile, tame, tired, uninspired, vapid, wan, waxen, waxy, whitish.
antonym ruddy.

palm *n.* hand, mitt, paw.
v. appropriate, conceal, grab, sneak, snitch.
palm off fob off, foist off, impose, offload, pass off, thrust, unload.

palpable *adj.* apparent, blatant, clear, conspicuous, evident, manifest, material, obvious, open, plain, real, solid, substantial, tangible, touchable, unmistakable, visible.
antonyms elusive, impalpable, imperceptible, intangible.

palpitate *v.* beat, flutter, pound, pulsate, quiver, shiver, throb, thump, tremble, vibrate.

palsied *adj.* arthritic, crippled, debilitated, disabled, helpless, paralysed, rheumatic, shaking, shaky, shivering, trembling.

paltry *adj.* derisory, inconsiderable, insignificant, low, meagre, mean, minor, miserable, negligible, petty, poor, puny, slight, small, sorry, trifling, trivial, unimportant, worthless, wretched.
antonyms significant, substantial, valuable.

pamper *v.* coddle, cosset, fondle, gratify, humour, indulge, mollycoddle, mother, over-indulge, pet, spoil.
antonyms ill-treat, neglect.

pamphlet *n.* booklet, brochure, folder, leaflet.

pan[1] *n.* casserole, container, fryer, pot, saucepan, vessel, wok.
pan out happen, result, turn out, work out, yield.

pan[2] *v.* circle, follow, move, scan, sweep, swing, track, traverse, turn.

panache *n.* dash, élan, enthusiasm, flair, flamboyance, flourish, grand manner, ostentation, spirit, style, verve, vigour, zest.

pandemonium *n.* chaos, commotion, confusion, din, disorder, frenzy, hubbub, hue and cry, hullaballoo, rumpus, to-do, tumult, turbulence, turmoil, uproar.
antonyms calm, order, peace.

pander *v.* cater to, gratify, indulge, pamper, please, provide, satisfy.

pang *n.* ache, agony, anguish, discomfort, distress, gripe, pain, prick, spasm, stab, sting, stitch, throe, twinge.

panic *n.* agitation, alarm, consternation, dismay, fear, fright, horror, hysteria, scare, terror, to-do.
antonyms assurance, confidence.
v. flap, go to pieces, lose one's nerve, overreact.
antonym relax.

panic-stricken *adj.* alarmed, fearful, frenzied, frightened, horrified, horror-stricken, hysterical, in a cold sweat, petrified, scared stiff, stunned, terrified.
antonyms confident, laid-back, relaxed.

panorama *n.* bird's-eye view, overview, perspective, prospect, scene, scenery, spectacle, survey, view, vista.

panoramic *adj.* bird's-eye, comprehensive, extensive, far-reaching, general, overall, scenic, sweeping, universal, wide, widespread.
antonyms limited, narrow, restricted.

pant *v.* ache, blow, breathe, crave, desire, gasp, heave, huff, hunger, long, palpitate, pine, puff, sigh, thirst, throb, wheeze, yearn.

pants *n.* briefs, drawers, knickers, panties, shorts, slacks, trousers, trunks, underpants, undershorts, Y-fronts.

paper *n.* **1** daily, journal, news, newspaper, organ. **2** authorisation, certificate, credential, deed, document. **3** article, composition, critique, dissertation, essay, report, study, thesis.

parable *n.* allegory, fable, lesson, story.

parade *n.* **1** cavalcade, ceremony, column, exhibition, march, motorcade, pageant, procession,

review, spectacle, train. **2** display, flaunting, show.
v. brandish, display, exhibit, flaunt, make a show of, march, show, show off, strut, swagger, vaunt.
paradise *n.* bliss, City of God, delight, Eden, Elysian fields, Garden of Eden, heaven, heavenly kingdom, Promised Land, utopia.
antonyms Hades, hell.
paradox *n.* absurdity, ambiguity, anomaly, contradiction, enigma, inconsistency, mystery, oddity, puzzle, riddle.
paradoxical *adj.* absurd, ambiguous, baffling, conflicting, confounding, contradictory, enigmatic, equivocal, illogical, impossible, improbable, incongruous, inconsistent, puzzling, self-contradictory.
paragon *n.* archetype, criterion, epitome, ideal, jewel, masterpiece, model, pattern, prototype, quintessence, standard.
paragraph *n.* clause, item, notice, part, passage, portion, section, subdivision, subsection.
parallel *adj.* aligned, alongside, analogous, co-extensive, corresponding, equidistant, like, matching, resembling, similar, uniform.
antonyms different, divergent, separate.
n. analogy, comparison, corollary, correlation, correspondence, counterpart, duplicate, equal, equivalent, likeness, match, parallelism, resemblance, similarity, twin.
v. agree, compare, conform, correlate, correspond, duplicate, equal, match.
antonyms differ, diverge, separate.
paralyse *v.* anaesthetise, cripple, debilitate, disable, freeze, halt, immobilise, incapacitate, lame, numb, stun, transfix.
paralysis *n.* arrest, break-down, halt, immobility, palsy, paraplegia, quadriplegia, shut-down, stagnation, standstill, stoppage, torpor.
paralytic *adj.* **1** crippled, disabled, immobilised, incapacitated, lame, numb, paralysed, quadriplegic. **2** canned, drunk, inebriated, intoxicated.
antonyms **1** able-bodied. **2** (stone-cold) sober.
parameter *n.* boundary, criterion, framework, guideline, indication, limit, limitation, restriction, specification, variable.
paramount *adj.* chief, eminent, first, foremost, highest, main, outstanding, predominant, pre-eminent, primary, prime, principal, superior, supreme, topmost, top-rank.
antonyms inferior, last, lowest.
paranoia *n.* delusions, megalomania, monomania, obsession, psychosis.
paraphernalia *n.* accessories, apparatus, baggage, belongings, bits and pieces, effects, equipment, gear, material, odds and ends, stuff, tackle, things.
paraphrase *n.* interpretation, rendering, rephrasing, restatement, rewording, translation, version.
v. interpret, render, rephrase, restate, reword, translate.
parasite *n.* bloodsucker, cadger, hanger-on, leech, scrounger, sponger, sucker.
parasitic *adj.* bloodsucking, cadging, leechlike, scrounging, sponging.
parcel *n.* **1** carton, pack, package, packet. **2** band, batch, bunch, collection, company, crew, crowd, gang, group, lot, plot, portion, quantity, set, tract.
v. bundle, collect, pack, package, tie up, wrap.
parcel out allocate, allot, apportion, carve up, deal out, disperse, distribute, divide, dole out, mete out, portion out, separate, share out.
parch *v.* bake, blister, burn, dehydrate, desiccate, dry up, roast, scorch, sear, shrivel, wither.
parched *adj.* arid, dehydrated, dried up, dry, scorched, shrivelled, thirsty, waterless, withered.
parchment *n.* certificate, charter, diploma, document, scroll, vellum.
pardon *v.* absolve, acquit, excuse, forgive, free, let off, liberate, overlook, release, remit, reprieve, vindicate.
antonyms discipline, punish, rebuke.
n. absolution, acquittal, allowance, amnesty, compassion, discharge, excuse, forgiveness, grace, humanity, indulgence, mercy, release, reprieve.
antonyms condemnation, punishment.
pardonable *adj.* allowable, excusable, forgivable, justifiable, minor, permissible, understandable, venial, warrantable.
antonym inexcusable.
pare *v.* clip, crop, cut, cut back, decrease, diminish, dock, lop, peel, prune, reduce, shear, skin, trim.
parent *n.* architect, author, begetter, cause, creator, father, forerunner, guardian, mother, origin, originator, procreator, prototype, root, source.
parentage *n.* affiliation, ancestry, birth, derivation, descent, extraction, family, line, lineage, origin, paternity, pedigree, race, source, stock.
parish *n.* brethren, church, churchgoers, community, congregation, district, flock, fold, parishioners.
park *n.* estate, garden, grounds, paddock, parkland, pleasure garden, reserve, woodland.
v. deposit, dump, leave, position, station.
parliament *n.* assembly, congress, convocation, council, diet, house, legislature, senate.
parliamentary *adj.* congressional, deliberative, governmental, law-making, legislative, senatorial.
parochial *adj.* blinkered, confined, insular, inward-looking, limited, narrow-minded, parish-pump, petty, provincial, restricted, small-minded.
antonyms international, national.
parochialism *n.* insularity, narrow-mindedness, pettiness, provincialism.
parody *n.* caricature, imitation, mimicry, satire, send-up, skit, spoof, take-off, travesty.
v. caricature, mimic, satirise, send up, spoof, take off.
paroxysm *n.* attack, convulsion, explosion, fit, flare-up, outbreak, outburst, seizure, spasm,

tantrum.

parrot *n.* ape, copy-cat, imitator, mimic.
v. ape, copy, echo, imitate, mimic, rehearse, reiterate, repeat.

parrot-fashion *adv.* automatically, by rote, mechanically, mindlessly, unthinkingly.

parry *v.* avert, avoid, block, deflect, divert, dodge, duck, evade, fence, fend off, field, rebuff, repel, shun, sidestep, ward off.

parson *n.* churchman, clergyman, cleric, incumbent, man of God, minister, padre, pastor, preacher, priest, rector, reverend, vicar.

part *n.* **1** bit, branch, component, constituent, district, division, factor, fraction, fragment, particle, piece, portion, region, scrap, section, sector, segment, share, side, territory. **2** behalf, capacity, character, duty, function, office, responsibility, role, task.
antonyms **1** totality, whole.
v. break, break up, come apart, detach, disband, disconnect, dismantle, disperse, disunite, divide, go away, leave, part company, scatter, separate, sever, split, split up, take leave, tear, withdraw.
part with abandon, discard, forgo, give up, jettison, let go of, relinquish, renounce, sacrifice, surrender, yield.

partial *adj.* **1** fragmentary, imperfect, incomplete, limited, part, uncompleted, unfinished. **2** affected, biased, coloured, discriminatory, one-sided, partisan, predisposed, prejudiced, tendentious, unfair, unjust.
antonyms **1** complete, exhaustive, total. **2** disinterested, fair, unbiased.
partial to crazy about, fond of, keen on, mad about.

partially *adv.* fractionally, in part, incompletely, somewhat, to some extent.

participant *n.* associate, contributor, co-operator, helper, member, participator, party, shareholder, worker.

participate *v.* be involved, co-operate, engage, enter, join in, partake, perform, share, take part.

participation *n.* a piece of the action, assistance, contribution, co-operation, involvement, partnership, sharing.

particle *n.* atom, bit, corn, crumb, drop, electron, grain, iota, jot, morsel, neutron, piece, proton, scrap, shred, sliver, speck, tittle, whit.

particular *adj.* **1** distinct, exact, marked, peculiar, precise, special, specific. **2** exceptional, notable, remarkable, thorough, uncommon, unusual. **3** choosy, discriminating, fastidious, finicky, fussy.
antonyms **1** general. **2** usual.
n. circumstance, detail, fact, feature, item, point, specific, specification.
in particular distinctly, especially, exactly, expressly, in detail, particularly, specifically.

particularise *v.* detail, enumerate, itemise, specify, spell out.

particularly *adv.* distinctly, especially, exceptionally, explicitly, extraordinarily, in particular, notably, noticeably, remarkably, specifically, surprisingly, uncommonly, unusually.

parting *n.* adieu, breaking, departure, divergence, division, farewell, going, goodbye, leave-taking, partition, rift, rupture, separation, split.
antonyms convergence, meeting.
adj. closing, concluding, departing, dying, farewell, final, last.
antonyms arriving, first.

partisan *n.* adherent, backer, champion, devotee, disciple, follower, guerrilla, irregular, party-man, stalwart, supporter.
adj. biased, discriminatory, interested, irregular, partial, predisposed, prejudiced, sectarian.

partition *n.* **1** barrier, divider, membrane, room-divider, screen, traverse, wall. **2** division, part, section, separation, severance, splitting.
v. **1** bar, divide, fence off, screen, separate, wall off. **2** divide, parcel out, segment, separate, share, split up.

partly *adv.* halfway, in part, incompletely, moderately, partially, relatively, slightly, somewhat, to a certain degree, to a certain extent, up to a point.
antonyms completely, totally.

partner *n.* accomplice, ally, associate, collaborator, colleague, companion, comrade, confederate, consort, co-partner, helper, husband, mate, participant, side-kick, spouse, team-mate, wife.

partnership *n.* affiliation, alliance, association, brotherhood, combination, companionship, company, conglomerate, connection, co-operation, co-operative, corporation, fellowship, firm, fraternity, house, interest, participation, sharing, society, syndicate, union.

party *n.* **1** assembly, at-home, celebration, do, entertainment, festivity, function, gathering, get-together, housewarming, reception, social. **2** band, bunch, company, crew, gang, group, squad, team. **3** alliance, association, combination, detachment, faction, gathering, grouping, league, side. **4** defendant, individual, litigant, person, plaintiff.

pass[1] *v.* **1** exceed, flow, go, go beyond, leave, move, outdo, outstrip, overtake, run, surpass, transfer, transmit. **2** fill, give, hand, occupy, spend, while away. **3** elapse, go by, go past, lapse, proceed, roll. **4** come up to scratch, get through, graduate, qualify, succeed. **5** adopt, approve, authorise, enact, ratify, sanction, validate.
n. **1** kick, lunge, move, play, swing, throw. **2** authorisation, identification, licence, passport, permission, permit, ticket, warrant.
pass away decease, die, expire, give up the ghost, pass on, pass over.
pass by disregard, forget, ignore, leave, miss, neglect, omit, overlook, pass over.
pass off **1** counterfeit, fake, feign, palm off. **2** go off, happen, occur, pass by, take place, turn out. **3** die away, disappear, fade out, vanish, vaporise.
pass out **1** black out, die, drop, faint, flake out, keel over, lose consciousness. **2** deal out, distribute, dole out, give out, hand out, share out.
pass over ignore, neglect, omit, overlook.

pass² *n.* canyon, col, defile, gap, gorge, ravine.

passable *adj.* **1** acceptable, adequate, all right, allowable, average, fair, mediocre, moderate, OK, ordinary, tolerable, unexceptional. **2** clear, navigable, open, unblocked, unobstructed.
antonyms **1** excellent. **2** blocked, obstructed.

passage *n.* **1** corridor, doorway, gallery, hall, hallway, lobby, passageway, vestibule. **2** avenue, entrance, exit, lane, opening, path, road, route, thoroughfare, way. **3** clause, excerpt, extract, paragraph, piece, quotation, section, text, verse. **4** crossing, journey, tour, trek, trip, voyage.

passageway *n.* aisle, alley, corridor, entrance, exit, hall, hallway, lane, lobby, passage.

passenger *n.* commuter, fare, hitch-hiker, pillion-rider, rider, traveller.

passer-by *n.* bystander, looker-on, onlooker, spectator, witness.

passing *adj.* brief, casual, cursory, ephemeral, fleeting, glancing, hasty, momentary, quick, shallow, short, short-lived, slight, superficial, temporary.
antonyms long-lasting, permanent.
n. death, decease, demise, end, finish, loss, termination.

passion *n.* adoration, affection, anger, ardour, attachment, craving, craze, desire, eagerness, emotion, enthusiasm, excitement, fancy, fascination, feeling, fervour, fire, fit, flare-up, fondness, fury, heat, idol, indignation, infatuation, intensity, itch, joy, keenness, love, lust, mania, obsession, outburst, rage, rapture, resentment, spirit, vehemence, warmth, wax, wrath, zeal, zest.
antonyms calm, coolness, self-possession.

passionate *adj.* ardent, aroused, desirous, eager, emotional, enthusiastic, erotic, excitable, excited, fervent, fierce, fiery, frenzied, hot-headed, hot-tempered, impetuous, impulsive, incensed, inflamed, intense, irate, irritable, loving, quick-tempered, sensual, sexy, stormy, strong, sultry, tempestuous, vehement, violent, wanton, warm, wild, zealous.
antonyms frigid, laid-back, phlegmatic.

passive *adj.* idle, inactive, indifferent, lifeless, long-suffering, non-participating, non-violent, patient, receptive, resigned, submissive, unassertive, unresisting.
antonyms active, involved, lively, responsive.

passport *n.* authorisation, pass, permit, visa.

password *n.* countersign, parole, signal, watchword.

past *adj.* ancient, completed, defunct, done, early, ended, extinct, finished, foregone, forgotten, former, gone, late, long-ago, no more, over, over and done with, preceding, previous, recent.
n. antiquity, background, experience, former times, history, life, olden days, track record.

paste *n.* adhesive, cement, glue, gum, mastic, putty.
v. cement, fasten, fix, glue, gum, hammer, stick, whitewash.

pastel *adj.* delicate, faint, gentle, light, pale, soft, soft-hued, subdued.
n. chalk, crayon, drawing, pastille, sketch.

pastime *n.* activity, amusement, distraction, diversion, entertainment, game, hobby, play, recreation, relaxation, sport.
antonyms business, employment, occupation, work.

pastor *n.* canon, churchman, clergyman, ecclesiastic, man of God, minister, parson, prebendary, priest, rector, vicar.

pastoral *adj.* **1** agrarian, country, idyllic, rural, rustic, simple. **2** clerical, ecclesiastical, ministerial, priestly.
antonym **1** urban.

pasty *adj.* anaemic, pale, pallid, sickly, unhealthy, wan.
antonyms healthy, ruddy.

pat *v.* caress, clap, dab, fondle, pet, rub, slap, stroke, tap, touch.
n. **1** caress, slap, stroke, tap, touch. **2** cake, dab, lump, piece, portion.
adv. exactly, faultlessly, flawlessly, fluently, just right, perfectly, precisely.
antonyms imprecisely, inaccurately, wrongly.
adj. appropriate, automatic, easy, glib, neat, ready, right, simplistic, slick, smooth, spot-on, suitable.

patch *n.* area, bit, ground, land, lot, parcel, piece, plot, scrap, spot, stretch, tract.
v. cover, fix, mend, reinforce, repair, sew up, stitch.

patchy *adj.* bitty, erratic, fitful, inconsistent, irregular, random, sketchy, spotty, uneven, variable, varying.
antonyms consistent, even, regular, uniform.

patent *adj.* apparent, blatant, clear, conspicuous, evident, explicit, flagrant, glaring, manifest, obvious, open, overt, palpable, transparent, unequivocal, unmistakable.
antonyms hidden, opaque.
n. certificate, copyright, invention, licence, privilege, registered trademark.

paternal *adj.* benevolent, concerned, fatherlike, fatherly, indulgent, protective, solicitous, vigilant.

pathetic *adj.* **1** contemptible, distressing, heart-breaking, heart-rending, lamentable, meagre, miserable, moving, pitiable, plaintive, poor, sad, sorry, touching. **2** crummy, deplorable, feeble, inadequate, trashy, useless, worthless.
antonyms **1** admirable, cheerful. **2** excellent, valuable.

patience *n.* calmness, composure, constancy, diligence, endurance, forbearance, fortitude, long-suffering, perseverance, persistence, resignation, restraint, self-control, stoicism, submission, tolerance, toleration.
antonyms exasperation, impatience, intolerance.

patient *adj.* accommodating, calm, composed, enduring, even-tempered, forbearing, forgiving, indulgent, lenient, long-suffering, mild, persevering, persistent, philosophical, quiet, resigned, restrained, self-controlled, self-

possessed, stoical, submissive, tolerant, uncomplaining, understanding.
antonyms exasperated, impatient, intolerant, restless.
n. case, client, invalid, sufferer.

patriot *n.* chauvinist, flag-waver, jingoist, loyalist, nationalist.

patrol *n.* defence, garrison, guard, policing, protecting, sentinel, surveillance, watch, watching, watchman.
v. cruise, go the rounds, guard, inspect, police, range, tour.

patron *n.* **1** advocate, backer, benefactor, champion, defender, friend, guardian, helper, philanthropist, protector, sponsor, subscriber, supporter, sympathiser. **2** buyer, client, customer, frequenter, regular, shopper.

patronise *v.* **1** assist, back, befriend, encourage, foster, fund, help, maintain, promote, sponsor, support. **2** frequent, shop at.

patronising *adj.* condescending, disdaining, haughty, high-handed, overbearing, snobbish, stooping, superior.
antonyms humble, lowly.

patter *v.* beat, pat, pelt, pitter-patter, scurry, scuttle, skip, spatter, tap, tiptoe, trip.
n. **1** pattering, pitter-patter, tapping. **2** chatter, gabble, jabber, jargon, line, lingo, pitch, spiel.

pattern *n.* **1** method, order, plan, system. **2** decoration, design, figure, motif, ornament, ornamentation, style. **3** guide, model, norm, original, prototype, standard, stencil, template.
v. copy, decorate, design, follow, form, imitate, match, model, mould, order, shape, stencil, style, trim.

patterned *adj.* decorated, figured, ornamented, printed, stamped.

paunch *n.* abdomen, beer-belly, belly, pot-belly.

paunchy *adj.* corpulent, fat, podgy, portly, pot-bellied, tubby.

pause *v.* break, cease, cut, delay, discontinue, halt, hesitate, interrupt, rest, take a break, wait, waver.
n. break, breather, delay, gap, halt, hesitation, interlude, interruption, interval, let-up, lull, respite, rest, slackening, stay, stoppage, wait.

pave *v.* asphalt, concrete, cover, floor, macadamise, slab, surface, tar, tile.

paw *v.* grab, manhandle, maul, mishandle, molest.
n. foot, forepaw, hand, pad.

pawn[1] *n.* dupe, instrument, plaything, puppet, stooge, tool, toy.

pawn[2] *v.* deposit, dip, hock, mortgage, pledge, pop, stake, wager.

pawnbroker *n.* lender, money-lender, uncle, usurer.

pay *v.* **1** pay out, recompense, reimburse, remit, remunerate, repay, reward, settle, spend, square up. **2** benefit, bring in, profit, return, yield.
n. allowance, compensation, earnings, emoluments, fee, honorarium, income, payment, recompense, reimbursement, remuneration, reward, salary, stipend, takings, wages.

pay back 1 recompense, refund, reimburse, repay, settle up, square. **2** avenge, chasten, get even with, get one's own back, punish, reciprocate, retaliate.

pay for answer for, atone, compensate, get one's deserts, make amends, suffer.

pay off 1 clear, discharge, settle, square. **2** dismiss, fire, lay off, sack. **3** succeed, work.

pay out disburse, expend, fork out, hand over, lay out, render, shell out, spend.

payable *adj.* due, in arrears, mature, outstanding, owed, owing, receivable, unpaid.

payment *n.* advance, consideration, deposit, discharge, fee, hire, instalment, outlay, paying, portion, premium, remittance, remuneration, reward, settlement, wage.

pay-off *n.* climax, conclusion, consequence, crunch, culmination, judgement, moment of truth, outcome, punch-line, result, reward, upshot.

peace *n.* agreement, armistice, calm, calmness, cease-fire, composure, conciliation, concord, contentment, harmony, hush, pacification, quiet, relaxation, rest, silence, stillness, tranquillity, treaty, truce.
antonyms disagreement, disturbance, war.

peaceable *adj.* amicable, compatible, conciliatory, easy-going, friendly, gentle, inoffensive, mild, pacific, peaceful, peace-loving, placid, unwarlike.
antonyms aggressive, belligerent, offensive.

peaceful *adj.* amicable, at peace, calm, friendly, gentle, halcyon, harmonious, non-violent, pacific, peaceable, peace-loving, placid, quiet, restful, serene, still, tranquil, unruffled, untroubled.
antonyms disturbed, noisy, troubled, violent.

peacemaker *n.* appeaser, arbitrator, conciliator, interceder, intercessor, mediator, pacifier, peacemonger.

peak *n.* climax, crest, crown, culmination, high point, maximum, pinnacle, point, summit, tip, top, zenith.
antonyms nadir, trough.
v. climax, come to a head, culminate, tower.

peal *n.* blast, chime, clamour, clang, clap, clash, crash, resounding, reverberation, ring, ringing, roar, rumble, sound.
v. chime, clash, crack, crash, resonate, resound, reverberate, ring, roar, roll, rumble, sound, toll, vibrate.

peasant *n.* boor, bumpkin, countryman, lout, oaf, provincial, rustic, yokel.

pebble *n.* chip, stone.

peck *n.* bite, food, jab, strike.
v. eat, jab, nibble.

peculiar *adj.* **1** abnormal, bizarre, curious, eccentric, exceptional, extraordinary, funny, odd, offbeat, outlandish, strange, uncommon, unconventional, unusual, way-out, weird. **2** appropriate, characteristic, distinctive, individual, local, particular, personal, private, special, specific, unique.
antonyms **1** normal, ordinary. **2** general,

uncharacteristic.

peculiarity *n.* abnormality, attribute, bizarreness, characteristic, distinctiveness, eccentricity, exception, feature, idiosyncrasy, mannerism, mark, oddity, particularity, quality, quirk, trait.

pedant *n.* hair-splitter, literalist, nit-picker, quibbler.

pedantic *adj.* academic, bookish, erudite, finical, fussy, hair-splitting, nit-picking, particular, perfectionist, precise, punctilious, stilted.
antonyms casual, imprecise, informal.

peddle *v.* flog, hawk, market, push, retail, sell, tout, trade, vend.

pedestal *n.* base, foot, foundation, mounting, pier, platform, plinth, podium, stand, support, understructure.

pedestrian *n.* foot-traveller, walker.
adj. banal, boring, commonplace, dull, flat, indifferent, mediocre, mundane, ordinary, plodding, run-of-the-mill, stodgy, uninspired.
antonyms brilliant, exciting, fascinating, imaginative.

pedigree *n.* ancestry, blood, breed, derivation, descent, dynasty, extraction, family, family tree, genealogy, line, lineage, parentage, race, stock, succession.

pedlar *n.* colporteur, gutter-man, hawker, seller, street-trader, vendor, walker.

peek *v.* glance, look, peep, peer, spy.
n. blink, glance, glimpse, look, peep.

peel *v.* flake (off), pare, scale, skin, strip (off).
n. peeling, rind, skin, zest.

peep *v.* blink, emerge, glimpse, issue, peek, peer.
n. blink, glimpse, look, peek.

peephole *n.* aperture, chink, cleft, crack, crevice, fissure, hole, keyhole, opening, pinhole, slit, spy-hole.

peer¹ *v.* appear, blink, emerge, examine, gaze, inspect, peep, scan, scrutinise, snoop, spy, squint.

peer² *n.* **1** aristocrat, baron, count, duke, earl, lord, marquess, marquis, noble, nobleman, viscount. **2** counterpart, equal, equivalent, fellow, like, match.

peerage *n.* aristocracy, lords and ladies, nobility, upper crust.

peeress *n.* baroness, countess, dame, duchess, lady, marchioness, noblewoman, viscountess.

peevish *adj.* acrimonious, cantankerous, childish, churlish, crabbed, cross, crotchety, crusty, fractious, grumpy, ill-tempered, irritable, perverse, petulant, querulous, ratty, short-tempered, snappy, sulky, sullen, surly, testy, touchy.
antonym good-tempered.

peg *v.* **1** attach, fasten, insert, join, secure, set. **2** control, fix, freeze, limit, mark, stabilise.
n. dowel, hook, knob, marker, pin, post, stake, toggle.
peg away apply oneself, beaver away, keep at it, persevere, persist, plod along, plug away, stick at it, work away.

pejorative *adj.* bad, belittling, damning, derogatory, disparaging, negative, slighting, uncomplimentary, unflattering, unpleasant.
antonym complimentary.

pelt¹ *v.* **1** assail, batter, beat, bombard, hit, strike, thrash, throw. **2** pour, rain cats and dogs, shower, teem. **3** belt, career, charge, dash, hurry, rush, speed, tear.

pelt² *n.* coat, fleece, fur, hide, skin.

pen¹ *v.* author, compose, draft, jot down, scribble, write.
pen name alias, nom de plume, pseudonym.

pen² *n.* cage, coop, crib, enclosure, fold, hutch, stall, sty.
v. cage, confine, coop, enclose, fence, hedge, hem in, hurdle, shut up.

penalise *v.* correct, discipline, handicap, punish.
antonym reward.

penalty *n.* fine, forfeit, handicap, price, punishment, retribution.
antonym reward.

penance *n.* atonement, mortification, penalty, punishment, sackcloth and ashes.

pendant *n.* locket, medallion, necklace.

pendent *adj.* dangling, drooping, hanging, pendulous, suspended, swinging.

pending *adj.* awaiting, forthcoming, hanging, imminent, impending, in the balance, in the offing, undecided.
antonyms definite, finished, settled.

penetrate *v.* affect, bore, enter, get through to, get to the bottom of, grasp, impress, infiltrate, permeate, pervade, pierce, prick, probe, seep, sink, strike, suffuse.

penetrating *adj.* acute, biting, critical, discerning, discriminating, harsh, incisive, intelligent, keen, observant, perceptive, piercing, profound, quick, searching, sharp, shrewd, shrill, stinging, strong.
antonyms blunt, gentle, soft.

peninsula *n.* cape, point.

penitence *n.* contrition, regret, remorse, repentance, self-reproach, shame, sorrow.

penitent *adj.* apologetic, atoning, conscience-stricken, contrite, humble, in sackcloth and ashes, regretful, remorseful, repentant, sorrowful, sorry.
antonyms callous, hard-hearted, unrepentant.

penniless *adj.* bankrupt, broke, bust, destitute, flat broke, impoverished, moneyless, needy, poor, poverty-stricken, ruined.
antonyms affluent, rich, wealthy.

pension *n.* allowance, annuity, benefit, maintenance, stipend, superannuation.

pensive *adj.* absent-minded, absorbed, contemplative, meditative, melancholy, preoccupied, reflective, serious, sober, solemn, thoughtful, wistful.
antonyms carefree, light-hearted.

pent-up *adj.* bottled-up, inhibited, repressed, restrained, stifled, suppressed.

people *n.* citizens, community, crowd, family, folk, general public, human beings, humanity, humans, inhabitants, mankind, multitude, nation, populace, population, public, race, rank

and file.
v. colonise, inhabit, occupy, populate, settle.

pep *n.* energy, exuberance, get-up-and-go, gusto, high spirits, life, liveliness, spirit, verve, vigour, vitality.
pep up excite, exhilarate, inspire, invigorate, jazz up, liven up, quicken, stimulate, vitalise, vivify.
antonym tone down.

peppery *adj.* **1** hot, piquant, pungent, sharp, spicy. **2** gruff, grumpy, hot-tempered, irritable, quick-tempered, testy.

perceive *v.* appreciate, apprehend, be aware of, catch sight of, conclude, deduce, discern, discover, distinguish, feel, gather, get, grasp, know, learn, make out, note, observe, realise, recognise, remark, see, sense, spot, understand, view.

perceptible *adj.* apparent, clear, conspicuous, detectable, discernible, distinguishable, evident, noticeable, observable, obvious, perceivable, visible.
antonyms imperceptible, inconspicuous.

perception *n.* apprehension, awareness, conception, consciousness, discernment, feeling, grasp, idea, impression, insight, observation, recognition, sense, taste, understanding.

perceptive *adj.* alert, astute, aware, discerning, observant, quick, responsive, sensitive, sharp.
antonym unobservant.

perch *v.* alight, balance, drop, land, rest, roost, settle, sit on.

percolate *v.* drain, drip, filter, leak, ooze, penetrate, permeate, pervade, seep, strain.

peremptory *adj.* abrupt, absolute, arbitrary, assertive, authoritative, autocratic, binding, bossy, categorical, commanding, compelling, curt, decisive, dictatorial, dogmatic, domineering, high-handed, imperious, incontrovertible, irrefutable, obligatory, overbearing, summary, undeniable.

perennial *adj.* constant, continual, continuing, enduring, eternal, everlasting, immortal, imperishable, incessant, lasting, lifelong, never-ending, permanent, perpetual, persistent, unceasing, unchanging, undying, unfailing, uninterrupted.

perfect *adj.* **1** blameless, excellent, faultless, flawless, immaculate, impeccable, pure, splendid, spotless, superb. **2** accurate, correct, exact, precise, right, true. **3** accomplished, complete, experienced, expert, ideal, model, skilful, ultimate. **4** absolute, complete, entire, sheer, utter.
antonyms **1** awful, blemished, flawed, imperfect. **2** inaccurate, wrong. **3** inexperienced, unskilled.
v. complete, elaborate, fulfil, polish, refine.
antonyms mar, spoil.

perfection *n.* acme, consummation, crown, exactness, excellence, flawlessness, ideal, paragon, pinnacle, superiority, wholeness.
antonyms flaw, imperfection.

perfectionist *n.* formalist, idealist, purist, stickler.

perfectly *adv.* absolutely, completely, correctly, entirely, faultlessly, flawlessly, fully, ideally, impeccably, quite, supremely, thoroughly, totally, utterly, wholly, wonderfully.
antonyms badly, imperfectly, partially.

perforate *v.* bore, drill, hole, penetrate, pierce, prick, punch, puncture, stab.

perforation *n.* bore, cut, dotted line, hole, prick, puncture, slit, space.

perform *v.* **1** accomplish, achieve, bring about, bring off, carry out, complete, discharge, do, execute, fulfil, function, manage, observe, produce, pull off, satisfy, transact, work. **2** act, appear as, enact, play, present, put on, render, represent, stage.

performance *n.* **1** act, acting, appearance, gig, interpretation, play, portrayal, presentation, production, rendition, representation, show. **2** accomplishment, achievement, action, carrying out, completion, discharge, execution, feat, fulfilment, functioning, implementation, operation. **3** bother, carry-on, fuss, rigmarole, to-do.

performer *n.* actor, actress, artiste, player.

perfume *n.* aroma, attar, balm, bouquet, cologne, essence, fragrance, incense, odour, scent, smell, sweetness, toilet water.

perhaps *adv.* conceivably, feasibly, maybe, possibly.

peril *n.* danger, hazard, imperilment, insecurity, jeopardy, menace, risk, threat, uncertainty.
antonyms safety, security.

perilous *adj.* chancy, dangerous, difficult, dire, exposed, hazardous, menacing, precarious, risky, threatening, unsafe, unsure, vulnerable.
antonyms safe, secure.

perimeter *n.* border, boundary, bounds, circumference, confines, edge, fringe, frontier, limit, margin.
antonyms centre, heart, middle.

period *n.* age, course, cycle, date, end, epoch, era, generation, interval, season, session, space, span, spell, stage, stop, stretch, term, time, turn, years.

periodic *adj.* infrequent, intermittent, occasional, periodical, recurrent, regular, repeated, seasonal, sporadic.

periodical *n.* journal, magazine, monthly, paper, publication, quarterly, review, serial, weekly.

peripatetic *adj.* itinerant, journeying, migrant, mobile, roaming, roving, travelling, wandering.
antonym fixed.

peripheral *adj.* **1** borderline, incidental, irrelevant, marginal, minor, secondary, superficial, surface, unimportant, unnecessary. **2** outer, outermost, outlying, outside.
antonyms **1** crucial, major. **2** central.

perish *v.* collapse, crumble, decay, decompose, decrease, die, disappear, disintegrate, end, expire, fall, pass away, rot, vanish, wither.

perishable *adj.* biodegradable, decomposable, destructible, fast-decaying, short-lived.
antonyms durable, imperishable.

perk *n.* benefit, bonus, dividend, extra, fringe benefit, gratuity, perquisite, plus, tip.
perk up brighten, buck up, cheer up, improve, liven up, look up, pep up, rally, recover, revive,

take heart.

perky *adj.* animated, bouncy, bright, buoyant, cheerful, cheery, jaunty, lively, spirited.
antonyms cheerless, dull, gloomy.

permanence *n.* constancy, continuity, durability, endurance, fixedness, imperishability, lastingness, perpetuity, stability.
antonyms impermanence, transience.

permanent *adj.* constant, enduring, fixed, imperishable, indestructible, lasting, long-lasting, perennial, perpetual, persistent, stable, standing, steadfast, unchanging, unfading.
antonyms ephemeral, fleeting, temporary.

permeable *adj.* absorbent, absorptive, penetrable, porous, spongy.
antonyms impermeable, watertight.

permeate *v.* dominate, fill, filter through, imbue, impregnate, infiltrate, pass through, penetrate, pervade, saturate, seep through, soak through.

permissible *adj.* acceptable, admissible, all right, allowable, allowed, authorised, lawful, legit, legitimate, permitted, proper, sanctioned.
antonyms banned, forbidden, prohibited.

permission *n.* allowance, approval, assent, authorisation, consent, dispensation, freedom, go-ahead, green light, leave, liberty, licence, permit, sanction.
antonym prohibition.

permissive *adj.* easy-going, forbearing, free, indulgent, lax, lenient, liberal, open-minded, overindulgent, tolerant.
antonyms rigid, strict.

permit *v.* admit, agree, allow, authorise, consent, give leave, grant, let, warrant.
antonyms forbid, prohibit.
n. authorisation, liberty, licence, pass, passport, permission, sanction, visa, warrant.
antonym prohibition.

pernickety *adj.* carping, fastidious, finicky, fussy, hair-splitting, nit-picking, over-precise, painstaking, particular, tricky.

perpendicular *adj.* sheer, straight, upright, vertical.
antonym horizontal.

perpetrate *v.* carry out, commit, do, execute, inflict, perform, practise, wreak.

perpetual *adj.* abiding, ceaseless, constant, continual, continuous, endless, enduring, eternal, everlasting, immortal, incessant, infinite, interminable, lasting, never-ending, perennial, permanent, persistent, recurrent, repeated, unceasing, unchanging, unending, unflagging, uninterrupted.
antonyms ephemeral, intermittent, temporary, transient.

perpetuate *v.* commemorate, continue, immortalise, keep alive, keep up, maintain, preserve.

perplex *v.* baffle, bewilder, confound, confuse, dumbfound, muddle, mystify, puzzle, stump.

perplexity *n.* bewilderment, confusion, difficulty, incomprehension, intricacy, involvement, puzzlement.

perquisite *n.* benefit, bonus, dividend, extra, fringe benefit, gratuity, perk, plus, tip.

persecute *v.* afflict, annoy, bother, crucify, distress, harass, hound, hunt, ill-treat, injure, maltreat, martyr, molest, oppress, pester, pursue, torment, torture, tyrannise, victimise, worry.
antonyms indulge, pamper, spoil.

persecution *n.* abuse, bashing, discrimination, maltreatment, molestation, oppression, punishment, subjugation, suppression, torture, tyranny.

perseverance *n.* constancy, dedication, determination, diligence, doggedness, endurance, indefatigability, persistence, resolution, stamina, steadfastness, tenacity.

persevere *v.* adhere, carry on, continue, endure, hang on, hold on, keep going, persist, plug away, pursue, remain, stand firm, stick at.
antonyms discontinue, give up, stop.

persist *v.* abide, carry on, continue, endure, insist, keep at it, last, linger, persevere, remain, stand fast, stand firm.
antonyms desist, stop.

persistence *n.* constancy, determination, diligence, doggedness, endurance, indefatigableness, perseverance, resolution, stamina, steadfastness, tenacity.

persistent *adj.* constant, continual, continuous, determined, dogged, endless, enduring, immovable, incessant, indefatigable, interminable, never-ending, obstinate, perpetual, persevering, relentless, repeated, resolute, steadfast, steady, stubborn, tenacious, tireless, unflagging, unrelenting, unremitting, zealous.

person *n.* being, body, character, human, human being, individual, soul, type.

personal *adj.* idiosyncratic, individual, intimate, own, particular, private, special.
antonyms general, public, universal.

personality *n.* **1** character, charisma, charm, disposition, individuality, lik(e)ableness, magnetism, make-up, nature, pleasantness, psyche, temperament, traits. **2** celebrity, notable, star.

personify *v.* embody, epitomise, exemplify, express, mirror, represent, symbolise, typify.

personnel *n.* crew, employees, helpers, human resources, manpower, members, people, staff, workers, workforce.

perspective *n.* angle, aspect, attitude, outlook, proportion, prospect, relation, scene, slant, view, vista.

perspiration *n.* moisture, sweat, wetness.

perspire *v.* drip, exude, secrete, sweat, swelter.

persuade *v.* advise, allure, bring round, cajole, coax, convert, convince, counsel, incite, induce, influence, lead on, lean on, prevail upon, prompt, satisfy, sway, talk into, urge, win over.
antonyms deter, discourage, dissuade.

persuasion *n.* **1** conversion, enticement, inducement, influence, power, pull, sweet talk, wheedling. **2** conviction, denomination, faction, opinion, party, school (of thought), sect, side, views.

persuasive *adj.* cogent, compelling, convincing, effective, forceful, influential, moving, potent, sound, telling, touching, valid, weighty.

antonym unconvincing.

pert *adj.* bold, brash, cheeky, flippant, forward, fresh, impertinent, impudent, insolent, presumptuous, saucy.
antonyms coy, restrained, shy.

pertinent *adj.* applicable, apposite, appropriate, apt, fitting, material, relevant, suitable, to the point.
antonyms inappropriate, irrelevant, unsuitable.

perturb *v.* alarm, bother, discompose, disconcert, disturb, fluster, muddle, ruffle, trouble, unsettle, upset, vex, worry.
antonyms compose, reassure.

peruse *v.* browse, check, examine, inspect, look through, pore over, read, scan, scrutinise, study.

pervade *v.* affect, charge, extend, fill, imbue, infuse, penetrate, percolate, permeate, saturate, suffuse.

pervasive *adj.* common, extensive, general, inescapable, permeating, prevalent, universal, widespread.

perverse *adj.* cantankerous, contrary, disobedient, headstrong, ill-tempered, improper, incorrect, obstinate, rebellious, stubborn, troublesome, unmanageable, unreasonable, unyielding, wayward, wilful, wrong-headed.
antonyms co-operative, obliging, reasonable.

perversion *n.* **1** abnormality, corruption, debauchery, depravity, deviance, distortion, immorality, kinkiness, vice, wickedness. **2** aberration, deviation, misapplication, misinterpretation, misrepresentation, misuse, travesty, twisting.

perversity *n.* contrariness, intransigence, waywardness.

pervert *v.* abuse, corrupt, debase, debauch, degrade, deprave, distort, falsify, garble, lead astray, misapply, misinterpret, misrepresent, misuse, twist, warp.
n. debauchee, degenerate, deviant, weirdo.

perverted *adj.* abnormal, corrupt, debased, debauched, depraved, deviant, distorted, evil, immoral, impaired, kinky, twisted, unhealthy, unnatural, warped, wicked.

pessimistic *adj.* bleak, cynical, defeatist, dejected, depressed, despairing, despondent, dismal, downhearted, fatalistic, gloomy, glum, hopeless, melancholy, morose, resigned, sad, worried.
antonym optimistic.

pest *n.* annoyance, bane, blight, bother, bug, curse, irritation, nuisance, scourge, trial, vexation.

pester *v.* annoy, badger, bother, disturb, fret, get at, harass, hassle, hound, irk, nag, pick on, plague, ride, torment, worry.

pet *n.* darling, favourite, idol, jewel, treasure.
adj. cherished, dearest, favoured, favourite, particular, personal, preferred, special.
v. **1** cosset, dote on, indulge, mollycoddle, pamper, spoil. **2** caress, cuddle, fondle, kiss, neck, snog, stroke.

peter out cease, dwindle, ebb, evaporate, fade, fail, stop, taper off, wane.

petite *adj.* dainty, delicate, dinky, little, slight, small.
antonyms big, large, massive.

petition *n.* address, appeal, application, entreaty, invocation, plea, prayer, request, round robin, solicitation, supplication.
v. appeal, ask, beg, beseech, bid, call upon, crave, entreat, implore, plead, pray, press, solicit, supplicate, urge.

pet-name *n.* diminutive, endearment, nickname.

petrify *v.* appal, confound, dumbfound, numb, paralyse, stun, terrify.

pettish *adj.* cross, fretful, grumpy, ill-humoured, irritable, petulant, sulky.

petty *adj.* **1** inconsiderable, insignificant, lesser, little, minor, negligible, paltry, secondary, slight, small, trifling, trivial, unimportant. **2** grudging, mean, small-minded, spiteful, stingy, ungenerous.
antonyms **1** important, significant, vital. **2** generous, large-hearted.

petulant *adj.* bad-tempered, cross, fretful, ill-humoured, irritable, moody, perverse, snappish, sour, sulky, sullen, ungracious.

phantom *n.* apparition, figment (of the imagination), ghost, hallucination, illusion, spectre, spirit, vision.

phase *n.* aspect, chapter, condition, development, period, point, position, season, spell, stage, state, step, time.
phase out close, dispose of, ease off, eliminate, get rid of, remove, replace, run down, taper off, terminate, wind down, withdraw.

phenomenal *adj.* amazing, exceptional, extraordinary, incredible, marvellous, remarkable, sensational, stupendous, uncommon, unusual.

phenomenon *n.* appearance, curiosity, episode, event, fact, happening, incident, marvel, miracle, occurrence, prodigy, rarity, sensation, sight, spectacle, wonder.

philanthropic *adj.* alms-giving, altruistic, benevolent, charitable, humanitarian, kind, public-spirited.
antonym misanthropic.

philanthropist *n.* alms-giver, altruist, benefactor, contributor, donor, giver, humanitarian, patron.
antonym misanthrope.

philanthropy *n.* alms-giving, altruism, benevolence, charity, generosity, humanitarianism, kind-heartedness, liberality, open-handedness, patronage, public-spiritedness, unselfishness.

philosophical *adj.* **1** abstract, analytical, erudite, learned, logical, metaphysical, rational, theoretical, wise. **2** calm, composed, patient, resigned, stoical, thoughtful, unruffled.

philosophy *n.* aesthetics, attitude, beliefs, convictions, doctrine, ideology, knowledge, logic, metaphysics, principle, rationalism, reason, thought, values, viewpoint, wisdom, world-view.

phlegmatic *adj.* impassive, indifferent, matter-of-fact, placid, stoical, stolid, unconcerned, undemonstrative, unemotional.

antonyms demonstrative, emotional, passionate.

phobia *n.* anxiety, aversion, dislike, dread, fear, hang-up, hatred, horror, loathing, neurosis, obsession, repulsion, revulsion, terror, thing.
antonyms liking, love.

phone *n.* handset, line, telephone.
v. buzz, call (up), contact, dial, get in touch, give someone a tinkle, ring (up), telephone.

phoney *adj.* affected, assumed, bogus, counterfeit, fake, false, forged, imitation, pseudo, put-on, sham, spurious, trick.
antonyms real, true.
n. counterfeit, fake, forgery, fraud, humbug, imposter, pretender, pseud, sham.

phosphorescent *adj.* bright, glowing, luminous, radiant.

photograph *n.* image, likeness, photo, picture, print, shot, slide, snap, snapshot, transparency.
v. film, record, shoot, snap, take, video.

photographic *adj.* accurate, detailed, exact, faithful, graphic, lifelike, natural, pictorial, precise, realistic, representational, retentive, visual, vivid.

phrase *n.* construction, expression, idiom, mention, motto, remark, saying, utterance.
v. couch, express, formulate, frame, present, pronounce, put, say, utter, word.

physical *adj.* actual, bodily, concrete, corporeal, earthly, incarnate, material, mortal, natural, real, solid, substantial, tangible, visible.
antonyms mental, spiritual.

physician *n.* doc, doctor, doctor of medicine, general practitioner, GP, healer, houseman, intern, medic, medical practitioner, registrar, specialist.

physique *n.* body, build, constitution, figure, form, frame, make-up, shape, structure.

pick *v.* **1** choose, decide on, opt for, select, settle on, single out. **2** collect, cull, gather, harvest, pluck. **3** break into, break open, crack, prise. **4** incite, instigate, provoke, start.
antonyms **1** reject. **2** leave. **3** close. **4** finish.
n. best, choice, cream, decision, elect, flower, option, preference, prize, selection.
pick at nibble, peck, play with, toy with.
pick off detach, drill, hit, kill, plug, remove, shoot, strike.
pick on bait, bully, get at, nag, needle, quibble with, torment.
pick out choose, distinguish, hand-pick, notice, perceive, recognise, select, separate, single out, spot, tell apart.
pick up **1** hoist, lift, raise. **2** call for, collect, fetch. **3** acquire, catch, gain, gather, grasp, learn, master, obtain. **4** improve, perk up, rally, recover. **5** buy, purchase. **6** arrest, nab, nick, run in. **7** catch, contract, get.

picket *n.* demonstrator, dissenter, patrol, peg, picketer, protester.
v. blockade, boycott, demonstrate, enclose, fence, hedge in, protest.

pickle *n.* crisis, difficulty, dilemma, fix, jam, pinch, predicament, quandary, scrape, spot, straits, tight spot.
v. conserve, cure, marinade, preserve, steep.

pictorial *adj.* diagrammatic, expressive, graphic, illustrated, picturesque, representational, scenic, schematic, striking, vivid.

picture *n.* **1** copy, drawing, effigy, engraving, film, illustration, image, likeness, motion picture, movie, painting, photograph, portrait, print, replica, representation, sketch. **2** account, depiction, description, impression, portrayal, report, scene. **3** archetype, embodiment, epitome, essence, personification.
v. **1** conceive of, envisage, envision, imagine, see, visualise. **2** depict, describe, draw, illustrate, paint, photograph, portray, render, represent, show, sketch.

picturesque *adj.* attractive, beautiful, charming, colourful, descriptive, graphic, pretty, scenic, striking, vivid.
antonyms dull, unattractive.

piece *n.* article, bit, chunk, component, constituent, creation, division, element, example, fraction, fragment, instance, item, morsel, mouthful, offcut, part, piecemeal, portion, quantity, sample, scrap, section, segment, share, shred, slice, snippet, specimen, stroke, study, work.
piece together assemble, attach, compose, fit, fix, join, mend, patch, repair, restore, unite.

pièce de résistance *n.* chef-d'oeuvre, magnum opus, masterpiece, masterwork, prize, showpiece.

piecemeal *adv.* at intervals, bit by bit, by degrees, intermittently, little by little, partially, slowly.
antonyms completely, entirely, wholly.
adj. fragmentary, intermittent, interrupted, partial, patchy, scattered, unsystematic.
antonyms complete, entire, whole, wholesale.

pier *n.* jetty, landing-place, promenade, quay, support, upright, wharf.

pierce *v.* bore, drill, enter, hurt, impale, pain, penetrate, perforate, prick, probe, puncture, run through, spike, stab, stick into, strike, thrust, transfix, wound.

piercing *adj.* **1** ear-splitting, high-pitched, loud, sharp, shrill. **2** penetrating, powerful, probing, searching. **3** biting, bitter, cold, fierce, freezing, frosty, keen, nippy, raw, severe, wintry. **4** excruciating, intense, painful, racking.

piety *n.* devotion, devoutness, faith, godliness, holiness, piousness, religion, reverence, saintliness, sanctity.
antonyms impiety, irreligion.

pig *n.* animal, beast, boor, brute, glutton, gormandiser, go(u)rmand, hog, sow, swine.

pigeonhole *n.* box, category, class, classification, compartment, cubbyhole, cubicle, locker, niche, place, section, slot.
v. alphabetise, catalogue, classify, compartmentalise, file, label, shelve, slot, sort.

pigment *n.* colour, colouring, dye, hue, paint, stain, tincture, tint.

pile[1] *n.* **1** accumulation, assortment, collection, heap, hoard, mass, mound, mountain, packet,

pot, stack, stockpile. **2** fortune, money, wealth. **3** building, edifice, structure.
v. accumulate, assemble, build up, charge, climb, collect, crowd, crush, flock, flood, gather, heap, hoard, jam, load up, mass, pack, rush, stack, store, stream.

pile[2] *n.* bar, beam, column, foundation, pier, post, support, upright.

pile[3] *n.* down, fur, fuzz, hair, nap, plush, shag.

pilfer *v.* filch, help oneself to, knock off, lift, nick, pinch, rob, steal, thieve.

pilgrim *n.* crusader, traveller, wanderer.

pilgrimage *n.* crusade, expedition, journey, mission, tour, trip.

pill *n.* capsule, contraceptive, tablet.

pillar *n.* bastion, column, leader, mainstay, mast, pier, post, prop, rock, shaft, support, supporter, tower of strength, upholder, upright, worthy.

pillory *v.* brand, denounce, mock, pour scorn on, ridicule, show up.

pilot *n.* airman, aviator, captain, conductor, coxswain, director, guide, helmsman, leader, navigator, steersman.
v. boss, conduct, control, direct, drive, fly, guide, handle, lead, manage, navigate, operate, run, steer.
adj. experimental, model, test, trial.

pimple *n.* black-head, boil, spot, swelling.

pin *v.* affix, attach, fasten, fix, hold down, hold fast, immobilise, join, nail, press, restrain, secure, tack.
n. bolt, brooch, clip, fastener, nail, peg, rivet, screw, spike, tack, tie-pin.
pin down 1 determine, home in on, identify, pinpoint, specify. **2** force, immobilise, make, nail down, press, pressurise.

pincers *n.* forceps, tweezers.

pinch *v.* **1** compress, grasp, nip, press, squeeze, tweak. **2** chafe, hurt. **3** nick, pilfer, rob, snatch, steal.
n. **1** nip, squeeze, tweak. **2** bit, dash, jot, mite, soupçon, speck, taste. **3** crisis, difficulty, emergency, hardship, oppression, predicament, pressure.

pinched *adj.* careworn, drawn, gaunt, haggard, narrowed, starved, thin, worn.

pine *v.* ache, crave, desire, grieve, hanker, hunger, long, sigh, thirst, weaken, wish, yearn.

pinnacle *n.* acme, cap, cone, crest, crown, eminence, height, needle, obelisk, peak, pyramid, spire, steeple, summit, top, turret, vertex.

pinpoint *v.* define, distinguish, identify, locate, place, spot, zero in on.

pioneer *n.* colonist, developer, explorer, founder, founding father, frontiersman, innovator, leader, settler, trail-blazer.
v. blaze a trail, create, develop, discover, establish, found, initiate, instigate, institute, invent, launch, lead, open up, originate, prepare, start.

pious *adj.* devout, godly, good, goody-goody, holier-than-thou, holy, hypocritical, moral, religious, reverent, righteous, saintly, sanctimonious, self-righteous, spiritual, virtuous.
antonyms impious, irreligious, irreverent.

pipe *n.* conduit, conveyor, duct, flue, horn, line, main, overflow, passage, pipeline, tube, whistle.
v. **1** carry, channel, conduct, convey, funnel, siphon, supply, transmit. **2** cheep, chirp, peep, play, sing, sound, tootle, trill, tweet, twitter, warble, whistle.

pipeline *n.* channel, conduit, conveyor, duct, line, passage, pipe, tube.

piquant *adj.* biting, interesting, lively, peppery, provocative, pungent, salty, savoury, sharp, sparkling, spicy, spirited, stimulating, stinging, tangy, zesty.
antonyms banal, bland, dull, jejune.

pique *n.* annoyance, displeasure, grudge, huff, irritation, miff, offence, resentment, vexation.

piqued *adj.* angry, annoyed, displeased, excited, incensed, irritated, miffed, offended, peeved, put out, resentful, riled, stirred, vexed.

pirate *n.* buccaneer, filibuster, infringer, marauder, plagiarist, raider, rover, sea-robber.
v. appropriate, borrow, copy, crib, nick, pinch, plagiarise, poach, reproduce, steal.

pirouette *n.* gyration, pivot, spin, turn, twirl, whirl.
v. gyrate, pivot, spin, turn, twirl, whirl.

pit *n.* abyss, cavity, chasm, coal-mine, crater, dent, depression, dimple, excavation, gulf, hole, hollow, indentation, mine, pothole, trench.
pit against match, oppose, set against.

pitch *v.* **1** chuck, fling, heave, hurl, lob, sling, throw, toss. **2** dive, drop, fall headlong, lurch, plunge, roll, tumble, wallow. **3** aim, direct, launch, place. **4** erect, fix, plant, set up, settle, station.
n. **1** ground, playing-field, sports field. **2** harmonic, modulation, sound, timbre, tone. **3** angle, degree, gradient, incline, level, steepness. **4** patter, sales talk.

pitcher *n.* bottle, can, container, crock, jar, jug, urn, vessel.

piteous *adj.* distressing, heart-rending, lamentable, mournful, moving, pathetic, pitiable, pitiful, plaintive, poignant, sad, sorrowful, touching, woeful, wretched.

pitfall *n.* catch, danger, difficulty, drawback, hazard, peril, snag, snare, stumbling-block, trap.

pith *n.* consequence, core, crux, essence, force, gist, heart, importance, kernel, marrow, matter, meat, moment, nub, point, power, quintessence, salient point, significance, strength, substance, value, weight.

pithy *adj.* brief, cogent, compact, concise, expressive, forceful, pointed, short, succinct, telling, terse, trenchant.
antonyms verbose, wordy.

pitiable *adj.* contemptible, distressing, doleful, grievous, lamentable, miserable, mournful, pathetic, piteous, poor, sad, sorry, woeful, wretched.

pitiful *adj.* contemptible, deplorable, despicable, distressing, heart-rending, hopeless, inadequate, insignificant, lamentable, low, mean, miserable, paltry, pathetic, piteous, pitiable, sad, shabby, sorry, vile, worthless, wretched.

pitiless *adj.* brutal, callous, cold-blooded, cold-hearted, cruel, hard-hearted, harsh, implacable, inexorable, inhuman, merciless, relentless, ruthless, uncaring, unfeeling, unsympathetic.
antonyms compassionate, gentle, kind, merciful.

pittance *n.* chicken-feed, crumb, drop (in the ocean), modicum, trifle.

pitted *adj.* blemished, dented, gouged, holey, indented, marked, nicked, notched, potholed, punctuated, riddled, rough, scarred, scratched.

pity *n.* **1** commiseration, compassion, fellow-feeling, forbearance, kindness, mercy, regret, sympathy, tenderness, understanding. **2** bad luck, misfortune, shame.
antonyms **1** anger, cruelty, disdain, scorn.
v. commiserate with, feel for, forgive, grieve for, pardon, sympathise with, weep for.

pivot *n.* axis, axle, centre, focal point, heart, hinge, hub, kingpin, linchpin, swivel.
v. depend, hang, hinge, lie, rely, revolve, rotate, spin, swing, swivel, turn.

placard *n.* advertisement, bill, poster, public notice, sandwich-board, sticker.

placate *v.* appease, assuage, calm, conciliate, lull, pacify, quiet, satisfy, soothe, win over.
antonyms anger, enrage, incense, infuriate.

placatory *adj.* appeasing, conciliatory, peace-making, propitiatory.

place *n.* apartment, area, city, district, dwelling, flat, home, house, locale, locality, location, neighbourhood, point, property, region, residence, room, seat, site, situation, space, spot, town, venue, village.
v. arrange, deposit, fix, lay, locate, plant, position, put, rest, set, settle, situate.
in place of as a replacement for, as a substitute for, as an alternative to, in exchange for, in lieu of, instead of.
out of place in disorder, inappropriate, tactless, topsy-turvy, unbecoming, unfitting, unseemly, unsuitable.
take place come about, come to pass, happen, occur.

placid *adj.* calm, composed, cool, equable, even, even-tempered, gentle, level-headed, mild, peaceful, quiet, restful, self-possessed, serene, still, tranquil, unruffled, untroubled.
antonyms agitated, disturbed, jumpy.

plagiarise *v.* appropriate, borrow, counterfeit, infringe, lift, reproduce, steal, thieve.

plagiarism *n.* borrowing, copying, counterfeiting, infringement, lifting, piracy, reproduction, theft.

plague *n.* **1** contagion, disease, epidemic, infection, pestilence. **2** affliction, aggravation, calamity, curse, nuisance, scourge, torment, trial.
v. afflict, annoy, bedevil, bother, distress, disturb, harass, haunt, hound, molest, pain, pester, tease, torment, torture, trouble, vex.

plain *adj.* **1** basic, modest, ordinary, restrained, simple, unadorned, unelaborate, unpretentious. **2** apparent, clear, evident, obvious, patent, understandable, unmistakable, visible. **3** blunt, candid, direct, forthright, frank, open, outspoken, straightforward, unambiguous. **4** ugly, unattractive, unbeautiful, unlovely, unprepossessing.
antonyms **1** elaborate, fancy, ostentatious, patterned. **2** obscure, unclear. **3** deceitful. **4** attractive, good-looking.
n. flat, grassland, lowland, plateau, prairie, steppe, tableland.

plain-spoken *adj.* blunt, candid, direct, explicit, forthright, frank, honest, open, outspoken, straightforward, truthful.
antonyms devious, equivocal.

plaintive *adj.* dismal, grief-stricken, heart-rending, high-pitched, melancholy, mournful, pitiful, sad, sorrowful, wistful.

plan *n.* blueprint, chart, design, diagram, drawing, idea, illustration, layout, map, method, plot, procedure, programme, project, proposal, proposition, representation, scenario, schedule, scheme, sketch, strategy, suggestion, system.
v. aim, arrange, contemplate, contrive, design, devise, draft, envisage, foresee, formulate, frame, intend, invent, organise, outline, plot, prepare, propose, represent, scheme.

plant *n.* **1** bush, flower, herb, shrub, vegetable, weed. **2** apparatus, equipment, factory, foundry, gear, machinery, mill, shop, works, workshop, yard.
v. bury, establish, fix, found, inlay, insert, inset, lodge, put in the ground, root, scatter, seed, set, settle, sow, transplant.

plaque *n.* badge, brooch, medal, medallion, panel, plate, shield, slab, tablet.

plaster *n.* bandage, dressing, plaster of Paris, sticking-plaster.
v. coat, cover, daub, smear, spread.

plastic *adj.* flexible, impressionable, malleable, manageable, mouldable, pliable, receptive, responsive, soft, supple.
antonyms inflexible, rigid.

plate *n.* **1** course, dish, helping, platter, portion, serving. **2** illustration, lithograph, print.
v. anodise, coat, cover, electroplate, face, galvanise, gild, laminate, nickel, overlay, platinise, silver, tin, veneer, zinc.

platform *n.* **1** dais, podium, rostrum, stage. **2** manifesto, objective(s), party line, policy, principle, programme, stand, tenet(s).

platitude *n.* banality, chestnut, cliché, inanity, truism.

platonic *adj.* ideal, idealistic, intellectual, non-physical, spiritual.

plausible *adj.* believable, convincing, credible, likely, persuasive, possible, probable, reasonable, smooth-talking.
antonyms implausible, improbable, unlikely.

play *v.* **1** amuse oneself, enjoy oneself, have fun, revel, romp, sport. **2** challenge, compete, participate, take on, take part, vie with. **3** bet, chance, gamble, risk, speculate, wager. **4** act, impersonate, perform, portray, represent.

antonym **1** work.
n. **1** amusement, diversion, entertainment, fun, game, hobby, pastime, recreation, sport. **2** comedy, drama, farce, performance, show, tragedy. **3** action, activity, movement. **4** give, latitude, leeway, margin, range, room, scope, space.
play around dally, flirt, fool, mess around, trifle, womanise.
play down gloss over, make light of, make little of, minimise, soft-pedal, underplay, undervalue.
play on capitalise on, exploit, misuse, profit by, take advantage of, trade on, turn to account, utilise.
play up 1 accentuate, emphasise, exaggerate, highlight, spotlight, stress. **2** annoy, bother, hurt, malfunction, misbehave, trouble.
play up to butter up, fawn, flatter, ingratiate oneself, soft-soap, suck up to, toady.

playboy *n.* debauchee, ladies' man, libertine, philanderer, rake, womaniser.

player *n.* actor, actress, artist(e), competitor, contestant, cricketer, entertainer, footballer, 'instrumentalist, musician, participant, performer, sportsman, sportswoman.

playmate *n.* buddy, chum, companion, comrade, friend, neighbour, pal, playfellow.

playwright *n.* dramatist, screen-writer, scriptwriter.

plea *n.* appeal, begging, claim, defence, entreaty, explanation, intercession, invocation, justification, petition, prayer, request, supplication.

plead *v.* appeal, ask, assert, beg, beseech, entreat, implore, maintain, petition, put forward, request.

pleasant *adj.* acceptable, agreeable, amiable, amusing, charming, cheerful, congenial, cool, delightful, enjoyable, fine, friendly, good-humoured, gratifying, likeable, lovely, nice, pleasing, refreshing, satisfying, welcome.
antonyms distasteful, nasty, unfriendly, unpleasant.

please *v.* amuse, captivate, charm, cheer, choose, content, delight, desire, entertain, go for, gratify, humour, indulge, like, opt, prefer, satisfy, suit, think fit, want, will, wish.
antonyms anger, annoy, displease, sadden.

pleased *adj.* contented, delighted, euphoric, glad, gratified, happy, satisfied, thrilled.
antonyms annoyed, displeased.

pleasing *adj.* acceptable, agreeable, attractive, charming, delightful, engaging, enjoyable, entertaining, good, gratifying, nice, satisfying, winning.
antonyms disagreeable, unpleasant.

pleasure *n.* amusement, comfort, command, contentment, delight, enjoyment, gratification, happiness, joy, satisfaction.
antonyms displeasure, pain, sorrow, trouble.

pleat *v.* crease, crimp, flute, fold, gather, plait, pucker, tuck.

plebeian *adj.* base, coarse, common, ignoble, low, lower-class, mean, peasant, proletarian, uncultivated, unrefined, vulgar, working-class.
antonyms aristocratic, noble.
n. common man, commoner, peasant, pleb, proletarian, worker.
antonyms aristocrat, noble.

pledge *n.* assurance, bail, bond, covenant, deposit, guarantee, oath, promise, security, surety, undertaking, vow, warrant, word of honour.
v. bind, contract, engage, guarantee, mortgage, promise, secure, swear, undertake, vouch, vow.

plenary *adj.* absolute, complete, entire, full, general, integral, whole.
antonyms limited, qualified, restricted.

plentiful *adj.* abundant, ample, bountiful, copious, fruitful, generous, lavish, liberal, overflowing, productive, profuse.
antonyms rare, scanty, scarce.

plenty *n.* abundance, enough, fund, heap(s), lots, mass, masses, mine, pile(s), plethora, profusion, quantities, quantity, stack(s), store, sufficiency, volume.
antonyms lack, need, scarcity, want.

pliable *adj.* accommodating, adaptable, bendable, compliant, docile, flexible, lithe, malleable, manageable, persuadable, plastic, pliant, receptive, responsive, supple, susceptible, tractable, yielding.
antonyms headstrong, inflexible, rigid.

pliant *adj.* adaptable, bendable, biddable, compliant, easily led, flexible, impressionable, influenceable, persuadable, plastic, pliable, supple, susceptible, tractable, yielding.
antonyms inflexible, intractable.

plight *n.* case, circumstances, condition, difficulty, dilemma, extremity, predicament, quandary, situation, state, straits, trouble.

plod *v.* drag, drudge, grind, labour, lumber, persevere, plough through, slog, soldier on, stomp, sweat, toil, tramp, tread, trudge.

plodder *n.* drudge, dullard, slogger, toiler.
antonym high-flier.

plot *n.* **1** conspiracy, intrigue, machination(s), scheme, stratagem. **2** narrative, outline, story, story line, subject, theme, thread. **3** allotment, area, green, ground, lot, parcel, patch, tract.
v. **1** conspire, contrive, cook up, design, devise, draft, draw, hatch, lay, manoeuvre, scheme. **2** calculate, chart, locate, map, mark, plan, project.

plotter *n.* conspirator, intriguer, machinator, schemer, strategist.

plough *v.* break, cultivate, dig, furrow, till.

ploy *n.* artifice, contrivance, device, dodge, game, manoeuvre, move, ruse, scheme, strategem, subterfuge, tactic, trick, wile.

pluck *n.* backbone, boldness, bravery, courage, determination, fortitude, grit, mettle, nerve, resolution, spirit.
v. **1** catch, collect, draw, gather, harvest, pick, pull, pull off, snatch, tug. **2** strum, twang.

plucky *adj.* bold, brave, courageous, daring, heroic, intrepid, spirited, unflinching, valiant.
antonyms cowardly, feeble, weak.

plug *n.* **1** bung, cork, spigot, stopper, wad. **2**

advertisement, good word, mention, publicity.
v. **1** block, bung, choke, close, cork, cover, fill, pack, seal, stop (up), stuff. **2** advertise, mention, promote, publicise, push.

plume *n.* crest, feather, pinion, quill, tuft.
plume oneself on boast about, congratulate oneself, exult in, pat oneself on the back, preen oneself, pride oneself.

plummet *v.* crash, descend, dive, drop, fall, hurtle, nose-dive, plunge, tumble.
antonym soar.

plump[1] *adj.* beefy, burly, buxom, chubby, dumpy, fat, fleshy, full, obese, podgy, portly, rotund, round, stout, tubby.
antonyms skinny, thin.

plump[2] *v.* collapse, descend, drop, dump, fall, flop, sink, slump.
plump for back, choose, favour, opt for, select, side with, support.

plunder *v.* devastate, loot, pillage, raid, ransack, ravage, rifle, rob, sack, spoil, steal, strip.
n. booty, ill-gotten gains, loot, pickings, pillage, prey, prize, spoils, swag.

plunge *v.* career, cast, charge, dash, descend, dip, dive, dive-bomb, drop, fall, go down, hurtle, immerse, jump, nose-dive, pitch, plummet, rush, sink, submerge, swoop, tear, throw, tumble.
n. collapse, descent, dive, drop, fall, immersion, jump, submersion, swoop, tumble.

plurality *n.* bulk, diversity, galaxy, majority, mass, most, multiplicity, numerousness, profusion, variety.

ply *n.* fold, layer, leaf, sheet, strand, thickness.

poach *v.* appropriate, infringe, pilfer, plunder, rob, steal, trespass.

pocket *n.* bag, compartment, envelope, hollow, pouch, receptacle, sack.
adj. abridged, compact, concise, little, mini, miniature, portable, potted, small.
v. appropriate, filch, help oneself to, lift, nick, pilfer, pinch, steal, take.

pockmark *n.* blemish, pit, pock, scar.

pod *n.* case, hull, husk, legume, shell.

poem *n.* *acrostic, ballad(e), ditty, elegy, idyll,* jingle, limerick, lyric, ode, rhyme, song, sonnet, verse.

poet *n.* bard, lyricist, minstrel, rhymer, versifier.

poetic *adj.* artistic, flowing, graceful, lyrical, metrical, moving, rhythmical.
antonym prosaic.

poignant *adj.* agonising, distressing, heart-rending, moving, painful, pathetic, penetrating, piercing, piquant, pointed, pungent, sad, stinging, tender, touching, upsetting.

point *n.* **1** aspect, attribute, detail, facet, feature, instance, item, particular. **2** aim, end, goal, intention, motive, object, objective, purpose, reason. **3** burden, core, crux, drift, essence, gist, meaning, pith, subject, thrust. **4** location, place, position, site, spot. **5** instant, juncture, moment, period, stage, time. **6** dot, full stop, mark, speck.
v. aim, denote, designate, direct, draw attention to, hint, indicate, level, show, signal, signify, suggest, train.
point of view angle, approach, attitude, belief, judgement, opinion, outlook, perspective, position, slant, standpoint, view, viewpoint.
point out allude to, bring up, call attention to, identify, indicate, mention, remind, reveal, show, specify.

point-blank *adj.* abrupt, blunt, categorical, direct, explicit, express, forthright, plain, straightforward, unreserved.
adv. bluntly, candidly, directly, explicitly, forthrightly, frankly, openly, plainly, straightforwardly.

pointed *adj.* barbed, biting, cutting, edged, incisive, keen, penetrating, sharp, telling, trenchant.

pointer *n.* advice, caution, guide, hand, hint, indication, indicator, information, needle, recommendation, suggestion, tip, warning.

pointless *adj.* absurd, aimless, fruitless, futile, irrelevant, meaningless, senseless, unproductive, unprofitable, useless, vague, vain, worthless.
antonyms beneficial, meaningful, profitable.

poise *n.* aplomb, assurance, calmness, composure, coolness, dignity, elegance, equanimity, equilibrium, grace, presence, presence of mind.
v. balance, hang, hold, hover, position, support, suspend.

poised *adj.* **1** calm, collected, composed, cool, dignified, expectant, graceful, self-confident, self-possessed, unruffled, waiting. **2** all set, prepared, ready.

poison *n.* bane, blight, cancer, contagion, contamination, corruption, malignancy, toxin, venom, virus.
v. adulterate, contaminate, corrupt, defile, deprave, infect, kill, pervert, pollute, taint, warp.

poisonous *adj.* deadly, evil, fatal, lethal, malicious, mortal, noxious, pernicious, toxic, venomous.

poke *v.* butt, dig, elbow, hit, interfere, intrude, jab, meddle, nudge, peek, prod, pry, punch, push, shove, stab, stick, tamper, thrust.
n. butt, dig, jab, nudge, prod, punch, shove, thrust.

pole[1] *n.* bar, lug, mast, post, rod, shaft, spar, staff, stake, standard, stick.

pole[2] *n.* antipode, extremity, limit, terminus.
poles apart at opposite extremes, incompatible, irreconcilable, like chalk and cheese, like night and day, worlds apart.

polemics *n.* argument, contention, controversy, debate, dispute.

police *n.* constabulary, law.
v. check, control, defend, guard, keep a check on, keep in order, keep the peace, monitor, observe, oversee, patrol, protect, regulate, stand guard over, supervise, watch.

policeman *n.* bobby, constable, copper, officer.

policy *n.* action, code, course, custom, guideline, line, plan, position, practice, procedure, programme, protocol, rule, scheme, stance, stratagem, theory.

polish *v.* **1** brighten, buff, burnish, clean, rub, shine, smooth, wax. **2** brush up, cultivate, enhance, finish, improve, perfect, refine, touch up.
antonyms **1** dull, tarnish.
n. **1** varnish, wax. **2** brightness, brilliance, finish, glaze, gloss, lustre, sheen, smoothness, sparkle, veneer. **3** breeding, class, cultivation, elegance, finesse, grace, poise, refinement, sophistication, style.
antonyms **2** dullness. **3 clumsiness.**
polish off bolt, consume, devour, dispose of, down, eat, eliminate, finish, gobble, put away, rub out, shift, stuff, wolf.

polished *adj.* **1** burnished, finished, glassy, gleaming, glossy, lustrous, shining, slippery, smooth. **2** accomplished, expert, faultless, flawless, impeccable, masterly, outstanding, perfected, professional, skilful, superlative. **3** cultivated, elegant, genteel, graceful, polite, refined, sophisticated, suave, urbane, well-bred.
antonyms **1** tarnished. **2** inexpert. **3** gauche.

polite *adj.* considerate, courteous, cultured, diplomatic, gentlemanly, gracious, ladylike, obliging, refined, respectful, tactful, thoughtful, well-behaved, well-mannered.
antonyms impolite, rude, uncultivated.

politic *adj.* advantageous, advisable, astute, expedient, opportune, sensible, tactful, wise.
antonym impolitic.

politics *n.* affairs of state, civics, diplomacy, government, ideology, political science, power-politics, statesmanship.

poll *n.* ballot, canvass, census, count, figures, plebiscite, returns, sampling, straw-poll, survey, tally, vote, voting.

pollute *v.* adulterate, contaminate, corrupt, debase, debauch, defile, deprave, desecrate, dirty, dishonour, foul, infect, mar, poison, profane, soil, spoil, stain, sully, taint, violate.

pollution *n.* adulteration, contamination, corruption, defilement, desecration, foulness, impurity, infection, profanation, stain, taint, violation, vitiation.
antonyms cleanness, purification, purity.

pomp *n.* ceremonial, ceremoniousness, ceremony, display, flourish, formality, grandeur, magnificence, ostentation, pageantry, parade, ritual, show, solemnity, splendour, state.
antonyms austerity, simplicity.

pompous *adj.* affected, arrogant, bombastic, grandiose, high-flown, imperious, magisterial, ostentatious, overbearing, overblown, pretentious, prosy, ranting, self-important, supercilious, windy.
antonyms modest, simple, unaffected, unassuming.

pool[1] *n.* lake, leisure pool, mere, pond, puddle, stank, swimming bath, swimming pool, tarn, watering-hole.

pool[2] *n.* accumulation, bank, cartel, collective, combine, consortium, funds, group, jackpot, kitty, pot, purse, reserve, ring, stakes, syndicate, team, trust.
v. amalgamate, chip in, combine, contribute, merge, muck in, put together, share.

poor *adj.* **1** badly off, bankrupt, broke, deficient, destitute, distressed, hard up, impoverished, in reduced circumstances, insufficient, lacking, meagre, miserable, needy, poverty-stricken, scanty, skimpy, skint, slight, sparse, stony-broke, straitened. **2** bad, below par, depleted, exhausted, faulty, feeble, fruitless, humble, imperfect, impoverished, inferior, infertile, insignificant, low-grade, mediocre, modest, pathetic, pitiful, plain, rotten, second-rate, shabby, shoddy, sorry, substandard, third-rate, trivial, unsatisfactory, weak, worthless. **3** ill-fated, luckless, miserable, pathetic, pitiable, star-crossed, unfortunate, unhappy, unlucky, wretched.
antonyms **1** affluent, rich, wealthy. **2** impressive, superior. **3** fortunate, lucky.

poorly *adj.* ailing, below par, frail, groggy, ill, indisposed, off colour, out of sorts, rotten, seedy, shaky, sick, under the weather, unhealthy, unwell.
antonyms healthy, robust, well.

pop *v.* **1** bang, burst, crack, explode, go bang, go off, go phut, snap. **2** bulge, protrude. **3** appear, come, insert, push, put. **4** call, go, slip, step, visit.
n. bang, burst, crack, explosion, noise, snap.

popular *adj.* accepted, approved, celebrated, common, conventional, current, famous, fashionable, favoured, favourite, general, household, idolised, in demand, in favour, liked, modish, overpopular, overused, prevailing, prevalent, sought-after, standard, stock, universal, well-liked, widespread.
antonyms despised, exclusive, unpopular, unusual.

popularise *v.* democratise, familiarise, give currency to, propagate, simplify, spread, universalise.
antonym discredit.

popularly *adv.* commonly, conventionally, customarily, generally, ordinarily, regularly, traditionally, universally, usually, widely.

populate *v.* colonise, establish oneself in, inhabit, live in, occupy, overrun, people, put down roots in, settle.

population *n.* citizens, community, folk, inhabitants, natives, occupants, people, residents, society.

populous *n.* crawling, crowded, frequented, overpopulated, packed, populated, swarming, teeming, thickly populated, thronged.
antonyms deserted, unfrequented.

pornographic *adj.* bawdy, blue, coarse, dirty, filthy, gross, indecent, lewd, obscene, off-colour, offensive, risqué.
antonyms innocent, inoffensive.

pornography *n.* dirt, erotica, filth, grossness, indecency, obscenity.

porous *adj.* absorbent, honeycombed, penetrable, permeable, pervious, pitted, sponge-like,

spongy.
antonyms impermeable, impervious.

portable *adj.* compact, convenient, handy, lightweight, manageable, movable, portatile, transportable.
antonyms fixed, immovable.

porter[1] *n.* baggage attendant, baggage man, bearer, caddie, carrier.

porter[2] *n.* caretaker, commissionaire, concierge, door-keeper, doorman, gatekeeper, janitor, porteress, portress.

portion *n.* allocation, allotment, allowance, assignment, bit, cup, division, fraction, fragment, helping, measure, morsel, parcel, part, piece, quantity, quota, ration, section, segment, serving, share, slice.
portion out allocate, allot, apportion, assign, deal, distribute, divide, dole, parcel, share out.

portly *adj.* ample, corpulent, dumpy, fat, full, heavy, large, obese, overweight, plump, rotund, round, stout.
antonyms slight, slim, thin.

portrait *n.* account, caricature, characterisation, depiction, description, icon, image, likeness, miniature, painting, photograph, picture, profile, representation, sketch, thumbnail, vignette.

portray *v.* characterise, depict, describe, draw, encapsulate, evoke, figure, illustrate, impersonate, paint, personate, personify, picture, play, present, render, represent, sketch, suggest.

portrayal *n.* characterisation, depiction, description, evocation, interpretation, performance, picture, presentation, rendering, representation, sketch.

pose *v.* **1** model, position, sit. **2** affect, feign, impersonate, masquerade, pass oneself off, pretend, profess to be, put on an act. **3** present, put forward, set.
n. act, affectation, air, attitude, bearing, façade, front, mark, masquerade, position, posture, pretence, role, sham, stance.

poser *n.* poseur, poseuse, posturer, show-off.

poseur *n.* charlatan, exhibitionist, impostor, masquerader, phoney, poser, poseuse, posturer, pseud, show-off.

posh *adj.* classy, de-luxe, exclusive, fashionable, grand, high-class, la-di-da, lavish, luxurious, luxury, refined, select, smart, stylish, swanky, swell, swish, up-market, upper-class.
antonyms cheap, inferior, vulgar.

position *n.* **1** location, niche, place, point, site, situation. **2** arrangement, disposition, posture. **3** duty, employment, function, job, occupation, office, post, role. **4** grade, level, rank, standing, status. **5** belief, opinion, outlook, point of view, stand, standpoint, view, viewpoint.
v. arrange, deploy, dispose, fix, lay out, locate, place, put, range, set, settle, stand.

positive *adj.* **1** certain, confident, convinced, sure. **2** constructive, helpful, hopeful, optimistic, practical, promising, useful. **3** clear, conclusive, decisive, definite, direct, explicit, express, firm, incontrovertible, indisputable, irrefutable, undeniable, unequivocal, unmistakable. **4** absolute, complete, perfect, sheer, utter.
antonyms **1** uncertain. **2** negative. **3** indecisive, indefinite, vague.

possess *v.* acquire, be endowed with, control, dominate, enjoy, have, hold, obtain, occupy, own, seize, take, take over, take possession of.

possessed *adj.* bewitched, consumed, crazed, cursed, demented, dominated, haunted.

possession *n.* **1** control, custody, enjoyment, hold, occupation, ownership, tenure, title. **2** colony, dependency, dominion, protectorate, province, territory.

possessions *n.* assets, belongings, chattels, effects, estate, goods, goods and chattels, movables, paraphernalia, property, riches, things, wealth.

possessive *adj.* acquisitive, clinging, covetous, dominating, domineering, grasping, jealous, overprotective, selfish.
antonyms generous, sharing, unassertive.

possibility *n.* chance, conceivability, feasibility, hope, likelihood, odds, plausibility, potentiality, practicability, probability, prospect, risk.
antonyms impossibility, impracticability.

possible *adj.* accomplishable, achievable, attainable, available, conceivable, feasible, hopeful, imaginable, likely, on, potential, practicable, probable, promising, realisable, tenable, viable, workable.
antonyms impossible, impracticable, unattainable, unthinkable.

possibly *adv.* at all, by any chance, by any means, hopefully, in any way, maybe, perhaps, very likely.

post[1] *n.* baluster, banister, column, leg, pale, palisade, picket, pillar, pole, shaft, stake, standard, support, upright.
v. advertise, announce, denounce, display, make known, placard, publicise, publish, report, stick up.

post[2] *n.* appointment, assignment, beat, employment, job, office, place, position, situation, station, vacancy.
v. appoint, assign, establish, locate, move, place, position, put, second, send, shift, situate, station, transfer.

post[3] *n.* collection, delivery, dispatch, mail, postal service.
v. acquaint, advise, brief, dispatch, fill in on, inform, keep posted, mail, notify, report to, send, transmit.

poster *n.* advertisement, announcement, bill, handbill, notice, placard, sign, sticker.

postmortem *n.* analysis, autopsy, dissection, examination, review.

postpone *v.* adjourn, defer, delay, freeze, hold over, pigeonhole, put back, put off, put on ice, shelve, suspend.
antonyms advance, forward.

postponement *n.* adjournment, deferment, deferral, delay, freeze, moratorium, put-off, stay, suspension.

postscript *n.* addendum, addition, afterthought, afterword, appendix, codicil, epilogue, supple-

ment.
antonyms introduction, prologue.
posture *n.* attitude, bearing, carriage, disposition, pose, position, stance.
v. affect, pose, put on airs, show off, strut.
posy *n.* bouquet, buttonhole, spray.
pot *n.* basin, beaker, bowl, coffee-pot, crock, crucible, cruse, flask, jar, pan, receptacle, teapot, test, urn, vase, vessel.
pot-bellied *adj.* bloated, corpulent, fat, obese, overweight, paunchy, portly, tubby.
potency *n.* authority, capacity, effectiveness, energy, force, influence, kick, might, muscle, persuasiveness, potential, power, punch, strength, sway, vigour.
antonyms impotence, weakness.
potent *adj.* authoritative, cogent, commanding, compelling, convincing, dominant, dynamic, effective, forceful, impressive, influential, mighty, moving, persuasive, powerful, pungent, strong, telling, vigorous.
antonyms impotent, weak.
potential *adj.* budding, concealed, dormant, embryonic, future, hidden, imaginable, in embryo, latent, likely, probable, promising, prospective, undeveloped, unrealised.
n. ability, aptitude, capability, capacity, flair, possibility, power, talent.
potion *n.* beverage, brew, concoction, cup, dose, draught, drink, medicine, mixture, tonic.
pot-pourri *n.* collection, combination, hotchpotch, jumble, medley, miscellany, mixture, motley, patchwork.
pottery *n.* ceramics, china, crockery, delf, earthenware, porcelain, stoneware, terra cotta, ware.
potty *adj.* barmy, crazy, daft, dotty, eccentric, foolish, nutty, silly, soft, touched.
pounce *v.* ambush, attack, dive on, drop, fall upon, grab, jump, leap at, snatch, spring, strike, swoop.
pound[1] *v.* **1** bang, bash, batter, beat, bruise, clobber, drum, hammer, pelt, smash, strike, thump. **2** crush, pulverise. **3** palpitate, pulsate, throb, thud. **4** march, stomp, tramp.
pound[2] *n.* compound, corral, enclosure, fold, pen, yard.
pour *v.* **1** decant, serve. **2** cascade, crowd, flow, gush, run, rush, spill, spout, stream, swarm, throng, tumble. **3** bucket, rain, teem.
pour out decant, discharge, emit, issue, serve, spew forth.
pout *v.* glower, grimace, mope, pull a face, scowl, sulk.
antonyms grin, smile.
n. glower, grimace, long face, scowl.
antonyms grin, smile.
poverty *n.* aridity, barrenness, dearth, deficiency, depletion, destitution, distress, exhaustion, hardship, impoverishment, inadequacy, insolvency, insufficiency, lack, meagreness, necessity, need, paucity, pennilessness, penury, poorness, privation, scarcity, shortage, thinness, unfruitfulness, want.
antonyms affluence, fertility, fruitfulness, richness.
poverty-stricken *adj.* bankrupt, broke, destitute, distressed, impoverished, needy, penniless, poor, stony-broke.
antonyms affluent, rich, wealthy.
powdery *adj.* chalky, crumbling, crumbly, dry, dusty, fine, grainy, granular, loose, powder, pulverised, sandy.
power *n.* **1** authority, command, control, dominion, influence, rule, sovereignty. **2** authorisation, prerogative, privilege, right, warrant. **3** energy, force, intensity, potency, strength, vigour. **4** ability, capability, competence, faculty, potential.
antonyms **1** subjection. **3** weakness. **4** inability.
powerful *adj.* **1** authoritative, commanding, compelling, convincing, dominant, effective, energetic, forceful, forcible, impressive, influential, leading, persuasive, potent, prevailing, telling, winning. **2** hefty, muscular, robust, stalwart, strapping, strong, sturdy.
antonyms **1** impotent, ineffective, weak. **2** weak.
powerless *adj.* defenceless, disabled, feeble, frail, helpless, impotent, incapable, incapacitated, ineffective, infirm, paralysed, prostrate, subject, tied, unarmed, vulnerable, weak.
antonyms able, commanding, potent, powerful.
practicable *adj.* achievable, attainable, feasible, negotiable, passable, performable, possible, viable, workable.
antonym impracticable.
practical *adj.* accomplished, active, applied, businesslike, commonsense, down-to-earth, efficient, everyday, experienced, factual, feasible, functional, hard-headed, hard-nosed, matter-of-fact, ordinary, pragmatic, proficient, qualified, realistic, sensible, serviceable, skilled, sound, trained, useful, utilitarian, workable, working.
antonyms impractical, theoretical, unskilled.
practicality *n.* basics, common sense, experience, feasibility, nitty-gritty, nuts and bolts, practicalities, practice, pragmatism, realism, sense, soundness, usefulness, utility.
practice *n.* **1** convention, custom, habit, method, policy, procedure, system, tradition, usage, way. **2** discipline, drill, dry run, dummy run, exercise, rehearsal, repetition, routine, run-through, study, training, work-out. **3** action, application, effect, experience, operation, performance, use.
antonyms **3** principle, theory.
practise *v.* **1** apply, carry out, do, engage in, execute, follow, implement, live up to, observe, perfect, perform, prepare, pursue, put into practice, undertake. **2** drill, exercise, rehearse, repeat, run through, study, train.
practised *adj.* able, accomplished, consummate, experienced, expert, finished, highly-developed, knowledgeable, proficient, qualified, refined, seasoned, skilled, trained, versed, veteran, well-trained.
antonyms inexperienced, inexpert, unpractised.
pragmatic *adj.* businesslike, efficient, factual, hard-headed, practical, realistic, sensible,

unsentimental, utilitarian.
antonyms idealistic, romantic, unrealistic.
pragmatism *n.* hard-headedness, opportunism, practicalism, practicality, realism, utilitarianism.
antonyms idealism, romanticism.
praise *n.* acclaim, accolade, adoration, adulation, applause, approval, cheering, commendation, compliment, congratulation, devotion, eulogy, flattery, glory, homage, honour, ovation, rave, recognition, testimonial, thanksgiving, tribute, worship.
antonyms criticism, revilement.
v. acclaim, acknowledge, admire, adore, applaud, approve, bless, celebrate, cheer, compliment, congratulate, exalt, extol, flatter, give thanks to, glorify, hail, honour, laud, magnify, pay tribute to, promote, rave over, recognise, wax lyrical, worship.
antonyms criticise, revile.
praiseworthy *adj.* admirable, commendable, deserving, estimable, excellent, fine, honourable, reputable, sterling, worthy.
antonyms discreditable, dishonourable, ignoble.
prank *n.* antic, caper, escapade, frolic, joke, lark, practical joke, stunt, trick.
pray *v.* ask, beg, beseech, call on, crave, entreat, implore, invoke, petition, plead, request, solicit, supplicate, urge.
prayer *n.* appeal, collect, communion, devotion, entreaty, invocation, litany, petition, plea, request, supplication.
preach *v.* address, admonish, advocate, evangelise, exhort, harangue, lecture, moralise, sermonise, urge.
precarious *adj.* chancy, dangerous, doubtful, dubious, hazardous, insecure, problematic, risky, shaky, slippery, tricky, uncertain, unpredictable, unreliable, unsafe, unstable, unsure, vulnerable.
antonyms certain, safe, secure.
precaution *n.* anticipation, caution, foresight, forethought, insurance, preparation, protection, providence, provision, prudence, safeguard, security.
precautionary *adj.* cautious, judicious, preliminary, preparatory, preventive, protective, prudent, safety.
precede *v.* come before, come first, front, go before, herald, introduce, lead, take precedence.
antonyms come after, follow, succeed.
precedence *n.* first place, lead, pre-eminence, preference, pride of place, priority, rank, seniority, superiority, supremacy.
precedent *n.* custom, example, instance, model, past instance, pattern, ruling, standard.
precinct *n.* area, bound, boundary, confine, district, division, enclosure, limit, quarter, section, sector, zone.
precious *adj.* adored, affected, beloved, cherished, choice, costly, darling, dear, dearest, expensive, favourite, fine, flowery, idolised, inestimable, loved, priceless, prized, rare, treasured, valuable, valued.
precipitate *v.* accelerate, advance, bring on, cause, expedite, further, hasten, hurry, induce, occasion, quicken, speed, trigger.
adj. abrupt, breakneck, brief, frantic, hasty, headlong, heedless, hot-headed, hurried, impatient, impetuous, impulsive, indiscreet, quick, rapid, rash, reckless, rushing, sudden, swift, unexpected, violent.
antonyms careful, cautious.
precipitous *adj.* **1** high, perpendicular, sheer, steep. **2** hasty, headless, rash, reckless.
antonyms **1** gradual, sloping. **2** careful, cautious.
précis *n.* abridgement, abstract, compendium, condensation, digest, outline, résumé, rundown, sketch, summary, synopsis.
precise *adj.* absolute, accurate, actual, authentic, blow-by-blow, careful, clear-cut, correct, definite, distinct, exact, explicit, express, factual, faithful, fixed, formal, identical, literal, meticulous, minute, nice, particular, punctilious, rigid, scrupulous, specific, strict, succinct, unequivocal, word-for-word.
antonyms ambiguous, careless, imprecise, inexact.
precisely *adv.* absolutely, accurately, correctly, distinctly, exactly, just, just so, literally, minutely, strictly, verbatim, word for word.
precision *n.* accuracy, care, correctness, definiteness, detail, exactness, expressness, faithfulness, meticulousness, neatness, particularity, rigour.
antonyms imprecision, inaccuracy.
precocious *adj.* advanced, ahead, bright, clever, developed, fast, forward, gifted, mature, premature, quick, smart.
antonym backward.
preconceive *v.* anticipate, assume, conceive, envisage, imagine, picture, presume, presuppose, project, visualise.
precondition *n.* essential, must, necessity, need, prerequisite, requirement, stipulation.
precursor *n.* antecedent, forebear, forerunner, harbinger, herald, messenger, pioneer, predecessor, sign, trail-blazer, usher, vanguard, way-maker.
antonyms follower, successor.
predecessor *n.* ancestor, antecedent, forebear, forefather, forerunner, precursor.
antonyms descendant, successor.
predestination *n.* destiny, election, fate, foreordination, lot, necessity, predetermination.
predestine *v.* destine, doom, fate, foreordain, intend, mean, preordain.
predicament *n.* crisis, dilemma, emergency, fix, impasse, mess, pinch, plight, quandary, situation, spot, trouble.
predict *v.* forecast, foresee, foretell, project, prophesy.
predictable *adj.* anticipated, certain, dependable, expected, finite, foregone, foreseeable, foreseen, imaginable, likely, probable, reliable, sure.
antonyms chance, uncertain, unpredictable.
prediction *n.* augury, divination, forecast, for-

tune-telling, prognosis, prophecy, soothsaying.

predispose *v.* affect, bias, dispose, head, incline, induce, influence, lead, lean, make, prejudice, prepare, prompt, sway.

predominance *n.* dominance, dominion, edge, hold, influence, leadership, mastery, numbers, power, preponderance, prevalence, superiority, supremacy, sway, upper hand, weight.
antonyms ineffectiveness, weakness.

predominant *adj.* capital, chief, controlling, dominant, forceful, important, influential, leading, main, paramount, potent, powerful, preponderant, prevalent, primary, prime, principal, prominent, ruling, strong, superior, supreme.
antonyms ineffective, lesser, minor, weak.

pre-eminence *n.* distinction, excellence, fame, incomparability, matchlessness, predominance, prestige, prominence, renown, repute, superiority, supremacy, transcendence.

pre-eminent *adj.* chief, distinguished, excellent, exceptional, foremost, incomparable, inimitable, leading, matchless, outstanding, passing, predominant, prominent, renowned, superior, superlative, supreme, surpassing, transcendent, unequalled, unmatched, unrivalled, unsurpassed.
antonyms inferior, undistinguished, unknown.

preface *n.* foreword, introduction, preamble, preliminaries, prelude, prologue.
antonyms epilogue, postscript.
v. begin, introduce, launch, lead up to, open, precede, prefix, prelude, start.
antonyms append, complete, finish.

prefer *v.* **1** adopt, advocate, back, be partial to, choose, desire, elect, fancy, favour, go for, incline towards, like better, opt for, pick, plump for, recommend, select, single out, support, want, wish, would rather, would sooner. **2** bring, file, lodge, place, present, press.
antonyms **1** discard, reject.

preferable *adj.* advantageous, advisable, better, choice, chosen, desirable, eligible, expedient, favoured, nicer, preferred, stronger, superior, worthier.
antonyms ineligible, inferior, undesirable.

preference *n.* **1** choice, desire, fancy, favourite, first choice, inclination, liking, option, partiality, pick, selection, wish. **2** favouritism, precedence, preferential treatment, special consideration, special treatment.

preferential *adj.* advantageous, better, biased, favourable, favoured, prior, privileged, special, superior.
antonym equal.

pregnancy *n.* child-bearing, conception, family way, fertilisation, gestation.

pregnant *adj.* **1** expecting, in the family way, with child. **2** charged, eloquent, expressive, full, loaded, suggestive, telling.

prehistoric *adj.* ancient, antediluvian, antiquated, archaic, earliest, early, obsolete, old, outmoded, out-of-date, primeval, primitive, primordial.
antonyms contemporary, modern.

prejudice *n.* **1** bias, bigotry, chauvinism, discrimination, injustice, intolerance, narrow-mindedness, partiality, partisanship, racism, sexism, unfairness. **2** damage, detriment, disadvantage, harm, hurt, impairment, injury, loss, ruin.
antonyms **1** fairness, tolerance. **2** advantage, benefit.
v. **1** bias, colour, condition, distort, influence, jaundice, load, predispose, slant, sway, weight. **2** damage, harm, hinder, hurt, impair, injure, mar, ruin, spoil, undermine, wreck.
antonyms **2** advance, benefit, help.

prejudiced *adj.* biased, bigoted, chauvinist, conditioned, discriminatory, distorted, influenced, intolerant, jaundiced, narrow-minded, one-sided, opinionated, partial, partisan, prepossessed, racist, sexist, subjective, unfair, warped, weighted.
antonyms fair, impartial, tolerant.

preliminaries *n.* basics, beginning, first round, formalities, foundations, groundwork, introduction, opening, preface, prelude, preparation, rudiments, start.

preliminary *adj.* earliest, early, embryonic, experimental, exploratory, first, inaugural, initial, introductory, opening, pilot, preparatory, primary, prior, qualifying, test, trial.
antonyms closing, final.

prelude *n.* beginning, commencement, curtain-raiser, foreword, introduction, opener, overture, preamble, precursor, preface, preliminary, preparation, prologue, start, taster.
antonyms epilogue, finale, postscript.

premature *adj.* abortive, early, embryonic, forward, green, half-formed, hasty, ill-considered, ill-timed, immature, impulsive, incomplete, inopportune, rash, raw, undeveloped, unfledged, unripe, untimely.
antonyms late, tardy.

premeditated *adj.* calculated, cold-blooded, conscious, considered, contrived, deliberate, intended, intentional, planned, prearranged, predetermined, preplanned, wilful.
antonyms spontaneous, unpremeditated.

premiere *n.* début, first night, opening night.

premise *n.* argument, assertion, assumption, hypothesis, postulate, presupposition, proposition, statement, stipulation, supposition, thesis.

premises *n.* building, establishment, estate, grounds, office, place, property, site.

premium *n.* bonus, extra, fee, incentive, recompense, reward.

premonition *n.* anxiety, apprehension, fear, feeling, foreboding, hunch, idea, intuition, misgiving, omen, presentiment, sign, suspicion, warning, worry.

preoccupation *n.* concern, distraction, enthusiasm, fixation, hang-up, hobby-horse, oblivion, obliviousness, obsession, raptness, reverie.

preoccupied *adj.* absent-minded, absorbed, abstracted, daydreaming, distracted, engrossed, faraway, heedless, immersed, intent, oblivious, obsessed, rapt, taken up, wrapped up.

preparation *n.* **1** arrangement, basics, foundation, groundwork, measure, plan, precaution, preliminaries, provision, readiness, rudiments, safeguard. **2** assignment, homework, prep, schoolwork, study, task. **3** application, composition, compound, concoction, lotion, medicine, mixture, potion.

preparatory *adj.* basic, elementary, fundamental, initial, introductory, opening, preliminary, primary, rudimentary.

prepare *v.* **1** adapt, adjust, anticipate, arrange, coach, do one's homework, get ready, make ready, train, warm up. **2** assemble, compose, concoct, construct, contrive, develop, devise, draft, draw up, make, produce. **3** equip, fit (out), provide, rig out, supply.

prepare oneself brace oneself, fortify oneself, gird oneself, limber up, ready oneself, steel oneself.

prepared *adj.* arranged, disposed, fit, inclined, planned, ready, set, waiting, well-rehearsed, willing, word-perfect.

antonyms unprepared, unready.

preponderant *adj.* controlling, extensive, foremost, greater, important, larger, overriding, overruling, predominant, prevailing, prevalent, significant, superior.

prepossessing *adj.* appealing, attractive, charming, delightful, fetching, good-looking, inviting, likable, lovable, magnetic, pleasing, striking, taking, winning, winsome.

antonyms unattractive, unprepossessing.

preposterous *adj.* absurd, crazy, extreme, foolish, impossible, inane, incredible, intolerable, ludicrous, monstrous, nonsensical, outrageous, ridiculous, shocking, unbelievable, unreasonable.

antonyms acceptable, reasonable, sensible.

prescribe *v.* appoint, assign, command, decree, define, dictate, direct, fix, impose, lay down, limit, ordain, order, require, rule, set, specify, stipulate.

prescription *n.* **1** direction, formula, instruction. **2** drug, medicine, mixture, preparation, remedy, treatment.

presence *n.* **1** attendance, company, existence, residence. **2** air, appearance, aura, bearing, carriage, demeanour, personality, poise, self-assurance. **3** closeness, nearness, proximity, vicinity.

antonyms **1** absence. **3** remoteness.

presence of mind alertness, calmness, composure, level-headedness, quickness, self-assurance, wits.

antonyms agitation, confusion.

present[1] *adj.* at hand, attending, available, contemporary, current, existent, here, immediate, instant, near, ready, there, to hand.

antonyms absent, out-of-date, past.

present[2] *v.* **1** acquaint with, demonstrate, display, exhibit, introduce, mount, put on, show, stage. **2** award, bestow, confer, donate, entrust, extend, give, grant, hand over, hold out, offer, submit, tender.

present[3] *n.* benefaction, boon, bounty, cadeau, compliment, donation, endowment, favour, gift, grant, gratuity, largess, nuzzer, offering, prezzie, refresher.

presentable *adj.* acceptable, becoming, clean, decent, neat, proper, respectable, satisfactory, suitable, tidy, tolerable.

antonyms shabby, unpresentable, untidy.

presentation *n.* **1** appearance, arrangement, delivery, demonstration, display, exposition, representation. **2** award, conferral, exhibition, investiture, pageant, performance, production, show, staging.

present-day *adj.* contemporary, current, existing, fashionable, living, modern, present, up-to-date.

antonyms future, past.

presenter *n.* anchorman, compère, frontman, host, master of ceremonies, MC.

presently *adv.* before long, by and by, directly, immediately, in a minute, shortly, soon.

preservation *n.* conservation, defence, keeping, maintenance, protection, retention, safekeeping, safety, security, storage, support, upholding, upkeep.

antonyms destruction, ruin.

preserve *v.* care for, conserve, continue, defend, guard, keep, maintain, perpetuate, protect, retain, safeguard, save, secure, shelter, shield, store, sustain, uphold.

antonyms destroy, ruin.

n. **1** confection, conserve, jam, jelly, marmalade. **2** area, domain, field, realm, speciality, sphere. **3** game park, game reserve, reservation, safari park, sanctuary.

preside *v.* administer, chair, conduct, control, direct, govern, head, lead, manage, officiate, run, supervise.

press *v.* **1** compress, crowd, crush, depress, push, squeeze, stuff, swarm, throng. **2** flatten, iron, smooth. **3** clasp, embrace, hug, squeeze. **4** campaign, compel, constrain, demand, force, harass, insist on, petition, plead, urge.

n. **1** bunch, bustle, crowd, crush, flock, herd, horde, mob, multitude, pack, push, swarm, throng. **2** pressure, strain, stress, urgency. **3** columnists, correspondents, Fleet Street, fourth estate, journalists, news media, newsmen, newspapers, papers, pressmen, reporters, the (mass) media, writers.

pressed *adj.* browbeaten, bullied, coerced, constrained, forced, harassed, pressured, pressurised, pushed, rushed, short.

antonyms unhurried, well-off.

pressing *adj.* burning, constraining, crowding, crucial, essential, high-priority, imperative, important, serious, thronging, urgent, vital.

antonyms trivial, unimportant, unnecessary.

pressure *n.* **1** compression, force, heaviness, load, power, press, squeezing, weight. **2** burden, difficulty, obligation, strain, stress, urgency.

pressurise *v.* browbeat, bulldoze, bully, coerce, compel, constrain, drive, force, lean on, oblige, persuade, press, pressure.

prestige *n.* authority, credit, distinction, eminence, esteem, fame, honour, importance, influence, kudos, regard, renown, reputation, standing, stature, status.
antonyms humbleness, unimportance.

prestigious *adj.* celebrated, eminent, esteemed, exalted, great, illustrious, important, imposing, impressive, influential, prominent, renowned, reputable, respected, up-market.
antonyms humble, modest.

presume *v.* assume, bank on, believe, count on, dare, depend on, go so far, infer, make so bold, presuppose, rely on, suppose, surmise, take for granted, take it, think, trust, undertake, venture.

presumption *n.* **1** anticipation, assumption, belief, chance, conjecture, grounds, guess, hypothesis, likelihood, opinion, plausibility, presupposition, probability, reason, supposition, surmise. **2** assurance, audacity, boldness, cheek, forwardness, impudence, insolence, nerve.
antonyms **2** humility, politeness.

presumptuous *adj.* arrogant, audacious, bold, conceited, foolhardy, forward, impertinent, impudent, insolent, over-confident, overfamiliar, pushy.
antonyms humble, modest.

presuppose *v.* accept, assume, consider, imply, postulate, presume, suppose, take for granted.

presupposition *n.* assumption, belief, preconception, premise, presumption, supposition, theory.

pretence *n.* acting, affectation, aim, allegation, appearance, charade, claim, cloak, cover, deceit, deception, display, excuse, fabrication, façade, faking, falsehood, feigning, garb, guise, invention, make-believe, mask, posing, posturing, pretext, profession, ruse, sham, show, simulation, trickery, veil, veneer, wile.
antonyms honesty, openness, reason.

pretend *v.* act, affect, allege, aspire, assume, claim, counterfeit, fake, falsify, feign, go through the motions, imagine, impersonate, make believe, pass oneself off, profess, put on, sham, simulate, suppose.

pretended *adj.* alleged, bogus, counterfeit, fake, false, feigned, fictitious, imaginary, ostensible, phoney, professed, pseudo, purported, sham, so-called, spurious, supposed.
antonyms actual, real, true.

pretender *n.* aspirant, claimant, claimer, pretendant.

pretension *n.* affection, airs, aspiration, claim, conceit, demand, hypocrisy, ostentation, pomposity, pretence, pretentiousness, profession, self-importance, show, showiness, snobbishness, vanity.
antonyms humility, modesty, simplicity, straightforwardness.

pretentious *adj.* affected, ambitious, assuming, conceited, euphemistic, exaggerated, extravagant, flaunting, high-sounding, inflated, magniloquent, mannered, ostentatious, overambitious, overassuming, pompous, showy, snobbish.
antonyms humble, modest, simple, straightforward.

pretext *n.* appearance, cloak, cover, excuse, guise, mask, ploy, pretence, ruse, semblance, show, simulation.

pretty *adj.* attractive, beautiful, bonny, charming, dainty, delicate, elegant, fair, fine, good-looking, graceful, lovely, neat, nice, tasteful, trim.
antonyms plain, tasteless, ugly, unattractive.
adv. fairly, moderately, quite, rather, reasonably, somewhat, tolerably.

prevail *v.* **1** abound, be present, predominate. **2** overcome, overrule, reign, rule, succeed, triumph, win.
antonyms **1** cease. **2** lose.
prevail upon convince, incline, induce, influence, persuade, prompt, sway, talk into, win over.

prevailing *adj.* common, controlling, current, customary, dominant, established, fashionable, general, in style, in vogue, influential, main, mainstream, popular, predominating, principal, set, usual, widespread.
antonyms minor, uncommon.

prevalent *adj.* accepted, common, compelling, current, customary, established, everyday, extensive, frequent, general, popular, powerful, predominant, prevailing, rampant, rife, universal, usual, widespread.
antonyms rare, subordinate, uncommon.

prevent *v.* anticipate, avert, avoid, bar, block, check, counteract, defend against, forestall, frustrate, hamper, head off, hinder, impede, inhibit, intercept, obstruct, restrain, stave off, stop, thwart, ward off.
antonyms allow, cause, encourage, foster, help.

prevention *n.* avoidance, bar, check, deterrence, elimination, forestalling, forethought, frustration, hindrance, impediment, interruption, obstacle, obstruction, precaution, safeguard, thwarting.
antonyms causing, fostering, help.

preventive *adj.* counteractive, deterrent, hindering, impeding, inhibitory, obstructive, precautionary, preventative, protective, shielding.
antonyms causative, fostering.

previous *adj.* earlier, ex-, foregoing, former, one-time, past, preceding, premature, prior, sometime.
antonyms following, later, subsequent.

previously *adv.* before, beforehand, earlier, formerly, once.
antonym later.

prey *n.* booty, dupe, fall guy, game, plunder, quarry, target, victim.
prey on **1** devour, feed on, gnaw at, hunt, live off, seize. **2** burden, distress, haunt, oppress, trouble, weigh down, worry.

price *n.* **1** amount, assessment, bill, charge, cost, estimate, expenditure, expense, fee, figure,

levy, outlay, payment, rate, reward, sum, toll, valuation, value, worth. **2** consequences, penalty, sacrifice.
v. assess, cost, estimate, evaluate, offer, put, rate, value.

priceless *adj.* **1** beyond price, costly, dear, expensive, incomparable, inestimable, irreplaceable, precious, prized, rich, treasured, without price. **2** a scream, amusing, comic, funny, hilarious, killing, ridiculous, riotous, side-splitting.
antonyms **1** cheap, run-of-the-mill.

prick *v.* bite, bore, itch, jab, jag, pain, perforate, pierce, point, prickle, punch, puncture, stab, sting, thorn, tingle, touch, trouble.
n. jag, pang, perforation, pinhole, puncture, spasm, sting, twinge, wound.

prickle *n.* barb, needle, point, spike, spine, spur, thorn, tickle, tingle.
v. itch, jab, nick, nip, prick, smart, sting, tingle.

prickly *adj.* **1** barbed, brambly, jaggy, sharp, thorny. **2** edgy, grumpy, irritable, short-tempered, touchy. **3** difficult, involved, tricky, troublesome.
antonyms **1** smooth. **2** easy-going, relaxed. **3** easy, simple.

pride *n.* **1** arrogance, big-headedness, boast, conceit, egotism, gratification, haughtiness, presumption, pretensiousness, self-importance, smugness, snobbery, superciliousness, vanity. **2** dignity, self-esteem, self-respect. **3** delight, honour, pleasure, satisfaction.
antonyms **1** humility, modesty. **2** shame.
pride (oneself on) boast, brag, congratulate oneself, exult, flatter oneself, glory, pat oneself on the back, revel, take pride, vaunt.
antonym humble.

priestly *adj.* canonical, clerical, ecclesiastical, pastoral, priestlike.

prig *n.* goody-goody, old maid, prude, puritan.

priggish *adj.* goody-goody, holier-than-thou, narrow-minded, pedantic, prim, prudish, puritanical, self-righteous, smug.
antonyms broad-minded, informal.

prim *adj.* demure, fastidious, formal, fussy, old-maidish, particular, precise, priggish, prissy, proper, prudish, strait-laced.
antonyms broad-minded, easy-going, relaxed.

primarily *adv.* at first, basically, chiefly, especially, essentially, fundamentally, mainly, mostly, originally, principally.
antonym secondarily.

primary *adj.* basic, beginning, best, capital, cardinal, chief, dominant, earliest, elementary, essential, first, first-made, fundamental, greatest, highest, initial, introductory, leading, main, original, paramount, primitive, principal, radical, rudimentary, simple, ultimate, underlying.
antonyms minor, secondary, subsidiary.

prime *adj.* basic, best, chief, choice, earliest, excellent, first-class, first-rate, fundamental, highest, leading, main, original, predominant, pre-eminent, primary, principal, quality, ruling, select, selected, senior, superior, top, underlying.
antonyms minor, secondary, second-rate.
n. beginning, flowering, height, heyday, maturity, morning, opening, peak, perfection, springtime, start.

primer *n.* introduction, manual, text-book.

primeval *adj.* ancient, earliest, early, first, old, original, prehistoric, primitive, primordial.
antonyms developed, later, modern.

primitive *adj.* **1** barbarian, crude, rough, savage, uncivilised, undeveloped, unsophisticated. **2** earliest, early, elementary, first, original, primary, rudimentary.
antonyms **1** advanced, civilised, developed, sophisticated.

princely *adj.* **1** imperial, majestic, noble, regal, royal, sovereign, stately. **2** grand, handsome, lavish, liberal, magnificent.

principal *adj.* cardinal, chief, dominant, essential, first, foremost, highest, key, leading, main, paramount, pre-eminent, primary, prime, strongest.
antonyms least, lesser, minor, subsidiary.
n. **1** boss, chief, dean, director, head, head teacher, headmaster, headmistress, lead, leader, master, superintendent. **2** assets, capital, capital funds, money.

principally *adv.* above all, chiefly, especially, mainly, mostly, particularly, predominantly, primarily.

principled *adj.* clear, clear-cut, conscientious, correct, decent, ethical, high-minded, honourable, just, logical, moral, rational, righteous, right-minded, scrupulous, sensible, upright, virtuous.
antonym unprincipled.

print *v.* engrave, impress, imprint, issue, mark, produce, publish, reproduce, run off, stamp, write.
n. **1** characters, lettering, letters, type, typeface. **2** copy, engraving, fingerprint, impression, photo, photograph, picture, reproduction. **3** book, magazine, newspaper, newsprint, periodical, publication, typescript.

prior *adj.* earlier, foregoing, former, preceding, previous.
antonym later.
prior to before, earlier than, preceding, preparatory to, previous to.
antonym after.

priority *n.* precedence, pre-eminence, rank, right of way, seniority, superiority, supremacy, the lead.
antonyms inferiority, subordinateness.

prise *v.* force (out), lever, open.

prison *n.* borstal, cage, cell, clink, confinement, cooler, dungeon, gaol, imprisonment, jail, lock-up, penal institution, penitentiary, prison-house.

prisoner *n.* convict, detainee, hostage, inmate, internee, jail-bird.

privacy *n.* concealment, confidentiality, isolation, quietness, retirement, seclusion, secrecy,

solitude.
antonym publicness.
private *adj.* concealed, confidential, exclusive, hush-hush, in camera, independent, individual, inside, intimate, inward, isolated, off the record, own, particular, personal, reserved, retired, secluded, secret, separate, solitary, unofficial, withdrawn.
antonyms disclosed, open, public, revealed.
in private behind closed doors, in camera, in confidence, in secret, privately, secretly.
antonym openly.
privatise *v.* denationalise.
antonym nationalise.
privilege *n.* advantage, benefit, concession, due, entitlement, franchise, freedom, immunity, liberty, licence, prerogative, right, sanction, title.
antonym disadvantage.
privileged *adj.* advantaged, élite, exempt(ed), favoured, honoured, powerful, ruling, sanctioned, special.
antonyms disadvantaged, under-privileged.
prize[1] *n.* accolade, aim, ambition, award, conquest, desire, gain, goal, honour, hope, jackpot, premium, purse, reward, stake(s), trophy, windfall, winnings.
adj. award-winning, best, champion, excellent, first-rate, outstanding, top, top-notch, winning.
antonym second-rate.
v. appreciate, cherish, esteem, hold dear, revere, set store by, treasure, value.
antonyms despise, undervalue.
prize[2] *see* **prise**.
prize-winner *n.* champion, cup-winner, medallist, winner.
probability *n.* assumption, chance, chances, expectation, likelihood, odds, prospect.
antonym improbability.
probable *adj.* apparent, feasible, likely, odds-on, on the cards, plausible, possible, reasonable, seeming.
antonyms improbable, unlikely.
probably *adv.* as likely as not, doubtless, in all likelihood, in all probability, most likely, perhaps, possibly, presumably.
antonym improbably.
probation *n.* apprenticeship, examination, proof, test, testing, trial, trial period.
probe *v.* examine, explore, go into, investigate, look into, pierce, poke, prod, query, scrutinise, search, sift, sound, test, verify.
n. bore, detection, drill, enquiry, examination, exploration, inquest, investigation, research, scrutiny, study, test.
problem *n.* brain-teaser, complication, conundrum, difficulty, dilemma, disagreement, dispute, enigma, predicament, puzzle, quandary, question, riddle, trouble.
adj. delinquent, difficult, uncontrollable, unmanageable, unruly.
antonyms manageable, well-behaved.
problematic *adj.* debatable, enigmatic, problematical, puzzling, questionable, tricky, uncertain, unsure.
antonyms certain, straightforward.
procedure *n.* action, conduct, course, custom, form, formula, method, move, operation, performance, plan of action, policy, practice, process, routine, scheme, step, strategy, system, transaction.
proceed *v.* advance, arise, carry on, come, continue, derive, ensue, flow, follow, go ahead, issue, move on, originate, press on, progress, result, set in motion, spring, start, stem.
antonyms retreat, stop.
proceedings *n.* account, action, affairs, annals, archives, business, course of action, dealings, deeds, doings, event(s), matters, measures, minutes, moves, records, report, steps, transactions, undertaking.
proceeds *n.* earnings, gain, income, produce, products, profit, receipts, returns, revenue, takings, yield.
antonyms expenditure, losses, outlay.
process *n.* action, advance, case, course, course of action, development, evolution, formation, growth, manner, means, measure, method, mode, movement, operation, performance, practice, procedure, proceeding, progress, progression, stage, step, system, transaction, trial, unfolding.
v. alter, deal with, dispose of, fulfil, handle, prepare, refine, transform, treat.
procession *n.* cavalcade, column, cortege, course, file, march, motorcade, parade, run, sequence, series, succession, train.
proclaim *v.* advertise, affirm, announce, blaze, circulate, declare, give out, indicate, make known, profess, publish, show, testify.
proclamation *n.* announcement, declaration, decree, edict, indiction, manifesto, notice, notification, proclaim, promulgation, pronouncement, publication.
procrastinate *v.* dally, defer, delay, dilly-dally, drag one's feet, gain time, play for time, postpone, prolong, protract, put off, retard, stall, temporise.
antonyms advance, proceed.
procure *v.* acquire, appropriate, come by, earn, find, gain, induce, lay hands on, obtain, pick up, purchase, secure, win.
antonym lose.
prodigy *n.* abnormality, child genius, curiosity, freak, genius, marvel, miracle, phenomenon, rarity, sensation, spectacle, talent, whiz kid, wizard, wonder, wonder child.
produce *v.* advance, afford, bear, beget, breed, bring about, bring forth, cause, compose, construct, create, deliver, demonstrate, develop, direct, effect, exhibit, fabricate, furnish, generate, give, give rise to, invent, make, manufacture, mount, occasion, offer, originate, present, provoke, put forward, put on, render, result in, show, stage, supply, throw, yield.
antonyms consume, result from.
n. crop, harvest, product, yield.
product *n.* artefact, commodity, concoction,

consequence, creation, fruit, goods, invention, issue, legacy, merchandise, offshoot, offspring, outcome, output, produce, production, result, returns, spin-off, upshot, work, yield.
antonym cause.

production *n.* assembly, construction, creation, direction, fabrication, facture, formation, making, management, manufacture, origination, preparation, presentation, producing, staging.
antonym consumption.

productive *adj.* constructive, creative, effective, energetic, fertile, fruitful, inventive, plentiful, producing, profitable, rewarding, rich, teeming, useful, valuable, vigorous, worthwhile.
antonyms fruitless, unfruitful, unproductive, useless.

productivity *n.* abundance, output, productiveness, work-rate, yield.

profane *adj.* abusive, blasphemous, coarse, crude, disrespectful, filthy, forbidden, foul, godless, heathen, idolatrous, impious, irreligious, irreverent, obscene, pagan, sacrilegious, secular, sinful, temporal, unclean, unconsecrated, ungodly, unhallowed, unholy, unsanctified, wicked.
antonyms religious, respectful, sacred.
v. abuse, contaminate, debase, defile, desecrate, misuse, pervert, pollute, prostitute, violate.
antonyms honour, revere.

profanity *n.* abuse, blasphemy, curse, expletive, four-letter word, irreverence, obscenity, sacrilege, swear-word.
antonyms politeness, reverence.

profess *v.* acknowledge, admit, affirm, allege, announce, assert, certify, claim, confess, confirm, declare, maintain, make out, own, pretend, proclaim, propose, state.

professed *adj.* acknowledged, confirmed, declared, pretended, proclaimed, self-confessed, self-styled, so-called, supposed, would-be.

profession *n.* **1** business, calling, career, employment, job, line (of work), métier, occupation, office, position, sphere, vocation, walk of life. **2** acknowledgement, affirmation, assertion, claim, confession, declaration, statement, testimony.

professional *adj.* competent, efficient, experienced, expert, finished, masterly, polished, practised, proficient, qualified, skilled, trained.
antonyms amateur, unprofessional.
n. authority, dab hand, expert, maestro, master, pastmaster, pro, specialist, virtuoso.

proficiency *n.* ability, accomplishment, aptitude, competence, dexterity, expertise, finesse, knack, know-how, mastery, skilfulness, skill, talent.
antonyms clumsiness, incompetence.

proficient *adj.* able, accomplished, capable, clever, competent, efficient, experienced, expert, gifted, masterly, qualified, skilful, talented, trained.
antonyms clumsy, incompetent, unaccomplished, unskilled.

profile *n.* analysis, biography, characterisation, chart, contour, diagram, drawing, examination, figure, form, graph, outline, portrait, review, shape, side view, silhouette, sketch, study, survey, thumbnail sketch, vignette.

profit *n.* advantage, avail, benefit, bottom line, earnings, fruit, gain, interest, percentage, proceeds, receipts, return, revenue, surplus, takings, use, value, winnings, yield.
antonym loss.
profit by/from capitalise on, cash in on, exploit, learn from, put to good use, reap the benefit of, take advantage of, turn to advantage, use, utilise.
antonym lose by.

profitable *adj.* advantageous, beneficial, commercial, cost-effective, fruitful, lucrative, money-making, paying, productive, remunerative, rewarding, successful, useful, valuable, worthwhile.
antonyms loss-making, unprofitable.

profiteer *n.* exploiter, extortioner, extortionist, racketeer.

profound *adj.* **1** deep, exhaustive, extensive, extreme, far-reaching, great, heartfelt, intense, marked, penetrating, weighty. **2** learned, philosophical, serious, thoughtful, wise.
antonyms **1** mild, shallow, slight.

profuse *adj.* abundant, ample, copious, excessive, extravagant, generous, immoderate, large-handed, lavish, liberal, open-handed, over the top, overflowing, plentiful.
antonyms inadequate, sparing, sparse.

profusion *n.* abundance, copiousness, cornucopia, excess, extravagance, glut, multitude, plethora, superfluity, surplus, wealth.
antonyms inadequacy, sparingness, sparsity.

prognosis *n.* diagnosis, expectation, forecast, outlook, prediction, prognostication, projection, prospect, speculation.

programme *n.* **1** agenda, curriculum, design, line-up, list, listing, order of events, performance, plan, presentation, procedure, production, project, schedule, scheme, show, syllabus. **2** broadcast, transmission.
v. arrange, bill, book, brainwash, design, engage, formulate, itemise, lay on, line up, list, map out, plan, schedule, work out.

progress *n.* advance, betterment, breakthrough, continuation, course, development, growth, headway, improvement, increase, journey, movement, passage, procession, progression, promotion, step forward, way.
antonyms decline, deterioration, recession, relapse.
v. advance, better, blossom, come on, continue, develop, forge ahead, gather momentum, grow, improve, increase, make headway, make strides, mature, proceed, prosper, travel.
antonyms decline, deteriorate.
in progress going on, happening, occurring, proceeding, under way.

progression *n.* advance, advancement, chain, course, cycle, development, furtherance, gain,

headway, order, progress, sequence, series, succession.
antonyms decline, deterioration.
progressive *adj.* advanced, advancing, avant-garde, continuing, developing, dynamic, enlightened, enterprising, forward-looking, go-ahead, growing, increasing, intensifying, liberal, modern, radical, reformist, revolutionary, up-and-coming.
prohibit *v.* ban, bar, forbid, hamper, hinder, impede, obstruct, outlaw, prevent, restrict, rule out, stop, veto.
antonyms allow, authorise, permit.
prohibitionist *n.* abolitionist, teetotaller.
project *n.* activity, assignment, conception, design, enterprise, idea, job, occupation, plan, programme, proposal, purpose, scheme, task, undertaking, venture, work.
v. **1** calculate, estimate, extrapolate, forecast, predict, reckon. **2** fling, hurl, propel, throw. **3** bulge, jut, overhang, protrude, stick out.
projection *n.* **1** bulge, ledge, overhang, protuberance, ridge, shelf, sill. **2** calculation, computation, estimate, extrapolation, forecast, prediction, reckoning. **3** diagram, representation.
proletariat *n.* common people, commoners, herd, hoi polloi, lower classes, masses, mob, plebs, rabble, working class.
proliferate *v.* breed, escalate, expand, increase, multiply, mushroom, snowball, spread.
antonym dwindle.
proliferation *n.* build-up, concentration, escalation, expansion, extension, increase, intensification, multiplication, spread.
antonym decrease.
prolific *adj.* abundant, copious, fertile, fruitful, productive, profuse.
antonym unproductive.
prologue *n.* foreword, introduction, preface, preliminary, prelude.
prolong *v.* continue, delay, drag out, draw out, extend, lengthen, perpetuate, protract, spin out, stretch.
antonym shorten.
prominence *n.* **1** celebrity, conspicuousness, distinction, eminence, fame, greatness, importance, name, notability, pre-eminence, prestige, rank, reputation, standing, visibility, weight. **2** bulge, bump, cliff, crag, crest, elevation, headland, height, hump, jutting, lump, mound, pinnacle, process, projection, promontory, protuberance, rise.
antonyms **1** inconspicuousness, insignificance, unimportance.
prominent *adj.* **1** celebrated, chief, conspicuous, distinguished, eminent, eye-catching, famous, foremost, important, leading, main, noted, noticeable, obvious, outstanding, popular, renowned, respected, striking, unmistakable, well-known. **2** bulging, jutting, obtrusive, projecting, protruding.
antonyms **1** inconspicuous, insignificant, unimportant, unknown.
promiscuity *n.* debauchery, depravity, dissipation, immorality, laxity, licentiousness, looseness, permissiveness, wantonness.
antonyms chastity, morality.
promiscuous *adj.* casual, dissolute, immoral, licentious, loose, of easy virtue, profligate.
antonyms chaste, moral.
promise *v.* **1** assure, contract, guarantee, pledge, swear, take an oath, undertake, vouch, vow, warrant. **2** augur, hint at, indicate, look like, suggest.
n. **1** assurance, bond, commitment, compact, covenant, engagement, guarantee, oath, pledge, undertaking, vow, word of honour. **2** ability, aptitude, capability, potential, talent.
promising *adj.* able, auspicious, bright, encouraging, favourable, hopeful, likely, talented, up-and-coming.
antonyms discouraging, inauspicious, unpromising.
promote *v.* **1** advertise, advocate, aid, assist, back, boost, champion, contribute to, develop, encourage, endorse, forward, foster, further, help, nurture, plug, popularise, publicise, push, recommend, sell, sponsor, stimulate, support, urge. **2** advance, elevate, exalt, honour, upgrade.
antonyms **1** hinder, obstruct. **2** demote.
promotion *n.* **1** advancement, elevation, exaltation, preferment, rise, upgrading. **2** advertising, backing, boosting, campaign, cultivation, development, encouragement, furtherance, honour, hype, plugging, progaganda, publicity, puffery, pushing, support.
antonyms **1** demotion. **2** disparagement, obstruction.
prompt[1] *adj.* alert, early, efficient, immediate, instant, on time, punctual, quick, rapid, ready, responsive, speedy, swift, timely, unhesitating, willing.
antonyms hesitant, late, slow.
adv. exactly, on the dot, promptly, punctually, sharp, to the minute.
prompt[2] *v.* advise, assist, call forth, cause, cue, elicit, evoke, give rise to, incite, inspire, instigate, motivate, move, occasion, prod, produce, provoke, remind, result in, spur, stimulate, urge.
antonyms deter, dissuade.
n. cue, help, hint, instigation, jog, jolt, prod, reminder, spur, stimulus.
promptly *adv.* directly, forthwith, immediately, instantly, on time, punctually, quickly, speedily, straightaway, swiftly, unhesitatingly.
prone *adj.* **1** apt, bent, disposed, given, inclined, liable, likely, predisposed, subject, susceptible, tending, vulnerable. **2** face down, flat, full-length, horizontal, prostrate, recumbent, stretched.
antonyms **1** unlikely. **2** upright.
prong *n.* fork, point, projection, spike, spur, tip.
pronounce *v.* **1** articulate, breathe, enunciate, say, sound, speak, stress, utter, vocalise, voice. **2** affirm, announce, assert, declare, decree, deliver, judge, proclaim.
pronounced *adj.* broad, clear, conspicuous,

decided, definite, distinct, evident, marked, noticeable, obvious, positive, striking, strong, unmistakable.
antonyms faint, unnoticeable, vague.

pronunciation *n.* accent, articulation, diction, elocution, enunciation, inflection, intonation, speech, stress.

proof *n.* confirmation, corroboration, demonstration, documentation, evidence, examination, experiment, substantiation, test, trial, verification.

prop *v.* bolster, buttress, lean, maintain, rest, set, shore, stand, stay, support, sustain, underpin, uphold.
n. brace, buttress, mainstay, stay, strut, support, truss.

propaganda *n.* advertising, brainwashing, hype, promotion, publicity.

propagate *v.* **1** broadcast, circulate, diffuse, disseminate, proclaim, promote, promulgate, publicise, publish, spread, transmit. **2** beget, breed, generate, increase, multiply, procreate, produce, proliferate, reproduce, spawn.

propel *v.* drive, force, impel, launch, push, send, shoot, shove, start, thrust.
antonyms slow, stop.

proper *adj.* **1** accurate, actual, correct, exact, genuine, precise, real, right, true. **2** accepted, appropriate, correct, decent, fitting, polite, respectable, suitable.
antonyms **1** wrong. **2** improper, indecent.

property *n.* **1** acres, assets, belongings, building(s), capital, chattels, effects, estate, freehold, goods, holding, holdings, house(s), land, means, possessions, real estate, resources, riches, wealth. **2** attribute, characteristic, feature, idiosyncrasy, mark, peculiarity, quality, trait, virtue.

prophecy *n.* forecast, prediction, prognosis, revelation.

prophesy *v.* forecast, foresee, foretell, forewarn, predict.

prophet *n.* clairvoyant, divinator, forecaster, foreteller, oracle, seer, soothsayer.

proportion *n.* amount, balance, correspondence, distribution, division, fraction, measure, percentage, quota, ratio, relationship, share, symmetry.
antonyms disproportion, imbalance.

proportional *adj.* commensurate, comparable, consistent, corresponding, equitable, even, proportionate.
antonym disproportionate.

proportions *n.* breadth, bulk, capacity, dimensions, expanse, extent, magnitude, measurements, range, scope, size, volume.

proposal *n.* bid, design, draft, manifesto, motion, offer, outline, plan, presentation, programme, project, proposition, recommendation, scheme, sketch, suggestion, tender, terms.

propose *v.* advance, aim, bring up, design, intend, introduce, invite, lay before, mean, move, name, nominate, plan, pop the question, present, purpose, put forward, put up, recommend, scheme, submit, suggest, table, tender.
antonyms oppose, withdraw.

proposition *n.* manifesto, motion, plan, programme, project, proposal, recommendation, scheme, suggestion, tender.

proprietor *n.* deed holder, freeholder, landlady, landlord, landowner, owner, possessor, proprietary, proprietress, title-holder.

prosecute *v.* bring to trial, indict, litigate, prefer charges, put on trial, sue, summon, take to court, try.
antonym defend.

prospect *n.* chance, expectation, future, hope, likelihood, odds, plan, possibility, probability, thought.
antonym unlikelihood.
v. explore, search, seek, survey.

prospective *adj.* anticipated, approaching, aspiring, awaited, coming, designate, destined, eventual, expected, forthcoming, future, imminent, intended, likely, possible, potential, soon-to-be, to come, -to-be, would-be.
antonym current.

prospectus *n.* account, announcement, catalogue, list, manifesto, outline, pamphlet, plan, platform, programme, scheme, syllabus, synopsis.

prosper *v.* advance, bloom, boom, flourish, flower, get on, grow rich, progress, succeed, thrive, turn out well.
antonym fail.

prosperity *n.* affluence, boom, fortune, good fortune, luxury, plenty, riches, success, the good life, wealth, well-being.
antonyms adversity, poverty.

prosperous *adj.* affluent, blooming, booming, flourishing, fortunate, lucky, rich, successful, thriving, wealthy, well-off, well-to-do.
antonyms poor, unfortunate.

prostrate *adj.* brought to one's knees, crushed, defenceless, dejected, depressed, desolate, fallen, flat, helpless, horizontal, inconsolable, overcome, overwhelmed, paralysed, powerless.
antonyms elated, happy, triumphant.
v. crush, depress, disarm, drain, exhaust, fatigue, lay low, overcome, overthrow, overturn, overwhelm, paralyse, reduce, ruin, shatter, tire, wear out.
antonym strengthen.
prostrate oneself abase oneself, bend the knee, bow down, cringe, grovel, kneel, kowtow, submit.
antonym exalt oneself.

protagonist *n.* advocate, champion, chief character, exponent, hero, heroine, lead, leader, prime mover, principal, proponent, supporter.

protect *v.* care for, cover, defend, escort, guard, harbour, keep, look after, preserve, safeguard, save, screen, secure, shelter, shield, stand guard over, support, watch over.
antonyms attack, threaten.

protective *adj.* careful, defensive, fatherly, insulating, maternal, motherly, paternal, possessive, sheltering, shielding, vigilant, watchful.
antonyms aggressive, threatening.

protector *n.* advocate, benefactor, bodyguard, champion, counsel, defender, father-figure, guard, guardian, patron, safeguard.
antonyms attacker, threat.

protest *n.* complaint, declaration, disapproval, dissent, formal complaint, objection, outcry, protestation.
antonym acceptance.
v. argue, assert, complain, contend, cry out, demonstrate, disagree, disapprove, insist, maintain, object, oppose, profess, take exception.
antonym accept.

protester *n.* agitator, demonstrator, dissenter, dissident, rebel.

protocol *n.* conventions, courtesies, customs, etiquette, formalities, good form, manners, procedure, propriety.

prototype *n.* archetype, example, mock-up, model, original, pattern, standard.

protracted *adj.* drawn-out, extended, interminable, lengthy, long, long-drawn-out, overlong, prolonged.
antonyms brief, shortened.

protrude *v.* bulge, come through, extend, jut out, point, pop, project, stand out, stick out.

protuberance *n.* bulge, bump, knob, lump, outgrowth, process, projection, prominence, protrusion, swelling, tumour, wart.

proud *adj.* **1** arrogant, boastful, complacent, conceited, egotistical, haughty, high and mighty, overbearing, presumptuous, self-important, smug, snobbish, snooty, stuck-up, supercilious, toffee-nosed, vain. **2** contented, gratified, honoured, pleased, satisfied. **3** dignified, noble, self-respecting.
antonyms **1** humble, modest, unassuming. **2** ashamed. **3** deferential, servile.

prove *v.* analyse, ascertain, attest, authenticate, bear out, check, confirm, corroborate, demonstrate, determine, document, establish, examine, experience, experiment, justify, show, substantiate, suffer, test, try, verify.
antonyms discredit, disprove, falsify.

proven *adj.* attested, authentic, certified, checked, confirmed, corroborated, definite, established, reliable, tested, tried, trustworthy, valid, verified.
antonyms doubted, unproven.

proverb *n.* aphorism, byword, dictum, maxim, precept, saying.

proverbial *adj.* accepted, acknowledged, archetypal, axiomatic, conventional, current, customary, famous, legendary, notorious, time-honoured, traditional, typical, well-known.

provide *v.* accommodate, add, afford, arrange for, bring, cater, contribute, determine, equip, furnish, give, lay down, lend, outfit, plan for, prepare for, present, produce, require, serve, specify, state, stipulate, stock up, suit, supply, take measures, take precautions, yield.
antonyms remove, take.
provide for endow, fend, keep, maintain, support, sustain.
antonyms ignore, neglect.

providence *n.* care, caution, divine intervention, far-sightedness, fate, foresight, fortune, presence of mind, prudence.
antonym improvidence.

providential *adj.* convenient, fortuitous, fortunate, happy, heaven-sent, lucky, opportune, timely, welcome.
antonym untimely.

provider *n.* benefactor, breadwinner, donor, earner, funder, giver, source, supplier, supporter, wage-earner.

providing *conj.* as long as, given, on condition, on the understanding, provided, subject to, with the proviso.

province *n.* **1** area, colony, county, department, dependency, district, region, territory, tract, zone. **2** concern, domain, duty, employment, field, function, line, orbit, responsibility, role, sphere.

provincial *adj.* country, home-grown, insular, inward-looking, limited, local, narrow, narrow-minded, parochial, rural, rustic, small-minded, small-town.
antonyms cosmopolitan, sophisticated, urban.

provincialism *n.* insularity, localism, narrow-mindedness, parochialism, provinciality, regionalism.
antonym sophistication.

provision *n.* **1** arrangement, equipping, fitting out, furnishing, plan, preparation, providing, supplying. **2** clause, condition, proviso, requirement, specification, stipulation, term.
antonyms **1** neglect, removal.

provisional *adj.* conditional, interim, limited, stop-gap, temporary.
antonyms definite, fixed, permanent.

provisions *n.* eatables, eats, food, foodstuff, groceries, rations, supplies, sustenance.

proviso *n.* clause, condition, limitation, provision, qualification, requirement, reservation, restriction, rider, small print, stipulation.

provocation *n.* affront, aggravation, annoyance, cause, challenge, dare, grievance, grounds, incitement, injury, instigation, insult, justification, motivation, motive, offence, reason, stimulus, taunt, vexation.

provocative *adj.* **1** abusive, aggravating, annoying, galling, insulting, offensive, outrageous. **2** challenging, disturbing, exciting, stimulating, suggestive. **3** alluring, arousing, erotic, inviting, seductive, sexy, tempting.
antonyms **1** conciliatory. **2** unprovocative.

provoke *v.* **1** aggravate, anger, annoy, enrage, exasperate, excite, incense, incite, infuriate, insult, irritate, madden, offend, rile. **2** cause, elicit, evoke, generate, give rise to, induce, inspire, instigate, motivate, move, occasion, produce, promote, prompt, stimulate, stir.
antonyms **1** pacify, please. **2** result.

prowess *n.* ability, accomplishment, aptitude, attainment, command, excellence, expertise, genius, mastery, skill, talent.
antonyms clumsiness, mediocrity.

proximity *n.* adjacency, closeness, juxtaposition,

nearness, neighbourhood, vicinity.
antonym remoteness.
proxy *n.* agent, attorney, delegate, deputy, factor, representative, stand-in, substitute.
prudence *n.* care, caution, common sense, discretion, far-sightedness, forethought, good sense, judgement, judiciousness, planning, precaution, providence, saving, thrift, wisdom.
antonyms carelessness, imprudence, rashness.
prudent *adj.* careful, cautious, circumspect, discerning, discreet, far-sighted, politic, sensible, shrewd, thrifty, vigilant, wary, wise.
antonyms careless, imprudent, rash, stupid.
prudish *adj.* demure, narrow-minded, old-maidish, overmodest, overnice, priggish, prim, prissy, proper, puritanical, squeamish, starchy, strait-laced, stuffy, Victorian.
antonyms easy-going, lax.
pseudonym *n.* alias, assumed name, false name, incognito, nom de plume, pen name, stage name.
psychic *adj.* clairvoyant, cognitive, extra-sensory, intellectual, mental, mystic, mystical, occult, psychological, spiritual, supernatural, telepathic.
psychological *adj.* cerebral, cognitive, emotional, intellectual, irrational, mental, psychosomatic, subconscious, subjective, unconscious, unreal.
antonyms physical, real.
puberty *n.* adolescence, maturity, teens, youth.
antonyms childhood, immaturity, old age.
public *adj.* **1** civil, common, communal, community, general, national, open, social, state, universal, unrestricted. **2** acknowledged, exposed, known, overt, plain, published, recognised, well-known, widespread.
antonyms **1** personal, private. **2** secret.
n. audience, buyers, citizens, clientèle, community, country, electorate, everyone, followers, following, masses, multitude, nation, patrons, people, populace, population, society, supporters, voters.
public house bar, inn, local, pub, tavern.
publican *n.* barman, inn-keeper, taverner.
publication *n.* advertisement, airing, announcement, appearance, book, booklet, brochure, declaration, disclosure, handbill, issue, leaflet, magazine, newspaper, notification, pamphlet, periodical, publishing, reporting.
publicise *v.* advertise, blaze, broadcast, plug, promote, push, spotlight, spread about, write off.
antonym keep secret.
publicity *n.* advertising, attention, boost, build-up, hype, plug, press, promotion, public notice, splash.
antonym secrecy.
public-spirited *adj.* altruistic, charitable, community-minded, conscientious, generous, humanitarian, unselfish.
antonym selfish.
publish *v.* advertise, announce, bring out, broadcast, circulate, communicate, declare, diffuse, disclose, distribute, divulge, issue, part, print, produce, publicise, reveal, spread.
antonym keep secret.
pucker *v.* compress, contract, crease, crinkle, crumple, furrow, gather, purse, ruffle, screw up, shrivel, tighten, wrinkle.
puerile *adj.* babyish, childish, foolish, immature, inane, infantile, irresponsible, juvenile, silly, trivial.
antonym mature.
puff *n.* blast, breath, drag, draught, flurry, gust, pull, smoke, waft, whiff.
v. blow, breathe, drag, draw, expand, gasp, gulp, inflate, pant, plug, pull, push, smoke, suck, swell, waft, wheeze, whiff.
puffed *adj.* breathless, done in, exhausted, gasping, out of breath, panting.
puffed up arrogant, big-headed, boastful, conceited, high and mighty, proud, swollen-headed, too big for one's boots.
antonyms humble, modest.
puffy *adj.* bloated, enlarged, inflamed, inflated, puffed up, swollen.
antonym flat.
pugnacious *adj.* aggressive, argumentative, contentious, hostile, hot-tempered, petulant, quarrelsome.
antonym easy-going.
pull *v.* **1** drag, draw, haul, jerk, stretch, tow, tug, yank. **2** cull, extract, gather, pick, pluck, remove, rip, take out, tear, uproot. **3** attract, entice, lure, magnetise. **4** dislocate, sprain, strain.
antonyms **1** press, push. **3** deter, discourage, repel.
n. **1** drag, jerk, tug, yank. **2** effort, exertion, force, muscle, power. **3** allurement, attraction, drawing power, influence, lure, magnetism, seduction, weight.
pull apart dismember, knock, lay into, part, separate.
antonym join.
pull down bulldoze, demolish, destroy, dismantle, knock down, remove.
antonyms build, construct, put up.
pull in 1 arrive, come in, park, stop. **2** arrest, nail, run in. **3** bring in, clear, earn, gross, make, net, take home. **4** attract, bring in, draw.
antonyms **1** pull away. **2** set free. **3** lose. **4** repel.
pull off accomplish, achieve, bring off, carry out, manage, succeed, swing.
antonym fail.
pull out abandon, depart, draw out, evacuate, leave, move out, quit, retreat, withdraw.
antonym join.
pull through rally, recover, recuperate, survive, weather.
antonym fail.
pull together collaborate, co-operate, team up, work together.
antonym fight.
pull up 1 brake, draw in, draw up, halt, stop. **2** criticise, rebuke, reprimand, take to task, tell off, tick off.

pulp *n.* flesh, marrow, mash, mush, paste, soft part.
v. crush, liquidise, mash, pulverise.

pulpit *n.* dais, platform, rostrum, soap-box.

pulse *n.* beat, beating, drumming, oscillation, pulsation, rhythm, stroke, throb, vibration.
v. beat, drum, pulsate, throb, thud, vibrate.

pulverise *v.* **1** crush, grind, mill, pound. **2** annihilate, defeat, demolish, destroy, flatten, smash, wreck.

pummel *v.* bang, batter, beat, hammer, knock, pound, punch, strike, thump.

pump *v.* drive, force, inject, pour, push, send, supply.
pump up blow up, inflate, puff up.

pun *n.* double entendre, play on words, quip, witticism.

punch[1] *v.* bash, box, clout, hit, pummel, slam, smash, strike, wallop.
n. **1** bash, blow, clout, hit, jab, knock, thump, wallop. **2** drive, effectiveness, force, impact, panache, pizzazz, verve, vigour.
antonym **2** feebleness.

punch[2] *v.* bore, cut, drill, perforate, pierce, prick, puncture, stamp.

punch-drunk *adj.* confused, dazed, dizzy, groggy, reeling, staggering, stupefied, unsteady.
antonyms fresh, steady.

punctilious *adj.* careful, conscientious, exact, finicky, formal, fussy, meticulous, particular, precise, proper, scrupulous, strict.
antonyms easy-going, informal, lax.

punctual *adj.* early, exact, in good time, on the dot, on time, precise, prompt, up to time.
antonyms late, unpunctual.

puncture *n.* break, cut, flat, flat tyre, hole, leak, nick, opening, slit.
v. bore, cut, deflate, discourage, disillusion, flatten, humble, nick, penetrate, perforate, pierce, prick, rupture, take down a peg or two.

pungent *adj.* acute, aromatic, biting, bitter, caustic, cutting, hot, incisive, keen, painful, penetrating, peppery, piercing, poignant, pointed, sarcastic, scathing, seasoned, sharp, sour, spicy, stinging, strong, tangy, telling.
antonyms bland, delicate, feeble, mild, tasteless.

punish *v.* beat, castigate, chasten, chastise, correct, discipline, flog, give a lesson to, harm, hurt, injure, lash, maltreat, manhandle, misuse, oppress, penalise, rough up.
antonym reward.

punishment *n.* abuse, beating, chastisement, correction, damnation, deserts, discipline, pain, pay-off, penalty, penance, retribution, sanction, torture, victimisation.
antonym reward.

punitive *adj.* penal, retaliatory, vindictive.

punter *n.* backer, better, bloke, chap, client, customer, fellow, gambler, individual, person.

puny *adj.* diminutive, feeble, frail, insignificant, little, meagre, minor, petty, stunted, tiny, trifling, trivial, undeveloped, weak.
antonyms important, large, strong, sturdy.

pupil *n.* beginner, catechumen, disciple, learner, novice, protégé, scholar, schoolboy, schoolgirl, student, tutee.
antonym teacher.

purchase *v.* acquire, attain, buy, earn, gain, invest in, obtain, pay for, ransom, realise, secure, win.
antonym sell.
n. acquisition, advantage, asset, buy, gain, investment, possession, property, ransoming, support.
antonym sale.

purchaser *n.* buyer, client, consumer, customer, hirer, shopper.
antonyms seller, vendor.

pure *adj.* **1** authentic, genuine, natural, neat, perfect, real, simple, true, unadulterated, unalloyed, unmixed. **2** antiseptic, clean, clear, disinfected, germ-free, hygienic, immaculate, sanitary, spotless, sterile, sterilised, uncontaminated, unpolluted. **3** absolute, sheer, thorough, unqualified, utter. **4** blameless, chaste, innocent, undefiled, unsullied, upright, virtuous. **5** abstract, academic, speculative, theoretical.
antonyms **1** adulterated, impure. **2** contaminated, polluted. **4** defiled, immoral. **5** applied.

pure-bred *adj.* blooded, full-blooded, pedigree, thoroughbred.
antonyms cross-bred, hybrid, mixed, mongrel.

purely *adv.* absolutely, completely, entirely, exclusively, just, merely, only, solely, thoroughly, totally, utterly, wholly.

purge *v.* absolve, clean out, cleanse, clear, dismiss, eject, eradicate, expel, exterminate, extract, get rid of, kill, oust, purify, remove, rid, root out, scour, wipe out.
n. ejection, elimination, eradication, expulsion, extermination, removal, witch hunt.

purist *n.* nit-picker, pedant, quibbler, stickler.

puritan *n.* disciplinarian, fanatic, kill-joy, moralist, prude, spoil-sport, zealot.
antonyms hedonist, libertarian.

puritanical *adj.* abstemious, ascetic, austere, bigoted, disapproving, disciplinarian, fanatical, narrow-minded, prim, proper, prudish, puritan, rigid, severe, stern, stiff, strait-laced, strict, stuffy, zealous.
antonyms broad-minded, hedonistic, indulgent, liberal.

purity *n.* **1** blamelessness, chasteness, chastity, cleanliness, clearness, decency, faultlessness, immaculateness, innocence, integrity, morality, rectitude, sanctity, untaintedness, uprightness, virtue, wholesomeness. **2** clarity, genuineness, simplicity, truth.
antonyms **1** immorality, impurity.

purpose *n.* **1** aim, design, end, function, goal, idea, intention, motive, object, objective, outcome, plan, point, principle, profit, rationale, reason, result, target, vision. **2** constancy, dedication, determination, devotion, drive, persistence, resolution, resolve, single-mindedness, steadfastness, tenacity, zeal.

on purpose deliberately, intentionally, expressly, knowingly, purposely, wilfully, wittingly.
antonyms accidentally, impulsively, spontaneously.

purposeful *adj.* decided, deliberate, determined, firm, fixed, motivated, persevering, persistent, positive, resolute, resolved, single-minded, steadfast, strong-willed, tenacious.
antonyms aimless, faltering, purposeless.

purse *n.* award, coffers, exchequer, finances, funds, means, money, money-bag, pouch, resources, reward, treasury, wallet, wealth.
v. close, compress, contract, draw together, pucker, tighten, wrinkle.

pursue *v.* **1** aim for, aspire to, carry on, conduct, continue, cultivate, desire, engage in, enquire into, follow, hold to, investigate, keep on, maintain, perform, persevere in, persist in, practise, proceed, seek, strive for, tackle, try for. **2** chase, dog, follow, go for, gun for, harass, harry, hound, hunt, persecute, tail, track, trail.

pursuit *n.* **1** chase, hounding, hue and cry, hunt, investigation, quest, search, seeking, tracking, trail. **2** activity, craft, hobby, interest, line, occupation, pastime, pleasure, side-line, speciality, vocation.

push *v.* **1** constrain, depress, drive, elbow, force, jostle, manoeuvre, poke, press, prod, propel, ram, shove, squeeze, thrust. **2** advertise, boost, bully, coerce, egg on, encourage, incite, influence, persuade, promote, publicise, spur, urge.
antonyms **1** pull. **2** discourage, dissuade.
n. **1** jolt, knock, nudge, poke, prod, shove, thrust. **2** advance, assault, attack, charge, impetus, impulse, offensive, onset, onslaught. **3** ambition, determination, drive, dynamism, effort, energy, enterprise, go, initiative, vigour, vitality, zip.

pushy *adj.* aggressive, ambitious, arrogant, assertive, assuming, bold, bossy, brash, forceful, forward, loud, obtrusive, offensive, overconfident, presumptuous, self-assertive.
antonyms quiet, restrained, unassertive, unassuming.

pussyfoot *v.* beat about the bush, equivocate, hedge, mess about, pad, prevaricate, sidestep, slink, tiptoe.

put *v.* **1** deposit, dispose, establish, fix, land, lay, place, plonk, position, post, set (down), settle, situate, station. **2** apply, assign, consign, enjoin, impose, inflict, levy, subject. **3** couch, express, formulate, offer, phrase, present, propose, state, submit, suggest, utter, voice, word, write.
put across bring home to, communicate, convey, explain, express, get through to, put over, spell out.
put aside 1 deposit, hoard, keep, lay by, put by, reserve, retain, salt away, save, set aside, stash, stockpile, store, stow. **2** abandon, bury, discard, dispense with, disregard, forget, ignore, set aside.
put away 1 consume, drink, eat. **2** certify, commit, imprison, institutionalise, lock up. **3** remove, return, save, store, tidy.
put back defer, delay, postpone, replace, reschedule, slow down.
antonyms bring forward, speed up.
put down 1 enter, log, note, record, register, report, state, transcribe, write down. **2** condemn, crush, defeat, deflate, degrade, destroy, dismiss, humble, humiliate, kill, mortify, put to sleep, quash, quell, reject, repress, shame, silence, slight, snub, squash, suppress, take down a peg, topple.
put forward advance, introduce, move, nominate, offer, present, press, propose, recommend, submit, suggest, table, tender.
put in enter, input, insert, key in, submit.
put off 1 defer, delay, postpone, reschedule. **2** confuse, daunt, demoralise, deter, disconcert, discourage, dishearten, dismay, dissuade, distract, unsettle.
antonym **2** encourage.
put on 1 add, affix, apply, attach, back, do, don, dress, gain, impose, increase by, mount, place, present, produce, provide, stage. **2** affect, assume, deceive, fake, feign, make believe, mislead, pretend, sham, simulate. **3** bet, stake, wager.
put out 1 announce, broadcast, circulate, publish. **2** extinguish, quench, smother. **3** anger, annoy, bother, confound, disconcert, disturb, douse, embarrass, exasperate, hurt, impose on, inconvenience, irk, irritate, offend, trouble, upset. **4** dismiss, expel, release.
antonym **2** light (up).
put through accomplish, achieve, bring off, complete, conclude, execute, finalise, manage.
put up 1 assemble, build, construct, erect, fabricate. **2** accommodate, house, shelter. **3** offer, present, propose, put forward, recommend, submit, supply. **4** advance, float, give, invest, pay, pledge, provide, raise.
put up to abet, encourage, goad, incite, instigate, prompt, urge.
antonyms discourage, dissuade.
put up with abide, allow, bear, endure, stand, stand for, stomach, suffer, take, take lying down, tolerate.
antonyms object to, protest against, reject.
put upon exploit, impose on, inconvenience, use.

putrid *adj.* addled, bad, contaminated, corrupt, decayed, decomposed, foul, mouldy, off, rancid, rank, rotten, rotting, stinking.
antonyms fresh, wholesome.

put-upon *adj.* abused, exploited, imposed on, inconvenienced, persecuted, used.

puzzle *v.* **1** baffle, bewilder, confound, confuse, floor, flummox, mystify, perplex. **2** brood, consider, deliberate, figure, meditate, mull over, ponder, rack one's brains, study, think, wonder.
n. **1** acrostic, anagram, brain-teaser, conundrum, crossword, enigma, knot, maze, mind-bender, mystery, paradox, poser, quandary, question, rebus, riddle, tickler.
puzzle out clear up, crack, decipher, decode,

figure out, resolve, see, solve, sort out, think out, unravel, untangle, work out.

puzzled *adj.* at a loss, at sea, baffled, beaten, bewildered, confounded, confused, disorientated, doubtful, flummoxed, in a haze, lost, mixed up, mystified, nonplussed, perplexed, stuck, stumped.
antonyms certain, clear.

puzzlement *n.* bafflement, bewilderment, confusion, disorientation, mystification, perplexity, surprise, uncertainty, wonder.
antonyms certainty, clarity, lucidity.

pygmy *n.* dwarf, midget, Tom Thumb.
antonym giant.

pyromaniac *n.* arsonist, firebug, fire-raiser, incendiary.

Q

quack *n.* charlatan, cowboy, fake, fraud, impostor, masquerader, pretender, swindler, trickster.
quagmire *n.* bog, fen, marsh, mire, morass, moss, quag, quicksand, swamp.
quail *v.* back away, cower, cringe, faint, falter, flinch, quake, recoil, shrink, shudder, shy away, tremble.
quaint *adj.* antiquated, bizarre, charming, curious, fanciful, odd, old-fashioned, old-time, picturesque, strange, unusual.
antonyms fashionable, modern.
quake *v.* convulse, jolt, move, quail, quiver, rock, shake, shiver, shudder, sway, throb, totter, tremble, vibrate, wobble.
qualification *n.* **1** ability, accomplishment, aptitude, attribute, capability, capacity, certification, competence, eligibility, fitness, skill, suitability, training. **2** caveat, condition, criterion, exception, exemption, limitation, modification, objection, provision, proviso, reservation, restriction, stipulation.
qualified *adj.* **1** able, accomplished, capable, certified, competent, efficient, eligible, equipped, experienced, expert, fit, knowledgeable, licensed, practised, proficient, skilful, talented, trained. **2** bounded, cautious, conditional, confined, contingent, equivocal, guarded, limited, provisional, reserved.
antonyms **1** unqualified. **2** whole-hearted.
qualify *v.* **1** authorise, empower, endow, equip, fit, graduate, permit, prepare, sanction, shape, train. **2** adjust, categorise, characterise, classify, define, delimit, describe, diminish, distinguish, ease, lessen, limit, mitigate, moderate, modify, reduce, regulate, restrain, restrict, soften, temper, vary, weaken.
antonym **1** disqualify.
quality *n.* **1** aspect, attribute, calibre, character, characteristic, class, condition, constitution, deal, description, essence, feature, grade, kind, make, mark, merit, nature, peculiarity, property, refinement, sort, standing, status, talent, tone, trait, value, worth. **2** distinction, excellence, pre-eminence, superiority.
qualm *n.* anxiety, apprehension, disquiet, doubt, fear, hesitation, misgiving, reluctance, scruple, twinge, uncertainty, uneasiness, worry.
quandary *n.* bewilderment, confusion, difficulty, dilemma, embarrassment, fix, hole, impasse, mess, perplexity, predicament, problem.
quantity *n.* aggregate, allotment, amount, breadth, bulk, capacity, content, expanse, extent, greatness, length, lot, magnitude, mass, measure, number, part, portion, proportion, quota, share, size, spread, sum, total, volume, weight.
quarantine *n.* detention, isolation, segregation.
quarrel *n.* argument, brawl, clash, commotion, conflict, contention, controversy, coolness, difference, disagreement, dispute, dissension, disturbance, fight, fracas, misunderstanding, row, schism, scrap, slanging match, squabble, strife, tiff, tumult, vendetta, wrangle.
antonyms agreement, harmony.
v. argue, be at loggerheads, be at variance, bicker, carp, clash, contend, differ, disagree, dispute, dissent, fall out, fight, row, squabble, take exception, wrangle.
antonym agree.
quarrelsome *adj.* argumentative, belligerent, contentious, cross, ill-tempered, irritable.
antonyms peaceable, placid.
quarry *n.* game, goal, kill, object, objective, prey, prize, target, victim.
quarter *n.* area, direction, district, division, locality, neighbourhood, part, place, point, position, province, region, section, sector, side, spot, station, territory, vicinity, zone.
v. accommodate, bed, billet, board, house, install, lodge, place, post, put up, shelter, station.
quarters *n.* accommodation, apartment, barracks, billet, digs, domicile, dwelling, habitation, lodgings, post, residence, rooms, station.
quash *v.* annul, cancel, crush, declare null and void, defeat, invalidate, nullify, overrule, overthrow, quell, repress, reverse, revoke, set aside, squash, subdue, suppress, void.
antonyms confirm, justify, reinstate, vindicate.
quaver *v.* break, crack, flicker, flutter, oscillate, pulsate, quake, quiver, shake, shudder, tremble, trill, twitter, vibrate, warble.
n. break, shake, throb, tremble, trembling, tremor, trill, vibration, warble.
quay *n.* dock, harbour, jetty, pier, wharf.
queasy *adj.* bilious, dizzy, faint, giddy, green, groggy, ill, nauseated, off-colour, queer, sick, sickened, squeamish, unwell.
queen *n.* beauty, belle, consort, doyenne, empress, goddess, idol, mistress, monarch, princess, ruler, sovereign, Venus.
queer *adj.* **1** bizarre, curious, mysterious, odd, puzzling, remarkable, strange, uncommon, unnatural, unusual, weird. **2** dizzy, faint, giddy, ill, queasy, reeling, unwell. **3** crazy, daft, eccentric, funny, light-headed, peculiar, unbalanced. **4** gay, homosexual, lesbian.
antonyms **1** common, ordinary, usual. **2** well.
quell *v.* allay, alleviate, calm, compose, conquer, crush, defeat, extinguish, hush, mitigate,

moderate, overcome, overpower, pacify, put down, quiet, reduce, silence, soothe, squash, stifle, subdue, suppress.

quench *v.* cool, sate, satisfy, slake.

querulous *adj.* cantankerous, captious, carping, complaining, critical, cross, discontented, dissatisfied, exacting, fault-finding, fretful, fussy, grouchy, grumbling, intolerant, irritable, quarrelsome.
antonyms contented, placid, uncomplaining.

query *v.* ask, be sceptical of, call in question, challenge, disbelieve, dispute, distrust, doubt, enquire, mistrust, quarrel with, question, suspect.
antonym accept.
n. doubt, enquiry, hesitation, misgiving, objection, problem, question, quibble, reservation, scepticism, suspicion, uncertainty.

quest *n.* adventure, crusade, enquiry, enterprise, expedition, exploration, hunt, investigation, journey, mission, pursuit, search, undertaking, venture, voyage.

question *v.* ask, challenge, cross-examine, debrief, disbelieve, dispute, distrust, doubt, enquire, examine, grill, interrogate, interview, investigate, mistrust, oppose, probe, pump, query, quiz.
n. **1** enquiry, examination, interrogation, investigation, query. **2** controversy, debate, difficulty, dispute, issue, motion, point, problem, proposal, proposition, subject, theme, topic.

questionable *adj.* arguable, controversial, debatable, disputable, doubtful, dubious, equivocal, fishy, iffy, problematical, queer, shady, suspect, suspicious, uncertain, undetermined, unproven, unsettled, vexed.
antonyms certain, indisputable, straightforward.

questioner *n.* agnostic, disbeliever, doubter, enquirer, examiner, interrogator, interviewer, investigator, sceptic.

questionnaire *n.* answer-sheet, form, quiz, test.

queue *n.* file, line, line-up, order, procession, sequence, series, string, succession, tail, tailback.

quibble *v.* carp, equivocate, prevaricate, split hairs.
n. complaint, criticism, niggle, objection, query.

quick *adj.* **1** brief, brisk, cursory, express, fast, fleet, hasty, hurried, immediate, instant, instantaneous, nimble, prompt, rapid, ready, speedy, sprightly, sudden, swift. **2** hot, quick-tempered, temperamental, touchy. **3** astute, clever, discerning, intelligent, keen, penetrating, perceptive, quick-witted, receptive, responsive, sharp, shrewd.
antonyms **1** lethargic, slow, sluggish. **2** easy-going. **3** dull, unintelligent.

quicken *v.* accelerate, activate, advance, animate, arouse, dispatch, energise, enliven, excite, expedite, galvanise, hasten, hurry, incite, inspire, invigorate, precipitate, reactivate, refresh, revive, rouse, sharpen, speed, stimulate, strengthen.
antonyms deaden, dull, retard.

quiet *adj.* **1** hushed, inaudible, noiseless, silent. **2** calm, composed, contented, even-tempered, gentle, peaceful, placid, reserved, retiring, serene, shy, still, subdued, thoughtful, tranquil, uncommunicative, undisturbed, unforthcoming, untroubled. **3** isolated, lonely, private, secluded, unfrequented.
antonyms **1** loud. **2** excitable, noisy. **3** conspicuous.
n. calm, ease, hush, lull, peace, quietness, repose, rest, serenity, silence, stillness, tranquillity.
antonyms bustle, disturbance, loudness, noise.

quieten *v.* calm, compose, deaden, diminish, dull, mitigate, mollify, mute, pacify, quell, quiet, reduce, silence, smooth, sober, soothe, stifle, still, stop, subdue.
antonyms agitate, discompose, disturb.

quilt *n.* bed quilt, bedcover, bedspread, counterpane, coverlet, duvet, eiderdown.

quip *n.* crack, gag, gibe, jest, joke, one-liner, quirk, retort, riposte, witticism.
v. gibe, jest, joke, quirk, retort, riposte.

quirk *n.* curiosity, eccentricity, foible, freak, habit, idiosyncrasy, mannerism, oddity, peculiarity, trait, turn, twist, warp, whim.

quit *v.* abandon, cease, decamp, depart, desert, disappear, discontinue, drop, end, exit, forsake, give up, go, halt, leave, pack in, relinquish, renege, renounce, repudiate, resign, retire, stop, surrender, suspend, vanish, withdraw.

quite *adv.* **1** comparatively, fairly, moderately, rather, relatively, somewhat. **2** absolutely, completely, entirely, exactly, fully, perfectly, precisely, totally, utterly, wholly.

quits *adj.* equal, even, level, square.

quiver *v.* agitate, bicker, convulse, flicker, flutter, oscillate, palpitate, pulsate, quake, quaver, shake, shiver, shudder, tremble, vibrate, wobble.
n. convulsion, flicker, flutter, oscillation, palpitation, shake, shiver, shudder, spasm, throb, tremble, tremor, vibration, wobble.

quiz *n.* catechism, examination, investigation, questioning, questionnaire, test.
v. ask, catechise, cross-examine, cross-question, debrief, examine, grill, interrogate, investigate, pump, question.

quizzical *adj.* amused, curious, enquiring, humorous, mocking, questioning, sardonic, satirical, sceptical, shrewd, teasing.

quota *n.* allocation, allowance, assignment, cut, part, percentage, portion, proportion, ration, share, slice.

quotation *n.* **1** citation, cutting, excerpt, extract, locus classicus, passage, piece, quote, reference. **2** charge, cost, estimate, figure, price, quote, rate, tender.

quote *v.* adduce, attest, cite, detail, echo, instance, name, recall, recite, recollect, refer to, repeat, reproduce.

quoted *adj.* above-mentioned, cited, forementioned, instanced, referred to, reported, reproduced, stated.

R

rabble *n.* crowd, herd, horde, masses, mob, populace, riffraff, throng.
rabble-rouser *n.* agitator, demagogue, fomenter, incendiary, ringleader, troublemaker.
rabid *adj.* berserk, bigoted, crazed, extreme, fanatical, fervent, frantic, frenzied, furious, hysterical, intolerant, irrational, mad, obsessive, raging, unreasoning, violent, wild, zealous.
race[1] *n.* chase, competition, contention, contest, marathon, pursuit, quest, rat race, regatta, rivalry, scramble, sprint, steeplechase.
v. career, compete, contest, dart, dash, fly, gallop, hasten, hurry, run, rush, speed, sprint, tear, zoom.
race[2] *n.* ancestry, blood, breed, clan, descent, family, folk, house, issue, kin, kindred, line, lineage, nation, offspring, people, progeny, seed, stock, tribe.
race-course *n.* circuit, circus, course, hippodrome, race-track, route, speedway, track, turf.
racial *adj.* ancestral, ethnic, folk, genealogical, genetic, inherited, national, tribal.
rack *n.* frame, framework, hack, shelf, stand, structure.
racket[1] *n.* **1** commotion, din, disturbance, fuss, hubbub, noise, outcry, pandemonium, row, shouting, uproar. **2** business, con, deception, dodge, fiddle, fraud, game, scheme, swindle, trick.
racket[2] *n.* bat, frame, net, web.
racy *adj.* animated, boisterous, breezy, broad, buoyant, dubious, dynamic, energetic, entertaining, enthusiastic, exciting, exhilarating, heady, indecent, indelicate, lively, naughty, ribald, rich, risqué, sharp, spicy, strong, suggestive.
antonyms dull, heavy.
radiance *n.* brightness, brilliance, delight, glare, gleam, glitter, glow, happiness, incandescence, joy, light, lustre, pleasure, rapture, resplendence, shine, splendour, warmth.
radiant *adj.* beaming, bright, brilliant, delighted, ecstatic, gleaming, glittering, glorious, glowing, happy, illuminated, joyful, joyous, luminous, resplendent, shining, sparkling, splendid, sunny.
antonyms dull, miserable.
radiate *v.* branch, diffuse, disseminate, diverge, emanate, emit, give off, gleam, glitter, issue, pour, scatter, shed, shine, spread (out).
radiation *n.* emanation, emission, rays.
radical *adj.* basic, complete, comprehensive, constitutional, deep-seated, entire, essential, excessive, extreme, extremist, fanatical, far-reaching, fundamental, innate, intrinsic, native, natural, primary, profound, revolutionary, severe, sweeping, thorough, thoroughgoing, total, violent.
antonym superficial.
n. extremist, fanatic, fundamentalist, left-winger, militant, reformer, reformist, revolutionary.
raffle *n.* draw, lottery, sweep, sweepstake, tombola.
rage *n.* **1** anger, frenzy, fury, tantrum, violence, wrath. **2** craze, enthusiasm, fad, fashion, obsession, passion, style, vogue.
v. explode, fume, ramp, rampage, rant, rave, seethe, storm, surge, thunder.
ragged *adj.* **1** down-at-heel, frayed, ripped, scraggy, scruffy, shabby, tattered, tatty, threadbare, torn, unkempt, worn-out. **2** disorganised, erratic, fragmented, irregular, jagged, notched, rough, serrated, uneven.
raid *n.* attack, break-in, bust, foray, incursion, inroad, invasion, onset, onslaught, seizure, sortie, strike, swoop.
v. attack, descend on, do, invade, loot, maraud, pillage, plunder, ransack, rifle, sack.
raider *n.* attacker, brigand, despoiler, forager, invader, looter, marauder, pirate, plunderer, ransacker, robber, sacker, thief.
railing *n.* balustrade, barrier, fence, paling, parapet, rail.
railway *n.* line, metro, permanent way, railroad, rails, subway, track, tramway, tube, underground.
rain *n.* cloudburst, deluge, downpour, drizzle, fall, flood, hail, precipitation, raindrops, rainfall, shower, squall, stream, thunderstorm, torrent.
v. bucket, deluge, drizzle, drop, fall, pour, shower, spit, teem.
rainy *adj.* damp, dripping, drizzly, showery, wet.
antonym dry.
raise *v.* **1** build, construct, elevate, erect, heave, hoist, lift. **2** amplify, boost, enhance, escalate, heighten, increase, intensify, magnify, promote, strengthen. **3** assemble, collect, gather, get, obtain, rally, recruit. **4** breed, bring up, cultivate, develop, grow, propagate, rear. **5** bring up, broach, introduce, moot, present, put forward, suggest.
antonyms **1** lower, wreck. **2** decrease, reduce. **5** suppress.
rake *v.* accumulate, amass, collect, comb, drag, examine, gather, graze, harrow, haul in, hoe, hunt, make, ransack, remove, scan, scour, scrape, scratch, scrutinise, search, strafe, sweep.
rally *v.* **1** assemble, collect, congregate, convene, gather, marshal, mass, mobilise, muster, organ-

ise, rally round, reassemble, re-form, regroup, reorganise, round up, summon, unite. **2** encourage, improve, pick up, recover, recuperate, revive.
n. **1** assembly, conference, congregation, convention, convocation, gathering, jamboree, meeting, regrouping, reunion. **2** comeback, improvement, recovery, recuperation, renewal, resurgence, revival.

ram *v.* beat, butt, cram, crash, crowd, dash, drive, drum, force, hammer, hit, jam, pack, pound, slam, smash, strike, stuff, thrust.

ramble *v.* **1** amble, dodder, meander, roam, rove, saunter, straggle, stray, stroll, traipse, walk, wander, wind, zigzag. **2** babble, chatter, digress, drift, expatiate.
n. excursion, hike, roaming, roving, saunter, stroll, tour, trip, walk.

rambler *n.* drifter, globe-trotter, hiker, roamer, rover, stroller, walker, wanderer, wayfarer.

rambling *adj.* circuitous, digressive, disconnected, incoherent, irregular, long-drawn-out, long-winded, sprawling, spreading, straggling, trailing, wordy.
antonyms deliberate, direct.

ramification *n.* branch, complication, consequence, development, implication, result, sequel, upshot.

ramp *n.* grade, gradient, incline, rise, slope.

rampage *v.* rage, rant, rave, run amuck, run riot, run wild, rush, storm, tear.
n. destruction, frenzy, fury, rage, storm, uproar, violence.
on the rampage amuck, berserk, out of control, violent, wild.

rampant *adj.* excessive, fierce, outrageous, prevalent, profuse, raging, rank, rife, riotous, standing, unbridled, unchecked, uncontrolled, unrestrained, violent, wanton, widespread, wild.

rampart *n.* barricade, bastion, bulwark, defence, earthwork, embankment, fence, fort, fortification, guard, parapet, security, stronghold, wall.

ramshackle *adj.* broken-down, crumbling, decrepit, derelict, dilapidated, haywire, jerry-built, rickety, shaky, tottering, tumbledown, unsafe, unsteady.
antonyms solid, stable.

ranch *n.* estate, farm, plantation, station.

rancid *adj.* bad, fetid, foul, musty, off, putrid, rank, rotten, sour, stale, strong-smelling.
antonym sweet.

random *adj.* accidental, aimless, arbitrary, casual, chance, fortuitous, haphazard, incidental, indiscriminate, purposeless, stray, unplanned.
antonyms deliberate, systematic.
at random accidentally, aimlessly, arbitrarily, casually, fortuitously, haphazardly, indiscriminately, irregularly, randomly, unsystematically.

range *n.* **1** amplitude, area, bounds, compass, distance, domain, extent, field, gamut, limits, orbit, parameters, province, reach, scale, scope, span, spectrum, sphere, sweep. **2** assortment, class, kind, order, selection, series, sort, string, variety.
v. **1** extend, fluctuate, reach, stretch, vary. **2** align, arrange, catalogue, classify, order. **3** cruise, go, ramble, roam, rove, stroll, wander.

rank¹ *n.* caste, class, classification, column, condition, degree, dignity, division, echelon, estate, file, formation, grade, group, level, line, order, position, range, row, series, sort, standing, station, status, tier, type.
v. arrange, class, classify, grade, locate, marshal, order, organise, place, position, range, rate, sort.

rank² *adj.* **1** absolute, arrant, bad, complete, crass, flagrant, glaring, gross, outrageous, sheer, thorough, total, unmitigated, utter. **2** disgusting, filthy, foul, pungent, putrid, rancid, repulsive, revolting, stale, stinking, strong-smelling.

rankle *v.* anger, annoy, fester, irk, irritate, nettle, rile.

ransack *v.* comb, despoil, explore, loot, pillage, plunder, raid, ravage, rummage, sack, scour, search, strip.

ransom *n.* deliverance, liberation, money, payment, pay-off, price, redemption, release, rescue.
v. buy out, deliver, free, liberate, redeem, release, rescue.

rant *v.* bellow, bluster, cry, declaim, rave, roar, shout, yell.

rap *v.* **1** hit, knock, strike, tap, thump. **2** chat, talk.
n. **1** blow, hit, knock, tap, thump. **2** blame, censure, punishment, rebuke, reprimand.

rape *n.* abuse, maltreatment, ravishment, violation.
v. ravish, violate.

rapid *adj.* brisk, express, fast, flying, hasty, headlong, hurried, precipitate, prompt, quick, speedy, swift.
antonyms leisurely, slow, sluggish.

rapidity *n.* briskness, dispatch, haste, hurry, promptness, quickness, rush, speed, swiftness.
antonyms slowness, tardiness.

rapport *n.* affinity, bond, compatibility, empathy, harmony, link, relationship, sympathy, understanding.

rapt *adj.* absorbed, bewitched, captivated, charmed, delighted, ecstatic, enchanted, engrossed, enraptured, enthralled, entranced, fascinated, gripped, held, intent, preoccupied, ravished, spellbound, transported.

rapture *n.* bliss, delight, ecstasy, enthusiasm, euphoria, exaltation, happiness, joy.

rare *adj.* **1** infrequent, scarce, sparse, sporadic, uncommon, unusual. **2** admirable, excellent, exceptional, exquisite, incomparable, precious, superb, superlative.
antonyms **1** abundant, common, usual.

rarefied *adj.* cliquish, esoteric, exclusive, high, noble, private, refined, select, sublime.

rarely *adv.* exceptionally, extraordinarily, hardly, infrequently, remarkably, seldom, singularly,

uncommonly, unusually.
antonyms frequently, often, usually.

raring *adj.* desperate, eager, enthusiastic, impatient, itching, keen, longing, ready, willing, yearning.

rarity *n.* **1** curio, curiosity, find, gem, one-off, pearl, treasure. **2** exquisiteness, infrequency, preciousness, scarcity, shortage, sparseness, strangeness, uncommonness, unusualness.
antonyms **1** commonness. **2** commonplace.

rascal *n.* devil, good-for-nothing, imp, rogue, scallywag, scamp, scoundrel, villain, wretch.

rascally *adj.* disreputable, good-for-nothing, reprobate, roguish, scoundrelly, unscrupulous, villainous, wicked.

rash[1] *adj.* adventurous, audacious, careless, foolhardy, hasty, headlong, headstrong, heedless, hot-headed, ill-advised, ill-considered, impetuous, imprudent, impulsive, indiscreet, reckless, unguarded, unthinking, unwary.
antonyms careful, cautious, considered, wary.

rash[2] *n.* epidemic, eruption, outbreak, plague.

rasp *n.* croak, grating, grinding, harshness, hoarseness, scrape, scratch.
v. **1** croak, grate. **2** file, grind, irk, irritate, rub, sand, scour, scrape.

rate *n.* **1** basis, class, classification, degree, figure, grade, measure, percentage, position, proportion, quality, rank, rating, ratio, reckoning, relation, scale, speed, standard, status, tempo, time, toll, velocity. **2** charge, cost, dues, duty, fee, hire, price, tariff, tax, value, worth.
v. **1** assess, class, classify, consider, count, esteem, estimate, evaluate, figure, grade, judge, measure (up), perform, rank, reckon, regard, weigh. **2** admire, respect, value. **3** deserve, merit.

rather *adv.* a bit, fairly, instead, moderately, noticeably, preferably, pretty, quite, relatively, significantly, slightly, somewhat, sooner, sort of, very.

ratify *v.* affirm, approve, authenticate, authorise, bind, certify, confirm, endorse, establish, legalise, recognise, sanction, sign, uphold, validate.
antonyms reject, repudiate.

rating *n.* class, classification, degree, designation, estimate, evaluation, grade, order, placing, position, rank, rate, sort, standing, status.

ratio *n.* arrangement, balance, correlation, correspondence, equation, fraction, percentage, proportion, rate, relation, relationship.

ration *n.* allocation, allotment, allowance, amount, helping, measure, part, portion, provision, quota, share.
v. allocate, allot, apportion, budget, conserve, control, deal, dispense, distribute, dole, issue, limit, restrict, save, supply.

rational *adj.* balanced, enlightened, intelligent, judicious, logical, lucid, normal, realistic, reasonable, reasoning, sane, sensible, sound, thinking, well-founded, well-grounded, wise.
antonyms crazy, illogical, insane, irrational.

rationale *n.* basis, exposition, grounds, logic, motivation, philosophy, principle, reasons, theory.

rationalise *v.* **1** excuse, justify, vindicate. **2** reorganise, streamline.

rations *n.* commons, food, provisions, stores, supplies.

rattle *v.* bounce, bump, clank, clatter, clitter, disturb, frighten, jangle, jolt, scare, shake, upset, vibrate.
rattle off list, recite, reel off, repeat, run through.
rattle on cackle, chatter, gab, gibber, jabber, prattle, rabbit on.

ratty *adj.* angry, annoyed, crabbed, cross, impatient, irritable, peeved, short-tempered, snappy, touchy.
antonyms calm, patient.

raucous *adj.* grating, harsh, hoarse, loud, noisy, rasping, rough, strident.

ravage *v.* demolish, desolate, despoil, destroy, devastate, lay waste, loot, pillage, plunder, ransack, raze, ruin, sack, shatter, spoil, wreck.
n. damage, demolition, desolation, destruction, devastation, havoc, pillage, plunder, ruin, waste, wreckage.

rave *v.* babble, rage, ramble, rant, roar, splutter, storm, thunder.
adj. enthusiastic, excellent, fantastic, favourable, trendy, wonderful.

ravenous *adj.* famished, greedy, starved, starving, voracious.

rave-up *n.* blow-out, celebration, do, orgy, party.

ravine *n.* canyon, gorge, gully, pass.

raving *adj.* berserk, crazed, crazy, delirious, frantic, frenzied, furious, hysterical, insane, mad, wild.

ravish *v.* **1** captivate, charm, delight, enchant, enrapture, entrance, fascinate, overjoy, spellbind. **2** abuse, rape, violate.

ravishing *adj.* alluring, beautiful, charming, dazzling, delightful, enchanting, gorgeous, lovely, radiant, seductive, stunning.

raw *adj.* **1** bloody, fresh, uncooked, unripe. **2** crude, natural, unprocessed, unrefined, untreated. **3** bare, basic, brutal, harsh, naked, plain, pure, realistic. **4** grazed, open, scraped, scratched, sensitive, sore, tender. **5** biting, bitter, bleak, chilly, cold, freezing, piercing. **6** callow, green, immature, inexperienced, new, unskilled, untrained.
antonyms **1** cooked, done. **2** processed, refined. **5** warm. **6** experienced, skilled.

raze *v.* bulldoze, demolish, destroy, dismantle, erase, extinguish, flatten, level, obliterate, remove, ruin.

re *prep.* about, concerning, regarding, with reference to, with regard to.

reach *v.* amount to, arrive at, attain, contact, drop, fall, get to, grasp, hand, land at, make, move, pass, rise, stretch, strike, touch.
n. capacity, command, compass, distance, extent, grasp, influence, jurisdiction, latitude, mastery, power, range, scope, spread, stretch, sweep.

react *v.* acknowledge, act, answer, behave,

function, operate, proceed, reply, respond, work.

reaction *n.* acknowledgement, answer, compensation, conservatism, counteraction, counterbalance, counter-revolution, feedback, recoil, reply, response.

reactionary *adj.* conservative, counter-revolutionary, obstructive, reactionist, rightist.
antonyms progressive, radical, revolutionary.
n. conservative, counter-revolutionary, die-hard, reactionist, rightist, right-winger.
antonyms progressive, radical, revolutionary.

read *v.* announce, comprehend, construe, decipher, declaim, deliver, discover, display, indicate, interpret, peruse, pore over, recite, record, refer to, register, scan, see, show, speak, study, understand, utter.

readable *adj.* clear, comprehensible, compulsive, decipherable, enjoyable, entertaining, gripping, intelligible, interesting, legible, pleasant, understandable, unputdownable.
antonyms illegible, unreadable.

readily *adv.* eagerly, easily, effortlessly, freely, gladly, promptly, quickly, smoothly, speedily, unhesitatingly, willingly.
antonyms reluctantly, unwillingly.

reading *n.* education, erudition, examination, grasp, inspection, interpretation, knowledge, learning, lecture, lesson, performance, perusal, recital, rendering, rendition, review, scholarship, scrutiny, sermon, study, treatment, understanding, version.

ready *adj.* **1** arranged, completed, fit, organised, prepared, set. **2** eager, game, happy, inclined, keen, willing. **3** accessible, available, convenient, handy, near, on tap, present. **4** alert, astute, perceptive, prompt, quick, sharp.
antonyms **1** unprepared. **2** disinclined, reluctant, unwilling. **3** inaccessible, unavailable.
v. alert, arrange, equip, order, organise, prepare, prime, set.

real *adj.* absolute, actual, authentic, bona fide, certain, essential, factual, genuine, heartfelt, honest, intrinsic, legitimate, positive, right, rightful, sincere, substantial, substantive, sure-enough, tangible, true, unaffected, unfeigned, valid, veritable.
antonyms false, imaginary, invented, unreal.

realise *v.* **1** appreciate, catch on, comprehend, grasp, imagine, recognise, take in, understand. **2** accomplish, achieve, fulfil, implement, perform, reproduce, translate. **3** earn, fetch, get, make, net, produce, sell for.

realism *n.* actuality, practicality, pragmatism, rationality, sanity, sensibleness.

realistic *adj.* authentic, businesslike, clear-eyed, clear-sighted, common-sense, detached, down-to-earth, faithful, genuine, graphic, hard-headed, level-headed, lifelike, matter-of-fact, natural, objective, practical, pragmatic, rational, real, real-life, representational, sensible, sober, true, truthful, unromantic, unsentimental.
antonyms fanciful, idealistic, impractical, irrational, unrealistic.

reality *n.* actuality, authenticity, certainty, fact, genuineness, materiality, realism, tangibility, truth, validity.

really *adv.* absolutely, actually, categorically, certainly, genuinely, honestly, indeed, positively, surely, truly, undoubtedly.

realm *n.* area, branch, country, department, domain, dominion, empire, field, jurisdiction, kingdom, land, monarchy, orbit, principality, province, region, sphere, state, territory, world, zone.

rear *n.* back, backside, behind, bottom, buttocks, end, posterior, rearguard, rump, stern, tail.
antonym front.
adj. back, following, hind, hindmost, last.
antonym front.
v. **1** breed, cultivate, educate, foster, grow, nurse, nurture, parent, raise, train. **2** loom, rise, soar, tower.

reason *n.* **1** aim, argument, basis, case, cause, defence, end, excuse, explanation, goal, ground, incentive, intention, justification, motive, object, purpose, rationale, warrant. **2** brains, common sense, gumption, intellect, judgement, logic, mind, rationality, reasoning, sense, understanding, wisdom.
v. conclude, deduce, infer, resolve, solve, think, work out.
reason with argue, debate, dispute, make representations, move, persuade, protest, remonstrate, talk, urge.

reasonable *adj.* **1** intelligent, logical, practical, rational, reasoned, sane, sensible, sound, well-advised, well-thought-out, wise. **2** acceptable, average, fair, inexpensive, just, moderate, modest, plausible, possible, satisfactory, tolerable, viable.
antonyms **1** crazy, irrational. **2** extravagant, outrageous.

reasoning *n.* analysis, argument, case, deduction, exposition, hypothesis, interpretation, logic, proof, reason, supposition, thinking, thought.

reassure *v.* brace, comfort, encourage, hearten, inspirit, nerve, rally.

rebate *n.* allowance, bonus, deduction, discount, reduction, refund, repayment.

rebel *v.* defy, disobey, dissent, mutiny, recoil, resist, revolt, rise up, run riot, shrink.
n. dissenter, heretic, insurrectionary, mutineer, nonconformist, revolutionary, schismatic.
adj. insubordinate, insurgent, rebellious, revolutionary.

rebellious *adj.* defiant, disloyal, disobedient, disorderly, insubordinate, insurgent, insurrectionary, intractable, mutinous, obstinate, resistant, revolutionary, seditious, ungovernable, unmanageable, unruly.
antonyms dutiful, obedient, submissive.

rebirth *n.* regeneration, reincarnation, rejuvenation, renaissance, renewal, restoration, resurrection, revitalisation, revival.

rebound *v.* backfire, boomerang, bounce, recoil, redound, resound, return, ricochet.

rebuff *v.* cold-shoulder, cut, decline, discourage, put someone's nose out of joint, reject, repulse, resist, slight, snub, spurn, turn down.
n. brush-off, check, cold shoulder, defeat, denial, discouragement, flea in one's ear, refusal, rejection, repulse, set-down, slight, snub.

rebuke *v.* admonish, blame, castigate, censure, chide, lecture, lesson, rate, reprimand, reproach, reprove, scold, tell off, tick off, trim, upbraid.
antonyms approve, compliment, praise.
n. admonition, blame, censure, dressing-down, lecture, reprimand, reproach, reproof, reproval, telling-off, ticking-off.
antonyms commendation, compliment, praise.

recall *v.* cast one's mind back, evoke, recognise, recollect, remember.
n. memory, recollection, remembrance.

recant *v.* deny, disclaim, disown, renounce, repudiate, retract, revoke, withdraw.

recapitulate *v.* give a resumé, recap, recount, reiterate, repeat, restate, review, summarise.

recede *v.* abate, decline, decrease, diminish, dwindle, ebb, fade, lessen, retire, retreat, return, shrink, sink, slacken, subside, wane, withdraw.
antonyms advance, proceed.

receipt *n.* acceptance, acknowledgement, counterfoil, delivery, receiving, reception, slip, stub, ticket, voucher.

receipts *n.* gains, income, proceeds, profits, return, take, takings.

receive *v.* accept, acquire, admit, apprehend, bear, collect, derive, encounter, entertain, experience, gather, get, greet, hear, meet, obtain, perceive, pick up, react to, respond to, suffer, sustain, take, undergo, welcome.
antonyms donate, give.

receiver *n.* **1** handset, radio, tuner, wireless. **2** beneficiary, fence, recipient.
antonym **2** donor.

recent *adj.* contemporary, current, fresh, late, latter, latter-day, modern, new, novel, present-day, up-to-date, young.
antonyms dated, old, out-of-date.

recently *adv.* currently, freshly, lately, newly.

receptacle *n.* container, holder, vessel.

reception *n.* **1** acceptance, acknowledgement, admission, greeting, reaction, receipt, receiving, recognition, response, treatment. **2** entertainment, function, party, welcome.

receptive *adj.* accessible, amenable, approachable, favourable, friendly, hospitable, interested, open, open-minded, perceptive, responsive, sensitive, suggestible, susceptible, sympathetic, welcoming.
antonyms narrow-minded, prejudiced, unresponsive.

recess *n.* **1** break, holiday, intermission, interval, respite, rest, vacation. **2** alcove, bay, cavity, corner, depression, hollow, indentation, niche.

recesses *n.* corner, depths, heart, interior, reaches.

recession *n.* decline, depression, downturn, slump.
antonyms boom, upturn.

recipe *n.* directions, formula, ingredients, instructions, method, prescription, procedure, process, programme, receipt, system, technique.

recipient *n.* beneficiary, receiver.
antonyms donor, giver.

reciprocal *adj.* alternate, complementary, correlative, corresponding, equivalent, give-and-take, interchangeable, interdependent, mutual, shared.

reciprocate *v.* alternate, correspond, equal, exchange, interchange, match, reply, respond, return, swap, trade.

recital *n.* account, description, interpretation, narration, performance, reading, rendition, repetition, statement, story, tale, telling.

recitation *n.* lecture, narration, party piece, passage, performance, piece, reading, recital, rendering, telling.

recite *v.* articulate, deliver, describe, detail, enumerate, itemise, narrate, perform, recapitulate, recount, relate, repeat, speak, tell.

reckless *adj.* careless, daredevil, foolhardy, hasty, heedless, ill-advised, imprudent, indiscreet, irresponsible, mindless, negligent, rash, thoughtless, wild.
antonyms calculating, careful, cautious, prudent, wary.

reckon *v.* account, add up, assess, assume, believe, calculate, compute, conjecture, consider, count, deem, enumerate, esteem, estimate, evaluate, expect, fancy, gauge, guess, hold, imagine, judge, number, rate, regard, suppose, surmise, tally, think, total.
reckon on bank on, calculate on, count on, depend on, figure on, hope for, rely on, trust in.
reckon with anticipate, bargain for, consider, cope, deal with, expect, face, foresee, handle, plan for, take into account, treat.

reckoning *n.* **1** account, addition, bill, calculation, charge, computation, counting, due, enumeration, estimate, score, settlement, working. **2** doom, judgement, retribution.

reclaim *v.* claim back, recapture, recover, redeem, reform, regain, regenerate, reinstate, rescue, restore, retrieve, salvage.

recognise *v.* accept, acknowledge, admit, allow, appreciate, approve, concede, confess, grant, greet, honour, identify, know, notice, own, perceive, place, realise, recall, recollect, remember, respect, salute, see, spot, understand.

recognition *n.* acceptance, acknowledgement, admission, allowance, appreciation, approval, awareness, confession, detection, discovery, gratitude, greeting, honour, identification, notice, perception, realisation, recall, recollection, remembrance, respect, salute, understanding.

recollect *v.* cast one's mind back, mind, recall, remember, reminisce.

recollection *n.* image, impression, memory, recall, remembrance, reminiscence, souvenir.

recommend *v.* advance, advise, advocate,

approve, commend, counsel, endorse, exhort, plug, praise, propose, suggest, urge, vouch for. *antonyms* disapprove, veto.

recommendation *n.* advice, advocacy, approval, blessing, commendation, counsel, endorsement, plug, praise, proposal, reference, sanction, suggestion, testimonial, urging. *antonyms* disapproval, veto.

recompense *v.* compensate, indemnify, pay, reimburse, remunerate, repay, requite, reward, satisfy.
n. amends, compensation, damages, indemnification, indemnity, pay, payment, remuneration, reparation, repayment, requital, restitution, return, reward, satisfaction, wages.

reconcile *v.* accept, accommodate, accord, adjust, appease, compose, conciliate, harmonise, pacify, placate, propitiate, resolve, reunite, settle, square, submit, yield. *antonyms* alienate, estrange.

reconciliation *n.* accommodation, adjustment, agreement, appeasement, compromise, conciliation, détente, forgiveness, harmony, pacification, propitiation, rapprochement, reunion, settlement, understanding. *antonyms* estrangement, separation.

reconnoitre *v.* examine, explore, inspect, investigate, observe, patrol, probe, scan, scrutinise, spy out, survey.

reconstruct *v.* reassemble, rebuild, recreate, re-establish, refashion, reform, reformulate, regenerate, remake, remodel, renovate, reorganise, restore.

record *n.* **1** account, annals, archives, diary, document, documentation, dossier, entry, evidence, file, history, journal, log, memoir, memorandum, memorial, minute, register, report, testimony, trace. **2** album, disc, forty-five, gramophone record, LP, recording, release, single. **3** best performance, performance, personal best, world record. **4** background, career, curriculum vitae, track record.
v. **1** chalk up, chronicle, contain, diarise, document, enrol, enter, indicate, inscribe, log, minute, note, preserve, read, register, report, say, score. **2** cut, tape, tape-record, transcribe, video, video-tape.
off the record confidentially, privately, unofficially.

recorder *n.* archivist, clerk, diarist, historian, registrar, score-keeper, scorer, scribe, stenographer.

recording *n.* cut, disc, gramophone record, performance, record, release, tape, video.

recount *v.* communicate, depict, describe, detail, enumerate, narrate, portray, recite, rehearse, relate, repeat, report, tell.

recoup *v.* compensate, indemnify, make good, recover, redeem, refund, regain, reimburse, remunerate, repay, retrieve.

recourse *n.* access, appeal, expedient, option, refuge, remedy, resort.

recover *v.* **1** convalesce, get over, heal, improve, mend, pick up, pull through, rally, recuperate. **2** recapture, reclaim, recoup, regain, repossess, restore, retake, retrieve, revive. *antonyms* **1** worsen. **2** forfeit, lose.

recovery *n.* convalescence, healing, improvement, mending, rally, recuperation, rehabilitation, restoration, retrieval, revival, upturn. *antonyms* forfeit, loss, worsening.

recreation *n.* amusement, distraction, diversion, enjoyment, entertainment, exercise, fun, games, hobby, leisure activity, pastime, play, pleasure, refreshment, relaxation, sport.

recrimination *n.* accusation, bickering, counterattack, countercharge, quarrel, retaliation, retort, squabbling.

recruit *v.* draft, engage, enlist, enrol, gather, headhunt, mobilise, obtain, procure, raise, reinforce, strengthen, supply.
n. apprentice, beginner, conscript, convert, helper, initiate, learner, novice, trainee.

rectify *v.* adjust, amend, correct, fix, improve, mend, refine, reform, remedy, repair, right.

recuperate *v.* convalesce, get better, improve, mend, pick up, rally, recover, revive. *antonym* worsen.

recur *v.* persist, reappear, repeat, return.

recurrent *adj.* continued, frequent, habitual, haunting, periodic, recurring, regular, repeated, repetitive.

recycle *v.* reclaim, reconstitute, reprocess, reuse, salvage, save.

red *adj.* bloodshot, bloodstained, bloody, blooming, blushing, carroty, cherry, chestnut, coral, crimson, embarrassed, flame-coloured, flaming, florid, flushed, glowing, healthy, inflamed, maroon, pink, reddish, rosy, ruby, ruddy, scarlet, shamefaced, suffused, vermilion.

redden *v.* blush, colour, crimson, flush, suffuse.

reddish *adj.* bloodshot, pink, rosy, ruddy, russet.

redeem *v.* absolve, acquit, atone for, cash (in), change, compensate for, defray, deliver, discharge, emancipate, exchange, free, fulfil, keep, liberate, make good, make up for, meet, offset, outweigh, perform, ransom, reclaim, recoup, recover, recuperate, regain, repossess, repurchase, rescue, retrieve, salvage, satisfy, save.

redemption *n.* atonement, compensation, deliverance, discharge, emancipation, exchange, expiation, fulfilment, liberation, ransom, reclamation, recovery, reinstatement, release, reparation, repurchase, rescue, retrieval, salvation.

reduce *v.* contract, curtail, cut, decrease, degrade, demote, depress, diminish, discount, downgrade, drive, force, humble, humiliate, impair, impoverish, lessen, lower, master, moderate, overpower, rebate, ruin, scant, shorten, slash, slim, subdue, trim, vanquish, weaken. *antonyms* boost, extend, increase, upgrade.

reduction *n.* compression, condensation, contraction, curtailment, cut, cutback, decline, decrease, deduction, deposal, depreciation, devaluation, diminution, discount, drop, ellipsis, limitation, loss, miniature, mitigation,

moderation, modification, narrowing, rebate, rebatement, refund, restriction, shortening, shrinkage, slackening, softening, subtraction, summarisation, summary.
antonyms enlargement, improvement, increase.

redundancy *n.* **1** dismissal, sacking, unemployment. **2** excess, repetition, superfluity, surplus, tautology, uselessness, wordiness.

redundant *adj.* **1** out of work, superfluous, supernumerary, surplus, unemployed, wordy. **2** excessive, extra, repetitious, unnecessary, unneeded, unwanted, verbose.
antonyms **2** concise, essential, necessary.

reel *v.* gyrate, lurch, pitch, revolve, rock, roll, spin, stagger, stumble, sway, swim, swirl, totter, twirl, waver, wheel, whirl, wobble.

refer *v.* allude, apply, ascribe, assign, attribute, belong, cite, commit, concern, consult, credit, deliver, direct, go, guide, hint, look up, mention, point, recommend, relate, send, speak of, submit, touch on, transfer, turn to.

referee *n.* adjudicator, arbiter, arbitrator, judge, ref, umpire.
v. adjudicate, arbitrate, judge, ref, umpire.

reference *n.* **1** allusion, citation, connection, consideration, illustration, instance, mention, note, quotation, regard, relation, remark, respect. **2** character, credentials, endorsement, recommendation, testimonial.

refined *adj.* civil, civilised, clarified, cultured, delicate, discriminating, elegant, exact, filtered, fine, genteel, gentlemanly, ladylike, polished, polite, precise, punctilious, pure, sensitive, sophisticated, sublime, subtle, urbane, well-bred, well-mannered.
antonyms brutish, coarse, earthy, rude, vulgar.

refinement *n.* **1** amendment, improvement, modification. **2** breeding, cultivation, fastidiousness, finesse, gentility, politeness, sophistication, style, subtlety, taste, urbanity.
antonyms **1** deterioration. **2** coarseness, earthiness, vulgarity.

reflect *v.* **1** communicate, demonstrate, depict, display, echo, exhibit, express, imitate, indicate, manifest, mirror, portray, reproduce, reveal, show. **2** consider, contemplate, deliberate, meditate, mull (over), muse, ponder, think.

reflection *n.* **1** criticism, echo, image, impression, observation, opinion, reproach, slur, view. **2** consideration, contemplation, deliberation, meditation, musing, pondering, study, thinking, thought.

reform *v.* amend, better, correct, improve, mend, purge, rebuild, reconstitute, reconstruct, rectify, regenerate, rehabilitate, remodel, renovate, reorganise, repair, restore, revamp, revolutionise.
n. amendment, correction, improvement, purge, rectification, rehabilitation, renovation, shake-out.

refrain[1] *v.* abstain, avoid, cease, desist, forbear, leave off, quit, renounce, stop, swear off.

refrain[2] *n.* chorus, melody, song, tune.

refresh *v.* brace, cheer, cool, enliven, freshen, jog, prod, prompt, reinvigorate, rejuvenate, renew, renovate, repair, replenish, restore, revitalise, revive, stimulate.
antonyms exhaust, tire.

refreshing *adj.* bracing, cooling, energising, fresh, inspiring, invigorating, new, novel, original, stimulating, thirst-quenching.
antonyms exhausting, tiring.

refreshment *n.* freshening, reanimation, reinvigoration, renewal, renovation, repair, restoration, revitalisation, revival, stimulation.

refuge *n.* asylum, harbour, haven, hide-away, hideout, protection, resort, retreat, sanctuary, security, shelter.

refugee *n.* absconder, deserter, displaced person, émigré, escapee, exile, fugitive, runaway.

refund *v.* rebate, reimburse, repay, restore, return.
n. rebate, reimbursement, repayment, return.

refusal *n.* **1** denial, negation, no, rebuff, rejection, repudiation. **2** choice, consideration, opportunity, option.
antonym **1** acceptance.

refuse[1] *v.* decline, deny, reject, repel, repudiate, spurn, withhold.
antonyms accept, agree, allow, permit.

refuse[2] *n.* chaff, dregs, dross, garbage, husks, junk, left-overs, litter, rubbish, scum, sediment, slops, trash, waste.

refute *v.* confute, counter, discredit, disprove, give the lie to, negate, rebut.

regain *v.* reattain, recapture, reclaim, recoup, recover, redeem, re-establish, repossess, retake, retrieve, return to.

regal *adj.* kingly, magnificent, majestic, monarchical, noble, princely, proud, queenly, royal, sovereign, stately.

regale *v.* amuse, captivate, delight, divert, entertain, fascinate, feast, gratify, refresh, serve.

regard *v.* believe, consider, deem, imagine, judge, mark, mind, note, notice, observe, rate, suppose, think, treat, value.
n. affection, attention, care, concern, consideration, deference, esteem, honour, reputation, repute, respect, sympathy.
antonyms contempt, disapproval, disregard.

regarding *prep.* about, as regards, as to, concerning, in respect of, on the subject of, with reference to, with regard to.

regardless *adj.* disregarding, heedless, inattentive, indifferent, neglectful, unconcerned, unmindful.
antonyms attentive, heedful, regardful.
adv. anyhow, anyway, come what may, despite everything, in any case, nevertheless, nonetheless.

regards *n.* compliments, greetings, respects.

regime *n.* administration, command, control, establishment, government, leadership, management, rule, system.

regiment *n.* band, battery, body, brigade, cohort, company, crew, group, platoon, squadron.

regimented *adj.* controlled, disciplined, methodical, ordered, organised, regulated,

severe, standardised, stern, strict, systematic.
antonyms disorganised, free, lax, loose.
region *n.* area, country, district, division, domain, expanse, field, land, neighbourhood, part, place, province, range, realm, scope, section, sector, sphere, terrain, territory, zone.
register *n.* almanac, annals, archives, catalogue, chronicle, diary, file, ledger, list, log, memorandum, record, roll, roster, schedule.
v. **1** catalogue, chronicle, enlist, enrol, enter, inscribe, list, log, mark, note, record, sign on. **2** betray, display, exhibit, express, indicate, manifest, read, reveal, say, show.
regret *v.* deplore, grieve, lament, miss, mourn, rue.
n. bitterness, contrition, disappointment, grief, lamentation, remorse, self-reproach, shame, sorrow.
regretful *adj.* apologetic, ashamed, conscience-stricken, contrite, disappointed, penitent, remorseful, repentant, rueful, sad, sorrowful, sorry.
antonyms impenitent, unashamed.
regrettable *adj.* deplorable, disappointing, distressing, ill-advised, lamentable, pitiable, sad, shameful, sorry, unfortunate, unhappy, unlucky, wrong.
antonyms fortunate, happy.
regular *adj.* **1** common, commonplace, conventional, correct, customary, daily, established, everyday, normal, official, ordinary, routine, standard, time-honoured, typical, usual. **2** balanced, constant, even, fixed, level, methodical, orderly, periodic, set, smooth, steady, symmetrical, systematic, uniform, unvarying.
antonyms **1** unconventional, unusual. **2** irregular, occasional.
regulate *v.* adjust, administer, arrange, balance, conduct, control, direct, fit, govern, guide, handle, manage, moderate, monitor, order, organise, rule, run, settle, square, tune.
regulation *n.* **1** commandment, decree, dictate, edict, law, order, ordinance, precept, procedure, requirement, rule, statute. **2** adjustment, administration, arrangement, control, direction, management, regimentation, supervision.
adj. accepted, customary, normal, official, orthodox, prescribed, required, standard, statutory, usual.
regurgitate *v.* disgorge, spew, throw up, vomit.
rehash *n.* rearrangement, rejigging, reshuffle, restatement, reworking, rewrite.
v. alter, change, rearrange, rejig, reshuffle, restate, rework, rewrite.
rehearsal *n.* account, catalogue, description, drill, dry-run, enumeration, list, narration, practice, preparation, reading, recital, relation, run-through, telling.
rehearse *v.* act, drill, practise, prepare, recite, recount, relate, repeat, review, study, train, try out.
reign *n.* command, control, dominion, empire, influence, monarchy, power, rule, sovereignty, supremacy, sway.
v. command, govern, influence, predominate, prevail, rule.
reimburse *v.* compensate, indemnify, recompense, refund, remunerate, repay, requite, restore, return, square up.
reinforce *v.* emphasise, fortify, harden, increase, prop, recruit, steel, stiffen, strengthen, stress, supplement, support, toughen, underline.
antonyms undermine, weaken.
reinforcements *n.* auxiliaries, back-up, reserves, support.
reinstate *v.* reappoint, recall, re-establish, reinstall, replace, restore, return.
reject *v.* condemn, deny, despise, disallow, discard, eliminate, exclude, jettison, jilt, rebuff, refuse, renounce, repel, repudiate, scrap, spurn, veto.
antonyms accept, choose, select.
n. cast-off, discard, failure, second.
rejection *n.* brush-off, denial, dismissal, elimination, exclusion, rebuff, refusal, renunciation, repudiation, veto.
antonyms acceptance, choice, selection.
rejoice *v.* celebrate, delight, glory, joy, jubilate, revel, triumph.
rejoicing *n.* celebration, cheer, delight, elation, exultation, festivity, gladness, happiness, joy, jubilation, merrymaking, revelry, triumph.
rejoin *v.* answer, quip, reply, respond, retort, riposte.
rejuvenate *v.* reanimate, recharge, refresh, regenerate, reinvigorate, rekindle, renew, restore, revitalise, revivify.
relapse *v.* backslide, degenerate, deteriorate, fail, lapse, regress, revert, sink, weaken, worsen.
n. backsliding, deterioration, lapse, recurrence, regression, reversion, setback, weakening, worsening.
relate *v.* **1** ally, associate, connect, correlate, couple, join, link. **2** appertain, apply, concern, refer. **3** describe, narrate, recite, recount, report, tell. **4** empathise, feel for, identify with, sympathise, understand.
related *adj.* accompanying, affiliated, akin, allied, associated, concomitant, connected, correlated, interconnected, joint, kin, kindred, linked.
antonyms different, unconnected, unrelated.
relation *n.* **1** affiliation, comparison, connection, correlation, interdependence, link, reference, regard, similarity. **2** bond, relationship. **3** kin, kindred, relative.
relations *n.* **1** family, kin, kindred, relatives. **2** affairs, associations, communications, connections, contact, dealings, doings, interaction, intercourse, liaison, meetings, rapport, relationship, terms.
relationship *n.* association, bond, communications, connection, contract, correlation, dealings, exchange, liaison, link, parallel, proportion, rapport, ratio, similarity, tie-up.
relative *adj.* applicable, appropriate, comparative, connected, corresponding, dependent, interrelated, proportionate, reciprocal, related,

relevant, respective.
antonym absolute.
n. family, kin, relation.

relax *v.* abate, diminish, ease, lessen, loosen, lower, mitigate, moderate, reduce, relieve, remit, rest, slacken, soften, tranquillise, unwind, weaken.
antonyms intensify, tighten.

relaxation *n.* **1** amusement, distraction, enjoyment, entertainment, fun, leisure, pleasure, recreation, refreshment, rest. **2** abatement, détente, easing, lessening, let-up, moderation, reduction, slackening, weakening.
antonyms **2** intensification, tension.

relaxed *adj.* calm, carefree, casual, collected, composed, cool, easy-going, even-tempered, happy-go-lucky, informal, laid-back, mild, unhurried.
antonyms edgy, nervous, stiff, tense, uptight.

relay *n.* broadcast, communication, dispatch, message, programme, relief, shift, transmission, turn.
v. broadcast, carry, communicate, rebroadcast, send, spread, supply, transmit.

release *v.* absolve, acquit, break, circulate, deliver, discharge, distribute, drop, emancipate, excuse, exempt, exonerate, extricate, free, issue, launch, liberate, loose, present, publish, unfasten, unleash, unloose, unveil.
antonyms check, detain, imprison.
n. absolution, acquittal, announcement, deliverance, delivery, discharge, emancipation, exemption, exoneration, freedom, issue, let-off, liberation, liberty, offering, proclamation, publication, relief.
antonyms detention, imprisonment.

relent *v.* capitulate, forbear, give in, relax, slacken, soften, unbend, weaken, yield.

relentless *adj.* cruel, fierce, grim, hard, harsh, implacable, incessant, inexorable, inflexible, merciless, persistent, pitiless, punishing, remorseless, ruthless, stern, unabated, uncompromising, unflagging, unforgiving, unremitting.
antonyms faltering, submissive, yielding.

relevant *adj.* admissible, applicable, apposite, appropriate, apt, fitting, material, pertinent, proper, related, relative, significant, suitable, suited.
antonyms inapplicable, inappropriate, irrelevant, unsuitable.

reliable *adj.* certain, constant, dependable, faithful, honest, predictable, regular, responsible, safe, solid, sound, stable, staunch, sure, true, trustworthy, unfailing, upright.
antonyms doubtful, suspect, unreliable, untrustworthy.

reliance *n.* assurance, belief, confidence, credit, dependence, faith, trust.

relic *n.* fragment, keepsake, memento, remembrance, remnant, scrap, souvenir, survival, token, trace, vestige.

relief *n.* abatement, aid, alleviation, assistance, balm, break, breather, comfort, cure, deliverance, diversion, ease, easement, help, let-up, refreshment, relaxation, release, remedy, remission, respite, rest, support, sustenance.

relieve *v.* aid, alleviate, assist, break, calm, comfort, console, cure, deliver, discharge, ease, free, help, interrupt, lighten, mitigate, relax, release, slacken, soften, soothe, stand in for, substitute for, support, sustain, take over from, take the place of, unburden, vary.
antonyms aggravate, intensify.

religious *adj.* church-going, devotional, devout, divine, doctrinal, faithful, God-fearing, godly, holy, pious, pure, reverent, righteous, sacred, scriptural, spiritual, strict, theological, unswerving.
antonyms irreligious, ungodly.

relinquish *n.* abandon, cede, desert, discard, drop, forgo, forsake, hand over, leave, release, renounce, repudiate, resign, surrender, vacate, waive, yield.
antonyms hold onto, keep, retain.

relish *v.* appreciate, enjoy, lap up, like, prefer, revel in, savour, taste.
n. appetiser, condiment, pickle, sauce, seasoning, spice.

reluctance *n.* aversion, disinclination, dislike, distaste, hesitancy, indisposition, loathing, unwillingness.
antonyms eagerness, readiness, willingness.

reluctant *adj.* averse, backward, disinclined, hesitant, indisposed, loath, slow, unenthusiastic, unwilling.
antonyms eager, ready, willing.

rely *v.* bank, count, depend, lean, reckon, swear by, trust.

remain *v.* abide, bide, cling, continue, dwell, endure, last, linger, persist, prevail, rest, sojourn, stand, stay, survive, wait.
antonyms depart, go, leave.

remainder *n.* balance, excess, remnant, rest, surplus, trace, vestige(s).

remaining *adj.* abiding, lasting, left, lingering, outstanding, persisting, residual, surviving, unfinished, unspent, unused.

remains *n.* ashes, balance, body, carcass, corpse, crumbs, debris, dregs, fragments, leavings, leftovers, oddments, pieces, relics, remainder, remnants, residue, rest, scraps, traces, vestiges.

remark *v.* comment, declare, heed, mention, note, notice, observe, regard, say, see, state.
n. acknowledgement, assertion, comment, consideration, declaration, mention, observation, opinion, statement, utterance.

remedy *n.* answer, antidote, corrective, countermeasure, cure, medicine, panacea, relief, restorative, solution, therapy, treatment.
v. correct, counteract, cure, ease, fix, heal, help, mitigate, put right, rectify, redress, reform, relieve, repair, restore, solve, soothe, treat.

remember *v.* commemorate, place, recall, recognise, recollect, reminisce, retain, summon up, think back.
antonyms disregard, forget, ignore.

remembrance *n.* commemoration, keepsake,

memento, memorial, memory, mind, monument, recall, recognition, recollection, regard, relic, reminder, reminiscence, retrospect, souvenir, testimonial, thought, token.

remind *v.* bring to mind, call to mind, call up, hint, jog one's memory, prompt, put in mind, refresh one's memory.

reminder *n.* hint, memo, memorandum, nudge, prompt(ing), suggestion.

reminiscence *n.* anecdote, memoir, memory, recall, recollection, reflection, remembrance, retrospection, review.

reminiscent *adj.* evocative, nostalgic, similar, suggestive.

remit *v.* dispatch, forward, mail, post, send, transfer, transmit.
n. authorisation, brief, guidelines, instructions, orders, responsibility, scope, terms of reference.

remittance *n.* allowance, consideration, dispatch, fee, payment, sending.

remnant *n.* balance, bit, end, fragment, hangover, left-overs, piece, remainder, remains, residue, residuum, rest, scrap, shred, survival, trace, vestige.

remorse *n.* anguish, bad conscience, compunction, contrition, grief, guilt, penitence, pity, regret, repentance, ruefulness, self-reproach, shame, sorrow.

remorseless *adj.* callous, cruel, hard, hard-hearted, harsh, inhumane, merciless, pitiless, relentless, ruthless, savage, stern, unforgiving, unmerciful, unrelenting, unstoppable.
antonyms forgiving, kind, merciful, sorry.

remote *adj.* **1** distant, far, faraway, far-off, god-forsaken, inaccessible, isolated, lonely, outlying, out-of-the-way, removed, secluded. **2** aloof, detached, indifferent, standoffish, uninvolved, withdrawn. **3** faint, negligible, slender, slight, slim, small, unlikely.
antonyms **1** accessible, close, nearby. **2** friendly. **3** significant.

removal *n.* dismissal, displacement, ejection, elimination, eradication, expulsion, extraction, flitting, move, purging, relocation, riddance, stripping, transfer, uprooting, withdrawal.

remove *v.* abolish, amputate, delete, depart, depose, detach, dethrone, discharge, dislodge, dismiss, displace, doff, efface, eject, eliminate, erase, expunge, extract, get rid of, move, oust, purge, quit, relegate, relocate, shear, shed, shift, sideline, strike, transfer, transport, unseat, vacate, withdraw.

remunerate *v.* compensate, fee, indemnify, pay, recompense, redress, reimburse, repay, requite, reward.

remuneration *n.* compensation, earnings, emolument, fee, income, indemnity, pay, payment, profit, recompense, reimbursement, remittance, reparation, repayment, retainer, return, reward, salary, stipend, wages.

render *v.* **1** cause to be, leave, make. **2** contribute, deliver, give, hand over, present, provide, submit, supply, tender. **3** clarify, explain, interpret, represent, reproduce, restate, transcribe, translate.

renew *v.* continue, extend, mend, modernise, overhaul, prolong, reaffirm, recommence, recreate, re-establish, refashion, refit, refresh, regenerate, rejuvenate, remodel, renovate, repair, repeat, replace, replenish, restate, restock, restore, revitalise, transform.

renewal *n.* kiss of life, reconditioning, reconstitution, reconstruction, recreation, refurbishment, reinvigoration, rejuvenation, renovation, repair, resuscitation, revitalisation.

renounce *v.* abandon, decline, deny, discard, disclaim, disown, forsake, put away, recant, reject, relinquish, repudiate, resign, spurn.

renovate *v.* do up, furbish, improve, modernise, overhaul, recondition, reconstitute, recreate, refit, reform, refurbish, remodel, renew, repair, restore, revamp.

renown *n.* acclaim, celebrity, distinction, eminence, fame, glory, honour, illustriousness, kudos, lustre, mark, note, reputation, stardom.
antonyms anonymity, obscurity.

renowned *adj.* acclaimed, celebrated, distinguished, eminent, esteemed, famed, famous, illustrious, notable, noted, pre-eminent, well-known.
antonyms anonymous, obscure, unknown.

rent *n.* fee, hire, lease, payment, rental, tariff.
v. charter, farm out, hire, lease, let, sublet, take.

repair *v.* fix, heal, mend, patch up, rectify, redress, renew, renovate, restore, retrieve.
n. adjustment, condition, form, improvement, mend, overhaul, patch, restoration, shape, state.

reparation *n.* amends, atonement, compensation, damages, indemnity, recompense, redress, renewal, repair, requital, restitution, satisfaction.

repartee *n.* banter, jesting, pleasantry, riposte, wit, witticism.

repay *v.* avenge, compensate, get even with, make restitution, reciprocate, recompense, refund, reimburse, remunerate, restore, retaliate, revenge, reward, settle the score, square.

repayment *n.* compensation, rebate, recompense, refund, reimbursement, remuneration, restitution, reward.

repeal *v.* abolish, annul, cancel, countermand, invalidate, nullify, quash, recall, rescind, reverse, revoke, set aside, void, withdraw.
antonyms enact, establish.
n. abolition, annulment, cancellation, invalidation, quashing, rescinding, reversal, withdrawal.
antonyms enactment, establishment.

repeat *v.* duplicate, echo, quote, rebroadcast, recapitulate, recite, re-do, reiterate, relate, renew, replay, reproduce, rerun, reshow, restate, retell.
n. duplicate, echo, rebroadcast, repetition, replay, reproduction, rerun, reshowing.

repeatedly *adv.* again and again, frequently, often, over and over, time after time, time and (time) again.

repel *v.* check, confront, decline, disadvantage,

disgust, fight, hold off, nauseate, offend, oppose, parry, rebuff, refuse, reject, repulse, resist, revolt, sicken, ward off.
antonyms attract, delight.
repent *n.* atone, deplore, lament, regret, rue, sorrow.
repentance *n.* compunction, contrition, grief, guilt, penitence, regret, remorse, sorrow.
repentant *adj.* apologetic, ashamed, chastened, contrite, penitent, regretful, remorseful, rueful, sorry.
antonym unrepentant.
repercussion *n.* backlash, consequence, echo, rebound, recoil, result, reverberation, side effect.
repertory *n.* collection, list, range, repertoire, repository, reserve, reservoir, stock, store, supply.
repetition *n.* duplication, echo, reappearance, recapitulation, recurrence, rehearsal, reiteration, restatement, return, tautology.
repetitive *adj.* boring, dull, mechanical, monotonous, recurrent, tedious, unchanging, unvaried.
replace *v.* deputise, follow, make good, oust, re-establish, reinstate, restore, substitute, succeed, supersede, supplant, supply.
replacement *n.* double, fill-in, proxy, stand-in, substitute, successor, surrogate, understudy.
replenish *v.* fill, furnish, provide, recharge, recruit, refill, reload, renew, replace, restock, restore, stock, supply, top up.
replica *n.* clone, copy, duplicate, facsimile, imitation, model, reproduction.
reply *v.* acknowledge, answer, counter, echo, react, reciprocate, rejoin, respond, retaliate, retort, return.
n. acknowledgement, answer, comeback, counter, echo, reaction, rejoinder, repartee, response, retaliation, retort, return, riposte.
report *n.* account, announcement, article, communication, communiqué, declaration, description, gossip, hearsay, information, message, narrative, news, note, paper, piece, record, relation, reverberation, rumour, statement, story, summary, tale, talk, version, word, write-up.
v. air, announce, appear, arrive, broadcast, circulate, communicate, cover, declare, describe, detail, document, mention, narrate, note, notify, proclaim, publish, recite, record, recount, relate, relay, state, tell.
reporter *n.* announcer, correspondent, hack, journalist, newscaster, newspaperman, newspaperwoman, pressman, writer.
represent *v.* act, amount to, appear as, be, constitute, denote, depict, describe, designate, embody, enact, evoke, exemplify, exhibit, express, illustrate, mean, outline, perform, personify, picture, portray, produce, render, reproduce, show, sketch, stage, stand for, symbolise, typify.
representation *n.* **1** committee, delegates, delegation, embassy. **2** account, bust, description, exhibition, explanation, exposition, idol, illustration, image, likeness, model, narration, performance, picture, play, portrait, portrayal, production, show, sight, sketch, spectacle, statue.
representative *n.* agent, commissioner, councillor, delegate, deputy, member, MP, proxy, rep, salesman, spokesman, spokesperson, spokeswoman, traveller.
adj. archetypal, characteristic, chosen, elected, evocative, exemplary, illustrative, normal, symbolic, typical, usual.
antonyms atypical, unrepresentative.
repress *v.* bottle up, chasten, check, control, crush, curb, hamper, hinder, impede, inhibit, master, muffle, overcome, overpower, quash, quell, restrain, silence, smother, stifle, subdue, subjugate, suppress, swallow.
repression *n.* authoritarianism, censorship, coercion, constraint, control, denial, despotism, domination, gagging, inhibition, restraint, suffocation, suppression, tyranny.
repressive *adj.* absolute, authoritarian, autocratic, coercive, despotic, dictatorial, harsh, iron-handed, oppressive, severe, tough, tyrannical.
reprieve *v.* abate, allay, alleviate, mitigate, pardon, redeem, relieve, rescue, respite.
n. abatement, abeyance, alleviation, amnesty, deferment, let-up, pardon, postponement, redemption, relief, remission, rescue, respite, suspension.
reprimand *n.* admonition, blame, censure, dressing-down, lecture, rebuke, reprehension, reproach, reproof, row, talking-to, telling-off, ticking-off.
v. admonish, blame, censure, chide, lecture, lesson, rebuke, reproach, reprove, scold, slate.
reprisal *n.* counter-stroke, requital, retaliation, retribution, revenge, vengeance.
reproach *v.* abuse, blame, censure, chide, condemn, criticise, defame, discredit, disparage, rebuke, reprehend, reprimand, reprove, scold, upbraid.
n. abuse, blame, blemish, censure, condemnation, contempt, disapproval, discredit, disgrace, dishonour, disrepute, ignominy, indignity, reproof, scorn, shame, slight, stain, stigma.
reproachful *adj.* abusive, censorious, critical, disappointed, disapproving, fault-finding, reproving, scolding, upbraiding.
antonym complimentary.
reproduce *v.* **1** copy, duplicate, echo, emulate, imitate, match, mirror, parallel, print, recreate, regurgitate, repeat, simulate, transcribe. **2** breed, generate, multiply, procreate, propagate, spawn.
reproduction *n.* **1** copy, duplicate, facsimile, imitation, increase, picture, print, replica. **2** breeding, generation, multiplication, procreation, propagation.
antonym **1** original.
reproductive *adj.* generative, genital, sex, sexual.

reproof *n.* admonition, blame, censure, condemnation, criticism, dressing-down, rebuke, reprimand, reproach, scolding, ticking-off, upbraiding.
antonym praise.

reprove *v.* abuse, admonish, blame, censure, condemn, rebuke, reprehend, reprimand, scold, upbraid.
antonym praise.

repugnance *n.* abhorrence, aversion, disgust, dislike, distaste, hatred, loathing, reluctance, repulsion, revulsion.
antonyms delight, liking, pleasure.

repugnant *adj.* abhorrent, disgusting, distasteful, foul, hateful, horrid, loathsome, nauseating, objectionable, offensive, repellent, revolting, sickening.
antonyms acceptable, delightful, pleasant.

repulse *v.* beat off, check, defeat, disregard, drive back, rebuff, refuse, reject, repel, snub, spurn.

repulsive *adj.* abhorrent, abominable, disagreeable, disgusting, distasteful, forbidding, hideous, loathsome, nauseating, objectionable, offensive, repellent, revolting, ugly, unpleasant, vile.
antonyms attractive, friendly, pleasant.

reputable *adj.* creditable, dependable, excellent, good, honourable, irreproachable, principled, reliable, respectable, trustworthy, upright, worthy.
antonyms disreputable, infamous.

reputation *n.* bad name, character, credit, distinction, fame, good name, honour, infamy, name, opinion, renown, repute, standing, stature.

repute *n.* celebrity, distinction, esteem, estimation, fame, good name, name, renown, reputation, standing, stature.

reputed *adj.* alleged, believed, considered, estimated, held, ostensible, reckoned, regarded, rumoured, said, seeming, supposed, thought.
antonyms actual, true.

reputedly *adv.* allegedly, apparently, ostensibly, seemingly, supposedly.
antonyms actually, really.

request *v.* ask for, beg, demand, desire, entreat, petition, pray, seek, supplicate.
n. appeal, application, asking, call, demand, desire, entreaty, petition, prayer, representation, solicitation, suit, supplication.

require *v.* ask, compel, constrain, demand, desire, direct, exact, force, instruct, involve, lack, make, miss, necessitate, need, oblige, order, request, take, want, wish.

requirement *n.* condition, demand, desideratum, lack, must, necessity, need, prerequisite, provision, qualification, specification, stipulation, term, want.
antonym inessential.

requisition *v.* appropriate, commandeer, confiscate, demand, occupy, put in for, request, seize, take.
n. application, appropriation, call, commandeering, demand, occupation, order, request, seizure, summons, takeover, use.

rescue *v.* deliver, free, liberate, ransom, recover, redeem, release, salvage, save.
antonyms capture, imprison.
n. deliverance, liberation, recovery, redemption, release, relief, salvage, salvation, saving.
antonym capture.

research *n.* analysis, enquiry, examination, experimentation, exploration, fact-finding, groundwork, investigation, probe, scrutiny, search, study.
v. analyse, examine, experiment, explore, investigate, probe, scrutinise, search, study.

researcher *n.* analyst, boffin, enquirer, field worker, inspector, investigator, student.

resemblance *n.* affinity, analogy, closeness, comparison, conformity, correspondence, facsimile, image, likeness, parallel, parity, sameness, similarity.
antonym dissimilarity.

resemble *v.* approach, be like, duplicate, echo, favour, mirror, parallel, take after.
antonym differ from.

resent *v.* begrudge, dislike, grudge, grumble at, object to, take amiss, take exception to, take offence at, take umbrage at.
antonyms accept, like.

resentful *adj.* aggrieved, angry, bitter, exasperated, grudging, huffy, hurt, incensed, indignant, irate, jealous, miffed, offended, put out, resentive, unforgiving, wounded.
antonyms contented, satisfied.

resentment *n.* anger, animosity, bitterness, displeasure, fury, grudge, huff, hurt, ill-feeling, ill-will, indignation, ire, irritation, malice, pique, rage, umbrage, vexation, vindictiveness, wrath.
antonyms contentment, happiness.

reservation *n.* **1** doubt, hesitation, scepticism, scruple, second thought. **2** proviso, qualification, stipulation. **3** enclave, homeland, park, preserve, reserve, sanctuary, territory, tract.

reserve *v.* **1** hold, keep, retain, save, set apart, stockpile, store. **2** book, engage, secure.
antonym use up.
n. **1** backlog, cache, stock, stockpile, store, supply. **2** capital, fund, hoard, savings. **3** park, preserve, reservation, tract. **4** replacement, substitute. **5** aloofness, coolness, formality, modesty, restraint, reticence, secretiveness, shyness.
antonyms **5** friendliness, informality, openness.
adj. additional, alternate, auxiliary, extra, secondary, spare, substitute.

reserved *adj.* **1** booked, bound, designated, destined, earmarked, engaged, held, intended, kept, meant, retained, set aside, spoken for, taken. **2** aloof, cautious, formal, modest, restrained, reticent, retiring, secretive, shy, silent, stand-offish, taciturn, unapproachable, uncommunicative, unforthcoming, unresponsive, unsociable.
antonyms **1** free, unreserved. **2** demonstrative, friendly, informal.

reshuffle *n.* change, realignment, rearrangement, redistribution, regrouping, reorganisation, restructuring, revision, shake-up, upheaval.
v. change, interchange, realign, rearrange, redistribute, regroup, reorganise, restructure, revise, shake up, shift, shuffle.
reside *v.* **1** dwell, inhabit, live, lodge, remain, settle, sojourn, stay. **2** consist, exist, inhere, lie.
residence *n.* abode, country-house, country-seat, dwelling, habitation, hall, home, house, household, lodging, manor, mansion, occupation, palace, place, quarters, seat, stay, villa.
resident *n.* citizen, inhabitant, local, lodger, occupant, tenant.
antonym non-resident.
residential *adj.* commuter, suburban.
antonyms business, industrial.
residential area commuter belt, dormitory town, suburbia, suburbs.
residual *adj.* left-over, net(t), remaining, unconsumed, unused.
resign *v.* abandon, abdicate, forgo, forsake, leave, relinquish, renounce, sacrifice, stand down, surrender, vacate, waive, yield.
antonyms join, maintain.
resign oneself accept, acquiesce, bow, comply, reconcile, submit, yield.
antonym resist.
resignation *n.* **1** abdication, departure, leaving, notice, relinquishment, renunciation, retirement. **2** acceptance, acquiescence, defeatism, forbearing, non-resistance, passivity, patience, submission.
antonym **2** resistance.
resigned *adj.* defeatist, patient, reconciled, stoical, submissive, unprotesting, unresisting.
antonym resisting.
resilient *adj.* adaptable, bouncy, buoyant, elastic, flexible, hardy, plastic, pliable, springy, strong, supple, tough, unshockable.
antonyms downcast, rigid.
resist *v.* avoid, combat, confront, counteract, defy, fight back, forgo, oppose, refuse, repel, weather, withstand.
antonyms accept, submit.
resistance *n.* battle, combat, contention, counteraction, defiance, fighting, obstruction, opposition, refusal, struggle.
antonyms acceptance, submission.
resistant *adj.* **1** antagonistic, defiant, dissident, opposed, unwilling, unyielding. **2** immune, impervious, -proof, strong, tough.
antonyms **1** compliant, yielding.
resolute *adj.* bold, determined, dogged, firm, fixed, obstinate, persevering, relentless, set, staunch, steadfast, strong-minded, strong-willed, stubborn, sturdy, tenacious, undaunted, unflinching, unwavering.
antonyms doubtful, irresolute, weak.
resolution *n.* **1** boldness, courage, dedication, determination, devotion, doggedness, earnestness, energy, firmness, perseverance, steadfastness, tenacity, will power, zeal. **2** decision, declaration, finding, intention, judgement, motion.
antonyms **1** half-heartedness, indecision, uncertainty.
resound *v.* boom, echo, re-echo, resonate, reverberate, ring, sound.
resounding *adj.* booming, conclusive, crushing, decisive, echoing, full, powerful, resonant, reverberating, rich, ringing, sonorous, sounding, thorough, vibrant, vocal.
antonyms faint, slight.
resource *n.* ability, capability, contrivance, course, device, ingenuity, initiative, inventiveness, means, reserve, resort, source, stockpile, supply, talent.
antonym unimaginativeness.
resourceful *adj.* able, bright, capable, clever, creative, fertile, imaginative, ingenious, innovative, inventive, originative, quick-witted, sharp, talented.
resources *n.* assets, capital, funds, holdings, materials, means, money, property, reserves, riches, supplies, wealth.
respect *n.* **1** admiration, appreciation, esteem, honour, recognition, reverence, veneration. **2** aspect, characteristic, connection, detail, facet, feature, matter, particular, point, reference, regard, relation, sense, way.
antonyms **1** disregard, disrespect.
v. **1** admire, appreciate, esteem, regard, value. **2** follow, honour, obey, observe.
antonyms **1** disrespect, scorn. **2** disobey, ignore.
respectable *adj.* **1** appreciable, clean-living, dignified, fair, honest, honourable, reasonable, respected, tolerable, upright, worthy. **2** acceptable, adequate, decent, passable.
antonyms **1** dishonourable, disreputable. **2** inadequate, paltry.
respectful *adj.* civil, courteous, deferential, humble, obedient, polite, reverential, well-mannered.
antonym disrespectful.
respective *adj.* corresponding, individual, own, particular, personal, relevant, separate, several, special, specific, various.
respects *n.* compliments, greetings, regards.
respond *v.* acknowledge, answer, come back, react, reply, retort, return.
response *n.* acknowledgement, answer, comeback, feedback, reaction, reply, respond, retort, return.
antonym query.
responsibility *n.* accountability, answerability, authority, blame, burden, care, charge, conscientiousness, culpability, dependability, duty, fault, guilt, importance, maturity, obligation, onus, power, reliability, sense, soberness, stability, trust, trustworthiness.
antonym irresponsibility.
responsible *adj.* **1** accountable, answerable, authoritative, chargeable, conscientious, culpable, dependable, guilty, liable, mature, rational, reliable, right, sensible, sober, sound, stable, steady, trustworthy. **2** decision-making,

executive, important.
antonyms **1** irresponsible, unreliable, untrustworthy.
responsive *adj.* alive, awake, forthcoming, impressionable, open, perceptive, receptive, respondent, sensitive, sharp, susceptible, sympathetic.
antonyms apathetic, silent, unresponsive.
rest[1] *n.* **1** calm, doze, idleness, inactivity, leisure, lie-down, lie-in, motionlessness, nap, relaxation, repose, siesta, sleep, snooze, standstill, stillness, tranquillity. **2** break, breather, breathing-space, cessation, halt, holiday, interlude, intermission, interval, lull, pause, recess, respite, vacation. **3** base, prop, stand, support, trestle.
antonyms **1** action, activity, restlessness. **2** business, work.
v. **1** cease, halt, pause, stay, stop. **2** doze, laze, lie down, recline, relax, repose, sit, sleep, snooze. **3** depend, hang, hinge, lie, rely, reside.
antonyms **1** continue. **2** work.
rest[2] *n.* balance, excess, left-overs, majority, others, remainder, remains, remnants, residue, surplus.
restaurant *n.* bistro, buffet, café, cafeteria, dining-car, dining-room, eating-house, grill-room, snack bar, steak-house.
restful *adj.* calm, comfortable, peaceful, quiet, relaxed, serene, soothing, tranquil, undisturbed, unhurried.
antonyms noisy, restless, wild.
restive *adj.* agitated, discontented, edgy, fractious, fretful, impatient, nervous, obstinate, restless, uneasy, unquiet, unruly.
antonyms calm, relaxed.
restless *adj.* active, agitated, anxious, disturbed, edgy, fidgety, fretful, hurried, inconstant, irresolute, jumpy, moving, nervous, roving, shifting, sleepless, troubled, turbulent, uneasy, unquiet, unresting, unruly, unsettled, unsteady, wandering, worried.
antonyms calm, comfortable, relaxed.
restoration *n.* reconstruction, recovery, recruit, re-establishment, refreshment, refurbishing, rehabilitation, reinstatement, renewal, renovation, repair, restitution, return, revitalisation, revival.
antonyms damage, removal, weakening.
restore *v.* fix, mend, rebuild, recondition, reconstruct, recover, recruit, re-enforce, re-establish, refresh, refurbish, rehabilitate, reinstate, reintroduce, rejuvenate, renew, renovate, repair, replace, retouch, return, revitalise, revive, strengthen.
antonyms damage, remove, weaken.
restrain *v.* arrest, bind, bridle, chain, check, confine, constrain, control, curb, curtail, debar, detain, fetter, govern, hamper, handicap, hinder, hold (back), imprison, inhibit, jail, keep, limit, prevent, repress, restrict, stay, subdue, suppress, tie.
antonyms encourage, liberate.
restrained *adj.* calm, controlled, low-key, mild, moderate, muted, quiet, reticent, self-controlled, soft, steady, subdued, tasteful, temperate, undemonstrative, unemphatic, unobtrusive.
antonym unrestrained.
restraint *n.* arrest, ban, bondage, bonds, bridle, captivity, chains, check, coercion, command, compulsion, confinement, confines, constraint, control, cramp, curb, curtailment, detention, embargo, fetters, grip, hindrance, hold, inhibition, limit, limitation, moderation, prevention, rein, restriction, self-control, self-discipline, straitjacket, suppression, taboo, tie.
antonyms freedom, liberty.
restrict *v.* bound, confine, constrain, contain, cramp, demarcate, hamper, handicap, impede, inhibit, limit, regulate, restrain, tie.
antonyms broaden, encourage, free.
restriction *n.* check, condition, confinement, constraint, control, curb, handicap, inhibition, limitation, regulation, restraint, rule, stipulation.
antonyms broadening, encouragement, freedom.
result *n.* conclusion, consequence, decision, development, effect, end-product, fruit, issue, outcome, produce, reaction, sequel, upshot.
antonyms beginning, cause.
v. appear, arise, bring about, culminate, derive, develop, emerge, end, ensue, finish, flow, follow, happen, issue, proceed, spring, stem, terminate.
antonyms begin, cause.
resume *v.* continue, pick up, proceed, recommence, reopen, restart, take up.
antonym cease.
resumption *n.* continuation, re-establishment, renewal, reopening, restart, resurgence.
antonym cessation.
resurrect *v.* bring to life, disinter, reactivate, reintroduce, renew, restore, revive.
antonyms bury, kill off, quash.
resurrection *n.* comeback, reactivation, reappearance, rebirth, renaissance, renewal, restoration, resurgence, resuscitation, return, revival.
antonyms burying, killing off, quashing.
resuscitate *v.* quicken, reanimate, reinvigorate, renew, rescue, restore, resurrect, revitalise, revive, save.
retain *v.* **1** hold back, keep, memorise, preserve, remember, reserve, save. **2** contain, hold. **3** commission, employ, engage, hire, pay.
antonyms **1** spend. **2** release. **3** dismiss.
retainer[1] *n.* attendant, dependant, domestic, footman, servant, supporter, valet.
retainer[2] *n.* advance, deposit, fee, retaining fee.
retaliate *v.* fight back, get back at, get even with, get one's own back, hit back, reciprocate, repay in kind, return like for like, revenge oneself, strike back, take revenge.
antonyms accept, submit.
reticent *adj.* close-lipped, quiet, reserved, restrained, secretive, silent, tight-lipped, uncommunicative, unforthcoming.

antonyms communicative, forward, frank.

retire *v.* depart, draw back, leave, recede, remove, retreat, withdraw.
antonyms enter, join.

retired *adj.* emeritus, ex-, former, past.

retirement *n.* loneliness, obscurity, privacy, retreat, seclusion, solitude, withdrawal.
antonyms company, limelight.

retiring *adj.* bashful, humble, meek, modest, quiet, reserved, reticent, self-effacing, shrinking, shy, timid, unassertive, unassuming.
antonyms assertive, bold, forward.

retort *v.* answer (back), counter, rejoin, reply, respond, retaliate, return.
n. answer, come-back, quip, rejoinder, repartee, reply, response, riposte.

retreat *v.* depart, draw back, leave, quit, recede, retire, shrink, turn tail, withdraw.
antonyms advance, move forward.
n. **1** departure, evacuation, flight, withdrawal. **2** asylum, den, haunt, haven, hideaway, privacy, refuge, sanctuary, seclusion, shelter.
antonyms **1** advance, charge. **2** company, limelight.

retrieve *v.* fetch, make good, recall, recapture, recoup, recover, redeem, regain, rescue, restore, return, salvage, save.
antonym lose.

retrograde *adj.* backward, declining, deteriorating, downward, negative, retrogressive, worsening.
antonym progressive.

retrospect *n.* afterthought, hindsight, recollection, re-examination, remembrance, reminiscence.
antonym prospect.

return *v.* **1** come back, go back, reappear, recur, retreat, revert. **2** deliver, give back, hand back, replace, restore. **3** reciprocate, recompense, refund, reimburse, repay, requite. **4** rebound, send, volley. **5** choose, elect.
antonyms **1** depart, leave. **2** take.
n. **1** comeback, home-coming, reappearance. **2** reciprocation, recompense, reinstatement, replacement, restoration. **3** advantage, benefit, gain, income, proceeds, profit, recurrence, revenue, reward, takings, yield.
antonyms **1** disappearance. **2** removal. **3** expense, loss, payment.

re-use *v.* reconstitute, recycle.

revamp *v.* amend, do up, modify, overhaul, recast, recondition, reconstruct, refit, refurbish, renovate, repair, restore, revise.

reveal *v.* announce, betray, broadcast, communicate, disclose, display, divulge, exhibit, expose, impart, manifest, open, proclaim, publish, show, tell, uncover, unearth, unveil.
antonyms conceal, hide, mask.

revelation *n.* announcement, broadcasting, communication, disclosure, discovery, display, exhibition, exposé, exposition, exposure, giveaway, leak, manifestation, news, proclamation, publication, telling, uncovering, unveiling.

reveller *n.* carouser, celebrator, merrymaker, party-goer, pleasure-seeker.

revelry *n.* carousal, celebration, debauchery, festivity, fun, merrymaking, party, riot.
antonym sobriety.

revenge *n.* a dose/taste of one's own medicine, reprisal, requital, retaliation, satisfaction, vengeance, vindictiveness.
v. avenge, even the score, get one's own back, get satisfaction, repay, retaliate, vindicate.

revenue *n.* gain, income, interest, proceeds, profits, receipts, returns, rewards, takings, yield.
antonym expenditure.

reverberate *v.* echo, recoil, re-echo, reflect, resound, ring, vibrate.

reverberation *n.* echo, recoil, re-echoing, reflection, resonance, resounding, ringing, vibration, wave.

reverberations *n.* consequences, effects, repercussions, results, ripples, shock wave.

revere *v.* adore, exalt, honour, pay homage to, respect, venerate, worship.
antonyms despise, scorn.

reverence *n.* admiration, adoration, awe, deference, devotion, homage, honour, respect, veneration, worship.
antonyms contempt, scorn.

reverent *adj.* adoring, awed, deferential, devout, dutiful, humble, loving, pious, respectful, solemn, submissive.
antonyms disrespectful, irreverent.

reversal *n.* annulment, cancellation, countermanding, defeat, delay, difficulty, disaster, misfortune, nullification, problem, repeal, rescinding, reverse, revocation, set-back, turnabout, turnround, upset, U-turn, volte-face.
antonyms advancement, progress.

reverse *v.* alter, annul, back, backtrack, cancel, change, countermand, invalidate, invert, negate, overrule, overset, overthrow, overturn, quash, repeal, retract, retreat, revert, revoke, transpose, undo, up-end, upset.
antonyms advance, enforce.
n. adversity, affliction, back, blow, check, contradiction, contrary, converse, defeat, disappointment, failure, hardship, inverse, misadventure, misfortune, mishap, opposite, rear, setback, trial, underside.
adj. backward, contrary, converse, inverse, inverted, opposite.

revert *v.* go back, lapse, recur, regress, relapse, resume, return, reverse.
antonym progress.

review *v.* assess, criticise, discuss, evaluate, examine, inspect, judge, reassess, recall, recapitulate, recollect, reconsider, re-evaluate, re-examine, remember, rethink, revise, scrutinise, study, weigh.
n. **1** analysis, assessment, commentary, criticism, critique, evaluation, examination, judgement, reassessment, recapitulation, re-evaluation, re-examination, report, revision, scrutiny, study, survey. **2** journal, magazine, periodical.

reviewer *n.* commentator, critic, judge, observer.

revise *v.* **1** alter, amend, change, correct, edit,

modify, recast, reconsider, reconstruct, re-examine, revamp, review, rewrite, update. **2** cram, memorise, study, swot up.

revision *n.* **1** alteration, amendment, change, correction, editing, modification, re-examination, review, rewriting, updating. **2** cramming, homework, memorising, studying, swotting.

revive *v.* animate, awaken, cheer, comfort, invigorate, quicken, rally, reactivate, recover, refresh, rekindle, renew, renovate, restore, resuscitate, revitalise, rouse.
antonyms suppress, weary.

revoke *v.* abrogate, annul, cancel, countermand, dissolve, invalidate, negate, nullify, quash, recall, renounce, repeal, repudiate, rescind, retract, reverse, withdraw.
antonym enforce.

revolt *n.* defection, insurrection, mutiny, putsch, rebellion, revolution, rising, secession, uprising.
v. **1** defect, mutiny, rebel, resist, riot, rise. **2** disgust, nauseate, offend, outrage, repel, scandalise, shock, sicken.
antonyms 1 submit. **2** delight, please.

revolting *adj.* abhorrent, appalling, disgusting, distasteful, foul, horrible, loathsome, nasty, nauseating, obnoxious, offensive, repellent, repulsive, shocking, sickening.
antonyms attractive, delightful, palatable, pleasant.

revolution *n.* **1** cataclysm, change, coup, coup d'état, innovation, insurgency, mutiny, putsch, rebellion, reformation, revolt, rising, transformation, upheaval, uprising. **2** circle, circuit, cycle, gyration, orbit, rotation, round, spin, turn, wheel, whirl.

revolutionary *n.* anarchist, insurgent, mutineer, rebel, revolutionist.
adj. **1** anarchistic, avant-garde, extremist, insurgent, mutinous, rebel, subversive. **2** different, drastic, innovative, new, novel, radical, thoroughgoing.
antonyms **1** establishment. **2** commonplace.

revolve *v.* circle, gyrate, orbit, rotate, spin, turn, whirl.

revolver *n.* air-gun, firearm, gun, hand-gun, pistol.

revulsion *n.* abhorrence, abomination, aversion, disgust, dislike, distaste, hatred, loathing, repugnance.
antonyms approval, delight, pleasure.

reward *n.* benefit, bonus, bounty, compensation, desert, gain, honour, meed, merit, payment, pay-off, premium, prize, profit, punishment, recompense, remuneration, repayment, requital, retribution, return, wages.
antonym punishment.
v. compensate, honour, pay, recompense, remunerate, repay, requite.
antonym punish.

rewarding *adj.* advantageous, beneficial, enriching, fruitful, fulfilling, gratifying, pleasing, productive, profitable, remunerative, rewardful, satisfying, valuable, worthwhile.
antonym unrewarding.

rewrite *v.* correct, edit, emend, recast, redraft, revise, reword, rework.

rhetoric *n.* eloquence, grandiloquence, hyperbole, oratory, pomposity, verbosity, wordiness.

rhetorical *adj.* artificial, bombastic, declamatory, flamboyant, florid, flowery, grand, high-flown, high-sounding, insincere, poetic, pompous, pretentious, showy.
antonym simple.

rhyme *n.* chime, ditty, jingle, limerick, ode, poem, poetry, song, verse.

rhythm *n.* accent, beat, cadence, cadency, flow, lilt, measure, metre, movement, pattern, pulse, rhythmicity, swing, tempo, time.

rhythmic *adj.* flowing, harmonious, lilting, melodious, metric, metrical, musical, periodic, pulsating, rhythmical, throbbing.
antonym unrhythmical.

ribbon *n.* band, cord, hair-band, head-band, sash, strip.

rich *adj.* **1** affluent, in the money, prosperous, wealthy, well-off, well-to-do. **2** abundant, ample, copious, full, plentiful, profuse, prolific. **3** fertile, fruitful, lush, productive. **4** creamy, delicious, fatty, full-bodied, full-flavoured, heavy, highly-flavoured, juicy, luscious, savoury, spicy, strong, sweet, tasty. **5** bright, deep, intense, vibrant, vivid, warm. **6** elaborate, elegant, expensive, fine, gorgeous, lavish, precious, splendid, sumptuous, valuable.
antonyms **1** impoverished, poor. **3** barren, unfertile. **4** bland, simple, tasteless. **5** dull, soft. **6** plain.

riches *n.* affluence, assets, fortune, gold, money, plenty, property, resources, substance, treasure, wealth.
antonym poverty.

rickety *adj.* broken-down, decrepit, derelict, dilapidated, flimsy, insecure, jerry-built, precarious, ramshackle, shaky, unstable, unsteady, wobbly.
antonyms stable, strong.

rid *v.* clear, deliver, expel, free, get rid of, purge, relieve, unburden.
antonym burden.

riddle[1] *n.* brain-teaser, charade, conundrum, enigma, mystery, poser, problem, puzzle.

riddle[2] *v.* corrupt, damage, fill, impair, infest, invade, mar, pepper, perforate, permeate, pervade, pierce, puncture, sieve, sift, spoil, strain, winnow.

ride *v.* control, dominate, drive, float, grip, handle, journey, manage, move, oppress, progress, sit, survive, travel, weather.
n. drive, jaunt, journey, lift, outing, spin, trip, whirl.

ridicule *n.* banter, chaff, derision, gibe, irony, jeering, jeers, laughter, mockery, sarcasm, satire, scorn, sneers, taunting.
antonym praise.
v. caricature, cartoon, crucify, deride, humiliate, jeer, mock, parody, pooh-pooh, queer, quiz, rib, satirise, scoff, send up, sneer at, take the mickey

out of, taunt.
antonym praise.

ridiculous *adj.* absurd, comical, contemptible, derisory, farcical, foolish, funny, hilarious, incredible, laughable, ludicrous, nonsensical, outrageous, preposterous, silly, stupid, unbelievable.
antonym sensible.

rife *adj.* abounding, abundant, common, commonplace, current, epidemic, frequent, general, prevailing, prevalent, raging, rampant, teeming, widespread.
antonym scarce.

rifle[1] *v.* burgle, despoil, loot, pillage, plunder, ransack, rob, rummage, sack, strip.

rifle[2] *n.* air-gun, carbine, firearm, gun, musket, shotgun.

rift *n.* alienation, breach, break, chink, cleft, crack, cranny, crevice, difference, disagreement, division, fault, flaw, fracture, gap, opening, quarrel, schism, separation, space, split.
antonym unity.

rig *n.* apparatus, equipment, fitments, fittings, fixtures, gear, machinery, outfit, tackle.
rig out clothe, costume, dress, dress up, equip, fit (out), furnish, kit out, outfit, supply.
rig up arrange, assemble, build, construct, erect, fix up, improvise, knock up.
antonym dismantle.

right *adj.* **1** accurate, actual, authentic, correct, exact, factual, precise, real, true. **2** admissible, advantageous, appropriate, becoming, desirable, favourable, fit, fitting, proper, reasonable, satisfactory, seemly, suitable. **3** due, equitable, ethical, fair, good, honest, honourable, just, lawful, moral, righteous, upright, virtuous. **4** conservative, right-wing, Tory.
antonyms **1** incorrect. **2** unsuitable. **3** wrong. **4** left, left-wing, socialist.
adv. **1** accurately, correctly, exactly, factually, fairly, genuinely, precisely, properly, satisfactorily, suitably, well. **2** directly, immediately, instantly, promptly, straight, straightaway.
antonyms **1** incorrectly, unfairly, wrongly.
n. **1** authority, business, claim, due, power, prerogative, privilege. **2** good, honour, integrity, justice, legality, morality, righteousness, uprightness, virtue.
antonyms **2** depravity, wrong.
v. avenge, correct, fix, rectify, redress, repair, righten, settle, stand up, straighten, vindicate.
right away at once, directly, forthwith, immediately, instantly, now, promptly, straightaway, without delay.
antonyms eventually, later.

rightful *adj.* authorised, bona fide, correct, due, just, lawful, legal, legitimate, prescribed, proper, real, suitable, true, valid.
antonyms incorrect, unlawful.

rigid *adj.* austere, cast-iron, firm, fixed, harsh, inflexible, invariable, rigorous, set, severe, stern, stiff, strict, stringent, tense, unalterable, unbending, uncompromising, unrelenting, unyielding.
antonyms alterable, elastic, flexible, tolerant.

rigmarole *n.* bother, carry-on, hassle, jargon, nonsense, palaver, performance, red tape, to-do.

rigorous *adj.* accurate, conscientious, demanding, exact, firm, meticulous, painstaking, precise, rigid, scrupulous, thorough.
antonyms lax, superficial.

rile *v.* anger, annoy, exasperate, get, irk, irritate, nettle, peeve, pique, provoke, put out, upset, vex.
antonyms calm down, soothe.

rim *n.* border, brim, brink, circumference, edge, lip, margin, skirt, verge.
antonyms centre, middle.

rind *n.* crust, husk, peel, skin, zest.

ring[1] *n.* **1** arena, band, circle, circuit, circus, collar, enclosure, halo, hoop, loop, rink, round. **2** association, cartel, cell, clique, coterie, crew, gang, group, mob, organisation, syndicate.
v. circumscribe, encircle, enclose, encompass, gird, surround.

ring[2] *v.* buzz, call, chime, clang, clink, peal, phone, resonate, resound, reverberate, sound, telephone, ting, tinkle.
n. buzz, call, chime, clang, clink, peal, phone-call, tang, ting, tinkle.

rinse *v.* bathe, clean, cleanse, dip, splash, swill, wash, wet.
n. bath, dip, dye, splash, tint, wash, wetting.

riot *n.* anarchy, boisterousness, commotion, confusion, disorder, disturbance, excess, fray, insurrection, lawlessness, quarrel, romp, rout, row, strife, tumult, turbulence, turmoil, uproar.
antonyms calm, order.
v. rampage, rebel, revolt, rise up, run riot, run wild.

rip *v.* burst, cut, gash, hack, rend, rupture, score, separate, slash, slit, split, tear.
n. cleavage, cut, gash, hole, rent, rupture, slash, slit, split, tear.
rip off cheat, con, defraud, diddle, do, dupe, exploit, fleece, lift, overcharge, pilfer, pinch, rob, steal, sting, swindle, swipe, thieve, trick.

ripe *adj.* **1** complete, developed, finished, grown, mature, mellow, perfect, ripened, seasoned. **2** auspicious, favourable, ideal, opportune, propitious, ready, right, suitable, timely.
antonyms **2** inopportune, untimely.

ripen *v.* age, develop, mature, mellow, prepare, season.

rip-off *n.* cheat, con, con trick, daylight robbery, diddle, exploitation, fraud, robbery, swindle, theft.

rise *v.* **1** ascend, climb, go up, grow, increase, intensify, mount, slope (up), soar, swell, tower. **2** arise, get up, spring up, stand up. **3** advance, improve, progress, prosper. **4** appear, emanate, emerge, flow, issue, originate, spring.
antonyms **1** descend, fall. **2** sit down.
n. **1** climb, elevation, hillock, incline, rising. **2** advance, advancement, improvement, increase, increment, progress, promotion, raise, upsurge,

upswing, upturn.
antonyms **1** valley. **2** descent, fall.

risk *n.* adventure, chance, danger, gamble, hazard, jeopardy, peril, possibility, speculation, uncertainty, venture.
antonyms certainty, safety.
v. adventure, chance, dare, endanger, gamble, hazard, imperil, jeopardise, venture.

risky *adj.* chancy, dangerous, dicey, hazardous, perilous, precarious, touch-and-go, tricky, uncertain, unsafe.
antonym safe.

risqué *adj.* bawdy, blue, coarse, crude, earthy, improper, indecent, indelicate, naughty, off colour, racy, suggestive.
antonyms decent, modest.

rite *n.* act, ceremonial, ceremony, custom, form, formality, liturgy, observance, ordinance, practice, procedure, ritual, sacrament, service, solemnity, worship.

ritual *n.* ceremony, convention, custom, form, formality, habit, liturgy, observance, ordinance, practice, prescription, procedure, rite, routine, sacrament, service, tradition, usage, wont.
adj. ceremonial, conventional, customary, formal, habitual, prescribed, procedural, routine, stereotyped.
antonyms informal, unusual.

rival *n.* adversary, antagonist, challenger, competitor, contender, contestant, equal, match, opponent, peer.
antonyms associate, colleague, co-worker.
adj. competing, competitive, conflicting, opposed, opposing.
antonyms associate, co-operating.
v. compete, contend, emulate, equal, match, oppose, vie with.
antonym co-operate.

rivalry *n.* antagonism, competition, competitiveness, conflict, contention, contest, duel, opposition, struggle, vying.
antonym co-operation.

river *n.* beck, creek, flood, flow, gush, rush, spate, stream, surge, tributary, waterway.

road *n.* avenue, boulevard, carriageway, clearway, course, crescent, direction, drive, driveway, freeway, highway, lane, motorway, roadway, route, street, thoroughfare, track, way.

roam *v.* drift, prowl, ramble, range, rove, squander, stray, stroll, travel, walk, wander.
antonym stay.

roar *v.* bawl, bay, bell, bellow, blare, clamour, crash, cry, guffaw, hoot, howl, rumble, shout, thunder, yell.
antonym whisper.
n. bellow, blare, clamour, crash, cry, guffaw, hoot, howl, rumble, shout, thunder, yell.
antonym whisper.

rob *v.* cheat, defraud, do, hold up, loot, plunder, raid, ransack, rifle, rip off, sack, swindle.
antonyms give, provide.

robbery *n.* burglary, embezzlement, filching, fraud, heist, hold-up, larceny, pillage, plunder, raid, rip-off, stealing, stick-up, swindle, theft.

robot *n.* automaton, Dalek, machine, zombie.

robust *adj.* athletic, fit, hardy, healthy, muscular, powerful, strong, sturdy, thick-set, tough, vigorous, well.
antonyms feeble, unhealthy, unrealistic, weak.

rock[1] *n.* boulder, bulwark, danger, foundation, hazard, mainstay, obstacle, pebble, stone, support.

rock[2] *v.* astonish, astound, daze, dumbfound, lurch, pitch, reel, roll, shake, shock, stagger, stun, surprise, sway, swing, tilt, tip, toss, wobble.

rocky[1] *adj.* craggy, flinty, hard, pebbly, rocklike, rough, rugged, stony.
antonyms smooth, soft.

rocky[2] *adj.* shaky, staggering, tottering, uncertain, unreliable, unsatisfactory, unstable, unsteady, weak, wobbly, wonky.
antonyms dependable, stable, steady, strong.

rogue *n.* cheat, con man, crook, deceiver, devil, fraud, miscreant, nasty piece/bit of work, ne'er-do-well, rascal, reprobate, scamp, scoundrel, swindler, villain.

roguish *adj.* cheeky, criminal, deceitful, dishonest, fraudulent, frolicsome, impish, mischievous, playful, shady, swindling, villainous.
antonyms honest, serious.

role *n.* capacity, character, duty, function, impersonation, job, part, portrayal, position, post, representation, task.

roll *v.* **1** billow, gyrate, lurch, pitch, reel, revolve, rock, rotate, spin, sway, swing, toss, turn, twirl, wallow, wheel, whirl. **2** bind, coil, curl, enfold, entwine, envelop, furl, twist, wind, wrap. **3** flow, move, pass, run, undulate. **4** flatten, level, press, smooth. **5** boom, resound, reverberate, roar, rumble, thunder.
n. **1** bobbin, cylinder, reel, roller, scroll, spool. **2** annals, catalogue, census, chronicle, directory, index, inventory, list, record, register, roster, schedule. **3** cycle, gyration, revolution, rotation, spin, turn, twirl, undulation, wheel, whirl. **4** boom, growl, resonance, reverberation, roar, rumble, thunder.
roll up arrive, assemble, cluster, congregate, convene, gather.
antonyms leave, scatter.

romance *n.* **1** adventure, affair(e), attachment, charm, excitement, fantasy, fascination, glamour, idyll, intrigue, liaison, love affair, melodrama, mystery, passion, relationship, sentiment. **2** fairy tale, fiction, legend, love story, novel, story, tale.
v. exaggerate, fantasise, invent, lie, overstate.

romantic *adj.* **1** dreamy, exciting, extravagant, fairy-tale, fanciful, fantastic, fascinating, fictitious, idealistic, idyllic, imaginary, imaginative, impractical, improbable, legendary, quixotic, unrealistic, utopian, visionary, wild. **2** amorous, fond, lovey-dovey, loving, mushy, passionate, sentimental, sloppy, soppy, starry-eyed, tender.
antonyms **1** practical, real. **2** unromantic, unsen-

timental.
n. dreamer, idealist, sentimentalist, utopian, visionary.
antonym realist.
roof *n.* canopy, ceiling, cover, top.
room *n.* **1** apartment, area, chamber, compartment, house-room, office, salon, saloon. **2** allowance, capacity, chance, elbow-room, extent, latitude, leeway, margin, occasion, opportunity, play, range, scope, space, territory, volume.
roomy *adj.* ample, broad, extensive, generous, large, sizable, spacious, wide.
antonyms cramped, tiny, uncomfortable.
root[1] *n.* base, basis, beginnings, bottom, cause, core, derivation, essence, fountainhead, fundamental, germ, heart, mainspring, nub, nucleus, occasion, origin, seat, seed, source, starting point, stem, tuber.
v. anchor, embed, entrench, establish, fasten, fix, ground, implant, moor, set, sink, stick.
root out abolish, clear away, destroy, dig out, discover, eliminate, eradicate, erase, exterminate, extirpate, produce, remove, root up, turn up, uncover, unearth, uproot.
antonyms cover, establish.
root[2] *v.* burrow, delve, dig, ferret, forage, grout, hunt, nose, poke, pry, rummage, sift.
rooted *adj.* confirmed, embedded, entrenched, established, fixed, grounded, ingrained, rigid, seated.
roots *n.* background, beginning(s), birthplace, family, heritage, home, origins.
rope *n.* cable, cord, lasso, line, strand.
v. bind, catch, fasten, hitch, lash, lasso, moor, tie.
rope in engage, enlist, involve, lure, persuade.
antonym keep out.
ropy *adj.* inadequate, inferior, off colour, poor, rough, substandard, unwell.
antonyms good, well.
roster *n.* list, listing, register, roll, rota, schedule.
rostrum *n.* dais, hustings, platform, podium, stage.
rot *v.* corrode, corrupt, crumble, decay, decompose, degenerate, deteriorate, disintegrate, fester, go bad, perish, putrefy, spoil, taint.
n. claptrap, drivel, nonsense, poppycock, rubbish.
rotary *adj.* gyrating, revolving, rotating, spinning, turning, whirling.
antonym fixed.
rotate *v.* gyrate, pivot, revolve, spell, spin, swivel, turn.
rotation *n.* cycle, gyration, orbit, revolution, sequence, spin, spinning, succession, turn, turning.
rotten *adj.* **1** addled, bad, decayed, decaying, decomposed, disintegrating, fetid, foul, mouldy, putrid, rank, stinking. **2** beastly, contemptible, corrupt, crooked, crummy, despicable, dirty, dishonest, dishonourable, dreadful, inadequate, inferior, lousy, low-grade, mean, nasty, ropy, vile, wicked. **3** grotty, poorly, rough, sick, unwell.
antonyms **1** fresh. **2** good, honest. **3** well.
rough *adj.* **1** bristly, bumpy, coarse, craggy, dishevelled, irregular, jagged, rugged, uneven. **2** austere, blunt, brusque, cruel, curt, drastic, extreme, hard, harsh, severe, sharp, tough. **3** approximate, crude, cursory, estimated, general, incomplete, preliminary, rudimentary, vague. **4** agitated, choppy, stormy, tempestuous, turbulent, violent, wild. **5** ill, off colour, poorly, ropy, sick, unwell.
antonyms **1** smooth. **2** mild. **3** accurate. **4** calm. **5** well.
rough-and-ready *adj.* adequate, approximate, crude, makeshift, primitive, provisional, sketchy, stop-gap, unpolished, unrefined.
antonyms exact, refined, well-thought-out.
roughen *v.* abrade, coarsen, graze, harshen, rough, scuff.
antonym smooth.
round *adj.* **1** ball-shaped, circular, curved, cylindrical, disc-shaped, globular, ring-shaped, rounded, spherical. **2** complete, entire, full, whole.
n. **1** ball, band, circle, disc, orb, ring, sphere. **2** bout, cycle, period, sequence, series, session, succession. **3** beat, circuit, compass, course, lap, routine. **4** bullet, cartridge, discharge, shell, shot.
v. bypass, circle, circumnavigate, encircle, flank, sail round, skirt.
round off cap, close, complete, conclude, crown, end, finish (off), settle.
antonym begin.
round on abuse, attack, lay into, retaliate, turn on.
round up assemble, collect, drive, gather, group, herd, marshal, rally.
antonyms disperse, scatter.
roundabout *adj.* circuitous, devious, evasive, indirect, oblique, tortuous, twisting, winding.
antonyms direct, straight, straightforward.
rouse *v.* agitate, anger, arouse, awaken, call, disturb, excite, galvanise, incite, inflame, instigate, move, provoke, rise, start, stimulate, stir, wake (up), whip up.
antonym calm.
rout *n.* beating, brawl, clamour, defeat, disturbance, fracas, fuss, overthrow, riot, ruin, stampede, thrashing.
antonyms calm, win.
v. beat, chase, conquer, crush, defeat, destroy, dispel, hammer, lick, overthrow, scatter, thrash.
route *n.* avenue, beat, circuit, course, direction, flightpath, itinerary, journey, passage, path, road, round, run, way.
v. convey, direct, dispatch, forward, send.
routine *n.* act, custom, formula, line, method, order, pattern, performance, piece, practice, procedure, programme, usage, way.
adj. banal, boring, clichéd, conventional, customary, day-by-day, dull, everyday, familiar, humdrum, normal, ordinary, predictable, run-of-the-mill, standard, tedious, tiresome, typical,

unimaginative, unoriginal, usual.
antonyms different, exciting, unusual.

row *n.* brawl, commotion, controversy, dispute, disturbance, fracas, fray, quarrel, racket, reprimand, reproof, rumpus, slanging match, squabble, tiff, trouble, uproar.
antonym calm.
v. argue, bicker, fight, scrap, squabble, wrangle.

rowdy *adj.* boisterous, disorderly, loud, noisy, rough, stroppy, unruly, wild.
antonyms peaceful, quiet, restrained.
n. brawler, hooligan, lout, ruffian, tearaway, thug, tough, yob.

royal *adj.* august, grand, imperial, impressive, kinglike, kingly, magnificent, majestic, monarchical, princely, queenlike, queenly, regal, sovereign, splendid, stately, superb, superior.

rub *v.* abrade, apply, caress, chafe, clean, fray, grate, knead, massage, polish, put, scour, scrape, shine, smear, smooth, spread, stroke, wipe.
rub out cancel, delete, erase, obliterate, remove.

rubbish *n.* balderdash, claptrap, cobblers, deadwood, debris, drivel, dross, flotsam and jetsam, garbage, gibberish, gobbledegook, junk, litter, nonsense, poppycock, refuse, rot, stuff, trash, twaddle, waste.
antonym sense.

ruddy *adj.* blooming, blushing, crimson, flushed, fresh, glowing, healthy, pink, red, reddish, rosy, ruby, scarlet, sunburnt.
antonyms pale, unhealthy.

rude *adj.* **1** abrupt, abusive, brusque, cheeky, curt, discourteous, disrespectful, impertinent, impolite, impudent, inconsiderate, insolent, insulting, sharp, short, uncivil, uncivilised, uneducated, unpolished, unrefined, untutored. **2** coarse, dirty, gross, low, naughty, obscene, uncouth, vulgar.
antonyms **1** graceful, polished, polite. **2** clean, decent.

rudimentary *adj.* basic, elementary, embryonic, fundamental, initial, introductory, primary, primitive, undeveloped.
antonyms advanced, developed.

rudiments *n.* ABC, basics, beginnings, elements, essentials, foundation, fundamentals, principles.

rugged *adj.* **1** bumpy, craggy, irregular, jagged, ragged, rocky, rough, stark, uneven, weather-beaten, weathered. **2** blunt, gruff, hard, harsh, muscular, robust, rude, severe, strong, tough, uncultured.
antonyms **1** smooth. **2** refined.

ruin *n.* bankruptcy, breakdown, collapse, crash, damage, decay, defeat, destruction, devastation, disintegration, disrepair, dissolution, downfall, failure, fall, havoc, heap, insolvency, overthrow, subversion, undoing, wreckage.
antonyms development, reconstruction.
v. bankrupt, botch, break, crush, damage, defeat, demolish, destroy, devastate, disfigure, impoverish, injure, mangle, mar, mess up, overthrow, overturn, overwhelm, raze, shatter, smash, spoil, wreck.
antonyms develop, restore.

ruins *n.* chaos, debris, devastation, havoc, shambles.

rule *n.* **1** axiom, canon, convention, criterion, decree, direction, formula, guide, guideline, law, maxim, order, ordinance, precept, principle, regulation, standard, tenet. **2** authority, command, control, domination, dominion, government, influence, leadership, mastery, power, regime, reign, supremacy. **3** custom, habit, practice, routine, wont.
v. adjudicate, administer, command, control, decide, decree, determine, direct, dominate, establish, find, govern, guide, judge, lead, manage, obtain, prevail, pronounce, regulate, reign.
as a rule generally, normally, ordinarily, usually.
rule out ban, disallow, dismiss, eliminate, exclude, forbid, preclude, prevent, prohibit, reject.

ruler *n.* commander, controller, emperor, empress, governor, head of state, king, leader, lord, monarch, potentate, prince, princess, queen, sovereign.
antonym subject.

ruling *n.* adjudication, decision, decree, finding, indiction, judgement, pronouncement, resolution, verdict.
adj. boss, chief, commanding, controlling, dominant, governing, leading, main, predominant, prevalent, principal, regnant, reigning, supreme.

rumour *n.* breeze, bush telegraph, fame, gossip, grapevine, hearsay, news, report, story, talk, whisper, word.
v. circulate, gossip, publish, put about, report, say, tell, whisper.

rump *n.* backside, bottom, buttocks, haunch, hindquarters, posterior, rear, seat.

run *v.* **1** abscond, bolt, dart, dash, depart, escape, flee, hurry, jog, race, rush, scarper, speed, sprint, tear. **2** go, issue, manoeuvre, move, pass, proceed, scud. **3** function, operate, work. **4** administer, control, direct, head, lead, manage, oversee, regulate, superintend, supervise. **5** challenge, compete, contend, stand. **6** continue, extend, last, range, reach, spread, stretch. **7** flow, gush, pour, stream.
n. **1** dash, gallop, jog, race, rush, sprint, spurt. **2** drive, excursion, journey, outing, ride, spin, trip. **3** chain, course, sequence, series, string.
run after chase, follow, pursue, stalk, tail.
antonym flee.
run away abscond, beat it, bolt, clear out, escape, flee.
antonym stay.
run down **1** belittle, criticise, defame, denigrate, disparage. **2** hit, knock over, run over, strike. **3** exhaust, tire. **4** curtail, cut, decrease, drop, reduce, trim, weaken.
run into bump into, encounter, hit, meet, strike.
antonym miss.

run off 1 abscond, bolt, elope, escape, make off, scarper. **2** duplicate, print, produce.
antonym **1** stay.
run out cease, close, dry up, end, expire, fail, finish, terminate.
run over 1 hit, knock down, run down, strike. **2** rehearse, reiterate, review, survey.
runaway *n.* absconder, deserter, escaper, fugitive, refugee, truant.
adj. escaped, fleeing, fugitive, loose, uncontrolled, wild.
rundown *n.* **1** cut, decline, decrease, drop, lessening, reduction. **2** briefing, outline, précis, recap, résumé, review, run-through, sketch, summary, synopsis.
run-down *adj.* broken-down, decrepit, dilapidated, dingy, drained, exhausted, fatigued, ramshackle, seedy, shabby, tumble-down, unhealthy, weak, weary, worn-out.
antonyms strong, well-kept.
runner *n.* **1** athlete, competitor, courier, jogger, messenger, participant, sprinter. **2** offshoot, shoot, sprout, stem.
running *adj.* consecutive, constant, continuous, current, flowing, incessant, moving, perpetual, successive, together, unbroken, unceasing, uninterrupted.
antonyms broken, occasional.
n. administration, charge, competition, conduct, contention, contest, control, co-ordination, direction, functioning, leadership, maintenance, management, operation, organisation, performance, regulation, superintendency, supervision, working.
runny *adj.* diluted, flowing, fluid, liquefied, liquid, melted, molten, watery.
antonym solid.
run-of-the-mill *adj.* average, common, everyday, fair, mediocre, ordinary, tolerable, undistinguished, unexceptional, unexciting, unimpressive, unremarkable.
antonyms exceptional, interesting.
rural *adj.* agrarian, agricultural, country, pastoral, rustic.
antonym urban.
rush *v.* accelerate, attack, bolt, capture, career, charge, dart, dash, dispatch, fly, hasten, hurry, press, push, quicken, race, run, scramble, shoot, speed (up), sprint, stampede, storm, tear, wallop.
n. assault, charge, dash, flow, haste, hurry, onslaught, push, race, scramble, speed, stampede, storm, surge, swiftness, tear, urgency.
adj. brisk, careless, cursory, emergency, fast, hasty, hurried, prompt, quick, rapid, superficial, swift, urgent.
rust *n.* corrosion, oxidation, stain.
v. corrode, decay, decline, degenerate, deteriorate, oxidise, tarnish.
rustic *adj.* agrarian, artless, awkward, boorish, bucolic, cloddish, clumsy, coarse, countrified, country, crude, oafish, pastoral, plain, provincial, rough, rude, rural, simple, sylvan, uncouth, uncultured, unrefined, unsophisticated, yokelish.
antonyms cultivated, polished, sophisticated, urban, urbane.
rustle *v.* crackle, swish, whisper, whoosh.
n. crackle, crinkling, rustling, swish, whisper, whispering.
rusty *adj.* ancient, antiquated, antique, corroded, creaking, croaking, croaky, dated, deficient, discoloured, dull, old-fashioned, outmoded, oxidised, rough, rust-covered, rusted, stale, stiff, tarnished, time-worn, unpractised, weak.
ruthless *adj.* brutal, callous, cruel, cut-throat, ferocious, fierce, hard, hard-hearted, harsh, heartless, implacable, inexorable, inhuman, merciless, pitiless, relentless, savage, severe, stern, unfeeling, unrelenting.
antonyms compassionate, forgiving, merciful.

S

sabotage *v.* cripple, damage, destroy, disable, disrupt, incapacitate, mar, scupper, thwart, undermine, vandalise, wreck.
n. damage, destruction, disruption, impairment, marring, subversion, treachery, treason, undermining, vandalism, wrecking.

sack *v.* axe, discharge, dismiss, fire, lay off, make redundant.
n. discharge, dismissal, notice, one's cards, the axe, the elbow, the push.

sacred *adj.* blessed, consecrated, dedicated, devotional, divine, ecclesiastical, godly, hallowed, heavenly, holy, inviolable, priestly, protected, religious, revered, sacrosanct, saintly, sanctified, secure, solemn, venerable.
antonyms mundane, profane, temporal.

sacrifice *v.* abandon, forego, forfeit, let go, lose, offer, relinquish, renounce, slaughter, surrender.
n. destruction, loss, offering, renunciation, surrender.

sacrilege *n.* blasphemy, defilement, desecration, disrespect, heresy, irreverence, mockery, outrage, profanity, violation.
antonyms piety, respect, reverence.

sacrosanct *adj.* hallowed, impregnable, inviolable, sacred, sanctified, untouchable.

sad *adj.* **1** crestfallen, dejected, depressed, despondent, downcast, down-hearted, gloomy, glum, grief-stricken, heavy-hearted, long-faced, low, low-spirited, melancholy, miserable, tearful, unhappy. **2** depressing, disastrous, dismal, distressing, grave, grievous, heart-rending, lamentable, painful, poignant, regrettable, serious, sorry, touching, tragic, unfortunate, upsetting.
antonyms **1** cheerful, happy. **2** fortunate, lucky.

sadden *v.* depress, discourage, dishearten, distress, grieve, hurt, upset.
antonyms cheer, delight, gratify, please.

saddle *v.* burden, charge, encumber, impose, load, lumber, tax.

sadism *n.* barbarity, bestiality, brutality, cruelty, inhumanity, malevolence, ruthlessness, sadomasochism, viciousness.

sadistic *adj.* barbarous, bestial, brutal, cruel, inhuman, perverted, savage, spiteful, unnatural, vicious.

safe *adj.* **1** harmless, innocuous, non- poisonous, non-toxic. **2** guarded, immune, impregnable, intact, invulnerable, protected, secure, uncontaminated, undamaged, unharmed, unhurt, uninjured, unscathed. **3** cautious, conservative, dependable, proven, prudent, reliable, sound, sure, tested, tried, trustworthy, unadventurous.
antonyms **1** dangerous, harmful. **2** exposed, vulnerable. **3** risky.
n. cash-box, chest, coffer, deposit box, repository, strongbox, vault.

safeguard *v.* assure, defend, guard, preserve, protect, screen, secure, shelter, shield.
antonyms endanger, jeopardise.
n. assurance, cover, defence, guarantee, insurance, long-stop, precaution, protection, security, shield, surety.

safekeeping *n.* care, charge, custody, guard, guardianship, keeping, protection, supervision, surveillance, trust.

safety *n.* assurance, cover, harmlessness, immunity, impregnability, protection, refuge, reliability, safeguard, sanctuary, security, shelter, sureness.
antonyms danger, jeopardy, risk.
adj. fail-safe, precautionary, preventative, protective.

sag *v.* bag, decline, dip, droop, drop, dwindle, fail, fall, flag, give, give way, hang, settle, sink, slide, slip, slump, weaken, wilt.
antonyms bulge, rise.

sail *v.* captain, cruise, embark, float, fly, glide, navigate, pilot, plane, put to sea, scud, shoot, skim, skipper, soar, steer, sweep, voyage, weigh anchor, wing.

sailor *n.* marine, mariner, navigator, rating, sea dog, seafarer, seaman.

saintly *adj.* angelic, blameless, blessed, celestial, devout, god-fearing, godly, holy, innocent, pious, pure, religious, righteous, sinless, spotless, upright, virtuous, worthy.
antonyms godless, unholy, unrighteous, wicked.

sake *n.* advantage, aim, behalf, benefit, cause, consideration, end, gain, good, interest, motive, object, objective, principle, profit, purpose, reason, regard, respect, welfare, wellbeing.

salacious *adj.* bawdy, coarse, erotic, improper, indecent, lascivious, lecherous, lewd, obscene, pornographic, raunchy, ribald, scurrilous, smutty.
antonyms clean, decent, proper.

salaried *adj.* paid, remunerated, waged.
antonyms honorary, unpaid, voluntary.

salary *n.* earnings, income, pay, remuneration, stipend, wages.

sale *n.* auction, deal, disposal, marketing, selling, trade, traffic, transaction, vending.

saleable *adj.* desirable, marketable, merchantable, sought-after.
antonyms unmarketable, unsaleable.

salesperson *n.* clerk, sales assistant, salesclerk, salesgirl, saleslady, salesman, saleswoman, shop assistant, shop-boy, shopgirl, shop-keeper.

salient *adj.* arresting, chief, conspicuous, important, jutting, main, marked, noticeable, obvious, outstanding, principal, projecting, prominent, pronounced, protruding, remarkable, significant, striking.

sallow *adj.* anaemic, bilious, colourless, pale, pallid, pasty, sickly, unhealthy, wan, yellowish.
antonyms healthy, rosy.

salt *n.* acuteness, bite, dryness, flavour, liveliness, piquancy, punch, pungency, relish, sarcasm, savour, seasoning, sharpness, taste, trenchancy, vigour, wit, zest, zip.
adj. brackish, briny, saline, salted.
antonym fresh.
salt away accumulate, amass, bank, cache, collect, hide, hoard, save, stash, stockpile, store up.
antonyms spend, squander.

salty *adj.* brackish, briny, piquant, pungent, salt, salted, spicy, tangy.

salutary *adj.* advantageous, beneficial, good, healthy, helpful, much-needed, practical, profitable, timely, useful, valuable.

salute *v.* acknowledge, address, bow, greet, hail, honour, nod, recognise, wave, welcome.
n. acknowledgement, address, bow, gesture, greeting, hail, handclap, handshake, nod, recognition, reverence, tribute, wave.

salvage *v.* conserve, glean, preserve, reclaim, recover, recuperate, redeem, repair, rescue, restore, retrieve, save.
antonyms abandon, lose, waste.

salvation *n.* deliverance, escape, liberation, preservation, reclamation, redemption, rescue, restoration, retrieval, safety, saving.
antonyms damnation, loss.

salve *n.* application, balm, cream, dressing, liniment, lotion, lubricant, medication, ointment, preparation.

same *adj.* alike, changeless, comparable, consistent, corresponding, duplicate, equal, equivalent, identical, indistinguishable, interchangeable, matching, mutual, reciprocal, selfsame, similar, substitutable, synonymous, twin, unchanged, uniform, unvarying, very.
antonyms changeable, different, inconsistent, variable.

sameness *n.* changelessness, consistency, duplication, identicalness, indistinguishability, likeness, monotony, predictability, repetition, similarity, standardisation, tedium, uniformity.
antonyms difference, variety.

sample *n.* cross section, demonstration, example, foretaste, free sample, illustration, indication, instance, model, pattern, representative, sign, specimen, swatch.
v. experience, inspect, investigate, sip, taste, test, try.
adj. demonstration, illustrative, pilot, representative, specimen, test, trial.

sanctify *v.* anoint, bless, cleanse, consecrate, dedicate, exalt, hallow, make holy, purify, sanction.
antonyms defile, degrade, desecrate.

sanctimonious *adj.* holier-than-thou, hypocritical, moralising, pharisaical, pious, self-righteous, smug, superior.
antonym humble.

sanction *n.* agreement, allowance, approval, authorisation, authority, backing, confirmation, endorsement, go-ahead, licence, OK, permission, ratification, support.
antonyms disapproval, veto.
v. accredit, allow, approve, authorise, back, confirm, endorse, license, permit, ratify, support, underwrite, warrant.
antonyms disapprove, forbid, veto.

sanctions *n.* ban, boycott, embargo, penalty, prohibition, restrictions.

sanctity *n.* devotion, godliness, goodness, grace, holiness, inviolability, piety, purity, religiousness, righteousness, sacredness, spirituality.
antonyms godlessness, impurity, secularity, unholiness, worldliness.

sanctuary *n.* altar, asylum, church, haven, protection, refuge, retreat, seclusion, shelter, shrine, tabernacle, temple.

sand *n.* arena, beach, grit, sands, shore, strand.

sandy *adj.* auburn, ginger, gritty, red, reddish, reddish-yellow, rusty, tawny, yellow, yellowish.

sane *adj.* all there, balanced, dependable, judicious, level-headed, moderate, normal, rational, reasonable, reliable, right-minded, sensible, sober, sound, stable.
antonyms crazy, foolish, mad.

sanitary *adj.* aseptic, clean, disinfected, germ-free, healthy, hygienic, pure, uncontaminated, unpolluted.
antonyms insanitary, unwholesome.

sanity *n.* balance of mind, common sense, judiciousness, level-headedness, normality, rationality, reason, reliability, sense, soundness, stability.
antonyms foolishness, insanity.

sap *v.* bleed, deplete, diminish, drain, exhaust, impair, reduce, rob, undermine, weaken.
antonyms build up, increase, strengthen.

sarcasm *n.* bitterness, contempt, cynicism, derision, irony, mockery, satire, scorn, sneering.

sarcastic *adj.* acid, biting, cutting, cynical, derisive, disparaging, incisive, ironical, mocking, satirical, scathing, sharp, sneering, taunting.

sardonic *adj.* biting, bitter, cynical, derisive, dry, heartless, jeering, malicious, mocking, sarcastic, scornful, sneering.

sash *n.* belt, girdle, waistband.

satanic *adj.* accursed, black, demonic, devilish, diabolic, evil, fiendish, hellish, infernal, inhuman, iniquitous, malevolent, satanical, wicked.
antonyms benevolent, divine, godlike, godly, heavenly, holy.

satire *n.* burlesque, caricature, irony, parody, ridicule, sarcasm, send-up, skit, spoof, takeoff, travesty, wit.

satirical *adj.* biting, bitter, caustic, cutting, cynical, derisive, incisive, ironical, irreverent, mocking, sarcastic, sardonic, taunting.

satirise *v.* abuse, burlesque, caricature, criticise, deride, lampoon, make fun of, mock, parody, ridicule, send up, take off.
antonyms acclaim, celebrate, honour.

satirist *n.* caricaturist, cartoonist, mocker, parodist, ridiculer.

satisfaction *n.* **1** comfort, contentment, ease, enjoyment, fulfilment, gratification, happiness, pleasure, sense of achievement, well-being. **2** amends, compensation, damages, indemnification, payment, recompense, redress, reimbursement, reparation, requital, settlement, vindication.
antonyms **1** displeasure, dissatisfaction.

satisfactory *adj.* acceptable, adequate, all right, average, competent, fair, OK, proper, sufficient, suitable, up to the mark.
antonyms inadequate, unacceptable, unsatisfactory.

satisfy *v.* **1** content, delight, gratify, indulge, please. **2** answer, discharge, fulfil, meet, qualify, serve, settle, suffice, surfeit. **3** assure, convince, persuade.
antonyms **1** dissatisfy. **2** fail. **3** disappoint.

saturate *v.* douse, drench, imbue, impregnate, infuse, permeate, soak, souse, steep, suffuse, waterlog.

saucy *adj.* cheeky, disrespectful, flippant, forward, fresh, impertinent, impudent, insolent, perky, presumptuous.
antonyms polite, respectful.

saunter *v.* amble, dally, dawdle, linger, loiter, meander, mooch, mosey, ramble, roam, rove, stroll, wander.
n. breather, constitutional, ramble, stroll, walk.

savage *adj.* barbarous, beastly, bloodthirsty, bloody, brutal, cruel, ferocious, fierce, harsh, inhuman, merciless, murderous, pitiless, primitive, ruthless, sadistic, uncivilised, undomesticated, untamed, vicious, wild.
antonyms civilised, humane, mild.
n. barbarian, brute, native, primitive.
v. attack, hammer, mangle, maul, tear.

save *v.* collect, conserve, cut back, deliver, economise, free, gather, guard, hinder, hoard, hold, keep, lay up, liberate, preserve, prevent, protect, put aside, put by, reclaim, recover, rescue, reserve, retain, safeguard, salvage, screen, shield, spare, stash, store.
antonyms discard, spend, squander, waste.

saving *adj.* careful, economical, extenuating, frugal, qualifying, redeeming, sparing, thrifty.
n. bargain, conservation, cut, discount, economy, preservation, reduction, rescue, salvage.
antonyms expense, loss, waste.

savings *n.* capital, fund, nest egg, reserve fund, reserves, resources, store.

saviour *n.* champion, defender, emancipator, guardian, liberator, messiah, preserver, protector, rescuer.
antonyms destroyer, enemy.

savour *n.* excitement, fascination, flavour, interest, piquancy, relish, salt, smack, smell, spice, tang, taste, zest.
v. appreciate, enjoy, like, relish, revel in.
antonyms shrink from, wince at.

savoury *adj.* **1** appetising, aromatic, delicious, full-flavoured, luscious, mouthwatering, palatable, piquant, spicy, tangy, tasty. **2** agreeable, decent, edifying, good, reputable, respectable.
antonyms **1** insipid, sweet, tasteless, unappetising. **2** disreputable, unsavoury.

say *v.* add, affirm, allege, announce, answer, assert, assume, claim, comment, communicate, convey, declare, deliver, disclose, divulge, enunciate, estimate, express, guess, imagine, imply, intimate, judge, maintain, mention, opine, orate, perform, presume, pronounce, read, recite, reckon, rejoin, remark, render, repeat, reply, report, respond, retort, reveal, rumour, signify, speak, state, suggest, surmise, tell, utter, voice.
n. authority, chance, influence, power, sway, turn, voice, vote, weight, word.

saying *n.* adage, aphorism, axiom, byword, dictum, expression, maxim, motto, precept, proverb, quotation, remark, slogan.

scald *v.* blister, burn, sear.

scale[1] *n.* calibration, compass, continuum, degree, extent, gamut, gradation, graduation, hierarchy, ladder, measure, order, progression, proportion, range, ranking, ratio, reach, register, scope, sequence, series, spectrum, spread, steps.
v. ascend, clamber, climb, mount, scramble, shin up, surmount.

scale[2] *n.* crust, encrustation, film, flake, lamina, layer, plate, shield.

scaly *adj.* branny, flaky, scabby, scabrous, scurfy.

scamp *n.* imp, losel, monkey, rascal, rogue, scallywag.

scamper *v.* dart, dash, fly, frolic, gambol, hasten, hurry, romp, run, rush, scoot, scurry, scuttle, sprint.

scan *v.* check, examine, glance through, investigate, scrutinise, search, skim, survey, sweep.
n. check, examination, investigation, probe, review, screening, scrutiny, search, survey.

scandal *n.* discredit, disgrace, dishonour, embarrassment, furore, gossip, ignominy, offence, outcry, outrage, reproach, rumours, shame, uproar.

scandalise *v.* affront, appal, disgust, dismay, horrify, offend, outrage, repel, revolt, shock.

scandalmonger *n.* busybody, defamer, gossip, gossip-monger, muck-raker, tale-bearer, tattler.

scandalous *adj.* abominable, atrocious, disgraceful, disreputable, improper, infamous, monstrous, outrageous, shameful, shocking, slanderous, unseemly, unspeakable, untrue.
antonyms kind, praising.

scant *adj.* bare, deficient, hardly any, inadequate, insufficient, limited, little, little or no, meagre, minimal, sparse.
antonyms adequate, ample, sufficient.

scanty *adj.* bare, deficient, inadequate, insub-

stantial, insufficient, meagre, narrow, poor, restricted, scant, short, skimpy, sparse, thin.
antonyms ample, plentiful, substantial.

scar *n.* blemish, injury, lesion, mark, stigma, trauma, wound.
v. brand, damage, disfigure, mark, stigmatise, traumatise.

scarce *adj.* deficient, few, infrequent, insufficient, lacking, rare, scanty, sparse, uncommon, unusual.
antonyms common, copious, plentiful.

scarcely *adv.* barely, hardly, not readily, not willingly, only just.

scarcity *n.* dearth, deficiency, infrequency, insufficiency, lack, paucity, poverty, rareness, rarity, scantiness, shortage, sparseness, uncommonness.
antonyms abundance, enough, glut, plenty, sufficiency.

scare *v.* alarm, appal, daunt, dismay, frighten, gally, intimidate, panic, shock, startle, terrify, terrorise, unnerve.
antonyms calm, reassure.
n. agitation, alarm, consternation, dismay, fright, hysteria, panic, shock, start, terror.
antonyms comfort, reassurance.

scared *adj.* anxious, appalled, dismayed, fearful, frightened, nervous, panicky, panic-stricken, shaken, startled, terrified, worried.
antonyms confident, reassured.

scary *adj.* alarming, bloodcurdling, chilling, creepy, disturbing, frightening, hair-raising, hairy, horrifying, intimidating, shocking, spine-chilling, spooky, terrifying.

scathing *adj.* acid, biting, bitter, brutal, caustic, critical, cutting, harsh, sarcastic, savage, scornful, trenchant, unsparing, vitriolic.
antonym complimentary.

scatter *v.* break up, broadcast, diffuse, disband, disintegrate, disject, dispel, disperse, disseminate, dissipate, disunite, divide, fling, propagate, separate, shower, sow, spatter, splutter, spread, sprinkle, squander, strew.
antonyms collect, concentrate.

scatter-brained *adj.* careless, empty-headed, feather-brained, forgetful, frivolous, inattentive, irresponsible, scatty, slap-happy, thoughtless, unreliable.
antonyms careful, efficient, sensible, sober.

scattering *n.* dispersal, few, handful, propagation, smattering, sprinkling.
antonyms abundance, mass.

scavenger *n.* cleaner, forager, raker, rummager, scrounger.

scenario *n.* outline, plan, plot, programme, projection, résumé, rundown, scene, scheme, sequence, situation, sketch, story line, summary, synopsis.

scene *n.* act, area, arena, backdrop, background, business, circumstances, display, division, drama, environment, episode, exhibition, focus, incident, landscape, locale, locality, location, milieu, pageant, panorama, part, performance, picture, place, position, prospect, representation, set, setting, show, sight, site, situation, spectacle, spot, stage, tableau, view, vista, whereabouts, world.

scenery *n.* backdrop, background, landscape, outlook, panorama, set, setting, sight, surroundings, terrain, view, vista.

scenic *adj.* awe-inspiring, beautiful, breathtaking, grand, impressive, magnificent, panoramic, picturesque, spectacular, striking, stupendous.
antonyms dreary, dull, unspectacular.

scent *n.* aroma, bouquet, fragrance, odour, perfume, smell, trace, track, waft.
antonym stink.
v. detect, discern, nose (out), perceive, recognise, sense, smell, sniff (out).

scented *adj.* aromatic, fragrant, perfumed, sweet-smelling.
antonyms malodorous, stinking.

sceptic *n.* agnostic, atheist, cynic, disbeliever, doubter, questioner, rationalist, scoffer, unbeliever.
antonym believer.

sceptical *adj.* cynical, disbelieving, distrustful, doubtful, doubting, dubious, hesitating, mistrustful, pessimistic, questioning, scoffing, suspicious, unbelieving, unconvinced.
antonyms convinced, naïve, trusting.

scepticism *n.* agnosticism, atheism, cynicism, disbelief, distrust, doubt, pessimism, rationalism, suspicion, unbelief.
antonyms belief, faith, naïvety.

schedule *n.* agenda, calendar, catalogue, diary, form, inventory, itinerary, list, plan, programme, scheme, table, timetable.
v. appoint, arrange, book, list, organise, plan, programme, slot, table, time.

schematic *adj.* diagrammatic, graphic, illustrative, representational, simplified, simplistic, symbolic.

scheme *n.* arrangement, blueprint, chart, configuration, conformation, design, device, diagram, draft, idea, lay-out, manoeuvre, method, outline, pattern, plan, plot, ploy, procedure, programme, project, proposal, proposition, schedule, schema, shape, shift, stratagem, strategy, suggestion, system, tactics, theory.
v. collude, conspire, contrive, devise, frame, imagine, intrigue, machinate, manipulate, manoeuvre, mastermind, plan, plot, project, pull strings, work out.

schemer *n.* conniver, deceiver, intriguer, machinator, mastermind, plotter, politician, wheeler-dealer, wire-puller.

schism *n.* breach, break, discord, disunion, division, estrangement, faction, quarrel, rift, rupture, sect, separation, severance, splinter group, split.

scholar *n.* academic, authority, expert, intellectual, pupil, scholastic, student.
antonyms dunce, ignoramus.

scholarly *adj.* academic, analytical, bookish, conscientious, critical, erudite, intellectual, knowledgeable, learned, lettered, scholastic,

scientific, studious, well-read.
antonyms illiterate, uneducated, unscholarly.

scholarship *n.* **1** attainments, book- learning, education, erudition, insight, knowledge, learnedness, learning, wisdom. **2** award, bursary, endowment, exhibition, fellowship, grant.

scholastic *adj.* academic, analytical, bookish, learned, lettered, literary, pedagogic, pedantic, precise, scholarly, subtle.

school *n.* academy, class, college, department, discipline, faculty, group, institute, institution, lycée, pupils, seminary, students, teaching.
v. coach, discipline, drill, educate, harden, indoctrinate, instruct, prepare, prime, train, tutor, verse.

schooling *n.* book-learning, booklore, coaching, drill, education, grounding, guidance, indoctrination, instruction, preparation, teaching, training, tuition.

schoolteacher *n.* educator, instructor, master, mistress, pedagogue, schoolmaster, schoolmistress, teacher.

science *n.* art, discipline, knowledge, proficiency, skill, specialisation, technique, technology.

scientific *adj.* accurate, analytical, controlled, exact, mathematical, methodical, precise, scholarly, systematic, thorough.

scintillating *adj.* animated, blazing, blinding, bright, brilliant, dazzling, ebullient, exciting, flashing, glittering, lively, shining, sparkling, stimulating, vivacious, witty.
antonym dull.

scoff[1] *v.* belittle, deride, despise, flout, jeer, knock, mock, poke fun, pooh-pooh, rail, revile, rib, ridicule, scorn, sneer, taunt.
antonyms compliment, flatter, praise.

scoff[2] *v.* bolt, consume, cram, devour, gobble, gulp, guzzle, put away, shift, wolf.
antonyms abstain, fast.

scoffing *adj.* cynical, fiendish, sarcastic.

scold *v.* admonish, blame, censure, chide, find fault with, lecture, nag, rebuke, reprimand, reproach, take to task, tell off, tick off, upbraid.
antonyms commend, praise.

scolding *n.* castigation, dressing-down, earful, lecture, rebuke, reprimand, reproof, row, talking-to, telling-off, ticking-off.
antonyms commendation, praise.

scoop *n.* **1** backhoe, bucket, dipper, lade, ladle, spoon. **2** coup, exclusive, exposé, inside story, latest, revelation, sensation.
v. bail, dig, dip, empty, excavate, gather, gouge, hollow, ladle, lift, pick up, remove, scrape, shovel, sweep.

scope *n.* ambit, application, area, breadth, capacity, compass, confines, coverage, elbow-room, extent, freedom, latitude, liberty, opportunity, orbit, outlook, range, reach, room, space, span, sphere, terms of reference.

scorch *v.* blacken, blister, burn, char, parch, roast, scald, sear, shrivel, singe, sizzle, wither.

scorching *adj.* baking, blistering, boiling, burning, fiery, flaming, parching, red-hot, roasting, scalding, searing, sizzling, sweltering, torrid, tropical.

score *n.* **1** points, result, sum total, total. **2** gash, line, mark, notch, scratch. **3** a bone to pick, grievance, grudge, injury, injustice, wrong.
v. **1** achieve, attain, be one up, chalk up, count, earn, gain, have the advantage, have the edge, make, notch up, record, register, total, win. **2** cut, deface, engrave, gouge, graze, groove, incise, indent, mark, nick, scrape, scratch, slash.

scorn *n.* contempt, derision, despite, disdain, disgust, disparagement, mockery, sarcasm, scornfulness, sneer.
antonyms admiration, respect.
v. deride, despise, disdain, dismiss, flout, hold in contempt, laugh at, laugh in the face of, look down on, refuse, reject, scoff at, slight, sneer at, spurn.
antonyms admire, respect.

scornful *adj.* arrogant, contemptuous, defiant, derisive, disdainful, dismissive, disparaging, haughty, insulting, jeering, mocking, sarcastic, scathing, scoffing, slighting, sneering, supercilious.
antonyms admiring, complimentary, respectful.

scot-free *adj.* clear, ininjured, safe, undamaged, unharmed, unhurt, unpunished, unscathed, without a scratch.
antonyms injured, punished.

scour[1] *v.* abrade, burnish, clean, cleanse, flush, polish, purge, rub, scrape, scrub, wash, whiten.

scour[2] *v.* beat, comb, drag, forage, go over, hunt, ransack, search, turn upside-down.

scourge *n.* affliction, bane, curse, evil, infliction, lash, menace, misfortune, penalty, plague, punishment, terror, thong, torment, whip.
antonyms benefit, blessing, boon, godsend.
v. afflict, beat, belt, cane, chastise, curse, devastate, discipline, flail, flog, harass, lash, plague, punish, terrorise, thrash, torment, wallop, whip.

scout *v.* case, check out, explore, hunt, investigate, look, observe, probe, reconnoitre, search, seek, snoop, spy, spy out, survey, track, watch.
n. emissary, escort, lookout, outrider, precursor, reconnoitrer, spy, vanguard.

scowl *v.* frown, glare, glower, grimace.
n. frown, glare, glower, grimace.
antonyms beam, grin, smile.

scrabble *v.* clamber, claw, dig, grope, grub, paw, root, scramble, scrape, scratch.

scraggy *adj.* angular, bony, emaciated, gaunt, lanky, lean, meagre, scrawny, skinny, undernourished, wasted.
antonyms plump, rounded, sleek.

scramble *v.* clamber, climb, contend, crawl, hasten, jostle, jumble, push, run, rush, scale, scrabble, shuffle, sprawl, strive, struggle, swarm, vie.
n. climb, commotion, confusion, contention, free-for-all, hustle, muddle, race, rivalry, rush, strife, struggle, tussle.

scrap[1] *n.* atom, bit, bite, crumb, fraction, fragment, grain, iota, mite, morsel, mouthful,

part, particle, piece, portion, remnant, shred, sliver, snippet, trace, vestige, waste.
v. abandon, axe, break up, cancel, demolish, discard, ditch, drop, jettison, shed, throw out, write off.
antonyms reinstate, restore, resume.

scrap[2] *n.* argument, barney, battle, brawl, disagreement, dispute, dust-up, fight, quarrel, row, ruckus, ruction, rumpus, scuffle, set-to, squabble, tiff, wrangle.
antonyms agreement, peace.
v. argue, bicker, clash, fall out, fight, squabble, wrangle.
antonym agree.

scrape *v.* abrade, bark, claw, clean, erase, file, grate, graze, grind, pinch, rasp, remove, rub, scour, scrabble, scratch, screech, skimp, skin, squeak, stint.

scrappy *adj.* bitty, disjointed, fragmentary, incomplete, piecemeal, sketchy, slapdash, slipshod, superficial.
antonyms complete, finished.

scraps *n.* bits, leavings, leftovers, remains, scrapings.

scratch *v.* claw, cut, damage, etch, grate, graze, incise, mark, rub, score, scrape.
n. blemish, claw mark, gash, graze, laceration, mark, scrape, streak.
up to scratch acceptable, adequate, satisfactory.

scrawl *n.* scratch, scribble, squiggle, writing.

scrawny *adj.* angular, bony, emaciated, lanky, lean, rawboned, scraggy, skinny, underfed, under-nourished.
antonyms fat, plump.

scream *v.* bawl, clash, cry, roar, screech, shriek, shrill, squeal, wail, yell, yelp.
n. howl, outcry, roar, screech, shriek, squeal, wail, yell, yelp.
antonym whisper.

screech *v.* cry, scream, shriek, squeal, yelp.
antonym whisper.

screen *v.* **1** broadcast, present, show. **2** cloak, conceal, cover, defend, evaluate, examine, filter, gauge, grade, guard, hide, mask, process, protect, safeguard, scan, shelter, shield, shroud, sieve, sift, sort, veil, vet.
n. awning, canopy, cloak, concealment, cover, divider, guard, hedge, mantle, mesh, net, partition, shade, shelter, shield, shroud, uncover.

screw *v.* adjust, compress, constrain, contract, distort, extort, extract, fasten, force, oppress, pressurise, squeeze, tighten, turn, twist, wind, wrest, wring, wrinkle.

screwy *adj.* batty, crackers, crazy, dotty, eccentric, mad, nutty, odd, queer, round the bend, weird.
antonym sane.

scribble *v.* dash off, doodle, jot, pen, scrawl, write.

scribe *n.* clerk, copyist, penman, secretary, writer.

scrimmage *n.* affray, brawl, disturbance, dust-up, fight, fray, free-for-all, riot, row, scrap, scuffle, set-to, skirmish, squabble, struggle.
antonym calmness.

scrimp *v.* curtail, economise, limit, reduce, restrict, save, scrape, shorten, skimp, stint.
antonyms spend, waste.

script *n.* book, calligraphy, copy, hand, handwriting, letters, lines, longhand, manuscript, text, words, writing.

scroll *n.* inventory, list, parchment, roll, volume.

scrounge *v.* beg, cadge, sponge, wheedle.

scrounger *n.* cadger, parasite, sponger.

scrub *v.* abandon, abolish, cancel, clean, cleanse, delete, discontinue, ditch, drop, forget, give up, rub, scour.

scruffy *adj.* disreputable, dog-eared, mangy, messy, ragged, run-down, seedy, shabby, slovenly, squalid, tattered, ungroomed, unkempt, untidy.
antonyms tidy, well-dressed.

scrunch *v.* crunch, crush, grate, grind.

scruple *n.* caution, difficulty, doubt, hesitation, misgiving, perplexity, qualm, reluctance, squeamishness, uneasiness.

scrupulous *adj.* careful, conscientious, exact, honourable, meticulous, minute, nice, painstaking, precise, principled, rigorous, strict, upright.
antonyms careless, reckless, superficial.

scrutinise *v.* analyse, examine, explore, inspect, investigate, probe, scan, search, sift, study.

scrutiny *n.* analysis, enquiry, examination, exploration, inspection, investigation, once-over, search, sifting, study.

scud *v.* blow, dart, fly, hasten, race, sail, shoot, skim, speed.

scuff *v.* abrade, brush, drag, graze, rub, scratch, shuffle, skin.

scuffle *v.* clash, contend, fight, grapple, jostle, struggle, tussle.
n. affray, brawl, commotion, disturbance, fight, fray, rumpus, scrap, set-to, tussle.

sculpt *v.* carve, chisel, cut, fashion, form, hew, model, mould, represent, sculpture, shape.

scum *n.* dregs, dross, film, froth, impurities, offscourings, rubbish, scruff, trash.

scupper *v.* defeat, demolish, destroy, overthrow, overwhelm, ruin, wreck.
antonyms advance, promote.

scurrilous *adj.* abusive, coarse, defamatory, foul, indecent, insulting, low, nasty, obscene, offensive, rude, salacious, scandalous, slanderous, vulgar.
antonyms complimentary, courteous, polite.

scurry *v.* dart, dash, fly, hurry, race, scamper, scoot, scud, scuttle, skelter, skim, sprint, trot, whisk.
antonym stroll.
n. flurry, whirl.

scuttle *v.* bustle, hasten, hurry, run, rush, scamper, scoot, scramble, scud, trot.
antonym stroll.

sea *n.* **1** briny, deep, ditch, ocean, waves. **2** abundance, mass, multitude, plethora, profusion.
adj. aquatic, marine, maritime, naval, ocean,

ocean-going, salt, saltwater, sea-going.
antonyms air, land.
at sea adrift, astray, baffled, bewildered, confused, insecure, lost, mystified, perplexed, puzzled.

seafaring *adj.* marine, maritime, nautical, naval, oceanic, sailing.
antonyms air, land.

seal *v.* close, conclude, cork, enclose, fasten, plug, secure, settle, shut, stamp, stop, stopper, waterproof.
antonym unseal.
n. assurance, attestation, authentication, confirmation, imprimatur, insignia, ratification, signet, stamp.
seal off block up, close off, cut off, fence off, isolate, quarantine, segregate, shut off.
antonym open up.

seam *n.* closure, crack, furrow, joint, layer, line, ridge, stratum, vein.

seamy *adj.* corrupt, dark, degraded, disreputable, low, nasty, rough, sleazy, sordid, squalid, unpleasant.
antonyms pleasant, respectable, wholesome.

sear *v.* brand, brown, burn, fry, harden, scorch, seal, shrivel, sizzle, wilt, wither.

search *v.* check, comb, enquire, examine, explore, frisk, inspect, investigate, look, probe, pry, ransack, rifle, rummage, scour, scrutinise, sift, test.
n. enquiry, examination, exploration, going-over, hunt, inspection, investigation, pursuit, quest, research, rummage, scrutiny.

searching *adj.* close, intent, keen, minute, penetrating, piercing, probing, severe, sharp, thorough.
antonyms superficial, vague.

season *n.* division, interval, period, span, spell, term, time.
v. colour, condition, flavour, harden, imbue, lace, mature, prepare, qualify, salt, spice, temper, toughen, train, treat.

seasonable *adj.* appropriate, convenient, fit, opportune, suitable, timely, welcome, well-timed.
antonyms inopportune, unseasonable.

seasoned *adj.* acclimatised, experienced, hardened, long-serving, mature, old, practised, time-served, veteran, weathered, well-versed.
antonyms inexperienced, novice.

seasoning *n.* condiment, dressing, flavouring, pepper, relish, salt, sauce, spice.

seat *n.* **1** bed, bench, chair, pew, stool, throne. **2** abode, house, mansion, residence. **3** axis, base, bottom, cause, centre, constituency, footing, foundation, ground, headquarters, heart, hub, location, membership, place, site, situation, source.
v. accommodate, assign, contain, deposit, fit, fix, hold, install, locate, place, set, settle, sit, slot, take.

seating *n.* accommodation, chairs, places, room, seats.

secede *v.* disaffiliate, leave, quit, resign, retire, separate, split off, withdraw.
antonyms join, unite with.

secluded *adj.* cloistered, cut off, isolated, lonely, out-of-the-way, private, remote, retired, sequestered, sheltered, solitary.
antonyms accessible, busy, public.

seclusion *n.* concealment, hiding, isolation, privacy, recluseness, remoteness, retirement, retreat, shelter, solitude.

second[1] *adj.* additional, alternate, alternative, double, duplicate, extra, following, further, inferior, lesser, lower, next, other, repeated, secondary, subordinate, subsequent, succeeding, supplementary, supporting, twin.
n. assistant, backer, helper, supporter.
v. advance, agree with, aid, approve, assist, back, encourage, endorse, forward, further, help, promote, support.

second[2] *n.* instant, jiffy, minute, moment, tick.

secondary *adj.* alternate, auxiliary, back-up, derivative, derived, extra, indirect, inferior, lesser, lower, minor, relief, reserve, resulting, second, spare, subordinate, subsidiary, supporting, unimportant.
antonyms main, major, primary.

second-class *adj.* indifferent, inferior, mediocre, second-best, second-rate, undistinguished, uninspired, uninspiring.

second-hand *adj.* borrowed, derivative, hand-me-down, old, used, vicarious, worn.
antonym new.

second-rate *adj.* cheap, inferior, low-grade, mediocre, poor, shoddy, substandard, tawdry, undistinguished, uninspired, uninspiring.
antonym first-rate.

secrecy *n.* concealment, confidence, confidentiality, covertness, furtiveness, mystery, privacy, retirement, seclusion, solitude, stealth, stealthiness, surreptitiousness.
antonym openness.

secret *adj.* back-door, backstairs, camouflaged, clandestine, classified, cloak-and-dagger, close, concealed, covered, covert, cryptic, deep, discreet, disguised, furtive, hidden, hole-and-corner, hush-hush, mysterious, occult, out-of-the-way, private, retired, secluded, secretive, shrouded, sly, stealthy, undercover, underhand, under-the-counter, undisclosed, unknown, unpublished, unrevealed, unseen.
antonyms open, public, well-known.
n. code, confidence, enigma, formula, key, mystery, recipe.

secretary *n.* assistant, clerk, girl Friday, man Friday, PA, person Friday, personal assistant, stenographer, typist.

secrete[1] *v.* appropriate, bury, cache, conceal, cover, disguise, harbour, hide, screen, secure, shroud, stash away, veil.
antonyms disclose, reveal, uncover.

secrete[2] *v.* emanate, emit, extrude, exude, give off, produce, separate.

secretion *n.* discharge, emission, exudation.

secretive *adj.* cagey, close, close-lipped, cryptic, deep, enigmatic, quiet, reserved, reticent, tight-

lipped, uncommunicative, unforthcoming, withdrawn.
antonyms communicative, forthcoming, open.
sect *n.* camp, denomination, division, faction, group, party, school, splinter group, subdivision, wing.
sectarian *adj.* bigoted, cliquish, doctrinaire, dogmatic, exclusive, factional, fanatical, insular, limited, narrow, narrow-minded, parochial, partisan, rigid.
antonyms broad-minded, cosmopolitan, nonsectarian.
section *n.* **1** area, article, component, department, district, division, fraction, fragment, instalment, part, passage, piece, portion, region, sample, sector, segment, slice, subdivision, wing, zone. **2** cross section, diagram, picture, representation.
antonym **1** whole.
sectional *adj.* class, divided, exclusive, factional, limited, local, localised, partial, racial, regional, sectarian, separate, separatist.
antonyms general, universal.
sector *n.* area, category, district, division, part, quarter, region, section, subdivision, zone.
antonym whole.
secular *adj.* civil, lay, non-religious, profane, state, temporal, worldly.
antonym religious.
secure *adj.* **1** certain, conclusive, definite, dependable, fast, fastened, firm, fixed, fortified, immovable, immune, impregnable, protected, reliable, safe, sheltered, shielded, solid, stable, steadfast, steady, sure, tight, undamaged, unharmed, well-founded. **2** assured, confident, reassured.
antonyms **1** insecure, vulnerable. **2** ill at east, uncertain, uneasy.
v. **1** acquire, gain, get, get hold of, guarantee, land, obtain. **2** attach, batten down, bolt, chain, fasten, fix, lash, lock (up), make fast, moor, nail, padlock, rivet.
antonyms **1** lose. **2** unfasten.
security *n.* **1** asylum, care, certainty, confidence, conviction, cover, custody, defence, guards, hostage, immunity, positiveness, precautions, preservation, protection, refuge, reliance, retreat, safeguards, safe-keeping, safety, sanctuary, surety, surveillance. **2** assurance, collateral, guarantee, insurance, pledge, warranty.
antonym **1** insecurity.
sedate *adj.* calm, collected, composed, cool, decorous, deliberate, demure, dignified, earnest, grave, imperturbable, proper, quiet, seemly, serene, serious, slow-moving, sober, solemn, staid, tranquil, unflappable, unruffled.
antonyms flippant, hasty, undignified.
sedative *adj.* allaying, anodyne, calming, depressant, lenitive, relaxing, soothing, soporific, tranquillising.
antonym rousing.
n. anodyne, narcotic, sleeping-pill, tranquilliser.
sedentary *adj.* desk, desk-bound, inactive, seated, sitting, stationary, still, unmoving.
antonym active.
sediment *n.* deposit, dregs, grounds, lees.
sedition *n.* agitation, disloyalty, rabble-rousing, rumpus, subversion, treason, tumult.
antonyms calm, loyalty.
seditious *adj.* disloyal, dissident, insubordinate, mutinous, rebellious, revolutionary, subversive, traitorous.
antonyms calm, loyal.
seduce *v.* allure, attract, beguile, betray, corrupt, deceive, dishonour, ensnare, entice, lure, mislead, ruin, tempt.
seduction *n.* come-on, corruption, enticement, lure, ruin, snare, temptation.
seductive *adj.* alluring, attractive, beguiling, bewitching, captivating, come-hither, come-on, enticing, inviting, irresistible, provocative, ravishing, seducing, sexy, tempting.
antonym unattractive.
see *v.* **1** discern, distinguish, glimpse, identify, look at, make out, mark, note, notice, observe, perceive, spot, view, watch. **2** anticipate, envisage, foresee, imagine, picture, visualise. **3** appreciate, comprehend, consider, deem, fathom, feel, follow, grasp, know, realise, recognise, understand. **4** ascertain, determine, discover, learn. **5** accompany, court, date, escort, go out with, lead, usher. **6** consult, interview, visit.
see to arrange, attend to, deal with, do, fix, look after, manage, organise, repair, sort out, take care of, take charge of.
seed *n.* beginning, children, descendants, egg, embryo, germ, grain, heirs, issue, kernel, nucleus, offspring, ovule, pip, progeny, quiverful, race, source, spawn, sperm, start, successors.
antonym ancestors.
seedy *adj.* ailing, crummy, decaying, dilapidated, faded, grotty, grubby, ill, mangy, off-colour, old, poorly, run-down, scruffy, shabby, sickly, sleazy, slovenly, squalid, tatty, unkempt, unwell, worn.
antonyms posh, well.
seek *v.* aim, ask, aspire to, attempt, desire, endeavour, enquire, entreat, follow, hunt, invite, petition, pursue, request, search for, solicit, strive, try, want.
seem *v.* appear, look, look like, pretend, sound like.
seeming *adj.* apparent, appearing, ostensible, outward, pseudo, quasi-, specious, surface.
antonym real.
seemingly *adv.* allegedly, apparently, as far as one can see, on the face of it, on the surface, outwardly, superficially.
antonym really.
seep *v.* exude, leak, ooze, percolate, permeate, soak, trickle, weep, well.
seethe *v.* boil, bubble, ferment, fizz, foam, foam at the mouth, froth, fume, rage, rise, saturate, simmer, smoulder, soak, steep, storm, surge, swarm, swell, teem.
see-through *adj.* filmy, flimsy, gauzy, gos-

samer(y), sheer, translucent, transparent.
antonym opaque.
segment *n.* bit, compartment, division, part, piece, portion, section, slice, wedge.
antonym whole.
segregate *v.* cut off, discriminate against, dissociate, isolate, quarantine, separate, set apart.
antonyms join, unite.
segregation *n.* apartheid, discrimination, isolation, quarantine, separation.
antonym unification.
seize *v.* abduct, annex, apprehend, appropriate, arrest, capture, catch, claw, clutch, collar, commander, confiscate, fasten, fix, get, grab, grasp, grip, hijack, impound, nab, snatch, take.
antonyms hand back, let go, release.
seizure *n.* **1** attack, convulsion, fit, paroxysm, spasm. **2** abduction, annexation, apprehension, arrest, attachment, capture, confiscation, grabbing, taking.
antonyms **2** liberation, release.
seldom *adv.* infrequently, occasionally, rarely, scarcely.
antonyms often, usually.
select *v.* choose, pick, prefer, single out.
adj. choice, élite, excellent, exclusive, first-class, first-rate, hand-picked, limited, picked, posh, prime, privileged, selected, special, superior, top.
antonyms general, second-rate, unremarkable.
selection *n.* anthology, assortment, choice, choosing, collection, line-up, medley, miscellany, option, pick, potpourri, preference, range, variety.
selective *adj.* careful, discerning, discriminating, eclectic, particular.
antonyms indiscriminate, unselective.
self *n.* ego, I, identity, person, personality, soul.
self-assertive *adj.* aggressive, bossy, commanding, dictatorial, domineering, forceful, heavy-handed, high-handed, overbearing, pushy.
antonym compliant.
self-assurance *n.* assurance, confidence, positiveness, self-confidence, self-possession.
antonyms humility, unsureness.
self-assured *adj.* assured, cocky, confident, self-possessed, sure of oneself.
antonyms humble, unsure.
self-centred *adj.* egotistic(al), narcissistic, self-absorbed, self-interested, selfish, self-seeking, self-serving.
antonym altruistic.
self-confidence *n.* aplomb, assurance, confidence, poise, self-assurance, self-possession, self-reliance.
antonyms humility, unsureness.
self-confident *adj.* assured, confident, fearless, secure, self-assured, self-possessed, self-reliant.
antonyms humble, unsure.
self-conscious *adj.* awkward, bashful, embarrassed, ill at ease, insecure, nervous, retiring, self-effacing, shamefaced, sheepish, shrinking, uncomfortable.
antonyms natural, unaffected.
self-control *n.* calmness, composure, cool, discipline, restraint, self-discipline, self-mastery, self-restraint, temperance, will-power.
self-denial *n.* abstemiousness, asceticism, moderation, renunciation, selflessness, self-sacrifice, temperance, unselfishness.
antonym self-indulgence.
self-evident *adj.* axiomatic, clear, incontrovertible, inescapable, manifest, obvious, undeniable, unquestionable.
self-government *n.* autonomy, democracy, home rule, independence, self-determination.
antonym subjection.
self-indulgent *adj.* dissolute, extravagant, intemperate, profligate.
antonym abstemious.
self-interest *n.* selfishness, self-love, self-serving.
antonym selflessness.
selfish *adj.* egotistic(al), greedy, mean, mercenary, narrow, self-centred, self-interested, self-seeking.
antonyms considerate, generous, unselfish.
selfless *adj.* altruistic, generous, self-denying, self-sacrificing, unselfish.
antonyms self-centred, selfish.
self-possessed *adj.* calm, collected, composed, confident, cool, self-assured, unruffled.
antonym worried.
self-respect *n.* dignity, pride, self-assurance, self-confidence.
self-righteous *adj.* complacent, goody-goody, holier-than-thou, hypocritical, pharisaical, pietistic, pious, sanctimonious, smug, superior.
self-sacrifice *n.* altruism, generosity, self-denial, selflessness, self-renunciation.
antonym selfishness.
self-satisfied *adj.* complacent, puffed up, self-congratulatory, self-righteous, smug.
antonym humble.
self-seeking *adj.* acquisitive, calculating, careerist, fortune-hunting, gold-digging, mercenary, on the make, opportunistic, self-interested, selfish, self-loving.
antonym altruistic.
self-styled *adj.* professed, self-appointed, so-called, would-be.
self-supporting *adj.* independent, self-financing, self-reliant, self-sufficient, self-sustaining.
antonym dependent.
self-willed *adj.* bloody-minded, headstrong, intractable, obstinate, opinionated, pig-headed, stiff-necked, stubborn, wilful.
antonyms flexible, persuadable.
sell *v.* barter, deal in, exchange, handle, hawk, impose on, market, merchandise, peddle, promote, retail, stock, surrender, trade, trade in, traffic in.
antonym buy.
seller *n.* agent, dealer, merchant, rep, representative, retailer, sales staff, salesgirl, saleslady, salesman, saleswoman, shopkeeper, tradesman, traveller, vendor.
antonyms buyer, purchaser.
selling *n.* advertising, dealing, marketing, mer-

chandising, promotion, salesmanship, trading, traffic, transactions.

semblance *n.* air, apparition, appearance, aspect, bearing, façade, figure, form, front, guise, image, likeness, mask, pretence, resemblance, show, similarity, veneer.

seminary *n.* academy, college, institute, institution, school, training-college.

send *v.* **1** consign, convey, deliver, dispatch, forward, mail, post, remit. **2** broadcast, communicate, electrify, transmit. **3** direct, discharge, drive, emit, fling, hurl, move, propel. **4** delight, excite, stir, thrill.

send for call for, call out, command, order, request, summon.

antonym dismiss.

send up imitate, mimic, mock, parody, ridicule, satirise, take off.

send-off *n.* departure, farewell, going-away, leave-taking, start.

antonym arrival.

send-up *n.* imitation, mockery, parody, satire, skit, spoof, take-off.

senile *adj.* aged, confused, decrepit, doddering, doting, failing, old.

senior *adj.* elder, first, higher, high-ranking, major, older, superior.

antonym junior.

seniority *n.* eldership, precedence, priority, rank, standing, superiority.

antonym juniority.

sensation *n.* **1** awareness, consciousness, emotion, feeling, impression, perception, sense, tingle, vibrations. **2** agitation, commotion, excitement, furore, hit, scandal, stir, surprise, thrill.

sensational *adj.* amazing, astounding, breathtaking, dramatic, electrifying, exceptional, exciting, hair-raising, horrifying, impressive, lurid, marvellous, melodramatic, mind-blowing, revealing, scandalous, shocking, smashing, spectacular, staggering, startling, thrilling.

antonyms ordinary, run-of-the-mill.

sense *n.* **1** appreciation, awareness, consciousness, faculty, feel, feeling, impression, perception, sensation. **2** brains, cleverness, discernment, intelligence, intuition, judgement, mind, opinion, reason, understanding, wisdom, wit(s). **3** advantage, definition, implication, interpretation, meaning, point, purpose, significance, substance.

antonyms **2** foolishness, nonsense.

v. appreciate, comprehend, detect, feel, grasp, notice, observe, perceive, realise, suspect, understand.

senseless *adj.* **1** absurd, crazy, daft, dotty, fatuous, foolish, futile, idiotic, illogical, imbecilic, irrational, ludicrous, mad, meaningless, mindless, moronic, nonsensical, pointless, ridiculous, silly, stupid, unreasonable, unwise. **2** anaesthetised, deadened, numb, out, stunned, unconscious, unfeeling.

antonyms **1** meaningful, sensible. **2** conscious.

sensibilities *n.* emotions, feelings, sensitivities, sentiments, susceptibilities.

sensibility *n.* appreciation, awareness, delicacy, discernment, insight, intuition, perceptiveness, responsiveness, sensitivity, susceptibility, taste.

antonyms deadness, insensibility, unresponsiveness.

sensible *adj.* appreciable, down-to-earth, far-sighted, intelligent, judicious, level-headed, practical, prudent, rational, realistic, reasonable, right-thinking, sane, shrewd, sober, solid, sound, visible, well-advised, well-thought-out, wise.

antonyms foolish, senseless, unwise.

sensitive *adj.* **1** impressionable, irritable, perceptive, responsive, sensitised, susceptible, temperamental, tender, thin-skinned, touchy. **2** delicate, exact, fine, precise.

antonyms **1** hard, insensitive, thick-skinned. **2** approximate, imprecise.

sensual *adj.* animal, bodily, carnal, erotic, fleshly, lecherous, lewd, licentious, lustful, physical, randy, self-indulgent, sexual, sexy, voluptuous, worldly.

antonym ascetic.

sensuous *adj.* gratifying, lush, luxurious, pleasurable, rich, sensory, sumptuous, voluptuous.

antonyms ascetic, plain, simple.

sentence *n.* **1** aphorism, clause, expression, maxim, opinion, saying. **2** condemnation, decision, decree, judgement, order, pronouncement, ruling, verdict.

v. condemn, doom, judge, pass judgement on, penalise, pronounce judgement on.

sentiment *n.* attitude, belief, emotion, feeling, idea, judgement, opinion, persuasion, romanticism, sensibility, slush, soft-heartedness, tenderness, thought, view.

antonyms hard-heartedness, straightforwardness.

sentimental *adj.* corny, drippy, emotional, gushing, gushy, impressionable, lovey-dovey, mawkish, mushy, nostalgic, pathetic, romantic, schmaltzy, sloppy, slushy, soft-hearted, soppy, tear-jerking, tender, touching, weepy.

antonyms down-to-earth, practical, realistic, unsentimental.

sentry *n.* guard, look-out, picket, sentinel, watch, watchman.

separable *adj.* detachable, distinct, distinguishable, divisible, partible, severable.

antonym inseperable.

separate *v.* abstract, departmentalise, detach, disaffiliate, disconnect, disentangle, diverge, divide, divorce, estrange, isolate, part, part company, remove, secede, segregate, sever, shear, split (up), uncouple, withdraw.

antonyms combine, join, unite.

adj. alone, apart, autonomous, detached, different, disconnected, discrete, disjointed, disparate, distinct, divided, divorced, independent, individual, isolated, particular, several, single, solitary, sundry, unattached, unconnected.

antonyms attached, together.

separated *adj.* apart, disconnected, disunited,

divided, isolated, parted, segregated, separate, split up.
antonyms attached, together.

separation *n.* break, break-up, detachment, disconnection, disengagement, dissociation, division, divorce, estrangement, farewell, gap, leave-taking, parting, rift, segregation, severance, solution, split, split-up.
antonyms togetherness, unification.

septic *adj.* festering, infected, poisoned, putrefying, putrid.

sequel *n.* conclusion, consequence, continuation, development, end, follow-up, issue, outcome, pay-off, result, upshot.

sequence *n.* arrangement, chain, consequence, course, cycle, order, procession, progression, series, set, succession, track, train.

serene *adj.* calm, composed, cool, peaceful, placid, tranquil, undisturbed, untroubled.
antonyms disturbed, troubled.

serenity *n.* calm, composure, cool, placidity, quietness, stillness, tranquillity.
antonyms anxiety, disruption.

series *n.* arrangement, chain, course, cycle, line, order, progression, run, scale, sequence, set, string, succession, train.

serious *adj.* **1** acute, critical, crucial, dangerous, deep, difficult, far-reaching, fateful, grave, grim, important, momentous, pressing, severe, significant, urgent, weighty, worrying. **2** earnest, humourless, long-faced, pensive, sincere, sober, solemn, stern, thoughtful, unsmiling.
antonyms **1** slight, smiling, trivial. **2** facetious, frivolous, smiling.

seriously *adv.* acutely, badly, critically, dangerously, earnestly, gravely, joking apart, severely, sincerely, solemnly, sorely, thoughtfully.
antonyms casually, slightly.

sermon *n.* address, exhortation, homily, lecture, talking-to.

serrated *adj.* notched, saw-toothed, toothed.
antonym smooth.

servant *n.* ancillary, attendant, boy, domestic, help, helper, hireling, lackey, maid, menial, retainer, skivvy, slave, steward, valet.
antonyms master, mistress.

serve *v.* **1** aid, assist, attend, benefit, further, help, minister to, oblige, wait on, work for. **2** act, answer, complete, discharge, fulfil, function, perform, satisfy. **3** arrange, deliver, distribute, present, provide, supply.

service *n.* **1** business, duty, employment, function, work. **2** advantage, assistance, benefit, help, labour, performance, use, usefulness, utility. **3** check, maintenance, overhaul, servicing. **4** ceremony, observance, rite, worship.
v. check, maintain, overhaul, recondition, repair, tune.

serviceable *adj.* advantageous, beneficial, convenient, dependable, durable, efficient, functional, hard-wearing, helpful, plain, practical, profitable, simple, strong, tough, unadorned, usable, useful, utilitarian.
antonyms unserviceable, unusable.

servile *adj.* abject, base, bootlicking, cringing, fawning, grovelling, humble, low, mean, menial, obsequious, slavish, subject, submissive, subservient, sycophantic, toadying.
antonyms aggressive, bold.

servitude *n.* bondage, bonds, chains, obedience, serfdom, slavery, subjugation.
antonyms freedom, liberty.

session *n.* assembly, conference, discussion, go, hearing, meeting, period, semester, sitting, term, year.

set *v.* **1** apply, arrange, deposit, establish, locate, lodge, park, place, position, prepare, put, situate, stick. **2** allocate, appoint, assign, conclude, decide, designate, determine, fix, impose, name, ordain, prescribe, resolve, schedule, settle, specify. **3** adjust, co-ordinate, direct, regulate, synchronise. **4** dip, disappear, go down, sink, subside, vanish. **5** congeal, crystallise, gelatinise, harden, jell, solidify, stiffen, thicken.
n. assortment, band, batch, circle, class, collection, company, compendium, crowd, faction, gang, group, kit, outfit, sect, sequence, series.
adj. agreed, appointed, arranged, artificial, conventional, customary, decided, definite, deliberate, established, firm, fixed, formal, hackneyed, immovable, inflexible, intentional, prearranged, prescribed, regular, rehearsed, rigid, routine, scheduled, settled, standard, stereotyped, stock, strict, traditional, unspontaneous, usual.
antonyms free, movable, spontaneous, undecided.
set about attack, begin, start, tackle, wade into.
set against balance, compare, contrast, disunite, divide, juxtapose, oppose, weigh.
set apart choose, distinguish, elect, put aside, reserve, separate.
set aside abrogate, annul, cancel, discard, dismiss, keep (back), lay aside, overrule, overturn, put aside, reject, repudiate, reserve, reverse, save, select, separate.
set back delay, hamper, hinder, hold up, impede, interrupt, retard, slow.
set off 1 depart, embark, leave, make tracks, set out. **2** detonate, explode, ignite, light, touch off, trigger off. **3** contrast, display, enhance, present, show off.
set on attack, beat up, fall upon, fly at, go for, lay into, pitch into, set upon, turn on.
set out 1 begin, make a move, set off, start (out). **2** arrange, describe, display, elaborate, exhibit, explain, lay out, present.
set up arrange, assemble, back, begin, boost, build, compose, construct, create, elevate, erect, establish, form, found, gratify, inaugurate, initiate, install, institute, introduce, organise, prepare, promote, raise, start, strengthen.

setback *n.* defeat, delay, disappointment, hiccup, hitch, hold-up, misfortune, problem, reverse, snag, throw-back, upset.
antonyms advance, advantage, boost, help.

setting *n.* background, context, environment,

frame, locale, location, milieu, mounting, period, perspective, position, scene, scenery, site, surroundings.

settle *v.* **1** adjust, arrange, complete, conclude, order, reconcile, resolve. **2** descend, drop, fall, sink, subside. **3** agree, appoint, choose, confirm, decide, determine, establish, fix. **4** colonise, inhabit, live, occupy, people, populate, reside. **5** clear, discharge, pay.

settlement[1] *n.* **1** agreement, arrangement, conclusion, confirmation, decision, establishment, resolution, satisfaction, termination. **2** clearance, clearing, defrayal, discharge, income, payment. **3** colonisation, colony, community, immigration, kibbutz, peopling, plantation, population.

settler *n.* coloniser, colonist, frontiersman, immigrant, incomer, newcomer, pioneer, planter, squatter.
antonym native.

set-to *n.* altercation, argument, brush, conflict, contest, disagreement, dust-up, exchange, fight, fracas, quarrel, row, scrap, scuffle, spat, squabble, wrangle.

set-up *n.* arrangement, business, circumstances, conditions, organisation, régime, structure, system.

sever *v.* alienate, cleave, cut, detach, disconnect, disjoin, dissociate, dissolve, disunite, divide, estrange, part, rend, separate, split, terminate.
antonyms attach, combine, join, unite.

several *adj.* assorted, different, distinct, diverse, individual, many, particular, separate, single, some, specific, various.

severe *adj.* **1** acute, arduous, biting, bitter, critical, cruel, cutting, dangerous, demanding, difficult, disapproving, distressing, extreme, fierce, forbidding, grave, grim, hard, harsh, inexorable, intense, oppressive, pitiless, punishing, relentless, rigid, rigorous, scathing, serious, shrewd, sober, stern, strait-laced, strict, tough, unbending, violent. **2** ascetic, austere, functional, plain, restrained, simple, unadorned, unembellished.
antonyms **1** compassionate, kind, lenient, mild, sympathetic. **2** decorated, ornate.

sex *n.* coitus, copulation, desire, fornication, gender, intercourse, intimacy, love, lovemaking, reproduction, sexual intercourse, sexual relations, sexuality, union.

sexual *adj.* carnal, coital, erotic, genital, intimate, reproductive, sensual, sex, venereal.

sexuality *n.* carnality, desire, eroticism, lust, sensuality, virility, voluptuousness.

sexy *adj.* arousing, cuddly, erotic, flirtatious, inviting, nubile, pornographic, provocative, provoking, seductive, sensual, sensuous, suggestive, voluptuous.
antonym sexless.

shabby *adj.* **1** dilapidated, dingy, dirty, dog-eared, faded, frayed, mangy, mean, moth-eaten, neglected, paltry, poky, poor, ragged, run-down, scruffy, seedy, shoddy, tattered, worn, worn-out. **2** cheap, contemptible, despicable, dishonourable, disreputable, low, rotten, shameful.
antonyms **1** smart. **2** fair, honourable.

shack *n.* cabin, hovel, hut, hutch, lean-to, shanty, shed.

shackle *n.* bond, bracelets, chain, fetter, hamper, handcuff, iron, leg-iron, manacle, rope, shackles.
v. bind, chain, constrain, embarrass, fetter, hamper, handcuff, handicap, impede, inhibit, limit, manacle, obstruct, restrain, restrict, secure, tether, thwart, tie, trammel.

shade *n.* **1** apparition, darkness, dimness, dusk, ghost, gloaming, gloom, gloominess, obscurity, phantom, semblance, semi-darkness, shadiness, shadow, spectre, spirit, twilight. **2** blind, canopy, cover, curtain, screen, shelter, shield, shroud, veil. **3** colour, hue, tinge, tint, tone. **4** amount, dash, degree, gradation, hint, nuance, suggestion, suspicion, trace, variety.
v. cloud, conceal, cover, darken, dim, hide, obscure, overshadow, protect, screen, shield, shroud, veil.

shadow *n.* cloud, cover, darkness, dimness, dusk, ghost, gloaming, gloom, hint, image, obscurity, phantom, protection, remnant, representation, sadness, shade, shelter, spectre, spirit, suggestion, suspicion, trace, vestige.
v. **1** darken, obscure, overhang, overshadow, screen, shade, shield. **2** dog, follow, stalk, tail, trail, watch.

shadowy *adj.* dark, dim, dreamlike, dusky, faint, ghostly, gloomy, hazy, illusory, imaginary, indistinct, intangible, murky, nebulous, obscure, spectral, undefined, unreal, unsubstantial, vague.

shady *adj.* **1** cool, dark, dim, leafy, shaded, shadowy. **2** crooked, dishonest, disreputable, dubious, fishy, questionable, slippery, suspect, suspicious, underhand, unethical, unscrupulous, untrustworthy.
antonyms **1** bright, sunlit, sunny. **2** honest, honourable, trustworthy.

shaft *n.* arrow, barb, beam, cut, dart, haft, handle, missile, pole, ray, rod, shank, stem, stick, thrust, upright.

shaggy *adj.* hairy, hirsute, long-haired, nappy, rough, unkempt, unshorn.
antonyms bald, close-cropped, shorn.

shake *n.* agitation, convulsion, disturbance, jerk, jolt, quaking, shiver, shock, shudder, trembling, tremor, twitch, vibration.
v. **1** brandish, convulse, flourish, fluctuate, heave, impair, joggle, jolt, move, oscillate, quake, quiver, rattle, rock, rouse, shiver, shudder, split, sway, totter, tremble, twitch, vibrate, wag, waggle, wave, waver, weaken, wobble. **2** agitate, discompose, distress, disturb, frighten, intimidate, shock, stir, unnerve, unsettle, upset.

shake off dislodge, elude, get rid of, give the slip, leave behind, lose, outdistance, outstrip.

shake-up *n.* disturbance, rearrangement, reorganisation, reshuffle, upheaval.

shaky *adj.* dubious, faltering, insecure, precar-

ious, questionable, quivery, rickety, rocky, suspect, tottery, uncertain, unreliable, unsound, unstable, unsteady, unsupported, weak, wobbly.
antonyms firm, strong.

shallow *adj.* empty, flimsy, foolish, frivolous, idle, ignorant, meaningless, simple, skin-deep, slight, superficial, surface, trivial, unintelligent, unscholarly.
antonyms analytical, deep, profound.

sham *n.* cheat, counterfeit, forgery, fraud, hoax, humbug, imitation, impostor, imposture, phoney, pretence, pretender.
adj. artificial, bogus, counterfeit, faked, false, feigned, imitation, mock, phoney, pretended, put-on, simulated, spurious, synthetic.
antonyms authentic, genuine, real.
v. affect, counterfeit, fake, feign, pretend, put on, simulate.

shambles *n.* chaos, confusion, disorganisation, havoc, mess, muddle, wreck.

shame *n.* degradation, discredit, disgrace, dishonour, disrepute, embarrassment, humiliation, ignominy, infamy, mortification, reproach, scandal, shamefacedness, stain, stigma.
antonyms credit, distinction, honour, pride.
v. abash, confound, debase, degrade, disconcert, discredit, disgrace, dishonour, embarrass, humble, humiliate, mortify, put to shame, reproach, ridicule, show up, stain, sully, taint.

shamefaced *adj.* abashed, apologetic, ashamed, blushing, conscience-stricken, contrite, embarrassed, humiliated, mortified, red-faced, remorseful, sheepish, shrinking, uncomfortable.
antonyms proud, unashamed.

shameful *adj.* abominable, atrocious, contemptible, disgraceful, embarrassing, humiliating, ignominious, indecent, infamous, low, mean, mortifying, outrageous, reprehensible, scandalous, unworthy, vile, wicked.
antonyms creditable, honourable, worthy.

shameless *adj.* audacious, barefaced, blatant, brash, brazen, corrupt, defiant, depraved, dissolute, flagrant, hardened, immodest, improper, incorrigible, indecent, insolent, unabashed, unashamed, unprincipled, wanton.
antonyms ashamed, contrite, shamefaced.

shanty *n.* cabin, hovel, hut, lean-to, shack, shed.

shape *n.* **1** build, contours, cut, dimensions, figure, form, format, frame, lines, make, model, mould, outline, pattern, physique, profile, silhouette. **2** appearance, aspect, guise, likeness, semblance. **3** condition, health, state, trim.
v. accommodate, adapt, construct, create, define, develop, devise, embody, fashion, forge, form, frame, guide, make, model, modify, mould, plan, prepare, produce, regulate, remodel.

shapeless *adj.* amorphous, characterless, dumpy, formless, irregular, misshapen, nebulous, undeveloped, unformed, unstructured.
antonym shapely.

shapely *adj.* comely, curvaceous, elegant, graceful, neat, pretty, trim, well-formed, well-proportioned, well-set-up, well-turned.
antonym shapeless.

share *v.* allot, apportion, assign, distribute, divide, go fifty-fifty, go halves, partake, participate, split, whack.
n. allotment, allowance, contribution, cut, dividend, division, due, finger, lot, part, portion, proportion, quota, ration, snap, snip, stint, whack.
share out allot, apportion, assign, distribute, divide up, give out, parcel out.

sharp *adj.* **1** barbed, cutting, edged, jagged, knife-edged, pointed, razor-sharp, serrated, spiky. **2** clear, clear-cut, crisp, distinct, marked, unblurred. **3** alert, artful, astute, clever, crafty, cunning, discerning, keen, observant, penetrating, perceptive, quick-witted, shrewd, sly. **4** abrupt, acute, extreme, fierce, intense, piercing, severe, sudden, violent. **5** acerbic, acid, bitter, pungent, sour, vinegary. **6** acrimonious, biting, caustic, harsh, incisive, sarcastic, sardonic, scathing, trenchant, vitriolic.
antonyms **1** blunt. **2** blurred. **3** slow, stupid. **4** gentle. **5** bland. **6** mild, polite.
adv. abruptly, exactly, on the dot, precisely, promptly, punctually, suddenly, unexpectedly.
antonyms approximately, roughly.

sharpen *v.* edge, file, grind, hone.
antonym blunt.

shatter *v.* blast, break, burst, crack, crush, demolish, destroy, devastate, disable, dumbfound, exhaust, explode, impair, overturn, overwhelm, ruin, smash, split, stun, torpedo, upset, wreck.

shave *v.* brush, crop, fleece, graze, pare, scrape, shear, touch, trim.

sheaf *n.* armful, bunch, bundle.

sheath *n.* armour, case, casing, coating, condom, covering, envelope, protective layer, rubber, safe, shell, sleeve.

shed¹ *v.* afford, cast (off), diffuse, discard, drop, emit, give, moult, pour, radiate, scatter, shower, slough, spill, throw.

shed² *n.* barn, hut, lean-to, lock-up, outhouse, shack.

sheen *n.* brightness, brilliance, burnish, gloss, lustre, polish, shimmer, shine, shininess.
antonyms dullness, tarnish.

sheepish *adj.* abashed, ashamed, chastened, embarrassed, foolish, mortified, self-conscious, shamefaced, silly, uncomfortable.
antonyms bold, brazen, unabashed.

sheer *adj.* **1** absolute, complete, downright, mere, out-and-out, pure, rank, thorough, thoroughgoing, total, unadulterated, unmitigated, unqualified, utter. **2** abrupt, perpendicular, precipitous, steep, vertical. **3** fine, flimsy, gauzy, gossamer, see-through, thin, translucent, transparent.
antonyms **2** gentle, gradual. **3** heavy, thick.

sheet *n.* **1** blanket, coat, covering, expanse, film, layer, leaf, membrane, overlay, pane, panel, piece, plate, shroud, skin, slab, stratum, surface, veneer. **2** broadsheet, broadside, circular, flyer, folio, handbill, handout, leaflet, news-sheet.

shelf *n.* bank, bar, bench, bracket, ledge, mantel, mantelpiece, platform, projection, reef, sandbank, step, terrace.

shell *n.* case, casing, chassis, covering, crust, frame, framework, hull, husk, pod, rind, skeleton, structure.
v. **1** hull, husk. **2** attack, barrage, batter, blitz, bomb, bombard.
shell out contribute, cough up, donate, expend, fork out, give, lay out, pay out, subscribe.

shelter *v.* accommodate, cover, defend, guard, harbour, hide, protect, put up, safeguard, screen, shade, shadow, shield, shroud.
antonym expose.
n. accommodation, cover, defence, guard, haven, lodging, protection, refuge, retreat, roof, safety, sanctuary, security, shade, shadow.
antonym exposure.

sheltered *adj.* cloistered, cosy, isolated, protected, quiet, reclusive, retired, secluded, shielded, snug, unworldly, warm, withdrawn.
antonym exposed.

shelve *v.* defer, dismiss, freeze, halt, mothball, pigeonhole, postpone, put aside, put in abeyance, put off, put on ice, suspend.
antonyms expedite, implement.

shepherd *n.* guardian, herdsman, protector, shepherd boy, shepherdess.
v. conduct, convoy, escort, guide, herd, lead, marshal, steer, usher.

shield *n.* aegis, buckler, bulwark, cover, defence, guard, protection, rampart, safeguard, screen, shelter, ward.
v. cover, defend, guard, protect, safeguard, screen, shade, shadow, shelter.
antonym expose.

shift *v.* adjust, alter, budge, change, dislodge, displace, fluctuate, manoeuvre, move, rearrange, relocate, remove, scoff, swallow, swerve, switch, transfer, transpose, vary, veer, wolf.
n. alteration, change, displacement, equivocation, evasion, fluctuation, manoeuvre, modification, move, rearrangement, removal, resource, shifting, switch, transfer, veering.

shifty *adj.* contriving, crafty, deceitful, devious, dishonest, dubious, evasive, fly-by-night, furtive, scheming, shady, slippery, tricky, underhand, untrustworthy, wily.
antonyms dependable, honest, open.

shilly-shally *v.* dilly-dally, falter, fluctuate, hesitate, prevaricate, shuffle, vacillate, waver.

shimmer *v.* gleam, glisten, glitter, scintillate, twinkle.
n. gleam, glimmer, glitter, glow, lustre.

shin *v.* ascend, clamber, climb, mount, scale, scramble, shoot, soar.

shine *v.* **1** beam, flash, glare, gleam, glimmer, glisten, glitter, glow, radiate, shimmer, sparkle, twinkle. **2** brush, buff, burnish, polish. **3** excel, stand out.
n. brightness, burnish, glare, glaze, gleam, gloss, glow, light, lustre, polish, radiance, sheen, shimmer, sparkle.

shining *adj.* **1** beaming, bright, brilliant, gleaming, glistening, glittering, glorious, glowing, radiant, resplendent, shimmering, sparkling, splendid, twinkling. **2** celebrated, conspicuous, distinguished, eminent, illustrious, leading, outstanding.

shiny *adj.* bright, burnished, gleaming, glistening, glossy, lustrous, polished, sheeny, shimmery, sleek.
antonyms dark, dull.

ship *n.* boat, craft, ferry, galleon, liner, steamer, tanker, trawler, vessel, yacht.

shipshape *adj.* businesslike, neat, orderly, spick-and-span, tidy, trim, well-organised, well-planned.
antonyms disorderly, untidy.

shirk *v.* avoid, dodge, duck, evade, shun, slack.

shirker *n.* absentee, clock-watcher, dodger, idler, layabout, loafer, skiver, slacker.

shiver *v.* palpitate, quake, quiver, shake, shudder, tremble, vibrate.
n. flutter, quiver, shudder, start, tremble, tremor, twitch, vibration.

shock *v.* agitate, appal, astound, confound, disgust, dismay, disquiet, horrify, jar, jolt, numb, offend, outrage, paralyse, revolt, scandalise, shake, sicken, stagger, stun, stupefy, unnerve, unsettle.
antonyms delight, gratify, please, reassure.
n. blow, bombshell, breakdown, clash, collapse, collision, concussion, consternation, dismay, distress, disturbance, encounter, fright, impact, jarring, jolt, thunderbolt, trauma, turn, upset.
antonyms delight, pleasure.

shocking *adj.* abhorrent, abominable, appalling, atrocious, deplorable, detestable, disgraceful, disgusting, distressing, dreadful, frightful, ghastly, hideous, horrible, horrifying, intolerable, monstrous, nauseating, offensive, outrageous, repulsive, revolting, scandalous, stupefying, unbearable, unspeakable.
antonyms acceptable, delightful, pleasant, satisfactory.

shoddy *adj.* cheap, flimsy, inferior, poor, rubbishy, second-rate, slipshod, tatty, tawdry, trashy, trumpery.
antonyms fine, well-made.

shoot *v.* **1** blast, discharge, fire, fling, gun down, hit, hurl, kill, launch, open fire, pick off, project, propel. **2** bolt, charge, dart, dash, hurtle, race, rush, speed, sprint, tear. **3** film, photograph, take.
n. branch, bud, offshoot, scion, slip, sprig, sprout, twig.

shore¹ *n.* beach, coast, lakeside, margin, offing, promenade, sands, seaboard, sea-front, seashore, strand, waterfront, water's edge.

shore² *v.* brace, buttress, hold, prop, reinforce, stay, strengthen, support, underpin.

shorn *adj.* bald, beardless, crew-cut, cropped, shaved, shaven, stripped.

short *adj.* **1** abbreviated, abridged, brief, compact, compressed, concise, curtailed, ephem-

eral, fleeting, momentary, pithy, précised, shortened, succinct, summarised, terse, transitory. **2** abrupt, blunt, brusque, curt, direct, discourteous, gruff, impolite, offhand, sharp, snappy, uncivil. **3** diminutive, dumpy, little, low, petite, small, squat. **4** deficient, inadequate, insufficient, lacking, meagre, poor, scant, sparse, wanting.
antonyms **1** lasting. **2** polite. **3** long, tall. **4** adequate, ample.
short of deficient in, except, lacking, less than, low on, missing, other than, pushed for, short on, wanting.

shortage *n.* absence, dearth, deficiency, deficit, failure, inadequacy, insufficiency, lack, paucity, poverty, scarcity, shortfall, sparseness, want.
antonyms abundance, sufficiency, surplus.

shortcoming *n.* defect, drawback, failing, fault, flaw, foible, frailty, imperfection, inadequacy, weakness.

shorten *v.* abbreviate, abridge, crop, curtail, cut, decrease, diminish, dock, lessen, prune, reduce, take up, trim, truncate.
antonyms amplify, enlarge, lengthen.

shortly *adv.* **1** anon, presently, soon. **2** abruptly, curtly, directly, sharply.

short-sighted *adj.* careless, hasty, ill-advised, ill-considered, impolitic, impractical, improvident, imprudent, injudicious, myopic, near-sighted, unimaginative.
antonyms far-sighted, long-sighted.

shot *n.* **1** ball, blast, bullet, cannon-ball, discharge, missile, pellet, projectile, slug. **2** attempt, bash, crack, effort, endeavour, go, guess, stab, try, turn.

shoulder *v.* **1** elbow, jostle, press, push, thrust. **2** accept, assume, bear, carry, sustain, take on.

shout *n.* bay, bellow, belt, call, cheer, cry, roar, scream, shriek, yell.
v. bawl, bay, bellow, call, cheer, cry, holler, roar, scream, shriek, yell.

shove *v.* barge, crowd, drive, elbow, force, jostle, press, propel, push, shoulder, thrust.

shovel *n.* bucket, scoop, spade.
v. convey, dig, dredge, heap, ladle, load, move, scoop, shift, spade, toss.

show *v.* **1** clarify, demonstrate, disclose, display, divulge, elucidate, exemplify, exhibit, explain, illustrate, indicate, instruct, manifest, offer, present, prove, register, reveal, teach. **2** accompany, attend, conduct, escort, guide, lead, usher.
antonyms **1** cover, hide.
n. **1** affectation, air, appearance, exhibitionism, façade, flamboyance, illusion, indication, ostentation, panache, pizzazz, pretence, pretext, profession, semblance, sight, swagger. **2** demonstration, display, entertainment, exhibition, exposition, extravaganza, fair, pageant, parade, performance, presentation, production, representation, spectacle.
show off advertise, boast, brag, brandish, demonstrate, display, enhance, exhibit, flaunt, parade, set off, strut, swagger, swank.
show up 1 appear, arrive, come, turn up. **2** disgrace, embarrass, humiliate, let down, mortify, shame. **3** expose, highlight, lay bare, pinpoint, reveal, show, unmask.

show-down *n.* clash, climax, confrontation, crisis, culmination.

shower *n.* **1** barrage, deluge, drift, hail, plethora, precipitation, rain, spout, stream, torrent, volley. **2** crew, gang, mob, rabble.
v. deluge, douse, heap, inundate, lavish, load, overwhelm, pour, rain, spray, sprinkle.

showing *n.* account, appearance, display, evidence, exhibition, impression, past performance, performance, presentation, record, representation, show, staging, statement, track record.

showman *n.* entertainer, impresario, performer, ring-master, self-advertiser, show-off.

show-off *n.* boaster, egotist, exhibitionist, peacock, self-advertiser, swaggerer, swanker.

showy *adj.* flamboyant, flash, flashy, garish, gaudy, loud, ostentatious, pompous, pretentious, specious, splashy, swanking, swanky, tawdry, tinselly.
antonyms quiet, restrained.

shred *n.* atom, bit, fragment, grain, iota, jot, mammock, mite, piece, rag, ribbon, scrap, snippet, tatter, trace, whit, wisp.

shrewd *adj.* acute, artful, astute, calculated, calculating, clever, crafty, cunning, discerning, discriminating, far-sighted, intelligent, judicious, keen, knowing, observant, perceptive, sharp, sly, smart, well-advised.
antonyms naïve, obtuse, unsophisticated, unwise.

shriek *v.* bellow, cry, holler, howl, scream, screech, shout, wail, yell.
n. bellow, cry, howl, scream, screech, shout, squeal, wail.

shrill *adj.* acute, ear-splitting, high, high-pitched, penetrating, piercing, screaming, screeching, sharp, strident, treble.
antonyms deep, gentle, low, soft.

shrine *n.* chapel, dome, sanctuary, tabernacle, temple.

shrink *v.* **1** contract, decrease, diminish, dwindle, lessen, narrow, shorten, shrivel, wither, wrinkle. **2** back away, balk, cower, cringe, flinch, quail, recoil, retire, shun, shy away, wince, withdraw.
antonyms **1** expand, stretch. **2** accept, embrace, warm to.

shrivel *v.* burn, dehydrate, desiccate, dwindle, frizzle, parch, pucker, scorch, sear, shrink, wilt, wither, wrinkle.

shroud *v.* blanket, cloak, conceal, cover, envelop, hide, screen, sheet, swathe, veil, wrap.
antonyms expose, uncover.
n. cloud, covering, grave-clothes, mantle, screen, veil.

shudder *v.* convulse, heave, quake, quiver, shake, shiver, tremble.
n. convulsion, horror, quiver, spasm, trembling, tremor.

shuffle *v.* **1** confuse, disorder, intermix, jumble,

mix, rearrange, reorganise, shift, shift around, switch around. **2** drag, hobble, limp, scrape, scuff, scuffle.

shun *v.* avoid, cold-shoulder, elude, evade, ignore, ostracise, shy away from, spurn, steer clear of.
antonyms accept, embrace.

shut *v.* bar, bolt, cage, close, fasten, latch, lock, seal, secure, slam, spar.
antonym open.
shut down cease, close, discontinue, halt, inactivate, shut up, stop, suspend, switch off, terminate.
shut in box in, confine, enclose, hedge round, hem in, imprison.
shut off cut off, isolate, remove, seclude, segregate, separate.
shut out banish, bar, conceal, cover, debar, exclude, hide, lock out, mask, ostracise, screen, veil.
shut up 1 clam up, hold one's tongue, hush up, pipe down, silence. **2** confine, coop up, gag, immure, imprison, incarcerate, intern, jail.

shuttle *v.* alternate, commute, go to and fro, ply, shunt, shuttlecock, travel.

shy *adj.* bashful, cautious, chary, coy, diffident, hesitant, inhibited, modest, nervous, reserved, reticent, retiring, self-conscious, self-effacing, shrinking, suspicious, timid.
antonyms assertive, bold, confident.
v. back away, balk, flinch, quail, rear, recoil, shrink, start, wince.

sick *adj.* **1** ailing, feeble, ill, indisposed, laid up, poorly, sickly, tired, under the weather, unwell, weak, weary. **2** nauseated, queasy, vomiting. **3** disgusted, fed up.
antonyms **1** healthy, well.

sicken *v.* disgust, nauseate, put off, repel, revolt, turn off.
antonyms attract, delight.

sickening *adj.* disgusting, distasteful, foul, loathsome, offensive, putrid, repulsive, revolting, vile.
antonyms attractive, delightful, pleasing.

sickly *adj.* ailing, bilious, delicate, faint, feeble, frail, indisposed, infirm, lacklustre, languid, nauseating, pallid, revolting, sweet, syrupy, unhealthy, wan, weak, weakly.
antonyms healthy, robust, strong, sturdy.

sickness *n.* affliction, ailment, complaint, disease, ill-health, illness, indisposition, infirmity, malady, nausea, queasiness, vomiting.
antonym health.

side *n.* **1** bank, border, boundary, brim, brink, edge, face, flank, fringe, hand, limit, margin, perimeter, periphery, rim, verge. **2** angle, aspect, quarter, region, stand, standpoint, view, viewpoint. **3** camp, cause, faction, gang, party, team.
adj. flanking, incidental, indirect, irrelevant, lateral, lesser, marginal, minor, oblique, roundabout, secondary, subordinate, subsidiary.
side with agree with, favour, support, team up with, vote for.

sidelong *adj.* covert, indirect, oblique, sideways.
antonyms direct, overt.

sidestep *v.* avoid, bypass, dodge, duck, elude, evade, find a way round, shirk, skirt.
antonyms deal with, tackle.

sidetrack *v.* deflect, distract, divert, head off.

sideways *adv.* edgeways, laterally, obliquely, sidelong, sidewards.
adj. oblique, side, sidelong, sideward, slanted.

sidle *v.* creep, edge, inch, slink, sneak, wriggle.

siesta *n.* catnap, doze, forty winks, nap, relaxation, rest, sleep, snooze.

sieve *v.* remove, separate, sift, strain.
n. colander, screen, sifter, strainer.

sift *v.* analyse, discuss, examine, filter, investigate, part, probe, review, riddle, screen, scrutinise, separate, sieve, sort, sprinkle, winnow.

sigh *v.* breathe, complain, grieve, lament, moan, sorrow.

sight *n.* **1** apprehension, eyesight, observation, seeing, vision. **2** field of vision, glance, glimpse, look, perception, range, view, viewing, visibility. **3** appearance, display, exhibition, eyesore, fright, monstrosity, pageant, scene, show, spectacle.
v. behold, discern, distinguish, glimpse, observe, perceive, see, spot.

sights *n.* amenities, beauties, curiosities, features, marvels, splendours, wonders.

sightseer *n.* excursionist, holidaymaker, tourist, tripper, visitor.

sign *n.* **1** badge, character, emblem, figure, insignia, logo, representation, symbol. **2** clue, evidence, gesture, hint, indication, manifestation, mark, note, signal, suggestion, trace. **3** board, notice, placard, warning. **4** foreboding, forewarning, omen, portent.
v. autograph, endorse, initial, write.
sign over consign, convey, deliver, entrust, make over, surrender, transfer, turn over.
sign up appoint, contract, employ, engage, enlist, enrol, hire, join (up), recruit, register, sign on, take on, volunteer.

signal *n.* alarm, alert, beacon, cue, flare, flash, gesture, go-ahead, impulse, indication, indicator, light, mark, password, rocket, sign, tip-off, token, transmitter, waft, warning, watchword.
adj. conspicuous, distinguished, eminent, exceptional, extraordinary, famous, impressive, memorable, momentous, notable, noteworthy, outstanding, remarkable, significant, striking.
v. beckon, communicate, gesticulate, gesture, indicate, motion, nod, sign, wave.

signature *n.* autograph, endorsement, initials, inscription, mark, sign.

significance *n.* consequence, consideration, force, implication, implications, importance, interest, matter, meaning, message, point, relevance, sense, weight.
antonyms insignificance, pettiness, unimportance.

significant *adj.* appreciable, critical, expressive, important, indicative, knowing, marked, mean-

ing, meaningful, momentous, noteworthy, ominous, serious, solemn, suggestive, symbolic, symptomatic, vital, weighty.
antonyms meaningless, petty, trivial, unimportant.

signify *v.* announce, communicate, convey, count, denote, evidence, exhibit, express, imply, indicate, intimate, matter, mean, represent, show, stand for, suggest, symbolise, transmit.

signpost *n.* clue, fingerpost, guidepost, handpost, pointer, sign.

silence *n.* calm, dumbness, hush, lull, muteness, noiselessness, peace, quiet, reserve, reticence, speechlessness, stillness, taciturnity, uncommunicativeness.
antonyms babble, noise, uproar.
v. deaden, dumbfound, extinguish, gag, muffle, muzzle, quell, quiet, quieten, stifle, still, subdue, suppress.

silent *adj.* dumb, hushed, inaudible, mum, mute, muted, noiseless, quiet, reticent, soundless, speechless, still, taciturn, tongue-tied, uncommunicative, understood, unexpressed, unsounded, unspeaking, unspoken, voiceless, wordless.
antonyms loud, noisy, talkative.

silhouette *n.* configuration, delineation, form, outline, profile, shadow-figure, shape.

silky *adj.* fine, satiny, silken, sleek, smooth, soft, velvety.

silly *adj.* absurd, childish, daft, foolish, idiotic, illogical, immature, imprudent, inappropriate, irrational, irresponsible, meaningless, mindless, pointless, preposterous, puerile, ridiculous, scatter-brained, senseless, stupid.
antonyms clever, collected, intelligent, mature, sane, sensible, wise.

silt *n.* deposit, mud, ooze, residue, sediment, sludge.
silt up block, choke, clog, dam.

similar *adj.* alike, analogous, close, comparable, compatible, corresponding, homogeneous, related, resembling, self-like, uniform.
antonyms clashing, contradictory, different, dissimilar.

similarity *n.* affinity, agreement, analogy, closeness, coincidence, comparability, compatibility, congruence, correspondence, equivalence, homogeneity, likeness, relation, resemblance, similitude, uniformity.
antonyms difference, disagreement, dissimilarity.

similarly *adv.* by analogy, by the same token, correspondingly, likewise, uniformly.
antonym differently.

simmer *v.* boil, burn, fizz, fume, rage, seethe, smoulder.
simmer down calm down, collect oneself, control oneself, cool down, settle down, take it easy.

simple *adj.* **1** clear, easy, elementary, lucid, natural, plain, single, straightforward, uncomplicated, understandable, uninvolved. **2** artless, feeble, foolish, frank, green, guileless, half-witted, ingenuous, innocent, naïve, silly, unsophisticated.
antonyms **1** complicated, difficult, intricate. **2** artful, devious, sophisticated, worldly.

simple-minded *adj.* artless, backward, brainless, feeble-minded, foolish, idiot, idiotic, imbecile, moronic, naïve, natural, simple, stupid, unsophisticated.
antonyms clever, sophisticated, subtle.

simplicity *n.* artlessness, candour, clarity, directness, ease, innocence, modesty, naturalness, openness, plainness, purity, restraint, simpleness, sincerity, straightforwardness, uncomplicatedness.
antonyms complexity, intricacy, sophistication.

simplify *v.* abridge, decipher, disentangle, reduce, streamline.
antonyms complicate, elaborate.

simplistic *adj.* naïve, oversimplified, shallow, simple, superficial, sweeping, unanalytical.
antonyms analytical, detailed.

simply *adv.* absolutely, clearly, completely, directly, easily, intelligibly, just, merely, modestly, naturally, obviously, only, plainly, purely, quite, really, solely, straightforwardly, totally, undeniably, unquestionably, utterly, wholly.

simulate *v.* act, affect, assume, counterfeit, duplicate, echo, fabricate, fake, feign, imitate, mimic, parrot, pretend, put on, reflect, reproduce, sham.

simultaneous *adj.* accompanying, coinciding, concurrent, parallel, synchronic, synchronous.
antonyms asynchronous, separate.

sin *n.* crime, debt, error, evil, fault, guilt, impiety, iniquity, lapse, misdeed, offence, sinfulness, transgression, trespass, ungodliness, unrighteousness, wickedness, wrong, wrongdoing.
v. err, fall, fall from grace, go astray, lapse, misbehave, offend, stray, transgress, trespass.

sincere *adj.* artless, candid, deep-felt, earnest, frank, genuine, guileless, heartfelt, honest, natural, open, plain-spoken, pure, real, serious, simple, simple-hearted, single-hearted, straightforward, true, true-hearted, truthful, unadulterated, unaffected, unmixed, wholehearted.
antonyms affected, feigned, insincere.

sincerely *adv.* earnestly, genuinely, honestly, in earnest, really, seriously, simply, truly, truthfully, unaffectedly, wholeheartedly.

sinewy *adj.* athletic, brawny, muscular, powerful, robust, stringy, strong, sturdy, vigorous, wiry.

sinful *adj.* bad, corrupt, criminal, depraved, erring, fallen, guilty, immoral, iniquitous, irreligious, ungodly, unholy, wicked, wrongful.
antonyms godly, pure, righteous, sinless.

sing *v.* chant, chirp, croon, hum, intone, lilt, melodise, pipe, purr, quaver, render, serenade, squeal, trill, vocalise, warble, whistle, yodel.
sing out bawl, bellow, call, cry, halloo, holler, shout, yell.

singe *v.* blacken, burn, char, scorch, sear.

singer *n.* bard, choirboy, choirgirl, chorister, crooner, minstrel, prima donna, troubadour, vocalist.

single *adj.* celibate, distinct, exclusive, free, individual, lone, man-to-man, one, one-fold, one-to-one, only, particular, separate, simple, sincere, single-minded, singular, sole, solitary, unattached, unbroken, uncombined, uncompounded, undivided, unique, unmarried, unmixed, unshared, wholehearted.
single out choose, distinguish, hand-pick, highlight, isolate, pick, pinpoint, select, separate, set apart.

single-handed *adj., adv.* alone, independently, solo, unaccompanied, unaided, unassisted.

sinister *adj.* dire, disquieting, evil, inauspicious, malevolent, menacing, ominous, threatening, unlucky.
antonyms auspicious, harmless, innocent.

sink *v.* abandon, abate, abolish, bore, collapse, conceal, decay, decline, decrease, defeat, degenerate, degrade, descend, destroy, dig, diminish, dip, disappear, drill, drive, droop, drop, drown, dwindle, ebb, engulf, excavate, fade, fail, fall, finish, flag, founder, lapse, lay, lessen, lower, merge, overwhelm, penetrate, plummet, plunge, relapse, ruin, sag, slip, slope, slump, stoop, submerge, subside, succumb, suppress, weaken, worsen.
antonyms float, rise, uplift.

sinner *n.* backslider, evil-doer, offender, reprobate, transgressor, trespasser, wrong-doer.

sinuous *adj.* coiling, crooked, curved, lithe, meandering, serpentine, slinky, tortuous, undulating, winding.
antonym straight.

sip *v.* sample, sup, taste.
n. drop, mouthful, spoonful, swallow, taste.

sissy *n.* baby, coward, mummy's boy, namby-pamby, pansy, softy, weakling, wet.
adj. cowardly, effeminate, feeble, namby-pamby, pansy, soft, unmanly, weak, wet.

sit *v.* accommodate, assemble, brood, contain, convene, deliberate, hold, meet, officiate, perch, pose, preside, reside, rest, seat, settle.

site *n.* ground, location, lot, place, plot, position, setting, spot, station.
v. dispose, install, locate, place, position, set, situate, station.

sitting *n.* assembly, consultation, get-together, hearing, meeting, period, seat, session, spell.

situation *n.* case, circumstances, condition, employment, job, lie of the land, locale, locality, location, office, place, position, post, predicament, rank, scenario, seat, setting, set-up, site, sphere, spot, state, state of affairs, station, status.

sizable *adj.* biggish, considerable, decent-sized, goodly, large, largish, respectable, significant, substantial.
antonyms small, tiny.

size *n.* amount, bigness, bulk, dimensions, extent, greatness, height, immensity, largeness, magnitude, mass, measurement(s), proportions, range, vastness, volume.
size up assess, evaluate, gauge, measure, weigh up.

sizzle *v.* crackle, frizzle, fry, hiss, scorch, sear, spit, sputter.

skeletal *adj.* drawn, emaciated, fleshless, gaunt, haggard, hollow-cheeked, shrunken, skin-and-bone, wasted.

skeleton *n.* bare bones, draft, frame, framework, outline, sketch, structure.

sketch *v.* block out, delineate, depict, draft, draw, outline, paint, pencil, plot, portray, represent, rough out.
n. delineation, design, draft, drawing, outline, plan, skeleton, vignette.

skilful *adj.* able, accomplished, clever, competent, experienced, expert, handy, masterly, nimble-fingered, practised, professional, proficient, quick, ready, skilled, tactical, trained.
antonyms awkward, clumsy, inept, unskilled.

skill *n.* ability, accomplishment, cleverness, competence, experience, expertise, expertness, facility, handiness, intelligence, knack, proficiency, quickness, readiness, savoir-faire, skilfulness, talent, technique, touch.

skilled *adj.* able, accomplished, crack, experienced, expert, masterly, practised, professional, proficient, schooled, skilful, trained.
antonyms inexperienced, unskilled.

skim *v.* brush, coast, cream, dart, float, fly, glide, plane, sail, scan, separate, skip, soar.

skimp *v.* conserve, cut corners, economise, pinch, scamp, scant, scrimp, stint, withhold.
antonyms squander, waste.

skimpy *adj.* beggarly, inadequate, insufficient, meagre, miserly, niggardly, scant, scanty, short, sketchy, sparse, thin, tight.
antonyms generous, lavish.

skin *n.* casing, coating, crust, fell, film, hide, husk, membrane, outside, peel, rind.
v. abrade, bark, flay, fleece, graze, peel, scrape, strip.

skinny *adj.* emaciated, lean, scragged, scraggy, scrawny, skeletal, skin-and-bone, thin, underfed, undernourished, weedy.
antonyms fat, plump.

skip *v.* bob, bounce, caper, cut, dance, flit, frisk, gambol, hop, miss, omit, prance, trip.

skirmish *n.* affair, affray, battle, brush, clash, combat, conflict, contest, dust-up, encounter, engagement, fracas, incident, scrap, set-to, tussle.
v. argue, clash, collide, fight, scrap, tussle.

skirt *v.* avoid, border, bypass, circle, circumnavigate, circumvent, edge, evade, flank, steer clear of.

skit *n.* caricature, parody, satire, sketch, spoof, take-off, travesty, turn.

skittish *adj.* excitable, fickle, fidgety, frivolous, jumpy, lively, nervous, playful, restive.

skulk *v.* creep, lie in wait, loiter, lurk, prowl, slink, sneak.

sky *n.* air, atmosphere, azure, blue, firmament, heavens, vault of heaven.

slab *n.* briquette, chunk, hunk, lump, piece, portion, slice, wedge, wodge.
slack *adj.* **1** baggy, lax, limp, loose, relaxed. **2** idle, inactive, lazy, quiet, slow, sluggish. **3** careless, easy-going, inattentive, neglectful, negligent, permissive, remiss.
antonyms **1** rigid, stiff, taut. **2** busy. **3** diligent.
n. excess, give, leeway, looseness, play, relaxation, room.
v. dodge, idle, neglect, relax, shirk, skive, slacken.
slacken off abate, decrease, diminish, fail, flag, lessen, loosen, moderate, reduce, relax, release, slow (down), tire.
antonyms increase, intensify, quicken.
slacker *n.* clock-watcher, dawdler, dodger, do-nothing, good-for-nothing, idler, layabout, shirker, skiver.
slake *v.* assuage, extinguish, gratify, moderate, moisten, quench, reduce, sate, satiate, satisfy.
slam *v.* **1** bang, clap, crash, fling, hurl, smash, throw. **2** criticise, damn, slate.
slander *n.* aspersion, backbiting, calumny, defamation, libel, misrepresentation, muck-raking, scandal, smear.
v. backbite, decry, defame, detract, disparage, libel, malign, scandalise, slur, smear, vilify.
antonyms compliment, glorify, praise.
slanderous *adj.* abusive, aspersive, damaging, defamatory, libellous, malicious.
slant *v.* angle, bend, bias, colour, distort, incline, lean, list, skew, slope, tilt, twist, warp, weight.
n. angle, attitude, bias, camber, diagonal, emphasis, gradient, incline, leaning, pitch, ramp, slope, tilt, viewpoint.
slap *n.* bang, blow, clap, smack, spank, wallop, whack.
v. bang, clap, clout, cuff, daub, hit, plaster, plonk, spank, spread, strike, whack.
adv. bang, dead, directly, exactly, plumb, precisely, right, slap-bang, smack.
slap-up *adj.* elaborate, excellent, first-class, first-rate, lavish, luxurious, magnificent, splendid, sumptuous, superb.
slash *v.* **1** cut, gash, rend, rip, slit. **2** cut, lash, lower, reduce.
n. cut, gash, incision, laceration, lash, rent, rip, slit.
slate *v.* berate, blame, censure, criticise, rebuke, reprimand, roast, scold, slam.
antonym praise.
slatternly *adj.* dirty, slipshod, sloppy, slovenly, sluttish, unclean, unkempt, untidy.
slaughter *n.* blood-bath, bloodshed, butchery, carnage, extermination, holocaust, killing, massacre, murder, slaying.
v. butcher, crush, defeat, destroy, exterminate, hammer, kill, liquidate, massacre, murder, overwhelm, rout, scupper, slay, thrash, vanquish.
slave *n.* captive, drudge, serf, servant, vassal, villein.
v. drudge, grind, labour, skivvy, slog, struggle, sweat, toil.
slaver *v.* dribble, drivel, drool, salivate, slobber.
slavery *n.* bondage, captivity, enslavement, impressment, serfdom, subjugation, thraldom, yoke.
antonyms freedom, liberty.
slavish *adj.* **1** imitative, literal, strict, unimaginative, uninspired, unoriginal. **2** abject, cringing, fawning, grovelling, low, mean, menial, servile, submissive, sycophantic.
antonyms **1** imaginative, original. **2** assertive, independent.
sleek *adj.* glossy, lustrous, shiny, smooth, well-groomed.
antonyms rough, unkempt.
sleep *v.* doss (down), doze, drop off, hibernate, nod off, repose, rest, slumber, snooze, snore.
n. doze, forty winks, hibernation, nap, repose, rest, shut-eye, siesta, slumber(s), snooze.
sleeping *adj.* asleep, daydreaming, dormant, hibernating, idle, inactive, inattentive, off guard, passive, slumbering, unaware.
antonyms alert, awake.
sleepless *adj.* alert, disturbed, insomniac, restless, unsleeping, vigilant, wakeful, watchful, wide-awake.
sleepy *adj.* drowsy, dull, heavy, hypnotic, inactive, lethargic, quiet, slow, sluggish, somnolent, soporific.
antonyms alert, awake, restless, wakeful.
slender *adj.* **1** graceful, lean, little, slight, slim, thin. **2** faint, feeble, flimsy, inadequate, inconsiderable, insufficient, meagre, poor, remote, scanty, tenuous.
antonyms **1** fat, tubby. **2** ample, appreciable, considerable.
slice *n.* cut, helping, piece, portion, rasher, section, segment, share, sheave, slab, sliver, tranche, wafer, wedge, whack.
v. carve, chop, cut, divide, segment, sever.
slick *adj.* adroit, deft, dexterous, plausible, polished, professional, sharp, skilful, sleek, smooth, trim.
antonyms amateurish, clumsy, coarse.
slide *v.* coast, glide, skate, skim, slip, slither, toboggan, veer.
slight *adj.* **1** feeble, inconsiderable, insignificant, insubstantial, minor, modest, negligible, paltry, trivial, unimportant. **2** delicate, slender, slim.
antonyms **1** considerable, major, noticeable, significant. **2** large, muscular.
v. affront, cold-shoulder, cut, despise, disdain, disparage, disrespect, ignore, insult, neglect, scorn, snub.
antonyms compliment, flatter, praise.
n. affront, contempt, discourtesy, disdain, disregard, disrespect, inattention, indifference, insult, neglect, rebuff, rudeness, slur, snub.
slighting *adj.* abusive, defamatory, derogatory, disdainful, disparaging, disrespectful, insulting, offensive, scornful, slanderous, uncomplimentary.
antonyms complimentary, flattering, respectful.
slim *adj.* **1** lean, slender, thin. **2** faint, poor, remote, slight.
antonyms **1** chubby, fat. **2** considerable, strong.

v. diet, lose weight, reduce.

slime *n.* filth, muck, mud, ooze.

sling *v.* catapult, chuck, dangle, fling, hang, heave, hurl, lob, pitch, suspend, swing, throw, toss.
n. band, bandage, catapult, loop, strap, support.

slink *v.* creep, prowl, pussyfoot, sidle, slip, sneak, steal.

slinky *adj.* clinging, close-fitting, figure-hugging, skin-tight, sleek.

slip[1] *v.* creep, disappear, elude, escape, fall, get away, glide, hide, skate, skid, slide, slink, slither, sneak, steal, trip.
n. bloomer, blunder, boob, error, failure, fault, indiscretion, mistake, omission, oversight, slip-up.

slip[2] *n.* certificate, coupon, cutting, piece, strip.

slipper *n.* flip-flop, moccasin, mule, pump, sandal.

slippery *adj.* **1** glassy, greasy, icy, perilous, skiddy, slippy, treacherous, unsafe. **2** crafty, cunning, devious, dishonest, duplicitous, evasive, false, smooth, two-faced, untrustworthy.
antonyms **1** rough. **2** reliable, trustworthy.

slippy *adj.* greasy, icy, slippery, smooth.

slipshod *adj.* careless, casual, loose, negligent, slap-dash, sloppy, slovenly, untidy.
antonyms careful, fastidious, neat, tidy.

slit *v.* cut, gash, lance, pierce, rip, slash, slice, split.
n. cut, gash, incision, opening, rent, split, tear, vent.

slither *v.* glide, slide, slink, slip, snake.

sliver *n.* chip, flake, fragment, paring, shaving, shiver, shred, slip, splinter.

slob *n.* brute, lout, oaf, yob.

slobber *v.* dribble, drivel, drool, salivate, slabber, slaver, splutter, water at the mouth.

slogan *n.* battle-cry, catch-phrase, catchword, chant, jingle, motto, rallying-cry, war cry, watchword.

slop *v.* overflow, slobber, slosh, spatter, spill, splash, splatter, wash away.

slope *v.* fall, incline, lean, pitch, rise, slant, tilt, verge.
n. descent, gradient, inclination, incline, ramp, rise, slant, tilt.

sloppy *adj.* amateurish, careless, clumsy, gushing, hit-or-miss, messy, mushy, schmaltzy, sentimental, slipshod, slovenly, sludgy, slushy, soppy, trite, unkempt, untidy, watery, weak, wet.
antonyms careful, exact, precise.

slosh *v.* flounder, pour, shower, slap, slop, slug, splash, spray, strike, swash, swipe, wade, wallop.

slot *n.* aperture, channel, gap, groove, hole, niche, opening, place, position, slit, space, time, vacancy.
v. adjust, assign, fit, insert, pigeonhole, place, position.

slouch *v.* droop, loll, shamble, shuffle, slump, stoop.

slovenly *adj.* careless, scruffy, slipshod, sloppy, untidy.
antonyms neat, smart.

slow *adj.* **1** creeping, dawdling, deliberate, gradual, inactive, late, lazy, leisurely, lingering, loitering, measured, plodding, slack, sleepy, slow-moving, sluggish, unhurried, unpunctual. **2** dim, slow-witted, stupid, thick. **3** boring, dull, long-drawn-out, prolonged, protracted, tedious, uneventful, uninteresting.
antonyms **1** fast, quick, rapid, speedy, swift. **2** clever, intelligent. **3** brisk, exciting, lively.
v. brake, check, curb, decelerate, delay, detain, handicap, hold up, lag, relax, restrict, retard.
antonyms accelerate, speed.

sludge *n.* dregs, mire, muck, mud, ooze, residue, sediment, silt, slag, slime, slush.

sluggish *adj.* dull, heavy, inactive, lethargic, lifeless, listless, slothful, slow, slow-moving, unresponsive.
antonyms brisk, dynamic, eager, quick, vigorous.

slump *v.* bend, collapse, crash, decline, deteriorate, droop, drop, fall, loll, plummet, plunge, sag, sink, slip, slouch, worsen.
n. collapse, crash, decline, depreciation, depression, downturn, drop, failure, fall, low, recession, reverse, stagnation, trough, worsening.
antonym boom.

sly *adj.* artful, astute, canny, clever, conniving, covert, crafty, cunning, devious, foxy, furtive, guileful, knowing, mischievous, roguish, scheming, secretive, shifty, stealthy, subtle, surreptitious, underhand, wily.
antonyms frank, honest, open, straightforward.

smack *v.* box, clap, cuff, hit, pat, slap, sock, spank, strike, tap, thwack, whack.
n. blow, box, crack, cuff, hit, pat, slap, spank, tap, thwack, whack.
adv. bang, directly, exactly, plumb, precisely, right, slap-bang, squarely, straight.

small *adj.* **1** diminutive, little, mini, miniature, minuscule, minute, petite, pint-size(d), pocket, pocket-sized, puny, short, slight, tiny, young. **2** inconsiderable, insignificant, mean, minor, petty, trifling, trivial, unimportant. **3** inadequate, insufficient, limited, meagre, negligible, paltry, scanty.
antonyms **1** big, huge, large. **2** considerable, great. **3** ample.

small-minded *adj.* bigoted, hidebound, insular, intolerant, mean, narrow-minded, petty, rigid, ungenerous.
antonyms broad-minded, liberal, tolerant.

small-time *adj.* inconsequential, insignificant, minor, no-account, petty, unimportant.
antonyms important, major.

smarmy *adj.* bootlicking, crawling, fawning, greasy, ingratiating, obsequious, oily, servile, smooth, soapy, sycophantic, toadying, unctuous.

smart *adj.* **1** chic, elegant, fashionable, modish, natty, neat, spruce, stylish, trim. **2** acute, astute, bright, clever, intelligent, sharp, shrewd, witty.

antonyms **1** dowdy, unfashionable, untidy. **2** slow, stupid.
v. burn, hurt, nip, pain, sting, throb, tingle, twinge.

smarten *v.* beautify, clean, groom, neaten, polish, prink, spruce up, tidy.

smash *v.* break, collide, crash, crush, defeat, demolish, destroy, lay waste, overthrow, prang, ruin, shatter, shiver, wreck.
n. accident, collapse, collision, crash, defeat, destruction, disaster, downfall, failure, pile-up, ruin, shattering, smash-up.

smattering *n.* basics, bit, dash, elements, rudiments, smatter, sprinkling.

smear *v.* **1** coat, cover, dab, daub, plaster, rub on, soil, spread over, streak. **2** blacken, dirty, drag (someone's) name through the mud, malign, stain, sully, tarnish, vilify.
n. **1** blot, blotch, daub, smudge, splodge, streak. **2** defamation, libel, mudslinging, slander.

smell *n.* aroma, bouquet, fragrance, malodour, odour, perfume, scent, sniff, stench, stink, whiff.
v. nose, pong, reek, scent, sniff, stink, whiff.

smelly *adj.* bad, evil-smelling, foul, foul-smelling, high, off, pongy, putrid, reeking, stinking, strong, strong-smelling, whiffy.

smirk *n.* grin, leer, sneer, snigger.

smitten *adj.* beguiled, besotted, bewitched, bowled over, captivated, charmed, enamoured, infatuated, plagued, struck, troubled.

smoke *n.* exhaust, fog, fume, gas, mist, reek, roke, smog, vapour.
v. cure, dry, fumigate, reek, smoulder, vent.

smoky *adj.* black, grey, grimy, hazy, murky, reeky, sooty, thick.

smooth *adj.* **1** even, flat, flush, horizontal, level, plane. **2** easy, effortless, flowing, frictionless, regular, rhythmic, steady, unbroken, uniform. **3** calm, glassy, mild, peaceful, polished, serene, shiny, silky, tranquil, undisturbed. **4** agreeable, ingratiating, persuasive, slick, smarmy, smug, suave, unctuous.
antonyms **1** coarse, lumpy, rough. **2** erratic, irregular, unsteady. **3** choppy, rough.
v. allay, alleviate, assuage, calm, ease, flatten, iron, level, mitigate, mollify, plane, polish, press, soften, unwrinkle.
antonym roughen.

smooth-talking *adj.* bland, facile, glib, persuasive, plausible, slick, smooth, suave.

smother *v.* choke, conceal, cover, envelop, extinguish, heap, hide, muffle, overwhelm, repress, shower, shroud, snuff, stifle, strangle, suffocate, suppress, surround.

smoulder *v.* boil, burn, fester, fume, rage, seethe, simmer, smoke.

smudge *v.* blur, daub, dirty, mark, smear, soil, spot, stain.
n. blemish, blot, blur, smear, smut, spot, stain.

smug *adj.* conceited, holier-than-thou, priggish, self-opinionated, self-righteous, self-satisfied, superior.
antonyms humble, modest.

smutty *adj.* bawdy, coarse, crude, dirty, filthy, gross, improper, indecent, indelicate, lewd, obscene, off colour, pornographic, racy, risqué, suggestive, vulgar.
antonyms clean, decent, inoffensive.

snack *n.* bite, break, elevenses, nibble, refreshment(s), titbit.

snag *n.* complication, difficulty, disadvantage, drawback, hitch, inconvenience, obstacle, problem, stick, stumbling block.
v. catch, hole, ladder, rip, tear.

snap *v.* bark, bite, break, catch, chop, crack, crackle, flash, grip, growl, nip, pop, retort, seize, separate, snarl, snatch.
n. bite, break, crack, crackle, fillip, flick, go, nip, pop, vigour.
adj. abrupt, immediate, instant, offhand, on-the-spot, sudden, unexpected.

snappy *adj.* **1** chic, fashionable, modish, natty, smart, stylish, trendy, up-to-the-minute. **2** brisk, energetic, hasty, lively, quick. **3** brusque, crabbed, cross, edgy, ill-natured, irritable, quick-tempered, testy, touchy.
antonyms **1** shabby. **2** slow, sluggish. **3** easy-going.

snare *v.* catch, ensnare, entrap, net, seize, trap, wire.
n. catch, cobweb, net, noose, pitfall, trap, wire.

snarl¹ *v.* complain, gnarl, growl, grumble.

snarl² *v.* complicate, confuse, embroil, enmesh, entangle, entwine, jam, knot, muddle, ravel, tangle.

snarl-up *n.* confusion, jumble, mess, mix-up, muddle, tangle, traffic jam.

snatch *v.* clutch, gain, grab, grasp, grip, kidnap, nab, pluck, pull, ramp, rap, rescue, seize, take, win, wrench, wrest.
n. bit, fraction, fragment, part, piece, section, segment, snippet.

sneak *v.* **1** cower, cringe, lurk, sidle, skulk, slink, slip, smuggle, spirit, steal. **2** grass on, inform on, split, tell tales.
n. informer, sneaker, telltale.

sneaking *adj.* grudging, hidden, intuitive, mean, nagging, niggling, persistent, private, secret, sly, sneaky, suppressed, surreptitious, uncomfortable, unexpressed, unvoiced, worrying.

sneer *v.* deride, disdain, gibe, jeer, laugh, look down on, mock, ridicule, scoff, scorn, sniff at, snigger.
n. derision, disdain, gibe, jeer, mockery, ridicule, scorn, smirk, snigger.

snide *adj.* base, cynical, derogatory, dishonest, disparaging, hurtful, ill-natured, malicious, mean, nasty, sarcastic, scornful, sneering, spiteful, unkind.

sniff *v.* breathe, inhale, nose, smell, snuff, snuffle, vent.

snigger *v., n.* giggle, laugh, sneer, snort, titter.

snip *v.* clip, crop, cut, nick, notch, shave, slit, trim.
n. **1** clipping, slit, snippet. **2** bit, fragment, piece, scrap, shred. **3** bargain, giveaway.

snippet *n.* fragment, part, particle, piece, portion, scrap, section, segment, snatch.

snivelling *adj.* blubbering, crying, grizzling, moaning, sniffling, weeping, whimpering, whining.
snobbery *n.* airs, arrogance, condescension, loftiness, pretension, pride, snobbishness, snootiness.
snobbish *adj.* arrogant, condescending, high and mighty, lofty, patronising, pretentious, snooty, stuck-up, superior, toffee-nosed, uppity.
snoop *v.* interfere, pry, sneak, spy.
snooze *v.* doze, kip, nap, nod off, sleep.
n. catnap, doze, forty winks, kip, nap, siesta, sleep.
snub *v.* check, cold-shoulder, cut, humble, humiliate, mortify, rebuff, rebuke, shame, slight, squash.
n. affront, brush-off, check, humiliation, insult, put-down, rebuff, rebuke, slap in the face.
snug *adj.* close, close-fitting, comfortable, compact, cosy, homely, intimate, neat, sheltered, trim, warm.
snuggle *v.* cuddle, embrace, hug, nestle.
soak *v.* bathe, damp, drench, immerse, infuse, marinate, moisten, penetrate, permeate, saturate, sog, steep, wet.
soaking *adj.* drenched, dripping, saturated, soaked, sodden, sopping, streaming, waterlogged, wringing.
antonym dry.
soar *v.* ascend, climb, escalate, fly, mount, plane, rise, rocket, tower, wing.
antonyms fall, plummet.
sober *adj.* **1** abstemious, abstinent, moderate, teetotal, temperate. **2** calm, clear-headed, composed, cool, dispassionate, level-headed, practical, quiet, rational, realistic, reasonable, restrained, sedate, serene, serious, severe, solemn, sound, steady, unexcited, unruffled. **3** drab, dull, plain, sombre, staid, subdued.
antonyms **1** drunk, intemperate. **2** excited, frivolous, irrational, unrealistic. **3** garish, gay.
so-called *adj.* alleged, nominal, ostensible, pretended, professed, self-styled, supposed.
sociable *adj.* accessible, affable, approachable, chummy, companionable, conversable, convivial, cordial, familiar, friendly, genial, gregarious, neighbourly, outgoing, social, warm.
antonyms hostile, unfriendly, unsociable, withdrawn.
social *adj.* collective, common, communal, community, companionable, friendly, general, gregarious, neighbourly, organised, public, sociable.
n. do, gathering, get-together, party.
socialise *v.* entertain, fraternise, get together, go out, hang out, mix.
socialism *n.* communism, leftism, Leninism, Marxism, Stalinism, Trotskyism.
socialist *adj.* communist, leftist, left-wing, Marxist, red, Trotskyist, Trotskyite.
n. communist, leftie, leftist, left-winger, Marxist, red, Trotskyist.
society *n.* association, brotherhood, camaraderie, circle, civilisation, club, companionship, company, corporation, culture, elite, fellowship, fraternity, friendship, gentry, group, guild, humanity, institute, league, mankind, organisation, people, population, sisterhood, the public, the smart set, the world, union, upper classes.
soft *adj.* **1** elastic, flexible, malleable, plastic, pliable, pulpy, spongy, squashy, yielding. **2** bland, delicate, diffuse, dim, dulcet, faint, gentle, light, low, mellow, melodious, mild, muted, pale, pastel, pleasant, quiet, soothing, subdued, sweet. **3** downy, furry, silky, smooth, velvety. **4** compassionate, easy-going, gentle, indulgent, kind, lax, lenient, permissive, sensitive, sentimental, spineless, sympathetic, tender, weak.
antonyms **1** hard. **2** harsh. **3** rough. **4** severe, strict.
soften *v.* abate, allay, alleviate, appease, assuage, calm, cushion, digest, diminish, ease, lessen, lighten, lower, melt, mitigate, moderate, modify, mollify, muffle, palliate, quell, relax, soothe, still, subdue, temper.
soften up disarm, melt, persuade, soft-soap, weaken, win over.
soft-hearted *adj.* benevolent, charitable, compassionate, generous, indulgent, kind, merciful, sentimental, sympathetic, tender, warm-hearted.
antonyms callous, hard-hearted.
soggy *adj.* boggy, dripping, heavy, moist, pulpy, saturated, soaked, sodden, sopping, soppy, spongy, waterlogged.
soil[1] *n.* clay, country, dirt, dust, earth, ground, humus, land, loam, region, terra firma.
soil[2] *v.* bedraggle, begrime, besmirch, defile, dirty, foul, muddy, pollute, smear, spatter, spot, stain, sully, tarnish.
soiled *adj.* dirty, grimy, manky, polluted, spotted, stained, sullied, tarnished.
antonyms clean, immaculate.
solace *n.* alleviation, comfort, consolation, relief, succour, support.
soldier *n.* fighter, man-at-arms, marine, redcoat, rifleman, serviceman, trooper, warrior.
sole *adj.* alone, exclusive, individual, one, only, single, singular, solitary, unique.
antonyms multiple, shared.
solemn *adj.* august, awed, awe-inspiring, ceremonial, ceremonious, devotional, dignified, earnest, formal, glum, grand, grave, hallowed, imposing, impressive, majestic, momentous, pompous, religious, reverential, ritual, sacred, sanctified, sedate, serious, sober, sombre, stately, thoughtful, venerable.
antonyms frivolous, light-hearted.
solemnity *n.* dignity, earnestness, gravity, impressiveness, momentousness, sacredness, sanctity, seriousness, stateliness.
antonyms frivolity, light-heartedness.
solicit *v.* ask, beg, beseech, canvass, crave, entreat, implore, petition, pray, seek, sue, supplicate.
solicitor *n.* advocate, attorney, barrister, law-

agent, lawyer, notary (public), QC.

solid *adj.* **1** compact, dense, firm, hard, sound, strong, sturdy, substantial, unshakeable. **2** continuous, unbroken, uninterrupted. **3** decent, dependable, level-headed, reliable, sensible, serious, sober, stable, trusty, upright, worthy. **4** concrete, genuine, pure, real, tangible.
antonyms **1** gaseous, hollow, insubstantial, liquid. **2** broken. **3** unstable. **4** flimsy, unreal.

solidarity *n.* accord, camaraderie, cohesion, concord, consensus, harmony, like-mindedness, soundness, stability, team spirit, unanimity, unification, unity.
antonyms discord, division, schism.

solidify *v.* cake, clot, coagulate, cohere, congeal, harden, jell, set.
antonyms dissolve, liquefy, soften.

solitary *adj.* alone, cloistered, desolate, friendless, hidden, isolated, lone, lonely, lonesome, out-of-the-way, remote, retired, secluded, separate, sequestered, single, sole, unfrequented, unsociable, unsocial, untrodden, unvisited.
antonyms accompanied, busy, gregarious.

solitude *n.* aloneness, emptiness, isolation, loneliness, privacy, reclusiveness, retirement, seclusion, waste, wasteland, wilderness.
antonym companionship.

solution *n.* **1** answer, explanation, key, remedy, result. **2** blend, compound, liquefaction, liquid, mixture, solvent, suspension.

solve *v.* answer, clarify, crack, decipher, disentangle, dissolve, explain, interpret, resolve, settle, unbind, unfold, unravel, work out.

sombre *adj.* dark, dim, dismal, drab, dull, funereal, gloomy, grave, joyless, melancholy, mournful, obscure, sad, shadowy, shady, sober.
antonyms bright, cheerful, happy.

someday *adv.* eventually, one day, sometime, ultimately.
antonym never.

somehow *adv.* by fair means or foul, come hell or high water, come what may, one way or another.

sometimes *adv.* at times, from time to time, now and again, now and then, occasionally, off and on, once in a while, otherwhiles.
antonyms always, never.

soon *adv.* before long, in a minute, in a short time, in the near future, presently, shortly.

soothe *v.* allay, alleviate, appease, assuage, calm, comfort, compose, ease, hush, lull, mitigate, mollify, pacify, quiet, relieve, salve, settle, soften, still, tranquillise.
antonyms aggravate, annoy, irritate, vex.

sophisticated *adj.* advanced, complex, complicated, cosmopolitan, cultivated, cultured, delicate, elaborate, highly-developed, intricate, jet-set, refined, seasoned, subtle, urbane, worldly, worldly-wise, world-weary.
antonyms artless, naïve, simple, unsophisticated.

sophistication *n.* culture, elegance, experience, poise, savoir-faire, worldliness.
antonyms naïvety, simplicity.

soporific *adj.* hypnotic, sedative, sleep-inducing, sleepy, tranquillising.
antonyms invigorating, stimulating.

soppy *adj.* cloying, corny, daft, gushy, lovey-dovey, mawkish, mushy, pathetic, schmaltzy, sentimental, silly, slushy, soft, weepy.

sorcerer *n.* enchanter, magician, necromancer, sorceress, warlock, witch, wizard.

sorcery *n.* black art, black magic, charm, divination, enchantment, incantation, magic, necromancy, spell, voodoo, witchcraft, wizardry.

sordid *adj.* corrupt, debauched, degenerate, degraded, despicable, dirty, disreputable, filthy, foul, grasping, low, mean, mercenary, miserly, niggardly, seamy, seedy, selfish, self-seeking, shabby, shameful, sleazy, slovenly, squalid, tawdry, unclean, ungenerous, vicious, vile, wretched.
antonyms honourable, pure, upright.

sore *adj.* **1** aching, hurt, inflamed, painful, raw, reddened, sensitive, smarting, stung, tender. **2** afflicted, aggrieved, angry, annoyed, grieved, irritated, resentful, touchy, upset, vexed. **3** critical, desperate, dire, distressing, extreme, pressing, severe, urgent.
antonyms **2** happy, pleased.
n. abscess, boil, carbuncle, chafe, inflammation, swelling, ulcer, wound.

sorrow *n.* affliction, anguish, distress, grief, hardship, heartache, heartbreak, misery, misfortune, mourning, regret, sadness, trial, tribulation, trouble, unhappiness, woe, worry.
antonyms gladness, happiness, joy.

sorry *adj.* **1** apologetic, contrite, guilt-ridden, penitent, regretful, remorseful, repentant, shamefaced. **2** dismal, miserable, pathetic, pitiful, poor, sad, unhappy, wretched.
antonyms **1** impenitent, unashamed. **2** cheerful, happy.

sort *n.* brand, breed, category, character, class, denomination, description, family, genre, genus, group, ilk, kind, make, nature, order, quality, race, species, stamp, style, type, variety.
v. arrange, catalogue, categorise, choose, class, classify, distribute, divide, grade, group, neaten, order, rank, screen, select, separate, systematise, tidy.
sort out clarify, clear up, divide, organise, resolve, segregate, select, separate, sift, tidy up.

soul *n.* **1** character, essence, inner being, intellect, life, mind, psyche, reason, spirit, vital force. **2** animation, courage, energy, feeling, fervour, force, inspiration, vitality, vivacity. **3** creature, individual, man, person, woman.

sound[1] *n.* description, din, earshot, hearing, idea, impression, noise, range, report, resonance, reverberation, tenor, tone, utterance, voice.
v. announce, appear, articulate, chime, declare, echo, enunciate, express, look, peal, pronounce, resonate, resound, reverberate, ring, seem, signal, toll, utter, voice.

sound[2] *adj.* **1** complete, firm, fit, healthy, intact, perfect, robust, solid, sturdy, unbroken, undamaged, unhurt, unimpaired, uninjured, vigorous, well, whole. **2** copper-bottomed, good,

logical, orthodox, proven, rational, reasonable, reliable, right, secure, substantial, thorough, tried-and-true, true, trustworthy, valid, well-founded.
antonyms **1** ill, shaky, unfit. **2** poor, unreliable, unsound.
sound[3] *n.* channel, estuary, firth, fjord, inlet, passage, strait.
sour *adj.* **1** acid, bitter, fermented, pungent, sharp, tart, unpleasant, vinegary. **2** acrimonious, crabbed, disagreeable, embittered, grouchy, ill-tempered, peevish.
antonyms **1** sugary, sweet. **2** generous, good-natured.
v. alienate, disenchant, embitter, exacerbate, exasperate, spoil, worsen.
source *n.* authority, beginning, cause, commencement, derivation, fountain-head, informant, mine, origin, originator, quarry, rise, spring, water-head, well-head.
souvenir *n.* gift, keepsake, memento, memory, relic, remembrance, reminder, token.
sovereign *n.* chief, emperor, empress, king, monarch, potentate, prince, queen, ruler, tsar.
adj. absolute, chief, dominant, excellent, imperial, kingly, majestic, monarch(ic)al, paramount, predominant, principal, queenly, regal, royal, ruling, supreme, unlimited.
sow *v.* disseminate, drill, implant, lodge, plant, scatter, seed, spread, strew.
space *n.* **1** accommodation, capacity, elbow-room, expanse, extension, extent, leeway, margin, place, play, room, scope, seat, volume. **2** blank, chasm, gap, interval, omission, span.
spacious *adj.* ample, big, broad, comfortable, expansive, extensive, huge, large, roomy, sizable, uncrowded, vast, wide.
antonyms confined, cramped, narrow, small.
span *n.* amount, compass, distance, duration, extent, length, period, reach, scope, spell, spread, stretch, term.
v. arch, bridge, cover, cross, extend, link, traverse, vault.
spank *v.* belt, cane, leather, slap, slipper, smack, tan, wallop, whack.
spar *v.* argue, bicker, contend, contest, dispute, fall out, scrap, skirmish, squabble, wrangle, wrestle.
spare *adj.* additional, emergency, extra, free, leftover, over, remaining, reserve, superfluous, supernumerary, surplus, unoccupied, unused, unwanted.
antonyms allocated, necessary, used, vital.
v. afford, allow, grant, leave, let off, pardon, part with, refrain from, release, relinquish.
sparing *adj.* careful, cost-conscious, economical, frugal, meagre, prudent, saving, thrifty.
antonyms lavish, liberal, unsparing.
spark *n.* atom, flake, flare, flash, flicker, gleam, glint, hint, jot, scrap, spit, trace, vestige.
v. cause, excite, inspire, kindle, occasion, prompt, provoke, set off, start, stimulate, stir, trigger.
sparkle *v.* beam, bubble, effervesce, fizz, fizzle, flash, gleam, glint, glisten, glitter, glow, shimmer, shine, spark, twinkle.
n. animation, brilliance, dash, dazzle, effervescence, flash, flicker, gleam, glint, glitter, life, panache, pizzazz, radiance, spark, spirit, twinkle, vitality, vivacity.
sparse *adj.* infrequent, meagre, scanty, scarce, scattered, sporadic.
antonyms crowded, dense, thick.
spartan *adj.* ascetic, austere, bleak, disciplined, extreme, frugal, joyless, plain, rigorous, self-denying, severe, stern, strict, temperate.
spasm *n.* burst, contraction, convulsion, eruption, fit, frenzy, jerk, outburst, seizure, twitch.
spasmodic *adj.* erratic, fitful, intermittent, irregular, jerky, occasional, sporadic.
antonyms continuous, uninterrupted.
spate *n.* deluge, flood, flow, outpouring, rush, torrent.
spatter *v.* daub, scatter, soil, speckle, splash, splodge, spray, sprinkle.
speak *v.* address, allude to, argue, articulate, comment on, communicate, converse, deal with, declaim, declare, discuss, express, lecture, mention, plead, pronounce, refer to, say, state, talk, tell, utter, voice.
speaker *n.* lecturer, orator, speech-maker, spokesman, spokesperson, spokeswoman.
special *adj.* characteristic, choice, detailed, distinctive, distinguished, exceptional, exclusive, extraordinary, festive, gala, important, individual, main, major, memorable, momentous, particular, peculiar, precise, primary, select, significant, specific, unique, unusual.
antonyms common, normal, ordinary, usual.
specialist *n.* authority, connoisseur, consultant, expert, master, professional.
speciality *n.* forte, pièce de résistance, scene, special, specialty, strength.
specific *adj.* clear-cut, definite, distinguishing, exact, explicit, express, limited, particular, peculiar, precise, special, unambiguous, unequivocal.
antonyms approximate, general, vague.
specification *n.* condition, description, detail, item, itemisation, listing, particular, qualification, requirement.
specify *v.* cite, define, delineate, describe, designate, detail, enumerate, indicate, itemise, list, mention, name, particularise, spell out, stipulate.
specimen *n.* copy, example, exhibit, illustration, individual, instance, model, paradigm, pattern, person, proof, representative, sample, type.
spectacle *n.* curiosity, display, event, exhibition, extravaganza, marvel, pageant, parade, performance, phenomenon, scene, show, sight, wonder.
spectacular *adj.* amazing, breathtaking, daring, dazzling, dramatic, eye-catching, fabulous, fantastic, grand, impressive, magnificent, marked, remarkable, sensational, splendid, staggering, striking, stunning.
antonyms ordinary, unimpressive, unspec-

tacular.

spectator *n.* bystander, eye-witness, looker-on, observer, onlooker, passer-by, viewer, watcher, witness.
antonyms contestant, participant, player.

spectre *n.* apparition, ghost, phantom, presence, shade, shadow, spirit, vision, wraith.

speculate *v.* conjecture, consider, contemplate, deliberate, gamble, guess, hazard, meditate, muse, reflect, risk, scheme, suppose, surmise, theorise, venture, wonder.

speculative *adj.* abstract, academic, conjectural, dicey, hazardous, hypothetical, notional, projected, risky, tentative, theoretical, uncertain, unpredictable.

speech *n.* address, articulation, communication, conversation, dialect, dialogue, diction, discourse, discussion, enunciation, harangue, jargon, language, lecture, oration, parlance, say, spiel, talk, tongue, utterance, voice.

speechless *adj.* aghast, amazed, astounded, dazed, dumb, dumbfounded, inarticulate, mum, mute, silent, thunderstruck, tongue-tied.

speed *n.* acceleration, celerity, dispatch, fleetness, haste, hurry, momentum, pace, quickness, rapidity, rush, swiftness, tempo, velocity.
antonyms delay, slowness.
v. advance, aid, assist, belt, boost, bowl along, career, dispatch, expedite, facilitate, fleet, further, gallop, hasten, help, hurry, impel, lick, press on, promote, put one's foot down, quicken, race, rush, sprint, step on it, tear, urge, zap, zoom.
antonyms delay, hamper, restrain, slow.

speedy *adj.* express, fast, fleet, hurried, immediate, nimble, precipitate, prompt, quick, rapid, summary, swift.
antonyms leisurely, slow, tardy.

spell[1] *n.* bout, course, innings, interval, patch, period, season, stint, stretch, term, time, turn.

spell[2] *n.* abracadabra, bewitchment, charm, enchantment, exorcism, fascination, glamour, incantation, love-charm, magic, open sesame, sorcery, trance, witchery.

spellbound *adj.* bemused, bewitched, captivated, charmed, enchanted, enthralled, entranced, fascinated, gripped, hooked, mesmerised, possessed, transfixed.

spend *v.* **1** consume, cough up, disburse, expend, fork out, fritter, invest, lay out, pay out, shell out, splash out, squander, use up, waste. **2** apply, devote, employ, fill, occupy, pass, use.
antonyms **1** hoard, save.

spendthrift *n.* prodigal, profligate, spender, squanderer, waster, wastrel.
antonyms hoarder, miser, saver.
adj. extravagant, improvident, prodigal, wasteful.

spent *adj.* all in, burnt out, bushed, dead beat, dog-tired, done in, drained, exhausted, expended, fagged (out), finished, knackered, shattered, tired out, used up, weary, whacked, worn out.

sphere *n.* ball, capacity, circle, compass, department, domain, employment, field, function, globe, orb, province, range, rank, realm, scope, territory.

spherical *adj.* globe-shaped, rotund, round.

spick and span clean, immaculate, neat, polished, scrubbed, spotless, spruce, tidy, trim, well-kept.
antonyms dirty, untidy.

spicy *adj.* **1** aromatic, fragrant, hot, piquant, pungent, seasoned, tangy. **2** improper, indecorous, indelicate, off-colour, pointed, racy, ribald, risqué, scandalous, sensational, suggestive, unseemly.
antonyms **1** bland, insipid. **2** decent.

spike *n.* barb, nail, point, prong, spine, spire.
v. impale, spear, stick.

spill *v.* discharge, disgorge, overflow, overturn, scatter, shed, slop, upset.
n. accident, cropper, fall, overturn, tumble, upset.

spin *v.* **1** gyrate, pirouette, reel, revolve, rotate, swirl, turn, twirl, twist, wheel, whirl. **2** concoct, develop, invent, narrate, recount, relate, tell, unfold.
n. **1** gyration, pirouette, revolution, roll, turn, twist, whirl. **2** agitation, commotion, flap, panic, state, tizzy. **3** drive, ride, run.
spin out amplify, delay, extend, lengthen, maintain, pad out, prolong, protract, sustain.

spindle *n.* axis, axle, pivot.

spindly *adj.* attenuate(d), gangling, lanky, leggy, skeletal, skinny, spidery, thin, weedy.
antonyms stocky, thickset.

spineless *adj.* cowardly, faint-hearted, feeble, inadequate, ineffective, irresolute, lily-livered, soft, squeamish, submissive, weak, weak-kneed, wet, wishy-washy, yellow.
antonyms brave, strong.

spiral *adj.* circular, coiled, corkscrew, helical, scrolled, voluted, whorled, winding.
n. coil, convolution, corkscrew, helix, screw, volution, whorl.

spire *n.* cone, peak, pinnacle, point, shoot, spike, sprout, stalk, steeple, summit, tip, top.

spirit *n.* **1** breath, life, psyche, soul. **2** angel, apparition, demon, fairy, faun, ghost, phantom, spectre, sprite. **3** animation, ardour, backbone, courage, energy, enterprise, enthusiasm, fire, liveliness, mettle, resolution, sparkle, vigour, vivacity, will power, zeal, zest. **4** character, essence, gist, meaning, quality, sense, substance, tenor. **5** attitude, disposition, feeling, humour, mood, morale, motivation, outlook, temper, temperament.
v. abduct, abstract, capture, carry, convey, kidnap, purloin, remove, seize, steal, whisk.

spirited *adj.* active, animated, ardent, bold, courageous, energetic, high-spirited, lively, mettlesome, plucky, sparkling, spunky, vigorous, vivacious.
antonyms lazy, spiritless, timid.

spirits *n.* alcohol, fire-water, liquor, strong drink, strong liquor, the hard stuff.

spiritual *adj.* devotional, divine, ecclesiastical,

holy, immaterial, otherwordly, pneumatic, pure, religious, sacred, unfleshly, unworldly.
antonyms material, physical.

spit *v.* discharge, eject, expectorate, hawk, hiss, spew, splutter, sputter.
n. drool, expectoration, phlegm, saliva, slaver, spittle, sputum.

spite *n.* animosity, bitchiness, gall, grudge, hate, hatred, ill-nature, malevolence, malice, malignity, rancour, spitefulness, venom, viciousness.
antonyms affection, compassion, goodwill.
v. annoy, gall, harm, hurt, injure, irk, irritate, offend, peeve, provoke, put out, vex.
in spite of despite, notwithstanding.

spiteful *adj.* barbed, bitchy, catty, cruel, ill-disposed, ill-natured, malevolent, malicious, malignant, nasty, snide, vengeful, venomous, vindictive.
antonyms affectionate, charitable.

splash *v.* **1** bathe, break, buffet, dabble, dash, paddle, plaster, plop, plunge, shower, slop, slosh, smack, spatter, splodge, spray, spread, sprinkle, squirt, strew, strike, surge, tout, wade, wallow, wash, wet. **2** flaunt, headline, publicise, trumpet.
n. **1** burst, dash, patch, spattering, splatter, splodge, splurge, touch. **2** display, effect, excitement, impact, ostentation, publicity, sensation, stir.
splash out invest in, lash out, push the boat out, spend, splurge.

splendid *adj.* admirable, beaming, bright, brilliant, dazzling, excellent, exceptional, fantastic, fine, first-class, glittering, glorious, glowing, gorgeous, grand, great, imposing, impressive, lavish, lustrous, luxurious, magnificent, marvellous, outstanding, radiant, rare, remarkable, renowned, resplendent, rich, sterling, sublime, sumptuous, superb, supreme, tiptop, top-hole, top-notch, topping, wonderful.
antonyms drab, ordinary, run-of-the-mill, squalid.

splendour *n.* brightness, brilliance, ceremony, dazzle, display, glory, grandeur, lustre, magnificence, majesty, pomp, radiance, renown, resplendence, richness, show, solemnity, spectacle.
antonyms drabness, ordinariness, squalor.

splice *v.* bind, braid, entwine, graft, interlace, interlink, intertwine, intertwist, interweave, join, knit, marry, mesh, plait, tie, unite, wed, yoke.

splinter *n.* chip, flake, fragment, paring, shaving, sliver.
v. disintegrate, fracture, fragment, shatter, shiver, smash, split.

split *v.* break, burst, cleave, crack, disband, distribute, disunite, diverge, divide, fork, gape, halve, open, parcel out, part, partition, rend, rip, separate, share out, slash, slice up, slit, sliver, snap, spell, splinter.
n. breach, break, break-up, cleft, crack, damage, difference, discord, disruption, dissension, disunion, divergence, division, fissure, gap, partition, race, rent, rift, rip, rupture, schism, separation, slash, slit, tear.
adj. ambivalent, bisected, broken, cleft, cloven, cracked, divided, dual, fractured, ruptured, twofold.
split up break up, disband, dissolve, divorce, part, part company, separate.

spoil *v.* **1** blemish, curdle, damage, debase, decay, decompose, deface, destroy, deteriorate, disfigure, go bad, go off, harm, impair, injure, mar, plunder, ruin, upset. **2** baby, coddle, cosset, indulge, mollycoddle, pamper, spoon-feed.

spoils *n.* acquisitions, booty, gain, haul, loot, pickings, plunder, prey, prizes, swag, winnings.

spoil-sport *n.* dog in the manger, killjoy, meddler, misery, wet blanket, wowser.

sponge *v.* cadge, scrounge.

sponger *n.* cadge, cadger, hanger-on, parasite, scrounger.

spongy *adj.* absorbent, cushioned, elastic, light, porous, springy.

sponsor *n.* backer, guarantor, patron, promoter, surety, underwriter.
v. back, finance, fund, guarantee, patronise, promote, subsidise, underwrite.

spontaneous *adj.* extempore, free, impromptu, impulsive, instinctive, natural, unforced, unhesitating, unpremeditated, unprompted, untaught, voluntary, willing.
antonyms deliberate, forced, planned, studied.

spoof *n.* bluff, caricature, deception, game, hoax, joke, leg-pull, mockery, parody, prank, satire, send-up, take-off, travesty, trick.

sporadic *adj.* erratic, infrequent, intermittent, irregular, isolated, occasional, random, scattered, spasmodic, uneven.
antonyms frequent, regular.

sport *n.* **1** activity, amusement, diversion, entertainment, exercise, game, pastime, play, plaything, recreation. **2** banter, frolic, fun, jest, joking, laughing-stock, mirth, mockery, ridicule, teasing.
v. display, exhibit, show off, wear.

sporty *adj.* athletic, casual, energetic, flashy, informal, jaunty, jazzy, loud, natty, outdoor, showy, snazzy, stylish, trendy.

spot *n.* **1** blemish, blot, blotch, daub, discoloration, flaw, mark, morsel, pimple, smudge, speck, splash, stain, stigma, taint. **2** locality, location, place, point, position, scene, site, situation. **3** difficulty, mess, plight, predicament, quandary, trouble.
v. detect, discern, identify, notice, observe, recognise, see.

spotless *adj.* blameless, chaste, faultless, gleaming, immaculate, innocent, irreproachable, pure, shining, spick and span, unblemished, unstained, unsullied, untarnished, virgin, white.
antonyms dirty, impure, spotted.

spotlight *v.* accentuate, emphasise, feature, focus on, highlight, illuminate, point up.
n. attention, emphasis, fame, interest, limelight,

notoriety, public eye.

spotted *adj.* dappled, dotted, flecked, mottled, pied, polka-dot, specked, speckled.

spotty *adj.* blotchy, pimpled, pimply, speckled, spotted.

spouse *n.* better half, companion, helpmate, husband, mate, partner, wife.

spout *v.* **1** discharge, emit, erupt, gush, jet, shoot, spray, spurt, squirt, stream, surge. **2** churn out, pontificate, rabbit on, ramble (on), rant, sermonise.

n. chute, fountain, gargoyle, geyser, jet, nozzle, outlet, rose, spray.

sprawl *v.* flop, loll, lounge, ramble, recline, repose, slouch, slump, spread, trail.

spray[1] *v.* diffuse, douse, drench, scatter, shower, sprinkle, wet.

n. aerosol, atomiser, drizzle, foam, froth, mist, moisture, sprinkler.

spray[2] *n.* bough, branch, garland, shoot, sprig, wreath.

spread *v.* **1** arrange, broaden, cover, dilate, escalate, expand, extend, fan out, lay, mushroom, open, proliferate, set, shed, sprawl, stretch, swell, unfold, unfurl, unroll, widen. **2** advertise, broadcast, circulate, disseminate, distribute, promulgate, propagate, publicise, publish, radiate, scatter, strew, transmit.

antonyms **1** close, fold. **2** suppress.

n. **1** compass, expanse, extent, reach, stretch, sweep. **2** advance, development, diffusion, dispersion, dissemination, escalation, expansion, increase, proliferation. **3** banquet, feast, meal, paste.

pree *n.* binge, bout, fling, orgy, revel, splurge.

prightly *adj.* active, agile, airy, alert, blithe, brisk, cheerful, energetic, hearty, jaunty, lively, nimble, spirited, spry, vivacious.

antonyms doddering, inactive, lifeless.

pring[1] *v.* **1** bounce, bound, hop, jump, leap, rebound, recoil, vault. **2** appear, arise, come, derive, descend, develop, emanate, emerge, grow, issue, mushroom, originate, proceed, sprout, start, stem.

n. bounce, bound, buoyancy, elasticity, flexibility, give, jump, leap, rebound, recoil, resilience, springiness, vault.

pring[2] *n.* beginning, cause, fountain-head, origin, root, source, well, well-spring.

pringy *adj.* bouncy, buoyant, elastic, flexible, resilient, rubbery, spongy, stretchy.

antonyms hard, rigid, stiff.

prinkle *v.* dot, dust, pepper, powder, scatter, seed, shower, spatter, spray, strew.

prinkling *n.* admixture, dash, dusting, few, handful, scatter, scattering, smattering, touch, trace.

print *v.* belt, dart, dash, hotfoot, race, run, scamper, shoot, tear, whiz.

prout *v.* bud, develop, germinate, grow, push, shoot, spring.

pruce *adj.* dapper, elegant, neat, sleek, slick, smart, trim, well-groomed, well-turned-out.

antonyms dishevelled, unkempt, untidy.

spruce up groom, neaten, primp, smarten up, tidy.

spry *adj.* active, agile, alert, brisk, energetic, nimble, quick, ready, sprightly.

antonyms doddering, inactive, lethargic.

spur *v.* animate, drive, goad, impel, incite, poke, press, prick, prod, prompt, propel, stimulate, urge.

antonyms curb, prevent.

n. fillip, impetus, impulse, incentive, incitement, inducement, motive, stimulus.

antonyms curb, hindrance.

spurious *adj.* artificial, bogus, contrived, counterfeit, deceitful, fake, false, feigned, forged, imitation, mock, phoney, pretended, sham, simulated.

antonyms authentic, genuine, real.

spurn *v.* cold-shoulder, despise, disdain, disregard, rebuff, reject, repulse, scorn, slight, snub, turn down.

antonyms accept, embrace.

spurt *v.* burst, erupt, gush, jet, shoot, spew, squirt, surge.

n. access, burst, effusion, fit, rush, spate, surge.

spy *n.* double agent, fifth columnist, foreign agent, mole, scout, secret agent, snooper, undercover agent.

v. discover, glimpse, notice, observe, spot.

squad *n.* band, brigade, company, crew, force, gang, group, outfit, team, troop.

squalid *adj.* broken-down, decayed, dirty, disgusting, filthy, foul, low, nasty, neglected, poverty-stricken, repulsive, run-down, seedy, slovenly, sordid, uncared-for, unclean, unkempt, untidy.

antonyms attractive, clean, pleasant.

squander *v.* blow, consume, dissipate, expend, fritter away, lavish, misspend, misuse, scatter, spend, throw away, waste.

square *v.* accord, adapt, adjust, agree, align, balance, correspond, corrupt, fit, fix, harmonise, level, match, reconcile, regulate, satisfy, settle, straighten, suit, tailor, tally, true.

adj. **1** even, exact, quadrilateral, right-angled, straight, true. **2** above-board, equitable, ethical, fair, genuine, honest, just, on the level, straightforward. **3** bourgeois, conservative, conventional, old-fashioned, strait-laced, stuffy, traditional.

n. conformer, conformist, conservative, conventionalist, die-hard, fuddy-duddy, (old) fogy, stick-in-the-mud, traditionalist.

squash *v.* annihilate, compress, crowd, crush, distort, flatten, humiliate, pound, press, pulp, quash, quell, silence, smash, snub, squelch, stamp, suppress, trample.

antonyms elongate, expand, stretch.

squat *adj.* chunky, dumpy, short, stocky, stubby, stumpy, thickset.

antonyms lanky, slender, slim.

v. bend, crouch, settle, stoop.

squawk *v.* cackle, complain, crow, cry, grouse, hoot, protest, screech, shriek, squeal, yelp.

squeak *v.* chirk, peep, pipe, shrill, squeal, whine,

yelp.

squeal *n.* scream, screech, shriek, wail, yell, yelp.
v. **1** scream, screech, shout, shriek, squawk, wail, yelp. **2** betray, blab, complain, grass, inform on, moan, protest, rat on.

squeamish *adj.* delicate, fastidious, nauseous, particular, prissy, prudish, punctilious, queasy, reluctant, sick, strait-laced.
antonym strong-stomached.

squeeze *v.* bleed, clasp, clutch, compress, cram, crowd, crush, cuddle, embrace, enfold, extort, force, grip, hug, jam, jostle, lean on, milk, nip, oppress, pack, pinch, press, ram, squash, strain, stuff, thrust, wedge, wrest, wring.
n. clasp, congestion, crowd, crush, embrace, grasp, hold, hug, jam, press, pressure, restriction, squash.

squint *adj.* askew, aslant, awry, cockeyed, crooked, indirect, oblique, off-centre, skew-whiff.
antonyms balanced, straight.

squirt *v.* discharge, ejaculate, eject, emit, expel, jet, shoot, spout, spurt.
n. jet, spray, spurt.

stab *v.* cut, gore, injure, jab, knife, pierce, puncture, spear, stick, thrust, wound.
n. ache, attempt, endeavour, gash, incision, jab, pang, prick, puncture, thrust, try, twinge, venture, wound.

stabbing *adj.* acute, piercing, shooting, stinging.

stability *n.* constancy, durability, firmness, permanence, solidity, soundness, steadfastness, steadiness, strength, sturdiness.
antonyms insecurity, instability, unsteadiness, weakness.

stable *adj.* abiding, constant, deep-rooted, durable, enduring, established, fast, firm, fixed, immutable, invariable, lasting, permanent, reliable, secure, sound, static, steadfast, steady, strong, sturdy, sure, unalterable, unchangeable, well-founded.
antonyms shaky, unstable, weak, wobbly.

staff *n.* **1** crew, employees, lecturers, officers, organisation, personnel, teachers, team, workers, workforce. **2** cane, pole, prop, rod, wand.

stage *n.* division, floor, juncture, lap, leg, length, level, period, phase, point, step.
v. arrange, do, engineer, give, mount, orchestrate, organise, perform, present, produce, put on, stage-manage.

stagger *v.* **1** falter, hesitate, lurch, reel, shake, shock, sway, teeter, totter, wobble. **2** amaze, astonish, astound, confound, dumbfound, flabbergast, overwhelm, stun, stupefy, surprise. **3** alternate, overlap.

stagnant *adj.* brackish, lethargic, motionless, sluggish, stale, standing, still, torpid.
antonyms fresh, lively.

stagnate *v.* decay, decline, degenerate, deteriorate, idle, languish, rot, rust, vegetate.

staid *adj.* calm, composed, demure, grave, quiet, sedate, self-restrained, serious, sober, solemn, steady.
antonyms adventurous, debonair, frivolous, jaunty.

stain *v.* blacken, blemish, blot, colour, contaminate, corrupt, defile, deprave, dirty, discolour, disgrace, dye, mark, smutch, soil, spot, sully, taint, tarnish, tinge.
n. blemish, blot, discoloration, disgrace, dishonour, reproach, shame, slur, smirch, soil, spot, tint.

stake *n.* pale, paling, picket, pole, post, spike, standard, stave, stick.
v. brace, fasten, pierce, prop, secure, support, tie (up).
stake out define, delimit, demarcate, keep an eye on, mark out, outline, reserve, survey, watch.

stale *adj.* **1** decayed, dry, flat, fusty, hard, insipid, musty, old, tasteless. **2** antiquated, banal, commonplace, drab, hackneyed, jaded, overused, repetitious, stereotyped, tedious, trite, unoriginal, worn-out.
antonyms **1** crisp, fresh. **2** imaginative.

stalemate *n.* deadlock, draw, halt, impasse, standstill, tie.
antonym progress.

stalk[1] *v.* approach, follow, haunt, hunt, march, pace, pursue, shadow, stride, strut, tail, track.

stalk[2] *n.* branch, shoot, stem, trunk.

stall *v.* delay, equivocate, hedge, obstruct, play for time, stonewall, temporise.
antonyms advance, progress.

stalwart *adj.* athletic, daring, dependable, determined, hefty, husky, indomitable, intrepid, manly, muscular, resolute, robust, rugged, staunch, stout, strapping, strong, sturdy, valiant, vigorous.
antonyms feeble, timid, weak.

stamina *n.* endurance, energy, force, grit, indefatigability, power, resilience, resistence, staying power, strength, vigour.
antonym weakness.

stammer *v.* falter, hesitate, splutter, stumble, stutter.

stamp *v.* **1** beat, crush, pound, strike, trample. **2** brand, categorise, characterise, engrave, exhibit, fix, identify, impress, imprint, inscribe, label, mark, mould, print.
n. attestation, authorisation, brand, breed, cast, character, cut, description, earmark, evidence, fashion, form, hallmark, impression, imprint, kind, mark, mould, sign, signature, sort, type.
stamp out crush, destroy, eliminate, end, eradicate, extinguish, kill, quench, suppress.
antonyms encourage, foster, promote.

stampede *n.* charge, dash, flight, rout, rush, scattering, sprint.
v. charge, dash, flee, fly, gallop, hightail it, run, rush, scurry, shoot, sprint, tear.
antonyms stop, walk, wander.

stance *n.* angle, attitude, bearing, carriage, deportment, point of view, position, posture, stand, standpoint, station, viewpoint.

stand *v.* **1** erect, place, put, rise, set. **2** abide, allow, bear, endure, experience, suffer, tolerate

undergo, weather, withstand.
n. **1** booth, frame, grandstand, place, platform, rack, stage, stall, support, table. **2** attitude, opinion, position, resistance, stance, standpoint.
stand by adhere to, back, champion, defend, hold to, reiterate, repeat, speak for, stick by, stick up for, support, uphold.
antonym let down.
stand down abdicate, give away, give up, quit, resign, step down, withdraw.
antonym join.
stand for 1 denote, exemplify, indicate, mean, personify, represent, signify, symbolise, typify. **2** bear, countenance, endure, tolerate.
stand in for cover for, deputise for, hold the fort for, replace, substitute for, understudy.
stand out catch the eye, jut out, project, stare one in the face, stick out.
stand up cohere, hold up, hold water, stand.
stand up for champion, defend, fight for, side with, speak for, speak up for, stick up for support, uphold.
antonym attack.
stand up to brave, confront, defy, endure, face, front, oppose, resist, withstand.
antonym give in to.

standard *n.* **1** average, bench-mark, criterion, example, gauge, grade, guide, guideline, level, measure, model, norm, pattern, principle, requirement, rule, sample, specification, touchstone, type, yardstick. **2** banner, colours, ensign, flag, pennant, pennon, rallying-point, streamer.
adj. accepted, approved, authoritative, average, basic, classic, customary, definitive, established, normal, official, orthodox, popular, prevailing, recognised, regular, set, staple, stock, typical, usual.
antonyms abnormal, irregular, unusual.

standardise *v.* equalise, institutionalise, mass-produce, normalise, stereotype.
antonym differentiate.

standards *n.* ethics, ideals, morals, principles.

stand-offish *adj.* aloof, cold, distant, remote, reserved, unapproachable, uncommunicative, unsociable.
antonyms approachable, friendly.

standpoint *n.* angle, point of view, position, stance, station, vantage-point, viewpoint.

standstill *n.* cessation, dead-finish, deadlock, hold-up, impasse, lapse, log-jam, lull, pause, reprieve, respite, rest, stalemate, stay, stop, stoppage, termination.
antonyms advance, progress.

staple *adj.* basic, chief, essential, fundamental, key, leading, main, major, necessary, predominant, primary, principle, standard.
antonym minor.

star *n.* **1** asterisk, asteroid, comet, meteor, meteorite, planet, pulsar, quasar, red dwarf, red giant, satellite, shooting-star, starlet, sun, supernova, white dwarf. **2** celebrity, idol, lead, leading lady, leading man, luminary, main attraction, name.
adj. brilliant, celebrated, illustrious, leading, major, paramount, pre-eminent, principal, prominent, talented, well-known.
antonyms minor, unknown.

starchy *adj.* ceremonious, conventional, formal, punctilious, stiff, strait-laced, stuffy.
antonyms informal, relaxed.

stare *v.* gape, gawk, gawp, gaze, glare, goggle, look, watch.
n. gaze, glare, glower, leer, look, ogle, scowl.

stark *adj.* **1** austere, bald, bare, barren, bleak, cold, depressing, dreary, forsaken, grim, harsh, plain, severe, simple. **2** absolute, arrant, consummate, downright, flagrant, out-and-out, patent, sheer, total, unmitigated, utter.
antonyms **1** attractive, pleasant.

start *v.* **1** activate, appear, arise, begin, commence, create, depart, establish, found, inaugurate, initiate, instigate, institute, introduce, issue, kick off, launch, leave, open, originate, pioneer, set off, set out, set up, shoot. **2** flinch, jerk, jump, recoil, spring forward, twitch.
antonyms **1** end, finish, stop.
n. **1** beginning, birth, break, commencement, dawn, foundation, inauguration, inception, initiation, introduction, kick-off, lead, onset, opening, opportunity, outburst, outset. **2** convulsion, fit, jump, spasm, twitch.
antonyms **1** cessation, finish, stop.

startle *v.* agitate, alarm, amaze, astonish, astound, electrify, flush, frighten, scare, shock, spook, start, surprise.
antonyms bore, calm.

startling *adj.* astonishing, astounding, dramatic, electrifying, extraordinary, remarkable, shocking, sudden, surprising, unexpected, unforeseen.
antonyms boring, calming, ordinary.

starvation *n.* hunger, malnutrition, undernourishment.
antonyms excess, plenty.

starve *v.* deny, deprive, die, diet, fast, hunger, perish, refuse.
antonyms feed, provide.

state *v.* affirm, articulate, assert, aver, declare, explain, expound, express, formalise, formulate, present, put, report, say, specify, voice.
n. **1** case, circumstances, condition, phase, position, shape, situation. **2** commonwealth, country, federation, government, kingdom, land, nation, republic, territory. **3** bother, flap, panic, plight, predicament, tizzy. **4** dignity, glory, grandeur, majesty, pomp, splendour.
adj. ceremonial, formal, governmental, magnificent, national, official, pompous, public, solemn.

stately *adj.* august, ceremonious, deliberate, dignified, elegant, grand, imperial, imposing, impressive, lofty, majestic, measured, noble, pompous, princely, regal, royal, solemn.
antonyms informal, unimpressive.

statement *n.* account, announcement, bulletin, communication, communiqué, declaration, explanation, proclamation, recital, relation,

report, testimony.
static *adj.* changeless, constant, fixed, immobile, inert, motionless, resting, stable, stationary, still, unmoving, unvarying.
antonyms active, dynamic, moving.
station *n.* base, depot, head-quarters, location, place, position, post, stopping-place.
v. appoint, assign, establish, garrison, install, locate, post, send, set.
stationary *adj.* fixed, immobile, inert, moored, motionless, parked, resting, settled, standing, static, unmoving.
antonyms mobile, moving, varying.
statue *n.* bronze, bust, carving, effigy, figure, head, idol, statuette.
status *n.* character, condition, consequence, degree, distinction, eminence, grade, importance, position, prestige, rank, standing, state, weight.
antonyms insignificance, unimportance.
statute *n.* act, decree, edict, law, ordinance, regulation, rule.
staunch *adj.* constant, dependable, faithful, firm, hearty, loyal, reliable, resolute, sound, steadfast, stout, strong, sure, true, trustworthy, trusty, zealous.
antonyms unreliable, wavering, weak.
v. arrest, block, check, halt, stay, stem, stop.
stay *v.* **1** abide, continue, endure, last, linger, remain. **2** defer, delay, dwell, halt, live, pause, reside, settle, sojourn, stop, wait.
antonyms **1** depart, leave.
n. holiday, sojourn, stopover, visit.
steady *adj.* balanced, calm, consistent, constant, dependable, equable, even, faithful, firm, fixed, immovable, imperturbable, incessant, level-headed, persistent, regular, reliable, rhythmic, safe, sensible, serious-minded, settled, stable, steadfast, unbroken, unchangeable, unfaltering, uniform, uninterrupted, unremitting, unswerving, unvarying, unwavering.
antonyms careless, unsteady, variable, wavering.
v. balance, brace, firm, fix, secure, stabilise, support.
steal *v.* **1** appropriate, embezzle, lift, nick, pilfer, pinch, plagiarise, poach, rip off, shoplift, snatch, swipe, take, thieve. **2** creep, slink, slip, sneak, tiptoe.
antonyms **1** give back, return.
stealth *n.* covertness, furtiveness, secrecy, slyness, surreptitiousness, unobtrusiveness.
antonym openness.
stealthy *adj.* cat-like, clandestine, covert, furtive, quiet, secret, secretive, sly, sneaking, sneaky, surreptitious, underhand.
antonym open.
steam *n.* condensation, dampness, haze, mist, moisture, vapour.
steel *v.* brace, fortify, harden, nerve, toughen.
antonym weaken.
steep[1] *adj.* **1** abrupt, headlong, precipitious, sheer. **2** excessive, exorbitant, extortionate, extreme, high, overpriced, stiff, unreasonable.
antonyms **1** gentle, moderate. **2** low.
steep[2] *v.* damp, drench, fill, imbue, immerse, infuse, marinate, moisten, permeate, pervade, pickle, saturate, seethe, soak, submerge.
steer *v.* conduct, control, direct, govern, guide, pilot.
stem[1] *n.* axis, branch, family, house, line, lineage, race, shoot, stalk, stock, trunk.
stem[2] *v.* check, contain, curb, dam, oppose, resist, restrain, stay, stop.
antonyms encourage, increase.
stench *n.* odour, reek, stink, whiff.
step *n.* **1** footprint, footstep, pace, print, stride, trace, track, walk. **2** act, action, deed, degree, means, measure, move, phase, procedure, proceeding, process, progression, stage. **3** doorstep, level, point, rank, rung, stair.
v. move, pace, stalk, stamp, tread, walk.
step down abdicate, bow out, leave, quit, resign, retire, stand down, withdraw.
antonym join.
step up accelerate, augment, boost, build up, escalate, increase, intensify, raise, speed up.
antonym decrease.
stereotype *n.* convention, formula, mould, pattern.
v. categorise, conventionalise, dub, mass-produce, pigeonhole, standardise, typecast.
antonym differentiate.
sterile *adj.* **1** antiseptic, aseptic, disinfected, germ-free, sterilised. **2** abortive, bare, barren, fruitless, pointless, unimaginative, unproductive.
antonyms **1** septic. **2** fruitful.
sterilise *v.* clean, cleanse, disinfect, fumigate, purify.
antonyms contaminate, infect.
stern *adj.* austere, authoritarian, bitter, cruel, forbidding, grim, hard, harsh, inflexible, relentless, rigid, rigorous, serious, severe, stark, strict, unrelenting, unsparing, unyielding.
antonyms gentle, kind, lenient, mild.
stew *v.* boil, braise, simmer.
n. goulash, hash, ragout.
stick[1] *v.* **1** gore, jab, penetrate, pierce, puncture, spear, stab, thrust, transfix. **2** affix, attach, bind, fasten, fix, fuse, glue, join, paste, pin. **3** adhere, cement, cling, hold, weld. **4** deposit, drop, install, lay, place, position, put, set. **5** clog, jam.
stick at continue, hang on in, keep at, persevere in, persist, plug away at.
antonym give up.
stick out extend, jut out, project, protrude.
stick to adhere to, cleave to, honour, keep to, persevere in, stand by.
antonyms give up, quit.
stick up for champion, defend, speak up for, stand up for, support, uphold.
antonym attack.
stick[2] *n.* **1** baton, birch, branch, cane, pole, rod, sceptre, staff, stake, twig, wand. **2** abuse, blame, criticism, flak, hostility, punishment, reproof.
antonym **2** praise.
stickler *n.* fanatic, fusspot, maniac, pedant, perfectionist, purist.

sticky *adj.* **1** adhesive, gluey, glutinous, gummy, tacky, viscous. **2** awkward, delicate, difficult, embarrassing, thorny, tricky, unpleasant. **3** clammy, close, humid, muggy, oppressive, sultry, sweltering.
antonyms **1** dry. **2** easy. **3** cool, fresh.

stiff *adj.* **1** firm, hard, hardened, inflexible, rigid, solid, solidified, taut, tense, tight, unbending, unyielding. **2** austere, ceremonious, cold, formal, pitiless, pompous, priggish, prim, severe, stand-offish, strict, unrelaxed. **3** arduous, awkward, difficult, exacting, laborious, rigorous.
antonyms **1** flexible. **2** informal. **3** easy.

stiffen *v.* brace, coagulate, congeal, crystallise, harden, jell, reinforce, set, solidify, starch, tense, thicken.

stifle *v.* asphyxiate, check, choke, curb, dampen, extinguish, hush, muffle, prevent, quell, repress, restrain, silence, smother, stop, strangle, suffocate, suppress.
antonym encourage.

stigma *n.* blemish, blot, brand, disgrace, dishonour, mark, reproach, shame, smirch, spot, stain.
antonyms credit, honour.

stigmatise *v.* brand, condemn, denounce, discredit, label, mark.
antonym praise.

still *adj.* calm, hushed, lifeless, motionless, noiseless, peaceful, placid, quiet, restful, serene, silent, smooth, stagnant, stationary, stilly, tranquil, undisturbed, unruffled.
antonyms agitated, busy, disturbed, noisy.
v. allay, alleviate, calm, hold back, hush, pacify, quiet, quieten, restrain, settle, silence, smooth, soothe, subdue, tranquillise.
antonyms agitate, stir up.
n. hush, peace, peacefulness, quiet, silence, tranquillity.
antonyms agitation, disturbance, noise.
adv. but, even so, even then, however, nevertheless, nonetheless, notwithstanding, yet.

stilted *adj.* artificial, constrained, forced, grandiloquent, high-flown, high-sounding, pedantic, pompous, pretentious, stiff, unnatural, wooden.
antonyms flowing, fluent.

stimulate *v.* animate, arouse, encourage, fire, goad, impel, incite, inflame, inspire, instigate, prompt, provoke, quicken, rouse, spur, trigger off, urge.
antonyms discourage, hinder, prevent.

sting *v.* **1** bite, burn, injure, pain, prick, smart, tingle, wound. **2** anger, gall, hurt, incense, infuriate, nettle, provoke, rile. **3** cheat, con, defraud, do, fleece, overcharge, rip off, swindle.
antonym **2** soothe.
n. bite, nip, prick, pungency, smarting, tingle.

stingy *adj.* covetous, mean, measly, mingy, miserly, niggardly, parsimonious, penny-pinching, scrimping, tightfisted.
antonyms generous, liberal.

stink *v.* pong, reek, smell, whiff.
n. **1** niff, odour, stench, whiff. **2** commotion, disturbance, fuss, hubbub, row, scandal, stir, to-do, uproar, upset.

stint *n.* assignment, bit, period, quota, share, shift, spell, stretch, term, time, trick, turn.

stipulate *v.* agree, contract, covenant, engage, guarantee, insist upon, lay down, pledge, postulate, promise, provide, require, settle, specify.
antonym imply.

stir *v.* affect, agitate, beat, budge, disturb, excite, fire, flutter, hasten, inspire, look lively, mix, move, quiver, rustle, shake, thrill, touch, tremble.
antonyms bore, calm, stay.
n. activity, ado, agitation, bustle, commotion, disorder, disturbance, excitement, ferment, flurry, fuss, hustle and bustle, movement, to-do, tumult, uproar.
antonym calm.
stir up animate, arouse, awaken, excite, incite, inflame, instigate, kindle, mix, prompt, provoke, quicken, raise, spur, stimulate, urge.
antonyms calm, discourage.

stock *n.* **1** assets, assortment, cache, capital, commodities, equipment, fund, funds, goods, hoard, inventory, investment, merchandise, range, repertoire, reserve, reservoir, source, stockpile, store, supply, variety, wares. **2** ancestry, breed, descent, extraction, family, forebears, house, kindred, line, lineage, parentage, pedigree, race, species, type. **3** cattle, flocks, herds, horses, livestock, sheep.
adj. banal, basic, conventional, customary, formal, hackneyed, ordinary, overused, regular, routine, run-of-the-mill, set, standard, stereotyped, traditional, trite, usual, worn-out.
antonyms original, unusual.
v. deal in, handle, keep, sell, supply, trade in.
stock up accumulate, amass, equip, fill, furnish, gather, hoard, lay in, pile up, provision, replenish, save, store (up), supply.

stocky *adj.* chunky, dumpy, short, solid, stubby, stumpy, sturdy, thickset.
antonyms skinny, tall.

stoical *adj.* calm, cool, dispassionate, impassive, indifferent, long-suffering, patient, resigned, stolid.
antonyms anxious, depressed, furious.

stoicism *n.* acceptance, calmness, fatalism, forbearance, fortitude, impassivity, imperturbability, indifference, long-suffering, patience, resignation.
antonyms anxiety, depression, fury.

stolid *adj.* beefy, blockish, dull, heavy, impassive, lumpish, phlegmatic, slow, stoic(al), stupid, unemotional, wooden.
antonyms interested, lively.

stomach *n.* abdomen, appetite, belly, desire, gut, inclination, inside(s), paunch, pot, potbelly, relish, taste, tummy.
v. abide, bear, endure, submit to, suffer, swallow, take, tolerate.

stony *adj.* adamant, blank, callous, expressionless, frigid, hard, heartless, hostile, icy, indifferent, inexorable, merciless, pitiless,

unfeeling, unresponsive.
antonyms forgiving, friendly, soft-hearted.

stoop *v.* bend, bow, couch, crouch, descend, duck, hunch, incline, kneel, lean, squat.
n. droop, inclination, round-shoulderedness, sag, slouch, slump.
stoop to condescend, deign, descend, go so far as, go so low as, lower oneself, resort, sink, vouchsafe.

stop *v.* **1** cease, conclude, desist, discontinue, end, finish, halt, interrupt, pack in, pack up, pause, quit, refrain, stall, terminate. **2** arrest, bar, check, frustrate, hinder, impede, intercept, obstruct, prevent, restrain. **3** block, close, plug, seal, staunch, stem. **4** lodge, remain, rest, sojourn, stay, visit, wait.
antonyms **1** advance, continue, start.
n. **1** depot, destination, station, terminus. **2** break, rest, sojourn, stage, stay, stop-over, visit. **3** cessation, conclusion, discontinuation, end, finish, halt, standstill, stoppage, termination.
antonyms **3** beginning, continuation, start.

stoppage *n.* abeyance, arrest, blockage, check, close, closure, curtailment, cut-off, deduction, desistance, halt, hindrance, interruption, lay-off, obstruction, shut-down, sit-in, standstill, stopping, strike, walk-out.
antonyms continuation, start.

stopper *n.* bung, cork, plug.

store *v.* accumulate, deposit, hoard, keep, lay by, lay up, put aside, reserve, salt away, save, stash, stock, stockpile, treasure.
antonym use.
n. abundance, accumulation, cache, cupboard, depository, fund, hoard, keeping, lot, market, mine, outlet, plenty, provision, quantity, repository, reserve, reservoir, shop, stock, stockpile, storehouse, storeroom, supermarket, supply, warehouse.
antonym scarcity.

storey *n.* deck, flight, floor, level, stage, tier.

storm *n.* **1** blizzard, cyclone, gale, gust, hurricane, roar, sandstorm, squall, tempest, tornado, whirlwind. **2** agitation, anger, assault, attack, commotion, disturbance, furore, outbreak, outburst, outcry, row, rumpus, stir, strife, tumult, turmoil, violence.
antonym **2** calm.
v. assail, assault, charge, complain, fly, fume, rage, rant, rave, rush, scold, stalk, stomp, thunder.

stormy *adj.* blustery, choppy, dirty, foul, gusty, raging, rough, squally, tempestuous, turbulent, wild, windy.
antonyms calm, gentle, peaceful.

story *n.* account, ancedote, article, chronicle, episode, fable, fairy-tale, falsehood, feature, fiction, history, legend, lie, myth, narrative, novel, plot, recital, record, relation, report, romance, tale, version.

storyteller *n.* author, bard, chronicler, narrator, novelist, romancer.

stout *adj.* athletic, beefy, big, bold, brave, brawny, bulky, burly, corpulent, courageous, dauntless, enduring, fat, fearless, fleshy, gallant, hardy, heavy, hulking, intrepid, lion-hearted, lusty, manly, muscular, overweight, plucky, plump, portly, resolute, robust, stalwart, strong, sturdy, substantial, thick, tough, valiant, vigorous.
antonyms cowardly, lean, slim, timid, weak.

stow *v.* bundle, cram, deposit, dump, load, pack, stash, store, stuff, tuck.
antonym unload.

straight *adj.* **1** aligned, direct, even, horizontal, level, right, true, undeviating, unswerving. **2** neat, orderly, organised, shipshape, tidy. **3** fair, honest, honourable, just, law-abiding, reliable, respectable, straightforward, trustworthy, upright. **4** blunt, candid, direct, forthright, frank, plain. **5** neat, unadulterated, undiluted, unmixed.
antonyms **1** bent, crooked. **2** untidy. **3** dishonest. **4** evasive. **5** diluted.
adv. candidly, directly, frankly, honestly, outspokenly, point-blank, upright.

straightaway *adv.* at once, directly, immediately, instantly, now, right away, there and then, this minute.
antonyms eventually, later.

straighten *v.* arrange, neaten, order.
antonyms bend, twist.
straighten out clear up, correct, disentangle, rectify, regularise, resolve, settle, sort out, work out.
antonyms confuse, muddle.

straightforward *adj.* **1** clear-cut, easy, elementary, simple, uncomplicated. **2** candid, direct, forthright, genuine, guileless, honest, open, sincere, truthful.
antonyms **1** complicated. **2** devious, evasive.

strain[1] *v.* compress, drive, embrace, endeavour, exert, express, extend, filter, injure, labour, overtax, overwork, pull, purify, restrain, screen, seep, separate, sieve, sift, sprain, squeeze, stretch, strive, struggle, tauten, tax, tear, tighten, tire, twist, weaken, wrench, wrest.
n. anxiety, burden, exertion, force, height, injury, pitch, pressure, pull, sprain, stress, struggle, tautness, tension, wrench.
antonym relaxation.

strain[2] *n.* **1** ancestry, blood, descent, extraction, family, lineage, pedigree, race, stem, stock. **2** streak, suggestion, suspicion, tendency, tone, trace, trait, vein.

strained *adj.* artificial, awkward, constrained, difficult, embarrassed, false, forced, laboured, self-conscious, stiff, tense, uncomfortable, uneasy, unnatural, unrelaxed.
antonyms natural, relaxed.

strains *n.* air, lay, measure, melody, song, theme, tune.

strait *n.* channel, narrows, sound.

straitened *adj.* difficult, distressed, embarrassed, limited, poor, reduced, restricted.
antonyms easy, well-off.

strait-laced *adj.* moralistic, narrow, narrow-minded, prim, proper, puritanical, strict, stuffy,

upright.
antonyms broad-minded, easy-going.
strand *n.* fibre, filament, length, lock, rope, string, thread, twist.
stranded *adj.* abandoned, aground, ashore, grounded, helpless, high and dry, homeless, in the lurch, marooned, shipwrecked, wrecked.
strange *adj.* **1** abnormal, bizarre, curious, eccentric, exceptional, extraordinary, funny, irregular, mystifying, odd, peculiar, perplexing, queer, remarkable, sinister, uncommon, unexplained, weird. **2** alien, exotic, foreign, new, novel, unacquainted, unfamiliar, unheard of, unknown, untried.
antonyms **1** common, ordinary. **2** familiar, well-known.
stranger *n.* alien, foreigner, guest, newcomer, non-member, unknown, visitor.
antonyms local, native.
strangle *n.* asphyxiate, choke, gag, inhibit, repress, smother, stifle, suffocate, suppress, throttle.
strap *n.* belt, leash, thong, tie.
v. beat, belt, bind, buckle, fasten, flog, lash, scourge, secure, tie, whip.
strapping *adj.* beefy, big, brawny, burly, hefty, hulking, husky, powerful, robust, stalwart, strong, sturdy, well-built.
antonym puny.
stratagem *n.* artifice, device, dodge, intrigue, manoeuvre, plan, plot, ploy, ruse, scheme, subterfuge, trick, wile.
strategic *adj.* calculated, critical, crucial, decisive, deliberate, diplomatic, important, key, planned, politic, tactical, vital.
antonym unimportant.
strategy *n.* design, manoeuvring, plan, planning, policy, procedure, programme, scheme, tactics, way.
stray *v.* deviate, digress, diverge, drift, err, get lost, meander, ramble, range, roam, rove, straggle, wander (off).
adj. **1** abandoned, homeless, lost, roaming, vagrant. **2** accidental, chance, erratic, freak, odd, random.
streak *n.* band, dash, element, freak, layer, line, smear, strip, stripe, stroke, touch, trace, vein.
v. **1** band, daub, fleck, slash, smear, stripe. **2** dart, flash, fly, gallop, hurtle, speed, sprint, sweep, tear, whistle, whizz, zoom.
stream *n.* beck, brook, creek, current, drift, flow, gill, gush, river, rivulet, run, tributary.
v. cascade, course, emit, flood, flow, glide, gush, issue, pour, run, shed, spill, spout, surge, well out.
streamer *n.* banner, ensign, flag, pennant, pennon, ribbon, standard.
streamlined *adj.* efficient, graceful, modernised, organised, rationalised, sleek, slick, smooth, smooth-running, superior, time-saving, up-to-the-minute, well-run.
antonyms clumsy, inefficient, old-fashioned.
strength *n.* brawn, cogency, concentration, courage, effectiveness, energy, firmness, force, fortitude, health, intensity, lustiness, might, muscle, potency, power, resolution, robustness, security, sinew, spirit, stamina, sturdiness, toughness, vehemence, vigour, virtue.
antonyms feebleness, timidness, weakness.
strengthen *v.* bolster, brace, buttress, confirm, consolidate, corroborate, edify, encourage, enhance, establish, fortify, harden, hearten, heighten, increase, intensify, invigorate, justify, nerve, nourish, reinforce, restore, steel, stiffen, substantiate, support, toughen.
antonyms undermine, weaken.
strenuous *adj.* active, arduous, bold, demanding, determined, eager, earnest, energetic, exhausting, hard, laborious, resolute, spirited, strong, taxing, tireless, tough, uphill, urgent, vigorous.
antonyms easy, effortless.
stress *n.* **1** anxiety, hassle, oppression, pressure, strain, tautness, tension, trauma, weight, worry. **2** accent, accentuation, beat, burden, emphasis, force, importance, significance.
antonym **1** relaxation.
v. accentuate, emphasise, repeat, strain, underline, underscore.
antonym relax.
stretch *n.* area, distance, exaggeration, expanse, extension, extent, period, reach, run, space, spell, spread, stint, strain, sweep, term, time, tract.
v. cover, elongate, expand, extend, inflate, lengthen, pull, rack, reach, spread, strain, swell, tauten, tighten, unfold, unroll.
antonyms relax, squeeze.
stretch out extend, hold out, lie down, put out, reach, relax, stretch forth.
antonym draw back.
strict *adj.* **1** austere, firm, harsh, rigid, rigorous, severe, stern, stringent, unsparing. **2** absolute, accurate, close, complete, exact, faithful, meticulous, no-nonsense, particular, precise, religious, scrupulous, thoroughgoing, total, true, utter.
antonyms **1** easy-going, flexible, mild. **2** loose.
strident *adj.* clamorous, clashing, discordant, grating, harsh, jangling, jarring, loud, rasping, raucous, screeching, shrill, unmusical, vociferous.
antonyms quiet, sweet.
strife *n.* animosity, battle, bickering, combat, conflict, contention, controversy, discord, dissension, friction, quarrel, rivalry, row, struggle, warfare, wrangling.
antonym peace.
strike *n.* **1** mutiny, refusal, stoppage, walk-out, work-to-rule. **2** attack, hit, raid, thump, wallop.
v. **1** down tools, mutiny, protest, revolt, walk out, work to rule. **2** afflict, attack, beat, box, buffet, clobber, clout, collide with, hammer, hit, impel, knock, pound, slap, smack, sock, thump, wallop. **3** affect, impress, register, seem, touch. **4** discover, encounter, find, reach, stumble upon, turn up, uncover, unearth.
strike down afflict, assassinate, destroy, kill,

murder, ruin, slay, smite.
strike out cancel, cross out, delete, erase, remove, score out, strike off, strike through.
antonyms add, include.
striking *adj.* arresting, astonishing, conspicuous, dazzling, extraordinary, impressive, memorable, noticeable, outstanding, salient, stunning, wonderful.
antonym unimpressive.
string *n.* bunch, chain, cord, fibre, file, line, number, procession, queue, row, sequence, series, strand, succession, train, twine.
v. festoon, hang, link, loop, stretch, suspend, thread, tie up.
stringent *adj.* binding, demanding, exacting, inflexible, mild, rigid, rigorous, severe, strict, tight, tough.
antonyms flexible, lax.
strings *n.* catches, conditions, limitations, provisos, qualifications, requirements, restrictions, stipulations.
stringy *adj.* chewy, fibrous, gristly, ropy, sinewy, tough, wiry.
antonym tender.
strip[1] *v.* bare, clear, denude, deprive, disadorn, disrobe, divest, empty, expose, gut, husk, lay bare, peel, pillage, plunder, ransack, rob, sack, skin, spoil, unclothe, uncover, undress.
antonyms cover, provide.
strip[2] *n.* band, belt, bit, piece, ribbon, sash, shred, slat, slip, strap, thong.
stripe *n.* band, bar, belt, chevron, flash, fleck.
strive *v.* attempt, compete, contend, endeavour, fight, labour, push oneself, strain, struggle, toil, try, work.
stroke *n.* **1** blow, caress, pat, rub. **2** apoplexy, attack, collapse, fit, seizure, shock. **3** flourish, move, movement, sweep.
v. caress, clap, fondle, pat, pet, rub.
stroll *v.* amble, dawdle, promenade, ramble, saunter, wander.
n. constitutional, dawdle, excursion, promenade, ramble, saunter, turn, walk.
strong *adj.* **1** aggressive, athletic, beefy, bold, brawny, burly, durable, firm, hard-wearing, hardy, healthy, heavy-duty, muscular, potent, powerful, resilient, resolute, robust, sinewy, sound, stalwart, stout, strapping, sturdy, substantial, tough, well-built. **2** capable, competent, concentrated, considerable, dedicated, deep, determined, eager, fervent, fierce, intense, keen, self-assertive, staunch, vehement, violent, vivid, zealous. **3** highly-flavoured, highly-seasoned, hot, piquant, pungent, sharp, spicy, undiluted. **4** cogent, compelling, convincing, effective, extreme, forceful, persuasive, severe, trenchant, urgent, weighty.
antonyms **1** feeble, frail, weak. **2** indecisive, weak. **3** bland, mild. **4** questionable, unconvincing.
stronghold *n.* bastion, bulwark, castle, centre, citadel, fort, fortress, keep, refuge.
strong-minded *adj.* determined, firm, independent, iron-willed, resolute, steadfast, strong-willed, tenacious, unbending, uncompromising, unwavering.
antonym weak-willed.
structural *adj.* configurational, constructional, design, formational, organisational.
structure *n.* arrangement, building, configuration, conformation, construction, contexture, design, edifice, erection, fabric, form, formation, make-up, organisation, set-up.
v. arrange, assemble, build, construct, design, form, organise, shape.
struggle *v.* agonise, battle, compete, contend, fight, grapple, labour, scuffle, strain, strive, toil, work, wrestle.
antonyms give in, rest, yield.
n. agony, battle, clash, combat, conflict, contest, effort, encounter, exertion, grind, hostilities, labour, pains, scramble, skirmish, strife, toil, tussle, work.
antonyms co-operation, ease, submission.
stub *n.* butt, counterfoil, dog-end, end, fag-end, remnant, snub, stump, tail, tail-end.
stubborn *adj.* difficult, dogged, fixed, headstrong, inflexible, intransigent, mulish, obstinate, persistent, pig-headed, refractory, rigid, self-willed, stiff, stiff-necked, tenacious, unbending, unmanageable, unyielding, wilful.
antonyms compliant, flexible, yielding.
stubby *adj.* bristling, bristly, chunky, dumpy, knobbly, knubbly, nubbly, prickly, rough, short, squat, stocky, stubbly, stumpy, thickset.
antonyms long, tall, thin.
stuck *adj.* **1** cemented, fast, fastened, firm, fixed, glued, joined. **2** baffled, nonplussed, stumped.
antonym **1** loose.
stuck on crazy about, enthusiastic about, infatuated with, keen on, mad on, obsessed with, wild about.
antonym indifferent to.
stuck-up *adj.* arrogant, big-headed, conceited, condescending, exclusive, haughty, high and mighty, proud, snobbish, snooty, toffee-nosed, uppity.
antonyms humble, modest.
student *n.* apprentice, disciple, fresher, freshman, learner, observer, pupil, scholar, sophomore, undergraduate.
studied *adj.* calculated, conscious, deliberate, forced, intentional, over-elaborate, planned, premeditated, purposeful, unnatural, wilful.
antonyms impulsive, natural, unplanned.
studio *n.* school, workroom, workshop.
studious *adj.* academic, assiduous, attentive, bookish, careful, diligent, eager, earnest, hard-working, industrious, intellectual, reflective, scholarly, serious, thoughtful.
antonyms idle, lazy, negligent.
study *v.* analyse, consider, contemplate, deliberate, dig, examine, investigate, learn, meditate, mug up, peruse, ponder, pore over, read, read up, research, revise, scan, scrutinise, survey, swot.
n. analysis, application, attention, consideration, contemplation, cramming, critique,

enquiry, examination, inclination, inspection, interest, investigation, learning, lessons, memoir, monograph, reading, report, research, review, scrutiny, survey, swotting, thesis, thought, zeal.

stuff *v.* compress, cram, crowd, fill, force, gobble, gorge, gormandise, guzzle, jam, load, overindulge, pack, pad, push, ram, sate, satiate, shove, squeeze, stow, wedge.
antonyms nibble, unload.
n. **1** essence, material, matter, pith, substance. **2** belongings, clobber, equipment, furniture, gear, goods, junk, kit, luggage, materials, objects, paraphernalia, possessions, tackle, things.

stuffing *n.* filler, filling, force-meat, packing, padding, quilting, wadding.

stuffy *adj.* **1** conventional, deadly, dreary, dull, old-fashioned, pompous, staid, stodgy, uninteresting. **2** airless, close, heavy, muggy, musty, oppressive, stale, stifling, suffocating, sultry, unventilated.
antonyms **1** informal, interesting, modern. **2** airy, well-ventilated.

stumble *v.* blunder, fall, falter, flounder, hesitate, lurch, reel, slip, stagger, stammer, stutter, trip.
stumble on blunder upon, chance upon, come across, discover, encounter, find, happen upon, light upon.

stumbling-block *n.* bar, barrier, crux, difficulty, hindrance, hurdle, impediment, obstacle, obstruction, snag.
antonyms boost, encouragement.

stump *v.* baffle, bamboozle, bewilder, confound, confuse, defeat, dumbfound, flummox, foil, lumber, mystify, outwit, perplex, plod, puzzle, stomp, stop.
antonym assist.
stump up contribute, cough up, donate, fork out, hand over, pay, shell out.
antonym receive.

stumpy *adj.* chunky, dumpy, dwarf, heavy, short, squat, stocky, stubby, thick, thickset.
antonyms long, tall, thin.

stun *v.* amaze, astonish, astound, bewilder, confound, confuse, daze, deafen, dumbfound, flabbergast, overcome, overpower, shock, stagger, stupefy.

stunning *adj.* amazing, beautiful, brilliant, dazzling, devastating, gorgeous, great, heavenly, impressive, lovely, marvellous, ravishing, remarkable, sensational, smashing, spectacular, striking, wonderful.
antonyms ghastly, poor, ugly.

stunt[1] *n.* act, campaign, deed, enterprise, exploit, feat, feature, performance, tour de force, trick, turn.

stunt[2] *v.* arrest, check, dwarf, hamper, hinder, impede, restrict, slow, stop.
antonyms encourage, promote.

stupefy *v.* amaze, astound, baffle, bewilder, confound, daze, dumbfound, numb, shock, stagger, stun.

stupendous *adj.* amazing, astounding, breathtaking, colossal, enormous, fabulous, fantastic, gigantic, huge, marvellous, overwhelming, phenomenal, prodigious, staggering, stunning, superb, tremendous, vast, wonderful.
antonyms ordinary, unimpressive, unsurprising.

stupid *adj.* **1** brainless, dim, dopey, dull, dumb, foolish, half-witted, idiotic, ill-advised, imbecilic, inane, indiscreet, irrelevant, irresponsible, laughable, ludicrous, meaningless, mindless, moronic, naïve, nonsensical, pointless, puerile, senseless, short-sighted, simple-minded, slow, thick. **2** dazed, groggy, semiconscious, sluggish, stunned, stupefied.
antonyms **1** clever, intelligent, sensible, wise. **2** alert.

stupidity *n.* absurdity, brainlessness, crassness, denseness, dullness, feeble-mindedness, folly, foolhardiness, futility, idiocy, imbecility, irresponsibility, ludicrousness, lunacy, madness, pointlessness, rashness, senselessness, silliness, simplicity, slowness, thickness.
antonyms alertness, cleverness, intelligence.

stupor *n.* coma, daze, inertia, insensibility, lethargy, numbness, stupefaction, torpor, trance, unconsciousness, wonder.
antonyms alertness, consciousness.

sturdy *adj.* athletic, determined, durable, firm, flourishing, hardy, hearty, muscular, powerful, resolute, robust, secure, solid, stalwart, staunch, steadfast, stout, strong, substantial, vigorous, well-built, well-made.
antonyms decrepit, flimsy, puny, weak.

stutter *v.* falter, hesitate, mumble, stammer, stumble.

style *n.* **1** appearance, approach, category, custom, cut, design, expression, fashion, form, genre, kind, manner, method, mode, pattern, phrasing, sort, technique, tenor, tone, treatment, type, variety, way, wording. **2** affluence, chic, comfort, dressiness, ease, elegance, fashion, fashionableness, flair, flamboyance, grace, grandeur, luxury, mode, panache, polish, refinement, smartness, sophistication, spirit, stylishness, taste, trend, urbanity, vogue.
antonyms **2** inelegance, tastelessness.
v. adapt, address, arrange, call, christen, create, cut, design, designate, dress, dub, entitle, fashion, label, name, shape, tailor, term, title.

stylish *adj.* á la mode, chic, classy, dressy, fashionable, in vogue, modish, natty, polished, smart, snappy, snazzy, trendy, urbane, voguish.
antonyms old-fashioned, shabby, unstylish.

suave *adj.* affable, agreeable, bland, charming, civilised, courteous, diplomatic, obliging, pleasing, polite, smooth, soft-spoken, sophisticated, unctuous, urbane, worldly.
antonyms rude, unsophisticated.

subconscious *adj.* hidden, inner, innermost, intuitive, latent, repressed, subliminal, suppressed, unconscious.
antonym conscious.
n. id, super-ego, unconscious.

subdue *v.* allay, break, check, conquer, control, crush, damp, dampen, defeat, discipline,

humble, master, mellow, moderate, overcome, overpower, overrun, quell, quieten, reduce, repress, soften, subject, suppress, tame, trample, vanquish.
antonyms arouse, awaken.

subdued *adj.* **1** crestfallen, dejected, downcast, repentant, sad. **2** dim, grave, hushed, low-key, muted, quiet, restrained, serious, shaded, sober, soft, solemn, sombre, subtle, unobtrusive.
antonyms **1** lively. **2** aroused.

subject *n.* **1** affair, business, case, ground, issue, matter, object, point, question, substance, theme, topic. **2** citizen, client, dependant, national, participant, patient, subordinate, victim.
antonyms **2** boss, lord, master.
adj. **1** conditional, contingent, dependent, disposed, liable, open, prone, susceptible, vulnerable. **2** answerable, bound, captive, inferior, obedient, subjugated, submissive, subordinate, subservient.
antonyms **1** insusceptible. **2** free, superior.
v. expose, lay open, subdue, submit, subordinate, treat.

subjection *n.* bondage, captivity, chains, crushing, defeat, domination, enslavement, mastery, oppression, quelling, shackles, slavery, subduing, subjugation.

subjective biased, emotional, idiosyncratic, individual, instinctive, introspective, intuitive, personal, prejudiced.
antonyms impartial, objective, unbiased.

sublime *adj.* elevated, eminent, exalted, glorious, grand, great, high, imposing, lofty, magnificent, majestic, noble, transcendent.
antonyms lowly, ordinary, trivial.

submerge *v.* deluge, dip, drown, duck, engulf, flood, immerse, inundate, overflow, overwhelm, plunge, sink, submerse, swamp.
antonym surface.

submerged *adj.* concealed, drowned, hidden, immersed, inundated, obscured, submarine, submersed, sunk, sunken, swamped, undersea, underwater, unseen.

submission *n.* **1** acquiescence, assent, capitulation, compliance, deference, meekness, obedience, passivity, resignation, surrender, yielding. **2** entry, presentation, proposal, suggestion, tendering.
antonyms **1** intractability, intransigence.

submissive *adj.* accommodating, deferential, docile, dutiful, humble, ingratiating, meek, obedient, passive, patient, resigned, subdued, subservient, uncomplaining, unresisting, yielding.
antonyms intractable, intransigent.

submit *v.* **1** agree, bend, bow, capitulate, comply, give in, knuckle under, stoop, succumb, surrender, yield. **2** argue, claim, present, propose, refer, state, suggest, table, tender.
antonyms **1** fight, struggle. **2** withdraw.

subordinate *adj.* ancillary, auxiliary, dependent, inferior, junior, lesser, lower, minor, secondary, subject, subsidiary, supplementary.
antonym superior.
n. aide, assistant, attendant, dependant, inferior, junior, second, underling.
antonyms boss, superior.

subscribe *v.* **1** advocate, agree, approve, endorse, support. **2** contribute, donate, give, receive regularly.

subscription *n.* contribution, donation, dues, fee, gift, offering, payment.

subsequent *adj.* after, consequent, consequential, ensuing, following, later, resulting, succeeding.
antonyms earlier, previous.

subside *v.* abate, collapse, decline, decrease, descend, die down, diminish, drop, dwindle, ease, ebb, fall, lessen, lower, moderate, quieten, recede, settle, sink, slacken, wane.
antonyms grow, increase.

subsidence *n.* abatement, decline, decrease, de-escalation, descent, diminution, ebb, lessening, settlement, sinking, slackening.
antonyms growth, increase.

subsidiary *adj.* ancillary, assistant, auxiliary, branch, contributory, co-operative, helpful, lesser, minor, secondary, subordinate, subservient, supplementary, useful.
antonyms chief, major, primary.
n. affiliate, branch, division, offshoot, part, section.

subsidise *v.* aid, back, finance, fund, promote, sponsor, support, underwrite.

subsidy *n.* aid, allowance, assistance, backing, contribution, finance, grant, help, sponsorship, support.

subsist *v.* continue, endure, exist, hold out, inhere, last, live, remain, survive.

subsistence *n.* existence, food, keep, livelihood, living, maintenance, nourishment, provision, rations, support, survival, sustenance, upkeep.

substance *n.* **1** actuality, body, burden, concreteness, element, entity, essence, fabric, force, foundation, gist, ground, material, matter, meaning, pith, reality, significance, solidity, stuff, subject, subject-matter, texture, theme. **2** affluence, assets, means, property, resources, wealth.

substandard *adj.* damaged, imperfect, inadequate, inferior, poor, second-rate, shoddy, tawdry, unacceptable.
antonyms first-rate, perfect, superior.

substantial *adj.* actual, ample, big, bulky, considerable, durable, enduring, firm, full-bodied, generous, hefty, important, large, massive, positive, significant, sizable, sound, stout, strong, sturdy, well-built, worthwhile.
antonyms insignificant, small, weak.

substantially *adv.* considerably, essentially, generally, largely, significantly, to all intents and purposes.
antonym slightly.

substantiate *v.* authenticate, confirm, corroborate, establish, prove, support, validate, verify.
antonyms disprove, refute.

substitute *v.* change, exchange, interchange, replace, swap, switch.
n. agent, alternate, deputy, equivalent, locum, makeshift, proxy, relief, replacement, reserve, stand-by, stop-gap, sub, supply, surrogate, temp.
adj. acting, additional, alternative, proxy, replacement, reserve, second, surrogate, temporary.

substitution *n.* change, exchange, interchange, replacement, swapping, switching.

subterfuge *n.* artifice, deception, deviousness, dodge, duplicity, evasion, excuse, machination, manoeuvre, ploy, pretence, quibble, ruse, scheme, stratagem, trick.
antonyms honesty, openness.

subtle *adj.* **1** delicate, faint, fine-drawn, implied, indirect, nice, profound, slight, tenuous. **2** astute, crafty, devious, scheming, shrewd, sly, sophisticated.
antonyms **1** blatant, obvious. **2** crude, direct, open, unsophisticated.

subtlety *n.* **1** cleverness, intricacy, nicety, refinement. **2** artfulness, astuteness, craftiness, cunning, delicacy, deviousness, discernment, discrimination, finesse, guile, sensitivity, slyness, sophistication, understatement.

subtract *v.* debit, deduct, detract, diminish, remove, withdraw.
antonyms add, add to.

subversive *adj.* destructive, disruptive, incendiary, inflammatory, overthrowing, perversive, riotous, seditious, treasonous, underground, undermining.
antonyms faithful, loyal.
n. dissident, fifth columnist, freedom fighter, quisling, saboteur, seditionist, terrorist, traitor.

succeed *v.* **1** flourish, get on, make good, make it, manage, prosper, thrive, triumph, work. **2** ensue, follow, result.
antonyms **1** fail, flop. **2** go before, precede.
succeed to accede, come into, enter upon, inherit, replace, supersede, take over.
antonyms abdicate, precede.

succeeding *adj.* coming, ensuing, following, later, next, subsequent, successive, to come.
antonyms earlier, previous.

success *n.* bestseller, celebrity, eminence, fame, fortune, happiness, hit, luck, prosperity, sensation, somebody, star, triumph, VIP, winner.
antonyms disaster, failure.

successful *adj.* acknowledged, bestselling, booming, favourable, flourishing, fortunate, fruitful, lucky, lucrative, moneymaking, paying, profitable, prosperous, rewarding, satisfactory, satisfying, thriving, top, unbeaten, victorious, wealthy, well-doing.
antonyms fruitless, unprofitable, unsuccessful, worthless.

succession *n.* accession, chain, continuation, course, cycle, flow, line, order, procession, progression, race, run, sequence, series, string, train.

successive *adj.* consecutive, following, in succession, succeeding.

succinct *adj.* brief, compact, concise, condensed, pithy, short, summary, terse.
antonyms lengthy, verbose, wordy.

succulent *adj.* fleshy, juicy, luscious, lush, mellow, moist, mouthwatering, rich.
antonym dry.

succumb *v.* capitulate, collapse, deteriorate, die, fall, give in, knuckle under, submit, surrender, yield.
antonyms master, overcome.

suck *v.* absorb, drain, draw in, extract, imbibe.

sudden *adj.* abrupt, hasty, hurried, impulsive, prompt, quick, rapid, rash, snap, startling, swift, unexpected, unforeseen, unusual.
antonyms expected, gradual, slow.

sue *v.* apply, charge, indict, prosecute, solicit, summon.

suffer *v.* ache, agonise, allow, bear, deteriorate, endure, experience, feel, go through, grieve, hurt, let, permit, sorrow, support, sustain, tolerate, undergo.

suffering *n.* ache, affliction, agony, anguish, discomfort, distress, hardship, misery, ordeal, pain, pangs, torment, torture.

sufficient *adj.* adequate, effective, enough, satisfactory, well-off.
antonyms inadequate, insufficient, poor.

suffocate *v.* asphyxiate, choke, smother, stifle, strangle, throttle.

suggest *v.* **1** advise, advocate, propose, recommend. **2** evoke, hint, imply, indicate, insinuate, intimate.

suggestion *n.* **1** motion, plan, proposal, proposition, recommendation. **2** hint, indication, innuendo, insinuation, intimation, suspicion, trace, whisper.

suggestive *adj.* **1** evocative, expressive, indicative, insinuating, meaning, reminiscent. **2** bawdy, immodest, improper, indecent, indelicate, off-colour, provocative, risqué, rude, smutty.
antonyms **1** inexpressive. **2** clean, decent.

suicide *n.* hara-kiri, self-destruction, self-immolation, self-murder, self-slaughter.

suit *v.* accommodate, adapt, adjust, agree, answer, become, befit, correspond, do, fashion, fit, gratify, harmonise, match, modify, please, proportion, satisfy, tailor, tally.
antonyms clash, displease.
n. **1** clothing, costume, dress, get-up, outfit. **2** action, appeal, case, cause, entreaty, lawsuit, proceeding, prosecution, trial.

suitable *adj.* acceptable, adequate, applicable, apposite, appropriate, apt, becoming, befitting, convenient, correspondent, due, fit, fitting, opportune, proper, relevant, right, satisfactory, seemly, suited.
antonyms inappropriate, unsuitable.

suitably *adv.* acceptably, accordingly, appropriately, fittingly, properly.
antonyms inappropriately, unsuitably.

sulk *v.* brood, grouch, grump, mope, pout.

sulky *adj.* aloof, bad-tempered, churlish, cross,

disgruntled, moody, morose, put out, resentful, sullen, surly.
antonyms cheerful, good-tempered.
sully *v.* besmirch, blemish, contaminate, darken, defile, dirty, disgrace, dishonour, mar, pollute, spoil, spot, stain, taint, tarnish.
antonyms cleanse, honour.
sultry *adj.* close, hot, humid, muggy, oppressive, sticky, stifling, stuffy, sweltering.
antonyms cold, cool.
sum *n.* aggregate, amount, culmination, entirety, height, quantity, reckoning, result, score, sum total, summary, tally, total, whole.
sum up close, conclude, recapitulate, review, summarise.
summarise *v.* abbreviate, abridge, condense, encapsulate, outline, précis, review, shorten, sum up.
antonym expand (on).
summary *n.* abridgement, abstract, compendium, digest, essence, extract, outline, précis, recapitulation, résumé, review, rundown, summing-up, synopsis.
adj. arbitrary, brief, cursory, direct, hasty, prompt, short, succinct, unceremonious.
antonyms careful, lengthy.
summit *n.* acme, apex, crown, culmination, head, height, peak, pinnacle, point, top, zenith.
antonyms bottom, foot, nadir.
summon *v.* arouse, assemble, beckon, bid, call, cite, convene, gather, invite, invoke, mobilise, muster, rally, rouse, send for.
antonym dismiss.
sumptuous *adj.* costly, dear, expensive, extravagant, gorgeous, grand, lavish, luxurious, magnificent, opulent, plush, posh, princely, rich, splendid, superb.
antonyms mean, plain, poor.
sun *n.* daystar, star, sunlight, sunshine.
v. bake, bask, brown, sunbathe, tan.
sunbathe *v.* bake, bask, brown, take the sun, tan.
sunburnt *adj.* blistered, bronzed, brown, burnt, peeling, red, tanned, weather-beaten.
antonyms colourless, pale.
sundry *adj.* a few, assorted, different, miscellaneous, separate, several, some, varied, various.
sunken *adj.* buried, concave, depressed, drawn, haggard, hollow, immersed, lower, recessed, submerged.
sunny *adj.* beaming, bright, brilliant, buoyant, cheerful, cheery, clear, cloudless, fine, happy, joyful, light-hearted, optimistic, pleasant, radiant, smiling, summery, sunlit, sunshiny.
antonyms dreary, dull, gloomy.
sunrise *n.* cock-crow, crack of dawn, dawn, daybreak, daylight, dayspring.
sunset *n.* dusk, evening, gloaming, nightfall, sundown, twilight.
super *adj.* excellent, fantastic, glorious, incomparable, magnificent, marvellous, matchless, outstanding, sensational, smashing, superb, superior, terrific, top-notch, wonderful.
antonyms awful, poor.
superb *adj.* admirable, breathtaking, choice, excellent, exquisite, fine, first-rate, gorgeous, grand, magnificent, marvellous, splendid, superior, unrivalled.
antonyms bad, poor.
superficial *adj.* apparent, casual, cosmetic, cursory, exterior, external, frivolous, hasty, hurried, lightweight, outward, passing, seeming, shallow, sketchy, skin-deep, slight, surface, trivial.
antonyms complete, deep, detailed, thorough.
superfluous *adj.* excess, excessive, extra, needless, redundant, remaining, residuary, spare, supernumerary, surplus, uncalled-for, unnecessary.
antonyms necessary, needed, wanted.
superintend *v.* administer, control, direct, guide, inspect, manage, overlook, oversee, run, steer, supervise.
superintendent *n.* administrator, boss, chief, conductor, controller, director, governor, inspector, manager, overseer, supervisor.
superior *adj.* **1** admirable, better, choice, de luxe, distinguished, excellent, exceptional, exclusive, fine, first-class, first-rate, good, grander, greater, high-class, higher, par excellence, predominant, preferred, prevailing, respectable, top-flight, top-notch, unrivalled. **2** condescending, disdainful, haughty, lordly, patronising, pretentious, snobbish, snooty, supercilious.
antonyms **1** average, inferior. **2** humble, inferior.
n. boss, chief, director, foreman, manager, principal, senior, supervisor.
antonyms assistant, inferior, junior.
superiority *n.* advantage, ascendancy, edge, excellence, lead, predominance, pre-eminence, prevalence, supremacy.
antonym inferiority.
superlative *adj.* consummate, excellent, greatest, highest, magnificent, matchless, outstanding, supreme, surpassing, transcendent, unbeatable, unbeaten, unparalleled, unrivalled, unsurpassed.
antonyms average, inadequate, poor.
supernatural *adj.* abnormal, dark, ghostly, hidden, metaphysical, miraculous, mysterious, mystic, occult, paranormal, phantom, psychic, spiritual, unnatural.
antonym natural.
supersede *v.* displace, oust, overrule, remove, replace, succeed, supplant, supplement, suspend, usurp.
superstition *n.* delusion, fable, fallacy, illusion, myth, old wives' tale.
superstitious *adj.* delusive, fallacious, false, groundless, illusory, irrational.
antonyms logical, rational.
supervise *v.* administer, conduct, control, direct, handle, inspect, manage, oversee, preside over, run, superintend.
supervision *n.* administration, care, charge, control, direction, guidance, instruction, management, oversight, stewardship, superintendence, surveillance.

supervisor *n.* administrator, boss, chief, foreman, inspector, manager, overseer, steward, superintendent.
supplant *v.* displace, oust, overthrow, remove, replace, supersede, topple, unseat.
supple *adj.* bending, double-jointed, elastic, flexible, fluid, lithe, loose-limbed, plastic, pliable, pliant.
antonyms inflexible, rigid, stiff.
supplement *n.* addendum, addition, appendix, complement, extra, insert, postscript, pull-out, sequel, supplemental, supplementary, suppletion.
v. add, add to, augment, complement, eke out, extend, fill up, reinforce, supply, top up.
antonyms deplete, use up.
supplementary *adj.* accompanying, additional, auxiliary, complementary, extra, secondary.
antonym core.
supplication *n.* appeal, entreaty, invocation, petition, plea, pleading, prayer, request, solicitation.
supplier *n.* dealer, provider, retailer, seller, shop-keeper, vendor, wholesaler.
supplies *n.* equipment, food, foodstuffs, materials, necessities, provisions, rations, stores.
supply *v.* afford, contribute, endow, equip, fill, furnish, give, grant, minister, outfit, produce, provide, replenish, satisfy, stock, store, yield.
antonyms receive, take.
n. cache, fund, hoard, materials, necessities, provisions, quantity, rations, reserve, reservoir, service, source, stake, stock, stockpile, store, stores.
antonym lack.
support *v.* **1** advocate, aid, assist, back, champion, comfort, defend, finance, foster, fund, help, promote, rally round, second, subsidise, underwrite. **2** bear, bolster, brace, buttress, carry, hold up, prop, reinforce, strengthen, sustain. **3** cherish, keep, maintain, nourish. **4** authenticate, confirm, corroborate, document, endorse, substantiate, verify.
antonyms **1** fight, oppose. **3** live off. **4** contradict, deny.
n. **1** aid, allegiance, approval, assistance, backing, comfort, encouragement, friendship, help, loyalty, patronage, protection, relief, sponsorship. **2** brace, crutch, foundation, mainstay, pillar, post, prop, stay, underpinning.
antonyms **1** antagonism, hostility, opposition.
supporter *n.* adherent, advocate, ally, champion, co-worker, defender, fan, follower, friend, helper, patron, seconder, sponsor, upholder, well-wisher.
antonym opponent.
supportive *adj.* attentive, caring, comforting, encouraging, helpful, reassuring, sympathetic, understanding.
antonym discouraging.
suppose *v.* assume, believe, calculate, conceive, conclude, conjecture, consider, expect, fancy, guess, imagine, infer, judge, postulate, presume, pretend, surmise, think.
antonym know.
supposed *adj.* accepted, alleged, assumed, hypothetical, imagined, presumed, professed, reported, reputed, rumoured.
antonyms certain, known.
supposition *n.* assumption, conjecture, guess, hypothesis, idea, notion, opinion, presumption, speculation, theory.
antonym knowledge.
suppress *v.* censor, check, conceal, contain, crush, extinguish, inhibit, quash, quell, repress, restrain, silence, smother, snuff out, stamp out, stifle, stop, strangle, subdue, submerge, withhold.
antonyms encourage, incite.
supreme *adj.* brilliant, chief, consummate, crowning, culminating, extreme, final, first, foremost, greatest, head, highest, incomparable, leading, matchless, predominant, pre-eminent, prevailing, prime, principal, second-to-none, sovereign, superlative, surpassing, top, transcendent, ultimate, unsurpassed, world-beating.
antonyms lowly, poor, slight.
sure *adj.* accurate, assured, bound, certain, clear, confident, convinced, decided, definite, dependable, effective, fast, firm, fixed, guaranteed, honest, indisputable, inevitable, infallible, irrevocable, persuaded, positive, precise, reliable, safe, satisfied, secure, solid, stable, steadfast, steady, trustworthy, undeniable, unerring, unfailing, unmistakable, unswerving, unwavering.
antonyms doubtful, uncertain, unsure.
surely *adv.* assuredly, certainly, confidently, definitely, doubtlessly, firmly, inevitably, undoubtedly, unquestionably.
surety *n.* bail, bond, certainty, deposit, guarantee, guarantor, hostage, indemnity, insurance, mortgagor, pledge, safety, security, sponsor, warranty.
surface *n.* covering, exterior, façade, face, outside, plane, side, skin, top, veneer, working-surface, worktop.
antonyms inside, interior.
adj. apparent, exterior, external, outer, outside, outward, superficial.
antonyms inside, interior.
v. appear, come to light, emerge, materialise, rise, transpire.
antonyms disappear, sink, vanish.
surly *adj.* bad-tempered, brusque, churlish, crabbed, cross, crusty, grouchy, gruff, grum, morose, perverse, sulky, sullen, ungracious.
antonyms pleasant, polite.
surplus *n.* balance, excess, remainder, residue, superfluity, surfeit.
antonyms lack, shortage.
adj. excess, extra, odd, redundant, remaining, spare, superfluous, unused.
antonym essential.
surprise *v.* amaze, astonish, astound, bewilder, confuse, disconcert, dismay, flabbergast, nonplus, stagger, startle.
n. amazement, astonishment, bewilderment,

bombshell, dismay, incredulity, revelation, shock, start, wonder.
antonym composure.
surprised *adj.* amazed, astonished, confounded, disconcerted, nonplussed, open-mouthed, shocked, speechless, staggered, startled, thunderstruck.
antonyms composed, unsurprised.
surprising *adj.* amazing, astonishing, astounding, extraordinary, incredible, marvellous, remarkable, staggering, startling, stunning, unexpected, unusual, wonderful.
antonyms expected, unsurprising.
surrender *v.* abandon, capitulate, cede, concede, forego, give in, give up, quit, relinquish, renounce, resign, submit, waive, yield.
antonym fight on.
n. appeasement, capitulation, relinquishment, renunciation, resignation, submission, white flag, yielding.
surreptitious *adj.* behind-door, clandestine, covert, fraudulent, furtive, secret, sly, sneaking, stealthy, unauthorised, underhand, veiled.
antonyms obvious, open.
surrogate *n.* deputy, proxy, replacement, representative, stand-in, substitute.
surround *v.* besiege, compass, encase, encircle, enclose, encompass, envelop, girdle, hem in, ring.
surrounding *adj.* adjacent, adjoining, bordering, encircling, enclosing, nearby, neighbouring.
surroundings *n.* ambience, background, environment, environs, locale, milieu, neighbourhood, setting, vicinity.
survey *v.* assess, consider, contemplate, estimate, examine, inspect, measure, observe, plan, plot, reconnoitre, research, review, scan, scrutinise, study, supervise, surview, view.
n. appraisal, assessment, enquiry, examination, inspection, measurement, overview, review, sample, scrutiny, study.
survive *v.* endure, exist, last (out), live (through), outlast, outlive, ride, stay, subsist, weather, withstand.
antonyms die, succumb.
susceptibility *n.* openness, predisposition, proneness, propensity, responsiveness, sensibility, sensitivity, suggestibility, tendency, vulnerability, weakness.
antonyms impregnability, resistance.
susceptible *adj.* disposed, given, impressionable, inclined, liable, open, predisposed, prone, receptive, sensitive, subject, suggestible, tender, vulnerable.
antonyms immune, impregnable, resistant.
suspect *v.* believe, call in question, conclude, conjecture, consider, distrust, doubt, fancy, feel, guess, infer, mistrust, speculate, suppose, surmise.
adj. debatable, dodgy, doubtful, dubious, fishy, questionable, suspicious, unreliable.
antonyms acceptable, innocent, reliable, straightforward.
suspend *v.* **1** attach, dangle, hang, swing. **2** adjourn, cease, defer, delay, discontinue, hold off, postpone, shelve, withhold. **3** debar, dismiss, expel.
antonyms **2** continue. **3** reinstate, restore.
suspense *n.* anticipation, anxiety, apprehension, excitement, expectancy, expectation, indecision, insecurity, tension, uncertainty.
antonyms certainty, knowledge.
suspension *n.* abeyance, adjournment, break, deferral, delay, intermission, interruption, moratorium, postponement, remission, respite, standstill, stay.
antonyms continuation, reinstatement, restoration.
suspicion *n.* **1** apprehension, distrust, doubt, misgiving, mistrust, scepticism, wariness. **2** glimmer, hint, shade, shadow, soupçon, strain, suggestion, tinge, touch, trace. **3** hunch, idea, notion.
antonyms **1** confidence, trust.
suspicious *adj.* **1** apprehensive, chary, distrustful, doubtful, mistrustful, sceptical, suspecting, unbelieving, uneasy, wary. **2** dodgy, dubious, fishy, irregular, peculiar, questionable, shady, suspect.
antonyms **1** confident, trustful. **2** innocent, unexceptionable.
sustain *v.* aid, assist, bear, carry, comfort, continue, endorse, endure, experience, feel, foster, help, hold, keep, keep going, maintain, nourish, nurture, prolong, provide for, relieve, stay, suffer, support, survive, undergo, uphold, withstand.
sustained *adj.* constant, continuous, long-drawn-out, non-stop, perpetual, prolonged, protracted, steady, unremitting.
antonyms broken, intermittent, interrupted, occasional, spasmodic.
sustenance *n.* fare, food, livelihood, maintenance, nourishment, provisions, subsistence.
swagger *v.* bluster, boast, brag, cock, crow, parade, prance, strut, swank.
n. arrogance, bluster, ostentation, show, showing off.
antonyms diffidence, modesty, restraint.
swallow *v.* absorb, accept, assimilate, believe, buy, consume, devour, down, drink, eat, engulf, gulp, knock back, quaff, stifle, suppress, swill, wash down.
swallow up absorb, consume, deplete, drain, eat up, engulf, envelop, exhaust, gobble up, guzzle, overrun, overwhelm, use up.
swamp *n.* bog, fen, marsh, mire, moss, quagmire, slough.
v. beset, besiege, deluge, drench, engulf, flood, inundate, overload, overwhelm, saturate, sink, submerge, waterlog.
swap, swop *v.* bandy, barter, exchange, interchange, substitute, switch, trade, traffic, transpose.
swarm *n.* army, crowd, drove, flock, herd, horde, host, mass, mob, multitude, myriad, shoal, throng.
v. congregate, crowd, flock, flood, mass, stream,

throng.

swarm with abound, bristle, crawl, hotch, teem.

swarthy *adj.* black, brown, dark, dark-complexioned, dark-skinned, dusky.
antonyms fair, pale.

sway *v.* affect, bend, control, direct, divert, dominate, fluctuate, govern, guide, incline, induce, influence, lean, lurch, oscillate, overrule, persuade, rock, roll, swerve, swing, veer, wave.

swear *v.* **1** affirm, assert, asseverate, attest, avow, declare, insist, promise, testify, vow, warrant. **2** blaspheme, curse.

swear-word *n.* bad language, blasphemy, curse, expletive, foul language, four-letter word, imprecation, oath, obscenity, profanity.

sweat *n.* **1** perspiration. **2** agitation, anxiety, flap, panic, strain, worry. **3** chore, drudgery, effort, toil.
v. **1** exude, perspire. **2** agonise, fret, worry.

sweaty *adj.* clammy, damp, glowing, moist, perspiring, sticky, sweating.
antonyms cool, dry.

sweep *v.* brush, clean, clear, dust, fly, glance, glide, hurtle, pass, remove, sail, scud, skim, tear, whisk, zoom.
n. arc, bend, clearance, compass, curve, expanse, extent, gesture, impetus, move, movement, range, scope, span, stretch, stroke, swing, vista.

sweeping *adj.* across-the-board, all-embracing, all-inclusive, blanket, broad, comprehensive, extensive, far-reaching, global, oversimplified, radical, simplistic, thoroughgoing, wholesale, wide, wide-ranging.
antonyms narrow, qualified, specific.

sweet *adj.* **1** honeyed, luscious, saccharine, sugary, sweetened, syrupy, toothsome. **2** affectionate, agreeable, amiable, appealing, attractive, beautiful, beloved, charming, cherished, darling, dear, dearest, delightful, fair, gentle, kind, lovable, mild, pleasant, precious, tender, treasured, unselfish, winsome. **3** aromatic, balmy, clean, fragrant, fresh, perfumed, pure, sweet-smelling, wholesome. **4** dulcet, euphonic, euphonious, harmonious, mellow, melodious, musical, soft, tuneful.
antonyms **1** acid, bitter, salty, sour. **2** bitter, nasty, unpleasant. **3** malodorous. **4** cacophonous, discordant, harsh.
n. **1** afters, dessert, pudding, second course, sweet course. **2** bonbon, candy, confection, confectionery.

sweeten *v.* cushion, honey, improve, mellow, soften, soothe, sugar, sugar-coat, take the sting out of, temper.
antonyms aggravate, embitter.

sweetheart *n.* admirer, beloved, boyfriend, darling, dear, girlfriend, love, lover, steady, sweetie, valentine.

swell *v.* aggravate, augment, billow, bloat, bulb, bulge, dilate, distend, enhance, enlarge, expand, extend, fatten, grow, heighten, increase, intensify, louden, mount, puff up, rise, surge.
antonyms contract, decrease, die down, dwindle, shrink.
n. billow, bulge, enlargement, loudening, rise, surge, swelling, undulation, wave.
adj. de luxe, exclusive, fashionable, flashy, grand, great, posh, ritzy, smart, stylish, swanky.
antonyms awful, seedy, shabby.

swelling *n.* blister, bruise, bulge, bump, distension, enlargement, gathering, inflammation, lump, protuberance, puffiness, tuber, tumour.

sweltering *adj.* airless, baking, burning, hot, humid, oppressive, scorching, steamy, stifling, suffocating, sultry, sweating, tropical.
antonyms airy, breezy, chilly, cold, cool, fresh.

swerve *v.* bend, carve, deflect, deviate, diverge, incline, sheer, shift, stray, sway, swing, turn, veer, wander, wind.

swift *adj.* agile, express, fast, flying, hurried, limber, nimble, nimble-footed, nippy, prompt, quick, rapid, ready, short, speedy, sudden, winged.
antonyms slow, sluggish, unhurried.

swimsuit *n.* bathing-costume, bathing-suit, bikini, swimming costume, swimwear, trunks.

swindle *v.* bamboozle, cheat, con, deceive, defraud, diddle, do, dupe, fleece, overcharge, rip off, trick.
n. con, deceit, deception, double-dealing, fiddle, fraud, racket, rip-off, sharp practice, swizz, trickery.

swindler *n.* cheat, con man, fraud, impostor, rascal, rogue, shark, trickster.

swing *v.* brandish, dangle, fix, fluctuate, hang, hurl, oscillate, rock, suspend, sway, swerve, vary, veer, vibrate, wave, whirl.
n. fluctuation, motion, oscillation, rhythm, stroke, sway, swaying, sweep, sweeping, vibration, waving.

swingeing *adj.* devastating, drastic, excessive, extortionate, harsh, heavy, huge, oppressive, punishing, severe, stringent, thumping.
antonyms gradual, harmless, mild.

swipe *v.* **1** hit, lunge, slap, slosh, sock, strike, thwack, wallop, whack. **2** lift, pilfer, pinch, snaffle, steal.
n. blow, clout, slap, smack, swing, thwack, wallop, whack.

swirl *v.* agitate, boil, eddy, scud, spin, surge, swish, twirl, twist, wheel, whirl.

switch *v.* change, change direction, deflect, deviate, divert, exchange, interchange, rearrange, replace, shift, shunt, substitute, swap, trade, turn, veer.
n. about-turn, alteration, change, change of direction, exchange, interchange, shift, substitution, swap.

switch off inactivate, put off, turn off.

swivel *v.* gyrate, pirouette, pivot, revolve, rotate, spin, swing round, turn, twirl.

swollen *adj.* bloated, bulbous, distended, enlarged, inflamed, puffed up, puffy, tumid.
antonyms contracted, emaciated, shrunken.

swoop *v.* descend, dive, drop, fall, lunge, pounce, rush, stoop, sweep.

n. attack, descent, drop, lunge, onslaught, plunge, pounce, rush, stoop, sweep.

swop *see* **swap**.

sword *n.* blade, broadsword, foil, machete, rapier, sabre, scimitar.

sworn *adj.* attested, confirmed, devoted, eternal, implacable, inveterate, relentless.

swot *v.* bone up, burn the midnight oil, cram, learn, memorise, mug up, pore over, revise, study, work.
n. bookworm, crammer, dig, worker.
antonym idler.

syllabus *n.* course, curriculum, plan, programme, schedule.

symbiotic *adj.* beneficial, co-operative, interactive, interdependent, synergetic.

symbol *n.* badge, character, emblem, figure, ideograph, image, logo, mark, representation, sign, token, type.

symbolic *adj.* allegorical, allusive, emblematic, figurative, metaphorical, representative, significant, symbolical, token, typical.

symbolise *v.* allude to, denote, exemplify, mean, personate, personify, represent, signify, stand for, typify.

symmetrical *adj.* balanced, corresponding, parallel, proportional, regular, well-balanced, well-proportioned, well-rounded.
antonyms asymmetrical, irregular, lop-sided.

symmetry *n.* agreement, balance, correspondence, evenness, form, harmony, order, parallelism, proportion, regularity.
antonyms asymmetry, irregularity.

sympathetic *adj.* affectionate, agreeable, appealing, appreciative, caring, comforting, commiserating, compassionate, compatible, concerned, congenial, consoling, feeling, friendly, interested, kind, like-minded, pitying, responsive, supportive, tender, understanding, warm-hearted, well-disposed, well-intentioned.
antonyms antipathetic, callous, indifferent, unsympathetic.

sympathise *v.* agree, commiserate, empathise, feel for, identify with, pity, respond to, side with, understand.
antonyms disapprove, dismiss, disregard, ignore, oppose.

sympathy *n.* **1** comfort, commiseration, compassion, condolence, condolences, congeniality, empathy, fellow-feeling, pity, rapport, responsiveness, tenderness, thoughtfulness, understanding, warmth. **2** affinity, agreement, correspondence, harmony.
antonyms **1** callousness, indifference, insensitivity. **2** disharmony, incompatibility.

symptom *n.* evidence, expression, feature, indication, manifestation, mark, note, sign, syndrome, token, warning.

synonymous *adj.* comparable, corresponding, equal, equivalent, exchangeable, identical, identified, interchangeable, parallel, similar, substitutable, tantamount, the same.
antonyms antonymous, dissimilar, opposite.

synopsis *n.* abridgement, abstract, condensation, digest, outline, précis, recapitulation, résumé, review, run-down, sketch, summary.

synthesise *v.* amalgamate, blend, combine, compound, fuse, integrate, manufacture, merge, unify, unite, weld.
antonyms analyse, resolve, separate.

synthetic *adj.* artificial, bogus, ersatz, fake, imitation, man-made, manufactured, mock, pseudo, put-on, sham, simulated.
antonyms genuine, natural, real.

system *n.* arrangement, classification, co-ordination, logic, method, methodology, mode, orderliness, organisation, plan, practice, procedure, process, regularity, routine, rule, scheme, set-up, structure, systematisation, technique, theory, usage.

systematic *adj.* businesslike, efficient, intentional, logical, methodical, ordered, orderly, organised, planned, precise, standardised, systematical, systematised, well-ordered, well-planned.
antonyms arbitrary, disorderly, inefficient, unsystematic.

T

tab *n.* docket, flag, flap, label, marker, sticker, tag, ticket.

tabby *adj.* banded, mottled, streaked, striped, stripy, variegated, wavy.

table *n.* **1** bench, board, counter, desk, slab, stand. **2** catalogue, chart, diagram, graph, inventory, list, paradigm, plan, record, register, schedule, syllabus, synopsis.
v. **1** propose, put forward, submit, suggest. **2** postpone, shelve.

tableau *n.* picture, portrayal, representation, scene, spectacle, vignette.

taboo *adj.* banned, forbidden, prohibited, proscribed, sacrosanct, unacceptable, unmentionable, unthinkable.
antonyms acceptable, permitted.
n. ban, curse, disapproval, interdiction, prohibition, restriction.

taciturn *adj.* aloof, antisocial, cold, distant, quiet, reserved, reticent, silent, uncommunicative, unforthcoming, withdrawn.
antonyms communicative, forthcoming, sociable, talkative.

tack *n.* **1** drawing-pin, nail, pin, staple, thumbtack, tin-tack. **2** approach, attack, bearing, course, direction, line, loop, method, path, plan, procedure, route, tactic, way.
v. add, affix, annex, append, attach, fasten, fix, join, nail, pin, staple, stitch, tag.

tackle *n.* **1** attack, block, challenge, interception, intervention, stop. **2** apparatus, equipment, gear, harness, implements, outfit, paraphernalia, rig, rigging, tackling, tools, trappings.
v. attempt, attend to, begin, block, challenge, confront, deal with, embark upon, encounter, engage in, face up to, grab, grapple with, grasp, halt, intercept, seize, set about, stop, take on, throw, try, undertake, wade into.
antonyms avoid, side-step.

tact *n.* adroitness, consideration, delicacy, diplomacy, discernment, discretion, finesse, grace, judgement, perception, prudence, sensitivity, skill, thoughtfulness, understanding.
antonyms clumsiness, indiscretion, tactlessness.

tactful *adj.* careful, considerate, delicate, diplomatic, discerning, discreet, judicious, perceptive, polished, polite, politic, prudent, sensitive, skilful, subtle, thoughtful, understanding.
antonyms careless, rude, tactless, thoughtless.

tactic *n.* approach, course, device, line, manoeuvre, means, method, move, ploy, policy, ruse, scheme, shift, stratagem, subterfuge, trick, way.

tactical *adj.* artful, calculated, clever, cunning, diplomatic, judicious, politic, prudent, shrewd, skilful, smart, strategic.
antonym impolitic.

tactician *n.* campaigner, co-ordinator, director, mastermind, orchestrator, planner, politician, strategist.

tactics *n.* approach, campaign, line of attack, manoeuvres, moves, plan, plan of campaign, ploys, policy, procedure, shifts, stratagems, strategy.

tactless *adj.* blundering, careless, clumsy, discourteous, hurtful, ill-timed, impolite, impolitic, imprudent, inappropriate, inconsiderate, indelicate, indiscreet, insensitive, rough, rude, thoughtless, undiplomatic, unfeeling, unkind.
antonyms careful, diplomatic, tactful.

tag *n.* docket, epithet, identification, label, mark, name, note, slip, sticker, tab, tally, ticket.
v. **1** call, christen, designate, dub, earmark, identify, label, mark, name, nickname, style, term. **2** add, adjoin, affix, annex, append, fasten.
tag along accompany, attend, follow, hang round, shadow, tail, trail.

tail *n.* **1** appendage, behind, posterior, rear, rear end, rump, tailpiece. **2** conclusion, end, extremity, queue, tailback.
v. dog, follow, keep with, shadow, spy on, stalk, track, trail.
tail off decrease, die (out), drop, dwindle, fade, fail, fall away, peter out, taper off, wane.
antonyms grow, increase.

tailor *n.* dressmaker, outfitter, seamstress.
v. accommodate, adapt, adjust, alter, convert, cut, fashion, fit, modify, mould, shape, style, suit, trim.

tailor-made *adj.* bespoke, custom-built, custom-made, fitted, ideal, made-to-measure, perfect, right, suitable, suited.
antonyms ill-adapted, unsuitable.

taint *v.* adulterate, blacken, blemish, blight, blot, brand, contaminate, corrupt, damage, defile, deprave, dirty, disgrace, dishonour, foul, infect, muddy, pollute, ruin, shame, smear, soil, spoil, stain, sully, tarnish.
n. blemish, blot, contamination, corruption, defect, disgrace, dishonour, fault, flaw, infamy, infection, pollution, shame, smear, smirch, spot, stain, stigma.

take *v.* **1** accept, acquire, adopt, assume, capture, catch, choose, derive, glean, grasp, grip, have, hold, obtain, pick, secure, seize, select, win. **2** abduct, appropriate, carry off, deduct, eliminate, fetch, filch, nick, pinch, pocket, purloin, remove, steal, subtract. **3** call for, demand, necessitate, need, require. **4** accompany, bring, carry, conduct, convey, escort, ferry, guide,

lead, transport, usher. **5** abide, bear, endure, stand, stomach, tolerate, undergo, withstand.
antonyms **1** leave, refuse. **2** bring, put back, replace. **5** avoid.
take aback astonish, astound, bewilder, disconcert, dismay, flabbergast, stagger, startle, stun, surprise, upset.
take apart analyse, disassemble, dismantle, resolve, take down, take to pieces.
take back deny, eat one's words, recant, reclaim, renounce, repossess, repudiate, retract, withdraw.
take down 1 deflate, demolish, disassemble, dismantle, humble, humiliate, level, lower, mortify, raze, reduce. **2** minute, note, put down, record, set down, transcribe, write.
take in 1 absorb, accommodate, admit, annex, appreciate, assimilate, comprehend, comprise, contain, cover, digest, embrace, enclose, encompass, grasp, imagine, include, incorporate, realise, receive, shelter, understand. **2** bamboozle, cheat, con, deceive, do, dupe, fool, hoodwink, kid, mislead, swindle, trick.
take off 1 beat it, decamp, depart, disappear, discard, divest, doff, drop, expand, flourish, go, leave, remove, soar. **2** caricature, imitate, mimic, mock, parody, satirise, send up.
take on accept, acquire, assume, complain, contend with, employ, engage, enlist, enrol, face, fight, hire, lament, oppose, retain, tackle, undertake, vie with.
take up absorb, accept, adopt, affect, arrest, assume, begin, borrow, carry on, consume, continue, cover, engage in, engross, fasten, fill, interrupt, lift, monopolise, occupy, proceed, raise, recommence, restart, resume, secure, start, use up.
take-off *n.* caricature, imitation, mimicry, parody, spoof, travesty.
takeover *n.* amalgamation, coalition, combination, coup, incorporation, merger.
takings *n.* earnings, gain, gate, income, pickings, proceeds, profits, receipts, returns, revenue, take, yield.
tale *n.* account, anecdote, fable, fabrication, falsehood, fib, fiction, legend, lie, myth, narrative, old wives' tale, report, romance, rumour, saga, spiel, story, superstition, tall story, tradition, untruth, yarn.
talent *n.* ability, aptitude, bent, capacity, endowment, faculty, feel, flair, forte, genius, gift, knack, power, strength.
antonyms inability, ineptitude, weakness.
talented *adj.* able, accomplished, adept, adroit, apt, artistic, brilliant, capable, clever, deft, gifted, ingenious, inspired, well-endowed.
antonyms clumsy, inept.
talisman *n.* amulet, charm, fetish, mascot.
talk *v.* articulate, blab, chat, chatter, communicate, confer, converse, gossip, inform, jaw, natter, negotiate, say, speak, utter.
n. address, chat, chatter, chitchat, conference, consultation, conversation, dialect, dialogue, discourse, discussion, gossip, hearsay, jargon, jawing, language, lecture, meeting, natter, negotiation, rumour, seminar, sermon, slang, speech, spiel, symposium, tittle-tattle, utterance, words.
talk into bring round, coax, convince, encourage, overrule, persuade, sway, win over.
antonyms dissuade, put off.
talk out of caution, deter, discourage, dissuade, head off, protest, put off, urge against.
antonyms convince, persuade.
talkative *adj.* chatty, communicative, expansive, forthcoming, garrulous, gossipy, unreserved, verbose, vocal, voluble, wordy.
antonyms quiet, reserved, taciturn.
talker *n.* chatterbox, communicator, conversationalist, lecturer, orator, speaker, speechmaker.
talking-to *n.* criticism, dressing-down, lecture, rebuke, reprimand, reproach, reproof, scolding, slating, telling-off, ticking-off.
antonyms commendation, congratulation, praise.
tall *adj.* big, elevated, giant, great, high, lanky, lofty, soaring, steep, towering.
antonyms low, short, small.
tally *v.* accord, agree, coincide, concur, conform, correspond, figure, fit, harmonise, mark, match, parallel, reckon, record, register, square, suit, tie in, total.
antonyms differ, disagree.
n. account, count, counterfoil, credit, duplicate, label, mark, match, notch, reckoning, record, score, stub, tab, tag, tick, total.
tame *adj.* **1** amenable, biddable, broken, disciplined, docile, domesticated, gentle, manageable, meek, obedient, submissive, tractable, unresisting. **2** bland, boring, dull, feeble, flat, humdrum, insipid, lifeless, spiritless, tedious, unadventurous, unenterprising, uninspired, uninteresting.
antonyms **1** rebellious, unmanageable, wild. **2** exciting.
v. break in, bridle, calm, conquer, curb, discipline, domesticate, house-train, humble, master, mellow, mitigate, pacify, quell, repress, soften, subdue, subjugate, suppress, temper, train.
tamper *v.* alter, bribe, cook, corrupt, damage, fiddle, fix, influence, interfere, juggle, manipulate, meddle, mess, rig, tinker.
tang *n.* aroma, bite, flavour, hint, overtone, piquancy, pungency, reek, savour, scent, smack, smell, suggestion, taste, tinge, touch, trace, whiff.
tangible *adj.* actual, concrete, definite, discernible, evident, manifest, material, objective, observable, palpable, perceptible, physical, positive, real, sensible, solid, substantial, touchable.
antonyms abstract, intangible, unreal.
tangle *n.* coil, complication, confusion, convolution, embroilment, entanglement, fix, jam, jumble, jungle, knot, labyrinth, mass, maze, mesh, mess, mix-up, muddle, snarl, snarl-up,

twist, web.
v. catch, coil, confuse, embroil, enmesh, ensnare, entangle, entrap, hamper, implicate, interlace, intertwine, interweave, involve, knot, mesh, muddle, snarl, trap, twist.
antonym disentangle.

tangled *adj.* complex, complicated, confused, convoluted, dishevelled, intricate, involved, jumbled, knotty, matted, messy, mixed-up, scrambled, snarled, tortuous, tousled, twisted.
antonyms clear, free.

tangy *adj.* biting, bitter, fresh, piquant, pungent, savoury, sharp, spicy, strong, tart.
antonyms insipid, tasteless.

tank *n.* **1** aquarium, basin, cistern, container, reservoir, vat. **2** armoured car, armoured vehicle, panzer.

tantalise *v.* baffle, bait, balk, entice, lead on, play upon, provoke, taunt, tease, thwart, torment, torture.
antonyms fulfil, gratify, satisfy.

tantamount *adj.* as good as, commensurate, equal, equivalent, synonymous, the same as, virtually.

tantrum *n.* fit, flare-up, fury, hysterics, outburst, rage, scene, storm, temper.

tap[1] *v.* beat, chap, drum, knock, pat, rap, strike, tat, touch.
n. beat, chap, knock, pat, rap, rat-tat, touch.

tap[2] *n.* bug, bung, faucet, plug, receiver, spigot, spout, stop-cock, stopper, valve.
v. bleed, drain, exploit, milk, mine, open, pierce, quarry, siphon, unplug, use, utilise.

tape *n.* band, binding, magnetic tape, ribbon, strip, tape-measure, video-tape.
v. assess, bind, measure, record, seal, secure, stick, tape-record, video, wrap.

taper *v.* attenuate, decrease, die away, die out, dwindle, fade, lessen, narrow, peter out, reduce, slim, subside, tail off, thin, wane, weaken.
antonyms increase, swell, widen.
n. candle, spill, wax-light, wick.

target *n.* aim, ambition, bull's-eye, butt, destination, end, goal, intention, jack, mark, object, objective, prey, purpose, quarry, scapegoat, victim.

tariff *n.* assessment, bill of fare, charges, customs, duty, excise, levy, menu, price list, rate, schedule, tax, toll.

tarnish *v.* blacken, blemish, blot, darken, dim, discolour, dull, mar, rust, soil, spoil, spot, stain, sully, taint.
antonyms brighten, enhance, polish up.

tart[1] *n.* pastry, pie, quiche, tartlet.

tart[2] *adj.* acerbic, acid, acrimonious, astringent, barbed, biting, bitter, caustic, cutting, incisive, piquant, pungent, sardonic, scathing, sharp, short, sour, tangy, trenchant, vinegary.

task *n.* assignment, burden, business, charge, chore, duty, employment, enterprise, exercise, imposition, job, job of work, labour, mission, occupation, toil, undertaking, work.

taste *n.* **1** flavour, palate, relish, savour, smack, tang. **2** bit, bite, dash, delicacy, drop, morsel, mouthful, nibble, sample, sip, soupçon, spoonful, titbit. **3** appetite, desire, experience, fondness, inclination, leaning, liking, preference. **4** appreciation, cultivation, culture, decorum, discernment, discrimination, elegance, finesse, grace, judgement, perception, polish, refinement, sensitivity, style, tastefulness.
antonyms **1** blandness. **3** disinclination. **4** tastelessness.
v. assay, differentiate, discern, distinguish, encounter, experience, feel, know, meet, nibble, perceive, relish, sample, savour, sip, smack, test, try, undergo.

tasteful *adj.* aesthetic, artistic, beautiful, charming, correct, cultivated, cultured, delicate, discriminating, elegant, exquisite, fastidious, graceful, harmonious, judicious, polished, refined, restrained, smart, stylish, well-judged.
antonyms disgusting, garish, tasteless.

tasteless *adj.* bland, boring, cheap, crass, crude, dilute, dull, flashy, flat, flavourless, garish, gaudy, graceless, improper, indiscreet, inelegant, insipid, low, mild, rude, stale, tatty, tawdry, uninspired, uninteresting, vapid, vulgar, watered-down, watery, weak, wearish.
antonyms attractive, elegant, tasteful.

tasting *n.* assessment, sampling, testing, trial.

tasty *adj.* appetising, delicious, flavoursome, luscious, mouthwatering, palatable, piquant, savoury, scrumptious, succulent, yummy.
antonyms disgusting, insipid, tasteless.

tattered *adj.* frayed, in shreds, ragged, raggy, rent, ripped, tatty, threadbare, torn.
antonyms neat, trim.

tatters *n.* rags, ribbons, shreds.

taunt *v.* bait, deride, flout, gibe, insult, jeer, mock, provoke, reproach, revile, rib, ridicule, sneer, tease, torment.
n. catcall, censure, derision, dig, gibe, insult, jeer, provocation, reproach, ridicule, sarcasm, sneer, teasing.

taut *adj.* contracted, rigid, strained, stressed, stretched, tense, tight, unrelaxed.
antonyms loose, relaxed, slack.

tautological *adj.* redundant, repetitive, superfluous.
antonyms economical, succinct.

tautology *n.* duplication, redundancy, repetition, repetitiveness, superfluity.
antonyms economy, succinctness.

tawdry *adj.* cheap, flashy, garish, gaudy, glittering, plastic, showy, tasteless, tinselly, vulgar.
antonyms excellent, fine, superior.

tawny *adj.* fawn, golden, sandy, tan, yellow.

tax *n.* assessment, burden, charge, contribution, customs, demand, duty, excise, imposition, levy, load, rate, tariff, toll.
v. assess, burden, censure, charge, demand, drain, exact, exhaust, impose, impugn, incriminate, load, push, sap, strain, stretch, try, weaken, weary.

teach *v.* accustom, advise, coach, counsel, demonstrate, direct, discipline, drill, edify, educate, enlighten, ground, guide, impart, implant, inculcate, inform, instruct, nurture, school, show, train, tutor, verse.

teacher *n.* coach, don, educator, guide, guru, instructor, lecturer, master, mentor, mistress, pedagogue, professor, pundit, school-teacher, trainer, tutor.

teaching *n.* doctrine, dogma, education, grounding, indoctrination, instruction, pedagogy, precept, principle, schooling, tenet, training, tuition.

team *n.* band, body, bunch, company, crew, gang, group, line-up, pair, set, shift, side, span, squad, stable, yoke.

team up band together, combine, co-operate, couple, join, link, match, unite.

teamwork *n.* collaboration, co-operation, co-ordination, esprit de corps, fellowship, joint effort, team spirit.

antonyms disharmony, disunity.

tear *v.* **1** divide, gash, grab, lacerate, mangle, mutilate, pull, rend, rip, rupture, scratch, seize, sever, shred, snatch, wrest, yank. **2** belt, bolt, career, charge, dart, dash, fly, hurry, race, run, rush, shoot, speed, sprint.

n. hole, laceration, rent, rip, run, rupture, scratch, snag, split.

tearful *adj.* blubbering, crying, distressing, emotional, lamentable, mournful, pathetic, pitiful, poignant, sad, sobbing, sorrowful, upsetting, weeping, weepy, whimpering.

tears *n.* blubbering, crying, distress, lamentation, mourning, pain, regret, sadness, sobbing, sorrow, wailing, weeping, whimpering.

tease *v.* aggravate, annoy, badger, bait, banter, gibe, irritate, mock, needle, pester, plague, provoke, rag, rib, ridicule, tantalise, taunt, torment, vex, worry.

technique *n.* approach, art, artistry, course, craft, craftsmanship, delivery, execution, expertise, facility, fashion, knack, know-how, manner, means, method, mode, performance, procedure, proficiency, skill, style, system, touch, way.

tedious *adj.* annoying, banal, boring, deadly, drab, dreary, dull, humdrum, laborious, lifeless, long-drawn-out, monotonous, tiresome, tiring, unexciting, uninteresting, wearisome.

antonyms exciting, interesting, lively.

teeming *adj.* abundant, alive, brimming, bristling, bursting, chock-full, crawling, fruitful, full, overflowing, packed, proliferating, replete, swarming, thick.

antonyms lacking, rare, sparse.

teenage *adj.* adolescent, immature, juvenile, young, youthful.

teenager *n.* adolescent, boy, girl, juvenile, minor, youth.

teeny *adj.* diminutive, microscopic, miniature, minuscule, minute, teeny-weeny, tiny, wee.

teeter *v.* balance, lurch, pitch, rock, seesaw, stagger, sway, totter, tremble, waver, wobble.

teetotaller *n.* abstainer, non-drinker.

telegram *n.* cable, telegraph, telemessage, telex, wire.

telegraph *n.* cable, telegram, teleprinter, telex, wire.

v. cable, send, signal, telex, transmit, wire.

telepathy *n.* clairvoyance, ESP, mind-reading, sixth sense, thought transference.

telephone *n.* handset, line, phone.

v. buzz, call (up), contact, dial, get in touch, give someone a tinkle, phone, ring (up).

telescope *v.* abbreviate, abridge, compress, condense, contract, crush, curtail, cut, reduce, shorten, shrink, squash, trim, truncate.

television *n.* goggle-box, idiot box, receiver, set, small screen, telly, the box, the tube, TV, TV set.

tell *v.* **1** acquaint, communicate, confess, disclose, divulge, inform, let know, notify, reveal, say, speak, state, utter. **2** announce, describe, mention, narrate, portray, recount, relate, report. **3** authorise, command, direct, instruct, order. **4** comprehend, differentiate, discern, discover, discriminate, distinguish, identify, see, understand.

tell off berate, censure, chide, dress down, lecture, rebuke, reprimand, reproach, reprove, scold, take to task, tear off a strip, tick off, upbraid.

temerity *n.* audacity, boldness, daring, forwardness, gall, impudence, impulsiveness, nerve, pluck, rashness, recklessness.

antonyms caution, prudence.

temper *n.* **1** attitude, character, constitution, disposition, humour, mind, mood, nature, temperament. **2** anger, annoyance, fury, ill-humour, irritability, passion, rage, resentment, surliness, tantrum. **3** calm, composure, self-control, tranquillity.

antonyms **2** calmness, self-control. **3** anger, rage.

v. allay, assuage, calm, harden, lessen, mitigate, moderate, modify, palliate, restrain, soften, soothe, strengthen, toughen.

temperament *n.* bent, character, complexion, constitution, disposition, humour, make-up, mood, nature, outlook, personality, quality, soul, spirit, stamp, temper, tendency.

temperamental *adj.* **1** capricious, emotional, excitable, explosive, fiery, highly-strung, hot-headed, impatient, irritable, moody, neurotic, over-emotional, passionate, sensitive, touchy, unpredictable, unreliable, volatile. **2** constitutional, inborn, ingrained, inherent, innate, natural.

antonyms **1** calm, level-headed, serene, steady.

temperance *n.* abstemiousness, abstinence, discretion, forbearance, moderation, prohibition, restraint, self-control, self-denial, self-discipline, self-restraint, sobriety, teetotalism.

antonyms excess, intemperance.

temperate *adj.* abstemious, abstinent, agreeable, balanced, balmy, calm, clement, composed, continent, controlled, equable, even-tempered, fair, gentle, mild, moderate, pleasant, reasonable, restrained, sensible, sober, soft, stable.

antonyms excessive, extreme, intemperate.

tempestuous *adj.* agitated, blustery, boisterous, breezy, emotional, excited, feverish, furious, gusty, heated, hysterical, impassioned, intense, passionate, raging, stormy, troubled, tumultuous, turbulent, uncontrolled, violent, wild, windy.
antonyms calm, quiet.

temple *n.* church, mosque, pagoda, sanctuary, shrine, tabernacle.

tempo *n.* beat, cadence, measure, metre, pace, pulse, rate, rhythm, speed, time, velocity.

temporal *adj.* **1** evanescent, fleeting, impermanent, momentary, passing, short-lived, temporary, transient, transitory. **2** carnal, earthly, fleshly, material, mortal, mundane, profane, secular, terrestrial, worldly.
antonyms **1** long-term, permanent. **2** spiritual.

temporary *adj.* brief, ephemeral, fleeting, interim, makeshift, momentary, passing, provisional, short-lived, stop-gap, transient, transitory.
antonyms everlasting, permanent.

tempt *v.* allure, attract, bait, coax, draw, entice, incite, invite, lure, provoke, risk, seduce, tantalise, test, woo.
antonyms discourage, dissuade, repel.

temptation *n.* allurement, appeal, attraction, bait, coaxing, draw, enticement, fascination, inducement, invitation, lure, persuasion, pull, seduction, snare.

tenable *adj.* arguable, believable, credible, defendable, defensible, justifiable, plausible, rational, reasonable, sound, supportable, viable.
antonyms indefensible, unjustifiable, untenable.

tenancy *n.* holding, lease, leasehold, occupancy, occupation, possession, renting, residence, tenure.

tenant *n.* inhabitant, landholder, leaseholder, lessee, occupant, occupier, renter, resident.

tend[1] *v.* affect, aim, bear, bend, contribute, go, gravitate, head, incline, influence, lead, lean, move, point, verge.

tend[2] *v.* attend, comfort, control, cultivate, feed, guard, handle, keep, maintain, manage, minister to, nurse, nurture, protect, serve, succour.
antonyms forget, ignore, neglect.

tendency *n.* bearing, bias, course, direction, disposition, drift, drive, heading, inclination, leaning, liability, movement, partiality, predisposition, propensity, readiness, susceptibility, tenor, thrust, trend, turning.

tender[1] *adj.* **1** affectionate, benevolent, caring, compassionate, considerate, emotional, fond, gentle, humane, kind, loving, merciful, romantic, sensitive, sentimental, soft-hearted, sympathetic, tender-hearted, touching, warm. **2** green, immature, impressionable, inexperienced, new, raw, vulnerable, young, youthful. **3** delicate, feeble, fragile, frail, soft, weak. **4** aching, bruised, inflamed, irritated, painful, raw, smarting, sore.
antonyms **1** callous, harsh, rough. **2** mature. **3** hard, tough.

tender[2] *v.* advance, extend, give, offer, present, propose, submit, suggest, volunteer.
n. **1** currency, money, payment. **2** bid, estimate, offer, proposal, proposition, submission, suggestion.

tenor *n.* aim, burden, course, direction, drift, essence, gist, meaning, point, purpose, sense, spirit, substance, tendency, theme, trend.

tense *adj.* anxious, apprehensive, edgy, exciting, fidgety, jittery, jumpy, moving, nervous, overwrought, restless, rigid, strained, stressful, stretched, strung up, taut, tight, uneasy, uptight, worrying.
antonyms calm, lax, loose, relaxed.
v. brace, contract, strain, stretch, tighten.
antonyms loosen, relax.

tension *n.* anxiety, apprehension, edginess, nervousness, pressure, restlessness, stiffness, strain, stress, stretching, suspense, tautness, tightness, worry.
antonyms calm(ness), laxness, looseness, relaxation.

tent *n.* big top, canvas, marquee, tepee, wigwam.

tentative *adj.* cautious, doubtful, experimental, faltering, hesitant, indefinite, provisional, speculative, uncertain, unconfirmed, undecided, unsure.
antonyms conclusive, decisive, definite, final.

tenuous *adj.* delicate, doubtful, dubious, fine, flimsy, insubstantial, nebulous, questionable, shaky, sketchy, slender, slight, slim, thin, weak.
antonyms significant, strong, substantial.

tenure *n.* habitation, holding, occupancy, occupation, possession, proprietorship, residence, tenancy, term, time.

tepid *adj.* apathetic, cool, half-hearted, lukewarm, unenthusiastic, warmish.
antonyms animated, cold, hot, passionate.

term *n.* **1** appellation, denomination, designation, epithet, expression, name, phrase, title, word. **2** course, duration, half, interval, limit, period, season, semester, session, space, span, spell, time, while.
v. call, denominate, designate, dub, entitle, label, name, style, tag, title.

terminal *adj.* bounding, concluding, deadly, extreme, fatal, final, incurable, killing, last, lethal, limiting, mortal, ultimate, utmost.
antonym initial.
n. boundary, depot, end, extremity, limit, termination, terminus.

terminate *v.* abort, cease, close, complete, conclude, cut off, discontinue, drop, end, expire, finish, issue, lapse, result, stop, wind up.
antonyms begin, initiate, start.

terminology *n.* jargon, language, nomenclature, phraseology, terms, vocabulary, words.

terminus *n.* boundary, close, depot, destination, end, extremity, garage, goal, limit, station, target, termination.

terms *n.* **1** language, phraseology, terminology. **2** conditions, particulars, provisions, provisos, qualifications, specifications, stipulations. **3** agreement, charges, compromise, fees, payment, price, rates. **4** footing, position, rela-

tions, relationship, standing, status.
terrain *n.* country, countryside, ground, land, landscape, territory, topography.
terrestrial *adj.* earthly, global, mundane, worldly.
antonyms cosmic, heavenly.
terrible *adj.* abhorrent, appalling, awful, bad, dangerous, desperate, disgusting, distressing, dreaded, dreadful, extreme, foul, frightful, gruesome, harrowing, hateful, hideous, horrible, horrid, horrific, monstrous, obnoxious, offensive, outrageous, repulsive, revolting, rotten, serious, severe, shocking, unpleasant, vile.
antonyms great, pleasant, superb, wonderful.
terribly *adv.* awfully, decidedly, exceedingly, extremely, frightfully, greatly, much, seriously, thoroughly, very.
terrific *adj.* amazing, breathtaking, brilliant, enormous, excellent, excessive, extreme, fabulous, fantastic, fine, gigantic, great, huge, intense, magnificent, marvellous, outstanding, sensational, smashing, stupendous, super, superb, tremendous, wonderful.
antonyms appalling, awful, terrible.
terrify *v.* alarm, appal, awe, dismay, frighten, horrify, intimidate, petrify, scare, shock, terrorise.
territorial *adj.* area, district, geographical, localised, regional, sectional, zonal.
territory *n.* area, country, dependency, district, domain, jurisdiction, land, park, preserve, province, region, sector, state, terrain, tract, zone.
terror *n.* alarm, anxiety, consternation, dismay, dread, fear, fright, horror, intimidation, panic, shock.
terrorise *v.* alarm, browbeat, bully, coerce, dismay, frighten, horrify, intimidate, menace, oppress, petrify, scare, shock, terrify, threaten.
terse *adj.* abrupt, brief, brusque, clipped, compact, concise, condensed, curt, epigrammatic, incisive, laconic, pithy, sententious, short, snappy, succinct.
antonyms long-winded, repetitious.
test *v.* analyse, assess, check, examine, experiment, investigate, prove, screen, try, verify.
n. analysis, assessment, attempt, check, evaluation, examination, investigation, ordeal, probation, proof, trial, try-out.
testify *v.* affirm, assert, attest, avow, certify, corroborate, declare, depose, show, state, swear, vouch, witness.
testimonial *n.* certificate, character, commendation, credential, endorsement, recommendation, reference, tribute.
testimony *n.* affidavit, affirmation, attestation, confirmation, declaration, demonstration, evidence, indication, information, manifestation, profession, proof, statement, submission, support, verification, witness.
tether *n.* bond, chain, cord, fastening, fetter, lead, leash, line, restraint, rope, shackle.
v. bind, chain, fasten, fetter, lash, leash, manacle, picket, restrain, rope, secure, shackle, tie.
text *n.* body, book, contents, matter, paragraph, passage, reading, script, sentence, source, subject, textbook, theme, topic, wording, words.
texture *n.* character, composition, consistency, constitution, fabric, feel, grain, quality, structure, surface, tissue, weave.
thank *v.* acknowledge, appreciate, be grateful, credit, recognise, say thank you.
thankful *adj.* appreciative, contented, grateful, indebted, obliged, pleased, relieved.
antonyms thankless, unappreciative, ungrateful.
thankless *adj.* fruitless, ungrateful, unprofitable, unrecognised, unrequited, useless.
antonyms rewarding, satisfying, worthwhile.
thanks *n.* acknowledgement, appreciation, credit, gratefulness, gratitude, recognition, thank-offering, thanksgiving.
thanks to as a result of, because of, by reason of, due to, in consequence of, on account of, owing to, through.
thaw *v.* defreeze, defrost, dissolve, liquefy, melt, soften, warm.
antonyms congeal, freeze.
theatre *n.* auditorium, hall, lyceum, odeon, opera house, playhouse.
theatrical *adj.* **1** dramatic, scenic. **2** affected, artificial, exaggerated, extravagant, histrionic, mannered, melodramatic, ostentatious, overdone, pompous, showy.
theft *n.* abstraction, embezzlement, fraud, kleptomania, larceny, pilfering, purloining, rip-off, robbery, stealing, thieving.
thematic *adj.* classificatory, conceptual, notional.
theme *n.* argument, burden, composition, dissertation, essay, exercise, idea, keynote, matter, paper, subject, subject-matter, text, thesis, topic.
theological *adj.* divine, doctrinal, ecclesiastical, religious.
theorem *n.* deduction, formula, hypothesis, principle, proposition, rule, statement, thesis.
theoretical *adj.* abstract, academic, doctrinaire, doctrinal, hypothetical, ideal, impractical, on paper, pure, speculative.
antonyms applied, concrete, practical.
theorise *v.* conjecture, formulate, guess, postulate, project, propound, speculate, suppose.
theory *n.* abstraction, assumption, conjecture, guess, hypothesis, philosophy, plan, presumption, proposal, scheme, speculation, supposition, surmise, system, thesis.
antonyms certainty, practice.
therapeutic *adj.* beneficial, corrective, curative, good, healing, recuperative, remedial, restorative, tonic.
antonyms damaging, detrimental, harmful.
therapy *n.* cure, healing, tonic, treatment.
therefore *adv.* as a result, consequently, for that reason, so, then.
thesaurus *n.* dictionary, encyclopedia, lexicon, repository, storehouse, synonymy, treasure-house, treasury, vocabulary, wordbook.
thesis *n.* argument, assumption, composition, contention, dissertation, essay, hypothesis, idea,

monograph, opinion, paper, proposal, proposition, statement, subject, surmise, theme, theory, topic, treatise, view.

thick *adj.* **1** broad, close, clotted, coagulated, compact, concentrated, condensed, deep, dense, fat, heavy, impenetrable, solid, wide. **2** abundant, brimming, bristling, bursting, chock-a-block, chock-full, crowded, full, numerous, packed, swarming, teeming. **3** brainless, dim-witted, dull, foolish, simple, slow, stupid.
antonyms **1** slender, slight, slim, thin. **2** sparse. **3** brainy, clever.
n. centre, focus, heart, hub, middle, midst.

thicken *v.* cake, clot, coagulate, condense, congeal, deepen, gel, jell, set.
antonym thin.

thicket *n.* clump, coppice, copse, covert, grove, spinney, wood, woodland.

thickness *n.* body, breadth, bulk, density, diameter, layer, ply, sheet, stratum, width.
antonym thinness.

thickset *adj.* beefy, brawny, bulky, burly, heavy, muscular, powerful, solid, squat, stocky, strong, stubby, sturdy, thick, well-built.
antonyms bony, lanky, thin.

thick-skinned *adj.* callous, hard-boiled, hardened, insensitive, stolid, tough, unfeeling.
antonyms sensitive, thin-skinned, touchy.

thief *n.* bandit, burglar, cheat, crook, embezzler, filcher, house-breaker, kleptomaniac, mugger, pickpocket, pilferer, plunderer, purloiner, robber, shop-lifter, stealer, swindler.

thin *adj.* **1** attenuated, bony, emaciated, gaunt, lanky, lean, narrow, scraggy, scrawny, shallow, skeletal, skinny, slender, slight, slim, spare, undernourished, underweight. **2** delicate, diluted, feeble, filmy, fine, flimsy, gossamer, light, runny, see-through, sheer, translucent, transparent, watery, weak. **3** deficient, inadequate, meagre, poor, scant, scanty, scarce, scattered, skimpy, sparse. **4** flimsy, insubstantial, tenuous, unconvincing, weak.
antonyms **1** broad, fat. **2** dense, solid, thick. **3** abundant, plentiful. **4** strong.
v. attenuate, dilute, diminish, extenuate, rarefy, reduce, refine, trim, water down, weaken, weed out.

thing *n.* **1** act, action, affair, apparatus, article, body, circumstance, concept, contrivance, creature, deed, detail, device, entity, event, eventuality, fact, factor, feat, feature, gadget, happening, implement, incident, instrument, item, liking, machine, means, mechanism, object, occurrence, part, particular, phenomenon, point, portion, possession, problem, proceeding, something, statement, substance, thought, tool. **2** dislike, fetish, fixation, hang-up, obsession, phobia, preoccupation.

things *n.* baggage, belongings, bits and pieces, clobber, clothes, effects, equipment, gear, goods, junk, luggage, odds and ends, paraphernalia, possessions, stuff, utensils.

think *v.* anticipate, be under the impression, believe, calculate, cogitate, conceive, conclude, consider, contemplate, deem, deliberate, design, determine, envisage, esteem, estimate, expect, foresee, hold, imagine, judge, meditate, mull over, muse, ponder, presume, purpose, reason, recall, reckon, recollect, reflect, regard, remember, revolve, suppose, surmise.
n. assessment, cogitation, consideration, contemplation, deliberation, meditation, reflection.
think over chew over, consider, contemplate, meditate, mull over, ponder, reflect upon, ruminate, weigh up.
think up conceive, concoct, contrive, create, design, devise, dream up, imagine, improvise, invent, visualise.

thinker *n.* brain, ideologist, intellect, mastermind, philosopher, theorist.

thinking *n.* assessment, conclusions, conjecture, idea, judgement, opinion, outlook, philosophy, position, reasoning, theory, thoughts, view.
adj. analytical, contemplative, cultured, intelligent, philosophical, rational, reasoning, reflective, sophisticated, thoughtful.

thin-skinned *adj.* irritable, sensitive, snappish, soft, susceptible, tender, touchy, vulnerable.
antonyms hardened, thick-skinned, tough, unfeeling.

third-rate *adj.* bad, cheap and nasty, cheap-jack, indifferent, inferior, low-grade, mediocre, poor, ropy, shoddy.
antonym first-rate.

thirst *n.* appetite, craving, desire, drought, dryness, eagerness, hankering, hunger, keenness, longing, lust, passion, thirstiness, yearning.

thirsty *adj.* arid, avid, burning, craving, dehydrated, desirous, dry, dying, eager, greedy, hankering, hungry, itching, longing, parched, thirsting, yearning.

thorn *n.* affliction, annoyance, barb, bother, curse, irritation, nuisance, prickle, scourge, spike, torment, torture, trouble.

thorough *adj.* absolute, all-embracing, all-inclusive, careful, complete, comprehensive, conscientious, deep-seated, downright, efficient, entire, exhaustive, full, in-depth, intensive, meticulous, out-and-out, painstaking, perfect, pure, scrupulous, sheer, sweeping, thoroughgoing, total, unmitigated, unqualified, utter.
antonyms careless, haphazard, partial.

though *conj.* allowing, although, even if, granted, notwithstanding, while.
adv. all the same, even so, for all that, however, in spite of that, nevertheless, nonetheless, notwithstanding, still, yet.

thought *n.* **1** attention, brainwork, consideration, contemplation, deliberation, expectation, heed, introspection, meditation, reflection, regard, scrutiny, study, thinking. **2** aim, anticipation, assessment, belief, concept, conception, conclusion, conjecture, conviction, design, dream, hope, idea, intention, judgement, notion, opinion, plan, purpose, view. **3** care, compassion, concern, gesture, kindness, sympathy, thoughtfulness, touch.

thoughtful *adj.* absorbed, astute, attentive, care-

ful, caring, cautious, considerate, contemplative, deliberate, discreet, heedful, helpful, introspective, kind, mindful, pensive, prudent, reflective, serious, studious, thinking, unselfish, wary, wistful.
antonyms insensitive, selfish, thoughtless.

thoughtless *adj.* absent-minded, careless, foolish, heedless, ill-considered, impolite, imprudent, inadvertent, inattentive, inconsiderate, insensitive, mindless, negligent, rash, reckless, remiss, rude, selfish, silly, stupid, uncaring, undiplomatic, unkind, unthinking.
antonyms careful, considerate, thoughtful.

thrash *v.* beat, belt, cane, clobber, crush, defeat, flail, flog, hammer, jerk, lay into, maul, overwhelm, plunge, punish, rout, scourge, slaughter, spank, squirm, swish, tan, thresh, toss, trim, trounce, wallop, whip.
thrash out debate, discuss, negotiate, resolve, settle, solve.

thread *n.* cotton, course, direction, drift, fibre, filament, film, line, motif, plot, story-line, strain, strand, string, tenor, theme, yarn.
v. ease, inch, pass, string, weave, wind.

threadbare *adj.* cliché-ridden, commonplace, conventional, corny, frayed, hackneyed, moth-eaten, old, overused, ragged, scruffy, shabby, stale, stereotyped, stock, tired, trite, used, worn.
antonyms fresh, luxurious, new, plush.

threat *n.* danger, foreboding, hazard, menace, omen, peril, portent, presage, risk, warning.

threaten *v.* browbeat, bully, endanger, forebode, foreshadow, impend, imperil, intimidate, jeopardise, menace, portend, presage, pressurise, terrorise, warn.

threatening *adj.* bullying, cautionary, grim, inauspicious, intimidatory, menacing, ominous, sinister, terrorising, warning.

threshold *n.* beginning, brink, dawn, door, doorstep, doorway, entrance, inception, minimum, opening, outset, start, starting-point, verge.

thrift *n.* carefulness, conservation, economy, frugality, husbandry, prudence, saving.
antonyms profligacy, waste.

thrifty *adj.* careful, conserving, economical, frugal, prudent, saving, sparing.
antonyms extravagant, prodigal, profligate, wasteful.

thrill *n.* adventure, charge, glow, kick, pleasure, quiver, sensation, shudder, stimulation, throb, tingle, tremble, tremor, vibration.
v. arouse, electrify, excite, exhilarate, flush, flutter, glow, move, quake, quiver, rouse, shake, shudder, stimulate, stir, throb, tingle, tremble, vibrate.
antonyms be tedious, bore.

thrive *v.* advance, bloom, blossom, boom, develop, flourish, gain, grow, increase, profit, prosper, succeed.
antonyms die, fail, languish, stagnate.

throat *n.* gorge, gullet, oesophagus, throttle, windpipe.

throb *v.* beat, palpitate, pound, pulse, thump, vibrate.
n. beat, palpitation, pounding, pulse, thumping, vibration.

throe *n.* convulsion, fit, pain, pang, paroxysm, seizure, spasm, stab.

throes *n.* agony, anguish, death-agony, distress, pain, suffering, torture, travail.

throttle *v.* asphyxiate, choke, control, gag, inhibit, silence, smother, stifle, strangle, suppress.

through *prep.* as a result of, because of, between, by, by means of, by way of, during, in, in consequence of, in the middle of, past, thanks to, throughout, using, via.
adj. completed, direct, done, ended, express, finished, non-stop, terminated.
through and through altogether, completely, entirely, from top to bottom, fully, thoroughly, to the core, totally, unreservedly, utterly, wholly.

throughout *adv.* everywhere, extensively, widely.

throw *v.* **1** cast, chuck, fling, heave, hurl, launch, lob, pitch, project, propel, sling, toss. **2** cast, direct, send, shed. **3** bring down, dislodge, fell, overturn, unhorse, unsaddle, unseat, upset. **4** astonish, baffle, confound, confuse, disconcert, dumbfound, floor, perplex.
n. **1** fling, heave, lob, pitch, sling, toss. **2** attempt, chance, gamble, hazard, try, venture, wager.
throw away blow, cast off, discard, dispense with, dispose of, ditch, dump, fritter away, jettison, lose, reject, scrap, squander, waste.
antonyms keep, preserve, rescue, salvage.
throw off abandon, cast off, confuse, discard, disconcert, disturb, drop, shake off, throw, unsaddle, unseat, unsettle, upset.
throw out confuse, discard, disconcert, dismiss, disturb, ditch, dump, eject, emit, evict, expel, give off, jettison, radiate, reject, scrap, turf out, turn down, unhouse, unsettle, upset, utter.
throw up **1** disgorge, heave, regurgitate, retch, spew, vomit. **2** leave, produce, reveal. **3** abandon, chuck, give up, jack in, quit, relinquish, renounce, resign.

thrust *v.* bear, butt, drive, force, impel, intrude, jab, jam, lunge, pierce, plunge, poke, press, prod, propel, push, ram, shove, stab, stick, wedge.
n. drive, impetus, lunge, momentum, poke, prod, prog, push, shove, stab.

thud *n.* clonk, clump, clunk, crash, knock, smack, thump, thwack, wallop, wham.
v. bash, clonk, clump, clunk, crash, knock, smack, thump, thunder, thwack, wallop, wham.

thug *n.* assassin, bandit, cut-throat, gangster, hooligan, killer, mugger, murderer, robber, ruffian, tough.

thump *n.* bang, blow, box, clout, clunk, crash, knock, rap, smack, thud, thwack, wallop, whack.
v. bang, batter, beat, box, clout, crash, cuff, hit, knock, pound, rap, smack, strike, thrash, throb, thud, thwack, wallop, whack.

thunder *n.* boom, booming, clap, cracking, crash, crashing, detonation, explosion, pealing, roll, rumble, rumbling.
v. blast, boom, clap, crack, crash, detonate, peal, rail, resound, reverberate, roar, rumble, shout, threaten, yell.
thundering *adj.* enormous, excessive, great, monumental, remarkable, tremendous, unmitigated.
thunderous *adj.* booming, deafening, ear-splitting, loud, noisy, resounding, reverberating, roaring, tumultuous.
thus *adv.* accordingly, as follows, consequently, hence, in this way, like so, like this, so, then, therefore, thuswise.
thwart *v.* baffle, check, defeat, foil, frustrate, hinder, impede, obstruct, oppose, prevent, stop, stymie.
antonyms abet, aid, assist.
tic *n.* jerk, spasm, twitch.
tick *n.* **1** click, clicking, stroke, tap, tick-tick. **2** flash, instant, jiffy, minute, moment, second.
v. **1** choose, indicate, mark (off), select. **2** beat, click, tap.
tick off censure, chide, haul over the coals, lecture, rebuke, reprimand, reproach, reprove, scold, take to task, tear off a strip, tell off, upbraid.
antonyms compliment, praise.
ticket *n.* card, certificate, coupon, docket, label, marker, pass, slip, sticker, tag, token, voucher.
tickle *v.* amuse, cheer, delight, divert, enchant, entertain, excite, gratify, please, thrill.
ticklish *adj.* awkward, critical, delicate, difficult, dodgy, hazardous, risky, sensitive, thorny, touchy, tricky, uncertain, unstable, unsteady.
antonyms easy, simple, straightforward.
tide *n.* course, current, direction, drift, ebb, flow, flux, movement, stream, tendency, tenor, trend.
tidy *adj.* **1** clean, methodical, neat, ordered, orderly, shipshape, spick-and-span, spruce, systematic, trim, uncluttered, well-kept. **2** ample, considerable, fair, generous, good, large, siz(e)-able, substantial.
antonyms **1** disorganised, messy, untidy. **2** insignificant, small.
v. arrange, clean, groom, neaten, order, spruce up, straighten.
tie *v.* attach, bind, confine, connect, draw, equal, fasten, hamper, hinder, hold, join, knot, lash, limit, link, match, moor, oblige, restrain, restrict, rope, secure, strap, unite.
n. **1** affiliation, allegiance, band, bond, commitment, connection, cord, duty, fastening, hindrance, joint, knot, liaison, limitation, link, obligation, relationship, restraint, restriction, rope, string. **2** contest, fixture, game, match. **3** dead heat, deadlock, draw, stalemate.
tie up attach, bind, conclude, end, engage, engross, finish off, lash, moor, occupy, restrain, rope, secure, settle, terminate, tether, truss, wind up, wrap up.
tier *n.* band, belt, echelon, floor, layer, level, line, rank, row, stage, storey, stratification, stratum, zone.
tiff *n.* barney, difference, disagreement, dispute, falling-out, huff, ill-humour, quarrel, row, scrap, set-to, squabble, sulk, tantrum, temper, words.
tight *adj.* **1** close, close-fitting, compact, constricted, cramped, fast, firm, fixed, rigid, secure, snug, stiff, stretched, taut, tense. **2** hermetic, impervious, -proof, sealed, watertight. **3** mean, miserly, niggardly, parsimonious, sparing, stingy, tight-fisted. **4** inflexible, rigorous, strict, stringent.
antonyms **1** loose, slack. **2** broken, open. **3** generous. **4** lax.
tighten *v.* close, constrict, cramp, crush, fasten, fix, narrow, secure, squeeze, stiffen, stretch, tauten, tense.
antonyms loosen, relax.
tight-fisted *adj.* grasping, mean, mingy, miserly, niggardly, parsimonious, penny-pinching, sparing, stingy, tight.
antonyms charitable, generous.
till *v.* cultivate, dig, dress, plough, work.
tilt *v.* incline, lean, list, pitch, slant, slope, tip.
n. angle, inclination, incline, list, pitch, slant, slope.
timber *n.* beams, boarding, boards, forest, logs, planking, planks, trees, wood.
time *n.* **1** age, chronology, date, day, duration, epoch, era, generation, heyday, hour, instance, interval, juncture, life, lifespan, lifetime, measure, occasion, peak, period, point, season, space, span, spell, stage, stretch, term, tide, while. **2** beat, metre, rhythm, tempo.
v. clock, control, count, judge, measure, meter, regulate, schedule, set.
timeless *adj.* ageless, changeless, endless, enduring, eternal, everlasting, immortal, permanent.
timely *adj.* appropriate, convenient, opportune, prompt, propitious, punctual, seasonable, suitable, well-timed.
antonyms ill-timed, inappropriate, unfavourable.
timetable *n.* agenda, calendar, curriculum, diary, list, listing, programme, roster, rota, schedule.
time-worn *adj.* ancient, cliché'd, dated, decrepit, hackneyed, hoary, outworn, passé, run-down, shabby, stale, threadbare, trite, weathered, worn.
antonyms fresh, new.
timid *adj.* afraid, apprehensive, bashful, cowardly, faint-hearted, fearful, irresolute, modest, nervous, retiring, shrinking, shy, spineless, timorous.
antonyms audacious, bold, brave.
tinge *n.* bit, colour, dash, drop, dye, flavour, pinch, shade, smack, smattering, sprinkling, stain, suggestion, tincture, tint, touch, trace, wash.
v. colour, dye, imbue, shade, stain, suffuse, tint.
tingle *v.* itch, ring, sting, thrill, throb, tickle, vibrate.
n. gooseflesh, goose-pimples, itch, itching, pins and needles, prickling, quiver, shiver, stinging, thrill, tickle, tickling.

tinker *v.* dabble, fiddle, meddle, monkey, play, potter, toy, trifle.

tint *n.* cast, colour, dye, hint, hue, rinse, shade, stain, streak, suggestion, tincture, tinge, tone, touch, trace, wash.
v. affect, colour, dye, rinse, stain, streak, taint, tinge.

tiny *adj.* diminutive, dwarfish, insignificant, little, microscopic, mini, miniature, minute, negligible, petite, pint-size(d), pocket, puny, slight, small.
antonyms enormous, huge, immense.

tip¹ *n.* acme, apex, cap, crown, end, extremity, head, nib, peak, pinnacle, point, summit, top.
v. cap, crown, finish, pinnacle, poll, pollard, prune, surmount, top.

tip² *v.* capsize, ditch, dump, empty, incline, lean, list, overturn, pour out, slant, spill, tilt, topple over, unload, up-end, upset.
n. dump, refuse-heap, rubbish-heap, slag-heap.

tip³ *n.* **1** clue, forecast, hint, information, inside information, pointer, suggestion, tip-off, warning, word, word of advice. **2** gift, gratuity, perquisite.
v. **1** advise, caution, forewarn, inform, suggest, tell, warn. **2** remunerate, reward.

tipple *v.* bib, drink, imbibe, indulge, swig.
n. alcohol, drink, liquor, wet.

tirade *n.* abuse, denunciation, lecture, outburst.

tire *v.* drain, enervate, exhaust, fatigue, jade, weary.
antonyms energise, enliven, exhilarate, invigorate, refresh.

tired *adj.* **1** all in, beat, bushed, dead-beat, dog-tired, drained, drowsy, exhausted, fagged, fatigued, flagging, knackered, shattered, sleepy, weary, whacked, worn out. **2** bored, fed up, sick. **3** conventional, corny, familiar, hackneyed, old, outworn, stale, stock, threadbare, trite, well-worn.
antonyms **1** active, energetic, fresh, lively, rested. **2** excited, interested. **3** new.

tireless *adj.* determined, diligent, energetic, indefatigable, industrious, resolute, unflagging, untiring, unwearied, vigorous.
antonyms tired, unenthusiastic, weak.

tiresome *adj.* annoying, boring, dull, exasperating, fatiguing, irritating, laborious, monotonous, tedious, troublesome, trying, uninteresting, wearisome.
antonyms easy, interesting, stimulating.

tiring *adj.* arduous, demanding, draining, exacting, exhausting, fatiguing, laborious, strenuous, wearying.

tissue *n.* agglomeration, collection, combination, fabric, fabrication, gauze, mass, mesh, network, pack, paper, series, structure, stuff, texture, tissue-paper, web.

titbit *n.* appetiser, dainty, delicacy, goody, morsel, scrap, snack, treat.

titillate *v.* arouse, captivate, excite, interest, intrigue, provoke, stimulate, tantalise, tease, thrill, tickle, turn on.

title *n.* **1** appellation, caption, denomination, designation, epithet, handle, heading, inscription, label, legend, letter-head, name, nickname, nom de plume, pseudonym, style, term. **2** championship, contest, winner. **3** claim, deeds, entitlement, ownership, prerogative, privilege, right.
v. call, christen, designate, dub, entitle, label, name, style, term.

titter *v.* chortle, chuckle, giggle, laugh, mock, snigger.

titular *adj.* formal, honorary, nominal, puppet, so-called, token.

toast *v.* brown, grill, heat, roast, warm.
n. **1** compliment, drink, health, pledge, salute, tribute. **2** darling, favourite, hero, heroine.

to-do *n.* agitation, bother, commotion, disturbance, excitement, flap, flurry, furore, fuss, performance, quarrel, rumpus, stew, stir, tumult, turmoil, unrest, uproar.

together *adv.* all at once, as one, at the same time, closely, collectively, consecutively, continuously, en masse, fixed, hand in glove, hand in hand, in a body, in a row, in concert, in co-operation, in succession, in unison, jointly, mutually, organised, settled, shoulder to shoulder, side by side, simultaneously, sorted out, straight, successively.
antonyms alone, apart, individually, separately.

toilet *n.* bathroom, cloakroom, convenience, lavatory, loo, powder-room, public convenience, rest-room, urinal, washroom, water-closet, WC.

token *n.* badge, clue, demonstration, evidence, expression, index, indication, keepsake, manifestation, mark, memento, memorial, note, proof, remembrance, reminder, representation, sign, souvenir, symbol, voucher, warning.
adj. hollow, minimal, nominal, perfunctory, superficial, symbolic.

tolerable *adj.* acceptable, adequate, all right, average, bearable, endurable, fair, indifferent, mediocre, not bad, OK, ordinary, passable, reasonable, run-of-the-mill, so-so, unexceptional.
antonyms insufferable, intolerable, unbearable.

tolerance *n.* **1** allowance, broad-mindedness, endurance, forbearance, indulgence, lenity, magnanimity, open-mindedness, patience, permissiveness, stamina, sympathy, toughness. **2** fluctuation, play, swing, variation. **3** resilience, resistance.
antonyms **1** bigotry, intolerance, narrow-mindedness, prejudice.

tolerant *adj.* broad-minded, charitable, easy-going, fair, forbearing, indulgent, kind-hearted, lax, lenient, liberal, long-suffering, open-minded, patient, permissive, soft, sympathetic, understanding, unprejudiced.
antonyms biased, bigoted, intolerant, prejudiced, unsympathetic.

tolerate *v.* abide, accept, admit, allow, bear, condone, countenance, endure, indulge, permit, put up with, receive, stand, stomach, suffer, swallow, take.

toll[1] *v.* announce, call, chime, clang, knell, peal, ring, send, signal, sound, strike, summon, warn.
toll[2] *n.* assessment, charge, cost, customs, demand, duty, fee, levy, loss, payment, penalty, rate, tariff, tax, tithe, tribute.
tomb *n.* burial-place, catacomb, cenotaph, crypt, grave, mausoleum, sepulchre, vault.
tone *n.* accent, air, approach, aspect, attitude, cast, character, colour, drift, effect, emphasis, feel, force, frame, grain, harmony, hue, inflection, intonation, manner, modulation, mood, note, pitch, quality, shade, spirit, strength, stress, style, temper, tenor, timbre, tinge, tint, tonality, vein, volume.
v. blend, harmonise, match, sound, suit.
tone down alleviate, assuage, dampen, dim, mitigate, moderate, modulate, play down, reduce, restrain, soften, soft-pedal, subdue, temper.
tongue *n.* argot, articulation, dialect, discourse, idiom, language, parlance, patois, speech, talk, utterance, vernacular, voice.
tongue-tied *adj.* dumb, dumbstruck, inarticulate, mute, silent, speechless, voiceless.
antonyms garrulous, talkative, voluble.
tonic *n.* boost, bracer, cordial, fillip, inspiration, livener, pick-me-up, refresher, restorative, shot in the arm, stimulant.
too *adv.* **1** also, as well, besides, further, in addition, likewise, moreover, what's more. **2** excessively, exorbitantly, extremely, inordinately, over, overly, ridiculously, to excess, to extremes, unduly, unreasonably, very.
tool *n.* **1** agency, agent, apparatus, appliance, contraption, contrivance, device, gadget, implement, instrument, intermediary, machine, means, medium, utensil, vehicle, weapon. **2** dupe, hireling, minion, pawn, puppet, stooge.
tooth *n.* fang, incisor, jag, molar, tusk.
top *n.* acme, apex, cap, cork, cover, crest, crown, culmination, head, height, high point, lead, lid, peak, pinnacle, stopper, summit, vertex, zenith.
antonyms base, bottom, nadir.
adj. best, chief, crowning, culminating, dominant, elite, finest, first, foremost, greatest, head, highest, lead, leading, maximum, pre-eminent, prime, principal, ruling, sovereign, superior, topmost, upmost, upper, uppermost.
antonyms bottom, inferior, lowest.
v. ascend, beat, best, better, cap, climb, command, cover, crown, decorate, eclipse, exceed, excel, finish (off), garnish, head, lead, outdo, outshine, outstrip, rule, scale, surmount, surpass, tip, transcend.
topic *n.* issue, matter, point, question, subject, subject-matter, talking-point, text, theme, thesis.
topical *adj.* contemporary, current, familiar, newsworthy, popular, relevant, up-to-date, up-to-the-minute.
topmost *adj.* dominant, foremost, highest, leading, maximum, paramount, principal, supreme, top, upper, uppermost.
antonyms bottom, bottommost, lowest.
topple *v.* capsize, collapse, oust, overbalance, overthrow, overturn, totter, tumble, unseat, upset.
torch *n.* brand, firebrand, flashlight.
torment *v.* afflict, annoy, bedevil, bother, crucify, distort, distress, excruciate, harass, harrow, hound, persecute, pester, plague, provoke, rack, tease, torture, trouble, vex, worry.
n. affliction, agony, anguish, annoyance, bane, bother, distress, harassment, hell, misery, nagging, nuisance, ordeal, pain, persecution, provocation, scourge, suffering, torture, trouble, vexation, worry.
tornado *n.* cyclone, gale, hurricane, monsoon, squall, storm, tempest, typhoon, whirlwind.
torrent *n.* cascade, deluge, downpour, flood, flow, gush, outburst, rush, spate, stream, tide, volley.
torture *v.* afflict, agonise, crucify, distress, martyr, pain, persecute, torment, wrack.
n. affliction, agony, anguish, distress, hell, martyrdom, misery, pain, persecution, suffering, torment.
toss *v.* agitate, cast, chuck, disturb, fling, flip, heave, hurl, jolt, lob, lurch, pitch, project, propel, rock, roll, shake, sling, thrash, throw, wriggle.
n. cast, chuck, fling, lob, pitch, throw.
total *n.* aggregate, all, amount, entirety, lot, mass, sum, totality, whole.
adj. absolute, all-out, complete, consummate, downright, entire, full, integral, outright, perfect, sheer, sweeping, thorough, thoroughgoing, unconditional, undisputed, unqualified, utter, whole.
antonyms limited, partial, restricted.
v. add (up), amount to, come to, count (up), reach, reckon, sum (up), tot up.
totalitarian *adj.* authoritarian, despotic, dictatorial, monolithic, omnipotent, one-party, oppressive.
antonym democratic.
totter *v.* falter, lurch, quiver, reel, rock, shake, stagger, stumble, sway, teeter, titter, tremble, waver.
touch *n.* **1** brush, caress, contact, feel, feeling, fondling, hand, pat, stroke, tap. **2** dash, hint, intimation, jot, pinch, smack, smattering, soupçon, speck, spot, suggestion, suspicion, tinge, trace. **3** approach, art, deftness, effect, manner, method, skill, style, technique.
v. **1** abut, adjoin, border, brush, caress, contact, feel, finger, fondle, graze, handle, hit, meet, pat, strike, stroke, tap. **2** affect, disturb, impress, influence, inspire, move, soften, stir, upset. **3** attain, better, compare with, concern, equal, hold a candle to, match, regard, rival. **4** consume, drink, eat.
touch off actuate, arouse, begin, cause, fire, ignite, inflame, initiate, light, provoke, set off, spark off, trigger (off).
touch on allude to, broach, cover, deal with, mention, refer to, remark on, speak of.
touched *adj.* barmy, batty, crazy, daft, disturbed,

dotty, eccentric, mad, nuts.

touching *adj.* affecting, emotional, heartbreaking, moving, pathetic, pitiable, pitiful, poignant, sad, stirring, tender.

touchy *adj.* bad-tempered, captious, crabbed, cross, grouchy, grumpy, huffy, irritable, peevish, pettish, quick-tempered, surly.
antonyms calm, imperturbable, serene, unflappable.

tough *adj.* **1** durable, firm, hard, hardy, inflexible, resilient, resistant, rigid, solid, stiff, strong, sturdy. **2** callous, hard-bitten, hardened, obstinate, rough, rugged, vicious, violent. **3** hard, leathery. **4** arduous, baffling, difficult, exacting, hard, knotty, laborious, perplexing, puzzling, thorny, troublesome. **5** determined, harsh, resolute, severe, stern, strict, tenacious.
antonyms **1** brittle, delicate, fragile, weak. **2** gentle, kind, soft. **3** tender. **4** easy. **5** weak.
n. brute, bully, hooligan, rough, rowdy, ruffian, thug, yob.

tour *n.* circuit, course, drive, excursion, expedition, journey, outing, progress, ride, round, trip.
v. drive, explore, journey, ride, sightsee, travel, visit.

tourist *n.* excursionist, globe-trotter, holidaymaker, journeyer, sightseer, traveller, tripper, voyager.

tournament *n.* championship, competition, contest, event, match, meeting, series.

tousled *adj.* dishevelled, messed up, ruffled, rumpled, tangled, untidy.

tow *v.* drag, draw, haul, lug, pull, trail, transport, tug.

towards *prep.* about, almost, approaching, close to, coming up to, concerning, for, getting on for, in the direction of, in the vicinity of, just before, nearing, nearly, on the way to, regarding, to, with regard to, with respect to.

tower *n.* barbican, bastille, bastion, belfry, castle, citadel, column, fort, fortification, fortress, keep, steeple, turret.
v. ascend, dominate, exceed, loom, mount, overlook, rear, rise, soar, surpass, top, transcend.

towering *adj.* colossal, elevated, extraordinary, extreme, gigantic, great, high, imposing, impressive, inordinate, lofty, magnificent, monumental, overpowering, soaring, sublime, supreme, surpassing, tall.
antonyms minor, small, tiny, trivial.

toxic *adj.* baneful, deadly, harmful, lethal, noxious, poisonous, unhealthy.
antonyms harmless, safe.

toy *n.* bauble, doll, game, knick-knack, plaything, trifle, trinket.
v. dally, fiddle, flirt, play, sport, tinker, trifle.

trace *n.* bit, dash, drop, evidence, footmark, footprint, footstep, hint, indication, jot, mark, path, record, relic, remains, remnant, shadow, sign, smack, soupçon, spot, suggestion, suspicion, tinge, token, touch, track, trail, vestige.
v. ascertain, chart, copy, delineate, depict, detect, determine, discover, draw, find, follow, map, mark, outline, pursue, record, seek, shadow, show, sketch, stalk, track (down), trail, unearth.

track *n.* course, drift, footmark, footprint, footstep, line, mark, orbit, path, pathway, rail, ridgeway, road, scent, sequence, slot, trace, trail, wake, wavelength, way.
v. chase, dog, follow, hunt, pursue, shadow, stalk, tail, trace, trail.
track down apprehend, capture, catch, dig up, discover, expose, ferret out, find, hunt down, run to earth, sniff out, trace, unearth.

tract[1] *n.* area, district, estate, expanse, extent, lot, plot, quarter, region, section, stretch, territory, zone.

tract[2] *n.* booklet, brochure, discourse, essay, leaflet, monograph, pamphlet, sermon, treatise.

trade *n.* barter, business, calling, clientele, commerce, commodities, custom, customers, deal, dealing, employment, exchange, job, market, occupation, patrons, profession, public, pursuit, shopkeeping, skill, traffic, transactions.
v. bargain, barter, commerce, deal, do business, exchange, peddle, swap, switch, traffic, transact.

trademark *n.* badge, brand, crest, emblem, hallmark, identification, insignia, label, logo, name, sign, symbol.

trader *n.* barrow-boy, broker, buyer, dealer, marketer, merchandiser, merchant, seller.

tradition *n.* convention, custom, folklore, habit, institution, lore, ritual, usage, way.

traditional *adj.* accustomed, ancestral, conventional, customary, established, fixed, folk, historic, long-established, new, old, oral, time-honoured, transmitted, unconventional, unwritten, usual.
antonyms contemporary, innovative, modern, new, unconventional.

traffic *n.* barter, business, commerce, communication, dealing, dealings, doings, exchange, freight, movement, passengers, relations, trade, transport, transportation, vehicles.
v. bargain, barter, deal, do business, exchange, market, merchandise, trade.

tragedy *n.* adversity, affliction, blow, calamity, catastrophe, disaster, misfortune, unhappiness.
antonyms prosperity, success, triumph.

tragic *adj.* appalling, awful, calamitous, catastrophic, deadly, dire, disastrous, dreadful, fatal, grievous, heartbreaking, ill-fated, miserable, mournful, pathetic, pitiable, sad, shocking, sorrowful, unfortunate, unhappy.
antonyms glorious, successful, triumphant.

trail *v.* chase, dawdle, drag, droop, extend, follow, hunt, lag, linger, loiter, pull, pursue, shadow, stalk, straggle, stream, sweep, tail, tow, trace, track, traipse.
n. footpath, footprints, marks, path, road, route, scent, tail, trace, track, way.

train *v.* aim, coach, direct, discipline, drill, educate, excercise, guide, improve, instruct, level, point, prepare, rear, school, teach, tutor.
n. **1** caravan, chain, convoy, cortege, file, order,

procession, progression, sequence, series, set, string, succession. **2** attendants, court, entourage, followers, following, household, retinue, staff.

trainer *n.* coach, handler, instructor, teacher, tutor.

training *n.* coaching, discipline, education, exercise, grounding, guidance, instruction, practice, preparation, schooling, teaching, tuition, upbringing, working-out.

trait *n.* attribute, characteristic, feature, idiosyncrasy, mannerism, peculiarity, quality, quirk.

traitor *n.* betrayer, deceiver, defector, deserter, double-crosser, informer, miscreant, quisling, rebel, renegade, turncoat.
antonyms defender, loyalist, supporter.

tramp *v.* crush, footslog, hike, march, plod, ramble, roam, rove, slog, stamp, stomp, stump, toil, traipse, trample, tread, trek, trudge, walk.
n. dosser, down-and-out, hobo, vagabond, vagrant.

trample *v.* crush, flatten, hurt, infringe, insult, squash, stamp, tread, violate.

trance *n.* daze, dream, ecstasy, rapture, reverie, spell, stupor, unconsciousness.

tranquil *adj.* at peace, calm, composed, cool, pacific, peaceful, placid, quiet, restful, sedate, serene, still, undisturbed, unexcited, untroubled.
antonyms agitated, disturbed, noisy, troubled.

tranquilliser *n.* barbiturate, downer, narcotic, sedative.

tranquillity *n.* calm, composure, coolness, equanimity, hush, imperturbability, peace, quiet, rest, restfulness, serenity, silence, stillness.
antonyms agitation, disturbance, noise.

transact *v.* accomplish, carry on, carry out, conclude, conduct, discharge, dispatch, do, enact, execute, handle, manage, negotiate, perform, settle.

transaction *n.* action, affair, arrangement, bargain, business, coup, deal, deed, enterprise, event, execution, matter, negotiation, occurrence, proceeding, undertaking.

transcend *v.* eclipse, exceed, excel, outdo, outrival, outshine, outstrip, overstep, surmount, surpass.

transcribe *v.* copy, note, record, render, reproduce, rewrite, take down, tape, tape-record, transfer, translate, transliterate.

transcript *n.* carbon, copy, duplicate, manuscript, note, record, recording, reproduction, transcription, translation, transliteration, version.

transfer *v.* carry, change, consign, convey, decant, grant, hand over, move, relocate, remove, shift, translate, transmit, transplant, transport, transpose.
n. change, changeover, crossover, displacement, handover, move, relocation, removal, shift, switch-over, transference, translation, transmission, transposition.

transfigure *v.* alter, change, convert, exalt, glorify, idealise, transform.

transfix *v.* **1** engross, fascinate, fix, hold, hypnotise, mesmerise, spellbind, stun. **2** impale, skewer, spear, spike, stick.
antonyms **1** bore, frighten, tire.

transform *v.* alter, change, convert, reconstruct, remodel, renew, revolutionise.
antonyms keep, preserve.

transformation *n.* alteration, change, conversion, renewal, revolution, transfiguration.
antonyms maintenance, preservation, retention.

transfuse *v.* imbue, instil, permeate, pervade, transfer.

transient *adj.* brief, ephemeral, fleeting, flying, momentary, passing, short, short-lived, short-term, temporary, transitory.
antonyms durable, long-lasting, permanent.

transition *n.* alteration, change, conversion, development, evolution, flux, passage, passing, progress, progression, shift, transformation.
antonyms beginning, end.

transitional *adj.* changing, developmental, fluid, intermediate, passing, provisional, temporary, unsettled.
antonyms final, initial.

translate *v.* alter, carry, change, convert, convey, decipher, decode, explain, improve, interpret, paraphrase, render, simplify, transcribe, transfer, transform, transpose, turn.

translation *n.* alteration, change, conversion, crib, explanation, gloss, interpretation, paraphrase, rendering, rephrasing, rewording, simplification, transcription, transformation, transliteration, version.

transmission *n.* broadcast, broadcasting, carriage, communication, conveyance, diffusion, dispatch, passage, programme, relaying, sending, shipment, show, showing, signal, spread, transfer, transit, transport.
antonym reception.

transmit *v.* bear, broadcast, carry, communicate, convey, diffuse, dispatch, disseminate, forward, impart, network, radio, relay, remit, send, spread, transfer, transport.
antonym receive.

transparency *n.* **1** photograph, picture, slide. **2** clarity, distinctness, openness, plainness, visibility.
antonyms **2** opacity, unclearness.

transparent *adj.* apparent, candid, clear, distinct, evident, explicit, lucid, manifest, obvious, open, patent, perspicuous, plain, recognisable, see-through, straightforward, translucent, unambiguous, understandable, undisguised, unequivocal, visible.
antonyms ambiguous, opaque, unclear.

transplant *v.* displace, pot, relocate, remove, repot, resettle, shift, transfer, uproot.
antonym leave.

transport *v.* bring, captivate, carry, carry away, convey, delight, deport, fetch, haul, move, remove, run, ship, take, transfer.
n. carriage, conveyance, removal, shipment, shipping, transference, transportation, vehicle.

transportation *n.* carriage, conveyance, haulage,

transfer, transport.

transpose *v.* alter, change, exchange, interchange, move, rearrange, relocate, reorder, shift, substitute, swap, switch, transfer.
antonym leave.

transverse *adj.* cross, crossways, crosswise, diagonal, oblique, transversal.

trap *n.* ambush, artifice, danger, deception, device, hazard, net, noose, pitfall, ruse, snare, spring, strategem, subterfuge, trap-door, trick, trickery, wile.
v. ambush, beguile, catch, corner, deceive, dupe, enmesh, ensnare, entrap, snare, take, trick.

trapped *adj.* ambushed, caught, cornered, deceived, duped, ensnared, stuck, surrounded, tricked.
antonym free.

trash *n.* balderdash, dregs, garbage, junk, litter, nonsense, offscourings, offscum, refuse, rot, rubbish, sweepings, tripe, twaddle, waste.
antonym sense.

trauma *n.* agony, anguish, damage, disturbance, hurt, injury, jolt, ordeal, pain, scar, shock, strain, suffering, torture, upheaval, upset, wound.
antonyms healing, relaxation.

traumatic *adj.* damaging, distressing, disturbing, frightening, hurtful, injurious, painful, shocking, unpleasant, upsetting, wounding.
antonyms healing, relaxed, relaxing.

travel *v.* carry, commute, cross, go, journey, move, proceed, progress, ramble, roam, rove, tour, traverse, trek, voyage, walk, wander, wend.
antonyms remain, stay.

traveller *n.* agent, excursionist, explorer, globetrotter, gypsy, hiker, holiday-maker, itinerant, journeyer, migrant, nomad, passenger, rep, representative, salesman, saleswoman, tinker, tourist, tripper, vagrant, voyager, wanderer, wayfarer.

travelling *adj.* itinerant, migrant, migratory, mobile, movable, moving, nomadic, on the move, peripatetic, roaming, roving, touring, vagrant, wandering, wayfaring.
antonyms fixed, stay-at-home.

travels *n.* excursion, expedition, globetrotting, journey, passage, ramble, tour, travel, trip, voyage, walk, wanderings, wayfare.

travesty *n.* apology, caricature, distortion, farce, mockery, parody, send-up, sham, take-off.

treacherous *adj.* **1** deceitful, disloyal, double-crossing, faithless, false, traitorous, unfaithful, unreliable, untrue, untrustworthy. **2** dangerous, hazardous, icy, perilous, precarious, risky, slippery, slippy.
antonyms **1** dependable, faithful, loyal. **2** safe, stable.

treachery *n.* betrayal, disloyalty, double-dealing, falseness, infidelity, treason.
antonyms dependability, loyalty.

treason *n.* disloyalty, duplicity, mutiny, perfidy, sedition, subversion, treachery.
antonym loyalty.

treasonable *adj.* disloyal, false, mutinous, perfidious, seditious, subversive, traitorous, treacherous.
antonyms faithful, loyal.

treasure *n.* **1** cache, cash, fortune, funds, gold, hoard, jewels, money, riches, wealth. **2** darling, gem, precious.
v. adore, cherish, esteem, idolise, love, preserve, prize, revere, value, worship.
antonyms belittle, disparage.

treasurer *n.* bursar, cashier, purser.

treat *n.* banquet, celebration, delight, enjoyment, entertainment, excursion, feast, fun, gift, gratification, joy, outing, party, pleasure, refreshment, satisfaction, surprise, thrill.
antonym drag.
v. **1** consider, deal with, discuss, handle, manage, negotiate, regard, use. **2** attend to, care for, heal, minister to, nurse. **3** entertain, feast, give, provide, regale, stand.

treatise *n.* dissertation, essay, exposition, monograph, pamphlet, paper, study, thesis, tract, work, writing.

treatment *n.* **1** care, cure, healing, medication, medicine, remedy, surgery. **2** conduct, dealing, discussion, handling, management, usage, use.

treaty *n.* agreement, alliance, bond, compact, contract, convention, covenant, negotiation, pact.

tree *n.* bush, conifer, evergreen, seedling, shrub.

trek *n.* expedition, hike, journey, march, migration, safari, slog, tramp, walk.
v. hike, journey, march, migrate, plod, roam, rove, slog, tramp, trudge.

tremble *v.* quake, quiver, rock, shake, shiver, shudder, vibrate, wobble.
n. heart-quake, quake, quiver, shake, shiver, shudder, tremor, vibration.
antonym steadiness.

tremendous *adj.* amazing, colossal, enormous, excellent, exceptional, extraordinary, fabulous, fantastic, formidable, gigantic, great, huge, immense, incredible, marvellous, sensational, spectacular, stupendous, super, terrific, towering, vast, wonderful.
antonyms appalling, dreadful, run-of-the-mill, tiny.

tremor *n.* agitation, earthquake, quake, quaver, quiver, shake, shiver, shock, thrill, tremble, vibration, wobble.
antonym steadiness.

trend *n.* course, current, direction, fashion, flow, inclination, leaning, look, mode, rage, style, tendency, vogue.

trendy *adj.* fashionable, in, latest, modish, stylish, up to the minute.
antonyms old-fashioned, unfashionable.

trespass *v.* encroach, infringe, intrude, invade, offend, poach, sin, transgress, violate, wrong.
antonyms keep to, obey.
n. **1** encroachment, infringement, intrusion, invasion, poaching. **2** contravention, crime, debt, error, evil-doing, fault, iniquity, mis-

demeanour, offence, sin, transgression, wrongdoing.

trespasser *n.* criminal, infringer, intruder, offender, poacher.

trial *n.* **1** enquiry, hearing, litigation, tribunal. **2** audition, check, contest, examination, experiment, proof, test. **3** adversity, affliction, distress, experience, grief, hardship, misery, nuisance, ordeal, pain, suffering, testing, tribulation, trouble, unhappiness, vexation.
antonyms **3** happiness, relief, rest.
adj. dry, dummy, experimental, exploratory, pilot, probationary, provisional, testing.

tribal *adj.* class, ethnic, family, group, native, parochial, primitive, savage, sectarian, sectional, uncivilised, uncultured.

tribe *n.* blood, branch, caste, clan, class, division, dynasty, family, group, house, nation, people, race, seed, stock.

tribute *n.* **1** accolade, acknowledgement, commendation, compliment, credit, gratitude, homage, honour, praise, recognition, respect, testimony. **2** charge, contribution, duty, excise, gift, offering, payment, subsidy, tax.

trick *n.* antic, artifice, caper, deceit, deception, dodge, feat, fraud, frolic, hoax, joke, leg-pull, practical joke, prank, ruse, secret, stunt, subterfuge, swindle, technique, trap, wile.
adj. artificial, bogus, counterfeit, ersatz, fake, false, feigned, forged, imitation, mock, pretend, sham.
antonyms authentic, genuine, real.
v. beguile, cheat, con, deceive, defraud, delude, diddle, dupe, fool, hoax, hoodwink, lead on, mislead, outwit, pull someone's leg, swindle, trap.

trickery *n.* cheating, chicanery, deceit, deception, dishonesty, double-dealing, fraud, funny business, guile, hoax, hocus-pocus, imposture, monkey business, pretence, skulduggery, sleight-of-hand, swindling.
antonyms honesty, openness, straightforwardness.

trickle *v.* dribble, drip, drop, exude, filter, leak, ooze, percolate, run, seep.
antonyms gush, stream.
n. dribble, drip, seepage.
antonyms gush, stream.

tricky *adj.* **1** awkward, complicated, difficult, knotty, problematic, sticky, thorny, ticklish. **2** artful, crafty, cunning, deceitful, devious, scheming, slippery, sly, subtle, wily.
antonyms **1** easy, simple. **2** honest.

trifle *n.* **1** bit, dash, drop, jot, little, spot, touch, trace. **2** bauble, knick-knack, nothing, plaything, toy, trinket, triviality.
v. dabble, dally, flirt, fool, fritter, meddle, play, sport, toy.

trifles *n.* inessentials, minor considerations, trivia, trivialities.
antonym essentials.

trifling *adj.* empty, frivolous, idle, inconsiderable, insignificant, negligible, petty, puny, silly, slight, small, tiny, trivial, unimportant, worthless.
antonyms important, serious, significant.

trigger *v.* activate, cause, elicit, generate, initiate, produce, prompt, provoke, set off, spark off, start.
n. catch, lever, release, spur, stimulus, switch.

trim *adj.* **1** dapper, natty, neat, orderly, shipshape, smart, spick-and-span, spruce, tidy. **2** compact, slender, slim, streamlined.
antonyms **1** scruffy, untidy.
v. adjust, arrange, array, balance, barber, clip, crop, curtail, cut, decorate, dock, dress, embellish, order, ornament, pare, prepare, prune, shave, tidy.
n. condition, form, health, order, shape, state.

trimmings *n.* accessories, additions, clippings, cuttings, ends, extras, frills, garnish, ornaments, parings, trappings.

trinket *n.* bauble, bijou, knick-knack, nothing, ornament, toy, trifle.

trio *n.* threesome, trilogy, trinity, triplet.

trip *n.* excursion, expedition, foray, journey, outing, ramble, run, skip, tour, travel, voyage.
v. blunder, confuse, disconcert, err, fall, flip, misstep, pull, slip up, stumble, trap, tumble, unsettle, voyage.

triple *adj.* three-branched, threefold, three-ply, three-way, treble, triplicate.
v. treble, triplicate.

triplet *n.* threesome, triad, trilogy, trinity, trio, triple, tripling, triumvirate, triune.

trite *adj.* banal, cliché'd, common, commonplace, corny, dull, hack, hackneyed, ordinary, overworn, routine, run-of-the-mill, stale, stereotyped, stock, threadbare, tired, unoriginal, well-trodden, worn.
antonyms exciting, fresh, inspired, new, original.

triumph *n.* accomplishment, achievement, conquest, coup, elation, exultation, feat, happiness, hit, joy, jubilation, masterstroke, rejoicing, sensation, smash-hit, success, victory, walkover, win.
antonyms disaster, failure.
v. celebrate, dominate, glory, overcome, overwhelm, prevail, prosper, rejoice, subdue, succeed, swagger, vanquish, win.
antonyms fail, lose.

triumphant *adj.* boastful, celebratory, conquering, dominant, elated, exultant, gloating, glorious, joyful, jubilant, proud, rejoicing, successful, swaggering, victorious, winning.
antonyms defeated, humble.

trivial *adj.* commonplace, everyday, frivolous, incidental, inconsequential, inconsiderable, insignificant, little, meaningless, minor, negligible, paltry, petty, small, trite, unimportant, worthless.
antonyms important, profound, significant.

triviality *n.* detail, frivolity, insignificance, meaninglessness, minor matter, nothing, pettiness, smallness, technicality, trifle, unimportance, worthlessness.
antonyms essential, importance.

troop *n.* assemblage, band, body, bunch, com-

pany, contingent, crew, crowd, division, flock, gang, gathering, group, herd, horde, multitude, pack, squad, squadron, swarm, team, throng, trip, unit.
v. crowd, flock, go, march, pack, parade, stream, swarm, throng, turn.

troops *n.* army, men, military, servicemen, soldiers.

trophy *n.* award, cup, memento, memorial, prize, souvenir.

tropical *adj.* equatorial, hot, humid, lush, luxuriant, steamy, stifling, sultry, sweltering, torrid.
antonyms arctic, cold, cool, temperate.

trot *v.* bustle, canter, jog, pace, run, scamper, scurry, scuttle.
n. canter, jog, jog-trot, lope, run.
trot out bring up, drag up, recite, reiterate, relate, repeat.

troubadour *n.* balladeer, minstrel, poet, singer.

trouble *n.* **1** affliction, agitation, annoyance, anxiety, bother, concern, difficulty, dissatisfaction, distress, grief, heartache, inconvenience, irritation, misfortune, nuisance, pain, problem, struggle, suffering, torment, trial, tribulation, uneasiness, woe, worry. **2** commotion, disorder, disturbance, strife, tumult, unrest, upheaval. **3** ailment, complaint, defect, disability, disease, disorder, illness. **4** attention, care, effort, exertion, pains, thought.
antonyms **1** calm, peace, relief. **2** order. **3** health.
v. afflict, agitate, annoy, bother, burden, discomfort, disconcert, distress, disturb, harass, inconvenience, pain, perplex, sadden, torment, upset, vex, worry.
antonyms help, reassure.

troublemaker *n.* agitator, incendiary, instigator, mischief-maker, rabble-rouser, ringleader, stirrer.
antonym peacemaker.

troublesome *adj.* annoying, bothersome, demanding, difficult, hard, insubordinate, irritating, laborious, oppressive, rebellious, rowdy, taxing, thorny, tiresome, tricky, trying, turbulent, unco-operative, unruly, upsetting, vexatious, violent, wearisome, worrying.
antonyms easy, helpful, polite, simple.

trough *n.* channel, conduit, depression, ditch, flume, furrow, gully, gutter, hollow, trench, tub.

trousers *n.* bags, bloomers, denims, dungarees, flannels, jeans, Levis®, pants, shorts, slacks.

truancy *n.* absence, dodging, shirking, skiving.
antonyms attendance, effort.

truant *n.* absentee, deserter, dodger, runaway, shirker, skiver.
adj. absent, missing, runaway, skiving.

truce *n.* armistice, break, cease-fire, cessation, intermission, interval, let-up, lull, moratorium, peace, respite, rest, stay, suspension.
antonyms hostilities, war.

truck[1] *n.* business, commerce, communication, connection, contact, dealings, exchange, relations, trade, traffic.

truck[2] *n.* barrow, bogie, cart, float, lorry, trailer, trolley, van, wag(g)on, wheelbarrow.

truculent *adj.* aggressive, antagonistic, bad-tempered, belligerent, contentious, cross, defiant, fierce, hostile, ill-tempered, obstreperous, pugnacious, quarrelsome, sullen, violent.
antonyms co-operative, good-natured.

trudge *v.* clump, hike, labour, lumber, march, mush, plod, slog, stump, tramp, trek, walk.
n. haul, hike, march, slog, traipse, tramp, trek, walk.

true *adj.* **1** accurate, actual, authentic, confirmed, correct, exact, factual, genuine, honest, legitimate, precise, proper, real, right, rightful, sincere, truthful, valid, veracious, veritable. **2** constant, dedicated, devoted, faithful, firm, honourable, loyal, staunch, true-hearted, trustworthy, trusty.
antonyms **1** false, inaccurate, incorrect, wrong. **2** faithless, false.

truism *n.* axiom, cliché, platitude, truth, verity.

truly *adv.* correctly, exactly, extremely, factually, faithfully, firmly, genuinely, greatly, honestly, in fact, in reality, in truth, indeed, indubitably, precisely, properly, really, rightly, steadfastly, truthfully, undeniably, very.
antonyms faithlessly, falsely, incorrectly, slightly.

trumpet *n.* bellow, blare, blast, bugle, call, clarion, cry, honk, horn, roar.
v. advertise, announce, bellow, blare, blast, broadcast, noise abroad, proclaim, publish, roar, shout.

truncate *v.* abbreviate, clip, crop, curtail, cut, cut short, lop, pare, prune, shorten, trim.
antonyms extend, lengthen.

trunk *n.* **1** bin, box, case, chest, coffer, crate, locker, suitcase. **2** body, frame, shaft, stalk, stem, stock, torso, tube. **3** nose, proboscis, snout.

truss *v.* bind, bundle, fasten, pack, pinion, secure, strap, tether, tie.
antonyms loosen, untie.
n. bandage, binding, brace, buttress, joist, prop, shore, stay, strut, support.

trust *n.* assurance, belief, care, certainty, charge, confidence, conviction, credence, credit, custody, duty, expectation, faith, fidelity, guard, guardianship, hope, protection, reliance, responsibility, safekeeping.
antonyms distrust, doubt, mistrust, scepticism.
v. assign, assume, bank on, believe, commit, confide, consign, count on, credit, delegate, depend on, entrust, expect, give, hope, imagine, presume, rely on, suppose, surmise, swear by.
antonyms disbelieve, doubt, mistrust.

trusting *adj.* confiding, credulous, gullible, innocent, naïve, simple, trustful, unguarded, unquestioning, unsuspecting, unwary.
antonyms cautious, distrustful, suspicious.

trustworthy *adj.* dependable, honest, honourable, principled, reliable, responsible, sensible, steadfast, true, upright.
antonyms dishonest, irresponsible, unreliable.

truth *n.* **1** accuracy, candour, certainty, constancy, exactness, faith, faithfulness, fidelity,

frankness, genuineness, honesty, integrity, legitimacy, loyalty, precision, realism, reality, truthfulness, uprightness, validity, veracity. **2** axiom, fact, facts, law, maxim, principle, truism.
antonyms **1** deceit, dishonesty, falseness. **2** error, falsehood, myth.

truthful *adj.* accurate, correct, exact, faithful, honest, precise, realistic, reliable, sincere, straight, straightforward, true, trustworthy, veracious, veritable.
antonyms deceitful, false, untrue, untruthful.

try *v.* **1** attempt, endeavour, seek, undertake, venture. **2** hear, put on trial. **3** evaluate, examine, experiment, inspect, investigate, sample, taste, test.
n. attempt, effort, endeavour, evaluation, experiment, go, inspection, sample, taste, test, trial.
try out check out, evaluate, inspect, sample, taste, test, try on.

trying *adj.* aggravating, annoying, arduous, difficult, distressing, exasperating, fatiguing, hard, irritating, taxing, testing, tough, troublesome, vexing, wearisome.
antonyms calming, easy.

tub *n.* barrel, basin, bath, bathtub, bucket, butt, cask, keg, pail, stand, tun, vat.

tubby *adj.* buxom, chubby, fat, obese, overweight, plump, podgy, portly, stout.
antonyms slender, slim, thin.

tube *n.* channel, conduit, cylinder, duct, hose, pipe, shaft, spout.

tubular *adj.* pipelike, tubelike.

tuck *v.* cram, crease, fold, gather, insert, push, stuff.
n. crease, fold, gather, pleat, pucker.

tuft *n.* beard, bunch, clump, cluster, collection, crest, flock, knot, tassle, truss.

tug *v.* drag, draw, haul, heave, jerk, lug, pluck, pull, tow, wrench.
n. drag, haul, heave, jerk, pluck, pull, tow, wrench.

tuition *n.* education, instruction, lessons, pedagogy, schooling, teaching, training, tutoring.

tumble *v.* disorder, drop, fall, flop, jumble, overthrow, pitch, plummet, roll, stumble, topple, toss, trip up.
n. collapse, drop, fall, flop, plunge, roll, stumble, toss, trip.

tumbledown *adj.* broken-down, crumbling, decrepit, dilapidated, ramshackle, rickety, shaky.
antonym well-kept.

tumult *n.* affray, agitation, brawl, bustle, clamour, coil, commotion, din, disorder, disturbance, excitement, fracas, hubbub, hullabaloo, outbreak, pandemonium, quarrel, racket, riot, rout, row, ruction, ruffle, stir, strife, turmoil, unrest, upheaval, uproar.
antonyms calm, composure, peace.

tumultuous *adj.* agitated, boisterous, confused, disorderly, disturbed, excited, fierce, hectic, irregular, noisy, raging, restless, riotous, rowdy, stormy, troubled, turbulent, unrestrained, unruly, violent, wild.
antonyms calm, peaceful, quiet.

tune *n.* air, concert, consonance, euphony, harmony, melody, motif, pitch, song, strain, theme, unison.

tuneful *adj.* catchy, euphonious, harmonious, mellow, melodic, melodious, musical, pleasant, sonorous.
antonyms clashing, tuneless.

tuneless *adj.* atonal, cacophonous, clashing, discordant, dissonant, harsh, unmelodious, unmusical.
antonyms harmonious, tuneful.

tunnel *n.* burrow, channel, chimney, drift, gallery, hole, passage, passageway, shaft, subway, underpass.
v. burrow, dig, excavate, mine, penetrate, sap, undermine.

turbulent *adj.* agitated, blustery, boisterous, choppy, confused, disordered, disorderly, foaming, furious, mutinous, obstreperous, raging, rebellious, riotous, rough, rowdy, stormy, tempestuous, tumultuous, unbridled, undisciplined, unruly, unsettled, unstable, violent, wild.
antonyms calm, composed.

turmoil *n.* agitation, bedlam, bustle, chaos, combustion, commotion, confusion, disorder, disquiet, disturbance, ferment, flurry, hubbub, noise, pandemonium, row, ruffle, stir, strife, trouble, tumult, turbulence, uproar, violence, welter.
antonyms calm, peace, quiet.

turn *v.* **1** circle, divert, gyrate, invert, move, pivot, return, reverse, revolve, roll, rotate, shift, spin, swerve, switch, swivel, twirl, twist, veer, whirl. **2** adapt, adjust, alter, apply, change, convert, fashion, fit, form, frame, make, modify, mould, remodel, shape, transform. **3** become, go, grow. **4** appeal, have recourse, resort. **5** curdle, go bad, go off, sour, spoil. **6** nauseate, sicken, upset.
n. **1** action, bend, circle, circuit, curve, cycle, gyration, reversal, revolution, rotation, round, spin, turning, twist. **2** alteration, change, deviation, shift. **3** chance, crack, go, occasion, opportunity, period, spell, stint. **4** act, performance, performer.
turn away avert, deflect, depart, deviate, discharge, dismiss, reject.
antonyms accept, receive.
turn back beat off, drive back, drive off, force back, go back, rebuff, repel, resist, retrace one's steps, return, revert.
antonyms go on, stay.
turn down 1 decline, rebuff, refuse, reject, repudiate, spurn. **2** lessen, lower, muffle, mute, quieten, soften.
antonyms **1** accept. **2** turn up.
turn in 1 go to bed, retire. **2** deliver, enter, give back, give up, hand in, hand over, register, return, submit, surrender, tender.
antonyms **1** get up. **2** give out, keep.
turn off 1 branch off, depart from, deviate,

divert, leave, quit. **2** cut out, shut down, stop, switch off, turn out, unplug. **3** alienate, bore, discourage, disenchant, disgust, displease, offend, put off, put out, repel, sicken, switch off. *antonyms* **1** join. **2** turn on. **3** turn on.

turn on **1** activate, energise, start (up), switch on. **2** arouse, attract, excite, please, stimulate, thrill. **3** depend on, hinge on, rest on. **4** attack, fall on, round on.
antonyms **1** turn off. **2** turn off.

turn out **1** become, come about, develop, emerge, end up, ensue, happen, result, transpire, work out. **2** switch off, turn off, unplug. **3** appear, clothe, dress, present. **4** assemble, fabricate, make, manufacture, produce. **5** banish, deport, discharge, dismiss, drive out, drum out, evict, expel, kick out, oust, sack, throw out. **6** clean out, clear, empty.
antonyms **2** turn on. **5** admit. **6** fill.

turn over **1** consider, contemplate, deliberate, examine, mull over, ponder, reflect on, think about, think over. **2** deliver, give over, hand over, pass on, surrender, transfer. **3** capsize, keel over, overturn, upend, upset.
antonym **3** stand firm.

turncoat *n.* apostate, backslider, blackleg, defector, deserter, rat, renegade, scab, traitor.

turning *n.* bend, crossroads, curve, fork, junction, turn, turn-off.

turning-point *n.* change, crisis, crossroads, crux, moment of truth, watershed.

turn-out *n.* **1** assembly, attendance, audience, company, congregation, crowd, gate, number. **2** appearance, dress, gear, get-up, outfit.

turnover *n.* business, change, flow, income, movement, output, production, productivity, profits, replacement, volume, yield.

tutor *n.* coach, director of studies, educator, governor, guardian, guide, guru, instructor, lecturer, master, mentor, supervisor, teacher.
v. coach, control, direct, discipline, drill, educate, guide, instruct, lecture, school, supervise, teach, train.

tutorial *n.* class, lesson, seminar, teach-in.
adj. coaching, didactic, guiding, instructional, teaching.

tweak *v., n.* jerk, nip, pull, punch, snatch, squeeze, tug, twist, twitch.

twee *adj.* affected, cute, dainty, precious, pretty, quaint, sentimental, sweet.

twiddle *v.* adjust, fiddle, finger, juggle, swivel, turn, twirl, twist, wiggle.

twilight *n.* dimness, dusk, evening, gloaming, half-light, sundown, sunset.

twin *n.* corollary, counterpart, double, duplicate, fellow, likeness, lookalike, match, mate.
adj. balancing, corresponding, double, dual, duplicate, identical, matched, matching, paired, parallel, symmetrical, twofold.
v. combine, couple, join, link, match, pair.

twine *n.* cord, string, twist, yarn.
v. bend, braid, coil, curl, encircle, entwine, knit, loop, plait, spiral, surround, tie, twist, weave, wind, wrap, wreathe, zigzag.

twinge *n.* pain, pang, pinch, prick, spasm, stab, stitch, throb, throe.

twinkle *v.* flash, flicker, glimmer, glint, glisten, glitter, shimmer, shine, sparkle, vibrate, wink.
n. amusement, flash, flicker, gleam, glimmer, glistening, glittering, light, scintillation, shimmer, shine, sparkle, wink.

twirl *v.* coil, gyrate, gyre, pivot, revolve, rotate, spin, swivel, turn, twiddle, twist, wheel, whirl, wind.
n. coil, convulution, gyration, pirouette, revolution, rotation, spin, spiral, turn, twist, whirl.

twist *v.* **1** coil, curl, entangle, entwine, intertwine, screw, spin, squirm, swivel, turn, twine, weave, wind, wrap, wreathe, wrest, wriggle, wring, writhe. **2** rick, sprain, strain, wrench. **3** alter, change, contort, distort, garble, misquote, misrepresent, pervert, warp.
n. **1** arc, bend, break, change, coil, convolution, curl, curve, roll, screw, spin, squiggle, swivel, tangle, turn, twine, variation, zigzag. **2** jerk, sprain, wrench. **3** contortion, distortion, perversion. **4** oddity, peculiarity, quirk, surprise.

twisted *adj.* deviant, distorted, perverse, unnatural, warped.
antonyms straight, straightforward.

twister *n.* blackguard, cheat, con man, crook, deceiver, fraud, phoney, scoundrel, swindler, trickster.

twitch *v.* blink, flutter, jerk, jump, pluck, pull, snatch, tug, tweak.
n. convulsion, flutter, jerk, jump, pull, tremor, tweak, twinge.

twitter *v.* chatter, cheep, chirp, chirrup, giggle, prattle, sing, titter, tweet, warble, whistle.

two-faced *adj.* deceitful, deceiving, devious, double-dealing, double-tongued, false, hypocritical, insincere, lying, treacherous, untrustworthy.
antonyms candid, frank, honest.

tycoon *n.* baron, capitalist, captain of industry, entrepreneur, financier, industrialist, magnate, mogul, supremo.

type *n.* **1** archetype, breed, category, class, classification, description, designation, emblem, embodiment, essence, example, form, genre, group, kind, mark, model, order, original, paradigm, pattern, prototype, sort, species, specimen, stamp, standard, strain, subdivision, variety. **2** characters, face, font, fount, lettering, print, printing.

typhoon *n.* cyclone, hurricane, squall, storm, tempest, tornado, twister, whirlwind.

typical *adj.* average, characteristic, conventional, distinctive, essential, illustrative, indicative, model, normal, orthodox, representative, standard, stock, usual.
antonyms atypical, untypical, unusual.

typify *v.* characterise, embody, encapsulate, epitomise, exemplify, illustrate, personify, represent, symbolise.

tyrannical *adj.* absolute, arbitrary, authoritarian, autocratic, despotic, dictatorial, domineering, high-handed, imperious, iron-handed, magis-

terial, oppressive, overbearing, overpowering, ruthless, severe, unjust, unreasonable.
antonyms liberal, tolerant.

tyrannise *v.* browbeat, bully, coerce, crush, dictate, domineer, enslave, intimidate, lord it, oppress, terrorise.

tyranny *n.* absolutism, authoritarianism, autocracy, coercion, despotism, dictatorship, harshness, imperiousness, injustice, oppression, ruthlessness.
antonyms democracy, freedom, liberality.

tyrant *n.* absolutist, authoritarian, autocrat, bully, despot, dictator, monarch, oppressor, slave-driver, taskmaster.

U

ubiquitous *adj.* all-over, common, commonly-encountered, ever-present, everywhere, frequent, global, omnipresent, pervasive, universal.
antonyms rare, scarce.
ugly *adj.* **1** hideous, ill-favoured, misshapen, monstrous, plain, unattractive, unsightly. **2** disagreeable, disgusting, frightful, horrid, nasty, objectionable, offensive, repulsive, revolting, terrible, unpleasant, vile.
antonyms **1** beautiful, charming, pretty. **2** good, pleasant.
ulcer *n.* abscess, canker, fester, sore.
ulterior *adj.* concealed, covert, hidden, personal, private, secondary, secret, selfish, undisclosed, unexpressed.
antonyms declared, overt.
ultimate *adj.* conclusive, eventual, extreme, final, fundamental, furthest, greatest, highest, last, perfect, primary, radical, remotest, superlative, supreme, terminal, utmost.
ultimately *adv.* after all, at last, basically, eventually, finally, fundamentally, in the end, originally, primarily, sooner or later.
ultra- *adv.* exceptionally, excessively, extra, extraordinarily, extremely, remarkably, unusually.
umpire *n.* adjudicator, arbiter, arbitrator, judge, linesman, mediator, moderator, ref, referee.
v. adjudicate, arbitrate, control, judge, moderate, ref, referee.
umpteen *adj.* a good many, a thousand, considerable, countless, innumerable, millions, numerous, plenty, uncounted.
antonym few.
unabashed *adj.* blatant, bold, brazen, composed, confident, unconcerned, undaunted, undismayed, unembarrassed.
antonyms abashed, sheepish.
unable *adj.* impotent, inadequate, incapable, incompetent, powerless, unequipped, unfit, unqualified.
antonyms able, capable.
unabridged *adj.* complete, entire, full, full-length, uncondensed, uncut, unexpurgated, unshortened, whole.
antonyms abridged, shorter.
unacceptable *adj.* inadmissible, intolerable, objectionable, offensive, undesirable, unpleasant, unsatisfactory, unwelcome.
antonyms acceptable, satisfactory.
unaccompanied *adj.* alone, lone, solo, unattended, unescorted.
antonym accompanied.
unaccountable *adj.* astonishing, baffling, extraordinary, impenetrable, incomprehensible, inexplicable, mysterious, odd, peculiar, puzzling, singular, strange, uncommon, unexplainable, unfathomable, unheard-of, unintelligible, unusual.
antonyms accountable, explicable.
unaccustomed *adj.* different, inexperienced, new, special, strange, surprising, unacquainted, uncharacteristic, uncommon, unexpected, unfamiliar, unpractised, unprecedented, unused, unusual.
antonyms accustomed, customary, familiar.
unacquainted *adj.* ignorant, strange, unaccustomed, unfamiliar.
unadorned *adj.* austere, outright, plain, restrained, severe, simple, stark, straightforward, undecorated, unornamented.
antonyms decorated, embellished, ornate.
unaffected *adj.* **1** impervious, unaltered, unchanged, unmoved, untouched. **2** artless, blasé, genuine, honest, indifferent, ingenuous, naïve, plain, simple, sincere, straightforward, unassuming, unconcerned, unpretentious, unsophisticated, unspoilt.
antonyms **1** affected, influenced. **2** affected, insincere, pretentious.
unafraid *adj.* confident, daring, dauntless, fearless, intrepid, unshakeable.
antonyms afraid, fearful.
unalterable *adj.* final, fixed, immutable, inflexible, invariable, permanent, rigid, steadfast, unchangeable, unchanging, unyielding.
antonyms alterable, flexible.
unanimity *n.* accord, agreement, concert, concord, concurrence, consensus, consent, correspondence, harmony, like-mindedness, unison, unity.
antonyms disagreement, disunity.
unanimous *adj.* at one, common, concerted, harmonious, in accord, in agreement, joint, united.
antonyms disunited, divided, split.
unanswerable *adj.* absolute, conclusive, final, incontestable, indisputable, irrefutable, unarguable.
antonyms answerable, refutable.
unappetising *adj.* disagreeable, insipid, off-putting, tasteless, unappealing, unattractive, uninviting, unpalatable, unpleasant.
antonyms appetising, exciting, tasty.
unapproachable *adj.* aloof, distant, forbidding, remote, reserved, stand-offish, unfriendly, unsociable, withdrawn.
antonyms approachable, friendly.
unarmed *adj.* defenceless, exposed, helpless,

open, unarmoured, unprotected, vulnerable, weak.
antonyms armed, protected.
unashamed *adj.* blatant, impenitent, open, shameless, unabashed, unconcealed, undisguised, unrepentant.
unasked *adj.* gratuitous, spontaneous, unbidden, undesired, uninvited, unrequested, unsolicited, unsought, unwanted, voluntary.
antonyms invited, solicited.
unassuming *adj.* humble, meek, modest, natural, quiet, restrained, retiring, self-effacing, simple, unassertive, unobtrusive, unpretentious.
antonyms assuming, presumptuous, pretentious.
unattached *adj.* available, fancy-free, footloose, free, independent, single, unaffilated, uncommitted, unmarried, unspoken for.
antonyms attached, committed, engaged.
unattended *adj.* abandoned, alone, disregarded, ignored, unaccompanied, unguarded, unsupervised, unwatched.
antonyms attended, escorted.
unauthorised *adj.* illegal, illicit, irregular, unlawful, unofficial, unsanctioned, unwarranted.
antonyms authorised, legal.
unavailing *adj.* abortive, barren, fruitless, futile, idle, ineffective, pointless, unprofitable, unsuccessful, useless, vain.
antonyms productive, successful.
unavoidable *adj.* certain, compulsory, fated, inescapable, inevitable, inexorable, mandatory, necessary, obligatory.
antonym avoidable.
unaware *adj.* blind, deaf, forgetful, heedless, ignorant, oblivious, unconscious, uninformed, unknowing, unmindful, unsuspecting.
antonyms aware, concious.
unawares *adv.* aback, by surprise, off guard, unprepared.
unbalanced *adj.* **1** crazy, demented, deranged, disturbed, insane, irrational, lunatic, mad, unsound. **2** asymmetrical, biased, lopsided, one-sided, partisan, prejudiced, unequal, uneven, unfair, unjust, unstable, unsteady.
antonyms **1** sane. **2** unbiased.
unbearable *adj.* excruciating, intolerable, unacceptable, unendurable, unspeakable.
antonyms acceptable, bearable.
unbeatable *adj.* excellent, invincible, matchless, nonpareil, supreme, unstoppable, unsurpassable.
antonyms inferior, weak.
unbelief *n.* agnosticism, atheism, disbelief, distrust, doubt, incredulity, scepticism.
antonyms belief, faith.
unbelievable *adj.* astonishing, extraordinary, far-fetched, implausible, impossible, improbable, inconceivable, incredible, preposterous, staggering, unconvincing, unimaginable, unlikely, unthinkable.
antonyms believable, credible.
unbeliever *n.* agnostic, atheist, disbeliever, doubter, infidel, sceptic.
antonyms believer, supporter.
unbelieving *adj.* disbelieving, distrustful, doubtful, doubting, dubious, incredulous, sceptical, suspicious, unconvinced, unpersuaded.
antonyms credulous, trustful.
unbend *v.* loosen up, relax, straighten, unbutton, uncoil, unfreeze.
antonyms stiffen, withdraw.
unbiased *adj.* disinterested, dispassionate, even-handed, fair, fair-minded, impartial, independent, just, neutral, objective, open-minded, uninfluenced, unprejudiced.
antonym biased.
unblemished *adj.* clear, flawless, immaculate, irreproachable, perfect, pure, spotless, unflawed, unimpeachable, unspotted, unstained, untarnished.
antonyms blemished, flawed, imperfect.
unblinking *adj.* assured, calm, fearless, impassive, steady, unafraid, unemotional, unfaltering, unflinching, unwavering.
antonyms cowed, faithful, fearful.
unborn *adj.* awaited, coming, embryonic, expected, future, hereafter, later, subsequent, succeeding.
unbounded *adj.* absolute, boundless, endless, immeasurable, infinite, lavish, limitless, unchecked, unlimited, unrestrained, vast.
antonyms limited, restrained.
unbreakable *adj.* durable, indestructible, lasting, permanent, proof, resistant, rugged, shatter-proof, solid, strong, tough, toughened.
antonyms breakable, fragile.
unbridled *adj.* excessive, immoderate, unchecked, uncontrolled, unrestrained.
unbroken *adj.* ceaseless, complete, constant, continuous, endless, entire, incessant, intact, perpetual, progressive, solid, successive, total, unbowed, unceasing, undivided, unimpaired, uninterrupted, unremitting, whole.
antonyms broken, fitful, intermittent.
uncalled-for *adj.* gratuitous, inappropriate, needless, unheeded, unjust, unjustified, unnecessary, unprovoked, unwarranted, unwelcome.
antonym timely.
uncanny *adj.* bizarre, creepy, eerie, extraordinary, fantastic, incredible, mysterious, queer, remarkable, scary, spooky, strange, supernatural, unaccountable, unearthly, unnatural, unusual, weird.
uncaring *adj.* callous, inconsiderate, indifferent, negligent, unconcerned, unfeeling, uninterested, unmoved, unresponsive, unsympathetic.
antonyms caring, concerned.
unceasing *adj.* constant, continual, continuous, endless, incessant, never-ending, non-stop, perpetual, persistent, relentless, unbroken, unending, unrelenting, unremitting.
antonyms intermittent, spasmodic.
uncertain *adj.* **1** ambivalent, doubtful, dubious, hesitant, unclear, undecided, unsure. **2** changeable, erratic, inconstant, irregular, shaky, unreliable, vacillating, variable, wavering. **3** iffy, indefinite, insecure, risky, unconfirmed,

undetermined, unfixed, unforeseeable, unpredictable, unresolved, unsettled, vague.
antonyms **1** certain, sure. **2** steady. **3** predictable.

uncertainty *n.* bewilderment, confusion, dilemma, doubt, hesitation, insecurity, irresolution, misgiving, perplexity, puzzlement, scepticism, unpredictability, vagueness.
antonym certainty.

unchangeable *adj.* changeless, eternal, final, immutable, irreversible, permanent, unalterable, unchanging.
antonyms alterable, changeable.

unchanging *adj.* abiding, constant, continuing, enduring, eternal, fixed, immutable, lasting, permanent, perpetual, steadfast, steady, unfading, unvarying.
antonyms changeable, changing.

uncharitable *adj.* callous, cruel, hard-hearted, inhumane, insensitive, mean, merciless, pitiless, stingy, unfeeling, unforgiving, unfriendly, ungenerous, unkind, unsympathetic.
antonyms charitable, generous, kind, sensitive.

uncharted *adj.* alien, foreign, mysterious, new, strange, undiscovered, unexplored, unfamiliar, unknown, unplumbed, virgin.
antonyms familiar, well-known.

uncivilised *adj.* antisocial, barbaric, gross, ill-bred, illiterate, primitive, savage, uncouth, uncultured, uneducated, unsophisticated, untamed, wild.
antonyms civilised, cultured.

unclean *adj.* contaminated, corrupt, defiled, dirty, evil, filthy, foul, impure, nasty, polluted, soiled, spotted, stained, sullied, tainted, unhygienic, unwholesome.
antonyms clean, hygienic.

unclear *adj.* ambiguous, dim, doubtful, dubious, equivocal, hazy, indefinite, indiscernible, indistinct, indistinguishable, obscure, uncertain, unintelligible, vague.
antonyms clear, evident.

uncomfortable *adj.* awkward, bleak, confused, conscience-stricken, cramped, disagreeable, discomfortable, disquieted, distressed, disturbed, embarrassed, hard, ill-fitting, irritating, painful, self-conscious, troubled, troublesome, uneasy.
antonyms comfortable, easy.

uncommitted *adj.* available, fancy-free, floating, free, neutral, non-aligned, non-partisan, unattached, undecided, uninvolved.
antonym committed.

uncommon *adj.* abnormal, atypical, bizarre, curious, distinctive, exceptional, extraordinary, infrequent, notable, noteworthy, odd, outstanding, rare, remarkable, scarce, special, strange, superior, unfamiliar, unprecedented, unusual.
antonyms common, normal, usual.

uncommunicative *adj.* brief, close, curt, reserved, reticent, retiring, secretive, shy, silent, taciturn, tight-lipped, unresponsive, unsociable, withdrawn.
antonyms communicative, forthcoming.

uncompromising *adj.* decided, die-hard, firm, hard-core, hard-line, inexorable, inflexible, intransigent, obstinate, rigid, steadfast, strict, stubborn, tough, unaccommodating, unyielding.
antonyms flexible, open-minded.

unconcealed *adj.* apparent, blatant, conspicuous, evident, frank, manifest, naked, noticeable, obvious, open, patent, self-confessed, unashamed, undistinguished, visible.
antonyms hidden, secret.

unconcern *n.* aloofness, apathy, callousness, detachment, indifference, negligence, remoteness, uninterestedness.
antonyms concern, interest.

unconcerned *adj.* aloof, apathetic, callous, carefree, careless, complacent, composed, cool, detached, dispassionate, distant, indifferent, nonchalant, oblivious, relaxed, uncaring, uninterested, uninvolved, unmoved, unruffled, unsympathetic, untroubled, unworried.
antonyms concerned, interested, worried.

unconditional *adj.* absolute, categorical, complete, downright, entire, full, implicit, outright, positive, thoroughgoing, total, unequivocal, unlimited, unqualified, unreserved, unrestricted, utter, whole-hearted.
antonyms conditional, limited, qualified.

uncongenial *adj.* antagonistic, disagreeable, displeasing, unappealing, unattractive, uninviting, unpleasant, unsympathetic.
antonyms attractive, congenial, pleasant.

unconnected *adj.* detached, disconnected, divided, illogical, incoherent, independent, irrational, irrelevant, separate, unattached, unrelated.
antonyms connected, relevant.

unconscious *adj.* **1** comatose, concussed, insensible, knocked out, out, out cold, out for the count, senseless, stunned. **2** blind to, deaf to, heedless, ignorant, oblivious, unaware, unmindful, unsuspecting. **3** accidental, automatic, inadvertent, innate, instinctive, involuntary; latent, reflex, repressed, subconscious, subliminal, suppressed, unintended, unintentional, unwitting.
antonyms **1** conscious. **2** aware. **3** intentional.

uncontrollable *adj.* frantic, furious, helpless, irrepressible, mad, strong, ungovernable, unmanageable, unruly, violent, wild.
antonyms controllable, manageable.

uncontrolled *adj.* furious, rampant, unbridled, unchecked, undisciplined, unrestrained, unruly, violent, wild.
antonyms contained, controlled.

unconventional *adj.* abnormal, alternative, bizarre, different, eccentric, idiosyncratic, individual, informal, irregular, nonconforming, odd, offbeat, original, unorthodox, unusual, way-out.
antonyms conventional, usual.

unconvincing *adj.* doubtful, dubious, feeble, flimsy, implausible, improbable, lame, questionable, suspect, unlikely, weak.
antonyms convincing, plausible.

unco-ordinated *adj.* awkward, bumbling, clumsy, disjointed, disorganised, inept, uncon-

certed, ungainly, ungraceful.
antonyms concerted, graceful, systematic.

uncouth *adj.* awkward, clumsy, coarse, crude, gauche, graceless, ill-mannered, rough, rude, uncivilised, uncultivated, unrefined, unseemly, vulgar.
antonyms polished, polite, refined, urbane.

uncover *v.* bare, detect, disclose, discover, disrobe, divulge, exhume, expose, leak, open, reveal, show, strip, unearth, unmask, unveil, unwrap.
antonyms conceal, cover, suppress.

uncritical *adj.* accepting, credulous, indiscriminate, naïve, superficial, trusting, undiscerning, undiscriminating, unquestioning, unselective, unthinking.
antonyms critical, discriminating, sceptical.

uncultivated *adj.* fallow, natural, rough, uncultured, wild.
antonym cultivated.

uncultured *adj.* awkward, boorish, coarse, crude, ill-bred, raw, rustic, uncivilised, uncouth, uncultivated, unrefined, unsophisticated.
antonyms cultured, sophisticated.

undaunted *adj.* bold, brave, courageous, dauntless, fearless, gallant, indomitable, intrepid, resolute, steadfast, unbowed, undeterred, undiscouraged, undismayed.
antonyms discouraged, dismayed, timorous.

undecided *adj.* ambivalent, debatable, dithering, doubtful, dubious, hesitant, in two minds, indefinite, irresolute, moot, open, tentative, torn, uncertain, uncommitted, unsettled, unsure, vague, wavering.
antonyms certain, decided, definite.

undemonstrative *adj.* aloof, cold, contained, cool, distant, formal, impassive, phlegmatic, reserved, restrained, reticent, stiff, unbending, uncommunicative, unemotional, withdrawn.
antonyms communicative, demonstrative, open.

undeniable *adj.* certain, clear, evident, incontrovertible, irrefutable, manifest, obvious, patent, proven, sound, sure, undoubted, unmistakable, unquestionable.

under *prep.* below, beneath, included in, inferior to, less than, lower than, secondary to, subject to, subordinate to, underneath.
antonyms above, over.
under way afoot, begun, going, in motion, in operation, in progress, launched, moving, on the go, on the move, started.

underclothes *n.* lingerie, undergarments, underwear.

undercover *adj.* clandestine, concealed, confidential, covert, furtive, hidden, hush-hush, intelligence, private, secret, spy, surreptitious, underground.
antonyms open, unconcealed.

undercurrent *n.* atmosphere, aura, crosscurrent, drift, eddy, feeling, flavour, hint, movement, murmur, overtone, rip, sense, suggestion, tendency, tenor, tide, tinge, trend, underflow, undertone, vibes, vibrations.

undercut *v.* excavate, gouge out, hollow out, mine, sacrifice, scoop out, underbid, undercharge, undermine, underprice, undersell.

underestimate *v.* dismiss, fail to appreciate, minimise, miscalculate, misjudge, sell short, underrate, undervalue.
antonyms exaggerate, overestimate.

undergo *v.* bear, endure, experience, stand, submit to, suffer, sustain, weather, withstand.

underground *adj.* alternative, avant-garde, buried, concealed, covered, covert, experimental, hidden, radical, revolutionary, secret, subterranean, subversive, surreptitious, undercover.
n. subway, tube.

undergrowth *n.* bracken, brambles, briars, brush, brushwood, ground cover, scrub, underbrush.

underhand *adj.* clandestine, crafty, crooked, deceitful, deceptive, devious, dishonest, fraudulent, furtive, immoral, improper, shady, shifty, sly, sneaky, stealthy, surreptitious, treacherous, unethical, unscrupulous.
antonyms above board, honest, open.

underline *v.* accentuate, emphasise, highlight, italicise, labour, mark, point up, press, reiterate, stress, urge.
antonyms play down, soft-pedal.

underling *n.* hireling, inferior, lackey, menial, minion, nobody, nonentity, retainer, servant, slave, subordinate, weakling.
antonyms boss, leader, master.

underlying *adj.* basic, elementary, essential, fundamental, hidden, intrinsic, latent, primary, prime, root, veiled.

undermine *v.* erode, impair, mar, mine, sabotage, shake, subvert, threaten, tunnel, vitiate, weaken, wear away.
antonyms fortify, strengthen.

underprivileged *adj.* deprived, destitute, disadvantaged, impoverished, needy, poor, poverty-stricken.
antonyms affluent, fortunate, privileged.

underrate *v.* belittle, depreciate, dismiss, disparage, underestimate, undervalue.
antonyms exaggerate, overrate.

undersized *adj.* dwarfish, miniature, minute, puny, pygmy, small, stunted, tiny, underdeveloped, underweight.
antonyms big, oversized, overweight.

understand *v.* **1** accept, appreciate, assume, believe, comprehend, conclude, cotton on, discern, fathom, follow, gather, get, get the message, grasp, hear, know, learn, make out, penetrate, perceive, presume, realise, recognise, see, suppose, take in, think. **2** commiserate, sympathise.
antonym **1** misunderstand.

understanding *n.* **1** awareness, belief, comprehension, discernment, grasp, idea, impression, insight, intellect, intelligence, interpretation, judgement, knowledge, notion, opinion, perception, sense, wisdom. **2** accord, agreement, arrangement, co-operation, pact. **3** appreciation, sympathy.

adj. accepting, compassionate, considerate, discerning, forbearing, forgiving, kind, loving, patient, sensitive, sympathetic, tender, tolerant.
antonyms impatient, insensitive, intolerant, unsympathetic.

understate *v.* belittle, dismiss, make light of, make little of, minimise, play down, soft-pedal, underplay.

understatement *n.* dismissal, minimisation, restraint, underplaying.

understood *adj.* accepted, assumed, implicit, implied, inferred, presumed, tacit, unspoken, unstated, unwritten.

understudy *n.* alternate, deputy, double, fill-in, replacement, reserve, stand-in, substitute.

undertake *v.* accept, agree, assume, attempt, bargain, begin, commence, contract, covenant, embark on, endeavour, engage, guarantee, pledge, promise, stipulate, tackle, take on, try.

undertaker *n.* funeral director, mortician.

undertaking *n.* **1** adventure, affair, attempt, business, effort, endeavour, enterprise, operation, project, task, venture. **2** assurance, commitment, pledge, promise, vow, word.

undertone *n.* atmosphere, current, feeling, flavour, hint, murmur, suggestion, tinge, touch, trace, undercurrent, whisper.

undervalue *v.* depreciate, dismiss, disparage, minimise, misjudge, underestimate, underrate.
antonyms exaggerate, overrate.

underwater *adj.* subaquatic, submarine, submerged, sunken, undersea.

underwear *n.* lingerie, underclothes, undergarments.

underweight *adj.* half-starved, puny, skinny, thin, undernourished, undersized.
antonym overweight.

underwrite *v.* approve, authorise, back, consent, countersign, endorse, finance, fund, guarantee, initial, insure, sanction, sign, sponsor, subscribe, subsidise, validate.

undesirable *adj.* disagreeable, disliked, distasteful, dreaded, objectionable, obnoxious, offensive, repugnant, unacceptable, unpleasant, unsuitable, unwanted, unwelcome.
antonyms desirable, pleasant.

undeveloped *adj.* embryonic, immature, latent, potential, stunted, unformed.
antonyms developed, mature.

undignified *adj.* foolish, improper, inappropriate, indecorous, inelegant, ungainly, unrefined, unsuitable.
antonyms dignified, elegant.

undisciplined *adj.* disobedient, disorganised, obstreperous, uncontrolled, unreliable, unrestrained, unruly, untrained, wayward, wild, wilful.
antonyms controlled, disciplined.

undisguised *adj.* apparent, blatant, confessed, evident, explicit, frank, genuine, manifest, naked, obvious, open, outright, overt, patent, stark, thoroughgoing, transparent, unadorned, unashamed, unconcealed, unmistakable, utter, whole-hearted.
antonyms concealed, hidden, secret.

undisputed *adj.* accepted, acknowledged, certain, conclusive, incontrovertible, indisputable, irrefutable, recognised, sure, unchallenged, uncontested, undeniable, undoubted, unmistakable, unquestioned.
antonyms debatable, dubious, uncertain.

undistinguished *adj.* banal, everyday, indifferent, inferior, mediocre, ordinary, run-of-the-mill, unexceptional, unexciting, unimpressive, unremarkable.
antonyms distinguished, exceptional.

undivided *adj.* combined, complete, concentrated, entire, exclusive, full, solid, thorough, tight-knit, unanimous, unbroken, united, whole, whole-hearted.

undo *v.* annul, cancel, defeat, destroy, invalidate, loose, loosen, mar, neutralise, nullify, offset, open, overturn, quash, reverse, ruin, separate, shatter, spoil, subvert, unbutton, undermine, unfasten, unlock, untie, unwind, unwrap, upset, vitiate, wreck.
antonyms fasten, tie.

undoing *n.* besetting sin, collapse, curse, defeat, destruction, disgrace, downfall, misfortune, overthrow, reversal, ruin, ruination, shame, trouble, weakness.

undone *adj.* **1** forgotten, incomplete, left, neglected, omitted, outstanding, unaccomplished, uncompleted, unfinished, unfulfilled. **2** loose, open, unbuttoned, unfastened, unlaced, unlocked, untied.
antonyms **1** accomplished, complete, done. **2** fastened, secured.

undoubted *adj.* acknowledged, certain, definite, incontrovertible, indisputable, indubitable, obvious, patent, sure, unchallenged, undisputed, unquestionable.

undreamed-of *adj.* astonishing, inconceivable, incredible, undreamt, unexpected, unforeseen, unheard-of, unhoped-for, unimagined, unsuspected.

undress *v.* disrobe, divest, peel off, remove, shed, strip, take off.

undue *adj.* disproportionate, excessive, extravagant, extreme, immoderate, improper, inordinate, needless, overmuch, uncalled-for, undeserved, unnecessary, unreasonable, unwarranted.
antonyms proper, reasonable.

undulate *v.* billow, heave, ripple, rise and fall, roll, surge, swell, wave.

unduly *adv.* disproportionately, excessively, extravagantly, immoderately, inordinately, over, too, unjustifiably, unnecessarily, unreasonably.
antonyms moderately, reasonably.

unearth *v.* detect, dig up, discover, disinter, dredge up, excavate, exhume, expose, find, reveal, uncover.

unearthly *adj.* **1** eerie, ghostly, haunted, spine-chilling, strange, supernatural, uncanny, weird. **2** outrageous, ungodly, unreasonable.
antonym **2** reasonable.

uneasy *adj.* agitated, anxious, apprehensive,

disturbed, edgy, impatient, insecure, jittery, nervous, restless, shaky, strained, tense, troubled, uncomfortable, unsettled, unsure, upset, worried.
antonyms calm, composed, sure.

uneconomic *adj.* loss-making, non-profit-making, uncommercial, unprofitable.
antonyms economic, profitable.

uneducated *adj.* benighted, ignorant, illiterate, philistine, uncultivated, uncultured, unread, unschooled, untaught.
antonym educated.

unemotional *adj.* apathetic, cold, cool, dispassionate, impassive, indifferent, objective, phlegmatic, reserved, undemonstrative, unexcitable, unfeeling, unresponsive.
antonyms emotional, excitable.

unemployed *adj.* idle, jobless, laid off, on the dole, out of work, redundant, unoccupied, workless.
antonyms employed, in work, occupied.

unending *adj.* ceaseless, constant, continual, endless, eternal, everlasting, incessant, interminable, never-ending, perpetual, unceasing, undying.
antonyms intermittent, transient.

unendurable *adj.* insufferable, intolerable, overwhelming, shattering, unbearable.
antonyms bearable, endurable.

unenviable *adj.* disagreeable, painful, thankless, uncomfortable, uncongenial, undesirable, unpleasant.
antonyms desirable, enviable.

unequal *adj.* asymmetrical, different, discriminatory, disproportionate, dissimilar, insufficient, irregular, unbalanced, uneven, unlike, unmatched, variable, varying.
antonym equal.

unequalled *adj.* exceptional, incomparable, inimitable, matchless, pre-eminent, supreme, surpassing, transcendent, unmatched, unparalleled, unrivalled, unsurpassed.

unequivocal *adj.* absolute, categorical, certain, clear, clear-cut, decisive, definite, direct, distinct, evident, explicit, express, incontrovertible, plain, positive, straight, unambiguous, unmistakable, unqualified, unreserved.
antonyms ambiguous, qualified, vague.

unerring *adj.* accurate, certain, exact, faultless, impeccable, infallible, perfect, sure, uncanny, unfailing.
antonym fallible.

uneven *adj.* **1** bumpy, rough. **2** asymmetrical, changeable, fluctuating, inequitable, lopsided, odd, one-sided, unbalanced, unequal, unfair. **3** erratic, fitful, inconsistent, intermittent, irregular, jerky, patchy, spasmodic, unsteady, variable.
antonyms **1** even, flat, level. **2** equal. **3** regular.

uneventful *adj.* boring, commonplace, dull, humdrum, monotonous, ordinary, quiet, routine, tedious, unexceptional, unexciting, uninteresting, unmemorable, unremarkable, unvaried.
antonyms eventful, memorable.

unexceptional *adj.* average, conventional, indifferent, insignificant, mediocre, normal, ordinary, typical, unimpressive, unmemorable, unremarkable, usual.
antonyms exceptional, impressive.

unexpected *adj.* abrupt, accidental, amazing, astonishing, chance, fortuitous, startling, sudden, surprising, unanticipated, unforeseen, unpredictable, unusual.
antonyms expected, normal, predictable.

unfair *adj.* arbitrary, biased, bigoted, crooked, discriminatory, dishonest, dishonourable, inequitable, one-sided, partial, partisan, prejudiced, uncalled-for, undeserved, unethical, unjust, unmerited, unprincipled, unscrupulous, unwarranted, wrongful.
antonyms deserved, fair, unbiased.

unfaithful *adj.* adulterous, deceitful, dishonest, disloyal, faithless, false, fickle, godless, inconstant, treacherous, treasonable, two-timing, unbelieving, unchaste, unreliable, untrue, untrustworthy.
antonyms faithful, honest, loyal.

unfamiliar *adj.* alien, curious, different, foreign, new, novel, strange, unaccustomed, unacquainted, uncharted, uncommon, unexplored, unknown, unpractised, unskilled, unusual, unversed.
antonyms conversant, customary, familiar.

unfashionable *adj.* antiquated, dated, obsolete, old-fashioned, out, out of date, outmoded, square, unpopular.
antonyms fashionable, popular.

unfasten *v.* detach, disconnect, loosen, open, separate, uncouple, undo, unlock, untie.
antonyms do up, fasten.

unfavourable *adj.* adverse, bad, contrary, disadvantageous, discouraging, hostile, ill-suited, inauspicious, inopportune, low, negative, ominous, poor, threatening, uncomplimentary, unfortunate, unfriendly, unlucky, unpromising, unseasonable, untimely.
antonyms auspicious, favourable, promising.

unfeeling *adj.* apathetic, callous, cold, cruel, hard, hard-hearted, harsh, heartless, inhuman, insensitive, pitiless, stony, uncaring, unsympathetic.
antonyms concerned, sympathetic.

unfinished *adj.* bare, crude, deficient, half-done, imperfect, incomplete, lacking, rough, sketchy, unaccomplished, uncompleted, undone, unfulfilled, wanting.
antonyms completed, finished.

unfit *adj.* debilitated, decrepit, feeble, flabby, ill-equipped, inadequate, inappropriate, incapable, incompetent, ineffective, ineligible, unequal, unhealthy, unprepared, unqualified, unsuitable, unsuited, untrained, useless.
antonyms competent, fit, suitable.

unflagging *adj.* constant, fixed, indefatigable, never-failing, persevering, persistent, single-minded, staunch, steady, tireless, unceasing, unfailing, unfaltering, unremitting, untiring.
antonyms faltering, inconstant.

unflattering *adj.* blunt, candid, critical, honest, outspoken, uncomplimentary, unfavourable, unprepossessing.
antonyms complimentary, flattering.

unfold *v.* **1** develop, evolve. **2** clarify, describe, disclose, elaborate, explain, illustrate, present, reveal, show. **3** disentangle, flatten, open, spread, straighten, stretch out, uncoil, uncover, undo, unfurl, unravel, unroll, unwrap.
antonyms **2** suppress, withhold. **3** fold, wrap.

unforeseen *adj.* startling, sudden, surprising, unanticipated, unavoidable, unexpected, unpredicted.
antonyms expected, predictable.

unforgettable *adj.* exceptional, extraordinary, historic, impressive, memorable, momentous, notable, noteworthy.
antonyms unexceptional, unmemorable.

unforgivable *adj.* deplorable, disgraceful, indefensible, inexcusable, reprehensible, shameful, unjustifiable, unpardonable.
antonyms forgivable, venial.

unfortunate *adj.* **1** luckless, poor, tactless, unhappy, unlucky, unsuccessful, wretched. **2** adverse, calamitous, deplorable, disastrous, doomed, hopeless, ill-advised, ill-fated, ill-timed, inappropriate, inopportune, lamentable, regrettable, ruinous, unfavourable, unsuitable, untimely.
antonyms **1** fortunate, happy. **2** appropriate, favourable.

unfortunately *adv.* regrettably, sad to say, sadly, unhappily, unluckily.
antonyms fortunately, happily, luckily.

unfounded *adj.* baseless, fabricated, false, gratuitous, groundless, idle, spurious, trumped-up, unjustified, unmerited, unproven, unsubstantiated, unsupported.
antonyms justified, substantiated.

unfrequented *adj.* deserted, desolate, godforsaken, isolated, lone, lonely, remote, secluded, solitary, uninhabited, unvisited.
antonyms busy, crowded, populous.

unfriendly *adj.* alien, aloof, antagonistic, chilly, cold, critical, disagreeable, distant, hostile, ill-disposed, inimical, quarrelsome, sour, stand-offish, surly, unapproachable, unbending, unfavourable, unneighbourly, unsociable, unwelcoming.
antonyms agreeable, amiable, friendly.

unfruitful *adj.* arid, barren, exhausted, fruitless, impoverished, infertile, sterile, unproductive, unprofitable, unrewarding.
antonym fruitful.

ungainly *adj.* awkward, clumsy, gauche, gawky, inelegant, lumbering, slouching, uncoordinated, uncouth, unwieldy.
antonyms elegant, graceful.

ungodly *adj.* **1** dreadful, intolerable, outrageous, unearthly, unreasonable, unsocial. **2** blasphemous, corrupt, depraved, godless, immoral, impious, irreligious, sinful, unseemly, vile, wicked.

ungovernable *adj.* disorderly, rebellious, refractory, uncontrollable, ungoverned, unmanageable, unrestrainable, unruly, wild.

ungracious *adj.* bad-mannered, churlish, disrespectful, graceless, ill-bred, impolite, offhand, rude, uncivil, unmannerly.
antonyms gracious, polite.

ungrateful *adj.* heedless, ill-mannered, selfish, thankless, unappreciative, ungracious, unmindful.
antonyms grateful, thankful.

unguarded *adj.* **1** careless, foolhardy, foolish, heedless, ill-considered, impolitic, imprudent, incautious, indiscreet, rash, thoughtless, undiplomatic, unheeding, unthinking, unwary. **2** defenceless, exposed, pregnable, undefended, unpatrolled, unprotected, vulnerable.
antonyms **1** cautious, guarded. **2** guarded, protected.

unhappy *adj.* **1** crestfallen, dejected, depressed, despondent, dispirited, down, downcast, gloomy, long-faced, luckless, melancholy, miserable, sad, sorrowful, sorry, uneasy. **2** awkward, clumsy, ill-chosen, ill-fated, inappropriate, inapt, infelicitous, tactless, unfortunate, unlucky, unsuitable.
antonyms **1** happy, satisfied. **2** fortunate, suitable.

unhealthy *adj.* **1** ailing, bad, feeble, frail, infirm, insanitary, invalid, poorly, sick, sickly, unhygienic, unwell, weak. **2** degrading, detrimental, harmful, morbid, undesirable, unnatural, unsound, unwholesome.
antonyms **1** healthy, hygienic, robust. **2** natural, wholesome.

unheard-of *adj.* **1** disgraceful, extreme, inconceivable, offensive, outrageous, preposterous, shocking, unacceptable, unbelievable, undreamed-of, unimaginable, unprecedented, unthinkable. **2** new, obscure, undiscovered, unfamiliar, unknown, unsung, unusual.
antonyms **1** normal, usual. **2** famous.

unheeded *adj.* disobeyed, disregarded, forgotten, ignored, neglected, overlooked, unnoticed, unobserved, unremarked.
antonyms heeded, noted, observed.

unheralded *adj.* surprise, unadvertised, unannounced, unexpected, unpublicised, unrecognised.
antonyms advertised, publicised, trumpeted.

unhesitating *adj.* automatic, immediate, implicit, instant, instantaneous, prompt, ready, spontaneous, unfaltering, unquestioning, unswerving, unwavering, whole-hearted.
antonyms hesitant, tentative, uncertain.

unholy *adj.* **1** appalling, corrupt, depraved, dishonest, evil, heinous, immoral, iniquitous, irreligious, sinful, vile, wicked. **2** outrageous, shocking, unearthly, ungodly, unreasonable.
antonyms **1** godly, holy, pious. **2** reasonable.

unhurried *adj.* calm, deliberate, easy, easy-going, laid-back, leisurely, relaxed, slow.
antonyms hasty, hurried, rushed.

uniform *n.* costume, dress, gear, insignia, livery, outfit, regalia, regimentals, rig, robes, suit.

adj. alike, consistent, constant, equable, equal, even, homogeneous, identical, like, monotonous, regular, same, similar, smooth, unbroken, unchanging, undeviating, unvarying.
antonyms changing, colourful, varied.

uniformity *n.* constancy, drabness, dullness, evenness, flatness, homogeneity, invariability, monotony, regularity, sameness, similarity, tedium.
antonyms difference, dissimilarity, variation.

unify *v.* amalgamate, bind, combine, confederate, consolidate, federate, fuse, join, marry, merge, unite, weld.
antonyms divide, separate, split.

unimaginable *adj.* fantastic, impossible, inconceivable, incredible, indescribable, mind-boggling, unbelievable, undreamed-of, unheard-of, unthinkable.

unimaginative *adj.* banal, barren, boring, dry, dull, hackneyed, lifeless, matter-of-fact, ordinary, predictable, routine, short-sighted, tame, uncreative, uninspired, unoriginal.
antonyms creative, imaginative, original.

unimpeachable *adj.* blameless, faultless, immaculate, impeccable, irreproachable, perfect, spotless, unblemished, unchallengeable.
antonyms blameworthy, faulty.

unimpeded *adj.* all-round, clear, free, open, unblocked, unchecked, unconstrained, unhampered, unhindered, uninhibited, unrestrained.
antonyms hampered, impeded.

unimportant *adj.* immaterial, inconsequential, insignificant, irrelevant, minor, negligible, petty, slight, trifling, trivial, worthless.
antonyms important, relevant, significant, vital.

unimpressive *adj.* average, commonplace, dull, indifferent, mediocre, undistinguished, unexceptional, uninteresting, unremarkable, unspectacular.
antonyms impressive, memorable, notable.

uninhibited *adj.* abandoned, candid, frank, free, informal, liberated, natural, open, relaxed, spontaneous, unconstrained, uncontrolled, unreserved, unrestrained, unrestricted, unselfconscious.
antonyms constrained, inhibited, repressed, restrained.

uninspired *adj.* boring, commonplace, dull, humdrum, indifferent, ordinary, stale, stock, trite, undistinguished, unexciting, unimaginative, uninspiring, uninteresting, unoriginal.
antonyms exciting, inspired, original.

unintentional *adj.* accidental, fortuitous, inadvertent, involuntary, unconscious, unintended, unpremeditated, unthinking.
antonyms deliberate, intentional.

uninterested *adj.* apathetic, blasé, bored, impassive, indifferent, listless, unconcerned, unenthusiastic, uninvolved, unresponsive.
antonyms concerned, enthusiastic, interested, responsive.

uninteresting *adj.* boring, commonplace, drab, dreary, dry, dull, flat, humdrum, monotonous, tame, tedious, tiresome, uneventful, unexciting, unimpressive, uninspiring, wearisome.
antonyms exciting, interesting.

uninterrupted *adj.* constant, continual, continuous, non-stop, peaceful, quiet, steady, sustained, unbroken, undisturbed, unending.
antonyms broken, intermittent.

uninvited *adj.* unasked, unsolicited, unsought, unwanted, unwelcome.
antonyms invited, solicited.

union *n.* alliance, amalgamation, association, blend, coalition, combination, confederacy, confederation, coupling, enosis, federation, fusion, harmony, junction, league, mixture, synthesis, unison, uniting, unity.
antonyms alienation, disunity, estrangement, separation.

unique *adj.* exceptional, incomparable, inimitable, lone, matchless, one-off, only, single, sole, solitary, unequalled, unexampled, unmatched, unparalleled, unprecedented, unrivalled.
antonym common.

unison *n.* accordance, aggreement, concert, concord, co-operation, harmony, unanimity, unity.
antonym disharmony.

unit *n.* assembly, component, constituent, detachment, element, entity, group, item, measure, measurement, member, module, one, part, piece, portion, quantity, section, segment, system, whole.

unite *v.* ally, amalgamate, associate, band, blend, coalesce, combine, consolidate, cooperate, couple, fuse, incorporate, join, link, marry, merge, pool, unify.
antonyms separate, sever.

united *adj.* affiliated, agreed, allied, collective, combined, concerted, corporate, in accord, in agreement, like-minded, one, pooled, unanimous, unified.
antonyms differing, disunited, separated, uncoordinated.

unity *n.* accord, agreement, community, concord, consensus, entity, harmony, integrity, oneness, peace, singleness, solidarity, unanimity, unification, union, wholeness.
antonyms disagreement, discord, disunity, strife.

universal *adj.* across-the-board, all-embracing, all-inclusive, all-round, common, entire, general, global, total, unlimited, whole, widespread, worldwide.

universe *n.* cosmos, creation, firmament, heavens, macrocosm, nature, world.

unjust *adj.* biased, inequitable, one-sided, partial, partisan, prejudiced, undeserved, unethical, unfair, unjustified, wrong.
antonyms fair, just, reasonable.

unjustifiable *adj.* excessive, immoderate, indefensible, inexcusable, outrageous, unacceptable, unforgivable, unjust, unreasonable, wrong.
antonyms acceptable, justifiable.

unkempt *adj.* dishevelled, disordered, messy, rumpled, scruffy, shabby, shaggy, slatternly, sloppy, slovenly, tousled, uncombed,

ungroomed, untidy.
antonyms neat, tidy.

unkind *adj.* callous, cruel, hard-hearted, harsh, inconsiderate, inhuman, inhumane, insensitive, malevolent, malicious, mean, nasty, spiteful, thoughtless, uncaring, uncharitable, unfeeling, unfriendly, unsympathetic.
antonyms considerate, kind, pleasant.

unknown *adj.* alien, anonymous, concealed, dark, foreign, hidden, incognito, mysterious, nameless, new, obscure, secret, strange, uncharted, undisclosed, undiscovered, undistinguished, unexplored, unfamiliar, unheard-of, unidentified, unnamed, unsung, untold.
antonyms familiar, known.

unlawful *adj.* banned, criminal, forbidden, illegal, illegitimate, illicit, outlawed, prohibited, unauthorised, unconstitutional.
antonyms lawful, legal.

unlike *adj.* contrasted, different, disparate, dissimilar, distinct, divergent, diverse, ill-matched, incompatible, opposed, opposite, unequal, unrelated.
antonyms related, similar.

unlikely *adj.* doubtful, dubious, faint, implausible, improbable, incredible, questionable, remote, slight, suspect, suspicious, tall, unbelievable, unconvincing, unexpected, unimaginable.
antonyms likely, plausible.

unlimited *adj.* absolute, all-encompassing, boundless, complete, countless, endless, extensive, full, great, illimitable, immeasurable, immense, incalculable, indefinite, infinite, limitless, total, unbounded, unconditional, unconstrained, unhampered, unqualified, unrestricted, vast.
antonyms circumscribed, limited.

unload *v.* discharge, dump, empty, offload, relieve, unburden, unpack.

unlock *v.* bare, disengage, free, open, release, unbar, unbolt, undo, unfasten, unlatch.
antonyms fasten, lock.

unlooked-for *adj.* chance, fortuitous, fortunate, lucky, surprise, surprising, unanticipated, undreamed-of, unexpected, unforeseen, unhoped-for, unpredicted, unthought-of.
antonyms expected, predictable.

unloved *adj.* detested, disliked, hated, loveless, neglected, rejected, spurned, uncared-for, unpopular, unwanted.
antonyms beloved, loved.

unlucky *adj.* cursed, disastrous, doomed, ill-fated, ill-starred, inauspicious, jinxed, luckless, miserable, ominous, unfavourable, unfortunate, unhappy, unsuccessful, wretched.
antonym lucky.

unmanageable *adj.* awkward, bulky, cumbersome, difficult, disorderly, inconvenient, uncontrollable, unhandy, unruly, unwieldy, wild.
antonyms controllable, manageable.

unmanly *adj.* cowardly, dishonourable, effeminate, feeble, namby-pamby, sissy, soft, weak, weak-kneed, weedy, wet, womanish, yellow.
antonym manly.

unmarried *adj.* available, celibate, fancy-free, footloose, single, unattached, unwed, unwedded.
antonym married.

unmask *v.* bare, detect, disclose, discover, dismask, expose, reveal, show, uncloak, uncover, unveil.

unmentionable *adj.* abominable, disgraceful, disreputable, immodest, indecent, scandalous, shameful, shocking, taboo, unnameable, unspeakable, unutterable.

unmistakable *adj.* certain, clear, crystal-clear, decided, distinct, evident, explicit, glaring, indisputable, manifest, obvious, patent, plain, positive, pronounced, sure, unambiguous, undeniable, undisputed, unequivocal, unquestionable.
antonyms ambiguous, unclear.

unmoved *adj.* adamant, cold, determined, dispassionate, dry-eyed, fast, firm, impassive, indifferent, inflexible, resolute, resolved, steadfast, steady, unaffected, unchanged, undeviating, unfeeling, unimpressed, unresponsive, unshaken, untouched, unwavering.
antonyms affected, moved, shaken.

unnatural *adj.* **1** abnormal, anomalous, bizarre, extraordinary, false, freakish, inhuman, irregular, odd, peculiar, perverse, perverted, phoney, queer, strange, supernatural, unaccountable, uncanny, unusual. **2** affected, artificial, contrived, feigned, forced, insincere, laboured, self-conscious, stiff, stilted, strained, unspontaneous.
antonyms **1** acceptable, natural, normal. **2** fluent, natural, sincere.

unnecessary *adj.* expendable, needless, nonessential, redundant, superfluous, tautological, uncalled-for, unneeded, useless.
antonyms indispensable, necessary, needed.

unnerve *adj.* confound, demoralise, disconcert, discourage, dismay, fluster, frighten, intimidate, rattle, scare, shake, unhinge, upset, worry.
antonyms brace, nerve, steel.

unnoticed *adj.* disregarded, ignored, neglected, overlooked, passed over, unconsidered, undiscovered, unheeded, unobserved, unrecognised, unremarked, unseen.
antonyms noted, remarked.

unobtrusive *adj.* humble, inconspicuous, low-key, modest, quiet, restrained, retiring, self-effacing, subdued, unassertive, unemphatic, unnoticeable, unostentatious, unpretentious.
antonyms obtrusive, ostentatious.

unoccupied *adj.* empty, free, idle, inactive, jobless, unemployed, uninhabited, untenanted, vacant, workless.
antonyms busy, occupied.

unofficial *adj.* confidential, illegal, informal, personal, private, unauthorised, unconfirmed, undeclared, wildcat.
antonym official.

unpaid *adj.* due, free, honorary, outstanding, overdue, owing, payable, unremunerative, unsalaried, unsettled, voluntary.
antonym paid.

unpalatable *adj.* **1** bitter, distasteful, inedible, insipid, unappetising, uneatable. **2** disagreeable, offensive, repugnant, unattractive, unenviable, unpleasant.
antonyms **1** palatable. **2** pleasant.

unparalleled *adj.* exceptional, incomparable, matchless, peerless, rare, superlative, supreme, surpassing, unequalled, unmatched, unprecedented, unrivalled, unsurpassed.

unpardonable *adj.* disgraceful, indefensible, inexcusable, outrageous, scandalous, shameful, shocking, unforgivable.
antonyms forgivable, understandable.

unpleasantness *n.* annoyance, bother, embarrassment, furore, fuss, ill-feeling, nastiness, scandal, trouble, upset.

unpopular *adj.* avoided, detested, disliked, hated, neglected, rejected, shunned, undesirable, unfashionable, unloved, unsought-after, unwanted, unwelcome.
antonyms fashionable, popular.

unprecedented *adj.* abnormal, exceptional, extraordinary, freakish, new, original, remarkable, revolutionary, unheard-of, unknown, unparalleled, unrivalled, unusual.
antonym usual.

unpredictable *adj.* chance, changeable, doubtful, erratic, fickle, inconstant, random, unforeseeable, unreliable, unstable, variable.
antonyms forseeable, predictable.

unprepared *adj.* ad-lib, half-baked, ill-considered, improvised, incomplete, off-the-cuff, spontaneous, surprised, unfinished, unplanned, unready, unrehearsed, unsuspecting.
antonyms prepared, ready.

unpretentious *adj.* honest, humble, modest, natural, plain, simple, straightforward, unaffected, unassuming, unimposing, unobtrusive, unostentatious, unpretending.
antonym pretentious.

unprincipled *adj.* corrupt, crooked, deceitful, devious, discreditable, dishonest, dishonourable, immoral, underhand, unethical, unprofessional, unscrupulous.
antonym ethical.

unproductive *adj.* arid, barren, dry, fruitless, futile, idle, ineffective, infertile, sterile, unfruitful, unprofitable, unremunerative, unrewarding, useless, vain, worthless.
antonyms fertile, productive.

unprofessional *adj.* amateur, amateurish, improper, inadmissible, incompetent, inefficient, inexperienced, inexpert, lax, negligent, unacceptable, unethical, unprincipled, unseemly, unskilled, untrained, unworthy.
antonyms professional, skilful.

unprotected *adj.* defenceless, exposed, helpless, liable, naked, open, unarmed, unattended, uncovered, undefended, unfortified, unguarded, unsheltered, unshielded, vulnerable.
antonyms immune, protected, safe, shielded.

unqualified *adj.* **1** ill-equipped, incapable, incompetent, ineligible, unprepared, untrained. **2** absolute, categorical, complete, consummate, downright, outright, thorough, total, unconditional, unmitigated, unmixed, unreserved, unrestricted, utter, whole-hearted.
antonyms **1** qualified. **2** conditional, tentative.

unquestionable *adj.* absolute, certain, clear, definite, incontestable, incontrovertible, irrefutable, obvious, patent, self-evident, sure, undeniable, unequivocal, unmistakable.
antonyms doubtful, dubious, questionable.

unquestioning *adj.* implicit, unconditional, unhesitating, unqualified, whole-hearted.
antonym doubtful.

unravel *v.* disentangle, explain, extricate, figure out, free, interpret, penetrate, puzzle out, resolve, separate, solve, sort out, undo, unknot, untangle, unwind, work out.
antonyms complicate, tangle.

unreal *adj.* artificial, fairy-tale, fake, false, fanciful, fantastic, fictitious, hypothetical, illusory, imaginary, immaterial, insincere, insubstantial, made-up, make-believe, mock, mythical, nebulous, ostensible, pretended, seeming, sham, synthetic, visionary.
antonyms genuine, real.

unrealistic *adj.* blinkered, half-baked, idealistic, impracticable, impractical, improbable, romantic, starry-eyed, theoretical, unworkable.
antonyms pragmatic, realistic.

unreasonable *adj.* **1** arbitrary, biased, blinkered, foolish, headstrong, irrational, mad, opinionated, perverse, unjust. **2** absurd, far-fetched, illogical, inconsistent, nonsensical, preposterous, senseless, silly, stupid, uncalled-for, undue, unfair, unjustifiable, unjustified, unwarranted. **3** excessive, exorbitant, extortionate, extravagant, immoderate, steep.
antonyms **1** fair, reasonable. **2** rational, sensible. **3** moderate.

unrecognisable *adj.* altered, changed, disguised, incognito, unidentifiable, unknowable.

unrefined *adj.* coarse, crude, imperfect, inelegant, raw, rude, uncultivated, uncultured, unfinished, unpolished, unsophisticated, untreated, vulgar.
antonyms finished, refined.

unrelated *adj.* different, disparate, dissimilar, distinct, extraneous, irrelevant, unassociated, unconnected, unlike.
antonyms related, similar.

unrelenting *adj.* ceaseless, constant, continual, continuous, cruel, endless, incessant, inexorable, insistent, merciless, perpetual, pitiless, relentless, remorseless, ruthless, steady, stern, tough, unabated, unalleviated, unbroken, unceasing, uncompromising, unmerciful, unremitting, unsparing.
antonyms intermittent, spasmodic.

unreliable *adj.* deceptive, erroneous, fallible,

false, implausible, inaccurate, inauthentic, irresponsible, mistaken, uncertain, unconvincing, undependable, unsound, unstable, untrustworthy.
antonyms dependable, reliable, trustworthy.

unrepentant *adj.* callous, hardened, impenitent, incorrigible, obdurate, shameless, unabashed, unashamed.
antonyms ashamed, penitent, repentant.

unreserved *adj.* absolute, complete, direct, entire, forthright, free, full, open, total, unconditional, unhesitating, unlimited, unqualified, unrestrained, whole-hearted.
antonyms qualified, tentative.

unresponsive *adj.* aloof, apathetic, cool, indifferent, unaffected, uninterested, unmoved, unsympathetic.
antonyms responsive, sympathetic.

unrestricted *adj.* absolute, all-round, clear, free, free-for-all, open, public, unbounded, unconditional, unhindered, unimpeded, unlimited, unobstructed, unopposed, unregulated.
antonyms limited, restricted.

unripe *adj.* green, immature, undeveloped, unready, unripened.
antonyms mature, ripe.

unrivalled *adj.* incomparable, inimitable, matchless, superlative, supreme, surpassing, unequalled, unmatched, unparalleled, unsurpassed, without equal.

unruffled *adj.* calm, collected, composed, cool, even, imperturbable, level, peaceful, serene, smooth, tranquil, undisturbed, unflustered, unmoved, untroubled.
antonyms anxious, troubled.

unruly *adj.* disobedient, disorderly, headstrong, insubordinate, intractable, lawless, mutinous, obstreperous, rebellious, riotous, rowdy, uncontrollable, ungovernable, unmanageable, wayward, wild, wilful.
antonyms manageable, orderly.

unsafe *adj.* dangerous, exposed, hazardous, insecure, perilous, precarious, risky, threatening, treacherous, uncertain, unreliable, unsound, unstable, vulnerable.
antonyms safe, secure.

unsaid *adj.* undeclared, unexpressed, unmentioned, unspoken, unstated, unuttered, unvoiced.
antonym spoken.

unsaleable *adj.* unmarketable, unsellable.
antonyms marketable, saleable.

unsatisfactory *adj.* deficient, disappointing, displeasing, dissatisfying, frustrating, inadequate, inferior, insufficient, mediocre, poor, unacceptable, unsatisfying, unsuitable, unworthy, weak.
antonyms pleasing, satisfactory.

unscathed *adj.* intact, safe, sound, unharmed, unhurt, uninjured, unscarred, unscratched, untouched, whole.
antonyms harmed, injured.

unscrupulous *adj.* corrupt, crooked, discreditable, dishonest, dishonourable, immoral, improper, ruthless, shameless, unethical, unprincipled.
antonyms ethical, proper, scrupulous.

unseasonable *adj.* ill-timed, inappropriate, inopportune, mistimed, unsuitable, untimely.
antonyms seasonable, timely.

unseat *v.* depose, dethrone, discharge, dismiss, dismount, displace, oust, overthrow, remove, throw, topple, unsaddle.

unseemly *adj.* discreditable, disreputable, improper, inappropriate, indelicate, shocking, unbecoming, undignified, undue, unrefined, unsuitable.
antonyms decorous, seemly.

unseen *adj.* concealed, hidden, invisible, obscure, overlooked, undetected, unnoticed, unobserved, unobtrusive, veiled.
antonyms observed, visible.

unselfish *adj.* altruistic, charitable, disinterested, generous, humanitarian, kind, liberal, magnanimous, noble, philanthropic, self-denying, selfless, self-sacrificing, single-eyed.
antonym selfish.

unsentimental *adj.* hard-headed, level-headed, practical, pragmatic, realistic, shrewd, tough.
antonyms sentimental, soft.

unsettle *v.* agitate, bother, confuse, discompose, disconcert, disorder, disturb, fluster, flutter, rattle, ruffle, shake, throw, trouble, unbalance, upset.
antonyms compose, settle.

unsettled *adj.* agitated, anxious, changeable, changing, confused, disorderly, disoriented, disturbed, doubtful, edgy, flustered, inconstant, insecure, open, outstanding, overdue, owing, payable, problematical, shaken, shaky, tense, troubled, uncertain, undecided, undetermined, uneasy, unnerved, unpredictable, unresolved, unstable, unsteady, upset, variable.
antonyms certain, composed, settled.

unshakable *adj.* absolute, adamant, constant, determined, firm, fixed, immovable, resolute, stable, staunch, steadfast, sure, unassailable, unswerving, unwavering, well-founded.
antonym insecure.

unskilled *adj.* amateurish, incompetent, inexperienced, inexpert, uneducated, unpractised, unprofessional, unqualified, untalented, untaught, untrained.
antonym skilled.

unsociable *adj.* aloof, chilly, cold, distant, hostile, inhospitable, introverted, reclusive, reserved, retiring, stand-offish, taciturn, uncommunicative, uncongenial, unforthcoming, unfriendly, unneighbourly, unsocial, withdrawn.
antonyms friendly, sociable.

unsolicited *adj.* gratuitous, spontaneous, unasked, uncalled-for, uninvited, unrequested, unsought, unwanted, unwelcome, voluntary.
antonyms invited, solicited.

unsophisticated *adj.* artless, childlike, guileless, inexperienced, ingenuous, innocent, naïve, natural, plain, simple, straightforward, unaffected, uncomplicated, uninvolved, unpreten-

tious, unrefined, unspecialised, unspoilt, unworldly.
antonyms complex, pretentious, sophisticated.

unsound *adj.* **1** defective, erroneous, fallacious, false, faulty, flawed, ill-founded, illogical, invalid. **2** ailing, deranged, diseased, frail, ill, unbalanced, unhealthy, unhinged, unwell, weak. **3** insecure, shaky, unsafe, unstable, unsteady, wobbly.
antonyms **1** sound. **2** well. **3** stable.

unspeakable *adj.* appalling, awful, dreadful, evil, frightful, horrible, inconceivable, inexpressible, loathsome, monstrous, shocking, terrible, unbelievable, unutterable.

unspoilt *adj.* natural, perfect, preserved, unaffected, unblemished, unchanged, undamaged, unharmed, unimpaired, unscathed, unsophisticated, unstudied, untouched, wholesome.
antonyms affected, spoilt.

unspoken *adj.* assumed, implicit, implied, inferred, silent, speechless, tacit, undeclared, understood, unexpressed, unsaid, unstated, untutered, voiceless, wordless.
antonyms explicit, expressed.

unstable *adj.* changeable, erratic, fitful, fluctuating, inconsistent, inconstant, insecure, irrational, precarious, rickety, risky, shaky, tottering, unbalanced, unpredictable, unsettled, unsteady, untrustworthy, vacillating, variable, volatile, wobbly.
antonyms stable, steady.

unstinting *adj.* abounding, abundant, ample, bountiful, full, generous, lavish, liberal, plentiful, profuse, unsparing.
antonyms grudging, mean.

unsubstantiated *adj.* debatable, dubious, questionable, unattested, unconfirmed, uncorroborated, unestablished, unproved, unproven, unsupported, unverified.
antonyms proved, proven.

unsuccessful *adj.* abortive, failed, fruitless, frustrated, futile, ill-fated, inadequate, ineffective, losing, luckless, sterile, thwarted, unavailing, unfortunate, unlucky, unproductive, unsatisfactory, useless, vain.
antonyms effective, fortunate, successful.

unsuitable *adj.* improper, inappropriate, inapt, incompatible, incongruous, inconsistent, unacceptable, unbecoming, unlikely, unsuited.
antonyms appropriate, suitable.

unsung *adj.* anonymous, disregarded, forgotten, neglected, obscure, overlooked, unacknowledged, unhonoured, unknown, unnamed, unrecognised.
antonyms famous, renowned, well-known.

unsure *adj.* agnostic, doubtful, dubious, hesitant, insecure, sceptical, suspicious, tentative, uncertain, unconvinced, undecided, unpersuaded.
antonyms confident, decided, sure.

unsurpassed *adj.* exceptional, incomparable, matchless, superlative, supreme, surpassing, transcendent, unequalled, unexcelled, unparalleled, unrivalled.

unsuspecting *adj.* childlike, confiding, credulous, gullible, inexperienced, ingenuous, innocent, naïve, trustful, trusting, unconscious, uncritical, unsuspicious, unwary.
antonyms conscious, knowing, suspicious.

unswerving *adj.* constant, dedicated, devoted, direct, firm, fixed, immovable, resolute, single-minded, staunch, steadfast, steady, true, undeviating, unflagging, untiring, unwavering.
antonyms irresolute, tentative.

unsympathetic *adj.* antagonistic, callous, cold, cruel, hard, hard-hearted, harsh, heartless, indifferent, inhuman, insensitive, soulless, stony, uncompassionate, unconcerned, unfeeling, unkind, unmoved, unpitying, unresponsive.
antonyms compassionate, sympathetic.

untangle *v.* disentangle, explain, extricate, resolve, solve, undo, unravel.
antonyms complicate, tangle.

unthinkable *adj.* absurd, illogical, implausible, impossible, improbable, inconceivable, incredible, insupportable, outrageous, preposterous, shocking, unbelievable, unheard-of, unimaginable, unlikely, unreasonable.

unthinking *adj.* automatic, careless, heedless, impulsive, inconsiderate, indiscreet, insensitive, instinctive, mechanical, negligent, rash, rude, selfish, senseless, tactless, thoughtless, unconscious, unguarded.
antonyms conscious, deliberate.

untidy *adj.* chaotic, cluttered, dishevelled, disorderly, jumbled, messy, muddled, scruffy, slipshod, sloppy, slovenly, topsy-turvy, unkempt, unsystematic.
antonyms systematic, tidy.

untie *v.* free, loosen, release, unbind, undo, unfasten, unknot, unloose, unloosen.
antonyms fasten, tie.

untimely *adj.* awkward, early, ill-timed, inappropriate, inauspicious, inconvenient, inopportune, mistimed, premature, unfortunate, unseasonable, unsuitable.
antonyms opportune, timely.

untiring *adj.* constant, dedicated, determined, devoted, dogged, incessant, indefatigable, patient, persevering, persistent, staunch, steady, tenacious, tireless, unfailing, unfaltering, unflagging, unremitting, unwearied.
antonyms inconstant, wavering.

untold *adj.* boundless, countless, hidden, incalculable, indescribable, inexhaustible, inexpressible, infinite, innumerable, measureless, secret, uncountable, uncounted, undisclosed, undreamed-of, unimaginable, unknown, unnumbered, unpublished, unreckoned, unrelated, unrevealed, unthinkable.

untouched *adj.* intact, safe, unaffected, unaltered, unconcerned, undamaged, unharmed, unhurt, unimpaired, unimpressed, uninjured, unmoved, unscathed.
antonyms affected, impaired, moved.

untrained *adj.* amateur, inexperienced, inexpert, uneducated, unprofessional, unqualified, unschooled, unskilled, untaught.

antonyms expert, trained.
untried *adj.* experimental, exploratory, innovative, innovatory, new, novel, unestablished, unproved, untested.
antonyms proven, tested.
untrue *adj.* **1** deceptive, erroneous, fallacious, false, inaccurate, incorrect, misleading, mistaken, wrong. **2** deceitful, deviant, dishonest, disloyal, lying, two-faced, unfaithful, untrustworthy.
antonyms **1** true. **2** honest, trustworthy.
untrustworthy *adj.* capricious, deceitful, devious, dishonest, disloyal, faithless, false, fickle, fly-by-night, shady, treacherous, two-faced, unfaithful, unreliable, untrue, untrusty.
antonyms reliable, trustworthy.
untruth *n.* deceit, fabrication, falsehood, fib, fiction, invention, lie, lying, perjury, story, tale, trick, untruthfulness, whopper.
antonym truth.
untruthful *adj.* crooked, deceitful, deceptive, dishonest, false, hypocritical, lying, untrustworthy.
antonym truthful.
unused *adj.* available, extra, fresh, idle, left, left-over, new, remaining, unaccustomed, unconsumed, unemployed, unexploited, unfamiliar, untouched.
unusual *adj.* abnormal, bizarre, curious, different, exceptional, extraordinary, odd, queer, rare, remarkable, strange, surprising, uncommon, unconventional, unexpected, unfamiliar.
antonyms normal, ordinary, usual.
unveil *v.* bare, disclose, discover, divulge, expose, reveal, uncover, unfold.
antonyms cover, hide.
unwanted *adj.* extra, outcast, rejected, superfluous, surplus, undesired, uninvited, unnecessary, unneeded, unrequired, unsolicited, unwelcome, useless.
antonyms necessary, needed, wanted.
unwarranted *adj.* groundless, inexcusable, uncalled-for, unjust, unjustified, unprovoked, unreasonable, wrong.
antonyms deserved, justifiable, warranted.
unwary *adj.* careless, hasty, heedless, imprudent, incautious, indiscreet, rash, reckless, thoughtless, unguarded, unthinking.
antonyms cautious, wary.
unwavering *adj.* consistent, dedicated, determined, resolute, single-minded, staunch, steadfast, steady, tenacious, undeviating, unfaltering, unflagging, unquestioning, unshakable, unswerving.
antonyms fickle, tentative, wavering.
unwelcome *adj.* **1** excluded, rejected, undesirable, uninvited, unpopular, unwanted. **2** disagreeable, displeasing, distasteful, thankless, unacceptable, unpalatable, unpleasant, upsetting, worrying.
antonyms **1** welcome. **2** desirable.
unwell *adj.* ailing, ill, indisposed, off-colour, poorly, sick, sickly, unhealthy.
antonyms healthy, well.
unwholesome *adj.* **1** bad, harmful, junk, unhealthy, unhygienic. **2** corrupting, degrading, demoralising, depraving, evil, immoral, insalubrious, insanitary, noxious, perverting, wicked.
antonyms **1** wholesome. **2** edifying, salubrious.
unwieldy *adj.* awkward, bulky, clumsy, cumbersome, hefty, hulking, inconvenient, massive, ponderous, ungainly, unmanageable, weighty.
antonyms dainty, neat, petite.
unwilling *adj.* averse, disinclined, grudging, indisposed, loath, loathful, opposed, reluctant, resistant, slow, unenthusiastic.
antonyms enthusiastic, willing.
unwind *v.* calm down, disentangle, quieten down, relax, slacken, uncoil, undo, unravel, unreel, unroll, untwine, untwist, unwrap, wind down.
antonyms twist, wind.
unwitting *adj.* accidental, chance, inadvertent, involuntary, unaware, unconscious, unintended, unintentional, unknowing, unplanned, unsuspecting, unthinking.
antonyms conscious, deliberate, knowing, witting.
unworldly *adj.* idealistic, impractical, inexperienced, innocent, metaphysical, naïve, otherworldly, religious, spiritual, transcendental, unearthly, unsophisticated, visionary.
antonyms materialistic, practical, worldly.
unworthy *adj.* base, contemptible, degrading, discreditable, disgraceful, dishonourable, disreputable, ignoble, improper, inappropriate, ineligible, inferior, shameful, unbecoming, undeserving, unfitting, unprofessional, unseemly, unsuitable, unsuited.
antonyms commendable, worthy.
unwritten *adj.* accepted, conventional, customary, implicit, oral, recognised, tacit, traditional, understood, unformulated, unrecorded, verbal, vocal, word-of-mouth.
antonyms recorded, written.
up-and-coming ambitious, eager, enterprising, go-getting, promising, pushing.
upbraid *v.* admonish, berate, blame, castigate, censure, chide, condemn, criticise, dress down, lecture, rebuke, reprimand, reproach, reprove, scold, take to task, tell off, tick off.
antonyms commend, praise.
upbringing *n.* breeding, bringing-up, care, cultivation, education, instruction, nurture, parenting, raising, rearing, tending, training.
update *v.* amend, correct, modernise, renew, renovate, revamp, revise.
upgrade *v.* advance, better, elevate, enhance, improve, promote, raise.
antonyms degrade, downgrade.
upheaval *n.* cataclysm, chaos, confusion, disorder, disruption, disturbance, earthquake, eruption, overthrow, revolution, shake-up, turmoil, upset.
uphill *adj.* arduous, ascending, climbing, difficult, exhausting, gruelling, hard, laborious, mounting, punishing, rising, strenuous, taxing, tough, upward, wearisome.

antonyms downhill, easy.
uphold *v.* advocate, aid, back, champion, countenance, defend, encourage, endorse, fortify, hold to, justify, maintain, promote, stand by, stengthen, support, sustain, vindicate.
antonyms abandon, reject.
upkeep *n.* care, conservation, keep, maintenance, preservation, repair, running, running costs, subsistence, support, sustenance.
antonym neglect.
upper *adj.* elevated, eminent, exalted, greater, high, higher, important, loftier, senior, superior, top, topmost, uppermost.
antonyms inferior, junior, lower.
upper-class *adj.* aristocratic, blue-blooded, educated, élite, exclusive, high-class, noble, well-bred.
antonyms humble, working-class.
uppermost *adj.* chief, dominant, first, foremost, greatest, highest, leading, main, paramount, predominant, pre-eminent, primary, principal, prominent, supreme, top, topmost, upmost.
antonyms bottommost, lowest.
upright *adj.* **1** erect, perpendicular, straight, vertical. **2** ethical, good, honest, honourable, incorruptible, just, noble, principled, righteous, trustworthy, unimpeachable, upstanding, virtuous.
antonyms **1** flat, horizontal. **2** dishonest.
uprising *n.* insurgence, insurgency, insurrection, mutiny, putsch, rebellion, revolt, revolution, rising, upheaval.
uproar *n.* brawl, clamour, commotion, confusion, din, disorder, furore, hubbub, hullabaloo, hurly-burly, noise, outcry, pandemonium, racket, riot, rumpus, tumult, turbulence, turmoil.
uproot *v.* destroy, disorient, displace, exile, remove, rip up, root out, weed out, wipe out.
upset *v.* **1** agitate, bother, change, confuse, discompose, disconcert, dismay, disorganise, distress, disturb, fluster, grieve, ruffle, shake, spill, trouble, unnerve, worry. **2** capsize, destabilise, overthrow, overturn, tip, topple, unsteady.
n. **1** agitation, bother, disruption, disturbance, reverse, shake-up, shock, surprise, trouble, upheaval, worry. **2** bug, complaint, disorder, illness, indisposition, sickness.
adj. agitated, bothered, confused, disconcerted, dismayed, disquieted, distressed, disturbed, grieved, hurt, ill, overwrought, poorly, queasy, shattered, sick, troubled, worried.
upshot *n.* conclusion, consequence, culmination, end, event, finale, finish, issue, outcome, result.
upside down at sixes and sevens, chaotic, confused, disordered, higgledy-piggledy, inverted, jumbled, muddled, overturned, topsy-turvy, upset, upturned, wrong side up.
uptight *adj.* anxious, edgy, hung-up, irritated, nervy, prickly, tense, uneasy.
antonyms calm, cool, relaxed.
upturn *n.* advancement, boost, improvement, increase, recovery, revival, rise, upsurge, upswing.
antonyms downturn, drop, setback.
urban *adj.* built-up, city, civic, inner-city, metropolitan, municipal, town, urbanised.
antonyms country, rural, rustic.
urchin *n.* brat, gutter-snipe, kid, ragamuffin, waif.
urge *v.* advise, advocate, beg, beseech, champion, compel, constrain, counsel, drive, encourage, entreat, exhort, force, goad, hasten, impel, implore, incite, induce, instigate, plead, press, propel, push, recommend, solicit, spur, stimulate, support, underline.
antonyms deter, discourage, dissuade, hinder.
n. compulsion, desire, drive, eagerness, fancy, impulse, inclination, itch, longing, wish, yearning.
antonym disinclination.
urgency *n.* extremity, gravity, hurry, imperativeness, importance, necessity, need, pressure, seriousness, stress.
urgent *adj.* compelling, critical, crucial, eager, earnest, exigent, immediate, imperative, important, insistent, instant, intense, persistent, persuasive, pressing, top-priority.
antonyms low-priority, unimportant, weak.
usable *adj.* available, current, exploitable, functional, operating, operational, practical, serviceable, valid, working.
antonyms unusable, useless.
usage *n.* application, control, convention, custom, employment, etiquette, form, habit, handling, management, method, operation, practice, procedure, regulation, routine, rule, running, tradition, treatment, use.
use *v.* apply, bring, consume, employ, enjoy, exercise, exhaust, expend, exploit, handle, manipulate, operate, practise, spend, treat, utilise, waste, wield, work.
n. advantage, application, avail, benefit, cause, custom, employment, end, exercise, good, habit, handling, help, mileage, necessity, need, object, occasion, operation, point, practice, profit, purpose, reason, service, treatment, usage, usefulness, utility, value, way, worth.
use up absorb, consume, deplete, devour, drain, eat into, exhaust, finish, fritter, sap, squander, swallow, waste.
used *adj.* **1** accustomed, familiar. **2** cast-off, dog-eared, hand-me-down, nearly new, second-hand, shop-soiled, soiled, worn.
antonyms **1** unaccustomed, unused. **2** fresh, new.
useful *adj.* advantageous, all-purpose, beneficial, convenient, effective, fruitful, handy, helpful, practical, productive, profitable, valuable, worthwhile.
antonyms ineffective, useless, worthless.
useless *adj.* clapped-out, effectless, fruitless, futile, hopeless, idle, impractical, incompetent, ineffective, inefficient, needless, of no use, pointless, stupid, unavailing, unproductive, unworkable, vain, valueless, weak, worthless.
antonyms effective, helpful, useful.
usher *n.* attendant, doorkeeper, escort, guide, usherette.

v. conduct, direct, escort, guide, lead, pilot, steer.

usher in announce, herald, inaugurate, initiate, introduce, launch, precede, ring in.

usual *adj.* accepted, accustomed, common, constant, conventional, customary, everyday, expected, familiar, fixed, general, habitual, normal, ordinary, recognised, regular, routine, standard, stock, typical, unexceptional.
antonyms strange, unheard-of, unusual.

usually *adv.* as a rule, by and large, chiefly, commonly, generally, generally speaking, mainly, mostly, normally, on the whole, ordinarily, regularly, traditionally, typically.
antonym exceptionally.

usurp *v.* annex, appropriate, arrogate, assume, commandeer, seize, steal, take, take over, wrest.

utilitarian *adj.* convenient, down-to-earth, effective, efficient, functional, practical, pragmatic, sensible, serviceable, unpretentious, useful.
antonyms decorative, impractical.

utility *n.* advantage, avail, benefit, convenience, efficacy, fitness, point, practicality, profit, service, serviceableness, use, usefulness, value.
antonym inutility.

utmost *adj.* extreme, farthest, final, first, greatest, highest, last, maximum, outermost, paramount, remotest, supreme, ultimate, uttermost.
n. best, hardest, maximum, most, uttermost.

Utopia *n.* bliss, Eden, Garden of Eden, heaven, paradise.

Utopian *adj.* airy, dream, fanciful, ideal, idealistic, illusory, imaginary, impractical, perfect, romantic, unworkable, visionary, wishful.

utter[1] *adj.* absolute, arrant, complete, consummate, dead, downright, entire, out-and-out, perfect, sheer, stark, thorough, thoroughgoing, total, unmitigated, unqualified.

utter[2] *v.* articulate, declare, deliver, divulge, enunciate, express, proclaim, pronounce, publish, reveal, say, sound, speak, state, tell, verbalise, vocalise, voice.

utterance *n.* announcement, articulation, comment, declaration, delivery, expression, opinion, pronouncement, remark, speech, statement.

utterly *adv.* absolutely, completely, entirely, extremely, fully, perfectly, thoroughly, totally, wholly.

U-turn *n.* about-turn, backtrack, reversal, volte-face.

V

vacancy *n.* accommodation, job, opening, opportunity, place, position, post, room, situation, space.

vacant *adj.* **1** available, empty, free, idle, to let, unemployed, unengaged, unfilled, unoccupied, void. **2** absent, absent-minded, blank, dreamy, expressionless, inane, inattentive, unthinking, vacuous.
antonyms **1** engaged, occupied.

vacate *v.* abandon, depart, evacuate, leave, quit, withdraw.

vacillate *v.* fluctuate, hesitate, oscillate, shuffle, sway, waver.

vacuous *adj.* apathetic, blank, empty, idle, inane, mindless, stupid, uncomprehending, unintelligent, vacant, void.

vacuum *n.* chasm, emptiness, gap, nothingness, space, vacuity, void.

vagary *n.* caprice, fancy, notion, prank, quirk, whim.

vague *adj.* ambiguous, blurred, dim, evasive, fuzzy, generalised, hazy, ill-defined, imprecise, indefinite, indistinct, inexact, lax, loose, misty, nebulous, obscure, shadowy, uncertain, unclear, undefined, undetermined, unknown, unspecific, woolly.
antonyms certain, clear, definite.

vain *adj.* **1** abortive, empty, fruitless, futile, groundless, hollow, idle, pointless, trivial, unavailing, unimportant, unproductive, unprofitable, useless, worthless. **2** affected, arrogant, bigheaded, conceited, egotistical, ostentatious, pretentious, proud, self-important, self-satisfied, stuck-up, swaggering, swollen-headed.
antonyms **1** fruitful, successful. **2** modest, self-effacing.
in vain fruitlessly, ineffectually, to no avail, unsuccessfully, uselessly, vainly.
antonym successfully.

valiant *adj.* bold, brave, courageous, dauntless, fearless, gallant, heroic, indomitable, intrepid, plucky, staunch, worthy.
antonyms cowardly, fearful.

valid *adj.* **1** cogent, conclusive, convincing, good, just, logical, powerful, reliable, sound, substantial, telling, weighty, well-founded, well-grounded. **2** authentic, binding, bona fide, genuine, lawful, legal, legitimate, official, proper.
antonyms **1** false, weak. **2** invalid, unofficial.

validate *v.* attest, authenticate, authorise, certify, confirm, corroborate, endorse, legalise, ratify, substantiate, underwrite.

valuable *adj.* advantageous, beneficial, cherished, costly, dear, esteemed, estimable, expensive, fruitful, handy, helpful, high-priced, important, invaluable, precious, prized, productive, profitable, serviceable, treasured, useful, valued, worthwhile, worthy.
antonyms useless, valueless, worthless.

valuation *n.* appraisement, assessment, computation, estimate, evaluation, survey.

value *n.* account, advantage, benefit, cost, desirability, equivalent, good, help, importance, merit, price, profit, rate, significance, use, usefulness, utility, worth.
v. **1** appreciate, cherish, esteem, hold dear, prize, respect, treasure. **2** assess, compute, estimate, evaluate, price, rate, survey.
antonyms **1** disregard, neglect. **2** undervalue.

values *n.* ethics, morals, principles, standards.

vanish *v.* depart, die out, disappear, disperse, dissolve, evaporate, exit, fade, fizzle out, melt, peter out.
antonyms appear, materialise.

vanity *n.* **1** affectation, airs, arrogance, bigheadedness, conceit, conceitedness, egotism, narcissism, ostentation, pretension, pride, self-conceit, self-love, self-satisfaction, swollen-headedness. **2** emptiness, fruitlessness, futility, hollowness, pointlessness, triviality, unreality, uselessness, worthlessness.
antonyms **1** modesty, worth.

vapour *n.* breath, damp, dampness, exhalation, fog, fumes, haze, mist, smoke, steam.

variable *adj.* changeable, fickle, fitful, flexible, fluctuating, inconstant, mutable, shifting, temperamental, unpredictable, unstable, unsteady, vacillating, varying, wavering.
antonyms fixed, invariable, stable.
n. factor, parameter.

variance *n.* conflict, difference, disagreement, discord, discrepancy, disharmony, dissension, dissent, divergence, division, inconsistency, quarrelling, strife, variation.
antonyms agreement, harmony.

variant *adj.* alternative, derived, deviant, different, divergent, exceptional, modified.
antonyms normal, standard, usual.
n. alternative, development, deviant, modification, variation.

variation *n.* alteration, change, departure, deviation, difference, discrepancy, diversification, diversity, elaboration, inflection, innovation, modification, modulation, variety.
antonyms monotony, uniformity.

varied *adj.* assorted, different, diverse, manifold, miscellaneous, mixed, sundry, various, wide-ranging.
antonyms similar, standardised, uniform.

variegated *adj.* diversified, freaked, many-

coloured, motley, mottled, multicoloured, particoloured, pied, streaked, varicoloured, veined.
antonyms monochrome, plain.

variety *n.* **1** array, assortment, collection, difference, diversity, intermixture, many-sidedness, medley, miscellany, mixture, multiplicity, potpourri, range. **2** brand, breed, category, class, kind, make, sort, species, strain, type.
antonyms **1** monotony, similitude, uniformity.

various *adj.* assorted, different, differing, distinct, diverse, diversified, heterogeneous, many, many-sided, miscellaneous, several, varied, varying.

varnish *n.* coating, glaze, gloss, lacquer, polish, resin, shellac.

vary *v.* alter, alternate, change, depart, differ, disagree, diverge, diversify, fluctuate, inflect, modify, modulate, permutate, reorder, transform.

vase *n.* container, jar, jug, pitcher, urn, vessel.

vast *adj.* colossal, enormous, extensive, far-flung, fathomless, gigantic, great, huge, immeasurable, immense, massive, monstrous, monumental, never-ending, stupendous, sweeping, tremendous, unlimited.

vat *n.* container, tank, tub.

vault[1] *v.* bound, clear, hurdle, jump, leap, leap-frog, spring.

vault[2] *n.* **1** cavern, cellar, crypt, depository, mausoleum, repository, strongroom, tomb, undercroft, wine-cellar. **2** arch, concave, roof, span.

vaunt *v.* boast, brag, crow, exult in, flaunt, parade, show off, trumpet.
antonyms belittle, minimise.

veer *v.* change, sheer, shift, swerve, tack, turn, wheel.

vegetate *v.* degenerate, deteriorate, go to seed, idle, languish, rust, rusticate, stagnate.

vehemence *n.* animation, ardour, eagerness, emphasis, energy, enthusiasm, fervency, fervour, fire, force, heat, impetuosity, intensity, keenness, passion, urgency, verve, vigour, violence, warmth, zeal.
antonyms apathy, indifference.

vehement *adj.* animated, ardent, eager, earnest, emphatic, enthusiastic, fervent, fierce, forceful, forcible, heated, impassioned, intense, passionate, powerful, strong, urgent, violent, zealous.
antonyms apathetic, indifferent.

vehicle *n.* apparatus, channel, conveyance, means, mechanism, medium, organ.

veil *v.* cloak, conceal, cover, disguise, hide, mask, obscure, screen, shade, shadow, shield.
antonyms expose, uncover.
n. blind, cloak, cover, curtain, disguise, film, mask, screen, shade, shroud.

vein *n.* **1** blood vessel, seam, stratum, streak, stripe, thread. **2** course, current, frame of mind, mode, mood, note, style, temper, tenor, tone.

veined *adj.* freaked, marbled, mottled, streaked, variegated.

velocity *n.* celerity, impetus, pace, quickness, rapidity, rate, speed.

venal *adj.* bent, bribable, corrupt, corruptible, crooked, grafting, mercenary.
antonyms incorruptible, pure.

vendetta *n.* bad blood, bitterness, blood-feud, enmity, feud, quarrel, rivalry.

veneer *n.* appearance, coating, façade, front, gloss, guise, layer, mask, pretence, show, surface.

venerable *adj.* aged, august, dignified, esteemed, grave, honoured, respected, revered, venerated, wise, worshipful.

venerate *v.* adore, esteem, hallow, honour, respect, revere, worship.
antonyms anathematise, disregard.

vengeance *n.* reprisal, requital, retaliation, retribution, revenge, tit for tat.
antonym forgiveness.

venial *adj.* excusable, forgivable, insignificant, minor, negligible, pardonable, slight, trifling, trivial.
antonyms mortal, unforgivable, unpardonable.

venom *n.* **1** poison, toxin. **2** acrimony, bitterness, grudge, hate, ill-will, malevolence, malice, rancour, spite, spitefulness, virulence.

venomous *adj.* baleful, baneful, hostile, malicious, malign, malignant, noxious, poison, poisonous, rancorous, savage, spiteful, toxic, vicious, vindictive, virulent, vitriolic.
antonyms affectionate, harmless, non-poisonous.

vent *n.* aperture, duct, hole, opening, orifice, outlet, passage, split.
v. air, discharge, emit, express, let fly, release, utter, voice.

ventilate *v.* air, broadcast, debate, discuss, examine, expound, express.
antonym suppress.

venture *v.* advance, dare, endanger, hazard, imperil, jeopardise, make bold, presume, put forward, risk, speculate, stake, suggest, take the liberty, volunteer, wager.
n. adventure, chance, endeavour, enterprise, fling, gamble, hazard, operation, project, risk, speculation, undertaking.

verbal *adj.* lexical, oral, spoken, unwritten, verbatim, word-of-mouth.

verbatim *adv.* exactly, literally, precisely, to the letter, word for word.

verbose *adj.* circumlocutory, diffuse, long-winded, phrasy, windy, wordy.
antonyms brief, economical, succinct.

verdict *n.* adjudication, assessment, conclusion, decision, finding, judgement, opinion, sentence.

verge *n.* border, boundary, brim, brink, edge, edging, extreme, limit, margin, roadside, threshold.
verge on approach, border on, come close to, near.

verify *v.* attest, authenticate, check, confirm, corroborate, prove, substantiate, support, testify, validate.
antonyms discredit, invalidate.

verity *n.* actuality, authenticity, factuality, soundness, truth, truthfulness, validity, veracity.

antonym untruth.
vernacular *adj.* colloquial, common, indigenous, informal, local, mother, native, popular, vulgar.
n. dialect, idiom, jargon, language, parlance, speech, tongue.
versatile *adj.* adaptable, adjustable, all-round, flexible, functional, general-purpose, handy, many-sided, multifaceted, multipurpose, resourceful, variable.
antonym inflexible.
verse *n.* doggerel, jingle, poesy, poetry, rhyme, stanza, verse-making.
versed *adj.* accomplished, acquainted, competent, conversant, experienced, familiar, knowledgeable, learned, practised, proficient, qualified, seasoned, skilled.
version *n.* account, adaptation, design, form, interpretation, kind, model, paraphrase, portrayal, reading, rendering, style, translation, type, variant.
vertical *adj.* erect, on end, perpendicular, upright, upstanding.
antonym horizontal.
vertigo *n.* dizziness, giddiness, light-headedness.
verve *n.* animation, dash, élan, energy, enthusiasm, force, gusto, life, liveliness, punch, relish, sparkle, spirit, vigour, vitality, vivacity, zeal.
antonyms apathy, lethargy.
very *adv.* absolutely, acutely, deeply, exceeding(ly), excessively, extremely, greatly, highly, noticeably, particularly, really, remarkably, surpassingly, terribly, truly, unusually, wonderfully.
antonyms hardly, scarcely, slightly.
adj. actual, appropriate, bare, exact, identical, mere, perfect, plain, precise, pure, real, same, selfsame, sheer, simple, unqualified, utter.
vestibule *n.* anteroom, entrance, entrance-hall, foyer, hall, lobby, porch.
vestige *n.* evidence, hint, indication, relic, remainder, remains, remnant, residue, scrap, sign, suspicion, token, trace, track, whiff.
vet *v.* appraise, audit, check, examine, inspect, investigate, review, scan, scrutinise, survey.
veteran *n.* master, old hand, old stager, old-timer, pastmaster, pro, war-horse.
antonyms novice, recruit.
adj. adept, battle-scarred, experienced, expert, long-serving, masterly, old, practised, professional, proficient, seasoned.
antonym inexperienced.
veto *v.* ban, disallow, forbid, kill, prohibit, reject, rule out, turn down.
antonyms approve, sanction.
n. ban, embargo, prohibition, rejection, thumbs down.
antonyms approval, assent.
vex *v.* afflict, aggravate, agitate, annoy, bother, distress, disturb, exasperate, fret, gall, harass, irritate, offend, pester, provoke, torment, trouble, upset, worry.
antonyms calm, soothe.
vexation *n.* aggravation, anger, annoyance, bore, bother, chagrin, difficulty, displeasure, dissatisfaction, exasperation, frustration, irritant, misfortune, nuisance, problem, trial, trouble, upset, worry.
vexed *adj.* **1** afflicted, aggravated, agitated, annoyed, bothered, confused, displeased, distressed, disturbed, exasperated, harassed, irritated, nettled, perplexed, provoked, put out, riled, ruffled, troubled, upset, worried. **2** contested, controversial, difficult, disputed.
viable *adj.* achievable, applicable, feasible, operable, possible, practicable, usable, workable.
antonyms impossible, unworkable.
vibrant *adj.* animated, bright, brilliant, colourful, dynamic, electric, electrifying, lively, oscillating, quivering, responsive, sensitive, sparkling, spirited, trembling, vivacious, vivid.
vibrate *v.* judder, oscillate, pulsate, quiver, resonate, reverberate, shake, shiver, shudder, sway, swing, throb, tremble, undulate.
vice *n.* bad habit, besetting sin, blemish, corruption, defect, degeneracy, depravity, evil, evil-doing, failing, fault, immorality, imperfection, iniquity, profligacy, shortcoming, sin, weakness, wickedness.
antonyms morality, virtue.
vicinity *n.* area, district, environs, locality, neighbourhood, precincts, proximity.
vicious *adj.* abhorrent, atrocious, bad, barbarous, bitchy, brutal, catty, corrupt, cruel, dangerous, debased, defamatory, depraved, diabolical, fiendish, foul, heinous, immoral, malicious, mean, nasty, perverted, profligate, savage, slanderous, spiteful, unprincipled, venomous, vile, vindictive, violent, virulent, wicked, worthless, wrong.
antonyms gentle, good, virtuous.
victim *n.* casualty, fatality, martyr, sacrifice, scapegoat, sufferer.
antonyms assailant, attacker, offender.
victimise *v.* bully, cheat, deceive, defraud, discriminate against, dupe, exploit, fool, gull, hoodwink, oppress, persecute, pick on, prey on, swindle, use.
victorious *adj.* champion, conquering, first, prize-winning, successful, top, triumphant, unbeaten, winning.
antonyms defeated, losing, unsuccessful.
victory *n.* conquest, mastery, prize, subjugation, success, superiority, triumph, vanquishment, win.
antonyms defeat, loss.
vie *v.* compete, contend, contest, fight, rival, strive, struggle.
view *n.* **1** attitude, belief, estimation, feeling, impression, judgement, notion, opinion, sentiment. **2** landscape, outlook, panorama, perspective, prospect, scene, sight, vision, vista. **3** glimpse, look, perception, scan.
v. **1** consider, contemplate, judge, regard, speculate, think about. **2** examine, explore, eye, inspect, observe, perceive, read, scan, survey, watch, witness.
viewer *n.* looker-in, observer, onlooker, specta-

..., watcher.

...ewpoint *n.* angle, attitude, feeling, opinion, perspective, position, slant, stance, standpoint.

vigil *n.* lookout, sleeplessness, wake, wakefulness, watch.

vigilance *n.* alertness, attentiveness, carefulness, caution, guardedness, observation, wakefulness, watchfulness.

vigilant *adj.* alert, attentive, careful, cautious, on one's guard, on the lookout, sleepless, unsleeping, watchful, wide-awake.
antonyms careless, forgetful, lax, negligent.

vigorous *adj.* active, brisk, dynamic, effective, efficient, energetic, enterprising, flourishing, forceful, forcible, full-blooded, healthy, intense, lively, lusty, powerful, robust, sound, spirited, stout, strenuous, strong, virile, vital, zippy.
antonyms feeble, lethargic, weak.

vigour *n.* activity, animation, dash, dynamism, energy, force, forcefulness, gusto, health, liveliness, might, potency, power, robustness, snap, soundness, spirit, stamina, strength, verve, virility, vitality.
antonyms impotence, sluggishness, weakness.

vile *adj.* appalling, bad, base, coarse, contemptible, corrupt, debased, degenerate, degrading, depraved, despicable, disgraceful, disgusting, evil, foul, horrid, humiliating, impure, loathsome, mean, miserable, nasty, nauseating, noxious, offensive, perverted, repugnant, repulsive, revolting, scandalous, shocking, sickening, sinful, ugly, vicious, vulgar, wicked, worthless, wretched.
antonyms lovely, pleasant, pure, refined, worthy.

villain *n.* criminal, devil, evil-doer, malefactor, miscreant, rascal, rogue, scoundrel.

villainous *adj.* atrocious, bad, criminal, cruel, degenerate, depraved, detestable, diabolical, disgraceful, evil, fiendish, hateful, infamous, inhuman, malevolent, mean, sinful, terrible, vicious, vile, wicked.
antonyms angelic, good, heroic.

vindicate *v.* absolve, acquit, advocate, assert, clear, defend, establish, excuse, exonerate, justify, maintain, rehabilitate, support, uphold, verify.
antonyms accuse, convict.

vindictive *adj.* implacable, malevolent, malicious, malignant, punitive, relentless, resentful, revengeful, spiteful, unforgiving, unrelenting, venomous.
antonyms charitable, forgiving, merciful.

vintage *n.* collection, crop, epoch, era, generation, harvest, origin, period, year.
adj. best, choice, classic, fine, mature, old, prime, rare, ripe, select, superior, venerable, veteran.

violate *v.* abuse, break, contravene, debauch, defile, dishonour, disobey, disregard, flout, infringe, invade, outrage, profane, transgress.
antonyms defend, obey, observe, uphold.

violence *n.* bloodshed, brutality, conflict, cruelty, destructiveness, ferocity, fierceness, fighting, force, frenzy, fury, harshness, hostilities, intensity, murderousness, passion, power, roughness, savagery, severity, sharpness, storminess, terrorism, tumult, turbulence, vehemence, wildness.
antonyms passivity, peacefulness.

violent *adj.* acute, agonising, berserk, biting, bloodthirsty, boisterous, brutal, cruel, destructive, devastating, excruciating, extreme, fiery, forceful, forcible, furious, harsh, headstrong, hot-headed, impetuous, intemperate, intense, maddened, murderous, outrageous, painful, passionate, powerful, raging, riotous, rough, ruinous, savage, severe, sharp, strong, tumultuous, turbulent, uncontrollable, ungovernable, unrestrained, vehement, vicious, wild.
antonyms calm, gentle, moderate, passive, peaceful.

VIP *n.* big name, celebrity, dignitary, heavyweight, luminary, notable, personage, somebody, star.
antonyms nobody, nonentity.

virginal *adj.* celibate, chaste, fresh, immaculate, maidenly, pristine, pure, spotless, stainless, uncorrupted, undefiled, untouched, white.

virile *adj.* forceful, lusty, macho, male, man-like, manly, masculine, potent, red-blooded, robust, rugged, strong, vigorous.
antonyms effeminate, impotent, weak.

virtually *adv.* almost, as good as, effectively, in effect, in essence, nearly, practically, to all intents and purposes.

virtue *n.* advantage, asset, chastity, credit, excellence, goodness, high- mindedness, honour, incorruptibility, innocence, integrity, justice, merit, morality, probity, purity, quality, rectitude, righteousness, strength, uprightness, virginity, worth, worthiness.
antonyms corruption, immorality, vice.

virtuoso *n.* ace, artist, expert, genius, maestro, master, prodigy, whiz, wizard.

virtuous *adj.* blameless, celibate, chaste, clean-living, ethical, excellent, exemplary, good, high-principled, honest, honourable, incorruptible, innocent, irreproachable, moral, pure, righteous, spotless, unimpeachable, upright, worthy.
antonyms bad, dishonest, immoral, vicious, wicked.

viscera *n.* bowels, entrails, innards, insides, intestines.

viscous *adj.* adhesive, gelatinous, gluey, glutinous, gummy, mucous, sticky, syrupy, tacky, thick, treacly, viscid.
antonyms runny, thin, watery.

visible *adj.* apparent, clear, conspicuous, detectable, discernible, discoverable, distinguishable, evident, manifest, noticeable, observable, obvious, open, palpable, patent, perceptible, plain, unconcealed, undisguised, unmistakable.
antonyms hidden, indiscernible, invisible.

vision *n.* **1** apparition, conception, daydream, delusion, dream, fantasy, ghost, hallucination, idea, ideal, illusion, image, insight, mirage, phantom, picture, revelation, spectre, view, wraith. **2** discernment, eyesight, far-sightedness, foresight, penetration, perception, seeing, sight.

visionary *adj.* dreamy, fanciful, idealistic, illusory, imaginary, impractical, prophetic, romantic, speculative, unreal, unrealistic, unworkable, utopian.
n. daydreamer, dreamer, enthusiast, idealist, mystic, prophet, rainbow-chaser, romantic, seer, theorist, utopian, zealot.
antonym pragmatist.

visit *v.* call in, call on, drop in on, look in, look up, pop in, see, stay at, stay with, stop by.
n. call, excursion, sojourn, stay, stop.

visitation *n.* appearance, blight, calamity, cataclysm, catastrophe, disaster, examination, infliction, inspection, manifestation, ordeal, punishment, retribution, scourge, trial, visit.

visitor *n.* caller, company, guest, holidaymaker, tourist.

vista *n.* panorama, perspective, prospect, view.

visual *adj.* discernible, observable, optical, perceptible, specular, visible.

visualise *v.* conceive, envisage, imagine, picture.

vital *adj.* **1** basic, critical, crucial, decisive, essential, forceful, fundamental, imperative, important, indispensable, key, life-or-death, necessary, requisite, significant, urgent. **2** alive, animated, dynamic, energetic, invigorating, life-giving, live, lively, quickening, spirited, vibrant, vigorous, vivacious.
antonyms **1** inessential, peripheral, unimportant.

vitality *n.* animation, energy, exuberance, go, life, liveliness, robustness, sparkle, stamina, strength, vigour, vivacity.

vitriolic *adj.* abusive, biting, bitter, caustic, destructive, malicious, sardonic, scathing, venomous, vicious, virulent.

vivacious *adj.* animated, bubbly, cheerful, ebullient, effervescent, high- spirited, light-hearted, lively, sparkling, spirited.
antonym languid.

vivacity *n.* animation, bubbliness, ebullience, effervescence, energy, high spirits, life, liveliness, pep, quickness, sparkle, spirit.
antonym languor.

vivid *adj.* **1** animated, bright, brilliant, colourful, dazzling, dramatic, expressive, flamboyant, glowing, intense, lifelike, lively, rich, spirited, strong, vibrant, vigorous. **2** clear, distinct, graphic, memorable, powerful, realistic, sharp, striking.
antonyms **1** colourless, dull. lifeless. **2** vague.

vocabulary *n.* dictionary, glossary, idiom, language, lexicon, thesaurus, word-book, words.

vocal *adj.* articulate, clamorous, eloquent, expressive, forthright, frank, free-spoken, noisy, oral, outspoken, plain-spoken, said, shrill, spoken, strident, uttered, voiced.
antonyms inarticulate, quiet.

vocation *n.* business, calling, career, employment, job, métier, mission, office, post, profession, pursuit, role, trade, work.

vociferous *adj.* clamorous, loud, noisy, obstreperous, shouting, strident, thundering, vehement, vocal.
antonyms quiet, silent.

vogue *n.* acceptance, craze, custom, fashion, mode, popularity, prevalence, style, the latest, the rage, the thing, trend, usage, use.
adj. current, fashionable, modish, now, popular, prevalent, stylish, trendy, up-to-the-minute.

voice *n.* **1** articulation, expression, inflection, instrument, intonation, language, medium, mouthpiece, organ, sound, speech, tone, utterance, words. **2** decision, opinion, say, view, vote, will, wish.
v. air, articulate, assert, convey, declare, disclose, divulge, enunciate, express, say, speak of, utter, ventilate.

void *adj.* bare, blank, cancelled, clear, dead, drained, emptied, empty, free, inane, ineffective, inoperative, invalid, unfilled, unoccupied, useless, vacant, vain, worthless.
antonyms full, valid.
n. blank, blankness, cavity, chasm, emptiness, gap, hollow, lack, opening, space, vacuity, vacuum, want.

volatile *adj.* airy, changeable, erratic, explosive, fickle, flighty, giddy, hot-headed, hot-tempered, inconstant, lively, sprightly, temperamental, unsettled, unstable, unsteady, variable, volcanic.
antonyms constant, steady.

volition *n.* choice, determination, discretion, option, preference, purpose, resolution, taste, will.

volley *n.* barrage, blast, bombardment, burst, discharge, explosion, hail, shower.

voluble *adj.* articulate, fluent, forthcoming, garrulous, glib, loquacious, talkative.

volume *n.* **1** aggregate, amount, amplitude, bigness, body, bulk, capacity, dimensions, mass, quantity, total. **2** book, publication, tome, treatise.

voluntary *adj.* conscious, deliberate, free, gratuitous, honorary, intended, intentional, optional, purposeful, purposive, spontaneous, unconstrained, unforced, unpaid, volunteer, wilful, willing.
antonyms automatic, compulsory, forced, involuntary, unwilling.

volunteer *v.* advance, communicate, extend, offer, present, propose, put forward, step forward, suggest, tender.
n. unpaid worker, willing horse, worker.

voluptuous *adj.* ample, buxom, enticing, erotic, licentious, luscious, luxurious, provocative, seductive, sensual, shapely.

vomit *v.* bring up, eject, heave, regurgitate, retch, throw up.

vote *n.* ballot, election, franchise, poll, referendum.
v. ballot, choose, declare, elect, judge, opt, plump for, pronounce, propose, recommend, return, suggest.

vouch for affirm, assert, attest to, back, certify, confirm, endorse, guarantee, speak for, support, swear to, uphold.

vow *v.* affirm, consecrate, dedicate, devote, maintain, pledge, profess, promise, swear.
n. oath, pledge, promise.

voyage *n.* crossing, cruise, expedition, journey, passage, travels, trip.

vulgar *adj.* **1** cheap and nasty, flashy, gaudy, tasteless, tawdry. **2** blue, coarse, common, crude, dirty, gross, ill-bred, impolite, indecent, indecorous, indelicate, nasty, naughty, risqué, rude, suggestive, uncouth, unmannerly, unrefined.
antonyms **1** elegant. **2** correct, decent, noble, polite, refined.

vulnerable *adj.* accessible, defenceless, exposed, sensitive, susceptible, tender, thin-skinned, unprotected, weak, wide open.
antonyms guarded, protected, strong.

W

wad *n.* ball, block, bundle, chunk, hunk, mass, plug, roll, wodge.
wadding *n.* cotton-wool, filler, lining, packing, padding, stuffing.
waddle *v.* rock, shuffle, sway, toddle, totter, wobble.
waffle *v.* jabber, prattle, rabbit on, spout, witter on.
n. blather, gobbledegook, hot air, jabber, nonsense, padding, prattle.
waft *v.* drift, float, ride, transmit, transport.
n. breath, breeze, current, draught, puff, scent, whiff.
wag *v.* bob, bobble, flutter, nod, oscillate, quiver, rock, shake, stir, vibrate, waggle, wave, wiggle.
wage *n.* allowance, compensation, earnings, emolument, fee, hire, pay, payment, recompense, remuneration, reward, salary, stipend, wage-packet, wages.
v. carry on, conduct, engage in, practise, pursue, undertake.
wagon *n.* buggy, carriage, cart, train, truck, van.
wail *v.* complain, cry, howl, moan, weep, yammer, yowl.
n. complaint, cry, grief, howl, moan, weeping, yowl.
wait *v.* delay, hang around, hang fire, hesitate, hold back, linger, pause, remain, rest, stay.
antonyms depart, go, leave.
n. delay, halt, hesitation, hold-up, interval, pause, rest, stay.
waiver *n.* abandonment, abdication, disclaimer, relinquishment, remission, renunciation, resignation, surrender.
wake[1] *v.* activate, animate, arise, arouse, enliven, excite, fire, galvanise, get up, kindle, provoke, quicken, rise, rouse, stimulate, stir.
antonyms relax, sleep.
n. death-watch, funeral, vigil, watch.
wake[2] *n.* aftermath, backwash, path, rear, track, trail, train, wash, waves.
wakeful *adj.* alert, alive, attentive, heedful, insomniac, observant, restless, sleepless, unsleeping, vigilant, wary, watchful.
antonyms inattentive, sleepy, unwary.
walk *v.* accompany, advance, amble, convoy, escort, hike, hoof it, march, move, pace, plod, promenade, saunter, step, stride, stroll, take, traipse, tramp, tread, trek, trudge.
n. **1** carriage, gait, pace, step, stride, traipse, trudge. **2** hike, march, ramble, saunter, stroll, trail, tramp, trek. **3** alley, avenue, esplanade, footpath, lane, path, pathway, pavement, promenade, sidewalk, walkway.
walk of life activity, area, arena, calling, career, course, field, line, métier, profession, pursuit, sphere, trade, vocation.
walker *n.* hiker, pedestrian, rambler.
walk-out *n.* industrial action, protest, rebellion, revolt, stoppage, strike.
walk-over *n.* child's play, cinch, doddle, piece of cake, pushover.
walkway *n.* esplanade, footpath, lane, path, pathway, pavement, promenade, sidewalk.
wall *n.* barricade, barrier, bulk-head, bulwark, dike, divider, embankment, enclosure, fence, fortification, hedge, impediment, membrane, obstacle, obstruction, palisade, panel, parapet, partition, rampart, screen, stockade.
wallet *n.* bill-fold, case, holder, note-case, pouch, purse.
wallop *v.* belt, clobber, crush, defeat, hammer, hit, pound, pummel, punch, smack, strike, swat, swipe, thrash, thump, thwack, whack.
n. bash, belt, blow, hit, kick, punch, slug, smack, swat, swipe, thump, thwack, whack.
wallow *v.* bask, delight, enjoy, flounder, glory, indulge, lie, loll, lurch, luxuriate, relish, revel, roll, splash, wade, welter.
wand *n.* baton, mace, rod, sceptre, sprig, staff, stick, twig, verge.
wander *v.* aberrate, cruise, depart, deviate, digress, diverge, drift, err, lapse, meander, mill around, ramble, range, rave, roam, rove, saunter, squander, straggle, stray, stroll, swerve, veer.
n. cruise, excursion, meander, ramble, saunter, stroll.
wanderer *n.* drifter, gypsy, itinerant, nomad, rambler, ranger, rolling stone, rover, straggler, stray, stroller, traveller, vagabond, vagrant, voyager.
wandering *n.* drifting, journeying, meandering, odyssey, travels, walkabout.
adj. aberrant, drifting, homeless, itinerant, migratory, nomadic, peripatetic, rambling, rootless, roving, strolling, travelling, vagabond, vagrant, voyaging, wayfaring.
wane *v.* abate, contract, decline, decrease, dim, diminish, droop, drop, dwindle, ebb, fade, fail, lessen, shrink, sink, subside, taper off, weaken, wither.
antonyms develop, increase, wax.
on the wane declining, degenerating, deteriorating, diminishing, dropping, dwindling, ebbing, fading, lessening, obsolescent, on its last legs, on the decline, subsiding, tapering off, weakening.
wangle *v.* arrange, contrive, engineer, fiddle, fix, manage, manipulate, manoeuvre, pull off, scheme, work.

want *v.* call for, covet, crave, demand, desire, fancy, hanker after, hunger for, lack, long for, miss, need, pine for, require, thirst for, wish, yearn for.
n. demand, desire, need, wish.

wanting *adj.* absent, defective, deficient, disappointing, faulty, imperfect, inadequate, inferior, insufficient, lacking, missing, patchy, poor, short, shy, sketchy, substandard, unsatisfactory, unsound.
antonyms adequate, sufficient.

wanton *adj.* arbitrary, cruel, evil, immoderate, immoral, malicious, needless, outrageous, rash, reckless, senseless, shameless, uncalled-for, unjustifiable, unprovoked, unrestrained, vicious, wicked, wild, wilful.

war *n.* battle, bloodshed, combat, conflict, contention, contest, enmity, fighting, hostilities, hostility, jihad, strife, struggle, warfare.
antonyms cease-fire, peace.
v. battle, clash, combat, contend, contest, fight, skirmish, strive, struggle, take up arms, wage war.
war cry battle cry, rallying-cry, slogan, watchword.

warble *v.* chirp, chirrup, quaver, sing, trill, twitter, yodel.
n. call, chirp, chirrup, cry, quaver, song, trill, twitter.

ward *n.* **1** apartment, room. **2** area, district, division, precinct, quarter, zone. **3** charge, dependant, minor, protégé.
ward off avert, avoid, beat off, block, deflect, evade, fend off, forestall, parry, repel, stave off, thwart, turn away.

warden *n.* administrator, captain, caretaker, curator, custodian, guardian, janitor, keeper, ranger, steward, superintendent, warder, watchman.

warder *n.* custodian, guard, jailer, keeper, prison officer, wardress.

wardrobe *n.* **1** closet, cupboard. **2** attire, clothes, outfit.

warehouse *n.* depository, depot, entrepot, repository, stockroom, store, storehouse.

wares *n.* commodities, goods, merchandise, produce, products, stock, stuff.

warfare *n.* arms, battle, blows, combat, conflict, contention, contest, discord, fighting, hostilities, passage of arms, strife, struggle, war.
antonyms harmony, peace.

warlike *adj.* aggressive, antagonistic, belligerent, bloodthirsty, combative, hostile, inimical, militaristic, military, pugnacious, unfriendly.
antonyms friendly, peaceable.

warm *adj.* **1** heated, lukewarm, tepid. **2** heavy, thermal, thick. **3** cheerful, intense, mellow, pleasant, relaxing, rich. **4** affable, affectionate, amiable, cordial, friendly, genial, hearty, hospitable, kindly, sympathetic, tender. **5** balmy, fine, sunny.
antonyms **1** cool. **2** cold, cool. **3** cold. **4** indifferent, unfriendly. **5** cool, stormy.
v. animate, excite, heat (up), interest, melt, put some life into, reheat, rouse, stimulate, stir, thaw, turn on.
antonym cool.

warm-hearted *adj.* affectionate, ardent, compassionate, cordial, generous, genial, kind-hearted, kindly, loving, sympathetic, tender, tender-hearted.
antonyms cold, unsympathetic.

warmth *n.* **1** heat, warmness. **2** affection, cheerfulness, cordiality, eagerness, enthusiasm, fervour, happiness, intensity, tenderness, vigour.
antonyms **1** coldness. **2** coolness, unfriendliness.

warn *v.* admonish, advise, alert, caution, counsel, inform, notify, put on one's guard, tip off.

warning *n.* admonition, advance notice, advice, alarm, alert, caution, hint, lesson, notice, notification, omen, premonition, presage, sign, signal, threat, tip-off, token, word.
adj. cautionary, ominous, threatening.

warp *v.* bend, contort, corrupt, deform, deviate, distort, kink, misshape, pervert, twist.
antonym straighten.
n. bend, bent, bias, contortion, defect, deformation, deviation, distortion, irregularity, kink, perversion, quirk, turn, twist.

warrant *n.* authorisation, authority, commission, guarantee, licence, permission, permit, pledge, sanction, security, voucher, warranty.
v. affirm, answer for, approve, assure, authorise, be bound, call for, certify, commission, declare, demand, entitle, excuse, guarantee, justify, license, necessitate, permit, pledge, require, sanction, secure, underwrite, uphold, vouch for.

warranty *n.* assurance, authorisation, certificate, contract, covenant, guarantee, pledge.

warrior *n.* champion, combatant, fighter, fighting man, soldier, war-horse.

wary *adj.* alert, apprehensive, attentive, cagey, careful, cautious, guarded, heedful, on one's guard, on the lookout, prudent, suspicious, vigilant, watchful, wide-awake.
antonyms careless, foolhardy, heedless, reckless, unwary.

wash *v.* bath, bathe, clean, cleanse, launder, moisten, rinse, scrub, shampoo, shower, swill, wet.
n. bath, bathe, cleaning, cleansing, flow, laundering, laundry, rinse, scrub, shampoo, shower, sweep, washing.

washed-out *adj.* all in, blanched, bleached, colourless, dog-tired, drained, drawn, exhausted, faded, fatigued, flat, haggard, lacklustre, mat, pale, pallid, spent, tired-out, wan, weary, worn-out.

wash-out *n.* disappointment, disaster, failure, fiasco, flop.
antonyms success, triumph.

waspish *adj.* bad-tempered, bitchy, cantankerous, crabbed, crabby, cross, crotchety, fretful, grouchy, grumpy, ill-tempered, irritable, peevish, pettish, petulant, prickly, snappish, testy, touchy, waxy.

waste *v.* consume, deplete, destroy, dissipate, drain, exhaust, fritter away, lavish, misspend,

misuse, spend, spoil, squander, throw away.
antonyms economise, preserve, save.
n. **1** abuse, dissipation, extravagance, loss, misapplication, misuse, prodigality, squandering, wastefulness. **2** debris, dregs, dross, effluent, garbage, leftovers, litter, offscouring(s), refuse, rubbish, scrap, slops, trash.
adj. bare, barren, desolate, devastated, dismal, dreary, empty, extra, left-over, superfluous, supernumerary, uncultivated, uninhabited, unprofitable, unused, unwanted, useless, wild, worthless.

wasted *adj.* **1** needless, unnecessary, useless. **2** abandoned, emaciated, finished, gaunt, shrivelled, shrunken, spent, washed-out, withered.
antonyms **1** necessary. **2** healthy, robust.

wasteful *adj.* extravagant, improvident, lavish, prodigal, profligate, ruinous, spendthrift, thriftless, uneconomical, unthrifty.
antonyms economical, frugal, thrifty.

wasteland *n.* barrenness, desert, solitude, void, waste, wilderness, wild(s).

waster *n.* good-for-nothing, idler, layabout, loafer, lounger, shirker, skiver, wastrel.
antonym worker.
adj. destroying, devastating, emaciating.
antonym strengthening.

watch *v.* **1** gaze at, look at, look on, mark, note, notice, observe, peer at, see, stare at, view. **2** guard, keep, keep an eye on, look after, mind, protect, superintend, take care of. **3** look out, pay attention, take heed.
n. **1** clock, ticker, tick-tock, timepiece, wristwatch. **2** alertness, attention, heed, inspection, lookout, notice, observation, supervision, surveillance, vigil, vigilance, watchfulness.
watch out keep one's eyes open, look out.
watch over defend, guard, keep an eye on, look after, mind, preserve, protect, shelter, shield, stand guard over.

watch-dog *n.* custodian, guard dog, guardian, house-dog, inspector, monitor, ombudsman, protector, scrutineer, vigilante.

watcher *n.* looker-on, lookout, observer, onlooker, spectator, spy, viewer, witness.

watchful *adj.* alert, attentive, cautious, guarded, heedful, observant, on one's guard, suspicious, unmistaking, vigilant, wary, wide awake.
antonyms careless, inattentive, unobservant.

watchman *n.* caretaker, custodian, guard, security guard, security man.

watchword *n.* battle-cry, buzz-word, byword, catch phrase, catchword, maxim, motto, password, rallying-cry, signal, slogan.

water *n.* lake, ocean, rain, river, saliva, sea, stream.
v. dampen, dilute, drench, flood, hose, irrigate, moisten, soak, spray, sprinkle, weaken.
antonyms dry out, parch.
water down adulterate, dilute, mix, qualify, soften, thin, tone down, water, weaken.
antonyms purify, strengthen.

watercourse *n.* channel, ditch, river, stream, water-channel.

waterfall *n.* cascade, cataract, chute, fall, torrent.

waterproof *adj.* coated, damp-proof, impermeable, impervious, proofed, rubberised, water-repellent, water-resistant.
antonym leaky.

watertight *adj.* airtight, firm, flawless, foolproof, hermetic, impregnable, incontrovertible, sound, unassailable, waterproof.
antonyms leaky, unsound.

watery *adj.* damp, diluted, flavourless, fluid, liquid, marshy, moist, runny, soggy, tasteless, thin, washy, watered-down, weak, wet, wishy-washy.
antonyms solid, strong.

wave *v.* brandish, direct, flap, flourish, flutter, gesticulate, gesture, indicate, quiver, ripple, shake, sign, signal, stir, sway, swing, waft.
n. billow, breaker, current, drift, flood, ground swell, movement, outbreak, rash, ripple, roller, rush, stream, surge, sweep, swell, tendency, tidal wave, trend, undulation, upsurge.

waver *v.* dither, falter, flicker, fluctuate, hesitate, reel, rock, seesaw, shake, sway, totter, tremble, vary, wobble.
antonyms decide, determine, stand.

wavy *adj.* curly, curvy, ridged, rippled, ripply, sinuous, undulated, winding, wrinkled, zigzag.
antonyms flat, smooth.

wax *v.* become, develop, dilate, enlarge, expand, fill out, grow, increase, magnify, mount, rise, swell.
antonyms decrease, diminish, wane.

waxen *adj.* anaemic, ashen, colourless, ghastly, livid, pale, pallid, pasty, wan, white.
antonym ruddy.

way *n.* **1** approach, fashion, manner, means, method, mode, procedure, system, technique. **2** characteristic, conduct, custom, habit, idiosyncrasy, nature, practice, style, trait, usage. **3** access, avenue, channel, course, direction, gate, highway, lane, passage, path, road, route, street, thoroughfare, track.
by the way in passing, incidentally.

wayward *adj.* capricious, changeable, contrary, disobedient, erratic, fickle, flighty, headstrong, incorrigible, insubordinate, intractable, obstinate, perverse, rebellious, refractory, self-willed, stubborn, ungovernable, unmanageable, unpredictable, unruly, wilful.
antonyms complaisant, good-natured.

weak *adj.* **1** debilitated, decrepit, delicate, exhausted, feeble, flimsy, fragile, frail, infirm, sickly, unguarded, unhealthy, unprotected, vulnerable. **2** cowardly, defective, deficient, faulty, impotent, inadequate, inconclusive, indecisive, ineffective, irresolute, lacking, lame, poor, powerless, spineless, unconvincing, untenable. **3** dull, faint, imperceptible, low, muffled, slight, soft. **4** diluted, insipid, runny, tasteless, thin, watery.
antonyms **1** safe, secure, strong. **2** powerful, substantial.

weaken *v.* cut, debilitate, depress, dilute, dimin-

ish, droop, dwindle, ease up, fade, fail, flag, give way, impair, lessen, lower, mitigate, moderate, reduce, sap, soften (up), temper, thin, tire, undermine, water down.
antonym strengthen.

weakling *n.* coward, drip, sissy, underdog, underling, weed, wet, wimp.
antonyms hero, stalwart.

weakness *n.* **1** debility, feebleness, frailty, impotence, infirmity, powerlessness, vulnerability. **2** blemish, defect, deficiency, failing, fault, flaw, foible, shortcoming. **3** fondness, inclination, liking, passion, penchant, soft spot.
antonyms **1** strength. **2** strength. **3** dislike.

weal *n.* mark, ridge, scar, stripe, wale, welt, wound.

wealth *n.* abundance, affluence, assets, bounty, capital, cash, estate, fortune, fullness, funds, goods, mammon, means, money, opulence, plenty, possessions, profusion, property, prosperity, resources, riches, store, substance.
antonyms deprivation, poverty.

wealthy *adj.* affluent, comfortable, filthy rich, flush, moneyed, opulent, prosperous, rich, rolling in it, well-heeled, well-off, well-to-do.
antonyms badly-off, impoverished, poor.

wear *v.* **1** bear, carry, display, don, dress in, have on, put on, show, sport. **2** abrade, consume, corrode, deteriorate, erode, fray, grind, rub, waste.
n. **1** attire, clothes, clothing, costume, dress, garments, outfit. **2** abrasion, corrosion, deterioration, erosion, friction, wear and tear.
wear down abrade, chip away at, consume, corrode, diminish, erode, grind down, lessen, overcome, reduce, rub away, undermine.
wear off abate, decrease, diminish, disappear, dwindle, ebb, fade, lessen, peter out, subside, wane, weaken.
antonym increase.
wear out deteriorate, erode, exhaust, fatigue, fray, impair, rub through, sap, tire (out), use up, wear through.
antonyms refresh, replenish.

wearing *adj.* abrasive, exasperating, exhausting, fatiguing, irksome, oppressive, taxing, tiresome, tiring, trying, wearisome.
antonym refreshing.

weary *adj.* all in, dead beat, dog-tired, drained, drowsy, exhausted, fagged out, fatigued, jaded, sleepy, tired, whacked, worn out.
antonyms fresh, lively, refreshed.

wearying *adj.* exhausting, fatiguing, taxing, tiring, trying, wearing, wearisome.
antonym refreshing.

weather *n.* climate, conditions, rainfall, temperature.
v. brave, come through, endure, expose, harden, live through, overcome, pull through, resist, ride out, rise above, season, stand, stick out, suffer, surmount, survive, toughen, withstand.
antonym succumb.

weave *v.* braid, contrive, create, criss-cross, entwine, fabricate, fuse, incorporate, intercross, interlace, intertwine, introduce, knit, mat, merge, plait, put together, spin, twist, unite, wind, zigzag.

web *n.* interlacing, lattice, mesh, net, netting, network, screen, snare, tangle, texture, trap, weave, webbing, weft.

wedding *n.* bridal, marriage, matrimony.
antonym divorce.
adj. bridal, marriage, matrimonial, nuptial.

wedge *n.* block, chock, chunk, lump, wodge.
v. block, cram, crowd, force, jam, lodge, pack, push, ram, squeeze, stuff, thrust.
antonyms dislodge, space out, take out.

weed *v.* hoe.
weed out eliminate, eradicate, get rid of, purge, remove, root out.
antonyms add, fix, infiltrate.

weedy *adj.* feeble, frail, insipid, lanky, puny, scrawny, skinny, thin, undersized, ungainly, weak, weak-kneed, wet, wimpish.
antonym strong.

weekly *adv.* by the week, every week, once a week.

weep *v.* blub, blubber, bubble, cry, drip, lament, moan, mourn, pour forth, pour out, snivel, sob, whimper.
antonym rejoice.
n. blub, bubble, cry, lament, moan, snivel, sob.

weepy *adj.* blubbering, crying, sobbing, tearful, teary, weeping.
antonym dry-eyed.

weigh *v.* **1** bear down, oppress, prey. **2** consider, contemplate, deliberate, evaluate, examine, meditate on, mull over, ponder, reflect on, think over.
weigh down afflict, bear down, burden, depress, get down, load, oppress, overload, press down, trouble, weigh upon, worry.
antonyms hearten, lighten, refresh.
weigh up assess, balance, chew over, consider, contemplate, deliberate, discuss, examine, mull over, ponder, ruminate on, size up, think over.

weight *n.* **1** ballast, burden, force, gravity, heaviness, load, mass, millstone, poundage, pressure, tonnage. **2** authority, clout, consequence, consideration, impact, importance, influence, moment, power, preponderance, significance, substance, value.
antonym **1** lightness.
v. bias, charge, handicap, load, prejudice, slant, unbalance, weigh down.

weightless *adj.* airy, insubstantial, light.
antonym heavy.

weighty *adj.* consequential, considerable, critical, crucial, demanding, difficult, exacting, grave, important, leading, momentous, serious, significant, solemn, substantial, taxing, worrying.
antonyms trivial, unimportant.

weir *n.* dam, fence, lash, wear.

weird *adj.* bizarre, creepy, eerie, freakish, ghostly, grotesque, mysterious, odd, outlandish, queer, spooky, strange, supernatural, uncanny, unnatural.

antonyms natural, normal, usual.

welcome *adj.* acceptable, agreeable, allowed, appreciated, delightful, desirable, free, gratifying, permitted, pleasant, pleasing, refreshing.
antonym unwelcome.
n. acceptance, greeting, hospitality, reception, red carpet, salutation.
v. accept, approve of, embrace, greet, hail, meet, receive, salute.
antonyms reject, snub.

weld *v.* bind, bond, cement, connect, fuse, join, link, seal, solder, unite.
antonym separate.
n. bond, join, joint, seal, seam.

welfare *n.* advantage, benefit, good, happiness, health, interest, profit, prosperity, success, well-being.
antonyms detriment, harm.

well[1] *n.* bore, cavity, fount, fountain, hole, lift-shaft, mine, pit, pool, shaft, source, spring, waterhole, well-spring.
v. brim over, flood, flow, gush, jet, ooze, pour, rise, run, seep, spout, spring, spurt, stream, surge, swell, trickle.

well[2] *adv.* ably, adequately, agreeably, carefully, clearly, comfortably, completely, considerably, correctly, deeply, easily, expertly, favourably, fully, greatly, happily, highly, justly, kindly, pleasantly, properly, readily, rightly, satisfactorily, skilfully, splendidly, substantially, successfully, sufficiently, suitably, thoroughly.
antonyms badly, inadequately, incompetently, wrongly.
adj. able-bodied, advisable, agreeable, bright, fine, fit, flourishing, fortunate, good, great, happy, healthy, in good health, lucky, pleasing, proper, prudent, right, satisfactory, sound, strong, thriving, useful.
antonyms bad, ill, weak.

well-balanced *adj.* harmonious, level-headed, rational, reasonable, sane, sensible, sober, sound, stable, symmetrical, together, well-adjusted.
antonym unbalanced.

well-being *n.* comfort, good, happiness, prosperity, welfare.
antonyms discomfort, harm.

well-bred *adj.* civil, cultured, polite, refined, well-brought-up, well-mannered.
antonym ill-bred.

well-disposed *adj.* agreeable, amicable, favourable, friendly, sympathetic, well-placed.
antonym ill-disposed.

well-dressed *adj.* neat, smart, spruce, tidy, trim, well-groomed.
antonym scruffy.

well-known *adj.* celebrated, famed, familiar, famous, illustrious, notable, noted, popular, renowned.
antonym unknown.

well-off *adj.* affluent, comfortable, fortunate, moneyed, prosperous, rich, successful, thriving, wealthy, well-to-do.
antonyms badly-off, poor.

well-thought-of *adj.* admired, esteemed, highly regarded, honoured, respected, revered.
antonym despised.

well-to-do *adj.* affluent, comfortable, loaded, moneyed, prosperous, rich, warm, wealthy, well-heeled, well-off.
antonym poor.

well-wisher *n.* fan, supporter, sympathiser.

well-worn *adj.* commonplace, hackneyed, overused, stale, stereotyped, threadbare, timeworn, tired, trite.
antonym original.

welsh *v.* cheat, defraud, diddle, do, swindle, welch.

welt *n.* contusion, mark, ridge, scar, streak, stripe, weal.

wet *adj.* **1** boggy, clammy, damp, dank, drenched, dripping, drizzling, humid, moist, pouring, raining, rainy, saturated, showery, soaked, soaking, sodden, soggy, sopping, spongy, teeming, waterlogged, watery. **2** feeble, ineffectual, irresolute, namby-pamby, sloppy, soft, soppy, spineless, weak, weedy.
antonyms **1** dry. **2** resolute, strong.
n. clamminess, condensation, damp, dampness, drizzle, humidity, liquid, moisture, rain, water, wetness.
antonym dryness.
v. damp, dampen, dip, drench, imbue, irrigate, moisten, saturate, soak, splash, spray, sprinkle, steep, water.
antonym dry.

whack *v.* bang, bash, beat, belt, biff, box, buffet, clobber, clout, hit, rap, slap, smack, sock, strike, thrash, thump, thwack, wallop.
n. bang, bash, belt, biff, bit, blow, box, clout, crack, cuff, hit, rap, shot, slap, slug, smack, stab, stroke, thump, thwack, wallop, wham.

wham *n.* bang, bash, blow, clout, hit, impact, slam, smack, splat, thump, wallop.

wharf *n.* dock, dockyard, jetty, landing-stage, marina, pier, quay, quayside.

wheedle *v.* cajole, charm, coax, court, draw, entice, flatter, inveigle, persuade.
antonym force.

wheel *n.* circle, gyration, pivot, revolution, roll, rotation, spin, turn, twirl, whirl.
v. circle, gyrate, orbit, pirouette, revolve, roll, rotate, spin, swing, swivel, turn, twirl, whirl.

wheelbarrow *n.* barrow, hand-cart.

wheeze *v.* cough, gasp, hiss, pant, rasp, whistle.

whereabouts *n.* location, place, position, site, situation, vicinity.

wherewithal *n.* capital, cash, funds, means, money, necessary, resources, supplies.

whet *v.* arouse, awaken, file, grind, hone, incite, increase, kindle, provoke, quicken, rouse, sharpen, stimulate, stir.
antonyms blunt, dampen.

whiff *n.* aroma, blast, breath, draught, gale, gust, hint, odour, puff, reek, scent, smell, sniff, stench, stink, trace.

whim *n.* caprice, conceit, fad, fancy, freak,

humour, notion, quirk, sport, urge, vagary.

whimper *v.* blub, blubber, cry, grizzle, mewl, moan, snivel, sob, weep, whine, whinge.
n. moan, snivel, sob, whine.

whimsical *adj.* capricious, curious, dotty, droll, eccentric, fanciful, funny, mischievous, odd, peculiar, playful, quaint, queer, unusual, weird.

whine *n.* beef, belly-ache, complaint, cry, gripe, grouch, grouse, grumble, moan, sob, wail, whimper.
v. beef, belly-ache, carp, complain, cry, gripe, grizzle, grouch, grumble, moan, sob, wail, whimper, whinge.

whip *v.* **1** beat, birch, cane, castigate, discipline, flog, lash, leather, lick, punish, scourge, strap, tan, thrash. **2** dart, dash, flash, flit, fly, jerk, pull, rush, snatch, tear, whisk. **3** agitate, drive, goad, incite, instigate, provoke, push, rouse, spur, stir, urge.
n. birch, cane, cat-o'-nine-tails, horsewhip, lash, riding-crop, scourge, switch, thong.
whip up agitate, arouse, excite, foment, incite, inflame, instigate, kindle, provoke, stir up, work up.
antonyms dampen, deter.

whirl *v.* birl, circle, gyrate, pirouette, pivot, reel, revolve, roll, rotate, spin, swirl, swivel, turn, twirl, twist, wheel.
n. agitation, bustle, circle, commotion, confusion, daze, flurry, giddiness, gyration, hubbub, hurly-burly, pirouette, reel, revolution, roll, rotation, round, series, spin, stir, succession, swirl, tumult, turn, twirl, twist, uproar, vortex, wheel.
antonym calm.

whirlpool *n.* maelstrom, vortex.

whirlwind *n.* cyclone, tornado, vortex.
adj. hasty, headlong, impetuous, impulsive, lightning, quick, rapid, rash, short, speedy, split-second, swift.
antonyms deliberate, slow.

whisk *v.* beat, brush, dart, dash, flick, fly, grab, hasten, hurry, race, rush, scoot, shoot, speed, sweep, swipe, tear, twitch, whip, wipe.
n. beater, brush.

whisker *n.* bristle, hair.

whisper *v.* breathe, buzz, divulge, gossip, hint, hiss, insinuate, intimate, murmur, rustle, sigh, tittle.
antonym shout.
n. breath, buzz, gossip, hint, hiss, innuendo, insinuation, murmur, report, rumour, rustle, shadow, sigh, sighing, soupçon, suggestion, suspicion, tinge, trace, underbreath, undertone, whiff, word.
antonym roar.

whistle *n.* call, cheep, chirp, hooter, siren, song, warble.
v. call, cheep, chirp, pipe, sing, warble, wheeze.

white *adj.* **1** ashen, colourless, pale, pallid, pasty, wan. **2** grey, light, silver, snowy.
antonyms **1** ruddy. **2** dark.

white-collar *adj.* clerical, executive, non-manual, office, professional, salaried.
antonyms blue-collar, manual.

whiten *v.* blanch, bleach, fade, pale, whitewash.
antonyms blacken, colour, darken.

whittle *v.* carve, consume, cut, destroy, diminish, eat away, erode, hew, pare, reduce, scrape, shape, shave, trim, undermine, wear away.

whole *adj.* **1** complete, entire, full, integral, total, unabridged, uncut, undivided, unedited. **2** fit, healthy, in one piece, intact, inviolate, mint, perfect, sound, strong, unbroken, undamaged, unharmed, unhurt, well.
antonyms **1** partial. **2** damaged, ill.
n. aggregate, all, ensemble, entirety, entity, everything, fullness, lot, piece, total, totality, unit, unity.
antonym part.
on the whole all in all, all things considered, as a rule, by and large, for the most part, generally, generally speaking, in general, mostly.

whole-hearted *adj.* committed, complete, dedicated, determined, devoted, earnest, emphatic, enthusiastic, genuine, passionate, real, sincere, true, unfeigned, unqualified, unreserved, unstinting, warm, zealous.
antonym half-hearted.

wholesale *adj.* broad, comprehensive, extensive, far-reaching, indiscriminate, mass, massive, outright, sweeping, total, wide-ranging.
antonym partial.

wholesome *adj.* advantageous, beneficial, clean, decent, edifying, good, healthy, helpful, honourable, hygienic, improving, invigorating, moral, nourishing, nutritious, pure, respectable, righteous, salubrious, salutary, sanitary, uplifting, virtuous, worthy.
antonyms unhealthy, unwholesome.

wholly *adv.* absolutely, all, altogether, completely, comprehensively, entirely, exclusively, fully, only, perfectly, solely, thoroughly, totally, utterly.
antonym partly.

whoop *v., n.* cheer, cry, hoot, hurrah, roar, scream, shout, shriek, yell.

whorl *n.* coil, convolution, corkscrew, helix, spiral, turn, twist, vortex.

wicked *adj.* abominable, agonising, atrocious, awful, bad, corrupt, debased, depraved, destructive, difficult, distressing, dreadful, evil, fearful, fierce, foul, guilty, harmful, heinous, immoral, iniquitous, injurious, intense, mischievous, nasty, offensive, painful, roguish, scandalous, severe, shameful, sinful, spiteful, terrible, troublesome, trying, ungodly, unpleasant, unprincipled, unrighteous, vicious, vile, worthless.
antonyms good, harmless, modest, upright.

wide *adj.* ample, baggy, broad, comprehensive, diffuse, dilated, distant, distended, expanded, expansive, extensive, far-reaching, full, general, immense, inclusive, large, loose, off-course, off-target, outstretched, remote, roomy, spacious, sweeping, vast.
antonyms limited, narrow, restricted.
adv. aside, astray, off course, off target, off the

mark, out.
antonym on target.
widen *v.* broaden, dilate, distend, enlarge, expand, extend, open out, spread, stretch.
antonym narrow.
widespread *adj.* broad, common, extensive, far-flung, far-reaching, general, pervasive, popular, prevailing, prevalent, rife, sweeping, universal, unlimited, wholesale.
antonyms limited, uncommon.
width *n.* amplitude, beam, breadth, compass, diameter, extent, girth, measure, range, reach, scope, span, thickness, wideness.
wield *v.* apply, brandish, command, control, employ, exercise, exert, flourish, handle, have, hold, maintain, manage, manipulate, ply, possess, swing, use, utilise, wave, weave.
wife *n.* better half, bride, mate, missus, partner, spouse, woman.
wiggle *v., n.* jerk, jiggle, shake, twist, twitch, waggle, wriggle.
wild *adj.* **1** barbaric, barbarous, desolate, feral, ferocious, fierce, natural, savage, uncivilised, uncultivated, undomesticated, uninhabited, untamed, waste. **2** blustery, boisterous, choppy, furious, lawless, riotous, rough, rowdy, rude, stormy, tempestuous, turbulent, undisciplined, unrestrained, unruly, violent. **3** dishevelled, messy, tousled, unkempt, untidy. **4** extravagant, foolhardy, foolish, frenzied, impracticable, imprudent, irrational, outrageous, preposterous, rash, reckless, wayward. **5** crazy, eager, enthusiastic, excited, mad.
antonyms **1** civilised, friendly, tame. **2** calm, peaceful. **3** orderly, tidy. **4** sane, sensible. **5** unenthusiastic, uninterested.
wilderness *n.* desert, jumble, jungle, mass, maze, muddle, tangle, waste, wasteland, wild.
wildlife *n.* animals, fauna.
wilds *n.* desert, outback, the middle of nowhere, the sticks, wasteland, wilderness.
wile *n.* cheating, chicanery, contrivance, craftiness, cunning, deceit, device, dodge, fraud, guile, lure, manoeuvre, ploy, ruse, stratagem, subterfuge, trick, trickery.
antonym guilelessness.
wilful *adj.* adamant, bloody-minded, conscious, deliberate, determined, dogged, headstrong, inflexible, intended, intentional, intransigent, obstinate, persistent, perverse, pig-headed, purposeful, self-willed, stubborn, uncompromising, unyielding, voluntary.
antonyms complaisant, good-natured.
will *n.* **1** determination, discretion, disposition, mind, resolution, resolve, volition, will-power. **2** aim, choice, command, decision, declaration, decree, desire, fancy, feeling, inclination, intention, option, preference, purpose, wish.
v. bequeath, confer, dispose of, hand down, leave, ordain, pass on, transfer.
willing *adj.* agreeable, amenable, biddable, consenting, content, disposed, eager, enthusiastic, favourable, happy, inclined, pleased, prepared, ready, so-minded, willing-hearted.
antonyms disinclined, reluctant, unwilling.
willowy *adj.* graceful, gracile, limber, lissom, lithe, slender, slim, supple.
antonym buxom.
will-power *n.* determination, drive, resolution, resolve, self-command, self-control, self-discipline, self-mastery, single-mindedness.
willy-nilly *adv.* compulsorily, forcibly, necessarily, of necessity.
wilt *v.* diminish, droop, dwindle, ebb, fade, fail, flag, flop, languish, melt away, sag, shrivel, sink, wane, weaken, wither.
antonym perk up.
wily *adj.* artful, astute, crafty, crooked, cunning, deceitful, deceptive, designing, fly, foxy, guileful, intriguing, scheming, shifty, shrewd, sly, tricky, underhand.
antonym guileless.
win *v.* accomplish, achieve, acquire, attain, capture, catch, collect, come away with, conquer, earn, gain, get, net, obtain, overcome, pick up, prevail, procure, receive, secure, succeed, triumph.
antonyms fail, lose.
n. conquest, mastery, success, triumph, victory.
antonym defeat.
win over allure, attract, carry, charm, convert, convince, influence, persuade, prevail upon, sway, talk round.
wince *v.* blench, cower, cringe, draw back, flinch, jerk, quail, recoil, shrink, start.
n. cringe, flinch, jerk, start.
wind[1] *n.* air, air-current, blast, bluster, breath, breeze, current, cyclone, draught, gale, gas, gust, hurricane, puff, tornado, whisper.
wind[2] *v.* bend, coil, curl, curve, deviate, encircle, furl, loop, meander, ramble, reel, roll, spiral, turn, twine, twist, wreath, zigzag.
n. bend, curve, meander, turn, twist, zigzag.
wind down decline, diminish, dwindle, lessen, quieten down, reduce, relax, slacken off, slow (down), subside, unwind.
antonym increase.
wind up close (down), conclude, end (up), excite, finalise, find oneself, finish (up), liquidate, settle, terminate, work up.
antonym begin.
winded *adj.* breathless, out of breath, panting, puffed (out).
antonym fresh.
windfall *n.* bonanza, find, godsend, jackpot, stroke of luck, treasure-trove.
window *n.* dormer, dormer-window, glass, light, opening, pane, rose- window, skylight.
windpipe *n.* pharynx, throat, trachea.
windy *adj.* **1** blowy, blustery, breezy, gusty, squally, stormy, tempestuous, windswept. **2** boastful, boisterous, bombastic, conceited, long-winded, pompous, rambling, verbose, wild, wordy.
antonyms **1** calm. **2** modest.
wine *n.* champagne, claret, port, rosé, vin ordinaire, vintage.
wine-glass *n.* flute, glass, goblet.

wing *n.* adjunct, annexe, arm, branch, circle, coterie, extension, faction, flank, group, grouping, protection, section, segment, set, side.

wink *v.* blink, flash, flicker, flutter, gleam, glimmer, glint, sparkle, twinkle.
n. blink, flash, flutter, gleam, glimmering, glint, hint, instant, second, sparkle, split second, twinkle.

winner *n.* champion, conqueror, cracker, first, master, vanquisher, victor, world-beater, wow.
antonym loser.

winning *adj.* alluring, amiable, attractive, captivating, charming, conquering, delightful, enchanting, endearing, engaging, fetching, lovely, pleasing, successful, sweet, triumphant, unbeaten, undefeated, victorious, winsome.
antonyms losing, unappealing.

winnings *n.* booty, gains, prize(s), proceeds, profits, spoils, takings.
antonym losses.

winnow *v.* cull, diffuse, divide, fan, part, screen, select, separate, sift, waft.

wintry *adj.* bleak, cheerless, chilly, cold, desolate, dismal, freezing, frosty, frozen, harsh, icy, snowy.

wipe *v.* brush, clean, clear, dry, dust, erase, mop, remove, rub, sponge, swab, take away, take off.
n. brush, lick, rub, swab.
wipe out abolish, annihilate, blot out, destroy, efface, eradicate, erase, expunge, exterminate, massacre, obliterate, raze.
antonym establish.

wiry *adj.* bristly, lean, sinewy, stiff, strong, tough, withy.
antonym puny.

wisdom *n.* astuteness, comprehension, discernment, enlightenment, erudition, experience, foresight, intelligence, judgement, judiciousness, knowledge, learning, penetration, prudence, reason, sagacity, understanding.
antonyms folly, stupidity.

wise *adj.* aware, clever, discerning, enlightened, erudite, experienced, informed, intelligent, judicious, knowing, long-sighted, perceptive, prudent, rational, reasonable, sagacious, sage, sensible, shrewd, sound, understanding, well-advised, well-informed.
antonyms foolish, stupid.

wisecrack *n.* funny, gag, jest, jibe, joke, one-liner, quip, witticism.

wish *v.* ask, aspire, bid, command, covet, crave, desire, direct, hanker, hope, hunger, instruct, long, need, order, prefer, require, thirst, want, yearn.
antonyms dislike, fear.
n. aspiration, command, desire, hankering, hope, hunger, inclination, intention, liking, order, preference, request, thirst, urge, want, whim, will, yearning.
antonyms dislike, fear.

wishy-washy *adj.* bland, feeble, flat, half-hearted, ineffective, insipid, tasteless, thin, vague, vapid, watered-down, watery, weak.
antonym strong.

wisp *n.* jag, lock, piece, shred, strand, thread, twist.

wispy *adj.* attenuated, delicate, ethereal, faint, fine, flimsy, fragile, frail, gossamer, insubstantial, light, straggly, thin.
antonym substantial.

wistful *adj.* contemplative, disconsolate, dreaming, dreamy, forlorn, longing, meditative, melancholy, mournful, musing, pensive, reflective, sad, thoughtful, wishful.

wit *n.* **1** banter, drollery, facetiousness, fun, humour, jocularity, levity, repartee. **2** brains, cleverness, common sense, insight, intellect, intelligence, judgement, reason, sense, understanding, wisdom. **3** humorist, joker, wag.
antonyms **1** seriousness. **2** ignorance, stupidity.

witch *n.* hag, magician, occultist, sorceress.

witchcraft *n.* black magic, conjuration, divination, enchantment, incantation, magic, necromancy, occultism, sorcery, spell, the black art, the occult, voodoo, wizardry.

withdraw *v.* abjure, absent oneself, back out, depart, disclaim, disengage, draw back, draw out, drop out, extract, fall back, go (away), hive off, leave, pull back, pull out, recall, recant, remove, repair, rescind, retire, retract, retreat, revoke, secede, subtract, take away, take back, unsay, waive.
antonyms advance, deposit, persist.

withdrawal *n.* abjuration, departure, disavowal, disclaimer, disengagement, exit, exodus, extraction, recall, recantation, removal, repudiation, retirement, retreat, revocation, secession, waiver.
antonyms advance, deposit, persistence.

withdrawn *adj.* aloof, detached, distant, hidden, introvert, isolated, out-of-the-way, private, quiet, remote, reserved, retiring, secluded, shrinking, shy, silent, solitary, taciturn, uncommunicative, unforthcoming, unsociable.
antonyms extrovert, outgoing.

wither *v.* decay, decline, disintegrate, droop, dry, fade, languish, perish, put down, shame, shrink, shrivel, snub, wane, waste, wilt.
antonyms boost, thrive.
wither away decrease, die, die off, disappear, dwindle, fade away, shrink, shrivel, wilt.

withering *adj.* contemptuous, deadly, death-dealing, destructive, devastating, humiliating, mortifying, scathing, scornful, searing, snubbing, wounding.
antonyms encouraging, supportive.

withhold *v.* conceal, deduct, detain, hide, keep back, refuse, repress, reserve, resist, restrain, retain, sit on, suppress, suspend.
antonyms accord, give.

withstand *v.* bear, brave, combat, confront, cope with, defy, endure, face, grapple with, hold off, hold one's ground, hold out, last out, oppose, put up with, resist, stand, stand fast, stand one's ground, stand up to, survive, take, take on, thwart, tolerate, weather.
antonyms collapse, give in, yield.

witness *n.* bystander, corroborator, eye-witness, looker-on, observer, onlooker, spectator, testifier, viewer, watcher, witnesser.
v. attend, attest, bear out, bear witness, confirm, corroborate, countersign, depose, endorse, look on, mark, note, notice, observe, perceive, see, sign, testify, view, watch.

wits *n.* alertness, brains, cleverness, comprehension, faculties, ingenuity, intelligence, judgement, reason, sense, understanding.
antonyms folly, stupidity.

witty *adj.* amusing, brilliant, clever, comic, droll, facetious, fanciful, funny, humorous, ingenious, jocular, lively, original, salty, sparkling, whimsical.
antonyms dull, unamusing.

wizard *n.* **1** conjurer, enchanter, magician, occultist, sorcerer, warlock, witch. **2** ace, adept, expert, genius, hotshot, maestro, master, prodigy, star, virtuoso, whiz.

wizened *adj.* dried up, gnarled, lined, shrivelled, shrunken, thin, withered, worn, wrinkled.
antonyms plump, smooth.

wobble *v.* dither, dodder, fluctuate, heave, hesitate, oscillate, quake, rock, seesaw, shake, shilly-shally, sway, teeter, totter, tremble, vacillate, vibrate, waver.
n. oscillation, quaking, rock, shake, tremble, tremor, unsteadiness, vibration.

wobbly *adj.* doddering, doddery, rickety, shaky, teetering, tottering, unbalanced, uneven, unsafe, unstable, unsteady, wonky.
antonyms stable, steady.

woman *n.* **1** adult, dame, female, individual, lady, person. **2** girl, girlfriend, mistress, partner, spouse, sweetheart, wife.

womanly *adj.* female, feminine, ladylike, maternal, motherly, womanish.

wonder *n.* admiration, amazement, astonishment, awe, bewilderment, curiosity, fascination, marvel, miracle, phenomenon, prodigy, rarity, sight, spectacle, surprise, wonderment.
antonyms disinterest, ordinariness.
v. **1** ask oneself, enquire, meditate, ponder, puzzle, query, question, speculate, stare, think. **2** be surprised, doubt, marvel.

wonderful *adj.* admirable, amazing, astonishing, astounding, brilliant, delightful, excellent, extraordinary, fabulous, fantastic, great, incredible, magnificent, marvellous, oustanding, remarkable, sensational, smashing, staggering, startling, strange, stupendous, superb, surprising, terrific, tremendous, unheard-of.
antonyms appalling, dreadful, ordinary.

wonky *adj.* shaky, skew-whiff, unsound, unsteady, weak, wobbly, wrong.
antonyms stable, straight.

woo *v.* attract, cultivate, encourage, look for, pursue, seek.

wood *n.* **1** lumber, planks, timber. **2** coppice, copse, forest, grove, plantation, thicket, trees, underwood, woodland, woods.

wooded *adj.* forested, silvan, timbered, tree-covered, woody.

wooden *adj.* **1** oaken, timber, woody. **2** awkward, blank, clumsy, colourless, deadpan, emotionless, empty, expressionless, inflexible, leaden, lifeless, rigid, slow, spiritless, stiff, stupid, thick, unbending, unemotional.
antonyms **2** bright, lively.

woodland *n.* forest, wood(s).

woody *adj.* forested, sylvan, tree-covered, wooded, wooden.
antonym open.

wool *n.* down, fleece, fluff, hair, yarn.

woolly *adj.* **1** fleecy, frizzy, fuzzy, hairy, shaggy, woollen, woolly-haired. **2** blurred, confused, hazy, ill-defined, indefinite, muddled, nebulous, unclear, vague.
antonyms **2** clear, distinct.
n. cardigan, jersey, jumper, pullover, sweater.

woozy *adj.* befuddled, bemused, blurred, confused, dazed, dizzy, fuddled, nauseated, tipsy, unsteady, wobbly.
antonyms alert, sober.

word *n.* **1** expression, name, term, utterance, vocable. **2** chat, conversation, discussion, talk. **3** account, advice, affirmation, assertion, bulletin, comment, communication, communiqué, consultation, declaration, dispatch, hint, information, intimation, message, news, notice, remark, report, rumour, statement, warning. **4** assurance, guarantee, oath, pledge, promise, vow. **5** command, commandment, decree, go-ahead, green light, order.
v. couch, explain, express, phrase, put, say, write.

words *n.* altercation, argument, bickering, contention, disagreement, dispute, quarrel, row, run-in, set-to, squabble, text.

wordy *adj.* diffuse, discursive, long- winded, loquacious, phrasy, rambling, verbose, windy.
antonyms concise, laconic.

work *n.* **1** business, calling, career, craft, employment, job, line, livelihood, métier, occupation, profession, pursuit, service, skill, trade, vocation. **2** assignment, chore, commission, duty, job, responsibility, task, undertaking. **3** drudgery, effort, elbow grease, exertion, graft, industry, labour, slog, toil. **4** achievement, composition, creation, production. **5** book, play, poem.
antonyms **1** hobby, play, rest.
v. **1** be employed, have a job. **2** drudge, labour, slave, toil. **3** control, function, go, handle, manage, operate, perform, run, use. **4** accomplish, achieve, bring about, cause, create, pull off. **5** cultivate, dig, farm, till. **6** fashion, form, knead, make, manipulate, mould, process, shape.
antonyms **1** be unemployed. **2** play, rest. **3** fail.
work on butter up, cajole, coax, influence, persuade, soft-soap, sweet-talk, talk round, wheedle.
work out **1** calculate, clear up, figure out, formulate, produce, puzzle out, resolve, solve, sort out, understand. **2** come to, develop, evolve, happen, pan out, result, turn out. **3**

arrange, construct, contrive, devise, invent, plan, put together. **4** add up to, amount to, come out.

work up agitate, animate, arouse, elaborate, excite, expand, generate, incite, increase, inflame, instigate, move, rouse, spur, stir up, wind up.

workable *adj.* feasible, possible, practicable, practical, realistic, viable.
antonym unworkable.

worker *n.* artisan, craftsman, employee, hand, labourer, proletarian, staffer, tradesman, work-horse, working man, working woman, workman, work-woman.
antonym idler.

workforce *n.* employees, labour, labour force, personnel, shop-floor, staff, workers, work-people.

working *n.* action, functioning, manner, method, operation, routine, running.
adj. active, employed, functioning, going, labouring, operational, operative, running.
antonyms idle, inoperative, retired, unemployed.

workman *n.* artisan, craftsman, employee, hand, journeyman, labourer, mechanic, navvy, operative, tradesman, worker.

workmanlike *adj.* careful, efficient, expert, masterly, painstaking, professional, proficient, satisfactory, skilful, skilled, thorough, workmanly.
antonym amateurish.

workmanship *n.* art, craft, craftsmanship, execution, expertise, finish, handicraft, handiwork, manufacture, skill, technique, work.

work-mate *n.* associate, chum, colleague, co-worker, fellow-worker, pal, work-fellow.

works *n.* **1** factory, foundry, mill, plant, shop, workshop. **2** actions, acts, books, doings, oeuvre, output, plays, poetry, productions, writings. **3** action, gearing, innards, insides, installations, machinery, mechanism, movement, parts, workings.

world *n.* **1** creation, earth, environment, globe, nature, planet, star, universe. **2** human race, humanity, humankind, man, mankind, people. **3** area, division, domain, field, kingdom, province, realm, society, sphere, system. **4** age, days, epoch, era, life, period, times.

worldly *adj.* **1** earthly, lay, mundane, physical, profane, secular, temporal, terrestrial, unspiritual. **2** cosmopolitan, experienced, knowing, sophisticated, urbane, worldly-wise. **3** ambitious, avaricious, covetous, grasping, greedy, materialistic, selfish.
antonyms **1** eternal, spiritual. **2** unsophisticated.

worldwide *adj.* general, global, international, ubiquitous, universal.
antonyms limited, local, provincial.

worn *adj.* **1** frayed, ragged, shabby, tattered, tatty, threadbare, worn-out. **2** careworn, drawn, exhausted, fatigued, haggard, jaded, spent, tired, weary.
antonyms **1** new, unused. **2** fresh.

worn out 1 all in, dog-tired, done in, exhausted, moth-eaten, on its last legs, ragged, shabby, tattered, tatty, threadbare, used, useless. **2** decrepit, frayed, knackered, tired out, weary.
antonyms **1** new, unused. **2** fresh.

worried *adj.* afraid, agonised, anxious, apprehensive, bothered, concerned, distracted, distraught, distressed, disturbed, fearful, fretful, frightened, ill at ease, nervous, on edge, overwrought, strained, tense, troubled, uneasy, upset.
antonyms calm, unconcerned, unworried.

worry *v.* **1** agonise, annoy, bother, distress, disturb, fret, harass, harry, hassle, irritate, nag, perturb, pester, plague, tease, torment, trouble, unsettle, upset, vex. **2** attack, go for, savage.
antonyms **1** comfort, reassure.
n. agitation, annoyance, anxiety, apprehension, care, concern, disturbance, fear, irritation, misery, misgiving, perplexity, problem, torment, trial, trouble, unease, vexation.
antonyms comfort, reassurance.

worrying *adj.* anxious, disquieting, distressing, disturbing, harassing, nail-biting, troublesome, trying, uneasy, unsettling, upsetting, worrisome.
antonym reassuring.

worsen *v.* aggravate, damage, decay, decline, degenerate, deteriorate, exacerbate, go downhill, sink.
antonym improve.

worsening *n.* decay, decline, degeneration, deterioration, exacerbation, retrogression.
antonym improvement.

worship *v.* adore, adulate, deify, exalt, glorify, honour, idolise, love, praise, pray to, respect, revere, reverence, venerate.
antonyms despise, hate.
n. adoration, adulation, deification, devotion(s), exaltation, glorification, glory, homage, honour, image-worship, laudation, love, praise, prayer(s), regard, respect, reverence.

worth *n.* aid, assistance, avail, benefit, cost, credit, desert(s), excellence, goodness, help, importance, merit, price, quality, rate, significance, use, usefulness, utility, value, virtue, worthiness.
antonym worthlessness.

worthless *adj.* abandoned, beggarly, contemptible, depraved, despicable, futile, good-for-nothing, insignificant, meaningless, miserable, paltry, pointless, poor, rubbishy, screwy, trashy, trifling, trivial, unavailing, unimportant, unusable, useless, valueless, vile, wretched.
antonyms important, profitable, valuable.

worthwhile *adj.* beneficial, constructive, gainful, good, helpful, justifiable, productive, profitable, useful, valuable, worthy.
antonyms pointless, useless, worthless.

worthy *adj.* admirable, appropriate, commendable, creditable, decent, dependable, deserving, excellent, fit, good, honest, honourable, laudable, praiseworthy, reliable, reputable, respectable, righteous, suitable, upright, valuable, worthwhile.

antonyms disreputable, unworthy, useless.

wound *n.* **1** cut, gash, injury, laceration, lesion, pain, scar, slash. **2** anguish, damage, distress, grief, harm, heartbreak, hurt, shock, torment, trauma.

v. annoy, cut, damage, distress, gash, grieve, harm, hit, hurt, injure, irritate, lacerate, offend, pain, pierce, shock, slash, sting.

wrangle *n.* argument, argy-bargy, bickering, brawl, clash, contest, controversy, dispute, quarrel, row, set-to, slanging match, squabble, tiff, tussle.

antonym agreement.

v. altercate, argue, bicker, brawl, contend, disagree, dispute, fall out, fight, quarrel, row, scrap, squabble.

antonym agree.

wrap *v.* bind, bundle up, cloak, cocoon, cover, enclose, envelop, fold, immerse, muffle, pack, package, roll up, shroud, surround, wind.

antonym unwrap.

wrap up **1** pack up, package, parcel, wrap. **2** bring to a close, complete, conclude, end, finish off, round off, terminate, wind up.

wrapper *n.* cover, dust-jacket, envelope, jacket, packaging, paper, sheath, sleeve, wrapping.

wrapping *n.* blister card, blister pack, bubble pack, carton, case, cellophane®, envelope, Jiffybag®, packaging, paper, silver-paper, tinfoil, wrappage.

wreak *v.* bestow, bring about, carry out, cause, create, execute, exercise, express, inflict, perpetrate, unleash, vent.

wreath *n.* band, coronet, crown, festoon, garland, loop, ring.

wreck *v.* break, demolish, destroy, devastate, mar, play havoc with, ravage, ruin, shatter, smash, spoil, write off.

antonyms conserve, repair, save.

n. derelict, desolation, destruction, devastation, disruption, hulk, mess, overthrow, ruin, ruination, shipwreck, write-off.

wreckage *n.* debris, flotsam, fragments, pieces, remains, rubble, ruin.

wrench *v.* distort, force, jerk, pull, rick, rip, sprain, strain, tear, tug, twist, wrest, wring, yank.

n. ache, blow, jerk, pain, pang, pull, sadness, shock, sorrow, sprain, tear, tug, twist, upheaval, uprooting.

wrestle *v.* battle, combat, contend, contest, fight, grapple, scuffle, strive, struggle, tussle, vie.

wretch *n.* good-for-nothing, miscreant, outcast, rascal, rogue, ruffian, scoundrel, vagabond, villain.

wretched *adj.* atrocious, awful, broken-hearted, contemptible, crestfallen, dejected, deplorable, depressed, despicable, disconsolate, distressed, doleful, downcast, forlorn, gloomy, hopeless, inferior, low, mean, melancholy, miserable, paltry, pathetic, pitiable, pitiful, poor, ratty, scurvy, shabby, shameful, sorry, unfortunate, unhappy, vile, worthless.

antonyms admirable, excellent, happy.

wriggle *v.* crawl, dodge, edge, extricate, jerk, manoeuvre, sidle, slink, snake, sneak, squiggle, squirm, talk one's way out, turn, twist, waggle, wiggle, worm, writhe, zigzag.

n. jerk, jiggle, squirm, turn, twist, twitch, wiggle.

wring *v.* coerce, distress, exact, extort, extract, force, hurt, mangle, pain, pierce, rack, rend, screw, squeeze, stab, tear, torture, twist, wound, wrench, wrest.

wrinkle *n.* corrugation, crease, crumple, fold, furrow, gather, line, pucker.

v. corrugate, crease, crinkle, crumple, fold, furrow, gather, line, pucker, shrivel.

wrinkled *adj.* creased, crinkled, crinkly, crumpled, furrowed, puckered, ridged, rumpled, wrinkly.

antonym smooth.

writ *n.* court order, decree, subpoena, summons.

write *v.* communicate, compose, copy, correspond, create, draft, draw up, inscribe, jot down, record, scribble, set down, take down, tell, transcribe.

write off **1** cancel, cross out, disregard, scrub. **2** crash, destroy, smash up, wreck.

writer *n.* author, clerk, columnist, copyist, crime writer, diarist, dramatist, essayist, hack, man of letters, novelist, pen, penman, penpusher, penwoman, playwright, prose-writer, scribbler, scribe, secretary, wordsmith.

writhe *v.* coil, contort, jerk, squirm, struggle, thrash, thresh, toss, twist, wiggle, wreathe, wriggle.

writing *n.* book, calligraphy, composition, document, hand, handwriting, letter, letters, literature, penmanship, print, publication, scrawl, scribble, script, work.

written *adj.* documentary, drawn up, recorded, set down, transcribed.

antonyms unwritten, verbal.

wrong *adj.* **1** amiss, awry, erroneous, fallacious, false, imprecise, in error, inaccurate, incorrect, mistaken, the matter. **2** improper, inappropriate, inapt, incongruous, indecorous, unconventional, unfitting, unhappy, unseemly, unsuitable. **3** bad, blameworthy, criminal, crooked, dishonest, evil, guilty, illegal, illicit, immoral, iniquitous, reprehensible, sinful, to blame, unacceptable, unethical, unfair, unjust, unlawful, wicked. **4** defective, faulty, out of order.

antonyms **1** accurate, correct, right. **2** suitable. **3** just, legal.

adv. amiss, askew, astray, badly, erroneously, faultily, improperly, inaccurately, incorrectly, mistakenly, wrongly.

antonym right.

n. abuse, crime, error, grievance, immorality, inequity, infringement, iniquity, injury, injustice, misdeed, offence, sin, sinfulness, transgression, trespass, unfairness, wickedness, wrongdoing.

antonym right.

v. abuse, cheat, discredit, dishonour, harm, hurt, ill-treat, ill-use, injure, malign, maltreat, misrepresent, mistreat, oppress.

wrong-doer *n.* criminal, culprit, delinquent, evil-doer, felon, law-breaker, miscreant, offender, sinner, transgressor, trespasser.

wrong-doing *n.* crime, delinquency, error, evil, fault, felony, immorality, iniquity, mischief, misdeed, offence, sin, sinfulness, transgression, wickedness.

wrongful *adj.* blameworthy, criminal, dishonest, dishonourable, evil, illegal, illegitimate, illicit, immoral, improper, reprehensible, unethical, unfair, unjust, unlawful, wicked, wrong.
antonym rightful.

wry *adj.* **1** droll, dry, ironic, mocking, sarcastic, sardonic. **2** contorted, crooked, deformed, distorted, twisted, uneven, warped.
antonym **2** straight.

Y

yank *v., n.* haul, heave, jerk, pull, snatch, tug, wrench.
yap *v.* babble, chatter, go on, gossip, jabber, jaw, prattle, talk, twattle, yammer, yatter, yelp.
yard *n.* court, court-yard, garden, quad, quadrangle.
yardstick *n.* benchmark, comparison, criterion, gauge, measure, standard, touchstone.
yarn *n.* **1** fibre, thread. **2** anecdote, cock-and-bull story, fable, fabrication, story, tale, tall story.
yawn *v.* gape, open, split.
yawning *adj.* cavernous, gaping, huge, vast, wide, wide-open.
antonym narrow.
yearly *adj.* annual, per annum, per year.
adv. annually, every year, once a year.
yearn for ache for, covet, crave, desire, hanker for, hunger for, itch for, languish for, long for, lust for, pant for, pine for, want, wish for.
antonyms dislike, hate.
yell *v.* bawl, bellow, holler, howl, roar, scream, screech, shout, shriek, squawl, squeal, whoop, yelp, yowl.
antonym whisper.
n. bellow, cry, holler, howl, roar, scream, screech, shriek, squawl, whoop, yelp.
antonym whisper.
yelp *v.* bark, bay, cry, squeal, yap, yell, yowl.
n. bark, cry, squeal, yap, yell, yip, yowl.
yen *n.* craving, desire, hunger, itch, longing, lust, passion, yearning.
antonym dislike.
yes-man *n.* bootlicker, crawler, creature, lackey, minion, sycophant.
yield *v.* **1** abandon, abdicate, accede, acquiesce, admit defeat, agree, allow, bow, capitulate, cave in, cede, comply, concede, consent, give (in), give way, go along with, grant, knuckle under, part with, permit, relinquish, resign oneself, submit, succumb, surrender. **2** afford, bring forth, bring in, earn, fruit, furnish, generate, give, net, pay, produce, provide, return, supply.
antonyms **1** hold, resist, retain, withstand.
n. crop, earnings, harvest, income, output, proceeds, produce, product, profit, return, revenue, takings.
yoke *n.* bond, bondage, burden, enslavement, oppression, service, servility, slavery, subjugation.
v. bracket, connect, couple, harness, hitch, join, link, tie, unite.
antonym unhitch.
young *adj.* adolescent, baby, cub, early, fledgling, green, growing, immature, inexperienced, infant, junior, juvenile, little, new, recent, unblown, unfledged, youthful.
antonyms adult, mature, old.
n. babies, brood, chicks, cubs, family, fledglings, issue, litter, little ones, offspring, progeny, quiverful.
antonym parents.
youngster *n.* boy, girl, kid, lad, lass, nipper, toddler, youth.
youth *n.* **1** adolescent, boy, juvenile, kid, lad, teenager, the young, young man, young people, younger generation, youngster. **2** adolescence, boyhood, girlhood, immaturity.
antonym **2** adulthood.
youthful *adj.* active, boyish, childish, fresh, girlish, immature, inexperienced, juvenile, lively, puerile, vigorous, vivacious, well-preserved, young.
antonym aged.

Z

zany *adj.* amusing, clownish, comical, crazy, droll, eccentric, funny, loony.
antonym serious.

zeal *n.* ardour, dedication, devotion, eagerness, earnestness, enthusiasm, fanaticism, fervour, fire, gusto, keenness, passion, spirit, verve, warmth, zest.
antonyms apathy, indifference.

zealous *adj.* ardent, burning, devoted, eager, earnest, enthusiastic, fanatical, fervent, fired, impassioned, keen, militant, passionate, spirited.
antonyms apathetic, indifferent.

zenith *n.* acme, apex, climax, culmination, height, high point, meridian, optimum, peak, pinnacle, summit, top, vertex.
antonym nadir.

zero *n.* bottom, cipher, duck, love, nadir, naught, nil, nothing, nought.
zero in on aim for, concentrate on, converge on, direct at, fix on, focus on, head for, home in on, level at, pinpoint, train on.

zest *n.* **1** appetite, charm, enjoyment, enthusiasm, flavour, gusto, interest, keenness, zeal. **2** peel, rind, savour, spice, taste.
antonym **1** apathy.

zigzag *v.* meander, snake, wind.
adj. meandering, sinuous, zigzagging, zigzaggy.
antonym straight.

zip *n.* drive, élan, energy, enthusiasm, get-up-and-go, go, gusto, life, liveliness, punch, sparkle, spirit, verve, vigour, vim, vitality, zest, zing.
antonym listlessness.
v. dash, flash, fly, gallop, hurry, race, rush, scoot, shoot, speed, tear, whoosh, zoom.

zone *n.* area, belt, district, region, section, sector, sphere, stratum, territory, tract.

zoom *v.* buzz, dash, dive, flash, fly, gallop, hurtle, race, rush, shoot, speed, streak, tear, whirl, zip.

Appendix

Lists of Related Words

air and space vehicles aerobus, aerodrome, aerodyne, aerohydroplane, aeroplane, aerostat, air-ambulance, air-bus, airship, all-wing aeroplane, amphibian, autogiro, balloon, biplane, blimp, bomber, cable-car, camel, canard, chopper, comsat, convertiplane, crate, delta-wing, dirigible, dive bomber, fan-jet, fighter, fire-balloon, flying boat, flying saucer, flying wing, glider, gondola, gyrocopter, gyroplane, helibus, helicopter, hoverbus, hovercar, hovercraft, hovertrain, hydro-aeroplane, hydrofoil, hydroplane, intercepter, jet, jetliner, jetplane, lem, microlight, module, monoplane, multiplane, plane, rocket, rocket-plane, runabout, sailplane, satellite, seaplane, space platform, space probe, space shuttle, spacecraft, spaceship, spitfire, sputnik, step-rocket, stol, strato-cruiser, stratotanker, swingtail cargo aircraft, swing-wing, tanker, taube, téléférique, tow-plane, tractor, triplane, troop-carrier, tube, tug, turbojet, turbo-jet, twoseater, UFO, warplane, zeppelin.

cattle breeds Africander, Alderney, Angus, Ankole, Ayrshire, Blonde d'Aquitaine, Brahman, Brown Swiss, cattabu, cattalo, Charol(l)ais, Chillingham, Devon, dexter, Durham, Friesian, Galloway, Guernsey, Hereford, Highland, Holstein, Jersey, Latvian, Limousin, Luing, Red Poll, Romagnola, Santa Gertrudis, short-horn, Simmenthaler, Teeswater, Ukrainian, Welsh Black.

cheeses Amsterdam, Bel Paese, Blarney, Bleu d'Auvergne, Blue Vinny, Boursin, Brie, Caboc, Caerphilly, Camembert, Carré, Cheddar, Cheshire, Chevrotin, Colwick, Coulommiers, Crowdie, Danish blue, Derby, Dolcelatte, Dorset Blue, double Gloucester, Dunlop, Edam, Emmental, Emment(h)al(er), Esrom, ewe-cheese, Feta, Fynbo, Gammelost, G(j)etost, Gloucester, Gorgonzola, Gouda, Grana, Grevé, Gruyère, Handkäse, Havarti, Herrgårdsost, Herve, Huntsman, Hushållsost, Islay, Jarlsberg, Killarney, Kryddost, Lancashire, Leicester, Limburg(er), Lymeswold, mouse-trap, mozzarella, Munster, Mysost, Neufchâtel, Parmesan, Petit Suisse, pipo creme, Pont-l'Éveque, Port(-du-)Salut, Prästost, Provolone, Pultost, Raclette, Red Windsor, Reggiano, ricotta, Romadur, Roquefort, sage Derby, Saint-Paulin, Samsø, sapsago, Stilton, stracchino, Tilsit(er), Vacherin, Wensleydale, Wexford.

collective nouns building of rooks, cast of hawks, cete of badgers, charm of goldfinches, chattering of choughs, clamour of rooks, clowder of cats, covert of coots, covey of partridges, down of hares, drift of swine, drove of cattle, dule of doves, exaltation of larks, fall of woodcock, fesnyng of ferrets, gaggle of geese, gam of whales, gang of elks, grist of bees, husk of hares, kindle of kittens, leap of leopards, leash of bucks, murder of crows, murmuration of starlings, muster of peacocks, mute of hounds, nide of pheasants, pace of asses, pod of seals, pride of lions, school of porpoises, siege (or sedge) of bitterns, skein of geese, skulk of foxes, sloth of bears, sounder of boars, spring of teals, stud of mares, team of ducks, tok of capercailzies, troop of kangaroos, walk of snipe, watch of nightingales.

dog-breeds affenpinscher, badger-dog, basenji, basset(-hound), Bedlington (terrier), Blenheim spaniel, boar-hound, Border terrier, borzoi, Boston terrier, Briard, Brussels griffon, bull mastiff, bulldog, bull-terrier, cairn terrier, Cavalier King Charles spaniel, chihuahua, chow, clumber spaniel, coach-dog, cocker spaniel, collie, corgi, dachshund, Dalmatian, Dandie Dinmont, Dane, deerhound, dhole, dingo, Doberman(n) pinscher, elkhound, Eskimo dog, foxhound, fox-terrier, German police dog, German Shepherd dog, Great Dane, greyhound, griffon, harlequin, (Irish) water-spaniel, Jack Russell, keeshond, King Charles spaniel, Labrador, laika, lhasa apso, lurcher, lyam-hound, malemute, Maltese, mastiff, peke, Pekin(g)ese, pinscher, pointer, Pomeranian, poodle, pug, pug-dog, retriever, Rottweiler, saluki, Samoyed(e), sausage-dog, schipperke, schnauzer, Scotch-terrier, Sealyham, setter, sheltie, Shetland sheepdog, shih tzu, shough, Skye (terrier), spaniel, Spartan, spitz, St Bernard, staghound, Sussex spaniel, talbot, teckel, terrier, vizsla, volpino, warragal, water-dog, Weimaraner, whippet, wire-hair(ed terrier), wolf-dog, wolf-hound, Yorkshire terrier, zorro.

herbs, spices amaracus, basil thyme, caraway seeds, cardamom, cassia, cayenne, chervil, chilli, chive, cinnamon, cloves, coriander, cum(m)in, dill, dittany, endive, eyebright, fennel, fenugreek, finoc(c)hio, galega, garlic, gentian, ginger, groundsel, hellebore, henbane, horehound, horseradish, Hyoscyamus, hyssop, isatis, juniper, lemon thyme, liquorice, lovage, lungwort, mace, marjoram, mint, motherwort, mustard, myrrh, nutmeg, oregano, orpine, paprika, parsley, peppermint, purslane, rampion, rape, rosemary, rue, saffron, sage, savory, stacte, tarragon, thyme, turmeric, vanilla, verbena, watercress, wintergreen, wormwood, woundwort, yerba.

jewels, gems agate, amber, amethyst, aquamarine, asteria, balas ruby, baroque, beryl, bloodstone, brilliant, cairngorm, cameo, carbuncle, chalcedony, chrysolite, coral, cornelian, crystal, diamond, draconites, emerald, fire-opal, garnet, girasol(e), grossular(ite), heliodor, hyacinth, hyalite, hydrophane, intaglio, jacinth, jade, jango(o)n, jasper, jet, lapis lazuli, ligure, marcasite, marquise, Mocha stone, moonstone, morganite, mother-of-pearl, nacre, olivet, olivine, onyx, opal, oriental amethyst, paragon, pearl, peridot(e), pyreneite, pyrope, Rhinestone, rhodolite, rose, rose-cut, rose-diamond, ruby, sapphire, sard, sardine, sardonyx, smaragd, topaz, tourmaline, turquoise, water-sapphire, wood-opal, yu, yu-stone, zircon.

wine-bottle sizes baby, balthasar, jeroboam, magnum, Methuselah, nebuchadnezzar, nip, rehoboam, Salmanazar.

zodiac signs Aquarius, Aries, Cancer, Capricorn, Gemini, Leo, Libra, Pisces, Sagittarius, Scorpio, Taurus, Virgo.